C000104611

the calorie carb & fat bible

The UK's Most Comprehensive Calorie Counter

the calorie, carb & fat bible 2005

Published by
Weight Loss Resources
Remus House
Peterborough
PE2 9JX

ISBN 1 904512 02 X

Authors
Dr Jeremy Sims MB BS FRIPH FRSH
Tracey Walton

Editor: Rebecca Walton
Design & Layout: Joanne Readshaw / Jonathan Slater

Printed and bound in Finland by
WS Bookwell Oy

Contents

INTRODUCTION

Losing Weight:
Taking Control & Winning

How do we achieve sustainable and ongoing success in our weight loss efforts?

"Success breeds success". So goes that well-known adage. That incredible tendency for small successes to lead on to even greater ones. We attain small goals and feel empowered to move on to even greater achievements. It can be true in many areas of our lives. And it can be just as applicable in our personal weight management efforts. We lose a few pounds, reach an early goal we have set ourselves, and we feel our confidence grow. We feel spurred on to our next weight goal. We have a growing sense of control.

But hey, wait up! I hear you cry. That doesn't sound like me. Yes I can lose a few pounds, feel great for a while, and then before I know it my confidence is blown sky high when next week I'm stuck at the same weight. Or, what about when I reach a healthier weight and then put it all back on again after a few months. You know, I'm not at all sure about all this success breeds success business.

And therein lies the problem, or to be more precise problems, for so many of us. How do we achieve sustainable and ongoing success in our weight loss efforts? And, then, having attained our ultimate goal of a healthier weight, how do we ensure it lasts? How do we ensure we maintain this healthy weight not just tomorrow, or next month, or next year even... but for a lifetime.

In recent years there has been much research attempting to find the answers to just these questions. How do the successful weight losers amongst us manage to lose their weight and then keep it off? What are the possible secrets that such individuals can reveal to the rest of us?

Many of the people in these studies have been dubbed "maintainers"- they have been able to lose weight successfully and then remain stable at their goal weight for the long term. These are the "winners" in the weight battles. Is it possible to learn from these individuals and use the knowledge gleaned to benefit others? Indeed we can. And what has been learnt has been invaluable.

Copying the positive actions of others is a proven technique, for success in achieving a goal. Who better to copy in our weight loss endeavours than those who have gone before us and triumphed? Research in this area has provided in depth information about the most effective strategies for weight control – both effective weight loss and maintenance. This information has highlighted many key factors common to most, if not all, successful weight losers:

The Secrets of Successful Weight Losers

1. They always eat a healthy breakfast which sets them up for the day, and boosts metabolism.

2. They maintain a low fat diet but never cut out fats altogether. They understand that all fats are not the same when it comes to health and are careful about saturated fat.

3. They never deny themselves the foods they enjoy – even those "naughties" – but ensure that they limit these foods.

4. They eat regular meals throughout the day – breakfast, lunch and dinner. They never skip meals. Also they always ensure that they eat a broad range of foods including plenty of fruit and veg.

5. They don't eat too many snacks, and they tend to choose healthy options.

6. They never deny themselves the opportunity to eat out but are very careful about consuming fast food.

7. They are regular monitors of what they eat. They have good knowledge of such essentials as calorie counting and the nutritional contents of food e.g. the saturated fat content.

8. They check their weight regularly but never go overboard. Once weekly is considered sufficient by most.

9. They maintain an active lifestyle. Many exercise for at least thirty minutes each day.

10. They are careful to lose weight gradually, in a healthy way. They set themselves small and achievable goals as steps towards their ultimate healthier weight.

11. They never berate themselves or feel guilty about lapses in their weight management programme. They have developed a self-belief that they can easily get back on track. They practice what is known as flexible restraint: they follow their programme but allow themselves the flexibility for occasional favourite foods or the enjoyment of a meal out.

We can easily conclude that these individuals have really taken control of their weight and, by following their example, you can take control of yours. But in order to do so you may also need change certain practices, attitudes and beliefs.

Never Rush Your Weight Loss

Muscle is the great calorie burning apparatus of the body, helping to set your metabolism

We live in a fast track world with seemingly fast track expectations. But trying to rush weight loss always fails. It simply does not work. Consider this: it may have taken you years to accumulate your extra weight. To expect that you can lose this weight in a matter of a few weeks is totally unrealistic. Research has shown that in general it is very difficult to lose more than 1-2 lbs of body fat weight per week – your body is highly protective of its fat stores and does not give them up readily.

When we crash diet we lose not just body fat but also water, glucose stores and protein. And the latter, in the form of muscle, you do not want to lose. Muscle is the great calorie burning apparatus of the body, helping to set your metabolism. As you lose muscle you also lose this calorie-burning capacity, removing one of the important factors in weight control.

Healthy weight loss should be gradual and careful. A steady weight loss of one or two pounds per week is best – ensuring body fat loss whilst retaining as much muscle weight as possible. You will also find it easier to stick to a steady weight loss programme with readily achievable weight loss goals.

Set Yourself Realistic & Achievable Goals

Successful weight losers are honest with themselves and set themselves readily achievable weight loss goals. They know that setting unrealistic goals is sure-fire way of demotivating themselves.

Learn from these experts and set yourself small steps to your own ultimate goal. These should be steps that you know with all confidence that you can achieve. Do go easy on yourself and likewise make your goals easy. For instance, as mentioned above, aim for one or two pounds weight reduction per week or, if you like, 5% of your weight in three months. Each small step will lead you further along the path to your ultimate goal of a healthier weight. And what's more you will find that the path is a far less arduous one than you ever expected it to be.

Visualize The New You

Before starting out on a weight loss programme try to sit down and visualize your new life as a slimmer, healthier you. Find somewhere quiet, where you cannot be disturbed. Sit in a comfortable chair and close your eyes. In your mind's eye see yourself as the slimmer you. How does it feel? How much more confident are you? What will you be doing in your new life? See yourself not only achieving a new healthier weight but also achieving all those ambitions which you have been storing up but have not felt confident enough to attempt.

*Take time to
develop your
personal weight
loss strategy –
this book is a
great start.*

Hold onto this image of the new you and, as you continue on your path to losing weight, take time to revisit it at regular intervals. The image will help you to stay focused and to boost your determination when things may not be going as well as you might hope.

Go Easy On Yourself

Weight loss should not be an ordeal. It should not be about denial, deprivation, and suffering. Look back at the key characteristics of our successful weight losers. Note that they never allow themselves to feel guilty about mistakes or lapses. They never deny themselves those little goodies that make our lives a happy experience. They still eat out and enjoy restaurant food. And they still lose weight and reach their goal weight. If they can do it without suffering and self-reproach then so can you.

Successful weight losers are smart with food. They ensure that they don't overindulge on the those "naughty" foods but they certainly don't remove them from their lives altogether. Everything in moderation.

By denying ourselves completely of the things we enjoy it is very easy to slip into feelings of deprivation. This can easily become self-loathing when we break down and binge on what we have denied ourselves, resulting in a big blow to our self-confidence and motivation. The answer is never to deny yourself, just moderate. You'll find your weight loss efforts a whole lot more gratifying.

Before closing this introduction to the latest edition of *The Calorie, Carb & Fat Bible* I'd like to spotlight some further observations of successful weight losers.

First of all, most will have devised their own weight loss programme. They will have taken time to arm themselves with information from a variety of sources and will have taken those aspects which fit their lifestyles and motivations. In short they have tailored a weight management programme to meet their personal needs. Remember no one programme will suit all. Take time to develop your personal weight loss strategy – this book is a great start.

Secondly, very few successful weight losers get it right first time. Like all of us they make mistakes; they suffer lapses; and they fail – very often more than once. However, what is highly important is that they never give up. They dust themselves off and learn from their mistakes – and try not to make the same errors twice.

You too must never see yourself as a failure if you have not achieved a goal or a desired weight. These are positive learning opportunities and as such your knowledge and personal understanding will have been invaluably reinforced. Learn from your mistakes or lapses, understand why these occurred, so that you can utilise this understanding to march on to success the next time.

Thirdly, and finally, because they have been careful and lost weight gradually, the new practices and attitudes they have acquired have become a lasting and rewarding part of their lives. Thus proving after all, that in weight management, success really can breed success when you take control.

Dr Jeremy Sims
MB BS FRIPH FRSH

Using this Book to Lose Weight

THE CALORIE BALANCE CONCEPT

*You only need
to eat or drink
a sausage roll
and a can of
cola more than
you need each
day to create
and store a
pound of fat in
a week*

Calories Consumed

greater than calories expended	= weight gain
equal to calories expended	= weight maintenance
less than calories expended	= weight loss

Making sure that calories consumed are less than calories expended is the best, if not the only, way to lose weight. After all, we put on weight by doing the exact opposite – eating a little more than we need each day, and becoming less active as each year passes.

You only need to eat or drink 500 calories (a sausage roll and a can of cola) more than you need each day to create and store a pound of fat in a week – 2 stones in just over six months. It's no wonder people say that excess weight tends to 'creep up on you'.

The good news is that the reverse is true. Eat 500 calories less than you need each day and you will lose a pound a week; a stone in 3 months, 2 stones in six months. If you combine this calorie cutting strategy with some exercise or activity that gets you moving, you'll lose weight more quickly.

How Much Weight To Lose

Use the body mass index chart and information on pages 16-17, to determine what is the right weight for you, and set a goal. You may find it helpful to set milestone goals of a stone, or half a stone, to measure your progress by; giving your confidence and motivation a boost as you go along. (Half a stone is the equivalent of 14 (½lb/250g) packs of butter!)

How Fast to Lose It

A pound a week is probably the best rate of loss for achieving sustained, healthy, permanent weight loss. If you have more than a couple of stones to lose, you could start out at 1½ – 2lb a week and see how you get on. If you begin to find this level too restrictive, slow your rate of loss down a bit – it's better to keep going at a pound a week than to give up because trying to lose 2lb a week is making you miserable! The following words may help you to keep your goal in perspective:

Never give up on a goal because of the time it will take to achieve it – the time will pass anyway.

How Many Calories

Use the calorie tables on pages 18-19 to find out how many calories you need to consume each day to maintain your current weight. Then subtract the 'calorie deficit' required to lose weight at your chosen rate, from the table below. This will give you a daily calorie allowance.

Rate of Loss	Calorie Deficit
½lb a week	250
1lb a week	500
1½lb a week	750
2lb a week	1000

Keep Track

Write down everything you eat and drink in a day – be as accurate as possible on serving sizes. Use the photocopiable Food and Exercise Diary on page 21 to help you keep track.

To start with, eat as you normally would for a few days. This will help you to see opportunities for cutting calories by substituting one food or drink item

Each time you lose half a stone- celebrate!

for another, and/or cutting portion sizes of high calorie foods, or eating them less often. Slowly introduce changes to your diet to bring your consumption within your chosen calorie allowance. Exercising will help you lose weight - not only does it burn extra calories (see page 20) but it will help you burn and maintain muscle tissue - which burns more calories, in the background, even when you are at rest.

Progressing

Each time you lose half a stone – celebrate! Treat yourself to a little luxury – something new to wear, a little pampering or some other (non-food!) treat. Review how well you've done, and set yourself up to lose the next half a stone by calculating a new calorie allowance based on your new weight.

Maintaining the Loss

I lost nearly three stones in just under a year of calorie counting. I reached my goal weight in February 2001, and have had no problem in keeping to that weight. The great thing about calorie counting is that you learn so much about what you eat, and make such important changes to your eating and drinking habits as you go along, that its difficult to go back to your old ways. The couple of times I have put on a pound or two, for example after a holiday, I've spent a few days calorie counting and got right back where I want to be. You can do it too – best of luck!

Tracey Walton
Founder www.weightlossresources.co.uk

Eating Healthily

Many people are unsure of what healthy eating means

As well as helping you to lose weight, a healthy and varied diet can also reduce the risk of a number of diseases including cancer, heart disease, stroke, osteoporosis and diabetes.

Many people are unsure of what healthy eating means - not surprising when you consider the variety of, often conflicting, advice given. The following guidelines are based on the UK Government's 'Balance of Good Health' and apply to most people over the age of 5. People under medical supervision or with special dietary requirements may have different needs and should check with their doctor.

The Balance of Good Health

Fruit & Vegetables
Eat at least 5 servings a day

This includes frozen, canned, dried and pure juices as well as fresh. Also included in this group are beans, including baked beans, pulses and lentils. The key for good health is to choose a wide variety - aiming for five different portions per day. A portion is approximately 80g, e.g. one medium apple or two medium plums.

Bread, Other Cereals & Potatoes
Eat 5 portions daily - about one third of of food intake

This group includes breakfast cereals, pasta, rice, noodles, oats and other cereals as well as bread and potatoes. You should aim to include at least one food from this group at each meal.

Milk & Dairy Foods
2-3 servings daily

Milk, cheese, yoghurt and fromage frais are included in this group, but not butter, eggs and cream. Serving sizes in this group vary, depending on how concentrated the food is, e.g. 1 serving of milk is 200ml, a serving of yoghurt is 150g and a serving of cheese is 30g.

Meat Fish & Alternatives
2-3 servings daily

This group includes eggs, poultry, and meat and fish products such as beefburgers and fishcakes. Some of these products can be high in fat - so it's best to choose lower fat versions of products, and trim visible fat from meat and poultry. Alternatives are non-meat sources of protein such as nuts, tofu, mycoprotein, textured vegetable protein (TVP) and kidney beans.

Food Containing Fat & Foods Containing Sugar
Eat in small quantities, 0-3 servings daily

These are foods high in fat and/or sugar. Butter, margarine, oil, mayonnaise, cream, crisps and fried foods are high in fat. Soft drinks, sweets and jam are high in sugar. Cakes, chocolate, biscuits, pastries and ice-cream are high in both. It is essential to include a small amount of fat in your diet, but most people need to eat less. The emphasis should be on unsaturated fat e.g. olive, sunflower and corn oil, rather than saturated fat which tends to come from animal products, cakes, biscuits and pastries.

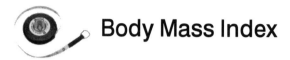

Body Mass Index

Body Mass Index is a number calculated from an individual's weight and height, that is used to determine whether a person is within, or outside of, a normal weight range. Use the Body Mass Index Chart to look up your BMI, and use the table below to see what range you fall into.

BMI	
Less than 20	Under Weight
20-25	Normal Weight
25-30	Over Weight
30-40	Obese
Over 40	Severely Obese

The spread from 20-25 shows that what is normal covers quite a big range. This is because 'normal' weight for height covers both men and women, and people of different shapes and body composition. A man would normally be expected to have a higher BMI than a woman of the same height, because men tend to have more muscle than women (women naturally have more fat) and muscle weighs more per square inch than fat. For the same reason a slim, muscular woman will have a higher BMI (i.e. weigh more) than a slim, not very muscular woman of the same height.

What's the Right Weight for You?

As a general rule women, unless they are very strong and muscular, will tend to look at their best at the lower end of the normal range, men around the middle to top of the range. 'Ideal weight' is a very individual thing, probably the best thing to do is set a goal within the normal range as described above and, as you get closer to it, adjust to a level at which you feel at your best.

BODY MASS INDEX CHART

WEIGHT IN STONES / LBS

	HEIGHT IN FEET / INCHES														
	4'6	4'8	4'10	5'0	5'2	5'4	5'6	5'8	5'10	6'0	6'2	6'4	6'6	6'8	6'10
6st 7	22.0	20.5	19.1	17.8	16.7	15.7	14.7	13.9	13.1	12.4	11.7	11.1	10.6	10.0	9.5
7st 0	23.7	22.1	20.6	19.2	18.0	16.9	15.9	15.0	14.1	13.3	12.6	12.0	11.4	10.8	10.3
7st 7	25.4	23.6	22.0	20.6	19.3	18.1	17.0	16.0	15.1	14.3	13.5	12.8	12.2	11.6	11.0
8st 0	27.1	25.2	23.5	22.0	20.6	19.3	18.1	17.1	16.1	15.2	14.4	13.7	13.0	12.3	11.8
8st 7	28.8	26.8	25.0	23.3	21.8	20.5	19.3	18.2	17.1	16.2	15.3	14.5	13.8	13.1	12.5
9st 0	30.5	28.4	26.4	24.7	23.1	21.7	20.4	19.2	18.1	17.2	16.2	15.4	14.6	13.9	13.2
9st 7	32.2	29.9	27.9	26.1	24.4	22.9	21.5	20.3	19.2	18.1	17.1	16.2	15.4	14.7	14.0
10st 0	33.9	31.5	29.4	27.4	25.7	24.1	22.7	21.4	20.2	19.1	18.0	17.1	16.2	15.4	14.7
10st 7	35.6	33.1	30.8	28.8	27.0	25.3	23.8	22.4	21.2	20.0	18.9	18.0	17.0	16.2	15.4
11st 0	37.3	34.7	32.3	30.2	28.3	26.5	24.9	23.5	22.2	21.0	19.8	18.8	17.9	17.0	16.2
11st 7	39.0	36.2	33.8	31.6	29.6	27.7	26.1	24.6	23.2	21.9	20.7	19.7	18.7	17.8	16.9
12st 0	40.7	37.8	35.2	32.9	30.8	28.9	27.2	25.6	24.2	22.9	21.6	20.5	19.5	18.5	17.6
12st 7	42.3	39.4	36.7	34.3	32.1	30.1	28.3	26.7	25.2	23.8	22.5	21.4	20.3	19.3	18.4
13st 0	44.0	41.0	38.2	35.7	33.4	31.4	29.5	27.8	26.2	24.8	23.5	22.2	21.1	20.1	19.1
13st 7	45.7	42.5	39.6	37.0	34.7	32.6	30.6	28.8	27.2	25.7	24.4	23.1	21.9	20.8	19.8
14st 0	47.4	44.1	41.1	38.4	36.0	33.8	31.7	29.9	28.2	26.7	25.3	23.9	22.7	21.6	20.6
14st 7	49.1	45.7	42.6	39.8	37.3	35.0	32.9	31.0	29.2	27.6	26.2	24.8	23.5	22.4	21.3
15st 0	50.8	47.3	44.0	41.2	38.5	36.2	34.0	32.0	30.2	28.6	27.1	25.7	24.4	23.2	22.0
15st 7	52.5	48.8	45.5	42.5	39.8	37.4	35.2	33.1	31.2	29.5	28.0	26.5	25.2	23.9	22.8
16st 0	54.2	50.4	47.0	43.9	41.1	38.6	36.3	34.2	32.3	30.5	28.9	27.4	26.0	24.7	23.5
16st 7	55.9	52.0	48.5	45.3	42.4	39.8	37.4	35.2	33.3	31.4	29.8	28.2	26.8	25.5	24.2
17st 0	57.6	53.6	49.9	46.6	43.7	41.0	38.6	36.3	34.3	32.4	30.7	29.1	27.6	26.2	25.0
17st 7	59.3	55.1	51.4	48.0	45.0	42.2	39.7	37.4	35.3	33.3	31.6	29.9	28.4	27.0	25.7
18st 0	61.0	56.7	52.9	49.4	46.3	43.4	40.8	38.5	36.3	34.3	32.5	30.8	29.2	27.8	26.4
18st 7	62.7	58.3	54.3	50.8	47.5	44.6	42.0	39.5	37.3	35.3	33.4	31.6	30.0	28.6	27.2
19st 0	64.4	59.9	55.8	52.1	48.8	45.8	43.1	40.6	38.3	36.2	34.3	32.5	30.8	29.3	27.9
19st 7	66.1	61.4	57.3	53.5	50.1	47.0	44.2	41.7	39.3	37.2	35.2	33.3	31.7	30.1	28.6
20st 0	67.8	63.0	58.7	54.9	51.4	48.2	45.4	42.7	40.3	38.1	36.1	34.2	32.5	30.9	29.4
20st 7	69.4	64.6	60.2	56.3	52.7	49.4	46.5	43.8	41.3	39.1	37.0	35.1	33.3	31.6	30.1
21st 0	71.1	66.2	61.7	57.6	54.0	50.6	47.6	44.9	42.3	40.0	37.9	35.9	34.1	32.4	30.9
21st 7	72.8	67.7	63.1	59.0	55.3	51.9	48.8	45.9	43.3	41.0	38.8	36.8	34.9	33.2	31.6
22st 0	74.5	69.3	64.6	60.4	56.5	53.1	49.9	47.0	44.4	41.9	39.7	37.6	35.7	34.0	32.3
22st 7	76.2	70.9	66.1	61.7	57.8	54.3	51.0	48.1	45.4	42.9	40.6	38.5	36.5	34.7	33.1
23st 0	77.9	72.5	67.5	63.1	59.1	55.5	52.2	49.1	46.4	43.8	41.5	39.3	37.3	35.5	33.8
23st 7	79.6	74.0	69.0	64.5	60.4	56.7	53.3	50.2	47.4	44.8	42.4	40.2	38.2	36.3	34.5
24st 0	81.3	75.6	70.5	65.9	61.7	57.9	54.4	51.3	48.4	45.7	43.3	41.0	39.0	37.0	35.3
24st 7	83.0	77.2	71.9	67.2	63.0	59.1	55.6	52.3	49.4	46.7	44.2	41.9	39.8	37.8	36.0
25st 0	84.7	78.8	73.4	68.6	64.2	60.3	56.7	53.4	50.4	47.6	45.1	42.8	40.6	38.6	36.7
25st 7	86.4	80.3	74.9	70.0	65.5	61.5	57.8	54.5	51.4	48.6	46.0	43.6	41.4	39.4	37.5
26st 0	88.1	81.9	76.3	71.3	66.8	62.7	59.0	55.5	52.4	49.5	46.9	44.5	42.2	40.1	38.2
26st 7	89.8	83.5	77.8	72.7	68.1	63.9	60.1	56.6	53.4	50.5	47.8	45.3	43.0	40.9	38.9
27st 0	91.5	85.1	79.3	74.1	69.4	65.1	61.2	57.7	54.4	51.5	48.7	46.2	43.8	41.7	39.7
27st 7	93.2	86.6	80.8	75.5	70.7	66.3	62.4	58.7	55.4	52.4	49.6	47.0	44.7	42.4	40.4
28st 0	94.9	88.2	82.2	76.8	72.0	67.5	63.5	59.8	56.4	53.4	50.5	47.9	45.5	43.2	41.1
28st 7	96.5	89.8	83.7	78.2	73.2	68.7	64.6	60.9	57.5	54.3	51.4	48.7	46.3	44.0	41.9
29st 0	98.2	91.4	85.2	79.6	74.5	69.9	65.8	62.0	58.5	55.3	52.3	49.6	47.1	44.8	42.6
29st 7	99.9	92.9	86.6	80.9	75.8	71.1	66.9	63.0	59.5	56.2	53.2	50.5	47.9	45.5	43.3

CALORIES REQUIRED TO MAINTAIN WEIGHT
ADULT MALES

AGE / ACTIVITY LEVEL

WEIGHT IN STONES / LBS	VERY SEDENTARY			MODERATELY SEDENTARY			MODERATELY ACTIVE			VERY ACTIVE		
	<30	30-60	60+	<30	30-60	60+	<30	30-60	60+	<30	30-60	60+
9st 0	1856	1827	1502	2010	1979	1627	2320	2284	1878	2784	2741	2254
9st 7	1913	1871	1547	2072	2026	1676	2391	2338	1933	2870	2806	2320
10st 0	1970	1914	1591	2134	2074	1724	2463	2393	1989	2955	2871	2387
10st 7	2027	1958	1636	2196	2121	1772	2534	2447	2045	3041	2937	2454
11st 0	2084	2001	1680	2258	2168	1820	2605	2502	2100	3127	3002	2520
11st 7	2141	2045	1724	2320	2215	1868	2677	2556	2156	3212	3067	2587
12st 0	2199	2088	1769	2382	2262	1916	2748	2611	2211	3298	3133	2654
12st 7	2256	2132	1813	2444	2310	1965	2820	2665	2267	3384	3198	2720
13st 0	2313	2175	1858	2506	2357	2013	2891	2719	2322	3470	3263	2787
13st 7	2370	2219	1902	2568	2404	2061	2963	2774	2378	3555	3329	2854
14st 0	2427	2262	1947	2630	2451	2109	3034	2828	2434	3641	3394	2920
14st 7	2484	2306	1991	2691	2498	2157	3106	2883	2489	3727	3459	2987
15st 0	2542	2350	2036	2753	2545	2205	3177	2937	2545	3813	3525	3054
15st 7	2599	2393	2080	2815	2593	2253	3248	2992	2600	3898	3590	3120
16st 0	2656	2437	2125	2877	2640	2302	3320	3046	2656	3984	3655	3187
16st 7	2713	2480	2169	2939	2687	2350	3391	3100	2711	4070	3721	3254
17st 0	2770	2524	2213	3001	2734	2398	3463	3155	2767	4155	3786	3320
17st 7	2827	2567	2258	3063	2781	2446	3534	3209	2823	4241	3851	3387
18st 0	2884	2611	2302	3125	2828	2494	3606	3264	2878	4327	3917	3454
18st 7	2942	2654	2347	3187	2876	2542	3677	3318	2934	4413	3982	3520
19st 0	2999	2698	2391	3249	2923	2591	3749	3373	2989	4498	4047	3587
19st 7	3056	2741	2436	3311	2970	2639	3820	3427	3045	4584	4112	3654
20st 0	3113	2785	2480	3373	3017	2687	3891	3481	3100	4670	4178	3721
20st 7	3170	2829	2525	3434	3064	2735	3963	3536	3156	4756	4243	3787
21st 0	3227	2872	2569	3496	3112	2783	4034	3590	3211	4841	4308	3854
21st 7	3285	2916	2614	3558	3159	2831	4106	3645	3267	4927	4374	3921
22st 0	3342	2959	2658	3620	3206	2880	4177	3699	3323	5013	4439	3987
22st 7	3399	3003	2702	3682	3253	2928	4249	3754	3378	5098	4504	4054
23st 0	3456	3046	2747	3744	3300	2976	4320	3808	3434	5184	4570	4121
23st 7	3513	3090	2791	3806	3347	3024	4392	3862	3489	5270	4635	4187
24st 0	3570	3133	2836	3868	3395	3072	4463	3917	3545	5356	4700	4254
24st 7	3627	3177	2880	3930	3442	3120	4534	3971	3600	5441	4766	4321
25st 0	3685	3220	2925	3992	3489	3168	4606	4026	3656	5527	4831	4387
25st 7	3742	3264	2969	4054	3536	3217	4677	4080	3712	5613	4896	4454
26st 0	3799	3308	3014	4116	3583	3265	4749	4135	3767	5699	4962	4521
26st 7	3856	3351	3058	4177	3630	3313	4820	4189	3823	5784	5027	4587
27st 0	3913	3395	3103	4239	3678	3361	4892	4243	3878	5870	5092	4654
27st 7	3970	3438	3147	4301	3725	3409	4963	4298	3934	5956	5158	4721
28st 0	4028	3482	3191	4363	3772	3457	5035	4352	3989	6042	5223	4787
28st 7	4085	3525	3236	4425	3819	3506	5106	4407	4045	6127	5288	4854
29st 0	4142	3569	3280	4487	3866	3554	5177	4461	4101	6213	5354	4921
29st 7	4199	3612	3325	4549	3913	3602	5249	4516	4156	6299	5419	4987
30st 0	4256	3656	3369	4611	3961	3650	5320	4570	4212	6384	5484	5054

CALORIES REQUIRED TO MAINTAIN WEIGHT
ADULT FEMALES

AGE / ACTIVITY LEVEL

WEIGHT IN STONES / LBS	VERY SEDENTARY			MODERATELY SEDENTARY			MODERATELY ACTIVE			VERY ACTIVE		
	<30	30-60	60+	<30	30-60	60+	<30	30-60	60+	<30	30-60	60+
7st 7	1425	1473	1304	1544	1596	1412	1781	1841	1630	2138	2210	1956
8st 0	1481	1504	1338	1605	1629	1450	1852	1880	1673	2222	2256	2008
8st 7	1537	1535	1373	1666	1663	1487	1922	1919	1716	2306	2302	2059
9st 0	1594	1566	1407	1726	1696	1524	1992	1957	1759	2391	2349	2111
9st 7	1650	1596	1442	1787	1729	1562	2062	1996	1802	2475	2395	2163
10st 0	1706	1627	1476	1848	1763	1599	2133	2034	1845	2559	2441	2214
10st 7	1762	1658	1511	1909	1796	1637	2203	2073	1888	2644	2487	2266
11st 0	1819	1689	1545	1970	1830	1674	2273	2111	1931	2728	2534	2318
11st 7	1875	1720	1580	2031	1863	1711	2344	2150	1975	2813	2580	2370
12st 0	1931	1751	1614	2092	1897	1749	2414	2188	2018	2897	2626	2421
12st 7	1987	1781	1648	2153	1930	1786	2484	2227	2061	2981	2672	2473
13st 0	2044	1812	1683	2214	1963	1823	2555	2266	2104	3066	2719	2525
13st 7	2100	1843	1717	2275	1997	1861	2625	2304	2147	3150	2765	2576
14st 0	2156	1874	1752	2336	2030	1898	2695	2343	2190	3234	2811	2628
14st 7	2212	1905	1786	2397	2064	1935	2766	2381	2233	3319	2858	2680
15st 0	2269	1936	1821	2458	2097	1973	2836	2420	2276	3403	2904	2732
15st 7	2325	1967	1855	2519	2130	2010	2906	2458	2319	3488	2950	2783
16st 0	2381	1997	1890	2580	2164	2047	2976	2497	2362	3572	2996	2835
16st 7	2437	2028	1924	2640	2197	2085	3047	2535	2405	3656	3043	2887
17st 0	2494	2059	1959	2701	2231	2122	3117	2574	2449	3741	3089	2938
17st 7	2550	2090	1993	2762	2264	2159	3187	2613	2492	3825	3135	2990
18st 0	2606	2121	2028	2823	2298	2197	3258	2651	2535	3909	3181	3042
18st 7	2662	2152	2062	2884	2331	2234	3328	2690	2578	3994	3228	3093
19st 0	2719	2182	2097	2945	2364	2271	3398	2728	2621	4078	3274	3145
19st 7	2775	2213	2131	3006	2398	2309	3469	2767	2664	4162	3320	3197
20st 0	2831	2244	2166	3067	2431	2346	3539	2805	2707	4247	3366	3249
20st 7	2887	2275	2200	3128	2465	2383	3609	2844	2750	4331	3413	3300
21st 0	2944	2306	2235	3189	2498	2421	3680	2882	2793	4416	3459	3352
21st 7	3000	2337	2269	3250	2531	2458	3750	2921	2836	4500	3505	3404
22st 0	3056	2368	2303	3311	2565	2495	3820	2960	2879	4584	3552	3455
22st 7	3112	2398	2338	3372	2598	2533	3890	2998	2923	4669	3598	3507
23st 0	3169	2429	2372	3433	2632	2570	3961	3037	2966	4753	3644	3559
23st 7	3225	2460	2407	3494	2665	2608	4031	3075	3009	4837	3690	3611
24st 0	3281	2491	2441	3554	2699	2645	4101	3114	3052	4922	3737	3662
24st 7	3337	2522	2476	3615	2732	2682	4172	3152	3095	5006	3783	3714
25st 0	3394	2553	2510	3676	2765	2720	4242	3191	3138	5091	3829	3766
25st 7	3450	2583	2545	3737	2799	2757	4312	3229	3181	5175	3875	3817
26st 0	3506	2614	2579	3798	2832	2794	4383	3268	3224	5259	3922	3869
26st 7	3562	2645	2614	3859	2866	2832	4453	3307	3267	5344	3968	3921
27st 0	3618	2676	2648	3920	2899	2869	4523	3345	3310	5428	4014	3973
27st 7	3675	2707	2683	3981	2932	2906	4594	3384	3353	5512	4060	4024
28st 0	3731	2738	2717	4042	2966	2944	4664	3422	3397	5597	4107	4076
28st 7	3787	2768	2752	4103	2999	2981	4734	3461	3440	5681	4153	4128

Calories Burned in Exercise

This table shows the approximate number of extra* calories that would be burned in a five minute period of exercise activity.

Activity	Calories Burned in 5 Minutes
Aerobics, Low Impact	25
Badminton, Recreational	17
Cross Trainer	30
Cycling, Recreational, 5mph	17
Dancing, Modern, Moderate	13
Fencing	24
Gardening, Weeding	19
Hill Walking, Up and Down, Recreational	22
Jogging	30
Kick Boxing	30
Netball Playing	23
Rebounding	18
Roller Skating	30
Rowing Machine, Moderate	30
Running, 7.5mph	48
Situps, Continuous	17
Skiing, Moderate	30
Skipping, Moderate	30
Squash Playing	39
Tennis Playing, Recreational	26
Toning Exercises	17
Trampolining	17
Volleyball, Recreational	10
Walking, Uphill, 15% Gradient, Moderate	43
Walking Up and Down Stairs, Moderate	34
Walking, 4mph	24
Weight Training, Moderate	12
Yoga	13

*Extra calories are those in addition to your normal daily calorie needs.

Food and Exercise Diary

DATE:

/   /

DAILY CALORIE ALLOWANCE [ ] **A**

FOOD/DRINK CONSUMED	SERVING SIZE	CALORIES

You are aiming for your Calorie Balance (Box D) to be as close to zero as possible - ie. you consume the number of calories you need.

Your Daily Calorie Allowance (Box A) should be set to lose 1-2lb a week, or maintain weight, depending on your goals.

Daily Calorie Allowance (A) *plus* Extra Calories used in Exercise (C) *minus* Total Calories Consumed (B) *equals* Calorie Balance (D)

$$A + C - B = D$$

TOTAL CALORIES CONSUMED [ ] **B**

EXERCISE/ACTIVITY	NO. MINS	CALORIES

CALORIES USED IN EXERCISE [ ] **C**

CALORIE BALANCE [ ] **D**

Food Information

Nutritional Information

Calorie values are given per serving, plus calorie and nutrition values per 100g of product. This makes it easy to compare the proportions of fat, protein, carbohydrate and fibre in each food.

The values given are for uncooked, unprepared foods unless otherwise stated.

Finding Foods

The Calorie, Carb & Fat Bible has a new, improved format for this edition. Most foods are grouped together by type, and then put in to alphabetical order. This makes it easy to compare different brands, and will help you to find lower calorie and/or fat alternatives where they are available.

This format also makes it easier to locate foods. Foods are categorised by their main characteristics so, for example, if it is bread, ciabatta or white sliced, you'll find it under "Bread".

There are, however, some foods which are not so easy to categorise, especially combination foods like ready meals. The following pointers will help you to find your way around the book until you get to know it a little better.

FILLED ROLLS AND SANDWICHES - Bagels, baguettes, etc which are filled are listed as "Bagels (filled)" etc. Sandwiches are under "Sandwiches".

Serving sizes vary greatly from person to person...it's very important to be accurate.

CURRIES - Popular types of curry, like Balti or Jalfrezi, are listed under their individual types. Unspecified or lesser known types are listed under their main ingredient.

BURGERS - All burgers, including chicken-type sandwiches from fast-food outlets, are listed under "Burgers".

CHIPS & FRIES - Are listed seperately, depending on the name of the particular brand. All other types of potato are listed under "Potatoes".

SWEETS & CHOCOLATES - Well-known brands, eg. Aero, Mars Bar, are listed under their brand names. Others are listed under "Chocolate" (for bars) and "Chocolates" (for individual sweets).

READY MEALS - Popular types of dishes are listed under their type, eg. "Chow Mein", "Casserole", "Hot Pot", etc. Others are listed by their main ingredient, eg. "Chicken With", "Chicken In", etc.

Serving Sizes

Many ready-meal type foods are given with calories for the full pack size, so that an individual serving can be worked out by estimating the proportion of the pack that has been consumed. For example, if you have eaten a quarter of a packaged pasta dish, divide the calorie value given for the whole pack by 4 to determine the number of calories you have consumed. Where serving sizes are not appropriate, or unknown, values are given per 1oz/28g. Serving sizes vary greatly from person to person and, if you are trying to lose weight, it's very important to be accurate – especially with foods that are very high in calories such as those that contain a fair amount of fat, sugar, cream, cheese, alcohol etc.

Food Data

Nutrition information for basic (non-branded) foods is from The Composition of Foods 5th Edition (1991) Reproduced under licence from the Controller of Her Majesty's Stationery Office.

Nutrition information for branded goods is from details supplied by retailers and manufacturers, and researched by Weight Loss Resources staff from packaging information. Calorie and nutrition data for all food and drink items are typical values.

The publishers gratefully acknowledge all the manufacturers and retailers who have provided information on their products. All product names, trademarks or registered trademarks belong to their respective owners and are used only for the purpose of identifying products.

Caution

The information in The Calorie, Carb and Fat Bible is intended as an aid to weight loss and weight maintenance, and is not medical advice. If you suffer from, or think you may suffer from a medical condition you should consult your doctor before starting a weight loss and/or exercise regime, If you start exercising after a period of relative inactivity, you should start slowly and consult your doctor if you experience pain, distress or other symptons.

Abbreviations

kcal	kilocalories / calories	tsp	teaspoon
prot	protein	tbsp	tablespoon
carb	carbohydrate	dtsp	desertspoon
sm	small		
med	medium		
lge	large		

Brand Abbreviations

Asda
Good for You .... GFY

English Provender Co. .. EPC

Marks & Spencer
Count on Us .... COU
Food to Go .... FTG

Morrisons
Better For You .... BFY

Sainsbury's
Be Good to Yourself .... BGTY
Taste the Difference .... TTD
Way to Five .... WTF

	Measure INFO/WEIGHT	per Measure KCAL	Nutrition Values per 100g / 100ml				
			KCAL	PROT	CARB	FAT	FIBRE
ACKEE,							
Canned, Drained	1oz/28g	42	151	2.9	0.8	15.2	0.0
ADVOCAAT,							
Average	1 Shot/25ml	65	260	4.7	28.4	6.3	0.0
AERO,							
Creamy White Centre, Nestle	1 Bar/46g	244	530	7.6	57.4	30.0	0.0
Honeycomb, Nestle*	1 Serving/40g	199	497	5.9	62.2	25.0	0.0
Minis, Nestle*	1 Bar/11g	57	518	6.8	58.1	28.7	0.8
Mint, Nestle*	1 Bar/48g	249	518	6.8	58.1	28.7	0.8
Nestle*	1 Bar/46g	238	518	6.8	58.1	28.7	0.8
ALCOPOPS,							
(Calculated Estimate)	1fl oz/30ml	22	73	0.3	5.0	0.0	0.0
Blue Original WKD	1 Bottle/330ml	244	74	0.3	5.1	0.0	0.0
Hooch*, Vodka, (Calculated Estimate)	1 Bottle/330ml	244	74	0.3	5.1	0.0	0.0
ALFALFA SPROUTS,							
Raw	1oz/28g	7	24	4.0	0.4	0.7	1.7
ALMONDS,							
Blanched, Average	1oz/28g	171	610	25.0	7.2	53.5	8.5
Ground, Average	1 Serving/10g	62	625	24.0	6.6	55.8	7.4
Smoked, Sainsbury's*	1 Serving/40g	264	660	26.0	9.0	57.8	7.5
Toasted, Average	1oz/28g	178	634	25.0	6.6	56.5	6.6
Whole, Average	1 Portion/20g	122	612	23.4	8.1	54.8	8.4
Yoghurt Coated, Holland & Barrett*	1 Pack/100g	536	536	10.9	45.3	37.0	2.8
ALOO TIKKI,							
Budgens*	1 Serving/25.2g	51	202	5.9	27.8	7.5	4.1
Mini, Indian Snack Selection, Occasions, Sainsbury's*	1 Tikki/17.9g	34	190	4.4	27.6	6.9	3.2
ANCHOVIES,							
Fillets, Flat, John West*	1 Can/50g	113	226	25.0	0.1	14.0	0.0
Fillets, Marinated, Waitrose*	1 Serving/5g	9	177	22.0	2.0	9.0	0.0
In Oil, Canned, Drained, Average	1 Serving/30g	58	194	22.9	0.0	11.3	0.0
Salted, Finest, Tesco*	1 Serving/10g	9	93	18.2	0.0	2.2	0.0
With Olives, Marinated, H Forman & Son*	1 Pack/200g	320	160	20.2	0.2	8.7	0.0
ANGEL DELIGHT,							
Banana Flavour, Kraft*	1 Sachet/59g	289	490	2.5	72.0	21.0	0.0
Banana Toffee Flavour, No Added Sugar, Kraft*	1 Sachet/59g	292	495	4.8	58.5	26.5	0.0
Butterscotch Flavour, Kraft*	1 Sachet/59g	280	475	2.4	73.5	19.0	0.0
Chocolate Flavour With Topples, Kraft*	1 Sachet/59g	274	465	5.0	67.0	20.0	0.5
Chocolate Flavour, Kraft*	1 Sachet/59g	266	450	6.3	56.5	22.0	0.6
Chocolate Flavour, No Added Sugar, Kraft*	1 Sachet/59g	266	450	6.3	56.5	22.0	0.0
Forest Fruit Flavour, Kraft*	1 Sachet/59g	289	490	2.5	71.5	21.5	0.0
Raspberry Flavour, Kraft*	1 Sachet/59g	289	490	2.5	72.0	21.0	0.0
Raspberry Flavour, No Added Sugar, Kraft*	1 Sachet/59g	292	495	4.8	59.5	26.0	0.0
Strawberry Flavour With Topples, Kraft*	1 Sachet/59g	266	450	2.8	74.5	14.0	0.0
Strawberry Flavour, Kraft*	1 Sachet/59g	286	485	2.5	71.0	21.0	0.0
Strawberry Flavour, No Added Sugar, Kraft*	1 Sachet/59g	289	490	4.8	59.0	26.5	0.0
Tangerine Flavour, No Added Sugar, Kraft*	1 Sachet/59g	292	495	4.8	58.0	27.0	0.9
Toffee Flavour, Kraft*	1 Sachet/59g	283	480	2.6	70.0	21.0	0.0
Vanilla Ice Cream Flavour, Kraft*	1 Sachet/59g	289	490	2.5	71.5	21.5	0.0
Vanilla Ice Cream Flavour, No Added Sugar, Kraft*	1 Sachet/59g	295	500	4.8	59.5	27.0	0.0
ANTIPASTO,							
Artichoke, Sainsbury's*	1 Serving/50g	68	135	2.0	3.6	12.5	2.3
Mixed Mushroom, Sainsbury's*	¼ Jar/72g	70	97	2.7	1.4	9.0	3.7
Mixed Pepper, Sainsbury's*	½ Jar/145g	183	126	1.5	11.0	8.4	1.8
Seafood, Drained, Sainsbury's*	½ Jar/84g	150	178	14.3	4.1	11.6	1.4

INFO/WEIGHT	Measure	per Measure KCAL	Nutrition Values per 100g / 100ml				
			KCAL	PROT	CARB	FAT	FIBRE
ANTIPASTO,							
Sun Dried Tomato, Sainsbury's*	1 Tomato/5g	12	232	4.7	15.5	16.8	6.6
Wild Mushroom, Sainsbury's*	1 Serving/100g	97	97	2.7	1.4	9.0	3.7
APPLES,							
Bites, Average	1 Pack/118g	58	49	0.3	11.7	0.1	2.2
Braeburn, Average	1 Apple/65g	31	48	0.4	11.3	0.1	1.8
Cape, Tesco*	1 Apple/100g	50	50	0.4	11.4	0.1	1.8
Cooking, Baked With Sugar, Flesh Only	1 Serving/140g	109	78	0.5	20.1	0.1	1.7
Cooking, Raw, Peeled	1oz/28g	10	35	0.3	8.9	0.1	1.6
Cooking, Stewed With Sugar	1 Serving/140g	104	74	0.3	19.1	0.1	1.2
Cooking, Stewed Without Sugar	1 Serving/140g	46	33	0.3	8.1	0.1	1.5
Dried, Average	1 Pack/250g	554	222	1.1	57.3	0.3	6.7
Empire, Tesco*	1 Apple/100g	50	50	0.4	11.8	0.1	1.8
English Cox, Average	1 Apple/108g	53	49	0.4	11.6	0.1	2.2
Gala, Average	1 Apple/152g	74	49	0.4	11.5	0.1	1.4
Golden Delicious, Average	1 Med Apple/102g	49	48	0.4	11.5	0.1	1.7
Granny Smith, Average	1 Apple/241g	120	50	0.4	11.9	0.1	2.0
Pink Lady, Average	1 Apple/125g	62	50	0.4	11.7	0.1	1.8
Red, Delicious, Asda*	1 Apple/170g	90	53	0.0	14.0	0.1	2.5
Rubinette, Tesco*	1 Apple/123g	62	50	0.4	11.8	0.1	1.8
Slices, Canned, Average	1oz/28g	8	27	0.2	6.4	0.1	1.5
Stewed, Sainsbury's*	¼ Can/100g	71	71	0.2	17.4	0.0	1.2
APPLETISE,							
Schweppes*	1 Glass/200ml	98	49	0.0	11.8	0.0	0.0
APRICOTS,							
Breakfast, In Fruit Juice, Average	1oz/28g	29	102	0.5	24.0	0.4	1.7
Canned, In Syrup	1oz/28g	18	63	0.4	16.1	0.1	0.9
Dried, Average	1/5 Pack/50g	86	171	3.6	37.4	0.5	6.3
Halves, In Fruit Juice, Average	1 Sm Can/221g	87	40	0.5	9.2	0.1	1.0
Raw, Average	1 Apricot/40g	13	34	1.0	7.5	0.1	1.5
ARCHERS*,							
Peach Aqua, Schnapps, Archers (Calculated Estimate)	1 Bottle/275ml	206	75	0.3	5.1	0.0	0.0
Peach Schnapps, (Calculated Estimate)	1 Shot/35ml	91	260	0.0	0.0	0.0	0.0
ARTICHOKE,							
Hearts, Canned, Drained, Average	½ Can/117g	35	30	1.9	5.5	0.1	2.2
Hearts, Chargrilled in Olive Oil, TTD, Sainsbury's*	¼ Jar/73g	150	205	1.0	3.4	20.8	0.0
Hearts, Marinated & Grilled, Waitrose*	1 Serving/50g	57	114	3.0	3.0	10.0	3.0
Raw, Fresh	1oz/28g	13	47	3.3	10.5	0.2	5.4
ASPARAGUS,							
Boiled in Salted Water	5 Spears/125g	33	26	3.4	1.4	0.8	1.4
Canned, Average	1 Can/250g	48	19	2.3	2.0	0.2	1.6
Raw, Average	1oz/28g	7	25	3.1	1.8	0.7	1.8
AUBERGINE,							
Baked Topped, Marks & Spencer*	1 Serving/150g	165	110	2.4	7.4	7.7	0.9
Fried, Average	1oz/28g	85	302	1.2	2.8	31.9	2.3
In Hot Sauce, Yarden*	1 Serving/35g	96	273	1.5	8.8	25.8	0.0
Marinated & Grilled, Waitrose*	½ Pack/100g	106	106	1.0	3.0	10.0	2.0
Parmigiana, Marks & Spencer*	1 Pack/350g	333	95	4.6	7.6	5.3	1.1
Raw, Fresh	1 Sm/120g	18	15	0.9	2.2	0.4	2.0
AUTHENTIC MIX,							
Bacon & Mushroom Taglietelle, Schwartz*	1 Pack/33g	112	340	9.0	73.8	0.6	0.1
Bombay Potatoes, Schwartz*	1 Pack/33g	110	332	15.3	61.7	2.7	0.2
Cajun Chicken, Schwartz*	1 Pack/38g	112	294	6.6	61.5	2.4	0.0
Chargrilled Chicken Pasta, Schwartz*	¼ Packet/9g	28	316	9.1	59.7	4.5	0.5

	Measure INFO/WEIGHT	per Measure KCAL	Nutrition Values per 100g / 100ml				
			KCAL	PROT	CARB	FAT	FIBRE
AUTHENTIC MIX,							
Chicken & White Wine, Schwartz*	½ Pack/35g	113	322	10.3	65.2	2.2	0.3
Chicken Balti, Schwartz*	1oz/28g	91	324	13.5	54.4	5.8	0.0
Chilli Con Carne, Schwartz*	1 Pack/40.9g	126	308	8.2	64.6	1.9	0.5
Creamy Pork & Mushroom, Schwartz*	¼ Pack/10g	30	302	9.9	63.3	1.0	1.0
Creamy Tikka Masala, Schwartz*	1oz/28g	97	346	13.7	63.6	4.1	0.2
For Chicken Fajitas, Schwartz*	1 Pack/35g	114	325	10.4	63.3	3.3	0.5
For Spagetti Bolognese, Schwartz*	1 Pack/40g	120	300	10.4	61.2	1.5	0.4
For Spaghetti Carbonara, Schwartz*	½ Pack/16g	70	436	9.5	56.0	19.3	0.3
Hot Chili Con Carne, Schwartz*	1 Pack/41g	126	308	10.6	61.8	0.8	0.2
Lamb Casserole, Schwartz*	1 Pack/35g	116	332	7.7	68.0	3.3	1.3
Lasagne, Schwartz*	1 Pack/36g	113	313	6.6	70.1	0.7	0.3
Mexican Chili Chicken, Schwartz*	1 Pack/35g	113	322	8.8	64.2	3.3	0.4
Thai Green Curry, Schwartz*	1 Serving/41g	141	344	11.2	67.6	3.2	0.2
Thai Lemon Chicken, Schwartz*	1 Serving/10g	37	365	3.6	78.3	4.2	0.0
Thai Red Curry, Schwartz*	1 Serving/20g	70	349	5.7	70.2	5.0	0.7
Thai Yellow Curry, Schwartz*	1 Packet/35g	126	360	7.3	64.2	8.2	0.8
Tuna Napolitana, Schwartz*	1 Serving/30g	107	357	10.3	49.7	13.0	0.3
AVOCADO,							
Average	1 Med/145g	276	190	1.9	1.9	19.5	3.4

A

INFO/WEIGHT	Measure	per Measure KCAL	Nutrition Values per 100g / 100ml				
			KCAL	PROT	CARB	FAT	FIBRE
BACARDI*,							
37.5% Volume	1 Shot/25ml	52	207	0.0	0.0	0.0	0.0
40% Volume	1 Shot/25ml	56	222	0.0	0.0	0.0	0.0
Bacardi & Diet Cola, Meadwestvaco*	1 Serving/275ml	85	31	0.0	1.0	0.0	0.0
Breezer (Calculated Estimate)	1 Bottle/275ml	198	72	0.3	5.0	0.0	0.0
Breezer, Lemon, Diet	1 Bottle/275ml	96	35	0.0	1.2	0.0	0.0
Breezer, Orange & Vanilla, Diet	1 Bottle/275ml	96	35	0.0	1.2	0.0	0.0
BACON,							
Average	1 Rasher/25g	74	295	15.0	22.9	16.1	0.9
Back, Dry Cured, Average	1 Rasher/31g	77	250	28.1	0.3	15.1	0.3
Back, Dry Fried Or Grilled, Average	1 Rasher/25g	76	304	26.5	0.1	21.9	0.0
Back, Lean, Average	1 Rasher/33g	57	174	16.3	0.1	12.0	0.5
Back, Smoked, Average	1 Rasher/25g	66	265	20.9	0.0	19.9	0.0
Back, Smoked, Lean, Average	2 Rashers/28g	46	163	28.2	1.1	5.0	0.2
Back, Smoked, Rindless, Average	1oz/28g	68	241	21.0	0.1	17.4	0.0
Back, Tendersweet, Average	1 Rasher/25g	63	251	29.8	0.5	14.4	0.1
Back, Unsmoked, Average	1 Rasher/32g	78	243	21.3	0.4	17.3	0.0
Back, Unsmoked, GFY, Asda*	1 Av Rasher/28g	30	107	21.0	0.0	2.5	0.0
Back, Unsmoked, Rindless, Average	1 Rasher/23g	56	241	22.5	0.0	16.9	0.0
Chops, Average	1oz/28g	62	222	22.3	0.0	14.8	0.0
Chops, BBQ Sainsbury's*	1 Chop/78g	184	236	21.2	4.6	14.8	0.1
Chops, in Cheese Sauce, Tesco*	1 Serving/185g	311	168	16.3	5.6	8.9	1.5
Collar Joint, Lean & Fat, Boiled	1oz/28g	91	325	20.4	0.0	27.0	0.0
Collar Joint, Lean & Fat, Raw	1oz/28g	89	319	14.6	0.0	28.9	0.0
Collar Joint, Lean Only, Boiled	1oz/28g	53	191	26.0	0.0	9.7	0.0
Fat Only, Cooked, Average	1oz/28g	194	692	9.3	0.0	72.8	0.0
Fat Only, Raw, Average	1oz/28g	209	747	4.8	0.0	80.9	0.0
Gammon Rasher, Lean Only, Grilled	1oz/28g	48	172	31.4	0.0	5.2	0.0
Joint, British, Sainburys*	1 Serving/100g	253	253	20.6	1.3	18.5	0.0
Joint, Smoked, Roasted, Asda*	1 Serving/100g	184	184	21.0	0.2	11.0	0.0
Lean Only, Fried, Average	1 Rasher/25g	83	332	32.8	0.0	22.3	0.0
Lean Only, Grilled, Average	1 Rasher/25g	73	292	30.5	0.0	18.9	0.0
Lean, Average	1oz/28g	40	142	19.6	0.9	6.7	0.2
Loin Rashers, Unsmoked, Less Than 3% Fat, Safeway*	1 Rasher/25g	22	87	19.6	0.0	0.9	0.0
Loin Steaks, Grilled	1 Serving/120g	229	191	25.9	0.0	9.7	0.0
Medallions, Average	1 Rasher/18g	27	151	29.4	0.9	3.3	0.1
Middle, Fried	1 Rasher/40g	140	350	23.4	0.0	28.5	0.0
Middle, Grilled	1 Rasher/40g	123	307	24.8	0.0	23.1	0.0
Middle, Raw	1 Rasher/43g	104	241	15.2	0.0	20.0	0.0
Rindless, Average	1 Rasher/20g	30	151	18.5	0.0	8.5	0.0
Smoked, Average	1oz/28g	46	166	24.8	0.3	7.4	0.0
Smoked, Back, Reduced Salt, Sainsbury's*	1 Rasher/20.3g	49	246	22.2	0.1	17.1	0.6
Smoked, Crispy, Cooked, Average	1 Serving/10g	46	460	53.0	2.1	26.9	0.0
Smoked, Rindless, Average	1 Rasher/20g	21	106	19.8	0.0	3.0	0.0
Streaky, Average	1 Serving/50g	135	270	20.0	0.0	21.0	0.0
Streaky, Cooked, Average	1 Rasher/20g	68	342	22.4	0.3	27.8	0.0
BACON BITS,							
Average	1oz/28g	66	235	19.6	0.0	17.4	0.0
BACON VEGETARIAN,							
Rashers, Morning Star*	2 Rashers/16.5g	59	345	11.5	13.4	27.6	3.9
Rashers, Redwood*	1 Serving/18g	33	185	23.8	12.4	4.4	4.4
Rashers, Tesco*	1 Rasher/20g	47	237	19.9	14.5	11.0	6.0
Realeat*	2 Rashers/35.7g	99	275	28.0	26.6	6.2	1.7

INFO/WEIGHT	Measure	per Measure KCAL	Nutrition Values per 100g / 100ml				
			KCAL	PROT	CARB	FAT	FIBRE
BAGEL,							
Bacon & Soft Cheese, Boots*	1 Serving/148g	481	325	12.0	31.0	17.0	2.2
Cheese & Jalapeno, Starbucks*	1 Bagel/115g	292	254	10.8	45.8	3.1	1.5
Chicken Caesar, Ixxy's*	1 Serving/213.8g	404	189	9.6	25.8	5.3	0.0
Chicken, Lemon & Watercress, Safeway*	1 Pack/153g	329	215	12.8	28.2	4.1	0.0
Cream Cheese & Crispy Bacon, Benjys*	1 Bagel/149g	329	221	7.1	35.1	5.9	0.0
Cream Cheese, Marks & Spencer*	1 Bagel/22.5g	81	352	7.8	31.0	21.8	1.8
Ham & Pesto, COU, Marks & Spencer*	1 Pack/173g	260	150	11.1	23.5	1.4	1.7
Smoked Salmon & Cream Cheese, Marks & Spencer*	1 Bagel/23g	64	280	10.9	31.7	12.2	2.9
Smoked Salmon & Soft Cheese, Shapers, Boots*	1 Pack/158g	344	218	12.0	29.0	6.0	0.9
Soft Cheese & Smoked Salmon, American, Sainsbury's*	1 Bagel/130.9g	356	272	8.3	31.8	12.4	1.7
Tuna & Sweetcorn Relish, Safeway*	1 Bagel/162g	284	175	11.5	26.2	2.7	0.0
Tuna Salad, BGTY, Sainsbury's*	1 Bagel/170g	325	191	10.4	26.0	4.2	1.0
Turkey, Pastrami & American Mustard, Shapers, Boots*	1 Bagel/146g	296	203	11.0	32.0	3.4	1.4
BAGUETTE,							
All Day Breakfast, Darwins Deli*	1 Serving/184g	498	271	13.4	31.9	11.7	0.0
Baton, Chicken & Bacon, Tesco*	1 Pack/201g	511	254	9.4	24.7	13.1	1.7
Cheddar & Baby Plum Tomato, Pret A Manger*	1 Baguette/300g	625	208	6.7	18.5	11.9	1.0
Cheese & Chive, Safeway*	¼ Baguette/65.5g	216	333	7.9	37.1	14.7	1.4
Cheese & Ham, French, Shell*	1oz/28g	82	292	8.9	37.2	12.0	0.0
Cheese & Onion, Asda*	1oz/28g	102	366	12.0	39.8	17.6	1.3
Cheese, Mixed, & Spring Onion, Asda*	1 Pack/190g	629	331	9.5	32.1	18.3	1.3
Cheese, Tomato & Basil, Asda*	¼ Bread/42g	138	329	10.0	40.8	14.0	1.3
Chicken & Mayonnaise, Asda*	1 Pack/190g	407	214	9.7	30.5	8.7	1.3
Chicken & Spicy Tomato, Snack, Sainsbury's*	1 Baguette/160g	344	215	14.1	31.2	3.7	2.2
Chicken & Stuffing, Hot, Sainsbury's*	1 Baguette/227g	543	239	13.7	29.6	7.2	0.0
Chicken Salad, Asda*	1 Serving/158.3g	325	206	9.0	29.0	6.0	2.1
Chicken Tikka, Asda*	1 Pack/190g	439	231	10.4	32.8	9.4	1.3
Chicken Tikka, Hot, Sainsbury's*	1 Pack/190g	386	203	8.5	28.4	6.1	0.0
Chicken, Honey & Mustard, BGTY, Sainsbury's*	1 Pack/186.8g	340	182	11.0	30.0	2.0	0.0
Egg & Tomato, Breakfast, Pret A Manger*	1 Av Pack/230g	281	122	5.4	15.9	5.3	2.5
Egg Mayonnaise & Cress, Cafe, Sainsbury's*	1 Pack/100g	480	480	13.8	60.2	20.4	0.0
Ham & Cheese, Snack 'n' Go, Sainsbury's*	1 Baguette/178g	381	215	12.6	29.6	5.1	1.9
Ham & Greve, Pret A Manger*	1 Av Pack/350g	535	153	9.8	16.1	5.4	1.2
Prawn Mayonnaise, Asda*	1 Pack/190g	399	210	9.1	32.5	4.9	1.3
Prawn, French, Shell*	1 Baguette/63g	171	272	9.7	32.4	11.5	0.0
Salmon & Egg, Pret A Manger*	1 Av Pack/230g	349	152	7.2	15.3	6.9	1.5
Steak & Onion, Snack 'n' Go, Sainsbury's*	1 Baguette/177g	396	225	14.3	30.6	5.0	2.2
Tuna Mayo, Pret A Manger*	1 Av Pack/230g	535	233	10.8	25.0	10.0	1.7
Tuna Melt, Sainsbury's*	1 Serving/204g	373	183	11.3	25.8	3.9	0.0
Turkey & Ham, Asda*	1 Baguette/360g	774	215	11.6	30.7	5.1	1.3
BAILEYS*,							
Irish Cream, Original	1 Glass/37g	130	350	3.2	20.0	15.7	0.0
BAKE,							
Aubergine & Spinach, BGTY, Sainsbury's*	1 Pack/360g	148	41	2.2	4.0	1.8	1.3
Bean & Pasta, Asda*	1 Pack/450g	599	133	5.0	17.0	5.0	1.7
Broccoli & Three Cheese, Marks & Spencer*	1 Serving/225g	315	140	6.3	6.3	9.7	1.8
Cauliflower & Broccoli Bake, Tesco*	½ Pack/250g	178	71	2.8	5.8	4.1	1.0
Cheese & Spinach, Tesco*	1 Serving/140g	258	184	4.8	22.4	8.3	1.6
Chicken & Mushroom, COU, Marks & Spencer*	1 Serving/360g	324	90	7.3	10.3	2.3	1.1
Chicken Arrabbbiata, Marks & Spencer*	1 Pack/450g	540	120	7.6	16.0	3.0	2.0
Chicken Spiralli, Marks & Spencer*	1 Serving/400g	400	100	7.9	9.1	3.8	1.1
Chicken, Broccoli & Mushroom, Safeway*	1 Serving/175g	425	243	8.9	22.4	13.1	3.0
Cod & Prawn, COU, Marks & Spencer*	1 Pack/400g	320	80	6.5	8.8	2.0	1.0

	Measure INFO/WEIGHT	per Measure KCAL	KCAL	PROT	CARB	FAT	FIBRE
BAKE,							
Fish & Vegetable, Youngs*	1 Serving/374.8g	446	119	5.6	10.0	6.3	1.3
Potato & Vegetable, Co-Op*	1 Bake/340g	425	125	4.0	11.0	8.0	1.0
Potato, Cheese, & Bacon, Homepride*	1 Serving/210g	277	132	1.6	3.2	12.5	0.0
Potato, Cheese, & Onion, Tesco*	1 Pack/400g	376	94	2.4	10.0	4.9	1.0
Potato, Mushroom & Leek, Marks & Spencer*	1 Serving/225g	225	100	3.5	10.0	5.9	2.0
Potato, Tomato & Mozzarella, Marks & Spencer*	1 Bake/450g	585	130	5.2	9.8	7.6	1.8
Roast Onion & Potato, COU, Marks & Spencer*	1 Pack/450g	338	75	1.9	13.6	1.3	1.5
Roast Potato, Cheese & Onion, Asda*	½ Pack/200g	288	144	4.2	14.0	8.0	1.1
Salmon & Broccoli, Weight Watchers*	1 Serving/330g	311	94	5.1	10.2	3.6	0.8
Salmon & Broccoli, Youngs*	1 Bake/375g	409	109	6.3	9.6	5.1	1.3
Salmon & Prawn, Marks & Spencer*	1 Bake/328.6g	461	140	7.4	6.6	9.5	0.7
Spicy Bean & Potato, Safeway*	1 Pack/385.7g	405	105	3.9	14.2	3.2	2.1
Spicy Chickpea & Apricot, Safeway*	1 Pack/400g	340	85	2.2	12.5	2.9	3.2
Tuna Conchiglie, Marks & Spencer*	1 Serving/400g	500	125	8.6	10.2	5.4	0.9
Vegetable & Lentil, Somerfield*	1 Pack/350g	319	91	4.9	13.8	1.8	2.5
Vegetable, Marks & Spencer*	1 Serving/300g	255	85	1.8	9.8	4.3	3.2
BAKE MIX,							
Potato, Creamy Cheddar Cheese, Colman's*	1 Pack/45g	189	420	11.5	34.8	26.0	9.6
Potato, Ham & Leek, Colman's*	1 Pack/44g	181	412	9.9	40.4	24.0	2.1
Quick Quisine, Atkins*	1 Serving/100g	286	286	44.0	16.0	2.7	19.8
BAKING POWDER,							
Average	1 Tsp/2g	3	163	5.2	37.8	0.0	0.0
BALTI,							
Chicken & Naan Bread, Somerfield*	1 Pack/335g	489	146	10.0	16.0	5.0	0.0
Chicken & Potato Wedges, Healthy Living, Tesco*	1 Pack/450g	387	86	6.0	10.8	2.1	1.1
Chicken & Rice, COU, Marks & Spencer*	1 Serving/400g	360	90	7.3	13.2	0.9	2.5
Chicken & Rice, Good Choice, Iceland*	1 Pack/400g	440	110	5.2	18.1	1.9	0.7
Chicken & Rice, Patak's*	1 Pack/370g	440	119	6.1	16.7	3.5	1.7
Chicken Ceylon, Finest, Tesco*	1 Pack/400g	588	147	14.4	0.9	9.5	5.0
Chicken Tikka & Wedges, Tesco*	1 Pack/450g	428	95	6.3	11.8	2.5	1.3
Chicken Tikka, Finest, Tesco*	½ Pack/200g	280	140	15.8	1.1	8.6	3.2
Chicken Tikka, Indian, Tesco*	1 Serving/350g	427	122	11.2	5.6	6.1	0.6
Chicken Tikka, Tesco*	1 Pack/350g	466	133	11.1	6.4	7.0	0.7
Chicken Tikka, Weight Watchers*	1 Pack/320g	224	70	4.8	10.2	1.1	0.6
Chicken With Naan Bread, Perfectly Balanced, Waitrose*	1 Pack/375g	450	120	12.1	9.7	3.6	2.8
Chicken With Naan Bread, Sharwood's*	1 Pack/375g	540	144	6.5	15.4	6.3	2.2
Chicken With Rice & Naan, Iceland*	1 Serving/148g	589	398	15.0	66.4	8.0	3.1
Chicken With Rice, Curry Break, Patak's*	1 Pack/220g	198	90	4.7	11.6	2.8	0.0
Chicken With Rice, Weight Watchers*	1 Pack/329g	253	77	4.8	10.7	1.7	0.5
Chicken, BGTY, Sainsbury's*	1 Pack/400g	356	89	5.1	15.8	0.6	0.7
Chicken, Blue Parrot Cafe, Sainsbury's*	1 Can/400g	308	77	8.9	4.6	2.5	0.8
Chicken, From Indian Meal For One, Sainsbury's*	1 Pack/300g	384	128	12.9	3.7	6.8	2.1
Chicken, Iceland*	1 Pack/544g	740	136	12.0	5.7	7.2	1.6
Chicken, Indian Takeaway, Iceland*	1 Pack/402.2g	362	90	7.8	4.0	4.8	0.7
Chicken, Marks & Spencer*	1 Pack/350g	350	100	10.8	3.9	4.8	1.3
Chicken, Ready Meals, Marks & Spencer*	1oz/28g	34	120	10.2	4.7	6.5	1.6
Chicken, Safeway*	1 Pack/350g	485	139	9.5	5.4	8.7	2.1
Chicken, Sainsbury's*	1 Serving/200g	230	115	12.8	4.2	5.2	3.5
Chicken, Takeaway, Sainsbury's*	1 Pack/400g	404	101	10.4	4.8	4.5	1.4
Chicken, Tesco*	1 Pack/460g	662	144	6.1	17.4	5.6	1.6
Chicken, Tin, Sainsbury's*	1 Serving/200g	168	84	9.4	4.0	3.4	1.0
Chicken, With Pilau Rice, Asda*	1 Pack/504g	625	124	5.0	15.0	4.9	1.2
Chunky Vegetable, Aldi*	1 Can/400g	404	101	1.5	9.3	6.4	1.4

INFO/WEIGHT	Measure	per Measure KCAL	Nutrition Values per 100g / 100ml KCAL	PROT	CARB	FAT	FIBRE
BALTI,							
Lamb With Rice & Naan, Iceland*	1 Pack/460g	1904	414	14.7	65.3	10.4	3.2
Prawn, Budgens*	1 Pack/350g	375	107	5.6	5.2	7.1	1.3
Vegetable & Rice, Tesco*	1 Pack/450g	378	84	2.0	15.6	1.6	1.3
Vegetable With Naan Bread & Raita, Eat Smart, Safeway*	1 Pack/371g	315	85	3.8	12.5	1.9	3.1
Vegetable, Asda*	½ Can/200g	206	103	2.2	10.0	6.0	2.5
Vegetable, GFY, Asda*	1 Pack/450g	324	72	1.9	14.0	0.9	1.5
Vegetable, Indian Meal for 2, Finest, Tesco*	½ Pack/150g	144	96	1.6	6.1	7.2	2.9
BAMBOO SHOOTS,							
Canned, Average	1 Sm Can/120g	11	9	1.1	0.9	0.1	0.9
BANANA,							
Chips	1oz/28g	143	511	1.0	59.9	31.4	1.7
Raw, Average	1 Med/118g	116	98	1.7	23.2	0.3	0.9
BANGERS & MASH,							
& Beans, Blue Parrot Cafe, Sainsbury's*	1 Pack/300g	354	118	5.3	14.8	4.2	2.1
Co-Op*	1 Pack/300g	375	125	4.0	13.0	6.0	0.8
Good Intentions, Somerfield*	1 Pack/447.7g	394	88	5.3	12.1	2.0	0.7
Meal for One, Marks & Spencer*	1 Pack/370g	481	130	4.7	9.5	7.9	1.1
Morrisons*	1 Pack/300g	306	102	3.0	12.3	4.9	0.8
Sausage, & Cabbage Mash, Eat Smart, Safeway*	1 Pack/400g	340	85	6.4	9.0	2.5	1.3
BARS,							
AM, Breakfast Muffin, Apple & Sultana, McVitie's*	1 Bar/45g	168	373	4.4	54.9	16.7	1.6
AM, Cereal, Apple, McVite's*	1 Bar/40g	160	400	4.3	65.4	13.5	3.1
AM, Cereal, Apricot, McVitie's*	1 Bar/30g	146	486	6.5	68.8	20.5	0.5
AM, Cereal, Berry, McVitie's*	1 Bar/30g	146	486	6.5	68.8	20.5	0.5
AM, Cereal, Fruit & Nut, McVitie's*	1 Bar/35g	167	477	6.6	64.9	21.4	3.4
AM, Cereal, Grapefruit, McVitie's*	1 Bar/35g	136	389	5.1	70.9	9.4	3.1
AM, Cereal, Orange Marmalade, McVitie's*	1 Bar/40g	151	378	4.5	53.3	18.0	1.8
AM, Cereal, Raisin & Nut, McVitie's*	1 Bar/35.1g	148	422	6.4	62.1	16.4	2.4
AM, Cereal, Strawberry, McVitie's*	1 Bar/35g	138	395	5.7	70.5	10.1	2.7
AM, Granola, Almond, Raisin & Cranberry, McVitie's*	1 Bar/35g	133	380	7.0	62.9	11.3	4.1
AM, Muesli Fingers, McVitie's*	1 Bar/35g	154	440	6.0	59.8	19.6	3.1
All Day Breakfast, Weight Watchers*	1 Bar/50g	179	358	6.8	72.2	4.6	3.2
All Fruit, Apple & Passionfruit, Jordans*	1 Bar/30g	89	295	1.2	71.0	0.7	5.2
All Fruit, Apple & Strawberry, Jordans*	1 Bar/30g	89	297	1.3	72.1	0.4	4.9
Almond, Apricot & Mango, Marks & Spencer*	1 Bar/50g	205	410	8.9	60.2	14.9	5.0
Alpen*, Apple & Blackberry With Yoghurt	1 Bar/29g	117	404	5.4	71.8	10.6	0.0
Alpen*, Fruit & Nut	1 Bar/28g	110	394	6.5	71.2	9.2	0.0
Alpen*, Fruit & Nut With Milk Chocolate	1 Bar/29g	125	431	7.0	68.0	14.5	0.0
Alpen*, Strawberry With Yoghurt	1 Bar/29g	119	409	5.7	72.6	10.6	0.0
Alpini, Continental Chocolate, Thorntons*	1 Bar/35.6g	194	539	7.0	55.1	32.2	2.1
Apple & Cinnamon, Breakfast Snack, Tesco*	1 Bar/37.5g	139	365	4.3	58.8	12.5	2.0
Apple & Cinnamon, Chewy, GFY, Asda*	1 Bar/27g	95	351	6.0	74.0	3.4	8.0
Apple & Raisin, Snack, Geobar, Traidcraft*	1 Bar/35g	127	362	3.3	76.4	4.8	2.3
Apple & Raspberry, Chewy & Crisp, Tesco*	1 Bar/27.0g	123	456	3.4	66.8	19.5	2.8
Apple, Geobar, Traidcraft*	1 Bar/35.1g	132	376	5.3	69.0	8.8	3.5
Apple, Granola, McVitie's*	1 Bar/35g	128	366	6.6	63.1	9.7	4.3
Apple, Lite, Leda*	1 Bar/50g	151	301	7.9	58.2	2.0	7.2
Apple, Pear & Berry, Shapers, Boots*	1 Bar/30g	78	261	1.2	64.0	0.1	10.0
Apricot & Almond, Chewy & Crisp, Tesco*	1 Bar/27g	122	452	6.2	60.0	20.8	2.6
Apricot & Coconut, Chewy & Crisp, Sainsbury's*	1 Bar/27g	123	457	5.2	58.8	22.3	4.0
Apricot & Raisin, Thorntons*	1 Bar/40g	185	462	8.0	46.0	27.3	3.5
Apricot, Dried Fruit, Sunsweet*	1 Bar/33g	96	292	3.6	72.5	0.1	0.0
Apricot, Fruity Grain, Tesco*	1 Bar/37g	50	134	1.3	25.3	3.0	0.9

B

BARS,

	Measure INFO/WEIGHT	per Measure KCAL	KCAL	PROT	CARB	FAT	FIBRE
			Nutrition Values per 100g / 100ml				
Apricot, Lite, Leda*	1 Bar/50g	143	285	8.1	54.0	2.0	7.6
Apricot, Oat Snack, Waitrose*	1 Bar/27g	121	447	4.9	65.2	18.5	2.4
Banana Break, Breakfast in a Bar, Jordans*	1 Bar/40g	152	381	5.7	69.1	9.1	5.0
Banana, Fruit Break, Lyme Regis Foods*	1 Bar/42g	162	385	9.0	51.9	15.7	3.9
Biscuit & Raisin, Reduced Fat, Tesco*	1 Bar/21g	85	406	4.9	68.5	12.5	1.8
Blue Riband, Double Choc, Nestle*	1 Bar/22g	113	513	5.1	63.1	26.7	1.1
Blue Riband, Nestle*	1 Bar/21.1g	108	516	5.2	64.1	26.6	1.1
Blueberrry, Fruit & Grain, Asda*	1 Bar/37g	123	332	3.3	64.0	7.0	2.7
Boohbah, Milk & White Chocolate, Marks & Spencer*	1 Bar/75g	405	540	7.9	54.7	32.3	1.2
Breakaway, Nestle*	1oz/28g	145	519	6.6	57.4	29.2	2.0
Breakfast, Apple Crisp, Morning Start, Atkins*	1 Bar/37g	145	392	29.2	25.4	21.4	13.8
Breakfast, Blueberry, Carbolite*	1 Bar/36g	105	295	8.4	62.0	8.0	2.3
Breakfast, Chocolate Chip Crisp, Morning Start, Atkins*	1 Bar/37g	137	370	31.8	22.5	18.8	15.0
Breakfast, Strawberry, Carbolite*	1 Bar/36g	105	295	8.4	62.0	8.0	2.3
Breakfast, Vitality, Fruit & Fibre, Asda*	1 Bar/29g	113	390	6.0	69.0	10.0	4.1
Breakfast, Vitality, Tropical Fruit, Asda*	1 Bar/28g	101	361	6.0	75.0	4.1	4.4
Breakfast, Vitality, With Cranberries, Asda*	1 Bar/27g	103	381	6.3	77.8	4.8	3.0
Breakfast, With Cranberries, Asda*	1 Bar/28g	105	376	6.0	77.0	4.9	3.0
Brunch, Cranberry & Orange, Cadbury's*	1 Bar/35g	154	440	5.9	67.7	15.9	0.0
Brunch, Hazelnut, Cadbury's*	1 Bar/35g	163	465	7.1	61.0	21.6	0.0
Brunch, Raisin, Cadbury's*	1 Bar/35g	151	430	5.7	66.7	15.8	0.0
Cappuccino Coll, Marks & Spencer*	1 Bar/35g	185	529	6.0	50.0	35.0	1.0
Caramel Crisp, Go Ahead, McVities*	1 Bar/33g	141	428	4.8	75.1	12.0	0.8
Caramel Crunch, Go Ahead, McVitie's*	1 Bar/24g	106	440	4.7	76.6	13.8	0.8
Caramel Shortcake, Jive, Aldi*	1 Bar/29g	135	467	4.6	56.0	25.0	1.4
Caramel, Asda*	1 Bar/29.5g	152	508	8.0	56.0	28.0	2.4
Caramel, Shapers, Boots*	1 Bar/25g	88	352	3.7	74.0	11.0	1.0
Caramel, Snack, SlimFast*	1 Bar/26g	94	360	3.1	66.3	11.2	0.0
Caramelised Nut & Raisin Crunch, TTD, Sainsbury's*	1 Bar/50g	206	412	8.3	64.4	13.5	5.3
Cereal & Milk, Rice Krispies, Kellogg's*	1 Bar/20g	84	421	7.0	70.0	13.0	0.3
Cereal & More, Marks & Spencer*	1 Bar/40g	154	385	20.0	58.2	7.8	2.9
Cereal, Apple & Blackberry, With Yoghurt, Alpen*	1 Bar/29g	122	419	5.5	73.8	11.1	0.0
Cereal, Apple & Cinnamonr, Fruit 'n' Grain, Asda*	1 Bar/37g	131	353	4.5	68.0	7.0	2.9
Cereal, Apple & Raisin, Harvest, Quaker*	1 Bar/22g	87	396	5.0	70.0	11.5	4.0
Cereal, Apple & Raspberry, Chewy & Crisp, Tesco*	1 Bar/27g	123	456	3.3	66.7	19.6	3.0
Cereal, Apple & Raspberry, Waitrose*	1 Bar/25g	90	359	5.0	77.1	3.4	4.6
Cereal, Apple & Sultana, Go Ahead, McVitie's*	1 Bar/35g	137	392	4.1	77.6	7.2	1.8
Cereal, Apple, Chewy, BGTY, Sainsbury's*	1 Bar/25g	85	340	4.8	76.0	2.0	2.0
Cereal, Apricot & Yoghurt, COU, Marks & Spencer*	1 Bar/20g	74	370	4.8	82.3	2.2	3.1
Cereal, Apricot & Yoghurt, Shapers, Boots*	1 Bar/27g	99	366	3.7	75.0	5.7	3.3
Cereal, Apricot Fruit & Cereal, Organic, Organix*	1 Bar/30g	122	408	7.2	55.3	20.4	6.2
Cereal, Apricot, Lyme Regis Foods*	1 Bar/35.1g	131	373	6.5	61.1	11.4	6.8
Cereal, Apricot, Perfectly Balanced, Waitrose*	1 Bar/25g	89	356	4.9	76.9	3.2	3.8
Cereal, Balance With Fruit, Sainsbury's*	1 Bar/25g	100	401	5.8	75.2	8.6	1.9
Cereal, Banoffee, COU, Marks & Spencer*	1 Bar/20g	75	375	4.5	82.5	2.0	2.5
Cereal, Benefit With Fruit, Harvest Morn*	1 Bar/27g	108	401	5.8	75.2	8.6	1.9
Cereal, Berry & Cream, COU, Marks & Spencer*	1 Bar/20g	72	360	5.3	79.7	2.3	3.1
Cereal, Blueberry Flavour, Breakfast, Sweet Mornings*	1 Bar/38g	152	399	4.5	66.0	13.0	2.5
Cereal, Brownie, COU, Marks & Spencer*	1 Bar/20g	70	350	5.0	79.5	2.5	4.5
Cereal, Cheerios & Milk Bar, Nestle*	1 Bar/24g	98	407	7.6	64.5	13.2	0.0
Cereal, Chewy & Crisp With Choc Chips, Tesco*	1 Bar/27g	125	463	9.2	54.0	23.4	3.8
Cereal, Chewy & Crisp With Roasted Nuts, Tesco*	1 Bar/27g	127	471	9.3	57.0	22.9	2.5
Cereal, Chewy Apple, Fruitus*	1 Bar/34.9g	132	378	5.4	64.8	10.8	5.4

BARS,

INFO/WEIGHT	Measure	per Measure KCAL	KCAL	PROT	CARB	FAT	FIBRE
Cereal, Chocolate & Orange, Healthy Living, Tesco*	1 Bar/25g	96	384	4.0	77.7	6.3	1.9
Cereal, Chocolate & Orange, Tesco*	1 Bar/25g	96	384	4.0	77.7	6.3	1.9
Cereal, Chocolate & Raisin, Seeds Of Change*	1 Bar/29g	109	375	4.6	69.8	8.5	0.0
Cereal, Chocolate Milk, Kellogg's*	1 Bar/26.7g	122	450	9.0	67.0	16.0	1.5
Cereal, Coco Pops & Milk Bar, Kellogg's*	1 Bar/20g	85	423	7.0	70.0	13.0	1.0
Cereal, Coconut Muesli, Kellogg's*	1 Bar/25g	108	430	5.0	65.0	17.0	5.0
Cereal, Cranberrry & Blackcurrant, Healthy Living, Tesco*	1 Bar/25g	79	316	5.5	68.2	2.3	8.6
Cereal, Cranberry & Orange, BGTY, Sainsbury's*	1 Bar/26g	93	358	2.7	75.8	4.9	2.3
Cereal, Cranberry & Orange, Weight Watchers*	1 Bar/28g	102	365	4.5	77.6	4.1	2.3
Cereal, Cranberry, Benefit, Aldi*	1 bar/27g	101	375	6.2	76.5	4.9	3.0
Cereal, Cranberry, Chewy, Safeway*	1 Bar/25g	86	345	4.7	75.7	2.3	3.9
Cereal, Cranberry, Eat Smart, Safeway*	1 Bar/25g	86	345	4.7	75.7	2.3	3.9
Cereal, Cranberry, Waitrose*	1 Bar/25g	91	363	4.5	78.3	3.5	2.9
Cereal, Crunchy Nut, Kelloggs*	1 Bar/25g	112	446	6.0	70.0	16.0	1.5
Cereal, Frosties & Milk, Kellogg's*	1 Bar/24.9g	103	413	6.0	71.0	12.0	1.5
Cereal, Frosties, Chocolate, Kellogg's*	1 Bar/25g	103	413	6.0	71.0	12.0	1.5
Cereal, Frosties, Kellogg's*	1 Bar/25g	103	411	7.0	72.0	11.0	1.0
Cereal, Fruit & Fibre, Harvest Morn*	1 Bar/29g	114	392	6.5	69.1	10.0	4.1
Cereal, Fruit & Fibre, Sainsbury's*	1 Bar/28g	111	397	5.7	70.9	10.1	3.8
Cereal, Fruit & Nut Break, Jordans*	1 Bar/37g	135	374	7.0	63.2	10.4	8.1
Cereal, Fruit & Nut, Alpen*	1 Bar/28g	110	394	6.5	71.2	9.2	0.0
Cereal, Fruit N Fibre, Kellogg's*	1 Serving/25g	96	384	4.0	72.0	10.0	4.0
Cereal, Ginger & Raisin, BGTY, Sainsbury's*	1 Bar/40g	91	228	2.0	48.5	2.8	0.0
Cereal, Ginger, Waitrose*	1 Bar/25g	92	367	4.9	79.3	3.3	3.3
Cereal, Golden Grahams, Nestle*	1 Bar/25g	106	425	6.5	68.8	13.7	0.0
Cereal, Granola, Starbucks*	1 Bar/90g	324	360	8.0	38.6	21.3	4.8
Cereal, Hazelnut & Pistachio, Go Ahead, McVitie's*	1 Bar/35g	147	419	5.4	68.3	13.8	2.3
Cereal, Hazelnut & Sultana, Organic, Seeds Of Change*	1 Bar/29g	118	407	6.3	65.9	13.1	0.0
Cereal, Hazelnuts & Raisins, Organic, Tesco*	1 Bar/30g	144	481	7.2	50.3	27.9	3.8
Cereal, Lemon & Sultana, Eat Smart, Safeway*	1 Bar/25g	89	355	4.2	78.4	2.2	2.6
Cereal, Lemon, Marks & Spencer*	1 Bar/25g	90	360	4.1	79.0	2.8	2.8
Cereal, Maple, Healthy Living, Tesco*	1 Bar/25g	93	372	5.5	76.6	4.9	2.0
Cereal, Milk Chocolate, Weetos*	1 Bar/20g	88	440	6.0	71.0	14.5	0.0
Cereal, Mixed Berry, Fruitus*	1 Bar/35g	132	376	5.7	63.8	13.8	6.6
Cereal, Mixed Berry, Go Ahead, McVitie's*	1 Bar/35g	134	383	4.6	77.1	6.3	3.1
Cereal, Muesli Break, Breakfast in a Bar, Jordans*	1 Bar/46g	178	387	5.9	66.6	10.8	4.3
Cereal, Muncho Chocolate & Coconut, Orco*	1 Bar/21g	93	441	5.0	71.4	15.0	0.0
Cereal, Nesquik, Nestle*	1 Bar/25g	108	433	6.2	68.7	14.9	0.0
Cereal, Nut & Chocolate, Chewy, Safeway*	1 Bar/27g	127	471	8.7	57.9	22.7	4.1
Cereal, Nutty, Free From, Sainsbury's*	1 Bar/25g	114	454	6.8	61.8	20.0	2.3
Cereal, Orange & Grapefruit, Healthy Eating, Tesco*	1 Bar/24.9g	90	361	4.1	79.9	2.8	2.2
Cereal, Orange, Lyme Regis Foods*	1 Bar/35g	132	377	4.6	73.4	9.5	5.2
Cereal, Pink Grapefruit, Chewy, BGTY, Sainsbury's*	1 Bar/25g	86	345	5.0	76.5	2.1	2.4
Cereal, Pure Points, Weight Watchers*	1 Bar/50g	179	358	6.8	72.2	4.6	3.2
Cereal, Raisin & Apricot, Weight Watchers*	1 Bar/28g	100	357	6.8	72.1	4.6	3.2
Cereal, Raisin & Nut Snack Bar, Benecol*	1 Bar/25g	98	390	3.9	68.5	11.1	2.0
Cereal, Redberry & Chocolate Sveltesse, Nestle*	1 Bar/25g	97	389	5.4	69.2	9.9	6.8
Cereal, Roast Hazelnut, Organic, Jordans*	1 Bar/33g	150	455	8.0	56.7	21.8	7.8
Cereal, Roasted Peanut, Weight Watchers*	1 Bar/26g	104	400	9.5	66.1	10.8	2.8
Cereal, Strawberry, BGTY, Sainsbury's*	1 Bar/26g	100	385	3.8	82.0	4.6	5.2
Cereal, Strawberry, Fruit `n` Grain, Asda*	1 Bar/37g	128	346	3.5	64.9	8.1	3.0
Cereal, Sultana & Honey, Jordans*	1 Bar/36g	130	361	6.0	65.9	8.2	9.2
Cereal, Toffee Apple, Chewy, Eat Smart, Safeway*	1 Bar/25g	89	355	4.0	78.3	2.8	2.9

BARS,

INFO/WEIGHT	Measure	per Measure KCAL	Nutrition Values per 100g / 100ml				
			KCAL	PROT	CARB	FAT	FIBRE
Cereal, White Choc Chip, Harvest*	1 Bar/22g	94	425	6.0	67.0	15.5	3.5
Cereal, White Chocolate Muesli, Kellogg's*	1 Bar/25g	110	440	5.0	70.0	16.0	2.0
Cereal, With Fig, Fitness, Nestle*	1 Bar/23.5g	88	366	4.3	71.5	6.8	5.5
Cereal, With Pink Grapefruit, Chewy, Sainsbury's*	1 Bar/25g	86	345	5.0	76.5	2.1	2.4
Choc Chip & Nut, Chewy & Crisp, Sainsbury's*	1 Bar/27.1g	129	476	8.8	51.8	26.0	4.4
Chocolate & Hazelnut, Meal Replacement, Tesco*	1 Bar/65g	250	385	24.2	41.0	11.0	6.3
Chocolate & Orange, Crispy, Free From, Sainsbury's*	1 Bar/30g	132	440	4.8	68.2	16.2	1.2
Chocolate & Orange, Shapers, Boots*	1 Bar/26g	98	378	4.2	73.0	13.0	1.5
Chocolate & Raisin Oat Snack, Waitrose*	1 Bar/27g	112	416	5.4	67.2	14.0	2.1
Chocolate & Raisin, Shapers, Boots*	1 Bar/27g	95	353	4.7	76.0	9.1	2.7
Chocolate & Raspberry, COU, Marks & Spencer*	1 Bar/25g	90	360	5.4	78.2	2.7	3.2
Chocolate & Toffee, Free From, Sainsbury's*	1 Bar/29.9g	140	465	4.8	71.0	18.0	0.8
Chocolate Brownie, Big Softies, To Go, Fox's*	1 Bar/25g	87	348	5.5	74.9	2.9	0.0
Chocolate Caramel, SlimFast*	1 Bar/26g	99	382	3.0	72.0	12.0	1.2
Chocolate Chip, SlimFast*	1 Bar/26g	98	378	4.9	70.4	11.4	1.8
Chocolate Chip, Snack, SlimFast*	1 Bar/26g	99	382	4.9	70.4	11.4	1.8
Chocolate Cookie Dough, Meal, SlimFast*	1 Bar/56g	220	393	14.3	64.3	8.9	3.6
Chocolate Crunch, SlimFast*	1 Bar/60g	215	359	23.4	47.8	10.3	6.7
Chocolate Decadence, Atkins*	1 Bar/60g	227	378	27.1	30.7	20.4	11.6
Chocolate Flavour Almond, Carbolite*	1 Bar/28g	124	438	8.7	52.0	36.0	3.8
Chocolate Flavour Coconut, Carbolite*	1 Bar/31g	110	355	3.3	54.0	24.0	5.1
Chocolate Flavour Crisp, Carbolite*	1 Bar/28g	123	438	11.0	55.0	32.0	2.5
Chocolate Flavour Truffle, Carbolite*	1 Bar/28g	124	438	6.0	58.0	28.0	4.1
Chocolate Hazelnut, Advantage, Atkins*	1 Bar/60g	236	393	32.3	29.0	20.3	8.3
Chocolate Heaven, Ainsley Harriott*	1 Bar/27.1g	147	543	7.0	56.0	32.0	2.5
Chocolate Muesli, SlimFast*	1 Bar/26g	97	373	4.6	53.8	14.2	6.5
Chocolate Muesli, Snack, SlimFast*	1 Bar/26g	99	379	4.7	64.5	13.3	6.5
Chocolate Peanut, SlimFast*	1 Bar/26g	97	373	5.4	63.1	12.7	1.2
Chocolate Truffle, Marks & Spencer*	1 Bar/35g	168	480	5.9	41.7	32.5	8.3
Chocolate, Crisp, Weight Watchers*	1 Bar/25g	92	369	5.4	75.1	10.2	0.8
Chocolate, Crispy, Sainsbury's*	1 Bar/24g	107	446	3.6	68.8	17.4	0.8
Chocolate, Digestive, Farmfoods*	1 Bar/21g	104	495	6.7	63.6	23.8	2.3
Chocolate, Double Cream, Nestle*	1 Bar/47g	250	531	8.5	54.8	30.9	0.0
Chocolate, Geobar, Traidcraft*	1 Bar/35g	126	360	5.2	72.6	5.4	4.8
Chocolate, Meal Replacement, SlimFast*	1 Bar/39g	122	314	19.9	46.2	9.4	5.5
Chocolate, Milk, Diabetic, Thorntons*	½ Bar/37g	174	470	7.3	43.0	33.1	2.2
Chocolate, SlimFast*	1 Bar/39g	107	274	20.6	35.3	9.0	5.5
Chocolate, Toffee Pecan, Marks & Spencer*	1 Bar/36g	179	498	4.9	58.3	27.3	0.7
Chocolate, Viennese, Continental, Thorntons*	1 Bar/38g	206	542	4.2	53.9	34.2	0.8
Cinnamon, Danish Pastry, Cafe Creations, Health Valley*	1 Bar/40g	130	325	5.0	67.5	6.3	5.0
Club, Fruit, Jacob's*	1 Biscuit/25g	124	496	5.6	62.2	25.0	2.3
Club, Milk Chocolate, Jacob's*	1 Biscuit/24g	123	511	5.8	62.6	26.4	2.0
Club, Mint, Jacob's*	1 Biscuit/24g	124	517	5.6	62.5	27.2	1.7
Club, Orange, Jacob's*	1 Biscuit/24g	125	519	5.6	62.2	27.6	1.7
Coconut Chocolate Crisp, Weight Watchers*	1 Bar/25g	89	356	3.6	71.2	10.4	3.2
Coconut, Cool, Tesco*	1 Bar/25g	121	484	3.9	60.4	25.2	2.8
Coconut, Mueslix, Kellogg's*	1 Bar/25g	105	420	5.0	67.0	16.0	5.0
Cookie, Apple Crumble, COU, Marks & Spencer*	1 Bar/27g	90	335	5.8	72.6	2.6	2.3
Cookie, Maryland*	1 Bar/24.1g	120	498	7.6	60.0	22.5	0.0
Cookie, Oreo, Nabisco*	1 Bar/35g	180	514	2.0	66.0	29.0	0.0
Cool Mint Nougat & Dark Chocolate, Shapers, Boots*	1oz/28g	101	360	2.8	75.0	13.0	1.4
Corn Flakes & Chocolate Milk, Kellogg's*	1 Bar/40g	176	440	9.0	66.0	16.0	2.0
Cranberry & Boysenberry, Altu*	1 Serving/40g	155	387	10.6	63.9	9.9	3.4

	Measure INFO/WEIGHT	per Measure KCAL	Nutrition Values per 100g / 100ml KCAL	PROT	CARB	FAT	FIBRE
BARS,							
Cranberry & Honey, Soft & Chewy, Sunny Crunch*	1 Bar/30g	115	382	6.0	73.1	8.3	3.1
Cranberry & Macadamia, Gold, Eat Natural*	1 Bar/45g	230	511	7.2	48.2	32.0	0.0
Cranberry & Raisin, Geobar, Traidcraft*	1 Bar/35g	131	374	3.6	72.5	8.1	2.3
Cranberry, Perfectly Balanced, Waitrose*	1 Bar/25g	91	363	4.5	78.3	3.5	2.9
Crazy Caramel, Tesco*	1 Treat Bar/20g	94	469	4.1	66.0	21.0	1.1
Creme Brulee Chocolate, Marks & Spencer*	1 Bar/36g	178	495	4.4	54.0	29.2	0.4
Crispy Caramel Flavour, Carbolite*	1oz/28g	97	345	11.0	65.0	15.0	1.0
Crispy Caramel, Shapers, Boots*	1 Bar/24g	96	400	3.9	67.0	17.0	0.4
Crispy Chocolate Peanut, Carb Minders*	1 Bar/60g	240	400	35.0	38.3	16.7	0.0
Crispy Lemon Yoghurt, Carb Minders*	1 Bar/60g	240	400	33.3	38.3	15.0	3.3
Crispy Orange, Reduced Fat, Tesco*	1 Bar/22g	95	431	3.6	75.5	12.7	0.6
Crispy Raspberry, Carb Minders*	1 Bar/60g	240	400	35.0	40.0	15.0	1.7
Crunchy Caramel, Tesco*	1 Bar/21g	98	467	4.6	56.0	25.0	1.4
Dairy Milk, Crispies, Cadbury's*	1 Bar/49g	250	510	7.6	58.6	27.4	0.0
Dark Chocolate, Diabetic, Thorntons*	1 Bar/75g	345	460	5.4	28.5	35.8	8.1
Dark Praline, Cavalier*	1 Bar/42g	202	482	5.0	46.3	38.9	7.2
Date & Fig, Lyme Regis Foods*	1 Bar/42g	169	402	7.3	58.2	15.5	8.9
Date & Fruit, Lyme Regis Foods*	1 Bar/42g	169	402	7.3	58.2	15.5	8.9
Date & Walnut, Eat Natural*	1 Bar/50g	220	440	8.0	57.2	20.0	0.0
Digestive, Milk Chocolate, Marks & Spencer*	1 Bar/23g	117	510	6.6	64.6	25.1	1.9
Digestive, Milk Chocolate, McVitie's*	1 Bar/23g	118	511	6.6	64.6	25.1	1.9
Digestive, Milk Chocolate, Value, Tesco*	1 Bar/24g	119	495	6.7	63.6	23.8	0.0
Double Caramel, GFY, Asda*	1 Bar/40g	92	231	5.0	47.0	2.6	0.0
Double Caramel, Go Ahead, McVitie's*	1 Cake/32g	97	302	4.0	65.3	4.4	0.7
Double Chocolate Treat, Shapers, Boots*	1 Bar/23g	92	400	3.6	74.0	9.9	0.7
Double Chocolate, Breakfast Snack, Tesco*	1 Bar/37.4g	142	385	5.3	52.7	17.0	3.3
Double Chocolate, Shapers, Boots*	1 Bar/23g	95	413	4.8	73.9	10.9	1.3
Fruit & Nut Crisp, Go Ahead, McVitie's*	1 Bar/23.0g	99	430	5.3	71.3	13.7	1.7
Fruit & Nut, Eat Natural*	1 Bar/50g	112	223	5.8	24.9	11.2	2.2
Fruit 'n Fibre, Kellogg's*	1 Bar/25g	96	383	4.5	72.0	9.0	4.5
Fruit, Apple, Hellema*	1 Bar/33.1g	127	384	4.5	74.0	7.5	2.0
Fruit, Kidz Organic, Lyme Regis Foods*	1 Bar/20g	73	364	9.5	67.3	7.4	1.4
Fruit, Nut & Seed Bars, The Village Bakery*	1 Bar/25g	93	373	5.7	73.7	6.2	0.1
Fruit, Organic, The Village Bakery*	1 Bar/42.6g	150	348	4.9	67.0	6.6	5.5
Fruits Of The Forest, Advantage, Atkins*	1 Bar/60g	224	374	31.0	32.9	17.4	7.7
Fruits Of The Forest, Meal, SlimFast*	1 Bar/60g	225	375	24.0	48.3	9.8	6.7
Fruitsome, Citrus, Rowntree's*	1 Bar/35g	140	400	4.1	65.1	13.7	2.3
Fruity Cereal Bar, Free From, Sainsbury's*	1 Bar/25.1g	100	399	4.4	79.3	10.2	2.6
Fruity Cereal, Banoffee, Go, Soreen*	1 Serving/40g	143	358	6.0	72.8	4.8	0.0
Fruity Cereal, Go, Soreen*	1 Bar/40g	133	332	5.5	68.1	4.2	0.0
Frusli, Absolutely Apricot, Jordans*	1 Bar/33g	120	365	5.0	63.8	10.0	6.3
Frusli, Blueberry Burst, Jordans*	1 Bar/33g	126	381	5.5	68.3	9.5	4.6
Frusli, Cranberry & Apple, Jordans*	1 Bar/33.3g	131	385	5.1	68.9	9.9	5.8
Frusli, Raisin & Hazelnut, Jordans*	1 Bar/34g	129	379	5.7	66.0	10.3	2.1
Frusli, Tangy Citrus, Jordans*	1 Bar/33g	124	376	4.4	67.7	9.8	4.8
Ginger Oat, Snack, Waitrose*	1 Bar/27.0g	119	441	4.8	63.5	18.6	2.2
Ginger, Perfectly Balanced, Waitrose*	1 Bar/25g	92	367	4.9	79.3	3.3	3.3
Gold Bar, McVitie's*	1 Bar/23g	121	524	6.0	64.6	26.8	0.6
Granola, Nature Valley*	1 Bar/42g	180	429	9.5	69.0	14.3	4.8
Granola, Peanut Butter, Quaker*	1 Bar/28g	110	393	7.1	64.3	12.5	3.6
Harvest Cheweee, Apple & Raisin, Quaker*	1 Bar/22g	89	405	5.5	68.0	12.0	3.0
Harvest Cheweee, Choc Chip, Quaker*	1 Bar/22g	95	430	5.5	68.0	16.0	3.5
Harvest Cheweee, Toffee, Quaker*	1 Bar/22g	94	427	5.0	68.2	15.0	3.2

BARS,	Measure INFO/WEIGHT	per Measure KCAL	Nutrition Values per 100g / 100ml				
			KCAL	PROT	CARB	FAT	FIBRE
Harvest Cheweee, White Chocolate Chip, Quaker*	1 Bar/22g	94	425	6.0	67.0	15.5	3.5
Honey & Almond, Crunchy, Jordans*	1 Bar/33g	153	465	8.8	56.1	22.8	5.8
Honey, Natural, Trail Mix, Kallo*	1 Bar/40g	196	490	15.7	40.9	33.2	5.7
Italian Tiramisu, Marks & Spencer*	1 Bar/35g	184	527	6.3	49.1	34.0	0.8
K-Time, Honey Nut Crunch, Kellogg's*	1 Bar/33.4g	126	382	5.0	82.7	2.5	1.8
K-Time, Mixed Berry, Kellogg's*	1 Bar/28g	104	372	4.9	80.1	2.2	3.8
Lemon, Sicilian, Continental, Thorntons*	1 Bar/40g	201	502	4.1	55.4	29.3	0.4
Mango & Brazil, Tropical Whole Foods*	1 Bar/40g	172	429	4.7	61.4	19.1	4.2
Maple & Pecan, Crunchy, Jordans*	1 Bar/33g	153	464	7.7	56.8	22.9	6.5
Mighty, Asda*	1 Bar/40.9g	201	491	8.0	54.0	27.0	0.0
Milk Choclate Flavour, Carbolite*	1 Bar/28g	124	438	7.0	57.0	34.0	2.7
Milk Chocolate Chip & Hazelnut, Snack, Benecol*	1 Bar/25g	99	395	4.7	64.5	13.1	2.5
Milk Chocolate Coated Orange Flavour, Energy, Boots*	1 Bar/70g	274	391	5.2	70.0	10.0	2.8
Milk Chocolate Whirls, Asda*	1 Bar/26g	116	447	3.7	72.0	16.0	0.8
Milk Chocolate, Mueslix, Kellogg's*	1 Bar/25g	110	440	6.0	63.0	18.0	2.0
Mint, Shapers, Boots*	1 Bar/25g	90	360	2.8	75.0	13.0	1.4
Mixed Nut Feast, Eat Natural*	1 Bar/50g	324	648	22.0	40.0	46.0	1.0
Muesli, The Cookie Coach Company*	1 Bar/75g	289	385	6.8	65.1	11.1	0.0
Muffin, Cadbury's*	1 Bar/68g	270	403	5.6	38.0	25.4	0.0
Nougat, Summer Strawberry, Shapers, Boots*	1 Bar/22g	76	345	2.7	77.3	10.9	0.9
Nuts & Choc Chip, Asda*	1 Bar/27g	127	471	8.0	58.0	23.0	2.8
Nutty Nougat Caramel, Tesco*	1 Bar/20g	99	493	8.5	54.0	27.0	2.4
Oat Crunchy, Blueberry & Cranberry, Waitrose*	1 Bar/60g	262	437	8.0	67.0	15.2	7.4
Oats, Raisins, Honet & Apricots, Geobar, Traidcraft*	1 Bar/35g	132	376	5.3	69.0	8.8	3.5
Orange Crunch, Go Ahead, McVitie's*	1 Bar/23g	99	430	4.1	78.0	12.8	0.8
Orange Truffle, Marks & Spencer*	1 Bar/33g	177	535	6.6	55.6	31.9	1.4
Peach, Apricot & Almond, Altu*	1 Bar/40g	158	395	7.9	65.2	11.4	4.3
Peanut Butter, Chewy, Granola, SlimFast*	1 Bar/56g	123	220	8.0	35.0	6.0	0.0
Peanut, Cashew & Thai Sweet Chilli, Altu*	1 Bar/40g	172	430	14.7	47.0	20.3	3.1
Pear & Ginger, Fruit Break, Lyme Regis Foods*	1 Bar/42g	160	381	2.7	45.4	20.9	9.9
Pecan Apricot & Peach, Marks & Spencer*	1 Bar/50g	255	510	9.3	38.2	35.5	4.9
Penguin, Chukka, McVitie's*	1 Bar/28g	135	481	6.1	65.1	21.8	0.0
Penguin, McVitie's*	1 Bar/25g	133	532	5.4	65.0	27.8	1.5
Penguin, Mint, McVitie's*	1 Bar/25g	133	531	5.4	65.0	27.7	1.5
Penguin, Orange, McVitie's*	1 Bar/25g	133	531	5.4	65.0	27.7	1.5
Penguin, Snack, McVitie's*	1 Bar/24g	121	504	5.2	54.6	29.5	0.0
Power, Pret A Manger*	1 Bar/65g	265	408	6.8	41.4	24.0	6.2
Protein, Ketoslim, Nature's Plus*	1 Bar/60g	230	383	35.0	40.0	16.7	1.7
Raisin & Apricot, Geobar, Traidcraft*	1 Bar/35g	132	376	5.3	69.0	8.8	3.5
Raisin & Chocolate, Traidcraft*	1 Bar/35.1g	127	362	4.2	75.0	5.0	1.8
Raisin & Hazelnut, Weight Watchers*	1 Bar/24g	95	396	5.0	71.3	10.0	2.9
Raisin & Oatmeal, Breakfast, Tesco*	1 Bar/37.5g	135	355	5.6	56.8	11.7	2.9
Rice Crisp, Cranberry & Orange, Go Ahead, McVitie's*	1 Bar/22.1g	92	417	3.9	77.0	10.4	1.0
Rice Crisp, With Honey, Go Ahead, McVitie's*	1 Bar/21.9g	91	415	4.1	76.1	10.5	0.8
Rice Krispies, Kellogg's*	1 Bar/20g	92	460	9.0	66.0	18.0	0.5
Roasted Nut, Chewy & Crisp, Sainsbury's*	1 Bar/27g	120	446	10.1	46.6	24.3	3.9
Roasted Nut, Chewy, Safeway*	1 Bar/26.9g	130	483	10.3	54.4	24.9	3.6
Rocky, Caramel, Fox's*	1 Bar/24g	115	480	6.1	60.7	23.8	0.8
Rocky, Fox's*	1 Bar/25g	129	516	8.2	58.8	27.5	1.4
Rocky, Funki Fudge, Fox's*	1 Biscuit/24.0g	125	520	6.9	60.3	27.7	1.1
Sandwich, Chocolate Viennese, Fox's*	1 Biscuit/14g	76	542	6.9	57.4	31.6	1.6
Sandwich, Chocolate, Rik & Rok*	1 Biscuit/22g	105	477	6.5	70.0	19.0	0.0
Sandwich, Milk Chocolate Orange, Farmfoods*	1 Biscuit/26g	131	503	6.1	65.7	24.1	1.4

	Measure INFO/WEIGHT	per Measure KCAL	Nutrition Values per 100g / 100ml				
			KCAL	PROT	CARB	FAT	FIBRE
BARS,							
Sandwich, Milk Chocolate Orange, Tesco*	1 Biscuit/25.3g	136	536	6.2	62.2	29.1	1.8
Sandwich, Milk Chocolate, SmartPrice, Asda*	1 Bar/25g	132	528	6.0	63.0	28.0	0.0
Sandwich, Milk Chocolate, Value, Tesco*	1 Biscuit/25.1g	132	529	4.8	64.5	28.0	1.3
School, Apricot, Fruit Bowl*	1 Bar/20g	72	361	0.5	83.0	3.0	0.0
School, Blackcurrant, Fruit Bowl*	1 Bar/19.9g	72	361	0.5	83.0	3.0	2.0
School, Strawberry, Fruit Bowl*	1 Bar/20g	72	360	0.5	83.0	3.0	0.0
Smarties, Nestle*	1 Bar/45g	238	528	6.2	58.2	30.0	0.9
Snack, Chocolate & Hazelnut, Benecol*	1 Bar/25g	99	397	4.7	64.5	13.1	2.5
Special K, Apple & Pear, Kellogg's*	1 Bar/23g	90	391	8.7	73.9	8.7	2.2
Special K, Kellogg's*	1 Bar/24g	94	390	7.0	75.0	7.0	2.0
Special K, Peach & Apricot, Kellogg's*	1 Bar/23g	90	391	8.0	73.0	9.0	2.5
Special K, Red Fruits, Kellogg's*	1 Bar/21.5g	86	390	8.0	78.0	5.0	1.5
Strawberry, Organic, Seeds Of Change*	1 Bar/26.2g	101	390	5.4	75.7	7.3	0.0
Strawberry, Shapers, Boots*	1 Bar/22g	75	343	2.5	77.0	11.0	0.9
Sultana & Honey, Breakfast, Jordans*	1 Bar/36.7g	134	361	6.0	65.9	8.2	9.2
Three Musketeer, Candy, Mars*	1 Bar/60.4g	258	430	3.3	76.2	13.2	1.7
Titan, Aldi*	1 Bar/55g	255	466	5.5	66.0	20.0	0.0
Toffee & Banana, Chewy, GFY, Asda*	1 Bar/27.3g	99	368	5.0	77.0	2.4	1.7
Toffee & Banana, Weight Watchers*	1 Bar/18g	67	372	6.1	77.2	3.9	1.7
Toffee Apple, Officially Low Fat, Fox's*	1 Bar/85g	90	106	1.6	22.8	0.8	0.7
Toffee Brazil Nut, Diabetic, Thorntons*	1 Serving/20g	93	467	3.2	49.0	35.1	0.5
Toffee Crisp, Nestle*	1 Bar/48g	245	511	4.3	60.6	27.9	0.0
Toffee Delight Meal Replacement, SlimFast*	1 Bar/78g	248	318	20.6	45.3	9.6	5.9
Toffee, SlimFast*	1 Bar/39g	122	314	19.7	47.1	8.5	5.6
Tracker, Breakfast, Banana, Mars*	1 Bar/37g	176	476	4.7	63.3	22.6	9.4
Tracker, Breakfast, Lemon, Mars*	1 Bar/26g	124	477	4.6	64.3	22.4	0.0
Tracker, Chocolate Chip, Mars*	1 Bar/37g	174	470	7.0	61.0	22.0	0.0
Tracker, Forest Fruits, Mars*	1 Bar/26g	123	474	4.6	64.1	22.2	0.0
Tracker, Roasted Nut, Mars*	1 Bar/27g	139	515	9.8	53.5	29.1	0.0
Tracker, Strawberry, Mars*	1 Bar/27g	129	479	4.7	63.6	22.8	0.0
Tracker, Yoghurt, Mars*	1 Bar/27g	133	491	6.3	64.2	23.2	0.0
Trophy, Organic Four Fruits, Village Bakery*	1 Bar/42.5g	150	348	5.0	67.0	6.6	5.3
Trophy, Organic, Four Seeds, Village Bakery*	1 Bar/42.6g	175	410	9.6	58.5	15.3	5.6
Turkish Delight, Co-Op*	1 Bar/53g	207	390	2.0	78.0	8.0	0.1
Turkish Delight, Diabetic, Thorntons*	1 Serving/37g	95	257	1.9	51.4	8.9	1.4
Vanilla Fudge, Diabetic, Thorntons*	1 Bar/34g	156	460	3.3	69.2	18.8	0.6
Very Berry, Cookie, Big Softies, Fox's*	1 Bar/26.2g	85	325	5.7	69.7	2.5	2.5
Wafer Biscuit, Milk Chocolate Coated, Value, Tesco*	1 Bar/24g	126	526	6.9	61.4	28.1	1.7
Wafer, Chocolate Flavour Crisp, Carbolite*	1 Bar/25g	120	482	8.5	52.3	34.8	2.0
White Chocolate, Mueslix, Kellogg's*	1 Bar/25g	110	440	6.0	64.0	18.0	3.0
Wild & Whippy, Tesco*	1 Treat Bar/17.5g	80	447	3.7	72.0	16.0	0.8
Yoghurt & Muesli, Meal, SlimFast*	1 Bar/60g	221	368	24.0	46.2	11.7	6.7
Yoghurt Coated Almond & Apricot, Eat Natural*	1 Bar/50g	278	556	9.4	55.4	33.8	0.0
BASIL,							
Dried, Ground	1 Tsp/1.4g	3	251	14.4	43.2	4.0	0.0
Fresh	1 Tbsp/5.3g	2	40	3.1	5.1	0.8	0.0
BASS,							
Sea, Raw, Average	1oz/28g	32	113	20.3	0.0	3.5	0.1
BATTER MIX,							
For Pancakes & Yorkshire Puddings, McDougalls*	1 Pancake/38g	83	218	6.3	24.8	10.4	1.9
For Yorkshire Puddings & Pancakes, Tesco*	1 Serving/17g	61	359	12.3	74.4	1.4	7.7
Greens*	1 Bag/125g	296	237	8.7	34.3	7.2	0.0
Made Up With Water & Egg, Safeway*	1 Serving/100g	143	143	6.4	23.1	2.8	4.1

B

	Measure INFO/WEIGHT	per Measure KCAL	Nutrition Values per 100g / 100ml				
			KCAL	PROT	CARB	FAT	FIBRE
BATTER MIX,							
Pancakes, Sainsbury's*	1 Pancake/63g	96	152	6.5	27.4	1.8	3.1
SmartPrice, Asda*	1 Pack/128g	421	329	11.0	69.0	1.0	3.3
Tesco*	1 Pack/130g	467	359	12.3	74.4	1.4	7.7
Value, Made Up, Tesco*	½ Pack/64g	92	143	6.4	23.1	2.8	4.1
BAY LEAVES,							
Dried	1oz/28g	88	313	7.6	48.6	8.4	0.0
BEAN SPROUTS,							
Average	½ Pack/100g	27	27	2.3	3.2	0.6	1.2
Bean Cuisine, Natura Organic*	1 Serving/100g	117	117	7.6	18.0	1.7	7.0
BEANFEAST,							
Bolognese, Batchelors*	1 Serving/65g	196	302	23.9	39.0	5.6	13.5
Mexican Chilli, Batchelors*	1 Serving/65g	203	312	24.3	42.7	4.9	13.6
Savoury Mince, Batchelors*	1 Serving/65g	205	316	24.7	39.5	6.6	12.7
BEANS,							
& Meatballs, In Tomato Sauce, Sainsbury's*	½ Can/200g	216	108	5.5	13.3	3.6	2.6
& Peas, Marks & Spencer*	1oz/28g	13	48	4.2	6.5	0.5	6.1
Aduki, Dried, Boiled in Unsalted Water	1 Tbsp/30g	37	123	9.3	22.5	0.2	5.5
Aduki, Dried, Raw	1 Tbsp/30g	82	272	19.9	50.1	0.5	11.1
Baked, & Jumbo Sausages, Asda*	1 Serving/210g	317	151	7.0	15.0	7.0	2.6
Baked, & Pork Sausages, Co-Op*	½ Can/210g	189	90	4.0	12.0	3.0	4.0
Baked, & Pork Sausages, Sainsbury's*	1 Serving/210g	248	118	5.7	13.9	4.4	3.4
Baked, & Sausage In Tomato Sauce, SmartPrice, Asda*	½ Can/203g	256	126	5.0	13.0	6.0	0.0
Baked, & Sausage, Asda*	½ Can/205g	252	123	6.0	16.0	3.9	3.0
Baked, & Sausage, GFY, Asda*	1 Serving/217g	178	82	4.7	10.0	2.6	1.8
Baked, & Vegetarian Sausages, In Tomato Sauce, Tesco*	1 Can/420g	538	128	6.7	13.6	3.4	2.7
Baked, Barbecue, Heinz*	½ Can/100g	82	82	4.9	14.9	0.3	4.0
Baked, Cheezy, Heinz*	1oz/28g	53	189	11.6	24.5	4.9	6.2
Baked, Curried, Average	½ Can/210g	203	97	4.9	17.2	0.9	3.6
Baked, In Tomato Sauce, Average	1 Can/400g	346	86	4.8	16.0	0.5	3.3
Baked, In Tomato Sauce, Healthy Range, Average	1oz/28g	19	68	3.9	12.8	0.2	2.8
Baked, In Tomato Sauce, Reduced Sugar & Salt, Average	½ Can/210g	159	76	4.6	13.7	0.3	3.8
Baked, With Chicken Nuggets, Heinz*	1 Can/200g	210	105	6.8	12.5	3.2	3.2
Baked, With Pork Sausages, Heinz*	½ Can/207g	184	89	5.5	11.2	2.5	2.6
Baked, With Pork Sausages, Tesco*	1 Can/220g	279	127	5.7	14.9	3.1	2.9
Baked, With Vegetable Sausages, Heinz*	1 Can/200g	212	106	6.1	12.2	3.6	2.9
Black, Canned In Salt, Drained, Zeta*	1 Can/250g	263	105	9.0	16.0	0.6	6.4
Blackeye, Canned, Average	1 Can/172g	206	120	8.5	19.8	0.8	3.3
Blackeye, Dried, Raw	1oz/28g	87	311	23.5	54.1	1.6	8.2
Borlotti, Canned, Average	1oz/28g	29	103	7.6	16.9	0.5	4.7
Broad, Canned, Average	1oz/28g	25	91	8.4	13.1	0.8	4.4
Broad, Dried, Raw	1oz/28g	69	245	26.1	32.5	2.1	27.6
Broad, Raw, Average	1 Can/195g	134	69	6.8	8.9	0.8	6.2
Butter, Canned, Average	1oz/28g	22	79	5.9	12.9	0.5	4.1
Butter, Dried, Boiled, Average	1oz/28g	30	106	7.2	18.7	0.6	5.2
Butter, Dried, Raw	1oz/28g	81	290	19.1	52.9	1.7	16.0
Cannellini, Canned, Average	1oz/28g	26	94	7.2	15.0	0.5	5.7
Cannellini, Dried, Boiled, Sainsbury's*	1 Pack/250g	243	97	6.8	16.6	0.5	7.4
Chilli, Canned, Average	1 Can/420g	381	91	5.2	15.9	0.7	4.4
Dwarf, Sainsbury's*	1oz/28g	7	25	1.9	3.1	0.5	2.2
Flageolet, Canned, Average	1 Can/265g	235	89	6.8	14.1	0.6	3.5
French, Canned, Average	1oz/28g	6	22	1.7	3.5	0.3	2.5
French, Raw	1oz/28g	7	24	1.9	3.2	0.5	2.2
Green, Cut, Average	1 Can/225g	50	22	1.7	3.7	0.2	2.1

INFO/WEIGHT	Measure	per Measure KCAL	Nutrition Values per 100g / 100ml				
			KCAL	PROT	CARB	FAT	FIBRE
BEANS,							
Green, Fine, Average	1 Serving/75g	18	25	1.8	3.4	0.4	2.6
Green, Sliced, Average	1oz/28g	6	23	1.9	3.5	0.2	2.1
Green, Sliced, Frozen, Average	1 Serving/50g	13	26	1.8	4.4	0.1	4.1
Green, Whole, Average	½ Can/110g	25	22	1.6	3.0	0.4	1.7
Haricot, Canned, In Salted Water, Safeway*	1 Can/265g	257	97	6.6	16.6	0.5	4.9
Haricot, Dried, Boiled in Unsalted Water	1oz/28g	27	95	6.6	17.2	0.5	6.1
Haricot, Dried, Raw	1oz/28g	80	286	21.4	49.7	1.6	17.0
Kidney, Red, Canned, Average	½ Can/90g	92	102	7.8	16.7	0.6	5.6
Kidney, Red, Dried, Boiled in Unsalted Water	1oz/28g	29	103	8.4	17.4	0.5	6.7
Kidney, Red, Dried, Raw	1oz/28g	74	266	22.1	44.1	1.4	15.7
Kidney, Red, In Chilli Sauce, Sainsbury's*	1 Can/420g	340	81	5.1	14.3	0.4	4.3
Kidney, White, Dry, Raw, Unico*	½ Cup Dry/80g	270	338	22.5	61.3	1.1	21.3
Mixed, Canned, Average	1 Can/300g	300	100	6.8	15.7	1.2	4.1
Mixed, In Spicy Pepper Sauce, Sainsbury's*	½ Can/210g	187	89	4.7	15.3	1.0	3.2
Mixed, In a Mild Chilli Sauce, Sainsbury's*	½ Can/208g	162	78	5.2	13.5	0.3	5.2
Mixed, Spicy, Average	1 Serving/140g	109	78	4.9	13.4	0.5	3.9
Mung, Whole, Dried, Boiled in Unsalted Water	1oz/28g	25	91	7.6	15.3	0.4	3.0
Mung, Whole, Dried, Raw	1oz/28g	78	279	23.9	46.3	1.1	10.0
Pinto, Dried, Boiled in Unsalted Water	1oz/28g	38	137	8.9	23.9	0.7	0.0
Pinto, Dried, Raw	1oz/28g	92	327	21.1	57.1	1.6	0.0
Pinto, In Water, Sugar & Salt Added, Sainsbury's*	½ Can/118g	124	105	7.7	17.5	0.7	5.0
Pinto, Re-fried Beans	1oz/28g	30	107	6.2	15.3	1.1	0.0
Refried, Average	1 Serving/215g	162	76	4.6	12.7	0.7	1.8
Runner & Carrots, Marks & Spencer*	1 Serving/240g	60	25	1.0	4.8	0.1	2.1
Runner, Raw, Average	1oz/28g	6	20	1.4	2.8	0.4	2.2
Soya, Dried, Average	1oz/28g	104	370	34.2	15.4	18.3	19.6
Soya, Dried, Boiled in Unsalted Water	1oz/28g	39	141	14.0	5.1	7.3	6.1
Stringless, Somerfield*	1 Serving/50g	12	23	1.6	3.2	0.4	2.0
Whole, Fine, Asda*	1 Serving/100g	25	25	1.7	4.4	0.1	4.1
BEEF,							
Brisket, Raw, Lean	1oz/28g	39	139	21.1	0.0	6.1	0.0
Brisket, Raw, Lean & Fat	1oz/28g	61	218	18.4	0.0	16.0	0.0
Cooked, From Supermarket, Average	1 Slice/35g	35	101	17.4	2.6	2.4	0.4
Escalope, Healthy Range, Average	1 Serving/170g	233	137	24.2	1.2	4.0	0.4
Flank, Pot-Roasted, Lean	1oz/28g	71	253	31.8	0.0	14.0	0.0
Flank, Pot-Roasted, Lean & Fat	1oz/28g	87	309	27.1	0.0	22.3	0.0
Flank, Raw, Lean	1oz/28g	49	175	22.7	0.0	9.3	0.0
Flank, Raw, Lean & Fat	1oz/28g	74	266	19.7	0.0	20.8	0.0
For Casserole, Lean, Diced, Average	1oz/28g	35	126	23.0	0.0	3.8	0.0
Fore Rib, Lean & Fat, Average	1oz/28g	40	144	21.7	0.1	6.3	0.2
Fore-Rib, Raw, Lean	1oz/28g	41	145	21.5	0.0	6.5	0.0
Fore-Rib, Roasted, Lean	1oz/28g	66	236	33.3	0.0	11.4	0.0
Fore-Rib, Roasted, Lean & Fat	1oz/28g	84	300	29.1	0.0	20.4	0.0
Grill Steak, Average	1 Steak/170g	501	295	19.3	2.1	23.2	0.1
Joint, For Roasting, Average	1oz/28g	38	134	24.5	1.4	3.5	0.2
Joint, Sirloin, Roasted, Lean	1oz/28g	53	188	32.4	0.0	6.5	0.0
Joint, Sirloin, Roasted, Lean & Fat	1oz/28g	65	233	29.8	0.0	12.6	0.0
Mince, Cooked, Average	1 Serving/75g	214	286	24.0	0.0	20.3	0.0
Mince, Extra Lean, Raw, Average	1oz/28g	49	175	22.0	0.0	9.7	0.0
Mince, Extra Lean, Stewed	1oz/28g	50	177	24.7	0.0	8.7	0.0
Mince, Lean, Raw, Average	1 Serving/100g	131	131	21.0	0.0	5.3	0.0
Mince, Raw, Average	1oz/28g	67	239	18.7	0.3	18.0	0.1
Mince, Steak, Extra Lean, Average	1oz/28g	37	131	20.5	0.4	5.6	0.0

B

BEEF,

	Measure INFO/WEIGHT	per Measure KCAL	KCAL	PROT	CARB	FAT	FIBRE
Mince, Steak, Lean, Average	1 Serving/100g	171	171	21.4	0.0	9.7	0.0
Mince, Steak, Raw, Average	1 Serving/125g	195	156	21.6	0.0	7.7	0.0
Mince, Stewed	1oz/28g	59	209	21.8	0.0	13.5	0.0
Peppered, Sliced, Average	1 Slice/20g	26	129	18.2	1.3	5.6	1.0
Roast, Sliced, Average	1 Slice/35g	48	136	26.1	0.4	3.6	0.2
Salt, Average	1 Serving/70g	80	114	21.7	1.0	2.5	0.1
Salted, Dried, Raw	1oz/28g	70	250	55.4	0.0	1.5	0.0
Silverside, Pot Roasted, Lean	1oz/28g	54	193	34.0	0.0	6.3	0.0
Silverside, Pot-Roasted, Lean & Fat	1oz/28g	69	247	31.0	0.0	13.7	0.0
Silverside, Raw, Lean	1oz/28g	38	134	23.8	0.0	4.3	0.0
Silverside, Raw, Lean & Fat	1oz/28g	60	215	20.4	0.0	14.8	0.0
Silverside, Salted, Boiled, Lean	1oz/28g	52	184	30.4	0.0	6.9	0.0
Silverside, Salted, Boiled, Lean & Fat	1oz/28g	63	224	27.9	0.0	12.5	0.0
Silverside, Salted, Raw, Lean	1oz/28g	39	140	19.2	0.0	7.0	0.0
Silverside, Salted, Raw, Lean & Fat	1oz/28g	64	227	16.3	0.0	18.0	0.0
Steak, Braising, Braised, Lean	1oz/28g	63	225	34.4	0.0	9.7	0.0
Steak, Braising, Braised, Lean & Fat	1oz/28g	69	246	32.9	0.0	12.7	0.0
Steak, Braising, Lean, Raw, Average	1oz/28g	40	145	24.8	0.0	5.0	0.0
Steak, Braising, Raw, Lean & Fat	1oz/28g	45	160	20.7	0.0	8.6	0.0
Steak, Economy, Average	1oz/28g	53	190	26.9	1.2	8.7	0.4
Steak, Fillet, Cooked, Average	1oz/28g	54	191	28.6	0.0	8.5	0.0
Steak, Fillet, Lean, Average	1oz/28g	42	150	21.0	0.0	7.3	0.0
Steak, Fillet, Lean, Cooked, Average	1oz/28g	52	186	28.7	0.0	8.0	0.0
Steak, Frying, Average	1 Steak/110g	128	116	23.7	0.0	2.5	0.0
Steak, Rump, Cooked, Average	1oz/28g	69	246	29.1	0.5	14.1	0.0
Steak, Rump, Lean, Cooked, Average	1oz/28g	50	179	31.0	0.0	6.1	0.0
Steak, Rump, Marinated Strips, Asda*	1oz/28g	66	235	17.6	0.1	18.3	0.1
Steak, Rump, Raw, Lean	1oz/28g	35	125	22.0	0.0	4.1	0.0
Steak, Rump, Raw, Lean & Fat	1oz/28g	49	174	20.7	0.0	10.1	0.0
Steak, Sirloin, Fried, Lean	1oz/28g	53	189	28.8	0.0	8.2	0.0
Steak, Sirloin, Fried, Lean & Fat	1oz/28g	65	233	26.8	0.0	14.0	0.0
Steak, Sirloin, Grilled, Medium-Rare, Lean	1oz/28g	49	176	26.6	0.0	7.7	0.0
Steak, Sirloin, Grilled, Medium-Rare, Lean & Fat	1oz/28g	60	213	24.8	0.0	12.6	0.0
Steak, Sirloin, Grilled, Rare, Lean	1oz/28g	46	166	26.4	0.0	6.7	0.0
Steak, Sirloin, Grilled, Rare, Lean & Fat	1oz/28g	60	216	25.1	0.0	12.8	0.0
Steak, Sirloin, Grilled, Well-Done, Lean	1oz/28g	63	225	33.9	0.0	9.9	0.0
Steak, Sirloin, Grilled, Well-Done, Lean & Fat	1oz/28g	72	257	31.8	0.0	14.4	0.0
Steak, Sirloin, Raw, Lean	1oz/28g	38	135	23.5	0.0	4.5	0.0
Steak, Sirloin, Raw, Lean & Fat	1oz/28g	56	201	21.6	0.0	12.7	0.0
Steak, Tender, Quick Cook, Average	1oz/28g	36	127	21.2	2.3	3.7	0.3
Stewed Steak, Average	1oz/28g	33	117	15.8	3.3	4.6	0.0
Stewing Steak, Lean & Fat, Raw, Average	1oz/28g	41	146	22.1	0.1	6.4	0.1
Stewing Steak, Raw, Lean	1oz/28g	34	122	22.6	0.0	3.5	0.0
Stewing Steak, Stewed, Lean	1oz/28g	52	185	32.0	0.0	6.3	0.0
Stewing Steak, Stewed, Lean & Fat	1oz/28g	57	203	29.2	0.0	9.6	0.0
Strips, For Stir Fry, Raw, Average	1 Serving/125g	146	117	23.6	0.0	2.5	0.3
Topside, Lean & Fat, Average	1oz/28g	61	220	27.5	0.0	12.2	0.0
Topside, Raw, Lean	1oz/28g	32	116	23.0	0.0	2.7	0.0
Wafer Thin Sliced, Cooked, Average	1 Slice/10g	13	129	24.5	0.5	3.2	0.2

BEEF &,

	Measure INFO/WEIGHT	per Measure KCAL	KCAL	PROT	CARB	FAT	FIBRE
Beer, Princes*	½ Can/205g	215	105	14.0	5.5	3.0	0.0
Chips, Steak, Healthy Eating, Tesco*	1 Pack/450g	473	105	6.3	13.8	2.7	0.5
Gravy, Lean Roast, Bird's Eye*	1 Portion/114g	111	97	13.3	3.0	3.5	0.1

	INFO/WEIGHT	KCAL	KCAL	PROT	CARB	FAT	FIBRE
BEEF &,							
Onions, Minced, Asda*	½ Can/196g	314	160	13.0	4.6	10.0	0.1
Yorkshire Pudding, Minced, Sainsbury's*	1 Pack/350g	375	107	8.4	10.7	3.4	1.1
BEEF BORDELAISE,							
Sainsbury's*	1 Pack/400.8g	525	131	8.7	9.7	6.4	1.0
BEEF BOURGUIGNON,							
Extra Special, Asda*	1 Serving/300g	*279	93	9.3	5.7	3.7	0.7
Finest, Tesco*	1 Serving/300g	351	117	15.5	3.5	4.5	1.2
BEEF BRAISED,							
& Mashed Potato, Sainsbury's*	1 Pack/450g	473	105	7.7	10.3	3.9	0.8
& Veg With Mashed Potato, Sainsbury's*	1 Pack/453g	331	73	6.5	8.9	1.3	1.2
& Vegetables With Mashed Potato, BGTY, Sainsbury's*	1 Pack/453g	331	73	6.5	8.9	1.3	1.2
Steak, & Cabbage, COU, Marks & Spencer*	1 Pack/380g	323	85	8.3	6.7	2.6	1.9
Steak, & Carrots, Mini Favourites, Marks & Spencer*	1 Serving/200g	140	70	8.0	4.2	2.5	1.3
Steak, & Mash, GFY, Asda*	1 Pack/400g	260	65	3.4	11.0	0.8	0.7
Steak, & Mash, Good Intentions, Somerfield*	1 Pack/400g	396	99	7.4	10.5	3.0	0.5
Steak, & Mash, Healthy Living, Tesco*	1 Pack/450g	419	93	7.0	10.2	2.7	0.7
Steak, & Mustard Mash, Healthy Eating, Tesco*	1 Pack/450g	392	87	7.4	9.5	2.1	0.7
Steak, COU, Marks & Spencer*	½ Pack/225g	180	80	11.9	3.6	2.2	0.7
Steak, With Colcannon Mash, Tesco*	1 Pack/450g	477	106	9.5	9.0	3.5	0.9
With Parsnip Mash, Eat Smart, Safeway*	1 Pack/400g	300	75	6.8	8.2	1.2	1.1
BEEF CANTONESE,							
Sainsbury's*	½ Pack/175g	200	114	5.5	20.1	1.3	0.5
BEEF CHASSEUR,							
& Potato Mash, BGTY, Sainsbury's*	1 Pack/450g	468	104	8.8	11.0	2.8	0.7
& Potato Mash, New, BGTY, Sainsbury's*	1 Pack/452g	411	91	7.6	9.6	2.5	0.8
Somerfield*	1 Serving/275g	287	104	14.8	5.2	2.7	2.1
BEEF DINNER,							
Roast, Bird's Eye*	1 Pack/283g	297	105	8.2	10.8	3.2	0.0
Roast, Iceland*	1 Serving/340g	354	104	8.5	9.1	3.7	1.6
Roast, New, Bird's Eye*	1 Pack/340g	374	110	8.4	11.1	3.6	1.4
Sliced, Farmfoods*	1 Serving/300g	195	65	4.0	10.6	0.7	1.7
Tesco*	1 Pack/400g	340	85	6.7	9.2	2.4	2.9
BEEF HOT & SOUR,							
Chef's Selection, Marks & Spencer*	1 Pack/329g	395	120	9.2	8.4	5.3	1.3
With Garlic Rice, BGTY, Sainsbury's*	1 Pack/400g	428	107	5.9	17.0	1.7	0.6
BEEF IN,							
Ale Gravy, Chunky, Bird's Eye*	1 Pack/340g	272	80	7.4	8.3	2.0	1.5
Ale With Mushrooms, BGTY, Sainsbury's*	1 Pack/250.6g	193	77	10.2	5.6	1.5	0.4
Black Bean Sauce, Chinese Takeaway, Sainsbury's*	1 Pack/386g	432	112	10.9	7.3	4.3	1.1
Black Bean Sauce, Marks & Spencer*	1 Pack/350g	350	100	7.8	9.1	3.4	1.1
Burgundy Red Wine, GFY, Asda*	1 Pack/405g	348	86	8.0	9.0	2.0	1.1
Creamy Peppercorn Sauce, Steak, Tesco*	1 Steak/150g	200	133	19.6	0.4	5.9	0.5
Gravy, Sliced, Sainsbury's*	1 Serving/125g	100	80	13.5	2.6	1.8	0.2
Gravy, Slices, Tesco*	1 Serving/200g	158	79	11.9	2.6	2.3	0.6
Madras Sauce, BGTY, Sainsbury's*	1 Can/400g	344	86	9.5	4.0	3.6	0.9
Oriental Sauce, Lean Cuisine, Findus*	1 Pack/350g	420	120	4.5	20.0	2.5	1.5
Red Wine Sauce, Marks & Spencer*	1oz/28g	34	120	13.2	3.6	5.9	0.3
Red Wine With Mashed Potato, Eat Smart, Safeway*	1 Serving/400g	340	85	4.6	12.6	1.4	0.7
Red Wine With Mashed Potato, Healthy Living, Tesco*	1 Pack/400g	288	72	3.4	10.2	1.9	1.7
Red Wine With Parsley Rice, Healthy Living, Tesco*	1 Serving/440g	431	98	4.9	16.9	1.4	0.6
Red Wine With Spinach Mash, Waitrose*	1 Pack/400g	304	76	6.7	9.6	1.2	1.3
Red Wine, Balanced Lifestyle, Aldi*	1 Pack/600g	426	71	10.5	2.4	2.1	1.8

B

	Measure INFO/WEIGHT	per Measure KCAL	Nutrition Values per 100g / 100ml				
			KCAL	PROT	CARB	FAT	FIBRE
BEEF MEAL,							
Roast, Mini Favourite, Marks & Spencer*	1 Pack/200g	140	70	9.1	6.0	1.3	0.7
BEEF PLATTER,							
Hillcrest, Aldi*	1 Pack/400g	312	78	7.7	7.2	2.0	2.4
BEEF SZECHUAN,							
Sizzling Hot Spicy, Oriental Express*	1 Pack/400g	380	95	6.4	13.2	1.9	2.0
BEEF TERIYAKI,							
With Noodles, BGTY, Sainsbury's*	1 Pack/400g	320	80	7.7	10.1	1.0	1.0
BEEF WELLINGTON,							
Extra Special, Asda*	1 Serving/218.4g	604	277	11.0	20.0	17.0	0.9
Finest, Tesco*	1/3 Pack/216g	525	243	13.0	12.3	15.7	1.5
Marks & Spencer*	1oz/28g	76	270	10.7	17.5	18.3	1.4
Sainsbury's*	1 Serving/175g	473	270	14.7	18.0	15.5	0.4
BEEF WITH,							
Black Bean Sauce, Chilli, Sainsbury's*	1 Pack/300g	336	112	8.7	8.6	4.8	1.0
Honey & Black Pepper, Waitrose*	1 Pack/350g	326	93	9.1	9.4	2.1	1.8
Onion & Gravy, Minced, Princes*	1 Serving/200g	342	171	9.9	5.5	12.2	0.0
Onions, Minced, Co-Op*	½ Can/196g	274	140	12.0	4.0	8.0	0.9
Oyster Sauce, Ooodles Of Noodles, Oriental Express*	1 Pack/425g	378	89	4.9	14.2	1.3	1.5
Peppercorn Sauce, Rib Eye Joint, Sainsbury's*	1 Serving/181.8g	300	165	22.2	3.4	7.0	0.1
Shiraz Wine Sauce, Roast, Finest, Tesco*	1 Pack/350g	350	100	14.1	5.1	2.6	0.9
Vegetable Rice, Hot & Sour, COU, Marks & Spencer*	1 Pack/400g	360	90	5.5	14.4	1.4	0.6
Vegetables & Gravy, Minced, Bird's Eye*	1 Pack/178g	155	87	9.1	5.1	3.4	0.6
Whisky, Collops, Sainsbury's*	1 Pack/450g	513	114	8.0	4.1	7.3	1.2
BEER,							
Bitter, Canned	1 Can/440ml	141	32	0.3	2.3	0.0	0.0
Bitter, Draught	1 Pint/568ml	182	32	0.3	2.3	0.0	0.0
Bitter, Keg	1 Pint/568ml	176	31	0.3	2.3	0.0	0.0
Bitter, Low Alcohol	1 Pint/568ml	74	13	0.2	2.1	0.0	0.0
Brown Ale, Bottled	1 Bottle/330ml	99	30	0.3	3.0	0.0	0.0
Extra Light, Sleeman Breweries*	1 Bottle/341ml	90	26	0.0	0.7	0.0	0.0
Ginger, Classic, Schweppes*	1 Can/330ml	115	35	0.0	8.4	0.0	0.0
Ginger, Diet, Sainsbury's*	1 Glass/200ml	2	1	0.0	0.1	0.0	0.0
Ginger, Light, Waitrose*	1 Glass/250ml	3	1	0.0	0.0	0.1	0.1
Ginger, Old Jamaica, Light, DG	1 Glass/200ml	6	3	0.1	0.1	0.1	0.0
Ginger, Sainsbury's*	1 Can/330ml	178	54	0.0	13.0	0.0	0.0
Ginger, Tesco*	1 Serving/200ml	70	35	0.1	8.2	0.1	0.0
Ginger, Traditional Style, Tesco*	1 Can/330ml	218	66	0.0	16.1	0.0	0.0
Guinness*, Draught	1 Pint/568ml	210	37	0.3	3.2	0.1	0.0
Guinness*, Stout	1 Pint/568ml	170	30	0.4	1.5	0.0	0.0
Mackeson, Stout	1 Pint/568ml	205	36	0.4	4.6	0.0	0.0
Mild, Draught	1 Pint/568ml	136	24	0.2	1.6	0.0	0.0
Ultra, Michelob*	1 Bottle/275ml	88	32	0.0	0.9	0.0	0.0
Weissbier, Alcohol Free, Erdinger*	1 Bottle/500ml	125	25	0.4	5.3	0.0	0.0
Wheat, Tesco*	1 Bottle/500ml	155	31	0.5	0.4	0.0	0.0
BEETROOT,							
& Roasted Red Onion, Marks & Spencer*	1 Serving/125g	94	75	1.5	12.6	2.1	2.5
Baby, Pickled, Average	1oz/28g	10	37	1.7	7.3	0.1	1.2
Pickled, In Sweet Vinegar, Average	1oz/28g	16	57	1.2	12.8	0.1	1.5
Pickled, In Vinegar, Average	1 Serving/50g	19	37	1.6	7.5	0.1	1.2
Raw, Average	1oz/28g	9	32	1.6	6.0	0.1	1.9
BHAJI,							
Aubergine & Potato	1oz/28g	36	130	2.0	12.0	8.8	1.7
Bhajia Selection, Occasions, Sainsbury's*	1 Serving/15g	32	211	4.8	19.7	12.6	0.0

	Measure INFO/WEIGHT	per Measure KCAL	Nutrition Values per 100g / 100ml				
			KCAL	PROT	CARB	FAT	FIBRE
BHAJI,							
Cabbage & Pea With Vegetable Oil	1oz/28g	50	178	3.3	9.2	14.7	3.4
Cauliflower	1oz/28g	60	214	4.0	4.0	20.5	2.0
Mushroom	1oz/28g	46	166	1.7	4.4	16.1	1.3
Mushroom, Marks & Spencer*	1 Pack/225g	293	130	3.6	5.1	10.4	3.9
Okra, Bangladeshi With Butter Ghee	1oz/28g	27	95	2.5	7.6	6.4	3.2
Onion, Asda*	1 Mini Bhaji/49g	96	196	6.0	20.0	10.0	2.0
Onion, Indian Starter Selection, Marks & Spencer*	1 Bhaji/22g	65	295	5.7	15.8	23.3	2.8
Onion, Indian Style Selection, Co-Op*	1 Bhaji/18.2g	40	220	8.0	29.0	8.0	6.0
Onion, Marks & Spencer*	1 Serving/115g	219	190	4.8	24.0	8.5	1.5
Onion, Marks & Spencer*	1 Serving/80g	164	205	5.2	25.8	9.1	1.6
Onion, Mini, Asda*	1 Bhaji/19.2g	56	297	9.0	36.0	13.0	4.5
Onion, Mini, Morrisons*	1 Bhaji/18g	58	320	5.7	36.3	16.8	3.2
Onion, Mini, Sainsbury's*	1 Serving/22g	43	196	5.9	18.7	10.8	3.4
Onion, Mini, Tesco*	1 Serving/23g	48	210	7.3	26.7	8.2	1.3
Onion, Mini, Waitrose*	1 Bhaji/21g	51	243	5.0	13.9	18.6	4.2
Onion, Morrisons*	1 Bhaji/50g	111	222	5.7	20.3	13.1	3.5
Onion, Safeway*	1 Bhaji/23g	40	175	5.7	20.3	7.5	3.5
Onion, Sainsbury's*	1 Bhaji/33g	75	226	6.0	31.7	8.3	1.1
Onion, Somerfield*	1 Bhaji/15g	39	262	5.0	15.0	20.0	0.0
Onion, Waitrose*	1 Bhaji/45g	100	223	5.6	17.7	14.4	4.3
Onion, With Tomato & Chilli Dip, Marks & Spencer*	2 Bhajis/107.5g	205	190	4.8	24.0	8.5	1.5
Potato & Onion	1oz/28g	45	160	2.1	16.6	10.1	1.6
Potato, Onion & Mushroom	1oz/28g	58	208	2.0	12.0	17.5	1.5
Potato, Spinach & Cauliflower	1oz/28g	47	169	2.2	7.1	15.1	1.4
Spinach	1oz/28g	23	83	3.3	2.6	6.8	2.4
Spinach & Potato	1oz/28g	53	191	3.7	13.4	14.1	2.3
Turnip & Onion	1oz/28g	36	128	1.3	7.1	10.9	2.2
Vegetable With Vegetable Oil	1oz/28g	59	212	2.1	10.1	18.5	2.4
BHUNA,							
Chicken & Rice, Sainsbury's*	1 Pack/500.7g	696	139	7.3	13.3	6.3	1.5
Chicken Tikka, Tesco*	1 Pack/350g	462	132	11.4	4.5	7.6	0.5
Prawn, Co-Op*	1 Pack/400g	300	75	3.0	6.0	4.0	1.0
BIERWURST,							
Average	1 Slice/10g	25	253	14.5	1.0	21.2	0.1
BILBERRIES,							
Fresh, Raw	1oz/28g	8	30	0.6	6.9	0.2	1.8
BILTONG,							
Average	1 Serving/25g	64	256	50.0	0.0	4.0	0.0
BIRYANI,							
Chicken Tikka With Basmati Rice, Sharwood's*	1 Pack/373g	481	129	6.3	16.2	4.3	0.9
Chicken Tikka With Pilau Rice, Iceland*	1 Pack/500g	520	104	4.3	15.8	2.6	1.4
Chicken Tikka, BGTY, Sainsbury's*	1 Pack/450g	491	109	9.7	13.2	1.9	1.3
Chicken Tikka, Healthy Eating, Tesco*	1 Pack/450g	482	107	6.4	18.6	0.8	1.0
Chicken Tikka, Northern Indian, Sainsbury's*	1 Pack/450g	698	155	9.4	16.5	5.7	1.2
Chicken With Rice, Tesco*	1 Pack/475g	518	109	7.2	12.1	3.5	1.0
Chicken, Easy Steam, Healthy Living, Tesco*	1 Pack/400g	424	106	7.0	15.5	1.8	0.6
Chicken, Healthy Choice, Nisa Heritage*	1 Pack/400g	380	95	6.6	12.0	2.3	1.0
Chicken, Healthy Eating, Tesco*	1 Pack/370g	289	78	8.5	10.0	0.5	0.4
Chicken, Indian, Asda*	1 Pack/450g	779	173	9.0	23.0	5.0	0.7
Chicken, Marks & Spencer*	1 Pack/400g	800	200	7.8	19.8	10.1	1.2
Chicken, Rice Bowl, Eat Smart, Safeway*	1 Pack/300g	255	85	5.5	11.3	1.6	2.4
Chicken, Tesco*	1 Pack/500g	640	128	6.0	15.0	4.9	0.6
Chicken, Waitrose*	1 Pack/450g	657	146	10.1	15.4	4.9	1.6

B

	Measure INFO/WEIGHT	per Measure KCAL	Nutrition Values per 100g / 100ml				
			KCAL	PROT	CARB	FAT	FIBRE
BIRYANI,							
Chicken, Weight Watchers*	1 Pack/330g	300	91	6.0	14.2	1.1	0.6
Vegetable & Rice, Patak's*	1 Pack/370g	481	130	2.5	18.8	5.5	0.7
Vegetable & Rice, Sainsbury's*	½ Pack/125.0g	229	183	4.4	32.4	4.0	0.7
Vegetable With Curry, Budgens*	1 Serving/250g	378	151	3.4	22.9	5.1	1.5
Vegetable, Healthy Living, Tesco*	1 Pack/450g	455	101	2.7	17.9	2.1	1.6
Vegetable, Sainsbury's*	1 Serving/225g	329	146	2.4	16.3	7.9	1.1
Vegetable, Waitrose*	1 Pack/450g	486	108	2.8	15.2	4.0	2.2
BISCUITS,							
Abbey Crunch, McVitie's*	1 Biscuit/9g	43	477	6.0	72.8	17.9	2.5
Abernethy, Simmers*	2 Biscuits/12.4g	59	490	5.7	69.2	21.9	0.0
Ace Milk Chocolate, McVitie's*	1 Biscuit/24g	122	510	6.1	66.2	24.5	1.6
After Eight, Nestle*	1 Biscuit/5g	26	525	6.5	62.6	27.7	1.5
All Butter Viennese, Marks & Spencer*	1 Biscuit/7g	40	571	7.1	71.4	31.4	1.4
All Butter, Asda*	1 Biscuit/9g	44	487	6.0	64.0	23.0	1.9
All Butter, Tesco*	1 Biscuit/9g	44	486	6.3	63.5	23.0	1.9
Almond Butter Thins, Extra Special, Asda*	1 Biscuit/4g	15	375	5.0	60.0	12.5	2.5
Almond Fingers, Tesco*	1 Finger/46g	180	391	6.2	58.4	14.7	1.0
Almond Thins, All Butter, Occasions, Sainsbury's*	1 Biscuit/3.1g	14	450	6.7	72.8	14.7	3.1
Almond Thins, Sainsbury's*	1 Biscuit/3g	13	430	7.0	80.3	9.0	1.0
Almond, Cantuccini*	1 Biscuit/8g	39	483	10.0	70.0	17.0	0.0
Amaretti, Doria*	1 Biscuit/4g	17	433	6.0	84.8	7.8	0.0
Amaretti, Marks & Spencer*	1 Biscuit/6g	30	480	9.6	71.3	17.2	3.8
Amaretti, Sainsbury's*	1 Biscuit/6g	27	450	6.5	80.5	11.3	1.1
Animal Bites, Cadbury's*	1 Pack/25g	120	480	7.1	69.8	19.0	0.0
Animals, Milk Chocolate, Cadbury's*	1 Biscuit/19g	94	493	6.6	69.8	20.9	0.0
Animals, Mini Packs, Cadburys*	1 Pack/25g	123	491	6.7	70.7	20.2	0.0
Animals, Minis, Cadbury's*	1 Biscuit/2.1g	10	480	6.5	68.5	20.1	0.0
Apple & Sultana, Go Ahead, McVitie's*	1 Biscuit/15g	56	386	6.0	72.7	7.9	3.3
Apple Crumble, Officially Low Fat, Fox's*	1 Biscuit/23.3g	84	365	5.4	80.4	2.4	2.5
Apple Strudel, Big Softies, Fox's*	1 Biscuit/23g	80	348	5.3	77.0	1.6	2.8
Apricot, Low Fat, Marks & Spencer*	1 Biscuit/23g	79	343	6.1	69.6	4.4	7.8
Arrowroot, Thin, Crawfords*	1 Biscuit/7.4g	33	473	7.4	76.7	15.2	2.2
BN, Chocolate Flavour, McVitie's*	1 Biscuit/18g	83	460	6.6	71.0	16.7	2.6
BN, Strawberry Flavour, McVitie's*	1 Biscuit/18g	71	395	5.6	78.0	6.8	0.0
BN, Vanilla Flavour, McVitie's*	1 Biscuit/18g	85	470	5.9	74.0	16.6	1.2
Banana Milk Shake, Creams, Safeway*	1 Biscuit/13.0g	60	460	5.6	70.9	16.8	1.8
Belgian Chocolate, Selection, Finest, Tesco*	1 Biscuit/10g	52	515	6.0	62.0	27.0	3.0
Bio*	1 Biscuit/10g	47	467	5.8	64.8	23.8	3.2
Bisc & Bounty, Masterfoods*	1 Bar/25g	132	526	4.8	52.3	33.0	0.0
Bisc & M&M's, Masterfoods*	1 Biscuit/25g	132	527	5.8	59.2	29.6	0.0
Bisc & Mars, Masterfoods*	1 Bar/27g	141	523	5.3	61.4	28.5	0.0
Bisc & Twix, Masterfoods*	1 Bar/27g	140	520	5.2	61.1	28.3	0.0
Biscotti, Almond, Pan Ducale*	1 Serving/30g	130	433	10.0	60.0	16.7	3.3
Biscotti, Starbucks*	1 Biscuit/27g	100	370	7.4	55.6	14.8	0.0
Blackcurrant With Wheat Bran, Bisca*	4 Biscuits/30g	126	420	6.0	72.0	12.0	5.5
Boasters, Hazelnut & Choc Chip, McVitie's*	1 Biscuit/16g	88	549	7.0	55.5	33.3	2.4
Bourbon Creams, Asda*	1 Biscuit/14g	70	485	6.0	68.0	21.0	2.2
Bourbon Creams, Crawfords*	1 Biscuit/12g	59	495	5.9	71.2	20.7	2.2
Bourbon Creams, Sainsbury's*	1 Biscuit/13g	60	476	5.7	70.4	19.1	1.7
Bourbon Creams, Tesco*	1 Biscuit/14g	68	485	5.6	67.8	21.3	2.2
Bourbon Creams, Value, Multipack, Tesco*	1 Biscuit/13g	62	494	5.9	68.0	22.8	1.7
Bourbon, Belmont, Aldi*	1 Biscuit/14g	68	490	5.6	68.8	21.4	1.9
Brandy Snaps, All Butter, Fox's*	1 Biscuit/12g	54	452	2.7	79.5	13.9	0.9

BISCUITS,

	Measure INFO/WEIGHT	per Measure KCAL	Nutrition Values per 100g / 100ml				
			KCAL	PROT	CARB	FAT	FIBRE
Breakfast, Aldi*	4 Biscuits/60g	213	355	13.7	69.5	2.5	7.5
Butter Crinkle Crunch, Fox's*	1 Biscuit/11g	52	470	5.7	70.2	18.2	1.9
Butter Puffs, Marks & Spencer*	1 Biscuit/10.5g	53	525	10.5	60.9	26.6	2.5
Butter Puffs, McVitie's*	1 Biscuit/10g	52	523	10.4	60.7	26.5	2.5
Butter Thins, Belgian Chocolate, The Best, Safeway*	1 Biscuit/10.1g	49	487	6.4	64.0	22.8	0.8
Butter, Dark Chocolate, Green & Black's*	1 Biscuit/8.3g	41	511	6.5	60.6	24.4	0.0
Cantuccini, Sainsbury's*	1 Biscuit/8g	35	440	10.4	63.1	16.2	4.4
Caramel Crunch, Go Ahead, McVitie's*	1 Bar/24g	106	440	4.7	76.6	13.8	0.8
Caramel Log, Tunnock's*	1 Biscuit/25g	118	472	4.2	64.3	24.0	0.0
Caramel Rocky Rounds, Fox's*	1 Biscuit/15g	72	480	6.2	62.3	22.9	1.1
Caramel Shortbread, Millionaires, Fox's*	1 Serving/16g	75	483	6.1	57.9	25.3	0.1
Caramel Shortcake, Aulds*	1 Slice/58g	286	493	4.4	52.9	29.7	0.8
Caramel Shortcake, Bobby's*	1 Slice/40g	201	502	4.7	50.5	31.2	0.0
Caramel Shortcake, Boots*	1 Piece/70g	317	453	4.8	59.0	22.0	1.0
Caramel Shortcake, Mr Kipling*	1 Shortcake/36g	177	506	4.2	57.6	28.8	1.3
Caramel Shortcake, Squares, Marks & Spencer*	1 Serving/40g	190	475	5.5	59.7	23.9	1.0
Caramel Shortcake, Tesco*	1 Shortcake/45g	217	482	4.6	57.8	25.8	0.5
Caramelised, Lotus*	1 Biscuit/9g	44	488	5.0	72.0	20.0	0.8
Caramels, Milk Chocolate, McVitie's*	1 Serving/17g	81	478	5.6	65.8	21.4	1.8
Cheese Savouries, Sainsbury's*	1 Serving/50g	268	536	11.6	53.3	30.6	2.5
Cherry Bakewell, Handfinished, Marks & Spencer*	1 Biscuit/40g	200	495	5.9	62.1	24.0	0.5
Chocahoops, Cadbury's*	1 Biscuit/12.7g	66	510	5.8	62.7	26.4	0.0
Choco Leibniz, Orange Flavour, Bahlsen*	1 Biscuit/14g	70	504	7.9	58.5	26.4	0.0
Chocolate & Coconut, Duchy Originals*	1 Biscuit/12.5g	71	543	6.3	52.1	34.4	2.6
Chocolate Fingers, Caramel, Cadbury's*	1 Finger/8g	39	490	5.8	63.2	23.8	0.0
Chocolate Fingers, Milk, Cadbury's*	1 Biscuit/6g	32	526	6.9	64.2	26.8	0.0
Chocolate Fingers, Milk, Extra Crunchy, Cadbury's*	1 Biscuit/5g	25	505	6.6	66.2	23.6	0.0
Chocolate Fingers, Milk, Mini, Marks & Spencer*	1 Finger/2.9g	15	515	7.1	59.5	27.9	3.4
Chocolate Fingers, Plain, Cadbury's*	1 Biscuit/6g	30	508	6.2	60.6	26.8	0.0
Chocolate Fingers, White, Cadbury's*	1 Biscuit/6g	32	530	6.7	62.4	28.2	0.0
Chocolate Flavour, Taillefine*	1 Biscuit/8g	33	408	5.8	70.8	10.8	5.8
Chocolate Ginger, Organic, Duchy Originals*	1 Biscuit/12.4g	62	518	4.6	59.7	29.0	2.1
Chocolate Ginger, Thorntons*	1 Biscuit/18.8g	97	512	5.9	58.2	28.4	0.0
Chocolate Kimberley, Jacob's*	1 Biscuit/20g	86	428	3.9	64.4	17.2	1.1
Chocolate Mousse Meringue, Occasions, Sainsbury's*	1 Biscuit/47g	245	522	5.6	55.7	30.7	3.2
Chocolate Orange, Thick Milk, Marks & Spencer*	1 Biscuit/13g	68	520	7.1	59.7	28.1	1.1
Chocolate Seville, Thorntons*	1 Biscuit/19g	97	512	5.7	59.0	28.1	0.0
Chocolate Teddy, Arnotts*	1 Biscuit/16.7g	81	478	6.6	69.3	19.2	2.0
Chocolate, Milk, Digestive, Homeblest*	1 Biscuit/12g	60	481	7.0	64.1	21.8	2.9
Chocolinis, Milk Chocolate, Go Ahead, McVitie's*	1 Biscuit/12g	56	466	7.7	77.2	14.0	2.0
Chocolinis, Plain Chocolate, McVitie's*	1 Biscuit/12g	56	468	6.9	77.0	14.7	2.6
Christmas Shapes, Assorted, Sainsbury's*	1 Biscuit/14.60g	77	525	5.2	59.0	29.8	1.7
Classic, Creams, Fox's*	1 Biscuit/14g	72	516	4.4	65.2	25.8	1.7
Classic, Fox's*	1 Biscuit/9g	43	480	4.6	68.6	20.8	2.2
Classic, Milk Chocolate, Fox's*	1 Biscuit/13g	67	517	6.1	64.9	24.0	1.6
Coconut Crinkle, Sainsbury's*	1 Biscuit/11g	54	500	6.4	59.6	26.2	3.7
Coconut Macaroon, Tesco*	1 Macaroon/30g	134	448	5.5	63.7	19.0	1.6
Coconut Ring, Asda*	1 Biscuit/7.6g	39	486	6.0	66.0	22.0	2.6
Coconut Rings, Happy Shopper*	1 Biscuit/8g	42	500	6.2	70.0	21.7	2.6
Coconut Rings, Tesco*	1 Biscuit/9g	44	485	6.2	66.1	21.7	2.6
Continental Chocolate, Parkwood, Aldi*	1 Biscuit/13g	65	499	7.5	62.5	24.3	2.6
Cranberry With Hip & Honey, Bisca*	4 Biscuits/30g	123	410	6.5	69.0	12.0	6.5
Crunchy Caramel, Tesco*	1 Bar/21g	98	467	4.8	56.2	25.2	1.4

BISCUITS,

INFO/WEIGHT	KCAL	KCAL	PROT	CARB	FAT	FIBRE
Curls, Marks & Spencer*	1 Curl/8g	43	540	5.0	63.8	30.0	1.3
Custard Creams, 25% Less Fat, Asda*	1 Biscuit/10g	47	474	6.0	72.0	18.0	1.2
Custard Creams, 25% Less Fat, Tesco*	1 Biscuit/12.5g	61	473	5.8	72.2	17.9	1.2
Custard Creams, BGTY, Sainsbury's*	1 Biscuit/12g	57	473	5.8	72.2	17.9	1.2
Custard Creams, Belmont, Aldi*	1 Biscuit/13g	63	501	5.1	66.7	23.8	1.6
Custard Creams, Belmont, Aldi*	1 Biscuit/13g	65	501	5.1	66.7	23.8	1.6
Custard Creams, Crawfords*	1 Biscuit/11g	57	517	5.9	69.2	24.1	1.5
Custard Creams, Jacob's*	1 Biscuit/16g	77	481	5.3	68.0	20.9	1.6
Custard Creams, Sainsbury's*	1 Cream/13g	64	496	6.0	67.3	22.6	1.6
Custard Creams, SmartPrice, Asda*	1 Biscuit/12.6g	63	486	6.0	69.0	21.0	1.6
Custard Creams, Somerfield*	1 Biscuit/11g	57	514	6.1	69.7	23.4	1.6
Custard Creams, Tesco*	1 Biscuit/12g	61	509	6.1	65.0	25.0	1.5
Custard Creams, Value, Multipack, Tesco*	1 Biscuit/13g	62	496	6.0	67.3	22.6	1.6
Custard Creams, Waitrose*	1 Biscuit/11.9g	62	514	5.5	70.4	23.4	1.6
Dark Chocolate All Butter, Marks & Spencer*	1 Biscuit/15g	72	480	6.9	52.4	27.2	11.4
Dark Chocolate Ginger, Marks & Spencer*	1 Biscuit/13.1g	64	495	5.6	68.2	22.3	1.6
Digestive, 25% Less Fat, Asda*	1 Biscuit/16g	73	455	7.3	69.8	16.3	2.6
Digestive, 25% Less Fat, Tesco*	1 Biscuit/14g	65	462	7.3	71.0	16.5	3.8
Digestive, BGTY, Sainsbury's*	1 Biscuit/15g	70	468	7.4	71.0	17.2	3.8
Digestive, Caramels, Milk Chocolate, McVitie's*	1 Biscuit/16g	76	477	5.6	65.7	21.4	1.8
Digestive, Caramels, Plain Chocolate, McVitie's*	1 Biscuit/17g	82	481	5.7	65.5	22.1	2.1
Digestive, Chocolate	1 Biscuit/ 17g	84	493	6.8	66.5	24.1	2.2
Digestive, Chocolate Chip, Asda*	1 Biscuit/13.8g	69	491	6.0	65.0	23.0	2.9
Digestive, Chocolate Chip, Co-Op*	1 Biscuit/14g	69	490	6.0	65.0	23.0	3.0
Digestive, Chocolate Chip, Waitrose*	1 Biscuit/15g	71	473	5.6	62.9	22.1	2.3
Digestive, Cracker Selection, Tesco*	1 Biscuit/12g	56	464	7.1	65.2	19.4	4.3
Digestive, Crawfords*	1 Biscuit/12g	58	484	7.1	68.8	20.0	3.4
Digestive, Creams, McVitie's*	1 Biscuit/12g	60	502	5.6	68.2	23.0	2.1
Digestive, Economy, Sainsbury's*	1 Biscuit/13g	65	498	6.8	66.3	22.8	3.3
Digestive, Family Selection, Elkes*	1 Biscuit/9g	43	475	7.1	64.6	20.9	3.3
Digestive, Finger, Reduced Fat, Sainsbury's*	1 Finger/8g	39	482	6.8	63.6	22.2	3.2
Digestive, GFY, Asda*	1 Biscuit/14g	65	461	6.0	71.0	17.0	3.6
Digestive, Good Intentions, Somerfield*	1 Biscuit/15.3g	64	426	7.3	71.0	16.5	3.8
Digestive, Happy Shopper	1 Biscuit/13g	64	498	6.8	66.3	22.8	3.3
Digestive, Hovis, Jacob's*	1 Biscuit/12g	56	469	7.8	66.0	19.3	2.9
Digestive, Jacob's*	1 Biscuit/14g	67	479	6.6	65.7	21.1	3.4
Digestive, Lemon & Ginger, McVitie's*	1 Biscuit/15g	72	480	6.7	66.7	20.7	2.7
Digestive, Light, McVitie's*	1 Biscuit/15g	70	466	7.3	72.9	16.2	3.0
Digestive, McVitie's*	1 Biscuit/15g	74	495	7.0	67.6	21.9	2.8
Digestive, Milk Chocolate Homewheat, McVitie's*	1 Biscuit/17g	86	505	6.8	65.8	23.9	2.3
Digestive, Milk Chocolate, 25% Less Fat, Tesco*	1 Biscuit/17g	79	466	7.4	69.0	17.8	2.6
Digestive, Milk Chocolate, BGTY, Sainsbury's*	1 Biscuit/17g	77	480	7.4	72.5	17.8	2.6
Digestive, Milk Chocolate, Belmont, Aldi*	1 Biscuit/17g	87	511	6.6	67.1	24.0	2.4
Digestive, Milk Chocolate, Budgens*	1 Biscuit/12.7g	66	511	6.8	66.4	24.2	2.4
Digestive, Milk Chocolate, GFY, Asda*	1 Biscuit/17g	79	466	7.0	69.0	18.0	2.6
Digestive, Milk Chocolate, Marks & Spencer*	1 Biscuit/17g	89	522	6.4	65.3	26.1	2.1
Digestive, Milk Chocolate, Mini, McVitie's*	1 Bag/40g	206	516	6.5	65.7	25.3	2.3
Digestive, Milk Chocolate, Safeway*	1 Biscuit/17g	86	504	7.0	61.5	25.5	2.2
Digestive, Milk Chocolate, Sainsbury's*	1 Biscuit/17g	87	511	6.9	65.9	24.5	2.5
Digestive, Milk Chocolate, Somerfield*	1 Biscuit/17g	87	513	7.0	67.0	24.0	0.0
Digestive, Milk Chocolate, Tesco*	1 Biscuit/17g	85	499	6.9	63.7	24.1	2.4
Digestive, Mini Milk Chocolate, Tesco*	1 Pack/30g	153	510	6.6	59.8	27.1	1.8
Digestive, Munch Bites, McVitie's*	1 Pack/40g	205	513	6.5	64.5	25.5	2.0

BISCUITS,

INFO/WEIGHT	Measure per Measure KCAL	Nutrition Values per 100g / 100ml KCAL	PROT	CARB	FAT	FIBRE
Digestive, Organic, Sainsbury's*	1 Biscuit/12.4g	58	483	6.6	60.9	23.7	5.8
Digestive, Organic, Tesco*	1 Biscuit/13g	60	464	7.7	66.3	20.8	4.6
Digestive, Organic, Waitrose*	1 Biscuit/12.6g	63	485	6.8	60.8	23.8	5.8
Digestive, Parkside, Lidl*	1 Biscuit/13g	64	498	6.8	66.3	22.8	3.3
Digestive, Plain	1 Biscuit/14g	66	471	6.3	68.6	20.9	2.2
Digestive, Plain Chocolate Homewheat, McVitie's*	1 Biscuit/17g	86	507	6.1	65.6	24.4	2.8
Digestive, Plain Chocolate, BGTY, Sainsbury's*	1 Biscuit/17g	81	478	6.8	72.6	17.8	3.1
Digestive, Plain Chocolate, Tesco*	1 Biscuit/17g	85	499	6.2	63.5	24.4	2.8
Digestive, Reduced Fat, Marks & Spencer*	1 Biscuit/15.6g	77	480	7.2	73.3	17.5	3.4
Digestive, Reduced Fat, McVitie's*	1 Biscuit/15g	70	467	7.1	72.8	16.3	3.4
Digestive, Reduced Fat, Safeway*	1 Biscuit/14g	66	469	6.5	73.4	22.9	2.8
Digestive, SmartPrice, Asda*	1 Biscuit/15g	71	474	7.0	62.0	22.0	5.0
Digestive, Sweetmeal, Aldi*	1 Biscuit/12.9g	64	497	6.8	66.3	22.8	3.3
Digestive, Sweetmeal, Asda*	1 Biscuit/13.6g	70	499	7.0	66.0	23.0	3.5
Digestive, Sweetmeal, Sainsbury's*	1 Biscuit/14g	72	498	6.0	66.4	23.1	3.3
Digestive, Sweetmeal, Tesco	1 Biscuit/18g	80	444	8.4	70.0	14.5	3.1
Digestive, Waitrose*	1 Biscuit/14g	67	469	6.5	73.4	16.6	0.0
Echo, Fox's*	1 Bar/25g	128	510	7.8	59.5	26.7	1.2
Festive Box, Cadbury's*	1oz/28g	139	495	6.8	65.2	23.2	0.0
First Class, Bahlsen*	1 Serving/125g	711	569	7.5	53.4	36.2	0.0
Florentines, Sainsbury's*	1 Florentine/8g	40	506	10.0	47.2	30.8	7.0
For Cheese, Bran Cracker, Christmas, Tesco*	1oz/28g	127	454	9.7	62.8	18.2	3.2
For Cheese, Chive Cracker, Christmas, Tesco*	1oz/28g	125	448	9.3	66.6	16.0	2.4
For Cheese, Cornish Water, Christmas, Tesco*	1oz/28g	147	526	8.3	53.5	31.0	2.3
For Cheese, Cream Cracker, Christmas, Tesco*	1oz/28g	123	438	10.2	66.7	14.5	2.8
For Cheese, Digestive, Hovis, Christmas, Tesco*	1oz/28g	132	470	7.8	66.0	19.4	2.9
For Cheese, Hovis Cracker, Christmas, Tesco*	1oz/28g	125	447	10.2	60.0	18.5	4.4
For Cheese, Poppy Snack, Christmas, Tesco*	1oz/28g	129	461	10.0	64.4	18.2	3.1
For Cheese, Sesame Carlton, Christmas, Tesco*	1oz/28g	133	476	9.1	61.5	21.5	2.7
For Cheese, Small High Bake Water, Christmas, Tesco*	1oz/28g	116	414	10.5	76.4	7.4	3.0
For Cheese, Whole Grain, Christmas, Tesco*	1oz/28g	128	458	9.0	63.9	18.5	4.1
Fruit Jambos, Rowntree's*	1 Biscuit/10.7g	47	435	4.7	73.6	13.4	1.7
Fruit Shortcake, Asda*	1 Biscuit/10g	45	445	6.0	67.0	17.0	4.6
Fruit Shortcake, McVitie's*	1 Biscuit/8g	39	483	5.9	69.6	20.1	2.1
Fruit Shortcake, Sainsbury's*	1 Biscuit/8g	39	483	5.9	69.6	20.1	2.1
Fruit Shortcake, Tesco*	1 Biscuit/9g	43	473	5.8	70.1	18.8	1.9
Fruit Shorties, Parkside, Aldi*	1 Biscuit/26g	120	461	6.4	69.1	17.7	2.1
Fruity Iced, Blue Parrot Cafe, Sainsbury's*	1 Pack/20g	83	415	6.0	82.0	7.0	1.1
Fruity Oat, Doves Farm*	1 Biscuit/16.7g	80	471	7.6	62.7	21.1	4.0
Fudge Flavour Choc Chip, Go Eat*	1 Biscuit/14.9g	77	510	6.5	59.2	27.4	1.7
Garibaldi, Crawfords*	1 Biscuit/10g	40	397	5.1	70.8	10.4	2.6
Garibaldi, Sainsbury's*	1 Biscuit/9g	35	389	5.7	67.1	10.9	3.3
Garibaldi, Tesco*	1 Section/10g	40	397	5.1	70.8	10.4	2.6
Ginger Crinkle, Sainsbury's*	1 Biscuit/11g	53	486	6.2	63.8	22.9	2.9
Ginger Crunch Creams, Fox's*	1 Biscuit/14g	73	518	4.6	64.8	26.7	0.0
Ginger Nuts, Asda*	1 Biscuit/10g	45	447	5.0	73.0	15.0	0.0
Ginger Nuts, McVitie's*	1 Biscuit/12g	57	473	5.6	75.3	16.6	1.7
Ginger Nuts, Milk Chocolate, McVitie's*	1 Biscuit/14g	68	489	5.8	71.8	19.9	1.5
Ginger Nuts, Tesco*	1 Biscuit/11g	49	447	5.5	73.3	14.6	1.7
Ginger Snap, BGTY, Sainsbury's*	1 Biscuit/12g	51	427	6.5	78.2	9.8	1.8
Ginger Snap, Fox's*	1 Biscuit/8g	35	443	4.6	77.1	12.8	1.5
Ginger Snap, Less Than 10% Fat, Sainsbury's*	1 Biscuit/12.0g	51	424	6.5	78.9	9.1	1.9
Ginger Snap, Marks & Spencer*	1 Biscuit/8g	36	445	5.4	76.7	12.9	1.5

BISCUITS,

	Measure INFO/WEIGHT	per Measure KCAL	KCAL	PROT	CARB	FAT	FIBRE
			Nutrition Values per 100g / 100ml				
Ginger Snap, Sainsbury's*	1 Biscuit/10g	46	461	5.5	76.9	14.6	1.7
Ginger Snap, Starbucks*	1 Biscuit/21g	89	426	7.9	73.1	11.3	0.0
Ginger Thins, Anna's*	1 Biscuit/2g	10	480	6.0	67.0	20.0	0.0
Ginger Thins, Asda*	1 Biscuit/5g	23	462	6.0	73.0	16.0	1.9
Ginger, Safeway*	1 Biscuit/12g	55	456	5.9	73.9	15.3	1.7
Ginger, Traditional, Fox's*	1 Biscuit/8.2g	32	404	4.4	70.1	11.7	1.4
Gingered, Duchy Originals*	1 Biscuit/15.7g	76	472	6.0	64.8	21.0	2.5
Gingernut	1 Biscuit/11g	50	456	5.6	79.1	15.2	1.4
Golden Crunch Creams, Fox's*	1 Biscuit/13g	66	511	4.3	65.6	25.7	1.2
Golden Crunch, Go Ahead, McVitie's*	1 Biscuit/9g	38	419	7.7	75.2	9.7	2.1
Golden Shortie, Jacob's*	1 Biscuit/11g	54	492	6.0	64.9	23.2	0.0
Golden Syrup, McVitie's*	1 Biscuit/12.4g	61	508	5.1	67.3	24.2	2.2
Happy Faces, Jacob's*	1 Biscuit/16g	78	485	4.8	66.1	22.3	1.6
Happy Hippos, Kinder, Nestle*	1 Hippo/22g	126	573	9.5	47.0	38.5	0.0
Hazelnut Crispies, Occasions, Sainsbury's*	1 Biscuit/6.9g	36	518	6.0	64.3	26.3	0.0
Hazelnut Meringue, Sainsbury's*	1 Biscuit/6g	24	404	5.0	43.0	23.5	1.1
Hob Nobs Munch Bites, McVitie's*	1 Pack/40g	203	508	6.8	63.4	25.2	2.8
Hob Nobs, Chocolate Creams, McVitie's*	1 Biscuit/12g	60	503	6.7	60.3	26.1	4.0
Hob Nobs, McVitie's*	1 Biscuit/14g	68	485	7.7	63.6	22.1	4.7
Hob Nobs, Milk Chocolate, McVitie's*	1 Biscuit/16g	79	496	7.3	63.0	24.0	3.7
Hob Nobs, Minis, McVitie's*	1 Bag/30g	150	499	6.8	64.0	23.9	3.8
Hob Nobs, Plain Chocolate, McVitie's*	1 Biscuit/16.2g	80	498	6.7	63.3	24.3	4.2
Hob Nobs, Vanilla Creams, McVitie's*	1 Biscuit/12g	60	501	6.1	62.3	25.2	3.6
Honey & Oatmeal, Walkers*	1 Biscuit/34g	158	465	6.7	64.1	22.4	3.8
Iced Gems, Jacob's*	1 Portion/30g	116	388	5.0	85.5	2.9	1.5
Jaffa Cakes, Asda*	1 Serving/11g	42	378	4.2	70.0	9.0	1.4
Jaffa Cakes, Co-Op*	1 Cake/12g	45	375	4.0	70.0	9.0	2.0
Jaffa Cakes, Dark Chocolate, Marks & Spencer*	1 Cake/11g	43	395	4.0	62.4	14.1	3.1
Jaffa Cakes, Lunch Box, McVitie's*	1 Cake/6.6g	28	395	4.2	74.3	9.0	1.4
Jaffa Cakes, McVitie's*	1 Biscuit/12g	45	375	4.1	70.0	8.5	2.0
Jaffa Cakes, Mini Roll XL, McVitie's*	1 Cake/44g	169	384	3.5	66.9	11.4	0.0
Jaffa Cakes, Mini, Asda*	1 Cake/5g	21	412	3.9	63.0	16.0	1.9
Jaffa Cakes, Mini, Co-Op*	1 Biscuit/5g	19	385	4.0	65.0	12.0	3.0
Jaffa Cakes, Mini, McVitie's*	1 Cake/5.9g	26	441	5.1	83.1	10.2	1.7
Jaffa Cakes, Mini, Morrisons*	1 Cake/5g	20	405	3.9	62.8	15.8	1.9
Jaffa Cakes, Morrisons*	1 Cake/13g	50	384	4.4	73.2	8.1	0.0
Jaffa Cakes, Plain Chocolate, Sainsbury's*	1 Cake/13g	46	384	4.4	73.3	8.1	1.3
Jaffa Cakes, SmartPrice, Asda*	1 Cake/11g	43	379	4.4	70.0	9.0	1.4
Jaffa Cakes, Tesco*	1 Cake/12g	45	378	4.2	70.4	8.8	1.4
Jaffa Cakes, Value, Tesco*	1 Cake/11g	42	386	4.2	72.7	8.7	0.6
Jaffa Viennese, Marks & Spencer*	1 Biscuit/17.2g	79	465	5.9	61.1	21.7	0.9
Jam Rings, Crawfords*	1 Biscuit/12g	56	470	5.5	73.0	17.2	1.9
Jam Sandwich Creams, Marks & Spencer*	1 Serving/15g	70	465	4.8	61.3	22.3	1.1
Jammie Dodgers, Bite Size, Burton's*	1 Pack/30g	134	448	5.1	74.1	14.2	0.0
Jammie Dodgers, Burton's*	1 Biscuit/19g	85	448	4.8	68.8	16.7	1.7
Jammie Dodgers, Mini, Burton's	1 Biscuit/29g	123	424	6.5	74.3	13.2	0.0
Jestives, Fruit & Nut, Cadbury's*	1 Biscuit/17g	85	500	6.7	60.7	25.6	0.0
Jestives, Milk Chocolate, Cadbury's*	1 Biscuit/17g	86	506	6.4	64.4	24.8	0.0
Lemon Curd Sandwich, Fox's*	1 Biscuit/14g	69	494	4.7	66.2	23.4	1.3
Lemon Puff, Jacob's*	1 Biscuit/13g	69	533	4.3	58.8	31.2	2.8
Lemon Thins, Sainsbury's*	1 Biscuit/10g	47	468	5.6	72.3	17.3	1.7
Lincoln, McVitie's*	1 Biscuit/8g	41	514	6.3	69.0	23.6	2.0
Lincoln, Sainsbury's*	1 Biscuit/8g	40	479	7.2	66.1	20.6	2.1

BISCUITS,

	Measure INFO/WEIGHT	per Measure KCAL	KCAL	PROT	CARB	FAT	FIBRE
				Nutrition Values per 100g / 100ml			
Malt, Basics*	1 Biscuit/8g	36	470	7.1	73.6	15.7	0.0
Malted Milk, Asda*	1 Biscuit/8g	39	490	7.0	66.0	22.0	2.0
Malted Milk, Family Selection, Elkes*	1 Biscuit/9g	42	490	7.2	65.8	22.0	2.0
Malted Milk, Milk Chocolate, Asda*	1 Biscuit/11g	56	509	7.0	64.0	25.0	1.7
Malted Milk, Sainsbury's*	1 Biscuit/8g	40	488	7.1	65.5	21.9	2.0
Malted Milk, Tesco*	1 Biscuit/8g	39	488	7.2	65.6	21.9	2.0
Marie, Crawfords*	1 Biscuit/7g	33	475	7.5	76.3	15.5	2.3
Milk Chocolate, All Butter, Marks & Spencer*	1 Biscuit/14g	70	500	7.5	58.3	26.4	4.6
Milk Chocolate, Tesco*	1 Biscuit/25.3g	134	535	6.4	62.1	29.0	1.8
Mini Assortment, Marks & Spencer*	4 Biscuits/10g	48	480	6.1	63.9	22.5	2.8
Mint, Plain Chocolate, Tesco*	1 Biscuit/25.3g	135	538	5.1	63.0	29.5	1.7
Morning Coffee, Asda*	1 Biscuit/4.8g	23	455	8.0	72.0	15.0	2.4
Morning Coffee, Co-Op*	1 Biscuit/5g	23	450	8.0	72.0	15.0	2.0
Morning Coffee, Spar*	1 Biscuit/5g	24	471	7.6	77.5	14.5	2.4
Morning Coffee, Tesco*	1 Biscuit/4.8g	23	450	7.6	72.3	14.5	2.4
Nice, Asda*	1 Biscuit/8g	38	480	6.0	68.0	21.0	2.4
Nice, Family Selection, Elkes*	1 Biscuit/8g	38	485	6.5	68.0	20.8	2.4
Nice, Fox's*	1 Biscuit/8g	38	474	5.9	65.9	20.4	3.8
Nice, Jacob's*	1 Biscuit/7g	33	471	6.1	68.5	19.2	1.8
Nice, Sainsbury's*	1 Biscuit/8g	34	485	6.5	68.0	20.8	2.4
Nice, Value, Multipack, Tesco*	1 Biscuit/8g	39	485	6.5	68.0	20.8	2.4
Nice, Value, Tesco*	1 Biscuit/5g	24	489	6.9	64.6	22.6	2.4
Oat & Wholemeal, Crawfords*	1 Biscuit/14g	67	482	7.7	64.2	21.6	4.8
Oat Crunch, Weight Watchers*	1 Biscuit/23g	103	449	7.2	65.3	17.7	6.1
Oat, Santiveri*	1 Biscuit/5.4g	21	428	10.0	58.8	17.0	7.0
Oaten, Organic, Duchy Originals*	1 Biscuit/16g	71	441	9.8	62.3	16.9	5.3
Oatmeal Crunch, Jacob's*	1 Biscuit/8g	37	458	6.8	65.9	18.6	3.6
Orange Chocolate, Organic, Duchy Originals*	1 Biscuit/12.6g	66	509	5.5	60.0	28.0	3.0
Orange Munchy Bites, Blue Riband, Nestle*	1 Box/125g	653	522	5.2	61.4	27.9	2.0
Party Rings, Fox's*	1 Biscuit/6g	27	453	4.3	77.8	13.8	1.3
Party Rings, Iced, Fox's*	1 Biscuit/6g	29	459	5.1	75.8	15.0	0.0
Peanut Butter Cups, Mini, Reese's*	5 Pieces/39g	220	564	10.3	56.4	30.8	2.6
Peanut Butter, American Style, Sainsbury's*	1 Biscuit/12.5g	66	504	5.2	68.7	23.1	2.2
Petit Beurre, Stella*	1 Biscuit/6g	26	440	9.0	73.0	15.0	0.0
Puffin, Chocolate, Asda*	1 Biscuit/25g	133	533	5.0	63.0	29.0	1.2
Puffin, Orange, Asda*	1 Biscuit/25g	133	529	5.0	62.0	29.0	2.2
Raisin & Honey, Doves Farm*	1 Biscuit/16.6g	85	501	4.7	59.5	27.1	4.2
Ratafias, Sainsbury's*	1 Biscuit/1.9g	9	450	6.5	80.5	11.3	1.1
Rich Shorties, Asda*	1 Biscuit/10.3g	49	486	6.0	66.0	22.0	2.0
Rich Shorties, Crawfords*	1 Biscuit/10g	50	501	6.4	69.8	21.8	0.0
Rich Tea Creams, Fox's*	1 Biscuit/11.4g	50	456	5.3	62.7	20.4	1.4
Rich Tea Finger, Marks & Spencer*	1 Biscuit/5g	24	471	7.4	77.9	14.4	0.4
Rich Tea Finger, Tesco*	1 Biscuit/5g	23	451	7.4	72.9	14.4	2.3
Rich Tea, 25% Less Fat, Tesco*	1 Biscuit/10g	44	435	7.1	77.0	11.0	1.3
Rich Tea, Asda*	1 Biscuit/10g	45	447	7.0	71.0	15.0	2.3
Rich Tea, BGTY, Sainsbury's*	1 Biscuit/10g	39	430	7.8	75.9	10.6	2.4
Rich Tea, Balanced Lifestyle, Parkwood, Aldi*	1 Biscuit/10g	42	421	7.3	75.5	10.0	2.1
Rich Tea, Belmont, Aldi*	1 Biscuit/10g	44	454	7.4	71.5	15.4	2.3
Rich Tea, Economy, Sainsbury's*	1 Biscuit/8g	33	470	7.8	77.5	14.3	2.4
Rich Tea, Marks & Spencer*	1 Biscuit/10g	46	460	6.9	71.6	15.7	2.4
Rich Tea, McVitie's*	1 Biscuit/8g	39	475	7.5	76.3	15.5	2.3
Rich Tea, Milk Chocolate, Sainsbury's*	1 Biscuit/13.1g	66	504	6.3	68.5	22.7	2.1
Rich Tea, Plain Chocolate, Sainsbury's*	1 Biscuit/13g	65	497	6.6	66.0	23.0	2.6

BISCUITS,	Measure INFO/WEIGHT	per Measure KCAL	Nutrition Values per 100g / 100ml				
			KCAL	PROT	CARB	FAT	FIBRE
Rich Tea, Reduced Fat, Marks & Spencer*	1 Biscuit/10g	43	430	7.8	75.9	10.6	2.4
Rich Tea, Safeway*	1 Biscuit/10g	45	454	7.4	71.5	15.4	2.3
Rich Tea, Sainsbury's*	1 Biscuit/10g	45	454	7.5	71.4	15.4	2.3
Rich Tea, Tesco*	1 Biscuit/10g	45	454	7.4	71.5	15.4	2.3
Rich Tea, Value, Tesco*	1 Biscuit/7.8g	37	462	7.4	70.2	16.8	2.2
Riva Milk, McVitie's*	1 Biscuit/25.2g	135	540	6.4	57.7	31.5	1.6
Rolo, Nestle*	1 Biscuit/22g	110	498	5.4	62.0	25.4	0.6
Rosemary & Raisin, Marks & Spencer*	1 Biscuit/7.1g	34	490	5.1	62.5	24.1	1.8
Sandwich, Viennese, Marks & Spencer*	1 Biscuit/15g	80	535	7.2	58.0	30.6	1.7
Savoury, Gluten, Wheat & Dairy Free, Sainsbury's*	1 Biscuit/16.5g	75	467	11.7	65.1	17.7	2.4
Savoury, Organic, Marks & Spencer*	1 Biscuit/7g	28	395	7.0	58.4	14.6	8.7
Shortbread, Organic, Waitrose*	1 Biscuit/12.5g	64	495	5.8	63.0	24.4	1.8
Shortcake, Asda*	1 Biscuit/14g	73	518	5.0	66.0	26.0	2.0
Shortcake, Caramel, Mini, Thorntons*	1 Piece/20.1g	98	492	4.8	46.3	31.6	0.6
Shortcake, Crawfords*	1 Biscuit/10.3g	52	518	6.4	68.1	24.4	2.0
Shortcake, Dairy Milk Chocolate, Cadbury's*	1 Bar/49g	252	515	7.5	59.2	27.5	0.0
Shortcake, Dutch, Marks & Spencer*	1 Biscuit/17g	90	530	5.7	58.2	30.6	0.9
Shortcake, Extremely Chocolatey, Marks & Spencer*	1 Biscuit/23g	120	522	7.8	60.0	28.7	0.9
Shortcake, Family Selection, Elkes*	1 Biscuit/11g	54	486	7.1	66.5	21.2	2.1
Shortcake, Farmfoods*	1 Biscuit/11g	56	506	6.9	63.1	25.1	1.9
Shortcake, Jacob's*	1 Biscuit/10g	49	485	6.7	65.6	21.8	2.0
Shortcake, Organic, Waitrose*	1 Biscuit/13g	64	495	5.8	63.0	24.4	1.8
Shortcake, Sainsbury's*	1 Biscuit/11g	53	484	7.2	66.6	21.0	2.0
Shortcake, Snack, Cadbury's*	1 Biscuit/8g	42	525	7.0	64.2	26.6	0.0
Shortcake, Value, Tesco*	1 Biscuit/10g	48	484	7.3	66.6	21.0	2.1
Shortcake, Waitrose*	1 Biscuit/13g	67	512	6.0	68.1	24.4	1.9
Shorties, Cadbury's*	1 Biscuit/15g	77	511	6.5	67.3	24.0	0.0
Shorties, Sainsbury's*	1 Biscuit/10g	50	500	6.4	69.8	21.8	2.0
Signature Collection, Cadbury's*	1 Biscuit/15g	80	530	6.2	60.1	29.5	0.0
Spiced, Whole Wheat, Prodia*	1 Biscuit/5g	17	339	7.1	41.4	19.4	8.5
Sports, Fox's*	1 Biscuit/7.1g	30	434	6.1	61.5	18.8	1.8
St Clements Big Softies, Fox's*	1 Biscuit/14g	50	355	6.0	75.2	2.1	3.3
Stem Ginger, Brakes*	2 Biscuits/25g	124	495	5.6	62.6	24.7	0.0
Strawberry Mallows, Go Ahead, McVitie's*	1 Biscuit/18g	69	385	4.3	70.6	9.5	0.9
Strawberry, Cream Tease, McVitie's*	1 Biscuit/19g	97	510	4.8	65.9	25.2	1.2
Sultana & Cinnamon, Weight Watchers*	2 Cookies/23g	101	441	4.3	72.3	15.0	3.0
Summer Fruits, Big Softies, Fox's	1 Bar/25g	89	356	5.9	77.8	2.6	0.0
Tangy Jaffa Viennese, Creations, Fox's*	1 Biscuit/17g	76	447	5.0	63.5	19.2	0.9
Taxi, McVitie's*	1 Biscuit/26.5g	131	504	4.2	63.3	26.0	0.7
Toffee Apple Flavoured, Officially Low Fat, Fox's*	1 Bar/25.7g	91	350	5.6	75.9	2.6	2.4
Toffee Chip Crinkle Crunch, Fox's*	1 Biscuit/11g	51	460	4.6	69.6	18.2	0.0
Toffee, Choc Dips, KP	1 Pot/32g	171	534	4.4	62.2	29.7	1.2
Treacle Crunch Creams, Fox's*	1 Biscuit/13g	65	502	4.5	65.3	24.8	1.4
Triple Chocolate, Fox's*	1 Biscuits/20.9g	100	478	5.7	57.3	25.1	2.5
Viennese Creams, Raspberry, Marks & Spencer*	1 Biscuit/17.3g	88	520	4.6	60.4	28.6	1.3
Viennese Creams, Strawberry, Marks & Spencer*	1 Biscuit/16.5g	78	485	6.4	63.0	22.2	1.7
Viennese Finger, Mr Kipling*	1 Finger/32g	167	523	4.3	54.9	31.8	0.0
Viennese Whirl, Chocolate, Border*	1 Biscuit/18.7g	97	513	6.4	61.2	28.6	0.0
Viennese Whirl, Fox's*	1 Biscuit/25g	130	518	6.7	60.1	27.8	0.0
Viscount* Mint	1 Biscuit/16g	83	521	4.8	62.7	27.9	1.3
Water, Asda*	1 Biscuit/5.8g	24	395	10.0	73.0	7.0	6.0
Water, Carr's*	1 Biscuit/8g	35	434	10.3	79.1	7.6	3.2
Water, High Bake, Jacob's*	1 Biscuit/5.3g	21	414	10.5	76.4	7.4	3.0

	Measure	per Measure		Nutrition Values per 100g / 100ml				
	INFO/WEIGHT	KCAL		KCAL	PROT	CARB	FAT	FIBRE
BISCUITS,								
Water, High Bake, Sainsbury's*	1 Biscuit/5g	21		412	9.8	76.3	7.5	3.2
Water, High Bake, Tesco*	3 Biscuits/16g	64		401	10.5	73.1	7.4	3.0
Water, High Bake, Waitrose*	1 Cracker/6g	24		408	10.3	75.0	7.4	2.6
Water, Table, Large, Carr's*	1 Biscuit/8g	35		434	10.3	79.1	7.6	3.2
Water, Table, Small, Carr's*	1 Biscuit/3.4g	13		438	10.4	80.0	7.7	3.3
Wheat Free, Mixed Berries, Nairn's*	1 Biscuit/10g	43		433	8.0	75.6	13.9	6.7
Wholemeal Brans, Fox's*	1 Biscuit/20g	90		451	8.5	58.8	20.2	7.5
Yorkie, Nestle*	1 Biscuit/25g	128		510	6.7	60.4	26.8	1.3
BITES,								
Apple & Cinnamon, All Butter, Marks & Spencer*	1 Biscuit/10g	50		510	5.5	64.6	25.2	2.1
Bacon Rice, Asda*	1 Pack/30g	136		452	7.0	70.0	16.0	0.4
Bacon, Crispy, Shapers, Boots*	1 Bag/23g	99		431	8.0	66.0	15.0	3.0
Bagel, Smokey Ham Flavour, COU, Marks & Spencer*	1 Pack/25g	91		365	10.5	75.6	2.5	5.2
Cheese & Ham, Sainsbury's*	1 Pack/21g	65		309	9.7	14.4	23.6	1.0
Mini Apricot & Orange, COU, Marks & Spencer*	1 Bag/25g	86		345	3.4	76.9	2.5	4.1
Mini, Raspberry, COU, Marks & Spencers*	1 Pack/27g	90		340	3.8	74.9	2.7	4.5
Oat & Cranberry, Yoghurt Coated, Marks Spencer*	1 Bite/12.5g	62		480	5.6	69.6	19.2	3.2
BITTER LEMON,								
Diet, Asda*	1 Glass/200ml	4		2	0.0	0.3	0.0	0.0
Low Calorie, Tesco*	1 Glass/200ml	6		3	0.0	0.8	0.0	0.0
Sainsbury's*	1 Glass/250ml	45		18	0.1	4.4	0.1	0.1
BLACK GRAM,								
Urad Gram, Dried, Raw	1oz/28g	77		275	24.9	40.8	1.4	0.0
BLACK PUDDING,								
Average	1 Pudding/40g	101		252	10.2	19.0	14.9	0.6
BLACKBERRIES,								
In Fruit Juice, Average	½ Can/145g	52		36	0.6	7.9	0.2	1.3
Raw, Average	1oz/28g	8		30	0.8	6.0	0.3	1.6
BLACKCURRANTS,								
Fresh, Raw	1oz/28g	8		28	0.9	6.6	0.0	3.6
In Fruit Juice, Average	1 Serving/30g	11		38	0.7	8.6	0.2	2.5
Stewed With Sugar	1oz/28g	16		58	0.7	15.0	0.0	2.8
Stewed Without Sugar	1oz/28g	7		24	0.8	5.6	0.0	3.1
BLUEBERRIES,								
Chocolate Covered, Waitrose*	1 Serving/25g	120		481	4.0	65.6	22.4	3.0
Dried, Whitworths*	1 Pack/75g	226		301	0.9	74.2	0.1	11.4
Raw, Average	1 Serving/125g	65		52	0.8	11.5	0.5	2.5
BOILED SWEETS,								
Average	1oz/28g	92		327	0.0	87.1	0.0	0.0
Blackcurrant & Liquorice, Co-Op*	1 Sweet/8g	32		405	0.9	91.0	5.0	0.0
Clear Fruits, Sainsbury's*	1 Sweet/7g	26		372	0.1	92.9	0.0	0.0
Cough Sweets, Fundays, Bassett's*	1oz/28g	107		383	0.0	94.9	0.0	0.0
Fruit Drops, Co-Op*	1 Sweet/6g	24		395	0.2	98.0	0.0	0.0
Fruit Rocks, Assorted, Marks & Spencer*	1oz/28g	107		381	0.0	95.2	0.0	0.0
Fruit Sherbets, Assorted, Marks & Spencer*	1 Sweet/8g	34		425	0.0	89.7	7.3	0.0
Lockets, Mars*	1 Pack/43g	165		383	0.0	95.8	0.0	0.0
Pear Drops, Marks & Spencer*	1oz/28g	109		390	0.0	96.9	0.0	0.0
BOK CHOY,								
Tesco*	1 Serving/100g	11		11	1.0	1.4	0.2	1.2
BOLOGNESE,								
Beef, Asda*	1 Pack/392g	412		105	8.0	7.0	5.0	0.0
Extra Meaty, Marks & Spencer*	1oz/28g	31		110	9.0	4.8	6.1	0.3
Fusilli, Ready Meals, Marks & Spencer*	1oz/28g	38		135	7.0	13.1	6.2	1.0

B

	Measure INFO/WEIGHT	per Measure KCAL	Nutrition Values per 100g / 100ml				
			KCAL	PROT	CARB	FAT	FIBRE
BOLOGNESE,							
Meat Free, Asda*	1 Serving/229g	179	78	6.0	11.0	1.1	0.6
Meatless, Granose*	1 Pack/400g	400	100	8.0	8.0	4.0	0.0
Medaglione, Rich Red Wine, Waitrose*	1 Serving/125g	253	202	11.6	29.6	4.1	3.1
Penne, BGTY, Sainsbury's*	1 Pack/400g	428	107	7.2	16.0	1.6	0.9
Penne, Heinz*	1 Pack/300g	213	71	3.8	11.8	0.9	0.6
Ravioli, Beef, Asda*	1 Serving/125g	206	165	7.0	28.0	2.8	1.2
Shells, BGTY, Sainsbury's*	1 Can/400g	340	85	5.0	11.8	2.0	0.7
Shells, Italiana, Weight Watchers*	1 Can/395g	284	72	5.3	9.8	1.3	0.8
Shells, Ready Meals, Marks & Spencer*	1 Pack/390g	585	150	7.8	11.4	8.3	0.9
Vegetarian, Marks & Spencer*	1 Pack/360g	360	100	4.5	12.5	3.5	2.1
BOMBAY ALOO,							
Marks & Spencer*	1oz/28g	20	70	1.8	9.5	2.7	2.0
BOMBAY MIX,							
Average	1oz/28g	141	503	18.8	35.1	32.9	6.2
BON BONS,							
Apple, Lemon & Strawberry, Co-Op*	¼ Bag/50g	203	405	1.0	88.0	5.0	0.0
Bassett's*	5 Bonbons/200g	834	417	1.1	85.4	7.5	0.0
BOOST,							
Cadbury's*	1 Bar/55g	297	540	5.9	62.3	29.3	0.0
Treat Size, Cadbury's*	1 Bar/24.3g	128	535	5.3	59.6	30.5	0.0
With Glucose & Guarana, Cadbury's*	1 Bar/61g	323	530	5.8	60.3	29.6	0.0
With Glucose, Cadbury's*	1 Bar/61g	326	535	5.3	59.6	30.5	0.0
BOUILLON,							
Beef, Benedicta*	1floz/30ml	22	73	7.5	9.5	0.5	0.0
Beef, Touch of Taste*	1 Serving/15ml	11	73	7.5	9.5	0.5	0.0
Chicken, Benedicta*	1fl oz/30ml	23	75	4.0	8.0	3.0	5.6
Fish, Benedicta*	1fl oz/30ml	21	69	7.5	9.0	0.3	0.0
Swiss Vegetable, Powder, Marigold*	1 teaspoon/4g	8	202	18.4	17.7	6.3	0.7
Vegetable, Benedicta*	1fl oz/30ml	30	101	7.5	17.0	0.3	0.0
Vegetable, Herbamare Concentre*	1 Serving/5g	15	298	4.6	13.5	25.4	0.3
BOUNTY,							
Calapuno, Mars*	1 Pack/175g	919	525	6.3	54.3	31.4	0.0
Dark, Mars*	1 Funsize/29g	137	471	3.2	54.1	26.8	0.0
Milk, Mars*	1 Funsize/29g	137	471	3.7	56.4	25.6	0.0
BOURNVITA,							
Powder, Made Up With Semi-Skimmed Milk	1 Mug/227ml	132	58	3.5	7.8	1.6	0.0
Powder, Made Up With Whole Milk	1 Mug/227ml	173	76	3.4	7.6	3.8	0.0
BOVRIL,							
Beef Extract, Bovril*	1 Tsp/5g	10	197	10.8	29.3	4.1	0.0
Chicken Savoury Drink, Bovril*	1 Serving/12.5g	15	129	9.7	19.4	1.4	2.1
BOYSENBERRIES,							
Canned, In Syrup	1oz/28g	25	88	1.0	20.4	0.1	1.6
BRAN,							
Wheat	1 Tbsp/7g	14	206	14.1	26.8	5.5	36.4
BRANDY,							
37.5% Volume	1 Shot/25ml	52	207	0.0	0.0	0.0	0.0
40% Volume	1 Shot/25ml	56	222	0.0	0.0	0.0	0.0
Cherry	1 Shot/25ml	64	255	0.0	32.6	0.0	0.0
BRATWURST,							
Frozen, Lidl*	1 Sausage/80g	235	294	12.8	0.5	26.8	0.0
BRAZIL NUTS,							
Average	6 Whole/20g	137	687	15.5	2.9	68.3	4.9

BREAD,

INFO/WEIGHT	Measure	per Measure KCAL	KCAL	PROT	CARB	FAT	FIBRE
10 Seed, Organic, The Village Bakery*	1 Slice/25g	66	263	9.0	43.8	5.7	3.8
Amazing Grain, Nimble*	1 Slice/22g	49	224	10.7	41.3	1.8	7.0
Apricot & Sesame Seed, LifeFibre*	1 Slice/43g	148	344	8.1	55.0	10.3	6.2
Bagel, Caramelised Onion & Poppyseed, Waitrose*	1 Bagel/86g	222	258	9.7	49.2	2.5	2.4
Bagel, Cinamon & Raisin, Starbucks*	1 Bagel/83g	190	229	44.8	9.4	1.4	1.3
Bagel, Cinnamon & Raisin, GFY, Asda*	1 Bagel/83.8g	223	266	10.0	52.0	2.0	2.7
Bagel, Cinnamon & Raisin, Marks & Spencer*	1 Bagel/85g	223	262	9.6	52.5	1.8	2.2
Bagel, Cinnamon & Raisin, Mr Bagels*	1 Bagel/85g	207	243	10.9	55.6	2.2	10.8
Bagel, Cinnamon & Raisin, New York Bagel Co*	1 Bagel/85g	240	282	10.5	56.0	1.8	2.2
Bagel, Cinnamon & Raisin, Tesco*	1 Bagel/85g	207	243	9.3	47.5	1.7	2.3
Bagel, Cinnamon & Raisin, Waitrose*	1 Bagel/86g	229	266	10.5	50.9	2.3	2.1
Bagel, Fruit & Spice, Sainsbury's*	1 Bagel/85.1g	234	275	9.7	54.3	2.1	3.8
Bagel, Multigrain, Sainsbury's*	1 Bagel/113g	293	259	10.0	49.6	3.1	2.0
Bagel, Onion & Poppy Seed, Marks & Spencer*	1 Roll/85g	223	262	9.6	52.5	1.8	2.2
Bagel, Onion & Poppy Seed, Tesco*	1 Bagel/85g	217	255	10.0	46.7	3.1	3.6
Bagel, Onion, New York Bagel Co*	1 Bagel/85g	233	274	11.1	53.9	1.6	2.1
Bagel, Onion, Tesco*	1 Bagel/85g	233	274	10.5	52.4	2.4	1.9
Bagel, Original, New York Bagel Co*	1 Bagel/85g	230	271	11.2	53.2	1.5	2.2
Bagel, Original, Organic, New York Bagel Co*	1 Bagel/85g	220	259	9.3	52.2	1.4	4.1
Bagel, Plain, GFY, Asda*	1 Bagel/84.2g	218	259	10.0	50.0	2.1	1.8
Bagel, Plain, Marks & Spencer*	1 Bagel/85g	230	270	10.4	51.7	2.1	1.3
Bagel, Plain, New York Bagel Co.*	1 Bagel/85g	216	254	10.6	49.2	1.7	3.6
Bagel, Plain, Organic, Waitrose*	1 Serving/86g	228	265	9.0	52.1	2.3	2.2
Bagel, Plain, Tesco*	1 Bagel/85g	214	252	9.9	48.6	2.0	1.8
Bagel, Plain, Waitrose*	1 Bagel/85g	226	266	10.4	50.7	2.4	1.5
Bagel, Poppy Seed, New York Bagel Co.*	1 Bagel/85g	233	274	11.4	50.8	2.8	3.2
Bagel, Sesame Seed, GFY, Asda*	1 Bagel/83.8g	228	271	11.0	51.0	2.5	2.6
Bagel, Sesame, New York Bagel Co*	1 Bagel/84g	228	272	11.4	52.7	1.8	2.2
Bagel, Simply Plain, Marks & Spencer*	1 Bagel/85g	230	270	10.4	51.7	2.1	1.3
Bagel, White, Asda*	1 Bagel/86g	227	264	10.0	49.0	3.1	0.0
Baguette, Budgens*	1 Baguette/125g	335	268	8.5	55.7	1.2	2.3
Baguette, Co-Op*	1 Baguette/125g	275	220	7.0	46.0	0.9	3.0
Baguette, French, Tesco*	1 Serving/150g	360	240	7.8	49.5	1.2	3.4
Baguette, Granary, Co-Op*	1 Baguette/105g	263	250	20.0	46.0	2.5	6.0
Baguette, Homebake, Half, Marks & Spencer*	1 Serving/125g	226	181	6.9	37.4	0.5	2.5
Baguette, Homebake, Half, Tesco*	1 Baguette/150g	353	235	7.8	49.1	0.8	1.2
Baguette, Marks & Spencer*	¼ Baguette/65g	187	287	9.8	58.6	1.4	3.2
Baguette, Mediterranean Herb, Sainsbury's*	1 Serving/85g	288	339	8.5	40.8	15.7	2.3
Baguette, Part Baked, Half, Tesco*	½ Baguette/150g	360	240	7.8	49.5	1.2	3.4
Baguette, Part Baked, Happy Shopper*	½ Baguette/55g	142	258	8.2	53.9	1.0	2.2
Baguette, Ready To Bake, Safeway*	¼ Baguette/56g	147	263	8.4	54.8	1.2	2.3
Baguette, Ready To Bake, Sainsbury's*	½ Baguette/62g	188	303	9.5	62.9	1.5	3.1
Baguette, Ready To Bake, St Pierre*	1 Baguette/150g	336	224	7.6	46.2	1.0	1.6
Baguette, Ready To Bake, Waitrose*	½ Baguette/65g	170	262	8.9	53.8	1.2	2.5
Baguette, Take & Bake, Budgens*	1 Baguette/110g	282	256	8.1	53.6	1.0	2.2
Baguette, White, Ready To Bake, Asda*	1 Baguette/115g	322	280	10.0	56.0	1.8	2.6
Baguette, White, Sainsbury's*	1 Serving/50g	132	263	9.3	53.1	1.5	2.7
Baguette, White, Sandwich, Somerfield*	1 Baguette/110g	285	259	9.4	52.1	1.4	1.7
Baltic Rye, Organic, The Village Bakery*	1oz/28g	68	243	8.0	50.3	1.4	2.9
Baps, Brown, Large, Asda*	1 Bap/58g	140	242	10.0	47.0	1.6	0.0
Baps, Brown, Malted Grain, Large, Tesco*	1 Bap/100g	238	238	8.5	44.0	3.1	1.9
Baps, Cheese Top, Sainsbury's*	1 Bap/75g	218	291	12.1	41.6	8.5	2.0
Baps, Cheese Topped, Marks & Spencer*	1 Bap/78.2g	215	275	11.6	34.1	11.1	1.8

B

BREAD,

	Measure INFO/WEIGHT	per Measure KCAL	KCAL	PROT	CARB	FAT	FIBRE
Baps, Cheese Topped, White, Tesco*	1oz/28g	86	307	12.2	48.0	7.0	0.7
Baps, Floured, Marks & Spencer*	1 Bap/60g	168	280	11.5	46.8	6.2	2.0
Baps, For Burger, Somerfield*	1oz/28g	77	276	10.0	48.0	4.0	0.0
Baps, Giant Malted, Sainsbury's*	1 Bap/108.5g	281	260	8.6	45.7	4.8	5.7
Baps, Multigrain, Tesco*	1 Serving/97.5g	239	244	8.7	45.1	3.2	1.9
Baps, White Sandwich, Kingsmill*	1 Bap/80g	209	261	10.1	46.2	4.0	2.2
Baps, White Soft, Giant, Somerfield*	1 Bap/105.2g	261	249	9.1	44.7	3.8	2.3
Baps, White Soft, Somerfield*	1oz/28g	69	248	11.0	44.0	3.0	0.0
Baps, White, Giant, Sainsbury's*	1 Bap/103g	267	259	9.0	49.9	2.6	2.7
Baps, White, Giant, Waitrose*	1 Bap/104g	261	251	8.8	45.3	3.8	2.1
Baps, White, Medium, Morrisons*	1 Bap/62g	152	245	8.6	48.5	2.0	2.4
Baps, White, Sliced, Large, Asda*	1 Bap/58g	148	255	10.0	50.0	1.7	0.0
Baps, White, Soft, Floured, Marks & Spencer*	1 Bap/63g	176	280	11.5	46.8	6.2	2.0
Baps, White, Warburton's*	1 Bap/57g	144	252	9.8	43.4	4.3	2.7
Baps, Wholemeal, Diet Choice, Waitrose*	1 Bap/68g	171	252	9.6	41.4	5.3	5.6
Baps, Wholemeal, Giant, Sainsbury's*	1 Bap/110g	275	250	11.7	43.5	3.2	6.1
Baps, Wholemeal, Large, Tesco*	1 Bap/95g	223	235	10.5	39.1	4.1	7.6
Baps, Wholemeal, Sainsbury's*	1 Bap/60g	151	252	9.6	41.4	5.3	5.6
Baps, Wholemeal, Somerfield*	1oz/28g	66	234	14.0	36.0	3.0	0.0
Baps, Wholemeal, Tesco*	1 Bap/46g	104	227	9.6	41.4	5.3	5.6
Batch, Seeded, Finest, Tesco*	1 Slice/65g	168	259	9.3	41.8	6.1	6.1
Batch, Seeded, Warburton's*	1 Thick Slice/46g	132	288	12.2	39.7	9.0	3.3
Batch, White, Warburton's*	1 Thick Slice/42g	98	233	9.8	43.6	2.1	2.7
Best Of Both, Hovis*	1 Slice/40g	88	219	9.0	40.8	2.3	4.5
Black Olive, Finest, Tesco*	1 Serving/72g	184	255	9.7	39.7	6.4	2.9
Bloomer, Multiseed, Sliced, Marks & Spencer*	1 Slice/53.6g	151	280	10.5	43.6	7.2	3.1
Bloomer, Soft Grain, Marks & Spencer*	1 Slice/34g	80	235	9.4	45.6	1.5	3.5
Bloomer, Vienna, Marks & Spencer*	1oz/28g	79	281	9.6	55.8	2.1	2.7
Bloomer, White, Bake Off, Somerfield*	1oz/28g	69	246	9.0	47.0	3.0	0.0
Bloomer, White, Seeded, Bake Off, Somerfield*	1oz/28g	68	243	9.0	46.0	3.0	0.0
Bloomer, Wholemeal, Organic, Marks & Spencer*	1 Slice/50g	120	240	8.7	35.5	8.0	5.2
Breadcakes, Big Brown, Morrisons*	1 Breadcake/63g	154	245	9.0	44.6	3.4	4.3
Brioche Loaf, Sainsbury's*	1/8 Loaf/50g	174	347	8.0	55.0	10.5	2.2
Brioche, Continental Classics*	1 Roll/35g	122	349	8.2	58.3	9.3	0.0
Brioche, Finest, Tesco*	1 Bun/52g	207	398	10.8	38.3	22.4	2.0
Brioche, Marks & Spencer*	1 Brioche/50g	182	363	7.8	40.2	20.5	1.5
Brown	1 Med Slice/34g	74	218	8.5	44.3	2.0	3.5
Brown, Brace's*	1 Serving/26.5g	57	219	10.1	38.0	3.0	3.7
Brown, Crusty Golden, Hovis*	1 Slice/44g	102	231	8.7	43.0	2.7	3.3
Brown, Danish, Sliced, Weight Watchers*	1 Slice/19g	41	215	11.0	38.8	2.0	7.3
Brown, Danish, Warburton's*	1 Slice/19g	38	200	8.6	37.7	1.6	9.6
Brown, Danish, Weight Watchers*	1 Slice/19g	38	200	8.6	37.7	1.6	9.6
Brown, Farmhouse, Linwoods*	1 Slice/25g	56	225	7.3	44.4	1.7	5.8
Brown, Fibre Rich, Allinson*	1 Slice/24g	51	212	13.2	33.6	2.8	8.0
Brown, Gluten & Wheat Free, Sliced, Dietary Specials*	1 Slice/25g	56	224	3.4	41.0	5.2	9.4
Brown, Good Health, Warburton's*	1 Slice/34.8g	79	226	10.3	39.6	2.9	7.2
Brown, Granary Malted, Waitrose*	1 Slice/40g	88	220	9.4	39.9	2.5	4.3
Brown, Harvest, Marks & Spencer*	1oz/28g	67	240	8.8	44.5	2.7	3.7
Brown, High Fibre, Ormo*	1 Slice/24g	57	239	9.2	42.9	2.6	7.5
Brown, Malted, Farmhouse Gold, Morrisons*	1 Slice/38g	96	253	10.3	49.9	1.4	3.1
Brown, Medium Sliced, Best Of Health, Hovis*	2 slices/76g	158	208	10.1	36.4	2.4	6.9
Brown, Medium Sliced, Bettabuy, Morrisons*	1 Slice/31g	66	212	8.6	42.0	1.3	3.6
Brown, Medium Sliced, Sainsbury's*	1 Slice/36g	81	225	8.2	43.8	1.9	3.9

BREAD,	Measure INFO/WEIGHT	per Measure KCAL	Nutrition Values per 100g / 100ml				
			KCAL	PROT	CARB	FAT	FIBRE
Brown, Medium Sliced, Tesco*	2 Slices/72g	157	218	8.0	41.6	2.2	4.5
Brown, Medium, Irwin's*	2 Slices/67g	143	213	9.7	42.9	0.3	4.4
Brown, Mixed Grain, Vogel*	1 Serving/45g	102	227	9.8	47.1	1.3	6.4
Brown, New Look, Weight Watchers*	1 Slice/12.2g	28	235	14.1	39.9	2.6	5.1
Brown, Original Wheatgerm, Medium Sliced, Hovis*	1 Slice/33g	77	233	10.8	40.1	3.3	3.7
Brown, Premium Gold Malted, TTD, Sainsbury's*	1 Slice/43g	93	217	8.5	40.3	2.4	2.4
Brown, Premium, Warburton's*	1 Slice/23.7g	60	249	10.6	43.2	3.7	5.1
Brown, Sainsbury's*	1 Slice/34g	81	239	8.4	46.8	2.1	4.2
Brown, Seeded Batch, Warburton's*	1 Slice/28.1g	78	279	11.3	39.4	8.5	3.2
Brown, Sliced, Medium, Asda*	1 Slice/36g	80	223	8.0	44.0	1.7	4.6
Brown, Soda, Marks & Spencer*	1 Slice/40g	92	229	9.2	43.6	3.6	4.9
Brown, Soya & Linseed, Vogel*	1 Slice/50g	119	238	12.2	34.0	5.9	5.4
Brown, Thick, Country Baked, Lidl*	1 Slice/38g	82	217	8.1	42.6	1.6	4.5
Brown, Thick, Warburton's*	1 Slice/37.9g	80	211	9.4	39.2	1.8	6.2
Brown, Thin Sliced, Sainsbury's*	1 Slice/28.9g	65	225	8.2	43.8	1.9	3.9
Brown, Toasted	1 Med Slice/24g	65	272	10.4	56.5	2.1	4.5
Brown, Toastie, Kingsmill*	1 Thick Slice/44g	101	230	9.5	40.5	3.3	4.7
Brown, Weight Watchers*	1 Slice/12g	25	209	11.9	36.5	1.8	6.3
Buns, Burger, Farmfoods*	1 Bun/53g	131	248	8.0	47.5	2.9	2.2
Buns, White, Burger, Waitrose*	1 Serving/64g	169	264	10.0	47.2	3.9	2.7
Carbs So Low, Nimble*	1 Slice/22g	45	204	11.6	34.4	2.2	5.9
Cheese & Onion, Somerfield*	1oz/28g	67	241	8.0	44.0	4.0	0.0
Cheese Onion & Garlic, Sainsbury's*	1 Baguette/190g	688	362	7.8	36.8	20.4	2.0
Cheese, Onion Mustard Seed, Cluster, Sainsbury's*	1 Cluster/100g	276	276	10.0	40.6	8.1	3.1
Cholla, Marks & Spencer*	1 Serving/67.9g	190	280	10.2	46.6	6.1	2.3
Ciabatta Stick, Organic, Marks & Spencer*	1 Stick/140g	315	225	8.9	48.5	1.4	4.2
Ciabatta, Black Olive, Part Baked, Sainsbury's*	¼ Ciabatta/67g	172	257	8.8	46.8	3.8	2.4
Ciabatta, Black Olive, Ready To Bake, Sainsbury's*	¼ Ciabatta/66g	170	257	8.8	46.8	3.8	2.4
Ciabatta, Finest, Tesco*	¼ Ciabatta/70g	185	264	9.3	42.5	6.3	2.3
Ciabatta, Garlic, Asda*	¼ Loaf/50g	173	345	9.5	41.6	15.6	1.1
Ciabatta, Garlic, BGTY, Sainsbury's*	½ Ciabatta/105g	306	291	8.7	36.2	12.4	2.7
Ciabatta, Garlic, Finest, Tesco*	1 Serving/65g	200	307	7.7	41.3	12.3	1.8
Ciabatta, Garlic, Healthy Living, Tesco*	¼ Bread/60g	151	251	8.6	44.6	4.2	2.6
Ciabatta, Garlic, Italiano, Tesco*	1 Serving/65g	211	324	7.7	40.9	14.4	2.2
Ciabatta, Garlic, Safeway*	¼ Ciabatta/53g	180	340	8.7	41.0	15.6	2.6
Ciabatta, Green Olive, Tesco*	¼ Loaf/70g	151	215	7.4	36.3	4.4	1.9
Ciabatta, Half, Marks & Spencer*	1 Loaf/135g	354	262	10.3	48.1	4.1	2.1
Ciabatta, Half, Organic, Sainsbury's*	½ Roll/63g	152	241	9.1	48.7	1.0	2.3
Ciabatta, Half, TTD, Sainsbury's*	½ Ciabatta/133g	346	260	8.9	47.7	3.7	2.2
Ciabatta, Italian Garlic, Sainsbury's*	1 Serving/145g	454	313	10.0	41.6	11.8	2.9
Ciabatta, Italian Style, Flutes, The Best, Safeway*	1 Flute/125g	319	255	8.8	47.2	3.5	2.2
Ciabatta, Italian Style, Safeway*	¼ Loaf/75g	194	258	8.9	47.7	3.5	2.2
Ciabatta, Marks & Spencer*	1 Ciabatta/130g	341	262	10.3	48.1	4.1	2.1
Ciabatta, Olive, Safeway*	1 Serving/25g	60	238	8.2	43.7	3.4	2.3
Ciabatta, Oregano & Feta, TTD, Sainsbury's*	½ Loaf/200g	574	287	10.4	36.5	11.0	2.4
Ciabatta, Organic, Marks & Spencer*	1oz/28g	59	209	7.8	42.5	0.9	1.9
Ciabatta, Organic, Tesco*	1/3 Loaf/100g	240	240	7.6	44.7	3.4	2.1
Ciabatta, Part Baked, Half, Sainsbury's*	½ Ciabatta/67g	174	260	8.9	47.7	3.7	2.2
Ciabatta, Ready To Bake, Marks & Spencer*	1 Serving/150g	393	262	10.3	48.1	4.1	2.1
Ciabatta, Ready To Bake, Sainsbury's*	½ Ciabatta/66g	172	260	8.9	47.7	3.7	2.2
Ciabatta, Spicy Topped, Finest, Tesco*	1 Serving/73g	163	223	9.2	34.0	5.5	1.7
Ciabatta, Sun Dried Tomato & Basil, Tesco*	¼ Loaf/75g	193	257	8.9	42.4	5.7	2.4
Ciabatta, Sun Dried Tomato & Olive, TTD, Sainsbury's*	1 Serving/62g	161	260	10.0	39.7	6.8	2.5

BREAD,

	Measure INFO/WEIGHT	per Measure KCAL	KCAL	PROT	CARB	FAT	FIBRE
Ciabatta, Sun Dried Tomato, Safeway*	1 Serving/127g	375	295	8.8	46.6	8.3	2.8
Ciabatta, Tomato & Basil, GFY, Asda*	1 Serving/55g	143	260	9.0	51.0	2.2	0.0
Ciabatta, Tomato & Mozzarella, Iceland*	1 Ciabatta/150g	374	249	10.0	29.6	10.1	3.3
Ciabatta, With Garlic & Herb Butter, Sainsbury's*	½ Loaf/105g	345	329	8.5	38.8	15.5	0.0
Cinnamon Swirl, Asda*	1 Serving/25g	87	349	6.0	52.0	13.0	1.6
Cobbles, Wholemeal, Hovis*	1 Serving/61g	143	235	9.7	31.7	3.4	6.3
Country Grain, COU, Marks & Spencer*	1 Slice/25g	58	233	11.0	42.8	2.0	5.6
Crusty Loaf, Harvest Blend, Warburton's*	1 Slice/28.6g	64	220	11.3	37.4	2.8	4.3
Farmhouse Loaf, Hovis*	1 Slice/44g	100	228	9.0	44.6	1.5	2.3
Fiery Green Pepper & Cheese, The Best, Safeway*	¼ Loaf/75g	180	240	12.3	38.4	4.1	3.4
Fig & Almond, Bröderna Cartwright*	4 Slices/100g	267	267	9.2	39.7	7.5	0.0
Focaccia, Garlic & Herb, Italian Style, Morrisons*	1/6 Bread/76g	259	341	8.5	44.7	14.3	2.5
Focaccia, Garlic & Herb, Safeway*	1/6 Bread /50g	154	308	9.1	42.9	11.1	2.1
Focaccia, Garlic & Onion, GFY, Asda*	¼ Bread/55g	150	272	12.0	47.0	4.0	0.0
Focaccia, Garlic Butter & Rosemary, Sainsbury's*	¼ Bread/75g	219	292	8.0	43.0	9.8	2.8
Focaccia, Mini, Sun Dried Tomato & Basil, Sainsbury's*	1oz/28g	90	321	8.0	41.8	13.6	0.0
Focaccia, Onion & Herb, Tesco*	½ Pack/190g	547	288	8.7	35.2	12.5	3.7
Focaccia, Oregano, The Best, Safeway*	1 Serving/55.6g	151	270	9.1	45.0	5.7	1.8
Focaccia, Roasted Onion & Cheese, Marks & Spencer*	1 Serving/88.9g	240	270	10.4	45.7	4.6	2.8
Focaccia, Safeway*	1/6 Slice/47g	131	279	9.5	46.9	5.9	3.4
Fougasse, Caramelised Onion & Cheese, Tesco*	1oz/28g	80	284	11.1	43.1	6.3	3.5
French Stick	2" Stick/40g	108	270	9.6	55.4	2.7	1.5
French Stick, Part Baked For Home Baking, Budgens*	1 Stick/200g	526	263	8.4	54.8	1.2	2.3
French's*	1 Serving/23g	57	247	11.0	46.0	3.0	6.0
French, Safeway*	1/5 Slice/41g	110	268	9.8	58.5	0.5	2.4
Fruit & Cinnamon Loaf, Finest, Tesco*	1 Slice/37g	134	363	6.4	54.6	13.2	1.5
Fruit Loaf, Apple & Cinnamon, Soreen*	1 Serving/10g	31	307	6.9	60.5	4.2	0.0
Fruit Loaf, Apple, Marks & Spencer*	1 Slice/39.2g	99	255	8.5	51.9	1.5	3.3
Fruit Loaf, Asda*	1 Slice/16g	45	280	8.0	54.0	3.5	2.1
Fruit Loaf, Banana, Soreen*	1 Slice/25g	78	313	6.8	60.9	4.7	0.0
Fruit Loaf, Co-Op*	1 Slice/36g	97	270	10.0	51.0	3.0	1.0
Fruit Loaf, Irish, Luxury, Crofters, Aldi*	1/12 Loaf/40g	119	298	7.0	56.8	4.8	3.9
Fruit Loaf, Luxury, Christmas, Soreen*	1 Serving/28g	85	303	4.5	66.6	2.1	0.0
Fruit Loaf, Marks & Spencer*	1 Slice/33g	79	240	14.7	52.7	1.4	2.2
Fruit Loaf, Mother's Pride*	1 Slice/36g	92	256	8.2	49.3	2.9	2.6
Fruit Loaf, Rich, Soreen*	1/10 Loaf/30g	93	310	7.4	60.7	4.1	0.0
Fruit Loaf, Sliced, Sainsbury's*	1 Slice/40g	104	260	8.9	47.9	3.6	2.4
Fruit Loaf, Sliced, Tesco*	1 Slice/27g	66	246	8.2	46.7	2.9	2.6
Fruit Loaf, With Orange, Warburton's*	1 Slice/33.3g	89	270	7.9	51.7	3.5	3.0
Fruit Loaf, With Strawberry, Summer, Warburton's*	1 Slice/35g	92	262	7.7	50.3	3.3	3.0
Fruit, Continental, Schneider Brot*	1 Slice/65g	198	305	5.4	57.0	5.4	0.0
Fruit, Raisin Swirl, Sun-Maid*	1 Slice/33.1g	95	287	8.3	50.4	5.8	2.6
Garlic & Herb, Giant Feast, Sainsbury's*	1 Serving/50g	159	317	8.0	42.1	12.9	2.6
Garlic Baguette, 50% Less Fat, Asda*	¼ Baguette/43g	126	294	9.2	45.8	8.2	1.3
Garlic Baguette, Asda*	¼ Baguette/42g	158	375	8.9	43.3	18.5	1.2
Garlic Baguette, BGTY, Sainsbury's*	1oz/28g	93	333	9.1	49.9	12.6	2.4
Garlic Baguette, Co-Op*	½ Baguette/80g	308	385	9.0	47.0	18.0	2.0
Garlic Baguette, Extra Strong, Sainsbury's*	½ Baguette/85g	278	327	8.4	40.0	14.8	3.4
Garlic Baguette, Frozen, Lidl*	1 Baguette/175g	555	317	7.6	44.7	12.0	0.0
Garlic Baguette, GFY, Asda *	¼ Baguette/43g	131	305	7.0	40.0	13.0	3.6
Garlic Baguette, Good Choice, Iceland*	1/3 Stick/54g	158	292	8.7	45.1	8.5	2.9
Garlic Baguette, Good Intentions, Somerfield*	½ Baguette/85g	209	246	7.0	37.8	7.4	1.6
Garlic Baguette, Healthy Eating, Tesco*	1 Serving/42g	111	264	8.0	41.1	7.5	2.6

BREAD,

	INFO/WEIGHT	KCAL	KCAL	PROT	CARB	FAT	FIBRE
Garlic Baguette, Iceland*	1 Serving/85g	302	355	7.5	38.2	19.1	1.8
Garlic Baguette, Italiano , Tesco*	1 Slice/19g	62	326	7.8	39.8	15.1	2.5
Garlic Baguette, Morrisons*	½ Baguette/95g	295	311	6.3	37.8	15.0	1.5
Garlic Baguette, Organic, Tesco*	1 Serving/43g	136	320	8.5	41.1	13.5	2.5
Garlic Baguette, Reduced Fat, Healthy Choice, Safeway*	½ Baguette/92g	306	333	7.3	45.4	13.6	2.1
Garlic Baguette, Reduced Fat, Waitrose*	½ Baguette/85g	230	270	8.1	41.5	8.0	2.7
Garlic Baguette, Sainsbury's*	1 Serving/50g	196	391	8.9	48.6	19.2	2.3
Garlic Baguette, Slices, Tesco*	1 Serving/35g	109	312	9.8	33.8	15.3	1.7
Garlic Baguette, Tesco*	1 Slice/19g	67	355	7.6	39.4	18.6	2.0
Garlic Baguette, Value, Asda*	½ Baguette/85g	252	297	9.0	47.0	8.0	1.6
Garlic Baguette, White, Homebake, Tesco*	3rd Baguette/55g	160	290	7.0	43.1	10.0	1.9
Garlic Flatbread, BGTY, Sainsbury's*	¼ Bread/56g	177	316	9.6	46.6	10.1	2.7
Garlic Flatbread, Tesco*	1 Serving/82.5g	251	302	6.7	45.3	10.4	3.0
Garlic Pizza Bread, Co-Op*	1 Pizza/240g	756	315	8.0	41.0	13.0	2.0
Garlic Pizza, Domino's Pizza*	1 Slice/40g	115	295	12.0	41.4	9.0	2.3
Garlic With Cheese, Asda*	1 Slice/34g	130	382	11.0	44.0	18.0	0.0
Garlic, 25% Less Fat, Sainsbury's*	½ Baguette/85g	268	315	7.8	39.4	14.0	3.1
Garlic, 30% Less Fat, Morrisons*	1 Serving/80g	226	283	5.9	41.1	10.8	1.9
Garlic, Asda*	½ Baguette/85g	302	355	7.6	39.4	18.6	2.0
Garlic, BGTY, Sainsbury's*	1 Serving/40g	126	315	7.8	39.4	14.0	3.1
Garlic, Baguette, 50% Less Fat, BGTY, Sainsbury's*	½ Baguette/80g	222	277	7.9	43.6	7.9	1.9
Garlic, Caramelised, TTD, Sainsbury's*	¼ Bread/75g	218	290	9.8	41.5	9.4	3.0
Garlic, Finest, Tesco*	¼ Loaf/60g	187	311	7.7	40.3	13.2	1.8
Garlic, GFY, Asda*	1 Slice/31g	104	337	11.0	53.0	9.0	1.1
Garlic, Good Choice, Iceland*	1 Slice/40g	156	389	7.7	43.9	22.8	0.0
Garlic, Herb, With Garlic & Herb Butter, Tesco*	1 Serving/73g	218	300	6.3	40.0	12.7	1.7
Garlic, Homebake, Tesco*	1 Serving/60g	209	348	7.1	33.7	20.5	1.5
Garlic, Italian Style Stone Baked, Morrisons*	½ Pack/115g	420	365	7.9	40.4	19.1	1.9
Garlic, Marks & Spencer*	1 Slice/20g	76	380	7.5	39.5	21.6	1.0
Garlic, Micro, McCain*	½ Bread/54g	202	374	7.8	45.1	18.0	0.0
Garlic, Organic, Waitrose*	1 Baguette/170g	536	315	8.7	39.1	13.7	1.8
Garlic, Pizza Hut*	1 Slice/24g	101	419	8.7	48.1	21.3	2.7
Garlic, Reduced Fat, Waitrose*	1 Pack/170g	551	324	6.9	49.4	11.0	0.9
Garlic, Safeway*	¼ Baguette/72g	242	336	8.2	45.9	13.3	2.7
Garlic, Slices, BGTY, Sainsbury's*	1 Slice/27g	82	305	9.4	48.9	8.0	2.9
Garlic, Slices, Farmfoods*	1oz/28g	106	379	8.8	37.9	21.4	3.3
Garlic, Slices, Frozen, Sainsbury's*	1 Slice/22.1g	104	471	9.6	52.3	24.9	2.4
Garlic, Slices, GFY, Asda*	1 Slice/31g	104	337	11.0	53.0	9.0	1.1
Garlic, Slices, Healthy Living, Tesco*	1 Slice/52g	131	251	8.6	44.6	4.2	2.6
Garlic, Slices, Morrisons*	1 Slice/30g	76	254	6.8	36.5	9.0	1.5
Garlic, Slices, Safeway*	1 Slice/27g	105	388	8.8	37.5	22.5	1.8
Garlic, Slices, Sainsbury's*	1 Slice/25g	108	433	8.5	39.2	26.9	2.3
Garlic, Stonebake, Marks & Spencer*	1 Loaf/85g	242	285	8.1	41.7	9.4	1.1
Garlic, To Share, Marks & Spencer*	¼ Loaf/82.1g	230	280	6.5	33.2	13.0	1.3
Garlic, With Cheese Slices, Asda*	1 Serving/32g	121	378	10.0	44.0	18.0	1.6
Ginger, Wheat Stem Sprouted, Organic, Sunnyvale*	1oz/28g	62	222	10.8	51.2	1.0	0.0
Granary	1 Slice/25g	59	235	9.3	46.3	2.7	4.3
Granary, COU, Marks & Spencer*	1 Slice/25g	62	246	11.7	45.1	2.1	5.7
Granary, Crusty, Farmhouse, Marks & Spencer*	1 Slice/50g	120	240	9.4	43.4	3.0	2.6
Granary, Hovis*	1 Serving/35g	79	225	9.1	42.7	2.0	3.3
Granary, Malted, Medium Brown, Asda*	1 Slice/35g	81	231	9.0	43.0	2.6	3.3
Granary, Medium Sliced, Hovis*	1 Slice/32.9g	81	246	9.6	45.8	2.7	5.3
Granary, Thick Sliced, COU, Marks & Spencer*	1 Slice/26g	65	250	11.7	45.1	2.1	5.7

B

BREAD,

INFO/WEIGHT	Measure	per Measure KCAL	KCAL	PROT	CARB	FAT	FIBRE
Granary, Thick Sliced, Hovis*	1 Slice/42.2g	95	225	9.1	42.7	2.0	3.3
Granary, Waitrose*	1 Slice/40g	88	220	9.4	39.9	2.5	4.3
Hi Bran, Burgen*	1 Slice/43.9g	94	214	13.2	33.5	3.0	7.9
Hi Bran, Marks & Spencer*	1 Slice/26.2g	55	210	12.6	32.5	3.0	6.3
Hi Bran, Medium Sliced, Allinson*	1 Slice/34g	72	212	13.2	33.6	2.8	8.0
Hi Fibre, Seed, LifeFibre Company*	1 Slice/35g	109	313	12.5	43.6	10.1	2.7
Hovis, Marks & Spencer*	1 Slice/21g	47	222	10.1	38.5	3.0	4.6
Irish Barm Brack, Tesco*	1 Serving/75g	233	310	16.0	47.6	6.9	3.0
Irish Brown Soda, Tesco*	1 Serving/50g	110	219	9.2	36.2	3.8	6.4
Irish Brown, Soda, Sainsbury's*	1 Serving/100g	208	208	8.8	36.4	3.0	5.3
Irish Cottage Wheaten, Tesco*	1 Serving/40g	79	198	9.1	35.4	1.9	6.1
Italian Style Pesto, TTD Sainsbury's*	¼ Bread/99g	247	249	9.1	39.4	6.1	4.4
Italian Style Red Pepper, Safeway*	1 Serving/80g	184	230	9.1	42.2	2.3	2.1
Italian Style, Cheese & Garlic, Morrisons*	½ Pack/135g	431	319	10.8	45.1	10.6	2.1
Juvela*	1 Slice/25g	60	240	3.3	50.0	3.0	1.7
Light Grain, Eat Smart, Safeway*	1 Slice/26.5g	66	245	9.7	45.5	2.5	3.5
Loaf, Crusty, Farmhouse, Poppy Seed, Marks & Spencer*	1 Slice/40g	104	260	9.4	47.6	3.3	2.3
Malt Loaf, Family, Asda*	1 Serving/20g	54	270	8.0	56.0	1.5	5.0
Malt Loaf, Fruit, Sainsbury's*	1oz/28g	86	308	7.9	63.8	2.4	2.4
Malt Loaf, Fruity, Sliced, 97% Fat Free, Soreen*	1 Slice/33g	103	312	7.7	65.9	2.0	0.0
Malt Loaf, Fruity, Soreen*	1 Serving/42g	130	310	7.4	65.6	2.0	0.0
Malt Loaf, Organic, Tesco*	1 Slice/28g	82	292	7.2	61.2	2.0	2.3
Malt Loaf, Ready Spread Snack, Soreen*	2 Slices/64g	220	344	6.4	57.0	10.0	3.0
Malt Loaf, Sticky, Marks & Spencer*	3 Slices/47.5g	139	295	6.9	64.9	2.3	3.1
Malt Loaf, Tesco*	1 Slice/50g	146	291	8.6	58.0	2.7	4.8
Malt Loaf, Value, Tesco*	1 Slice/25g	72	289	8.9	60.2	1.4	3.3
Malted Brown, Granary, Hovis*	1 Med Slice/35g	79	225	9.1	42.7	2.0	3.3
Malted Brown, Kingsmill*	1 slice/44g	103	234	9.4	43.4	2.5	2.7
Malted Brown, Morrisons*	1 Slice/38g	96	253	10.3	49.9	1.4	3.1
Malted Brown, Slice, BGTY, Sainsbury's*	1 Slice/22g	53	239	12.1	41.4	2.8	5.8
Malted Brown, TTD, Sainsbury's*	1 Slice/44g	103	234	8.8	42.9	3.0	3.1
Malted Brown, Thick Sliced, Organic, Tesco*	1 Slice/44g	116	264	7.8	53.8	2.0	3.3
Malted Danish, Nimble*	1 Slice/22g	49	222	8.3	43.7	1.6	5.3
Malted Danish, Weight Watchers, Warburton's*	1 Slice/19.1g	46	241	12.3	44.5	1.7	4.3
Malted Grain, Co-Op*	1 Slice/43g	99	230	8.0	46.0	2.0	3.0
Malted Oat, Duchy Originals*	1 Serving/80g	195	244	8.8	43.6	3.8	3.7
Malted Wheat Country, Kingsmill Gold*	1 Slice/41g	96	234	9.4	43.4	2.5	2.7
Malted Wheat Loaf, Thick Sliced, Village Green, Aldi*	1 Slice/38g	96	253	10.3	49.9	1.4	3.1
Malted Wheat, Eat Smart, Safeway*	1 Slice/26g	60	230	10.0	42.8	1.8	5.3
Malted Wheat, Gold, Kingsmill*	1 Slice/45g	108	240	9.8	43.8	2.9	3.6
Malted Wheat, The Best, Safeway*	1 Slice/44g	103	235	9.1	45.6	1.8	4.7
Malted, Crusty, Sainsbury's*	1 Slice/42.1g	109	259	8.6	48.6	3.3	4.4
Malted, Danish, Sliced, Warburton's*	1 Slice/19g	41	218	10.2	41.3	1.4	6.9
Malted, Danish, Weight Watchers*	1 Slice/19g	41	218	10.2	41.3	1.4	6.9
Malted, Floury Batch, Sainsbury's*	1 Roll/68g	190	280	8.7	51.6	4.3	4.2
Malted, Sunblest*	1 Serving/45g	115	256	9.9	49.1	2.2	3.8
Malted, Wheat Loaf, Crusty, Finest, Tesco*	1 Slice/50g	115	230	9.8	44.2	1.5	4.4
Mediterranean Olive, Waitrose*	1 Slice/30g	82	273	7.4	40.1	9.2	4.9
Mediterranean Style Seed, Safeway*	1 Slice/25g	65	259	11.4	37.2	7.2	9.1
Mediterranean Style, Marks & Spencer*	1/6 Loaf/47.6g	151	315	10.9	42.5	11.1	1.2
Milk Roll, Warburton's*	1 Slice/18g	46	253	11.0	45.1	2.7	2.7
Mixed Seed Loaf, Organic, Marks & Spencer*	1oz/28g	73	261	9.3	37.5	8.7	5.1
Mixed Seed, Organic, Duchy Originals*	2 Slices/85g	229	269	10.9	39.1	8.1	5.3

	Measure	per Measure	Nutrition Values per 100g / 100ml				
	INFO/WEIGHT	KCAL	KCAL	PROT	CARB	FAT	FIBRE
BREAD,							
Multigrain, Bakers Choice, Marks & Spencer*	1 Slice/25g	61	242	13.4	33.7	6.0	6.4
Multigrain, Batch, Finest, Tesco*	1 Slice/50g	127	254	9.8	47.7	2.7	4.2
Multigrain, Farmhouse Baker's, Marks & Spencer*	1 Slice/51.1g	115	225	13.0	31.2	5.4	5.1
Multigrain, Gluten Free, Sainsbury's*	1 Slice/17g	39	229	5.1	40.8	5.0	5.6
Multigrain, Sliced Loaf, Gluten-Free, Dietary Specials*	2 Slices/66.4g	151	229	5.1	40.8	5.1	5.6
Multigrain, Soft Batch, Sainsbury's*	1 Slice/44g	106	242	11.3	34.5	6.5	5.6
Multigrain, Sunblest*	1 Slice/30g	76	254	9.0	47.0	2.5	4.5
Multigrain, Sunflower, Allinson*	1 Slice/47g	113	240	9.8	36.9	4.7	3.9
Multigrain, TTD, Sainsbury's*	1 Slice/44g	106	242	10.2	35.9	6.4	5.3
Multigrain, Tesco*	1 Slice/31g	66	214	11.1	36.8	3.2	8.9
Multigrain, Thick Sliced, Tesco*	1 Slice/50g	113	225	8.4	42.2	2.5	3.9
Naan	1 Naan/160g	538	336	8.9	50.1	12.5	1.9
Naan Garlic & Coriander, Mini, Safeway*	1 Naan/56.4g	154	275	9.0	42.8	7.5	3.8
Naan, Co-Op*	1oz/28g	60	216	7.7	36.9	4.2	1.3
Naan, Fresh, BGTY, Sainsbury's*	1 Serving/150g	368	245	9.4	44.9	3.1	2.2
Naan, Fresh, Sharwood's*	1oz/28g	70	251	7.3	48.0	3.3	2.0
Naan, Garlic & Coriander, Asda*	½ Naan/74g	260	352	7.0	45.0	16.0	2.3
Naan, Garlic & Coriander, Fresh, Sharwood's*	1oz/28g	71	252	7.7	47.8	3.3	2.2
Naan, Garlic & Coriander, Large, Sainsbury's*	½ Naan/75g	209	279	7.1	46.3	7.3	2.9
Naan, Garlic & Coriander, Mini, Asda*	1 Naan/49.7g	165	330	7.0	44.0	14.0	1.2
Naan, Garlic & Coriander, Mini, Long Life, Sharwood's*	1oz/28g	71	255	7.4	45.3	4.9	2.3
Naan, Garlic & Coriander, Mini, Sainsbury's*	1 Naan/50g	148	295	8.6	44.2	9.3	3.7
Naan, Garlic & Coriander, Mini, Sharwood's*	1 Naan/59g	144	244	7.1	46.2	3.4	2.0
Naan, Garlic & Coriander, Mini, Tesco*	1 Naan/60g	178	296	7.6	47.0	8.6	2.5
Naan, Garlic & Coriander, Spar*	1 Naan/122g	376	308	6.7	49.9	9.1	0.0
Naan, Garlic & Coriander, Tesco*	1 Naan/150g	374	249	7.1	36.5	8.3	2.1
Naan, Healthy Eating, Tesco*	1 Naan/70g	165	236	8.0	46.1	2.1	2.6
Naan, Indian Meal For One, BGTY, Sainsbury's*	1 Serving/45g	115	257	10.3	44.2	4.3	2.1
Naan, Indian Meal For One, Sainsbury's*	1 Serving/50g	145	289	9.7	47.6	6.6	2.1
Naan, Indian Style, Lidl*	1 Naan/140g	332	237	8.7	44.2	2.5	0.0
Naan, Indian Style, Mini, Asda*	1 Naan/50g	152	304	8.0	50.0	8.0	2.8
Naan, Keema Filled, Mini, Indian Takeaway, Safeway*	1 Naan/23g	58	253	10.1	38.3	6.6	2.1
Naan, King Prawn, Marks & Spencer*	1 Serving/185g	360	195	9.1	25.3	6.3	2.5
Naan, Long Life, Sharwood's*	1oz/28g	72	258	7.3	45.8	5.1	2.0
Naan, Marks & Spencer*	1 Bread/84g	260	310	12.0	43.8	9.8	2.1
Naan, Mini, Plain, Tesco*	1 Naan/60g	175	292	9.3	47.6	7.2	2.5
Naan, Mini, Sainsbury's*	1 Serving/50g	157	314	8.7	41.5	12.4	4.3
Naan, Northern Indian,, Sainsbury's*	1 Serving/125.3g	356	285	8.7	45.9	7.4	1.9
Naan, Onion & Mint, Marks & Spencer*	½ Naan/135g	351	260	8.9	35.8	8.7	2.5
Naan, Onion Bhaji, Sharwood's*	1 Pack/130g	378	291	7.3	48.4	7.6	2.2
Naan, Onion Bhajia, Marks & Spencer*	1 Naan/140.4g	399	285	9.5	34.2	12.1	2.0
Naan, Peshwari, Fresh, Sharwood's*	1oz/28g	67	240	6.8	41.9	5.0	2.5
Naan, Peshwari, Long Life, Sharwood's*	1oz/28g	71	252	6.2	42.0	6.6	2.6
Naan, Peshwari, Marks & Spencer*	1 Serving/127g	394	310	9.2	45.8	10.1	1.9
Naan, Peshwari, Northern Indian, Sainsbury's*	1 Bread/160g	458	286	6.3	49.7	6.9	2.8
Naan, Peshwari, Tesco*	1 Naan/215.0g	544	253	6.8	38.8	7.8	3.0
Naan, Plain, Mini, Asda*	1 Nann/50g	144	288	7.0	47.0	8.0	1.5
Naan, Plain, Mini, Fresh, Sharwood's*	1oz/28g	70	251	7.3	48.0	3.3	2.0
Naan, Plain, Mini, Tesco*	1 Serving/60g	158	263	7.5	43.9	6.4	2.1
Naan, Plain, Nisa Heritage*	1 Naan/150g	401	267	9.0	44.2	6.2	1.9
Naan, Plain, Original, Mild, Patak's*	1 Serving/130g	399	307	9.5	48.0	8.6	0.0
Naan, Plain, Sainsbury's*	½ Naan/74.9g	209	279	7.3	46.7	7.0	2.7
Naan, Plain, Sharwood's*	1 Bread/120g	294	245	10.1	43.1	3.6	3.4

B

	Measure	per Measure	Nutrition Values per 100g / 100ml				
	INFO/WEIGHT	KCAL	KCAL	PROT	CARB	FAT	FIBRE
BREAD,							
Naan, Plain, Tesco*	1 Naan/150g	429	286	7.8	47.6	7.2	2.5
Naan, Plain, Value, Tesco*	1 Naan/135g	363	269	8.1	42.9	7.2	1.6
Naan, Plain, Waitrose*	1 Naan/144.8g	473	326	7.2	49.9	10.8	2.4
Naan, Safeway*	1 Naan/120g	346	288	8.4	51.4	5.4	2.6
Naan, Smartprice, Asda*	1 Naan/131g	439	335	10.0	49.0	11.0	2.1
Naan, Tandoor Baked, Waitrose*	1 Naan/139.8g	372	266	9.8	49.6	3.1	2.9
Naan, Tandoori, Large, The Bombay Brasserie, London*	1 Naan/110g	270	245	10.1	43.1	3.6	3.4
Naan, Tandoori, Sharwood's*	1 Bread/130g	330	254	7.3	45.0	5.0	2.4
Oat, Waitrose*	1oz/28g	71	253	8.5	44.9	4.4	3.6
Oatmeal, Batch, Tesco*	1 Slice/50g	135	269	9.3	50.1	3.5	4.0
Oatmeal, Farmhouse, Soft, Marks & Spencer*	1 Slice/45g	110	245	11.1	39.5	4.4	5.2
Oatmeal, Farmhouse, Waitrose*	1 Slice/40g	110	276	9.4	47.9	5.2	4.6
Oatmeal, Sliced Loaf, Tesco*	1 Slice/50g	111	222	7.4	40.5	3.4	2.8
Olive, Waitrose*	1 Slice/28g	86	306	9.0	43.6	10.6	2.0
Panettone, Bauli*	1 Serving/75g	314	418	5.9	53.5	20.1	0.0
Panettone, Marks & Spencer*	1/8 Loaf/51g	184	360	6.5	53.4	13.2	2.0
Petit Pain, Harvester, Somerfield*	1 Serving/70g	188	269	10.6	52.2	2.0	3.2
Petit Pain, Homebake Mini, Tesco*	1 Roll/50g	118	235	7.8	49.1	0.8	1.2
Petit Pain, Homebake, Mini, Tesco*	1 Serving/50g	118	235	7.8	49.1	0.8	0.0
Petit Pain, Organic, Tesco*	1 Roll/100g	235	235	7.8	49.1	0.8	1.2
Petit Pain, Ready To Bake, Sainsbury's*	1 Petit Pain/44g	132	299	9.4	61.6	1.7	3.2
Petit Pain, Ready to Bake, Co-Op*	1 Petit Pain/33g	73	220	7.0	46.0	1.0	3.0
Petit Pain, Waitrose*	1 Roll/69g	190	275	9.3	55.9	1.6	3.1
Petit Pain, White, Part Baked, Asda*	1 Roll/128g	330	258	8.0	53.0	1.6	2.0
Petit Pain, White, Soft Bake, Somerfield*	1 Roll/70g	174	248	9.2	49.9	1.3	1.8
Pitta, Brown, Organic, Waitrose*	1 Pitta/61g	138	226	6.4	47.5	1.4	6.6
Pitta, Cypriana Supreme*	1oz/28g	67	239	8.5	48.6	1.2	0.0
Pitta, Feta, Sun Dried Tomato, TTD, Sainsbury's*	1 Pitta/71g	235	331	10.7	48.6	10.4	3.2
Pitta, Garlic & Coriander, Asda*	1 Bread/57g	149	261	8.0	53.0	1.9	0.0
Pitta, Garlic & Herb, Tesco*	1 Pitta/56g	138	246	8.4	50.3	1.2	2.1
Pitta, Garlic, Co-Op*	1 Pitta/63g	161	255	9.0	53.0	1.0	2.0
Pitta, Garlic, Morrisons*	1 Pitta/60g	149	249	9.7	51.1	1.8	0.0
Pitta, Garlic, Sainsbury's*	1 Pitta/60g	153	255	9.5	52.0	1.0	2.5
Pitta, Iceland*	1 Pitta/50g	126	251	8.6	50.0	1.8	2.3
Pitta, Mexican, Santa Maria*	1 Pitta/66g	165	250	7.5	52.0	1.0	0.0
Pitta, Mini, Marks & Spencer*	1 Pitta/13g	34	260	9.2	52.1	2.4	1.8
Pitta, Mini, Safeway*	1 Pitta/25g	53	212	7.6	47.6	1.2	2.0
Pitta, Organic, Tesco*	1 Pitta/60g	124	206	8.3	40.2	1.4	5.7
Pitta, Pockets, Pride Valley*	1 Pitta/63g	151	239	9.3	48.4	0.9	3.2
Pitta, Pockets, Sainsbury's*	1 Serving/75g	188	250	8.5	52.0	1.0	3.5
Pitta, Sesame, Sainsbury's*	1 Pitta/59g	156	264	9.8	50.8	2.4	3.1
Pitta, Somerfield*	1 Pitta/56g	141	251	8.6	50.0	1.8	2.3
Pitta, Tesco*	1oz/28g	69	247	8.4	50.7	1.2	2.6
Pitta, Value, Tesco*	1oz/28g	64	227	6.0	48.8	0.9	2.0
Pitta, White	1 Pitta/75g	199	265	9.2	57.9	1.2	2.2
Pitta, White Picnic, Waitrose*	1 Pitta/30g	75	249	10.3	49.3	1.2	3.5
Pitta, White, Asda*	1 Pitta/56g	141	252	9.0	50.0	1.8	2.3
Pitta, White, Co-Op*	1 Pitta/63g	151	240	10.0	47.0	1.0	3.0
Pitta, White, Greek Style, Asda*	1 Pitta/50g	127	253	8.0	51.0	1.9	0.0
Pitta, White, Iceland*	1 Pitta/50g	126	251	8.6	50.0	1.8	2.3
Pitta, White, Marks & Spencer*	1 Pitta/61g	156	255	8.9	51.6	2.4	0.0
Pitta, White, Mini, Safeway*	1 Pitta/54g	119	220	8.0	49.4	1.2	1.9
Pitta, White, Mini, Sainsbury's*	1 Pitta/30g	75	249	10.3	49.3	1.2	3.5

BREAD,

INFO/WEIGHT	Measure	per Measure KCAL	KCAL	PROT	CARB	FAT	FIBRE
Pitta, White, Mini, Tesco*	1 Pitta/18g	47	262	10.1	51.2	1.9	2.6
Pitta, White, Morrisons*	1 Pitta/60g	157	262	10.1	51.2	1.9	0.0
Pitta, White, Organic, Sainsbury's*	1 Pitta/59g	150	254	10.3	50.7	1.1	2.5
Pitta, White, Safeway*	1 Pitta/54g	119	220	8.0	49.4	1.2	1.9
Pitta, White, Sainsburys*	1 Pittta/59g	147	249	10.3	49.3	1.2	3.5
Pitta, White, Somerfield*	1 Pitta/55.8g	141	251	8.6	50.0	1.8	2.3
Pitta, White, Tesco*	1 Pitta/56g	147	262	10.1	51.2	1.9	2.6
Pitta, White, Waitrose*	1 Pitta/60g	149	249	10.3	49.3	1.2	3.5
Pitta, Wholemeal, Arnaouti*	1 Pitta/88.5g	199	226	11.5	43.0	1.7	7.2
Pitta, Wholemeal, Asda*	1oz/28g	64	229	11.0	41.0	2.3	0.0
Pitta, Wholemeal, Healthy Eating, Co-Op*	1 Pitta/63g	135	215	12.0	37.0	2.0	9.0
Pitta, Wholemeal, Lemon, TTD, Sainsbury's*	1 Pitta/83g	207	249	10.0	38.0	6.3	6.8
Pitta, Wholemeal, Marks & Spencer*	1 Pitta/60.9g	140	230	10.7	40.6	2.8	7.2
Pitta, Wholemeal, Morrisons*	1 Pitta/60g	135	225	11.9	46.4	2.0	0.0
Pitta, Wholemeal, Safeway*	1 Pitta/54g	125	232	9.7	44.2	1.9	6.5
Pitta, Wholemeal, Sainsbury's*	1 Pitta/59g	146	247	12.4	46.0	1.5	5.3
Pitta, Wholemeal, Somerfield*	1 Pitta/55.9g	127	227	10.6	41.0	2.3	6.2
Pitta, Wholemeal, Tesco*	1 Pitta/55g	138	251	11.9	46.4	2.0	6.6
Pitta, Wholemeal, Waitrose*	1 Pitta/60g	151	251	11.3	53.4	0.6	0.0
Plum Loaf, Lincolnshire, Soreen*	1/10 Loaf/29.1g	88	302	8.1	57.8	4.3	0.0
Potato & Rosemary, Marks & Spencer*	1 Serving/40g	108	270	9.4	42.2	6.8	2.3
Potato & Rosemary, Tesco*	1oz/28g	67	241	8.2	42.0	4.5	2.2
Pumpernickel Rye, Kelderman*	1 Slice/50g	93	185	6.0	38.0	1.0	0.0
Pumpkin Seed, Raisin & Sunflower Seed, Sainsbury's*	1 Slice/30g	77	255	11.6	45.9	2.8	3.4
Raisin & Pumpkin Seed, Organic, Tesco*	1 Slice/30g	76	253	9.7	40.6	5.8	3.8
Raisin Loaf With Cinnamon, Warburton's*	1 Slice/33g	91	276	7.5	52.9	3.8	4.2
Roasted Onion, Marks & Spencer*	1 Slice/50g	125	250	9.0	46.7	3.3	2.1
Roasted Shallot & Gruyere, Safeway*	¼ Loaf/52.6g	151	285	11.2	43.1	7.3	9.1
Rolls, American Style Deli, Tesco*	1 Roll/65g	162	249	7.8	46.8	3.4	1.6
Rolls, Batch, Seeded, Marks & Spencer*	1 Roll/76g	220	290	10.6	39.7	9.6	4.0
Rolls, Batched Sandwich, Warburton's*	1 Roll/60g	148	246	9.6	42.7	4.1	0.0
Rolls, Best Of Both, Square, Hovis*	1 Roll/52g	120	231	10.8	35.7	5.0	4.6
Rolls, Best of Both, Hovis*	1 Roll/29g	68	235	9.8	39.5	4.2	4.2
Rolls, Blackpool Milk, Warburton's*	1 Slice/18g	45	251	10.8	45.3	3.0	2.8
Rolls, Brioche, Sainsbury's*	1 Roll/32g	116	362	8.5	56.0	11.5	3.6
Rolls, Brown, Crusty	1 Roll/50g	128	255	10.3	50.4	2.8	3.5
Rolls, Brown, Large, Asda*	1 Roll/57g	138	242	10.0	47.0	1.6	0.0
Rolls, Brown, Malted Grain, Somerfield*	1 Roll/60g	147	245	8.7	45.2	3.2	3.0
Rolls, Brown, Malted Grain, Tesco*	1 Roll/58g	142	244	8.7	45.1	3.2	1.9
Rolls, Brown, Marks & Spencer*	1 Roll/105g	242	230	9.2	37.3	6.1	4.4
Rolls, Brown, Mini, Marks & Spencer*	1 Serving/32.7g	81	245	9.8	35.5	7.6	3.8
Rolls, Brown, Morning, Farmfoods*	1 Roll/50g	135	269	12.0	47.0	3.7	4.2
Rolls, Brown, Old Fashioned, Waitrose*	1 Roll/63g	152	241	9.6	41.3	4.1	4.7
Rolls, Brown, Soft	1 Roll/50g	134	268	10.0	51.8	3.8	3.5
Rolls, Brown, Soft, Marks & Spencer*	1 Roll/45.7g	106	230	8.7	44.0	2.2	5.2
Rolls, Brown, Soft, Somerfield*	1oz/28g	68	243	9.0	42.0	3.0	0.0
Rolls, Brown, Soft, Tesco*	1 Roll/50g	118	235	9.0	41.6	3.6	4.5
Rolls, Brown, Spar*	1 Roll/60g	151	252	9.1	46.8	3.2	4.2
Rolls, Brown, Square, Marks & Spencer*	1 Roll/105g	242	230	9.2	37.3	6.1	4.4
Rolls, COU, Marks & Spencer*	1 Serving/51.1g	120	235	9.8	44.0	2.3	3.4
Rolls, Cheese Topped, Village Green*	1 Roll/56g	159	284	13.1	41.2	7.4	4.8
Rolls, Ciabatta, Cheese Topped, Mini, Finest, Tesco*	1 Roll/30g	85	282	11.5	40.9	8.1	3.8
Rolls, Ciabatta, Finest, Tesco*	1 Roll/45g	93	206	7.7	33.5	4.6	2.3

BREAD,

INFO/WEIGHT	Measure	per Measure KCAL	KCAL	PROT	CARB	FAT	FIBRE
			Nutrition Values per 100g / 100ml				

	Measure INFO/WEIGHT	per Measure KCAL	KCAL	PROT	CARB	FAT	FIBRE
Rolls, Ciabatta, Marks & Spencer*	1 Roll/80g	210	262	10.3	48.1	4.1	2.1
Rolls, Ciabatta, Mini, Finest, Tesco*	1 Roll/30g	89	297	9.9	49.1	6.8	4.1
Rolls, Ciabatta, Ready To Bake, Sainsbury's*	1 Roll/75g	198	264	9.1	48.9	3.6	2.3
Rolls, Ciabatta, Ready to Bake, TTD, Sainsbury's*	1 Roll/72g	187	260	8.9	47.7	3.7	2.2
Rolls, Ciabatta, Sun Dried Tomato, Mini, Finest, Tesco*	1 Roll/30g	79	262	8.7	42.3	6.4	2.6
Rolls, Ciabatta, Tesco*	1 Serving/80g	194	242	9.8	41.8	3.9	2.4
Rolls, Country Grain, Mini, Marks & Spencer*	1 Serving/30.9g	85	275	10.2	38.9	9.7	3.8
Rolls, Crisp, Original, Organic, Kallo*	1 Roll/8.7g	35	390	11.0	74.0	5.6	3.0
Rolls, Crusty, French, Marks & Spencer*	1 Roll/65g	159	245	8.1	50.5	1.2	3.3
Rolls, Crusty, Part-Baked, Budgens*	1 Roll/50g	148	296	9.4	61.4	1.4	2.5
Rolls, Finger, Morrisons*	1 Roll/46g	119	259	10.7	50.0	1.8	2.3
Rolls, Finger, Sainsbury's*	1 Roll/40g	102	256	10.3	47.9	2.6	2.4
Rolls, For Hamburgers	1 Roll/50g	132	264	9.1	48.8	5.0	1.5
Rolls, Granary Malted Wheatgrain, Soft, Marks & Spencer*	1 Roll/80g	208	260	9.3	47.2	3.9	2.3
Rolls, Granary, Bakers Premium, Tesco*	1 Roll/65g	158	243	9.9	47.8	1.3	2.3
Rolls, Granary, Waitrose*	1 Roll/59g	160	271	10.0	47.2	6.4	3.8
Rolls, Green Olive, Marks & Spencer*	1 Roll/75g	210	280	11.2	44.0	6.0	1.8
Rolls, Hot Dog, Farmfoods*	1 Roll/53g	125	235	8.1	47.0	1.7	2.2
Rolls, Hot Dog, Sliced, Asda*	1 Roll/84g	197	234	7.0	44.0	3.3	0.0
Rolls, Hot Dog, Tesco*	1 Roll/85g	200	235	7.3	44.0	3.3	1.9
Rolls, Lidl*	1 Roll/75g	209	279	11.0	51.0	3.0	2.3
Rolls, Malted Grain Submarine, Marks & Spencer*	1 Serving/109.1g	300	275	8.9	53.6	4.3	3.0
Rolls, Malted Grain, Soft, Weight Watchers*	1 Roll/42g	95	226	9.8	42.2	2.0	4.5
Rolls, Malted Wheat & Poppy Seed, Safeway*	1 Roll/54g	140	260	10.6	48.7	2.8	3.4
Rolls, Malted, Sainsbury's*	1 Roll/68g	190	280	8.7	51.6	4.3	4.2
Rolls, Mediterranean Style, TTD, Sainsbury's*	1 Roll/75g	192	256	8.5	41.9	6.0	5.8
Rolls, Mini Submarine, Marks & Spencer*	1 Roll/23g	63	275	11.4	47.7	4.9	1.1
Rolls, Mini, Mixed, Marks & Spencer*	1 Roll/32g	71	221	9.6	43.4	5.0	1.9
Rolls, Morning Breakfast, Marks & Spencer*	1 Roll/55g	160	290	10.3	53.8	4.3	0.6
Rolls, Morning, Tesco*	1 Roll/48g	117	243	10.4	44.8	2.5	4.7
Rolls, Multigrain, Torpedo, Sainsbury's*	1 Roll/111.9g	328	293	10.5	47.7	6.7	6.3
Rolls, Oatmeal, Soft, Marks & Spencer*	1 Roll/80g	224	280	12.3	43.4	6.4	2.7
Rolls, Pain Raisin, Mini, Marks & Spencer*	1oz/28g	87	310	5.3	42.3	13.6	1.3
Rolls, Panini, Marks & Spencer*	1 Roll/86g	211	245	8.3	39.3	6.2	1.6
Rolls, Poppy Seeded Knot, Waitrose*	1 Roll/65g	179	275	9.3	55.9	1.6	3.1
Rolls, Rye, Toasting, Good & Hot*	1 Roll/65g	143	220	7.3	44.6	1.1	7.1
Rolls, Sandwich, Kids, Warburton's*	1 Roll/40g	99	248	9.8	43.0	4.1	3.7
Rolls, Scottish, White, Tesco*	1 Roll/48g	117	243	10.4	44.8	2.5	4.7
Rolls, Seeded, Sandwich, Warburton's*	1 Roll/77g	240	312	13.3	41.2	10.4	0.0
Rolls, Snack, Mini, Tesco*	1 Roll/35g	95	271	19.0	43.0	6.0	4.0
Rolls, Square, Hovis*	1 Roll/47g	116	247	8.4	44.8	3.8	2.0
Rolls, Sun Dried Tomato, Homebake, Tesco*	1 Roll/50g	123	246	11.3	44.0	3.0	0.0
Rolls, Sunflower Seed, Toasting, Good & Hot*	1 Roll/65g	163	250	8.5	41.0	5.0	8.0
Rolls, Tomato & Basil, Sub, COU, Marks & Spencer*	1 Roll/32.5g	87	265	11.0	48.7	2.7	2.4
Rolls, White, BGTY, Sainsbury's*	1 Roll/50g	114	227	9.1	45.3	1.0	3.0
Rolls, White, Basics, Somerfield*	1 Roll/44g	107	243	8.9	48.2	1.6	2.1
Rolls, White, Big Square, Hovis*	1 Roll/73g	183	250	8.4	45.2	3.9	2.1
Rolls, White, Cheese Topped, Asda*	1 Roll/46g	121	264	10.0	46.0	4.4	2.0
Rolls, White, Cheese Topped, Sainsbury's*	1 Roll/75g	218	291	12.1	41.6	8.5	2.0
Rolls, White, Co-Op*	1 Roll/55g	138	250	8.0	46.0	4.0	2.0
Rolls, White, Crusty	1 Roll/50g	140	280	10.9	57.6	2.3	1.5
Rolls, White, Deli Tesco*	1 Roll/65g	180	277	8.7	52.0	3.8	2.7
Rolls, White, Finger, Co-Op*	1 Roll/46g	129	280	10.0	52.0	4.0	2.0

BREAD,

INFO/WEIGHT	Measure per Measure KCAL		Nutrition Values per 100g / 100ml				
			KCAL	PROT	CARB	FAT	FIBRE
Rolls, White, Finger, SmartPrice, Asda*	1 Roll/50g	121	242	9.0	48.0	1.6	2.1
Rolls, White, Finger, Tesco*	1 Roll/50g	125	251	9.7	55.5	0.4	1.5
Rolls, White, Finger, Waitrose*	1 Roll/49g	121	247	9.4	45.6	3.0	2.7
Rolls, White, Floured, Warburton's*	1 Roll/50g	124	247	9.8	43.3	3.8	2.7
Rolls, White, Floury Batch, Sainsbury's*	1 Roll/65g	167	257	8.7	46.6	4.0	3.1
Rolls, White, Floury, Roberts*	1 Roll/63.0g	160	254	8.4	49.5	2.5	2.0
Rolls, White, Golden Sun, Lidl*	1 Roll/36g	89	248	8.3	48.6	2.3	0.0
Rolls, White, Good Health, Warburton's*	1 Roll/54g	122	226	9.6	42.0	2.0	4.1
Rolls, White, Hot Dog, Safeway*	1 Roll/52.8g	131	248	8.6	46.1	3.2	2.5
Rolls, White, Hot Dog, Sainsbury's*	1 Roll/85g	235	277	7.3	48.8	5.8	2.4
Rolls, White, Hot Dog, Tesco*	1 Roll/85g	200	235	7.3	44.0	3.3	1.9
Rolls, White, Kingsmill*	1 Roll/60g	151	252	9.3	44.5	4.1	2.4
Rolls, White, Large, Sliced, Warburton's*	1 Serving/89g	223	250	10.2	45.0	3.2	2.5
Rolls, White, Low Price, Sainsbury's*	1 Roll/44g	107	243	8.9	48.2	1.6	2.1
Rolls, White, Milk, Warburton's*	1 Serving/18.3g	45	251	10.8	45.3	3.0	2.8
Rolls, White, Morning, Co-Op*	1 Roll/47g	134	285	12.0	53.0	3.0	2.0
Rolls, White, Morning, Marks & Spencer*	1 Roll/50g	136	272	8.8	53.8	1.5	2.7
Rolls, White, Old Fashioned, Waitrose*	1 Roll/57g	157	275	8.8	49.8	4.5	2.8
Rolls, White, Organic, Sainsbury's*	1 Roll/65g	170	262	8.7	49.9	3.0	1.0
Rolls, White, Part Baked, Morrisons*	1 Roll/75g	227	303	9.6	63.0	1.4	2.6
Rolls, White, Ploughman's, Sainsbury's*	1 Roll/65g	185	285	8.6	54.1	3.8	2.3
Rolls, White, Premium Soft, Rathbones*	1 Roll/65g	190	293	9.3	50.3	6.0	2.7
Rolls, White, Savers, Safeway*	1 Roll/40g	113	283	10.4	54.6	1.8	20.0
Rolls, White, Scottish, Morning, Safeway*	1 Roll/40g	113	283	10.4	56.4	1.8	1.6
Rolls, White, Seeded, Sainsbury's*	1 Roll/80g	217	271	10.9	43.4	5.9	4.8
Rolls, White, Seeded, Soft, Marks & Spencer*	1 Roll/72g	205	285	11.7	46.2	5.7	1.8
Rolls, White, SmartPrice, Asda*	1 Roll/44g	106	242	9.0	48.0	1.6	2.1
Rolls, White, Snack, Sainsbury's*	1 Roll/67g	159	237	7.9	49.2	1.0	2.3
Rolls, White, Soft	1 Roll/45g	121	268	9.2	51.6	4.2	1.5
Rolls, White, Soft, Boulders, Hovis*	1 Roll/74g	206	279	11.0	51.5	3.0	2.3
Rolls, White, Soft, COU, Marks & Spencer*	1 Roll/37g	94	255	10.7	47.1	2.7	1.5
Rolls, White, Soft, Farmhouse, Warburton's*	1 Roll/59g	148	250	9.7	43.0	4.4	2.5
Rolls, White, Soft, Finger, Marks & Spencer*	1 Roll/64g	189	295	10.1	47.5	7.2	2.2
Rolls, White, Soft, Marks & Spencer*	1 Roll/49g	120	245	9.7	45.8	2.8	2.0
Rolls, White, Soft, Morrisons*	1 Roll/42g	100	238	9.1	46.4	1.9	2.4
Rolls, White, Soft, Premium, Village Green, Aldi*	1 Roll/65g	168	259	8.3	47.5	4.0	1.9
Rolls, White, Soft, Sandwich, Warburtons*	1 Roll/79g	209	264	11.0	45.0	4.4	0.0
Rolls, White, Soft, Somerfield*	1 Roll/40g	104	260	10.0	48.0	3.0	0.0
Rolls, White, Softgrain, GFY, Asda*	1 Roll/54.0g	128	237	9.0	46.0	1.9	2.9
Rolls, White, Spar*	1 Roll/45g	113	251	8.6	46.6	3.4	2.4
Rolls, White, Split, Asda*	1 Roll/45g	113	251	10.0	45.0	3.4	2.8
Rolls, White, Submarine, Marks & Spencer*	1 Serving/109.1g	300	275	11.0	47.0	5.0	1.0
Rolls, White, Value, Tesco*	1 Roll/35g	81	231	8.0	45.7	1.8	2.3
Rolls, White, Warburton's*	1 Roll/57g	141	248	9.7	42.8	4.2	0.0
Rolls, White, Weight Watchers*	1 Roll/54g	137	254	12.6	47.3	1.6	3.2
Rolls, Wholemeal	1 Roll 45g	108	241	9.0	48.3	2.9	5.9
Rolls, Wholemeal With Cracked Wheat, Allinson*	1 Roll/58g	134	231	11.0	38.0	3.9	7.0
Rolls, Wholemeal, Asda*	1 Roll/58g	131	225	11.0	39.0	2.8	6.0
Rolls, Wholemeal, Budgens*	1 Roll/55.2g	147	268	11.7	48.1	3.2	4.0
Rolls, Wholemeal, COU, Marks & Spencer*	1 Roll/110g	226	205	11.3	33.4	2.8	7.1
Rolls, Wholemeal, Deli, With Cracked Wheat, Tesco*	1 Roll/65g	156	240	9.0	40.2	4.8	5.7
Rolls, Wholemeal, Finger, Soft, Marks & Spencer*	1 Roll/69g	179	260	11.9	37.4	6.8	4.4
Rolls, Wholemeal, Floury Batch, Sainsbury's*	1 Roll/68g	150	220	10.7	36.0	3.7	6.6

BREAD,	Measure INFO/WEIGHT	per Measure KCAL	Nutrition Values per 100g / 100ml				
			KCAL	PROT	CARB	FAT	FIBRE
Rolls, Wholemeal, Food Explorers, Waitrose*	1 Roll/32.0g	74	231	10.6	40.2	3.1	5.7
Rolls, Wholemeal, Healthy Eating, Co-Op*	1 Roll/60g	141	235	13.0	37.0	4.0	8.0
Rolls, Wholemeal, Healthy Eating, Tesco*	1 Roll/67g	135	202	8.9	37.4	1.9	7.0
Rolls, Wholemeal, Kingsmill*	1 Roll/68g	167	245	10.7	41.5	4.0	5.1
Rolls, Wholemeal, Milk, Warburton's*	1 Roll/22g	51	231	12.5	38.1	3.2	7.0
Rolls, Wholemeal, Mini, Assorted, Waitrose*	1 Roll/35.6g	85	236	9.0	38.1	5.3	5.2
Rolls, Wholemeal, Mini, Tesco*	1 Roll/34g	82	240	10.9	36.4	5.6	5.8
Rolls, Wholemeal, Old Fashioned, Waitrose*	1 Roll/57g	135	236	11.1	37.2	4.8	6.6
Rolls, Wholemeal, Organic, Sainsbury's*	1 Roll/66g	152	230	10.7	41.0	2.7	6.6
Rolls, Wholemeal, Ploughman's, Sainsbury's*	1 Roll/65g	171	263	9.0	45.9	4.8	5.7
Rolls, Wholemeal, Sainsbury's*	1 Serving/64.8g	153	236	10.7	40.8	3.3	7.4
Rolls, Wholemeal, Sandwich Warburton's*	1 Roll/58g	132	228	10.8	37.7	3.8	0.0
Rolls, Wholemeal, Soft, Marks & Spencer*	1 Roll/55g	128	233	12.4	36.6	4.1	5.8
Rolls, Wholemeal, Square, Hovis*	1 Roll/52g	118	227	11.1	36.3	4.2	6.1
Rolls, Wholemeal, Submarine, Warburton's*	1 Serving/94g	231	246	10.9	40.6	4.4	6.3
Rolls, Wholemeal, Sunflower & Honey, Sainsbury's*	1 Roll/85g	225	265	9.2	45.4	5.1	4.5
Rolls, Wholemeal, Tasty, Kingsmill*	1 Roll/53g	125	236	10.7	39.2	4.0	7.4
Rolls, Wholewhite, Kingsmill*	1 Roll/63g	158	251	9.5	43.7	4.2	3.5
Rolls, Wholmeal, Deli, Tesco*	1 Roll/65g	156	240	9.0	40.2	4.8	5.7
Rye	1 Slice/25g	55	219	8.3	45.8	1.7	4.4
Rye With Sesame Seeds, Ryvita*	1 Slice/9g	31	339	10.5	58.5	7.0	16.0
Rye With Sunflower Seeds, Organic, Sunnyvale*	1 Slice/25g	50	198	5.1	30.3	6.3	0.0
Rye, Dark, Sliced, Trianon*	1 Slice/41g	74	180	6.5	35.0	1.5	0.0
Rye, German Style, Kelderman*	1 Slice/62g	96	155	5.6	30.2	1.4	7.7
Rye, Swedish Style, Kelderman*	1 Slice/50g	93	185	7.2	31.5	3.2	4.3
Rye, Wholemeal, Organic, House Of Westphalia*	1 Slice/75g	122	162	5.1	32.8	1.2	7.8
Rye, Wholemeal, Organic, Mestemacher*	1 Serving/71g	127	179	5.7	33.5	2.5	8.1
Rye, Wholemeal, With Sunflower Seeds, Organic, Biona*	1 Slice/72g	144	202	7.1	35.0	3.7	0.0
Scottish Plain, Mothers Pride*	1oz/28g	64	227	8.7	44.6	1.5	3.0
Sfilatino, Ready to Bake, TTD, Sainsbury's*	1 Sfilatino/126g	327	260	8.9	47.7	3.7	2.2
Soda	1oz/28g	72	258	7.7	54.6	2.5	2.1
Soda Farls, Marks & Spencer*	1 Farl/110g	267	243	9.6	50.1	2.7	2.3
Soda Farls, Tesco*	1 Farl/142g	325	229	7.1	42.2	3.2	2.6
Soda, Fruit, Marks & Spencer*	1 Slice/40.4g	104	260	5.9	51.3	4.6	2.5
Soda, Marks & Spencer*	1 Slice/40g	82	205	8.7	39.2	1.6	4.2
Softgrain, Farmhouse, Marks & Spencer*	1 Slice/25g	60	238	8.4	42.8	3.7	3.2
Softgrain, Medium Sliced, GFY, Asda*	1 Slice/35g	79	226	7.0	46.0	1.5	3.7
Softgrain, Mighty White*	1 Slice/36g	81	224	7.2	45.5	1.5	3.7
Sourdough, Flax Corn Rice, Sunnyvale*	1oz/28g	51	182	4.7	41.8	2.8	7.4
Soya & Linseed, Burgen*	1 Slice/36g	89	246	14.7	29.5	7.7	5.6
Submarine, Malted Grain, Marks & Spencer*	1 Roll/109g	300	275	8.9	53.8	4.3	3.0
Submarine, Sainsbury's*	1 Roll/117g	381	326	10.6	60.2	4.8	2.8
Sunflower & Honey, Marks & Spencer*	1 Serving/67g	206	308	12.9	34.0	13.4	5.6
Sunflower & Pumpin Seed, Batched, Organic, Tesco*	1 Slice/30g	73	243	11.0	33.1	7.4	5.2
Sunny, Hovis*	1 Slice/44g	110	250	8.2	41.5	5.7	2.0
Three Grain, Organic, Schneider Brot*	1 Slice/71.5g	119	165	5.8	30.4	2.2	0.0
Toaster, White, Rathbones*	2 Slices/76g	185	243	9.1	48.6	1.3	2.3
Tomato & Chilli, BGTY, Sainsbury's*	¼ Bread/65g	155	238	11.9	36.9	4.7	2.8
Tomato & Garlic, Morrisons*	1 Serving/125g	271	217	5.9	31.4	7.6	2.5
Veda Malt, St Michael*	1 Serving/45g	99	219	7.1	45.3	1.1	2.2
Walnut, Waitrose*	1 Slice/33g	104	315	10.8	43.2	11.0	4.3
Wheat Free, Organic, The Stamp Collection*	1 Slice/35g	66	188	6.5	39.5	0.4	0.4
Wheat, Tasty, Kingsmill*	1 Serving/38g	84	221	10.1	37.6	3.4	6.8

	Measure	per Measure	Nutrition Values per 100g / 100ml				
	INFO/WEIGHT	KCAL	KCAL	PROT	CARB	FAT	FIBRE
BREAD,							
Wheaten, Marks & Spencer*	1 Slice/33g	74	225	9.3	42.9	3.5	3.9
Wheaten, Sliced, Healthy, Irwin's*	2 Slices/80g	152	190	9.0	40.5	1.9	6.2
Wheatgerm Brown, Original, Medium, Hovis*	1 Slice/33g	77	233	10.8	40.1	3.3	3.7
Wheatgerm, Thin Sliced, Hovis*	1 Slice/21g	47	222	10.1	38.5	3.0	4.6
Wheatgerm, Thin Sliced, Marks & Spencer*	1 Slice/23g	50	220	10.1	38.5	3.0	4.6
Wheatgrain, Robertson*	1 Slice/30g	90	300	9.3	57.3	4.0	4.0
White	1 Slice/25g	59	235	8.4	49.3	1.9	1.5
White, Aldi*	1 Serving/60g	143	239	9.5	47.3	1.3	2.2
White, Batch Loaf, Extra Special, Asda*	1 Slice/47g	109	233	9.0	45.0	1.9	2.2
White, Big & Bouncy, Hovis*	1 Slice/50g	117	233	8.3	46.3	1.6	2.2
White, Brace's*	1 Med Sl/31.7g	73	227	9.6	43.4	1.7	2.2
White, COU, Marks & Spencer*	1 Slice/26g	60	231	10.6	41.9	2.3	4.6
White, Classic Cut, Thick, Hovis*	1 Slice/42g	95	226	7.5	46.0	1.3	2.4
White, Country Maid*	1 Slice/33.2g	76	229	8.5	44.1	2.1	3.0
White, Crusty, Gold, Kingsmill*	1 Slice/27g	70	258	9.4	48.5	2.9	2.7
White, Crusty, Hovis*	1 Slice/44g	103	233	8.8	44.3	2.2	2.1
White, Crusty, Sliced Loaf, Tesco*	1 Slice/50g	117	233	7.4	46.0	2.1	2.0
White, Crusty, Sliced, Finest, Tesco*	1 Slice/113g	255	226	9.5	44.3	1.2	2.7
White, Crusty, Sliced, Harvestime*	1 Slice/44g	98	222	6.6	45.6	1.5	1.9
White, Crusty, Sliced, Premium, Budgens*	1 Slice/50g	121	242	8.8	46.9	2.2	2.2
White, Danish, Medium Sliced, Morrisons*	1 Slice/17g	42	245	10.2	49.1	1.8	2.2
White, Danish, Soft & Light, Thick Cut, Asda*	1 Slice/26g	60	230	9.0	45.0	1.6	2.1
White, Danish, Tesco*	1 Slice/22g	56	254	9.4	49.7	1.9	2.8
White, Danish, Thick Sliced, Iceland*	1 Slice/22g	51	232	8.9	45.4	1.6	2.1
White, Danish, Thick Sliced, Tesco*	2 Slices/47g	105	223	7.4	45.3	1.3	2.6
White, Danish, Warburton's*	1 Slice/25g	61	244	10.8	46.8	1.6	2.8
White, Danish, Weight Watchers*	1 Slice/19g	42	222	8.7	43.9	1.3	2.8
White, Eat Smart, Safeway*	1 Slice/26g	60	230	8.8	45.0	1.8	2.3
White, Extra Thick Sliced, Kingsmill*	1 Slice/58g	135	232	8.8	43.8	2.4	2.8
White, Farmhouse Crusty, Marks & Spencer*	1 Slice/34g	85	250	8.8	48.0	2.6	2.3
White, Farmhouse Gold Premium, Morrisons*	1 Slice/38g	91	239	9.5	47.3	1.3	2.2
White, Farmhouse, Hovis	1 Slice/37g	84	228	9.0	44.6	1.5	2.3
White, Farmhouse, Seeded, Waitrose*	1 Serving/75g	192	256	10.8	40.9	5.5	5.6
White, Farmhouse, Sliced, Enjoy Organic Co.*	1 Slice/33g	81	246	8.7	45.9	3.0	3.6
White, Farmhouse, Soft, Warburton's*	1 Slice/26g	63	241	10.2	44.3	2.5	2.7
White, Farmhouse, The Best, Safeway*	1 Slice/44.3g	104	237	8.4	47.5	1.5	3.1
White, Farmhouse, Waitrose*	1 Slice/40g	94	235	9.5	45.4	1.7	2.6
White, Fibre, Morrisons*	2 Slices/80g	192	240	8.0	48.4	1.7	0.3
White, Floury Batch, Sainsbury's*	1 Serving/62g	166	267	8.0	48.8	4.5	2.3
White, Fried in Blended Oil	1 Slice/28g	141	503	7.9	48.5	32.2	1.6
White, Gluten & Wheat Free, Free From, Sainsbury's*	1 Serving/70g	159	227	1.9	35.5	8.6	1.0
White, Gluten Free, Bakers Delight*	1 Serving/28g	64	227	1.9	35.5	8.6	1.0
White, Gold Seeded, Kingsmill*	1 Slice/44g	108	245	9.7	38.8	5.7	3.5
White, Gold Toastie, Kingsmill*	1 Slice/44g	103	234	9.3	42.3	3.1	0.6
White, Golden, Square Cut, Marks & Spencer*	1 Med Sl/39.5g	86	215	8.9	40.7	2.1	6.1
White, Good Health, Warburton's*	1 Slice/38g	84	220	9.4	41.6	1.8	4.1
White, Great, Hovis*	1 Slice/40g	90	226	8.8	44.4	1.5	2.2
White, Harvest Crust Premium, Ormo*	1 Slice/40g	92	229	9.4	47.4	1.5	2.7
White, Loaf, Crusty, Premium, Warburton's*	1 Slice/28.6g	72	247	10.4	46.1	2.3	2.7
White, Loaf, Danish, Asda*	1 Serving/22.5g	52	236	9.0	45.0	2.2	2.0
White, Loaf, Mini, Medium Sliced, Warburton's*	1 Slice/23.5g	57	237	10.2	44.9	1.8	2.7
White, Medium Sliced	1 Med Slice/39g	93	238	7.5	48.5	1.6	1.8
White, Medium Sliced, Asda*	1 Slice/37g	84	226	7.0	46.0	1.5	2.8

BREAD,

INFO/WEIGHT	Measure	per Measure KCAL	Nutrition Values per 100g / 100ml				
			KCAL	PROT	CARB	FAT	FIBRE
White, Medium Sliced, BGTY, Sainsbury's*	1 Slice/20g	45	225	10.2	43.9	0.9	4.6
White, Medium Sliced, Budgens*	1 Slice/35.8g	82	229	8.0	45.6	1.6	3.0
White, Medium Sliced, Co-Op*	1 Slice/36g	83	230	8.0	46.0	2.0	2.0
White, Medium Sliced, Economy, Sainsbury's*	1 Slice/44g	104	236	7.6	48.6	1.3	1.8
White, Medium Sliced, Hovis*	1 Slice/35g	78	223	8.4	44.5	1.2	2.0
White, Medium Sliced, Keep Fresh, Safeway*	1 Slice/34g	76	224	7.3	44.3	1.9	2.7
White, Medium Sliced, Long Life, Asda*	1 Slice/36g	82	228	8.0	45.0	1.8	2.7
White, Medium Sliced, Longer Life, Co-Op*	1 Slice/44g	99	225	8.0	45.0	2.0	2.0
White, Medium Sliced, Longerlife, Sainsbury's*	1 Slice/36g	87	243	8.3	47.6	2.2	1.7
White, Medium Sliced, Makes Sense, Somerfield*	1 Slice/36.3g	81	226	7.5	46.4	1.2	2.4
White, Medium Sliced, Marks & Spencer*	1 Slice/35g	81	230	7.4	45.9	1.7	2.4
White, Medium Sliced, Mother's Pride*	1 Slice/36g	82	229	8.0	45.6	1.6	3.0
White, Medium Sliced, Nimble*	1 Slice/20g	46	232	9.7	44.3	1.8	2.9
White, Medium Sliced, Sainsbury's*	1 Slice/36g	83	231	8.0	46.4	1.5	2.1
White, Medium Sliced, SmartPrice, Asda*	1 Slice/36g	81	226	7.0	46.0	1.5	2.8
White, Medium Sliced, Soft & Light, Danish, Safeway*	1 Slice/20.2g	47	233	8.7	45.1	2.0	2.2
White, Medium Sliced, Soft, Danish, Somerfield*	1 Slice/21g	48	229	8.6	44.8	1.4	2.4
White, Medium Sliced, Spinaca, Aldi*	1 Slice/25g	59	237	7.2	46.7	1.8	2.3
White, Medium Sliced, Square, Kingsmill*	1 Slice/66g	88	133	5.0	25.2	1.4	1.7
White, Medium Sliced, Superlife, Morrisons*	1 Slice/30g	79	263	9.6	47.4	3.9	2.5
White, Medium Sliced, Tesco*	1 Slice/37g	84	228	8.0	45.5	1.6	3.0
White, Medium Sliced, Value, Tesco*	1 Slice/36g	81	225	7.9	46.1	1.0	2.1
White, Medium Sliced, Warburton's*	1 Slice/24g	57	237	10.2	44.9	1.8	2.7
White, Medium Sliced, Weight Watchers*	1 Slice/12g	27	226	10.3	42.6	1.6	3.6
White, Nimble*	1 Slice/20g	49	245	9.9	46.4	2.2	2.1
White, Organic, Marks & Spencer*	1 Slice/36g	94	261	7.6	52.5	2.4	2.2
White, Organic, Sainsbury's*	1 Slice/35.9g	84	234	8.9	45.5	1.8	2.3
White, Premium Farmhouse, Lidl*	1 Slice/44g	99	225	7.4	45.4	1.5	2.5
White, Premium Gold, TTD, Sainsbury's*	1 Slice/44g	103	233	8.4	45.6	1.9	2.2
White, Premium, Marks & Spencer*	1 Slice/40.4g	94	235	8.5	45.8	1.9	2.7
White, Sandwich, Bakery, Sainsbury's*	1 Slice/50g	121	242	10.3	49.0	0.6	2.9
White, Sandwich, Premier, Irwin's*	1 Slice/44g	98	222	8.4	45.6	1.5	2.7
White, Scottish, Sunblest*	1 Slice/57g	133	233	10.1	42.3	2.6	2.8
White, Sliced, Brennans*	1 Serving/39g	80	205	8.5	42.0	1.4	2.7
White, Soft Batch, Sliced, Sainsbury's*	1 Slice/44.0g	102	232	8.2	45.4	1.9	2.3
White, Soft Crusty, Marks & Spencer*	1 Slice/25g	64	256	9.3	49.0	2.5	2.4
White, Soft, Batch Loaf, Sliced, Tesco*	1 Slice/50g	117	233	7.5	46.1	2.1	2.1
White, Soft, Farmhouse, Marks & Spencer*	1 Slice/25g	60	239	9.8	42.6	3.3	2.5
White, Soft, Gold, Kingsmill*	1 Slice/47g	111	236	8.9	42.9	3.2	2.8
White, Soft, Medium Slice, Warburton's*	1 Slice/27g	88	326	12.2	61.5	3.3	4.1
White, Soft, Medium Sliced, Kingsmill*	1 Slice/38g	88	232	8.8	43.8	2.4	2.8
White, Soft, Milk Roll, Warburton's*	1 Slice/18g	46	251	10.8	45.3	3.0	2.8
White, Soft, Organic, Warburton's*	1 Slice/26.7g	62	228	9.7	44.6	3.0	2.6
White, Softgrain, Sliced, Tesco*	1 Med Slice/36g	81	224	7.2	45.5	1.5	3.7
White, Square Cut, Extra Thick Sliced, Hovis*	1 Slice/67g	163	244	8.3	49.2	1.6	2.8
White, Square Cut, Hovis*	1 Med Slice/40g	90	226	8.8	44.4	1.5	2.2
White, Square Cut, Kingsmill*	1 Med Slice/38g	88	232	8.8	43.8	2.4	2.8
White, Stay Fresh, Tesco*	1 Slice/40g	100	249	8.6	48.3	2.4	1.5
White, Sunblest*	1 Med Slice/33g	77	232	7.4	46.4	1.9	2.1
White, Super Toastie, Warburton's*	1 Serving/57g	134	235	10.1	44.6	1.8	2.7
White, Superior English Quality, Thin Cut, Hovis*	1 Serving/73g	169	232	9.2	42.8	1.5	3.8
White, Thick Cut, Lidl*	1 Slice/35g	87	249	8.6	45.4	2.4	2.9
White, Thick Sliced, Aldi*	1 Slice/38g	90	237	7.2	46.7	1.8	2.3

BREAD,	Measure INFO/WEIGHT	per Measure KCAL	Nutrition Values per 100g / 100ml KCAL	PROT	CARB	FAT	FIBRE
White, Thick Sliced, Bakers Gold, Asda*	1 Slice/44g	101	229	8.0	45.0	1.9	2.3
White, Thick Sliced, Co-Op*	1 Slice/43g	99	230	8.0	46.0	2.0	2.0
White, Thick Sliced, Family Favourite*	1 Slice/37g	83	225	8.5	44.5	1.4	2.3
White, Thick Sliced, Fine Lady*	1 Slice/44.4g	112	254	7.8	53.1	1.2	2.3
White, Thick Sliced, Gold, Co-Op*	1 Slice/44g	99	225	7.0	45.0	2.0	3.0
White, Thick Sliced, Golden Sun*	1 Slice/44g	100	228	7.5	46.1	1.5	2.4
White, Thick Sliced, Healthy, Warburtons*	1 Slice/38g	84	222	10.3	41.2	1.8	4.1
White, Thick Sliced, Hovis*	1 Serving/50g	122	244	8.4	49.2	1.6	2.8
White, Thick Sliced, Kingsmill*	1 Slice/42g	98	233	8.8	44.1	2.4	2.5
White, Thick Sliced, Long Life, Somerfield*	1 Slice/44g	100	227	7.5	44.9	1.9	2.4
White, Thick Sliced, Marks & Spencer*	1 Slice/42g	96	228	7.3	46.7	1.3	2.8
White, Thick Sliced, Organic, Tesco*	1 Slice/44g	110	249	7.4	51.3	1.6	2.1
White, Thick Sliced, Premium, Tesco*	1 Slice/44.4g	98	222	8.7	45.2	0.7	1.5
White, Thick Sliced, Sainsbury's*	1 Slice/44g	100	228	7.1	46.4	1.5	2.8
White, Thick Sliced, SmartPrice Asda*	1 Slice/47g	106	226	7.0	46.0	1.5	2.8
White, Thick Sliced, Square Cut, Asda*	1 Slice/43.9g	101	230	8.0	46.0	1.5	2.1
White, Thick Sliced, Staysoft, Rathbones*	2 Slices/76g	173	228	8.5	45.5	1.3	2.7
White, Thick Sliced, Sunblest*	1 Slice/40g	91	228	8.0	45.7	1.5	2.8
White, Thick Sliced, Tesco*	1 Slice/44g	100	228	7.1	46.4	1.5	2.8
White, Thick Sliced, Value, Tesco*	1 Slice/44g	109	248	8.4	49.3	1.9	1.5
White, Thick Sliced, Warbuton's*	1 Slice/28g	65	233	9.8	43.6	2.1	2.7
White, Thick Sliced, Woolworths*	1 Slice/38g	93	246	7.9	47.6	2.4	3.0
White, Thin Sliced, Sainsbury's*	1 Slice/29g	66	228	7.1	46.4	1.5	2.8
White, Thin Sliced, Tesco*	2 Slices/59g	135	228	9.5	44.5	1.3	3.4
White, Toast, Gamle Mølle*	1 Slice/32g	83	260	8.0	52.0	2.0	3.0
White, Toasted	1 Med Slice/33g	87	265	9.3	57.1	1.6	1.8
White, Toastie, Thick Cut, Hovis*	1 Slice/50g	113	226	8.8	44.4	1.5	2.2
White, Toastie, Thick Sliced, Warburton's*	1 Slice/44.5g	107	237	10.1	44.3	2.1	2.8
White, Toastie, Thick, Kingsmill*	1 Slice/38g	89	234	9.3	42.3	3.1	3.1
White, Weight Watchers*	1 Serving/5g	12	246	12.3	45.1	1.6	3.3
White, Whole, Extra Thick, Kingsmill*	1 Slice/57g	130	228	9.0	42.3	2.5	4.0
White, Whole, Kingsmill*	1 Slice/38g	87	230	9.0	42.9	2.5	3.4
White, Wholesome, Medium Sliced, Asda*	1 Slice/35.0g	78	223	7.0	43.0	2.6	5.0
White, Wholesome, Medium Sliced, Tesco*	1 Slice/36.6g	86	232	8.9	43.9	2.3	4.2
White, With Wheatgerm, Best of Both, Hovis*	1 Slice/40g	89	223	8.8	42.3	2.0	3.8
Whole & White, Kingsmill*	1 Slice/38.2g	87	228	9.0	42.3	2.5	4.0
Whole Grain, Batch, Finest, Tesco*	1 Slice/127g	323	254	9.8	47.7	2.7	4.2
Whole Wheat, Nature's Own*	1 Slice/28g	66	236	14.3	39.3	3.6	10.7
Wholemeal	1 Slice/25g	54	215	9.2	41.6	2.5	5.8
Wholemeal, American Sandwich, Harry's*	2 Slices/85g	220	259	9.0	45.0	5.0	5.0
Wholemeal, BGTY, Sainsburys*	1 Slice/20g	41	207	12.6	36.8	1.0	7.3
Wholemeal, Bake Off, Somerfield*	1oz/28g	62	222	11.0	40.0	2.0	0.0
Wholemeal, Batch Loaf, Organic, Marks & Spencer*	1 Serving/30g	60	200	10.4	32.1	3.2	7.4
Wholemeal, Batch Loaf, Village Green, Aldi*	1 Slice/30g	67	224	9.8	40.6	2.5	5.8
Wholemeal, Batch, Organic, Waitrose*	1 Slice/40g	88	219	10.0	38.8	2.6	7.2
Wholemeal, Batch, Stoneground, Warburton's*	1 Slice/42g	91	217	9.8	39.3	2.3	7.2
Wholemeal, COU, Marks & Spencer*	1 Slice/21g	45	213	13.6	33.7	2.6	7.0
Wholemeal, Country Grain, Hovis*	1 Slice/44.1g	97	220	11.2	37.9	2.6	6.2
Wholemeal, Crusty, Finest, Tesco*	1 Slice/50g	103	206	10.8	37.0	1.7	6.9
Wholemeal, Crusty, Kingsmill*	1 Slice/42g	104	247	11.2	41.1	4.2	7.0
Wholemeal, Danish, Better For You, Morrisons*	1 Slice/17g	39	228	11.2	47.9	1.8	6.2
Wholemeal, Danish, Warburton's*	1 Slice/25g	57	229	13.3	38.5	2.4	7.2
Wholemeal, Dove's Farm*	1 Slice/40g	83	208	8.5	40.5	2.5	6.4

B

BREAD,

INFO/WEIGHT	Measure	per Measure KCAL	Nutrition Values per 100g / 100ml KCAL	PROT	CARB	FAT	FIBRE
Wholemeal, Economy, Sainsbury's*	1 Slice/28g	61	217	10.3	38.4	2.5	6.5
Wholemeal, Family Loaf, Safeway*	1 Slice/45g	96	213	9.5	37.4	2.8	6.0
Wholemeal, Farmhouse Gold, Morrisons*	1 Slice/38g	78	204	9.2	38.3	1.6	6.0
Wholemeal, Farmhouse Soft Golden, Marks & Spencer*	1 Slice/30g	65	215	11.0	35.1	3.1	7.4
Wholemeal, Farmhouse, Hovis*	1 Slice/44g	91	206	10.2	36.6	2.1	5.3
Wholemeal, Farmhouse, Organic, Marks & Spencer*	1oz/28g	63	224	11.2	42.7	4.2	7.4
Wholemeal, Farmhouse, Split Top, Hovis*	1 Thick Slice/44g	97	221	11.3	37.1	3.1	6.4
Wholemeal, Fresher For Longer, Sainsbury's*	1 Slice/44.1g	98	222	10.9	36.2	3.7	6.5
Wholemeal, Gold, Kingsmill*	1 Slice/44g	95	217	10.9	36.8	2.9	7.0
Wholemeal, Golden Wheat, Kingsmill*	1 Slice/44g	97	221	10.9	37.8	2.9	6.0
Wholemeal, Good Health, Warburton's*	1 Slice/35.2g	82	233	10.9	41.0	2.7	7.2
Wholemeal, Great Tasting, Warburton's*	1 Serving/42.2g	95	227	10.4	40.0	2.8	6.3
Wholemeal, Greggs*	1 Slice/36g	77	215	9.2	41.6	2.5	5.8
Wholemeal, Hearty, Hovis*	1 Slice/36g	78	217	11.1	38.4	2.1	6.4
Wholemeal, Heavenly, Hovis*	1 Slice/40.1g	87	217	11.4	38.0	2.2	6.5
Wholemeal, Hovis*	1 Med Slice/36g	78	217	11.1	38.4	2.1	6.4
Wholemeal, Iceland*	1 Slice/35.9g	78	217	10.3	38.4	2.5	6.5
Wholemeal, Keep Fresh, Medium Sliced, Safeway*	1 Slice/37g	75	204	9.1	36.6	2.4	6.2
Wholemeal, Kingsmill*	1 Slice/45g	99	221	10.9	37.8	2.9	6.0
Wholemeal, Loaf, Crusty, Farmhouse, Marks & Spencer*	1 Serving/32.6g	76	230	10.1	40.7	2.7	6.3
Wholemeal, Longer Life, Medium Sliced, Sainsbury's*	1 Slice/36g	73	203	8.6	37.6	2.1	5.1
Wholemeal, Longer Life, Sainsbury's*	1 Med Slice/36g	85	237	10.7	41.0	3.4	6.2
Wholemeal, Longer Life, Thick Slice, Sainsbury's*	1 Slice/45g	101	224	10.6	37.4	3.6	5.9
Wholemeal, Marks & Spencer*	1 Med Slice/38g	82	215	11.4	36.0	2.6	7.1
Wholemeal, Medium Cut, Allinson*	1 Slice/36g	78	216	9.5	39.2	2.4	6.5
Wholemeal, Medium Cut, Small Sliced, Allinson*	1 Slice/23g	50	219	10.3	38.3	2.7	6.1
Wholemeal, Medium Sliced, Stay Fresh, Tesco*	1 Slice/36g	55	156	7.3	29.2	1.1	4.1
Wholemeal, Medium Sliced, Asda*	1 Slice/36g	80	223	9.0	39.0	3.4	6.0
Wholemeal, Medium Sliced, Co-Op*	1 Slice/36g	77	215	11.0	38.0	2.0	6.0
Wholemeal, Medium Sliced, Fresh For A Week, Asda*	1 Slice/35g	82	233	9.0	39.0	3.4	6.0
Wholemeal, Medium Sliced, Hearty, Hovis*	1 Slice/36g	78	217	11.1	38.4	2.1	6.4
Wholemeal, Medium Sliced, Kingsmill*	1 Slice/38g	87	228	10.1	39.2	3.4	5.2
Wholemeal, Medium Sliced, Longerlife, Sainsbury's*	1 Slice/36g	73	203	8.6	37.6	2.1	5.1
Wholemeal, Medium Sliced, Morrisons*	1 Slice/32g	68	214	9.9	38.0	2.5	5.8
Wholemeal, Medium Sliced, Organic, Asda*	1 Slice/43.3g	93	217	9.0	40.0	2.3	6.0
Wholemeal, Medium Sliced, Organic, Tesco*	2 Slices/53g	111	209	9.2	37.2	2.8	6.0
Wholemeal, Medium Sliced, Premium, Waitrose*	1 Med Slice/35g	83	237	10.7	41.0	3.4	6.2
Wholemeal, Medium Sliced, Safeway*	1 Slice/36g	73	204	9.1	36.6	2.4	6.2
Wholemeal, Medium Sliced, Sainsbury's*	1 Slice/36g	80	221	10.8	38.1	2.8	5.9
Wholemeal, Medium Sliced, Somerfield*	1 Slice/23.7g	53	219	10.3	38.3	2.7	6.1
Wholemeal, Medium Sliced, Stay Fresh, Somerfield*	1 Slice/36g	72	200	9.2	36.6	1.8	0.5
Wholemeal, Medium Sliced, Tesco*	1 Slice/36g	81	226	9.2	41.6	2.5	5.8
Wholemeal, Medium Sliced, Warburton's*	1 Slice/36g	84	234	10.3	40.1	3.6	7.2
Wholemeal, Medium Sliced, Xtra Life, Waitrose*	1 Slice/36g	85	237	10.7	41.0	3.4	6.2
Wholemeal, Medium, Square, Tasty, Kingsmill*	1 Serving/38g	84	221	10.1	37.6	3.4	6.8
Wholemeal, Multigrain, Country, Hovis*	1 Slice/36g	80	222	11.2	37.4	3.1	5.7
Wholemeal, Multigrain, Premium Gold, TTD, Sainsbury's*	1 Slice/44g	106	242	10.2	35.9	6.4	5.3
Wholemeal, Multigrain, Sliced, Finest, Tesco*	1 Serving/50g	123	246	10.1	42.1	4.1	6.5
Wholemeal, Multigrain, Soft Batch, Sainsbury's*	1 Slice/44g	106	242	11.3	34.5	6.5	5.6
Wholemeal, Nimble*	1 Slice/20g	43	216	11.2	36.9	2.7	6.9
Wholemeal, Premium, Marks & Spencer*	1 Med Sl/32.5g	66	200	10.5	32.9	3.1	6.7
Wholemeal, Rathbones*	1 Slice/27g	57	211	9.4	39.2	1.8	7.1
Wholemeal, Sandwich, Warburton's*	1 Slice/31g	72	232	10.7	40.2	3.1	7.2

B

	Measure INFO/WEIGHT	per Measure KCAL	Nutrition Values per 100g / 100ml				
			KCAL	PROT	CARB	FAT	FIBRE
BREAD,							
Wholemeal, Savers, Safeway*	1 Slice/36.5g	78	211	8.8	38.2	2.5	1.2
Wholemeal, Sliced, Gluten Free, Glutano*	1 Slice/56g	107	191	7.0	34.0	3.0	0.0
Wholemeal, Sliced, McCambridge*	1 Slice/38g	90	237	7.9	44.7	1.8	0.0
Wholemeal, Sliced, Organic, Harvestime*	2 Slices/88g	190	216	9.0	38.8	2.7	5.6
Wholemeal, Sliced, Organic, Warburton's*	1 Slice/27g	57	212	11.2	34.6	3.2	7.2
Wholemeal, Sliced, Premium, Budgens*	1 Slice/45g	101	224	9.3	39.1	3.3	8.2
Wholemeal, Small Sliced, Warburton's*	1 Slice/23.5g	57	238	10.6	41.7	3.0	7.2
Wholemeal, Small, Allinson*	1 Slice/23g	49	213	10.1	37.3	2.6	7.5
Wholemeal, Small, Kingsmill*	1 Slice/25g	56	224	10.7	38.0	3.2	5.8
Wholemeal, Soft Crusty, Marks & Spencer*	1 Slice/25g	58	230	11.4	39.1	3.1	6.5
Wholemeal, Soft, Medium Sliced, Morrisons*	1 Slice/32g	68	214	9.9	38.0	2.5	5.8
Wholemeal, Square, Tasty, Kingsmill*	1 Slice/42g	96	228	10.1	39.2	3.4	5.2
Wholemeal, Stay Fresh, Tesco*	2 Slices/88g	209	237	10.7	41.0	3.4	6.2
Wholemeal, Stoneground, Organic, Sainsbury's*	1 Slice/29g	63	217	7.9	39.9	2.9	5.8
Wholemeal, Stoneground, Organic, Waitrose*	1 Slice/40g	95	237	10.7	41.0	3.4	6.2
Wholemeal, Stoneground, Warburton's*	1 Slice/45.8g	98	213	9.9	37.4	2.7	7.1
Wholemeal, Tasty, Kingsmill*	1 Slice/40g	88	220	10.7	37.0	3.2	6.9
Wholemeal, Tesco*	1 Slice/36g	71	198	7.6	37.6	1.9	5.1
Wholemeal, Thick Cut, Allinson*	1 Slice/44g	94	213	10.1	37.3	2.6	7.5
Wholemeal, Thick Sliced Loaf, Tesco*	1 Slice/45g	90	201	8.8	36.4	2.3	5.3
Wholemeal, Thick Sliced, Asda*	1 Slice/45g	97	215	10.0	38.0	2.5	6.0
Wholemeal, Thick Sliced, Bakers Gold, Asda*	1 Slice/44g	99	225	12.0	37.0	3.2	6.0
Wholemeal, Thick Sliced, COU, Marks & Spencer*	1 Slice/26g	56	215	13.6	33.7	2.6	7.0
Wholemeal, Thick Sliced, Healthy Living, Co-Op*	1 Slice/44g	95	215	11.0	38.0	2.0	7.0
Wholemeal, Thick Sliced, Hearty, Hovis*	1 Slice/44g	95	217	11.1	38.4	2.1	6.4
Wholemeal, Thick Sliced, Keep Fresh, Safeway*	1 Slice/45g	92	204	9.1	36.6	2.4	6.0
Wholemeal, Thick Sliced, Kingsmill*	1 Slice/42g	96	228	10.1	39.2	3.4	5.2
Wholemeal, Thick Sliced, Organic, Sainsbury's*	1 Slice/44g	92	210	10.0	40.1	1.0	6.7
Wholemeal, Thick Sliced, Organic, Tesco*	1 Slice/44g	101	229	9.0	42.2	2.7	5.8
Wholemeal, Thick Sliced, Organic, Warburton's*	1 Slice/26.5g	57	219	11.0	36.4	3.3	7.2
Wholemeal, Thick Sliced, Sainsbury's*	1 Slice/44g	94	214	10.3	37.8	2.4	7.4
Wholemeal, Thick Sliced, Stayfresh, Tesco, *	1 Slice/34g	69	204	10.2	34.5	2.9	6.0
Wholemeal, Thick Sliced, Waitrose*	1 Slice/44g	111	252	10.9	36.0	7.2	5.8
Wholemeal, Toasted	1 Med Slice/26g	58	224	8.6	42.3	2.2	5.8
Wholemeal, Toastie, Warburton's*	1 Slice/44g	101	230	10.3	40.2	2.9	7.2
Wholemeal, Unsliced, Organic, Dove's Farm*	1 Med Slice/35g	73	208	8.5	40.5	2.5	6.4
Wholemeal, Value, Tesco*	1 Slice/36g	78	217	10.3	38.4	2.5	6.5
Wholemeal, Warburton's*	2 Slices/47g	112	239	10.8	41.9	3.1	7.2
Wholemeal, With Kibbled Malted Wheat, Kingsmill*	1 Slice/42g	96	228	10.1	39.2	3.4	5.2
Wholemeal, With Oat Flakes & Seeds, Waitrose*	1 Slice/44.4g	111	252	10.9	36.0	7.2	5.8
Wholemeal, With Pumpkin & Sunflower Seeds, Tesco*	1 Slice/25g	61	243	11.0	33.1	7.4	5.2
BREAD & BUTTER PUDDING,							
5% Fat, Marks & Spencer*	1 Pudding/237g	367	155	4.4	24.8	4.2	0.4
Asda*	1 Serving/125g	280	224	4.9	24.0	12.0	0.0
BGTY, Sainsbury's*	1 Serving/120g	161	134	5.6	23.0	2.2	0.8
COU, Marks & Spencer*	1 Pot/140g	189	135	5.5	24.6	1.7	0.6
Co-Op*	½ Pudding/170g	425	250	7.0	28.0	13.0	1.0
Finest, Tesco*	1 Serving/153g	379	248	4.9	24.6	14.4	0.9
GFY, Asda*	1 Serving/125g	153	122	7.0	20.0	1.6	1.3
Good Choice, Iceland*	1 Pudding/130g	242	186	6.1	27.7	5.6	2.4
Healthy Eating, Tesco*	1 Serving/125g	153	122	7.0	20.0	1.6	1.3
Healthy Living, Tesco*	1 Pudding/125g	146	117	5.8	9.8	6.1	0.3
Iceland*	½ Pack/160g	413	258	4.7	25.4	16.8	3.4

B

	Measure INFO/WEIGHT	per Measure KCAL	Nutrition Values per 100g / 100ml				
			KCAL	PROT	CARB	FAT	FIBRE
BREAD & BUTTER PUDDING,							
Individual, Marks & Spencer*	1 Pudding/130g	280	215	4.4	21.4	12.6	0.5
Individual, Waitrose*	1 Pudding/116g	247	213	5.4	24.4	10.4	0.3
Marks & Spencer*	1 Serving/125g	359	287	5.3	24.1	19.4	0.8
Reduced Fat, Waitrose*	1 Serving/205g	299	146	7.4	23.3	2.6	2.0
Sainsbury's*	1 Pudding/230g	446	194	4.8	21.9	9.7	0.4
BREAD MIX,							
Ciabatta, Wright's*	1 Serving/45g	154	343	14.2	71.0	3.0	0.0
Crusty White, Made Up, Tesco*	1 Slice/126g	316	251	9.4	49.3	1.8	2.5
Focaccia, Garlic & Herb, Asda*	1 Serving/125g	385	308	11.0	48.0	8.0	3.3
Focaccia, Garlic & Rosemary, Wrights*	1 Loaf/250g	820	328	14.5	70.0	2.6	0.0
Italian Ciabatta, Sainsbury's*	1 Slice/45g	96	213	8.7	40.0	2.0	2.4
Italian Sun Dried Tomato & Parmesan, Sainsbury's*	1 Serving/100g	247	247	8.1	50.1	1.7	2.5
Mixed Grain, Sainsbury's*	1 Serving/45g	103	228	7.7	46.0	1.5	4.4
White Loaf, Asda*	1 Slice/60g	150	250	10.0	49.0	1.5	3.1
Wholemeal, Crusty, Tesco*	1 Bag/500g	1120	224	9.7	40.7	2.4	7.6
BREADCRUMBS,							
Average	1oz/28g	98	350	10.8	74.8	1.9	2.6
BREADFRUIT,							
Boiled in Unsalted Water	1oz/28g	33	119	1.6	29.0	0.4	0.0
Canned, Drained	1oz/28g	18	66	0.6	16.4	0.2	1.7
Raw	1oz/28g	27	95	1.3	23.1	0.3	0.0
BREADSTICKS,							
Asda*	1 Serving/5g	21	412	12.0	73.0	8.0	2.9
Cheese, Italian, Tesco*	4 Breadsticks/21g	84	399	14.2	67.5	8.0	3.4
Classic, Somerfield*	1 Breadstick/6g	24	396	10.0	82.5	2.9	1.0
Farleys*	1 Serving/12g	50	414	14.0	76.5	5.8	1.1
Grissini, Italian, Sainsbury's*	1 Breadstick/5g	20	408	11.6	72.9	7.8	2.9
Grissini, Thin, With Olive Oil, Forno Bianco*	1 Stick/5g	21	420	11.0	77.0	7.5	0.0
Grissini, Waitrose*	1 Breadstick/6.3g	24	397	12.0	72.5	6.2	3.1
Mini, Wheat & Gluten Free, Tesco*	1 Stick/2.7g	12	414	4.0	72.1	12.2	2.2
Olive, Italian, Finest, Tesco*	1 Stick/40g	170	424	10.5	65.0	13.6	4.8
Onion, Marks & Spencer*	1 Serving/40g	166	415	12.6	59.6	14.1	4.8
Original, Italian, Tesco*	1 Pack/125g	510	408	11.6	72.9	7.8	2.9
Original, Organic, Kallo*	1 Breadstick/6g	24	393	11.8	69.5	7.6	4.7
Pesto Flavour, Safeway*	1 Stick/6g	24	394	13.4	67.5	7.8	5.2
Plain, Asda*	1 Stick/5g	21	412	12.0	73.0	8.0	0.0
Safeway*	1 Breadstick/6.3g	24	395	12.9	72.7	9.3	4.3
Sesame Seed Grissini, Sainsbury's*	1 Breadstick/5g	21	419	12.7	65.5	11.8	3.2
Thin, Healthy Eating, Primo D'Oro*	1 Breadstick/3g	11	400	10.0	75.0	6.5	1.1
BREAKFAST,							
All Day, Kershaws*	1 Pack/280g	392	140	7.3	9.6	8.0	1.6
All Day, With Baked Beans, Heinz*	1 Pack/403g	463	115	5.8	13.3	4.3	2.4
Big Breakfast Bun, McDonald's*	1 Bun/242g	571	236	13.0	15.1	13.3	0.9
Big Breakfast, McDonald's*	1 Breakfast/256g	591	231	10.2	15.6	14.2	1.6
Farmhouse, Ready Meals, Waitrose*	½ Pack/250g	385	154	2.9	11.0	10.0	1.2
Pack, Fruit Pudding, Asda*	1 Serving/44g	45	103	1.4	15.0	4.2	0.0
Pack, Lorne, Sausage, Asda*	1 Serving/54g	96	178	6.0	7.0	14.0	0.0
BREAKFAST CEREAL,							
Advantage, Weetabix*	1 Serving/30g	105	350	10.2	72.0	2.4	9.0
All Bran Splitz, Kellogg's*	1 Serving/40g	130	325	9.0	69.0	2.0	9.0
All Bran, Apricot Bites, Kellogg's*	1 Serving/45g	126	280	10.0	56.0	3.0	17.0
All Bran, Flakes, Kellogg's*	1 Serving/28g	90	320	10.0	66.0	2.5	15.0
All Bran, Kellogg's	1 Serving/40g	108	270	13.0	45.0	4.0	29.0

B

BREAKFAST CEREAL,

	Measure INFO/WEIGHT	per Measure KCAL	Nutrition Values per 100g / 100ml				
			KCAL	PROT	CARB	FAT	FIBRE
Almond, Low Carb, Atkins*	1 Serving/30g	100	333	50.0	26.7	5.0	0.0
Alpen*, Blackberry & Apple	1 Serving/40g	140	349	9.2	69.4	3.8	8.3
Alpen*, Caribbean Crunch	1 Serving/40g	155	388	8.8	67.9	9.0	4.6
Alpen*, Crunchy Bran	1 Serving/40g	120	299	11.8	52.3	4.7	24.8
Alpen*, Mixed Cereal, With Fruit & Nuts, No Added Sugar	1 Serving/40g	142	354	10.5	64.6	6.0	7.7
Alpen*, No Added Sugar	1 Serving/40g	143	357	12.1	61.3	7.1	9.0
Alpen*, Nutty Crunch	1 Serving/40g	159	398	10.7	63.6	11.2	6.5
Alpen*, Original	1 Serving/40g	146	365	10.0	66.0	6.8	7.7
Alpen*, Strawberry	1 Serving/40g	144	359	9.4	69.5	4.8	7.9
Alpen*, Wheat Flakes	1 Serving/40g	140	350	10.2	72.0	2.4	9.0
Apple & Cinnamon Flakes, Marks & Spencer*	1 Serving/30g	111	370	6.0	82.7	1.9	3.4
Apple & Cinnamon, Crisp, Sainsbury's*	1 Serving/50g	217	433	6.2	69.1	14.7	3.4
Apple, Balckberry & Raspberry Flakes, GFY, Asda	1 Serving/40g	138	344	9.0	73.0	1.8	11.0
Apricot Bites, Kellogg's*	1 Serving/45g	126	280	12.0	51.0	3.5	21.0
Apricot Wheats, Asda*	1 Serving/50g	165	330	8.0	71.0	1.5	8.0
Apricot Wheats, Tesco*	1 Serving/40g	132	330	7.8	71.4	1.5	8.0
Apricot Wheats, Whole Grain, Sainsbury's*	1 Serving/50g	165	330	7.8	71.4	1.5	8.0
Balance With Red Fruit, Sainsbury's*	1 Serving/40g	148	369	9.9	78.1	1.9	3.1
Banana & Toffee Crisp, Mornflake*	1 Serving/30g	133	443	5.7	68.8	16.1	5.4
Banana, Papaya & Honey Oat, Crunchy, Waitrose*	1 Serving/40g	170	426	9.6	69.8	12.0	5.5
Barley Crisp, Cocoa, Pertwood*	1 Serving/30g	105	350	8.1	84.0	2.1	9.3
Barley Crisp, Plain, Pertwood*	1 Serving/40g	142	356	9.4	82.7	2.3	8.2
Barley Crisp, With Maple Syrup, Pertwood*	1 Serving/50g	168	335	7.1	86.0	1.7	6.2
Benefit Flakes, Harvest Morn*	1 Serving/40g	148	370	11.4	77.7	1.5	3.2
Berries, Cherries & Flakes, COU, Marks & Spencer*	1 Serving/40g	152	380	8.5	82.2	1.9	3.2
Berry Crunchy, Sainsbury's*	1 Serving/30g	122	408	7.7	67.3	12.0	4.8
Blueberry & Cranberry, Oat Crunchy, Waitrose*	1 Serving/60g	262	437	8.0	67.0	15.2	7.4
Bran Flakes, Asda*	1 Serving/47g	157	333	11.0	65.0	3.2	14.0
Bran Flakes, Co-Op*	1 Serving/30g	99	330	11.0	65.0	3.0	15.0
Bran Flakes, Harvest Home, Nestle*	1 Serving/30g	99	331	10.2	67.1	2.4	14.1
Bran Flakes, Healthy Living, Tesco*	1 Serving/30g	99	331	10.2	67.1	2.4	14.1
Bran Flakes, Honey & Nut, Safeway*	1 Serving/47g	168	358	9.6	70.0	4.4	11.0
Bran Flakes, Honey Nut, Asda*	1 Serving/50g	179	358	9.6	70.0	4.4	11.0
Bran Flakes, Honey Nut, Morrisons*	1 Serving/40g	143	358	9.6	70.0	4.4	11.0
Bran Flakes, Honey Nut, Sainsbury's*	1 Serving/40g	143	358	9.6	70.0	4.4	11.0
Bran Flakes, Honey Nut, Tesco*	1 Serving/40g	143	358	9.6	70.0	4.4	11.0
Bran Flakes, Kellogg's*	1 Serving/30g	96	320	10.0	66.0	2.5	15.0
Bran Flakes, Little Man, Lidl*	1 Serving/30g	99	331	11.0	65.0	3.0	14.5
Bran Flakes, Morrisons*	1 Serving/25g	83	331	11.1	64.6	3.2	14.5
Bran Flakes, Oat With Apple & Raisin, Kellogg's*	1 Serving/40g	140	350	10.0	66.0	5.0	10.0
Bran Flakes, Organic, Asda*	1 Serving/30g	99	330	10.0	67.0	2.4	14.0
Bran Flakes, Organic, Sainsbury's*	1 Serving/30g	100	332	10.2	67.4	2.4	14.1
Bran Flakes, Organic, Tesco*	1 Serving/30g	99	330	10.2	67.0	2.4	14.1
Bran Flakes, Safeway*	1 Serving/40g	132	331	10.2	67.1	2.4	14.1
Bran Flakes, Somerfield*	1 Serving/50g	166	331	10.2	67.1	2.4	14.1
Bran Flakes, Tesco*	1 Serving/30g	99	331	10.2	67.1	2.4	14.1
Bran Flakes, Value, Tesco*	1 Serving/50g	160	320	11.4	63.2	2.4	17.1
Bran Flakes, Waitrose*	1 Serving/30g	100	333	10.1	67.7	2.4	12.7
Bran Flakes, Whole Grain, Sainsbury's*	1 Serving/30g	99	331	10.2	67.1	2.4	14.1
Cheerios, Honey Nut, Nestle*	1 Serving/40g	150	374	7.0	78.9	3.4	5.2
Cheerios, Nestle*	1 Serving/40g	146	366	8.1	74.6	3.9	6.5
Cheerios, Whole Grain, Nestle*	1 Serving/30g	110	366	8.1	74.6	3.9	6.5
Choc & Nut Crisp, Tesco*	1 Serving/40g	185	462	8.3	62.5	19.9	4.8

B

BREAKFAST CEREAL,

	Measure INFO/WEIGHT	per Measure KCAL	KCAL	PROT	CARB	FAT	FIBRE
			Nutrition Values per 100g / 100ml				
Choco Crackles, Morrisons*	1 Serving/30g	115	383	5.5	84.8	2.4	1.9
Choco Flakes, Asda*	1 Serving/50g	187	374	6.0	86.0	0.7	2.6
Choco Flakes, Kellogg's*	1 Serving/30g	114	380	5.0	84.0	3.0	2.5
Choco Flakes, Sainsbury's*	1 Serving/30g	111	370	5.5	85.4	0.7	3.0
Choco Flakes, Tesco*	1 Serving/30g	112	374	5.6	86.3	0.7	2.6
Choco Hoops, Aldi*	1 Serving/30g	116	385	7.0	79.1	4.5	0.0
Choco Hoops, Asda*	1 Serving/40g	154	385	7.0	79.0	4.5	4.0
Choco Hoops, Co-Op*	1 Serving/30g	116	385	7.0	80.0	4.0	5.0
Choco Hoops, Kids, Tesco*	1 Serving/30g	116	387	7.6	79.1	4.5	4.5
Choco Snaps, Asda*	1 Serving/30g	115	382	5.0	85.0	2.4	1.9
Choco Snaps, Sainsbury's*	1 Serving/30g	115	383	5.5	84.8	2.4	1.9
Choco Snaps, Tesco*	1 Serving/30g	114	379	5.5	83.9	2.4	2.3
Choco Snaps, Value, Tesco*	1 Serving/30g	112	372	7.0	79.7	2.8	3.3
Choco Squares, Asda*	1 Serving/30g	130	434	10.0	67.0	14.0	4.0
Chocolate Cereal, Tesco*	1 Serving/40g	169	423	8.0	66.3	14.0	6.0
Cinnamon & Apple, Sensations, Asda*	1 Serving/30g	112	373	10.0	72.0	5.0	7.0
Cinnamon Grahams, Nestle*	1 Serving/40g	166	416	4.6	75.1	10.9	4.2
Clusters, Nestle*	1 Serving/40g	153	382	10.0	70.2	6.8	8.5
Coco Pops Crunchers, Kellogg's*	1 Serving/30g	114	380	7.0	81.0	3.5	3.0
Coco Pops, Kellogg's*	1 Serving/30g	114	380	4.5	85.0	2.5	2.0
Cookie Crunch, Nestle*	1 Serving/40g	154	385	4.6	85.3	2.8	1.8
Corn Flakes, Asda*	1 Serving/30g	111	370	7.0	84.0	0.7	3.0
Corn Flakes, Banana Crunch, Kellogg's*	1 Serving/40g	159	398	6.0	80.0	7.0	2.5
Corn Flakes, Co-Op*	1 Serving/30g	113	375	8.0	84.0	1.0	1.0
Corn Flakes, Crispy Nut, Asda*	1 Serving/30g	117	390	7.0	81.0	4.2	2.5
Corn Flakes, Crunchy Nut, Kellogg's*	1 Serving/30g	117	390	7.0	82.0	3.5	3.0
Corn Flakes, Harvest Home, Nestle*	1 Serving/25g	92	367	7.3	82.7	0.8	3.6
Corn Flakes, Honey Nut With Cranberries, Sainsbury's*	1 Serving/40g	166	416	7.4	74.4	9.9	0.0
Corn Flakes, Honey Nut With Cranberries, Tesco*	1 Serving/50g	208	416	7.4	74.4	9.9	3.1
Corn Flakes, Honey Nut, Co-Op*	1 Serving/40g	154	385	7.0	81.0	4.0	1.0
Corn Flakes, Honey Nut, Harvest Home, Nestle*	1 Serving/30g	118	392	7.4	81.1	4.2	2.5
Corn Flakes, Honey Nut, Morrisons*	1 Serving/30g	116	387	7.1	80.0	4.3	3.0
Corn Flakes, Honey Nut, Rumblers*	1 Pack/40g	207	518	17.3	91.3	8.8	3.0
Corn Flakes, Honey Nut, Sainsbury's*	1 Serving/30g	116	387	7.3	80.0	4.2	2.9
Corn Flakes, Honey Nut, Tesco*	1 Serving/30g	116	387	7.3	80.0	4.2	2.0
Corn Flakes, Kellogg's*	1 Serving/30g	111	370	7.0	84.0	0.8	2.5
Corn Flakes, Safeway*	1 Serving/25g	92	367	7.3	82.7	0.8	3.6
Corn Flakes, Sainsbury's*	1 Serving/25g	92	367	7.3	82.7	0.8	3.6
Corn Flakes, Tesco*	1 Serving/25g	93	371	7.3	83.8	0.7	3.0
Corn Pops, Kellogg's*	1 Serving/40g	152	380	6.0	87.0	1.0	2.0
Cornflakes, Organic, Lima*	1 Serving/50g	178	355	8.3	77.7	1.0	6.4
Cornflakes, Organic, Whole Earth*	1 Serving/40g	154	386	8.6	84.2	1.0	3.0
Cornflakes, With Semi Skimmed Milk, Bowl, Kellogg's*	1 Serving/30g	170	567	20.0	106.7	8.3	3.0
Counrty Crisp With Whole Raspberries, Jordans*	1 Serving/50g	219	438	7.4	64.6	16.8	6.0
Country Crisp Four Nut Combo, Jordans*	1 Serving/50g	240	480	8.9	54.2	25.3	5.9
Country Crisp Wild About Berries, Jordans*	1 Serving/50g	222	443	7.5	68.0	15.7	5.7
Country Crisp With Strawberries, Jordans*	1 Serving/40g	176	440	7.3	65.3	16.6	6.9
Country Crisp With Whole Raspberries, Jordans*	1 Serving/40g	175	438	7.3	64.6	16.7	6.0
Cranberry Wheats, Tesco*	1 Serving/40g	130	325	7.3	70.9	1.4	7.7
Cranberry, Cherry & Almond, Dorset Cereals*	1 Serving/25g	89	355	9.2	60.5	8.5	8.4
Crispy Rice & Wheat Flakes, Asda*	1 Serving/50g	185	370	11.0	78.0	1.5	3.2
Crunchy Bran Curls, Weetabix*	1 Serving/40g	120	299	11.8	52.3	4.7	24.8
Crunchy Cereal, Safeway*	1 Serving/45g	207	459	9.2	65.4	17.8	6.3

	Measure	per Measure		Nutrition Values per 100g / 100ml			
	INFO/WEIGHT	KCAL	KCAL	PROT	CARB	FAT	FIBRE

BREAKFAST CEREAL,

Crunchy Choco, Crisp & Square, Tesco*	1 Serving/50g	212	423	8.0	66.3	14.0	6.0
Crunchy Chocolate, Carrefour*	1 Serving/40g	176	440	9.0	62.0	17.0	8.0
Crunchy Nut Clusters, Kellogg's*	1 Serving/40g	178	444	7.0	68.0	16.0	4.0
Crunchy Nut Clusters, Milk Chocolate Curls, Kellogg's*	1 Serving/40g	185	463	6.0	66.0	19.0	3.5
Crunchy Nut, Red, Kellogg's*	1 Serving/40g	164	410	7.0	73.0	10.0	3.0
Crunchy Oat With Raisins, Almonds & Honey, Tesco*	1 Serving/50g	213	425	9.1	62.8	15.3	4.7
Crunchy Oat, Golden Sun, Lidl*	1 Serving/50g	206	411	8.6	65.0	12.9	6.2
Crunchy Rice & Wheat Flakes, Co-Op*	1 Serving/30g	111	370	11.0	78.0	2.0	3.0
Eat My Shorts, Kellogg's*	1 Serving/30g	173	577	20.0	103.3	10.0	2.0
Eat Natural*	1 Serving/40g	180	450	12.0	45.0	25.0	6.0
Fibre 1, Nestle*	1 Serving/40g	107	267	10.8	50.2	2.6	30.5
Fibre Bran, Safeway*	1 Serving/48.3g	124	259	13.3	43.4	3.6	31.0
Fitness & Fruits, Nestle*	1 Serving/40g	140	350	5.6	77.0	2.2	5.6
Fitnesse, Nestle*	1 Serving/30g	111	369	6.3	83.7	1.0	3.7
Flakes & Grains, Exotic Fruit, BGTY, Sainsbury's*	1 Serving/30g	113	377	6.8	76.4	4.9	5.9
Flakes & Orchard Fruits, BGTY, Sainsbury's*	1 Serving/40g	154	385	13.0	80.6	1.2	4.5
Force, Nestle*	1 Serving/40g	138	344	10.6	70.3	2.3	9.2
Four Berry Crisp, Organic, Jordans*	1 Serving/50g	221	442	7.7	67.1	15.8	5.4
Frosted Flakes, Sainsbury's*	1 Serving/30g	112	374	4.9	87.8	0.4	2.4
Frosted Flakes, Tesco*	1 Serving/30g	112	374	4.9	87.8	0.4	2.4
Frosted Wheats, Kellogg's*	1 Serving/30g	105	350	10.0	72.0	2.0	9.0
Frosties, Caramel, Kellogg's*	1 Serving/30g	113	377	5.0	88.0	0.6	2.0
Frosties, Chocolate, Kellogg's*	1 Serving/40g	156	390	4.5	82.0	4.5	2.0
Frosties, Kellogg's*	1 Serving/30g	114	380	5.0	88.0	0.6	2.0
Fruit & Fibre, Asda*	1 Serving/30g	112	372	9.0	66.0	8.0	8.0
Fruit & Fibre, Flakes, Waitrose*	1 Serving/40g	140	350	8.2	65.7	6.0	10.1
Fruit & Fibre, Harvest Morn, Aldi*	1 Serving/40g	149	372	8.9	68.9	6.8	8.0
Fruit & Fibre, Kellogg's*	1 Serving/40g	140	350	9.0	69.0	4.5	9.0
Fruit & Fibre, Lidl*	1 Serving/25g	91	363	8.8	70.9	4.9	8.0
Fruit & Fibre, Morrisons*	1 Serving/30g	110	366	8.8	66.5	7.2	8.5
Fruit & Fibre, Organic, Sainsbury's*	1 Serving/40g	147	367	10.0	72.4	4.1	7.8
Fruit & Fibre, Safeway*	1 Serving/40g	143	358	9.0	66.4	6.4	9.0
Fruit & Fibre, Sainsbury's*	1 Serving/30g	108	361	8.1	68.5	6.1	8.9
Fruit & Fibre, Tesco*	1 Serving/30g	113	375	8.5	66.3	8.4	7.8
Fruit & Fibre, Value, Tesco*	1 Serving/40g	144	359	11.4	65.7	5.6	8.0
Fruit Nuts & Flakes, Marks & Spencer*	1 Serving/30g	117	391	9.1	69.6	8.5	3.5
Golden Balls, Asda*	1 Serving/30g	112	374	5.0	85.0	1.5	1.5
Golden Grahams, Nestle*	1 Serving/40g	152	381	5.6	81.6	3.6	3.2
Golden Honey Puffs, Tesco*	1 Serving/30g	115	382	6.6	86.3	1.2	3.0
Golden Nuggets, Nestle*	1 Serving/40g	152	381	6.2	87.4	0.7	1.5
Golden Puffs, Sainsbury's*	1 Serving/28g	107	383	6.6	86.3	1.2	3.0
Grape Nuts, Kraft*	1 Serving/30g	104	345	10.5	72.5	1.9	8.6
Harvest Crunch, Nut, Quaker*	1 Serving/40g	184	459	8.0	62.5	19.5	6.0
Harvest Crunch, Real Red Berries, Quaker*	1 Serving/50g	224	447	7.0	66.0	17.0	4.5
Harvest Crunch, Soft Juicy Raisins, Quaker*	1 Serving/50g	221	442	6.0	67.0	16.0	4.0
Hawaiian Crunch, Mornflake*	1 Serving/60g	247	411	8.1	66.8	12.4	6.8
Healthy Flakes, Safeway*	1 Serving/30g	111	371	11.0	78.4	1.5	4.3
High Fibre Bran, Asda*	1 Serving/50g	137	273	13.0	44.0	5.0	29.0
High Fibre Bran, Co-Op*	1 Serving/40g	108	270	13.0	44.0	5.0	29.0
High Fibre Bran, New, Tesco*	1 Serving/30g	73	242	14.0	38.4	3.5	31.0
High Fibre Bran, Sainsbury's*	1 Serving/40g	114	286	13.4	50.7	3.3	23.6
High Fibre Bran, Tesco*	1 Serving/40g	108	271	13.0	43.6	5.0	29.0
High Fibre Bran, Waitrose*	1 Serving/40g	112	281	14.4	47.2	3.8	26.0

B

BREAKFAST CEREAL,

	Measure INFO/WEIGHT	per Measure KCAL	Nutrition Values per 100g / 100ml KCAL	PROT	CARB	FAT	FIBRE
Honey Loops, Kellogg's*	1 Serving/30g	111	370	8.0	77.0	3.0	7.0
Honey Nut & Flakes, Marks & Spencer*	1 Serving/40g	164	411	9.8	73.4	8.7	2.6
Honey Nut Flakes With Red Berries, Somerfield*	1 Serving/30g	126	419	8.6	70.4	11.4	1.9
Honey Nut, Corn Flakes, Somerfield*	1 Serving/30g	118	392	7.4	81.2	4.2	2.5
Honey Raisin & Almond, Crunchy, Waitrose*	1 Serving/40g	170	425	10.5	68.8	12.0	5.7
Hot Cereal, Flax O Meal*	1 Serving/40g	130	325	52.5	2.5	15.0	30.0
Hot Oat, Harvest Morn, Aldi*	1 Serving/40g	142	356	11.6	58.8	8.3	8.9
Hot Oats, Instant, Tesco*	1 Serving/30g	107	356	11.5	58.8	8.3	8.9
Hot Oats, Safeway*	1 Serving/20g	71	356	11.6	58.8	8.3	8.9
Hunny B's, Kellogg's*	1 Serving/28g	106	380	6.0	83.0	2.5	3.0
Just Right, Kellogg's*	1 Serving/40g	144	360	7.0	78.0	2.5	4.5
Malt Bites, Safeway*	1 Serving/40g	137	343	10.0	69.2	2.9	10.0
Malt Crunchies, Co-Op*	1 Serving/50g	168	335	10.0	69.0	2.0	10.0
Malted Wheaties, Asda*	1 Serving/50g	171	342	10.0	69.0	2.9	10.0
Malted Wheaties, New Day*	1 Serving/30g	101	336	10.0	69.2	2.1	0.0
Malties, Sainsbury's*	1 Serving/40g	137	343	10.0	69.2	2.9	10.0
Malty Flakes With Peach & Raspberry, BGTY, Sainsbury's*	1 Serving/40g	146	364	10.8	76.4	1.7	3.3
Malty Flakes With Red Berries, Tesco*	1 Serving/30g	111	369	9.9	78.1	1.9	3.1
Malty Flakes, Tesco*	1 Serving/40g	148	371	11.0	78.4	1.5	4.3
Maple & Pecan Crisp, Sainsbury's*	1 Serving/50g	226	452	7.9	61.3	19.5	5.4
Maple & Pecan, Crisp, Asda*	1 Serving/30g	135	451	8.0	62.0	19.0	6.0
Maple & Pecan, Crisp, Tesco*	1 Serving/60g	277	461	8.2	60.6	20.6	6.2
Maple & Pecan, Luxury Crunchy, Jordans*	1 Serving/50g	224	448	9.9	59.9	18.7	6.5
Maple & Pecan, Sainsbury's*	1 Serving/60g	318	530	13.3	69.7	22.0	5.3
Maple Frosted Flakes, Whole Earth*	1 Serving/30g	113	375	6.2	85.6	1.0	1.6
Mini Crunch, Banana, Weetabix*	1 Serving/36g	134	371	9.0	71.9	5.3	8.3
Mini Crunch, Weetabix*	1 Serving/36.1g	130	360	9.4	70.4	4.5	7.7
Mini Wheats, Sainsbury's*	1 Serving/45g	157	348	11.8	69.9	2.3	11.8
Minibix, Banana, Weetabix*	1 Serving/40g	148	370	8.8	73.0	5.0	8.1
Minibix, Chocolate, Weetabix*	1 Serving/39g	149	383	8.4	73.3	6.2	6.7
Minibix, Fruit & Nut, Weetabix*	1 Serving/40g	141	353	8.8	71.2	3.8	8.1
Minibix, Honey, Weetabix*	1 Serving/40g	144	359	8.8	76.1	2.2	0.0
Minibix, Weetabix*	1 Serving/40g	134	335	8.8	71.2	3.8	8.1
Muddles, Kellogg's*	1 Serving/30g	110	368	8.0	76.0	3.5	8.0
Muesli, 12 Fruit & Nut, Sainsbury's*	1 Serving/50g	166	332	8.1	64.2	4.7	7.8
Muesli, Apricot, Traidcraft*	1 Serving/30g	103	344	8.0	68.0	6.0	5.0
Muesli, BGTY, Sainsbury's*	1 Serving/64.8g	211	324	6.7	70.8	1.6	6.2
Muesli, Base, Nature's Harvest*	1 Serving/50g	179	358	11.0	71.2	5.1	7.4
Muesli, COU, Marks & Spencer*	1 Serving/60g	201	335	7.6	70.2	2.5	8.1
Muesli, Cranberry & Almond, Dorset*	1 Serving/50g	165	329	10.0	54.8	7.7	7.5
Muesli, Creamy Tropical Fruit, Finest, Tesco*	1 Serving/80g	283	354	7.2	68.8	5.6	6.9
Muesli, Crunchy Bran, Nature's Harvest*	1 Serving/50g	176	352	8.8	62.9	9.9	6.4
Muesli, Crunchy, Organic, Sainsbury's*	1 Serving/40g	168	420	10.6	62.0	14.4	9.2
Muesli, De Luxe, No Added Salt or Sugar, Sainsbury's*	1 Serving/40g	161	403	11.9	57.6	13.9	8.4
Muesli, Eat Smart, Safeway*	1 Serving/40g	134	335	8.7	68.6	2.8	7.4
Muesli, Fruit & Bran, Unsweetened, Marks & Spencer*	1 Serving/40g	128	320	8.1	68.0	2.7	9.4
Muesli, Fruit & Nut, 55%, Asda*	1 Serving/40g	151	378	9.0	54.0	14.0	7.0
Muesli, Fruit & Nut, COU, Marks & Spencer*	1 Serving/40g	128	320	7.4	74.5	2.8	7.4
Muesli, Fruit & Nut, Iceland*	1 Serving/30g	105	350	9.3	61.0	7.5	8.1
Muesli, Fruit & Nut, Jordans*	1 Serving/50g	189	378	7.3	60.6	11.8	6.7
Muesli, Fruit & Nut, Luxury, Co-Op*	1 Serving/50g	150	375	8.0	64.0	10.0	7.0
Muesli, Fruit & Nut, Luxury, Marks & Spencer*	1 Serving/50g	175	349	7.7	62.2	7.7	7.3
Muesli, Fruit & Nut, Luxury, Waitrose*	1 Serving/40g	145	363	9.0	60.3	9.5	6.5

	Measure	per Measure	Nutrition Values per 100g / 100ml				
	INFO/WEIGHT	KCAL	KCAL	PROT	CARB	FAT	FIBRE

BREAKFAST CEREAL,

	Measure	per Measure KCAL	KCAL	PROT	CARB	FAT	FIBRE
Muesli, Fruit & Nut, Marks & Spencer*	1 Serving/40g	128	320	7.4	74.5	2.8	7.4
Muesli, Fruit & Nut, Organic, Marks & Spencer*	1 Serving/50g	167	333	8.2	61.6	6.0	7.6
Muesli, Fruit & Nut, Sainsbury's*	1 Serving/30g	121	402	10.4	51.3	17.2	9.2
Muesli, Fruit & Nut, Somerfield*	1 Serving/50g	176	352	7.4	60.1	9.1	5.8
Muesli, Fruit & Nut, Tesco*	1 Serving/65g	237	365	7.4	57.9	11.5	8.0
Muesli, Fruit & Nut, Traidcraft*	1 Serving/28g	100	358	10.0	63.0	8.0	6.0
Muesli, Fruit & Nut, Whole Wheat, Organic, Asda*	1 Serving/50g	172	343	10.0	60.0	7.0	7.0
Muesli, Fruit & Spice, Sainsbury's*	1 Serving/50g	184	368	7.4	69.4	6.8	7.7
Muesli, Fruit Sensation, Marks & Spencer*	1 Serving/50g	158	315	6.0	66.0	3.0	7.4
Muesli, Fruit, 55%, Asda*	1 Serving/35g	111	318	6.0	67.0	2.9	7.0
Muesli, Fruit, GFY, Asda*	1 Serving/50g	152	304	8.0	64.0	1.8	10.0
Muesli, Fruit, Healthy Eating, Tesco*	1 Serving/40g	129	322	7.0	66.6	4.2	6.9
Muesli, Fruit, Luxury, Weight Watchers*	1 Serving/40g	127	318	7.2	67.7	2.0	8.1
Muesli, Fruit, Sainsbury's*	1 Serving/40g	132	330	8.1	64.3	4.5	9.6
Muesli, Fruit, Tesco*	1 Serving/50g	167	333	7.0	66.0	4.2	6.9
Muesli, Fruit, The Best, Safeway*	1 Serving/40g	138	346	5.3	71.3	4.3	5.0
Muesli, Gluten Free, Nature's Harvest, Holland & Barrett*	1 Serving/60g	234	390	14.1	54.1	13.0	3.3
Muesli, Golden Sun, Lidl*	1 Serving/40g	144	360	8.0	60.0	9.8	7.5
Muesli, Healthy Living, Tesco*	1 Serving/40g	133	333	6.9	71.1	2.3	5.3
Muesli, Luxury Fruit, Perfectly Balanced, Waitrose*	1 Serving/50g	162	324	7.1	66.4	3.3	7.0
Muesli, Luxury Fruit, Safeway*	1 Serving/40g	139	347	7.1	74.3	1.0	2.2
Muesli, Luxury Fruit, Sainsbury's*	1 Serving/50g	162	324	7.1	66.4	3.3	7.0
Muesli, Luxury Fruit, Waitrose*	1 Serving/30g	101	337	7.7	66.3	4.5	6.9
Muesli, Luxury, Dorset Cereals*	1 Serving/28g	92	328	8.4	63.0	6.5	9.0
Muesli, Luxury, Jordans*	1 Serving/40g	154	384	9.6	58.4	12.5	8.2
Muesli, Luxury, Sainsbury's*	1 Serving/40g	144	359	8.5	57.1	10.7	7.7
Muesli, Natural, Jordans*	1 Serving/40g	141	352	10.4	62.4	6.7	8.9
Muesli, No Added Sugar or Salt, Organic, Jordans*	1 Serving/50g	191	381	9.9	62.3	10.2	9.3
Muesli, No Added Sugar, Waitrose*	1 Serving/40g	146	364	12.0	64.9	6.3	6.7
Muesli, Orchard Fruit, Luxury, Cape*	1 Serving/30g	98	328	7.6	67.0	2.5	5.7
Muesli, Organic, Pertwood Farm*	1 Serving/30g	106	353	8.6	70.7	4.0	7.1
Muesli, Organic, Waitrose*	1 Serving/50g	179	358	10.8	59.1	8.7	7.8
Muesli, Organic, Whole Earth*	1 Serving/25g	87	347	10.5	61.0	6.4	8.0
Muesli, Original, Holland & Barrett*	1 Serving/30g	105	351	11.1	61.2	8.4	7.1
Muesli, Original, Sainsbury's*	1 Serving/60g	226	376	9.3	65.7	8.4	7.1
Muesli, Rich, Nature's Harvest*	1 Serving/40g	143	358	10.0	60.5	9.2	7.6
Muesli, Special, Jordans*	1 Serving/40g	154	384	9.6	58.4	12.5	8.2
Muesli, Swiss Style, Bettabuy, Morrisons*	1 Serving/50g	170	340	11.0	62.8	5.0	9.4
Muesli, Swiss Style, Co-Op*	1 Serving/40g	148	370	11.0	67.0	6.0	6.0
Muesli, Swiss Style, Harvest Morn, Aldi*	1 Serving/50g	180	359	9.8	65.3	6.5	8.3
Muesli, Swiss Style, No Added Salt Or Sugar, Sainsbury's*	1 Serving/40g	143	358	10.7	64.3	6.4	7.0
Muesli, Swiss Style, No Added Sugar or Salt, Asda*	1 Serving/50g	182	363	11.0	64.0	7.0	8.0
Muesli, Swiss Style, SmartPrice, Asda*	1 Serving/60g	222	370	9.0	70.0	6.0	10.0
Muesli, Swiss Style, Somerfield*	1 Serving/50g	180	359	11.0	64.0	6.5	8.0
Muesli, Swiss Style, Tesco*	1 Serving/40g	141	353	10.9	65.1	5.4	8.2
Muesli, Swiss Style, Waitrose*	1 Serving/40g	146	364	10.2	66.1	6.5	7.6
Muesli, Tropical Fruit, Holland & Barrett*	1 Bowl/60g	197	328	7.5	69.8	3.2	5.1
Muesli, Tropical, Tesco*	1 Serving/50g	173	346	7.8	68.2	4.7	9.1
Muesli, Tropical, Traidcraft*	1 Serving/60g	212	353	7.0	70.0	6.0	4.0
Muesli, Unsweetened Whole Wheat, Safeway*	1 Serving/50g	180	360	7.7	68.0	6.3	7.2
Muesli, Unsweetened, Marks & Spencer*	1 Serving/40g	129	322	8.1	68.0	2.7	9.4
Muesli, Value, Tesco*	1 Serving/50g	171	342	7.5	67.6	4.6	8.6
Muesli, Whole Wheat, Co-Op*	1 Serving/40g	140	350	11.0	61.0	7.0	7.0

	Measure INFO/WEIGHT	per Measure KCAL	Nutrition Values per 100g / 100ml				
			KCAL	PROT	CARB	FAT	FIBRE
BREAKFAST CEREAL,							
Muesli, Whole Wheat, No Added Sugar & Salt, Tesco*	1 Serving/40g	152	379	9.6	60.2	11.1	8.1
Muesli, Whole Wheat, No Added Sugar, Tesco*	1 Serving/40g	154	386	9.5	59.1	12.4	7.4
Muesli, Whole Wheat, Sainsbury's*	1 Serving/40g	136	339	8.5	60.6	6.9	7.6
Multi Fruit & Flake, COU, Marks & Spencer	1 Serving/39g	142	365	6.5	81.8	1.1	4.0
Multi Fruit & Flake, Perfectly Balanced, Waitrose*	1 Serving/40g	134	335	8.2	68.8	3.0	14.0
Multigrain Flakes With Apple, Eat Smart, Safeway*	1 Serving/45g	160	355	8.0	74.7	2.5	7.0
Multigrain, Balanced Lifestyle, Aldi*	1 Serving/30g	108	360	7.5	77.1	2.4	4.5
Multigrain, Start, Kellogg's*	1 Serving/40g	144	360	8.0	79.0	2.0	6.0
Natural Wheatgerm, Jordans*	1 Serving/40g	138	345	26.5	39.6	9.0	13.7
Natures Whole Grains, Jordans*	1 Serving/25g	98	390	9.4	61.7	11.7	7.7
Nesquik, Nestle*	1 Serving/30g	118	394	5.0	83.6	4.4	2.4
Nutty Crunch, Deliciously, Marks & Spencer*	1 Serving/50g	238	476	8.8	59.6	22.5	4.4
Oat & Bran Flakes, Sainsbury's*	1 Serving/50g	172	344	12.6	60.0	5.9	15.0
Oat Bran, Crispies, Quaker*	1 Serving/40g	153	383	11.0	69.0	6.5	9.0
Oat Krunchies, Quaker*	1 Serving/30g	118	393	9.5	72.0	7.0	5.5
Oat With Tropical Fruits, Crunchy, Tesco*	1 Serving/35g	157	448	8.7	66.0	16.6	3.2
Oat, Crunchy, Sainsbury's*	1 Serving/50g	227	453	8.2	59.3	20.3	6.6
Oatbran Flakes, Nature's Path*	1 Serving/30g	124	414	8.7	83.0	4.7	6.7
Oatmeal, Instant, Quaker*	1 Serving/35g	126	360	13.6	57.0	8.7	9.7
Oatmeal, Quick Oats, Dry, Quaker*	1/3 Cup/30g	114	380	14.0	66.7	6.7	10.0
Oats, Ready, Asda*	1 Serving/30g	107	356	12.0	59.0	8.0	9.0
Oatso Easy, Jungle*	1oz/28g	83	296	11.0	45.2	9.0	14.4
Oatso Simple, Apple & Cinnamon, Quaker*	1 Satchet/38g	136	358	8.0	68.0	5.5	2.5
Oatso Simple, Baked Apple Flavour, Quaker*	1 Serving/38g	141	370	8.0	70.0	6.0	5.5
Oatso Simple, Berry Burst, Quaker*	1 Serving/39g	146	374	8.0	71.0	6.0	5.5
Oatso Simple, Country Honey, Quaker*	1 Serving/36g	134	373	8.5	69.0	6.5	6.0
Oatso Simple, Fruit Muesli, Quaker*	1 Sachet/39g	140	360	7.5	69.0	6.0	7.0
Oatso Simple, Golden Syrup Flavour, Quaker*	1 Serving/39g	147	376	7.5	72.0	6.0	5.0
Oatso Simple, Quaker*	1 Serving/39g	145	372	7.5	71.0	6.0	6.0
Oatso Simple, Toffee Flavour, Quaker*	1 Serving/30g	122	407	6.5	67.0	12.0	5.5
Optimum Power, Nature's Path*	1 Serving/30g	109	363	15.3	60.0	6.7	12.6
Perfect Balance, Weight Watchers*	1 Serving/30g	90	300	7.8	63.3	1.7	15.6
Porridge Flakes, Organic, Barkat*	1 Serving/30g	109	362	8.5	74.1	3.0	0.0
Porridge Oats & Bran, Co-Op*	1 Serving/40g	141	353	12.5	60.0	7.0	12.0
Porridge Oats & Bran, Somerfield*	1 Serving/40g	154	385	12.0	68.0	7.0	0.0
Porridge Oats, Jordans*	1 Serving/40g	145	363	12.5	61.5	7.4	8.0
Porridge Oats, Organic, Evernat*	1 Serving/40g	167	418	13.0	69.0	9.6	7.4
Porridge Oats, Organic, Jordans*	1 Serving/45g	163	363	12.5	61.5	7.4	8.0
Porridge Oats, Organic, Tesco*	1 Serving/28g	100	357	13.5	57.8	8.0	9.0
Porridge Oats, Quick & Easy, Morrisons*	1 Serving/28g	103	367	11.8	62.0	8.0	7.0
Porridge Oats, Safeway*	1 Serving/35g	127	364	11.8	62.0	7.6	7.2
Porridge Oats, Scot's, Quaker*	1 Serving/30g	110	368	11.0	62.0	8.0	7.0
Porridge Oats, Scott, Co-Op*	1 Serving/40g	146	364	11.8	62.0	7.6	7.2
Porridge Oats, Scottish, Asda*	1 Serving/50g	192	383	10.0	75.0	4.8	7.0
Porridge Oats, Scottish, Organic, Sainsbury's*	1 Serving/45g	172	383	10.0	74.4	5.0	7.9
Porridge Oats, Scottish, Tesco*	1 Serving/50g	182	364	11.8	62.0	7.6	7.2
Porridge Oats, SmartPrice, Asda*	1 Serving/50g	178	356	11.0	60.0	8.0	8.0
Porridge Oats, So-Easy, Scotts*	1 Serving/30g	109	364	11.0	60.0	8.5	9.0
Porridge Oats, Somerfield*	1 Serving/40g	154	385	12.0	68.0	7.0	0.0
Porridge Oats, Value, Tesco*	1 Serving/50g	192	384	11.8	68.0	7.2	7.2
Porridge Oats, Whole Rolled, Scottish, Sainsbury's*	1 Serving/50g	191	381	9.7	74.7	4.8	7.0
Porridge, COU, Marks & Spencer*	1 Pot/200g	180	90	3.9	13.3	2.2	0.9
Porridge, Instant, Quakers*	1 Serving/34g	125	368	12.8	66.7	7.6	5.0

BREAKFAST CEREAL,	Measure INFO/WEIGHT	per Measure KCAL	Nutrition Values per 100g / 100ml				
			KCAL	PROT	CARB	FAT	FIBRE
Porridge, Quick, Marks & Spencer*	1 Serving/40g	159	398	15.5	55.1	12.8	5.9
Porridge, Weight Watchers*	1 Pack/220g	114	52	1.1	9.5	1.1	0.9
Precise, Sainsbury's*	1 Serving/40g	148	371	6.4	79.9	2.9	3.5
Puffed Rice, Kallo*	1 Serving/25g	95	380	8.0	80.0	3.0	9.0
Puffed Wheat, Quaker*	1 Serving/15g	49	328	15.3	62.4	1.3	5.6
Puffed Wheat, Tesco*	1 Serving/28g	104	373	13.9	72.2	3.2	5.7
Quaker Oats Crunch, Quaker*	1 Serving/40g	178	445	8.0	66.5	16.0	5.0
Quaker Oats, Quaker*	1 Serving/45g	160	356	11.0	60.0	8.0	9.0
Raisin & Almond, Crunchy, Jordans*	1 Serving/56g	230	411	8.4	66.0	12.5	5.0
Raisin & Coconut, Crunchy, Organic, Jordans*	1 Serving/40g	168	419	8.1	66.3	13.5	6.4
Raisin Wheats, Kellogg's*	1 Serving/30g	96	320	9.0	69.0	2.0	9.0
Raisin Wheats, Sainsbury's*	1 Serving/50g	166	332	8.2	71.5	1.5	8.0
Raisin, Bran Flakes, Asda*	1 Serving/50g	166	331	7.0	69.0	3.0	10.0
Raisin, Honey & Almond Crunch, Asda*	1 Serving/60g	265	442	8.0	62.0	18.0	6.0
Rasberry Crisp, Mornflake*	1 Serving/50g	214	428	6.5	68.2	14.3	6.8
Ready Brek, Banana, Weetabix*	1 Serving/40g	146	365	8.9	68.0	6.4	6.7
Ready Brek, Chocolate, Weetabix*	1 Serving/40g	144	360	9.6	63.7	7.4	8.1
Ready Brek, Oatmeal, Readybrek*	1 Serving/40g	150	375	11.5	58.8	8.3	9.0
Ready Brek, Strawberry, Weetabix*	1 Serving/40g	146	365	8.7	68.6	6.2	6.8
Ready Brek, Weetabix*	1 Serving/40g	142	356	11.6	58.8	8.3	8.9
Red Berries Crisp, Sommerfield*	1 serving/30g	134	448	7.3	67.0	16.8	4.3
Red Berry & Almond Luxury Crunch, Jordans*	1 Serving/40g	176	441	8.2	60.5	18.5	6.6
Rice & Wheat Flake, Special Choice, Waitrose*	1 Serving/30g	111	370	11.4	77.7	1.5	3.2
Rice Krispies, Honey, Kellogg's*	1 Serving/30g	114	380	4.0	89.0	0.7	1.0
Rice Krispies, Kellogg's*	1 Serving/30g	114	380	6.0	87.0	1.0	1.0
Rice Pops, Blue Parrot Cafe, Sainsbury's*	1 Serving/30g	111	370	7.2	82.3	1.3	2.2
Rice Pops, Organic, Dove's Farm*	1 Serving/30g	107	357	6.8	86.1	0.8	2.0
Rice Pops, Sainsbury's*	1 Serving/30g	113	378	7.4	84.2	1.3	1.5
Rice Snaps, Asda*	1 Serving/28g	105	376	7.0	84.0	1.3	1.5
Rice Snaps, Harvest Home, Nestle*	1 Serving/25g	95	378	7.4	84.2	1.3	1.5
Rice Snaps, Healthy Eating, Tesco*	1 Pack/25g	93	370	7.2	82.3	1.3	2.2
Rice Snaps, Tesco*	1 Serving/30g	113	378	7.3	84.2	1.3	1.5
Ricicles, Kellogg's*	1 Serving/30g	114	380	4.0	90.0	0.7	0.9
Right Balance, Morrisons*	1 Serving/50g	181	362	6.9	78.6	2.2	5.3
Shredded Wheat, Bitesize, Nestle*	1 Serving/45g	158	350	11.8	69.9	2.6	11.9
Shredded Wheat, Fruitful, Nestle*	1 Serving/50g	177	353	8.4	66.9	5.8	10.3
Shredded Wheat, Honey Nut, Nestle*	1 Serving/40g	151	378	10.9	68.8	6.6	10.4
Shredded Wheat, Nestle*	1 Piece/22g	72	325	11.2	65.2	2.1	12.4
Shredded Wheat, Triple Berry, Nestle*	1 Serving/40g	138	344	10.6	70.6	2.1	11.1
Shreddies, Coco, Nestle*	1 Serving/50g	177	353	8.0	76.1	1.9	9.2
Shreddies, Frosted, Kellogg's*	1 Serving/50g	162	323	0.7	78.5	1.8	4.7
Shreddies, Frosted, Nestle*	1 Serving/50g	178	356	7.3	78.5	1.4	8.3
Shreddies, Frosted, Variety Pack, Nestle*	1 Pack/45g	163	363	6.7	81.1	1.3	6.8
Shreddies, Malt Wheats, Tesco*	1 Serving/45g	151	335	8.3	70.7	2.1	9.7
Shreddies, Nestle*	1 Serving/45g	158	350	9.9	73.4	1.9	9.8
Smart Start, Kellogg's*	1 Serving/70g	252	360	6.0	86.0	1.0	4.0
Smoothies, Strawberry, Quaker*	1 Sachet/29g	117	402	6.5	67.0	12.0	5.5
Smoothies, Toffee, Quaker*	1 Serving/30g	122	407	6.5	66.0	13.0	5.0
Special K, Apricot & Peach, Kellogg's*	1 Serving/30g	111	369	15.0	75.0	1.0	3.0
Special K, Choco, Kellogg's*	1 Serving/40g	160	400	14.0	70.0	7.0	3.5
Special K, Kellogg's*	1 Serving/30g	111	369	16.0	74.0	1.0	3.0
Special K, Red Berries, Kellogg's*	1 Serving/30g	111	370	14.0	75.0	1.0	3.0
Start Right, Asda*	1 Serving/40g	150	376	8.0	74.0	6.0	5.0

	Measure INFO/WEIGHT	per Measure KCAL	Nutrition Values per 100g / 100ml				
			KCAL	PROT	CARB	FAT	FIBRE
BREAKFAST CEREAL,							
Strawberry & Almond Crunch, Marks & Spencer*	1 Serving/40g	186	465	8.0	66.0	18.6	4.9
Strawberry & Maltiflakes, COU, Marks & Spencer*	1 Serving/40g	146	365	12.7	73.8	2.3	3.5
Strawberry Crisp, Asda*	1 Serving/30g	134	445	8.0	65.0	17.0	5.0
Sugar Puffs, Quaker*	1 Serving/30g	116	387	6.5	86.5	1.0	3.0
Sultana Bran, Asda*	1 Serving/30g	98	327	9.0	66.0	3.0	11.0
Sultana Bran, Co-Op*	1 Serving/40g	130	325	9.0	66.0	3.0	11.0
Sultana Bran, Healthwise, Kellogg's*	1 Serving/40g	128	320	8.0	68.0	2.0	12.0
Sultana Bran, Healthy Eating, Tesco*	1 Serving/48g	156	326	8.1	69.0	1.9	9.8
Sultana Bran, Healthy Living, Tesco*	1 Serving/30g	87	290	9.8	58.1	2.0	11.7
Sultana Bran, Morrisons*	1 Serving/30g	98	325	8.8	65.8	3.0	11.4
Sultana Bran, Safeway*	1 Serving/50g	162	324	8.2	68.6	1.9	11.6
Sultana Bran, Sainsbury's*	1 Serving/30g	97	324	8.2	68.6	1.9	11.6
Sultana Bran, Somerfield*	1 Serving/30g	97	324	8.2	68.6	1.9	11.6
Super High Fibre, Dorset Cereals*	1 Serving/60g	214	357	8.0	60.1	9.4	8.4
Superfast Oats, Mornflake*	1 Serving/40g	144	359	11.0	60.4	8.1	8.5
Toasted Multi-Grain Flakes With Apple, Weight Watchers*	1 Serving/30g	97	323	10.4	67.8	1.1	14.4
Triple Chocolate Crisp, Sainsbury's*	1 Serving/40g	180	451	7.7	63.8	18.3	6.0
Tropical Fruit & Bran Multi Flakes, Marks & Spencer*	1 Serving/50g	175	350	7.1	81.2	2.3	7.0
Tropical, Crunchy, Jordans*	1 Serving/40g	169	423	9.0	66.0	13.8	5.0
Tropicana, Weight Watchers*	1 Serving/50g	120	240	5.1	52.0	1.0	7.0
Vitality, Asda*	1 Serving/30g	111	370	11.0	78.0	1.5	3.2
Vitality, With Red Fruit, Asda*	1 Serving/30g	110	366	11.0	77.0	1.6	3.8
Vitality, With Tropical Fruit, Asda*	1 Serving/30g	112	373	9.0	73.0	5.0	4.9
Weetabix*	2 Biscuits/37.5g	128	340	11.2	67.6	2.7	10.5
Weetabix, Organic, Weetabix*	2 Biscuits/35g	117	335	10.9	66.2	3.0	11.3
Weetos, Weetabix*	1 Serving/30g	115	384	6.2	78.4	5.0	5.6
Wheat Biscuits, Healthy Eating, Tesco*	2 Biscuits/55g	191	348	11.0	70.0	2.7	8.0
Wheat Biscuits, Morrisons*	2 Biscuits/37.5g	129	340	11.2	67.6	2.7	10.5
Wheat Biscuits, Nature's Own, Organic, Weetabix*	1 Biscuit/17g	58	339	10.3	69.2	2.4	10.4
Wheat Biscuits, Somerfield*	2 Biscuits/37.5g	129	339	11.2	67.6	2.7	10.5
Wheat Biscuits, Value, Tesco*	2 Biscuits/30g	103	342	13.7	69.5	1.0	7.5
Wheat Bisks, Asda*	1 Bisk/19g	65	340	11.0	68.0	2.7	10.0
Whole Wheat Biscuits, Sainsbury's*	1 Biscuit/36g	122	340	11.2	67.6	2.7	10.5
Whole Wheat Biscuits, Waitrose*	2 Biscuits/37g	124	336	11.8	68.0	1.9	10.1
Yoghurt & Raspberry, Crisp, Sainsbury's*	1 Serving/45g	199	442	7.5	66.0	16.4	5.4
Yoghurty, Special K, Kellogg's*	1 Serving/30g	115	383	14.0	75.0	3.0	2.5
BREAKFAST COMPOTE,							
In Apple Juice, Tesco*	1 Can/300g	219	73	0.4	17.0	0.4	2.1
Sainsbury's*	1 Can/300g	327	109	1.7	24.4	0.5	3.1
BREAM,							
Sea, Raw	1oz/28g	27	96	17.5	0.0	2.9	0.0
BRESAOLA,							
Della Valtellina, Sainsbury's*	1 Slice/14g	23	163	34.7	0.1	2.6	0.1
Finest, Tesco*	1 Serving/35g	64	182	36.0	0.5	4.0	0.0
Finest, Tesco*	1 Slice/8.8g	16	182	36.0	0.5	4.0	0.0
Marks & Spencer*	1oz/28g	56	200	34.6	0.0	6.8	0.0
BROCCOLI,							
& Cauliflower, Floret Mix, Frozen, Tesco*	1 Serving/150g	50	33	4.0	2.3	0.9	2.2
& Cheese, Morrisons*	1 Pack/350g	406	116	6.2	6.6	7.1	0.8
Baby Courgette & Baby Leeks, Safeway*	1oz/28g	7	24	2.4	2.1	0.8	2.0
Carrot & Mange Tout, Marks & Spencer*	1oz/28g	10	35	2.9	5.6	0.2	2.1
Cauliflower & Baby Carrots, Safeway*	1 Serving/150g	38	25	2.0	3.0	0.6	2.3
Cauliflower & Carrots, Frozen, Great Value, Asda*	1 Serving/100g	25	25	2.2	2.6	0.6	5.0

	Measure INFO/WEIGHT	per Measure KCAL	Nutrition Values per 100g / 100ml				
			KCAL	PROT	CARB	FAT	FIBRE
BROCCOLI,							
Courgette & Peppers, COU, Marks & Spencer*	1 Pack/283g	156	55	1.7	2.7	4.1	1.7
Green, Boiled, Average	1 Serving/90g	22	24	3.1	1.1	0.8	2.3
Green, Raw, Average	1 Serving/17g	5	31	3.7	2.1	0.8	2.4
Mornay, Asda*	1 Pack/434g	434	100	4.5	7.0	6.0	0.3
Purple Sprouting, Boiled, Average	1 Serving/90g	17	19	2.1	1.3	0.6	2.3
Purple Sprouting, Raw	1oz/28g	10	35	3.9	2.6	1.1	3.5
BROWNIE,							
Chocolate Chip, McMini, McDonald's*	1 Brownie/18.9g	68	360	4.9	58.8	12.7	1.9
Chocolate, Chewy, Marks & Spencer*	1 Cake/28.6g	132	455	6.5	59.8	21.1	2.0
Chocolate, Chunky, Marks & Spencer*	1 Serving/30g	126	420	6.3	56.9	18.6	2.5
Chocolate, Fudgy, Marks & Spencer*	1 Brownie/87g	400	460	4.8	56.9	25.2	3.0
Chocolate, Sainsbury's*	1 Brownie/60g	265	442	4.6	55.0	22.6	1.6
Chocolate, Slices, Marks & Spencer*	1 Brownie/36g	158	440	5.3	51.1	24.1	1.3
Chocolate, Tesco*	1 Serving/46g	189	411	5.2	61.1	16.2	0.7
Chocolate, Topped With M&M's Minis, McVitie's*	1 Cake/92.5g	424	456	4.6	59.4	22.2	0.0
Chocolate, Waitrose*	1 Brownie/45g	192	426	6.3	55.6	19.8	2.7
Chocolate, Weight Watchers*	1 Serving/47g	143	304	4.8	62.5	3.8	3.2
Pret A Manger*	1 Av Pack/50g	328	656	7.2	81.0	33.8	1.0
BRUSCHETTA,							
Pane Italia*	1 Serving/75g	367	489	12.4	53.6	25.1	1.4
Safeway*	¼ Pack/115g	420	365	11.8	65.5	5.8	2.8
Toasted, Olive Oil & Sea Salt, Tesco*	1 Serving/30g	126	420	11.5	58.7	15.5	4.5
BRUSSELS SPROUTS,							
Boiled, Average	1 Serving/90g	32	35	3.1	3.2	1.3	3.5
Canned, Drained	1oz/28g	8	28	2.6	2.4	1.0	2.6
Raw, Average	1oz/28g	10	37	3.5	3.3	1.1	3.0
BUBBLE & SQUEAK,							
Aunt Bessie's*	1 Serving/100g	145	145	2.7	17.5	7.1	1.3
Fried in Vegetable Oil	1oz/28g	35	124	1.4	9.8	9.1	1.5
Safeway*	1 Serving/200g	160	80	1.8	10.7	3.3	1.4
Tesco*	1 Pack/325g	325	100	1.3	13.5	4.5	1.3
Waitrose*	½ Pack/225g	216	96	1.6	13.4	4.0	1.8
BUCKWHEAT,							
Average	1oz/28g	102	364	8.1	84.9	1.5	2.1
BULGUR WHEAT,							
Average	1oz/28g	99	353	9.7	76.3	1.7	0.0
BUNS,							
American, Safeway*	1 Bun/60.1g	152	253	8.9	44.5	4.4	3.7
Bath, Marks & Spencer*	1 Bun/71g	217	305	8.3	49.8	8.0	1.9
Bath, Tesco*	1 Bun/80g	262	328	8.0	48.9	11.1	5.8
Belgian, Asda*	1 Bun/133g	464	350	4.8	49.0	15.0	2.2
Belgian, Co-Op*	1 Bun/118g	413	350	5.0	54.0	13.0	2.0
Belgian, Dairy Cream, Somerfield*	1 Serving/120.8g	401	331	5.2	52.6	11.1	2.0
Belgian, Tesco*	1 Bun/125g	451	361	4.4	56.7	12.9	2.7
Burger, Giant, Sainsbury's*	1 Bun/95.0g	249	262	8.7	45.2	5.2	2.9
Burger, Sainsbury's*	1 Bun/56g	162	289	7.8	49.4	6.7	2.4
Burger, Sliced, Tesco*	1 Bun/60g	168	280	7.9	47.3	6.6	2.1
Burger, Sliced, Waitrose*	1 Bun/61g	158	264	10.0	47.2	3.9	1.8
Burger, With Sesame Seeds, Co-Op*	1 Bun/55g	143	260	9.0	44.0	5.0	2.0
Chelsea	1 Bun/78g	285	366	7.8	56.1	13.8	1.7
Chelsea, Sainsbury's*	1 Bun/85g	239	281	6.9	51.6	5.2	2.9
Chelsea, Tesco*	1 Bun/85g	269	316	7.9	53.9	7.6	2.3
Currant	1 Bun/60g	178	296	7.6	52.7	7.5	0.0

B

	Measure INFO/WEIGHT	per Measure KCAL	Nutrition Values per 100g / 100ml				
			KCAL	PROT	CARB	FAT	FIBRE
BUNS,							
Currant, Healthy Eating, Tesco*	1 Bun/62g	157	253	6.6	50.8	2.6	3.2
Currant, Healthy Living, Tesco*	1 Bun/63g	155	246	6.6	51.8	1.4	2.4
Currant, Safeway*	1 Bun/65.0g	178	274	7.0	50.0	5.1	2.8
Currant, Sainsbury's	1 Bun/72g	197	274	7.0	50.0	5.1	2.8
Currant, Somerfield*	1 Bun/52.7g	150	283	8.0	50.8	5.3	2.4
Custard Choux, Marks & Spencer*	1 Bun/85g	234	275	4.2	15.0	22.0	0.3
Dairy Cream, Somerfield*	1 Bun/98g	304	310	6.0	46.9	10.9	0.0
Fruit, Waitrose*	1 Bun/54g	171	316	7.8	55.7	6.9	1.6
Hevva, Somerfield*	1 Bun/75g	298	397	5.4	57.8	16.0	1.5
Hot Cross	1 Bun/50g	155	310	7.4	58.5	6.8	1.7
Hot Cross, 25% Reduced Fat, Asda*	1 Bun/60.5g	152	253	9.0	49.0	2.3	3.0
Hot Cross, Apple & Cinnamon, Marks & Spencer*	1 Bun/71g	170	240	8.1	46.9	2.1	3.7
Hot Cross, Asda*	1 Bun/60g	190	317	10.0	55.0	6.3	3.3
Hot Cross, BGTY, Sainsbury's*	1 Bun/70g	176	252	9.3	48.7	1.6	2.0
Hot Cross, Budgens*	1 Bun/64g	201	314	7.9	54.2	7.3	2.9
Hot Cross, Chocolate & Raisin, Mini, Tesco*	1 Bun/40g	127	318	8.1	47.0	10.9	2.8
Hot Cross, Chocolate, Mini, Sainsbury's*	1 Bun/39g	127	325	7.7	48.1	11.3	2.5
Hot Cross, Co-Op*	1 Bun/60g	165	275	8.0	47.0	6.0	3.0
Hot Cross, Extra Spicy, Marks & Spencer*	1 Bun/76g	175	230	8.6	44.1	1.9	4.2
Hot Cross, Finest, Tesco*	1 Bun/75g	203	270	6.9	49.0	5.2	2.6
Hot Cross, Golden Wholemeal, 3% Fat, Marks & Spencer*	1 Bun/67g	144	215	8.9	39.6	2.2	6.7
Hot Cross, Golden Wholemeal, Sainsbury's*	1 Bun/65g	180	277	9.9	45.4	6.2	4.3
Hot Cross, Healthy Eating, Tesco*	1 Bun/60g	155	258	8.6	50.3	2.5	2.6
Hot Cross, Healthy Living, Tesco*	1 Bun/62g	155	250	6.7	51.4	1.9	2.3
Hot Cross, Less Than 3% Fat, Marks & Spencer*	1 Bun/70g	175	250	8.1	49.8	1.8	2.2
Hot Cross, Low Fat, Good Intentions, Somerfield*	1 Bun/50g	135	270	10.0	51.8	2.6	2.8
Hot Cross, Luxury White, Safeway*	1 Bun/75.5g	186	245	8.0	39.4	5.9	3.7
Hot Cross, Luxury, Cafe, Marks & Spencer*	1 Bun/78g	199	255	8.6	46.2	4.0	2.1
Hot Cross, Luxury, Marks & Spencer*	1 Bun/79g	201	255	8.6	46.2	4.0	2.1
Hot Cross, Mini, Marks & Spencer*	1 Bun/37.3g	94	255	8.0	52.1	1.7	1.7
Hot Cross, Mini, Tesco*	1 Bun/36g	99	274	7.9	48.1	5.5	2.7
Hot Cross, Morning Fresh, Safeway*	1 Bun/64g	170	265	6.0	50.9	4.1	1.7
Hot Cross, Morrisons*	1 Bun/60g	163	272	8.5	47.4	5.4	3.3
Hot Cross, Perfectly Balanced, Waitrose*	1 Bun/68g	166	244	7.6	48.7	2.1	3.2
Hot Cross, Reduced Fat, GFY, Asda*	1 Bun/67g	179	267	7.0	53.0	3.0	2.1
Hot Cross, Reduced Fat, Waitrose*	1 Bun/67g	171	255	8.1	54.3	2.1	3.3
Hot Cross, Safeway*	1 Bun/65g	174	268	7.9	46.9	5.4	2.2
Hot Cross, Sainsbury's*	1 Bun/70g	205	293	7.6	53.2	5.5	2.1
Hot Cross, Square, Marks & Spencer*	1 Bun/110.4g	264	240	8.5	49.1	1.8	2.2
Hot Cross, Tesco*	1 Bun/55g	144	262	7.4	46.8	5.0	2.8
Hot Cross, White, Kingsmill*	1 Bun/24.9g	71	286	7.0	51.1	6.0	3.0
Hot Cross, White, Low Fat, Safeway*	1 Bun/65g	161	248	8.7	47.4	2.6	3.0
Hot Cross, White, Waitrose*	1 Bun/67.5g	175	258	8.1	49.5	3.1	3.9
Hot Cross, Wholemeal, Asda*	1 Bun/69.5g	181	262	9.0	43.0	6.0	6.0
Hot Cross, Wholemeal, Organic, Tesco*	1 Bun/55g	140	254	7.6	44.8	4.9	4.5
Hot Cross, Wholemeal, Tesco*	1 Bun/62g	166	268	9.9	43.6	6.0	4.7
Hot Cross, Wholemeal, Waitrose*	1 Bun/64g	177	276	8.8	45.2	6.7	4.9
Iced & Spiced Soft, Marks & Spencer*	1 Bun/42g	118	280	7.9	55.0	2.9	1.9
Iced Finger, Tesco*	1 Finger/69g	241	349	6.4	58.3	10.0	1.7
Iced Fruit, Marks & Spencer*	1 Bun/95g	285	300	8.5	57.9	4.3	1.3
Iced Lemon, Tesco*	1 Bun/48g	156	325	5.2	56.5	8.7	1.9
Iced, Marks & Spencer*	1 Bun/42g	138	328	8.3	53.7	8.9	2.0
Iced, Tesco*	1 Bun/35g	113	323	7.0	58.9	6.6	2.1

B

	Measure INFO/WEIGHT	per Measure KCAL	Nutrition Values per 100g / 100ml				
			KCAL	PROT	CARB	FAT	FIBRE
BUNS,							
Saffron, Somerfield*	1 Bun/70g	266	380	6.4	50.9	16.7	1.9
Spiced, Perfectly Balanced, Waitrose*	1 Bun/65g	177	272	8.0	52.3	3.4	2.9
Swiss, Sainsbury's*	1 Bun/90g	314	349	5.1	49.3	14.6	1.3
Vanilla, Soft Iced, Marks & Spencer*	1 Bun/41g	131	320	8.2	55.5	7.6	1.8
BURGERS,							
Aberdeen Angus Beef, Mega, Bird's Eye*	1 Burger/101g	279	276	16.3	2.4	22.4	0.1
Aberdeen Angus, Virgin Trains*	1 Serving/239.7g	696	290	13.5	23.8	15.7	0.0
American Style, Asda*	1 Burger/41.7g	157	374	25.0	10.0	26.0	1.1
American Style, Tesco*	1 Burger/125g	250	200	13.0	20.4	7.3	3.9
BGTY, Sainsbury's*	1 Burger/110g	177	161	20.8	7.1	5.5	1.1
Bacon Double Cheeseburger, Bunless, Burger King*	1 Burger/138g	607	440	30.0	4.0	31.0	0.0
Bacon McDouble, With Cheese, McDonald's*	1 Burger/141g	372	264	16.1	19.6	13.5	2.2
Bean, Quarter Pounders, Mexican Style, Tesco*	1 Burger/101g	215	213	4.3	25.0	10.6	2.8
Beef With Onion, Bird's Eye*	1 Burger/41g	114	278	15.3	3.5	22.5	0.2
Beef With Onion, Sainsbury's*	1 Burger/42g	102	243	20.7	6.9	14.8	1.0
Beef, 100%, Bird's Eye*	1 Burger/41g	120	292	17.3	0.0	24.8	0.0
Beef, 100%, Half Pounders, Sainsbury's*	1 Burger/147.6g	463	313	26.0	1.7	22.4	0.2
Beef, 100%, Mega, Bird's Eye*	1 Burger/95.6g	281	293	17.3	0.0	24.9	0.0
Beef, 100%, Quarter Pounders, Aldi*	1 Burger/114g	320	282	24.3	0.1	20.5	1.3
Beef, 100%, Quarter Pounders, Bird's Eye*	1 Burger/100g	250	250	20.0	0.0	19.0	0.0
Beef, 100%, Quarter Pounders, Prime, Asda*	1 Burger/86g	254	299	26.0	1.6	21.0	0.0
Beef, 100%, Quarter Pounders, Ross*	1 Serving/73.8g	223	301	16.8	1.1	25.5	0.0
Beef, 100%, Sainsbury's*	1 Burger/44g	133	302	21.4	0.9	23.6	0.9
Beef, 100%, Somerfield*	1 Burger/113.5g	329	289	17.0	1.0	24.0	0.0
Beef, 100%, With Seasoning, No Onion, Bird's Eye*	1 Burger/41g	134	326	16.1	0.2	29.0	0.0
Beef, 100%, Without Onion, Sainsbury's*	1 Burger/43g	133	308	21.9	0.8	24.1	0.8
Beef, Aberdeen Angus, Asda*	1 Burger/112g	244	218	16.0	4.8	15.0	0.1
Beef, Aberdeen Angus, Marks & Spencer*	1 Burger/142g	298	210	18.3	4.1	13.3	0.1
Beef, Aberdeen Angus, Waitrose*	1 Burger/114g	269	236	18.2	0.3	18.0	0.0
Beef, Asda*	1 Burger/114g	259	227	22.2	5.7	12.8	0.6
Beef, Barbecue, Tesco*	1 Burger/113.5g	259	227	16.4	1.3	17.4	1.2
Beef, Chargrill, Tesco*	1 Burger/113.5g	247	217	17.0	0.8	16.2	2.5
Beef, Farmfoods*	1 Burger/50g	128	255	14.4	5.4	19.6	0.1
Beef, Flame Grilled, Dalepak*	1 Burger/44g	131	304	15.3	2.1	26.0	0.4
Beef, Frozen, Safeway*	1 Burger/44g	123	279	21.3	1.3	20.2	0.0
Beef, Giant Chargrilled, Farmfoods*	1 Burger/170g	352	207	17.3	5.6	12.8	1.2
Beef, Herbs, Finest, Tesco*	1 Burger/170g	284	167	16.9	3.6	9.4	0.3
Beef, Iceland*	1 Serving/115g	148	129	19.2	3.6	4.1	0.1
Beef, In a Bun, Healthy Eating, Tesco*	1 Pack/189g	282	149	13.6	20.7	1.3	2.1
Beef, Mega, Bird's Eye*	1 Burger/109g	300	275	14.3	2.7	23.0	0.3
Beef, Morrisons*	1 Burger/56.7g	170	298	12.3	5.5	25.2	0.6
Beef, Organic, Marks & Spencer*	1 Burger/110g	239	217	18.2	0.0	16.0	0.2
Beef, Organic, Tesco*	1 Burger/56.8g	148	260	15.5	4.2	20.1	0.5
Beef, Quarter Pounders, Bird's Eye*	1 Burger/139g	386	278	15.3	3.5	22.5	0.2
Beef, Quarter Pounders, Farmfoods*	1 Burger/113g	289	256	14.4	5.4	19.6	0.1
Beef, Quarter Pounders, Flame Grilled, Rustlers*	1 Burger/190g	557	293	14.9	24.3	15.1	0.0
Beef, Quarter Pounders, Flame Grilled, Tesco*	1 Burger/88g	246	280	13.1	4.8	23.2	0.8
Beef, Quarter Pounders, Good Intentions, Somerfield*	1 Burger/96.3g	183	191	18.9	1.9	12.0	0.8
Beef, Quarter Pounders, Grilled, Bird's Eye*	1 Burger/113.5g	231	203	14.1	2.7	15.0	0.3
Beef, Quarter Pounders, Morrisons*	1 Burger/113.5g	340	298	12.3	5.5	25.2	0.6
Beef, Quarter Pounders, Reduced Fat, Tesco*	1 Burger/95g	171	180	14.0	1.8	13.0	0.8
Beef, Quarter Pounders, Safeway*	1 Burger/100g	227	227	22.2	5.7	12.8	0.6
Beef, Quarter Pounders, Somerfield*	1 Burger/113.9g	319	280	14.7	5.6	22.1	1.2

B

	Measure INFO/WEIGHT	per Measure KCAL	Nutrition Values per 100g / 100ml				
			KCAL	PROT	CARB	FAT	FIBRE
BURGERS,							
Beef, Quarter Pounders, Steak Country, Lidl*	1 Burger/68g	188	276	16.3	2.4	22.2	0.1
Beef, Quarter Pounders, Tesco*	1 Burger/113g	292	258	17.8	0.7	20.4	1.3
Beef, Quarter Pounders, With Fresh Onion, Bird's Eye*	1 Burger/100g	230	230	16.0	5.9	16.0	0.4
Beef, Quarter Pounders, With Onion, Sainsbury's*	1 Burger/91.1g	247	271	18.0	5.1	19.8	1.5
Beef, Sainsbury's*	1 Burger/57g	150	267	29.6	1.3	15.9	1.5
Beef, Spicy Jalapeno, Finest, Tesco*	1 Burger/170g	277	163	17.2	2.4	9.4	0.4
Beef, Tesco*	1 Burger/47g	110	234	22.3	8.7	12.1	1.1
Beef, With Onion, Cooked, Ross*	1 Burger/41.2g	116	284	14.7	2.8	23.8	0.4
Beef, With Peppermix, Danish Crown*	1 Burger/100g	250	250	19.0	0.0	19.0	0.0
Big Mac, McDonald's*	1 Big Mac/215g	492	229	12.4	20.5	10.7	2.7
Big Tasty, McDonald's*	1 Burger/348g	804	231	11.7	14.6	14.5	1.6
Cheeseburger, American, Tesco*	1 Burger/275g	660	240	13.6	24.9	9.6	1.6
Cheeseburger, Bacon Double, Burger King*	1 Pack/191g	510	267	19.0	16.0	14.0	1.0
Cheeseburger, Beef, British, Tesco*	1 Burger/275g	666	242	12.6	23.0	11.2	0.8
Cheeseburger, Burger King*	1 Burger/141g	379	269	15.6	30.0	13.4	1.4
Cheeseburger, Double, McDonalds*	1 Burger/171g	438	256	15.5	19.4	11.7	1.8
Cheeseburger, McDonald's*	1 Burger/122g	300	246	13.0	27.2	9.5	2.1
Cheeseburger, SmartPrice, Asda*	1 Burger/150g	374	249	13.3	28.0	9.3	1.4
Cheeseburger, With Relish, American Style, Tesco*	1 Burger/61.4g	131	215	14.2	17.5	9.8	4.2
Chicken Crunch & Fries, Marks & Spencer*	1 Pack/425g	915	215	8.8	20.8	11.2	2.1
Chicken Fillet, KFC*	1 Burger/213g	469	220	15.0	19.0	9.2	1.6
Chicken Flamer, Burger King*	1 Serving/162g	308	190	12.6	18.6	7.3	1.9
Chicken Royale, Burger King*	1 Serving/204g	560	275	12.3	25.5	13.7	1.5
Chicken Sandwich, Burger King*	1 Serving/224g	659	294	11.2	23.6	17.4	1.3
Chicken Whopper, Lite, Burger King*	1 Whopper/159g	339	213	15.3	18.4	8.7	0.0
Chicken, Bird's Eye*	1 Burger/57g	147	258	13.6	16.8	15.2	0.4
Chicken, Breaded, Asda*	1 Burger/54.8g	145	263	14.0	18.0	15.0	0.0
Chicken, Crispy Crumb, Farmfoods*	1 Burger/242g	707	292	10.5	20.2	18.8	1.1
Chicken, Crunch Crumb, Tesco*	1 Burger/57g	161	282	12.3	15.6	18.9	0.0
Chicken, Quarter Pounders, Bird's Eye*	1 Burger/117g	280	239	13.5	15.2	13.8	0.6
Chicken, Sainsbury's*	1 Serving/46g	115	247	15.6	12.2	15.1	1.3
Chicken, Southern Fried, Sainsbury's*	1 Burger/52g	154	297	12.6	17.2	19.8	1.3
Chicken, Spar*	1 Burger/67g	163	244	16.1	20.8	11.2	1.5
Chicken, With Sesame Seed Bun, Breaded, Tesco*	1 Burger/205g	588	287	10.2	26.2	15.7	2.9
Chicken, Without Mayo, Nando's*	1 Burger/100g	399	399	32.3	45.2	9.5	0.0
Chilli, Quarter Pounders, Asda*	1 Burger/87.7g	222	252	25.0	2.0	16.0	0.0
Chilli, Quarter Pounders, Farmfoods*	1 Burger/115g	285	248	13.5	2.9	20.3	0.9
Chilli, Quarter Pounders, Iceland*	1 Burger/84g	265	316	18.6	6.5	23.9	0.4
Double Cheeseburger, McDonald's*	1 Burger/171g	438	256	15.5	19.4	12.9	1.8
Double Whopper With Cheese, Burger King*	1 Pack/378g	934	247	14.0	13.0	16.0	1.0
Double Whopper, Burger King*	1 Serving/353g	918	260	13.5	15.0	16.1	1.1
Economy, SmartPrice, Asda*	1 Burger/48.5g	141	293	14.0	12.0	21.0	1.1
Filet-O-Fish, McDonald's*	1 Burger/161g	386	240	9.9	25.2	11.1	1.2
Fillet Towermeal, KFC*	1 Pack/283g	656	232	13.0	19.8	11.2	1.5
Grilled Chicken Caprese, McDonald's*	1 Burger/275g	470	171	12.5	15.0	7.7	2.1
Hamburger, Burger King*	1 Burger/128g	339	265	14.8	23.4	12.5	1.5
Hamburger, McDonald's*	1 Burger/108g	254	235	12.2	30.6	7.1	2.3
Lamb, Quarter Pounders, Bird's Eye*	1 Burger/112g	232	207	13.9	3.8	15.1	0.3
Lamb, Quarter Pounders, Farmfoods*	1oz/28g	76	272	12.3	6.6	21.8	1.0
Less Than 7% Fat, Sainsbury's*	1 Burger/102g	164	161	20.8	7.1	5.5	1.1
Low Fat, Iceland*	1 Serving/85g	148	174	27.8	5.0	4.8	1.1
McChicken Grill With BBQ Sauce, McDonald's*	1 Pack/215g	309	144	12.1	18.1	2.6	2.2
McChicken Premiere, McDonald's*	1 Burger/244g	537	220	12.1	21.4	9.5	1.6

BURGERS,	Measure INFO/WEIGHT	per Measure KCAL	Nutrition Values per 100g / 100ml				
			KCAL	PROT	CARB	FAT	FIBRE
McChicken Sandwich, McDonald's*	1 Burger/167g	376	225	9.9	23.2	10.3	2.3
Mushroom & Red Onion, Tesco*	1 Burger/87.1g	135	155	5.4	21.3	5.4	1.6
Nacho, Chicken & Sweetcorn, Asda*	½ Pack/143.9g	249	173	14.0	9.0	9.0	2.3
Pork, Quarter Pounders, Bird's Eye*	1 Burger/122g	292	239	13.9	3.2	19.0	0.2
Prime Beef, Asda*	1 Burger/45g	123	274	22.0	6.0	18.0	0.6
Quarter Pounder With Cheese & Buns, Sainsbury's*	1 Burger/198g	471	238	15.6	19.1	11.5	1.4
Quarter Pounder, Deluxe, McDonald's*	1 Burger/253g	521	206	11.4	16.1	10.6	1.7
Quarter Pounder, McDonald's*	1 Burger/178g	424	238	14.5	20.9	10.7	2.1
Quarter Pounder, With Cheese, McDonald's*	1 Burger/206g	515	250	15.1	18.2	13.0	1.8
Quarter Pounders, 95% Fat Free, Good Choice, Iceland*	1 Burger/86g	150	174	27.8	5.0	4.8	1.1
Quarter Pounders, BGTY, Sainsbury's*	1 Serving/97g	161	166	16.9	6.1	8.2	1.0
Quarter Pounders, Big Country*	1 Burger/90g	271	301	22.1	1.8	23.1	0.0
Quarter Pounders, Chargrilled, BGTY, Sainsbury's*	1 Burger/114g	184	161	20.8	7.1	5.5	1.1
Quarter Pounders, Healthy Living, Tesco*	1 Burger/114g	188	165	18.7	3.6	8.4	0.6
Quarter Pounders, Highlander*	1 Burger/113.5g	335	295	21.7	4.2	23.2	0.0
Quarter Pounders, Iceland*	1 Burger/83g	253	305	20.4	5.1	22.6	0.6
Quarter Pounders, Scotch Beef, Sainsbury's*	1 Burger/113.5g	257	225	22.2	3.5	13.6	0.5
Quarter Pounders, TTD, Sainsbury's*	1 Burger/100g	182	182	22.6	5.5	7.7	1.5
Salmon, Quarter Pounders, Morrisons*	1 Burger/109.8g	235	214	21.4	5.5	11.8	1.7
Spicy Bean, Burger King*	1 Burger/239g	504	211	7.9	26.2	8.3	3.9
Spicy Bean, Dalepak*	1 Burger/118g	242	205	4.6	22.8	10.6	3.0
Spicy Bean, Quarter Pounders, Asda*	1 Serving/108g	257	238	4.5	28.0	12.0	3.0
Spicy Bean, Sainsbury's*	1 Burger/110g	262	240	5.0	27.1	12.4	2.0
Steak Premiere, McDonald's*	1 Burger/229g	453	198	14.9	19.4	6.2	1.6
Tuna, Bird's Eye*	1 Burger/50g	125	250	15.0	16.2	14.0	0.8
Tuna, Quarter Pound, Asda*	1 Burger/113g	212	188	21.0	3.4	10.0	0.0
Tuna, Sainsbury's*	1 Serving/105g	194	185	20.8	3.4	9.8	1.2
Turkey Cheese, Somerfield*	1oz/28g	79	281	14.0	16.0	18.0	0.0
Turkey Cheeseburgers, Tesco*	1 Burger/105g	252	240	15.4	12.8	14.1	1.3
Turkey, Crispy Crumb, Bernard Matthews*	1 Burger/71g	222	313	11.3	19.3	19.8	0.9
Value, Farmfoods*	1 Burger/49g	138	282	11.4	9.6	22.1	0.9
Whopper Junior With Cheese, Burger King*	1 Burger/167g	421	252	12.0	18.0	14.0	1.0
Whopper With Cheese, Burger King*	1 Pack/299g	724	242	11.0	16.0	15.0	1.0
Whopper With Mayo, Burger King*	1 Whopper/278g	678	244	10.4	19.0	14.0	1.4
Whopper, Burger King*	1 Whopper/274g	641	234	11.0	17.0	14.0	1.0
Zinger Fillet, KFC*	1 Serving/185g	445	241	13.9	22.4	10.6	1.4
Zinger Tower, KFC*	1 Serving/256g	620	242	12.4	20.2	12.5	1.3
Zinger, Meal, KFC*	1 Meal/305g	735	241	22.4	10.6	14.0	1.4
BURGERS MEAT FREE,							
Asda*	1 Burger/60g	138	230	24.0	11.0	10.0	0.3
Sainsbury's*	1 Burger/57g	92	161	19.6	3.9	7.4	4.8
BURGERS VEGETABLE,							
& Cheese, Tesco*	1 Burger/85g	167	197	7.7	19.5	9.8	1.4
Captains, Bird's Eye*	1 Burger/48g	96	200	4.7	25.5	8.8	2.0
Deluxe, McDonald's*	1 Burger/210g	475	226	5.1	28.8	10.0	4.9
Organic, Goodlife*	1 Burger/67.1g	114	170	3.2	26.3	5.8	2.6
Organic, Tesco*	1 Burger/90g	108	120	2.6	17.6	4.3	2.1
Quarter Pounders, Bird's Eye*	1 Burger/100g	166	166	4.3	19.8	8.0	1.6
Quarter Pounders, Dalepak*	1 Burger/114g	251	220	4.4	20.8	13.2	2.7
Spicy Bean, BGTY, Sainsbury's*	1 Burger/76g	119	156	5.6	24.3	3.2	3.3
Spicy, Asda*	1 Burger/56g	108	193	3.4	20.0	11.0	0.0
With Tofu, Organic, Evernat*	1oz/28g	52	186	7.9	16.9	8.3	0.0

BURGERS VEGETARIAN,

INFO/WEIGHT	Measure	per Measure KCAL	KCAL	PROT	CARB	FAT	FIBRE
Bean, Mexican Style Quarter Pounders, Tesco*	1 Burger/101g	215	213	4.3	25.0	10.6	2.8
Burger King*	1 Burger/223g	433	194	6.6	24.9	7.6	3.4
Chargrilled Style, Safeway*	1 Burger/57g	95	167	18.8	3.7	8.5	4.0
Cheeseburger, Chicken Style, Safeway*	1 Burger/100g	234	234	16.6	11.4	13.5	3.0
Chilli Flavour Brown Rice & Tofu, Cauldron Foods*	1 Burger/75g	185	246	16.2	13.5	14.1	4.3
Flame Grilled, Linda McCartney*	1 Burger/60g	80	134	22.6	2.9	3.6	1.6
Juicy Mushroom & Sweet Onion, Cauldron Foods*	1 Burger/87.5g	99	113	6.4	9.9	5.3	2.7
Mushroom & Red Onion, Tesco*	1 Burger/78g	105	135	4.7	18.6	4.6	1.4
Mushroom, Cauldron Foods*	1 Burger/87.5g	135	153	7.1	15.1	7.1	2.7
Mushroom, Tesco*	1 Burger/87g	144	166	2.8	20.4	8.1	3.1
Quarter Pounders, Chargrilled, Tesco*	1 Burger/113.5g	187	164	16.0	7.0	8.0	2.5
Spicy Bean, Linda McCartney*	1 Burger/85g	190	223	4.3	26.2	11.2	2.9
Spicy Black Bean, Cauldron Foods*	1 Burger/88g	158	180	10.8	13.4	9.2	5.1
Tesco*	1 Burger/56g	92	164	16.0	7.0	8.0	2.5
Tofu, Savoury, Cauldron Foods*	1 Burger/75g	162	216	14.8	13.2	11.5	3.5
Vegeburger, Linda McCartney*	1 Burger/59g	79	134	22.6	2.9	3.6	1.6
Vegeburger, Retail, Grilled	1oz/28g	55	196	16.6	8.0	11.1	4.2

BUTTER,

INFO/WEIGHT	Measure	per Measure KCAL	KCAL	PROT	CARB	FAT	FIBRE
Brandy, With Cognac, Sainsbury's*	1/8 Pot/25g	137	549	0.2	44.1	37.6	0.0
Creamery, Average	1 Serving/10g	74	736	0.5	0.4	81.4	0.0
Fresh, Average	1 Serving/25g	184	735	0.6	0.4	81.3	0.0
Garlic, Somerfield*	1oz/28g	192	686	1.0	2.0	75.0	0.0
Reduced Fat, Fresh, Average	1 Serving/15g	55	368	2.3	1.2	39.4	0.2
Salted, Average	1oz/28g	204	729	0.4	0.3	81.1	0.0
Slightly Salted, Organic, Sainsbury's*	1 Serving/10g	72	724	0.5	0.6	80.0	0.0
Slightly Salted, Very Low Fat, Bri, Delight*	Thin Spread/7g	19	265	0.9	10.0	25.0	0.0
Spreadable, Fresh, Average	Thin Spread/7g	51	730	0.4	0.3	80.8	0.0
Spreadable, Reduced Fat, Average	1 Serving/5g	27	540	0.5	0.5	60.0	0.0
With Crushed Garlic, Lurpak*	1 Serving/10g	70	700	1.0	4.0	75.0	0.0

BUTTERMILK,

INFO/WEIGHT	Measure	per Measure KCAL	KCAL	PROT	CARB	FAT	FIBRE
Average	1 Mug/400ml	177	44	4.2	5.9	0.3	0.0
Low Fat, Yoplait*	1 Pot/284ml	133	47	5.2	6.0	0.2	0.0

BUTTON SPROUTS,

INFO/WEIGHT	Measure	per Measure KCAL	KCAL	PROT	CARB	FAT	FIBRE
Raw, Average	1oz/28g	10	37	3.5	2.9	1.3	3.2

BUTTONS,

INFO/WEIGHT	Measure	per Measure KCAL	KCAL	PROT	CARB	FAT	FIBRE
Milk Chocolate, Cadbury's*	1 Treat Pack/14g	74	525	7.6	56.2	29.9	0.0
White, Cadbury's*	1 Bag/32g	171	535	8.8	56.5	30.3	0.0

	Measure INFO/WEIGHT	per Measure KCAL	Nutrition Values per 100g / 100ml				
			KCAL	PROT	CARB	FAT	FIBRE
CABBAGE,							
Boiled, Average	1 Serving/90g	14	15	1.0	2.2	0.3	1.7
Chinese, Raw	1oz/28g	3	12	1.0	1.4	0.2	1.2
Greens, Trimmed, Average	1oz/28g	8	29	2.9	3.0	0.5	3.4
Mash, Eat Smart, Safeway*	½ Pack/225g	146	65	2.0	9.2	1.8	1.7
Medley, Marks & Spencer*	1 Serving/300g	270	90	1.7	2.7	8.2	1.5
Medley, Safeway*	1oz/28g	6	20	1.2	2.1	0.5	1.9
Raw, Average	1oz/28g	6	21	1.3	3.2	0.5	1.9
Red & Cranberry Slaw, Tesco*	½ Pack/125g	75	60	0.7	11.3	1.3	0.0
Red, Average	1 Serving/90g	19	21	1.0	3.7	0.3	2.2
Red, Braised With Red Wine, Marks & Spencer*	½ Pack/150g	180	120	1.4	17.1	4.8	1.0
Red, Pickled, Average	1oz/28g	7	27	0.9	4.6	0.2	1.6
Red, With Apple & Cranberry, TTD, Sainsbury's*	½ Pack/200g	166	83	1.3	12.8	2.9	1.4
Red, With Wine & Cranberies, Waitrose*	1 Serving/200g	210	105	1.2	16.0	4.0	2.3
Savoy, Boiled in Salted Water	1 Serving/90g	15	17	1.1	2.2	0.5	2.0
Savoy, Raw	1 Serving/90g	24	27	2.1	3.9	0.5	3.1
White, Raw, Average	1oz/28g	8	27	1.4	5.0	0.2	2.1
CAKE,							
Action Man, Birthday, Memory Lane Cakes*	1/12 Portion/83g	322	388	3.0	57.0	16.4	0.8
Alabama Chocolate Fudge, Farmfoods*	1/6 Cake/61g	201	329	4.7	55.7	9.7	2.7
Almond Flavour Slices, GFY, Asda*	1 Slice/25g	67	268	4.0	56.0	3.1	0.7
Almond Slices, Lyons*	1 Slice/26.8g	115	426	7.1	41.3	25.8	1.6
Almond Slices, Mr Kipling*	1 Slice/35g	128	366	6.3	53.8	14.0	1.9
Angel Layer, Somerfield*	1 Serving/37.0g	146	395	4.1	51.9	19.0	0.6
Angel Layer, Tesco*	1 Serving/25g	101	403	4.5	57.4	17.3	0.9
Angel Slices, Mr Kipling*	1 Slice/38g	156	410	3.8	58.8	18.2	0.5
Angel, Asda*	1 Serving/46.1g	184	399	4.5	57.0	17.0	0.9
Angel, Co-Op*	1/8 Cake/35g	131	375	4.0	52.0	17.0	0.7
Angel, Sainsbury's*	1/8 Cake/41g	171	417	4.1	55.7	19.8	0.8
Apple & Cinnamon, Oat Break, Go Ahead, McVitie's*	1 Serving/35g	122	349	5.2	67.2	6.6	2.6
Apple Bakes, Go Ahead, McVitie's*	1 Cake/35g	129	368	2.8	74.7	8.3	1.2
Apple Sponge, Marks & Spencer*	1 Serving/95g	247	260	3.7	30.6	13.9	0.8
Apple, Bramley, & Blackberry Crumble, Marks & Spencer*	1/8 Cake/56g	221	395	4.4	54.1	17.9	1.5
Apple, Home Style, Marks & Spencer*	1 Cake/54g	189	350	5.3	49.4	14.7	1.5
Apple, Pret A Manger*	1 Av Pack/120g	432	360	5.3	38.8	21.9	2.1
Apricot & Apple, Trimlyne*	1 Cake/50g	134	267	4.3	58.4	2.7	1.9
Assorted Cup, Sainsbury's*	1 Cake/38g	130	341	2.2	69.3	6.1	0.4
Bakewell Slices, Mr Kipling*	1 Slice/35g	146	416	4.2	53.7	20.5	1.0
Banana & Date Loaf, Starbucks*	1 Slice/105g	292	278	5.9	57.1	2.9	2.7
Banana Loaf, Waitrose*	1 Slice/70g	236	337	5.0	55.2	10.7	1.7
Banana, Date & Walnut Slices, BGTY, Sainsbury's*	1 Slice/28g	78	280	5.3	56.1	4.9	2.2
Battenberg, Lyons*	1 Serving/26g	112	431	6.9	70.3	13.7	1.3
Battenberg, Mini, Mr Kipling*	1 Serving/35g	138	393	3.7	75.0	8.7	0.9
Best Chocolate Orange Explosion, Safeway*	1 Serving/59g	248	421	4.1	48.8	23.3	0.9
Birthday Present, Tesco*	1 Serving/79g	347	439	3.5	66.6	17.6	0.4
Birthday, Marks & Spencer*	1 Serving/60g	240	400	2.3	70.9	11.9	0.8
Birthday, McDonald's*	1 Portion/158g	640	405	2.7	65.4	14.3	1.0
Bites, Jaffa Cake Roll, Mini, McVitie's*	1 Cake/15.9g	62	389	3.7	66.7	12.0	1.4
Butterfly, Mr Kipling*	1 Cake/29g	114	392	4.4	43.4	22.2	0.6
Buttons, Cadbury's*	1 Cake/25g	110	440	7.2	50.0	22.8	0.0
Cadbury Byte, McMini, McDonald's*	1 Byte/14.0g	67	478	6.5	64.7	20.7	1.7
Cafe Latte, Extra Special, Asda*	1 Slice/64.7g	234	360	2.6	38.0	22.0	0.3
Cappuccino, Finest, Tesco*	1oz/28g	105	374	2.8	40.4	22.3	0.2
Caramel Slice, Marks & Spencer*	1 Slice/64g	304	475	4.9	60.4	25.2	2.6

CAKE,

INFO/WEIGHT	Measure	per Measure KCAL	KCAL	PROT	CARB	FAT	FIBRE
Carrot & Apple, Safeway*	1 Serving/50g	158	315	3.2	50.4	11.2	0.8
Carrot & Mango Slices, Eat Smart, Safeway*	1 Slice/31g	95	305	3.4	65.3	2.9	2.3
Carrot & Orange Slices, GFY, Asda*	1 Serving/23.1g	77	334	3.4	74.0	2.7	1.0
Carrot & Orange Slices, Good Intentions, Somerfield*	1 Cake/27g	85	315	4.1	68.0	3.0	1.5
Carrot & Orange Slices, Healthy Eating, Tesco*	1 Slice/29g	75	257	3.0	56.4	2.7	1.9
Carrot & Orange Slices, Healthy Living, Tesco*	1 Slice/29g	80	276	3.1	56.6	2.8	2.1
Carrot & Orange, Extra Special, Asda*	1/6 Cake/65.0g	240	369	4.7	47.0	18.0	0.9
Carrot & Orange, Finest, Tesco*	1 Serving/50g	171	342	4.1	49.1	14.3	1.0
Carrot & Orange, Safeway*	1 Serving/120g	265	221	4.9	26.8	10.0	0.7
Carrot & Orange, Waitrose*	1/6 Cake/47g	165	350	5.3	46.8	15.7	1.8
Carrot & Pecan, Marks & Spencer*	1 Slice/90.4g	329	365	6.4	48.7	16.2	2.3
Carrot & Walnut, Marks & Spencer*	1/6 Cake/82g	279	340	5.8	34.8	19.5	1.5
Carrot Loaf, Starbucks*	1 Slice/100g	352	352	4.7	38.4	19.9	2.3
Carrot Slices, BGTY, Sainsbury's*	1 Slice/27g	81	313	3.4	68.7	2.7	2.4
Carrot Slices, Weight Watchers*	1 Slice/27g	71	263	3.0	56.7	2.7	1.9
Carrot Wedge, Tesco*	1 Pack/175g	576	329	4.6	41.7	16.0	1.5
Carrot, Entenmann's*	1 Serving/40g	156	391	4.1	47.4	20.5	1.5
Carrot, Farmfoods*	1/8 Cake/59g	187	317	3.7	35.4	17.8	1.6
Carrot, Pret A Manger*	1 Av Pack/120g	288	240	2.9	41.6	6.9	0.2
Carrot, Ultimate, Entenmann's*	1/8 Cake/63.8g	235	367	4.7	51.4	15.8	0.3
Champagne Bottle, Tesco*	1 Serving/79.1g	310	393	1.9	75.5	9.3	0.8
Cherry Bakewell Slices, GFY, Asda*	1 Slice/29.1g	98	337	3.5	75.0	2.5	0.8
Cherry Bakewell, Gluten Free, Bakers Delight*	1 Cake/50g	211	422	2.9	66.1	16.3	0.4
Cherry Bakewell, Layer, Asda*	1/8 Cake/50g	210	420	4.4	51.0	22.0	0.6
Cherry Bakewell, Marks & Spencer*	1 Cake/44g	185	420	4.5	61.7	17.7	1.0
Cherry Bakewell, Mini, Sainsbury's*	1 Tart/27.3g	100	370	3.4	62.2	12.0	0.4
Cherry Bakewell, Mr Kipling*	1 Cake/45g	186	414	3.9	59.3	17.9	1.2
Cherry Bakewell, Safeway*	1 Bakewell/47g	203	432	3.5	58.7	20.3	3.9
Cherry Bakewell, Sara Lee*	1/5 Slice/69.9g	228	326	4.1	51.9	11.3	1.4
Cherry Bakewell, Savers, Safeway*	1 Cake/45g	176	391	3.6	60.6	14.9	0.1
Cherry Bakewell, SmartPrice, Asda*	1 Cake/38g	157	413	2.7	60.0	18.0	2.6
Cherry Bakewell, Somerfield*	1 Cake/50g	216	431	3.5	58.7	20.3	3.9
Cherry Bakewell, Tesco*	1 Cake/39g	171	439	3.2	63.3	19.2	1.1
Cherry Bakewell, Waitrose*	1 Tart/43.9g	184	419	3.8	57.4	19.3	2.1
Cherry Bakewell, Weight Watchers*	1 Cake/43g	156	363	3.7	65.1	11.6	3.3
Cherry Genoa, Marks & Spencer*	1oz/28g	99	355	4.5	59.3	10.9	1.6
Cherry, Asda*	1 Slice/37.3g	130	351	4.7	56.0	12.0	0.6
Cherry, Co-Op*	1/8 Cake/47g	195	415	5.0	49.0	22.0	0.5
Cherry, Marks & Spencer*	1 Serving/75g	285	380	5.0	60.6	12.7	0.8
Chewy Fruity Corn Flake, Doves Farm*	1 Bar/40g	155	388	5.8	64.5	14.0	4.5
Chewy Rice Pop & Chocolate, Doves Farm*	1 Bar/35g	156	447	3.9	69.9	20.2	2.3
Chocolate	1oz/28g	128	456	7.4	50.4	26.4	0.0
Chocolate & Brandy Butter, Entenmann's*	1 Portion/38.5g	146	374	3.4	53.5	17.5	2.8
Chocolate & Orange Rolls, Marks & Spencer*	1 Roll/60g	228	380	3.6	27.0	28.4	1.3
Chocolate & Orange Slices, GFY, Asda*	1 Serving/30.2g	95	315	3.2	70.0	2.5	1.3
Chocolate Birthday, Asda*	1/10 Cake/61.1g	281	460	6.0	46.0	28.0	0.9
Chocolate Birthday, Marks & Spencer*	1 Serving/68g	279	410	4.5	43.7	24.1	1.3
Chocolate Birthday, Tesco*	1 Serving/58g	276	475	6.3	50.3	27.6	0.9
Chocolate Box, Asda*	1 Serving/60g	263	439	5.0	53.0	23.0	0.7
Chocolate Brownie, Fudge, Entenmann's*	1/8 Cake/55g	168	306	4.0	62.7	4.4	1.5
Chocolate Caramel Mini Bites, Marks & Spencer*	1 Bite/20.7g	97	460	5.6	53.5	24.6	1.6
Chocolate Chip, Co-Op*	1/6 Cake/62.5g	273	440	5.0	44.0	27.0	0.5
Chocolate Cup, 5% Fat, Sainsbury's*	1 Cake/38g	133	349	2.5	74.8	4.4	1.7

CAKE,	Measure INFO/WEIGHT	per Measure KCAL	Nutrition Values per 100g / 100ml				
			KCAL	PROT	CARB	FAT	FIBRE
Chocolate Cup, BGTY, Sainsbury's*	1 Cake/38g	121	318	2.5	66.5	4.6	0.8
Chocolate Cup, Fabulous Bakin' Boys*	1 Cake/40g	164	410	3.0	44.0	24.0	1.0
Chocolate Cup, Lyons*	1 Cake/39g	125	321	2.4	67.5	4.6	0.8
Chocolate Cupcake, COU, Marks & Spencer*	1 Cake/45g	130	290	4.6	62.2	2.8	4.3
Chocolate Flavour Slice, Eat Smart, Safeway*	1 Slice/28g	95	340	5.3	73.6	2.4	4.0
Chocolate Flavour Slices, GFY, Asda*	2 Slices/55g	141	257	4.3	54.0	2.6	1.4
Chocolate Flavour Slices, Healthy Eating, Tesco*	1 Slice/25g	79	314	4.7	65.5	2.4	3.7
Chocolate Flower Pot, Marks & Spencer*	1 Serving/68.6g	297	430	3.8	60.8	19.3	1.5
Chocolate Fudge & Vanilla Cream, Marks & Spencer*	1/6 Cake/69g	306	450	5.2	49.8	26.0	1.3
Chocolate Fudge Slice, Waitrose*	1 Slice/60g	230	383	4.7	54.6	16.2	1.5
Chocolate Fudge, Classic, Marks & Spencer*	1 Serving/70.9g	195	275	2.8	42.8	10.6	1.1
Chocolate Fudge, Entenmann's*	1 Serving/48g	173	361	4.4	51.8	15.1	0.9
Chocolate Fudge, Safeway*	1 Serving/93.1g	375	403	4.0	53.2	19.3	1.8
Chocolate Fudge, Sainsbury's*	1/8 Cake/98g	402	410	5.5	47.3	22.3	1.9
Chocolate Fudge, Tea Time Treats, Asda*	1 Cake/37.0g	157	424	3.6	53.0	22.0	1.7
Chocolate Heaven, Extra Special, Asda*	1/6 Cake/65.7g	256	388	4.0	48.0	20.0	1.0
Chocolate Indulgence, Finest, Tesco*	1 Slice/52g	203	390	3.8	47.8	20.4	0.4
Chocolate Log, Iceland*	1 Cake/31g	157	505	5.3	48.0	32.4	1.2
Chocolate Orange Slices, BGTY, Sainsbury's*	1 Slice/30g	90	301	3.9	62.8	4.8	1.3
Chocolate Orange Slices, Weight Watchers*	1 Slice/27g	80	297	5.6	63.9	2.1	2.8
Chocolate Orange, Sponge, Asda*	1 Serving/70g	298	425	4.9	42.9	26.0	3.0
Chocolate Party, Marks & Spencer*	1 Serving/60.8g	241	395	4.6	46.9	20.8	1.1
Chocolate Party, Tesco*	1 Slice/62g	244	394	4.6	46.3	21.2	0.9
Chocolate Roll, Sainsbury's*	1 Slice/50g	210	420	5.0	54.0	20.4	3.3
Chocolate Sensation, Sainsbury's*	1 Serving/92.0g	320	348	3.7	40.0	19.2	2.3
Chocolate Slice, Go Ahead, McVitie's*	1 Slice/32g	94	293	4.5	49.4	8.2	1.9
Chocolate Sponge Roll, Marks & Spencer*	¼ Cake/66g	251	380	3.9	50.5	18.4	1.8
Chocolate Sponge Sandwich, Co-Op*	1/6 Cake/37g	131	355	5.0	51.0	15.0	2.0
Chocolate Sponge, Less Than 5% Fat, Asda*	1 Sponge/110g	198	180	4.4	32.0	3.8	1.1
Chocolate Tiffin, Sainsbury's*	1 Cake/61g	184	301	2.7	29.8	19.0	1.3
Chocolate Truffle, Extra Special, Asda*	1 Serving/103g	402	390	5.0	34.0	26.0	1.8
Chocolate Victoria Sponge, Co-Op*	1 Slice/61g	201	330	5.0	42.0	16.0	1.0
Chocolate With Butter Icing	1oz/28g	135	481	5.7	50.9	29.7	0.0
Chocolate, Double Dream, Nestle*	1 Serving/150g	638	425	5.0	44.7	25.1	0.9
Chocolate, Fudge, The Cake Shop*	1 Cake/37.1g	178	480	3.7	50.5	29.2	1.3
Chocolate, Low Fat, Safeway*	1 Slice/73.4g	176	241	5.8	45.0	4.8	1.3
Chocolate, Mini Roll, Safeway*	1 Roll/40g	180	450	0.0	53.5	23.9	2.2
Chocolate, Morrisons*	1 Serving/31.5g	157	505	5.3	48.0	32.4	1.2
Chocolate, Part Of Tea Time Selection, Iceland*	1 Cake/31g	144	464	4.5	54.1	25.5	2.0
Chocolate, Sainsbury's*	1 Serving/30g	119	395	4.1	52.6	18.5	1.3
Chocolate, Sara Lee*	¼ Cake/88g	339	385	4.1	54.3	16.8	0.0
Chocolate, Smarties*	Per Slice/60g	261	435	5.8	53.8	21.8	0.5
Chocolate, Thorntons*	1 Serving/87g	408	469	5.2	47.1	28.8	0.6
Chocolate, Viennese, Marks & Spencer*	1oz/28g	105	375	4.4	54.1	13.6	1.6
Chocolate, White Button, Asda*	1 Cake/30g	117	390	5.0	44.0	21.0	2.0
Chocolate, With White Chocolate, The Cake Shop*	1 Cake/29g	146	503	4.6	49.2	32.0	1.2
Chorley, Asda*	1 Cake/60g	269	449	6.0	59.0	21.0	2.2
Choux Buns, Fresh Cream, Tesco*	1 Bun/95g	340	358	4.9	28.5	24.9	0.9
Choux Buns, Marks & Spencer*	1oz/28g	89	317	5.4	25.6	22.2	0.3
Christmas Slices, Weight Watchers*	1 Slice/40.1g	136	339	4.4	66.0	6.4	3.0
Christmas, Conoisseur, Marks & Spencer*	1 Slice/60g	216	360	4.1	64.7	9.2	3.3
Christmas, Iced, Slices, Tesco*	1 Slice/45g	168	369	2.9	67.6	9.6	1.2
Christmas, Marks & Spencer*	1 Slice/60g	219	365	3.8	67.3	8.8	2.6

CAKE,

INFO/WEIGHT	Measure	per Measure KCAL	KCAL	PROT	CARB	FAT	FIBRE
Christmas, Rich Fruit, All Iced, Sainsbury's*	1/16 Cake/85g	307	361	4.0	66.4	8.9	1.5
Christmas, Rich Fruit, Organic, Tesco*	1 Serving/75.5g	284	374	3.9	67.1	10.0	2.0
Christmas, TTD, Sainsbury's*	1/16 Cake/85g	315	371	3.7	67.1	8.9	1.3
Classic Lemon Drizzle, Marks & Spencer*	1/6 Cake/67.5g	255	375	4.7	55.0	15.3	0.6
Coconut	1 Slice/70g	304	434	6.7	51.2	23.8	2.5
Coconut Delight, Burton's*	1 Cake/25.1g	104	415	4.1	65.0	15.4	1.6
Coconut Macaroons, Sainsbury's*	1 Macaroon/33g	144	436	4.8	65.1	17.3	1.6
Coconut Snowball, Bobby's*	1 Cake/18.3g	78	436	2.2	57.3	22.1	0.0
Coconut Sponge, Mini Classics, Mr Kipling*	1 Cake/38g	155	409	3.7	47.0	22.9	0.9
Coffee & Walnut Slices, Healthy Eating,Tesco*	1 Slice/23g	69	301	4.4	65.7	2.3	2.8
Coffee & Walnut, Classic, Marks & Spencer*	1 Serving/70.8g	309	435	4.3	50.3	24.3	1.6
Coffee Sponge Roll, Marks & Spencer*	1 Serving/40g	150	375	3.5	51.1	17.3	0.6
Coffee, Entenmann's*	1 Portion/41g	159	388	4.0	54.7	17.3	0.6
Coffee, Iced, Marks & Spencer*	1 Slice/33g	135	410	4.4	54.5	19.6	1.6
Colin The Caterpillar, Marks & Spencer*	1 Slice/60g	234	390	5.3	57.2	21.3	1.3
Country Slices, Good Intentions, Somerfield*	1 Cake/22g	70	318	5.5	70.0	1.8	1.8
Country Slices, Mr Kipling*	1oz/28g	108	385	4.3	56.5	15.7	1.1
Cream Oysters, Marks & Spencer*	1 Oyster/72g	227	315	3.6	27.5	21.2	3.0
Cream Slices, Marks & Spencer*	1 Slice/80g	310	387	2.3	45.7	22.9	0.6
Crispy Fruit Slices, Apple & Sultana, Go Ahead, McVitie's*	1 Slice/14g	54	386	6.0	72.7	7.9	3.3
Crispy Fruit Slices, Forest Fruit, Go Ahead, McVitie's*	1 Biscuit/14g	56	400	5.5	73.0	8.8	3.7
Cup, Marks & Spencer*	1 Cake/55g	195	355	2.8	71.5	6.5	0.5
Custard Slices, Tesco*	1 Slice/108g	320	296	2.4	37.5	15.2	0.5
D'Oh Nuts, Asda*	1 Cake/50g	186	372	4.0	47.0	19.0	0.0
Date & Walnut Loaf, Sainsbury's*	1/10 Slice/40g	148	371	6.7	40.1	20.4	1.0
Date & Walnut Slices, Healthy Living, Tesco*	1 Slice/24g	74	308	5.4	67.0	2.0	1.4
Date & Walnut, Trimlyne*	1 Slice/50g	135	269	5.7	53.8	4.9	1.8
Double Chocolate Brownies, Weight Watchers*	1 Pot/83g	153	184	4.5	33.3	3.6	2.2
Double Chocolate Ganache, Marks & Spencer*	1/12 Cake/61g	281	460	5.9	46.1	27.6	2.5
Double Chocolate Wedge, Tesco*	1 Piece/100g	416	416	5.0	53.4	20.3	0.9
Dundee, Co-Op*	1/8 Cake/71g	238	335	5.0	53.0	11.0	2.0
Dundee, Somerfield*	1/10 Cake/75g	254	339	5.0	57.0	11.0	0.0
Easter Lemon Bakewells, Morrisons*	1 Cake/45g	186	413	3.1	64.8	15.7	1.8
Eccles	1 Cake/45g	214	475	3.9	59.3	26.4	1.6
Eccles, Weight Watchers*	1 Cake/48g	190	396	4.4	57.5	16.5	2.0
Fairy, Iced, Somerfield*	1 Cake/15.1g	59	392	4.9	62.9	13.4	1.4
Fairy, Mini, Tesco*	1 Cake/13g	53	424	6.1	54.6	20.1	1.3
Fairy, SmartPrice, Asda*	1 Cake/15g	66	438	6.0	54.0	22.0	1.0
Fairy, Value,Tesco*	1 Cake/16g	70	436	6.1	53.7	21.9	1.0
Farmhouse Fruit, Bakers Delight*	1oz/28g	107	381	5.2	55.5	15.3	2.1
Farmhouse Slice, Weight Watchers*	1 Slice/23g	73	317	5.5	64.9	4.0	1.3
Figfuls, Go Ahead, McVitie's*	1 Figful/15g	56	365	4.2	76.8	4.6	2.9
Flake, Cadbury's*	1 Cake/26g	114	439	6.0	54.1	22.1	0.7
Fondant Fancies, Marks & Spencer*	1 Cake/34.5g	148	435	2.4	76.5	13.4	0.5
Fondant Fancies, Sainsbury's*	1 Cake/27g	95	353	2.4	65.7	9.0	0.4
French Fancies, Mr Kipling*	1 Cake/28g	100	356	2.3	65.1	9.6	0.4
Fresh Cream Bramley Apple Sponge, Tesco*	1/6 Slice/43g	130	303	3.6	35.4	16.3	1.0
Fruit Cake With Marzipan & Icing, Asda*	1/12 Slice/76g	280	369	3.9	68.0	9.0	0.0
Fruit Slice, Value, Tesco*	1 Slice/22.6g	85	372	4.0	48.7	17.7	1.3
Fruit, Fully Iced, Luxury Rich, Co-Op*	1oz/28g	99	355	3.0	64.0	9.0	4.0
Fruit, Healthy Selection, Somerfield*	1oz/28g	73	260	5.0	55.0	2.0	0.0
Fruit, Plain, Retail	1 Slice/90g	319	354	5.1	57.9	12.9	0.0
Fruit, Rich, Connoisseur, Somerfield*	1oz/28g	91	326	4.0	54.0	10.0	0.0

CAKE,

	Measure INFO/WEIGHT	per Measure KCAL	Nutrition Values per 100g / 100ml				
			KCAL	PROT	CARB	FAT	FIBRE
Fruit, Rich, Iced	1 Slice/70g	249	356	4.1	62.7	11.4	1.7
Fruit, Rich, Retail	1 Slice/70g	225	322	4.9	50.7	12.5	1.7
Fudge, Pret A Manger*	1 Pack/140g	537	384	4.1	46.1	20.3	1.3
Fudgy Chocolate Slices, COU, Marks & Spencer*	1 Slice/36g	95	265	4.6	66.4	2.2	2.1
Genoa, Home Bake, McVitie's*	1oz/28g	107	383	4.7	55.9	15.6	1.4
Genoa, Tesco*	1 Serving/50g	162	324	4.0	58.6	8.2	3.2
Ginger Drizzle, Iced, Co-Op*	1/6 Cake/64.5g	226	350	3.0	58.0	12.0	1.0
Ginger, Marks & Spencer*	1/6 Cake/41g	156	380	6.3	62.3	11.5	1.7
Glitzy Bag, Birthday, Tesco*	1 Serving/81g	314	388	2.1	75.9	8.5	0.6
Happy Birthday, Sainsbury's*	1 Slice/50g	207	414	2.8	64.5	16.1	0.6
Heavenly Chocolate Brownie, Safeway*	1 Pack/300g	900	300	6.2	38.5	13.4	0.8
Iced Madeira, Sainsbury's*	1/8 Cake/47g	182	388	3.6	61.6	14.1	0.7
Jamaica Ginger With Lemon Filling, McVitie's*	1 Cake/32.9g	143	434	4.0	48.3	25.0	0.8
Jamaica Ginger, McVitie's*	1 Serving/75g	291	388	3.4	61.2	14.4	1.2
Jammy Strawberry Rolls, Mini, Cadbury's*	1 Roll/29g	119	411	4.9	59.8	16.5	0.5
Lemon Bakewell, Mr Kipling*	1 Cake/48.0g	195	407	2.6	65.0	15.2	0.7
Lemon Buttercream & Lemon Curd, The Cake Shop*	1 Cake/28g	124	444	3.5	43.4	27.8	0.6
Lemon Cup Cakes, COU, Marks & Spencer*	1 Cake/42.6g	131	305	3.3	68.1	2.1	2.0
Lemon Drizzle Cake, Asda*	1 Serving/50g	150	299	2.8	45.0	12.0	0.4
Lemon Drizzle, Marks & Spencer*	1/6 Cake/63g	230	365	4.2	55.8	13.9	1.4
Lemon Iced Madeira, Co-Op*	1 Cake/290g	1131	390	4.0	53.0	18.0	0.6
Lemon Madeira, Half Moon, Dan Cake*	1 Slice/50g	215	430	3.5	59.0	20.0	0.0
Lemon Slices, BGTY, Sainsbury's*	1 Slice/26.0g	84	323	3.7	74.0	1.4	1.3
Lemon Slices, Healthy Eating, Tesco*	1 Slice/26g	86	329	3.4	69.1	2.6	3.0
Lemon Slices, Mr Kipling*	1oz/28g	117	417	4.1	58.2	16.3	0.0
Lemon Slices, Sponge, Mr Kipling*	1 Slice/30g	119	397	4.1	58.5	16.2	0.0
Lemon Smoothie Bake, Go Ahead, McVitie's*	1 Bar/35g	130	372	3.0	75.1	8.1	1.0
Lemon Tartlette, Go Ahead, McVitie's*	1 Cake/45g	161	357	3.7	67.9	9.5	1.1
Lemon, Entenmann's*	1 Serving/55.6g	214	383	3.7	56.9	15.7	1.1
Lemon, Half Moon, Bobby's*	1/6 Cake/60g	244	406	4.1	55.7	18.4	0.0
Lemon, Home Bake, McVitie's*	1oz/28g	108	384	4.6	53.9	18.2	1.0
Lemon, Low Fat, Weight Watchers*	1 Cake/26g	79	304	3.7	68.8	1.6	3.5
Leo the Lion, Birthday, Asda*	1 Slice/80.8g	326	402	2.6	62.0	16.0	0.5
Madeira	1 Slice/40g	157	393	5.4	58.4	16.9	0.9
Madeira, All Butter, Sainsbury's*	1 Serving/30g	116	388	5.2	47.4	19.7	0.8
Madeira, Coffee Iced, Tesco*	1 Serving/50g	215	429	3.8	62.1	18.4	0.9
Madeira, Tesco*	1 Serving/50g	197	394	5.5	57.9	15.6	1.2
Manor House, Mr Kipling*	1 Serving/69.2g	276	400	5.3	49.7	20.0	1.4
Marble, Home Bake, McVitie's*	1oz/28g	115	411	3.7	56.9	18.8	0.9
Mini Eggs, Cadbury's*	1 Cake/26.2g	109	420	5.3	52.9	21.1	0.0
Mini Rolls, Blackforest, Weight Watchers*	1 Cake/23.8g	90	374	5.3	58.9	14.2	4.4
Mini Rolls, Cadbury's*	1 Roll/26g	113	434	5.5	55.6	20.6	0.6
Mini Rolls, Chocolate & Vanilla, Somerfield*	1oz/28g	112	399	5.0	62.0	15.0	0.0
Mini Rolls, Chocolate, Tesco*	1 Roll/31g	137	442	6.0	56.3	21.4	0.8
Mini Rolls, Chocolate, Weight Watchers*	1 Cake/23g	85	371	5.3	61.9	15.0	2.0
Mini Rolls, Jaffa Cake, McVitie's*	1 Cake/28g	106	379	3.5	67.5	10.5	0.0
Mini Rolls, Juicy Orange, Cadbury's*	1 Cake/28g	110	390	5.0	55.0	16.8	0.0
Mini Rolls, Milk Chocolate Orange, Shapers, Boots*	1 Roll/25g	97	386	4.6	64.0	12.0	2.4
Mini Rolls, Rolo, Nestle*	1 Cake/29g	111	388	4.8	49.5	19.0	1.0
Orange & Ginger, Oat Break, Go Ahead, McVitie's*	1 Cake/35g	121	347	5.2	67.1	6.4	2.6
Orange & Lemon, Frozen, Iceland*	1/4 Cake/57g	85	150	1.6	18.0	7.9	0.1
Orange Marmalade Loaf, Aldi*	1 Slice/33.0g	88	267	4.5	57.4	2.2	1.8
Orange Marmalade, Marks & Spencer*	1 Slice/50g	195	390	3.6	53.2	18.3	1.8

CAKE,

INFO/WEIGHT		Measure per Measure KCAL	Nutrition Values per 100g / 100ml KCAL	PROT	CARB	FAT	FIBRE
Party Bake, Marks & Spencer*	1/15 Cake/59.7g	231	385	4.0	46.6	20.2	0.9
Party, Asda*	1 Serving/56.5g	240	421	2.3	67.0	16.0	0.4
Pecan Pie, Pret A Manger*	1 Av Pack/70g	333	476	6.1	44.4	30.3	0.7
Piece Of Cake, Birthday, Marks & Spencer*	1 Serving/85g	395	465	4.3	39.7	28.7	0.9
Pink Cup Cakes, Marks & Spencer*	1 Cake/39g	160	410	2.5	81.3	8.5	0.6
Raisin, Dernys*	1 Cake/45g	175	388	5.0	54.0	17.0	0.0
Raspberry Smoothie Bake, Go Ahead, McVitie's*	1 Bar/35g	131	373	3.1	74.9	8.2	1.4
Raspberry Sponge, Marks & Spencer*	1oz/28g	58	207	1.0	18.6	14.3	0.8
Rich Choc' Roll, Cadbury's*	1/6 Portion/39g	149	381	4.8	50.2	15.6	1.0
Rock	1 Sm Cake/40g	158	396	5.4	60.5	16.4	1.5
Rollers, Culi d'Or*	1 Roll/20.8g	69	330	5.8	50.0	12.0	0.0
Rum Baba	1oz/28g	62	223	3.5	32.2	8.1	0.8
Seriously Chocolatey Celebration, Sainsbury's*	1/8 Cake/77g	336	437	6.3	45.0	25.7	0.3
Shrek Birthday, Tesco*	1/16 Cake/72g	248	344	3.3	64.0	12.2	0.5
Snowball, Chocolate, Tunnock's*	1 Snowball/25g	97	388	3.9	47.0	21.8	0.0
Snowballs, Sainsbury's*	1 Snowball/18g	80	445	2.5	55.6	23.0	3.6
Sponge	1 Slice/53g	243	459	6.4	52.4	26.3	0.9
Sponge With Butter Icing	1 Slice/65g	319	490	4.5	52.4	30.6	0.6
Sponge, Jam Filled	1 Slice/65g	196	302	4.2	64.2	4.9	1.8
Spooky, Birthday, Memory Lane*	1 Slice/75g	295	393	3.5	50.8	19.5	0.7
St. Clements, Finest, Tesco*	1 Serving/49g	194	395	3.1	47.2	21.5	0.4
Stem Ginger, 96% Fat Free, Trimlyne*	¼ Cake/62.5g	170	273	4.4	58.1	3.6	1.2
Sticky Toffee Slices, Eat Smart, Safeway*	1 Cake/85g	259	305	3.6	65.8	2.7	1.3
Stollen, Christmas Range, Tesco*	1oz/28g	99	355	5.0	52.9	13.7	1.8
Stollen, Marks & Spencer*	2 Slices/175g	656	375	7.3	46.3	17.0	2.4
Strawberry Sponge Roll, Marks & Spencer*	1/6 Cake/48.5g	158	330	2.8	58.0	9.5	0.8
Sultana & Cherry Slice, Co-Op*	1oz/28g	87	310	3.0	48.0	12.0	2.0
Sultana & Cherry, Tesco*	1 Cake/37g	124	334	4.7	54.4	10.8	2.5
Sultana, Apple & Cranberry, 99% Fat Free, Trimlyne*,	1/6 Cake/66.6g	130	195	4.6	45.5	0.9	3.3
Summer Fruit Cream, GFY, Asda*	1 Serving/74.0g	165	223	3.6	41.0	4.9	2.5
Summer Strawberry Bakes, Go Ahead, McVitie's*	1 Bar/35g	128	367	2.7	75.1	8.0	1.0
Swiss Roll	1oz/28g	77	276	7.2	55.5	4.4	0.8
Swiss Roll, Chocolate Flavour, Value, Tesco*	1 Slice/20g	79	394	5.5	49.2	19.5	1.4
Swiss Roll, Chocolate, Individual	1 Roll/26g	88	337	4.3	58.1	11.3	0.0
Swiss Roll, Chocolate, Jumbo, Safeway*	1/12 Roll/35g	129	369	4.1	47.1	18.2	0.9
Swiss Roll, Chocolate, Lyons*	1 Serving/50g	190	379	4.3	47.0	19.3	0.9
Swiss Roll, Chocolate, Mini, Tesco*	1 Roll/22g	87	396	4.6	61.0	14.8	0.0
Swiss Roll, Chocolate, Somerfield*	¼ Roll/43.5g	167	384	6.0	55.0	16.0	0.0
Swiss Roll, Raspberry & Vanilla, Morrisons*	1 Serving/28g	98	350	4.2	61.8	9.5	0.0
Swiss Roll, Raspberry, Lyons*	1 Swiss Roll/175g	485	277	5.2	60.6	1.4	0.0
Swiss Roll, Raspberry, Sainsbury's*	1 Serving/35g	105	301	3.5	67.0	2.1	1.1
Swiss Roll, Raspberry, Somerfield*	1 Swiss Roll/80g	245	306	5.0	66.0	3.0	0.0
Swiss Roll, Strawberry, Luxury, Somerfield*	1oz/28g	84	301	4.0	62.0	4.0	0.0
Syrup & Ginger, Tesco*	1 Serving/32g	134	420	4.5	51.4	21.8	0.7
Tangy Lemon Trickle, Marks & Spencer*	1 Slice/75g	281	375	4.7	47.4	18.8	1.1
The Ultimate Carrot Passion, Entenmann's*	1 Slice/52g	206	403	4.6	42.4	24.3	1.0
Toffee & Pecan Loaf, Safeway*	1/6 Cake/62g	225	363	3.6	35.5	22.9	0.5
Toffee & Pecan Slices, Marks & Spencer*	1 Slice/36g	160	445	4.7	54.0	23.7	1.3
Toffee Flavour Slices, Low Fat, Weight Watchers*	1 Slice/27g	80	297	4.2	63.9	2.6	3.2
Toffee Fudge, Entenmann's*	1 Serving/65g	274	421	3.4	53.0	21.7	0.5
Toffee Temptation, Tesco*	1 Slice/67g	228	340	2.9	39.1	19.1	0.3
Toffee, Slices, Healthy Living, Tesco*	1 Cake/24g	76	315	4.5	65.0	2.6	1.6
Toffee, Thorntons*	1/6 Cake/70.1g	302	431	4.6	49.2	24.0	0.8

C

	Measure	per Measure	Nutrition Values per 100g / 100ml				
	INFO/WEIGHT	KCAL	KCAL	PROT	CARB	FAT	FIBRE
CAKE,							
Triple Chocolate, TTD, Sainsbury's*	1/8 Cake/52g	210	412	4.7	42.6	24.7	0.5
Turkish Delight, Fry's*	1 Cake/26g	96	371	4.5	62.4	10.8	0.5
Vanilla Slices, Marks & Spencer*	1 Slice/89g	336	377	2.6	42.6	18.5	0.5
Victoria Ring, Asda*	1 Serving/50g	153	305	6.0	59.0	5.0	1.3
Victoria Sandwich, Classic, Large, Marks & Spencer*	1/10 Cake/65.8g	261	395	5.1	49.5	19.6	2.3
Victoria Sponge Sandwich, Somerfield*	1oz/28g	112	400	4.0	53.0	19.0	0.0
Victoria Sponge, Fresh Cream, Tesco*	1 Slice/46.7g	157	334	3.9	40.8	17.3	0.7
Victoria Sponge, Lemon, Co-Op*	1 Slice/42g	151	360	4.0	44.0	19.0	0.7
Victoria Sponge, Mini, Mr Kipling*	1 Cake/37g	142	383	3.8	48.7	19.2	0.6
Viennese Whirl, Lemon, Mr Kipling*	1 Cake/28g	115	409	4.2	62.2	15.9	0.7
Viennese Whirl, Mr Kipling*	1 Whirl/28g	139	497	4.1	51.5	30.5	1.2
Viennese Whirl, Tesco*	1 Cake/39g	181	465	4.0	53.2	26.2	1.2
Viennese, Marks & Spencer*	1 Cake/50.5g	252	495	4.1	58.9	28.0	2.8
Walnut & Coffee, Co-Op*	¼ Cake/65g	254	390	5.0	47.0	20.0	0.7
Walnut Layer, Somerfield*	¼ Cake/77.5g	295	381	6.0	45.0	20.0	0.0
Welsh	1oz/28g	121	431	5.6	61.8	19.6	1.5
Wild Blueberry & Apple, Bakers Delight*	1oz/28g	99	354	4.6	48.8	15.6	1.5
Xmas Pudding, Tesco*	1 Cake/16.7g	59	349	3.3	60.5	9.3	1.4
Yoghurt & Berry Loaf, Low Fat, Starbucks*	1 Cake/94g	254	270	5.3	50.8	5.1	1.7
Yoghurt Berry Burst, Finest, Tesco*	1 Slice/47.6g	204	426	4.6	48.4	23.8	0.9
Yorkshire Parkin, Bakers Delight*	1oz/28g	111	395	5.1	60.3	14.8	1.5
Yum Yum, Marks & Spencer*	1 Cake/37g	155	420	5.8	42.2	25.6	1.8
Yum Yums, Tesco*	1 Cake/61g	232	380	6.1	51.6	16.6	1.7
CAKE BAR,							
Blueberry, Trimlyne*	1 Cake/50g	142	283	3.9	64.0	2.2	2.2
Bounty, McVitie's*	1 Cake/36g	166	461	5.1	55.2	24.5	0.0
Caramel, Cadbury's*	1 Bar/26g	107	411	6.4	57.0	16.8	0.0
Choc Chip, Go Ahead, McVitie's*	1 Bar/28g	100	356	6.4	56.9	12.1	1.0
Choc Chip, Mini, Go Ahead, McVitie's	1 Bar/27g	93	343	5.7	55.3	12.1	0.9
Chocolate & Orange, Go Ahead, McVitie's*	1 Cake Bar/33g	109	330	4.3	64.9	6.0	1.0
Chocolate Chip, Mr Kipling*	1 Bar/33g	147	444	5.7	45.7	26.5	0.6
Chocolate Chip, Sainsbury's*	1 Cake Bar/25g	108	430	6.1	51.2	22.3	0.6
Chocolate Dream, Go Ahead, McVitie's*	1 Bar/36g	141	391	4.6	63.2	13.4	0.9
Crunchie, Cadbury's*	1 Cake Bar/32g	147	460	5.9	58.3	22.6	0.0
Double Chocolate, Free From, Sainsbury's*	1 Cake/50.1g	196	391	4.2	58.2	15.7	1.0
Flake, Cadbury's*	1 Cake/22g	97	442	6.5	51.8	23.3	0.5
Fruit & Nut Crisp, Go Ahead, McVitie's*	1 Bar/22g	95	430	5.3	71.3	13.7	1.7
Fudge, Cadbury's*	1 Pack/52.4g	218	420	5.7	60.3	17.6	0.0
Galaxy, McVitie's*	1oz/28g	138	494	5.1	57.5	27.0	0.3
Golden Syrup, McVitie's*	1 Mini Cake/33g	127	385	3.6	60.2	14.4	1.2
Jaffa Cake, McVitie's	1 Bar/31g	126	408	3.9	59.0	17.4	0.0
Jamaica Ginger, McVitie's*	1 Mini Cake/33g	128	388	3.5	60.2	14.7	1.2
Milk Chocolate, Cadbury's*	1 Bar/35g	140	401	6.8	48.8	19.8	0.8
Milky Way, McVitie's*	1 Bar/26g	138	530	5.3	53.8	32.6	0.2
Rich Chocolate, Trimlyne*	1 Serving/40g	115	288	5.3	59.3	4.3	2.3
CAKE MIX,							
Cheesecake, Strawberry, Real, Green's*	1 Serving	254	253	3.9	30.6	12.8	0.6
Chocolate, Greens*	¼ Cake/259g	3750	361	5.8	54.6	13.3	1.4
Dennis, Greens*	1 Cake/17.3g	54	319	4.6	57.8	7.7	0.0
Free From, Sainsbury's*	1 Serving/50g	173	346	1.3	84.4	0.3	2.2
CALAMARI,							
Battered With Tartar Sauce Dip, Tesco*	1 Pack/210g	573	273	8.9	15.4	19.5	0.6
Battered, Marks & Spencer*	1 Pack/160g	424	265	14.3	15.8	16.1	0.7

	Measure INFO/WEIGHT	per Measure KCAL	Nutrition Values per 100g / 100ml				
			KCAL	PROT	CARB	FAT	FIBRE
CALAMARI,							
Marks & Spencer*	1oz/28g	65	231	13.9	11.5	14.4	0.5
Rings In Batter, Waitrose*	½ Pack/85g	227	267	13.9	14.2	17.2	0.6
CALZONE,							
Bolognese, Weight Watchers*	1 Calzone/88.1g	178	202	11.7	31.2	3.4	4.3
Cheese & Tomato, Weight Watchers*	1 Calzone/88.0g	191	217	11.3	33.4	4.3	3.4
Ham & Gruyere, Asda*	1 Serving/280g	661	236	10.0	31.0	8.0	2.7
CAMPINO,							
Oranges & Cream, Bendicks*	1oz/28g	116	416	0.1	85.8	8.1	0.0
Strawberries & Cream, Bendicks*	1oz/28g	117	418	0.1	86.2	8.1	0.0
CANAPES,							
Caponata, Puff Pastry, Occasions, Sainsbury's*	1 Square/12g	30	249	4.1	22.9	15.7	2.1
Spinach & Ricotta, Puff Pastry, Occasions, Sainsbury's*	1 Square/12g	35	290	10.1	19.3	19.1	1.5
CANNELLONI,							
Beef, BGTY, Sainsbury's*	1 Pack/300g	249	83	5.5	10.1	2.3	1.7
Beef, Geat Value, Asda*	1 Pack/400g	384	96	6.0	12.0	2.7	1.6
Beef, Healthy Living, Tesco*	1 Pack/340g	323	95	6.4	11.9	2.4	1.5
Beef, Italiano, Tesco*	1 Serving/340g	442	130	5.3	12.4	6.6	0.7
Chicken & Pesto, Italian, Sainsbury's*	1 Pack/450g	675	150	6.1	14.4	7.5	1.1
Findus*	1 Pack/342g	445	130	5.6	11.1	6.7	1.0
Five Cheese & Spinach, Finest, Tesco*	½ Pack/300g	468	156	7.0	9.6	9.9	1.7
Iceland*	1 Pack/400g	584	146	7.2	13.0	7.2	0.6
Marks & Spencer*	1 Pack/400g	540	135	7.4	7.8	8.1	2.1
Mediterranean Vegetable, Waitrose*	1 Serving/170g	330	194	9.7	18.7	9.0	1.9
Mushroom, Italian, Sainsbury's*	1 Pack/449.6g	599	133	5.2	12.5	6.9	0.5
Parmesan & Basil, Marks & Spencer*	1 Pack/360g	504	140	5.9	11.4	7.9	0.8
Pork, Marks & Spencer*	1 Pack/400g	460	115	6.2	8.7	6.2	1.1
Ricotta & Spinach, COU, Marks & Spencer*	1 Pack/360g	288	80	5.8	9.7	1.9	1.5
Ricotta & Spinach, Co-Op*	1 Pack/340g	357	105	5.0	10.0	5.0	3.0
Ricotta & Spinach, Waitrose*	½ Pack/170g	323	190	10.2	21.9	6.9	1.2
Roasted Vegetable, Morrisons*	1 Pack/350g	312	89	3.9	12.5	2.5	2.3
Safeway*	1 Serving/100g	144	144	7.5	13.4	6.7	1.5
Smoked Salmon & Spinach, Sainsbury's*	1 Pack/450g	599	133	5.7	13.5	6.2	0.4
Spinach & Ricotta, BGTY, Sainsbury's*	1 Serving/300g	297	99	4.9	15.9	1.7	1.0
Spinach & Ricotta, Eat Smart, Safeway*	1 Pack/350g	333	95	6.2	12.0	2.2	1.3
Spinach & Ricotta, Frozen, Sainsbury's*	1 Pack/350g	536	153	6.4	14.5	7.7	1.1
Spinach & Ricotta, GFY, Asda*	1 Pack/303g	418	138	6.0	21.0	3.3	0.5
Spinach & Ricotta, Good Intentions, Somerfield*	1 Serving/400g	366	92	5.3	12.2	2.4	2.1
Spinach & Ricotta, Healthy Choice, Asda*	1 Pack/400g	448	112	4.0	15.0	4.0	0.5
Spinach & Ricotta, Healthy Eating, Tesco*	1 Pack/340g	326	96	4.5	13.7	2.6	1.3
Spinach & Ricotta, Healthy Living, Tesco*	1 Pack/340g	296	87	4.7	12.3	2.1	1.1
Spinach & Ricotta, Italiano, Tesco*	1 Serving/340g	377	111	4.2	12.5	4.9	1.2
Spinach & Ricotta, Italiano, Tesco*	1 Pack/425g	510	120	4.7	12.4	5.7	0.9
Spinach & Ricotta, Ross*	1 Pack/300g	300	100	4.3	13.7	3.1	0.5
Spinach & Ricotta, Safeway*	1 Pack/401g	565	141	6.5	14.4	6.4	0.4
Spinach & Ricotta, Sainsbury's*	1 Pack/288g	372	129	5.1	10.5	7.4	1.2
Spinach & Ricotta, Somerfield*	1 Pack/300g	393	131	5.0	13.0	7.0	0.0
Spinach & Ricotta, Tesco*	1 Pack/340g	490	144	4.5	6.4	11.2	0.5
Spinach & Wild Mushroom, Linda McCartney*	1 Pack/340g	381	112	4.9	14.1	4.0	1.7
Value, Tesco*	1 Serving/250g	320	128	6.6	10.0	6.8	1.4
Vegetarian, Tesco*	1 Pack/400g	552	138	5.3	9.8	8.6	1.5
CAPPELLETTI,							
Cheese & Tomato, Tesco*	¼ Pack/125g	405	324	14.5	52.3	6.3	2.5
Chicken & Ham, Fresh, Safeway*	½ Pack/177g	320	181	9.7	27.7	3.5	1.8

	Measure INFO/WEIGHT	per Measure KCAL	Nutrition Values per 100g / 100ml				
			KCAL	PROT	CARB	FAT	FIBRE
CAPPELLETTI,							
Fresh, Sainsbury's*	1 Serving/125g	294	235	12.9	33.5	5.5	2.7
Meat, Italian, Somerfield*	½ Pack/125g	331	265	13.6	38.5	6.3	2.4
CARAMAC,							
Nestle*	1 Bar/30g	163	563	5.8	54.4	35.8	0.0
CARAMBOLA,							
Average	1oz/28g	9	32	0.5	7.3	0.3	1.3
CARAMEL,							
Cadbury's*	1 Bar/50g	240	480	4.3	61.3	24.3	0.0
Egg, Cadbury's*	1 Egg/39g	191	490	4.3	58.9	26.1	0.0
Mighty, Asda*	1 Serving/40g	186	464	5.0	66.0	20.0	1.5
CAROB POWDER,							
Average	1 Tsp/2g	3	159	4.9	37.0	0.1	0.0
CARROT & SWEDE,							
Diced, For Mashing, Average	½ Pack/250g	58	23	0.6	4.7	0.3	1.9
Mash, From Supermarket, Average	1oz/28g	26	92	1.3	10.4	5.0	1.3
Mash, Healthy Range, Average	1 Serving/150g	98	66	1.3	8.6	2.8	2.1
CARROTS,							
& Cauliflower, Marks & Spencer*	1 Serving/335g	74	22	0.6	4.4	0.4	2.3
& Mange Tout, Tendersteam, Marks & Spencer*	½ Pack/100g	35	35	2.9	5.6	0.2	2.1
& Peas, Sainsbury's*	1 Serving/200g	100	50	3.3	8.3	0.5	3.8
Baby Corn, & Mange Tout, Safeway*	1 Pack/200g	48	24	2.1	3.2	0.3	0.0
Baby, Canned, Average	1 Can/195g	40	21	0.5	4.2	0.3	2.1
Baby, Fresh, Average	1 Serving/60g	17	29	0.7	5.8	0.3	1.7
Baby, With Fine Beans, Tesco*	1 Pack/200g	58	29	1.3	4.7	0.5	2.3
Batons, Fresh, Average	1 Pack/300g	83	28	0.6	5.7	0.3	2.6
Boiled, Average	1oz/28g	6	22	0.6	4.4	0.4	2.3
Broccoli & Cauliflower Florets, Marks & Spencer*	1oz/28g	8	30	1.8	6.1	0.0	2.8
Canned, Average	1oz/28g	6	22	0.6	4.4	0.3	2.1
Cauliflower & Broccoli Florets, Safeway*	1 Serving/125g	44	35	2.6	4.6	0.7	2.3
Cauliflower & Broccoli, Tesco*	1oz/28g	10	35	2.5	4.9	0.6	2.3
Crunchies, Blue Parrot Cafe, Sainsbury's*	1 Pack/80g	28	35	0.6	7.5	0.3	3.0
Crunchies, With Dip, Shapers, Boots*	1 Pack/80g	28	35	0.6	7.5	0.3	3.0
Crunchies, With Dip, Shapers, Improved, Boots*	1 Pack/121.1g	69	57	2.3	7.1	2.2	2.3
Sliced, Canned, Average	1 Serving/180g	36	20	0.7	4.1	0.1	1.5
Sliced, Fresh, Average	1 Serving/60g	17	28	0.7	5.7	0.3	2.0
Whole, Raw, Average	1oz/28g	8	29	0.6	6.3	0.3	2.2
With Parsley & English Butter, Marks & Spencer*	½ Pack/100g	65	65	0.6	7.1	3.9	2.4
CASHEW NUTS,							
Honey Roasted, Waitrose*	½ Pack/50g	298	595	17.8	35.0	42.6	3.2
Plain, Average	1oz/28g	164	585	15.7	18.8	48.9	3.4
Roasted & Salted, Average	1 Serving/50g	306	612	18.8	19.6	51.1	3.1
Roasted Unsalted, Sainsbury's*	1/3 Pack/50g	298	595	18.3	18.7	49.7	3.3
CASHEWS & PEANUTS,							
Honey Roasted, Average	1 Serving/50g	290	579	21.6	26.6	42.9	4.2
Salted, Sainsbury's*	¼ Pack/50g	314	627	25.5	12.1	52.3	5.4
CASSAVA,							
Baked	1oz/28g	43	155	0.7	40.1	0.2	1.7
Boiled in Unsalted Water	1oz/28g	36	130	0.5	33.5	0.2	1.4
Chips	1oz/28g	99	353	1.8	91.4	0.4	4.0
Gari	1oz/28g	100	358	1.3	92.9	0.5	0.0
Raw	1oz/28g	40	142	0.6	36.8	0.2	1.6
Steamed	1oz/28g	40	142	0.6	36.8	0.2	1.6

C

	Measure INFO/WEIGHT	per Measure KCAL	Nutrition Values per 100g / 100ml				
			KCAL	PROT	CARB	FAT	FIBRE
CASEROLE,							
Bean & Lentil, Morrisons*	1 Can/410g	287	70	4.1	12.5	0.4	0.0
Beef & Ale, Finest, Tesco*	½ Pack/300g	222	74	12.2	3.9	1.1	0.4
Beef & Dumplings, Marks & Spencer*	1 Pack/454g	522	115	10.5	7.7	4.7	1.0
Beef & Red Wine, BGTY, Sainsbury's*	1 Pack/300g	192	64	8.0	6.7	0.6	0.9
Beef Bourguignon, Finest, Tesco*	1 Serving/300g	258	86	10.8	1.9	3.9	0.8
Beef With Dumplings, COU, Marks & Spencer*	½ Pack/226g	215	95	9.0	9.1	2.4	0.6
Beef With Dumplings, Eat Smart, Safeway*	1 Pack/390.9g	215	55	1.6	7.3	1.9	1.2
Beef With Dumplings, GFY, Asda*	1 Pack/400g	416	104	11.0	10.0	2.2	0.9
Beef With Potatoes, Tesco*	1 Pack/475g	470	99	5.0	10.2	4.2	0.7
Beef, Diced, Lean, Sainsbury's*	½ Pack/250g	340	136	22.5	0.0	5.1	0.0
Beef, Marks & Spencer*	1 Serving/200g	240	120	8.1	9.2	5.7	1.0
Beef, Mini Favourites, Marks & Spencer*	1 Serving/200g	250	125	7.3	9.2	6.7	1.1
Beef, Ready Meals, Marks & Spencer*	1 Meal/454g	622	137	11.1	9.9	6.4	0.7
Braised Beef With Horseradish Dumplings, Finest, Tesco*	1 Pack/350g	588	168	9.7	12.6	8.7	0.8
Chicken & Asparagus in White Wine, Finest, Tesco*	1 Pack/350.3g	683	195	10.0	11.6	12.1	0.3
Chicken & Asparagus in White Wine, Tesco*	½ Pack/300g	444	148	11.5	7.7	7.9	0.8
Chicken & Dumplings, Healthy Eating, Tesco*	1 Pack/450g	441	98	7.4	11.1	2.7	0.6
Chicken & Dumplings, Healthy Living, Tesco*	1 Pack/450g	441	98	7.4	11.1	2.7	0.6
Chicken & Dumplings, Morrisons*	1 Pack/300g	333	111	3.9	14.0	4.4	0.8
Chicken & Herb Dumplings, BGTY, Sainsbury's*	1 Pack/450g	446	99	6.1	9.5	4.1	0.6
Chicken & Tomato, Asda*	¼ Pack/273g	569	208	16.0	2.2	15.0	0.5
Chicken & White Wine, BGTY, Sainsbury's*	1 Serving/300g	216	72	7.2	5.9	2.2	1.3
Chicken Filled Yorkshire Pudding, Farmfoods*	1 Pack/280g	347	124	6.5	19.3	2.3	1.3
Chicken Fillets, Safeway*	½ Pack/172.2g	155	90	15.6	2.9	1.3	0.6
Chicken Mediterranean, Tesco*	1 Pack/400g	260	65	6.7	4.5	2.3	0.9
Chicken With Dumplings, Marks & Spencer*	½ Pack/227g	261	115	9.7	9.0	4.4	0.9
Chicken With Dumplings, Somerfield*	1 Pack/450g	581	129	7.7	9.6	6.6	1.0
Chicken With Herb Dumplings, COU, Marks & Spencer*	½ Pack/227.8g	205	90	10.6	7.2	1.9	0.6
Chicken, GFY, Asda*	1 Pack/400g	280	70	5.0	8.0	2.0	1.5
Chicken, Leek & Mushroom, Tesco*	1 Pack/350g	382	109	4.5	8.6	6.3	1.0
Chicken, Marks & Spencer*	1 Pack/200g	230	115	7.4	10.9	4.4	0.9
Chicken, Mini Favourites, Marks & Spencer*	1 Serving/200g	230	115	7.4	10.9	4.4	0.9
Chicken, Perfectly Balanced, Waitrose*	1 Pack/400g	392	98	6.6	9.8	3.6	1.2
Chunky Vegetables, Marks & Spencer*	1 Bag/450g	90	20	0.7	3.4	0.3	1.4
Country Vegetable, Sainsbury's*	1 Can/400g	300	75	2.2	11.0	2.5	1.1
Cowboy, Iceland*	1 Pack/400g	500	125	5.8	10.9	6.5	1.7
Lamb & Rosemary, BGTY, Sainsbury's*	1 Serving/300g	192	64	7.1	6.8	0.9	0.6
Lamb & Rosemary, Marks & Spencer*	1 Pack/454g	409	90	9.7	5.5	3.3	1.0
Lamb, BGTY, Sainsbury's*	1 Serving/200g	242	121	20.7	0.1	4.3	0.1
Lamb, Braised, British Classics, Tesco*	1 Pack/350g	333	95	7.5	4.6	5.2	1.2
Lamb, Marks & Spencer*	1 Pack/200g	260	130	6.2	10.6	6.8	1.2
Lentil & Vegetable, Granose*	1 Pack/400g	220	55	2.8	7.9	1.4	0.0
Minced Beef & Onion, British Classics, Tesco*	1 Pack/340g	367	108	5.0	9.3	5.6	0.8
Minced Lamb With Mint Dumplings, Sainsbury's*	1 Pack/450g	558	124	5.4	10.4	6.8	1.1
Mushroom & Onion, Iceland*	1 Pack/400g	272	68	1.3	8.8	3.1	1.9
Normandy Style Pork, Finest, Tesco*	1 Pack/450g	405	90	7.6	4.1	4.8	2.3
Pork With Apple & Cider, Safeway*	1 Pack/450g	729	162	8.3	13.4	8.4	1.1
Prime Steak, Sainsbury's*	1oz/28g	34	122	22.6	0.1	3.5	0.1
Rabbit	1oz/28g	29	102	11.6	2.6	5.1	0.4
Sausage	1oz/28g	46	165	11.9	5.1	10.9	0.9
Sausage & Potato, Marks & Spencer*	1 Serving/200g	190	95	3.3	7.5	5.9	0.9
Scottish Wild Venison & Beaujolais, Tesco*	1 Pack/425g	366	86	11.9	4.9	2.1	0.6
Spicy Bean, BGTY, Sainsbury's*	1 Pack/300g	171	57	3.0	9.1	0.9	4.2

	Measure INFO/WEIGHT	per Measure KCAL	Nutrition Values per 100g / 100ml				
			KCAL	PROT	CARB	FAT	FIBRE
CASSEROLE,							
Steak & Ale, Sainsbury's*	1 Pack/300g	288	96	10.6	5.6	3.5	0.4
Steak & Mushroom With Mustard Mash, Finest, Tesco*	1 Pack/550g	523	95	5.9	9.0	3.9	1.1
Steak & Mushroom, Asda*	½ Pack/304.4g	410	135	7.0	4.2	10.0	0.3
Vegetable & Chicken, Long Life, Sainsbury's*	1 Pack/300g	186	62	4.6	7.4	1.5	0.8
Vegetable With Dumplings, Asda*	1 Pack/350g	343	98	2.7	12.0	4.3	2.1
Vegetable With Herb Dumplings, COU, Marks & Spencer*	1 Pack/450g	270	60	1.6	10.1	1.2	1.0
Vegetable With Potato Crush, Safeway*	1 Pack/450g	293	65	1.3	7.7	3.1	2.0
Vegetable, Tesco*	1 Serving/220g	66	30	0.8	6.1	0.3	1.5
Vegetables, Ready To Cook, Sainsbury's*	½ Pack/217g	50	23	0.8	4.2	0.3	1.4
CASSEROLE MIX,							
Beef Bourguignon, Colman's*	1 Pack/40g	113	283	4.1	65.9	0.4	2.9
Beef, Authentic, Schwartz*	1 Pack/43g	111	257	7.4	54.5	1.0	0.4
Beef, Colman's*	1 Pack/40g	119	297	5.2	67.0	0.6	0.0
Beef, Schwartz*	½ Pack/21g	58	276	9.9	53.9	2.3	0.0
Chicken Chasseur, Asda*	1 Pack/80g	273	341	9.0	74.0	1.0	1.4
Chicken, Colman's*	1 Pack/40g	109	272	5.3	60.0	0.7	0.0
Chicken, Schwartz*	½ Pack/18g	55	304	10.6	62.8	1.2	0.0
Farmhouse Sausage, Schwartz*	1 Pack/39g	124	317	8.1	64.6	2.9	0.5
Liver & Bacon, Colman's*	1 Pack/40g	116	289	9.3	59.0	1.2	0.0
Peppered Beef, Schwartz*	1 Serving/80g	254	318	8.7	63.1	3.5	0.8
Pork, Colman's*	1 Serving/40g	117	293	5.3	65.5	1.1	3.4
Sausage, Asda*	¼ Pack/25g	80	321	6.0	65.0	4.1	3.0
Sausage, Colman's*	1 Serving/40g	122	304	8.1	65.7	1.0	5.4
Turkey, Colman's*	1 Pack/50g	148	296	7.2	63.4	1.5	4.9
CATFISH,							
Cooked	1 Fillet/87g	199	229	18.0	8.0	13.3	0.7
CAULIFLOWER,							
Boiled, Average	1oz/28g	8	28	2.9	2.1	0.9	1.6
Florets, In A Cheese Sauce, Healthy Living, Tesco*	½ Pack/250g	160	64	6.5	3.8	2.6	1.0
Florets, In Cheese Sauce, Tesco*	1 Pack/500g	345	69	5.9	4.8	2.9	1.9
Peas & Carrots, Bird's Eye*	1oz/28g	9	32	2.2	4.8	0.4	2.6
Raw, Average	1oz/28g	9	31	3.3	2.7	0.8	1.6
CAULIFLOWER CHEESE,							
2% Fat, Healthy Eating, Tesco*	1 Pack/400g	164	41	3.8	3.0	1.5	1.9
Asda*	1 Pack/454g	431	95	4.8	3.1	7.0	0.7
BGTY, Sainsbury's*	1 Pack/403g	238	59	5.4	6.5	1.3	1.0
Better For You, Morrisons*	1 Pack/300g	231	77	4.5	5.4	4.1	1.2
Bird's Eye*	1 Pack/329g	354	108	4.8	7.7	6.4	0.8
COU, Marks & Spencer*	1 Pack/300g	195	65	5.3	5.7	2.2	1.3
Eat Smart, Safeway*	1 Pack/300g	165	55	4.5	4.0	2.1	1.0
Finest, Tesco*	1 Serving/250g	318	127	6.5	6.1	8.5	0.4
Frozen, Tesco*	1 Pack/400g	224	56	2.9	6.0	2.3	1.3
Great Value, Asda*	1 Pack/396g	352	89	3.9	4.9	6.0	0.8
Grills, Tesco*	1 Grill/91.9g	226	246	4.6	20.1	16.4	2.6
Healthy Eating, Tesco*	1 Pack/500g	345	69	5.9	4.8	2.9	1.9
Healthy Living, Co-Op*	1 Pack/300g	155	52	5.3	4.7	1.3	1.3
Healthy Living, Tesco*	½ Pack/250g	160	64	6.5	3.8	2.6	1.0
Iceland*	1 Pack/500g	350	70	3.4	7.9	2.8	1.1
Improved Recipe, Marks & Spencer*	½ Pack/225g	214	95	6.4	5.2	5.6	2.4
Lattice Bake, Asda*	1 Serving/132g	355	269	6.0	23.0	17.0	1.1
Made With Semi-Skimmed Milk	1oz/28g	28	100	6.0	5.2	6.4	1.3
Made With Skimmed Milk	1oz/28g	27	97	6.0	5.2	6.0	1.3
Made With Whole Milk	1oz/28g	29	105	6.0	5.2	6.9	1.3

C

C

CAULIFLOWER CHEESE,	Measure INFO/WEIGHT	per Measure KCAL	KCAL	PROT	CARB	FAT	FIBRE
Marks & Spencer*	1 Serving/300g	300	100	6.9	3.7	6.6	3.1
Morrisons*	1 Pack/350g	361	103	5.9	5.1	6.9	0.6
Ready Meal, Tesco*	1 Pack/300g	264	88	4.2	5.2	5.6	1.2
Ross*	1 Pack/300g	300	100	4.9	5.5	6.6	0.1
Safeway*	½ Pack/185g	205	111	5.7	3.7	8.1	1.5
Sainsbury's*	1 Pack/300g	357	119	6.4	7.8	6.9	0.9
Somerfield*	1 Serving/402.5g	322	80	4.6	3.1	5.5	1.8
TTD, Sainsbury's*	½ Pack/150g	252	168	6.9	8.0	12.0	0.9
Vegetable Recipes, Less Than 5% Fat, Ross*	1 Pack/300g	213	71	3.1	5.6	4.0	1.1
Vegetarian, Safeway*	1 Serving/150g	138	92	4.7	5.2	5.8	1.4
Waitrose*	1 Pack/450g	419	93	5.0	5.3	5.8	0.9
With Crispy Bacon, Finest, Tesco*	1/3 Pack/166g	211	127	6.5	6.1	8.5	0.4
With Half Fat Cheese, Healthy Eating, Tesco*	½ Pack/250g	160	64	6.5	3.8	2.6	1.0
With Roasted Potatoes, Marks & Spencer*	1 Pack/200g	290	145	5.4	9.6	9.6	1.2
CAVATELLI,							
King Prawn & Scallop, Marks & Spencer*	1 Pack/400g	600	150	6.4	18.0	5.6	1.3
CAVIAR,							
Average	1oz/28g	26	92	12.0	0.5	4.7	0.0
CELERIAC,							
Boiled in Salted Water	1oz/28g	4	15	0.9	1.9	0.5	3.2
Raw	1oz/28g	5	18	1.2	2.3	0.4	3.7
CELERY,							
Boiled in Salted Water	1 Med Serving/50g	4	8	0.5	0.8	0.3	1.2
Raw, Average	1 Med Stalk/40g	3	8	0.7	1.0	0.2	1.7
CHAMPAGNE,							
Average	1 Glass/120ml	89	76	0.3	1.4	0.0	0.0
CHANNA MASALA,							
Indian, Sainsbury's*	1 Serving/149g	165	111	4.2	12.4	4.9	3.3
Marks & Spencer*	1 Pack/225g	360	160	5.6	11.2	10.5	8.2
Safeway*	1 Pack/400g	540	135	5.3	16.2	5.4	2.5
CHAPATIS,							
Brown Wheat Flour, Waitrose*	1 Chapatis/42g	128	305	8.6	49.4	8.0	4.6
Elephant*	1 Serving/44.9g	129	287	7.5	53.1	6.4	3.2
Gujarati Style, Safeway*	1 Chapatis/40g	111	277	8.1	50.0	4.9	2.8
Indian Style, Asda*	1 Chapatis/43g	121	282	7.0	50.0	6.0	0.0
Made With Fat	1 Chapatis/60g	197	328	8.1	48.3	12.8	0.0
Made Without Fat	1 Chapatis/55g	111	202	7.3	43.7	1.0	0.0
Morrisons*	1 Chapatis/40g	105	269	8.6	49.8	6.9	0.0
Patak's*	1 Chapatis/42g	121	287	7.5	53.1	6.4	3.2
Spicy, Safeway*	1 Chapatis/41g	115	280	8.9	47.6	6.6	4.5
Wholemeal, Patak's*	1 Chapatis/42g	130	310	11.2	44.9	9.5	9.0
Wrap, Plain, Patak's*	1 Serving/35g	109	310	11.2	44.9	9.5	0.0
CHARD,							
Swiss, Boiled in Unsalted Water	1oz/28g	6	20	1.9	3.2	0.1	0.0
Swiss, Raw	1oz/28g	5	19	1.8	2.9	0.2	0.6
CHEDDARS,							
Cheese & Ham, Mini, McVitie's*	1 Bag/30g	160	534	11.0	55.5	29.8	2.0
McVitie's*	1 Biscuit/4g	19	509	11.6	53.2	27.7	2.7
Mini, McVitie's*	1 Bag/30g	161	535	11.0	54.4	30.3	2.0
Peperami, Mini, McVitie's	1 Bag/30g	160	532	9.7	55.2	30.2	2.0
Smokey BBQ, Cheddars, McVitie's*	1 Pack/30g	160	533	9.5	56.3	29.9	2.0
Tangy Salsa, Mini, McVitie's*	1 Bag/50g	266	532	11.0	54.7	29.9	2.1
Totally Cheesy, Crinkly's, Mini, McVitie's*	1 Pack/28g	143	512	9.9	57.0	27.1	1.9

CHEESE,

	Measure INFO/WEIGHT	per Measure KCAL	Nutrition Values per 100g / 100ml				
			KCAL	PROT	CARB	FAT	FIBRE
Ail & Fines Herbes, Boursin*	1oz/28g	116	414	7.0	2.0	42.0	0.0
Alternative To, Vegetarian, Average	1oz/28g	103	368	28.2	0.0	28.1	0.0
Appenzellar, Sainsbury's*	1 Serving/25g	97	386	25.4	0.0	31.6	0.0
Applewood, Somerfield*	1oz/28g	119	426	28.0	0.0	35.0	0.0
Asiago, Marks & Spencer*	1oz/28g	105	375	33.0	0.1	27.0	0.0
Aufschnitt in Scheiben Gouda, Edam, Tilsiter, Du Darfst*	1 Slice/19g	51	269	29.0	0.0	17.0	0.0
Austrian Smoked Flavour, Sainsbury's*	½ Pack/50g	143	286	17.4	0.0	24.0	0.0
Babybel, Fromageries Bel*	1 Cheese/20g	62	308	23.0	0.0	24.0	0.0
Babybel, Light, Fromageries Bel*	1 Pack/40g	85	212	26.0	0.0	12.0	0.0
Babybel, Light, Mini, Fromageries Bel*	1 Cheese/20g	43	214	26.5	0.0	12.0	0.0
Babybel, Mini, Fromageries Bel*	1/120g	359	299	23.0	0.0	23.0	0.0
Babybel, With Cheddar, Mini, Fromageries Bel*	1 Cheese/25g	94	374	25.0	1.0	30.0	0.0
Bavarian Smoked, Processed, Somefield*	1oz/28g	85	302	29.0	0.0	21.0	0.0
Bleu d' Auvergne, Sainsbury's*	1 Serving/25g	84	335	22.0	2.0	26.5	0.0
Bresse Bleu, Marks & Spencer*	1oz/28g	99	355	19.0	0.3	31.0	0.0
Brie, Average	1oz/28g	83	296	19.7	0.3	24.0	0.0
Brie, Creamy, Average	1 Serving/50g	180	360	18.1	0.1	31.9	0.0
Brie, Reduced Fat, Average	1 Serving/50g	99	198	23.0	0.8	11.4	0.0
Caerphilly, Average	1 Serving/50g	187	374	23.0	0.1	31.3	0.0
Cambozola Blue Brie, Somerfield*	1oz/28g	122	434	14.0	1.0	42.0	0.0
Camembert, Average	1 Serving/50g	141	283	20.5	0.1	22.2	0.0
Camembert, Breaded With Cranberry Dip, Sainsbury's*	1 Serving/80g	265	331	15.6	10.1	25.4	2.8
Camembert, Breaded, Average	1 Serving/90g	307	342	16.7	14.3	23.3	0.5
Camembert, Half, Fat, Coeur De Lion*	1 Serving/125g	261	209	23.5	0.5	12.5	0.0
Cantal, French, Sainsbury's*	1 Serving/30g	106	353	23.0	0.1	29.0	0.0
Cantenaar, Marks & Spencer*	1 Serving/28g	84	300	32.2	0.1	19.2	0.0
Chaumes, Marks & Spencer*	1oz/28g	85	305	20.2	1.0	26.0	0.0
Cheddar, Canadian, Average	1oz/28g	114	409	25.0	0.1	34.3	0.0
Cheddar, Davidstow, Mature, Average	1 Serving/28g	115	410	25.0	0.1	34.4	0.0
Cheddar, Extra Mature, Average	1oz/28g	115	410	25.1	0.1	34.4	0.0
Cheddar, Grated, Average	1 Serving/50g	206	413	24.4	1.5	34.3	0.0
Cheddar, Mature, Average	1 Serving/10g	41	410	25.0	0.1	34.4	0.0
Cheddar, Mature, Grated, Average	1 Serving/28g	113	404	24.7	1.6	33.2	0.0
Cheddar, Mature, Reduced Fat, Average	1 Serving/25g	68	271	30.0	0.1	16.7	0.0
Cheddar, Medium, Average	1oz/28g	115	411	24.9	0.2	34.5	0.0
Cheddar, Mild, Average	1oz/28g	114	409	25.0	0.1	34.3	0.0
Cheddar, Reduced Fat, Average	1oz/28g	71	255	32.2	0.1	14.0	0.0
Cheddar, Smoked, Average	1oz/28g	115	411	25.3	0.1	34.4	0.0
Cheddar, Vintage Truckle, Marks & Spencer*	1oz/28g	115	410	25.0	0.1	34.4	0.0
Cheddar, West Country Farmhouse, Average	1 Serving/28g	115	410	25.0	0.1	34.4	0.0
Cheddar, Wexford, Average	1 Serving/20g	82	410	25.0	0.1	34.4	0.0
Cheddar, With Caramelised Onion, Sainsbury's*	1 Serving/28g	109	391	22.8	5.1	31.0	0.0
Cheddar, With Caramelised Onion, Tesco*	1 Serving/50g	183	366	21.4	7.1	28.0	0.4
Cheddar, With Onion & Chives, Davidson*	1 Serving/25g	100	400	24.3	0.6	33.3	0.0
Cheestrings, Golden Vale*	1 Stick/21g	69	328	28.0	0.0	24.0	0.0
Cheshire	1oz/28g	106	379	24.0	0.1	31.4	0.0
Chevre Pave d'Affinois, Finest, Tesco*	1 Pack/150g	404	269	18.5	0.0	21.7	0.0
Coloured, Low Fat, Weight Watchers*	1oz/28g	51	182	34.2	0.1	5.0	0.0
Coloured, Medium Fat, Average	1oz/28g	74	259	30.3	0.1	15.3	0.0
Cotswold, Full Fat With Herbs, Somerfield*	1oz/28g	113	405	25.0	0.0	34.0	0.0
Cottage, Arla*	1 Serving/25g	23	90	12.0	2.0	4.0	0.0
Cottage, BGTY, Sainsbury's*	1oz/28g	25	91	12.1	8.4	0.9	0.2
Cottage, Bettabuy, Morrisons*	1 Tub/200g	210	105	11.0	5.0	5.0	0.0

C

CHEESE,	Measure INFO/WEIGHT	per Measure KCAL	Nutrition Values per 100g / 100ml				
			KCAL	PROT	CARB	FAT	FIBRE
Cottage, Better For You, Morrisons*	1 Pot/125g	110	88	13.0	6.9	0.9	0.0
Cottage, Crunchy Vegetable, GFY, Asda*	1 Serving/50g	37	74	11.0	4.5	1.3	0.6
Cottage, Garlic & Herb, Diet, Yoplait*	1 Pot/225g	180	80	12.0	3.9	1.9	0.0
Cottage, Healthy Choice, Nisa Heritage*	1 Pot/227g	175	77	11.8	3.4	1.8	0.3
Cottage, Healthy Choice, Asda*	1oz/28g	25	88	13.0	4.0	2.0	0.0
Cottage, Jocca, Kraft*	1 Serving/50g	55	109	9.3	5.0	5.5	0.0
Cottage, Less Than 5% Fat, Sainsbury's*	½ Pot/125g	131	105	12.3	4.4	4.2	0.0
Cottage, Lidl*	1 Pot/200g	204	102	13.2	2.0	4.6	0.0
Cottage, Low Fat, Loseley*	1 Pot/125g	148	118	13.3	2.0	6.0	0.0
Cottage, Low Fat, Westacre, Aldi*	1 Pot/100g	85	85	14.6	3.6	1.3	0.1
Cottage, Low Fat, With Onion & Chive, Safeway*	1 Pot/250g	210	84	12.0	4.2	1.9	0.1
Cottage, Natural	1oz/28g	29	105	12.0	4.0	4.0	0.0
Cottage, Natural, 95% Fat Free, Marks & Spencer*	1oz/28g	28	99	11.6	3.5	4.0	0.0
Cottage, Natural, Asda*	¼ Pot/113g	118	104	12.0	4.0	4.2	0.0
Cottage, Natural, BGTY, Sainsbury's*	1oz/28g	25	88	13.0	6.9	0.9	0.0
Cottage, Natural, COU, Marks & Spencer*	½ Pot/125g	100	80	11.9	3.3	1.8	0.3
Cottage, Natural, Deliciously Creamy, Marks & Spencer	1 Serving/50g	48	95	12.5	4.1	2.9	0.0
Cottage, Natural, Diet Choice, Waitrose*	1oz/28g	27	98	11.4	3.6	4.2	0.0
Cottage, Natural, Eat Smart, Safeway*	1 Pot/115g	93	81	11.8	3.4	1.8	0.3
Cottage, Natural, GFY, Asda*	1 Serving/113g	97	86	12.0	4.3	2.0	0.0
Cottage, Natural, Good Intentions, Somerfield*	1 Pot/125g	110	88	13.0	6.9	0.9	0.0
Cottage, Natural, Healthy Choice, Safeway*	1oz/28g	24	87	12.7	4.0	2.0	0.0
Cottage, Natural, Healthy Eating, Tesco*	1 Pot/125g	98	78	11.9	3.6	1.8	0.0
Cottage, Natural, Healthy Living, Co-Op*	1 Pot/250g	188	75	10.0	4.0	2.0	0.0
Cottage, Natural, Kwik Save*	1 Serving/25g	21	85	13.8	4.4	1.4	0.0
Cottage, Natural, Less Than 5% Fat, Sainsbury's*	½ Pot/131g	138	105	12.3	4.4	4.2	0.0
Cottage, Natural, Organic, Loseley*	1 Pot/250g	265	106	13.7	1.5	5.0	0.0
Cottage, Natural, Organic, Sainsbury's*	1 Pot/201g	185	92	12.8	6.3	1.8	0.0
Cottage, Natural, Organic, Tesco*	½ Pot/100g	78	78	11.9	3.6	1.8	0.0
Cottage, Natural, Perfectly Balanced, Waitrose*	1 Serving/250g	198	79	11.9	3.8	1.8	0.0
Cottage, Natural, Simply, Kwik Save*	1 Pot/200g	158	79	11.7	5.5	1.1	0.0
Cottage, Natural, SmartPrice, Asda	½ Pot/100g	86	86	12.0	4.3	2.0	0.0
Cottage, Natural, Tesco*	1 Serving/50g	49	97	11.2	3.5	4.2	0.0
Cottage, Natural, Waitrose*	½ Pot/125g	113	90	10.0	3.1	4.2	0.0
Cottage, Pineapple, Perfectly Balanced, Waitrose*	1 Pot/125g	105	84	10.4	6.7	1.7	0.2
Cottage, Plain	1oz/28g	27	98	13.8	2.1	3.9	0.0
Cottage, Plain, Reduced Fat	1oz/28g	22	78	13.3	3.3	1.4	0.0
Cottage, Slimline*	1 Serving/70g	43	62	12.0	3.0	0.2	0.0
Cottage, Tuna & Sweetcorn, GFY, Asda*	½ Pot/113g	104	92	12.4	5.3	2.4	0.3
Cottage, Very Low Fat, Nisa Heritage*	1 Tub/227g	193	85	13.8	4.4	1.4	0.0
Cottage, Virtually Fat Free, Eden Vale*	1oz/28g	22	80	12.9	6.5	0.3	0.0
Cottage, Virtually Fat Free, Longley Farm*	½ Pot/125g	84	67	13.4	3.0	0.1	0.0
Cottage, Virtually Fat Free, Sainsbury's*	1oz/28g	22	80	12.9	6.5	0.3	0.0
Cottage, With Black Pepper, Healthy Eating, Tesco*	1 Pot/125g	101	81	12.1	4.0	1.8	0.0
Cottage, With Chargrilled Vegetables, BGTY, Sainsbury's*	1oz/28g	25	88	12.1	7.8	0.9	0.6
Cottage, With Chives, Good Intentions, Somerfield*	1 Pot/125g	101	81	10.8	3.2	2.8	0.0
Cottage, With Chives, Low Fat, Westacre, Aldi*	1 Pot/100g	81	81	13.7	3.5	1.4	1.2
Cottage, With Chives, Marks & Spencer*	1oz/28g	28	100	11.9	3.5	3.9	0.0
Cottage, With Chives, Somerfield*	1oz/28g	29	105	12.0	5.0	4.0	0.0
Cottage, With Coronation Chicken, BGTY, Sainsbury's*	1oz/28g	25	91	11.3	8.7	1.2	0.1
Cottage, With Cucumber & Mint, BGTY, Sainsbury's*	½ Pot/125g	103	82	12.0	6.6	0.9	0.0
Cottage, With Cucumber & Mint, COU, Marks & Spencer*	1 Pot/113g	85	75	11.6	3.1	1.5	0.2
Cottage, With Cucumber & Mint, Healthy Eating, Tesco*	½ Pot/125g	91	73	10.7	3.8	1.7	0.1

CHEESE,

	Measure INFO/WEIGHT	per Measure KCAL	Nutrition Values per 100g / 100ml				
			KCAL	PROT	CARB	FAT	FIBRE
Cottage, With Cucumber & Mint, GFY, Asda*	1 Serving/75g	54	72	11.0	4.1	1.3	0.5
Cottage, With Lime & Coriander, Low Fat, Safeway*	½ Pot/126g	113	90	12.2	5.2	2.0	0.0
Cottage, With Mango & Peach, Healthy Eating, Tesco*	1 Pot/250g	188	75	10.4	4.8	1.6	0.1
Cottage, With Mango & Pineapple, BGTY, Sainsbury's*	½ Pot/125g	113	90	10.7	10.4	0.7	0.2
Cottage, With Mango & Pineapple, Morrisons*	1 Pot/125g	113	90	10.7	10.4	0.7	0.0
Cottage, With Onion & Chive, BGTY, Sainsbury's*	1 Serving/50g	42	83	12.4	6.4	0.9	0.1
Cottage, With Onion & Chive, GFY, Asda*	1 Serving/50g	43	85	12.0	4.4	1.9	0.1
Cottage, With Onion & Chive, Healthy Choice, Asda*	1oz/28g	23	82	12.0	4.0	2.0	0.1
Cottage, With Onion & Chive, Healthy Choice, Safeway*	1 Pot/125g	105	84	12.0	4.2	1.9	0.1
Cottage, With Onion & Chive, Healthy Eating, Tesco*	1oz/28g	22	77	11.0	4.5	1.7	0.2
Cottage, With Onion & Chive, Iceland*	½ Pot/100g	81	81	8.5	8.9	1.3	0.3
Cottage, With Onion & Chive, Tesco*	1 Serving/250g	235	94	10.9	3.7	4.0	0.0
Cottage, With Onion & Chives, Low Fat, Sainsbury's*	1oz/28g	28	99	11.6	4.4	4.0	0.1
Cottage, With Onion & Chives, Marks & Spencer*	¼ Pot/65g	88	135	10.4	4.0	8.5	0.1
Cottage, With Onion & Chives, Nisa Heritage*	1 Pot/227g	168	74	11.1	3.8	1.6	0.3
Cottage, With Peach & Mango, COU, Marks & Spencer*	1 Pot/113g	96	85	9.1	9.7	1.0	0.4
Cottage, With Pineapple, Asda*	1oz/28g	31	109	10.0	8.0	3.9	0.0
Cottage, With Pineapple, BGTY, Sainsbury's*	1oz/28g	24	84	10.5	8.9	0.7	0.1
Cottage, With Pineapple, Balanced Lifestyle, Aldi*	1 Serving/200g	140	70	11.0	4.4	0.9	1.5
Cottage, With Pineapple, GFY, Asda*	1 Serving/200g	184	92	10.0	9.0	1.6	0.2
Cottage, With Pineapple, Good Intentions, Somerfield*	1 Pot/125g	105	84	10.5	8.9	0.7	0.1
Cottage, With Pineapple, Healthy Choice, Safeway*	1oz/28g	25	89	10.8	6.9	1.8	0.0
Cottage, With Pineapple, Healthy Eating, Tesco*	1oz/28g	21	75	10.1	5.3	1.5	0.1
Cottage, With Pineapple, Healthy Living, Tesco*	½ Pot/125g	119	95	10.0	9.0	2.0	0.2
Cottage, With Pineapple, Iceland*	½ Pot/100g	81	81	8.5	8.9	1.3	0.3
Cottage, With Pineapple, Low Fat, Waitrose*	1 Serving/40g	34	84	10.4	6.7	1.7	0.2
Cottage, With Pineapple, Sainsbury's*	½ Pot/125g	121	97	9.9	6.8	3.4	2.1
Cottage, With Pineapple, Shape*	1oz/28g	20	73	9.8	8.0	0.2	0.1
Cottage, With Pineapple, Somerfield*	1oz/28g	27	97	10.0	7.0	3.0	0.0
Cottage, With Pineapple, Tesco*	1 Serving/150g	158	105	9.1	9.8	3.3	0.1
Cottage, With Poached Salmon & Dill, GFY, Asda*	1/3 Pot/75g	65	86	12.0	2.3	2.7	0.6
Cottage, With Prawn & Cucumber, Safeway*	1 Serving/200g	184	92	12.0	4.7	2.5	0.1
Cottage, With Prawn Cocktail, BGTY, Sainsbury's*	1oz/28g	25	91	12.3	8.3	0.9	0.1
Cottage, With Prawn, GFY, Asda*	1oz/28g	25	91	13.0	6.0	1.5	0.0
Cottage, With Roasted Vegetables, Low Fat, Safeway*	1 Pot/125g	96	77	10.5	4.3	1.7	1.8
Cottage, With Salmon & Dill, Healthy Eating, Tesco*	1oz/28g	25	89	12.0	4.7	2.5	0.5
Cottage, With Smoked Cheese & Onion, GFY, Asda*	1 Serving/50g	39	78	12.0	3.9	1.6	0.4
Cottage, With Smoked Salmon & Dill, BGTY, Sainsbury's*	1oz/28g	25	89	13.8	6.4	0.9	0.1
Cottage, With Sweet Chilli Chicken, Marks & Spencer*	1 Serving/200g	190	95	13.8	4.7	2.1	0.5
Cottage, With Tomato & Cracked Black Pepper, Asda*	½ Pot/113g	86	76	10.0	3.1	2.1	1.3
Cottage, With Tuna & Cucumber, Safeway*	1 Serving/40g	35	87	12.0	3.7	2.5	0.1
Cottage, With Tuna & Pesto, Asda*	1 Serving/170g	184	108	10.0	3.5	6.0	0.7
Cottage, With Tuna & Sweetcorn, BGTY, Sainsbury's*	1oz/28g	25	91	12.1	8.4	0.9	0.2
Cottage, With Tuna & Sweetcorn, Healthy Living, Tesco*	1 Serving/150g	113	75	10.6	4.9	1.5	0.4
Cream	1 Portion/30g	132	439	3.1	0.0	47.4	0.0
Cream, Garlic & Herbs, Light, Boursin*	1 Portion/20g	28	140	12.0	2.5	9.0	0.0
Cream, Light, Benecol*	1 Serving/34g	58	170	7.8	3.3	14.0	0.7
Cream, Reduced Fat, Average	1oz/28g	33	117	13.0	4.0	5.3	0.1
Cream, With Onion & Chives, Morrisons*	1 Serving/20g	38	190	11.0	3.0	15.0	0.0
Cream, With Pineapple, Asda*	1 Serving/40g	77	193	8.0	11.0	13.0	0.0
Cream, With Red Peppers & Onion, GFY, Asda*	1 Serving/32.3g	42	130	13.0	6.0	6.0	0.0
Creamy Chaumes, Marks & Spencer*	1oz/28g	80	287	17.6	1.0	23.6	0.0
Danish Blue, Average	1oz/28g	99	352	20.8	0.0	29.1	0.0

CHEESE,	Measure INFO/WEIGHT	per Measure KCAL	Nutrition Values per 100g / 100ml				
			KCAL	PROT	CARB	FAT	FIBRE
Demi Pont L'eveque, Finest, Tesco*	1 Serving/46g	138	301	21.1	0.4	23.0	0.0
Dolcelatte, Average	1oz/28g	102	366	17.8	0.4	32.3	0.4
Double Gloucester, Average	1oz/28g	113	405	24.5	0.1	34.0	0.0
Dubliner, Kerrygold*	1oz/28g	110	392	26.0	0.1	32.0	0.0
Edam, Average	1 Serving/10g	33	326	25.3	0.0	24.9	0.0
Edam, Dutch, Garlic & Herb Wedge, Asda*	1 Serving/60g	197	329	26.0	0.0	25.0	0.0
Edam, Reduced Fat, Average	1oz/28g	64	230	32.4	0.1	11.1	0.0
Edam, Slices, Average	1 Slice/30g	96	320	25.0	0.4	24.1	0.0
Emmental, Average	1 Serving/10g	37	369	28.4	0.0	28.4	0.0
Farmhouse, Healthy Range, Average	1oz/28g	73	261	30.4	0.1	15.4	0.0
Feta, Average	1oz/28g	74	262	16.3	1.0	21.5	0.0
Feta, Light, Salakis*	¼ Pack/38g	61	161	20.3	2.1	8.0	0.0
Feta, Marinated, Jar, Discover*	1oz/28g	75	267	19.0	1.0	21.0	0.0
Feta, With Green Olives, For Salad, Discover*	1oz/28g	75	267	19.0	1.0	21.0	0.0
Feta, With Herbs & Spices, For Salad, Discover*	1oz/28g	75	267	19.0	1.0	21.0	0.0
Feta, With Kalamata Olives, For Salad, Discover*	1oz/28g	75	267	19.0	1.0	21.0	0.0
Feta, With Red Pepper, For Salad, Discover*	1oz/28g	75	267	19.0	1.0	21.0	0.0
For Pizza, Grated, Average	1 Serving/50g	163	326	25.0	1.6	24.4	0.0
Garlic & Parsley Roule, Light, BGTY, Sainsbury's*	1 Pack/100g	176	176	17.6	1.6	11.0	0.0
Garlic Roule With Herbs, Somerfield*	1oz/28g	92	329	10.0	3.0	31.0	0.0
Goats Camembert, Marks & Spencer*	1oz/28g	85	304	20.0	2.0	24.0	0.0
Goats With Roasted Vegetables, Somerfield*	1oz/28g	55	196	8.0	26.0	7.0	0.0
Goats, Average	1 Tsp/10g	26	262	13.8	3.8	21.2	0.0
Goats, Breaded, Bites, Sainsbury's*	1 Bite/24.9g	84	337	13.0	15.1	25.0	0.8
Goats, French, Mild, Average	1 Serving/30g	49	163	11.3	3.0	11.8	0.0
Goats, Premium, Average	1 Pack/100g	327	327	20.5	0.6	26.1	0.0
Gorgonzola, Average	1oz/28g	94	334	20.0	0.1	27.0	0.0
Gouda, Average	1oz/28g	105	376	24.0	0.0	31.5	0.0
Gouda, Crispies, Occasions, Sainsbury's*	4 Crispies/10g	59	587	15.3	33.3	43.6	1.3
Grana Padano, Italian Cheese, Waitrose*	1 Serving/14g	54	388	33.0	0.0	28.4	0.0
Gruyere	1oz/28g	115	409	27.2	0.0	33.3	0.0
Halloumi, Average	1 Serving/80g	253	316	20.8	1.6	24.7	0.0
Italian, Grated, Average	1 Serving/10g	48	481	44.0	1.1	33.4	0.0
Jarlsberg, Marks & Spencer*	1oz/28g	98	351	27.0	0.1	27.0	0.0
Lancashire	1oz/28g	104	373	23.3	0.1	31.0	0.0
Leerdammer* Wedge	1 Wedge/250g	933	373	28.3	0.0	28.6	0.0
Light Salad, Discover	1oz/28g	61	216	24.0	1.0	13.0	0.0
Light, Boursin*	1oz/28g	43	153	12.5	4.5	9.5	0.0
Mascarpone, 25% Less Fat, Sainsbury's*	1 Portion/30g	95	316	6.7	4.8	30.0	0.0
Mascarpone, Average	1oz/28g	122	437	5.6	4.1	43.6	0.0
Mild, Reduced Fat, Grated, Average	1oz/28g	66	235	31.5	2.2	11.1	0.0
Monterey Jack, Shredded, Kraft*	¼ Cup/28g	101	360	22.0	3.6	28.8	0.0
Mozzarella, Average	1 Pack/125g	343	275	21.2	1.2	20.6	0.0
Mozzarella, Breaded, Asda*	1 Serving/24.5g	66	274	17.0	11.0	18.0	0.7
Mozzarella, Buffalo, Marks & Spencer*	1oz/28g	80	284	18.0	0.1	23.5	0.0
Mozzarella, Grated, Average	1 Serving/25g	76	303	25.1	1.4	22.0	0.0
Mozzarella, Reduced Fat, Average	1oz/28g	51	184	21.2	1.0	10.3	0.0
Mozzarella, Sticks, Breaded, With Tomato Dip, D'esir, Aldi*	1 Pack/200g	462	231	12.0	21.0	11.0	0.0
Norvegia, Sliced Light, Tine*	1 Slice/10g	27	272	32.0	0.0	16.0	0.0
Parmesan, Average	1 Serving/25g	100	401	35.2	0.0	29.4	0.0
Parmesan, Grated, Average	1 Serving/10g	40	395	33.3	0.1	29.1	0.0
Parmigiano Reggiano, Sainsbury's*	1 Serving/30g	116	388	33.0	0.1	28.4	0.1
Pastrami Flavour, Sandwich, Swiss Processed, Gerber*	2 Slices/25g	87	348	24.0	0.0	28.0	0.0

CHEESE,

	Measure INFO/WEIGHT	per Measure KCAL	KCAL	PROT	CARB	FAT	FIBRE
Pecorino, Italian, Tesco*	1 Serving/30g	119	397	22.0	0.0	33.0	0.0
Poivre, Boursin*	1oz/28g	116	414	7.0	2.0	42.0	0.0
Port Salut, Marks & Spencer*	1oz/28g	90	322	21.0	1.0	26.0	0.0
Quark, Average	1 Serving/20g	13	66	11.9	4.0	0.2	0.0
Red Leicester, Average	1oz/28g	112	400	23.8	0.1	33.7	0.0
Red Leicester, Reduced Fat, Average	¼ Pack/75g	196	261	30.2	0.1	15.4	0.0
Ricotta, Average	1 Serving/50g	67	134	9.3	2.9	9.5	0.0
Roquefort	1oz/28g	105	375	19.7	0.0	32.9	0.0
Roule, French, Sainsbury's*	1 Serving/30g	96	321	8.5	3.0	30.5	0.0
Sage Derby	1oz/28g	113	402	24.2	0.1	33.9	0.0
Saint Agur, Marks & Spencer*	1 Serving/25g	91	363	16.0	0.2	33.5	0.0
Scheese, Animal-Free, Isle Of Bute Foods*	1oz/28g	103	369	14.5	1.2	29.0	4.3
Shropshire, Blue, Average	1oz/28g	109	391	21.1	0.1	34.3	0.0
Soft, & Creamy With Onions & Garlic, GFY, Asda*	1 Serving/25g	32	126	13.0	5.0	6.0	0.0
Soft, & Creamy With Pineapple, Asda*	1 Serving/32.1g	62	193	8.0	11.0	13.0	0.0
Soft, Creamy, With Onion & Chives, BGTY, Sainsbury's*	1 Serving/20g	23	115	13.5	4.0	5.0	1.0
Soft, Creamy, With Shallots & Chives, BGTY, Sainsbury's*	1 Serving/20g	47	235	5.8	2.2	22.5	0.0
Soft, Double Gloucester, & Chives, Marks & Spencer*	1oz/28g	100	358	20.0	9.2	26.8	0.0
Soft, Extra Light, Average	1oz/28g	35	125	14.3	3.6	5.9	0.1
Soft, Fruit & Rum Halo, Discover*	1oz/28g	116	416	8.6	11.7	34.1	0.0
Soft, Full Fat, Average	1 Serving/50g	156	312	8.2	1.7	30.3	0.0
Soft, Garlic & Herb, Lite, Somerfield*	½ Pot/100g	191	191	9.0	4.9	15.0	0.0
Soft, Garlic & Herb, Marks & Spencer*	1oz/28g	58	206	8.5	2.7	18.0	0.0
Soft, Garlic & Herb, Medium Fat, Safeway*	1 Serving/10g	20	195	9.3	4.9	15.0	0.0
Soft, Garlic & Herb, Soft & Creamy, Extra Light, Asda*	¼ Pack/50g	65	130	13.0	6.0	6.0	0.0
Soft, Garlic, Aldi*	1 Serving/50g	94	188	8.0	3.0	16.0	0.1
Soft, Goats Milk	1oz/28g	55	198	13.1	1.0	15.8	0.0
Soft, Herbs & Garlic, Creamery, Light, Sainsbury's*	1 Serving/30g	54	180	7.2	3.4	15.5	0.3
Soft, Light, Average	1 Serving/30g	54	179	12.1	3.2	13.1	0.0
Soft, Medium Fat, Average	1oz/28g	58	207	8.4	3.0	17.9	0.0
Soft, Onion & Chive, Low Fat, BGTY, Sainsbury's*	1 Serving/30g	35	115	13.5	4.0	5.0	1.0
Soft, Orange Halo, Discover*	1oz/28g	110	394	8.1	7.9	35.3	0.0
Soft, Philadelphia, & Breadsticks, Light, Kraft*	1 Portion/50g	119	238	8.5	24.5	12.0	1.1
Soft, Philadelphia, Blue, Kraft*	1 Serving/28g	76	270	6.8	3.4	25.5	0.2
Soft, Philadelphia, Extra Light, Kraft*	1oz/28g	28	101	11.0	3.0	5.0	0.6
Soft, Philadelphia, Garlic & Herb, Light, Kraft*	1oz/28g	50	180	7.2	3.4	15.5	0.2
Soft, Philadelphia, Kraft*	1oz/28g	78	280	6.0	2.5	27.5	0.1
Soft, Philadelphia, Light, Kraft*	1oz/28g	53	190	7.6	3.4	16.0	0.3
Soft, Philadelphia, Light, Snack, Kraft*	1 Pack/50g	123	246	8.4	23.0	13.2	1.6
Soft, Philadelphia, Mini Tubs, Extra Light, Kraft*	1 Mini Tub/35g	39	111	11.0	4.8	5.2	0.0
Soft, Philadelphia, Mini Tubs, Light, Kraft*	1 Tub/35g	57	163	7.1	2.9	14.0	0.0
Soft, Philadelphia, Tomato & Basil, Light, Kraft*	1 Tbsp/20g	38	190	7.6	4.3	16.0	0.5
Soft, Philadelphia, With Chive & Onion, Kraft*	1 Serving/25g	73	290	6.5	6.5	29.0	0.0
Soft, Philadelphia, With Chives, Light, Kraft*	1oz/28g	52	185	7.5	3.4	15.5	0.3
Soft, Philadelphia, With Ham, Light, Kraft*	1oz/28g	52	184	7.9	4.3	15.0	0.2
Soft, Pineapple Halo, Discover*	1oz/28g	107	383	7.0	16.7	30.9	0.0
Soft, Pineapple, Light, Safeway*	1 Serving/25g	48	190	7.6	10.8	12.5	0.0
Soft, With Cracked Pepper, Marks & Spencer*	1 Serving/40g	44	110	13.0	4.2	4.5	0.3
Soft, With Onion & Chives, Extra Light, Tesco*	1 Serving/30g	36	121	12.9	5.0	5.5	0.0
Soft, With Onion & Chives, Marks & Spencer*	¼ Pack/37.5g	38	100	10.7	4.4	4.7	1.2
Somerset Camembert, Safeway*	½ Pack/110g	341	310	22.0	0.5	24.0	0.0
Soya	1oz/28g	89	319	18.3	0.0	27.3	0.0
St Agur*	1 Serving/45g	163	363	16.0	0.2	33.5	0.0

CHEESE,	Measure INFO/WEIGHT	per Measure KCAL	KCAL	PROT	CARB	FAT	FIBRE
Stilton, Average	1 Serving/30g	123	410	22.4	0.1	35.5	0.0
Stilton, Blue, Average	1oz/28g	115	412	22.8	0.1	35.7	0.0
Stilton, White	1oz/28g	101	362	19.9	0.1	31.3	0.0
Stilton, White, & Apricot, Marks & Spencer*	1oz/28g	94	337	13.8	18.5	23.1	0.0
Stilton, White, & Cranberry, Marks & Spencer*	1oz/28g	101	362	18.2	15.5	25.3	0.0
Stilton, White, With Apricot, Somerfield*	1oz/28g	103	369	16.0	8.0	30.0	0.0
Stilton, White, With Cranberries, Tesco*	1 Serving/50g	184	368	15.8	9.5	29.7	0.7
Taleggio, Tesco*	1 Serving/25g	74	297	18.0	0.0	25.0	0.0
Vinney, Blue, BGTY, Sainsbury's*	1oz/28g	90	320	30.4	0.1	22.0	0.0
Wensleydale With Cranberries, Co-Op*	1 Serving/25g	91	365	18.0	12.0	27.0	3.0
Wensleydale With Cranberries, Sainsbury's*	1 Serving/50g	180	359	20.7	6.4	27.8	0.0
Wensleydale, Average	1 Serving/25g	92	369	22.5	0.1	31.0	0.1
CHEESE ON TOAST,							
Average	1oz/28g	106	380	13.8	23.8	26.3	0.7
CHEESE PUFFS,							
Farmfoods*	1 Bag/18g	96	532	7.0	54.3	31.9	1.0
Sainsbury's*	1 Pack/100g	530	530	9.1	51.4	32.0	1.9
Shapers, Boots*	1 Bag/16g	84	523	6.4	59.0	29.0	1.6
SmartPrice, Asda*	1 Bag/18g	92	512	7.0	58.0	28.0	1.3
Value, Tesco*	1 Bag/18g	90	498	7.7	54.1	27.9	1.7
CHEESE SINGLES,							
50% Less Fat, Asda*	1 Slice/20g	38	190	19.0	6.0	10.0	0.0
50% Less Fat, BGTY, Sainsbury's*	1 Slice/20g	38	190	18.0	7.0	10.0	0.0
American, 2% Milk, Kraft*	1 Slice/19g	45	237	21.0	5.3	15.8	0.0
Half Fat, Co-Op*	1 Slice/20g	47	235	25.0	7.0	12.0	0.0
Healthy Living, Tesco*	1 Slice/20g	39	194	21.7	4.2	10.0	0.0
Kraft*	1 Single/20g	52	260	13.5	7.6	18.5	0.0
Light, Kraft*	1 Slice/20g	41	205	20.0	6.0	11.0	0.0
Light, Safeway*	1 Slice/20g	38	192	21.2	4.2	10.0	0.0
CHEESE SLICES,							
40% Less Fat, Iceland*	1 Slice/20.1g	41	204	18.0	6.0	12.0	0.0
97% Fat Free, Kraft*	1 Slice/20g	31	155	23.3	9.9	2.3	0.0
Bavarian Smoked, Asda*	1 Slice/18g	50	277	17.0	0.4	23.0	0.0
Bettabuy, Morrisons*	1 Slice/17g	47	274	14.0	4.0	22.5	0.0
Better For You, Morrisons*	1 Slice/20g	39	196	21.0	5.4	10.0	0.0
Cheddar, Mature, Marks & Spencer*	1 Slice/30g	124	412	25.5	0.1	34.4	0.0
Cheddar, Mild, Marks & Spencer*	1 Slice/30g	124	412	25.5	0.1	34.4	0.0
Cheddar, Mild, Tesco*	1 Slice/30g	123	410	25.0	0.1	34.4	0.0
Cheddar, Reduced Fat, Weight Watchers*	1 Slice/21g	50	239	21.9	5.0	14.7	0.0
Cheese Food, Asda*	1 Slice/20g	58	289	18.0	7.0	21.0	0.0
Cheese Food, Sainsbury's*	1 Slice/20g	52	260	14.5	5.4	20.0	0.0
Dairylea*	1 Slice/25g	76	305	13.0	8.0	24.5	0.0
Farmfoods*	1 Slice/17g	49	286	18.0	4.0	22.0	0.0
Good Intentions, Somerfield*	1 Slice/20g	39	195	19.2	7.1	10.0	0.0
Gruyere, Switzerland, Natural, Le Superbe*	1 Slice/20g	82	410	27.0	0.0	32.0	0.0
Half Fat, Asda*	1 Slice/20g	39	194	20.6	5.4	10.0	0.0
Half Fat, Co-Op*	1 Slice/20g	47	235	25.0	7.0	12.0	0.0
Half Fat, Marks & Spencer*	1 Slice/30g	83	277	31.0	0.1	17.0	0.0
Jarlsberg*	1 Slice/15g	54	360	27.0	0.0	27.0	0.0
Kraft*	1 Slice/20g	56	280	13.5	6.6	21.5	0.0
Leerdammer*	1 Slice/28g	101	360	27.1	0.0	27.7	0.0
Light & Fine, Milbona*	1 Slice/20g	37	183	19.0	4.3	10.0	0.0
Light, Aldi*	1 Slice/19.9g	41	206	20.1	8.1	10.4	0.9

	Measure INFO/WEIGHT	per Measure KCAL	Nutrition Values per 100g / 100ml				
			KCAL	PROT	CARB	FAT	FIBRE
CHEESE SLICES,							
Light, Dairylea*	1 Slice/25g	55	220	18.5	7.0	12.5	0.0
Light, Laughing Cow*	1 Slice/20g	41	203	21.0	6.0	10.5	0.0
Light, Thick, Dairylea*	1 Slice/25g	51	205	17.3	8.6	10.5	0.0
Lightlife, Leerdammer*	1 Slice/20g	55	273	30.6	0.0	16.4	0.0
Low Fat, Healthy Living, Tesco*	1 Slice/27g	52	193	36.1	6.0	2.7	0.0
Mature Cheddar, Tesco*	1 Slice/30g	123	410	25.0	0.1	34.4	0.0
Mature, Asda*	1 Slice/20g	52	259	31.0	0.1	15.0	0.0
Mature, BGTY, Sainsbury's*	1 Slice/24g	63	261	31.5	0.1	15.0	0.0
Mature, Medium Fat, Healthy Eating, Tesco*	1 Slice/30g	78	259	30.9	0.0	15.0	0.0
Mature, White, Half Fat, Healthy Living, Co-Op*	1 Slice/30g	78	260	31.0	0.1	15.0	0.0
Reduced Fat, GFY, Asda*	1 Slice/19.9g	38	191	21.0	4.2	10.0	0.0
Safeway*	1 Slice/20.1g	56	279	15.2	7.2	21.0	0.0
Singles, Half Fat, Healthy Living, Tesco*	1 Slice/20g	39	195	19.2	7.1	10.0	0.0
Singles, Lite, Somerfield*	1 Slice/20g	42	212	20.0	6.0	12.0	0.0
Singles, Tesco*	1 Slice/20g	55	273	13.2	7.9	21.0	0.0
Singles, Value, Tesco*	1 Slice/17g	46	273	12.7	5.0	22.5	0.0
SmartPrice, Asda*	1 Slice/16.6g	48	283	14.0	5.0	23.0	0.0
Smoked, Bavarian, Marks & Spencer*	1oz/28g	85	305	14.0	0.1	24.0	0.0
Somerfield*	1 oz/28g	84	300	19.0	2.0	24.0	0.0
Swiss, Leerdammer*	1 Slice/25g	90	360	27.1	0.0	27.7	0.0
Thick, Dairylea*	1 Slice/25g	70	280	13.0	9.5	21.0	0.0
CHEESE SPREAD,							
60% Less Fat, Asda*	1 Serving/30g	52	174	16.0	7.3	9.0	0.0
Asda*	1 Serving/33g	92	280	9.0	7.0	24.0	0.0
BGTY, Sainsbury's*	1 Serving/25g	28	111	11.0	4.3	5.5	0.4
Better for You, Morrisons*	1 Serving/25g	43	172	13.5	6.5	8.5	0.0
Cheese & Garlic, Primula*	1 Serving/20g	49	247	15.7	4.3	18.6	0.0
Cheese & Salmon With Dill, Primula*	3 Inches/10g	26	261	17.6	3.8	19.5	0.0
Cheez Whiz, Original, Light, 41% Less Fat, Kraft*	2 Tbsp/30g	63	210	15.7	11.7	11.3	0.0
Chunky Triangles, BGTY, Sainsbury's*	1 Triangle/25g	43	171	14.8	10.0	8.0	0.0
Chunky, Triangles, Kerrygold*	2 Triangles/47g	119	254	9.1	9.5	20.0	0.0
Cream, Light, Sainsbury's*	1 Serving/50g	94	187	7.8	4.1	15.5	0.3
Creamery, Light, Sainsbury's*	1 Serving/25g	46	185	9.0	3.5	15.0	0.0
Dairylea*	1oz/28g	71	255	7.6	8.0	21.5	0.0
Flavoured	1oz/28g	72	258	14.2	4.4	20.5	0.0
Garlic & Herbs, Light, Benecol*	1 Serving/20g	35	174	7.8	4.2	14.0	0.7
Happy Shopper*	1 Serving/30g	64	213	11.0	8.5	15.0	0.0
Healthy Eating, Tesco*	¼ Pot/25g	47	187	20.0	6.5	9.0	0.0
Kerrygold*	1oz/28g	60	213	11.0	8.5	15.0	0.0
Light, Half Fat, Dairylea*	1 Serving/25g	40	161	12.0	8.2	8.7	0.0
Light, Laughing Cow*	1 Triangle/18g	25	141	13.5	6.5	7.0	0.0
Light, New, Dairylea*	1 Serving/22.5g	34	149	15.0	6.3	7.0	0.0
Light, Primula*	1oz/28g	48	171	16.0	6.6	9.0	0.0
Light, Tub, Dairylea*	1oz/28g	52	186	14.0	7.3	11.0	0.0
Low Fat, Weight Watchers*	1 Serving/50g	56	112	18.1	3.4	2.9	1.2
Mediterranean Soft & Creamy, Extra Light, Asda*	1 Serving/32g	42	130	13.0	6.0	6.0	0.0
Original, Primula*	1oz/28g	72	257	16.0	1.0	21.0	0.0
Portions, GFY, Asda*	1 Triangle/22.4g	35	161	14.0	6.0	9.0	0.0
Soft, Low Fat, Marks & Spencer*	1 Pack/100g	111	111	13.0	4.2	4.5	0.3
The Laughing Cow*	1 Portion/17.5g	46	269	10.0	6.5	22.5	0.0
With Chives, Primula*	1oz/28g	71	253	15.0	1.0	21.0	0.0
With Ham, Primula*	1oz/28g	71	253	15.0	1.0	21.0	0.0
With Shrimp, Primula*	1 Tbsp/15g	38	253	15.0	1.0	21.0	0.0

C

	Measure INFO/WEIGHT	per Measure KCAL	Nutrition Values per 100g / 100ml				
			KCAL	PROT	CARB	FAT	FIBRE
CHEESE STRAWS,							
Cheddar, Marks & Spencer*	1 Straw/11g	59	535	14.9	40.1	34.9	2.4
Finest, Tesco*	1 Straw/7g	39	558	13.3	41.5	37.6	1.5
Selection, Sainsbury's*	1 Straw/7g	41	558	16.6	34.5	39.3	2.8
Selection, Somerfield*	1 Straw/7g	39	558	13.3	41.5	37.6	1.5
CHEESE STRIPS,							
Dairylea*	1 Pack/21g	72	345	23.5	0.4	27.0	0.0
CHEESE THINS,							
Cheddar, The Planet Snack Co*	1 Serving/30g	153	509	11.5	50.1	29.2	2.1
Mini, Snack Rite, Aldi*	1 Bag/30g	144	480	12.9	55.9	22.7	2.5
Waitrose*	1 Biscuit/4g	21	545	11.9	52.6	31.9	2.5
CHEESE TRIANGLES,							
Average	1 Triangle/14g	35	247	10.6	6.6	19.9	0.0
Reduced Fat, Average	1 Triangle/18g	30	170	14.8	7.4	9.0	0.0
CHEESE TWISTS,							
All Butter, Marks & Spencer*	½ Pack/62.6g	312	495	14.0	46.4	28.0	4.2
Asda*	1 Stick/8g	42	500	14.0	48.0	28.0	5.0
Safeway*	2 Twists/11.8g	60	496	13.6	46.2	28.5	5.6
CHEESECAKE,							
American Red White & Blueberry, Sainsbury's*	1/6th/83g	264	318	3.8	35.1	18.5	0.4
Apple & Cinnamon, Baked, Marks & Spencer*	1 Portion/116.4g	389	335	3.7	39.7	18.9	2.1
Apricot, Healthy Living, Tesco*	1 Pot/100g	179	179	4.9	34.7	2.3	1.6
Average	1oz/28g	119	426	3.7	24.6	35.5	0.4
Blackcurrant Devonshire, McVitie's*	1/6 Cake/67g	190	288	3.8	29.7	17.1	1.7
Blackcurrant Swirl, Heinz*	1/5 Portion/87g	241	277	4.1	30.3	15.4	3.6
Blackcurrant, Marks & Spencer*	1oz/28g	82	293	3.3	29.4	17.9	0.9
Blackcurrant, Sainsbury's*	1oz/28g	75	267	3.2	29.5	15.1	1.1
Blackcurrant, Tesco*	1 Cake/100g	252	252	3.9	32.2	12.0	0.7
Blackcurrant, Value, Tesco*	1 Serving/70g	174	248	2.8	31.4	12.3	1.0
Blueberry & Lemon Flavour Wedges, Sainsbury's*	1 Serving/80g	262	327	5.1	29.2	21.1	1.2
Boysenberry, Chateau, KFC*	1 Cake/85g	196	230	4.0	30.0	11.0	0.0
Caramel Crunch, Pret A Manger*	1 Serving/150g	395	263	3.7	14.7	21.1	0.9
Caramel Swirl, Cadbury's*	1 Slice/91g	373	410	6.0	40.1	25.8	0.0
Cheery, Reduced Fat, Safeway*	¼ Cake/137.5g	302	219	3.7	40.8	4.5	1.5
Cherry, BGTY, Sainsbury's*	1 Serving/91g	181	199	4.6	35.5	4.3	0.5
Cherry, Low Fat, Tesco*	1 Serving/91g	185	203	3.4	38.0	4.1	0.9
Chocolate & Hazelnut, Sara Lee*	1 Serving/65g	224	345	6.5	31.2	21.4	1.2
Chocolate & Hazlenut, Gold, Sara Lee*	1 Slice/65g	205	316	5.9	28.7	19.7	1.1
Chocolate & Vanilla, Reduced Fat, Marks & Spencer*	1 Portion/114g	319	280	7.0	37.9	12.0	1.5
Chocolate Brownie, Tesco*	1 Serving/101g	400	396	4.8	31.8	27.7	0.8
Chocolate Chip, Marks & Spencer*	1oz/28g	109	391	5.1	39.7	23.6	0.2
Chocolate Swirl, Deeply Delicious, Heinz*	1/5 Slice/81.5g	221	271	4.6	37.4	11.5	4.7
Chocolate, American Style, Asda*	1 Cake/390g	1486	381	5.0	43.0	21.0	6.0
Chocolate, Baked, Ultimate, Entenmann's*	1 Cake/100g	331	331	5.7	34.2	19.0	2.8
Chocolate, Family, Safeway*	1/6 Cake/100g	385	385	7.2	35.0	23.8	1.6
Chocolate, Marks & Spencer*	1oz/28g	106	380	6.5	40.3	21.5	0.4
Chocolate, Pure Indulgence, Thorntons*	1 Serving/75g	308	410	5.6	44.3	23.4	0.6
Chocolate, Starbucks*	1 Serving/185g	723	391	6.9	30.5	26.8	0.8
Chocolate, Weight Watchers*	1 Cake/95g	143	151	7.5	20.7	4.0	0.7
Citrus, Good Choice, Iceland*	1 Cake Mini/111g	198	178	3.5	31.6	4.2	0.4
Devonshire Strawberry, McVitie's*	1/6 Portion/66g	192	291	4.4	31.8	16.2	3.6
Domino's Pizza*	1 Serving/132g	396	300	5.0	28.5	18.6	0.0
Double Chocolate Wedge, Sainsbury's*	1 Portion/75g	327	436	5.7	29.0	33.0	1.7
Homestyle Chocolate, Marks & Spencer*	1oz/28g	105	376	6.0	38.0	22.2	0.7

CHEESECAKE,	Measure INFO/WEIGHT	per Measure KCAL	Nutrition Values per 100g / 100ml				
			KCAL	PROT	CARB	FAT	FIBRE
Irish Cream, McVitie's*	¼ Slice/190g	616	324	4.4	33.0	19.4	0.4
Lemon Creamy & Light, Marks & Spencer*	1/6 Cake/67.5g	238	350	3.5	32.3	20.4	0.4
Lemon Meringue, Tesco*	1 Wedge/94g	353	375	3.8	30.1	26.6	0.3
Lemon, BGTY, Sainsbury's*	1/6 Cake/71g	142	200	4.4	37.0	3.8	0.5
Lemon, Marks & Spencer*	1oz/28g	92	330	5.7	38.7	17.1	0.2
Lemon, Pret A Manger*	1 Pot/150g	382	255	1.8	14.6	20.9	0.2
Lemon, Value, Tesco*	1 Serving/78.6g	222	281	4.3	32.2	15.0	4.2
Mandarin, Co-Op*	1 Slice/99g	297	300	4.0	32.0	17.0	0.3
Mandarin, GFY, Asda*	1 Serving/97g	194	200	4.0	36.0	4.4	0.8
Mandarin, Healthy Choice, Safeway*	1 Serving/92g	189	205	3.8	37.1	4.6	0.4
Mandarin, Low Fat, Tesco*	1 Serving/70g	145	207	3.3	37.0	4.7	1.4
Pizza Express*	1 Slice/100g	347	347	5.9	24.8	24.8	0.0
Praline, Asda*	1/8 Cake/62g	226	364	7.0	30.0	24.0	3.2
Raspberry Brulee, Marks & Spencer*	1 Serving/100g	255	255	5.7	29.7	12.9	2.1
Raspberry Rapture, Tesco*	1 Serving/109.5g	332	302	3.8	25.4	20.6	0.6
Raspberry Ripple, Marks & Spencer*	1oz/28g	84	300	5.9	32.8	15.6	0.3
Raspberry, Marks & Spencer*	1 Slice/105g	331	315	5.0	32.2	20.5	1.0
Raspberry, Perfectly Balanced, Waitrose*	1 Serving/106g	212	200	4.0	36.2	3.5	1.7
Rhubarb Crumble, Sainsbury's*	1 Serving/114g	268	235	3.1	34.8	9.3	2.4
Sticky Toffee, Iceland*	1 Pack/116g	331	285	3.8	33.9	14.9	0.1
Sticky Toffee, Tesco*	1 Slice/66g	248	375	4.0	35.3	24.2	0.5
Strawberry Shortcake, Sara Lee*	1/6 Slice/68.2g	229	337	4.9	27.6	23.0	0.5
Strawberry, 95% Fat Free, Marks & Spencer*	1 Slice/98g	187	191	5.1	33.8	4.0	0.3
Strawberry, Co-Op*	1 Cake/100g	225	225	4.0	27.0	11.0	1.0
Strawberry, Deep Dish, Iceland*	¼ Cake/120g	292	243	4.2	32.3	10.8	2.0
Strawberry, Fresh, Marks & Spencer*	¼ Cake/125g	300	240	2.8	23.1	15.4	1.1
Strawberry, Heinz*	1 Pack/245g	588	240	3.4	28.1	12.7	2.4
Strawberry, Iceland*	1 Cake/101g	226	224	3.5	31.0	9.5	0.1
Strawberry, Individual, Weight Watchers*	1 Cake/103g	199	193	5.5	33.9	3.2	1.8
Strawberry, Sainsbury's*	1 Serving/90g	221	246	3.5	24.4	14.9	4.6
Strawberry, SmartPrice, Asda*	1 Cake/90g	239	265	5.0	32.0	13.0	1.1
Summerfruit, GFY, Asda*	¼ Cake/130g	259	199	2.8	36.0	4.7	2.0
The Ultimate New York Baked, Entenmann's*	1 Cake/100g	347	347	4.2	35.7	21.3	0.9
Toffee & Banana, Marks & Spencer*	1oz/28g	88	315	5.0	35.7	16.7	0.2
Toffee & Pecan, Wedge, Sainsbury's*	1 Serving/75g	296	395	5.4	28.1	29.0	3.1
Toffee, American Style, Asda*	1 Serving/75g	269	359	4.5	38.0	21.0	3.8
Toffee, Asda*	1 Cake/87g	295	339	4.3	31.0	22.0	3.5
Toffee, Co-Op*	1oz/28g	74	265	5.0	35.0	11.0	1.0
Toffee, Marks & Spencer*	1 Serving/105g	357	340	5.2	37.2	21.5	0.9
Triple Chocolate, Waitrose*	1/6 Cake/76g	262	349	5.4	38.3	19.3	1.2
Ultimate Vanilla New York Baked, Entenmann's*	1 Cake/100g	327	327	4.1	34.2	19.3	1.7
Vanilla, Tesco*	1 Serving/115g	417	363	5.7	29.4	24.7	0.6
CHEETOS,							
Cheese, Walkers*	1 Bag/24g	120	500	6.5	61.0	26.0	1.3
CHEEZLY,							
Cheddar Style, Garlic & Herb Flavoured, Redwood Foods*	1 Pack/190g	473	249	3.6	19.4	17.4	0.0
Cream, Garlic & Herb Flavour, Redwood Foods*	1 Pack/113g	360	319	5.8	5.4	30.5	0.0
Cream, Original Flavour, Redwood Foods*	1 Pack/113g	357	316	5.6	4.8	30.5	0.0
Cream, Sour Cream & Chive Flavour, Redwood Foods*	1 Pack/113g	359	318	5.7	5.1	30.5	0.0
Feta Style, In Oil, Redwood Foods*	1 Pack/190g	903	475	2.5	10.6	47.0	0.0
Grated Cheddar Style, Redwood Foods*	1 Pack/150g	242	161	3.1	21.5	7.5	0.0
Mature Cheddar Style, Redwood Foods*	1 Pack/190g	490	258	3.9	19.2	18.4	0.0
Mature Cheddar Style, With Cranberries, Redwood Foods*	1 Pack/190g	454	239	3.2	24.3	14.3	0.0

	Measure	per Measure		Nutrition Values per 100g / 100ml			
	INFO/WEIGHT	KCAL	KCAL	PROT	CARB	FAT	FIBRE
CHEEZLY,							
Nacho Style, Redwood Foods*	1 Pack/190g	321	169	3.3	21.1	7.9	0.0
White Cheddar Style, Redwood Foods*	1 Pack/190g	321	169	3.3	21.1	7.9	0.0
CHERRIES,							
Black, In Syrup, Average	1 Serving/242g	160	66	0.6	16.0	0.0	0.7
Glace, Average	1oz/28g	79	281	0.4	71.2	0.2	1.1
Raw, Average	1oz/28g	14	49	0.9	11.3	0.1	1.5
Stewed With Sugar	1oz/28g	23	82	0.7	21.0	0.1	0.7
Stewed Without Sugar	1oz/28g	12	42	0.8	10.1	0.1	0.8
CHESTNUTS,							
Average	1 Nut/10g	17	170	2.0	36.6	2.7	4.1
CHEWING GUM,							
Airwaves, Wrigleys*	1 Piece/1g	2	150	0.0	62.0	0.0	0.0
Big Red, Wrigley's*	1 Stick/3g	10	333	0.0	66.7	0.0	0.0
Extra Peppermint Maltitol, Wrigleys*	1 Piece/1g	2	165	0.0	63.0	0.0	0.0
Juicy Fruit, Wrigley's*	1 Stick/3g	10	333	0.0	66.7	0.0	0.0
Orbit, Spearmint, Wrigleys*	1 Piece/3g	6	190	0.0	62.0	0.0	0.0
Spearmint, Wrigleys*	1 Piece/3g	9	295	0.0	73.0	0.0	0.0
Very Berry, Sugar Free, Marks & Spencer*	1 Piece/1.4g	2	165	0.1	68.4	0.0	1.9
CHICK PEAS,							
& Lentils, In Tomata & Onion Sauce, Asda*	1 Serving/200g	204	102	4.3	14.0	3.2	2.9
Dried, Average	1oz/28g	89	319	21.7	47.4	5.4	8.0
Dried, Boiled, Average	1oz/28g	32	114	7.3	16.4	2.2	2.6
In Salted Water, Canned, Average	1 Can/179g	204	114	7.2	14.9	2.9	4.1
In Water, Canned, Average	1 Can/250g	283	113	7.2	15.3	2.6	4.8
CHICKEN,							
Balls, Chinese, Marks & Spencer*	1 Ball/16g	45	280	10.8	29.2	13.6	2.1
Balls, Crispy, Marks & Spencer*	1 Ball/16g	35	220	13.3	23.7	8.1	0.5
Balls, Lemon, Asda*	1 Ball/15g	42	279	14.0	19.0	17.0	1.6
Bites, Mexican, Somerfield*	1 Pack/227g	508	224	26.0	15.0	7.0	0.0
Bites, Roast, Bird's Eye*	5 Bites/80g	160	200	15.0	3.4	13.8	0.1
Bites, Southern Fried, Tesco*	1 Pack/300g	720	240	18.1	16.9	11.1	2.1
Bites, Tikka, Average	1 Serving/50g	96	193	20.7	3.8	10.5	1.9
Breast, Chargrilled, Average	1 Slice/19g	24	124	24.4	0.5	2.7	0.4
Breast, Chunks, Marks & Spencer*	1 Pack/360g	648	180	7.5	22.0	6.9	1.3
Breast, Diced, Average	1 Serving/188g	215	114	25.0	0.1	2.0	0.1
Breast, Eastern Spices, Bird's Eye*	1 Portion/175g	308	176	13.5	3.8	11.9	1.5
Breast, Escalope, Plain, Average	1 Serving/100g	110	110	22.3	0.7	2.2	0.5
Breast, Fajita, Sliced, Sainsbury's*	½ Pack/70g	91	130	24.0	4.1	2.0	0.0
Breast, Fillets, Barbecue Chargrill, Iceland*	1 Fillet/80g	106	132	26.1	3.5	1.5	0.0
Breast, Fillets, Breaded, Average	1 Fillet/112g	246	220	17.5	14.0	10.4	1.3
Breast, Fillets, Breaded, Lemon & Pepper, Average	1 Fillet/89g	133	150	22.0	10.1	2.3	1.3
Breast, Fillets, Cajun, Raw, Average	1 Fillet/93g	118	127	25.4	3.1	1.5	0.3
Breast, Fillets, Cheesy Salsa, Safeway*	½ Pack/163.6g	180	110	17.9	2.2	3.0	1.1
Breast, Fillets, Cordon Bleu, Sainsbury's*	1 Serving/150g	304	203	17.5	11.5	9.5	1.6
Breast, Fillets, Crunchy Coated, Mini, Marks & Spencer*	1 Serving/150g	345	230	15.8	18.1	10.5	2.0
Breast, Fillets, Korma Style, Average	1 Serving/100g	132	132	27.4	0.8	2.8	0.6
Breast, Fillets, Lemon & Pepper, Mini, Marks & Spencer*	½ Pack/150g	338	225	15.6	17.0	10.5	1.3
Breast, Fillets, Lemon Parsley, Marks & Spencer*	½ Pack/145g	232	160	14.3	20.7	2.4	4.3
Breast, Fillets, Mini, Raw, Average	1oz/28g	34	121	26.9	0.2	1.5	0.1
Breast, Fillets, Organic, Average	1 Serving/150g	153	102	24.0	0.0	0.8	0.0
Breast, Fillets, Red Thai Style, Mini, Tesco*	½ Pack/100g	135	135	26.8	2.8	1.8	0.5
Breast, Fillets, Skinless & Boneless, Raw, Average	1 Serving/100g	126	126	25.1	1.2	2.3	0.2
Breast, Fillets, Sliced, BBQ, Safeway*	1 Serving/80g	120	150	28.1	3.2	2.2	0.6

CHICKEN,

INFO/WEIGHT	Measure	per Measure KCAL	KCAL	PROT	CARB	FAT	FIBRE
			Nutrition Values per 100g / 100ml				
Breast, Garlic & Herb Flavour, Co-Op*	1 Serving/170g	281	165	19.0	2.0	9.0	0.3
Breast, Golden Roasted, Bernard Matthews*	1oz/28g	31	110	23.4	0.6	1.5	0.0
Breast, Joint, Free Range, Marks & Spencer*	1oz/28g	36	130	22.0	3.9	4.1	0.6
Breast, Joint, Lemon & Tarragon, Finest, Tesco*	1 Serving/175g	247	141	18.8	2.3	6.3	0.2
Breast, Mediterranean Style Coating, Tesco*	1 Breast/195g	283	145	20.4	0.7	6.7	0.0
Breast, Original Recipe, KFC*	1 Breast/161g	596	370	40.0	11.0	19.0	0.0
Breast, Original, KFC*	1 Breast/161g	370	230	24.8	6.8	11.8	0.0
Breast, Pieces, Tikka, Average	1 Serving/100g	154	154	28.2	2.8	3.4	0.4
Breast, Roast, Average	1oz/28g	42	149	25.4	1.1	4.7	0.2
Breast, Roast, Sliced, Average	1 Slice/13g	17	139	25.0	1.8	3.5	0.2
Breast, Roll, Average	1 Slice/10g	17	167	16.1	3.2	10.0	0.2
Breast, Sage & Onion, Slices, Sainsbury's*	1 Pack/140g	158	113	23.1	1.0	1.8	0.5
Breast, Seasoned, Marks & Spencer*	1oz/28g	35	126	20.5	2.6	3.8	0.0
Breast, Sliced, Chargrilled, Sainsbury's*	1 Pack/140g	202	144	32.0	0.8	1.4	0.0
Breast, Sliced, Flamegrilled, Co-Op*	1 Pack/170g	187	110	26.0	0.0	0.9	0.0
Breast, Smoked, Average	1 Slice/20g	22	110	20.7	0.9	2.6	0.1
Breast, Steaks, Garlic, Crunchy, Iceland*	1 Steak/95.1g	255	268	15.1	15.7	16.1	1.2
Breast, Strips, Raw, Average	1 Serving/280g	358	128	27.1	0.4	2.1	0.3
Breast, Tandoori Style, Average	1 Serving/180g	237	132	22.3	2.3	3.8	1.0
Breast, Tikka, Sliced, Average	1oz/28g	34	120	24.9	2.0	1.7	0.6
Breast, Wafer Thin, Sage & Onion, Bernard Matthews*	1 Serving/25g	30	120	19.8	3.5	3.0	0.0
Breast, With Skin, Raw, Average	1oz/28g	51	181	24.3	4.9	7.2	0.6
Breasts, Chargrilled, Bird's Eye*	1 Piece/93.8g	196	208	22.2	2.5	12.1	0.1
Breasts, Honey & Mustard, Bird's Eye*	1 Portion/97g	175	180	19.6	4.2	9.4	0.1
Chargrilled Style, Slices, Asda*	1 Slice/24.6g	29	114	24.0	0.8	1.6	0.0
Chargrills, Garlic, Bird's Eye*	1 Piece/76g	169	222	19.2	1.2	15.6	0.0
Chargrills, Original, Birds Eye*	1 serving/94g	195	208	22.2	2.5	12.1	0.1
Chunky, Chargrilled, Tesco*	1oz/28g	32	116	25.5	0.9	1.1	0.0
Chunky, Marks & Spencer*	1oz/28g	46	163	12.2	3.6	11.4	0.5
Chunky, SmartPrice, Asda*	½ Can/206.2g	332	161	12.0	3.5	11.0	0.0
Cooked, Sliced, Average	1oz/28g	33	118	22.4	1.6	2.4	0.1
Corn Fed, Sainsbury's*	1 Serving/200g	450	225	23.5	0.1	14.5	0.0
Cracked Pepper, Bird's Eye*	1 Portion/94.7g	196	206	21.0	3.9	11.8	0.1
Crispy, Bird's Eye*	1 Piece/98g	231	236	15.0	10.2	15.0	0.3
Dippers, Crispy, Average	5 Dippers/93g	231	249	13.2	14.4	15.4	0.6
Dippers, Tikka, Tesco*	1oz/28g	54	193	21.5	5.0	9.7	1.0
Drumsticks, BBQ Flavour, Average	1 Serving/200g	348	174	22.6	3.1	8.0	0.4
Drumsticks, Breaded, Fried, Average	1oz/28g	70	248	19.6	9.9	14.6	0.6
Drumsticks, Chinese Style, Average	1 Drumstick/100g	178	178	22.6	3.6	8.1	0.7
Drumsticks, Roast, Without Skin, Average	1 Serving/100g	163	163	22.6	0.5	7.8	0.2
Drumsticks, With Skin, Average	1 Drumstick/125g	269	215	22.1	1.8	13.3	0.3
Dunkers, Domino's Pizza*	1oz/28g	62	220	23.5	1.5	13.3	0.5
Escalope, Breaded, Average	1 Escalope/128g	361	282	13.4	19.1	16.9	0.7
Escalope, Cheese Topped, Asda*	1 Serving/173.4g	410	237	12.0	18.0	13.0	1.9
Escalope, Tomato & Basil, Safeway*	1 Escalope/150g	242	161	21.2	2.2	7.5	1.2
Fillets, Barbecue, Mini, Marks & Spencer*	1oz/28g	36	130	25.3	5.9	0.6	0.8
Fillets, Battered, Average	1oz/28g	62	221	16.1	13.3	11.5	0.5
Fillets, Breaded, Average	1 Piece/98g	214	219	14.2	15.9	10.7	1.9
Fillets, Burger King*	1 Serving/72g	101	140	27.9	0.4	3.1	0.0
Fillets, Chargrilled, Sliced, Marks & Spencer*	1 Serving/140g	182	130	29.8	0.6	1.0	0.5
Fillets, Chinese Style, Average	1oz/28g	37	132	24.4	4.6	1.8	0.5
Fillets, Coronation, BGTY, Sainsbury's*	1 Fillet/100g	136	136	27.1	2.4	2.6	1.0
Fillets, Hickory Barbecue & Chilli, BGTY, Sainsbury's*	1 Fillet/100g	133	133	26.9	3.6	1.2	0.9

CHICKEN,

INFO/WEIGHT	Measure	per Measure KCAL	KCAL	PROT	CARB	FAT	FIBRE
Fillets, Honey & Maple, Roast, Mini, Waitrose*	½ Pack/100g	131	131	23.0	8.6	0.5	1.5
Fillets, Honey & Mustard, Mini, Marks & Spencer*	1 Serving/105g	142	135	24.9	3.9	2.0	1.3
Fillets, Hot & Spicy, Average	1oz/28g	58	206	16.4	10.5	11.0	1.1
Fillets, Indian, Style, Sainsbury's*	1 Pack/200g	233	112	13.7	4.4	4.4	1.2
Fillets, Lime & Coriander, Mini, Average	1 Fillet/42g	49	118	24.3	2.6	1.3	0.6
Fillets, Red Thai, Mini, Average	1oz/28g	36	128	21.7	5.5	2.1	0.6
Fillets, Southern Fried, Average	1oz/28g	62	222	16.4	12.2	12.0	1.1
Fillets, Sweet Chilli & Lime, Mini, Marks & Spencer*	1 Serving/210g	284	135	24.5	5.6	1.8	1.1
Fillets, Tandoori Style, Mini, Average	1oz/28g	36	128	24.7	2.6	2.1	0.4
Fillets, Thai, COU, Marks & Spencer*	1 Fillet/120g	160	133	19.5	10.4	1.6	1.3
Fillets, Tikka, Average	1oz/28g	39	141	22.4	1.7	5.0	1.1
Fillets, Tikka, Mini, Average	1oz/28g	35	124	25.1	1.3	2.2	1.2
Fillets, Tomato & Basil, Mini, Average	1oz/28g	34	123	23.5	2.5	2.1	0.4
Fillets,Cheese & Ham, Safeway*	½ Pack/162.5g	261	160	20.0	1.2	8.1	0.6
Fingers, Average	1 Serving/75g	188	250	13.7	18.8	13.3	1.2
Fresh, Healthy Eating, Tesco*	1 Fillet/110g	128	116	21.8	0.0	3.2	0.0
Fresh, Large, Asda*	1 Serving/169g	373	221	26.0	0.0	13.0	0.1
Garlic, Frozen, Tesco*	1 Serving/94.9g	242	255	12.9	14.7	16.1	1.3
Golden Drummers, Bernard Matthews*	1 Drummer/54g	138	256	12.2	10.1	18.6	0.0
Goujons, Breaded, Average	1 Serving/114g	293	258	15.8	15.2	15.0	1.0
Goujons, Breast, Fresh, Average	1oz/28g	36	127	28.0	0.0	1.7	0.0
Goujons, Caesar, Marks & Spencer*	½ Pack/128g	250	195	18.6	9.2	9.2	2.0
Goujons, Cracked Black Pepper, American, Asda*	1 Serving/150g	333	222	16.0	8.0	14.0	2.5
Goujons, Garlic & Herb, Breaded, American, Asda*	½ Pack/150g	377	251	17.0	12.0	15.0	2.1
Goujons, Hot & Spicy, Sainsbury's*	½ Pack/125g	253	202	20.0	13.1	7.7	1.2
Griddlers, BBQ, Mini, Bird's Eye*	½ Pack/50g	109	217	15.8	6.7	14.1	0.2
Griddles, BBQ, Bird's Eye*	1 Serving/48g	105	217	15.8	6.7	14.1	0.2
Grilled, Tulip*	1 Serving/50g	50	100	19.0	2.0	2.0	0.0
Half, Roasted, Marks & Spencer*	1oz/28g	60	215	24.8	0.3	12.8	0.0
Leg Or Thigh, Hot & Spicy, Average	1oz/28g	50	179	19.4	1.0	10.8	0.4
Leg Portion, Roast, Average	1 Quarter/120g	244	203	21.6	0.3	12.7	0.2
Leg, With Skin, Raw, Average	1oz/28g	48	172	19.1	0.0	10.4	0.0
Leg, With Skin, Roasted, Avrage	1oz/28g	66	234	21.5	0.1	16.4	0.0
Lemon Pepper, Bird's Eye*	1 Piece/113g	273	242	15.4	17.5	12.3	0.6
Light Meat, Raw	1oz/28g	30	106	24.0	0.0	1.1	0.0
Light Meat, Roasted	1oz/28g	43	153	30.2	0.0	3.6	0.0
Meat & Skin Portions, Deep Fried	1oz/28g	73	259	26.9	0.0	16.8	0.0
Meat & Skin, Raw	1oz/28g	64	230	17.6	0.0	17.7	0.0
Meat & Skin, Roasted	1oz/28g	60	216	22.6	0.0	14.0	0.0
Meat, Roasted, Average	1oz/28g	50	177	27.3	0.0	7.5	0.0
Mince, Average	1oz/28g	39	140	20.9	0.1	6.0	0.2
Nibbles, Marks & Spencer*	1 Bag/24.7g	111	445	8.9	70.5	13.9	3.4
Nuggets, Battered, Average	1oz/28g	70	251	13.5	16.9	14.4	0.9
Nuggets, Breaded, Average	1 Nugget/14g	37	263	14.8	19.8	13.8	1.9
O's, Bird's Eye*	10 O's/48g	125	260	13.1	14.6	16.6	0.7
Pieces, Garlic, Crunchy, Bird's Eye*	1 Piece/99g	259	262	14.4	16.9	15.2	0.9
Pieces, Sainsbury's*	1 Serving/89g	190	214	13.6	13.5	11.7	0.5
Pieces, Spicy, Mexican, Bird's Eye*	1 Piece/103g	254	247	14.6	16.5	13.6	0.6
Popcorn, Large, KFC*	1 Serving/170g	1054	620	30.0	36.0	40.0	0.0
Popcorn, Small, KFC*	1 Serving/99g	358	362	17.0	21.0	23.0	0.2
Quarters, Roast, Farmfoods*	1oz/28g	41	148	24.8	0.0	5.4	0.0
Roast, In Sugar Marinade, Marks & Spencer*	1 Portion/200g	370	185	26.4	0.4	8.6	0.1
Schnitzel, Chicky World*	1 Piece/60g	134	223	14.0	11.0	15.0	0.0

	Measure	per Measure	Nutrition Values per 100g / 100ml				
	INFO/WEIGHT	KCAL	KCAL	PROT	CARB	FAT	FIBRE
CHICKEN,							
Seasoned & Basted, Marks & Spencer*	1oz/28g	38	137	17.3	6.7	4.5	0.5
Selects, McDonald's*	2 Selects/82.1g	184	224	13.7	14.8	11.7	1.3
Sliced, Honey Roast, Average	1 Slice/13g	15	117	21.6	2.2	2.5	0.1
Slices, BBQ, Morrisons*	1 Serving/170g	218	128	25.5	3.9	1.4	0.6
Southern Style, Barbecue, GFY, Asda*	1 Serving/165g	213	129	19.0	5.0	3.7	1.0
Spicy, Fried, Sainsbury's*	1 Serving/150g	414	276	28.8	2.9	16.6	2.1
Steaks, Average	1oz/28g	57	205	21.1	9.0	9.4	0.7
Strippers, Domino's Pizza*	1oz/28g	61	219	23.3	13.4	8.0	1.0
Strips Or Tenders, Chinese Style, Average	1oz/28g	41	145	19.7	8.0	4.1	1.1
Strips, Crispy, KFC*	1 Strip/50g	134	268	18.6	14.5	15.1	1.5
Strips, Mexican, Sliced, Marks & Spencer*	½ Pack/70g	77	110	24.3	2.3	0.6	0.5
Strips, Southern Fried, Tesco*	1 Pack/300g	699	233	18.7	18.3	9.4	1.4
Tenders, Tex Mex, Jumbo, Marks & Spencer*	1 Serving/200g	250	125	22.8	0.7	3.4	0.6
Thigh, BBQ, Asda*	1oz/28g	60	216	22.6	0.0	14.0	0.0
Thigh, Meat & Skin, Average	1oz/28g	61	218	21.4	0.0	14.7	0.0
Thigh, Meat & Skin, Casseroled	1oz/28g	65	233	21.5	0.0	16.3	0.0
Thigh, Meat Only, Diced, Casseroled	1oz/28g	50	180	25.6	0.0	8.6	0.0
Thigh, Meat Only, Raw, Average	1 Thigh/90g	113	126	19.4	0.0	5.5	0.0
Thigh, Original Recipe, Kentucky Fried, KFC*	1 Serving/126g	360	286	17.5	9.5	19.8	0.0
Thigh, Roast, Average	1oz/28g	67	238	23.9	0.4	15.7	0.0
Thigh, Southern Fried, Tesco*	1oz/28g	68	242	14.7	10.1	15.9	0.5
Wafer Thin, Average	1oz/28g	34	120	19.0	2.8	3.6	0.2
Wafer Thin, Coronation, Sainsbury's*	½ Pack/50g	68	135	19.1	4.5	4.5	0.1
Whole, Roast, Average	1oz/28g	59	211	21.2	1.5	13.4	0.2
Wing Quarter, Meat Only, Casseroled	1oz/28g	46	164	26.9	0.0	6.3	0.0
Wing, Breaded, Fried, Average	1oz/28g	82	294	18.4	14.0	18.5	0.4
Wing, Meat & Skin, Cooked, Average	1oz/28g	67	241	23.3	1.9	15.6	0.3
Wings, BBQ Flavour, Average	1oz/28g	61	220	20.3	6.6	12.5	0.6
Wings, Chinese Style, Average	1oz/28g	72	256	24.2	5.1	15.5	0.6
Wings, Hot & Spicy, Average	1oz/28g	65	231	21.9	5.2	13.7	0.9
Wings, Meat & Skin, Raw, Average	1oz/28g	52	184	19.0	0.5	11.8	0.2
CHICKEN &,							
Apricot Rice, COU, Marks & Spencer*	1 Pack/400g	360	90	9.4	10.6	0.9	0.7
Asparagus, BGTY, Sainsbury's*	1 Pack/450g	504	112	8.5	17.4	1.0	0.8
Asparagus, In A Champagne Sauce, Finest, Tesco*	1 Pack/500g	615	123	8.8	7.0	6.7	0.9
Asparagus, Long Grain & Wild Rice, BGTY, Sainsbury's*	1 Pack/451g	555	123	9.2	17.1	2.0	0.8
Bacon Parcels, Finest, Tesco*	1 Pack/232.5g	380	163	16.1	3.7	9.3	0.5
Bacon Parcels, Sainsbury's*	½ Pack/170g	406	239	21.9	0.1	16.8	0.0
Bacon, Al Forno, Safeway*	½ Pack/400g	420	105	6.1	13.3	2.9	1.1
Black Bean Noodles, Sainsbury's*	1 Serving/130g	155	119	4.3	23.9	0.7	0.8
Black Bean Sauce, & Egg Fried Rice, BGTY, Sainsbury's*	1 Pack/450g	527	117	7.2	14.7	3.3	0.5
Black Bean, Chinese Takeaway, Tesco*	1 Serving/200g	190	95	8.3	8.0	3.3	0.5
Black Bean, Safeway*	1 Pack/350g	263	75	10.3	4.4	1.6	2.5
Black Bean, With Chinese Rice, COU, Marks & Spencer*	1 Pack/400g	320	80	7.4	7.6	2.4	1.1
Black Bean, With Egg Fried Rice, New, BGTY, Sainsbury's*	1 Pack/450g	446	99	6.4	16.6	0.8	0.6
Black Bean, With Noodles, Tesco*	1 Pack/475g	470	99	7.6	13.6	1.6	0.2
Black Bean, With Rice, Good Intentions, Somerfield*	1 Pack/400g	352	88	7.0	13.4	0.7	0.6
Black Bean, With Rice, Healthy Living, Tesco*	1 Pack/450g	464	103	6.9	19.6	1.6	0.6
Broccoli, With Rigatoni Pasta, BGTY, Sainsbury's*	1 Pack/450g	590	131	15.3	15.2	3.1	0.7
Cashew Nuts, & Vegetable Rice, COU, Marks & Spencer*	1 Pack/400g	360	90	7.5	9.7	2.6	1.1
Cashew Nuts, Asda*	1 Pack/400g	528	132	8.2	4.2	9.1	0.8
Cashew Nuts, Cantonese, Sainsbury's*	1 Pack/350g	350	100	9.4	3.8	5.2	1.8
Cashew Nuts, Chinese, Sainsbury's*	1 Pack/350g	312	89	7.8	5.7	4.0	1.2

C

	Measure INFO/WEIGHT	per Measure KCAL	Nutrition Values per 100g / 100ml				
			KCAL	PROT	CARB	FAT	FIBRE
CHICKEN &,							
Cashew Nuts, Chinese, Tesco*	1 Pack/350g	378	108	9.5	4.9	5.6	0.6
Cashew Nuts, Marks & Spencer*	1 Pack/300g	300	100	10.3	5.0	4.0	1.2
Cashew Nuts, Ready Meals, Waitrose*	1 Pack/400g	416	104	11.3	8.2	2.9	1.0
Cashew Nuts, With Egg Fried Rice, Healthy Living, Tesco*	1 Pack/450g	441	98	8.9	12.7	1.3	1.3
Cashew Nuts, With Egg Fried Rice, Somerfield*	1 Pack/340g	435	128	7.0	13.0	5.0	0.0
Cashew Nuts, With Egg Rice, GFY, Asda*	1 Pack/396g	384	97	6.0	16.0	1.0	6.0
Cashew Nuts, With Rice, Eat Smart, Safeway*	1 Serving/400g	400	100	6.6	12.6	2.3	2.0
Chargrilled Vegetable Roll, Healthy Living, Tesco*	1 Pack/221.1g	336	152	10.1	21.8	2.7	2.3
Cous Cous, Healthy Eating, Tesco*	1 Pack/351g	263	75	10.3	7.3	0.5	1.4
Cranberry, Perfectly Balanced, Waitrose*	1 Pack/240g	161	67	11.8	4.1	0.4	1.1
Gravy, COU, Marks & Spencer*	1 Pack/300g	216	72	7.2	7.8	1.3	1.6
King Prawn Special Fried Rice, Finest, Tesco*	1 Pack/450g	734	163	7.7	17.0	7.1	0.7
Mushroom, Chinese, Iceland*	1 Pack/400g	276	69	8.2	3.8	2.3	0.4
Mushroom, Chinese, Sainsbury's*	½ Pack/175g	116	66	7.6	4.4	2.0	0.9
Mushroom, Chinese, Tesco*	1 Pack/460g	474	103	5.7	13.8	2.8	1.0
Mushroom, In Oyster Sauce, Tesco*	1 Pack/350g	252	72	8.0	6.3	1.6	0.7
Mushroom, In White Wine Sauce, GFY, Asda*	1 Pack/400g	272	68	6.0	7.0	1.8	1.2
Mushroom, With Egg Fried Rice, Iceland*	1 Pack/500g	410	82	4.9	13.0	1.2	0.7
Mushroom, With Vegetable Rice, BGTY, Sainsbury's*	1 Pack/400g	376	94	6.4	13.0	1.8	0.9
Mushroom, With Vegetable Rice, BGTY, Sainsbury's*	1 Pack/400g	376	94	6.4	13.0	1.8	0.9
Noodles, Chinese Style, Healthy Eating, Tesco*	1 Pack/370g	422	114	8.5	15.9	1.7	1.5
Peppers, In A Black Bean Sauce, Marks & Spencer*	1 Pack/320g	256	80	9.4	7.3	1.5	1.2
Peppers, Marks & Spencer*	1 Serving/240g	264	110	14.7	2.3	4.5	0.6
Pineapple, Chilled, Tesco*	1 Pack/350g	364	104	9.6	11.1	2.4	5.5
Pineapple, With Egg Fried Rice, Healthy Living, Tesco*	1 Pack/450g	414	92	6.0	15.4	0.7	0.6
Pineapple, With Egg Fried Rice, Tesco*	1 Pack/450g	450	100	7.6	12.1	2.4	1.2
Pineapple, With Rice, Healthy Living, Tesco*	1 Pack/450g	401	89	6.6	12.0	1.6	1.0
Pineapple, With Vegetable Rice, Marks & Spencer*	1 Pack/450g	400	100	7.2	13.0	1.9	1.6
Prawn Yaki Udan Noodles, Marks & Spencer*	1 Pack/395g	435	110	8.1	11.9	3.6	0.8
Red Pepper Dressing, Simple Solutions, Tesco*	1 Serving/140g	228	163	19.2	0.1	9.5	0.5
Tomato & Basil, COU, Marks & Spencer*	½ Pack/200g	180	90	14.3	3.4	2.3	0.8
Tomato Saag, With Pilau Rice, BGTY, Sainsbury's*	1 Pack/400g	404	101	7.3	15.6	1.0	1.0
Tomato Sauce, With Basil Mash, COU, Marks & Spencer*	1 Pack/400g	360	90	7.9	9.3	2.3	0.9
Vegetable Medley, Chargrilled, Healthy Eating, Tesco*	1 Pack/450g	270	60	6.5	5.8	1.2	0.9
Vegetable Savoury Rice, Safeway*	½ Pack/185g	231	125	2.9	25.9	1.1	0.8
White Wine, With Rice, Healthy Eating, Tesco*	1 Pack/450g	450	100	7.1	14.8	1.4	1.0
CHICKEN A L' ORANGE,							
Lean Cuisine, Findus*	1 Pack/334g	384	115	5.6	18.0	2.1	0.4
CHICKEN ALFREDO,							
BGTY, Sainsbury's*	1 Serving/200g	208	104	18.0	1.9	2.7	0.5
CHICKEN ARRABBIATA,							
Al Forno, Sainsbury's*	1 Pack/900g	1026	114	6.5	16.4	2.5	1.4
Bistro, Waitrose*	½ Pack/175g	156	89	12.9	2.5	3.0	0.5
Easy Steam, Healthy Living, Tesco*	1 Pack/400g	284	71	8.4	7.6	0.8	1.2
GFY, Asda*	1 Pack/400g	256	64	5.0	9.0	0.9	0.7
Perfectly Balanced, Waitrose*	1 Serving/240g	211	88	12.4	4.0	2.4	0.6
CHICKEN BBQ,							
& Chips, Sainsbury's*	1 Serving/380g	422	111	7.9	15.9	1.8	2.5
Chunky, Ready To Eat, Tesco*	½ Pack/85g	118	139	29.0	3.2	1.1	0.3
CHICKEN BANG BANG,							
Oriental Express*	½ Pack/200g	170	85	6.4	11.0	1.7	3.2
Waitrose*	1 Pack/350g	368	105	9.4	5.9	4.9	1.2

	Measure INFO/WEIGHT	per Measure KCAL	Nutrition Values per 100g / 100ml				
			KCAL	PROT	CARB	FAT	FIBRE
CHICKEN BARBECUE,							
Asda*	1 Serving/165g	213	129	19.0	5.0	3.7	1.0
CHICKEN BOMBAY,							
GFY, Asda*	½ Pack/168.1g	158	94	16.0	2.1	2.4	4.3
Style, GFY, Asda*	1 Serving/185g	158	85	14.6	1.9	2.2	3.8
CHICKEN BUTTER,							
Safeway*	1 Pack/350g	473	135	12.0	4.1	7.3	2.5
Sainsbury's*	1 Pack/400g	592	148	12.1	4.4	9.1	1.2
CHICKEN CAJUN,							
& Pasta, Safeway*	1 Pack/455g	501	110	8.6	10.5	3.4	2.1
& Potato Hash, Healthy Eating, Tesco*	1 Pack/450g	428	95	6.6	11.7	2.4	0.9
& Potato Hash, Healthy Living, Tesco*	1 Pack/450g	414	92	8.0	10.0	2.2	0.9
Asda*	1 Serving/150g	327	218	22.0	7.0	11.0	0.4
Fettuccine, Marks & Spencer*	1 Pack/500g	600	120	8.7	11.4	4.4	0.9
Healthy Eating, Tesco*	1 Pack/365g	412	113	7.9	17.3	1.3	0.7
Somerfield*	1 Pack/149g	282	189	6.2	24.4	7.5	1.1
CHICKEN CALIFORNIAN,							
Creamy Lime & Wedges, Safeway*	1 Pack/400g	460	115	8.8	9.2	4.5	2.5
CHICKEN CALYPSO,							
With Turmeric Rice, BGTY, Sainsbury's*	1 Pack/450g	495	110	6.7	16.3	2.1	1.0
CHICKEN CANTONESE,							
Honey Pepper, Sainsbury's*	½ Pack/175g	124	71	6.6	6.1	2.2	0.9
Honey, Sesame, Sainsbury's*	1/3 Pack/135g	116	86	9.8	5.5	2.7	0.8
CHICKEN CARBONARA,							
Steam Cuisine, Marks & Spencer*	1 Pack/400g	560	140	10.4	9.8	6.9	1.2
CHICKEN CARIBBEAN,							
Fruity, With Rice & Peas, BGTY, Sainsbury's*	1 Pack/400g	412	103	7.3	14.8	1.6	1.5
Fruity, With Rice & Peas, New, BGTY, Sainsbury's*	1 Pack/400g	352	88	6.9	13.1	0.9	2.2
Somerfield*	1 Pack/400g	554	139	8.7	16.5	4.2	1.7
Style Curry, With Rice & Beans, Eat Smart, Safeway*	1 Pack/380g	342	90	6.2	12.5	1.3	1.8
With Potato & Toasted Coconut Rosti, TTD, Sainsbury's*	½ Pack/200g	320	160	13.8	9.7	7.3	0.6
Style, Breasts, COU, Marks & Spencer*	1 Serving/205g	205	100	14.6	7.3	1.5	1.3
CHICKEN CHASSEUR,							
& Colcannon, Healthy Living, Tesco*	1 Pack/400g	348	87	9.7	6.7	2.4	0.6
BGTY, Sainsbury's*	1 Pack/320g	243	76	6.8	9.5	1.1	1.0
Finest, Tesco*	1 Serving/200g	266	133	12.6	1.6	8.4	0.4
CHICKEN CHILLI,							
& Ginger, Breasts, COU, Marks & Spencer*	1 Breast/120g	156	130	19.5	8.6	2.0	1.7
& Ginger, Fillets, Marks & Spencer*	1 Serving/120g	156	130	19.5	8.6	2.0	1.7
& Lemongrass, With Egg Noodles, BGTY, Sainsbury's*	1 Pack/450g	500	111	10.0	10.2	3.4	1.2
Grande, Stagg*	1oz/28g	27	95	10.0	10.4	0.4	2.0
Quick To Cook, BGTY, Sainsbury's*	1 Serving/420g	336	80	7.4	10.2	1.1	1.0
Sweet, COU, Marks & Spencer*	1 Pack/400g	380	95	9.9	11.0	1.1	1.1
Sweet, Findus*	1 Pack/350g	420	120	6.0	15.0	3.5	1.5
Sweet, Roast, Fillets, Mini, Waitrose*	1 Pack/200g	216	108	23.0	3.8	0.2	0.9
With Beans, Grand, Stagg*	1oz/28g	27	95	10.0	10.4	0.4	2.0
With Lime, Breast, Simple Solutions, Tesco*	1 Pack/400g	564	141	22.5	0.8	5.3	1.4
CHICKEN CHINESE,							
Marks & Spencer*	1 Serving/140g	182	130	22.8	8.5	0.3	0.8
Oriental Express*	1 Pack/350g	326	93	5.7	15.9	0.7	2.2
Style, & Noodles, Healthy Eating, Tesco*	1 Pack/370g	278	75	6.9	9.4	1.1	0.7
Style, GFY, Asda*	1 Serving/200g	220	110	18.0	3.5	2.7	0.5
With Szechuan Pepper, Bird's Eye*	1 Breast/97g	189	195	21.9	3.9	10.2	0.1

C

	Measure INFO/WEIGHT	per Measure KCAL	Nutrition Values per 100g / 100ml				
			KCAL	PROT	CARB	FAT	FIBRE
CHICKEN CIDER,							
COU, Marks & Spencer*	1 Pack/400g	300	75	7.2	6.7	2.3	0.8
With Colcannon, Perfectly Balanced, Waitrose*	1 Pack/401.1g	353	88	6.2	8.9	3.1	1.1
CHICKEN CORDON BLEU,							
TTD, Sainsbury's*	1 Fillet/140g	339	242	21.3	14.1	11.2	1.1
CHICKEN CORONATION,							
COU, Marks & Spencer*	1oz/28g	34	120	16.3	8.6	2.2	0.7
Marks & Spencer*	1 Serving/200g	420	210	12.6	10.6	13.2	1.3
CHICKEN DIJONNAISE,							
Steam Cuisine, Marks & Spencer*	1 Pack/400g	320	80	9.6	4.2	2.6	2.0
CHICKEN DINNER,							
Roast, Bird's Eye*	1 Pack/368g	316	86	8.9	9.1	3.1	1.0
Tesco*	1 Serving/400g	388	97	9.2	10.9	1.8	1.2
CHICKEN EN CROUTE,							
Breast, Tesco*	1 Serving/215g	555	258	9.4	20.4	15.4	0.6
Sainsbury's*	1 Serving/180g	481	267	16.8	15.9	15.3	0.4
CHICKEN ESCALOPE,							
Creamy Peppercorn, Sainsbury's*	1 Serving/150g	367	245	13.3	11.2	16.3	1.1
Spinach & Ricotta, Sainsbury's*	1 Escalope/150g	354	236	13.1	11.5	15.3	0.9
Topped With Cheese, Ham & Mushrooms, Asda*	½ Pack/149.4g	259	174	25.0	0.6	8.0	0.0
CHICKEN FLORENTINE,							
Asda*	1 Serving/200g	322	161	18.0	2.1	9.0	0.9
Finest, Tesco*	1 Serving/225g	297	132	17.6	3.3	5.4	0.7
Healthy Living, Tesco*	1 Pack/400g	340	85	12.1	3.0	2.7	0.9
CHICKEN FORRESTIERE,							
GFY, Asda*	½ Pack/225g	205	91	15.0	2.5	2.3	0.3
Marks & Spencer*	1 Serving/220g	230	105	14.4	0.6	4.8	0.4
CHICKEN FU YUNG,							
Chinese Takeaway, Tesco*	1 Pack/350g	315	90	5.6	14.5	1.0	0.8
CHICKEN GINGER,							
& Lemon, With Apricot Rice, BGTY, Sainsbury's*	1 Pack/401.8g	438	109	9.7	14.5	1.4	0.3
& Lemon, With Basmati Rice, East Smart, Safeway*	1 Pack/395g	395	100	7.3	13.4	1.7	1.4
& Lemon, With Rice, COU, Marks & Spencer*	1 Pack/400g	320	80	7.9	9.7	0.9	2.0
& Plum, With Rice, Perfectly Balanced, Waitrose*	1 Pack/400g	492	123	6.3	23.5	0.5	1.0
& Spring Onion, With Rice, Sharwood's*	1 Pack/375g	347	93	5.1	14.2	1.7	1.7
CHICKEN GLAZED,							
Balsamic, Healthy Living, Tesco*	1 Pack/400g	288	72	5.1	10.8	0.9	0.9
CHICKEN HARISSA,							
BGTY, Sainsbury's*	1 Serving/250g	211	84	10.4	8.0	1.2	1.5
CHICKEN HAWAIIAN,							
With Rice, Bird's Eye*	1 Pack/350g	406	116	5.5	20.2	1.5	0.6
CHICKEN HERB,							
Steam Cuisine, Marks & Spencer*	1 Pack/400g	280	70	8.2	6.0	1.6	0.9
CHICKEN HONEY & MUSTARD,							
Bird's Eye*	1 Piece/87g	185	213	18.2	3.0	14.2	0.0
GFY, Asda*	1 Pack/402g	478	119	7.0	17.0	2.5	0.1
Shapers, Boots*	1 Pack/241g	304	126	7.0	19.0	2.4	1.7
With Baby Potatoes, BGTY, Sainsbury's*	1 Pack/450g	392	87	8.5	11.7	0.7	0.8
With Spring Vegetable Rice, Slim Fast*	1 Pack/375g	375	100	5.8	15.5	1.4	0.8
With Vegetable Medley, BGTY, Sainsbury's*	1 Pack/400g	288	72	8.4	8.1	0.7	0.8
CHICKEN IN,							
A Curry Sauce, Fillets, Safeway*	1 Serving/124g	180	145	17.2	3.9	6.4	0.6
Asparagus Sauce & New Potatoes, Sainsbury's*	1 Pack/495g	545	110	7.4	9.5	4.7	0.9
BBQ Sauce, Breast, Sainsbury's*	1 Serving/170g	199	117	14.5	13.1	0.7	1.3

CHICKEN IN,

	Measure INFO/WEIGHT	per Measure KCAL	KCAL	PROT	CARB	FAT	FIBRE
BBQ Sauce, Breast, Weight Watchers*	1 Pack/339g	336	99	5.8	11.0	3.5	0.9
BBQ Sauce, Chargrilled, Breast, GFY, Asda*	1 Serving/166g	214	129	19.0	5.0	3.7	1.0
BBQ Sauce, GFY, Asda*	1 Pack/380g	414	109	13.0	13.0	0.5	1.3
Bacon, Mushroom & Red Wine Sauce, Asda*	1 Serving/151g	145	96	16.0	2.2	2.6	0.5
Barbecue Sauce, COU, Marks & Spencer*	1 Pack/352g	370	105	8.6	13.8	1.6	1.2
Barbeque Sauce, Breasts, COU, Marks & Spencer*	1 Pack/350g	420	120	8.5	20.6	1.9	0.6
Barbeque Sauce, Healthy Eating, Tesco*	1 Breast/170g	177	104	18.3	4.5	1.4	0.9
Black Bean Sauce, & Rice, Morrisons*	1 Pack/400g	408	102	3.9	16.4	2.3	1.2
Black Bean Sauce, BGTY, Sainsbury's*	1 Can/400g	308	77	9.3	7.9	0.9	0.7
Black Bean Sauce, Budgens*	1 Pack/350g	333	95	9.9	4.9	4.0	0.9
Black Bean Sauce, Chinese Takeaway, Iceland*	1 Pack/400g	348	87	9.3	5.3	3.2	0.7
Black Bean Sauce, Marks & Spencer*	1 Pack/350g	298	85	8.7	8.0	2.0	1.1
Black Bean Sauce, Safeway*	1 Pack/350g	284	81	9.4	7.9	1.3	1.0
Black Bean Sauce, Sainsbury's*	1 Pack/465g	484	104	5.0	17.3	1.7	0.3
Black Bean Sauce, Somerfield*	½ Pack/175g	133	76	10.7	6.1	1.0	1.9
Black Bean Sauce, Tesco*	1 Pack/450g	387	86	7.4	12.4	0.7	1.6
Black Bean Sauce, Waitrose*	1 Pack/300g	243	81	10.9	6.6	1.2	0.8
Black Bean Sauce, With Egg Fried Rice, GFY, Asda*	1 Serving/416g	320	77	5.0	12.0	1.0	0.9
Black Bean Sauce, With Egg Fried Rice, Somerfield*	1 Pack/340g	384	113	7.0	13.0	4.0	0.0
Black Bean Sauce, With Rice, Asda*	1 Pack/400g	500	125	7.0	20.0	1.9	0.6
Black Bean Sauce, With Rice, BGTY, Sainsbury's*	1 Pack/450g	446	99	6.4	16.6	0.8	0.6
Black Bean Sauce, With Rice, Iceland*	1 Pack/400g	388	97	5.1	15.8	1.5	0.8
Black Bean, & Rice, Healthy Eating, Tesco*	1 Pack/450g	387	86	7.4	12.4	0.7	1.6
Broccoli & Mushroom, Good Choice, Iceland*	1 Pack/500g	590	118	6.4	18.1	2.2	0.6
Broccoli & Mushroom, With Rice, Healthy Eating, Tesco*	1 Pack/400g	440	110	7.5	17.1	1.2	0.7
Cheese, Leek & Ham, Breast Fillets, Asda*	1 Serving/190g	291	153	19.0	1.2	8.0	2.0
Cheesy Salsa, Fillets, Safeway*	½ Pack/175g	193	110	17.9	2.2	3.0	1.1
Chilli & Lemon Grass With Rice, Sainsbury's*	1 Pack/450g	527	117	6.2	17.4	2.5	0.7
Coriande & Lime Marinade, Chargrilled, Asda*	½ Pack/163.4g	285	175	23.0	0.5	9.0	0.0
Coriander, Lime & Chilli Dressing, Fillets, Aldi*	1 Serving/140g	258	184	8.5	11.4	11.6	0.0
Creamy Mushroom Sauce, Healthy Living, Tesco*	1 Pack/400g	296	74	13.2	1.8	1.5	0.5
Creamy Mushroom Sauce, Weight Watchers*	1 Pack/330g	264	80	6.8	7.5	2.5	0.5
Creamy Mustard Sauce, GFY, Asda*	1 Pack/400g	468	117	6.0	18.0	2.3	0.4
Creamy Thai Sauce, Somerfield*	1 Pack/440g	748	170	22.0	2.0	8.0	0.0
Creamy Tikka Style Sauce, Tesco*	1 Breast/190g	215	113	15.1	0.7	5.5	0.8
Creamy White Wine Sauce, Sainsbury's*	1 Pack/324g	285	88	8.9	4.7	3.7	1.0
Garlic & Herbs, Breast, Sainsbury's*	1 Serving/200g	316	158	28.3	5.4	2.6	0.1
Ginger & Chilli With Veg Noodles, COU, Marks & Spencer*	1 Pack/400g	300	75	6.4	10.7	0.6	1.1
Gravy, Chunky, Marks & Spencer*	1 Can/489g	465	95	13.6	1.4	3.9	0.8
Gravy, With Stuffing & Potatoes, British Classics, Tesco*	1 Pack/450.5g	482	107	7.8	12.1	3.0	0.8
Hot Ginger Sauce, With Jasmine Rice, BGTY, Sainsbury's*	1 Pack/400g	400	100	6.6	15.4	1.4	0.5
Hot Ginger Sauce, With Thai Sticky Rice, Sainsbury's*	1 Pack/450g	603	134	6.8	16.3	4.6	0.5
Italian Style Tomato & Herb Sauce, Tesco*	1 Serving/180g	144	80	15.8	1.6	1.2	0.6
Leek & Bacon Sauce, Chilled, Co-Op*	1 Pack/400g	460	115	15.0	2.0	5.0	0.2
Lemon Flavour Sauce, Breast Fillets, Safeway*	1 Fillet/92g	200	217	17.0	16.0	9.4	1.4
Lemon Sauce With Rice, Sainsbury's*	1 Pack/450g	513	114	8.1	17.0	1.5	0.7
Lemon Sauce, Breast, Healthy Eating, Tesco*	1 Pack/385g	385	100	15.9	4.7	1.9	0.5
Mango Ginger Marinade, Breast, Chargrilled, GFY, Asda*	½ Pack/190g	234	123	17.0	11.0	1.2	0.5
Mediterranean Sauce, Iceland*	1 Pack/500g	640	128	7.4	21.8	1.2	0.5
Mediterranean Style Sauce, Breasts, BGTY, Sainsbury's*	½ Pack/170g	148	87	14.5	2.7	2.0	0.9
Mexican Salsa, Tesco*	1 Pack/320g	368	115	19.5	3.1	2.7	0.6
Mild & Fruity Curry, Breasts, Healthy Eating, Tesco*	2 Breasts/345g	321	93	15.8	4.1	1.5	0.5
Mushroom & Ham Sauce With Rice, BGTY, Sainsbury's*	1 Pack/450g	581	129	9.7	18.9	1.6	0.3

	Measure	per Measure	Nutrition Values per 100g / 100ml				
	INFO/WEIGHT	KCAL	KCAL	PROT	CARB	FAT	FIBRE
CHICKEN IN,							
Mushroom Sauce With Mash, Healthy Living, Tesco*	1 Pack/400g	384	96	9.9	8.0	2.7	0.6
Peppercorn Sauce, GFY, Asda*	1 Serving/399.1g	431	108	6.0	17.0	1.8	0.5
Peppercorn Sauce, Safeway*	1 Pack/395.2g	415	105	8.8	12.2	2.2	1.6
Peppers, Fillets, Sainsbury's*	1 Pack/360g	378	105	13.7	4.2	3.7	1.1
Pesto Style Dressing, Asda*	1 Serving/150g	210	140	18.7	1.3	6.7	0.0
Pesto Style Dressing, Simple Solutions, Tesco*	1 Serving/142g	268	189	20.1	2.5	11.0	1.6
Red Pepper Sauce, Eat Smart, Safeway*	1 Serving/175g	166	95	18.4	2.3	1.3	1.4
Red Pepper Sauce, Tesco*	1 Serving/140g	228	163	19.2	0.1	9.5	0.5
Red Thai Marinade, Breasts, Mini, Healthy Eating, Tesco*	1 Serving/200g	276	138	26.8	2.0	2.5	0.5
Red Thai Sauce, Breasts, Healthy Eating, Tesco*	1 Pack/350g	368	105	17.0	3.1	2.7	0.2
Red Wine & Bacon Sauce, Breast, Somerfield*	1 Breast/150g	131	87	14.0	3.0	2.0	0.0
Red Wine & Mushrooms, Asda*	½ Pack/190g	174	92	17.0	1.8	1.9	0.5
Red Wine & Potato Grattin, Healthy Eating, Tesco*	1 Pack/450g	410	91	7.7	8.9	2.7	2.2
Red Wine Sauce, Breast, Tesco*	1 Serving/180g	164	91	15.9	2.2	2.1	0.6
Red Wine Sauce, Breasts, Tesco*	1 Pack/360g	328	91	15.9	2.2	2.1	0.6
Red Wine Sauce, Fillets, Safeway*	1 Serving/175g	210	120	17.7	2.9	3.9	0.7
Red Wine With Mash, Eat Smart, Safeway*	1 Pack/400g	300	75	9.1	6.1	1.3	1.4
Satay Sauce, Safeway*	1 Serving/250g	363	145	10.5	7.1	8.0	1.4
Shiraz Wine Sauce, Finest, Tesco*	1 Pack/600g	420	70	10.9	2.9	1.6	1.3
Spicy Chilli Sauce, Topped With Cheese, Breast, Asda*	½ Pack/190g	241	127	20.0	3.4	3.7	0.0
Sun Dried Tomato & Basil Sauce, Breast, Iceland*	1 Serving/155.8g	134	86	14.6	3.3	1.6	1.0
Sweet & Sour Sauce, Breasts, Good Choice, Iceland*	1 Pack/340g	350	103	15.3	8.8	0.7	0.8
Sweet & Sour Sauce, GFY, Asda*	1 Pack/400g	424	106	6.0	19.0	0.7	1.2
Sweet & Sour With Noodles, Feeling Great, Findus*	1 Pack/350g	385	110	5.0	17.0	2.5	1.5
Tarragon Sauce, Breast, Glazed, Feeling Great, Findus*	1 Pack/350g	270	77	4.0	10.9	1.9	1.4
Tarragon Sauce, Lean Cuisine*	1 Pack/337.5g	270	80	4.0	11.0	2.0	1.5
Tikka Masala Sauce, Breast, GFY, Asda*	1 Pack/380g	426	112	13.0	6.0	4.0	0.7
Tomato & Basil Sauce, Asda*	1 Breast/189.3g	231	122	22.0	1.2	3.2	2.0
Tomato & Basil Sauce, Breast, GFY, Asda*	1 Pack/392g	447	114	12.0	9.0	3.4	1.5
Tomato & Basil Sauce, Chargrilled, Marks & Spencer*	1 Serving/235g	223	95	12.9	2.1	3.8	1.3
Tomato & Basil Sauce, Eat Smart, Safeway*	1 Serving/235.7g	165	70	10.3	2.4	1.6	1.3
Tomato & Basil Sauce, Good Choice, Iceland*	½ Pack/170g	153	90	13.3	3.3	2.6	0.6
Tomato & Basil Sauce, Safeway*	1 Serving/175g	201	115	16.7	3.8	3.6	1.1
White Sauce, BGTY, Sainsbury's*	1 Can/200g	250	125	14.5	2.5	6.3	1.0
White Sauce, Chunky, Marks & Spencer*	½ Can/209g	303	145	13.0	3.7	8.6	0.5
White Sauce, Low Fat, Breast, Safeway*	1 Serving/200g	190	95	11.5	2.1	4.5	0.2
White Wine & Asparagus Panzerotti, Asda*	½ Pack/150g	239	159	8.0	28.0	1.7	0.0
White Wine & Mushrooauce, COU, Marks & Spencer*	1 Serving/400g	400	100	9.6	13.0	1.6	1.3
White Wine & Mushrooauce, Marks & Spencer*	1 Serving/200g	260	130	15.6	1.6	6.8	1.0
White Wine & Mushroom Sauce, Breasts, Asda*	1 Breast/167.9g	272	162	23.0	1.8	7.0	0.0
White Wine & Tarragon Sauce, Breasts, Finest, Tesco*	½ Pack/200g	326	163	16.8	1.3	10.1	0.0
White Wine Sauce, Simple Solutions, Tesco*	½ Pack/200g	198	99	19.3	0.9	2.0	0.5
White Wine, With Rice, Eat Smart, Safeway*	1 Serving/400g	400	100	8.9	13.6	1.0	1.1
Wild Mushroom Sauce, Breasts, Healthy Living, Tesco*	1 Serving/212g	191	90	15.1	2.1	2.4	1.5
Wild Mushroom Sauce, Extra Special, Asda*	1 Serving/225g	319	142	14.2	2.2	8.4	0.3
Zesty Orange Sauce, Asda*	1 Serving/200g	340	170	16.0	13.0	6.0	0.4
Zesty Orange Sauce, Breast, Asda*	1 Serving/200g	326	163	16.0	9.0	7.0	0.0
CHICKEN ITALIAN,							
Good Choice, Iceland*	1 Pack/400g	388	97	4.7	18.3	0.5	0.6
Iceland*	1 Pack/250g	208	83	13.6	4.8	1.0	0.5
Ready Meal, Slim Fast*	1 Pack/375g	390	104	7.1	16.6	1.1	0.4
Style, BGTY, Sainsbury's*	1 Pack/400g	364	91	6.0	14.5	1.1	0.9
Style, Dinner, Asda*	1 Pack/400g	244	61	6.0	7.0	1.0	1.1

	Measure INFO/WEIGHT	per Measure KCAL	Nutrition Values per 100g / 100ml				
			KCAL	PROT	CARB	FAT	FIBRE
CHICKEN ITALIAN,							
Style, Meal, Asda*	1 Pack/408g	241	59	6.0	7.0	0.8	0.8
Style, Sainsbury's*	½ Pack/190g	222	117	16.3	3.9	4.0	0.1
With a Spicy Tomato, Chilli & Herb Sauce, Slim Fast*	1 Pack/371.4g	390	105	7.1	16.6	1.1	0.4
CHICKEN JEERA,							
Sainsbury's*	½ Pack/200.8g	247	123	10.5	4.6	7.0	1.8
CHICKEN KUNG PO,							
Sainsbury's*	½ Pack/175g	131	75	9.2	4.0	2.5	1.0
Waitrose*	1 Pack/350g	319	91	8.2	12.1	1.1	1.2
With Egg Fried Rice, Asda*	1 Pack/450g	689	153	6.0	21.0	5.0	1.0
CHICKEN LAKSA,							
COU, Marks & Spencer*	1 Pack/450g	360	80	7.5	7.0	2.2	1.1
CHICKEN LEMON,							
& Ginger With Apricot Rice, COU, Marks & Spencer*	1 Pack/400g	320	80	7.9	9.7	0.9	2.0
Battered, Chinese Meal For Two, Tesco*	½ Portion/175g	294	168	6.6	18.8	7.4	2.0
Battered, Healthy Eating, Tesco*	1 Pack/350g	399	114	8.8	13.9	2.6	0.4
Battered, Sainsbury's*	1 Pack/350g	462	132	8.9	16.0	3.6	0.5
Breast, Fillets, BGTY, Sainsbury's*	1 Fillet/112.5g	195	173	18.4	19.9	2.1	1.9
COU, Marks & Spencer*	1 Pack/150g	150	100	17.9	5.6	0.9	0.8
Cantonese Style, With Egg Fried Rice, Farmfoods*	1 Pack/324g	486	150	4.9	21.8	4.8	0.1
Cantonese, Sainsbury's*	½ Pack/140g	217	156	11.0	13.9	6.3	0.6
Chargrilled, COU, Marks & Spencer*	½ Pack/175g	158	90	16.1	5.5	0.6	0.9
Cream, With Rice, Perfectly Balanced, Waitrose*	1 Pack/400g	592	148	7.6	21.7	3.4	0.3
Crispy, Take It Away, Marks & Spencer*	1 Carton/227g	329	145	9.4	19.2	3.4	0.7
Steam Cuisine, COU, Marks & Spencer*	1 Pack/400g	420	105	9.8	11.8	2.2	2.0
Tesco*	½ Pack/175g	214	122	11.0	10.1	4.2	0.6
With Rice, Healthy Living, Tesco*	1 Pack/450g	477	106	5.9	14.4	2.7	0.9
With Vegetable Rice, BGTY, Sainsbury's*	1 Pack/400g	428	107	6.5	16.8	1.6	0.8
CHICKEN LUNCH,							
Light, French Style, John West*	1 Pack/240.4g	226	94	7.2	6.7	4.3	2.1
Light, Italian Style, John West*	1 Pack/240g	247	103	7.1	9.6	4.1	0.8
CHICKEN MEAL,							
American, Fillets, Asda*	1 Pack/345g	838	243	9.0	27.0	11.0	2.3
Raost, Marks & Spencer*	1 Pack/250g	375	150	14.6	5.3	7.7	0.1
CHICKEN MEDITERRANEAN,							
Style, Somerfield*	1 Pot/215g	455	212	7.4	16.0	13.1	1.0
CHICKEN MEXICAN,							
Style, BGTY, Sainsbury's*	1 Serving/260g	255	98	6.9	12.1	2.5	2.2
Style, Combo, Asda*	1 Pack/380g	927	244	19.0	15.0	12.0	0.0
Style, GFY, Asda*	½ Pack/200g	256	128	17.0	3.7	5.0	0.3
Style, With Rice, Better For You, Morrisons*	1 Pack/400g	360	90	5.1	14.1	1.3	0.8
CHICKEN MOROCCAN,							
Style, With Spicy Cous Cous, BGTY, Sainsbury's*	1 Serving/225g	304	135	9.2	20.6	1.7	0.0
With Apricots & Pine Nuts, TTD, Sainsbury's*	½ Pack/200g	210	105	10.6	3.4	5.4	1.3
With Cous Cous & Fruity Sauce, BGTY, Sainsbury's*	1 Pack/400g	440	110	10.0	13.1	2.0	2.6
CHICKEN MUSTARD,							
With Creme Fraiche Mash, Perfectly Balanced, Waitrose*	1 Pack/400g	408	102	7.2	9.4	4.0	0.8
With Gratin Potatoes, Healthy Living, Tesco*	1 Pack/450g	464	103	9.0	10.7	2.7	2.5
CHICKEN ORIENTAL,							
Slim Fast*	1 Pack/385g	385	100	5.7	18.6	0.6	0.6
CHICKEN PAPRIKA,							
& Savoury Rice, BGTY, Sainsbury's*	1 Pack/401g	441	110	6.8	19.2	0.7	0.4
COU, Marks & Spencer*	1 Pack/400g	380	95	9.0	11.7	1.6	2.0
With Savoury Vegetables & Rice, BGTY, Sainsbury's*	1 Pack/451g	555	123	7.2	17.8	2.6	0.8

C

	Measure INFO/WEIGHT	per Measure KCAL	Nutrition Values per 100g / 100ml				
			KCAL	PROT	CARB	FAT	FIBRE
CHICKEN PARMESAN,							
& Sun Dried Tomato, Fillets, Mini, Sainsbury's*	1 Pack/200g	278	139	22.1	6.0	2.9	0.5
Sun Dried Tomato, Fillets, BGTY, Sainsbury's*	½ Pack/100g	138	138	22.1	6.0	2.9	0.5
With Pasta, Steam Cuisine, Marks & Spencer*	1 Pack/400g	400	100	10.1	8.1	3.0	1.3
CHICKEN PEPPER,							
Fry, Sainsbury's*	1 Pack/400g	508	127	15.0	2.9	6.2	1.6
Hot, With Minted Mash, BGTY, Sainsbury's*	1 Serving/450g	333	74	7.3	8.4	1.2	1.3
CHICKEN PEPPERCORN,							
BGTY, Sainsbury's*	1 Pack/251.8g	214	85	11.0	4.5	2.6	0.9
CHICKEN PICCATA,							
Healthy Eating, Tesco*	1 Pack/405g	518	128	15.7	7.7	3.8	0.5
CHICKEN PIRI PIRI,							
GFY, Asda*	1 Pack/400g	360	90	4.7	17.0	0.4	0.5
Marks & Spencer*	1 Pack/300g	420	140	10.0	7.3	7.7	1.3
Safeway*	1 Serving/350g	455	130	11.6	4.7	7.0	2.4
Sainsbury's*	½ Pack/200g	248	124	14.0	4.8	5.4	0.5
Tesco*	1 Serving/290g	307	106	15.8	1.4	4.1	0.5
With Rice, BGTY, Sainsbury's*	1 Serving/399g	395	99	10.3	11.9	1.1	1.6
CHICKEN PROVENCAL,							
Marks & Spencer*	1 Serving/280g	350	125	11.4	4.8	6.8	1.5
CHICKEN RENDANG,							
Sainsbury's*	1 Pack/350g	690	197	9.6	5.1	15.3	1.7
CHICKEN ROAST,							
In A Pot, Sainsbury's*	1 Pack/450g	477	106	9.6	10.3	2.9	0.7
Meal, Blue Parrot Cafe, Sainsbury's*	1 Pack/285g	259	91	6.9	8.1	3.4	1.5
CHICKEN ROLL,							
Broccoli & Mushroom, Sainsbury's*	½ Roll/175g	441	252	8.7	24.3	13.3	1.0
Value, Tesco*	1 Slice/13g	30	223	15.4	3.9	16.2	0.1
With Pork, Sage & Onion Stuffing, Value, Tesco*	1 Roll/125g	166	133	9.4	7.8	7.1	0.5
CHICKEN SAFFRON,							
& Rice, Marks & Spencer*	1 Pack/400g	360	90	7.6	11.6	1.2	1.1
CHICKEN SALSA,							
BGTY, Sainsbury's*	1 Pack/250g	178	71	9.7	4.7	1.5	1.2
Breast, Chunks, Roast, Waitrose*	1oz/28g	36	127	25.9	3.6	1.0	1.1
Mango, Breast, Sainsbury's*	1 Breast/178g	271	152	26.2	6.4	2.4	0.1
CHICKEN SATAY,							
Stuffed, Asda*	½ Pack/168.1g	242	144	22.0	6.0	3.6	0.8
CHICKEN SICILIAN,							
Somerfield*	1 Serving/400g	384	96	7.5	7.8	3.9	1.0
CHICKEN SPANISH,							
Style, Asda*	½ Pack/275.2g	322	117	14.0	4.1	4.9	0.7
CHICKEN SPATCHOCK,							
Poussin, Sainsbury's*	1 Serving/122g	168	138	21.1	0.1	5.4	0.2
CHICKEN STUFFED,							
Asparagus & Ricotta, With Herb Rice, BGTY, Sainsbury's*	1 Pack/400g	444	111	8.1	13.8	2.6	0.3
Breast, With Mushrooms, Healthy Eating, Tesco*	1 Serving/175g	152	87	16.3	1.5	1.8	0.2
With Moroccan Style Cous Cous, GFY, Asda*	½ Pack/180g	259	144	20.0	10.0	2.7	0.0
With Mushrooms, Finest, Tesco*	1 Serving/150g	177	118	15.9	2.0	5.1	0.6
CHICKEN SUPREME,							
BGTY, Sainsbury's*	1 Pack/350g	417	119	9.4	17.2	1.4	0.5
Breast, Sainsbury's*	1 Serving/187g	421	225	20.6	0.3	15.8	0.6
With Rice, Asda*	1 Pack/450g	549	122	6.0	18.0	2.9	0.5
With Rice, Bird's Eye*	1 Pack/375g	499	133	6.7	19.1	3.3	0.5
With Rice, Healthy Eating, Tesco*	1 Pack/400g	384	96	4.9	15.6	1.6	1.5

	Measure	per Measure		Nutrition Values per 100g / 100ml				
	INFO/WEIGHT	KCAL	KCAL	PROT	CARB	FAT	FIBRE
CHICKEN SUPREME,							
With Rice, Weight Watchers*	1 Pack/300g	255	85	5.6	11.9	1.6	0.5
CHICKEN SZECHUAN,							
Chilli & Peppercorn, Sainsbury's*	1 Pack/400g	352	88	9.9	3.2	4.0	0.5
With Noodles, Sainsbury's*	1 Pack/450g	423	94	6.0	10.4	3.1	0.9
CHICKEN TANDOORI,							
GFY, Asda*	1 Pack/420g	420	100	9.0	8.0	3.6	1.4
Healthy Choice, McCain*	1 Pack/270g	297	110	7.5	17.5	1.0	0.0
Masala, Asda*	1 Pack/400g	580	145	7.0	18.0	5.0	1.3
Safeway*	1 Pack/350g	595	170	13.7	5.7	10.3	1.3
Sizzler, Sainsbury's*	1 Pack/400g	536	134	12.8	4.3	7.3	1.7
Sizzler, Tesco*	1 Serving/175g	243	139	10.0	10.0	6.6	1.0
Tesco*	1 Serving/175g	198	113	10.6	6.7	4.9	1.0
With Spicy Potatoes & Dip, Healthy Eating, Tesco*	1 Pack/370g	322	87	9.7	10.3	0.8	1.3
With Spicy Vegatable Rice, Eat Smart, Safeway*	1 Serving/350g	368	105	9.7	11.1	2.2	7.0
CHICKEN TERIYAKI,							
Asda*	1 Pack/360g	299	83	9.1	8.6	1.4	0.8
Japanese, With Ramen Noodles, Sainsbury's*	1 Pack/450g	482	107	6.5	15.5	2.1	0.8
CHICKEN THAI,							
Bird's Eye*	1 Portion/86g	189	220	18.1	3.1	15.0	0.1
Chiang Mai, & Noodles, BGTY, Sainsbury's*	1 Pack/448g	484	108	6.9	11.0	4.0	1.7
Coconut, & Noodles, Marks & Spencer*	1 Pack/400g	320	80	7.2	8.1	1.8	0.7
Green, Fillets, Mini, Sainsbury's*	½ Pack/100g	130	130	27.9	0.9	1.6	0.8
Style Marinade, Breast, Chargrilled, GFY, Asda*	½ Pack/178g	178	100	17.0	1.3	3.0	0.5
Style, Steam Cuisine, Marks & Spencer*	1 Pack/400g	440	110	8.8	10.4	3.8	1.7
Style, With Noodles, Tesco*	1 Pack/400g	332	83	7.5	9.5	1.7	1.0
With Lemongrass & Rice, Slim Fast*	1 Pack/375g	413	110	5.7	18.2	1.3	0.8
CHICKEN TIKKA,							
& Cous Cous, Boots*	1 Pack/160g	307	192	6.2	17.0	11.0	1.3
& Lemon Rice, Deli Meal, Marks & Spencer*	1 Pack/360g	342	95	9.8	10.2	2.0	0.7
& Rice Salad, COU, Marks & Spencer*	1 Pack/390g	351	90	5.9	14.6	0.7	0.6
BGTY, Sainsbury's*	1 Serving/188g	265	141	10.5	21.2	1.6	0.0
Bird's Eye*	1 Serving/98g	195	199	22.1	3.5	10.7	0.1
Breasts, Summer Eating, Asda*	1 Serving/170g	238	140	25.9	5.9	1.4	0.2
Chunky, Tesco*	1 Pack/170g	221	130	27.4	0.5	2.1	0.3
Fillets, Mini, Eat Smart, Safeway*	1 Serving/100g	120	120	27.9	1.2	0.3	0.8
Pinwheels, BGTY, Sainsbury's*	1 Serving/213.9g	261	122	9.6	16.0	2.2	0.0
Sliced, Asda*	1 Serving/140g	274	196	40.0	2.3	3.0	0.0
Sliced, Ready To Eat, Asda*	1 Pack/140g	188	134	24.0	3.2	2.8	1.3
With Basmati Rice, GFY, Asda*	1 Pack/400g	592	148	9.0	24.0	1.8	1.6
CHICKEN VINDALOO,							
Asda*	1 Pack/411g	649	158	7.0	19.0	6.0	0.0
Sainsbury's*	1 Pack/400g	460	115	14.6	4.8	4.2	0.6
Waitrose*	1 Pack/340g	398	117	10.6	6.4	5.4	1.6
CHICKEN WITH,							
A Sea Salt & Black Pepper Crust, Breasts, Asda*	1 Serving/153.7g	186	121	19.0	5.0	2.8	0.0
A Sticky Honey & Chilli Sauce, Breast, Asda*	1 Serving/175g	247	141	20.0	8.0	3.2	0.0
Apricots & Almonds, Healthy Eating, Tesco*	1 Pack/500g	465	93	11.8	7.3	1.9	0.5
Asparagus & Rice, BGTY, Sainsbury's*	1 Pack/400g	428	107	9.1	14.5	1.4	0.9
Bacon & Leeks, GFY, Asda*	1 Pack/400g	328	82	13.0	3.0	2.0	0.6
Bacon & Leeks, With Mashed Potato, BGTY, Sainsbury's*	1 Pack/450g	437	97	8.4	10.1	2.5	0.7
Bacon & Sweetcorn, Safeway*	½ Pot/85g	366	430	15.1	3.3	39.3	2.3
Black Bean Sauce & Noodles, Eat Smart, Safeway*	1 Pack/369g	295	80	7.2	10.5	0.7	1.2
Broccoli & Pesto Pasta, BGTY, Sainsbury's*	1 Pack/300.9g	328	109	10.3	13.2	1.7	2.5

C

CHICKEN WITH,	Measure INFO/WEIGHT	per Measure KCAL	Nutrition Values per 100g / 100ml				
			KCAL	PROT	CARB	FAT	FIBRE
Cheddar & Bacon Filling, Breast, Just Cook, Sainsbury's*	1 Serving/180g	346	192	23.2	6.5	8.1	0.1
Cheese & Bacon, Tesco*	1 Pack/475g	546	115	8.1	9.6	4.9	0.4
Cheese Croutons & Onion, Asda*	1 Serving/200g	200	100	16.0	2.0	3.2	0.9
Cheese, Leek & Bacon, Breasts, Stuffed, Safeway*	½ Pack/159.0g	310	195	24.3	1.0	9.9	0.6
Chunky Tomato Sauce, COU, Marks & Spencer*	1 Pack/400g	360	90	7.9	9.3	2.3	0.9
Coriander & Lime, Asda*	1 Serving/105g	122	116	24.0	2.9	0.9	0.2
Cranberry & Orange Stuffing, Sainsbury's*	1 Serving/100g	201	201	23.0	4.1	10.3	0.8
Cranberry Stuffing, Breast, Finest, Tesco*	½ Pack/200g	252	126	16.2	9.9	2.4	0.9
Creamy Mushroom Sauce & Mash, Healthy Living, Tesco*	1 Pack/400g	384	96	10.0	8.0	2.7	0.6
Creamy Mushroom Sauce, Eat Smart, Safeway*	1 Serving/250g	213	85	12.8	2.7	2.4	0.9
Garlic & Herbs, Asda*	1 Slice/25g	29	114	23.9	1.1	1.5	0.0
Garlic & Mushrooms, Somerfield*	½ Pack/190g	287	151	17.3	0.9	8.7	0.8
Garlic Mushrooms, Asda*	1 Serving/320g	403	126	16.0	2.0	6.0	2.6
Garlic Mushrooms, Breasts, Tesco*	1 Serving/175g	263	150	19.2	0.3	8.0	0.2
Grapes & Asparagus, Sainsbury's*	½ Pack/200g	240	120	13.3	1.8	6.6	1.0
Ham & Vegetables, Creamy, Eat Smart, Safeway*	1 Pack/370g	241	65	6.5	5.5	1.8	1.4
Ham, Cheese & Mushrooms, Breasts, Tesco*	1 Serving/175g	222	127	17.5	0.9	5.9	0.2
Hoi Sin Sauce, Ooodles Of Noodles, Oriental Express*	1 Pack/425g	400	94	5.3	13.2	2.2	1.7
Leek & Bacon Sauce, Good Intentions, Somerfield*	1 Pack/400g	284	71	5.4	7.2	2.3	2.9
Leek, Cheese & Bacon, Breasts, Simple Solutions, Tesco*	1 Serving/200g	296	148	17.6	0.5	8.4	0.3
Lime & Coriander Marinade, Chargrilled, Asda*	1 Portion/163.4g	285	175	23.0	0.5	9.0	0.0
Lime & Coriander, Chargrilled, Asda*	1 Serving/190g	352	185	24.0	2.0	9.0	1.1
Lime & Coriander, Marks & Spencer*	1 Pack/140g	168	120	25.8	2.0	1.2	0.3
Lyonnaise Potatoes, Marks & Spencer*	½ Pack/260g	286	110	12.6	8.0	3.1	0.9
Mango Salsa & Potato Wedges, BGTY, Sainsbury's*	1 Pack/400g	336	84	7.0	10.4	1.6	1.5
Mango Salsa & Potato Wedges, Sainsbury's*	1 Pack/400g	336	84	7.0	10.4	1.6	1.5
Mascapone, Bacon & Roasted Onions, Finest, Tesco*	1 Serving/200g	312	156	14.5	4.7	8.8	0.5
Mushroom & Garlic Butter, Breasts, Sainsbury's*	½ Pack/180g	388	199	20.0	4.6	10.3	0.1
Mushroom & Garlic, Breast Fillets, Just Cook, Sainsbury's*	½ Pack/165.8g	330	199	20.0	4.6	10.3	0.1
Mushroom & Madeira Ragout, TTD, Sainsbury's*	½ Pack/225g	218	97	13.6	3.7	3.1	0.1
Mushroom & Tomato Sauce, GFY, Asda*	1 Serving/175g	180	103	19.0	2.0	2.1	2.7
Mushroom In Madeira Sauce, Healthy Eating, Tesco*	½ Pack/200g	182	91	15.0	5.4	1.0	0.4
Mushrooms & Creamy Chardonnay Sauce, Finest, Tesco*	1 Serving/195.4g	254	130	13.0	3.5	7.1	0.0
Mushrooms in Oyster Sauce, Tesco*	1 Pack/350g	189	54	8.0	3.5	0.9	0.8
Olive Oil, Coriander & Lemon, Chargrilled, Sainsbury's*	1 Serving/122g	310	254	22.7	2.2	17.1	0.7
Pancakes & Pluauce, COU, Marks & Spencer*	1 Pack/245g	257	105	7.9	12.7	2.3	0.3
Pancetta & Mozzarella, Finest, Tesco*	1 Serving/150g	297	198	11.6	11.5	11.8	0.9
Pasta & Spicy Arrabbiata Sauce, COU, Marks & Spencer*	1 Pack/360g	252	70	5.2	8.7	1.4	1.3
Plum Tomatoes & Basil, Breasts, Bird's Eye*	1 Portion/172.4g	200	116	13.3	5.0	4.7	0.6
Pork, Stuffing & Chipolatas, Breast Joint, Tesco*	½ Pack/340g	524	154	16.7	3.4	8.2	0.5
Potato & Smoked Bacon Topping, Marks & Spencer*	1 Serving/175g	228	130	17.8	3.2	4.8	1.2
Potato Wedges, BBQ, Eat Smart, Safeway*	1 Pack/350g	368	105	9.6	14.0	0.9	1.8
Prosciutio, Dolcelatte & 3 Cheese Sauce, Asda*	½ Pack/195g	355	182	30.0	1.9	6.0	1.2
Rice 'n' Peas, Sainsbury's*	1 Pack/300g	489	163	12.5	14.4	6.1	2.1
Rice, Breast, Chargrilled, Spicy, Asda*	1 Pack/400g	372	93	6.0	16.0	0.6	1.0
Rice, Fiesta, Weight Watchers*	1 Pack/330g	307	93	6.1	12.8	2.0	0.4
Roast Potatoes, Eat Smart, Safeway*	1 Serving/363.2g	345	95	8.5	10.1	1.8	1.5
Salsa & Spicy Potato Wedges, GFY, Asda*	1 Pack/400g	332	83	6.0	11.0	1.7	1.8
Sour Cream & Chive Dip, Wings, Pizza Hut*	1 Pack/178g	680	382	22.8	1.9	31.5	1.3
Spinach, Honey Mustard, American Style, Asda*	1 Serving/240g	394	164	14.0	4.4	10.0	0.3
Stuffing & Roast Potatoes, Tesco*	1 Pack/440g	480	109	10.1	11.5	2.5	1.0
Stuffing, Butter Basted, Co-Op*	1 Slice/23.1g	30	130	21.0	2.0	4.0	1.0
Sun Dried Tomato & Basil Butter, Sainsbury's*	1 Breast/185g	363	196	25.0	2.5	9.5	0.2

	Measure INFO/WEIGHT	per Measure KCAL	Nutrition Values per 100g / 100ml				
			KCAL	PROT	CARB	FAT	FIBRE
CHICKEN WITH,							
Sun Dried Tomato & Basil Sauce, Bistro, Waitrose*	½ Pack/175g	254	145	14.2	3.7	8.1	0.3
Tagine, Cous Cous, BGTY, Sainsbury's*	1 Pack/450g	626	139	10.1	15.9	3.9	1.5
Tagine, Cous Cous, Perfectly Balanced, Waitrose*	1 Pack/400g	516	129	8.2	16.2	3.5	1.0
Tangy Lemon Sauce, Breasts, Just Cook, Sainsbury's*	1 Serving/164g	244	149	16.2	16.9	1.8	0.1
Thai Green Curry, Breasts, Finest, Tesco*	1 Serving/200g	292	146	16.5	2.0	8.0	0.7
Tomato & Basil Pasta, Marks & Spencer*	1 Serving/190g	171	90	6.8	10.6	2.1	1.4
Tomato & Basil Sauce, Breasts, Healthy Living, Tesco*	1 Serving/200g	136	68	11.0	3.9	0.9	0.5
Tomato & Basil, Healthy Eating, Tesco*	1 Serving/225g	189	84	11.2	6.1	1.7	1.2
Tomato & Basil, Steam Cuisine, Marks & Spencer*	1 Pack/400g	460	115	9.6	11.6	3.4	2.0
Tomato & Basil, Weight Watchers*	1 Pack/330g	317	96	7.4	13.9	1.2	0.3
Tomato & White Wine Sauce, Bird's Eye*	1 Pack/382.4g	325	85	9.4	9.7	0.9	0.8
Tomato, Chargrilled, Tesco*	1 Pot/300g	381	127	6.0	14.6	4.9	1.0
With Caramelised Peppers, Chargrilled, Marks & Spencer*	½ Pack/237g	225	95	12.9	2.1	3.8	1.3
With Cous Cous, Lemon & Herb, Finest, Tesco*	1 Pack/370g	492	133	10.5	11.5	5.0	0.9
CHILLI,							
& Lemongrass Prawns With Noodles, BGTY, Sainsbury's*	1 Pack/400g	328	82	5.0	13.8	0.7	1.3
& Potato Wedges, Good Choice, Iceland*	1 Pack/400g	368	92	5.5	9.8	3.4	1.2
& Potato Wedges, Sainsbury's*	1 Pack/370g	393	106	7.2	10.1	4.1	2.2
& Rice, Bird's Eye*	1 Serving/285g	305	107	3.4	17.2	2.7	1.0
& Rice, Frozen, Sainsbury's*	1 Pack/400g	436	109	4.8	18.4	1.9	0.6
& Rice, GFY, Asda*	1 Pack/400g	352	88	5.0	16.0	0.4	1.8
& Spicy Wedges, Good Intentions, Somerfield*	1 Serving/400g	340	85	5.6	10.5	2.3	1.1
& Wedges, BBQ, Healthy Living, Tesco*	1 Pack/420g	391	93	5.4	12.2	2.6	1.9
Beef & Potato Wedges, Superbowl, GFY, Asda*	1 Pack/450g	477	106	6.0	14.0	2.9	1.5
Beef Jacket, Marks & Spencer*	1 Pack/360g	288	80	5.9	9.6	2.0	0.9
Beef, Asda*	½ Pack/200g	190	95	7.0	8.0	3.9	1.2
Beef, Crispy, Sainsbury's*	1 Pack/400g	628	157	12.8	4.9	9.6	1.2
Beef, With Rice, GFY, Asda*	1 Serving/402.3g	354	88	4.7	14.0	1.5	0.9
Beef, With Rice, Sainsbury's*	1 Serving/300g	360	120	5.6	20.6	1.7	1.1
Bowl, American Style, Sainsbury's*	½ Pack/300g	255	85	8.8	4.6	3.5	2.0
Bowl, Safeway*	1 Pack/300g	327	109	8.8	8.3	4.5	2.7
Chicken Grande, Stagg*	1 Serving/204.9g	168	82	9.7	9.4	0.6	1.6
Chicken With Fettucini, Marks & Spencer*	1 Pack/350g	368	105	7.9	13.9	2.1	1.1
Con Carne & Rice, Co-Op*	1 Pack/300g	195	65	4.0	8.0	2.0	1.0
Con Carne & Rice, Healthy Eating, Tesco*	1 Pack/450g	446	99	9.1	10.9	2.1	1.6
Con Carne & Rice, Healthy Living, Tesco*	1 Pack/450.5g	473	105	5.5	14.8	2.6	1.2
Con Carne & Rice, Somerfield*	1 Pack/500g	490	98	5.0	18.0	1.0	0.0
Con Carne With Rice, BGTY, Sainsbury's*	1 Pack/400g	432	108	6.2	16.9	1.7	1.0
Con Carne With Rice, Eat Smart, Safeway*	1 Pack/400g	340	85	5.3	12.2	1.3	1.4
Con Carne With Rice, GFY, Asda*	1 Serving/400g	456	114	6.0	19.0	1.6	0.9
Con Carne With Rice, Healthy Choice, Asda*	1 Pack/400g	412	103	6.0	15.0	2.1	0.9
Con Carne With Rice, Organic, Sainsbury's*	1 Pack/400g	472	118	5.0	18.5	2.7	1.8
Con Carne With Rice, Perfectly Balanced, Waitrose*	1 Pack/400g	508	127	5.6	19.9	2.8	0.9
Con Carne, Asda*	1 Can/392g	376	96	7.0	9.0	3.5	0.0
Con Carne, Baked Bean, Heinz*	1 Can/390g	324	83	7.0	10.3	1.5	2.8
Con Carne, Bird's Eye*	1 Pack/300g	324	108	3.9	17.8	2.3	1.6
Con Carne, Classic, Stagg*	1 Can/410g	521	127	8.8	8.6	6.4	2.3
Con Carne, Co-Op*	1 Serving/200g	240	120	7.0	15.0	3.3	0.0
Con Carne, Dynamite Hot, Stagg*	1 Serving/250g	310	124	7.6	9.6	6.2	2.5
Con Carne, Frozen, Co-Op*	1 Pack/340g	306	90	6.0	15.0	1.0	1.0
Con Carne, Good Choice, Iceland*	1 Pack/400g	476	119	5.5	21.9	1.0	1.0
Con Carne, Homepride*	1 Can/390g	234	60	2.5	11.2	0.6	0.0
Con Carne, Marks & Spencer*	1 Pack/285g	285	100	8.7	7.4	3.7	2.0

C

	Measure INFO/WEIGHT	per Measure KCAL	Nutrition Values per 100g / 100ml				
			KCAL	PROT	CARB	FAT	FIBRE
CHILLI,							
Con Carne, Morrisons*	1 Tin/197g	227	115	8.1	11.5	4.1	1.7
Con Carne, New Lower Fat, BGTY, Sainsbury's*	1 Pack/400g	400	100	5.5	18.4	0.5	1.0
Con Carne, Sainsbury's*	1 Pack/376.2g	459	122	7.4	19.6	1.6	1.0
Con Carne, Silverado Beef, Stagg*	1 Can/410g	406	99	7.8	10.9	2.7	1.5
Con Carne, Slim Fast*	1 Pack/375g	394	105	5.5	16.2	1.9	1.5
Con Carne, Tesco*	1 Can/392g	463	118	8.0	10.5	4.9	2.4
Con Carne, With Rice, Tesco*	1 Serving/400g	404	101	4.2	15.3	2.6	1.5
Crispy Beef, Tesco*	1 Pack/250g	455	182	11.4	19.8	6.3	1.2
Medium, Uncle Ben's*	1 Jar/500g	305	61	1.8	11.1	0.8	0.0
Mexican Chilli With Potato Wedges, Weight Watchers*	1 Pack/300g	252	84	5.1	10.3	2.5	1.7
Mixed Vegetable, Tesco*	1 Pack/400g	352	88	3.9	11.0	2.9	3.2
Non Carne, Linda McCartney*	1 Pack/340g	252	74	5.8	9.2	2.3	1.7
Spicy Bean & Vegetable, Safeway*	1 Pack/311g	196	63	3.3	9.6	1.3	2.5
Three Bean & Potato Wedges, Safeway*	1 Pack/415.8g	395	95	3.2	13.1	3.0	3.5
Vegetable	1oz/28g	16	57	3.0	10.8	0.6	2.6
Vegetable & Rice, BGTY, Sainsbury's*	1 Pack/450g	401	89	3.4	17.8	0.5	2.4
Vegetable & Rice, Good Intentions, Somerfield*	1 Serving/400g	336	84	2.7	15.8	1.1	2.1
Vegetable & Rice, Healthy Eating, Tesco*	1 Pack/450g	392	87	2.8	16.1	1.2	1.5
Vegetable & Rice, Safeway*	1 Pack/500g	530	106	3.4	21.2	0.8	1.7
Vegetable Garden, Stagg*	1 Can/410g	254	62	3.6	10.8	0.5	2.3
Vegetable, 99% Fat Free, Stagg*	1oz/28g	16	58	3.1	9.3	0.5	3.1
Vegetable, Retail	1oz/28g	20	70	4.0	9.4	2.1	0.0
Vegetable, Waitrose*	1 Can/392g	227	58	2.9	6.6	2.2	0.0
Wedge Bowl, COU, Marks & Spencer*	1 Pack/400g	380	95	7.2	11.3	2.3	1.8
With Potatoes Wedges, GFY, Asda*	1 Pack/450g	419	93	6.0	12.0	2.3	1.5
CHILLI MEAT FREE,							
Mexican Style, Asda*	1 Serving/60g	54	90	8.0	12.0	1.1	2.4
Sainsbury's*	1 Pack/400g	308	77	4.0	4.1	5.0	5.2
CHILLI POWDER,							
Average	1 Tsp/4g	16	405	12.3	54.7	16.8	34.2
CHILLIES,							
Green, Tesco*	1oz/28g	4	16	0.8	2.6	0.3	1.6
Mixed, Tesco*	1oz/28g	8	27	1.8	4.2	0.3	1.6
Red, Raw, Tesco*	1 Serving/28g	8	27	1.8	4.2	0.3	0.0
Very Lazy, EPC*	1 serving/10g	11	114	4.2	15.3	4.0	0.5
CHINESE MEAL,							
For One, GFY, Asda*	1 Pack/570g	946	166	7.0	28.0	2.9	0.0
For One, Safeway*	1 Serving/584g	993	170	5.5	25.8	4.7	1.3
For One, Safeway*	1 Serving/600g	605	101	5.3	17.1	1.2	1.2
For Two, Tesco*	1 Pack/500g	480	96	4.4	16.0	1.6	1.1
House Special, Healthy Living, Tesco*	1 Pack/450g	369	82	6.5	10.5	1.6	1.1
House Special, With Egg Fried Rice, Tesco*	1 Pack/450g	563	125	7.2	19.7	1.9	0.8
My Very Own, Asda*	1 Pack/297g	416	140	7.0	24.0	1.8	0.6
CHIPS,							
11mm Fresh, Deep Fried, McCain*	1oz/28g	66	235	3.2	31.8	10.6	0.0
14mm Fresh, Deep Fried, McCain*	1oz/28g	59	209	2.7	34.2	6.8	0.0
14mm Friers Choice, Deep Fried, McCain*	1oz/28g	56	199	3.5	29.3	8.0	0.0
3 Way Cook, Somerfield*	1 Serving/96g	145	151	2.5	24.0	5.0	1.6
9/16" Straight Cut Caterpack, Deep Fried, McCain*	1oz/28g	63	225	3.1	32.1	9.4	0.0
American Style, Oven, Co-Op*	1 Serving/150g	255	170	2.0	26.0	6.0	3.0
American Style, Oven, Safeway*	1 Serving/125g	288	230	4.1	38.2	6.8	3.0
American Style, Oven, Sainsbury's*	1 Serving/165g	314	190	5.4	23.6	8.3	1.3
American Style,Thin, Oven, Tesco*	1 Serving/125g	210	168	2.7	24.6	6.5	2.1

CHIPS,

INFO/WEIGHT	Measure	per Measure KCAL	KCAL	PROT	CARB	FAT	FIBRE
			Nutrition Values per 100g / 100ml				
Beefeater, Deep Fried, McCain*	1oz/28g	71	253	3.3	37.7	9.9	0.0
Beefeater, Oven Baked, McCain*	1oz/28g	55	195	4.0	32.2	5.6	0.0
Chippy, Deep Fried, McCain*	1oz/28g	51	182	3.0	27.8	6.5	0.0
Chunky Oven, Harry Ramsden's*	1 Serving/150g	185	123	2.8	19.9	3.6	1.6
Chunky, COU, Marks & Spencer*	1 Serving/150g	135	90	1.6	17.6	1.7	1.5
Chunky, Eat Smart, Safeway*	1 Serving/158g	150	95	1.6	18.3	1.6	1.4
Chunky, Ready To Bake, Marks & Spencer*	1 Serving/200g	310	155	2.2	26.8	4.2	2.0
Crinkle Cut Oven, 5% Fat, McCain*	1 Serving/100g	163	163	2.9	30.2	5.4	2.9
Crinkle Cut, Frozen, Fried in Corn Oil	1oz/28g	81	290	3.6	33.4	16.7	2.2
Crinkle Cut, Marks & Spencer*	1 Serving/150g	270	180	3.3	29.5	5.4	2.4
Crinkle Cut, Oven Baked, McCain*	1oz/28g	51	182	3.3	29.7	5.6	0.0
Family Fries Oven, Tesco*	1 Serving/125g	164	131	2.0	22.4	3.7	1.8
Homefries, Crinkle Cut, Oven Baked, McCain*	1 Serving/225g	448	199	3.2	34.8	6.9	0.0
Homefries, Jacket Oven, McCain*	1 Serving/100g	220	220	3.9	37.9	7.4	0.0
Homefries, Straight Cut, Frozen, McCain*	1 Serving/200g	282	141	2.0	26.1	4.4	0.0
Homemade, Fried in Blended Oil	1oz/28g	53	189	3.9	30.1	6.7	2.2
Homemade, Fried in Corn Oil	1oz/28g	53	189	3.9	30.1	6.7	2.2
Homemade, Fried in Dripping	1oz/28g	53	189	3.9	30.1	6.7	2.2
Homestyle Oven, Sainsbury's*	1 Serving/125g	206	165	2.4	29.2	4.3	2.1
Just Bake, Low Fat, Marks & Spencer*	1oz/28g	37	133	2.0	24.7	3.7	1.7
Low Fat, Good Choice, Iceland*	1oz/28g	41	147	2.0	25.3	2.6	1.8
Micro, Asda*	1 Serving/112g	221	197	3.5	30.0	7.0	4.0
Micro, McCain*	1oz/28g	54	194	3.3	27.3	7.9	0.0
Microwave, Cooked	1oz/28g	62	221	3.6	32.1	9.6	2.9
Oven Baked, Crinke Cut, New, McCain*	1oz/28g	55	198	3.5	33.4	5.6	0.0
Oven Baked, McCain*	1oz/28g	48	173	2.8	29.3	4.9	0.0
Oven Baked, Straight Cut, New, McCain*	1oz/28g	51	182	3.6	31.4	4.7	0.0
Oven, 3% Fat, BGTY, Sainsbury's*	1 Serving/165g	185	112	2.4	19.2	2.8	1.9
Oven, American Style, Champion, Aldi*	1 Serving/200g	372	186	2.2	28.2	7.2	2.0
Oven, BGTY, Sainsbury's*	1oz/28g	42	151	2.7	27.1	3.5	2.1
Oven, Best in the World, Iceland*	1 Serving/175g	333	190	3.4	28.9	6.7	3.5
Oven, Champion, Aldi*	1oz/28g	44	158	2.5	27.0	4.5	0.0
Oven, Cooked, Value, Tesco*	1 Serving/125g	308	246	4.5	39.5	7.8	2.9
Oven, Crinkle Cut, Co-Op*	1oz/28g	38	135	2.0	22.0	4.0	3.0
Oven, Crinkle Cut, Safeway*	1 Serving/130g	234	180	3.3	29.5	5.4	2.4
Oven, Crinkle Cut, Sainsbury's*	1 Serving/165g	297	180	3.3	29.5	5.5	2.4
Oven, Crinkle Cut, Tesco*	1oz/28g	40	142	2.1	23.3	4.5	2.0
Oven, Curly, Safeway*	1 Serving/125g	376	301	3.8	34.0	16.6	4.1
Oven, Frozen, Baked	1oz/28g	45	162	3.2	29.8	4.2	2.0
Oven, Frozen, McCain*	1oz/28g	39	138	2.5	26.2	4.0	1.9
Oven, Good Choice, Iceland*	1 Serving/150g	171	114	2.5	20.3	2.5	1.9
Oven, Healthy Choice, Safeway*	1 Serving/150g	227	151	2.8	27.1	3.5	2.1
Oven, New, BGTY, Sainsbury's*	1 Serving/165g	185	112	2.4	19.2	2.8	1.9
Oven, Organic, Waitrose*	1 Serving/165g	233	141	1.5	25.1	3.8	1.6
Oven, Original, McCain*	1 Serving/84g	144	172	3.4	32.4	4.9	2.3
Oven, Reduced Fat, Waitrose*	1oz/28g	37	133	2.3	24.3	3.0	1.6
Oven, Safeway*	1oz/28g	42	151	2.8	27.1	3.5	2.1
Oven, Steak Cut, Sainsbury's*	1 Serving/165g	266	161	2.6	27.1	4.7	2.8
Oven, Steakhouse, Tesco*	1 Serving/125g	165	132	2.7	22.7	3.4	1.7
Oven, Straight Cut, 4% Fat, Healthy Eating, Tesco*,	1oz/28g	35	124	2.3	21.8	3.1	1.9
Oven, Straight Cut, 5% Fat, Sainsbury's*	1 Serving/165g	281	170	3.4	28.0	4.9	2.5
Oven, Straight Cut, Better For You, Morrisons*	1 Serving/165g	249	151	2.8	27.1	3.5	2.1
Oven, Straight Cut, Budgens*	1 Portion/180g	205	114	2.3	21.9	1.9	2.7

CHIPS,	Measure INFO/WEIGHT	per Measure KCAL	Nutrition Values per 100g / 100ml				
			KCAL	PROT	CARB	FAT	FIBRE
Oven, Straight Cut, GFY, Asda*	1oz/28g	42	150	2.6	27.0	3.5	2.4
Oven, Straight Cut, Great Value Asda*	1 Serving/100g	199	199	3.5	35.0	5.0	3.0
Oven, Straight Cut, Healthy Eating, Tesco*	1oz/28g	35	124	2.3	21.8	3.1	1.9
Oven, Straight Cut, Reduced Fat, Tesco*	1 Serving/100g	127	127	2.3	22.7	3.0	2.1
Oven, Straight Cut, Safeway*	1 Serving/125g	226	181	3.6	30.0	5.2	2.5
Oven, Straight Cut, Tesco*	1oz/28g	46	166	2.6	27.8	4.9	1.7
Oven, Stringfellows, McCain*	1oz/28g	72	256	4.1	37.0	10.2	0.0
Oven, Thick Cut, Frozen, Baked	1oz/28g	44	157	3.2	27.9	4.4	1.8
Oven, Thin Cut, American Style, Asda*	1 Serving/100g	240	240	3.4	34.0	10.0	3.0
Oven, Weight Watchers*	1 Serving/100g	150	150	2.8	33.7	3.0	5.9
Steak Cut, 3 Way Cook, Somerfield*	1 Serving/200g	294	147	2.4	23.0	5.0	1.5
Steak Cut, Oven, Tesco*	1 Serving/165.2g	233	141	2.0	24.4	3.9	2.0
Steak, Cut Frying, Safeway*	1 Serving/125g	289	231	3.3	27.1	12.1	2.2
Straight Cut, Low Fat, Tesco*	1 Serving/125g	159	127	2.3	22.7	3.0	2.1
Straight Cut, Microwave Baked, McCain*	1oz/28g	70	251	3.5	35.0	10.7	0.0
Thick Cut, Caterpack, Deep Fried, McCain*	1oz/28g	60	215	3.1	28.8	9.7	0.0
Thick Cut, Frozen, Fried in Corn Oil	1oz/28g	66	234	3.6	34.0	10.2	2.4
Three Way Cook, Skinny, Co-Op*	1 Serving/100g	175	175	2.0	26.0	7.0	3.0
Vending 3/8" Straight Cut, Deep Fried, McCain*	1oz/28g	62	220	3.3	29.6	9.8	0.0
Waffle, Bird's Eye*	1 Serving/75g	156	208	2.5	24.3	11.2	2.6
CHIPSTICKS,							
Ready Salted, Smiths, Walkers*	1 Bag/22g	105	476	6.8	59.5	23.5	0.0
Salt & Vinegar, Smiths, Walkers*	1 Bag/22g	105	476	6.8	59.5	23.5	0.0
CHIVES,							
Fresh	1oz/28g	6	23	2.8	1.7	0.6	1.9
CHOC ICES,							
Average	1 Ice/50g	139	277	3.5	28.1	17.5	0.0
Chocolate, Real Milk, Sainsbury's*	1 Ice/48.4g	150	312	3.5	30.3	19.7	0.8
Chunky, Wall's*	1 Ice/81g	162	200	2.6	18.9	13.1	0.0
Dark, Sainsbury's*	1 Ice/43.2g	135	315	3.8	25.5	22.0	0.4
Dark, Somerfield*	1 Ice/62ml	186	300	3.0	25.0	21.0	0.0
Dark, Tesco*	1 Ice/43.4g	136	316	3.0	27.4	21.4	0.7
Light, Safeway*	1 Choc Ice/43.5g	136	310	2.8	25.9	21.6	0.9
Light, Sainsbury's*	1 Ice/43g	135	313	3.2	27.0	21.4	0.3
Light, Tesco*	1 Ice/43g	138	322	3.4	27.1	22.1	0.5
Milk Chocolate, Marks & Spencer*	1oz/28g	86	306	4.1	28.7	19.4	0.5
Morrisons*	1 Ice/31g	86	279	3.0	24.7	19.3	0.4
Neapolitan Chocolate, Co-Op*	1 Ice/62g	120	194	2.0	16.9	13.2	0.4
Neapolitan, Safeway*	1 Ice/41.4g	119	290	2.6	25.4	19.5	0.3
Real Milk, Sainsbury's*	1 Ice/71ml	133	187	2.0	20.0	11.0	0.1
Real Plain, Sainsbury's*	1 Ice/48.4g	149	310	2.9	29.5	20.0	2.2
Real White, Tesco*	1 Ice/54g	185	343	4.2	27.4	24.1	0.1
Rum & Rasin, Safeway*	1 Ice/45g	136	303	3.3	28.9	19.3	1.1
Safeway*	1 Ice/70g	217	310	2.8	25.9	21.6	0.9
SmartPrice, Asda*	1 Ice/31g	81	262	2.8	20.0	19.0	0.0
Value, Tesco*	1 Ice/31g	87	281	2.6	24.8	19.0	0.6
Vanilla, Co-Op*	1 Ice/70g	130	186	3.6	3.6	17.1	0.0
CHOCOLATE,							
A Darker Shade of Milk, Green & Black's*	1 Serving/20g	108	542	9.5	54.0	32.0	0.0
Animal Bar, Nestle*	1 Bar/19g	97	513	5.8	63.6	26.1	0.0
Assortment, Diabetic, Thorntons*	1oz/28g	108	385	4.3	57.0	24.0	2.5
Assortment, Occasions, Tesco*	1 Serving/150g	705	470	4.6	65.8	20.9	0.5
Beans, Coffee, Solid Dark Chocolate, Marks & Spencer*	1 Serving/10g	53	532	4.7	42.4	37.6	11.6

CHOCOLATE,

	Measure INFO/WEIGHT	per Measure KCAL	KCAL	PROT	CARB	FAT	FIBRE
Beans, Plain, Carl Brandt, Aldi*	4 Beans/5g	25	501	5.7	54.6	28.9	0.0
Belgian Assortment, Waitrose*	1oz/28g	127	453	6.3	45.5	27.3	3.8
Belgian Dark, Extra Special, Asda*	2 Squares/20g	102	508	11.0	26.0	40.0	16.0
Belgian Milk, TTD, Sainsbury's*	2 Squares/20g	108	540	9.8	50.9	33.0	2.3
Belgian Plain With Ginger, TTD, Sainsbury's*	2 Squares/20g	114	571	7.2	31.2	46.4	10.9
Belgian Plain, Diabetic, Boots*	1oz/28g	109	391	5.3	44.0	30.0	14.0
Belgian Plain, Organic, Waitrose*	1 Bar/100g	505	505	9.6	32.0	37.6	5.6
Belgian White With Coffee, TTD, Sainsbury's*	2 Squares/20g	110	548	6.5	56.9	32.7	0.0
Belgian White With Lemon, TTD, Sainsbury's*	2 Squares/20g	109	546	5.7	61.2	30.9	0.1
Belgian White, No Added Sugar, Boots*	1 Serving/30g	146	488	6.0	47.8	36.0	7.0
Belgian, Finest, Tesco*	1 Chocolate/12g	62	520	5.9	55.6	28.4	5.2
Belgian, Petit Fours, Safeway*	1 Serving/10.5g	53	525	6.2	49.9	33.2	1.8
Belgian, Thins, Extra Special, Asda*	1 Biscuit/8.7g	45	503	7.0	67.0	23.0	0.2
Big Purple One, Nestle*	1 Chocolate/39g	191	489	5.0	60.2	25.4	0.6
Black Magic, Nestle*	1oz/28g	128	456	4.4	62.6	20.8	1.6
Bournville, Cadbury's*	1 Bar/50g	248	495	4.6	59.6	26.7	0.0
Bournville, Extra Dark, Cadbury's*	1 Square/10g	56	560	8.5	30.8	44.8	0.0
Brandy Liqueurs, Asda*	1 Chocolate/8.3g	33	409	4.0	60.0	17.0	0.8
Brazil Nut Assortment, Marks & Spencer*	1oz/28g	163	581	9.6	37.5	45.3	1.5
Bubble Bar, Marks & Spencer*	1 Bar/25g	136	542	9.5	51.8	33.1	2.2
Cafe au Lait, Thorntons*	1 Chocolate/16g	77	481	5.3	58.1	25.0	0.6
Cappuccino Bar, Thorntons*	1 Bar/38g	201	529	5.2	49.7	34.7	0.5
Cappuccino Mountain Bar, Marks & Spencer*	1oz/28g	149	533	8.4	52.0	32.5	2.6
Chocolat Noir, Lindt*	1/6 Bar/17g	87	510	6.0	50.0	32.0	0.0
Chocolate Favourites, Tesco*	1 Box/454g	2029	447	4.2	64.3	19.2	0.3
Chomp, Cadbury's*	1 Treatsize/12g	56	465	3.5	67.9	19.8	0.6
Chunky Hazelnut Bar, Marks & Spencer*	1 Bar/52g	293	563	8.8	48.1	37.3	1.7
Classic Chocolate Bar, Cadbury's*	1 Bar/26g	134	514	6.5	62.3	26.5	0.8
Cocoa, Organic, Green & Black's*	1 Serving/5g	16	321	20.0	13.0	21.0	0.0
Coconut, White, Excellence, Lindt*	1 Square/10g	61	610	6.0	48.0	44.0	0.0
Coins, Milk, Sainsbury's*	1 Coin/5g	26	502	5.5	58.8	27.1	2.5
Continental, Cappuccino, Thorntons*	1 Bar/38.0g	201	529	5.2	49.7	34.7	0.1
Cool & Delicious, Dairy Milk, Cadbury's*	1 Bar/21g	110	525	7.6	56.1	30.1	0.0
Cream, Fry's*	1 Serving/50g	215	430	2.6	68.6	15.4	0.0
Creamy Vanilla White, Green & Black's*	1 Serving/20g	115	577	7.5	52.5	37.5	0.0
Credit Card, Solid Milk, Marks & Spencer*	1 Bar/20g	108	540	8.1	54.1	32.4	1.3
Creme Egg, Cadbury's*	1 Egg/39g	174	445	3.0	71.0	16.0	0.0
Crispy, Sainsbury's*	4 Squares/19g	99	521	9.1	56.9	28.5	2.1
Dairy Milk, Advent Calendar, Cadbury's*	1 Piece/4.2g	21	525	7.6	56.1	30.1	0.0
Dairy Milk, Bubbly, Cadbury's*	1 Bar/35.2g	184	525	7.6	56.4	29.7	0.0
Dairy Milk, Cadbury's*	1 Bar/25g	131	525	7.6	56.1	30.1	0.0
Dairy Milk, Caramel Centre, Cadbury's*	1 Square/10g	50	495	5.7	61.1	25.3	0.0
Dairy Milk, Mint Chips, Cadbury's*	1 Serving/49g	247	505	6.5	61.2	26.1	0.0
Dairy Milk, Snack Size, Cadbury's*	1 Bar/30g	159	530	7.8	57.1	29.9	0.0
Dairy Milk, With Shortcake Biscuit, Cadbury's*	1 Square/6g	31	520	7.5	59.0	28.0	0.0
Dark, Bar, Thorntons*	1 Sm Bar/48g	245	511	9.3	31.6	38.8	15.9
Dark, Belgian, Luxury Continental, Sainsbury's*	1 Bar/100g	490	490	11.1	24.2	38.7	7.4
Dark, Fair Trade, Co-Op*	1 Square/4.7g	25	500	4.0	55.0	29.0	7.0
Dark, Mint, Thorntons*	1 Box/115g	544	473	4.4	58.8	24.7	5.3
Dark, Orange With Slivered Almonds, Excellence, Lindt*	1 Square/10g	50	500	6.0	46.0	30.0	0.0
Dark, Organic, Green & Black's*	1 Bar/20g	114	571	10.0	51.0	37.0	0.0
Dark, Smooth, Safeway*	4 Squares/25g	128	512	4.3	54.9	29.4	6.3
Dark, TTD, Sainsbury's*	1 Square/10g	57	569	7.2	31.2	46.3	10.9

	Measure	per Measure	Nutrition Values per 100g / 100ml				
	INFO/WEIGHT	KCAL	KCAL	PROT	CARB	FAT	FIBRE
CHOCOLATE,							
Dark, With 70% Cocoa Solids, Organic, Green & Black's*	1 Serving/20g	115	576	7.5	45.5	40.5	0.0
Dark, With Cherries, Green & Black's*	1 Serving/75g	390	520	7.0	57.3	32.8	0.0
Dark, With Hazelnuts & Currants, Green & Black's*	1 Serving/60g	323	539	8.4	51.6	36.4	0.0
Dark, With a Soft Mint Centre, Green & Black's*	4 Squares/30g	136	452	4.8	56.0	23.2	0.0
Divine, Milk, Co-Op*	1 Bar/45g	243	540	7.0	57.0	32.0	2.0
Drops, Plain, Sainsbury's*	1 Serving/125g	638	510	5.3	60.1	27.6	4.0
Egg, Double Cream, Nestle*	1 egg/28.0g	163	582	6.9	49.2	39.7	0.4
Eggs, Party, Mini, Safeway*	1 Egg/20.3g	64	320	11.2	18.4	21.9	0.7
Excellence, 85% Cocoa Solids, Lindt*	1 Square/8.3g	44	530	11.0	32.0	46.0	0.0
Extremely Chocolatey Mini Bites, Marks & Spencer*	1 Cake/17g	76	445	5.5	51.4	24.6	2.0
Ferrero Rocher, Ferrero*	1 Chocolate/12.5g	74	593	7.0	49.0	41.0	0.0
Florentine, Marks & Spencer*	1 Serving/39g	195	500	7.4	64.5	24.9	1.7
Football, Thorntons*	1 Football/200g	1088	544	7.6	52.9	33.5	1.0
Freddo, Dairy Milk, Cadbury's*	1 Frog/20g	106	530	7.8	57.1	29.9	0.0
Fruit & Nut Assortment, Marks & Spencer*	1oz/28g	148	527	7.6	49.8	34.3	1.3
Fruit & Nut, Cadbury's*	1 Bar/49g	240	490	8.0	55.7	26.3	0.0
Fruit & Nut, Dark, Tesco*	4 Squares/25g	124	494	5.8	54.8	27.9	6.5
Fudge, Keto Bar*	1 Serving/65g	250	385	36.9	36.9	10.8	32.3
Ginger, Dark, Thorntons*	1 Bar/100g	509	509	5.8	44.3	35.1	8.8
Ginger, Terry's*	1oz/28g	111	395	2.6	68.0	12.4	3.4
Ginger, Traidcraft*	1 Bar/50g	212	424	3.9	68.2	14.8	0.0
Jazz Orange Bar, Thorntons*	1 Bar/56g	304	543	6.8	55.7	32.3	1.2
Kinder Bueno, Ferrero*	1 Twin Bar/43g	245	570	8.5	47.6	38.5	0.0
Kinder Maxi, Ferrero*	1 Bar/21g	116	550	10.0	51.0	34.0	0.0
Kinder Surprise, Ferrero*	1 Egg/20g	110	550	10.0	51.0	34.0	0.4
Kinder, Ferrero*	1 Bar/12.5g	69	550	10.0	51.0	34.0	0.0
Kinder, Riegel, Ferrero*	1 Bar/21g	117	558	10.0	53.0	34.0	0.0
Lemon Mousse, Bar, Thorntons*	1oz/28g	141	503	4.1	55.3	29.3	0.0
Luxury Dark Continental, Tesco*	1 Bar/100g	571	571	11.3	46.5	37.8	0.1
Marble, Cadbury's*	1 Bar/46g	246	535	8.4	54.8	31.2	0.0
Matchmakers, Mint, Nestle*	1oz/28g	134	477	4.3	69.7	20.1	0.9
Maya Gold, Green & Black's*	1 Bar/20g	110	552	6.0	56.5	33.5	0.0
Milk	1oz/28g	146	520	7.7	56.9	30.7	0.8
Milk & White Belgian, Shells, Waitrose*	1 Serving/15g	77	511	5.0	53.1	31.0	2.8
Milk & White, Winnie The Pooh, Marks & Spencer*	1 Bar/13.9g	76	540	7.9	54.7	32.3	1.0
Milk Caramel, Green & Black's*	1 Serving/20g	92	461	5.9	57.5	22.9	0.0
Milk Chocolate Excellence, Lindt*	1 Bar/100g	570	570	6.6	48.9	39.6	0.0
Milk, Co-Op*	1 Sm Bar/50g	265	530	9.0	55.0	31.0	2.0
Milk, Extra Fine Swiss, Marks & Spencer*	1oz/28g	155	553	8.9	50.4	35.3	2.4
Milk, Extra au Lait, Milch Extra, Lindt*	½ Bar/50g	268	535	6.5	57.0	31.0	0.0
Milk, Honey, Traidcraft*	1 Bar/50g	273	545	6.0	54.0	33.0	0.0
Milk, Organic, Green & Black's*	1oz/28g	147	524	9.5	54.0	32.0	0.0
Milk, Sainsbury's*	4 Squares/25g	133	533	9.2	54.6	30.8	2.2
Milk, Santa, Tesco*	1 Bag/90g	433	481	4.5	61.4	24.2	1.4
Milk, SmartPrice, Asda*	1 Square/6g	32	536	8.0	54.0	32.0	2.4
Milk, Swiss Made, Organic, Traidcraft*	4 Squares/16.6g	94	550	7.0	50.0	34.0	0.0
Milk, Tesco*	1 Serving/25g	133	533	9.5	54.7	30.7	2.2
Milk, Thorntons*	1 Sm Bar/50g	269	538	7.5	54.8	32.0	1.0
Milk, With Whole Almonds, Green & Black's*	1 Serving/20g	114	572	11.5	41.5	40.0	0.0
Mini Bites, Chunky, Moments, Fox's*	1 Roll/20g	90	450	5.7	52.4	24.6	2.2
Mini Eggs, Marks & Spencer*	Pack Of 4/80g	244	305	11.0	15.7	21.8	1.3
Mini Eggs, Milk, Cadbury's*	1 Egg/3g	15	495	5.6	67.7	22.2	0.0
Mint Crisp, Cadbury's*	1oz/28g	141	505	6.4	70.3	22.2	0.0

CHOCOLATE,	Measure INFO/WEIGHT	per Measure KCAL	Nutrition Values per 100g / 100ml KCAL	PROT	CARB	FAT	FIBRE
Mint Crisp, Sainsbury's*	4 Squares/19g	95	501	5.0	63.7	25.0	3.6
Mint Crisps, Marks & Spencer*	1 Mint/8g	40	494	5.4	54.8	29.6	3.1
Mint Thins, Plain, Safeway*	1 Thin/10g	48	480	2.3	67.5	22.3	0.7
Neapolitans, Terry's*	1oz/28g	146	522	6.0	57.3	29.7	4.1
Nuts About Caramel, Cadbury's*	1 Bar/55g	272	495	5.8	56.6	27.4	0.0
Old Jamaica, Cadbury's*	1oz/28g	129	460	5.8	56.9	23.3	0.0
Orange Cream, Cadbury's*	1 Bar/51g	217	425	2.6	68.6	15.4	0.0
Orange Mini Bites, Marks & Spencer*	1 Bite/22g	95	430	5.5	54.6	21.6	1.8
Peppermint Cream, Fry's*	1 Bar/51g	217	425	2.6	68.8	15.4	0.0
Peppermint Patty, Hershey*	3 Patties/41g	160	390	2.4	80.5	7.3	0.0
Plain	1oz/28g	143	510	5.0	63.5	28.0	2.5
Plain, 72%, Finest, Tesco*	1 Square/10g	60	603	7.7	44.0	44.0	3.7
Plain, Cocoa Solids, Finest, Tesco*	1 Square/10g	58	581	7.7	38.5	44.0	5.8
Plain, Organic, Tesco*	1 oz/28g	145	519	6.4	44.7	34.9	9.6
Plain, With Hazelnuts, Tesco*	4 Squares/25g	135	539	6.1	48.3	35.7	6.5
Praline, Marks & Spencer*	1 Bar/34g	185	545	7.3	49.6	35.2	3.1
Refrigerator Squares, Marks & Spencer*	1 Square/24g	180	750	5.0	113.8	30.4	3.3
Rich Dark Fruit & Nut Plain, Sainsbury's*	4 Squares/25g	117	489	5.2	53.9	27.9	5.7
Rich Dark Plain, Co-Op*	1 Bar/200g	1010	505	4.0	57.0	29.0	6.0
Rich Dark Plain, Sainsbury's*	1oz/28g	144	514	3.7	65.0	29.5	0.9
Rocher, Thorntons*	1 Chocolate/15g	76	507	6.8	45.3	33.3	2.0
Roulade, Sainsbury's*	1 Serving/72g	264	367	5.7	36.9	21.8	1.8
Shots, Cadbury's*	1 Pack/160g	752	470	5.9	59.7	23.2	0.0
Speckled Eggs, Marks & Spencer*	1 Egg/5.7g	26	440	6.6	63.1	18.2	1.5
Swiss Dark Extra Fine, Marks & Spencer*	1 Bar/150g	773	515	6.4	46.7	34.5	9.7
Swiss Milk Chocolate & Hazelnut Bar, Marks & Spencer*	1oz/28g	156	556	6.4	51.9	36.0	3.3
Swiss Milk, Marks & Spencer*	1oz/28g	150	535	5.1	60.9	30.1	1.9
Swiss Mountain Bar, Marks & Spencer*	1 Bar/100g	555	555	6.5	55.2	35.3	0.2
Swiss Mountain Bar, Orange, Marks & Spencer*	½ Bar/50g	268	535	8.0	52.2	32.8	3.2
Swiss Plain With Ginger, Waitrose*	4 Squares/17g	88	519	5.3	58.3	29.4	2.0
Swiss White, Bar, Marks & Spencer*	1oz/28g	152	543	8.0	58.3	30.9	0.0
Tasters, Dairy Milk, Cadbury's*	1 Bag/45g	239	530	7.6	56.4	30.5	0.0
Taz Chocolate Bar, Cadbury's*	1 Bar/25g	121	485	4.8	62.0	24.0	0.0
Teddy, Milk, Thorntons*	1 Teddy/250g	1358	543	7.6	52.6	33.5	1.0
Triple Crunch, Marks & Spencer*	1 Serving/60g	280	467	6.8	66.3	19.4	3.4
White	1oz/28g	148	529	8.0	58.3	30.9	0.0
White, Creamy, Safeway*	4 Squares/21g	113	537	6.9	59.9	29.5	0.0
White, Crispy, Fair Trade, Co-Op*	½ Bar/50g	278	555	9.0	51.0	35.0	0.1
White, Double Berry, Nestle*	¼ Bar/30g	167	556	6.6	54.9	34.5	0.0
White, Nestle*	4 Pieces/40g	220	550	7.5	55.0	32.5	0.0
White, Organic, Green & Black's*	1 Bag/30g	173	577	7.5	52.5	37.5	0.0
White, Organic, Waitrose*	1oz/28g	160	572	6.1	53.9	36.8	0.0
White, SmartPrice, Asda*	1 Serving/25g	137	549	7.0	56.0	33.0	0.0
White, Thorntons*	1 Bar/50g	273	546	6.7	59.4	31.4	0.0
White, With Honey & Almond Nougat, Toblerone*	1 Serving/25g	133	530	6.2	60.5	29.0	0.2
Whole Nut, Cadbury's*	1 Bar/49g	270	550	9.3	48.8	35.2	0.0
Whole Nut, Plain, Belgian, Waitrose*	4 Squares/25g	135	540	6.3	45.4	38.0	7.8
Wholenut, SmartPrice, Asda*	½ Bar/16.4g	90	562	8.0	47.0	38.0	3.3
Wildlife Bar, Cadbury's*	1 Bar/21g	109	520	7.8	56.8	29.3	0.0
Winnie The Pooh, Solid Shapes, Marks & Spencer*	1 Chocolate/6g	32	540	8.1	54.1	32.4	1.3
With Almonds, Dark, Organic, Evernat*	1oz/28g	169	604	16.3	37.4	43.2	0.0
With Orange & Spices, Green & Black's*	1 Serving/20g	110	552	6.0	56.5	33.5	0.0

	Measure INFO/WEIGHT	per Measure KCAL	Nutrition Values per 100g / 100ml				
			KCAL	PROT	CARB	FAT	FIBRE
CHOCOLATE DRINK,							
Finest, Tesco*	1 Serving/200ml	242	121	4.9	10.7	6.5	0.8
Flavia*	1 Serving/18g	64	368	15.6	67.2	4.0	0.0
Instant Break, Milk, Cadbury's*	4 Tsp/28g	119	425	10.9	64.2	14.0	0.0
Orange, Clipper*	1 Packet/28g	98	350	14.6	69.7	1.5	0.0
CHOCOLATE DROPS,							
White, For Cooking & Decorating, Sainsbury's*	1oz/28g	152	544	6.5	60.3	30.8	0.0
CHOCOLATE ECLAIRS,							
Asda*	1 Eclair/50g	192	383	6.0	20.0	31.0	0.5
Cadbury's*	1 Sweet/8g	39	485	4.6	75.0	18.8	0.0
Dairy Cream, Co-Op*	1 Eclair/29g	122	420	6.0	23.0	34.0	0.6
Dairy Cream, Safeway*	1 Eclair/27g	101	373	4.1	32.1	26.2	0.4
Fresh Cream, Co-Op*	1 Eclair/8g	38	470	3.0	71.0	19.0	0.1
Fresh Cream, Jumbo, Co-Op*	1 Eclair/94g	357	380	4.0	27.0	28.0	2.0
Fresh Cream, Marks & Spencer*	1 Eclair/62g	234	378	4.1	18.8	32.3	0.2
Fresh Cream, Mini, Tesco*	1 Cake/28g	111	397	4.8	33.6	27.0	0.4
Fresh Cream, Safeway*	1 Eclair/59g	210	356	4.1	24.8	26.7	0.4
Fresh Cream, Sainsbury's*	1 Eclair/59g	218	370	4.4	27.1	27.2	0.5
Fresh, Cream, Tesco*	1 Eclair/66g	244	370	4.0	31.2	25.5	0.4
Marks & Spencer*	1 Sweet/7g	34	482	1.9	73.9	20.1	0.0
Mini, Iceland*	1 Eclair/13g	55	426	4.9	21.5	35.6	0.4
Sainsbury's*	½ Eclair/30g	104	347	4.0	31.7	22.7	0.3
Tesco*	1 Eclair/66.0g	260	394	4.6	31.2	27.9	0.4
Weight Watchers*	1 Serving/30g	83	278	4.1	36.7	12.7	7.0
CHOCOLATE ORANGE,							
Crunchball, Terry's*	1 Segment/8.7g	47	520	6.9	59.8	28.1	2.0
Dark, Terry's	1 Segment/9g	45	511	4.3	57.0	29.3	6.2
Egg & Spoon, Terry's*	1 Egg/33.9g	196	575	5.5	51.6	38.0	1.7
Milk Bar, Terrys*	1 Bar/40g	212	531	7.2	57.5	30.2	0.4
Milk, Mini Segments, Terry's*	1 Segment/8g	42	527	7.7	57.9	29.4	2.1
Milk, Terry's*	1 Orange/175g	928	530	7.5	57.3	30.0	2.1
Plain, Terry's*	1 Orange/175g	889	508	3.8	56.8	29.4	6.2
Segsations, Terry's*	1 Segsation/8.2g	42	530	5.8	58.5	30.0	2.6
Snowball, Terry's*	1 Segment/8.5g	48	534	6.6	61.3	29.2	0.0
White, Terry's*	1 Segment/11.4g	59	535	6.3	60.9	29.4	0.0
CHOCOLATE PEANUTS,							
Assorted, Thorntons*	1 Bag/140g	785	561	13.8	34.8	40.8	3.6
Belgian Coated, Marks & Spencer*	1 Serving/20g	109	545	14.7	35.6	38.0	5.8
Milk, Tesco*	1 Bag/227g	1221	538	17.5	31.8	37.9	4.4
CHOCOLATE RAISINS,							
Assorted, Thorntons*	1 Bag/140g	601	429	4.2	58.8	19.7	2.9
Belgian Coated, Marks & Spencer*	1 Bag/100g	450	450	4.3	60.6	20.9	0.8
Californian, Tesco*	¼ Bag/56.8g	268	472	5.2	66.2	20.7	1.3
Co-Op*	¼ Pack/50g	205	410	4.0	64.0	15.0	1.0
Coated, Californian, Marks & Spencer*	1 Bag/130g	520	400	4.3	63.2	14.7	1.9
Marks & Spencer*	1oz/28g	116	414	4.5	66.5	14.6	1.2
Milk, Sainsbury's*	1oz/28g	117	418	4.7	62.7	16.5	1.4
Milk, Tesco*	1 Lge Bag/227g	933	411	4.8	63.3	15.4	0.9
CHOCOLATE SPREAD,							
Average	1 Tsp/12g	68	569	4.1	57.1	37.6	0.0
Cadbury's*	1 Tsp/12g	69	575	4.5	55.0	38.0	0.0
Hazelnut, Asda*	1 Tbsp/15g	86	574	5.0	53.0	38.0	0.0
Hazelnut, Nutella, Ferrero*	1oz/28g	149	533	6.5	57.0	31.0	0.0
Milk, Belgian, Sainsbury's*	1 Serving/10g	56	559	11.9	47.2	35.8	1.4

	Measure	per Measure		Nutrition Values per 100g / 100ml				
	INFO/WEIGHT	KCAL		KCAL	PROT	CARB	FAT	FIBRE
CHOCOLATE SPREAD,								
Milk, SmartPrice, Asda*	1 Tbsp/16g	92		573	4.0	56.0	37.0	2.0
Nutella, Ferrero*	1 Tsp/12g	64		533	6.5	57.0	31.0	0.0
Snickers, Mars*	1 Serving/7g	38		548	8.7	43.3	37.8	0.0
Value, Tesco*	1 Serving/20g	116		581	3.0	54.5	39.0	1.5
With Nuts	1 Tsp/12g	66		549	6.2	60.5	33.0	0.8
CHOCOLATES,								
All Gold, Dark, Terry's*	1oz/28g	136		487	3.6	60.9	25.2	4.0
All Gold, Milk, Terry's*	1 Serving/50g	248		496	5.6	61.4	25.2	1.7
All Gold, Plain, Terry's*	1oz/28g	134		477	3.8	60.9	24.0	1.1
Almond Mocca Mousse, Thorntons*	1 Chocolate/14g	76		543	8.5	40.7	37.9	2.9
Alpini, Thorntons*	1 Chocolate/13g	70		538	7.0	54.6	32.3	2.3
Bittermint, Bendicks*	1 Mint/18.2g	74		411	4.4	63.0	17.6	0.0
Buttons, Milk, Asda*	1 Bag/70g	368		526	7.0	57.0	30.0	1.5
Buttons, Milk, Marks & Spencer*	1 Pack/75g	375		500	8.6	59.8	25.3	1.9
Buttons, Milk, Somerfield*	1 Pack/75g	390		520	8.0	58.0	28.0	0.0
Buttons, White, Co-Op*	1 Pack/70g	382		545	7.0	61.0	31.0	0.0
Cappuccino, Thorntons*	1 Chocolate/13g	70		538	5.9	48.5	36.2	0.8
Celebrations, Mars*	1 Bounty/8.3g	36		438	0.0	75.0	18.8	0.0
Champagne, Thorntons*	1 Chocolate/16g	76		475	6.9	43.1	29.4	2.5
Chocolate Mousse, Thorntons*	1 Chocolate/13g	67		515	7.5	40.0	36.2	3.1
Coffee Creme, Dark, Thorntons*	1 Chocolate/13g	52		400	3.0	71.5	10.8	0.8
Coffee Creme, Milk, Thorntons*	1 Chocolate/13g	52		400	2.8	74.6	10.0	0.8
Continental, Belgian, Thorntons*	1 Chocolate/13g	67		514	5.8	53.5	30.3	2.9
Continental, Thorntons*	1 Chocolate/15g	76		506	5.6	54.5	29.3	2.7
Country Caramel, Milk, Thorntons*	1 Chocolate/9g	45		500	4.6	62.2	26.7	0.0
Dairy Box, Milk, Nestle*	1 Sm Box/227g	1085		478	5.7	60.8	23.5	0.8
Dark, Elegant, Elizabeth Shaw*	1 Chocolate/8g	38		469	2.9	62.5	23.1	0.0
Italian Collection, Amaretto, Marks & Spencer*	1 Chocolate/13g	62		480	4.4	59.7	25.1	2.3
Italian Collection, Favourites, Marks & Spencer*	1 Chocolate/14g	74		530	5.7	50.4	33.7	1.6
Italian Collection, Panna Cotta, Marks & Spencer*	1 Chocolate/13g	71		545	5.3	49.4	36.4	0.1
Liquers, Cognac Truffle, Thorntons*	1 Chocolate/14g	65		464	7.3	40.0	27.1	2.9
Liqueur, Elizabeth Shaw*	1 Chocolate/8g	36		447	2.7	56.5	20.7	0.0
Milk Tray, Cadbury's*	1oz/28g	139		495	5.2	60.5	26.0	0.0
Mingles, Bendicks*	1 Chocolate/5g	26		528	6.5	55.0	32.9	0.0
Mint Crisp, Bendicks*	1 Mint/7.7g	40		494	5.2	55.0	29.9	0.0
Mint Crisp, Dark, Elizabeth Shaw*	1 Chocolate/6g	27		458	1.9	68.0	20.7	0.0
Mint Crisp, Milk, Elizabeth Shaw*	1 Chocolate/6g	30		493	4.0	70.9	21.4	0.0
Mint Crisp, Thorntons*	1 Chocolate/7g	34		486	7.7	40.0	31.4	4.3
Misshapes, Assorted, Cadbury's*	1 Chocolate/8g	41		515	5.2	57.5	29.1	0.0
Orange Crisp, Elizabeth Shaw*	1 Chocolate/6g	29		478	2.9	68.2	21.5	0.0
Praline, Coffee, Thorntons*	1 Chocolate/7g	37		529	7.0	47.1	34.3	2.9
Praline, Roast Hazelnut, Thorntons*	1 Chocolate/13g	70		538	6.0	51.5	33.8	3.1
Praline, Hazelnut, Thorntons*	1 Chocolate/5g	27		540	7.0	48.0	36.0	4.0
Praline, Marzipan, Thorntons*	1 Chocolate/14g	63		450	5.9	58.6	21.4	2.1
Quality Street, Nestle*	1 Serving/25g	117		466	4.0	66.0	20.7	0.8
Roses, Cadbury's*	1oz/28g	136		485	4.8	60.9	24.8	0.0
Strawberrys & Cream, Thorntons*	1 Chocolate/12g	64		533	5.1	54.2	32.5	0.8
Swiss Milk Discs, Marks & Spencer*	1 Disc/5g	28		553	8.9	50.4	35.3	2.4
Tartufo, Thorntons*	1 Chocolate/15g	77		513	7.4	40.0	36.0	3.3
Truffle, Lemon, White, Thorntons*	1 Chocolate/14g	63		450	4.6	64.3	25.0	0.7
Truffle, Seville, Thorntons*	1 Chocolate/14g	76		543	7.1	53.6	33.6	1.4
Truffle, Swiss, Somerfield*	1 Pack/125g	640		512	4.0	52.0	32.0	0.0
Truffle, Amaretto, Thorntons*	1 Chocolate/14g	66		471	5.5	55.0	25.7	2.9

C

	Measure	per Measure	Nutrition Values per 100g / 100ml				
	INFO/WEIGHT	KCAL	KCAL	PROT	CARB	FAT	FIBRE
CHOCOLATES,							
Truffle, Balls, Red, Lindt Lindor*	1 Ball/12g	70	583	0.0	41.7	50.0	0.0
Truffle, Brandy, Thorntons*	1 Chocolate/14g	68	486	6.1	52.1	27.1	0.7
Truffle, Caramel, Thorntons*	1 Chocolate/14g	67	479	4.2	57.9	25.7	2.1
Truffle, Champagne, Petit, Thorntons*	1 Chocolate/6g	31	517	7.5	48.3	31.7	3.3
Truffle, Champagne, Premier, Thorntons*	1 Chocolate/17g	88	518	6.9	45.3	32.9	2.4
Truffle, Cherry, Thorntons*	1 Chocolate/14g	58	414	4.2	50.7	21.4	1.4
Truffle, Continental Champagne, Thorntons*	1 Chocolate/16g	78	488	6.1	51.3	28.0	0.6
Truffle, Grand Marnier, Thorntons*	1 Chocolate/15g	77	513	7.2	40.7	34.0	4.0
Truffle, Irish Milk Chocolate Cream, Elizabeth Shaw*	1 Chocolate/12g	57	477	3.9	63.4	22.8	0.0
Truffle, Rum, Thorntons*	1 Chocolate/13g	63	485	4.8	58.5	24.6	4.8
Truffle, Thorntons*	1 Chocolate/7g	33	471	6.0	48.6	27.1	1.4
Truffle, Vanilla, Thorntons*	1 Chocolate/13g	64	492	4.8	57.7	26.9	1.5
Truffle, Viennese, Dark, Thorntons*	1 Chocolate/10g	53	530	5.9	47.0	36.0	3.0
Truffle, Viennese, Milk, Thorntons*	1 Chocolate/10g	56	560	4.9	54.0	36.0	0.0
Truffles, Mint, Marks & Spencer*	1 Bar/35g	190	543	6.8	55.9	32.4	1.2
Truffles, Rum	1oz/28g	146	521	6.1	49.7	33.7	1.9
Valentine, Thorntons*	1 Chocolate/11g	60	542	5.7	52.0	34.5	2.1
Winter Selection, Thorntons*	1 Chocolate/10g	51	506	6.2	51.3	30.6	3.8
CHOCOLATINE,							
All Butter, Sainsbury's*	1 Serving/58.1g	241	415	7.9	42.5	23.7	3.3
Mini, Sainsbury's*	1 Serving/30g	120	400	7.7	41.0	23.0	3.3
Sainsbury's*	1 Serving/58g	263	454	8.5	42.3	27.9	2.1
CHOP SUEY,							
Chicken, With Noodles, Sainsbury's*	1 Pack/300g	300	100	5.7	13.6	2.5	1.2
CHOW MEIN,							
Beef, Sainsbury's*	1 Pack/450g	500	111	6.6	15.5	2.5	0.8
Cantonese Chicken, Sainsbury's*	1 Pack/450g	455	101	6.5	11.5	3.2	1.7
Cantonese Vegetable Stir Fry, Sainsbury's*	¼ Pack/100g	85	85	2.2	10.6	3.8	1.2
Char Sui, Cantonese, Sainsbury's*	½ Pack/225g	205	91	5.7	10.0	3.1	1.1
Chicken Stir Fry, Oriental Express*	1 Pack/350g	347	99	5.8	14.9	1.8	2.9
Chicken With Vegetable Spring Roll, Oriental Express*	1 Pack/300g	213	71	5.5	12.4	0.6	1.9
Chicken, Ainsley Harriott*	1 Serving/250g	447	179	14.0	21.2	4.7	2.0
Chicken, Asda*	1 Pack/460g	488	106	5.0	13.0	3.8	2.1
Chicken, BGTY, Sainsbury's*	1 Pack/450g	410	91	6.9	11.5	1.9	1.2
Chicken, COU, Marks & Spencer*	1 Pack/200g	180	90	9.3	8.1	2.3	1.1
Chicken, Cantonese, Sainsbury's*	½ Pack/225g	198	88	5.7	11.7	2.0	1.2
Chicken, Chinese Takeaway, Sainsbury's*	1 Pack/316g	338	107	9.1	11.6	2.7	0.7
Chicken, Co-Op*	1 Pack/300g	270	90	8.0	9.0	3.0	0.9
Chicken, Frozen, Sainsbury's*	1 Pack/403.8g	424	105	6.1	13.4	3.0	0.9
Chicken, Great Value, Asda*	1 Pack/400g	408	102	5.0	14.0	2.9	0.8
Chicken, Healthy Living, Tesco*	1 Pack/450g	392	87	8.2	10.8	1.2	0.4
Chicken, New Improved Recipe, Sainsbury's*	1 Pack/449g	395	88	5.7	11.7	2.0	1.2
Chicken, New, BGTY, Sainsbury's*	1 Pack/450g	374	83	6.0	11.4	1.4	1.1
Chicken, Oriental Express*	1 Pack/300g	210	70	4.4	13.1	0.6	1.9
Chicken, Oriental, Healthy Living, Tesco*	1 Pack/450g	288	64	7.2	7.6	0.5	3.5
Chicken, Sizzling Stir Fry, Oriental Express*	1 Pack/375g	360	96	7.3	10.7	2.7	2.2
Chicken, Tesco*	1 Pack/350g	322	92	5.1	14.5	1.5	0.8
Chicken, Waitrose*	1 Serving/400g	384	96	6.0	11.4	2.9	1.3
Chinese Style, Safeway*	1 Serving/150g	167	111	4.0	13.0	4.4	1.1
GFY, Asda*	1 Pack/400g	236	59	6.0	8.0	0.3	1.2
Pork, Perfectly Balanced, Waitrose*	½ Pack/310g	332	107	7.6	17.2	0.9	1.6
Special Chinese, Farmfoods*	1 Pack/400g	276	69	4.3	6.7	2.8	0.8
Special, COU, Marks & Spencer*	1 Pack/400g	320	80	7.4	9.9	1.0	1.0

	Measure INFO/WEIGHT	per Measure KCAL	Nutrition Values per 100g / 100ml KCAL	PROT	CARB	FAT	FIBRE
CHOW MEIN,							
Special, GFY, Asda*	1 Pack/400g	360	90	7.0	14.0	0.7	1.2
Special, Marks & Spencer*	1 Pack/340g	289	85	6.6	8.2	2.7	1.2
Stir Fry With Veg & Noodles, Somerfield*	1 Serving/200g	234	117	2.8	12.9	6.0	1.3
Stir Fry, Asda*	1 Pack/350g	270	77	2.1	6.0	5.0	0.0
Stir Fry, Somerfield*	1 Pack/300g	474	158	6.0	32.0	1.0	0.0
Stir Fry, Tesco*	1 Pack/500g	335	67	2.5	10.8	1.5	1.0
Vegetable & Cashew Nut, Eat Smart, Safeway*	1 Pack/380g	323	85	7.0	11.4	1.2	1.1
Vegetable, Asda*	1oz/28g	25	90	2.9	15.5	1.8	1.2
Vegetable, Healthy Eating, Tesco*	1 Pack/350g	221	63	6.8	7.9	0.5	1.3
Vegetables & Noodles in Sauce, Safeway*	1 Serving/200g	110	55	3.7	9.5	0.2	1.3
With Vegetable Spring Roll, Oriental Express*	1 Roll/120g	196	163	5.3	28.5	3.2	3.0
CHRISTMAS PUDDING,							
Average	1oz/28g	81	291	4.6	49.5	9.7	1.3
BGTY, Sainsbury's*	1 Serving/113g	302	266	2.8	58.2	2.5	4.6
Black Cherry & Ameretto, Cole's*	1 Pudding/450g	1647	366	2.7	56.9	6.2	1.1
Iceland*	¼ Pudding/100g	352	352	3.3	63.0	9.6	7.6
Less Than 5% Fat, GFY, Asda*	½ Pudding/100g	279	279	2.6	58.0	4.1	1.6
Luxury, Safeway*	1/8 Pudding/114g	316	277	3.1	47.9	8.1	1.3
Retail	1oz/28g	92	329	3.0	56.3	11.8	1.7
Rich Fruit, Tesco*	1 Serving/114g	331	290	2.4	55.0	5.9	0.0
Sticky Toffee, Tesco*	¼ Pudding/114g	372	326	2.5	64.5	6.4	0.8
Tesco*	1 Serving/113g	305	270	2.4	55.0	5.9	1.5
Toffee Sauce Coated, Morrisons*	1 Pudding/100g	324	324	2.5	64.5	6.4	0.0
Traditional Style, Asda*	1 Pudding/100g	296	296	2.6	58.0	6.0	1.6
Vintage, Marks & Spencer*	1/8 Pudding/113g	335	295	2.6	59.8	5.6	1.4
With Cider, Value, Tesco*	1 Serving/100g	312	312	2.7	59.6	7.0	3.3
CHUTNEY,							
Albert's Victorian, Baxters*	1 Serving/25g	38	150	35.0	6.0	0.1	0.0
Apricot & Ginger, Safeway*	1 Tsp/15g	24	162	1.4	38.0	0.2	2.0
Apricot, Sharwood's*	1 Tsp/16g	21	131	0.6	32.0	0.1	2.3
Bengal Hot, Sharwood's*	1oz/28g	56	200	0.5	48.7	0.3	1.1
Bengal Spice Mango, Sharwood's*	1 Tsp/5g	12	236	0.5	58.0	0.2	1.2
Caramalised Onion, Sainsbury's*	1 Serving/25g	28	111	1.1	23.5	1.4	1.1
Cranberry & Caramelised Red Onion, Baxters*	1 Serving/20g	31	154	0.3	38.0	0.1	0.3
Flame Roasted Tomato & Pepper, TTD, Sainsbury's*	1 Serving/5g	9	189	1.0	45.3	0.4	1.1
Fruit, Spiced, Baxters*	1 Tsp/16g	23	143	6.0	34.8	0.1	0.0
Fruit, Traditional, Marks & Spencer*	1oz/28g	43	155	0.9	37.2	0.3	1.7
Hot Mango, TTD, Sainsbury's*	1 Tbs/15g	36	240	0.7	54.7	2.0	2.0
Lime & Chilli, Geeta's*	1 Serving/25g	69	277	2.0	64.0	1.4	1.9
Major Grey Mango, Patak's*	1oz/28g	71	255	0.4	66.0	0.2	0.7
Mango & Apple, Sharwood's*	1oz/28g	65	233	0.4	57.6	0.1	1.1
Mango & Ginger, Baxters*	1 Jar/320g	598	187	5.0	45.7	0.2	0.9
Mango & Lime, Sharwood's*	1oz/28g	58	206	0.4	50.5	0.3	0.8
Mango, Green Label, Sharwood's*	1 Serving/10g	23	234	0.3	57.8	0.2	0.9
Mango, Hot, Patak's*	1oz/28g	72	258	0.4	67.1	0.2	0.7
Mango, Somerfield*	1oz/28g	40	143	1.0	35.0	0.0	0.0
Mango, Sweet	1 Heaped Tsp/16g	30	189	0.7	48.3	0.1	0.0
Mixed Fruit	1 Heaped Tsp/16g	25	155	0.6	39.7	0.0	0.0
Peach Fruit, Sharwoods*	1oz/28g	48	172	0.4	42.3	0.1	0.9
Ploughman's Plum, EPC*	1 Tsp/10g	16	160	1.3	38.1	0.2	1.6
Spicy Fruit, Safeway*	1 Tsp/16g	16	109	0.5	25.5	0.1	0.1
Spicy Mango, Marks & Spencer*	1oz/28g	52	185	0.1	46.1	0.3	1.8
Sweet Mango, Marks & Spencer*	1oz/28g	67	240	0.3	58.8	0.2	1.5

C

	Measure	per Measure	Nutrition Values per 100g / 100ml				
	INFO/WEIGHT	KCAL	KCAL	PROT	CARB	FAT	FIBRE
CHUTNEY,							
Sweet Mango, Patak's*	1oz/28g	73	259	0.3	67.4	0.1	0.7
Tomato	1 Heaped Tsp/16g	20	128	1.2	31.0	0.2	1.3
Tomato & Red Pepper, Baxters*	1 Jar/312g	512	164	2.0	38.0	0.4	1.5
Tomato, TTD, Sainsbury's*	1 Tbsp/15g	29	193	2.0	44.7	1.3	2.7
Tomato, Waitrose*	1 Pot/100g	195	195	1.3	46.8	0.3	0.0
CIABATTA,							
Chicken Tomato & Basil, Boots*	1 Pack/207g	499	241	11.0	20.0	13.0	3.0
CIDER,							
Diamond White*	1fl oz/30ml	11	36	0.0	2.6	0.0	0.0
Dry	1 Pint/568ml	205	36	0.0	2.6	0.0	0.0
Low Alcohol	1 Pint/568ml	97	17	0.0	3.6	0.0	0.0
Medium Sweet, Somerfield*	1 Pint/568ml	233	41	0.0	5.0	0.0	0.0
Sweet	1 Pint/568ml	239	42	0.0	4.3	0.0	0.0
Value, Tesco*	1 Pint/568ml	153	27	0.0	0.8	0.0	0.0
Vintage	1 Pint/568ml	574	101	0.0	7.3	0.0	0.0
CINNAMON,							
Powder	1 Tsp/3g	8	261	3.9	55.5	3.2	0.0
CLAMS,							
In Brine, Average	1oz/28g	22	79	16.0	2.5	0.6	0.0
CLEMENTINES,							
Raw, Average	1 Med/60g	23	38	0.9	8.7	0.1	1.2
COCKLES,							
Boiled	1 Cockle/4g	2	53	12.0	0.0	0.6	0.0
Bottled in Vinegar, Drained	1oz/28g	17	60	13.3	0.0	0.7	0.0
Van Smirren*	1 Jar/100g	81	81	9.0	9.0	1.0	0.0
COCOA BUTTER,							
Average	1oz/28g	251	896	0.0	0.0	99.5	0.0
COCOA POWDER,							
Cadbury's*	1 Tbsp/16g	52	322	23.1	10.5	20.8	0.0
Made Up With Semi-Skimmed Milk	1 Mug/227ml	129	57	3.5	7.0	1.9	0.2
Made Up With Skimmed Milk	1 Mug/227ml	100	44	3.5	7.0	0.5	0.0
Made Up With Whole Milk	1 Mug/227ml	173	76	3.4	6.8	4.2	0.2
Organic, Green & Black's*	1oz/28g	115	412	24.5	42.0	22.0	0.0
COCONUT,							
Creamed, Average	1oz/28g	186	666	6.0	6.7	68.4	7.0
Desiccated	1oz/28g	169	604	5.6	6.4	62.0	13.7
Fresh	1oz/28g	98	351	3.2	3.7	36.0	7.3
Ice	1oz/28g	104	371	1.7	66.7	12.7	2.6
Juice, With Pulp, My Way*	1 Can/330ml	130	39	0.0	9.1	0.0	0.0
Milk, Amoy*	1oz/28g	39	140	1.9	1.1	17.0	0.0
Milk, BGTY, Sainsbury's*	¼ Can/100ml	96	96	1.0	3.6	8.6	0.0
Milk, Blue Dragon*	1 Can/400ml	640	160	2.2	2.2	15.7	0.0
Milk, Light, Reduced Fat, Blue Dragon*	1 Can/400ml	408	102	0.9	2.4	9.8	0.0
Milk, Low Fat, Blue Dragon*	1 Can/400ml	272	68	0.7	1.0	6.7	0.0
Milk, Rich Creamy, Amoy*	1 Can/400ml	684	171	2.0	2.5	17.0	0.0
COD,							
Baked	1oz/28g	27	96	21.4	0.0	1.2	0.0
Cakes, Big Time, Bird's Eye*	1 Cake/114g	223	196	8.3	17.8	10.2	1.0
Captains Coins, Bird's Eye*	1 Coin/20g	34	168	10.1	13.3	8.3	0.9
Dried, Salted, Boiled	1oz/28g	39	138	32.5	0.0	0.9	0.0
Fillets, Battered, Average	1 Serving/135g	237	176	12.6	13.0	8.2	1.1
Fillets, Breaded, Average	1 Portion/97g	200	206	13.0	16.7	9.7	1.0
Fillets, Breaded, Chunky, Average	1 Piece/135g	204	151	13.7	10.9	5.9	1.4

COD,	Measure INFO/WEIGHT	per Measure KCAL	KCAL	PROT	CARB	FAT	FIBRE
Fillets, Breaded, Light, Healthy Range, Average	1 Fillet/135g	209	154	13.6	13.3	5.1	1.2
Fillets, Chargrilled, Sainsbury's*	1 Fillet/112g	184	164	15.4	0.8	11.0	0.0
Fillets, Chunky, Average	1 Fillet/198g	267	135	17.1	8.2	3.7	0.8
Fillets, Skinless & Boneless, Raw, Average	1 Portion/92g	90	98	17.8	2.7	1.7	0.4
Fillets, Smoked, Average	1 Serving/150g	152	101	21.6	0.0	1.6	0.0
Fritters, Cafe Culture, Marks & Spencer*	½ Pack/68.6g	121	175	8.5	10.8	11.1	1.2
Loins, Average	1 Serving/145g	116	80	17.9	0.1	0.8	0.2
Poached	1oz/28g	26	94	20.9	0.0	1.1	0.0
Portions, Low Fat, Tesco*	1 Portion/92g	63	68	15.6	0.0	0.6	0.0
Smoked, Raw	1oz/28g	22	79	18.3	0.0	0.6	0.0
Steaks, Battered, Chip Shop Style, Average	1 Serving/150g	321	214	12.5	14.3	12.0	1.1
Steamed	1oz/28g	23	83	18.6	0.0	0.9	0.0
COD &,							
Chips, Oven Baked, Safeway*	1 Pack/250g	523	209	8.4	25.0	8.4	3.5
Parsley Sauce, Frozen, Marks & Spencer*	1 Pack/184g	156	85	11.1	1.9	3.9	1.0
Salmon, Steam Cuisine, COU, Marks & Spencer*	1 Pack/400g	340	85	6.8	8.9	1.8	1.2
COD IN,							
A Sweet Red Pepper Sauce, Fillets, GFY, Asda*	½ Pack/170g	143	84	15.0	2.3	1.6	0.1
Butter Sauce, Portions, Asda*	1 Serving/151g	134	89	10.0	3.5	3.9	0.1
Butter Sauce, Ross*	1 Serving/150g	126	84	9.1	3.2	3.9	0.1
Butter Sauce, Sainsbury's*	1 Serving/170g	184	108	10.5	3.1	5.9	0.3
Butter Sauce, Steaks, Bird's Eye*	1 Pack/170g	185	109	9.8	5.0	5.5	0.1
Butter Sauce, Steaks, Frozen, Asda*	1 Pouch/152.3g	163	107	16.0	5.0	2.6	0.8
Butter Sauce, Steaks, Morrisons*	1 Steak/170g	153	90	10.9	4.1	3.3	0.4
Butter Sauce, Tesco*	1 Pack/150g	123	82	9.4	2.9	3.6	0.5
Cheese Sauce, BGTY, Sainsbury's*	1 Serving/170g	145	85	12.8	3.1	2.4	0.0
Cheese Sauce, Steaks, Bird's Eye*	1 Pack/182g	175	96	10.9	5.2	3.5	0.1
Mushroom Sauce, BGTY, Sainsbury's*	1 Serving/170g	112	66	9.9	2.8	1.7	0.1
Parsley Sauce, BGTY, Sainsbury's*	1 Pack/170g	143	84	11.4	2.4	3.2	0.3
Parsley Sauce, COU, Marks & Spencer*	1 Pack/185g	130	70	10.6	1.4	2.5	0.6
Parsley Sauce, Eat Smart, Safeway*	1 Serving/200g	150	75	11.5	2.4	1.9	0.9
Parsley Sauce, Fillets, BGTY, Sainsbury's*	1 Pack/351g	316	90	11.6	1.3	4.3	0.7
Parsley Sauce, GFY, Asda*	½ Pack/149g	124	83	12.0	1.5	3.5	0.6
Parsley Sauce, Marks & Spencer*	1oz/28g	30	107	11.5	3.9	5.1	0.5
Parsley Sauce, Portions, Asda*	1 Serving/150g	116	77	11.0	3.8	2.0	0.1
Parsley Sauce, Portions, Sainsbury's*	1 Pack/170g	143	84	11.4	2.4	3.2	0.3
Parsley Sauce, Steaks, Bird's Eye*	1 Pack/176g	150	85	10.4	5.0	2.6	0.1
Parsley Sauce, Steaks, Frozen, Bird's Eye*	1 Pack/172.2g	155	90	10.5	5.6	2.8	0.1
Parsley Sauce, Steaks, Iceland*	1 Serving/151.2g	130	86	9.1	2.1	4.6	0.7
Parsley Sauce, Steaks, Sainsbury's*	1 Serving/150g	126	84	11.4	2.4	3.2	0.3
Parsley Sauce, Tesco*	1 Serving/150g	122	81	10.0	3.3	3.1	0.3
Zesty Sauce, COU, Marks & Spencer*	1 Serving/400g	260	65	7.2	5.2	1.7	1.2
COD MEDITERRANEAN,							
COU, Marks & Spencer*	1 Pack/400g	320	80	6.5	11.2	0.7	2.3
Style, Fillets, GFY, Asda*	1 Serving/200g	138	69	9.0	2.5	2.5	0.9
Style, Fillets, Herb, Tesco*	1 Serving/115g	190	165	14.5	1.3	11.3	0.6
COD MORNAY,							
Fillets, In A Rich Creamy Cheese Sauce, Sainsbury's*	1 Pack/360g	472	131	12.9	1.9	8.0	0.8
Fillets, Sainsbury's*	1 Serving/153g	236	154	15.2	2.2	9.4	0.9
COD WITH,							
A Mediterranean Pepper Sauce, Fillets, Waitrose*	1 Pack/370g	241	65	12.2	1.1	1.3	0.9
A Thai Crust, Perfectly Balanced, Waitrose*	1 Pack/280g	249	89	15.1	1.6	2.5	0.6
Mediterranean Butter, Sainsbury's*	1 Pack/170.4g	196	115	17.0	0.1	5.2	0.1

C

	Measure INFO/WEIGHT	per Measure KCAL	Nutrition Values per 100g / 100ml				
			KCAL	PROT	CARB	FAT	FIBRE
COD WITH,							
Parma Ham & Sardinian Chick Peas, Marks & Spencer*	½ Pack/255g	268	105	9.8	5.3	4.9	0.5
Parsley Sauce, Somerfield*	1 Serving/200g	276	138	13.3	3.3	7.9	0.5
Roasted Vegetables, Marks & Spencer*	1 Serving/280g	238	85	8.0	4.9	3.8	1.7
Salsa & Rosemary Potatoes, BGTY, Sainsbury's*	1 Pack/450g	356	79	4.7	13.1	0.9	1.6
Sunblush Tomato Sauce, GFY, Asda*	½ Pack/177.3g	117	66	13.0	0.1	1.5	1.6
Sweet Chilli, COU, Marks & Spencer*	1 Pack/400g	360	90	7.7	13.1	0.5	1.6
COFFEE,							
Black	1 Mug/270ml	5	2	0.2	0.3	0.0	0.0
Cafe Latte, Dry, Douwe Egberts*	1 Serving/12g	58	480	10.0	60.0	22.0	0.0
Cafe Latte, Skimmed Milk, Starbucks*	1 Serving/260ml	88	34	3.4	5.0	0.1	0.0
Cafe Latte, Whole Milk, Grande, Starbucks*	1 Serving/16floz	260	57	3.1	4.6	3.1	0.0
Cafe Latte, Whole Milk, Tall, Starbucks*	1 Serving/12floz	200	59	3.2	4.7	3.2	0.0
Cafe Mocha, Skimmed Milk, Starbucks*	1 Tall Mug/350ml	170	49	3.1	9.4	0.4	0.3
Cafe Vanilla, Nescafe*	1 Sachet/18.5g	82	432	9.7	73.0	11.4	0.0
Caffe Mocha, Starbucks*	1 Tall/200ml	278	139	4.9	15.0	7.9	0.7
Cappuccino, Asda*	1 Sachet/15g	60	399	13.0	53.0	15.2	0.9
Cappuccino, Cafe Mocha, Dry, Maxwell House*	1 Serving/23g	100	434	4.3	78.2	10.8	0.0
Cappuccino, Cafe Specials, Dry, Marks & Spencer*	1 Serving/14g	55	395	14.0	59.0	11.5	0.7
Cappuccino, Cappio, Kenco*	1 Sachet/18g	79	439	11.7	73.9	10.6	0.6
Cappuccino, Chocolate, Pret A Manger*	1 Serving/340g	106	31	1.7	2.2	1.7	0.0
Cappuccino, Chocolate, Safeway*	1 Serving/120g	222	185	5.1	32.9	3.7	0.6
Cappuccino, Co-Op*	1 Serving/12.5g	55	440	16.0	64.0	16.0	8.0
Cappuccino, Dry, Maxwell House*	1 Mug/15g	53	350	12.0	64.0	9.6	0.4
Cappuccino, For Filter Systems, Kenco*	1 Sachet/6g	23	375	19.0	44.0	13.5	0.0
Cappuccino, Instant, Kenco*	1 Sachet/20g	80	401	13.5	55.7	13.8	0.0
Cappuccino, Instant, Made Up, Maxwell House*	1 Serving/280g	123	44	0.6	5.8	1.9	0.0
Cappuccino, Instant, Unsweetened, Douwe Egberts*	1 Serving/12g	48	400	11.0	53.0	16.0	0.0
Cappuccino, Low Sugar, Tesco*	1 Serving/13g	55	425	18.4	43.3	19.8	0.4
Cappuccino, Marks & Spencer*	1 Serving/164g	66	40	1.5	4.4	1.6	0.1
Cappuccino, McDonald's*	1 Reg Cup/25ml	92	365	22.4	20.6	14.4	0.0
Cappuccino, No Chocolate, Pret A Manger*	1 Serving/340g	102	30	1.7	2.0	1.7	0.0
Cappuccino, Nonfat Milk, Starbucks*	1 Tall/480ml	80	17	1.5	2.3	0.0	0.0
Cappuccino, Organic Chocolate, Traidcraft*	1 Serving/25g	139	555	7.0	43.0	38.0	0.0
Cappuccino, Original Mugsticks, Maxwell House*	1 Serving/18g	73	406	14.4	52.8	15.6	0.0
Cappuccino, Sachets, Nescafe*	1 Serving/12.5g	52	400	11.2	66.4	9.6	0.0
Cappuccino, Sainsbury's*	1 Serving/12g	49	411	14.9	52.9	15.5	0.4
Cappuccino, Short, Non Fat Milk, Starbucks*	1oz/28g	17	59	5.6	8.4	0.3	0.0
Cappuccino, Skimmed Milk, EAT*	1 Tall/355ml	85	24	2.6	3.1	0.1	0.0
Cappuccino, Soy Milk, Starbucks*	1 Serving/480ml	120	25	1.3	3.5	0.6	0.1
Cappuccino, Swiss Chocolate, Nescafe*	1 Sachet/20g	81	404	10.5	65.3	11.5	2.9
Cappuccino, Unsweetened Taste, Maxwell House*	1 Serving/15g	65	434	17.4	47.6	19.3	0.3
Cappuccino, Unsweetened, Cappio, Kenco*	1 Serving/18g	73	406	12.2	66.7	10.0	0.6
Cappuccino, Unsweetened, Dry, Nescafe*	1 Sachet/12g	51	427	14.9	54.7	16.6	0.0
Cappuccino, Venti, Non Fat Milk, Starbucks*	1oz/28g	33	118	11.0	17.0	0.6	0.0
Cappuccino, Whip, Marks & Spencer*	1 Serving/28g	140	500	7.0	57.1	27.0	1.4
Cappucino, Regular, Burger King*	1 Serving/200ml	36	18	1.0	3.0	0.1	0.1
Compliment*	1 Serving/14ml	20	143	1.4	6.4	12.9	0.0
Frappe Iced, Nestle*	1 Serving/25g	96	384	15.0	72.0	4.0	0.5
Frappuccino, Blended Coffee, Starbucks*	1 Serving/454ml	260	57	1.1	11.5	0.8	0.0
Frappuccino, Caramel, Coffee Based, Starbucks*	1 Grande/473ml	279	59	1.0	11.6	0.7	0.0
Frappuccino, Mango Citrus Tea, Starbucks*	1 Tall/220ml	180	82	0.5	18.2	0.0	0.0
Frappuccino, Starbucks*	1 Drink/281ml	190	68	2.1	13.9	1.1	0.0
Frappuccino, Strawberries & Cream, Starbucks*	1 Grande/473ml	581	123	3.2	19.5	3.6	0.0

	Measure		Nutrition Values per 100g / 100ml				
	INFO/WEIGHT	per Measure KCAL	KCAL	PROT	CARB	FAT	FIBRE

COFFEE,

Ice Mocha Drink, Nescafe, Nestle*	1 Bottle/280ml	160	57	1.1	10.5	1.2	0.0
Infusion, Average With Semi-Skimmed Milk	1 Cup/220ml	14	7	0.6	0.7	0.2	0.0
Infusion, Average With Single Cream	1 Cup/220ml	31	14	0.4	0.3	1.2	0.0
Infusion, Average With Whole Milk	1 Cup/220ml	15	7	0.5	0.5	0.4	0.0
Infusion, Average, Made With Skimmed Milk	1 Cup/220ml	13	6	0.6	0.7	0.0	0.0
Instant, Made With Skimmed Milk	1 Serving/270ml	15	6	0.6	0.8	0.0	0.0
Instant, Made With Water & Semi-Skimmed Milk	1 Serving/350ml	25	7	0.4	0.5	0.4	0.0
Latte, 'A' Mocha, Cafe Met*	1 Bottle/290ml	174	60	3.2	9.0	1.4	0.0
Latte, Cafe, Marks & Spencer*	1 Serving/190g	143	75	4.3	8.3	2.8	0.0
Latte, McDonald's*	1 Cup/16.2ml	59	364	22.3	20.3	14.3	0.0
Latte, Nescafe*	1 Sachet/21g	98	469	14.5	52.4	22.5	0.0
Latte, Pret A Manger*	1 Serving/336g	194	58	3.1	3.9	3.3	2.1
Latte, Skimmed Milk, Tall, 12 oz, Starbucks*	1 12 oz Cup/360g	123	34	3.3	4.7	0.2	0.0
Mocha, Pret A Manger*	1 Serving/340ml	243	71	2.8	7.6	3.4	0.0
Mocha, Skimmed Milk, Pret a Manger*	1 Serving/340ml	91	27	2.6	3.6	0.2	0.0
Regular, Ground or Instant	1 Cup (6fl oz)/177g	6	4	0.2	0.7	0.0	0.0

COFFEE MATE,

French Vanilla, Nestle*	1 Tbsp/15ml	25	167	0.0	33.3	0.0	0.0
Lite, Carnation*	1 Serving/5g	20	398	2.5	83.9	6.9	0.0
Lite, Nestle*	2 Tsps/5g	20	398	2.5	83.9	6.9	0.0
Nestle*	2 Tsp/7g	36	520	1.2	60.5	30.3	0.0
Original, Fat Free, Nestle*	1 Tbsp/15ml	10	67	0.0	13.3	0.0	0.0

COFFEE WHITENER,

Half Fat, Co-Op*	1 Tsp/5g	22	430	0.9	78.0	13.0	0.0
Light, Healthy Eating, Tesco*	1 Tsp/6g	27	449	3.5	71.0	16.8	0.0
Light, Tesco*	1 serving/3g	13	429	0.9	77.7	12.7	0.0
Tesco*	1 Tsp/3g	16	533	1.2	61.3	31.4	0.0

COGNAC,

40% Volume	1 Shot/25ml	56	222	0.0	0.0	0.0	0.0

COINTREAU,

Liqueur Specialite De France	1 Serving/37g	80	215	0.0	0.0	0.0	0.0

COKE,

Average	1 Can/330ml	135	41	0.0	10.9	0.0	0.0
Burger King*	1 Med/400g	172	43	0.0	10.6	0.0	0.0
Cherry, The Coca Cola Co*	1fl oz/30ml	13	42	0.0	10.0	0.0	0.0
Coca Cola, Diet, McDonald's*	1 Med/400ml	2	0	0.0	0.0	0.0	0.0
Coca Cola, McDonald's*	1 Med/400ml	172	43	0.0	10.5	0.0	0.0
Cola, Marks & Spencer*	1 Bottle/500ml	225	45	0.0	11.0	0.0	0.0
Diet, Caffeine Free, The Coca Cola Co*	1 Can/330ml	1	0	0.0	0.1	0.0	0.0
Diet, Classic, Sainsbury's*	1 Can/330ml	1	0	0.0	0.0	0.0	0.0
Diet, Just, Asda*	1 Bottle/250ml	1	0	0.0	0.0	0.0	0.0
Diet, Just, Lemon & Lime, Asda*	1 Serving/250ml	1	0	0.0	0.0	0.0	0.0
Diet, Marks & Spencer*	1 Can/330ml	3	1	0.0	0.3	0.0	0.0
Diet, Pepsi*	1 Can/330ml	1	0	0.0	0.0	0.0	0.0
Diet, Tesco*	1 Glass/200ml	2	1	0.1	0.1	0.1	0.0
Diet, The Coca Cola Co*	1 Can/330ml	1	0	0.0	0.0	0.0	0.0
Diet, Virgin*	1 Glass/250ml	1	0	0.1	0.1	0.1	0.0
Pepsi Max*	1fl oz/30ml	0	1	0.1	0.1	0.0	0.0
Pepsi-Cola, Pepsi*	1 Can/330ml	145	44	0.0	11.1	0.0	0.0
The Coca Cola Co*	1 Can/330ml	142	43	0.0	10.7	0.0	0.0
Twist, Light, Pepsi*	1 Bottle/500ml	5	1	0.0	0.1	0.0	0.0
Twist, Pepsi*	1 Bottle/500ml	235	47	0.0	11.7	0.0	0.0
Vanilla, The Coca Cola Co*	1 Serving/500ml	215	43	0.0	10.7	0.0	0.0

C

	Measure	per Measure	Nutrition Values per 100g / 100ml				
	INFO/WEIGHT	KCAL	KCAL	PROT	CARB	FAT	FIBRE
COKE,							
With Lemon, Diet, Coca Cola*	1 Can/330ml	5	1	0.0	0.0	0.0	0.0
With Vanilla, Diet, The Coca Cola Co*	1 Glass/200ml	1	0	0.0	0.1	0.0	0.0
COLCANNON,							
Co-Op*	1 Pack/500g	325	65	2.0	10.0	2.0	2.0
Healthy Eating, Tesco*	1 Pack/330g	244	74	2.1	12.2	1.9	1.0
Mash, Healthly Living, Tesco*	1 Serving/250g	188	75	1.7	11.6	2.4	0.9
Tesco*	1 Serving/250g	245	98	2.3	11.7	4.7	1.7
Waitrose*	½ Pack/150g	138	92	1.7	12.8	3.8	1.4
COLESLAW,							
3% Fat, Marks & Spencer*	1oz/28g	47	167	1.3	9.0	14.0	1.4
50% Less Fat, Asda*	1oz/28g	17	61	2.1	6.8	2.8	0.9
99% Fat Free, Kraft*	1 Serving/40ml	50	126	1.0	28.9	1.0	0.0
Apple, Marks & Spencer*	1oz/28g	53	190	1.4	9.2	16.6	1.4
BGTY, Sainsbury's*	1oz/28g	19	69	0.9	6.6	4.3	1.9
Better For You, Morrisons*	1oz/28g	17	62	1.5	6.7	3.5	0.0
Betterbuy, Morrisons*	1 Serving/20g	23	113	0.8	9.2	8.1	0.0
Budgens*	1 Serving/50g	103	206	1.2	9.5	18.1	2.0
COU, Marks & Spencer*	½ Pack/125g	75	60	1.3	7.4	2.7	1.7
Cheese, Co-Op*	1 Serving/125g	344	275	6.0	6.0	25.0	1.0
Cheese, Marks & Spencer*	1 Serving/57g	165	290	4.5	4.7	28.1	2.0
Cheese, Somerfield*	1oz/28g	48	171	3.0	7.0	14.0	0.0
Chunky, Asda*	1oz/28g	54	194	1.0	7.1	18.0	1.6
Classic, Marks & Spencer*	1 Pot/190g	124	65	1.9	8.8	2.3	1.3
Co-Op*	1 Serving/50g	65	130	1.0	7.0	11.0	2.0
Creamy, Asda*	1oz/28g	55	195	1.0	7.8	17.7	1.0
Creamy, Healthy Eating, Tesco*	1 Serving/30g	29	95	2.4	6.8	6.4	1.4
Creamy, Sainsbury's*	1oz/28g	69	245	1.3	4.6	24.6	1.6
Creamy, Tesco*	1oz/28g	52	186	1.1	7.6	16.8	1.5
Deli Style, Marks & Spencer*	½ Pack/150g	285	190	1.6	3.9	18.5	1.3
Eat Smart, Safeway*	¼ Pack/50g	30	60	1.8	7.2	2.6	1.9
Finest, Tesco*	1 Serving/50g	107	214	1.2	6.1	20.5	1.6
Fruity, Asda*	½ Pot/125g	101	81	1.3	8.0	4.9	1.7
Fruity, Marks & Spencer*	1 Serving/63g	151	240	1.1	8.3	22.7	3.1
GFY, Asda*	1 Serving/50g	48	96	1.4	9.0	6.0	1.6
Garlic & Herb, Asda*	1oz/28g	60	216	1.1	7.2	20.3	1.5
Good Intentions, Somerfield*	1 Serving/50g	36	72	1.6	7.6	3.9	1.5
Half Fat, Safeway*	1 Serving/70g	60	86	1.5	7.4	5.7	1.6
Healthy Choice, Safeway*	1 Pot/250g	215	86	1.5	7.4	5.7	1.6
Healthy Living, Tesco*	1 Serving/60g	51	85	1.3	7.0	5.8	1.6
Heinz*	1oz/28g	38	135	1.6	9.4	10.2	1.2
Iceland*	1 Serving/110g	112	102	0.7	7.8	7.5	1.6
KFC*	1 Portion/142g	231	163	1.4	18.3	9.5	2.1
Less Than 3% Fat, BGTY, Sainsbury's*	¼ Pot/63.3g	31	49	1.3	6.7	1.9	1.9
Less Than 3% Fat, Marks & Spencer*	1oz/28g	18	65	1.9	8.8	2.3	1.3
Less Than 5% Fat, Marks & Spencer*	1 Serving/225g	169	75	1.8	6.9	4.4	2.8
Light, Morrisons*	1oz/28g	33	118	1.1	8.3	7.8	0.0
Low Fat Mayonnaise, Tesco*	1oz/28g	18	64	1.4	4.7	4.4	1.4
Luxury, Asda*	1 Serving/50g	109	217	0.9	6.0	21.0	0.0
Luxury, Marks & Spencer*	1oz/28g	43	152	1.0	6.0	13.8	1.0
Luxury, Morrisons*	1 Serving/50g	137	273	1.2	6.4	27.0	0.0
Marks & Spencer*	1oz/28g	50	180	1.7	6.1	16.5	1.1
Organic, Marks & Spencer*	1oz/28g	41	145	1.1	7.3	12.4	1.0
Perfectly Balanced, Waitrose*	1 Serving/84g	46	55	1.8	6.8	2.3	1.5

C

	Measure INFO/WEIGHT	per Measure KCAL	Nutrition Values per 100g / 100ml				
			KCAL	PROT	CARB	FAT	FIBRE
COLESLAW,							
Prawn, Asda*	1oz/28g	54	192	2.4	6.6	17.3	1.4
Prawn, Safeway*	1 Serving/113g	156	139	3.1	6.3	10.0	1.0
Premium, Safeway*	1 Serving/125g	334	267	1.9	3.8	27.2	2.3
Reduced Calorie, Budgens*	½ Pot/125g	124	99	1.0	8.3	6.9	2.3
Reduced Calorie, Iceland*	1 Serving/50g	51	102	0.7	7.8	7.5	1.6
Reduced Calorie, Waitrose*	1 Serving/125g	74	59	2.3	5.5	3.1	1.7
Reduced Fat, Asda*	1 Pot/250g	218	87	1.5	6.0	6.3	1.6
Reduced Fat, Co-Op*	1 Serving/50g	45	90	0.9	6.0	7.0	2.0
Reduced Fat, Healthy Living, Co Op*	1 Serving/50g	48	95	0.8	8.0	7.0	2.0
Reduced Fat, Sainsbury's*	1/3 Pot/87g	89	102	1.2	7.3	8.0	1.7
Reduced Fat, Traditional, Marks & Spencer*	1oz/28g	57	205	1.1	5.4	20.0	2.8
Safeway*	1 Serving/75g	128	170	0.7	6.7	15.6	0.0
Sainsbury's*	1/3 Pot/75g	108	144	1.3	6.8	12.5	1.7
Salad, Reduced Fat, Sainsbury's*	1 Serving/250g	255	102	1.2	7.3	8.0	1.7
Savers, Safeway*	1 Serving/114g	122	107	1.1	6.6	8.5	0.0
SmartPrice, Asda*	1oz/28g	30	107	0.8	8.0	8.0	2.0
So Good, Somerfield*	1 Serving/10g	21	210	1.3	6.5	19.9	1.2
Supreme, Waitrose*	1oz/28g	53	190	1.8	4.9	18.1	1.7
TTD, Sainsbury's*	1oz/28g	74	263	1.6	6.1	25.8	1.5
Tesco*	1 Serving/50g	79	158	2.2	5.2	14.3	1.6
The Best, Safeway*	1 Serving/10g	30	296	1.0	7.2	29.2	0.8
Three Cheese, Asda*	1oz/28g	54	192	5.0	7.4	16.4	1.2
Three Cheese, Asda*	1 Serving/78g	203	260	5.0	6.0	24.0	1.7
Three Cheese, Safeway*	½ Pot/113g	189	168	4.5	6.2	14.2	1.1
Three Cheese, Tesco*	½ Pot/125g	230	184	4.0	4.8	16.5	1.2
Traditional, Marks & Spencer*	1 Pack/225g	675	300	1.2	3.9	31.2	1.7
Value, Tesco*	1oz/28g	32	115	1.2	6.8	9.2	1.6
With 60% Less Fat, GFY, Asda*	1 Serving/41g	36	88	1.5	7.0	6.0	1.7
With Mayonnaise, Retail	1oz/28g	72	258	1.2	4.2	26.4	1.4
With Reduced Calorie Dressing, Retail	1oz/28g	19	67	0.9	6.1	4.5	1.4
COLESLAW MIX,							
Tesco*	1 Pack/400g	124	31	1.1	6.2	0.2	2.1
COLEY,							
Portions, Raw, Average	1 Portion/92g	75	82	18.4	0.0	0.7	0.0
Steamed	1oz/28g	29	105	23.3	0.0	1.3	0.0
CONCHIGLIE,							
Cooked, Average	1 Serving/185g	247	134	4.9	26.7	0.9	0.6
Dry, Average	1 Serving/100g	352	352	12.5	71.6	1.7	2.6
Shells, Dry, Average	1 Serving/100g	346	346	12.3	70.4	1.5	3.0
Whole Wheat, Dry, Average	1 Serving/75g	237	316	12.6	62.0	2.0	10.7
CONSERVE,							
Apricot, Average	1 Tbsp/15g	37	244	0.5	59.3	0.2	1.5
Apricot, Reduced Sugar, Streamline*	1 Tbsp/20g	37	184	0.5	45.0	0.2	0.0
Blackcurrant, Average	1 Tbsp/15g	37	245	0.6	60.1	0.1	1.9
Blueberry, Marks & Spencer*	1 Tsp/7.5g	16	206	0.3	51.1	0.1	1.3
Raspberry, Average	1 Tbsp/15g	37	249	0.6	61.0	0.3	1.3
Red Cherry, Finest, Tesco*	1 Tbsp/15g	42	277	0.6	67.6	0.1	0.8
Rhubarb & Ginger, Marks & Spencer*	1 Tbsp/15g	29	194	0.3	47.9	0.1	1.0
Strawberry, Average	1 Tbsp/15g	37	250	0.4	61.6	0.1	0.5
CONSOMME,							
Average	1oz/28g	3	12	2.9	0.1	0.0	0.0
COOKIES,							
All Butter Chocolate Chunk, Marks & Spencer*	1 Cookie/26g	130	500	5.2	62.4	25.2	2.6

C

COOKIES,	Measure INFO/WEIGHT	per Measure KCAL	Nutrition Values per 100g / 100ml				
			KCAL	PROT	CARB	FAT	FIBRE
All Butter Fruity Flapjack, Marks & Spencer*	1 Cookie/24.1g	100	415	4.6	53.4	20.2	4.2
All Butter Melting Moment, Marks & Spencer*	1 Cookie/23.4g	108	470	4.5	51.5	27.5	3.4
All Butter Sultana, Marks & Spencer*	1 Cookie/16g	73	455	5.2	66.0	19.0	2.7
All Butter, Italian Style Sorrento Lemon, Marks & Spencer*	1 Cookie/24g	120	500	4.9	60.4	26.7	2.1
Apple & Raisin, Go Ahead, McVitie's*	1 Cookie/15g	66	443	5.3	76.8	12.7	3.4
Apple Crumble, Marks & Spencer*	1 Cookie/26g	90	345	4.6	76.8	2.0	2.9
Apple Pie, The Biscuit Collection*	1 Biscuit/19g	90	474	3.9	65.0	22.1	0.0
Apricot, COU, Marks & Spencer*	1 Cookie/26g	88	340	5.4	75.0	2.4	2.0
Brazil Nut, Organic, Traidcraft*	1 Cookie/16.6g	93	547	5.8	57.7	32.6	2.1
Butter & Sultana, Sainsbury's*	1 Cookie/13g	61	473	4.5	68.4	20.1	1.6
Cherry Bakewell, COU, Marks & Spencer*	1 Cookie/25.4g	89	355	6.0	77.2	2.5	3.4
Choc Chip & Coconut, Maryland*	1oz/28g	143	512	5.1	62.9	23.7	0.0
Choc Chip & Hazelnut, Maryland*	1oz/28g	140	500	5.4	65.2	24.2	0.0
Choc Chip, Asda*	1 Cookie/11g	56	506	5.0	63.0	26.0	1.8
Choc Chip, Cadbury's*	1oz/28g	138	493	6.5	66.1	22.6	0.0
Choc Chip, Lyons*	1oz/28g	142	506	5.3	68.3	23.5	0.0
Choc Chip, Maryland*	1 Cookie/11g	56	511	6.2	68.0	23.9	0.0
Choc Chunk & Hazelnut, Co-Op*	1 Cookie/17g	89	525	6.0	56.0	31.0	3.0
Choc Chunk & Hazelnut, Luxury, Cadbury's*	1oz/28g	146	521	6.3	60.0	28.7	0.0
Choc Chunk, Fabulous Bakin Boys*	1 Cookie/60g	270	450	5.0	59.0	21.0	3.0
Chocolate & Ginger, The Best, Safeway*	1 Cookie/135g	709	525	5.5	62.0	28.0	2.6
Chocolate & Nut, Organic, Evernat*	1 Cookie/69g	337	489	7.2	64.1	22.6	0.0
Chocolate & Orange, COU, Marks & Spencer*	1 Cookie/25.7g	91	350	5.7	77.2	2.6	3.2
Chocolate & Roasted Hazelnut, TTD, Sainsbury's*	1 Cookie/17g	89	521	6.4	56.3	30.3	2.2
Chocolate Chip & Hazelnut, Asda*	1 Cookie/12g	62	516	6.0	60.0	28.0	0.0
Chocolate Chip & Peanut, Trufree*	1 Cookie/11g	55	496	4.0	66.0	24.0	2.0
Chocolate Chip, BGTY, Sainsbury's*	1 Cookie/16.8g	73	428	4.5	75.6	11.9	2.5
Chocolate Chip, Co-Op*	1 Cookie/11g	55	500	5.0	65.0	24.0	1.0
Chocolate Chip, GFY, Asda*	1 Cookie/10.4g	46	463	5.0	68.0	19.0	3.5
Chocolate Chip, Handbaked, Border*	1 Cookie/15g	72	480	5.9	67.4	22.6	0.0
Chocolate Chip, Low Price, Sainsbury's*	1 Cookie/10.8g	55	500	7.0	70.1	21.3	2.5
Chocolate Chip, Lyons*	1 Cookie/12g	56	483	5.6	66.5	21.6	1.7
Chocolate Chip, Marks & Spencer*	1 Cookie/12g	61	506	6.0	62.1	25.9	1.2
Chocolate Chip, McVitie's*	1 Serving/17g	88	527	5.4	62.4	28.5	2.1
Chocolate Chip, Mini, McVitie's*	1 Pack/50g	260	520	5.7	66.7	25.6	1.9
Chocolate Chip, Mini, Shapers, Boots*	1 Pack/30g	141	471	6.8	70.0	18.0	1.4
Chocolate Chip, Mini, Tesco*	1 Bag/30g	148	493	5.4	64.6	23.7	1.7
Chocolate Chip, Organic, Sainsbury's*	1 Cookie/16.8g	90	530	5.0	61.8	29.2	0.3
Chocolate Chip, Organic, Tesco*	1 Cookie/17g	88	520	0.0	63.3	27.4	2.8
Chocolate Chip, Sainsbury's*	1 Cookie/11g	55	508	6.2	67.0	23.9	1.3
Chocolate Chip, SmartPrice, Asda*	1 Cookie/10g	52	508	5.0	68.0	24.0	0.0
Chocolate Chip, Tesco*	1oz/28g	139	496	5.4	63.6	24.4	2.0
Chocolate Chip, The Decadent, President's Choice*	2 Cookies/31g	159	513	6.1	61.3	26.5	3.5
Chocolate Chunk & Hazelnut, Tesco*	1 Cookie/22g	118	538	6.2	60.2	30.3	1.9
Chocolate Chunk & Hazelnut, So Good, Somerfield*	1 Cookie/22.3g	117	530	6.3	55.7	31.3	2.4
Chocolate Chunk, Cadbury's*	1 Cookie/22g	119	540	6.5	58.0	31.2	0.0
Chocolate Chunk, Fresh, Finest, Tesco*	1 Cookie/75g	325	433	5.7	62.4	16.6	2.7
Chocolate Coated, Wheatfree, Sunstart*	1 Cookie/20.0g	103	516	5.6	54.4	30.7	4.1
Chocolate Fruit & Nut, Extra Special, Asda*	1 Cookie/24.6g	127	509	6.0	56.0	29.0	2.0
Chocolate Orange, Half Coated, Finest, Tesco*	1 Cookie/22g	107	488	4.9	59.6	25.5	1.2
Chocolate, Belgian, Extra Special, Asda*	1 Cookie/25.8g	139	535	6.0	58.0	31.0	2.0
Chocolate, Half Coated Triple, Finest, Tesco*	1 Cookie/25g	129	517	5.8	58.8	28.7	2.2
Chocolate, Soft, American Style, Budgens*	1 Cookie/50g	216	431	5.1	60.8	18.6	2.2

	Measure	per Measure	Nutrition Values per 100g / 100ml				
	INFO/WEIGHT	KCAL	KCAL	PROT	CARB	FAT	FIBRE

COOKIES,

	Measure INFO/WEIGHT	per Measure KCAL	KCAL	PROT	CARB	FAT	FIBRE
Coconut & Raspberry, Gluten Free, Sainsbury's*	1 Cookie/20g	102	511	5.9	56.0	29.3	6.7
Coconut, Gluten-Free, Sainsbury's*	1 Cookie/20g	103	516	5.6	54.4	30.7	4.1
Coconut, TTD, Sainsbury's*	1 Cookie/16.7g	92	539	4.8	49.8	35.6	3.8
Cranberry & Orange, Go Ahead, McVitie's*	1 Cookie/17g	77	452	5.3	78.0	13.2	2.4
Cranberry & Orange, Weight Watchers*	2 Cookies/23g	103	448	4.3	72.2	15.7	3.0
Crunchy Muesli, Mini, Shapers, Boots*	1 Pack/30g	134	448	6.7	71.0	15.0	1.8
Danish Butter, Tesco*	1oz/28g	144	516	4.7	66.7	25.6	1.3
Dark Treacle, Weight Watchers*	2 Cookies/23g	97	423	5.2	66.7	15.1	1.7
Double Choc Chip, Mini, Marks & Spencer*	1 Cookie/22g	108	490	5.3	63.6	23.7	1.8
Double Choc Chip, Weight Watchers*	2 Cookies/23g	102	445	4.7	69.7	16.4	5.0
Double Choc Chunk, Luxury, Cadbury's*	1oz/28g	146	521	5.7	59.0	29.0	0.0
Double Choc, Cadbury's*	Per Biscuit/11g	55	485	7.3	64.3	22.2	0.0
Double Choc, Maryland*	1 Cookie/10g	46	510	5.2	64.4	25.7	0.0
Double Chocolate Chip, Co-Op*	1 Cookie/17g	87	510	5.0	63.0	27.0	2.0
Double Chocolate Chip, Organic, Waitrose*	1 Cookie/18g	96	535	5.1	58.6	31.0	1.9
Double Chocolate Chip, Somerfield*	1 Cookie/11g	56	513	5.2	64.9	25.8	1.3
Double Chocolate Chip, Traidcraft*	1 Cookie/22g	114	520	5.8	64.1	26.7	2.4
Fruit & Oat, Starbucks*	1 Cookie/80g	359	449	7.8	72.3	14.4	0.0
Fruit, Giant, Cookie Coach Co*	1 Cookie/60g	280	466	4.9	62.0	22.0	0.0
Fudge Brownie American Cream, Sainsbury's*	1 Cookie/12g	60	499	4.8	67.9	23.2	2.2
Ginger & Lemon, Weight Watchers*	2 Cookies/23g	104	452	4.3	73.9	15.7	2.2
Ginger Crunch, Hand Baked, Border*	1 Cookie/11.5g	52	470	4.7	71.4	20.4	0.0
Ginger, Low Fat, Marks & Spencer*	1 Cookie/23g	82	358	5.1	74.9	4.3	2.4
Ginger, Safeway*	1 Cookie/22g	106	480	4.7	66.5	22.7	2.4
Glace Cherry, Border*	1 Cookie/15.0g	74	493	5.4	64.3	25.6	0.0
Lemon Meringue, COU, Marks & Spencer*	1 Cookie/25g	89	355	5.6	77.6	2.6	3.0
Milk Chocolate, Millie's Cookies*	1 Cookie/65g	280	431	4.6	58.5	20.0	1.5
Oat & Cranberry, BGTY, Sainsbury's*	1 Cookie/28g	126	449	6.8	65.0	18.0	5.1
Oat & Raisin, Health Matters*	1 Cookie/8g	33	414	7.0	76.6	8.8	3.3
Oat & Raisin, Safeway*	1 Cookie/12g	50	414	7.5	77.5	8.8	0.0
Oatflake & Honey, Organic, Sainsbury's*	1 Cookie/17g	82	480	6.3	66.0	21.2	2.6
Oatflake & Raisin, Waitrose*	1 Cookie/17g	80	469	5.8	61.7	22.1	4.7
Oreo, Nabisco*	3 Cookies/34g	160	470	6.0	71.0	21.0	3.0
Peanut, Hellema*	1 Cookie/16g	81	509	11.8	47.3	30.3	0.7
Pecan & Maple, Mini, Bronte*	1 Pack/100g	509	509	5.4	60.3	27.3	1.6
Praline Nougatine, Belle France*	1 Cookie/16.6g	86	506	8.0	63.0	25.0	0.0
Raisin & Cinnamon, Low Fat, Marks & Spencer*	1 Cookie/22g	78	355	6.2	73.0	4.1	3.2
Raspberry Spritz, Heaven Scent*	1 Serving/19g	90	474	5.3	52.6	31.6	0.0
Real Chocolate Chip, Weight Watchers*	2 Cookies/23g	98	427	5.3	66.1	15.7	1.6
Shortbread Rings, Handbaked, Border*	1 Cookie/16.5g	88	520	6.2	61.2	29.5	0.0
Shortbread, Organic, Evernat*	1oz/28g	149	532	5.9	56.7	31.3	0.0
Spiced Apple, COU, Marks & Spencer*	1 Cookie/25g	83	330	5.0	72.8	2.5	2.1
Spiced Apple, Marks & Spencer*	1 Cookie/25g	90	360	5.2	75.6	2.8	2.0
Stem Ginger, BGTY, Sainsbury's*	1 Cookie/17g	78	458	5.3	68.2	18.2	2.2
Stem Ginger, Half Coated, Finest, Tesco*	1 Cookie/25g	127	508	4.4	62.4	26.8	3.6
Stem Ginger, Less Than 5% Fat, Marks & Spencer*	1 Cookie/22g	79	360	6.2	73.9	4.3	3.0
Stem Ginger, Reduced Fat, Waitrose*	1 Cookie/16.7g	76	448	4.5	71.0	16.2	1.6
Stem Ginger, TTD, Sainsbury's*	1 Cookie/17g	84	496	4.5	63.4	24.9	1.7
Stem Ginger, Tesco*	1 Cookie/20g	98	489	4.2	64.0	24.0	2.0
Strawberries & Cream, TTD, Sainsbury's*	1 Cookie/17g	84	504	4.7	62.7	26.0	1.9
Sultana & Cinnamon, Weight Watchers*	2 Cookies/23g	92	398	5.0	67.1	12.1	1.8
Sultana, All Butter, Reduced Fat, Marks & Spencer*	1 Cookie/16.7g	71	420	4.9	68.6	14.2	2.6
Tennessee American Style, Stiftung & Co, Lidl*	1 Cookie/19g	96	504	6.0	66.0	24.0	0.0

	Measure	per Measure	Nutrition Values per 100g / 100ml				
	INFO/WEIGHT	KCAL	KCAL	PROT	CARB	FAT	FIBRE
COOKIES,							
Toffee, Weight Watchers*	2 Cookies/23g	105	457	4.8	72.2	16.5	2.2
White Chocolate & Raspberry, McVitie's*	1 Cookie/17g	88	518	4.8	65.1	26.5	1.8
White Chocolate, Asda*	1 Cookie/54g	256	474	5.0	64.0	22.0	2.1
COQ AU VIN,							
Finest, Tesco*	1 Serving/273g	251	92	14.3	0.7	3.6	1.8
Healthy Living, Tesco*	½ Pack/200g	172	86	15.2	2.1	1.9	0.4
Marks & Spencer*	1 Serving/295g	398	135	14.2	1.5	7.7	1.0
Perfectly Balanced, Waitrose*	1 Pack/500g	445	89	12.6	2.7	3.1	0.6
Sainsbury's*	1 Pack/400g	484	121	16.8	3.5	4.4	0.2
CORDIAL,							
Elderflower, Bottle Green*	1 Glass/200ml	46	23	0.0	5.6	0.0	0.0
Elderflower, Undiluted, Waitrose*	1 Cordial/20ml	22	110	0.0	27.5	0.0	0.0
Honey & Lemonbalm, With Chamomile, Bottle Green*	1fl oz/30ml	8	27	0.0	6.8	0.0	0.0
Lime Juice, Concentrated	1floz/30ml	34	112	0.1	29.8	0.0	0.0
Lime Juice, Diluted	1 Glass/250ml	55	22	0.0	6.0	0.0	0.0
Lime Juice, Diluted, Co-Op*	1fl oz/30ml	8	25	0.0	4.0	0.0	0.0
Lime Juice, Sainsbury's*	1 Glass/250ml	24	9	0.1	1.9	0.1	0.1
Lime Juice, Tesco*	1 Serving/75ml	14	18	0.1	2.1	0.0	0.0
Lime With Aromatic Bitters & Ginger, Sainsbury's*	1 Serving/40ml	12	29	0.0	6.9	0.3	0.3
CORIANDER,							
Leaves, Dried	1oz/28g	78	279	21.8	41.7	4.8	0.0
Leaves, Fresh	1oz/28g	6	20	2.4	1.8	0.6	0.0
CORN,							
Baby, & Asparagus Tips, Tesco*	1 Pack/150g	38	25	2.6	2.5	0.5	1.9
Baby, & Sugar Snap Peas, Safeway*	½ Pack/100g	27	27	2.9	3.3	0.2	0.0
Baby, Average	1oz/28g	7	26	2.5	3.1	0.4	1.7
Baby, Fine Beans & Baby Carrots, Tesco*	1 Pack/250g	68	27	1.7	4.0	0.5	2.2
Creamed, Green Giant*	1 Can/418g	238	57	1.2	11.9	0.5	3.0
On The Cob, Average	1 Serving/75g	44	59	2.1	10.4	1.1	1.0
On The Cob, Boiled in Salted Water, Average	1oz/28g	18	66	2.5	11.6	1.4	1.3
CORN CAKES,							
Marks & Spencer*	½ Pack/85g	238	280	6.4	19.8	20.0	3.4
Organic, Kallo*	1 Cake/5g	16	340	12.7	74.3	4.1	11.2
Thick Slices, Orgran*	1 Cake/11g	42	385	13.2	79.0	3.7	14.2
CORN SNACKS,							
Crispy, Bugles*	1 Bag/20g	102	508	4.8	60.7	28.0	1.4
Light Bites, Cheese Flavour, Special K, Kellogg's*	1 Packet/28g	116	416	9.0	77.0	8.0	1.0
Light Bites, Tikka Flavour, Special K, Kellogg's*	1 Packet/28g	116	416	7.0	79.0	8.0	1.5
Light Bites, Tomato & Basil Flavour, Special K, Kellogg's*	1 Packet/28g	116	416	7.0	79.0	8.0	1.5
Paprika Flavour, Shapers, Boots*	1 Pack/13g	64	494	8.7	54.0	27.0	2.2
Rings, Cheese & Onion, Crunchy, Shapers, Boots*	1 Serving/15g	56	374	5.9	81.0	2.9	20.0
CORNED BEEF,							
Average	1 Slice/35g	75	215	25.9	0.7	12.2	0.0
Lean, Healthy Range, Average	1oz/28g	53	191	27.0	1.0	8.7	0.0
Sliced, Premium, Average	1 Slice/31g	69	222	26.6	0.5	12.6	0.0
CORNFLAKE CAKES,							
Bites, Chocolate, Mini, Marks & Spencers*	1 Bite/8g	40	475	6.2	66.5	20.7	1.0
Bobby's*	1/6 Cake/45g	207	461	3.9	65.5	20.4	0.0
Nest, Crunchy Chocolate, Marks & Spencer*	1 Nest/14.7g	71	475	6.3	67.2	20.2	2.2
CORNFLOUR,							
Average	1oz/28g	99	355	0.7	86.9	1.2	0.1
COURGETTE,							
& Sweetcorn, Fresh 'n' Ready, Sainsbury's*	1oz/28g	12	42	2.3	6.7	0.9	1.3

	Measure INFO/WEIGHT	per Measure KCAL	Nutrition Values per 100g / 100ml				
			KCAL	PROT	CARB	FAT	FIBRE
COURGETTE,							
Boiled In Unsalted Water	1oz/28g	5	19	2.0	2.0	0.4	1.2
Fried, Average	1oz/28g	18	63	2.6	2.6	4.8	1.2
Raw, Average	1oz/28g	5	18	1.8	1.8	0.4	0.9
COUS COUS,							
& Chargrilled Vegetables, Marks & Spencer*	1 Serving/200g	200	100	3.9	17.3	1.5	1.6
& Vegetables, Chargrilled, Sainsbury's*	1 Serving/56g	88	158	5.2	23.7	4.7	3.4
& Wok Oriental, Findus*	½ Pack/300g	510	170	4.5	19.0	8.5	0.0
Chargrilled Red & Yellow Pepper, Tesco*	1 Pack/200g	212	106	4.6	17.8	1.8	0.5
Citrus Kick, Ainsley Harriott*	½ Pack/134.3g	184	137	4.3	28.5	0.6	2.4
Cooked, Average	1 Cup/157g	249	159	4.3	31.4	1.9	1.3
Coriander & Lemon, GFY, Asda*	½ Pack/145g	189	130	4.2	27.0	0.6	1.8
Coriander & Lemon, Sainsbury's*	½ Pack/165g	200	121	4.8	23.5	0.7	0.8
Dry, Average	1 Serving/50g	178	356	13.7	72.8	1.5	2.6
Garlic & Coriander, Dry, Waitrose*	1 Serving/70g	235	336	11.7	64.2	3.6	6.2
Indian Style, Sainsbury's*	½ Pack/143g	204	143	4.5	25.1	2.7	1.0
Lemon & Coriander, Tesco*	1 Serving/137g	207	151	4.0	28.3	2.4	2.0
Mediterranean Style, Dry, Tesco*	1 Pack/110g	369	335	11.9	65.1	3.0	5.6
Mediterranean Tomato, GFY, Asda*	½ Pack/141g	192	136	5.0	27.0	0.9	1.7
Mediterranean, Safeway*	½ Pack/55g	87	158	4.8	25.9	3.9	1.1
Mint & Coriander Flavour, Dry, Amazing Grains, Aldi*	1 Sachet/99g	349	353	12.2	70.0	2.7	3.2
Moroccan Style, Sainsbury's*	½ Pack/150g	195	130	5.0	21.5	2.7	1.0
Morroccan Chicken, Shapers, Boots*	1 Serving/218g	311	143	6.9	21.1	3.4	2.4
Mushroom, Safeway*	1 Serving/139g	232	167	4.9	23.9	5.7	1.6
Mushrooms, Onion, Garlic & Herbs, Dry, Tesco*	½ Pack/50g	167	333	11.3	66.2	2.6	4.9
Red Pepper & Chilli, Waitrose*	1 Pack/200g	344	172	4.5	23.0	6.9	1.3
Roast Garlic & Olive Oil, Dry, Sammy's*	1 Serving/49.9g	170	339	12.0	71.5	3.0	0.0
Roasted Vegetable, Finest, Tesco*	1 Serving/175g	263	150	4.0	17.4	7.1	1.3
Roasted Vegetables, Waitrose*	1 Serving/200g	324	162	5.2	22.4	5.7	0.0
Salad Bar, BGTY, Sainsbury's*	1 Md Bowl/28g	29	103	3.7	18.5	1.6	0.0
Spice Sensation, Cooked, Ainsley Harriott*	½ Pack/100g	123	123	4.3	24.5	0.9	3.4
Spice Sensation, Uncooked, Ainsley Harriott*	½ Sachet/50g	166	332	11.6	66.2	2.4	9.2
Spicy Moroccan Chicken & Veg, COU, Marks & Spencer*	1 Pack/400g	380	95	9.1	10.3	1.7	1.9
Spicy Vegetable, GFY, Asda*	½ Pack/141g	183	130	5.0	25.0	1.1	2.0
Spicy Vegetable, Morrisons*	1 Serving/50g	85	170	5.1	26.2	5.0	2.9
Spicy, Healthy Eating, Tesco*	1 Pot/250g	325	130	3.6	25.1	1.7	0.6
Sun Dried Tomato, Somerfield*	1 Jar/110g	176	160	3.0	25.0	5.0	0.0
Tangy Tomato, Dry, Ainsley Harriot*	1 Serving/50g	166	332	12.2	67.2	1.6	8.8
Tomato & Onion, Dry, Waitrose*	½ Pack/55g	188	342	12.6	64.9	3.6	5.1
Tomato & Vegetable, Snack Pack, Dry, Sammy's*	1 Serving/70g	228	326	12.0	67.9	3.5	6.3
Tomato tango, Ainsley Harriott*	½ Pack/132.8g	166	125	4.6	25.3	0.6	3.3
Tomato, & Mediterranean Herb, Co-Op*	½ Pack/55g	256	465	12.7	72.7	12.7	3.6
Wild Mushroom & Garlic, Sainsbury's*	1 Serving/166g	239	144	4.2	22.9	4.0	0.6
With Lemon & Garlic, Dry, Waitrose*	½ Pack/55g	188	341	11.8	65.5	3.3	4.5
CRAB,							
Boiled	1oz/28g	36	128	19.5	0.0	5.5	0.0
Claws, Asda*	1oz/28g	25	89	11.0	9.0	1.0	0.2
Dressed, Average	1 Can/43g	66	154	16.8	4.1	7.9	0.2
Meat, In Brine, Average	½ Can/60g	46	76	17.2	0.9	0.4	0.1
Meat, Raw, Average	1oz/28g	28	100	20.8	2.8	0.6	0.0
CRAB CAKES,							
Finest, Tesco*	1 Serving/170g	836	492	3.2	3.7	51.6	0.0
Iceland*	1 Serving/18g	52	288	7.2	25.6	18.0	1.3
Marks & Spencer*	1 Pack/170g	340	200	9.5	10.9	12.9	2.2

C

	Measure	per Measure	Nutrition Values per 100g / 100ml				
	INFO/WEIGHT	KCAL	KCAL	PROT	CARB	FAT	FIBRE
CRAB CAKES,							
Tesco*	1 Serving/130g	281	216	11.0	15.4	12.3	1.1
CRAB STICKS,							
Average	1oz/28g	26	94	9.1	13.9	0.3	0.0
CRACKERBREAD,							
Golden Wheat, Ryvita*	1 Slice/6g	19	317	8.3	65.0	3.3	3.3
High Fibre, Ryvita*	1oz/28g	90	321	12.6	61.3	2.8	16.8
Multi Grain Rye, Ryvita*	1 Slice/11.1g	37	332	11.0	58.6	6.0	17.3
Original Wheat, Ryvita*	1 Serving/5g	19	380	10.3	76.9	3.5	3.5
Rice, Asda*	1 Serving/5g	19	374	9.1	79.4	2.2	1.9
Wholemeal, Ryvita*	1 Slice/5.6g	19	319	10.8	71.5	4.2	6.5
CRACKERS,							
99% Fat Free, Rakusen's*	1 Cracker/5g	18	366	10.9	88.9	0.9	0.0
Bath Oliver, Jacob's*	1 Cracker/12g	52	432	9.6	67.6	13.7	2.6
Biscuits For Cheese, TTD, Sainsbury's*	1 Cracker/8g	39	493	8.6	61.0	23.8	3.1
Black Olive, Marks & Spencer*	1 Cracker/4.1g	19	485	8.3	59.4	23.5	4.3
Blazing BBQ, JacoBites, Jacob's*	1 Pack/9g	41	461	5.2	55.8	24.2	1.7
Bran, Jacob's*	1 Cracker/7g	32	454	9.7	62.8	18.2	3.2
Butter Puff, Sainsbury's*	1 Cracker/10g	54	523	10.4	60.7	26.5	2.5
Cheddars, McVitie's*	1 Cracker/4g	22	543	10.0	55.1	31.3	2.6
Cheese Biscuit Thins, Safeway*	1 Cracker/4g	22	545	11.9	52.6	31.9	2.5
Cheese Melts, Carr's*	1 Cracker/4g	19	468	9.4	58.0	22.1	3.0
Cheese Thins, Asda*	1 Cracker/4g	21	532	12.0	49.0	32.0	0.0
Cheese Thins, Co-Op*	1 Cracker/4g	21	530	12.0	49.0	32.0	3.0
Chinese, Pop Pan*	2 Crackers/15g	80	533	13.3	53.3	33.3	0.0
Chives, Jacob's*	1 Cracker/6.1g	27	457	9.5	67.5	16.5	2.7
Choice Grain, Jacob's*	1 Cracker/7g	30	435	9.2	65.4	15.0	4.7
Corn Thins, 97% Fat Free, Real Foods*	1 Cracker/6g	19	378	10.2	81.7	3.0	8.6
Corn Thins, Real Foods*	1 Serving/5.8g	25	414	10.3	82.8	3.4	8.6
Cornish Wafer, Jacob's*	1 Cracker/9g	48	528	8.0	54.4	31.2	2.4
Cream	1 Cracker/7g	31	440	9.5	68.3	16.3	2.2
Cream With Flaked Salt, TTD, Sainsbury's*	1 Cracker/7.4g	35	500	8.5	64.8	22.9	2.7
Cream, Asda*	1 Cracker/8g	35	443	10.0	67.0	15.0	0.0
Cream, BGTY, Sainsbury's*	1 Cracker/8g	32	400	10.9	71.7	7.7	3.1
Cream, Better For You, Morrisons*	1 Cracker/8g	32	406	10.9	74.4	7.2	2.8
Cream, Biscuits For Cheese, Tesco*	1 Cracker/8g	35	438	10.2	66.7	14.5	2.8
Cream, Half Fat, Safeway*	1 Cracker/8g	32	406	74.4	2.4	7.2	2.9
Cream, Jacob's*	1 Cracker/8g	35	438	10.2	66.9	14.4	2.9
Cream, Lower Fat, Tesco*	1 Cracker/5g	20	393	11.0	72.4	6.6	3.1
Cream, Roasted Onion, Jacob's*	1 Cracker/8g	35	441	10.2	66.8	14.8	2.9
Cream, Sainsbury's*	1 Cracker/8.3g	34	422	9.5	66.7	15.2	2.8
Cream, Sun Dried Tomato Flavour, Jacob's*	1 Cracker/8g	35	434	10.2	66.7	14.0	3.0
Cream, Tesco*	1 Cracker/7.7g	34	447	9.0	69.0	15.0	3.0
Crispy Cheese, Marks & Spencer*	1oz/28g	134	478	10.2	57.8	22.6	2.9
Extra Wheatgerm, Hovis*	1 Serving/6g	27	447	10.2	60.0	18.5	4.4
Garden Herbs, Jacob's*	1 Cracker/6g	28	457	9.5	67.5	16.5	2.7
Glutafin*	1 Serving/11g	52	470	2.4	70.0	20.0	0.7
Harvest Grain, Sainsbury's*	1 Cracker/6g	27	458	8.5	64.5	18.4	4.1
Herb & Onion, 99% Fat Free, Rakusen's*	1 Cracker/4g	14	361	10.0	78.0	1.0	0.0
Herb & Onion, Trufree*	1 Cracker/6g	25	418	2.5	75.0	12.0	10.0
Herb & Spice, Jacob's*	1 Cracker/6g	27	457	9.5	67.5	16.5	2.7
Herbs & Spice Selection, Jacob's*	1 Cracker/6g	27	451	9.5	68.0	15.7	2.7
Hovis, Jacob's*	1 Cracker/6g	27	447	10.2	60.0	18.5	4.4
Italian, Doriano, Doria*	1 Sm Cracker/4g	19	464	9.5	69.8	16.4	0.0

	Measure INFO/WEIGHT	per Measure KCAL	Nutrition Values per 100g / 100ml				
			KCAL	PROT	CARB	FAT	FIBRE
CRACKERS,							
Krackawheat, McVitie's*	1 Cracker/7g	36	515	9.1	62.4	25.4	4.8
Light & Crispy, Sainsbury's*	1 Cracker/11g	42	384	11.3	61.0	10.5	13.0
Lightly Salted, Crispy, Sainsbury's*	1 Cracker/4.7g	27	533	7.8	62.6	27.9	2.1
Lightly Salted, Italian, Jacob's*	1 Cracker/6g	26	429	10.3	67.6	13.0	2.9
Matzo, Rakusen's*	1 Cracker/4g	15	370	8.8	80.2	1.5	4.0
Mediterranean, Jacob's*	1 Cracker/6g	27	450	9.7	66.5	16.1	2.7
Melts, Carr's*	1 Cracker/4g	18	451	10.2	57.0	20.2	5.0
Multigrain, Tesco*	1 Cracker/6g	27	458	8.5	64.5	18.4	4.1
Olive Oil & Oregano, Italian, Jacob's*	1 Cracker/6g	26	437	10.3	66.3	14.5	4.0
Oriental Style, Safeway*	1 Serving/25g	88	350	1.5	82.2	1.2	6.2
Oriental, Asda*	1 Serving/30g	146	485	1.0	62.0	26.0	3.5
Passionately Pizza, JacoBites, Jacob's*	1 Pack/150g	708	472	5.7	55.3	25.4	1.7
Peking Spare Rib & Five Spice, Sensations, Walkers*	1 Bag/24g	116	485	1.3	62.0	26.0	3.5
Pesto, Jacob's*	1 Cracker/6g	27	450	9.7	66.5	16.1	2.7
Poppy & Sesame Thins Savoury, Somerfield*	1oz/28g	147	524	9.0	58.0	28.0	0.0
Ritz, Original, Jacob's*	1 Cracker/3g	15	509	6.9	55.6	28.8	2.0
Rye, Organic, Doves Farm*	1 Cracker/7.1g	28	393	7.0	58.4	14.6	8.7
Salt & Black Pepper, Jacob's*	1 Cracker/6g	27	457	9.5	67.5	16.5	2.7
Sesame & Poppy, Tesco*	1 Cracker/3g	15	506	9.4	53.7	28.2	3.4
Spicy Indonesian Vegetable, Waitrose*	1 Pack/60g	295	492	1.2	60.6	27.2	2.2
Spicy Vegetable, Tesco*	1 Serving/60g	340	566	2.6	52.4	38.4	1.2
Tangy Malaysian Chutney, Oriental, Sensations, Walkers*	1 Serving/35g	170	485	0.9	62.0	26.0	3.5
Tempting Tandoori, JacoBites, Jacob's*	1 Pack/150g	711	474	5.7	55.5	25.5	1.7
Thai Rice, Marks & Spencers*	1 Serving/55g	209	380	7.0	80.2	3.3	1.2
Thai Spicy Vegetable, Sainsbury's*	1 Pack/50g	231	462	7.2	61.5	20.8	2.6
Tuc, Jacob's*	1 Cracker/4.5g	23	512	7.8	57.7	27.8	2.1
Tuc, McVitie's*	1 Cracker/4g	21	530	7.8	62.2	27.8	2.1
Wheaten, Marks & Spencer*	1 Cracker/4.4g	18	450	10.2	57.0	20.2	5.0
Wholemeal, Tesco*	1 Cracker/7g	29	414	9.4	60.6	14.9	10.4
Wholmeal, Organic, Nairn's*	1 Cracker/14g	58	413	9.0	61.4	14.6	8.7
CRANBERRIES,							
& Raisins, Dried, Sweetened, Ocean Spray*	1 Serving/50g	163	326	0.1	80.3	0.5	4.6
Dried & Sweetened, Whitworths*	1 Serving/25g	81	325	0.1	76.8	1.4	5.6
Dried, Sainsbury's*	1 Pack/75g	253	337	0.1	81.1	1.4	5.1
Fresh, Raw	1oz/28g	4	15	0.4	3.4	0.1	3.0
CRAYFISH,							
Raw	1oz/28g	19	67	14.9	0.0	0.8	0.0
Tails, Chilli & Garlic, Asda*	1 Serving/140g	133	95	16.0	1.1	3.1	0.8
Tails, In Brine, Luxury, The Big Prawn Co*	½ Tub/90g	46	51	10.1	1.0	0.7	0.0
CREAM,							
Aerosol, Average	1oz/28g	87	309	1.8	6.2	30.9	0.0
Aerosol, Reduced Fat, Average	1 Serving/55ml	33	60	0.6	2.0	5.5	0.0
Clotted, Fresh, Average	1 Serving/28g	162	579	1.6	2.3	62.7	0.0
Double, Average	1 Serving/25ml	110	438	1.8	2.7	46.7	0.0
Double, Reduced Fat, Average	1 Serving/30g	73	243	2.7	5.7	23.3	0.1
Single, Average	1 Serving/50ml	62	123	2.7	4.4	10.5	0.1
Single, Extra Thick, Average	1 Serving/37.5ml	73	192	2.7	4.1	18.4	0.0
Soured, Fresh, Average	1 Tbsp/15ml	29	191	2.7	3.9	18.4	0.0
Swirls Light, Half Fat, Anchor*	1 Serving/30ml	14	45	0.6	1.8	3.9	0.0
Thick, Sterilised, Average	1 Tbsp/15ml	35	233	2.6	3.6	23.1	0.0
UHT, Double, Average	1 Tbsp/15g	41	275	2.2	7.4	26.3	0.0
UHT, Reduced Fat, Average	1 Serving/25ml	16	62	0.6	2.3	5.7	0.0
UHT, Single, Average	1 Tbsp/15ml	29	194	2.6	4.0	18.8	0.0

	Measure INFO/WEIGHT	per Measure KCAL	Nutrition Values per 100g / 100ml				
			KCAL	PROT	CARB	FAT	FIBRE
CREAM,							
Whipping, Average	1 Tbsp/15ml	52	348	2.1	3.2	36.4	0.1
CREAMER,							
Non Dairy, Cremora, Borden*	1 Tsp/2g	10	500	0.0	50.0	25.0	0.0
CREME BRULEE,							
Marks & Spencer*	1 Pot/100g	360	360	3.3	13.0	32.6	0.0
Somerfield*	1 Pot/100g	316	316	4.0	15.0	27.0	0.0
CREME CARAMEL,							
Asda*	1 Pot/100g	113	113	2.4	20.0	2.6	0.0
Average	1oz/28g	31	109	3.0	20.6	2.2	0.0
Carmelle, Green's*	1 Pack/70g	82	117	3.0	17.0	4.0	0.0
La Laitiere*	1 Pot/100g	135	135	5.0	20.0	4.0	0.0
Marks & Spencer*	1oz/28g	48	172	4.5	18.9	8.7	0.0
Sainsbury's*	1 Pot/100g	102	102	2.5	21.1	0.9	0.0
SmartPrice, Asda*	1 Pot/100g	87	87	2.5	18.0	0.5	0.0
Somerfield*	1 Pot/100g	114	114	3.0	24.0	1.0	0.0
Tesco*	1 Pot/100g	113	113	2.4	20.0	2.6	0.0
CREME FRAICHE,							
Average	1 Pot/295g	1067	362	2.2	2.6	38.0	0.0
Extra Light, President*	1 Tub/200g	182	91	2.7	8.7	5.0	0.0
Half Fat, Average	1 Dtsp/30g	54	181	3.1	5.5	16.3	0.0
CREPES,							
Chicken, Asda*	1 Crepe/204.4g	369	181	14.0	11.0	9.0	3.6
Cream Cheese & Onion, Mini, Marks & Spencer*	1 Crepe/2g	10	510	8.3	55.9	28.0	1.0
Lobster, Finest, Tesco*	1 Serving/160g	250	156	10.7	14.0	6.4	1.2
Mushroom, Marks & Spencer*	1 Pack/186g	195	105	5.7	17.1	2.4	2.5
CRISPBAKES,							
Bubble & Squeak, Marks & Spencer*	1 Crispbake/46.5g	78	170	2.7	19.6	8.8	1.5
Cheese & Chive, Sainsbury's*	1 Serving/108g	273	253	7.1	24.5	14.8	1.7
Cheese & Onion, Marks & Spencer*	1 Crispbake/114g	285	250	6.4	19.4	16.2	1.7
Cheese & Onion, Tesco*	1 Crispbake/109g	275	252	7.9	19.6	15.8	2.1
Chicken & Broccoli, Marks & Spencer*	1 Crispbake/114g	225	197	6.1	16.5	11.9	1.9
Dutch, Asda*	1 Toast/10g	39	394	14.0	77.0	3.3	3.9
Dutch, Safeway*	1 Bake/10g	39	394	14.0	77.0	3.3	3.9
Dutch, Tesco*	1 Slice/8g	30	371	17.0	72.0	1.7	4.0
Minced Beef, Marks & Spencer*	1 Crispbake/113g	226	200	10.0	15.6	10.9	1.5
Mushroom & Garlic, Ovenbaked, Iceland*	1 Crispbake/140g	241	172	4.3	23.7	6.7	2.9
Organic, Trimlyne*	1 Bake/10g	38	380	16.0	73.0	2.0	6.0
Sainsbury's*	1 Serving/9g	35	392	14.5	72.3	5.0	5.8
Spinach, Feta & Soft Cheese, Mini, Safeway*	1 Pack/191.5g	449	235	6.6	20.8	13.4	2.5
Tuna & Sweetcorn, Lakeland*	1 Serving/170g	391	230	11.3	20.1	11.6	0.0
Vegetable, Marks & Spencer*	1 Crispbake/114g	160	140	2.8	14.9	7.7	1.8
Vegetable, Sainsbury's*	1 Serving/114g	246	216	2.0	26.2	11.4	2.0
CRISPBREAD,							
Bran, Scandinavian, GG*	2 Crispbread/16g	36	223	14.9	29.0	5.3	42.1
Breaks, Ryvita*	1 Crispbread/14g	47	333	8.0	69.5	2.5	12.0
Corn, Orgran*	1 Crispbread/5g	18	360	7.5	83.0	1.8	3.0
Crisp N Light, Wasa*	1 Crispbread/7g	24	360	12.0	73.0	2.2	5.3
Currant Crunch, Ryvita*	1oz/28g	94	334	8.7	69.9	2.5	12.8
Dark Rye, Morrisons*	1 Slice/13g	39	300	11.5	61.5	3.1	16.9
Dark Rye, Ryvita*	1 Serving/9g	28	308	8.5	65.0	1.5	18.5
Emmental Cheese & Pumpkin Seed, Dr Kracker*	1 Serving/25g	101	404	20.0	43.2	16.8	15.2
Gluten Free, Dietary Specials*	1 Serving/8g	25	331	6.4	72.9	1.5	0.0
Harvest Wheat, Finn Crisp*	1 Serving/50g	195	390	10.0	72.0	6.7	5.8

INFO/WEIGHT	per Measure KCAL	KCAL	PROT	CARB	FAT	FIBRE
CRISPBREAD,						
Hi-Fibre Rye, Organic, Finn Crisp*	1 Crispbread/12.9g 40	310	9.8	63.0	1.8	16.0
Light, Marks & Spencer*	1 Crispbread/4.2g 14	360	10.7	69.2	4.6	7.6
Light, Ryvita*	1 Slice/5g 19	383	9.8	79.3	3.0	2.6
Milky, Grafschafter*	1 Slice/9g 29	316	11.4	64.0	1.6	15.0
Multigrain, Finn Crisp*	1 Bread/8g 26	320	11.0	58.0	4.7	18.0
Multigrain, Ryvita*	1 Slice/11g 37	332	11.0	58.6	6.0	17.3
Multigrain, Wasa*	1 Crispbread/13g 43	320	12.0	62.0	2.6	14.0
Organic, Trimlyne*	1 Crispbake/10g 38	380	16.0	73.0	2.3	6.0
Original Rye, Wasa*	1 Crispbread/11g 35	315	9.0	67.0	1.4	14.0
Original, Rye, Hi Fibre, Finn Crisp*	1 Serving/14g 42	300	8.5	61.5	0.8	16.2
Original, Rye, Trimlyne*	1 Crispbread/11g 36	325	10.3	65.4	2.5	12.8
Original, Ryvita*	1 Crispbread/9g 27	305	9.4	63.3	1.6	17.4
Pagen*	1 Crispbread/3g 11	370	12.0	65.0	7.0	9.5
Poppyseed, Wasa*	1 Crispbread/13g 46	350	13.0	56.0	8.0	14.0
Provita*	1 Biscuit/6g 26	416	12.5	68.4	9.9	0.0
Rice, & Cracked Pepper, Orgran*	4 Slices/19g 74	388	8.4	81.9	1.8	2.0
Rice, Original, Sakata*	1 Serving/25g 103	410	6.9	88.0	2.6	1.3
Rye, Harvest Slims, Finn Crisp*	3 Slices/18g 58	320	11.0	63.0	2.3	16.0
Rye, Original, Ryvita*	1 Crispbread/9g 28	315	8.5	67.2	1.4	16.5
Rye, Somerfield*	1 Crispbread/11g 35	320	9.0	66.0	2.2	13.0
Sesame Rye, Ryvita*	1 Crispbread/9g 30	338	9.5	60.3	6.5	16.5
Sesame, Ryvita*	1oz/28g 95	339	10.5	58.5	7.0	16.0
Trufree*	1 Crispbread/6g 22	370	6.0	82.0	2.0	1.0
Wheat, Cracottes*	1 Slice/6.9g 26	367	9.8	75.2	3.0	3.2
Wholemeal Rye, Kallo*	1 Crispbread/10g 31	314	9.7	65.0	1.7	15.4
Wholemeal, Light, Allinson*	1 Slice/5g 17	349	11.7	69.7	2.6	11.0
Wholemeal, Organic, Allinson*	1 Crispbread/5g 17	336	14.2	66.0	1.7	12.2
With Currants, Oats & Honey, Ryvita*	1 Crisp/14.8g 50	333	8.0	69.5	2.5	12.0
CRISPS,						
Apple, Thyme & Sage, Marks & Spencer*	1 Bag/55g 253	460	5.5	55.3	24.3	6.1
BBQ Chilli & Mesquite, Pan-Fried, TTD, Sainsbury's*	1 Sm Pack/50g 239	478	8.0	51.3	26.7	5.4
Bacon Bites, Eat Smart, Safeway*	1 Bag/12g 41	340	10.8	70.3	1.6	3.5
Bacon Crispies, Sainsbury's*	1 Bag/25g 117	468	19.9	45.8	22.8	4.8
Bacon Flavour Rashers, BGTY, Sainsbury's*	1 Pack/10g 34	340	10.8	70.3	1.6	3.5
Bacon Pillows, Light, Shapers, Boots*	1 Pack/12g 44	367	3.7	83.0	2.3	4.0
Bacon Rashers, Blazin, Tesco*	1 Bag/25g 119	477	15.4	44.7	26.3	4.4
Bacon Rashers, COU, Marks & Spencer*	1 Bag/20g 72	360	9.4	77.5	2.9	3.5
Bacon Rashers, Iceland*	1 Bag/75g 330	440	8.3	61.9	17.6	2.9
Bacon Rashers, Marks & Spencer*	1 Bag/40g 192	480	8.1	59.9	22.9	2.2
Bacon Rice Bites, Asda*	1 Bag/30g 136	452	7.0	70.0	16.0	0.4
Bacon, Shapers, Boots*	1 Bag/23g 99	431	8.0	66.0	15.0	3.0
Bagels, Sour Cream & Chive, Shapers, Boots*	1 Bag/25g 94	377	9.7	78.0	2.9	1.9
Baked Beans, Walkers*	1 Bag/35g 184	525	6.5	50.0	33.0	4.0
Baked Potato, COU, Marks & Spencer*	1 Bag/25g 88	350	8.5	76.4	2.3	5.7
Banging BBQ, Shots, Walkers*	1 Pack/17.9g 87	485	5.5	60.0	25.0	1.3
Barbecue, Handcooked, Tesco*	1 Bag/40g 187	468	6.6	53.8	25.1	5.2
Barbecue, Snack Rite, Aldi*	1 Bag/25g 131	524	5.1	51.3	33.2	0.0
Barbecue, Walkers*	1 Bag/35g 184	525	6.5	50.0	33.0	4.0
Beef & Onion, Asda*	1 Bag/25g 135	539	7.0	49.0	35.0	4.5
Beef & Onion, Potato, Marks & Spencer*	1 Bag/24.5g 133	530	6.6	48.2	34.5	5.0
Beef & Onion, Safeway*	1 Bag/25g 125	501	5.2	55.7	31.5	0.0
Beef & Onion, Walkers*	1 Bag/35g 184	525	6.5	50.0	33.0	4.0
Beefy, Smiths, Walkers*	1 Bag/25g 133	531	4.3	45.2	37.0	0.0

	Measure INFO/WEIGHT	per Measure KCAL	Nutrition Values per 100g / 100ml				
			KCAL	PROT	CARB	FAT	FIBRE
CRISPS,							
Beefy, Square, Walkers*	1 Bag/25g	105	420	6.0	59.0	18.0	4.6
Butter & Chive, COU, Marks & Spencer*	1 Bag/26g	95	365	7.7	77.3	1.9	4.6
Chargrilled Chicken Crinkles, Shapers, Boots*	1 Bag/20g	96	482	6.6	60.0	24.0	4.0
Chargrilled Steak, Max, Walkers*	1 Bag/55g	289	525	6.5	50.0	33.0	4.0
Cheddar & Chive, Pret A Manger	1 Bag/40g	187	468	7.0	53.8	24.8	6.0
Cheddar & Onion, McCoy's*	1 Bag/50g	258	516	7.0	53.2	30.6	3.9
Cheese & Branston Pickle Flavour, Walkers*	1 Bag/34.5g	176	510	7.0	49.0	32.0	4.5
Cheese & Chive Flavour, GFY, Asda*	1 Bag/25g	119	476	6.0	59.0	24.0	6.0
Cheese & Chives, Walkers*	1 Bag/35g	186	530	6.5	50.0	33.0	4.1
Cheese & Onion, Asda*	1 Bag/25g	133	530	6.0	50.0	34.0	4.5
Cheese & Onion, 30% Less Fat, Sainsbury's*	1 Pack/25g	115	459	7.5	58.1	21.8	5.4
Cheese & Onion, BGTY, Sainsbury's*	1 Bag/25g	120	479	7.0	57.0	24.8	5.7
Cheese & Onion, Big Eat, Walkers*	1 Bag/55g	289	525	6.5	50.0	33.0	4.0
Cheese & Onion, Flavour Crinkles, Shapers, Boots*	1 Bag/20g	96	482	6.6	60.0	24.0	4.0
Cheese & Onion, GFY, Asda*	1 Pack/26g	122	471	7.0	59.0	23.0	6.0
Cheese & Onion, Golden Wonder*	1 Bag/25g	131	524	6.1	49.2	33.6	2.0
Cheese & Onion, KP*	1 Bag/25g	134	534	6.6	48.7	34.8	4.8
Cheese & Onion, Lites, Walkers*	1 Bag/28g	130	465	7.5	61.0	21.0	5.0
Cheese & Onion, Lower Fat, Asda*	1 Bag/25g	120	481	6.0	58.0	25.0	4.8
Cheese & Onion, Marks & Spencer*	1 Bag/25g	134	535	5.5	48.8	35.5	5.0
Cheese & Onion, Max, Walkers*	1 Bag/55g	289	525	6.5	50.0	33.0	4.0
Cheese & Onion, Morrisons*	1 Bag/30g	152	508	7.1	50.5	30.8	4.6
Cheese & Onion, Organic, Tesco*	1 Bag/25g	129	514	5.2	49.9	32.6	7.0
Cheese & Onion, Safeway*	1 Bag/25g	143	570	5.8	52.5	37.5	0.0
Cheese & Onion, Sainsbury's*	1 Bag/25g	132	527	4.6	48.8	34.8	3.9
Cheese & Onion, Select, Tesco*	1 Bag/25g	134	535	6.6	48.5	34.9	4.8
Cheese & Onion, Sky Snacks, Safeway*	1 Packet/15g	74	495	4.9	59.8	26.2	3.7
Cheese & Onion, Smiths, Walkers*	1 Bag/25g	133	531	4.3	45.2	37.0	0.0
Cheese & Onion, Snack Rite, Aldi*	1 Bag/25g	132	527	5.3	51.3	33.4	0.0
Cheese & Onion, SnackRite*	1 Pack/25g	132	527	5.3	51.3	33.4	0.0
Cheese & Onion, Sprinter, Aldi*	1 Bag/25g	137	549	5.4	49.4	36.6	0.0
Cheese & Onion, Square, Smiths, Walkers*	1 Bag/25g	113	452	6.9	62.5	19.4	0.0
Cheese & Onion, Square, Walkers*	1 Bag/25g	106	425	6.5	59.0	18.0	4.4
Cheese & Onion, Tayto*	1 Bag/25g	137	546	4.8	51.9	38.5	0.0
Cheese & Onion, Value, Tesco*	1 Bag/20g	108	541	6.0	48.3	36.0	4.8
Cheese & Onion, Walkers*	1 Bag/35g	184	525	6.5	50.0	33.0	4.0
Cheese Curls, Asda*	1 Bag/14g	71	507	4.3	50.0	32.1	2.9
Cheese Curls, Morrisons*	1 Bag/14g	71	510	4.5	51.0	32.0	2.6
Cheese Curls, Shapers, Boots*	1 Pack/13.9g	68	489	4.5	57.0	27.0	2.7
Cheese Curls, Sprinters, Aldi*	1 Bag/14g	68	483	4.1	56.4	26.8	0.0
Cheese Flavour Puffs, Morrisons*	1 Bag/25g	136	542	6.7	50.2	34.9	1.1
Cheese Tasters, Marks & Spencer*	1 Sm Bag/30g	156	520	8.5	51.0	31.0	3.2
Cheese XL, Golden Wonder*	1 Bag/30g	155	516	6.2	50.6	32.1	4.2
Cheesy Puffs, Co-Op*	1 Bag/60g	321	535	3.0	54.0	34.0	2.0
Chicken & Thyme, Sensations, Oven Roasted, Walkers*	1 Bag/40g	194	485	6.5	54.0	27.0	4.5
Chicken Flavour, Healthy Eating, Tesco*	1 Bag/12g	43	357	5.1	81.0	1.4	3.4
Chicken Tikka Masala, Great British Takeaways, Walkers*	1 Bag/25g	131	525	6.5	50.0	33.0	4.0
Chicken, Firecracker, McCoy's*	1 Bag/35g	177	506	6.2	54.0	29.5	4.0
Chill, Coriander & Lime, Marks & Spencer*	1 Bag/40g	194	485	6.4	53.6	27.1	5.0
Chinese Sizzling Beef, McCoys*	1 Bag/35g	178	506	6.9	51.8	30.2	4.0
Chinese Spare Rib, Walkers*	1 Bag/25g	131	525	6.5	50.0	33.0	4.0
Cool Cheese Curly, Tesco*	1 Bag/14g	71	510	4.5	51.0	32.0	2.6
Coronation Chicken, Walkers*	1 Bag/25g	131	525	6.5	50.0	33.0	4.0

CRISPS,

INFO/WEIGHT	Measure	per Measure KCAL	KCAL	PROT	CARB	FAT	FIBRE
Creme Fraiche, Red Onion & Chive, TTD, Sainsbury's*	1 Serving/50g	226	452	7.8	50.8	24.2	6.3
Crinkle Cut, Lower Fat, No Added Salt, Waitrose*	1 Bag/40g	193	483	6.5	58.0	25.0	3.9
Crispy Bacon Bites, Shapers, Boots*	1 Bag/21g	97	464	13.0	58.0	20.0	1.8
Crunchy Claws, Sprinters, Aldi*	1 Serving/30g	152	508	6.0	55.7	29.0	0.0
Double Cheddar & Chives, Deli Style, Brannigans*	1oz/28g	148	529	7.6	49.5	33.4	3.8
Feta Cheese Flavour, Mediterranean, Walkers*	1 Pack/25g	128	510	6.5	49.0	33.0	4.5
Flame Grilled Steak, McCoy's*	1 Bag/50g	252	504	6.4	53.8	29.2	3.9
Four Cheese & Red Onion Sensations, Walkers*	1 Bag/40g	194	485	6.5	54.0	27.0	4.5
Garlic & Herbs Creme Fraiche, Kettle Chips*	1 Bag/50g	249	497	6.0	54.7	28.3	4.2
Golden Lights, Golden Wonder*	1 Bag/21g	91	435	5.4	64.5	17.2	0.0
Greek Kebab, Mediterranean, Walkers*	1 Pack/25g	128	510	6.0	49.0	33.0	4.5
Handcooked, Marks & Spencer*	1 Bag/40g	198	495	5.4	56.9	27.2	4.5
Hint Of Garlic, Doritos*	1 Serving/35g	175	500	7.0	61.0	25.0	3.5
Honey Roast Ham, Marks & Spencer*	1 Bag/24.5g	133	530	6.6	49.0	34.1	4.6
Honey Roasted Ham, Sensations, Walkers*	1 Bag/40g	196	490	6.5	55.0	27.0	4.0
Hot & Spicy Salami, Tesco*	1 Bag/50g	216	431	26.2	0.7	35.9	0.0
Lamb & Mint, Sensations, Walkers*	1 Bag/35g	170	485	6.5	54.0	27.0	4.5
Lant Chips, Ikea*	1 Serving/25g	126	505	8.3	55.9	27.6	4.5
Lightly Salted, COU, Marks & Spencer*	1 Bag/26g	91	350	8.5	76.4	2.3	5.7
Lightly Salted, Crinkle Cut, Potato, Lower Fat, Waitrose*	1 Bag/40g	193	483	6.5	58.0	25.0	3.9
Lightly Salted, Crinkles, Shapers, Boots*	1 Pack/20g	96	482	6.6	60.0	24.0	4.0
Lightly Salted, Golden Lights, Golden Wonder*	1 Bag/21g	92	440	5.1	64.3	18.0	4.3
Lightly Salted, Kettle Chips*	1 Bag/50g	124	247	6.4	51.5	3.0	6.0
Lightly Salted, Pret A Manger*	1 Bag/40g	198	495	5.8	58.0	28.5	4.3
Lightly Salted, Traditional Pan Fried, TTD, Sainsbury's*	1 Bag/50g	236	472	6.2	53.6	25.8	5.1
Lightly Sea Salted, Jonathan Crisp*	1 Bag/35g	176	503	6.5	52.0	29.0	5.4
Marmite Flavour, Walkers*	1 Bag/34.5g	176	510	6.5	49.0	32.0	4.0
Mature Cheddar & Chive, Kettle Chips*	1 Serving/50g	239	478	8.1	54.4	25.4	5.0
Mediterranean Baked Potato, COU, Marks & Spencer*	1 Pack/25g	90	360	7.6	74.0	2.4	6.8
Mexican Chilli, McCoys*	1 Bag/35g	177	511	7.1	52.8	30.2	4.1
Mixed Pepper Flavour Burst, Marks & Spencer*	1 Bag/55g	286	520	6.0	50.1	33.5	4.0
New York Cheddar, Kettle Chips*	1 Bag/50g	242	483	6.7	53.9	26.7	4.5
Nicely Spicy, Shots, Walkers*	1 Bag/18g	87	485	5.5	60.0	25.0	1.5
Paprika, Handcooked, Shapers, Boots*	1 Bag/20g	99	493	7.2	62.0	24.0	5.0
Paprika, Max, Walkers*	1 Bag/29g	152	525	6.5	50.0	33.0	4.0
Paprika, Mini Hoops, Shapers, Boots*	1 Bag/13.0g	64	494	8.7	54.0	27.0	2.2
Pastrami & Cheese, Crinkle, Marks & Spencer*	1 Bag/24.7g	121	485	6.5	61.0	24.0	3.5
Pickled Onion Flavour Rings, BGTY, Sainsbury's*	1 Serving/10g	35	345	5.0	81.7	1.5	3.7
Pickled Onion, Beastie Bites, Asda*	1 Bag/20g	100	498	6.0	60.0	26.0	0.0
Pickled Onion, Golden Wonder*	1 Bag/25g	131	524	5.6	49.0	34.0	2.0
Pickled Onion, Marks & Spencer*	1 Bag/20.3g	69	345	5.0	81.7	1.5	3.7
Pickled Onion, Monster Bites, Sainsbury's*	1 Bag/20g	107	535	5.2	53.5	33.3	1.0
Pickled Onion, Pret A Manger*	1 Bag/40g	177	443	7.5	52.0	22.8	7.3
Pickled Onion, Tesco*	1 Bag/20g	104	520	6.5	50.0	35.0	1.0
Pickled Onion, Walkers*	1 Bag/35g	184	525	6.5	50.0	33.0	4.0
Potato	1oz/28g	148	530	5.7	53.3	34.2	5.3
Potato Sticks, Ready Salted, Marks & Spencer*	1 Packet/40g	210	525	6.5	52.0	33.0	4.0
Potato, Low Fat	1oz/28g	128	458	6.6	63.5	21.5	5.9
Prawn Cocktail Flavour, Morrisons*	1 Bag/25g	132	528	8.0	48.8	32.8	5.2
Prawn Cocktail, 30% Less Fat, Sainsbury's*	1 Pack/25g	118	470	6.3	58.9	23.6	5.7
Prawn Cocktail, Asda*	1 Bag/25g	134	535	6.0	49.0	35.0	4.3
Prawn Cocktail, BGTY, Sainsbury's*	1 Bag/25g	118	473	6.3	58.6	23.7	5.7
Prawn Cocktail, Golden Wonder*	1 Bag/25g	130	521	5.8	49.0	33.5	2.0

C

CRISPS,

	Measure INFO/WEIGHT	per Measure KCAL	Nutrition Values per 100g / 100ml				
			KCAL	PROT	CARB	FAT	FIBRE
Prawn Cocktail, KP*	1 Bag/25g	133	531	5.9	48.4	34.9	4.7
Prawn Cocktail, Lites, Shapers, Boots*	1 Bag/21g	92	438	5.1	64.0	18.0	4.1
Prawn Cocktail, Marks & Spencer*	1 Bag/30g	155	515	3.2	60.1	29.3	1.3
Prawn Cocktail, Sainsbury's*	1 Bag/25g	130	521	4.3	47.5	34.9	3.9
Prawn Cocktail, Seabrook*	1 Bag/31.8g	182	569	5.3	54.4	36.8	3.9
Prawn Cocktail, Select, Tesco*	1 Bag/25g	134	535	6.2	49.1	34.9	4.3
Prawn Cocktail, Smiths, Walkers*	1 Bag/25g	133	531	4.3	45.2	37.0	0.0
Prawn Cocktail, Snack Rite, Aldi*	1 Bag/25g	129	516	5.0	49.2	33.2	0.0
Prawn Cocktail, Walkers*	1 Bag/35g	184	525	6.5	50.0	33.0	4.0
Prawn Crackers, Tesco's*	1 Bag/60g	316	527	3.2	62.8	29.2	0.8
Punching Paprika, Max, Walkers*	1 Bag/55g	256	465	7.5	61.0	21.0	4.0
Ready Salted Crinkle, Reduced Fat, Marks & Spencer*	1 Bag/40g	190	475	6.5	58.0	24.0	6.5
Ready Salted, 30% Less Fat, Sainsbury's*	1 Serving/25g	111	444	7.0	55.0	21.8	5.1
Ready Salted, BGTY, Sainsbury's*	1 Bag/25g	122	486	6.8	55.7	26.2	6.6
Ready Salted, Betterbuy, Morrisons*	1 Bag/22g	118	538	6.5	49.3	35.0	4.2
Ready Salted, GFY, Asda*	1 Bag/25g	118	471	6.0	60.0	23.0	6.0
Ready Salted, Golden Lights, Golden Wonder*	1 Bag/21g	92	440	5.1	64.3	18.0	0.0
Ready Salted, Golden Wonder*	1 Bag/25g	135	539	5.5	49.9	35.3	2.0
Ready Salted, KP*	1 Bag/24g	131	545	5.6	47.9	36.8	4.9
Ready Salted, Lites, Walkers*	1 Bag/28g	132	470	7.5	60.0	22.0	5.0
Ready Salted, Lower Fat, Asda*	1 Bag/25g	120	481	6.0	58.0	25.0	4.8
Ready Salted, Lower Fat, Sainsbury's*	1 Bag/25g	111	444	7.0	55.0	21.8	5.1
Ready Salted, Made With Sunflower Oil, Walkers*	1 Bag/24g	113	470	7.5	60.0	22.0	5.0
Ready Salted, Marks & Spencer*	1 Bag/25g	136	545	5.6	47.8	36.6	4.9
Ready Salted, McCoy's*	1 Bag/49g	253	517	6.0	52.3	31.5	4.9
Ready Salted, Morrisons*	1 Bag/25g	134	536	4.9	50.9	34.8	4.3
Ready Salted, Organic, Tesco*	1 Bag/25g	130	520	4.3	49.0	34.1	7.3
Ready Salted, Potato Chips, Tesco*	1 Bag/25g	132	526	5.6	51.7	33.0	3.8
Ready Salted, Potato Squares, Sainsbury's*	1 Bag/50g	192	384	6.5	53.8	15.9	7.8
Ready Salted, Reduced Fat, Tesco*	1 Pack/25g	114	456	6.3	52.0	24.7	5.9
Ready Salted, Safeway*	1 Serving/50g	264	528	5.6	52.2	33.0	3.8
Ready Salted, Sainsbury's*	1 Bag/25g	135	538	4.3	47.4	36.8	4.1
Ready Salted, Savers, Safeway*	1 Packet/20g	110	549	5.6	51.3	35.7	0.0
Ready Salted, Select, Tesco*	1 Bag/25g	136	544	6.2	47.9	36.6	4.5
Ready Salted, SmartPrice, Asda*	1 Bag/20g	111	553	5.0	50.0	37.0	3.0
Ready Salted, Smiths, Walkers*	1 Bag/25g	133	531	4.3	45.2	37.0	0.0
Ready Salted, Snack Rite, Aldi*	1 Bag/25g	136	545	4.9	50.3	36.0	0.0
Ready Salted, Square, Smiths, Walkers*	1 Bag/25g	106	425	6.0	58.0	19.0	4.6
Ready Salted, Squares, Marks & Spencer*	1 Bag/35g	151	430	6.8	63.5	18.1	3.9
Ready Salted, Value, Tesco*	1 Bag/21g	115	548	6.0	50.0	36.0	0.0
Ready Salted, Walkers*	1 Bag/35g	186	530	6.5	49.0	34.0	4.0
Red Leicester & Spring Onion, Marks & Spencer*	1 Bag/40g	194	485	6.2	58.7	27.2	4.9
Reduced Fat, Lay's*	1 Serving/25g	118	470	7.5	60.0	22.0	5.0
Roast Beef & Mustard, Thick Cut, Brannigans*	1 Bag/40g	203	507	7.6	51.7	30.0	3.7
Roast Beef, KP*	1 Bag/25g	134	534	6.6	47.5	35.3	4.7
Roast Chicken & Sage Flavour, Marks & Spencer*	1 Bag/25g	135	540	5.9	50.6	34.6	4.6
Roast Chicken Flavour, BGTY, Sainsbury's*	1 Bag/25g	118	473	6.2	58.9	23.6	5.7
Roast Chicken, 30% Less Fat, Sainsbury's*	1 Pack/25g	115	460	7.4	58.3	21.9	5.2
Roast Chicken, Golden Wonder*	1 Bag/25g	131	522	6.2	48.6	33.6	2.0
Roast Chicken, Highlander*	1 Bag/25g	139	554	5.3	46.0	38.9	5.1
Roast Chicken, Select, Tesco*	1 Bag/25g	134	536	6.6	48.6	35.0	4.4
Roast Chicken, Smiths, Walkers*	1 Bag/25g	133	531	4.3	45.2	37.0	0.0
Roast Chicken, Snack Rite, Aldi*	1 Bag/25g	132	526	5.3	51.3	33.3	0.0

CRISPS,

	Measure INFO/WEIGHT	per Measure KCAL	Nutrition Values per 100g / 100ml				
			KCAL	PROT	CARB	FAT	FIBRE
Roast Chicken, Walkers*	1 Bag/35g	184	525	6.5	50.0	33.0	4.0
Roast Turkey & Paxo, Walkers*	1 Bag/34.5g	184	525	6.4	50.1	33.0	4.1
Salsa With Mesquite, Kettle Chips*	1 Bag/50g	229	458	6.1	54.0	24.3	5.7
Salt & Black Pepper, Handcooked, Marks & Spencer*	1 Bag/40g	180	450	5.7	55.0	22.9	5.2
Salt & Malt Vinegar Flavour, Sainsbury's*	1 Bag/25g	135	538	4.9	50.3	35.2	2.3
Salt & Malt Vinegar, McCoy's*	1 Bag/50g	256	512	6.8	52.8	30.4	3.9
Salt & Shake, Walkers*	1 Bag/24g	127	530	6.5	49.0	34.0	4.5
Salt & Vinegar Flavour, Asda*	1 Bag/25g	133	530	6.0	50.0	34.0	4.5
Salt & Vinegar Flavour, Half Fat, Marks & Spencer*	1 Bag/40g	168	420	5.8	61.0	17.0	7.7
Salt & Vinegar Flavour, Sprinters, Aldi*	1 Bag/25g	133	532	4.8	49.1	35.2	0.0
Salt & Vinegar Fries, COU, Marks & Spencer*	1 Bag/25g	85	340	5.0	80.0	1.6	4.0
Salt & Vinegar, 30% Less Fat, Sainsbury's*	1 Bag/25g	115	458	7.2	58.3	21.8	5.1
Salt & Vinegar, BGTY, Sainsbury's*	1 Bag/25g	121	482	6.5	57.3	25.2	5.2
Salt & Vinegar, Big Eat, Walkers*	1 Bag/55.0g	289	525	6.5	50.0	33.0	4.0
Salt & Vinegar, Crinkle Cut, Seabrook*	1 Bag/31.8g	182	569	5.4	54.4	36.7	3.9
Salt & Vinegar, Crinkle, Marks & Spencer*	1 Pack/24.7g	121	485	6.5	61.0	24.0	3.5
Salt & Vinegar, Crinkles, Shapers, Boots*	1 Pack/20g	96	482	6.6	60.0	24.0	4.0
Salt & Vinegar, Everyday, Co-Op*	1 Bag/17g	77	455	6.0	62.0	20.0	2.0
Salt & Vinegar, Fish Shapes, Food Explorers, Waitrose*	1 Bag/20g	86	430	2.4	69.1	16.0	1.3
Salt & Vinegar, Fries, Safeway*	1 Bag/20g	75	375	5.1	80.9	1.6	2.3
Salt & Vinegar, GFY, Asda*	1 Bag/25.7g	121	467	6.0	59.0	23.0	10.0
Salt & Vinegar, Golden Lights, Golden Wonder*	1 Bag/21g	91	435	4.9	64.1	17.8	4.3
Salt & Vinegar, Golden Wonder*	1 Bag/25g	131	522	5.4	48.5	34.0	2.0
Salt & Vinegar, Healthy Eating, Tesco*	1 Bag/17g	61	357	3.2	82.4	1.6	3.0
Salt & Vinegar, Hoops, Safeway*	1 Bag/15g	65	430	4.2	66.3	16.1	5.3
Salt & Vinegar, KP*	1 Bag/25g	133	532	5.5	48.7	35.0	4.7
Salt & Vinegar, Lites, Walkers*	1 Bag/28g	130	465	7.5	61.0	21.0	4.0
Salt & Vinegar, Lower Fat, Asda*	1 Bag/25g	120	481	5.0	58.0	25.0	4.8
Salt & Vinegar, Marks & Spencer*	1 Bag/25g	131	525	5.4	48.8	34.5	4.6
Salt & Vinegar, Max, Walkers*	1 Bag/55g	289	525	6.5	50.0	33.0	4.0
Salt & Vinegar, Morrisons*	1 Bag/25g	124	497	7.2	48.7	30.4	4.5
Salt & Vinegar, Pret A Manger*	1 Bag/40g	186	465	6.8	55.0	25.3	6.0
Salt & Vinegar, Red Mill*	1 Bag/40g	174	436	3.9	65.8	17.5	2.4
Salt & Vinegar, Reduced Fat, Marks & Spencer*	1 Bag/40g	190	475	7.0	58.0	24.0	6.5
Salt & Vinegar, Rough Cuts, Tayto*	1 Bag/30g	152	506	4.6	56.8	30.8	0.0
Salt & Vinegar, Sainsbury's*	1 Bag/25g	131	522	4.1	46.9	35.3	3.9
Salt & Vinegar, Select, Tesco*	1 Bag/25g	132	529	5.9	47.8	34.9	4.3
Salt & Vinegar, Smiths, Walkers*	1 Bag/25g	133	531	4.3	45.2	37.0	0.0
Salt & Vinegar, Snack Rite, Aldi*	1 Bag/25g	127	508	4.7	48.1	33.0	0.0
Salt & Vinegar, Square, Smiths, Walkers*	1 Bag/25g	113	452	6.9	62.5	19.4	0.0
Salt & Vinegar, Square, Walkers*	1 Bag/25g	105	420	6.0	58.0	18.0	4.5
Salt & Vinegar, Value, Tesco*	1 Bag/20g	109	547	5.7	47.7	37.0	4.8
Salt & Vinegar, Waitrose*	1 Bag/25g	134	535	6.2	40.5	34.2	4.3
Salt & Vinegar, Walkers*	1 Bag/35g	184	525	6.5	50.0	33.0	4.1
Salt'n'Shake, Smiths, Walkers*	1 Bag/25g	136	543	4.1	44.2	38.9	0.0
Salted Tubes, Shapers, Boots*	1 Bag/15g	67	448	5.1	62.0	20.0	3.6
Sausage & Tomato Flavour, Golden Wonder*	1 Bag/34.5g	177	505	6.1	51.3	30.6	4.5
Screaming Salt & Vinegar, Max, Walkers*	1 Bag/55g	256	465	7.5	61.0	21.0	4.0
Sea Salt & Balsamic Vinegar, Kettle Chips*	1 Bag/50g	234	468	5.6	60.9	24.4	4.4
Sea Salt & Black Pepper, GFY, Asda*	1 Bag/100g	476	476	6.0	59.0	24.0	6.0
Sea Salt & Black Pepper, Highlander*	1 Serving/25g	141	564	5.6	44.0	38.4	4.8
Sea Salt & Black Pepper, Pret A Manger*	1 Bag/40g	180	450	5.8	55.0	23.0	5.3
Sea Salt & Black Pepper, Shapers, Boots*	1 Bag/19.9g	96	482	6.6	60.0	24.0	4.0

CRISPS,	Measure INFO/WEIGHT	per Measure KCAL	Nutrition Values per 100g / 100ml KCAL	PROT	CARB	FAT	FIBRE
Sea Salt & Cracked Black Pepper, Sensations, Walkers*	1 Bag/40g	194	485	6.5	54.0	27.0	4.5
Sea Salt & Malt Vinegar, Sensations, Walkers*	1 Bag/40g	194	485	6.5	54.0	27.0	4.5
Sea Salt & Vinegar, Bagels, Shapers, Boots*	1 Pack/25g	95	378	11.0	77.0	2.9	3.1
Sea Salt With Crushed Black Peppercorns, Kettle Chips*	1 Bag/50g	225	449	5.7	55.0	22.9	5.2
Sea Salt, Handcooked, Extra Special, Asda*	1 Pack/31g	149	477	7.0	56.0	25.0	4.1
Sea Salt, Original, Crinkle Cut, Seabrook*	1 Bag/31.8g	182	569	5.4	54.4	36.7	3.9
Sizzling Beef, Spice, McCoy's*	1 Bag/35g	175	501	6.4	51.7	29.8	4.0
Smoked Ham & Pickle, Thick Cut, Brannigans*	1 Bag/40g	203	507	7.0	52.8	29.8	3.8
Smokey Bacon, Budgens*	1 Bag/25g	130	519	6.2	49.3	33.0	4.8
Smokey Bacon, Seabrook*	1 Bag/32g	181	569	5.4	54.4	36.7	3.9
Smokey Bacon, Select, Tesco*	1 Bag/25g	134	536	6.4	49.0	34.9	4.3
Smokey Bacon, Smiths, Walkers*	1 Bag/25g	133	531	4.3	45.2	37.0	0.0
Smoky Bacon, 30% Lower Fat, Sainsbury's*	1 Bag/25g	118	471	6.5	58.4	23.6	5.7
Smoky Bacon, Asda*	1 Bag/25g	133	530	6.0	50.0	34.0	4.5
Smoky Bacon, BGTY, Sainsbury's*	1 Bag/25g	118	472	6.5	58.5	23.6	5.7
Smoky Bacon, Golden Wonder*	1 Bag/25g	131	523	5.9	49.1	33.7	2.0
Smoky Bacon, Sainsbury's*	1 Bag/25g	132	529	5.7	49.5	34.2	4.4
Smoky Bacon, Snack Rite, Aldi*	1 Bag/25g	131	525	5.5	51.2	33.1	0.0
Smoky Bacon, Walkers*	1 Bag/34g	179	525	6.5	50.0	33.0	4.0
Snax, Tayto*	1 Pack/17g	82	483	2.4	70.0	21.5	1.6
Sour Cream & Chive Crinkles, Shapers, Boots*	1 Bag/20g	96	482	6.6	60.0	24.0	4.0
Sour Cream & Chive, Healthy Eating, Tesco*	1 Bag/19.9g	72	362	6.7	81.1	3.8	3.4
Sour Cream & Chive, Reduced Fat, Marks & Spencer*	1 Bag/40g	192	480	6.5	60.0	24.0	6.5
Sour Cream & Chives, Jordans*	1 Bag/30g	125	417	7.3	69.9	12.0	2.7
Sour Cream & Onion, Lights, Golden Wonder*	1 Bag/21g	91	435	5.4	64.5	17.2	5.9
Spare Rib Flavour, Chinese, Walkers*	1 Bag/34.5g	184	525	6.5	50.0	33.0	4.0
Spiced Chilli, McCoy's*	1 Bag/35g	175	500	6.1	54.2	28.8	4.2
Spring Onion Flavour, Marks & Spencer*	1 Bag/40g	210	525	5.9	48.7	34.3	5.1
Spring Onion, Seabrook*	1 Bag/32g	182	569	5.4	54.4	36.7	3.9
Strawberry Raisin Snack, Fruitwonders, Golden Wonder*	1 Bag/29.5g	115	383	3.8	62.9	12.9	0.0
Strong Cheese & Onion, Starbucks*	1 Bag/50g	228	455	7.1	56.2	22.6	4.0
Sun Dried Tomato & Basil, Jonathan Crisp*	1 Pack/35g	176	503	5.6	52.0	29.0	5.4
Sun Dried Tomato & Chilli, Asda*	1 Pack/150g	701	467	7.0	58.0	23.0	4.1
Sweet & Sour, Great British Takeaways, Walkers*	1 Bag/25g	131	525	6.5	50.0	33.0	4.0
T Bone Steak, Roysters*	1 Bag/31g	160	516	5.7	52.6	31.4	3.6
Tangy Malaysian Chutney, Sensations, Walkers*	1 Bag/24g	116	485	0.9	62.0	26.0	0.0
Tangy Tomato & Red Pepper Salsa, Sensations, Walkers*	1 Bag/35g	168	480	6.5	53.0	27.0	4.5
Tangy Toms, Red Mill*	1 Bag/15g	76	507	6.0	60.0	27.3	0.7
Thai Curry & Coriander, Tyrrell's*	1 Pack/50g	261	522	6.1	56.5	27.9	5.4
Thai Curry Flavour Curls, Marks & Spencer*	1 Bag/25g	90	360	1.3	82.5	2.5	3.1
Thai Green Curry, TTD, Sainsbury's*	1 Bag/50g	235	470	5.5	55.6	24.8	5.2
Thai Sweet Chicken, McCoys*	1 Bag/35g	178	509	6.6	53.0	30.1	4.0
Thai Sweet Chilli, Sensations, Walkers*	1 Bag/40g	194	485	6.5	54.0	27.0	4.5
Tomato & Basil, Mediterranean, Walkers*	1 Pack/25g	128	510	6.5	49.0	33.0	4.5
Tomato & Herb, Shapers, Boots*	1 Bag/20g	94	468	3.7	66.0	21.0	3.9
Tomato Ketchup, Walkers*	1 Bag/35g	179	510	6.5	49.0	32.0	4.0
Tomato Sauce, Golden Wonder*	1 Bag/25g	130	521	5.7	49.2	33.5	2.0
Tomato, Olive Oil & Basil, TTD, Sainsbury's*	1 Bag/50g	235	469	7.5	51.4	26.0	5.4
Traditional, Hand Cooked, Finest, Tesco*	1 Bag/150g	708	472	6.4	52.9	26.1	5.1
Tubes, Salt & Vinegar, Healthy Living, Tesco*	1 Bag/17g	61	357	3.2	82.4	1.6	3.0
Vegetable Chips, Pret A Manger*	1 Bag/25g	126	504	5.6	37.2	36.8	10.0
Vegetable, Pan Fried, Sainsbury's*	¼ Bag/25g	102	407	4.6	36.5	27.0	6.4
Waffles, Bacon Flavour, BGTY, Sainsbury's*	1 Serving/12g	41	345	6.4	79.7	1.4	2.9

	Measure INFO/WEIGHT	per Measure KCAL	Nutrition Values per 100g / 100ml				
			KCAL	PROT	CARB	FAT	FIBRE
CRISPS,							
Wild Chilli, McCoy's*	1 Bag/50g	255	510	6.0	53.2	30.3	4.8
Wild Paprika Flavour, Croky*	1 Pack/45g	234	521	6.0	58.0	29.0	0.0
Worcester Sauce, Walkers*	1 Bag/25g	131	525	6.5	50.0	33.0	4.0
Worcester Sauce Flavour, Hunky Dorys*	1 Bag/45g	211	469	6.3	49.3	28.7	0.0
Yoghurt & Green Onion, Kettle Chips*	1 Serving/50g	237	473	6.6	54.1	26.1	5.4
CRISPY PANCAKE,							
Beef Bolognese, Findus*	1 Pancake/65g	104	160	6.6	25.0	4.3	1.2
Chicken & Bacon, Findus*	1 Pancake/62g	90	145	6.1	23.6	2.8	0.9
Chicken, Bacon & Sweetcorn, Findus*	1 Pancake/63g	101	160	5.8	24.8	4.1	1.1
Three Cheeses, Findus*	1 Pancake/62g	118	190	7.0	25.0	6.5	0.9
CROISSANT,							
All Butter, BGTY, Sainsbury's*	1 Croissant/44g	176	401	9.8	44.2	20.5	2.2
All Butter, Budgens*	1 Croissant/45g	185	412	7.9	39.7	24.6	3.3
All Butter, Finest, Tesco*	1 Croissant/77g	328	426	8.6	44.9	23.6	1.9
All Butter, Marks & Spencer*	1 Croissant/54g	227	420	7.2	44.4	25.0	1.6
All Butter, Mini, Sainsbury's*	1 Croissant/35g	156	446	9.3	38.2	28.4	2.0
All Butter, Mini, Tesco*	1 Croissant/35g	151	430	9.3	45.2	23.5	2.0
All Butter, Reduced Fat, Marks & Spencer*	1 Croissant/54g	181	335	6.8	38.4	16.9	1.5
All Butter, Reduced Fat, Tesco*	1 Croissant/52g	164	315	7.5	47.4	10.6	1.8
All Butter, Sainsbury's*	1 Croissant/44g	196	446	9.3	38.2	28.4	2.0
All Butter, TTD, Sainsbury's*	1 Croissant/75g	362	483	8.3	40.2	32.1	2.9
All Butter, Tesco*	1 Croissant/77g	297	386	6.5	40.4	22.1	1.9
Almond Filled, Starbucks*	1 Croissant/92g	330	359	0.0	42.4	19.6	2.2
Almond, Pret A Manger*	1 Croissant/50g	365	730	17.6	69.8	42.2	2.2
Asda*	1 Croissant/47g	186	405	9.0	45.0	21.0	0.0
Average	1 Croissant/50g	180	360	8.3	38.3	20.3	1.6
Butter, Asda*	1 Croissant/46g	191	416	8.0	42.0	24.0	1.9
Butter, GFY, Asda*	1 Croissant/44g	151	352	6.0	46.0	16.0	2.0
Butter, Mini, Waitrose*	1 Croissant/35g	156	446	9.3	38.2	28.4	2.0
Butter, Part Bake, Morrisons*	1 Croissant/45g	179	397	7.3	49.6	18.8	1.9
Butter, Part Baked, De Graaf*	1 Croissant/45g	170	378	7.3	45.2	18.7	0.0
Butter, Starbucks*	1 Croissant/82g	289	352	5.9	34.9	21.1	0.0
Chocolate, Pret A Manger*	1 Croissant/70g	322	460	9.3	35.6	31.3	0.0
Flaky Pastry With A Plain Chocolate Filling, Tesco*	1 Croissant/78g	318	408	6.5	41.0	24.3	2.0
Heart Shaped, Breakfast In Bed, Marks & Spencer*	1 Croissant/54g	228	430	8.2	43.7	25.5	1.2
Low Fat, Marks & Spencer*	1 Croissant/45g	180	400	8.2	46.0	20.2	1.8
Mini, Lidl*	1 Croissant/30g	112	373	7.8	48.0	16.6	0.0
Reduced Fat Butter, Tesco*	1 Croissant/52g	165	318	6.6	45.0	12.4	2.1
Reduced Fat, Sainsbury's*	1 Croissant/44g	173	393	9.8	49.2	17.5	2.2
Smoked Ham & Cheese, Marks & Spencer*	1 Croissant/105g	341	325	13.4	22.2	21.6	3.9
CROQUETTE,							
Morrisons*	1 Serving/150g	231	154	3.3	23.1	5.4	1.1
Parsnip, Finest, Tesco*	1 Croquette/37g	77	207	5.9	26.2	8.7	1.3
Potato, Asda*	1 Pack/127g	224	176	2.3	26.0	7.0	1.8
Potato, Bird's Eye*	1 Croquette/29g	44	152	2.6	22.6	5.7	1.2
Potato, Farmfoods*	1oz/28g	28	101	2.3	22.6	0.2	2.2
Potato, Fried in Blended Oil	1oz/28g	60	214	3.7	21.6	13.1	1.3
Potato, Frozen, Tesco*	1 Croquette/30g	58	193	3.7	23.0	9.7	1.0
Potato, Marks & Spencer*	1 Serving/125g	206	165	2.4	19.3	8.8	2.2
Potato, Sainsbury's*	1 Croquette/28g	50	180	3.9	23.0	8.0	1.0
Potato, Tesco*	1 Croquette/30g	43	142	3.0	19.2	5.9	1.5
Potato, Waitrose*	1 Croquette/29.9g	47	157	3.0	17.9	8.1	1.5
Vegetable, Sainsbury's*	1 Serving/175g	392	224	5.8	23.3	11.9	2.2

C

	Measure INFO/WEIGHT	per Measure KCAL	Nutrition Values per 100g / 100ml				
			KCAL	PROT	CARB	FAT	FIBRE
CROUTONS,							
Cracked Black Pepper & Sea Salt, Safeway*	1 Serving/20g	77	385	11.8	61.6	10.2	4.4
Fresh, Marks & Spencer*	1 Serving/10g	53	530	11.4	50.0	32.8	3.2
Herb & Garlic, Rochelle*	¼ Pack/18g	106	587	6.9	49.8	40.0	2.1
Herb, Sainsbury's*	1 Serving/15g	64	429	13.4	68.2	11.4	2.8
Italian Salad, Sainsbury's*	1 Pack/40g	204	510	8.5	62.7	25.0	2.5
McDonald's*	1 Sachet/14g	58	414	14.6	70.8	8.0	3.0
Sun Dried Tomato For Salad, Safeway*	1/5 packet/15g	59	395	13.3	59.4	11.5	8.8
Sun Dried Tomato, Sainsbury's*	¼ Pack/15g	75	497	11.7	55.2	25.5	2.5
CRUMBLE,							
Apple & Blackberry, Asda*	1 Serving/175g	427	244	2.7	38.0	9.0	1.2
Apple & Blackberry, Marks & Spencer*	1 Serving/135g	398	295	3.5	44.9	11.2	1.6
Apple & Blackberry, Sainsbury's*	1 Serving/110g	232	211	3.0	37.1	5.6	2.1
Apple & Blackberry, Tesco*	1 Crumble/335g	667	199	2.6	40.1	3.1	1.9
Apple & Custard, Asda*	1 Serving/125g	250	200	2.3	32.0	7.0	0.0
Apple & Toffee, Weight Watchers*	1 Pot/98g	206	210	2.1	37.6	5.7	1.6
Apple With Custard, Individual, Sainsbury's*	1 Pudding/120g	286	238	2.0	31.4	11.6	2.4
Apple, Co-Op*	¼ Crumble/110g	0	565	6.0	84.0	23.0	2.0
Apple, Co-Op*	1/8 Cake/52g	151	290	4.0	41.0	12.0	2.0
Apple, Dietary Specialists*	1 Pot/240g	497	207	0.9	40.5	5.0	1.1
Apple, Eat Smart, Safeway*	1 Serving/28g	85	305	5.2	64.5	2.4	1.2
Apple, Farmfoods*	½ Pack/185g	411	222	2.9	39.3	5.9	2.3
Apple, Frozen, Iceland*	1 Portion/97g	240	247	2.1	36.9	10.1	1.8
Apple, Iceland*	1 Pie/45g	175	389	4.0	58.4	15.6	2.0
Apple, Sara Lee*	1 Serving/200g	606	303	2.3	53.3	9.0	1.2
Apple, Somerfield*	1 Serving/195g	454	233	2.5	36.8	8.4	1.1
Apple, Tesco*	1 Serving/150g	342	228	2.0	33.6	9.5	1.2
Apple, Waitrose*	1 Serving/125g	310	248	2.2	54.5	2.3	1.2
Apple, With Sultanas, Weight Watchers*	1 Dessert/110g	196	178	1.4	34.2	3.9	1.3
Bramley Apple, Favourites, Marks & Spencer*	1 Serving/140g	390	279	4.6	43.2	9.9	1.2
Bramley Apple, Marks & Spencer*	1 Serving/149g	387	260	4.4	40.3	9.2	1.1
Fish & Prawn, Youngs*	1 Pie/375g	476	127	5.8	9.7	7.2	1.3
Fruit	1oz/28g	55	198	2.0	34.0	6.9	1.7
Fruit, Marks & Spencer*	1 Serving/9g	34	380	0.0	93.8	0.0	0.0
Fruit, Wholemeal	1oz/28g	54	193	2.6	31.7	7.1	2.7
Gooseberry, Marks & Spencer*	1 Serving/133g	379	285	3.5	43.3	10.7	1.7
Ocean, Good Choice, Iceland*	1 Pack/340g	377	111	7.2	14.4	2.7	1.1
Ocean, Low Fat, Ross*	1 Crumble/300g	219	73	5.1	11.4	0.8	0.4
Ocean, Youngs*	1 Pack/340g	306	90	4.8	11.3	2.8	1.1
Rhubarb, Co-Op*	¼ Crumble/110g	0	245	2.0	42.0	7.0	1.0
Rhubarb, Farmfoods*	1oz/28g	54	192	2.0	35.0	4.9	2.3
Rhubarb, Marks & Spencer*	1 Serving/133g	366	275	3.4	42.6	9.9	1.4
Rhubarb, Sainsbury's*	1 Serving/50g	112	224	3.1	40.4	5.6	1.8
Rhubarb, Somerfield*	¼ Crumble/130g	281	216	3.0	38.0	6.0	0.0
Rhubarb, Tesco*	1/6 Crumble/117g	228	195	2.8	27.3	8.3	1.7
Rhubarb, With Custard, Sainsbury's*	1 Serving/120g	288	240	2.4	31.4	11.6	2.3
Salmon, Youngs*	1 Pie/339g	380	112	4.6	13.0	4.6	0.7
CRUMBLE MIX,							
Co-Op*	2/50g	225	450	5.0	70.0	17.0	2.0
Luxury, Tesco*	1 Pack/225g	992	441	5.7	67.9	16.3	3.2
Topping, Morrisons*	1 Serving/40g	179	448	5.4	69.5	16.5	2.8
Topping, Sainsbury's*	1 Serving/47g	188	401	5.9	50.3	19.6	5.3
CRUMPETS,							
Asda*	1 Crumpet/45g	94	208	6.0	44.0	0.9	0.0

	Measure INFO/WEIGHT	per Measure KCAL	Nutrition Values per 100g / 100ml				
			KCAL	PROT	CARB	FAT	FIBRE
CRUMPETS,							
Co-Op*	1 Crumpet/55g	102	185	8.0	36.0	1.0	2.0
Finger, Safeway*	1 Crumpet/30g	55	182	6.9	36.7	0.1	1.8
Finger, Sainsbury's*	1 Crumpet/30g	55	182	7.0	36.6	0.8	1.8
Iceland*	1 Crumpet/46.6g	97	206	6.1	43.8	0.7	1.8
Less Than 1% Fat, Warburton's*	1 Crumpet/45.6g	71	155	5.6	31.7	0.7	0.0
Less Than 2% Fat, Marks & Spencer*	1 Crumpet/61g	116	190	8.0	36.9	1.3	2.1
Morning Fresh*	1 Crumpet/20g	36	180	7.3	34.8	1.3	5.2
Morrisons*	1 Crumpet/41g	78	191	6.1	38.6	1.4	0.0
Mother's Pride*	1 Crumpet/48g	90	187	5.6	38.9	1.0	1.7
Perfectly Balanced, Waitrose*	1 Crumpet/55g	94	171	6.1	36.1	0.3	4.4
Premium, Safeway*	1 Crumpet/60g	111	185	7.5	36.3	1.1	2.4
Premium, Sainsbury's*	1 Crumpet/50g	96	191	6.1	38.6	1.4	1.7
Premium, TTD, Sainsbury's*	1 Crumpet/56g	101	180	7.3	34.8	1.3	5.2
Safeway*	1 Crumpet/44g	80	182	7.0	36.6	0.8	1.8
Sainsbury's*	1 Crumpet/44g	91	207	5.6	44.0	0.9	0.5
Scrumptious, Kingsmill*	1 Crumpet/55g	99	180	6.1	37.2	0.8	1.7
SmartPrice, Asda*	1 Crumpet/42g	84	199	6.0	42.0	0.8	1.7
Soldier, Mother's Pride*	1 Crumpet/30g	58	193	7.8	37.1	1.6	1.6
Somerfield*	1 Crumpet/25g	48	192	5.9	39.9	1.0	2.5
Square, Tesco*	1 Crumpet/60g	101	168	6.3	33.8	0.8	2.7
Sunblest*	1 Serving/100g	87	87	2.8	18.1	0.5	1.2
Tesco*	1 Crumpet/46g	92	201	6.0	42.6	0.7	1.8
Toasted	1 Crumpet/40g	80	199	6.7	43.4	1.0	2.0
Toaster, Organic, Waitrose*	1 Crumpet/55g	95	172	7.3	34.4	0.6	4.6
Value, Tesco*	1 Crumpet/35g	59	168	6.4	33.9	0.8	1.8
Waitrose*	1 Crumpet/55g	99	180	7.3	34.8	1.3	5.2
Warburton's*	1 Crumpet/50g	89	178	7.1	35.8	0.7	0.0
CRUNCHERS,							
BBQ, Atkins*	1 Bag/28g	100	357	46.4	28.6	10.7	14.3
Nacho Cheese, Atkins*	1 Bag/28g	100	357	46.4	28.6	10.7	10.7
Original, Atkins*	1 Bag/28g	90	321	46.4	28.6	10.7	14.3
Sour Cream & Onion, Atkins*	1 Bag/28g	100	357	42.9	28.6	14.3	10.7
CRUNCHIE,							
Cadbury's	1 Std Bar/41g	193	470	4.4	72.1	18.1	0.0
Nuggets, Cadbury's*	1 Bag/125g	569	455	3.8	73.1	16.4	0.0
CRUNCHY STICKS,							
Ready Salted, Marks & Spencer*	1 Pack/75g	398	530	5.6	52.2	33.0	3.8
Ready Salted, Tesco*	1 Serving/25g	119	475	5.6	60.3	23.5	3.0
Salt & Vinegar, BGTY, Sainsburys*	1 Bag/15g	51	340	6.0	80.1	1.5	4.1
Salt & Vinegar, Sainsbury's*	1 Bag/25g	119	474	5.9	58.0	24.3	2.4
Salt & Vinegar, Shapers, Boots*	1 Bag/23g	99	430	7.8	66.0	15.0	3.1
Salt & Vinegar, Value, Tesco*	1 Bag/22g	109	497	6.3	58.7	26.3	2.4
CRUSH,							
Grapefruit, Organic, Tesco*	1 Can/330ml	139	42	0.0	9.8	0.0	0.0
Morello Cherry, Finest, Tesco*	1 Bottle/250ml	115	46	0.0	11.2	0.0	0.0
Orange & Raspberry, Freshly Squeezed, Finest, Tesco*	1fl oz/30ml	17	56	0.5	12.6	0.1	0.2
Orange & Strawberry, Finest, Tesco*	1 Bottle/250ml	115	46	0.4	10.5	0.1	0.4
Orange, Cool, Diet, Sainsbury*	1 Can/330ml	10	3	0.1	0.6	0.1	0.1
Pineapple & Grapefruit, No Added Sugar, Morrisons*	1 Glass/250ml	25	10	0.2	1.2	0.0	0.0
CUCUMBER,							
Average	1 Serving/14g	1	10	0.7	1.5	0.1	0.6
CURACAO,							
Average	1 Shot/25ml	78	311	0.0	28.3	0.0	0.0

C

	Measure INFO/WEIGHT	per Measure KCAL	Nutrition Values per 100g / 100ml				
			KCAL	PROT	CARB	FAT	FIBRE
CURLY KALE,							
Boiled in Salted Water	1oz/28g	7	24	2.4	1.0	1.1	2.8
Raw	1oz/28g	9	33	3.4	1.4	1.6	3.1
CURLY WURLY,							
Cadbury's*	1 Bar/28g	126	450	4.8	69.9	16.7	0.0
Squirlies, Cadbury's*	1 Squirl/3g	14	450	3.9	69.0	17.8	0.0
CURRANTS,							
Average	1oz/28g	75	267	2.3	67.8	0.4	1.9
CURRY,							
& Chips, Curry Sauce, Chipped Potatoes, Kershaws*	1 Sering/330g	391	119	10.0	14.0	2.5	2.0
Aubergine	1oz/28g	33	118	1.4	6.2	10.1	1.5
Beef & Rice, Iceland*	1 Pack/400g	492	123	8.7	16.0	2.6	0.6
Beef With Rice, Asda*	1 Pack/406g	547	135	6.0	19.0	3.9	1.2
Beef With Rice, Bird's Eye*	1 Pack/388g	524	135	6.9	20.8	2.8	0.8
Beef With Rice, Healthy Choice, Asda*	1 Pack/400g	476	119	6.0	18.0	2.6	0.9
Beef With Rice, Tesco*	1 Pack/400g	456	114	4.5	16.7	3.3	0.6
Beef With Rice, Weight Watchers*	1 Pack/328g	249	76	4.2	12.5	1.0	0.3
Beef, Hot, Canned, Marks & Spencer*	1 Can/425g	446	105	12.2	2.8	5.1	1.0
Beef, Marks & Spencer*	1oz/28g	34	120	12.2	3.9	6.1	1.0
Beef, Sainsbury's*	1 Serving/400g	552	138	10.7	5.4	8.2	0.9
Beef, SmartPrice, Asda*	1 Serving/392g	223	57	4.0	9.0	0.5	1.0
Bhuna Chicken, Tesco*	1 Serving/300g	396	132	11.4	4.5	7.6	0.5
Blackeye Bean, Gujerati	1oz/28g	36	127	7.2	16.1	4.4	2.8
Butter Chicken, Fresh, Tesco*	1 Pack/350g	487	139	11.8	7.1	7.0	1.8
Cabbage	1oz/28g	23	82	1.9	8.1	5.0	2.1
Cauliflower & Potato	1oz/28g	17	59	3.4	6.6	2.4	1.8
Chick Pea, Whole	1oz/28g	50	179	9.6	21.3	7.5	4.5
Chick Pea, Whole & Tomato, Punjabi With Vegetable	1oz/28g	31	112	5.6	12.4	4.9	2.9
Chick Pea, Whole, Basic	1oz/28g	30	108	6.0	14.2	3.6	3.3
Chicken & Rice, Asda*	1 Pack/300g	351	117	4.7	15.0	4.2	0.3
Chicken & Rice, Fresh, Co-Op*	1 Pack/300g	270	90	3.0	13.0	3.0	1.0
Chicken & Rice, Iceland*	1 Pack/399g	455	114	7.5	13.6	3.3	0.9
Chicken Malaysian With Rice, Bernard Matthews*	1 Pack/400g	512	128	6.1	17.0	3.9	0.0
Chicken With Naan Bread, Iceland*	1 Portion/260g	484	186	10.1	22.3	6.3	1.4
Chicken With Rice, Asda*	1 Pack/400g	440	110	5.0	17.0	2.4	1.0
Chicken With Rice, Bird's Eye*	1 Pack/380g	475	125	5.8	20.5	2.2	0.8
Chicken With Rice, Frozen, Tesco*	1 Pack/400g	488	122	4.6	17.2	3.9	0.7
Chicken With Rice, Morrisons*	1 Pack/300g	345	115	5.5	18.7	2.0	0.4
Chicken With Rice, Ross*	1 Serving/320g	272	85	3.4	14.7	1.3	0.5
Chicken With Rice, Sainsbury's*	1 Pack/400g	500	125	5.4	17.5	3.7	0.8
Chicken With Rice, Tesco*	1 Pack/300g	300	100	5.7	14.4	2.2	0.4
Chicken With Rice, Weight Watchers*	1 Pack/300g	273	91	4.8	14.3	1.7	0.5
Chicken With Vegetables, Morrisons*	1 Can/392g	392	100	9.0	7.0	4.0	1.0
Chicken With Vegetables, Value, Tesco*	1 Serving/196g	123	63	3.1	7.2	2.4	0.7
Chicken, & Potato Wedges, Healthy Eating, Tesco*	1 Pack/450g	428	95	7.6	10.3	2.7	1.1
Chicken, Asda*	1 Can/200g	210	105	10.0	5.0	5.0	0.0
Chicken, COU, Marks & Spencer*	1 Pack/400g	360	90	7.3	13.2	0.9	2.5
Chicken, Extra Strong, Marks & Spencer*	1oz/28g	28	100	13.8	2.5	3.9	1.4
Chicken, Fruity With Rice, Healthy Living, Tesco*	1 Pack/450g	495	110	6.5	18.2	1.2	1.2
Chicken, Hot, Can, Tesco*	1 Can/418g	514	123	9.7	6.9	6.3	0.9
Chicken, Hot, Canned, Asda*	1 Can/398g	462	116	10.0	5.5	6.0	0.0
Chicken, Medium Hot, Marks & Spencer*	1 Serving/200g	310	155	7.8	14.3	7.1	0.8
Chicken, Mild, Asda*	½ Can/189.7g	239	126	11.0	7.0	6.0	0.5
Chicken, Mild, BGTY, Sainsbury's*	1 Serving/200g	184	92	10.0	7.2	2.6	0.5

CURRY,

INFO/WEIGHT	Measure	per Measure KCAL	Nutrition Values per 100g / 100ml KCAL	PROT	CARB	FAT	FIBRE
Chicken, Mild, Bilash, Aldi*	½ Can/200g	180	90	9.5	4.5	3.8	0.7
Chicken, Mild, Iceland*	½ Can/200g	234	117	10.6	8.5	4.5	0.7
Chicken, Mild, Marks & Spencer*	1oz/28g	28	100	13.8	2.5	3.9	1.4
Chicken, Mild, Sainsbury's*	1 Can/400g	472	118	10.5	3.5	6.9	1.3
Chicken, Reduced Fat, Asda*	1 Pack/400g	476	119	6.0	18.0	2.6	0.9
Chicken, SmartPrice, Asda*	1 Can/392g	282	72	4.0	11.0	1.3	1.0
Chicken, Value, Tesco*	1 Pack/300g	399	133	5.5	15.9	5.2	1.7
Chicken, With Rice, Asda*	1 Serving/400g	492	123	6.0	18.0	3.0	1.0
Chicken, With Rice, Big Value, Safeway*	1 Serving/500g	645	129	4.2	20.7	3.3	0.5
Chicken, With Rice, Bird's Eye*	1 Box/400g	520	130	6.4	21.7	2.0	4.0
Chinese Chicken With Vegetable Rice, Marks & Spencer*	1 Pack/400g	320	80	7.1	8.4	2.0	1.3
Chinese Chicken, Morrisons*	1 Pack/340g	347	102	10.3	5.0	4.6	0.8
Chinese Chicken, Oriental Express*	1 Pack/340g	286	84	4.8	16.2	0.6	0.8
Courgette & Potato	1oz/28g	24	86	1.9	8.7	5.2	1.2
Dudhi, Kofta	1oz/28g	32	113	2.6	9.4	7.4	2.8
Fish & Vegetable, Bangladeshi	1oz/28g	33	117	9.1	1.4	8.4	0.5
Fish, Bangladeshi	1oz/28g	35	124	12.2	1.5	7.9	0.3
Gobi Aloo Sag, Retail	1oz/28g	27	95	2.2	7.1	6.9	1.4
Green Bean	1oz/28g	37	131	1.7	3.6	12.7	1.6
Green Salmon, Waitrose*	1 Pack/400.7g	581	145	9.1	4.5	10.1	2.7
Green Thai Style, Chicken & Sticky Rice, Asda*	1 Pack/450g	585	130	7.0	20.0	2.4	0.1
Green Thai, & Rice, GFY, Asda*	1 Pack/400g	460	115	5.0	19.0	2.1	0.5
Green Thai, Chicken, Safeway*	1 Pack/350g	490	140	12.5	3.5	8.0	1.4
Green Thai, Chicken, Sainsbury's*	1 Serving/200g	306	153	13.6	3.0	9.6	1.6
Hot Chicken With Rice, Asda*	1 Pack/400g	440	110	5.0	18.0	2.0	1.1
King Prawn, Goan, Eat Smart, Safeway*	1 Pack/400g	340	85	3.7	12.7	1.7	2.1
Lamb With Rice, Bird's Eye*	1 Pack/382g	520	136	5.6	20.8	3.4	0.9
Lamb, Extra Strong, Marks & Spencer*	1oz/28g	35	125	11.5	4.6	6.9	0.9
Malai Prawn, Sainsbury's*	1 Serving/171g	299	175	7.7	1.4	15.4	1.1
Potato & Pea	1oz/28g	26	92	2.9	13.0	3.8	2.4
Prawn & Mushroom	1oz/28g	47	168	7.3	2.5	14.4	1.0
Prawn With Rice, Asda*	1 Pack/400g	420	105	3.5	17.0	2.6	1.1
Prawn With Rice, Bird's Eye*	1 Pack/375g	443	118	3.5	20.6	0.0	0.0
Prawn, With Rice, Iceland*	1 Pack/400g	360	90	3.2	13.8	2.4	0.9
Red Kidney Bean, Punjabi	1oz/28g	30	106	4.7	10.1	5.6	3.8
Red Thai Style, Chicken, Healthy Eating, Tesco*	1 Pack/420g	462	110	6.0	17.7	1.7	0.2
Red Thai, Chicken, New Recipe, Waitrose*	1 Pack/350g	389	111	8.9	5.0	6.2	0.9
Red Thai, Fish, Waitrose*	1 Pack/500g	275	55	5.2	3.7	2.2	1.0
Red Thai, Oriental, Tesco*	1 Pack/350g	315	90	5.4	10.7	2.8	0.7
Red Thai, Safeway*	1 Pack/324g	369	114	10.0	4.8	6.1	1.6
Thai Green, Chicken, BGTY, Sainsbury's*	1 Pack/400g	376	94	9.3	6.1	3.6	0.4
Thai Green, Chicken, Bird's Eye*	1 Pack/450g	536	119	4.7	15.2	4.4	0.3
Thai Green, Chicken, Marks & Spencer*	½ Pack/107g	171	160	12.3	1.8	11.6	0.6
Thai Green, Chicken, Weight Watchers*	1 Pack/340g	262	77	4.4	10.9	1.7	0.6
Thai Green, With Sticky Rice, Healthy Living, Tesco*	1 Pack/450g	518	115	7.7	14.9	2.7	0.6
Thai Red, Chicken, 97% Fat Free, Bird's Eye*	1 Pack/366g	425	116	5.7	19.0	1.9	0.5
Thai Red, Chicken, Asda*	1 Pack/360g	461	128	9.1	5.5	7.7	1.0
Thai Red, Chicken, COU, Marks & Spencer*	1 Pack/400g	420	105	7.1	13.4	2.3	1.4
Thai Red, Chicken, Sainsbury's*	1 Serving/200g	300	150	14.3	5.5	7.9	1.0
Thai Red, Chicken, With Fragrant Rice, Somerfield*	1 Pack/340g	503	148	8.0	18.0	5.0	0.0
Thai Red, Chicken, With Jasmine Rice, BGTY, Sainsbury's*	1 Pack/400g	428	107	6.9	16.0	1.7	0.2
Thai Red, Chicken, With Jasmine Rice, New, Sainsbury's*	1 Pack/400g	448	112	6.2	16.6	1.4	0.8
Thai Yellow, Vegetable, Sainsbury's*	1 Pack/400g	624	156	2.2	9.4	12.2	1.1

	Measure INFO/WEIGHT	per Measure KCAL	Nutrition Values per 100g / 100ml				
			KCAL	PROT	CARB	FAT	FIBRE
CURRY,							
Thai Yellow, Vegetable, Sainsbury's*	½ Pack/200g	256	128	1.7	7.1	10.3	1.5
Thai, Chicken, COU, Marks & Spencer*	1 Pack/400g	320	80	7.2	8.8	1.9	1.0
Thai, Chicken, Tom Yum, Sainsbury's*	1 Pot/400g	416	104	11.1	3.5	5.1	1.9
Thai, Chicken, With Rice, Oriental Express*	1 Pack/340g	303	89	4.1	15.3	1.3	1.2
Thai, Mango Chicken, Sainsbury's*	½ Pack/200g	288	144	11.2	4.8	8.9	1.9
Thai, Peanut Chicken, Sainsbury's*	½ Pack/200g	314	157	12.8	4.9	9.6	1.2
Thai, Prawn, With Jasmine Rice, Sainsbury's*	1 Serving/401g	353	88	4.2	14.5	1.5	2.0
Vegetable With Pilau Rice, BGTY, Sainsbury's*	1 Pack/450g	441	98	2.4	16.9	2.3	0.5
Vegetable With Pilau Rice, Linda McCartney*	1 Pack/339g	224	66	1.6	13.5	0.6	0.5
Vegetable With Rice, Asda*	1 Pack/392.7g	432	110	2.6	18.0	3.1	1.4
Vegetable With Rice, Co-Op*	1 Pack/340g	289	85	2.0	17.0	1.0	0.7
Vegetable With Rice, Tesco*	1 Pack/400g	440	110	2.1	18.7	3.0	1.0
Vegetable With Yoghurt	1oz/28g	17	62	2.6	4.6	4.1	1.4
Vegetable, Asda*	1 Pack/350g	329	94	1.9	8.0	6.0	1.9
Vegetable, Frozen, Mixed Vegetables	1oz/28g	25	88	2.5	6.9	6.1	0.0
Vegetable, Health Eating, Tesco*	1 Pack/350g	280	80	4.5	13.6	0.8	1.3
Vegetable, Indian Meal For One, Tesco*	1 Serving/200g	220	110	1.9	10.5	6.7	1.4
Vegetable, Marks & Spencer*	1 Pack/250g	300	120	2.1	7.1	9.5	2.5
Vegetable, Medium, Tesco*	1 Pack/350g	326	93	2.3	7.1	6.2	1.9
Vegetable, Mild, Tesco*	1 Can/425g	315	74	2.1	10.7	2.5	1.7
Vegetable, Pakistani	1oz/28g	17	60	2.2	8.7	2.6	2.2
Vegetable, Ready Meals, Marks & Spencer*	1 Pack/300g	495	165	2.4	7.2	14.2	2.1
Vegetable, Retail With Rice	1oz/28g	29	102	3.3	16.4	3.0	0.0
Vegetable, Safeway*	1 Pack/275g	239	87	2.4	7.3	5.4	2.8
Vegetable, SmartPrice, Asda*	½ Can/203g	132	65	2.0	13.0	0.5	1.7
Vegetable, Takeaway	1oz/28g	29	105	2.5	7.6	7.4	0.0
Vegetable, Tesco*	½ Can/200g	278	139	3.4	10.5	9.3	3.2
Vegetable, Tinned, Asda*	½ Can/200g	206	103	2.2	10.0	6.0	2.5
Vegetable, Tinned, Tesco*	1 Can/400g	312	78	2.4	10.5	2.9	1.7
Vegetable, Waitrose*	1 Pack/352g	285	81	3.5	4.9	5.3	2.1
Vegetable, Way to Five, Sainsbury's*	½ Pack/344g	227	66	2.5	11.6	1.1	1.4
Vegetable, With Rice, Bird's Eye*	1 Pack/413.6g	455	110	2.3	19.6	2.3	1.1
Vegetable, in Sweet Sauce	1 Serving/330g	162	49	1.4	6.7	2.1	1.3
Yellow Thai Style, Chicken, Healthy Living, Tesco*	1 Pack/450g	504	112	9.3	12.6	2.7	0.5
Yellow Vegetable, Tesco*	1 Pack/355.6g	324	91	1.9	9.9	4.9	1.4
CURRY LEAVES,							
Fresh	1oz/28g	27	97	7.9	13.3	1.3	0.0
CURRY PASTE,							
Balti, Patak's*	1 Tbsp/15g	59	393	5.0	20.3	31.8	3.1
Balti, Sharwood's*	¼ Pack/72.5g	328	453	5.0	19.2	39.6	3.1
Balti, Tomato & Coriander, Patak's*	1 Serving/30g	117	391	4.1	17.2	34.0	2.2
Garam Masala, Cinnamon & Ginger, Hot, Patak's*	1 Tbsp/25g	101	403	3.2	17.9	35.4	0.6
Hot, Marks & Spencer*	1oz/28g	69	245	4.2	13.4	19.2	3.3
Hot, Sharwood's*	1oz/28g	123	439	5.1	18.6	38.3	2.6
Korma, Patak's*	1 Tbsp/10g	54	535	4.2	13.0	51.8	2.6
Madras, Patak's*	½ Jar/50g	293	586	4.3	21.6	53.6	5.2
Medium, Marks & Spencer*	1oz/28g	64	230	2.5	10.7	19.5	4.9
Medium, Sharwood's*	1oz/28g	122	434	4.5	16.8	38.8	2.7
Mild, Original, Patak's*	1oz/28g	155	552	4.9	14.3	52.8	6.2
Mild, Sharwood's*	1oz/28g	78	279	3.6	17.7	21.5	3.4
Rogan Josh, Patak's*	1 Serving/30g	119	397	4.1	12.7	36.7	5.9
Tandoori, Patak's*	1 Tbsp/25g	28	111	3.1	20.7	1.8	2.6
Tandoori, Sharwood's*	1oz/28g	64	228	5.9	15.5	15.8	1.9

	Measure INFO/WEIGHT	per Measure KCAL	Nutrition Values per 100g / 100ml				
			KCAL	PROT	CARB	FAT	FIBRE
CURRY PASTE,							
Thai Green, Mild, Sainsbury's*	1 Tbsp/15g	23	156	2.2	14.5	9.9	2.7
Thai Red, Sainsbury's*	1oz/28g	43	154	2.0	8.0	12.0	3.0
Tikka Masala, Patak's*	1oz/28g	101	361	3.4	16.2	31.4	3.2
Tikka Masala, Sharwood's*	1oz/28g	53	191	3.2	9.9	15.4	2.6
Vindaloo, Patak's*	1 Tbsp/15g	84	557	4.8	16.0	52.6	6.1
CURRY POWDER,							
Average	1 Tsp/2g	7	325	12.7	41.8	13.8	0.0
Medium, Schwartz*	1 Tsp Heaped/4g	14	348	12.0	50.0	11.0	15.0
CUSTARD,							
Chocolate, COU, Marks & Spencer*	1 Pot/140g	147	105	3.1	18.6	2.2	1.0
Dairy Free, Sainsbury's*	1 Serving/250g	210	84	3.0	14.2	1.7	0.2
Instant, Better For You, Morrisons*	1 Serving/35g	142	407	6.0	73.2	10.0	2.6
Instant, Bird's*	1oz/28g	119	425	4.5	76.0	11.5	0.0
Instant, Low Fat, Bird's*	Per serving/25g	101	405	4.4	78.5	8.3	0.4
Instant, No Added Sugar, Tesco*	1 Serving/Dry/18g	73	406	5.3	77.0	8.5	0.0
Instant, Sainsbury's*	1 Serving/141g	109	77	0.8	14.0	2.0	0.0
Low Fat, Average	1/3 Pot/141g	116	82	2.9	15.0	1.2	0.0
Mix, Instant, Co-Op*	1 Pack/76g	340	448	4.5	68.5	17.3	0.0
Mix, Instant, Made Up, Co-Op*	½ Pack/140ml	118	84	0.7	13.9	2.9	0.0
Mix, Reduced Sugar, Asda*	1 Serving/145ml	103	71	0.7	14.0	1.4	0.1
Pot, Forest Fruits Flavour, Hot 'n' Fruity, Bird's*	1 Pot/174g	171	98	0.9	18.5	2.4	0.1
Pot, Strawberry Flavour, Hot 'n' Fruity, Bird's*	1oz/28g	28	99	1.0	18.5	2.4	0.1
Powder	1oz/28g	99	354	0.6	92.0	0.7	0.1
Powder, Original Flavour, Bird's*	1oz/28g	99	355	0.4	87.0	0.5	0.0
Strawberry Style, Shapers, Boots*	1 Pot/148g	83	56	4.0	8.2	0.8	0.1
Summer, Ambrosia*	1 Pack/500g	490	98	2.7	15.0	3.0	0.0
Vanilla With Apple Crunch, Ambrosia*	1 Pack/193g	276	143	3.4	22.4	4.5	0.8
Vanilla, COU, Marks & Spencer*	1 Pot/140g	147	105	4.3	16.6	2.5	0.6
CUTLETS,							
Nut, Goodlife*	1 Serving/88g	248	282	10.2	27.4	14.6	3.0
Nut, Grilled, Cauldron Foods*	1 Cutlet/87g	250	287	10.2	26.8	15.4	4.6
Nut, Retail, Fried in Vegetable Oil	1oz/28g	81	289	4.8	18.7	22.3	1.7
Nut, Retail, Grilled	1oz/28g	59	212	5.1	19.9	13.0	1.8
Vegetable & Nut, Asda*	1 Cutlet/88.4g	295	335	10.0	22.0	23.0	4.6
Vegetable, Nut, Tesco*	1 Serving/88g	271	308	7.7	22.0	21.0	3.5
CUTTLEFISH,							
Raw	1oz/28g	20	71	16.1	0.0	0.7	0.0

C

	Measure INFO/WEIGHT	per Measuring KCAL	Nutrition Values per 100g / 100ml				
			KCAL	PROT	CARB	FAT	FIBRE
DAB,							
Fillets, Lightly Dusted, Marks & Spencer*	1 Fillet/111.8g	190	170	13.3	8.2	9.1	1.3
Raw	1oz/28g	21	74	15.7	0.0	1.2	0.0
DAIRYLEA DUNKERS,							
Jumbo Munch, Dairylea*	1 Serving/50g	150	300	7.2	26.5	18.5	1.2
Salt & Vinegar, Dairylea*	1 Tub/42g	116	275	6.7	17.5	19.5	0.3
Smokey Bacon, Dairylea*	1 Pack/45g	135	300	7.3	24.0	19.5	0.0
DAIRYLEA LUNCHABLES,							
Cheese & Pizza Crackers, Dairylea*	1oz/28g	105	375	10.5	24.5	27.0	1.4
Chicken, Fun Pack, Dairylea*	1 Pack/311g	454	146	5.5	15.0	6.2	0.2
Double Cheese, Dairylea*	1 Pack/110g	413	375	18.0	17.0	26.0	0.3
Ham & Cheese Pizza, Dairylea*	1 Pack/97g	247	255	11.5	26.0	11.0	1.6
Harvest Ham, Dairylea*	1 Pack/110g	314	285	16.5	16.5	17.0	0.3
Tasty Chicken, Dairylea*	1 Pack/110g	314	285	17.0	17.5	16.5	0.3
DAMSONS,							
Raw, Weighed With Stones	1oz/28g	10	34	0.5	8.6	0.0	1.6
Raw, Weighed Without Stones	1oz/28g	11	38	0.5	9.6	0.0	1.8
DANISH PASTRY,							
Apple & Sultana, Tesco*	1 Pastry/72g	293	407	5.4	45.0	22.8	1.4
Custard Danish Bar, Sara Lee*	¼ Bar/100g	228	228	6.6	36.1	6.4	0.8
Danish Apple Bar, Sara Lee*	1/6 Bar/70g	160	229	4.3	42.1	5.7	1.7
Danish Twist, Apple & Cinnamon, Entenmann's*	1 Serving/52g	150	288	5.6	62.0	1.9	1.5
Danish Twist, Toasted Pecan, Entenmann's*	1 Slice/48g	171	351	7.0	47.2	15.6	1.4
Pastry	1 Pastry/110g	411	374	5.8	51.3	17.6	1.6
Pecan, Marks & Spencer*	1 Serving/67g	287	428	6.2	45.0	26.0	1.3
DATES,							
Dried, Average	1 Date/20g	54	272	2.8	65.4	0.4	4.2
Raw, Average	1 Date/30g	35	116	1.4	29.1	0.1	1.7
DELI FILLER,							
Chinese, Princes*	1 Serving/50g	47	94	3.6	15.6	1.9	0.3
King Prawn & Avocado, Marks & Spencer*	1 Pack/170g	425	250	9.5	1.4	22.8	0.5
Prawn & Mayonnaise, Marks & Spencer*	1 Serving/60g	150	250	11.3	1.0	23.0	0.5
Smoked Salmon & Soft Cheese, Marks & Spencer*	1 Serving/85g	208	245	11.7	3.3	20.4	0.5
DELIGHT,							
Butterscotch Flavour, No Added Sugar, Tesco*	½ Pack/25g	109	434	4.8	66.5	16.5	0.0
Butterscotch, Dessert, Safeway*	1 Pack/69g	302	438	1.8	81.5	11.6	0.3
Chocolate Flavour, Dry, Tesco*	1 Pack/49g	204	417	6.3	63.0	15.5	0.5
Ravishing Raspberry, Made Up, Asda*	1/3 Pack/100g	112	112	3.2	16.0	3.9	0.0
Strawberry Flavour, No Added Sugar, Dry, Tesco*	½ Pack/25g	110	440	4.8	67.0	17.0	0.0
Strawberry, Shapers, Boots*	1 Pot/121g	96	79	4.5	13.0	1.0	0.1
DESSERT,							
Apple Rice, Classic Desserts, Marks & Spencer*	1 Pot/200g	210	105	2.5	20.0	1.7	0.3
Baklava	1 Serving/100g	393	393	5.0	46.0	21.0	0.0
Banana Flavour Custard, Ambrosia*	1 Pack/135g	136	101	2.6	16.2	2.9	0.1
Banoffee Layered, Sainsbury's*	1 Pot/115g	270	235	2.2	27.8	12.8	1.0
Banoffee, Frozen, Healthy Living, Tesco*	1 Serving/60g	92	153	2.5	29.9	2.6	0.6
Banoffee, Shape*	1 Pot/120g	175	146	3.3	28.0	2.3	0.5
Banoffee, Weight Watchers*	1 Pot/80g	154	192	4.5	35.3	3.7	0.8
Black Cherry & Chocolate, COU, Marks & Spencer*	1 Pack/115g	132	115	3.6	22.6	1.4	1.2
Black Forest, Tesco*	1 Pot/100g	287	287	3.5	35.8	14.4	2.4
Blackcurrant, Yoghurt & Sorbet, Mini, Eat Smart, Safeway*	1 Pot/75g	90	120	2.2	25.8	0.7	1.8
Blissful Banana, Asda*	1/3 Pack/100g	122	122	3.7	17.0	4.3	0.0
Blueberry Muffin, Tesco*	1 Pot/91g	265	291	2.0	24.5	20.6	3.0
Bounty, Mars*	1 Pot/110g	253	230	5.3	23.2	13.6	0.0

DESSERT,	Measure INFO/WEIGHT	per Measure KCAL	Nutrition Values per 100g / 100ml KCAL	PROT	CARB	FAT	FIBRE
Bread & Butter, Eat Smart, Safeway*	1 Pudding/117g	140	120	5.1	20.4	1.8	0.8
Butterscotch Flavour Whip, Co-Op*	1 Pack/64g	241	377	0.6	93.4	0.1	0.1
Buttons, Cadbury's*	1 Pot/100g	295	295	6.4	34.9	14.7	0.0
Cafe Latte, COU, Marks & Spencer*	1 Pot/120g	162	135	5.0	24.0	2.2	0.9
Cafe Latte, Iced, BGTY, Sainsbury's*	1 Serving/75g	104	139	2.9	23.7	3.6	3.3
Cafe Mocha, COU, Marks & Spencer*	1 Dessert/115g	155	135	5.5	21.8	2.7	1.0
Cappuccino, BGTY, Sainsbury's*	1 Pot/119g	224	188	3.3	25.2	8.1	0.8
Cappuccino, Italian, Co-Op*	1 Pack/90g	257	285	5.0	39.0	12.0	0.1
Caramel, Marks & Spencer*	1oz/28g	41	147	3.9	22.3	4.1	0.0
Cherry & Vanilla, BGTY, Sainsbury's*	1 Pot/115g	225	196	1.6	32.6	6.6	1.0
Chocolate & Cherry, COU, Marks & Spencer*	1 Pot/130g	156	120	2.6	24.5	1.6	0.9
Chocolate & Coconut, COU, Marks & Spencer*	1 Pot/125g	169	135	3.6	25.6	2.2	0.7
Chocolate & Honeycomb, Weight Watchers*	1 Pot/57.9g	92	159	3.1	26.2	4.3	0.8
Chocolate & Mallow Iced, GFY, Asda*	1 Pot/150ml	140	93	2.0	18.7	1.2	2.3
Chocolate & Mallow, Weight Watchers*	1 Pot/150ml	140	93	2.0	18.7	1.2	2.3
Chocolate & Marshmallow Swirls, Iced, BGTY, Sainsbury's	¼ Pot/75g	130	173	3.9	33.8	2.5	2.8
Chocolate & Orange Sorbet, Weight Watchers*	1 Dessert/105g	137	130	1.1	24.6	2.1	0.2
Chocolate & Vanilla Caramel, Dairy, Petits Filous, Yoplait*	1 Pot/60g	101	169	4.8	23.6	6.2	0.0
Chocolate Brownie, Asda*	1/6 Brownie/63.5g	171	271	5.0	38.0	11.0	4.4
Chocolate Brownie, Marks & Spencer*	¼ Pack/143.5g	612	425	4.7	39.6	27.5	1.0
Chocolate Creme, Somerfield*	1 Pot/125g	180	144	4.0	22.0	4.0	0.0
Chocolate Dream, Delicious Dessert Co-Op*	1 Pot/110g	184	167	4.1	22.0	7.0	0.0
Chocolate Fudge Brownie, Tesco*	1 Pot/125g	374	299	4.6	40.2	13.3	1.3
Chocolate Honeycomb Crisp, COU, Marks & Spencer*	1 Serving/71g	110	155	4.6	27.6	2.9	1.0
Chocolate Mint Crisp, Iced, Marks & Spencer*	¼ Pot/85.2g	115	135	5.4	21.9	2.9	1.0
Chocolate Mocha, BGTY, Sainsbury's*	1 Pot/100g	115	115	3.8	19.2	2.6	2.8
Chocolate Muffin, COU, Marks & Spencer*	1 Serving/110g	149	135	4.6	26.5	1.9	0.9
Chocolate Muffin, Tesco*	1 Serving/104g	354	340	3.5	35.5	20.4	2.1
Chocolate Orange, Eat Smart, Safeway*	1 Pot/90g	153	170	4.5	32.5	1.9	0.5
Chocolate Profiterole, Sainsbury's*	1/6 Pot/95.0g	192	202	5.4	25.1	8.9	0.8
Chocolate Profiterole, Tesco*	1 Serving/76g	281	370	4.3	27.9	26.7	0.4
Chocolate Toffee, Weight Watchers*	1 Pot/90.1g	164	182	4.9	35.0	3.5	1.8
Chocolate, COU Marks & Spencers*	1 Serving/120g	168	140	5.6	26.4	2.1	1.1
Chocolate, Campina*	1 Pot/125g	186	149	3.2	18.5	6.9	0.0
Chocolate, Frozen, Healthy Eating, Tesco*	1 Serving/52g	68	131	3.5	23.7	2.5	0.9
Chocolate, Value, Tesco*	1 Pot/115g	112	97	2.8	15.7	2.6	0.0
Chocolate, Weight Watchers*	1 Serving/82g	145	177	5.2	32.3	3.0	2.9
Crema Catalana, Cafe Culture, Marks & Spencer*	1 Pot/110g	385	350	3.5	12.2	31.7	0.4
Creme Caramel, Sainsbury's*	1 Pot/100g	102	102	2.5	21.1	0.9	0.0
Crunchie, Nuggets, Mousse, Meringue, Cadbury's*	1 Serving/55g	180	325	3.8	49.5	0.0	12.2
Dairy Vanilla Iced, Sainsbury's*	1 Serving/65g	77	119	3.0	19.9	3.0	3.7
Double Chocolate Brownie, Weight Watchers*	1 Serving/82.5g	145	177	5.2	32.3	3.0	2.9
Double Chocolate Fudge, Marks & Spencer*	1 Pot/119g	387	325	3.0	30.6	21.4	1.6
Double Chocolate, Eat Smart, Safeway*	1 Pot/90g	144	160	3.9	31.0	2.2	2.0
Dreaming of, Cherry Rice, Marks & Spencer*	1 Pot/200g	220	110	2.4	19.7	2.2	0.1
Dreamy Vanilla, BGTY, Sainsbury's*	1 Serving/58g	146	252	3.5	27.6	14.2	5.3
Flake, Milk Chocolate, Cadbury's*	1 Pot/100g	290	290	6.3	34.7	14.1	0.0
Fruit & Nut, Cadbury's*	1 Pot/100g	285	285	6.4	36.3	12.5	0.0
Galaxy, Mars*	1 Pot/75g	166	221	4.9	22.7	12.3	0.0
Gulabjam Indian, Waitrose*	1 Pot/180g	476	266	4.8	42.9	8.6	0.6
Irish Cream Cafe Latte, COU, Marks & Spencer*	1 Pot/120g	160	133	5.0	24.0	2.2	0.9
Jaffa Cake, COU, Marks & Spencer*	1 Serving/120g	138	115	2.4	20.1	2.6	1.0
Lemon & Sultana Sponge, COU, Marks & Spencer*	1 Pot/130g	169	130	2.8	26.5	1.2	0.5

D

DESSERT,

	Measure INFO/WEIGHT	per Measuring KCAL	Nutrition Values per 100g / 100ml				
			KCAL	PROT	CARB	FAT	FIBRE
Lemon Meringue, Weight Watchers*	1 Pot/170g	321	189	2.4	43.1	0.5	0.6
Lemoncello, Italian, Co-Op*	1 Pot/90g	266	295	3.0	34.0	16.0	0.1
Lemoncillo, Tesco*	1 Pot/100g	273	273	4.2	41.8	9.9	0.8
Luxurious Chocolate Marshmallow, Weight Watchers*	1 Serving/50g	97	194	3.2	34.5	4.7	1.3
Mandarin, COU, Marks & Spencer*	1 Serving/150g	195	130	1.0	22.0	3.8	0.1
Maple & Pecan, American Style, Sainsbury's*	1 Pot/110g	287	261	2.6	30.6	14.2	1.2
Mars, Mars*	1 Pot/110g	215	195	6.0	28.2	6.7	0.7
Natural Rice, Shape*	1 Pot/175g	149	85	3.5	15.4	1.0	0.1
Passion Fruit & Mango, Weight Watchers*	¼ Tub/70g	103	147	1.8	29.1	2.6	0.6
Peach & Raspberry, COU, Marks & Spencer*	1 Pot/90g	135	150	2.6	30.5	1.6	1.0
Peach, Iced, So-Lo, Iceland*	1 Lolly/92ml	98	107	2.3	23.5	0.0	2.2
Pineapple & Passionfruit, Marks & Spencer*	1 Pot/100g	130	130	0.8	21.7	3.8	0.3
Profiterole, Marks & Spencer*	1 Pot/61g	209	342	5.5	29.1	22.1	0.5
Raspberry & Chardonnay, COU, Marks & Spencer*	1 Serving/135g	155	115	1.6	25.5	0.5	2.7
Raspberry Flavour Whip, Co-Op*	1 Whip/64g	241	377	1.2	92.5	0.2	0.1
Raspberry Swirl, Iced, Weight Watchers*	1 Scoop/60g	74	124	1.7	23.4	2.5	0.3
Raspberry With Light Lemon Sponge, Weight Watchers*	1 Dessert/85.2g	155	182	3.9	32.0	4.3	1.8
Red Devil, Simpsons, St Ivel*	1oz/28g	38	134	2.8	24.3	2.8	0.4
Rice, Lite, Muller*	1 Pot/150g	116	77	3.5	13.6	0.9	0.0
Rolo, Nestle*	1 Pot/78g	191	245	3.1	30.3	12.2	0.3
Simply Strawberry, Sainsbury's*	1 Pot/150g	126	84	0.6	19.3	0.1	0.9
Strawberries & Cream, Better for You, Morrisons*	1 Serving/200g	244	122	2.2	26.0	1.1	0.1
Strawberry & Rhubarb, COU, Marks & Spencer*	1 Pot/110g	105	95	1.5	20.1	0.7	0.9
Strawberry Flavour, SmartPrice, Asda*	1 Pot/115g	113	98	2.4	17.0	2.3	0.0
Strawberry Flavour, With Cream, Somerfield*	1 Pot/100g	119	119	2.0	16.0	5.0	0.4
Strawberry Panna Cotta, COU, Marks & Spencer*	1 Pot/145g	145	100	2.6	15.7	2.6	0.8
Strawberry, SmartPrice, Asda*	1 Pot/100g	120	120	2.3	16.0	5.0	0.0
Strawberry, Value, Tesco*	1 Pot/115g	113	98	2.4	16.9	2.3	0.0
Summer Fruits, COU, Marks & Spencer*	1 Serving/105g	110	105	2.1	21.6	1.1	1.2
Summer Fruits, Yoghurt, Iced, BGTY, Sainsbury's*	¼ Pot/85g	105	124	3.3	25.6	0.9	0.5
Summerberry, Healthy Living, Tesco*	1 Pot/102g	133	130	2.8	24.5	2.3	1.5
Supreme, No Added Sugar, Sainsbury's*	¼ Pack/91g	98	108	3.5	13.6	4.4	0.0
Tantalising Toffee Flavour, Weight Watchers*	1 Serving/57g	93	163	2.7	26.2	4.8	0.2
Tantalising Toffee, COU, Marks & Spencer*	¼ Pot/85g	145	170	3.1	32.8	2.9	0.5
Toffee & Vanilla, Weight Watchers*	1 Pot/67g	107	159	3.1	34.8	0.8	3.9
Toffee Apple, Eat Smart, Safeway*	1 Pot/100g	145	145	2.4	29.1	1.7	2.6
Toffee Chocolate, Weight Watchers*	1 Pot/100g	164	164	4.4	31.5	3.2	1.6
Toffee Flavour & Toffee Sauce, Weight Watchers*	1 Pot/57g	93	163	2.7	26.2	4.8	0.2
Toffee Flavour Custard, Ambrosia*	1 Pack/135g	139	103	2.7	16.4	2.9	0.1
Toffee Flavour Fudge Swirl, Weight Watchers*	1 Pot/57g	82	143	2.5	22.6	4.4	0.4
Toffee Flavoured Dairy, Iced, BGTY, Sainsbury's*	1 Serving/70g	103	147	2.7	24.0	4.5	0.2
Toffee Iced, 3% Fat, Marks & Spencer*	1oz/28g	51	183	3.1	37.2	2.4	0.5
Toffee, Frozen, BGTY, Sainsbury's*	1 Pot/73.8g	96	130	3.3	26.0	1.4	4.2
Toffee, With Biscuit Pieces, Weight Watchers*	1 Pot/57.1g	93	163	2.7	26.2	4.8	0.2
Triple Chocolate Layered, BGTY, Sainsbury's*	1 Pot/105g	147	140	4.2	24.4	2.8	0.5
Vanilla & Chocolate Iced, Healthy Living, Tesco*	1 Pot/73g	104	143	3.0	26.9	2.6	0.7
Vanilla & Raspberry Swirl, Weight Watchers*	1 Serving/100ml	81	81	1.5	13.3	2.2	0.2
Vanilla & Strawberry Compote, Weight Watchers*	1 Pot/57g	81	142	2.5	23.4	3.9	0.2
Vanilla & Toffee, Heavenly Swirls, Healthy Living. Tesco*	1 Pot/73g	106	145	2.8	28.1	2.5	0.5
Vanilla Flavour, Iced, Healthy Eating, Tesco*	1 Serving/50g	67	134	3.9	24.1	2.4	4.6
Vanilla Supreme, Sainsbury's*	1 Pot/95g	116	122	3.0	18.0	4.0	0.0
Vanilla With Strawberries Swirl, Weight Watchers*	1 Pot/57g	81	142	2.5	23.4	3.9	0.2
Vanilla, Frozen, BGTY, Sainsbury's*	1 Serving/75g	89	119	3.0	19.9	3.0	3.7

D

	Measure INFO/WEIGHT	per Measure KCAL	Nutrition Values per 100g / 100ml				
			KCAL	PROT	CARB	FAT	FIBRE
DESSERT,							
Vanilla, Frozen, GFY, Asda*	1 Serving/52g	72	139	2.7	22.0	4.5	0.0
Vanilla, Iced, 3% Fat, Marks & Spencer*	1oz/28g	40	143	3.5	25.9	2.8	0.7
Vanilla, Iced, Non-Dairy, Swedish Glace*	1 Serving/100g	200	200	2.5	25.0	10.0	1.0
Vanilla, Too Good To Be True, Frozen, Wall's*	1 Serving/50ml	35	70	2.0	14.9	0.4	0.1
Wild Blueberry & White Peach, Extra Special, Asda*	1 Pot/120g	180	150	1.8	20.0	7.0	1.0
DESSERT MIX,							
Instant Powder, Made Up With Skimmed Milk	1oz/28g	27	97	3.1	14.9	3.2	0.2
Instant Powder, Made Up With Whole Milk	1oz/28g	35	125	3.1	14.8	6.3	0.2
DHAL,							
Black Gram	1oz/28g	21	74	4.2	7.0	3.4	1.7
Blackeye Bean, Patak's*	1oz/28g	29	102	3.6	12.4	4.6	1.8
Chick Pea	1oz/28g	42	149	7.4	17.7	6.1	3.8
Chick Pea, Asda*	1 Serving/400g	404	101	4.5	14.0	3.0	3.0
Chick Pea, Sainsbury's*	½ Can/200g	432	216	10.8	22.7	9.1	7.1
Lentil, Patak's*	1 Can/283g	156	55	2.8	9.3	1.0	1.0
Lentil, Red Masoor & Tomato With Butter	1oz/28g	26	94	4.0	9.7	4.9	0.9
Lentil, Red Masoor & Vegetable	1oz/28g	31	110	5.8	14.7	3.8	1.8
Lentil, Red Masoor With Vegetable Oil	1oz/28g	48	172	7.6	19.2	7.9	1.8
Lentil, Red Masoor, Punjabi	1oz/28g	39	139	7.2	19.2	4.6	2.0
Lentil, Red Masoorl & Mung Bean	1oz/28g	32	114	4.8	9.9	6.7	1.6
Lentil, Red, Way To Five, Sainsbury's*	½ Pack/94g	87	93	5.5	14.4	1.5	1.4
Lentil, Tesco*	1 Serving/200g	248	124	5.1	10.6	6.6	2.5
Mung Bean, Bengali	1oz/28g	20	73	4.2	7.4	3.3	1.7
Mung Beans, Dried, Boiled in Unsalted Water	1oz/28g	26	92	7.8	15.3	0.4	0.0
Mung Beans, Dried, Raw	1oz/28g	81	291	26.8	46.3	1.1	0.0
Split Peas, Yellow, Chana, Asda*	1 Serving/275g	300	109	2.6	9.0	7.0	1.8
Toor, Cooked Dish	1oz/28g	31	109	4.6	13.3	4.6	0.0
DHANSAK,							
Chicken With Bagara Rice, Waitrose*	1 Pack/450g	549	122	8.2	18.2	1.8	1.2
Chicken, Ready Meals, Marks & Spencer*	1oz/28g	50	180	12.4	6.6	11.5	1.6
Vegetable, Sainsbury's*	1 Pack/400g	416	104	2.6	7.2	7.2	1.3
DILL,							
Dried	1 Tsp/1g	3	253	19.9	42.2	4.4	13.6
Fresh	1oz/28g	7	25	3.7	0.9	0.8	2.5
DIME,							
Mini, Terry's*	1 Bag/100g	550	550	4.2	61.0	32.0	0.7
Single, Terry's*	1oz/28g	154	550	3.9	61.6	32.1	0.6
Terry's*	1oz/28g	154	550	4.6	68.5	33.8	0.6
DIP,							
Applewood Cheddar & Onion, Fresh, BGTY, Sainsbury's*	½ Pot/85g	85	100	7.3	7.3	4.6	0.5
Aubergine, Fresh, Waitrose*	1 Serving/85g	159	187	2.5	10.5	15.0	1.7
Barbeque Sauce, Pot, Burger King*	1 Serving/25g	31	125	0.6	28.7	0.3	0.4
Bean & Cheese, Asda*	1 Serving/50g	79	157	7.0	12.0	9.0	1.7
Blue Cheese, Fresh, Sainsbury's*	1/5 Pot/34g	115	337	3.6	3.1	34.5	0.1
Cajun Red Pepper, Sainsbury's*	1 Serving/50g	25	50	1.4	7.0	1.8	1.4
Caramelised Onion & Garlic, Waitrose*	½ Pot/85g	389	458	1.7	5.8	47.6	0.5
Celery, Marks & Spencer*	1 pot/130g	163	125	1.8	4.4	11.0	1.2
Cheddar & Onion, Marks & Spencer*	1oz/28g	88	315	5.1	7.5	29.5	0.5
Cheddar & Spring Onion, Marks & Spencer*	1 Pack/125g	581	465	3.6	4.7	48.3	0.5
Cheese & Bacon With Breadsticks, Weight Watchers*	1 Pack/50g	98	196	16.0	24.0	4.2	1.4
Cheese & Chive, 50% Less Fat, Asda*	1 Pot/125g	261	209	4.5	9.0	17.2	0.0
Cheese & Chive, 50% Less Fat, Morrisons*	1 Serving/50g	86	172	8.8	5.2	12.7	0.2
Cheese & Chive, Asda*	1 Serving/42.5g	192	447	4.9	3.4	46.0	0.0

D

	Measure INFO/WEIGHT	per Measure KCAL	Nutrition Values per 100g / 100ml				
			KCAL	PROT	CARB	FAT	FIBRE
DIP,							
Cheese & Chive, Classic, Tesco*	1 Serving/32g	164	511	3.3	3.1	54.0	0.1
Cheese & Chive, Fresh, Safeway*	1 Pot/170g	877	516	4.1	3.0	54.2	0.0
Cheese & Chive, Fresh, Sainsbury's*	1oz/28g	109	390	3.9	2.7	40.4	0.0
Cheese & Chive, Healthy Choice, Safeway*	1 Pack/100g	137	137	10.2	6.0	8.0	1.3
Cheese & Chive, Healthy Eating, Tesco*	1 Tsp/10g	23	228	5.7	6.4	19.9	0.0
Cheese & Chive, Healthy Selection, Somerfield*	1oz/28g	67	239	6.0	5.0	22.0	0.0
Cheese & Chive, Marks & Spencer*	1oz/28g	120	430	4.5	3.9	44.1	0.5
Cheese & Chive, Sainsbury's*	1 Pot/300g	1296	432	3.6	4.6	44.5	0.2
Cheese & Chive, Tesco*	1 Pack/170g	811	477	3.3	5.1	49.2	0.1
Cheese & Spring Onion, Weight Watchers*	1 Serving/50g	98	196	16.0	24.0	4.2	1.4
Chilli Cheese, Asda*	1 Serving/50g	131	262	8.0	8.0	22.0	1.1
Chilli Cheese, Max, Walkers*	1 Jar/300g	390	130	3.3	9.4	9.1	0.3
Chilli, Marks & Spencer*	1 Pot/35g	103	295	0.4	73.2	0.2	0.4
Chunky Tomato Salsa, Tesco*	1 Pot/170g	68	40	1.1	5.9	1.3	1.1
Cranberry, Asda*	½ Pot/40g	53	132	0.4	29.0	1.6	0.8
Cucumber & Mint, Eat Smart, Safeway*	½ Pot/85g	55	65	7.3	4.9	1.3	0.8
Cucumber & Mint, Fresh, Sainsbury's*	1oz/28g	34	123	4.5	3.7	10.0	0.0
Doritos Hot Salsa, Walkers*	1 Jar/326g	130	40	0.9	8.5	0.2	2.2
Doritos Mild Salsa, Walkers*	1oz/28g	11	40	0.9	8.5	0.2	2.2
Feta Cheese, Fresh, Tesco*	1oz/28g	81	288	6.8	7.9	25.5	0.7
Garlic & Herb, Marks & Spencer*	1oz/28g	88	315	2.4	7.1	30.6	0.5
Garlic & Herb, Reduced Fat, Marks & Spencer*	1 Serving/10g	10	95	6.0	8.1	4.0	0.5
Garlic & Herb, Tesco*	¼ Pack/42.5g	260	604	0.9	3.2	65.4	0.3
Garlic Herb & Rocket, Marks & Spencer*	1 Serving/25g	104	415	2.4	4.5	43.0	0.5
Garlic& Herb, Domino's Pizza*	1 Pot/28g	194	693	1.4	2.5	75.4	0.4
Garlic, Olive Oil & Butter, Pizza Express*	½ Pot/17g	106	621	1.5	2.8	67.4	0.5
Mature Cheddar Cheese & Chive, Fresh, Waitrose*	½ Pot/85g	393	462	5.8	2.4	47.7	1.7
Mexican Bean, Doritos*	1 Tbsp/20g	18	89	2.7	12.1	3.3	2.4
Mustard & Honey, Fresh, Sainsbury's*	1oz/28g	100	356	2.2	5.1	36.3	0.1
Mustard Mash, Marks & Spencer*	1oz/28g	25	90	2.6	12.7	3.1	1.0
Nacho Cheese, Marks & Spencer*	1oz/28g	76	270	9.8	3.8	23.7	0.4
Nacho Cheese, Sainsbury's*	1 Serving/50g	244	487	4.8	3.9	50.2	0.0
Onion & Garlic, 50% Less Fat, Asda*	1oz/28g	59	209	4.5	9.0	17.2	0.0
Onion & Garlic, Classic, Tesco*	1 Serving/30g	133	442	1.7	4.6	46.3	0.2
Onion & Garlic, Fresh, BGTY, Sainsbury's*	1oz/28g	56	201	4.4	4.8	18.2	0.8
Onion & Garlic, GFY, Asda*	1/5 Pot/34g	56	166	2.1	8.0	14.0	0.2
Onion & Garlic, Half Fat, Safeway*	½ Pot/85g	170	200	3.2	7.4	17.2	0.1
Onion & Garlic, Healthy Eating, Tesco*	1 Pot/170g	345	203	3.3	7.9	17.6	0.1
Onion & Garlic, Healthy Living, Tesco*	1 Serving/42.5g	81	188	2.5	6.3	17.0	0.1
Onion & Garlic, Healthy Selection, Somerfield*	1oz/28g	62	222	3.0	5.0	21.0	0.0
Onion & Garlic, Safeway*	¼ Pack/45g	216	480	1.7	4.7	50.4	0.1
Onion & Garlic, Tesco*	1oz/28g	177	632	2.5	4.4	67.2	0.1
Peanut, Satay Selection, Occasions, Sainsbury's*	1 Serving/2g	4	186	7.1	13.8	11.4	1.1
Pecorino, Basil & Pine Nut, Fresh, Waitrose*	½ Pot/85g	338	398	5.1	5.1	39.7	0.0
Red Pepper, Sainsbury's*	1 Pot/100g	103	103	2.3	14.6	4.0	0.0
Roast Onion, Garlic & Rocket, Reduced Fat, Waitrose*	1 Serving/25g	51	202	2.7	5.4	18.8	1.5
Salsa, GFY, Asda*	1 Pot/170g	68	40	1.2	8.0	0.4	1.5
Salsa, Kettle*	1 Serving/25g	10	39	1.7	8.0	0.0	0.0
Salsa, Less Than 5% Fat, Safeway*	½ Pot/85g	47	55	1.5	6.1	2.4	0.9
Smoked Salmon & Dill, Fresh, Waitrose*	½ Pot/85g	373	439	5.1	4.1	44.7	0.1
Smoked Salmon & Dill, Reduced Fat, Waitrose*	½ Pot/85g	184	217	3.9	6.1	19.7	1.1
Sour Cream & Chive, Asda*	1/5 Pot/33g	116	350	2.4	4.0	36.0	0.1
Sour Cream & Chive, BGTY, Sainsbury's	1oz/28g	46	165	4.9	3.4	14.6	0.7

	Measure	per Measure	Nutrition Values per 100g / 100ml				
	INFO/WEIGHT	KCAL	KCAL	PROT	CARB	FAT	FIBRE

DIP,

	Measure	per Measure	KCAL	PROT	CARB	FAT	FIBRE
Sour Cream & Chive, Doritos*	1 Tbsp/20g	64	322	2.5	3.1	33.3	0.1
Sour Cream & Chive, Fresh, Tesco*	½ Pot/75g	305	407	2.1	4.1	42.4	0.0
Sour Cream & Chive, Primula*	1oz/28g	97	346	5.0	1.8	35.3	0.0
Sour Cream & Chive, Reduced Fat, Asda*	1oz/28g	55	197	2.3	7.1	17.9	0.1
Sour Cream & Chive, Sainsbury's*	1 Serving/50g	157	314	2.2	2.5	32.8	0.1
Sour Cream, Co-Op*	1oz/28g	137	490	2.0	3.0	52.0	0.0
Soured Cream & Chive, 95% Fat Free, Marks & Spencer*	1oz/28g	25	90	6.5	9.6	2.8	0.5
Soured Cream & Chive, BGTY, Sainsbury's*	1 Serving/170g	131	77	6.0	6.6	2.9	0.3
Soured Cream & Chive, Classic, Tesco*	1 Serving/25g	81	323	1.7	3.2	33.7	0.2
Soured Cream & Chive, Reduced Fat, Tesco*	1 Serving/85g	159	187	3.6	6.1	16.5	0.4
Spiced Mango, Ginger & Chilli Salsa, Weight Watchers*	1 Serving/56g	48	85	1.0	19.9	0.2	2.6
Spicy Moroccan, BGTY, Sainsbury's*	½ Pot/84.8g	56	66	2.1	10.0	2.0	1.7
Sun Dried Tomato, Somerfield*	1oz/28g	155	552	1.0	5.0	59.0	0.0
Sweet & Sour, Marks & Spencer*	1oz/28g	36	130	0.7	31.4	0.1	0.5
Sweet & Zesty, Doritos*	1 Jar/375g	150	40	1.3	8.0	0.5	1.4
Sweet Chilli, Oriental Selection, Waitrose*	½ Pot/35.2g	88	250	1.3	59.4	0.8	0.4
Sweet Pepper & Ricotta, Asda*	1 Serving/20g	74	370	1.0	12.0	35.0	0.0
Tangy Barbecue, Marks & Spencer*	1oz/28g	28	100	1.1	22.2	0.6	0.6
Taramasalata, Sainsbury's	½ Pot/85g	407	479	4.0	7.5	48.1	0.1
Thousand Island, Marks & Spencer*	1oz/28g	69	245	2.1	9.4	22.2	0.7
Tikka, Classic, Fresh, Healthy Choice, Safeway*	1oz/28g	38	137	10.2	6.0	8.0	1.3
Tomato Ketchip, Asda*	1 Pack/25g	18	71	1.6	16.0	0.1	1.0
Tomato Salsa, Fresh, Waitrose*	1 Serving/50g	24	47	1.5	5.0	2.3	1.7
Tzatzaki, Somerfield*	1oz/28g	37	131	6.0	3.0	11.0	0.0
Yoghurt & Cucumber Mint, Tesco*	1oz/28g	34	121	7.0	7.2	7.1	0.6

DISCOS,

Cheese & Onion, KP*	1 Pack/28g	144	514	5.4	57.5	29.3	2.9
Pickled Onion, KP*	1 Bag/31g	155	500	3.7	58.6	27.8	2.9
Salt & Vinegar, KP*	1 Bag/31g	153	493	3.8	57.2	27.6	2.8

DOLLY MIXTURES,

Marks & Spencer*	1 Pack/125g	479	383	1.5	90.7	1.5	0.0
SmartPrice, Asda*	1 Sweet/2.9g	11	380	0.5	91.0	1.6	0.0

DOPIAZA,

Chicken, Safeway*	1 Pack/326g	450	138	10.4	5.3	8.4	1.4
Chicken, Tesco*	1 Pack/350g	448	128	10.8	5.3	7.1	0.6
Chicken, With Pilau Rice, Sharwood's*	1 Pack/375g	473	126	5.3	15.8	4.6	0.8
Chicken, With Pilau Rice, Tesco*	1 Pack/400g	424	106	5.7	12.3	3.8	1.5
Mushroom, Retail	1oz/28g	19	69	1.3	3.7	5.7	1.1
Mushroom, Tesco*	1 Pack/350g	291	83	3.0	6.7	4.9	1.3
Mushroom, Waitrose*	½ Pack/150g	81	54	2.2	4.3	3.1	2.3

DORITOS,

Chargrilled BBQ, Walkers*	1 Bag/35g	170	485	5.5	59.0	25.0	3.5
Cheesy 3D's, Walkers*	1 Pack/20g	89	445	7.0	68.0	16.0	3.0
Chilli Heatwave, Walkers*	1 Pack/33g	162	490	6.5	58.0	26.0	3.0
Cool Original, Walkers*	1 Bag/40g	202	505	7.5	58.0	27.0	3.0
Cool Spice 3Ds, Walkers*	1 Bag/24g	108	450	8.0	64.0	18.0	4.4
Corn Chips, Cool Original, Doritos*	1 Serving/200g	1010	505	7.5	58.0	27.0	3.0
Dippas Dipping Chips, Doritos*	1 Bag/35g	172	490	7.5	63.0	23.0	3.5
Hint Of Chilli Dippas, Walkers*	1 Bag/35g	173	495	7.0	61.0	25.0	3.5
Hint of Lime, Walkers*	1 Bag/35g	173	495	7.0	60.0	25.0	3.5
Latinos, Mexican Grill, Walkers*	1 Serving/35g	170	485	6.5	59.0	25.0	3.5
Latinos, Sour Cream & Sweet Pepper, Walkers*	1 Pack/40g	194	485	5.5	60.0	25.0	3.5
Lightly Salted Dippas, Walkers*	1 Bag/50g	245	490	7.5	63.0	23.0	3.5

D

	Measure INFO/WEIGHT	per Measure KCAL	Nutrition Values per 100g / 100ml KCAL	PROT	CARB	FAT	FIBRE
DORITOS,							
Mexican Hot, Walkers*	1 Bag/40g	202	505	8.0	57.0	27.0	3.5
Roast Onion & Garlic Dippas, Walkers*	1 Tsp/25g	83	333	3.2	8.7	31.7	0.9
Tangy Cheese Flavour Corn Chips, Doritos*	1 Bag/35g	177	505	8.5	57.0	27.0	3.5
Tangy Cheese, Walkers*	1 Bag/40g	202	505	8.5	57.0	27.0	3.5
DOUBLE DECKER,							
Cadbury's*	1 Bar/51g	237	465	5.2	64.9	20.7	0.0
With Nuts, Cadbury's*	1 Bar/60g	291	485	7.9	58.6	24.5	0.0
DOUGH BALLS,							
Cheese & Garlic, Occasions, Sainsbury's*	1 Ball/12g	41	341	10.3	33.4	18.5	2.1
Garlic & Herb, Occasions, Sainsbury's*	1 Ball/12g	41	343	8.4	38.7	17.2	2.2
Garlic, GFY, Asda*	1 Dough Ball/8.4g	20	250	9.0	49.0	2.0	2.0
Garlic, Healthy Living, Tesco*	1 Serving/40g	110	274	8.8	42.0	7.9	2.3
Pizza Express*	8 Balls/50g	200	400	14.3	85.0	3.2	0.0
Sainsbury's*	1 Ball/12g	41	343	8.4	38.7	17.2	2.2
DOUGHNUTS,							
Chocolate Donut, McDonald's*	1 Donut/79g	345	437	5.7	43.8	20.5	1.0
Chocolate Donut, McMini, McDonald's*	1 Donut/17.1g	64	375	6.8	46.9	17.8	1.6
Chocolate, Somerfield*	1 Doughnut/57g	203	356	7.8	43.8	16.6	1.7
Cinnamon Donut, McDonald's*	1 Donut/72g	302	419	5.1	43.1	25.1	3.8
Cream & Jam, Tesco*	1 Doughnut/90g	324	360	4.1	39.7	20.5	1.3
Custard & Bramley Apple, Sainsbury's*	1 Doughnut/91g	256	282	4.5	34.6	13.9	1.0
Custard, Tesco*	1 Doughnut/91g	266	292	4.1	33.4	15.8	1.0
Custard-Filled	1 Doughnut/75g	269	358	6.2	43.3	19.0	0.0
Dairy Cream & Jam, Somerfield*	1 Doughnut/80g	296	370	4.6	35.8	23.1	1.3
Dairy Cream Finger, Safeway*	1 Doughnut/98g	342	349	5.5	36.4	20.1	1.8
Dairy Cream, Marks & Spencer*	1oz/28g	87	310	4.9	40.8	14.1	1.3
Finger, Co-Op*	1 Doughnut/82g	299	365	4.0	45.0	18.0	2.0
Jam	1 Doughnut/75g	252	336	5.7	48.8	14.5	0.0
Jam, Marks & Spencer*	1 Doughnut/49g	141	287	5.0	57.6	4.0	1.3
Jam, Somerfield*	1 Doughnut/70.1g	213	304	6.8	47.9	9.5	1.6
Mini Donuts, Crunchie, Cadbury's*	1oz/28g	105	375	4.8	49.8	17.0	0.0
Original Glazed, Krispy Kreme*	1 Doughnut/52g	200	384	3.9	42.3	23.1	1.9
Ring	1 Doughnut/60g	238	397	6.1	47.2	21.7	0.0
Ring, Iced	1 Doughnut/70g	268	383	4.8	55.1	17.5	0.0
Ring, Waitrose*	1 Doughnut/107g	396	370	4.2	43.5	19.9	0.7
Strawberry Jam & Cream, Sainsbury's	1 Doughnut/80g	299	374	5.3	36.2	23.2	1.3
Sugared Donut, McDonald's*	1 Donut/72g	303	421	5.0	42.6	25.6	3.7
Toffee, Tesco*	1 Doughnut/75g	235	313	8.0	44.2	11.6	1.6
DOVER SOLE,							
Raw	1oz/28g	25	89	18.1	0.0	1.8	0.0
DR PEPPER*,							
Coca-Cola*	1 Bottle/500ml	210	42	0.0	10.9	0.0	0.0
Soda, Diet	1fl oz/30ml	0	1	0.0	0.1	0.0	0.0
DRAMBUIE,							
39% Volume	1 Shot/25ml	68	272	0.0	0.0	0.0	0.0
DREAM,							
Cadbury's*	1 Bar/45g	250	555	4.5	59.7	33.3	0.0
Double Fudge, Cadbury's*	1oz/28g	139	495	6.3	61.4	25.2	0.0
Snowbites, Cadbury's*	1 Serving/31.2g	169	545	3.1	59.7	32.7	0.0
White Chocolate, Cadbury's*	1 Piece/8g	44	555	4.5	59.7	33.3	0.0
DREAM TOPPING,							
Dry, Bird's*	1oz/28g	193	690	6.7	32.5	58.5	0.5
Made Up, Skimmed Milk, Bird's*	1oz/28g	21	75	2.0	4.8	5.3	0.0

	Measure INFO/WEIGHT	per Measure KCAL	Nutrition Values per 100g / 100ml				
			KCAL	PROT	CARB	FAT	FIBRE
DREAM TOPPING,							
Sugar Free, Dry, Bird's*	1oz/28g	195	695	7.3	30.5	60.5	0.5
DRESSING,							
Balsamic & Orange, Organic, Simply Delicious*	1 Serving/15ml	16	104	0.1	23.9	0.0	0.0
Balsamic Bliss, Ainsley Harriot*	1Tbsp/15g	41	272	0.8	19.3	21.1	0.0
Balsamic Vinegar & Oregano, Waitrose*	1 Serving/25g	101	404	0.6	8.2	41.0	0.4
Balsamic Vinegar & Smoked Garlic, Safeway*	1 Tbsp/15ml	19	125	0.1	28.3	0.9	0.5
Balsamic Vinegar, Asda*	1 Pack/44ml	121	275	0.9	7.0	27.0	0.0
Balsamic Vinegar, COU, Marks & Spencer*	1 Serving/30g	18	60	0.4	9.3	2.6	0.8
Balsamic With Garlic & Herbs, Finest, Tesco*	1 Serving/10g	13	133	0.3	3.4	13.1	0.1
Balsamic With Olive Oil, Pizza Express*	1 Serving/10g	42	421	0.3	10.3	41.2	0.0
Balsamic, Extra Virgin Olive Oil, TTD, Sainsbury's*	1 Tsp/5ml	19	376	0.5	12.8	36.0	0.4
Balsamic, Marks & Spencer*	1 Tbsp/15g	74	490	0.3	9.7	48.0	0.5
Balsamic, McDonald's*	1 Serving/32ml	73	226	0.3	11.6	7.5	0.0
Balsamic, New, Sainsbury's*	1 Tbsp/15g	58	389	0.6	18.3	34.8	0.8
Balsamic, Sainsbury's*	1 Tbsp/15ml	47	316	0.4	13.8	28.8	0.4
Blue Cheese, BGTY, Sainsbury's*	1 Tbsp/15ml	16	108	2.9	3.6	6.0	0.7
Blue Cheese, Fresh, Sainsbury's*	1 Dtsp/10ml	42	423	2.3	0.5	45.7	0.1
Blue Cheese, Healthy Eating, Tesco*	1 Tsp/5g	4	82	4.4	9.0	3.1	0.1
Blue Cheese, Hellmann's*	1 Tbsp/15g	69	459	0.7	6.3	47.2	1.1
Blue Cheese, Low Fat, Weight Watchers*	1oz/28g	17	59	1.5	5.8	3.4	0.0
Caesar Salad, Finest, Tesco*	1 Serving/25ml	119	477	1.9	2.8	50.9	0.2
Caesar Salad, Marks & Spencer*	1 Serving/10ml	52	515	1.8	2.2	55.2	0.5
Caesar Salad, Safeway*	1 Serving/25g	122	488	3.7	13.7	48.5	0.1
Caesar Style, GFY, Asda*	1 Sachet/44ml	34	77	5.0	9.0	2.3	0.0
Caesar Style, Kraft*	1 Tbsp/15ml	15	102	2.1	15.0	3.5	0.1
Caesar Style, Low Fat, Weight Watchers*	1 Tsp/6g	4	60	1.6	5.8	3.4	0.0
Caesar, 95% Fat Free, Tesco*	1 Tsp/6g	5	88	4.1	8.9	3.7	0.3
Caesar, BGTY, Sainsbury's*	1 Serving/25ml	27	108	1.3	8.3	7.8	0.9
Caesar, Chilled, Reduced Fat, Tesco*	1 Tsp/5ml	13	252	6.5	3.1	23.7	0.1
Caesar, Finest, Tesco*	1 Tbsp/15ml	72	477	1.9	2.8	50.9	0.4
Caesar, Fresh, Asda*	1 Dtsp/10ml	45	445	2.5	0.7	48.0	0.0
Caesar, Fresh, Marks & Spencer*	1 Tsp/6g	32	525	2.0	1.8	56.4	0.2
Caesar, Fresh, Sainsbury's*	1 Tsp/6g	29	479	3.0	1.1	51.4	0.2
Caesar, Gourmet, Fresh, Waitrose*	1 Tbsp/15ml	72	479	4.5	0.9	50.8	0.5
Caesar, Healthy Eating, Tesco*	1 Tbsp/15ml	11	74	3.0	8.4	2.8	0.2
Caesar, Hellmann's*	1 Tsp/6g	30	499	2.5	4.5	51.7	0.3
Caesar, Marks & Spencer*	1 Tsp/6g	31	523	2.0	1.8	56.4	0.2
Caesar, Reduced Fat, Marks & Spencer*	1 Tbsp/15ml	30	200	3.5	5.3	18.3	0.5
Caesar, Somerfield*	1 Serving/50ml	274	547	1.3	2.2	59.2	0.0
Caesar, Weight Watchers*	1 Serving/20g	16	80	3.3	14.7	0.9	0.2
Caesar, With Parmigiano Cheese, Marks & Spencer*	1 Serving/15g	72	480	3.5	3.1	50.4	0.0
Ceasar Salad, McDonald's*	1 Serving/50g	143	285	4.2	7.5	26.5	1.0
Citrus Salad, BGTY, Sainsbury's*	1 Tbsp/15ml	14	90	0.3	14.4	3.1	0.3
Classic Caesar, Sainsbury's*	1 Tsp/5ml	22	442	2.7	4.6	45.9	0.5
Classic French, Fresh, Marks & Spencer*	1 Serving/10ml	52	515	0.6	8.2	53.1	0.2
Classic French, Vinaigrette, Get Dressed, Kraft*	1 Tbsp/15ml	6	39	0.1	8.7	0.0	0.5
Classic Italian, Fat Free, Kraft*	1fl oz/30ml	10	32	0.1	6.8	0.0	0.6
Classic Italian, Get Dressed, Kraft*	1 Serving/25ml	30	120	0.1	5.6	10.3	0.5
Cream Cheese & Chive, Creamy Ranch, Kraft*	1 Serving/15ml	31	205	1.2	11.0	17.0	0.0
Creamy Caesar, Get Dressed, Kraft*	1 Serving/66.7g	68	102	2.1	15.0	3.5	0.1
Creamy Caesar, Waistline, Crosse & Blackwell*	1 Dtsp/11g	15	135	1.5	11.1	9.2	0.3
Creamy Ranch, 95% Fat Free, Kraft*	1 Tsp/6ml	7	111	1.4	14.5	5.0	0.3
Creamy Roasted Garlic, GFY, Asda*	1 Tbsp/15g	11	70	0.8	8.0	3.9	0.6

D

D

DRESSING,

	Measure INFO/WEIGHT	per Measuring KCAL	KCAL	PROT	CARB	FAT	FIBRE
			Nutrition Values per 100g / 100ml				
Creamy, Waistline, 93% Fat Free, Crosse & Blackwell*	1 Tsp/6g	7	120	1.0	14.4	6.4	0.2
Creme Fraiche, Salad, Kraft*	2 Tbsp/30ml	23	78	0.8	12.5	2.5	0.0
Extra Virgin Olive Oil & Balsamic Vinegar, Fresh, Safeway*	1 Serving/20ml	86	432	0.5	6.8	44.7	0.0
Fire Roasted Garlic & Thyme, Tesco*	1 Serving/10ml	45	447	0.9	4.7	47.2	0.0
Fire Roasted Red Pepper, Marks & Spencer*	1 Serving/30g	14	45	0.5	10.7	0.1	0.9
For Caesar Salad, McDonald's*	1 Serving/77ml	145	188	2.6	10.0	15.3	0.5
For Ranch Salad, McDonald's*	1 Serving/79ml	107	136	3.1	12.3	8.3	0.8
For Tuna, Coronation Style, Weight Watchers*	1 Can/80g	122	152	10.2	6.5	9.5	0.6
French Classic, Marks & Spencer*	1 Tbsp/15ml	77	516	0.6	8.2	53.1	0.2
French Dressing, Fresh, Co-Op*	1 Tbsp/15ml	70	467	0.0	0.0	46.7	0.0
French Salad, Marks & Spencer*	1 Serving/25ml	156	625	0.5	3.8	67.3	0.1
French Style Calorie-Wise Salad, Kraft*	1 Tbsp/15ml	24	160	0.0	18.7	10.7	0.0
French Style, Eat Smart, Safeway*	1 Serving/15ml	22	145	0.7	28.9	2.5	0.7
French Style, Oil Free, Healthy Eating, Tesco*	1 Tbsp/15g	5	30	0.3	6.0	0.2	1.4
French, BGTY, Sainsbury's*	1 Tbsp/15ml	12	79	1.1	8.8	4.4	0.5
French, COU, Marks & Spencer*	1/3 Bottle/105g	74	70	0.7	11.5	2.6	0.7
French, Chilled, Tesco*	1 Tbsp/15ml	63	421	1.1	15.1	39.6	0.0
French, Classic, Fat Free, Kraft*	1 Tsp/5ml	2	39	0.1	8.7	0.0	0.5
French, Fresh, Healthy Eating, Tesco*	1 Tbsp/15ml	8	56	1.1	6.7	2.8	0.0
French, Fresh, Organic, Sainsbury's*	1 Tbsp/15ml	45	301	0.4	5.5	31.0	0.4
French, Fresh, Safeway*	1 Tbsp/15ml	77	510	1.5	13.8	49.9	0.0
French, Fresh, Sainsbury's*	1 Tbsp/15ml	64	429	0.6	6.6	44.6	0.6
French, Fresh, Somerfield*	1 Tbsp/15ml	74	490	1.0	7.0	51.0	0.0
French, GFY, Asda*	1 Tbsp/15g	8	50	0.7	7.0	2.1	0.1
French, Good Intentions, Somerfield*	1 Serving/15ml	12	83	0.7	12.1	3.5	0.3
French, Healthy Eating, Tesco*	1 Tbsp/15ml	3	23	0.8	3.1	0.8	0.0
French, Less Than 3% Fat, Marks & Spencer*	1 Tbsp/15ml	10	68	0.7	11.5	2.6	0.7
French, Low Fat, Hellmann's*	1 Tbsp/15g	9	62	0.1	10.8	1.6	0.5
French, Low Fat, McDonald's*	1 Serving/22g	13	58	0.5	7.1	2.6	1.0
French, Luxury, Hellmann's*	1 Tbsp/15g	45	297	0.4	14.9	25.9	0.3
French, Oil Free, Perfectly Balanced, Waitrose*	1 Serving/15ml	11	72	2.2	12.2	1.6	1.1
French, Organic, Marks & Spencer*	1 Tbsp/15g	98	655	0.2	7.5	69.4	0.3
French, Organic, Sainsbury's*	1 Tbsp/15ml	11	71	0.2	8.3	4.1	0.5
French, Organic, Tesco*	1 Tsp/5ml	23	451	0.6	11.0	44.9	0.2
French, Reduced Fat, Marks & Spencer*	1 Tbsp/15g	11	70	0.7	11.5	2.8	0.7
French, Sainsbury's*	1 Tbsp/15ml	33	219	0.6	9.8	19.1	0.5
French, Virtually Fat Free, Aldi*	1 Serving/10g	3	33	0.9	6.7	0.3	1.1
Garlic & Herb, Perfectly Balanced, Waitrose*	1 Serving/50ml	68	135	0.6	29.9	1.4	0.8
Garlic & Herb, Reduced Calorie, Hellmann's*	1 Tbsp/15ml	35	232	0.6	12.8	19.3	0.4
Green Olive, Marks & Spencer*	1oz/28g	40	144	1.5	2.2	14.4	1.3
Green Thai, Coconut & Lemon Grass, Loyd Grossman*	1oz/28g	49	174	0.2	19.3	10.6	0.5
Healthy Choice, Safeway*	1 Tbsp/15ml	4	29	0.2	6.3	0.3	0.0
Herb & Garlic, 5% Fat, Get Dressed, Kraft*	1 Serving/25ml	29	116	1.3	15.5	5.1	0.2
Herb 'n' Garlic, Kraft*	1 Tbsp/15ml	17	116	1.3	15.5	5.1	0.2
Herb, Eat Smart, Safeway*	1 Tbsp/15ml	9	60	0.5	9.5	2.0	0.5
Honey & Mustard, Burger King*	1 Sachet/40g	32	80	1.5	14.5	2.0	0.8
Honey & Mustard, Eat Smart, Safeway*	1 Tbsp/15ml	25	165	0.8	37.5	0.9	0.3
Honey & Mustard, Finest, Tesco*	1 Serving/25ml	72	288	1.7	19.6	22.5	0.7
Honey & Mustard, Fresh, Marks & Spencer*	1 Serving/10ml	43	430	1.7	9.7	42.4	0.5
Honey & Mustard, Fresh, Safeway*	1 Serving/80ml	309	386	1.3	13.4	36.3	0.0
Honey & Mustard, GFY, Asda*	1 Tbsp/15g	13	89	1.5	13.0	3.4	0.8
Honey & Mustard, Healthy Eating, Tesco*	1 Tbsp/15g	12	79	1.5	12.1	2.7	0.9
Honey & Mustard, Kraft*	1 Serving/30ml	39	131	1.3	19.0	5.0	1.2

DRESSING,

INFO/WEIGHT	Measure	per Measure KCAL	Nutrition Values per 100g / 100ml				
			KCAL	PROT	CARB	FAT	FIBRE
Honey & Mustard, Low Fat, Marks & Spencer*	1 Serving/28g	31	110	1.5	20.0	2.5	0.8
Honey & Mustard, Marks & Spencer*	1 Tbsp/15ml	64	427	1.7	9.7	42.4	0.6
Honey & Mustard, Sainsbury's*	1 Serving/10ml	37	366	1.0	15.4	33.0	0.1
Honey Mustard, 5% Fat, Get Dressed, Kraft*	1 Serving/15ml	20	131	1.3	19.0	5.0	1.2
Honey, Orange & Mustard, BGTY, Sainsbury's*	1 Tbsp/15ml	16	105	1.8	18.6	2.5	1.8
Hot Lime & Coconut, BGTY, Sainsbury's*	1 Tbsp/15ml	8	51	0.7	5.7	2.9	1.2
Italian Balsamic, Loyd Grossman*	1 Serving/10g	36	357	0.9	13.1	33.5	0.1
Italian Salad, Hellmann's*	1 Serving/50g	103	206	0.7	12.8	16.7	0.0
Italian, Marks & Spencer*	1 Tbsp/15ml	62	415	0.9	8.9	41.5	1.0
Italian, Reduced Calorie, Hellmann's*	1 Serving/25ml	65	269	0.5	19.5	20.8	0.3
Italian, Waistline, 99% Fat Free, Crosse & Blackwell*	1 Tsp/6g	2	39	0.7	7.0	0.9	0.3
Lemon & Black Pepper, Good Intentions, Somerfield*	1 Tbsp/15ml	36	241	2.6	10.5	21.0	0.4
Lemon & Cracked Black Pepper, GFY, Asda*	1 Tbsp/15g	9	57	0.2	14.0	0.0	0.3
Lemon & Tarragon, Healthy Eating, Tesco*	1 Serving/10ml	11	113	1.1	21.6	2.4	0.0
Lemon & Watercress, COU, Marks & Spencer*	1 Serving/28g	14	50	0.4	8.5	1.8	0.5
Lemon, Feta & Oregano, Marks & Spencer*	1 Tbsp/15ml	24	160	1.3	8.2	13.4	0.6
Lime & Coriander, EPC*	1 Serving/50g	29	57	0.3	13.3	0.3	0.0
Lime & Coriander, Oil Free, Safeway*	1 Serving/25ml	18	70	1.5	13.2	1.2	0.0
Lime & Coriander, Oil Free, Waitrose*	1 Tsp/5ml	3	65	1.5	11.9	1.3	0.4
Lime & Coriander, Sainsbury's*	1 Tbsp/15ml	61	409	0.4	10.0	40.8	0.5
Lime Sublime Creamy, Ainsley Harriott*	1 Serving/28g	95	338	0.0	10.0	32.5	0.0
Mayonnaise Style, 90% Fat Free, Weight Watchers*	1 Tsp/11g	14	125	1.7	8.9	9.2	0.0
Mild Mustard, Low Fat, Weight Watchers*	1 Tbsp/10g	6	63	2.0	5.7	3.6	0.0
Miracle Whip, Fat Free, Kraft*	1 Tbsp/16g	15	94	0.0	18.8	0.0	0.0
Miracle Whip, Kraft*	1 Tbsp/15ml	60	400	0.3	11.0	39.0	0.1
Mustard & Dill, Perfectly Balanced, Waitrose*	1 Tbsp/15ml	24	159	1.1	31.5	3.2	1.1
Oil & Lemon	1 Tbsp/15g	97	647	0.3	2.8	70.6	0.0
Oil Free, Safeway*	1 Serving/30ml	23	75	1.6	14.0	1.4	0.0
Olive Oil & Balsamic Vinegar, Sainsbury's*	1 Serving/25ml	104	415	0.9	9.4	41.8	0.2
Olive Oil, Pizza Express*	2 Tsp/5g	29	573	1.4	3.4	63.0	0.0
Orange & Cracked Pepper, Tesco*	1 Tbsp/15ml	17	114	0.5	27.8	0.1	0.3
Orange & Honey, Luxury, Hellmann's*	1 Serving/15ml	17	110	0.8	17.5	3.5	0.8
Parmesan & Peppercorn, Loyd Grossman*	1oz/28g	98	349	2.1	5.9	35.2	0.5
Passion Fruit & Mango, Healthy Eating, Tesco*	1 Tbsp/15ml	25	169	0.6	36.7	2.2	0.4
Porcini Mushroom, TTD, Sainsbury's*	1 Tbsp/15g	46	308	1.3	3.3	32.1	5.4
Provencal Roasted Vegetable, Healthy Eating, Tesco*	1 Serving/10ml	8	75	1.0	12.1	2.5	0.4
Ranch Style, Asda*	1 Serving/44ml	37	85	3.5	9.0	3.9	0.0
Raspberry Balsamic Vinegar, EPC*	1 Serving/50g	34	67	0.4	15.7	0.1	0.6
Red Pepper, Marks & Spencer*	1 Tbsp/15ml	58	385	0.6	7.6	39.2	0.5
Roasted Red Pepper, TTD, Sainsbury's*	1 Tbsp/15ml	52	347	1.3	10.0	34.0	1.3
Salad Cream Style, Weight Watchers*	1 Tbsp/10g	12	115	1.5	16.2	4.4	0.0
Salad, BGTY, Sainsbury's*	1 Tbsp/15g	21	140	0.8	10.8	9.9	0.3
Salad, Healthy Eating, Tesco*	1 Tbsp/15g	22	144	0.8	12.9	9.9	0.3
Salad, Italian, Light, Calorie-Wise, Kraft*	1 Tbsp/15ml	6	40	0.0	5.3	2.7	0.0
Salad, Kickin' Mango, Oil Free, Ainsley Harriott*	1 Tbsp/15ml	14	92	0.1	21.1	0.1	0.0
Salad, Light, Heinz*	1 Serving/9.8g	24	244	1.8	13.5	19.9	0.0
Salad, Low Fat, Weight Watchers*	1 Tbsp/10g	11	106	1.5	15.4	4.3	0.0
Salad, Luxury Caesar, Hellmann's*	1 Serving/10ml	50	498	2.5	4.4	51.7	0.3
Salad, Pizza Express*	1 Serving/5g	29	573	1.4	3.4	63.0	0.0
Salad, Raspberry Balsamic, GFY, Asda*	1 Tbsp/15ml	6	40	0.7	9.3	0.7	1.3
Salad, Sun Dried Tomato & Chilli, Loyd Grossman*	1 Tsp/5g	18	361	0.9	5.3	37.3	0.9
Salad, Thousand Island, 95% Fat Free, Asda	1 Tsp/6g	6	99	1.6	12.6	4.7	0.5
Salad, Thousand Island, Hellmann's*	1oz/28g	97	347	0.9	15.2	31.0	1.0

INFO/WEIGHT	Measure	per Measure KCAL	Nutrition Values per 100g / 100ml				
			KCAL	PROT	CARB	FAT	FIBRE
DRESSING,							
Salad, Thousand Island, Reduced Calorie, Hellmann's*	1oz/28g	73	259	1.0	19.0	19.4	0.9
Salad, Vinaigrette Style, 95% Fat Free, Asda*	1 Tbsp/15ml	6	42	0.1	10.6	0.0	0.3
Seafood, Marks & Spencer*	1 Tsp/7g	39	555	0.9	4.9	59.3	0.9
Smoked Garlic & Parmesan, Sainsbury's*	1 Serving/20ml	83	415	3.0	4.0	41.1	0.3
Sun Dried Tomato, Safeway*	1 Serving/40ml	126	314	1.1	13.8	28.3	0.0
Sun Dried Tomato, Sainsbury's	1 Serving/15ml	27	179	1.5	10.9	14.4	0.6
Sweet Chilli, COU, Marks & Spencer*	1 Tbsp/15ml	9	60	0.5	14.5	0.5	0.4
Sweetfire Pepper, Healthy Eating, Tesco*	1 Serving/10ml	7	67	0.6	15.7	0.3	0.1
Texas Ranch, Frank Cooper*	1 Pot/28g	128	457	1.9	9.4	45.8	0.2
Thai Lime & Coriander, EPC*	1 Serving/25g	26	104	1.6	22.3	0.9	1.1
Thousand Island	1 Tsp/6g	19	323	1.1	12.5	30.2	0.4
Thousand Island, BGTY, Sainsbury's*	1 Serving/50g	53	105	1.2	21.6	1.1	2.9
Thousand Island, COU, Marks & Spencer*	1 Serving/30g	26	85	1.4	14.2	2.6	1.1
Thousand Island, Fat Free, Kraft*	1floz/30ml	27	90	0.5	20.5	0.2	2.8
Thousand Island, Healthy Eating, Tesco*	1 Serving/25ml	47	189	2.9	10.0	15.1	0.0
Thousand Island, Original, Kraft*	1oz/28g	102	365	0.9	19.0	31.5	0.4
Thousand Island, Reduced Calorie	1 Tsp/6g	12	195	0.7	14.7	15.2	0.0
Thousand Island, Tesco*	1 Serving/30ml	130	433	1.0	12.3	42.2	0.0
Tomato & Basil, Fresh, Somerfield*	1 Tbsp/15ml	52	348	2.0	7.0	35.0	0.0
Tomato & Basil, Healthy Eating, Tesco*	1 Serving/10ml	7	73	0.5	12.9	2.0	0.5
Tomato & Herb, Less Than 1% Fat, Asda*	1 Tbsp/15g	6	43	0.7	8.0	0.9	0.4
Tomato & Olive, Eat Smart, Safeway*	1 Tbsp/15ml	15	100	0.7	22.8	0.7	1.8
Tomato & Red Pepper, BGTY, Sainsbury's*	1 Serving/50ml	42	83	1.1	10.0	4.3	0.6
Tuna Mayonnaise & Sweetcorn Style, Weight Watchers*	1 Can/80g	114	142	11.5	6.2	8.0	0.1
Tuna, Tomato & Herb, Weight Watchers*	1 Can/80g	79	99	11.6	5.1	3.6	0.5
Vinaigrette, BGTY, Sainsbury's*	1 Serving/10ml	5	47	0.1	11.7	0.0	0.3
Waistline, Reduced Fat, Crosse & Blackwell*	1oz/28g	29	105	0.8	11.6	6.0	0.3
Whole Grain Dijon Mustard & Honey, Loyd Grossman*	1oz/28g	93	331	1.2	9.9	31.8	1.3
Yoghurt & Mint, GFY, Asda*	1 Tbsp/15ml	9	60	3.9	8.0	1.4	0.0
Yoghurt & Mint, Healthy Eating, Tesco*	1 Tbsp/15g	20	135	1.5	26.2	2.7	0.0
Yoghurt Mint Cucumber, Marks & Spencer*	1 Tsp/5ml	6	115	1.0	8.7	8.0	0.0
Yogurt & Mint, Safeway*	1 Serving/15ml	54	360	3.3	6.7	35.3	0.0
DRIED FRUIT,							
& Nut, The Mix, Whitworths*	1 Pot/90g	341	379	4.1	63.1	14.6	7.3
& Nuts, Marks & Spencer*	1 Serving/28g	126	450	12.4	44.3	25.3	6.0
5 Fruits, Ready To Eat, Sundora*	½ Pack/100g	233	233	1.6	58.4	0.4	6.8
Baby Mix, Somerfield*	1 Packet/250g	520	208	3.1	47.2	0.7	5.3
Exotic Mix, Sundora*	1 Sm Pack/50g	138	276	2.3	60.6	2.7	3.8
Exotic, Ready To Eat, Sainsbury's*	1/3 Pack/85g	241	284	0.2	70.6	0.1	2.4
Luxury Mixed, Co-Op*	1 Serving/40g	114	285	2.0	68.0	0.6	4.0
Mix, Taste Of New England, Asda*	1 Serving/50g	158	316	2.2	74.0	1.2	5.0
Mixed	1 Tbsp/25g	67	268	2.3	68.1	0.4	2.2
Mixed, Tesco*	1 Tbsp/25g	71	284	2.3	67.9	0.4	2.2
Salad, Whitworths*	1 Serving/62g	113	183	2.9	41.8	0.5	6.6
DRIFTER,							
Nestle*	1 Finger/31g	143	478	3.7	67.3	21.5	0.8
DRINKING CHOCOLATE,							
Cadbury's*	3 Heaped Tsp/25g	91	365	6.4	72.4	5.8	0.0
Dry Powder, Cocodirect*	1 Serving/18g	67	372	8.9	65.1	8.4	0.0
Dry, Asda*	1 Serving/30g	111	370	6.0	73.0	6.0	0.0
Dry, Cadbury's*	1 Serving/18g	66	367	6.4	72.4	5.8	0.0
Dry, Tesco*	3 Heaped Tsps/25g	92	368	6.4	72.6	5.8	4.2
Dry, Waitrose*	3 Tsp/12g	48	403	7.2	79.9	6.1	2.9

	Measure INFO/WEIGHT	per Measure KCAL	Nutrition Values per 100g / 100ml				
			KCAL	PROT	CARB	FAT	FIBRE
DRINKING CHOCOLATE,							
Made Up, BGTY, Sainsbury's*	1 Serving/178.1g	114	64	3.9	11.4	0.2	0.7
Maxpax, Light, Suchard*	1 Cup/10.5g	39	355	20.0	56.0	5.5	9.3
Powder, Made Up With Skimmed Milk	1 Mug/227ml	134	59	3.5	10.8	0.6	0.0
Powder, Made Up With Whole Milk	1 Mug/227ml	204	90	3.4	10.6	4.1	0.0
DRIPPING,							
Beef	1oz/28g	249	891	0.0	0.0	99.0	0.0
DUCK,							
Breast, Meat Only, Cooked, Average	1oz/28g	48	173	25.3	1.8	7.1	0.0
Breast, Meat Only, Raw, Average	1 Serving/160g	206	129	22.6	0.1	4.3	0.2
Leg, Meat & Skin, Average	1oz/28g	80	286	17.2	9.5	20.0	0.4
Raw, Meat, Fat & Skin	1oz/28g	109	388	13.1	0.0	37.3	0.0
Roasted, Meat, Fat & Skin	1oz/28g	118	423	20.0	0.0	38.1	0.0
DUCK &,							
Orange Sauce, Gressingham Fillets, TTD, Sainsbury's*	½ Pack/250g	633	253	24.9	0.1	17.0	1.0
Plum Sauce, Roasted, Sainsbury's*	½ Pack/150g	272	181	12.0	13.5	8.8	0.7
DUCK A L' ORANGE,							
Roast, Marks & Spencer*	½ Pack/270g	554	205	12.5	4.1	15.6	0.6
DUCK AROMATIC,							
Crispy, Asda*	1/3 Pack/165.7g	470	283	19.0	18.0	15.0	0.8
Crispy, Ready Meals, Marks & Spencer*	1 Pack/275g	591	215	12.6	10.3	13.6	1.2
Crispy, Somerfield*	1 Serving/265g	782	295	18.1	14.0	18.5	0.7
Crispy, Tesco*	1 Serving/61g	131	214	14.6	12.3	11.8	0.9
With Plum Sauce, Tesco*	½ Pack/250g	350	140	9.3	15.2	4.6	0.3
With a Plum Sauce, Finest, Tesco*	1 Serving/250g	400	160	16.1	11.3	5.6	4.6
DUCK CANTONESE,							
Style, Roast, Tesco*	1 Pack/300g	375	125	8.2	17.9	2.3	0.5
DUCK IN,							
A Pluauce, Crispy, Marks & Spencer*	1 Pack/325g	569	175	10.7	11.2	9.6	0.9
Orange Sauce, Iceland*	1 Serving/200g	336	168	11.3	7.4	10.4	1.2
Oriental Sauce, Iceland*	1 Pack/201.1g	352	175	12.0	6.3	11.3	1.5
Red Wine Sauce, Free Range Fillets, Waitrose*	½ Pack/250g	378	151	16.4	4.1	7.7	2.2
DUCK PEKING,							
Crispy, Sainsbury's*	½ Pack/300g	1236	412	19.5	0.6	36.9	0.0
DUCK WITH,	0.8						
Apple & Calvados, Goujons, GFY, Asda*	1 Pack/320g	362	113	16.0	6.0	2.8	0.8
Diuelection, Marks & Spencer*	1 Serving/67g	194	290	7.2	34.8	13.4	2.2
Noodles, Shanghai Roast, Sainsbury's*	1 Pack/450g	581	129	5.6	18.0	3.8	1.2
Orange Sauce, Fillet, Waitrose*	½ Pack/250g	418	167	12.0	7.1	9.9	3.9
Pancakes, Shredded, Iceland*	1 Pack/220g	471	214	20.4	27.0	2.7	1.5
Pancakes, With Hoisin Sauce, Marks & Spencer*	1 Pack/80g	136	170	13.0	19.9	4.0	0.9
DUMPLINGS,							
Average	1oz/28g	58	208	2.8	24.5	11.7	0.9
Homestyle, Aunt Bessie's*	1 Dumpling/49g	187	382	8.5	39.5	21.1	2.1
Prawn Sui Mai, Marks & Spencer*	1 Serving/25g	29	115	14.6	5.4	3.7	0.6
Prawn, Cantonese, Crispy, Sainsbury's*	1 Dumpling/11g	27	241	9.3	20.9	13.4	1.1

D

INFO/WEIGHT	Measure per Measuring KCAL	Nutrition Values per 100g / 100ml KCAL	PROT	CARB	FAT	FIBRE
EASTER EGG,						
Buttons, Cadbury's*	1 Pack/105g	557	530	7.8	56.9	30.0	0.0
Disney, Nestle*	1 Egg/65g	342	526	6.3	59.7	29.1	0.6
Kit Kat, Chunky, Nestle*	1 Pack/245g	1279	522	6.0	60.0	28.7	0.8
Mars*	1 Serving/62.6g	283	449	4.2	69.0	17.4	0.0
Milk Chocolate, Nestle*	½ Egg/42g	205	489	5.0	65.2	23.1	0.5
Milky Bar, Nestle*	1 Egg/40g	182	454	4.2	70.8	17.2	0.0
Smarties, Nestle*	½ Egg/37.5g	182	478	4.8	69.6	20.0	0.7
ECLAIR,						
Chocolate & Caramel, Finest, Tesco*	Eclair/100g	389	389	4.0	32.1	27.2	0.5
Chocolate, Healthy Living, Tesco*	1 Serving/77g	192	249	6.8	27.1	12.6	0.9
Dairy Cream, Safeway*	1 Eclair/59.3g	210	356	4.1	24.9	26.7	0.4
EEL,						
Jellied	1oz/28g	27	98	8.4	0.0	7.1	0.0
Raw	1oz/28g	47	168	16.6	0.0	11.3	0.0
EGGS,						
Dried	1oz/28g	159	568	48.4	0.0	41.6	0.0
Duck, Boiled & Salted	1 Egg/75g	149	198	14.6	0.0	15.5	0.0
Duck, Whole, Raw	1 Egg/75g	122	163	14.3	0.0	11.8	0.0
Free Range, Large, Average	1 Egg/65g	95	147	12.4	0.0	10.8	0.0
Free Range, Medium, Average	1 Serving/56g	82	147	12.3	0.1	10.9	0.0
Fried	1 Med/60g	107	179	13.6	0.0	13.9	0.0
Large, Average	1 Serving/63g	92	147	12.5	0.1	10.8	0.1
Medium, Average	1 Egg/56g	82	148	12.5	0.0	10.8	0.0
Medium, Boiled, Average	1 Size One/67g	98	147	12.5	0.0	10.8	0.0
Poached	1 Med/50g	74	147	12.5	0.0	10.8	0.0
Quail, Whole, Raw	1oz/28g	42	151	12.9	0.0	11.1	0.0
Scrambled	1 Egg/68g	100	147	12.5	0.0	10.8	0.0
Scrambled With Milk	2 Med Eggs/120g	296	247	10.7	0.6	22.6	0.0
Turkey, Whole, Raw	1oz/28g	46	165	13.7	0.0	12.2	0.0
White, Dried	1oz/28g	83	295	73.8	0.0	0.0	0.0
Whites, Raw, Average	1oz/28g	12	44	10.0	0.2	0.3	0.0
Whole, Raw	1 Size Three/57g	84	147	12.5	0.0	10.8	0.0
Yolks, Raw	1oz/28g	95	339	16.1	0.0	30.5	0.0
ELDERBERRIES,						
Average	1oz/28g	10	35	0.7	7.4	0.5	0.0
ENCHILADAS,						
Chicken, Asda*	1 Serving/500g	690	138	10.0	17.0	6.0	1.0
Chicken, In A Spicy Salsa & Bean Sauce, Asda*	½ Pack/211.9g	373	176	10.0	16.0	8.0	0.0
Chicken, Marks & Spencer*	1 Serving/225g	405	180	9.2	11.5	10.6	2.2
Chicken, Perfectly Balanced, Waitrose*	1 Pack/450g	482	107	6.9	12.7	3.2	1.1
Chicken, Safeway*	1 Serving/230g	384	167	7.9	22.9	4.9	1.0
Chilli Beef, Asda*	1 Serving/225g	428	190	12.0	13.0	10.0	1.1
Vegetable, GFY, Asda*	1 Pack/350g	399	114	4.4	14.0	4.5	1.3
ENDIVE,						
Raw	1oz/28g	4	13	1.8	1.0	0.2	2.0
ENERGY DRINK,						
Explosade, Sportisotonic, Aldi*	1 Can/500ml	140	28	0.0	6.6	0.0	0.0
Isotonic, Citrus, Sports, Asda*	1 Bottle/500ml	150	30	0.0	7.0	0.0	0.0
Orange, Iso, Body Fortress*	1 Serving/43g	154	362	0.0	90.4	0.0	0.0
Red Rooster, Hi Energy Mixer, Cott Beverages Ltd*	1 Can/250ml	113	45	0.6	10.3	0.0	0.0
Red Thunder, Aldi*	1 Can/250ml	113	45	0.6	10.3	0.0	0.0
Redcard, Britvic*	1 Can/330ml	96	29	0.1	7.0	0.0	0.0
V, Frucor Beverages*	1 Can/250ml	113	45	0.0	11.2	0.0	0.0

	Measure INFO/WEIGHT	per Measure KCAL	Nutrition Values per 100g / 100ml				
			KCAL	PROT	CARB	FAT	FIBRE
FAGGOTS,							
In Rich Gravy, Iceland*	1 Faggot/81g	116	143	6.5	15.9	6.4	1.1
Mushy Peas & Mash, Sainsbury's*	1 Pack/450g	576	128	6.0	16.3	4.3	1.6
Pork, Mr Brains*	1 Serving/189g	242	128	5.3	11.9	6.6	0.6
FAGOTTINI,							
Mushroom, Sainsbury's*	½ Pack/155g	339	219	10.2	27.7	7.5	2.7
FAJITA,							
Beef, GFY, Asda*	½ Pack/208g	354	170	11.0	21.0	4.7	1.6
Chicken With Salsa & Sour Cream Dips, Safeway*	1 Pack/242g	390	161	9.8	16.7	6.1	1.9
Chicken With Sour Cream, Asda*	1 Pack/440g	713	162	10.3	17.1	8.3	1.3
Chicken, American Style, Tesco*	1 Pack/275g	388	141	9.5	14.2	5.1	1.0
Chicken, Asda*	½ Pack/225g	371	165	11.0	20.0	4.5	3.5
Chicken, BGTY, Sainsbury's*	1 Pack/299g	389	130	11.0	18.3	1.4	1.6
Chicken, Boots*	1 Pack/223g	448	201	9.1	25.0	7.2	3.9
Chicken, COU, Marks & Spencer*	1 Pack/230g	288	125	10.0	16.5	2.3	1.5
Chicken, Char Grilled Style, Safeway*	½ Pack/234.8g	588	250	17.2	40.5	2.3	1.9
Chicken, Eat Smart, Safeway*	1 Serving/248g	290	117	10.6	14.8	1.7	1.6
Chicken, GFY, Asda*	1 Serving/225g	297	132	10.0	17.0	2.7	1.1
Chicken, Healthy Eating, Tesco*	½ Pack/225g	248	110	9.2	15.3	1.3	0.5
Chicken, Just Cook, Sainsbury's*	½ Pack/200g	200	100	18.5	3.1	1.5	2.0
Chicken, Marks & Spencer*	1 Pack/230g	345	150	8.6	17.7	5.3	1.0
Chicken, Sainsbury's*	½ Pack/250g	360	144	11.5	13.8	4.8	1.2
Chicken, Salt Balanced, COU, Marks & Spencer*	1 Pack/230g	253	110	9.5	13.2	2.3	1.7
Chicken, Shapers, Boots*	1 Pack/192g	307	160	9.3	24.0	3.0	1.7
Chicken, Tesco*	1 Serving/275g	388	141	9.5	14.2	5.1	1.0
Chicken, Weight Watchers*	1 Pack/175g	271	155	8.6	24.1	2.7	1.2
Dinner Kit, With Tortillas, Old El Paso*	1 Serving/163g	559	343	10.0	60.0	7.0	0.0
Gammon Steaks, Tesco*	1 Serving/250g	368	147	17.5	5.3	6.2	0.0
Steak, Marks & Spencer*	1oz/28g	53	190	8.9	17.2	9.1	0.6
Texan, Seasoning & Sauce, Discovery*	1 Jar/360g	328	91	2.7	13.2	2.6	3.3
Tuna, Eat Smart, Safeway*	1 Pack/263g	302	115	9.7	15.0	1.8	1.4
Tuna, Sainsbury's*	1 Pack/450g	752	167	11.4	18.2	5.4	1.6
Vegetable, Somerfield*	1 Pack/500g	640	128	3.0	17.0	5.0	0.0
Vegetable, Tesco*	1 Wrap/112g	133	119	4.2	14.3	5.0	1.1
FALAFEL,							
Cauldron Foods*	1 Falafel/25g	37	149	7.6	15.3	6.4	7.1
Fried in Vegetable Oil	1oz/28g	50	179	6.4	15.6	11.2	3.4
Marks & Spencer*	1 Serving/165g	388	235	8.3	19.2	13.7	8.4
Mini, Marks & Spencer*	1 Falafel/13g	40	310	7.9	28.1	18.4	2.6
Mini, Sainsbury's*	1 Serving/168g	499	297	8.0	26.8	17.6	3.2
Vegetarian, Organic, Waitrose*	1 Felafel/25g	55	220	8.0	23.3	10.5	7.6
FANTA,							
Apple Splash, The Coca Cola Co*	1 Bottle/500ml	100	20	0.0	4.7	0.0	0.0
Fruit Twist, The Coca Cola Co*	1 Serving/250ml	133	53	0.0	13.0	0.0	0.0
Lemon, The Coca Cola Co*	1 Can/330ml	165	50	0.0	12.0	0.0	0.0
Light, The Coca Cola Co*	1 Glass/250ml	5	2	0.0	0.5	0.0	0.0
Orange, Diet, The Coca Cola Co*	1 Serving/250ml	8	3	0.0	0.5	0.0	0.0
Orange, McDonald's*	1 Reg/250ml	108	43	0.0	10.4	0.0	0.0
Orange, The Coca Cola Co*	1 Can/330ml	142	43	0.0	10.4	0.0	0.0
FARFALLE,							
Bows, Dry, Average	1 Serving/75g	265	353	11.4	72.6	1.9	1.9
Dry, Average	1 Serving/50g	178	357	11.7	73.5	1.8	2.7
Salmon & Broccoli, Eat Smart, Safeway*	1 Pack/380g	361	95	6.4	11.6	2.4	1.1

F

	Measure INFO/WEIGHT	per Measure KCAL	Nutrition Values per 100g / 100ml				
			KCAL	PROT	CARB	FAT	FIBRE
FENNEL,							
Florence, Boiled in Salted Water	1oz/28g	3	11	0.9	1.5	0.2	2.3
Florence, Raw	1oz/28g	3	12	0.9	1.8	0.2	2.4
FENUGREEK LEAVES,							
Raw	1oz/28g	10	35	4.6	4.8	0.2	0.0
FETTUCINI,							
Cajun Chicken, COU, Marks & Spencer*	1 Pack/350g	370	106	7.9	13.9	2.1	1.1
Chicken Mushroom, GFY, Asda*	1 Pack/400g	359	90	7.3	11.3	1.8	0.7
Dry, Buitoni*	1oz/28g	101	362	12.2	74.4	1.7	0.0
Garlic Mushroom, GFY, Asda*	1 Pack/450g	347	77	3.3	12.0	1.7	0.9
FIG ROLLS,							
Asda*	1 Biscuit/19g	71	372	4.8	68.0	9.0	0.0
Go Ahead, McVitie's*	1 Roll/15g	55	365	4.2	76.8	4.6	2.9
Jacob's*	1 Biscuit/17g	61	357	3.5	67.7	8.0	3.9
Sainsbury's*	1 Biscuit/18g	70	377	4.8	68.3	9.4	2.6
Vitalinea, Jacob's*	1 Biscuit/18g	61	339	3.7	68.2	5.8	3.8
FIGS,							
Dried, Average	1 Fruit/14g	32	232	3.6	53.2	1.1	8.7
Raw, Average	1 Fig/35g	16	45	1.3	9.8	0.2	1.5
FIORELLI,							
Egg, Marks & Spencer*	1 Serving/100g	355	355	13.9	68.5	2.8	3.0
FISH,							
Balls, Gefilte, Marks & Spencer*	1 Pack/200g	280	140	14.1	11.9	3.9	1.0
Balls, Steamed	1oz/28g	21	74	11.8	5.5	0.5	0.0
Battered, Portion, Ross*	1 Fish/100g	203	203	10.4	16.1	10.8	0.8
Breaded, Asda*	1 Serving/150g	351	234	15.0	12.0	14.0	0.5
Breaded, Fishysaurus, Young'uns, Youngs*	1 Fishysaurus/70g	143	204	11.4	15.5	10.7	1.5
Breaded, Pollock, Asda*	1 Portion/97g	200	206	12.0	17.0	10.0	1.0
Dried, Small, Ogura*	1 Serving/10g	32	320	69.0	0.3	3.0	0.0
Fillets, Breaded, White, Tesco*	1 Piece/95g	205	216	10.0	20.9	10.3	1.1
Fillets, Crunch Crumb, Steaks, Bird's Eye*	1 Steak/110g	264	240	15.0	18.0	12.0	0.9
Fillets, Garlic & Herb, Youngs*	1 Fillet/117.6g	262	222	11.0	16.2	12.6	1.4
Fillets, Lemon & Pepper, Young's*	1 Fillet/130g	283	218	10.3	15.3	12.9	4.3
Fillets, White, Natural, Tesco*	1 Fillet/100g	72	72	16.6	0.0	0.6	0.0
In Batter, Morrisons*	1 Fish/140g	235	168	14.0	15.0	5.8	0.2
Nuggets, Battered, Farmfoods*	1oz/28g	60	214	10.9	16.0	11.8	0.7
Salted, Chinese, Steamed	1oz/28g	43	155	33.9	0.0	2.2	0.0
Simply, Bird's Eye*	1 Serving/123.7g	246	198	12.6	14.2	10.1	0.6
Steaks, Chip Shop, Youngs*	1 Portion/100g	198	198	11.0	14.9	10.4	0.9
Steaks, Skinless & Boneless, Youngs*	1 Serving/104.7g	225	214	10.5	16.6	11.8	0.8
FISH & CHIPS,							
Breaded, Budgens*	1 Pack/340g	544	160	8.6	19.3	5.3	1.5
Co-Op*	1 Pack/250g	388	155	6.0	18.0	6.0	2.0
Cod, Asda*	1 Serving/279.5g	451	161	8.0	21.0	5.0	1.1
Cod, Waitrose*	1 Pack/283g	849	300	14.4	33.7	12.0	4.8
Haddock, Marks & Spencer*	1oz/28g	52	187	7.0	22.6	7.6	2.1
Haddock, Scottish, & Chunky Chips, Marks & Spencer*	1 Pack/343.3g	515	150	7.3	16.0	6.5	2.1
Safeway*	1 Pack/249g	518	208	8.0	25.0	8.4	3.5
Somerfield*	1 Serving/283g	495	175	8.0	22.0	6.0	0.0
Tesco*	1 Serving/300g	489	163	5.5	21.2	6.2	1.6
FISH BAKE,							
Cheese & Leek, Healthy Living, Tesco*	1 Pack/400g	340	85	11.0	5.8	2.0	0.8
Cheese Pastry, Bird's Eye*	1 Piece/171g	390	228	9.3	17.2	13.6	1.9
Haddock & Prawn, COU, Marks & Spencer*	1 Bake/340g	289	85	7.3	7.3	2.8	0.4

F

	Measure INFO/WEIGHT	per Measure KCAL	Nutrition Values per 100g / 100ml				
			KCAL	PROT	CARB	FAT	FIBRE
FISH BAKE,							
Italiano, Bird's Eye*	½ Pack/205g	180	88	11.5	3.6	3.1	0.3
Mediterranean, Healthy Living, Tesco*	½ Pack/200g	158	79	10.3	5.9	1.6	1.4
Vegetable Tuscany, Bird's Eye*	½ Pack/204.3g	235	115	13.1	4.3	5.0	0.2
FISH CAKES,							
Breaded, Sainsbury's*	1 Cake/42g	75	179	10.0	16.2	8.1	0.7
Bubbly Batter, Youngs*	1 Fish Cake/44g	109	247	7.1	20.5	15.1	1.4
Captain's Coins, Mini, Bird's Eye*	1 Fish Cake/20g	34	168	10.1	13.3	8.3	0.9
Cod, & Pancetta, Cafe Culture, Marks & Spencer*	1 Fish Cake/85g	166	195	9.2	7.2	15.5	2.0
Cod, & Parsley, Waitrose*	1 Fish Cake/85g	157	185	10.7	13.1	10.0	2.0
Cod, Asda*	1 Fish Cake/72g	163	227	7.0	25.0	11.0	2.3
Cod, Fresh, Asda*	1 Serving/75g	164	219	7.0	23.0	11.0	1.6
Cod, Homemade	1 Fish Cake/50g	121	241	9.3	14.4	16.6	0.7
Cod, In Crunch Crumb, Bird's Eye*	1 Fish Cake/52g	85	163	8.8	16.2	7.0	0.7
Cod, Marks & Spencer*	1 Fish Cake/85g	162	190	8.4	15.7	10.1	1.6
Cod, Sainsbury's*	1 Fish Cake/90g	176	195	9.5	17.5	9.0	0.8
Cod, Tesco*	1 Fish Cake/49g	110	224	8.9	23.8	10.4	0.2
Cod, Youngs*	1 Cake/75g	144	192	7.6	22.1	8.3	1.1
Crab, & Prawn, Thai, Tesco*	1 Fish Cake/115g	269	234	8.8	17.4	14.4	1.2
Crab, Marks & Spencer*	1oz/28g	63	225	8.0	18.0	13.2	1.4
Great Value, Iceland*	1 Fish Cake/42.3g	74	175	9.1	20.3	6.4	1.6
Grilled	1 Fish Cake/50g	77	154	9.9	19.7	4.5	0.0
Haddock, Asda*	1 Fish Cake/88g	181	206	8.0	21.0	10.0	1.5
Haddock, Marks & Spencer*	1 Pack/170g	289	170	8.6	13.7	9.2	1.3
Haddock, Sainsbury's*	1 Fish Cake/90g	173	192	11.7	18.1	8.1	0.7
Haddock, Smoked, Asda*	1 Fish Cake/90g	185	206	10.0	19.0	10.0	1.4
Haddock, Smoked, Frozen, Waitrose*	1 Fish Cake/85g	157	185	11.0	12.4	10.1	2.1
Haddock, Smoked, Marks & Spencer*	1 Cake/85g	153	180	10.6	13.4	9.4	2.6
Haddock, Smoked, Sainsbury's*	1 Fish Cake/63g	127	201	11.0	17.8	9.5	2.1
Haddock, Smoked, Tesco*	1 Cake/85g	128	151	5.8	17.1	6.6	1.3
Haddock, Smoked, Waitrose*	1 Serving/170g	372	219	8.9	19.5	11.7	2.1
Halibut Cod Loin, Finest, Tesco*	1 Serving/115g	213	185	8.8	21.3	7.2	1.4
Halibut, TTD, Sainsbury's*	1 Cake/115g	289	251	10.0	17.6	15.6	1.3
Makes Sense, Somerfield*	1 Fish Cake/42.2g	70	166	8.2	18.7	6.5	1.5
Marks & Spencer*	1 Fish Cake/80g	180	225	8.0	18.0	13.3	0.0
Prawn, Battered, Asda*	1 Serving/90g	182	202	10.0	15.6	11.1	1.0
Prawn, Sainsbury's*	1 Fish Cake/90g	154	171	10.3	15.6	7.5	0.7
Prawn, Tesco*	1 Fish Cake/90g	209	232	8.2	29.2	9.1	1.8
Salmon, & Broccoli, Morrisons*	1 Fish Cake/60g	126	210	9.8	17.2	11.9	1.3
Salmon, & Broccoli, With Bubble & Squeak, Safeway*	1 Pack/389g	513	132	3.9	15.0	6.3	1.0
Salmon, & Dill, Waitrose*	1 Fish Cake/85g	179	211	9.1	17.6	11.6	2.2
Salmon, & Tarragon, Waitrose*	1 Fish Cake/85g	179	211	11.9	14.3	11.8	2.2
Salmon, Asda*	1 Fish Cake/86g	215	250	8.0	23.0	14.0	1.4
Salmon, Bird's Eye*	1 Fish Cake/50g	84	168	9.5	12.2	9.0	1.4
Salmon, Homemade	1 Fish Cake/50g	137	273	10.4	14.4	19.7	0.7
Salmon, In Crunch Crumb, Bird's Eye*	2 Cakes/99g	214	216	9.7	15.0	13.0	1.4
Salmon, Marks & Spencer*	1 Fish Cake/86g	181	210	9.1	15.1	12.7	1.7
Salmon, Morrisons*	1 Fish Cake/90g	241	268	10.1	27.6	13.1	1.5
Salmon, Sainsbury's*	1 Fish Cake/90g	167	186	13.2	17.4	7.1	1.2
Salmon, Tesco*	1 Fishcake/90g	239	266	11.4	21.3	15.0	0.0
Salmon, With Lemon Butter Sauce, Finest, Tesco*	1 Cake/220g	524	238	7.3	10.9	18.3	1.0
Salmon, With Lemon Butter Sauce, Marks & Spencer*	1 Serving/215g	420	195	9.3	7.6	13.9	2.3
Salmon, With Parsley Sauce, Finest, Tesco*	½ Pack/170g	350	206	8.6	11.7	13.9	1.0
SmartPrice, Asda*	1 Fish Cake/41.5g	77	188	7.0	22.0	8.0	0.9

F

FISH CAKES,	Measure INFO/WEIGHT	per Measure KCAL	KCAL	PROT	CARB	FAT	FIBRE
Thai Style, Sainsbury's*	1 Fish Cake/49g	69	141	12.0	13.8	4.2	1.7
Thai, Frozen, Sainsbury's*	1 Cake/15g	28	187	21.3	9.3	7.3	0.7
Thai, Oriental Selection, Waitrose*	1 Cake/11.2g	18	161	17.8	15.8	3.0	1.5
Thai, Tesco*	4 Cakes/88.9g	148	166	17.4	12.8	5.0	1.1
Tuna, & Red Pepper, Waitrose*	1 Fish Cake/85g	175	206	9.5	15.4	11.8	1.6
Tuna, Asda*	1 Fish Cake/87g	171	196	9.0	22.0	8.0	1.3
Tuna, Marks & Spencer*	1 Fish Cake/85g	170	200	10.0	14.9	11.0	1.6
Tuna, Sainsbury's*	1 Cake/90g	197	219	14.4	26.7	6.1	0.9
Tuna, Tesco*	1 Fishcake/90g	222	247	12.8	25.4	10.5	0.2
Value, Tesco*	1 Fish Cake/40.4g	73	183	7.1	21.2	7.8	1.2
FISH FINGERS,							
Chip Shop, Youngs*	1 Finger/30g	75	251	9.3	16.6	16.4	1.2
Cod, Fillet, 100%, Bird's Eye*	1 Finger/30g	56	186	13.0	15.6	7.9	0.7
Cod, Fillet, Asda*	1 Finger/31g	66	214	13.0	18.0	10.0	0.0
Cod, Fillet, Chunky, Marks & Spencer*	1 Finger/40g	70	175	12.0	17.3	6.0	1.0
Cod, Fillet, Iceland*	1 Finger/30g	62	205	13.0	19.5	8.3	1.4
Cod, Fillet, Waitrose*	1 Finger/30g	55	183	11.9	16.9	7.5	0.7
Cod, Fried in Blended Oil	1 Finger/28g	67	238	13.2	15.5	14.1	0.6
Cod, Frozen	1 Finger/28g	48	170	11.6	14.2	7.8	0.6
Cod, Grilled	1 Finger/28g	56	200	14.3	16.6	8.9	0.7
Cod, Morrisons*	1 Finger/30g	54	180	11.7	16.4	7.5	1.1
Cod, Tesco*	1 Finger/30g	56	188	12.3	16.8	7.9	1.6
Economy, Sainsbury's*	1 Finger/26g	51	198	12.6	17.7	8.5	1.3
Free From, Sainsbury's*	1 Finger/30g	56	188	11.4	18.0	7.8	0.7
Haddock, Fillet, Asda*	1 Finger/30g	62	205	14.0	17.0	9.0	0.0
Haddock, Fillet, Bird's Eye*	1 Finger/29g	48	167	12.4	13.2	7.2	0.9
Haddock, In Crunchy Crumb, Morrisons*	1 Finger/30g	57	190	13.1	16.3	8.0	1.1
Hoki, Fillet, Bird's Eye*	1 Finger/30g	58	193	12.6	15.6	8.9	0.7
Iceland*	1 Finger/23g	44	192	11.5	17.3	8.5	1.3
In Batter, Crispy, Bird's Eye*	1 Finger/29g	63	218	10.4	15.8	12.6	0.4
In Batter, Crispy, Jumbo, Morrisons*	1 Finger/71g	146	205	11.3	12.2	12.5	0.6
McDonald's*	3 Fingers/74g	164	221	13.5	20.2	9.6	3.1
Sainsbury's*	1 Finger/27g	52	194	13.4	16.0	8.5	0.7
SmartPrice, Asda*	1 Finger/25g	46	184	12.0	16.0	8.0	1.1
Value, Tesco*	1 Finger/25g	42	166	11.5	11.9	8.1	1.7
FISH IN,							
Butter Sauce, Steaks, Ross*	1 Serving/150g	126	84	9.1	3.2	3.9	0.1
Parsley Sauce, Steaks, Ross*	1 Serving/150g	123	82	9.1	3.1	3.7	0.1
FIVE SPICE,							
Powder, Sharwood's*	1oz/28g	48	172	12.2	11.6	8.6	23.4
FLAKE,							
Cadbury's*	1 Bar/34g	180	530	8.1	55.7	30.7	0.0
Dipped, Cadbury's*	1 Bar/44.3g	233	530	7.0	55.3	31.0	0.0
Snow, Cadbury's*	1 Bar/36g	198	550	7.2	60.1	30.9	0.0
FLAN,							
Cauliflower Cheese, Safeway*	1 Sm Flan/150g	420	280	7.3	25.0	16.5	2.0
Cauliflower, Cheese & Broccoli, Hot, Sainsbury's*	¼ Flan/100g	303	303	6.4	24.7	19.8	1.2
Cheese & Onion, Marks & Spencer*	1oz/28g	81	290	6.1	25.1	18.7	1.4
Cheese & Potato, Hot, Tesco*	¼ Flan/100g	282	282	6.0	20.0	19.7	2.3
Chicken & Smoked Bacon, Hot, Sainsbury's*	¼ Flan/100g	293	293	10.2	21.5	18.5	1.2
Mediterranean Vegetable, Co-Op*	¼ Flan/87.5g	189	215	4.0	22.0	12.0	3.0
Parsnip, Broccoli & Gruyere, Safeway*	½ Flan/200g	534	267	7.0	23.0	16.4	2.8
Pastry, With Fruit	1oz/28g	33	118	1.4	19.3	4.4	0.7

F

	Measure INFO/WEIGHT	per Measure KCAL	Nutrition Values per 100g / 100ml				
			KCAL	PROT	CARB	FAT	FIBRE
FLAN,							
Potato, Cheddar & Onion, Safeway*	1 Serving/150g	420	280	6.4	25.6	16.7	2.7
Smoked Ham Cheese & Leek, Safeway*	½ Flan/200g	520	260	8.0	20.0	16.4	2.0
Sponge With Fruit	1oz/28g	31	112	2.8	23.3	1.5	0.6
FLAN CASE,							
Sponge, Average	1oz/28g	90	320	7.0	62.5	5.4	0.7
FLAPJACK,							
All Butter, Blackcurrant Jam, Marks & Spencer*	1 Serving/65g	280	430	4.8	60.5	18.6	2.2
All Butter, Marks & Spencer*	1 Flapjack/31.8g	141	440	6.1	56.1	21.2	4.4
All Butter, Organic, Sainsbury's*	1 Serving/35g	156	446	5.3	54.5	23.0	2.7
All Butter, Sainsbury's*	1 Flapjack/35g	156	446	5.7	54.5	22.8	2.7
Apple & Raspberry, Fox's*	1 Flapjack/26g	105	403	4.8	52.5	19.4	3.7
Apple & Sultana, Mr Kipling*	1 Flapjack/27g	123	456	4.6	59.0	22.4	3.6
Apricot & Raisin, Waitrose*	1 Flapjack/38g	143	376	4.7	64.3	11.1	5.8
Apricot, COU, Marks & Spencer*	1oz/28g	96	342	5.4	77.1	2.1	2.0
Apricot, Food To Go, Marks & Spencer*	1 Bar/86g	348	405	4.7	64.4	16.2	4.3
Apricot, Sweet, Shapers, Boots*	1 Flapjack/55g	188	341	5.7	65.0	11.0	4.1
Average	1oz/28g	136	484	4.5	60.4	26.6	2.7
Cherry & Sultana, Marks & Spencer*	1oz/28g	111	395	5.4	63.7	13.0	5.1
Chewy Nutty, Coffee Republic*	1 Flapjack/33g	145	440	7.1	50.9	23.2	2.0
Chocolate & Hazelnut, Marks & Spencer*	1 Flapjack/71g	330	465	7.3	55.6	25.5	3.8
Chocolate Chip, Boots*	1 Flapjack/75g	313	417	5.6	65.0	15.0	3.5
Chocolate Chunk, Boots*	1 Slice/75g	351	468	5.7	55.0	25.0	3.0
Chocolate Dipped, Marks & Spencer*	1 Flapjack/96g	442	460	6.1	61.3	22.4	3.0
Chocolate, McVitie's*	1 Flapjack/85g	422	496	6.6	56.6	27.1	3.2
Chunky Chocolate, Marks & Spencer*	1 Flapjack/32.5g	152	460	5.7	57.5	22.9	2.1
Co-Op*	1 Flapjack/37.6g	177	465	5.0	54.0	25.0	4.0
Crazy Raizin, Fabulous Bakin' Boys*	1 Pack/90g	378	420	6.0	60.0	17.0	4.0
Fingers, GFY, Asda*	1 Finger/37g	130	350	5.0	60.0	10.0	3.5
Fruit & Nut, Organic, Evernat*	1oz/28g	136	484	4.5	60.4	26.6	0.0
Fruit With Raisins, Boots*	1 Pack/75g	329	439	5.4	57.0	21.0	3.5
Fruit, GFY, Asda*	1 Flapjack/45g	173	384	6.0	72.0	8.0	3.4
Fruit, Mr Kipling*	1 Flapjack/24g	103	430	4.8	51.4	22.9	0.0
Fruit, Somerfield*	1 Flapjack/45g	182	405	6.3	57.9	16.5	5.0
Fruit, Weight Watchers*	1 Slice/30g	106	354	6.1	68.2	6.3	4.5
Fruity, Waitrose*	1 Serving/50g	199	398	6.1	62.9	13.5	3.9
Golden Oaty Fingers, Tesco*	1 Finger/25g	113	450	5.7	59.6	21.1	3.4
Marks & Spencer*	1 Flapjack/53g	228	430	6.0	59.1	19.0	3.5
Mini Bites, Mark & Spencer*	1 Bite/14g	70	500	6.4	62.8	25.0	2.6
Mixed Fruit, Fabulous Bakin' Boys*	1 Serving/90g	351	390	5.0	67.0	10.0	3.0
Mixed Fruit, Organic, Evernat*	1oz/28g	136	484	4.5	60.4	26.6	0.0
Really Raspberry, Fabulous Bakin' Boys*	1 Flapjack/90g	378	420	6.0	60.0	18.0	0.0
Safeway*	1 Flapjack/60g	255	425	5.9	55.1	20.1	2.7
Snickers, McVitie's*	1 Flapjack/65g	320	492	9.5	47.6	29.3	0.0
Sultana, Tesco*	1 Flapjack/50g	173	346	5.0	36.2	20.1	3.7
Syrup, McVitie's*	1 Flapjack/85g	417	490	6.5	56.0	26.7	3.4
Toffee, Finest, Tesco*	1 Piece/35g	156	446	4.9	63.6	19.1	1.3
Tropical Mix, Reduced Fat, Fabulous Bakin' Boys*	1 Flapjack/90g	347	385	6.0	63.0	12.0	3.0
Weight Watchers*	1 Slice/30g	109	364	6.5	71.0	6.0	3.9
With Sultanas, Tesco*	1 Flapjack/49g	217	442	5.3	57.9	21.0	3.7
FLATBREAD,							
BBQ Chicken, Improved, Shapers, Boots*	1 Pack/165.4g	267	162	10.0	25.0	2.3	1.2
BBQ Style Chicken, Shapers, Boots*	1 Serving/108g	187	173	10.0	23.0	4.6	2.8
Cajun Style Chicken, GFY, Asda*	1 Wrap/176.3g	231	131	9.0	21.0	1.2	0.9

FLATBREAD,	Measure INFO/WEIGHT	per Measure KCAL	Nutrition Values per 100g / 100ml				
			KCAL	PROT	CARB	FAT	FIBRE
Chargrilled Chicken, COU, Marks & Spencer*	1 Pack/163.3g	245	150	10.8	23.0	1.9	5.2
Cheese & Garlic, Sainsbury's*	¼ Bread/100g	340	340	9.3	39.3	16.2	2.2
Cheese & Onion Swedish Style, Shapers, Boots*	1 Flatbread/127g	265	209	10.0	24.0	8.1	1.3
Chicken & Black Bean Sauce, Shapers, Boots*	1 Pack/204g	249	122	8.7	20.0	0.8	1.7
Chicken Caesar, Shapers, Boots*	1 Serving/160g	254	159	13.0	22.0	2.1	2.0
Chicken Fajita, Improved, Shapers, Boots*	1 Pack/201.3g	302	150	11.0	21.0	2.6	1.8
Chicken Fajita, Shapers, Boots*	1 Serving/200g	276	138	9.0	20.0	2.4	2.6
Chicken Tikka, BGTY, Sainsbury's*	1 Flatbread/188g	241	128	10.3	18.5	1.4	2.0
Chicken Tikka, Shapers, Boots*	1 Flatbread/164g	282	172	11.0	24.0	3.6	1.4
Chinese Chicken, COU, Marks & Spencer*	1 Flatbread/156g	281	180	13.9	24.3	2.8	2.2
Chinese Chicken, Shapers, Boots*	1 Pack/159.3g	273	172	11.0	29.0	1.3	1.8
Falafel & Houmous, Starbucks*	1 Pack/232.8g	405	174	5.9	28.8	3.9	2.5
Feta Cheese, Shapers, Boots*	1 Pack/165.6g	256	154	6.7	23.0	3.9	1.4
Garlic & Parsley, BGTY, Sainsbury's*	¼ Bread/62.6g	160	254	9.5	40.3	6.1	3.7
Garlic & Rosemary, Accompaniments, Sainsbury's*	¼ Flatbread/60g	184	306	8.7	40.3	12.2	2.7
Greek Feta Salad, Boots*	1 Pack/157.5g	242	153	6.4	24.0	3.6	1.2
Greek Style Salad, Waitrose*	1 Pack/171.8g	280	163	7.4	22.3	4.9	3.3
Greek Style, GFY, Asda*	1 Flatbread/165g	256	155	7.0	22.0	4.3	2.1
Greek, McDonald's*	1 Flatbread/100g	433	433	21.2	47.3	20.7	3.8
Italian Chicken, Improved, Shapers, Boots*	1 Pack/151.1g	263	174	11.0	22.0	4.5	1.8
Italian Chicken, Shapers, Boots*	1 Pack/168.4g	265	158	10.0	22.0	3.3	1.3
Japapeno & Sweet Pepper, Sainsbury's*	1 Serving/100g	263	263	10.9	40.9	6.2	2.6
Mediterranean Chicken, Ginsters*	1 Pack/167.8g	302	180	10.6	25.5	4.0	0.0
Mediterranean Tuna, Ginsters*	1 Pack/166.9g	297	178	10.3	25.6	3.8	0.0
Mexican Style Chicken, Safeway*	1 Pack/150g	248	165	11.6	24.7	2.1	1.9
Peking Duck, Less Than 3% Fat, Shapers, Boots*	1 Pack/155.7g	246	158	7.2	27.0	2.4	1.9
Prawn Korma, Shapers, Boots*	1 Pack/169.0g	267	158	8.8	22.0	3.9	1.3
Rancher's Chicken, COU, Marks & Spencer*	1 Pack/174g	270	155	10.9	23.0	2.0	1.5
Ranchers Chicken, Shapers, Boots*	1 Pack/194.2g	303	156	12.0	22.0	2.2	1.5
Salsa Chicken, Shapers, Boots*	1 Pack/190.7g	329	172	11.0	22.0	4.4	1.6
Spicy Chicken & Salsa, Healthy Living, Tesco	1 Flatbread/183g	251	137	10.1	21.1	1.4	1.2
Spicy Chicken, Shapers, Boots*	1 Pack/181.4g	291	161	11.0	23.0	2.5	0.0
Spicy Mexican, New, Shapers, Boots*	1 Pack/183.7g	282	153	8.0	24.0	2.7	1.9
Spicy Mexican, Shapers, Boots*	1 Pack/190g	296	156	7.0	23.0	4.0	3.7
Sticky BBQ Style Chicken, Shapers, Boots*	1 Pack/158.4g	273	173	10.0	23.0	4.6	2.8
Tomata & Chilli, Sainsbury's*	¼ Bread/65g	155	238	11.9	36.9	4.7	2.8
Tomato & Chilli, BGTY, Sainsbury's*	¼ Flatbread/100g	155	155	7.7	24.0	3.1	1.8
Tomato & Garlic, Italian Style, Iceland*	1 Serving/75g	195	260	6.3	32.3	11.8	2.4
Vegetable & Salsa, Healthy Living, Tesco*	1 Flatbread/193g	262	136	7.9	22.2	1.8	1.2
FLOUR,							
Brown, Chapati	1 Tbsp/20g	67	333	11.5	73.7	1.2	0.0
Brown, Wheat	1oz/28g	90	323	12.6	68.5	1.8	6.4
Chick Pea	1oz/28g	88	313	19.7	49.6	5.4	10.7
Corn, Tesco*	1 Serving/90g	316	351	0.4	87.0	0.1	0.1
Millet	1oz/28g	99	354	5.8	75.4	1.7	0.0
Plain, Average	1oz/28g	98	349	10.3	73.8	1.5	2.2
Potato	1oz/28g	92	328	9.1	75.6	0.9	5.7
Rice	1oz/28g	102	366	6.4	80.1	0.8	2.0
Rye, Whole	1oz/28g	94	335	8.2	75.9	2.0	11.7
Soya, Full Fat, Average	1oz/28g	118	422	37.9	19.8	21.8	11.6
Soya, Low Fat	1oz/28g	99	352	45.3	28.2	7.2	13.5
Speciality Gluten Free, Doves Farm*	1 Serving/100g	353	353	4.7	85.2	1.8	2.7
Strong, Brown Bread, Average	1 Serving/100g	311	311	14.0	61.0	1.8	6.4

	Measure INFO/WEIGHT	per Measure KCAL	Nutrition Values per 100g / 100ml				
			KCAL	PROT	CARB	FAT	FIBRE
FLOUR,							
Strong, Canadian, Waitrose*	1oz/28g	94	337	12.6	68.6	1.4	3.1
Strong, Wholemeal, Average	1 Serving/100g	315	315	13.3	60.6	2.2	9.0
White, Average	1oz/28g	89	319	9.8	66.8	1.0	2.9
White, Chapati,	1 Tbsp/20g	67	335	9.8	77.6	0.5	0.0
White, Self Raising, Average	1oz/28g	94	336	9.9	71.8	1.3	2.9
White, Wheat, Average	1oz/28g	95	341	10.5	76.5	1.4	3.1
Wholemeal, Average	1 Serving/25g	78	312	12.6	61.9	2.2	9.0
Wholemeal, Self Raising, Tesco*	1oz/28g	89	317	11.5	62.9	2.2	9.0
FLYING SAUCERS,							
Co-Op*	1 Sweet/1g	4	370	0.5	90.0	1.0	0.6
FLYTE,							
Mars*	1 Bar/45g	196	435	3.6	72.3	14.7	0.0
Snacksize, Mars*	1 Bar/22.5g	98	436	3.8	72.5	14.5	0.0
FOOL,							
Apricot, BGTY, Sainsbury's*	1 Pot/113g	87	77	3.5	8.0	3.4	0.3
Apricot, Fruit, Tesco*	1 Pot/113g	200	177	2.6	16.4	11.2	0.3
Blackcurrant, Asda*	1 Serving/114g	89	78	3.6	10.0	2.6	0.6
Blackcurrant, BGTY, Sainsbury's*	1 Pot/113g	89	79	3.5	10.4	2.6	0.6
Fruit	1oz/28g	46	163	1.0	20.2	9.3	1.2
Fruit, Better for You, Morrisons*	1 Pot/114g	96	84	3.4	10.1	3.4	0.3
Gooseberry, Better For You, Morrison's*	1 Pot/114g	99	87	3.4	10.7	3.4	0.4
Gooseberry, Fruit, BGTY, Sainsbury's*	1 Pot/121g	93	77	2.9	10.0	2.8	0.8
Gooseberry, Fruit, Co-Op*	1 Pot/114g	211	185	3.0	22.0	10.0	1.0
Gooseberry, Fruit, Somerfield*	1 Pot/114g	215	189	3.0	19.0	11.0	0.0
Gooseberry, Real Fruit, Safeway*	1 Pot/114g	215	189	2.8	19.1	11.3	0.5
Lemon, Better For You, Morrison's*	1 Pot/114g	96	84	3.4	10.1	3.4	0.3
Lemon, Fruit, BGTY, Sainsbury's*	1 Pot/113g	94	83	3.4	9.7	3.4	0.3
Lemon, Fruit, Shapers, Boots*	1 Pot/113g	105	93	3.8	11.0	3.8	0.0
Raspberry, Fruit, Tesco*	1 Pot/113g	234	207	2.6	23.6	11.3	0.3
Raspberry, Pret A Manger*	1 Pot/140g	188	134	1.7	12.4	8.9	0.4
Rhubarb, Fruit, BGTY, Sainsbury's*	1 Pot/120g	90	75	2.9	9.5	2.8	0.3
Rhubarb, Fruit, Somerfield*	1 Pot/114g	201	176	3.0	16.0	11.0	0.0
Rhubarb, Fruit, Waitrose*	1 Pot/114g	182	160	2.7	11.9	11.3	0.3
Strawberry, Fruit, BGTY, Sainsbury's*	1 Pot/120g	100	83	3.0	11.5	2.8	1.0
Strawberry, Fruit, Co-Op*	1 Pot/114g	188	165	2.0	18.0	9.0	0.8
Strawberry, Fruit, Shapers, Boots*	1 Pot/112g	90	81	3.5	9.2	3.4	0.3
Strawberry, Fruit, Somerfield*	1 Pot/114g	201	176	3.0	16.0	11.0	0.0
Strawberry, GFY, Asda*	1 Pot/114g	95	83	3.8	11.0	2.6	0.8
Strawberry, Real Fruit, Safeway*	1 Pot/114g	197	173	2.7	15.4	11.2	0.3
FOR MILK,							
Peachy Banana, Robinson's*	1 Serving/50ml	79	158	0.0	39.0	0.0	0.0
Strawberry & Raspberry, Robinson's*	1 Serving/50ml	69	137	0.0	34.0	0.0	0.0
FRANKFURTERS,							
Average	1 Frankfurter/42g	123	292	12.0	1.3	26.6	0.0
Vegetarian, Tivall*	3 Sausages/90g	220	244	18.0	7.0	16.0	3.0
FRAZZLES,							
Bacon, Smiths, Walkers*	1 Bag/23g	108	470	8.0	59.0	22.4	0.0
FRENCH FRIES,							
Cheese & Onion, Walkers*	1 Bag/22g	95	430	4.8	64.0	17.0	4.2
Fish & Chips, Walkers*	1 Bag/19.0g	79	415	4.2	64.0	16.0	4.3
Ready Salted, Walkers*	1 Bag/22g	97	440	4.6	65.0	18.0	4.2
Salt & Vinegar, BGTY, Sainsbury's*	1 Bag/15g	50	335	5.5	75.3	1.4	2.7
Salt & Vinegar, COU, Marks & Spencer*	1 Bag/25g	88	350	5.1	80.9	1.6	2.3

F

	Measure INFO/WEIGHT	per Measure KCAL	Nutrition Values per 100g / 100ml				
			KCAL	PROT	CARB	FAT	FIBRE
FRENCH FRIES,							
Salt & Vinegar, Eat Smart, Safeway*	1 Bag/20g	75	375	5.1	80.9	1.6	2.3
Salt & Vinegar, Walkers*	1 Bag/22g	94	425	4.6	64.0	17.0	4.1
Scampi, Smiths, Walkers*	1 Bag/27g	134	496	13.0	52.5	26.0	0.0
Spicy Curly, Asda*	1 Serving/75g	134	179	2.3	29.0	6.0	2.5
Walkers*	1 Pack/22g	94	425	4.5	64.0	17.0	4.1
Worcester Sauce, Walkers*	1 Bag/22g	92	420	5.1	64.0	16.0	4.2
FRENCH TOAST,							
Asda*	1 Slice/8g	30	381	10.0	74.0	5.0	4.0
Co-Op*	1 Serving/8g	31	385	10.0	72.0	6.0	5.0
Sainsbury's*	1 Serving/8g	31	382	10.0	72.0	6.6	5.0
FRIES,							
9/16" Straight Cut Home, Deep Fried, McCain*	1oz/28g	65	233	3.2	32.7	9.9	0.0
9/16" Straight Cut Home, Oven Baked, McCain*	1oz/28g	53	188	3.2	31.5	5.5	0.0
American Style, Frozen, Thin, Tesco*	1 Serving/125g	208	166	2.2	21.1	8.1	1.9
American, 3 Way Cook, Somerfield*	1oz/28g	43	155	3.0	25.0	5.0	0.0
American, Oven, Asda*	1 Serving/180g	432	240	3.4	34.0	10.0	3.0
Cafe Frites, Marks & Spencer*	1 Pack/200g	440	220	3.0	32.7	8.7	2.4
Chips, Retail	1oz/28g	78	280	3.3	34.0	15.5	2.1
Crinkle, Home, McCain*	1 Serving/135g	248	184	2.3	25.5	9.0	0.0
Crispy French, McCain*	1 Serving/100g	165	165	2.1	24.3	6.6	0.0
Crispy Savoury Seasoning Southern, McCain*	1 Serving/100g	179	179	2.8	26.4	6.9	0.0
Home Oven Chips, McCain*	1oz/28g	53	188	3.2	31.5	5.5	0.0
Home, Frozen, McCain*	1 Serving/100g	141	141	2.0	26.1	4.4	0.0
Home, Oven Cooked, McCain*	1 Serving/100g	202	202	3.2	37.5	6.1	0.0
King Size, Salted, Burger King*	1 Bag/170g	539	317	3.5	42.3	14.7	2.9
McDonald's *	1 Regular/78g	207	265	3.8	36.3	11.5	3.6
Medium, KFC*	1 Serving/100g	294	294	3.8	36.4	14.8	3.1
Medium, Salted, Burger King*	1 Bag/116g	369	318	3.4	42.2	14.6	3.4
Oven, Straight Cut, Morrisons*	1 Serving/100g	149	149	2.8	24.6	4.3	2.6
Regular, Burger King*	1 Serving/150g	483	322	3.0	43.0	16.0	0.0
Small, Salted, Burger King*	1 Bag/74g	229	310	2.7	41.8	14.8	2.7
Southern Spicy Spiral, Deep Fried, McCain*	1oz/28g	58	208	2.7	26.4	10.2	0.0
Southern Spicy Spiral, Oven Baked, McCain*	1oz/28g	46	165	1.7	24.6	6.6	0.0
Southern, Oven Cook, McCain*	1 Serving/80g	146	182	2.7	26.1	8.4	0.0
Southern, Straight Cut, Oven Baked, McCain*	1oz/28g	74	263	4.1	37.1	10.9	0.0
Wimpy*	1 Serving/100g	295	295	3.7	42.4	12.1	3.5
FRISPS,							
Tangy Salt & Vinegar, Frisps*	1 Bag/30g	160	532	5.0	52.6	33.5	2.9
Tasty Cheese & Onion, Frisps*	1 Bag/28g	166	537	5.5	53.2	33.6	3.2
FROMAGE FRAIS,							
Apple Pie, Low Fat, Sainsbury's*	1 Pot/90g	108	120	6.7	17.3	2.6	0.3
Apple Strudel, Safeway*	1 Pot/100g	116	116	6.6	14.8	3.4	0.7
Apricot, Makes Sense, Somerfield*	1 Pot/60g	67	112	5.9	13.2	4.0	0.0
Apricot, Tesco*	1 Pot/100g	77	77	6.5	6.0	3.0	1.3
Apricot, Weight Watchers*	1 Pot/100g	47	47	6.2	5.4	0.1	0.2
Bakewell Tart Flavour, BGTY, Sainsbury's*	1 Pot/100g	54	54	7.6	5.5	0.2	1.1
Banana, Organic, Yeo Valley*	1 Pot/90g	118	131	6.6	12.6	6.0	0.2
Banoffee Pie Flavour, Low Fat, Safeway*	1 Pot/100g	135	135	6.8	17.6	4.1	0.2
Banoffee Toffee, Thick & Creamy, Weight Watchers*	1 Pot/100g	59	59	5.2	9.3	0.1	1.0
Banoffee Toffee, Weight Watchers*	1 Pot/100g	64	64	5.7	10.0	0.1	1.1
Black Cherry, Asda*	1 Pot/100g	113	113	4.1	13.0	5.0	0.0
Black Cherry, GFY, Asda*	1 Pot/100g	54	54	6.0	7.0	0.2	0.0
Blackcurrant, Eat Smart, Safeway*	1 Pot/100g	60	60	7.9	6.1	0.2	0.5

FROMAGE FRAIS,	INFO/WEIGHT	KCAL	KCAL	PROT	CARB	FAT	FIBRE
Blackcurrant, GFY, Asda*	1 Pot/100g	43	43	6.0	4.2	0.2	0.0
Blackcurrant, Healthy Eating, Tesco*	1 Pot/100g	59	59	7.7	6.5	0.2	0.6
Blackcurrant, Healthy Living, Tesco*	1 Pot/100g	56	56	6.2	7.4	0.2	0.4
Blackcurrant, Safeway*	1 Pot/100g	121	121	6.7	15.8	3.4	0.9
Blue Parrot Cafe, Sainsbury's*	1 Serving/50g	49	98	6.6	11.0	3.1	0.2
COU, Marks & Spencer*	1 Pot/100g	48	48	7.8	4.5	0.1	0.5
Cherries & Chocolate, Finest, Tesco.*	1 Serving/165g	299	181	5.4	20.1	8.8	0.7
Cherry Pie Flavour, BGTY, Sainsbury's*	1 Pot/100g	54	54	7.6	5.5	0.2	1.1
Cherry, 0% Fat, Vitalinea, Danone*	1 Serving/150g	89	59	6.1	8.0	0.2	1.6
Chocolate & Orange, Thick & Creamy, Weight Watchers*	1 Pot/100g	59	59	5.2	9.3	0.1	1.0
Chocolate & Orange, Weight Watchers*	1 Pot/100g	64	64	5.7	10.0	0.1	1.1
Chocolate Fudge, Smooth & Creamy, Tesco*	1 Pot/100g	136	136	6.7	13.3	6.2	0.2
Eat Smart, Safeway*	1 Pot/100g	55	55	7.7	5.1	0.2	1.6
Exotic Fruits, Eat Smart, Safeway*	1 Pot/100g	60	60	7.9	6.6	0.2	0.4
Fabby, Loved By Kids, Marks & Spencer*	1 Pot/42.9g	45	105	6.2	12.3	3.7	0.0
Fruit On The Bottom, Better For You, Morrisons*	1 Pot/100g	66	66	5.6	10.6	0.2	0.0
Fruit, Balanced Lifestyle, Aldi*	1 Pot/100g	52	52	5.4	7.1	0.2	0.7
Fruit, Weight Watchers*	1 Pot/100g	48	48	5.4	6.3	0.1	0.3
Good Intentions, Somerfield*	1 Pot/100g	49	49	7.6	4.5	0.1	0.0
Kids, Yeo Valley*	1 Serving/90g	111	123	6.6	12.6	5.3	0.0
Lemon Pie, Low Fat, Sainsbury's*	1 Pot/90g	108	120	6.7	17.3	2.7	0.2
Lemon Sponge Flavour, BGTY, Sainsbury's*	1 Pot/100g	52	52	7.6	5.0	0.2	1.1
Low Fat, Aldi*	1 Pot/100g	52	52	5.4	7.1	0.3	0.7
Mandarin, Eat Smart, Safeway*	1 Pot/100g	55	55	7.7	5.2	0.2	1.6
Mango & Papaya, Healthy Living, Tesco*	1 Pot/100g	55	55	6.2	7.0	0.2	0.1
Mango, Eat Smart, Safeway*	1 Pot/100g	55	55	7.7	5.1	0.2	1.6
Morello Cherries, Perfectly Balanced, Waitrose*	½ Pot/250ml	260	104	2.5	19.1	1.9	1.8
Morrisons*	1 Serving/28g	17	59	9.8	4.8	0.0	0.0
Munch Bunch, Nestle*	1 Pot/42g	50	119	7.6	14.8	2.9	0.0
Natural, Creamy, Co-Op*	1 Pot/200g	204	102	6.1	2.9	7.3	0.0
Natural, French, Virtually Fat Free, Waitrose*	1 Serving/46g	21	46	7.3	3.7	0.2	0.0
Natural, GFY, Asda*	1oz/28g	13	45	8.0	3.3	0.0	0.0
Natural, Healthy Eating, Tesco*	1 Serving/65g	30	46	7.8	3.3	0.2	0.0
Natural, Normandy, BGTY, Sainsbury's*	1 Serving/15g	7	47	7.5	3.9	0.2	0.0
Natural, Virtually Fat Free, Safeway*	1 Serving/50g	23	46	7.3	3.7	0.2	0.0
Normandy, Sainsbury's*	1 Serving/25g	29	116	7.7	3.4	8.1	0.0
Orange & Mandarin, Tesco*	1 Pot/100g	75	75	6.5	5.6	3.0	2.3
Peach & Apricot, Healthy Eating, Tesco*	1 Pot/100g	54	54	6.2	6.8	0.2	0.1
Peach, BGTY, Sainsburys*	1 Pot/100g	53	53	7.2	5.5	0.2	0.5
Peach, Weight Watchers*	1 Pot/100g	48	48	5.4	6.4	0.1	0.2
Petit Dessert, Co-Op*	1 Pot/60g	74	123	6.3	14.5	4.4	0.0
Petits Filous, Yoplait*	1 Pot/60g	76	127	6.5	14.5	4.7	0.0
Pineapple & Passion Fruit, Healthy Living, Tesco*	1 Pot/100g	55	55	6.2	7.1	0.2	0.1
Pineapple, Eat Smart, Safeway*	1 Pot/100g	60	60	7.9	6.3	0.2	0.3
Plain	1oz/28g	32	113	6.8	5.7	7.1	0.0
Raspberry & Redcurrant, BGTY, Sainsbury's*	1 Pot/100g	49	49	7.2	4.5	0.2	1.9
Raspberry & Strawberry, Weight Watchers*	1 Pot/100g	48	48	5.4	6.2	0.1	0.3
Raspberry, COU, Marks & Spencer*	1 Pot/100g	49	49	7.8	4.9	0.1	0.4
Raspberry, Eat Smart, Safeway*	1 Pot/100g	50	50	7.6	4.5	0.2	1.8
Raspberry, GFY, Asda*	1 Pot/100g	43	43	6.0	4.2	0.2	0.0
Raspberry, Healthy Choice, Asda*	1 Pot/100g	41	41	6.0	3.8	0.2	0.0
Raspberry, Healthy Eating, Tesco*	1 Pot/100g	53	53	6.2	6.6	0.2	0.3
Raspberry, Low Fat, Sainsbury's*	1 Pot/90g	96	107	5.8	15.1	2.6	0.1

F

	Measure INFO/WEIGHT	per Measure KCAL	Nutrition Values per 100g / 100ml				
			KCAL	PROT	CARB	FAT	FIBRE
FROMAGE FRAIS,							
Raspberry, Makes Sense, Somerfield*	1 Pot/60g	69	115	5.3	14.8	3.8	0.0
Raspberry, Muller*	1 Pot/50g	68	135	6.1	13.5	6.3	0.0
Raspberry, Organic, Yeo Valley*	1 Pot/100g	127	127	6.1	11.1	6.5	0.4
Raspberry, Value, Tesco*	1 Serving/60g	56	93	7.2	13.5	1.3	0.0
Raspberry, Weight Watchers*	1 Pot/100g	49	49	5.3	6.9	0.1	1.2
Real Fruit, Tesco*	1 Pot/100g	54	54	5.6	7.6	0.1	0.1
Red Cherry, Healthy Eating, Tesco*	1 Pot/100g	55	55	6.2	7.2	0.2	0.1
Red Cherry, Tesco*	1 Pot/100g	75	75	6.5	5.5	3.0	2.3
Rhubarb & Crumble, Low Fat, Sainsbury's*	1 Pot/90g	96	107	6.7	14.1	2.6	0.4
Strawberry & Rasberry, Organic, Yeo Valley*	1 Pot/90g	118	131	6.3	12.9	6.0	0.2
Strawberry Cheesecake, Dessert Selection, Sainsbury's*	1 Pot/90g	95	106	5.8	15.3	2.5	0.1
Strawberry Tart, Sainsbury's*	1 Pot/100g	54	54	7.6	5.5	0.2	1.1
Strawberry, 0% Fat, Vitalinea, Danone*	1 Serving/150g	83	55	6.0	7.4	0.2	1.6
Strawberry, 99.9% Fat Free, Onken*	1 Serving/50g	46	91	6.9	15.3	0.1	0.0
Strawberry, BGTY, Sainsbury's*	1 Pot/100g	48	48	7.2	4.3	0.2	1.4
Strawberry, BGTY, Sainsbury's*	1 Pot/90g	46	51	7.0	5.8	0.1	1.4
Strawberry, COU, Marks & Spencer*	1 Pot/100g	50	50	7.7	4.6	0.1	0.5
Strawberry, GFY, Asda*	1 Pot/100g	58	58	6.0	8.0	0.2	0.0
Strawberry, Healthy Choice, Asda*	1 Pot/100g	41	41	6.0	3.7	0.2	0.0
Strawberry, Healthy Eating, Tesco*	1 Pot/100g	54	54	6.2	6.8	0.2	0.1
Strawberry, Low Fat, St Ivel*	1 Pot/100g	69	69	6.9	6.8	1.2	0.0
Strawberry, Organic, Yeo Valley*	1 Pot/90g	116	129	6.3	12.5	6.0	0.2
Strawberry, Puree, Somerfield*	1 Pot/50g	60	120	7.0	14.0	4.0	0.0
Strawberry, Tesco*	1 Pot/100g	75	75	6.5	5.5	3.0	2.5
Strawberry, Thomas The Tank Engine, Yoplait*	1 Pot/50g	51	101	6.8	15.4	1.3	0.0
Strawberry, Weight Watchers*	1 Pot/100g	47	47	5.4	6.2	0.1	0.2
Summer Fruits, Weight Watchers*	1 Pot/100g	48	48	5.4	6.3	0.1	0.4
Toffee & Pecan Pie, Smooth & Creamy, Tesco*	1 Pot/100g	148	148	6.9	14.8	6.8	0.2
Toffee, BGTY, Sainsbury's*	1 Pot/100g	60	60	7.2	7.0	0.3	0.2
Toffee, Weight Watchers*	1 Pot/100g	64	64	5.7	10.0	0.1	1.1
Tropical Fruit, COU, Marks & Spencer*	1 Pot/100g	50	50	7.8	4.5	0.1	0.5
Tropical Fruits, BGTY, Sainsbury's*	1 Pot/100g	54	54	7.3	5.8	0.2	0.3
Vanilla Flavour With Fruit, Thick & Fruity, Weight Watchers*	1 Pot/100g	49	49	5.3	6.9	0.0	1.2
Vanilla, Danone*	1 Serving/200g	274	137	5.3	19.6	4.1	0.0
Very Low Fat	1oz/28g	16	58	7.7	6.8	0.2	0.0
Virtually Fat Free, Safeway*	1 Pot/100g	41	41	6.7	3.2	0.2	0.0
Virtually Fat Free, Tesco*	1 Pot/100g	56	56	5.6	8.2	0.1	0.0
Wildlife, Yoplait*	1 Pot/50g	48	96	7.0	14.0	1.3	0.0
With Cereal, Shape Rise, Danone*	1 Serving/165g	205	124	6.5	23.9	1.3	0.5
With Real Fruit Puree, Nestle*	1 Serving/50g	65	130	7.1	18.9	2.7	0.2
FRUIT,							
& Yoghurt, McDonald's*	1 Serving/144g	138	96	2.8	15.9	1.9	1.1
A Croquer, McDonald's*	1 Serving/80g	47	59	0.4	13.5	0.4	2.3
Bag, Happy Meal, McDonald's*	1 Bag/80g	43	54	0.3	13.0	0.1	2.3
Bites, Apple & Grape, Food Explorers, Waitrose*	1 Pack/80g	44	55	0.4	13.2	0.1	1.4
Bowl, Sainsbury's*	1oz/28g	12	42	0.6	9.1	0.1	0.1
Collection, Fresh, Marks & Spencer*	1 Pack/240g	108	45	0.6	10.3	0.2	1.3
Deluxe, Fresh, Rindless, Shapers, Boots*	1 Pack/168g	64	38	0.7	8.3	0.2	0.7
Exotic, Marks & Spencer*	1 Pack/425g	213	50	0.7	11.8	0.3	0.0
Fantasy, Strawberries & Cranberries, Sundora*	1 Serving/25g	70	280	2.5	67.0	0.6	5.4
Grapefruit & Orange Segments, Breakfast, Del Monte*	1 Can/411g	193	47	1.0	10.2	0.1	1.0
Just Fruit, Shapers, Boots*	1 Pot/140g	60	43	0.6	10.0	0.1	1.5
Melon & Grape Selection, Food To Go, Marks & Spencer*	1oz/28g	10	35	0.5	8.6	0.1	0.7

F

	Measure	per Measure	Nutrition Values per 100g / 100ml				
FRUIT,	INFO/WEIGHT	KCAL	KCAL	PROT	CARB	FAT	FIBRE
Melon, Kiwi, & Strawberry, Fully Prepared, Sainsbury's*	1 Pack/245g	74	30	0.8	6.3	0.2	1.3
Mixed, Fresh, 5 A Day, Tesco*	1 Pack/400g	136	34	0.8	7.4	0.2	1.4
Mixed, Fresh, Tesco*	1 Pack/200g	70	35	0.8	7.4	0.2	1.4
Mixed, Fruitime, Pieces, Tesco*	1 Can/140g	84	60	0.4	14.0	0.0	1.0
Mixed, Melon, Kiwi & Strawberry, Sainsbury's*	1oz/28g	9	33	0.8	6.3	0.2	1.3
Mixed, Pieces, In Juice, Fruitini*	1 Can/140g	77	55	0.4	13.0	0.1	0.0
Mixed, Pieces, In Orange Jelly, Fruitini*	1 Can/140g	94	67	0.3	15.8	0.1	0.0
Mixed, Somerfield*	1oz/28g	80	285	2.0	68.0	1.0	0.0
Mixed, Tropical, Fruit Express, Del Monte*	1 Pot/185g	89	48	0.2	11.2	0.1	1.2
Peaches & Pears, Fruit Express, Del Monte*	1 Serving/185g	87	47	0.4	10.8	0.1	0.9
Pieces, Mixed In Fruit Juice, Fruiyini, Del Monte*	1 Serving/120g	61	51	0.4	12.0	0.1	0.5
Pineapple, Grape & Kiwi, Asda*	1 Serving/200g	98	49	0.6	11.0	0.3	1.7
Seeds & Nuts, Waitrose*	1 Serving/20g	90	452	13.5	36.5	28.0	5.5
Snack Pack, Fresh, Sainsbury's*	1 Serving/120g	54	45	0.1	11.0	0.1	1.3
Snack, Apple & Grape, Blue Parrot Cafe, Sainsbury's*	1 Pack/80g	42	53	0.4	12.5	0.1	2.1
To Go, Del Monte*	1 Can/113g	80	71	0.0	17.7	0.0	0.0
Tropical Mix, Sainsbury's*	1 Serving/50g	203	406	3.6	54.8	19.2	6.4
Tropical Mix, Somerfield*	1 Bag/50g	306	611	71.1	68.4	5.9	3.7
Tropical, Fresh, Marks & Spencer*	1 Pack/425g	213	50	0.7	11.8	0.3	2.0
Tropical, In Juice, Dole*	1 Pot/113g	59	52	0.3	14.2	0.0	1.8
Tropical, Tesco*	1 Pack/180g	85	47	0.6	10.8	0.2	1.9
FRUIT & NUT MIX,							
Exotic, Waitrose*	1 Serving/50g	207	414	9.0	54.6	17.7	4.6
Luxury, Asda*	1 Serving/50g	226	451	9.0	33.5	30.5	7.4
Organic, Waitrose*	1 Pack/100g	489	489	15.0	33.8	32.6	5.4
TTD, Sainsbury's*	1 Bag/250g	900	360	5.1	49.5	15.7	5.9
FRUIT COCKTAIL,							
Fresh & Ready, Sainsbury's*	1 Pack/300g	117	39	0.6	9.0	0.1	1.2
In Apple Juice, Asda*	1/3 Can/80g	40	50	0.3	12.0	0.1	1.6
In Fruit Juice, Morrisons*	1 Can/140g	64	46	0.4	11.0	0.0	0.0
In Fruit Juice, Safeway*	1 Serving/220g	68	31	0.4	7.2	0.0	1.0
In Fruit Juice, Sainsbury's*	1 Serving/198g	97	49	0.3	11.9	0.1	1.3
In Fruit Juice, Waitrose*	1 Can/142g	71	50	0.4	12.0	0.0	1.0
In Grape Juice, Tesco*	1oz/28g	12	43	0.4	10.0	0.0	1.0
In Juice, Del Monte*	1 Can/415g	203	49	0.4	11.2	0.1	0.0
In Light Syrup, Makes Sense, Somerfield*	½ Can/205g	127	62	0.4	15.0	0.0	1.0
In Light Syrup, Sainsbury's*	½ Can/125g	73	58	0.4	14.0	0.1	1.3
In Syrup, Del Monte*	1 Can/420g	315	75	0.4	18.0	0.1	0.0
In Syrup, Morrisons*	½ Can/205g	129	63	0.3	14.9	0.1	0.0
In Syrup, SmartPrice, Asda*	1 Tin/411g	173	42	0.3	10.0	0.1	1.6
In Syrup, Tesco*	1 Serving/135g	85	63	0.4	15.0	0.0	1.0
In Very Light Syrup, Value, Tesco*	1 Can/410g	123	30	0.4	7.3	0.0	1.0
No Added Sugar, Asda*	1 Serving/134g	67	50	0.3	12.0	0.1	1.6
Safeway*	1 Serving/205g	117	57	0.4	14.0	0.0	1.0
Tropical, Asda*	½ Can/135g	81	60	0.0	15.0	0.0	1.6
Tropical, In Syrup, Sainsbury's*	½ Can/130g	95	73	0.5	17.6	0.1	1.4
Tropical, Morrisons*	½ Can/212g	144	68	0.0	17.0	0.0	0.0
Tropical, Safeway*	½ Can/214g	154	72	0.5	17.6	0.0	1.4
FRUIT COMPOTE,							
& Vanilla Sponge, Weight Watchers*	1 Pack/140.3g	202	144	2.2	29.0	2.1	1.8
Apple, Strawberry & Blackberry, Organic, Yeo Valley*	½ Pot/112g	73	65	0.5	15.5	0.1	1.9
Apricot & Prune, Yeo Valley*	1 Pot/225g	207	92	0.6	22.3	0.1	1.6
Black Cherry & Creme Fraiche, Extra Special, Asda*	1 Pot/118g	188	159	1.7	20.0	8.0	0.8

F

	Measure INFO/WEIGHT	per Measure KCAL	Nutrition Values per 100g / 100ml				
			KCAL	PROT	CARB	FAT	FIBRE
FRUIT COMPOTE,							
Healthy Eating, Tesco*	1 Pot/140g	113	81	0.9	19.1	0.2	1.6
Orchard Fruits, GFY, Asda*	1 Pot/180g	113	63	0.5	15.0	0.1	0.0
Organic, Yeo Valley*	1oz/28g	13	47	0.5	11.2	0.0	0.0
Spiced, Tesco*	1 Serving/112g	122	109	1.7	24.4	0.5	3.1
Strawberry & Raspberry, Marks & Spencer*	1 Serving/80g	72	90	0.7	23.5	0.1	2.3
Summerfruit, Marks & Spencer*	¼ Pot/125g	119	95	0.9	22.7	0.6	0.8
FRUIT DRINK,							
Alive Tropical Torrent, The Coca Cola Co*	1 Glass/200ml	88	44	0.0	11.0	0.0	0.0
Apple & Blackcurrant, No Added Sugar, Safeway*	1fl oz/30ml	2	8	0.1	1.0	0.0	0.0
Blackcurrant & Apple, Shapers, Boots*	1 Bottle/500ml	10	2	0.0	0.2	0.0	0.0
Herbal, Crisp Dry, Ame*	1 Glass/200ml	46	23	0.0	4.2	0.0	0.0
Infusion, Peach, Lime & Ginger, Marks & Spencer*	1 Serving/250ml	88	35	0.0	8.5	0.0	0.0
FRUIT FILLING,							
Apricot, Sainsbury's*	1 Can/400g	316	79	0.5	19.1	0.1	0.9
Bramley Apple, Morton*	1 Serving/197.5g	168	85	0.2	21.1	0.1	0.0
Cherry & Amaretto, Asda*	¼ Pack/100g	105	105	0.9	23.0	0.2	0.0
Red Cherry, Morton*	1 Serving/70g	69	98	0.4	23.9	0.0	0.0
FRUIT GUMS,							
Multi Vitamin, Aldi*	1 Serving/50g	168	336	6.7	76.9	0.2	0.0
No Added Sugar, Boots*	1 Sweet/1.6g	2	88	0.0	22.0	0.0	0.0
Red & Black, Marks & Spencer*	1 Bag/113g	362	320	5.2	75.8	0.1	0.1
Rowntree's*	1 Pack/48g	164	342	4.7	80.8	0.2	0.0
FRUIT LOLLY,							
Exotic Fruit, Mini, Healthy Living, Tesco*	1 Lolly/31.3g	41	131	1.0	26.4	2.0	1.0
No Added Sugar, Tesco*	1 Lolly/32.4g	26	80	0.1	20.0	0.0	0.1
FRUIT MEDLEY,							
Citrus, Somerfield*	1 Serving/80.6g	25	31	0.6	6.9	0.1	0.4
Dried Fruit Mix, Shapers, Boots*	1 Serving/50g	131	262	3.2	61.0	0.6	5.5
Exotic, Co-Op*	1 Serving/120g	54	45	0.6	10.0	0.2	0.0
Exotic, Waitrose*	1 Medley/300g	126	42	0.6	9.5	0.2	1.1
Fresh, Marks & Spencer*	½ Pack/200g	100	50	0.7	12.3	0.1	1.6
Fresh, Waitrose*	1 Pack/300g	114	38	0.6	8.7	0.1	1.4
Freshly Prepared, Waitrose*	1 Pack/300g	135	45	0.7	10.2	0.1	2.1
In Fresh Orange Juice, Co-Op*	1 Serving/140g	49	35	0.5	9.0	0.0	0.0
Marks & Spencer*	1oz/28g	7	25	0.6	7.1	0.2	1.1
Shapers, Boots*	1 Pack/140g	55	39	0.7	8.6	0.2	1.0
Summer, Waitrose*	1 Bowl/300g	84	28	0.8	5.9	0.1	1.3
FRUIT MIX,							
Mango & Cranberry, Way To Five, Sainsbury's*	1 Serving/50g	166	331	1.8	79.4	0.7	4.8
TTD, Sainsbury's*	1 Serving/50g	69	137	0.3	36.4	0.4	1.6
Tropical Dried, & Coconut, Safeway*	1 Pack/50g	185	369	3.0	69.0	9.0	4.3
FRUIT SALAD,							
Autumn, Marks & Spencer*	1 Bowl/400g	220	55	0.4	13.2	0.1	1.8
Chunky, In Grape Juice, Tesco*	1 Serving/135g	63	47	0.4	11.0	0.2	0.8
Citrus, Asda*	1 Serving/265g	88	33	0.9	7.2	0.1	1.5
Classic, Fresh, Marks & Spencer*	1oz/28g	11	40	0.6	8.4	0.1	1.2
Dried, Marks & Spencer*	½ Pack/125g	269	215	1.8	51.4	0.4	5.9
Dried, Nature's Harvest*	½ Pack/125g	231	185	3.1	40.9	1.0	8.0
Dried, Safeway*	1 Serving/50g	109	217	1.7	51.6	0.3	5.1
Exotic, Fully Prepared, Sainsbury's*	1 Serving/200g	74	37	0.6	8.3	0.2	1.3
Exotic, Prepared, Sainsbury's*	1 Serving/400g	148	37	0.6	8.3	0.2	1.3
Exotic, Safeway*	½ Pot/159.6g	75	47	0.6	10.5	0.3	1.1
Exotic, Sainsbury's*	½ Tub/200g	80	40	0.6	9.1	0.3	1.0

F

	Measure INFO/WEIGHT	per Measure KCAL	Nutrition Values per 100g / 100ml				
			KCAL	PROT	CARB	FAT	FIBRE
FRUIT SALAD,							
Exotic, Somerfield*	1 Pot/350g	140	40	0.6	9.0	0.2	1.3
Exotic, Tesco*	1 Serving/225g	86	38	0.7	8.4	0.2	1.5
Exotic, Waitrose*	1 Pack/300g	126	42	0.6	9.5	0.2	1.1
Fresh, Asda*	½ Pot/215g	95	44	0.7	10.0	0.1	2.0
Fresh, Golden, Asda*	1 Pot/146.8g	69	47	0.6	11.0	0.1	1.6
Fresh, Marks & Spencer*	1oz/28g	10	36	0.6	9.5	0.2	0.9
Fresh, Morrisons*	1 Pot/180g	77	43	0.7	9.9	0.1	0.0
Fresh, Safeway*	1 Pack/300g	135	45	0.7	10.0	0.2	1.5
Fresh, Sainsbury's*	1 Serving/120g	55	46	0.6	10.5	0.2	1.4
Fresh, Somerfield*	1 Bowl/200g	94	47	0.6	11.0	0.1	1.5
Fresh, Sweet, Ripe & Moist, Tesco*	1 Serving/750g	345	46	0.7	10.6	0.1	1.6
Fresh, Tesco*	1oz/28g	13	45	0.6	10.5	0.1	1.4
Fresh, Washed, Ready To Eat, Tesco*	1 Pack/200g	92	46	0.7	10.6	0.1	1.6
Fruit, Mediterranean Style, Shapers, Boots*	1 Pack/141.9g	61	43	0.6	10.0	0.1	1.5
Fully Prepared, Fresh, Sainsbury's*	½ Pack/150g	65	43	0.7	9.9	0.1	2.0
Grapefruit & Orange, Fresh, Marks & Spencer*	1 Serving/250g	88	35	0.9	7.4	0.1	1.6
Green, Marks & Spencer*	1 Bowl/400g	200	50	0.6	10.9	0.2	1.2
Homemade	1oz/28g	15	55	0.7	13.8	0.1	1.5
Luxury, Marks & Spencer*	1oz/28g	11	40	0.6	9.2	0.1	1.1
Mediterranean Style, Budgens*	1 Serving/250g	95	38	0.6	8.5	0.2	0.8
Melon, Kiwi, Strawbery, Way to Five, Sainsbury's*	1 Pack/245g	74	30	0.8	6.3	0.2	1.3
Mixed, Food To Go, Marks & Spencer*	1 Pack/400g	400	100	0.9	23.3	0.3	2.8
Mixed, New Improved, Tesco*	1 Pot/225g	79	35	0.8	7.6	0.2	1.2
Mixed, Prepared, Sainsbury's*	½ Pack/230g	97	42	0.7	8.9	0.2	1.2
Mixed, Sainsbury's*	1 Bowl/480g	211	44	0.6	10.2	0.1	1.1
Mixed, Tesco*	1 Salad/225g	86	38	0.7	8.3	0.2	1.3
Mixed, Way To Five, Sainsbury's*	1 Pack/430g	168	39	0.7	8.6	0.2	1.2
Pineapple, Mandarin & Grapefruit, Asda*	1 Serving/200g	86	43	0.6	10.0	0.1	0.0
Pret a Manger*	1 Av Pack/300g	120	40	0.5	9.2	0.2	1.2
Sainsbury's*	1 Serving/300g	129	43	0.7	9.9	0.1	2.0
Seasonal, Asda*	1 Pack/125g	55	44	0.5	10.4	0.1	1.2
Seasonal, Marks & Spencer*	1 Serving/200g	100	50	0.5	11.8	0.2	2.1
Shapers, Boots*	1 Pack/140g	55	39	0.7	8.6	0.2	1.0
Summer, Sainsbury's*	1 Pack/240g	84	35	0.7	7.8	0.2	1.3
Tesco*	1 Serving/200g	70	35	0.8	7.4	0.2	1.4
Tropical Fruit, In Light Syrup, Fast Fruit, Safeway*	1 Pot/125g	90	72	0.6	17.2	0.0	1.0
Tropical, Asda*	1oz/28g	10	36	0.6	8.8	0.2	1.2
Tropical, Budgens*	1 Pack/250g	128	51	0.6	11.7	0.2	1.8
Tropical, Co-Op*	1 Serving/150g	90	60	1.5	11.0	1.0	0.0
Tropical, Fresh, Asda*	1 Pack/400g	164	41	0.7	9.0	0.2	1.8
Tropical, Fresh, Marks & Spencer*	1 Pack/425g	213	50	0.7	11.8	0.3	2.0
Tropical, Fresh, Sainsbury's*	1 Pack/230g	104	45	0.7	10.2	0.2	2.0
Tropical, Fruit Snacks, Frozen, Sainsbury's*	1 Serving/175g	79	45	0.7	10.4	0.1	1.6
Tropical, In Light Syrup, Passion Fruit Juice, Tesco*	½ Can/216g	130	60	0.3	14.1	0.1	1.1
Tropical, Marks & Spencer*	1oz/28g	12	44	0.8	9.6	0.3	1.8
Weight Watchers*	1 Serving/135g	50	37	0.2	9.0	0.1	0.7
FRUIT SELECTION,							
Fresh, Marks & Spencer*	1 Pack/400g	180	45	0.6	10.1	0.2	1.3
New, Shapers, Boots*	1 Pack/160g	72	45	0.6	11.0	0.1	1.8
Shapers, Boots*	1 Pack/235g	96	41	0.5	9.2	0.2	0.8
FRUIT SHOOT,							
Apple & Blackcurrant, Robinson's*	1 Bottle/200ml	10	5	0.1	0.8	0.0	0.0
Orange & Peach, Robinson*	1 Bottle/200ml	10	5	0.1	0.8	0.0	0.0

F

	Measure INFO/WEIGHT	per Measure KCAL	Nutrition Values per 100g / 100ml				
			KCAL	PROT	CARB	FAT	FIBRE
FRUIT SPREAD,							
Apricot, Pure, Organic, Whole Earth*	1 Serving/20g	33	167	0.8	40.0	0.4	0.9
High, Blueberry, St Dalfour*	1 Tsp/15g	34	228	0.5	56.0	0.2	2.2
Pear & Apricot, Sunwheel*	1oz/28g	59	209	1.5	65.3	0.2	3.0
Raspberry, Weight Watchers*	1 Tsp/15g	17	111	0.4	27.1	0.1	0.9
Seville Orange, Weight Watchers*	1 Tsp/15g	17	111	0.2	27.5	0.0	0.3
Strawberry, Weight Watchers*	1 Tsp/15g	17	115	0.2	28.4	0.0	0.4
FU YUNG,							
Egg	1oz/28g	67	239	9.9	2.2	20.6	1.3
FUDGE,							
All Butter, TTD, Sainsbury's*	1 Pack/125g	536	429	1.3	73.4	14.5	0.0
Average	1oz/28g	123	441	3.3	81.1	13.7	0.0
Butter Tablet, Thorntons*	1oz/28g	116	414	0.9	77.6	11.1	0.0
Butter, Milk, Thorntons*	1 Chocolate/13g	60	462	3.7	68.5	19.2	0.0
Cadbury's*	1 Std Bar/26g	116	445	2.8	72.3	16.3	0.0
Cherry & Almond, Thorntons*	1 Bag/100g	464	464	3.2	70.5	19.1	0.4
Chocolate, Thorntons*	1 Bag/100g	459	459	3.1	69.0	19.1	0.6
Clotted Cream, Marks & Spencer*	1oz/28g	133	474	1.7	67.6	22.1	0.0
Dairy, Co-Op*	1 Sweet/9g	39	430	2.0	76.0	13.0	0.0
Devon, Somerfield*	1 Pack/250g	1060	424	2.0	78.9	11.1	0.0
Double Chocolate Bar, Marks & Spencer*	1 Bar/43g	202	470	4.2	66.9	21.0	0.7
Pure Indulgence, Thorntons*	1 Bar/45g	210	466	1.8	65.9	21.9	0.0
Vanilla, Bar, Marks & Spencer*	1 Bar/43g	205	476	3.7	63.0	23.3	0.4
Vanilla, Thorntons*	1 Bag/100g	465	465	1.8	65.9	21.9	0.0
Vanilla, Whipped, Marks & Spencer*	1 Serving/42.9g	211	490	3.8	65.4	23.9	0.3
FUSE,							
Cadbury's*	1 Std Bar/49g	238	485	7.6	58.2	24.8	0.0
FUSILLI,							
Cooked, Average	1 Serving/210g	248	118	4.2	23.8	0.7	1.2
Corn Rice, Free From, Sainsbury's*	1 Serving/75g	262	349	7.6	73.9	2.6	3.6
Dry, Average	1 Serving/90g	316	352	12.3	72.0	1.6	2.2
Fresh, Cooked, Average	1 Serving/200g	329	165	6.4	30.7	1.8	1.8
Fresh, Dry, Average	1 Serving/250g	692	277	10.9	53.4	2.7	2.1
Microwaveable, Express, Dolmio*	1 Serving/220g	299	136	5.3	26.3	1.0	0.0
Tomato, Weight Watchers*	1 Can/388g	198	51	1.9	10.1	0.4	0.8
Tricolore, Dry, Average	1 Serving/75g	264	351	12.2	71.8	1.7	2.7
Tuna, BGTY, Sainsbury's*	1 Pack/400g	304	76	6.0	8.6	2.0	0.5
Whole Wheat, Dry, Average	1 Serving/90g	290	322	13.1	62.3	2.3	9.0
With Chicken & Courgettes, Sainsbury's*	1 Pack/450g	675	150	8.6	14.6	6.4	0.5

F

	Measure INFO/WEIGHT	per Measure KCAL	Nutrition Values per 100g / 100ml				
			KCAL	PROT	CARB	FAT	FIBRE
GALAXY,							
Amicelli, Mars*	1 Serving/13g	66	507	6.2	59.7	27.1	0.0
Caramel, Mars*	1 Bar/49g	238	485	5.4	60.3	24.7	0.0
Chocolate, Mars*	1 Bar/47g	250	532	9.0	56.6	30.0	0.0
Fruit & Hazelnut, Milk, Mars*	1 Bar/47g	235	501	7.1	55.2	28.0	0.0
Liaison, Mars*	1 Bar/48g	233	485	5.4	60.3	24.7	0.0
Ripple, Mars*	1 Bar/33g	169	528	6.9	59.3	29.3	0.0
Swirls, Mars*	1 Bag/150g	747	498	4.9	60.2	26.5	0.0
GAMMON,							
& Pineapple, Roast, Dinner, Iceland*	1 Meal/400g	360	90	6.2	12.7	1.6	1.7
Breaded, Average	1oz/28g	34	120	22.5	1.0	3.1	0.0
Dry Cured, Ready To Roast, Marks & Spencer*	½ Joint/255g	255	100	20.5	0.5	1.5	0.5
Honey & Mustard, Average	½ Pack/190g	294	155	19.1	3.6	7.1	0.1
Joint, Lean Only, Boiled	1oz/28g	47	167	29.4	0.0	5.5	0.0
Joint, Unsmoked, Danish, Marks & Spencer*	1oz/28g	34	122	16.6	0.0	6.2	0.0
Steaks, Average	1 Steak/97.1g	157	161	23.3	0.4	7.4	0.0
Steaks, Healthy Range, Average	1 Serving/110g	107	97	18.0	0.4	3.2	0.2
Steaks, Honey Roast, Average	1oz/28g	40	142	21.5	2.3	5.3	0.1
Steaks, Smoked, Average	1 Steak/250g	342	137	22.7	0.1	5.0	0.1
Wiltshire, Traditional British Roast, Marks & Spencer*	1 Serving/70g	133	190	24.7	0.0	9.8	0.0
GARAM MASALA,							
Average	1oz/28g	106	379	15.6	45.2	15.1	0.0
GARLIC,							
Powder	1 Tsp/3g	7	246	18.7	42.7	1.2	9.9
Raw	1 Clove/3g	3	98	7.9	16.3	0.6	4.1
Very Lazy, English Provender Company*	1 Tsp/3g	1	38	3.0	6.1	0.2	1.4
GARLIC PUREE,							
Asda*	1 Tbsp/15g	63	423	2.7	13.0	40.0	6.0
Average	1 Tbsp/18g	61	380	3.5	16.9	33.6	0.0
Organic, Tesco*	1 Serving/10g	12	119	6.6	22.8	0.2	3.2
Sharwood's*	1 Tbsp/18g	9	63	3.4	13.3	0.3	2.4
GATEAU,							
Black Forest, Tesco*	1 Serving/55g	141	257	3.2	29.9	13.8	0.1
Blackforest, Sainsbury's*	1/8 Gateau/63g	163	259	3.9	27.7	17.1	3.5
Chocolate Layer, Marks & Spencer	1 Serving/86g	278	323	4.2	35.9	18.3	0.9
Chocolate Orange, Co-Op*	1 Slice/97g	320	330	5.0	37.0	18.0	1.0
Chocolate, Swirl, Tesco*	1 Serving/83g	230	277	3.8	29.3	16.0	0.2
Double Chocolate, Light, Sara Lee*	1/5 Gateau/58.6g	140	237	5.7	43.3	4.6	2.0
Double Chocolate, Sara Lee*	1oz/28g	93	331	5.6	41.3	16.5	0.9
Double Chocolate, Tesco*	1 Serving/45g	124	276	4.4	32.1	14.4	2.2
Double Strawberry, Sara Lee*	1/8 Slice/199g	533	268	3.2	36.2	12.2	0.6
Ice Cream, Chocolate & Vanilla, Iceland*	1 Serving/130g	252	194	3.3	24.1	9.4	0.6
Orange & Lemon, Iceland*	1 Serving/90g	221	245	2.6	33.8	11.0	0.3
Profiterole, TTD, Sainsbury's*	1/6 Gateau/112g	410	365	3.9	26.2	27.2	1.1
Strawberry, Co-Op*	1 Slice/77g	222	288	5.1	29.2	16.7	1.0
Swiss, Cadbury's*	1/6/60g	228	380	5.2	52.0	16.8	0.9
Triple Chocolate, Tesco*	1 Serving/64g	187	292	3.9	31.1	16.9	0.4
GELATINE,							
Average	1oz/28g	95	338	84.4	0.0	0.0	0.0
GHEE,							
Butter	1oz/28g	251	898	0.0	0.0	99.8	0.0
Palm	1oz/28g	251	897	0.0	0.0	99.7	0.0
Vegetable	1oz/28g	251	895	0.0	0.0	99.4	0.0

G

	Measure INFO/WEIGHT	per Measure KCAL	Nutrition Values per 100g / 100ml				
			KCAL	PROT	CARB	FAT	FIBRE
GHERKINS,							
Pickled, Average	1 Gherkin/36g	5	14	0.9	2.6	0.1	1.2
GIN,							
37.5% Volume	1 Shot/25ml	52	207	0.0	0.0	0.0	0.0
40% Volume	1 Shot/25ml	56	222	0.0	0.0	0.0	0.0
GINGER,							
Crystallised, Nature's Harvest*	1 Tbsp/15g	50	330	0.3	82.0	0.1	16.0
Fresh	1oz/28g	14	49	1.7	9.5	0.7	0.0
Ground	1 Tsp/2g	5	258	7.4	60.0	3.3	0.0
Lazy, EPC*	1 Tbsp/10g	2	15	0.2	3.2	0.2	1.5
Root, Raw	1oz/28g	11	38	1.4	7.2	0.6	0.0
Stem, In Sugar Syrup, Sainsbury's*	1oz/28g	76	271	0.2	67.3	0.1	1.4
GINGER ALE,							
American, Finest, Tesco*	1 Serving/150ml	68	45	0.0	11.0	0.0	0.0
American, Low Calorie, Somerfield*	1fl oz/30ml	0	1	0.0	0.0	0.0	0.0
Dry	1 Glass/250ml	38	15	0.0	3.9	0.0	0.0
GINGERBREAD,							
Average	1oz/28g	106	379	5.7	64.7	12.6	1.2
Men, Mini, Marks & Spencer*	1 Biscuit/16.6g	80	470	6.2	63.9	18.6	1.7
GNOCCHI,							
Di Patati, Safeway*	1 Serving/150g	255	170	4.5	37.3	0.3	0.4
Dry, Buitoni*	1 Serving/150g	528	352	11.2	72.6	1.9	0.0
GOOSE,							
Raw, Meat, Fat & Skin	1oz/28g	101	361	16.5	0.0	32.8	0.0
Roast, Meat Only	1oz/28g	89	319	29.3	0.0	22.4	0.0
Roasted, Meat, Fat & Skin	1oz/28g	84	301	27.5	0.0	21.2	0.0
GOOSEBERRIES,							
Dessert, Raw	1oz/28g	11	40	0.7	9.2	0.3	2.4
GOULASH,							
Beef, Bistro Range, Tesco*	1 Pack/450g	545	121	7.9	14.6	3.4	0.6
Beef, With Tagliatelle, COU, Marks & Spencer*	1 Pack/360g	414	115	8.5	14.5	2.3	1.0
Hungarian, Pret a Manger*	1 Serving/455g	240	53	3.2	6.7	1.7	1.2
GRANOLA,							
Cranberry & Apple, Good Intentions, Somerfield*	1 Serving/30g	109	363	9.0	71.0	4.8	10.2
Low Fat, Sweet Home Farm*	1 Serving/55g	180	328	7.3	69.0	5.4	9.0
Sultana, Crunchy, Organic, Marks & Spencer*	1oz/28g	120	430	8.6	53.9	15.7	6.4
GRAPEFRUIT,							
In Juice, Average	1oz/28g	13	46	0.5	10.6	0.0	0.4
In Syrup, Average	1oz/28g	19	69	0.5	16.8	0.1	0.5
Raw, Average	1 Med/340g	85	25	0.7	5.7	0.1	1.1
Ruby Red, In Juice, Average	1 Serving/135g	54	40	0.6	9.4	0.1	0.5
GRAPES,							
Green, Average	1oz/28g	17	62	0.4	15.2	0.1	0.7
Red & Green Selection, Average	1 Bag/80g	50	63	0.4	15.2	0.1	0.9
Red, Average	1 Serving/79g	53	67	0.5	16.5	0.1	0.8
GRATIN,							
Cauliflower, Findus*	1 Pack/400g	340	85	3.5	7.0	5.0	0.0
Creamy Potato, Marks & Spencer*	½ Pack/225g	360	160	2.2	11.9	11.1	0.9
Leek & Carrot, Findus*	1 Pack/400g	440	110	3.5	9.5	6.5	0.0
Potato, Somerfield*	½ Pack/225g	356	158	2.0	11.0	12.0	0.0
Spinach & Mushroom, Safeway*	1 Packet/520g	728	140	4.8	10.3	8.4	1.5
Vegetable, Somerfield*	1 Pack/300g	417	139	1.0	5.0	13.0	0.0
GRAVADLAX,							
Finest, Tesco*	1 Serving/70g	125	178	22.1	0.2	9.9	0.0

	Measure INFO/WEIGHT	per Measure KCAL	Nutrition Values per 100g / 100ml				
			KCAL	PROT	CARB	FAT	FIBRE
GRAVADLAX,							
Marks & Spencer*	1 Serving/140g	294	210	18.4	5.3	11.4	0.5
Scottish Salmon, Marks & Spencer*	1 Serving/70g	147	210	18.4	5.3	11.4	0.5
GRAVY,							
Beef, Fresh, Sainsbury's*	1 Serving/83ml	47	56	2.4	4.5	3.2	0.6
Beef, Heat Serve, Morrisons*	1 Serving/150g	27	18	0.3	3.9	0.3	0.5
Beef, With Winter Berry Shallot, Made Up, Oxo*	1 Serving/105ml	24	23	0.6	4.3	0.3	0.1
Chicken, Fresh, Marks & Spencer*	1oz/28g	10	35	2.5	5.0	0.1	0.3
Chicken, KFC*	1oz/28g	39	138	5.2	7.0	9.8	0.0
Chips & Onion, Asda*	1 Pack/357.6g	329	92	2.1	15.0	2.6	1.2
For Poultry, Marks & Spencer*	1 Jar/400g	136	34	2.5	5.0	0.4	0.3
Fresh, Somerfield*	1 Pack/300g	69	23	0.0	4.0	1.0	0.0
Granules For Chicken, Dry, Bisto*	1 Serving/4g	15	385	3.2	57.9	15.6	1.4
Granules For Chicken, Made Up, Bisto*	1 Serving/50ml	15	30	0.2	4.2	1.2	0.2
Granules For Vegetarian Dishes, Dry Weight, Bisto*	1 Serving/50ml	184	367	2.6	59.5	13.2	1.3
Granules With Onion, Dry, Bisto*	1 Serving/4g	15	365	2.9	56.1	14.3	1.8
Granules for Turkey, Dry, Bisto*	1 Serving/4g	15	367	3.3	53.9	15.3	1.2
Granules, Beef, Dry, Tesco*	1 Serving/6g	29	480	5.5	36.4	34.7	1.5
Granules, Beef, Made Up, Tesco*	1 Serving/140ml	41	29	0.3	4.0	1.3	0.0
Granules, Chicken & Hint of Sage & Onion, Oxo*	3/4 Pint Made/30g	95	316	11.1	54.2	6.1	0.7
Granules, Chicken, Dry, Oxo*	1oz/28g	83	296	11.1	54.2	4.9	0.7
Granules, Chicken, Made Up, Oxo*	1fl oz/30ml	5	18	0.7	3.3	0.3	0.0
Granules, Chicken, Tesco*	½ Pint Gravy/20g	100	501	4.5	38.4	36.7	0.0
Granules, Chip Shop Curry, Dry Weight, Bisto*	1 Serving/50ml	234	468	4.3	72.6	17.8	2.7
Granules, Dry, Bisto*	1 Serving/10g	38	384	3.1	56.4	16.2	1.5
Granules, Dry, Value, Tesco*	1oz/28g	111	397	3.2	54.4	18.5	1.0
Granules, Instant, Dry	1oz/28g	129	462	4.4	40.6	32.5	0.0
Granules, Instant, Made Up	1oz/28g	10	34	0.3	3.0	2.4	0.0
Granules, Lamb, Made Up, Oxo*	1 Serving/100ml	25	25	0.7	4.3	0.5	0.0
Granules, Made Up, Bisto*	1 Serving/50ml	15	30	0.2	4.2	1.4	0.2
Granules, Made Up, Oxo*	1 Serving/150ml	29	19	0.6	3.4	0.3	0.0
Granules, Onion, Dry, Morrisons*	1 Serving/25g	124	495	3.4	44.0	34.7	0.0
Granules, Onion, Dry, Oxo*	1oz/28g	92	328	8.2	62.3	4.8	0.8
Granules, Onion, Made Up, Bisto*	1 Serving/140ml	39	28	0.2	4.2	1.0	0.2
Granules, Onion, Made Up, Oxo*	1fl oz/30ml	6	20	0.5	3.7	0.3	0.0
Granules, Original, Dry, Oxo*	1oz/28g	88	313	10.2	57.2	4.8	1.0
Granules, Vegetable, Dry, Bisto*	1 Serving/4g	15	367	2.6	59.5	13.2	1.3
Granules, Vegetable, Dry, Oxo*	1oz/28g	88	316	8.4	59.5	4.9	0.9
Granules, Vegetable, Dry, Tesco*	½ Pint/20g	94	470	3.8	38.5	33.4	3.7
Granules, Vegetarian, Dry, Asda*	½ Pint/20g	100	498	3.8	42.0	35.0	2.1
Granules, Vegetarian, Dry, Bisto*	1 Serving/28g	110	394	2.6	54.9	18.2	1.3
Granules, Vegetarian, Made Up, Bisto*	1 Serving/140ml	39	28	0.2	4.4	1.0	0.0
Instant Mix, Better for You, Morrisons*	1 Serving/25g	80	320	3.5	77.0	0.3	1.2
Mix, Instant, Made Up, BGTY, Sainsbury's*	1fl oz/30ml	10	32	0.3	7.4	0.1	0.1
Onion, Fresh, Asda*	1/6 Pot/77g	30	39	1.7	3.3	2.1	0.4
Onion, Fresh, Somerfield*	1 Pack/300g	195	65	1.0	7.0	4.0	0.0
Onion, Rich, Marks & Spencer*	½ Pack/150g	60	40	2.0	5.9	1.2	0.3
Powder For Pork, Dry, Best, Bisto*	1 Serving/100g	303	303	5.1	62.3	3.7	0.8
Powder, Dry, Tesco*	1 Serving/20g	57	286	7.2	61.0	1.5	2.0
Roast Beef Flavour, Made Up, Best, Bisto*	1 Serving/50ml	13	26	0.4	5.4	0.4	0.2
Roast Beef, Dry, Schwartz*	1 Pack/27g	90	333	12.7	65.2	2.4	0.0
Roast Chicken, Dry, Schwartz*	1 Pack/26g	95	365	10.2	65.7	6.8	0.0
Roast Pork & Sage, Dry, Schwartz	1 Serving/25g	90	359	10.2	65.7	6.2	0.0
Roast Turkey, Dry, Schwartz*	1 Serving/6g	21	355	12.0	60.2	7.4	0.0

G

	Measure INFO/WEIGHT	per Measure KCAL	Nutrition Values per 100g / 100ml				
			KCAL	PROT	CARB	FAT	FIBRE
GREENGAGES,							
Raw, Average	1oz/28g	11	40	0.8	9.5	0.1	2.1
GRILLS,							
Cauliflower Cheese, Dalepak*	1 Grill/94g	231	246	4.6	20.0	14.8	2.6
Cheese & Bacon, Danepak*	1 Grill/84.9g	241	284	15.0	13.4	18.9	1.2
London, Heinz*	1 Can/400g	404	101	7.1	10.9	3.2	3.1
Tikka, Organic, Waitrose*	1 Grill/100g	185	185	6.9	18.5	9.3	3.4
Vegetable, Dalepak*	1 Grill/85g	170	200	5.2	17.2	12.3	3.2
Vegetable, Ross*	1 Grill/114g	252	221	4.3	25.5	11.3	0.9
Vegetable, Tesco*	1 Grill/72.2g	129	179	4.2	18.0	10.0	2.2
Vegetarian, Mushroom & Oregano, Organic, Waitrose*	1 Grill/100g	160	160	8.8	12.8	8.2	2.4
GROUSE,							
Meat Only, Roasted	1oz/28g	36	128	27.6	0.0	2.0	0.0
GUACAMOLE,							
Asda*	½ Pot/56.5g	105	184	1.6	4.0	18.0	0.0
Average	1oz/28g	36	128	1.4	2.2	12.7	2.5
Chunky, Marks & Spencer*	1 Serving/50g	65	130	1.5	5.1	11.3	3.7
Chunky, Sainsbury's*	½ Pot/64.9g	120	185	1.6	3.2	18.4	3.8
Doritos*	1 Tbsp/20g	32	159	1.2	2.6	16.0	0.1
Fresh, Sainsbury's*	1oz/28g	59	210	1.8	5.3	20.2	2.5
Fresh, Waitrose*	½ Pot/85.1g	172	202	1.7	3.3	20.2	3.4
GFY, Asda*	1 Pack/113g	144	127	2.8	4.3	11.0	2.2
Reduced Fat, Sainsburys*	½ Pot/65g	86	133	1.5	3.5	12.6	4.0
Reduced Fat, Tesco*	1 Pot/113g	142	126	2.9	5.7	10.2	2.3
Reduced Fat, Waitrose*	1 Serving/25g	32	129	3.0	2.7	11.8	4.7
Tesco*	1 Serving/35g	67	190	1.9	4.1	18.4	2.5
Somerfield*	1oz/28g	53	188	2.0	5.0	18.0	0.0
GUAVA,							
Canned, In Syrup	1oz/28g	17	60	0.4	15.7	0.0	3.0
Raw, Average	1oz/28g	7	25	0.8	4.8	0.5	3.5
GUINEA FOWL,							
Boned & Stuffed, Fresh, FayreGame*	1 Serving/325g	650	200	19.1	3.3	12.1	0.5
GUMBO,							
Cajun Vegetable, Sainsbury's*	1 Serving/450g	266	59	1.4	7.7	2.5	1.5
Louisiana Chicken, Perfectly Balanced, Waitrose*	1 Serving/235g	207	88	12.2	3.5	2.8	1.3
GUMS,							
American Hard, Asda*	1 Serving/50g	173	345	0.1	86.0	0.0	0.0
American Hard, Sainsbury's*	1 Sweet/6g	22	360	0.1	90.0	0.1	0.0
Milk Bottles, Bassett's*	1 Pack/25g	88	353	6.2	78.3	1.6	0.0
Milk Bottles, Milk Flavour, Asda*	1 Pack/100g	369	369	7.0	80.0	2.3	0.4
Percy Pig & Pals, Soft, Marks & Spencer*	1 Sweet/7.6g	28	344	5.8	80.0	0.1	0.0

G

	Measure INFO/WEIGHT	per Measure KCAL	Nutrition Values per 100g / 100ml				
			KCAL	PROT	CARB	FAT	FIBRE
HADDOCK,							
Fillets, Battered, Average	1oz/28g	64	228	13.4	16.3	12.2	1.1
Fillets, In Breadcrumbs, Average	1oz/28g	57	203	13.5	14.9	9.9	1.2
Fillets, Raw, Average	1oz/28g	22	80	18.0	0.2	0.9	0.0
Fillets, Smoked, Cheese & Mustard, Tesco*	1 Serving/120g	185	154	17.8	0.0	9.2	0.0
Fillets, Smoked, Cooked, Average	1 Pack/300g	337	112	21.9	0.4	2.6	0.1
Fillets, Smoked, Raw, Average	1 Pack/227g	194	86	20.3	0.1	0.5	0.2
Flour, Fried in Blended Oil	1oz/28g	39	138	21.1	4.5	4.1	0.2
Goujons, Batter, Crispy, Marks & Spencer*	1 Serving/100g	250	250	11.7	18.5	14.1	0.8
HADDOCK EN CROUTE,							
Youngs*	1 Serving/170.1g	432	254	8.0	17.1	16.9	4.3
HADDOCK FLORENTINE,							
Eat Smart, Safeway*	1 Serving/250g	200	80	12.0	2.5	1.8	1.3
Healthy Eating, Tesco*	1 Pack/370g	303	82	8.2	10.0	1.0	0.5
HADDOCK IN,							
Butter Sauce, Steaks, Youngs*	1 Portion/150g	134	89	9.9	4.0	3.7	0.5
Cheese & Chive Sauce, Healthy Living, Tesco*	1 Serving/400g	304	76	11.6	2.2	2.3	0.7
Smoked Leek & Cheese Sauce, Asda*	½ Pack/200g	232	116	14.0	3.7	5.0	1.5
Tomato Herb Sauce, Fillets, BGTY, Sainsbury's*	½ Pack/165g	150	91	12.9	3.6	2.8	0.1
Watercress Sauce, GFY, Asda*	1 Pack/400g	268	67	6.0	7.0	1.7	1.4
HADDOCK MORNAY,							
COU, Marks & Spencer*	1 Pack/200g	160	80	14.0	0.7	2.5	0.3
Fillets, In Mornay Cheese Sauce, Marks & Spencer*	½ Pack/190g	219	115	13.5	1.8	6.1	0.1
Iceland*	½ Pack/179g	179	100	13.6	4.3	3.2	0.7
Meal for One, Marks & Spencer*	1 Pack/400g	340	85	6.6	7.4	3.3	2.3
Somerfield*	1 Serving/200g	266	133	13.6	5.1	6.5	0.5
Waitrose*	1 Serving/180g	140	78	14.2	1.9	1.6	0.7
With Leek Mash, Eat Smart, Safeway*	1 Pack/369.9g	307	83	7.1	7.9	2.5	1.0
Youngs*	½ Pack/190g	236	124	12.1	1.3	7.8	0.6
HADDOCK RAREBIT,							
Smoked, Finest, Tesco*	1 Rarebit/180g	326	181	5.6	19.1	9.2	0.4
HADDOCK TOPPED,							
Potato, Cumberland, Marks & Spencer*	1 Pack/300g	390	130	8.2	10.6	6.0	0.4
HADDOCK WITH,							
A Rich Cheese Crust, Smoked, Sainsbury's*	1 Serving/199g	295	148	13.0	2.5	9.5	0.9
Cheese & Chive, Smoked, GFY, Asda	½ Pack/185.7g	195	105	15.0	3.1	3.6	0.3
HAGGIS,							
Neeps & Tatties, Marks & Spencer*	1 Pack/300g	330	110	3.8	12.3	4.8	0.8
Traditional, McSween*	1 Haggis/454g	1149	253	11.1	19.1	15.6	2.1
HAKE,							
Fillets, In Breadcrumbs, Average	1oz/28g	66	235	12.9	16.0	13.4	1.0
Goujons, Average	1 Serving/150g	345	230	12.4	18.7	11.9	1.3
Raw, Average	1oz/28g	29	102	20.4	0.0	2.2	0.0
HALIBUT,							
Cooked, Average	1oz/28g	38	135	24.6	0.4	4.0	0.0
Raw	1oz/28g	29	103	21.5	0.0	1.9	0.0
HALWA,							
Average	1oz/28g	107	381	1.8	68.0	13.2	0.0
HAM,							
Applewood Smoked, Average	1 Slice/28g	31	112	21.3	0.6	2.8	0.3
Baked, Average	1 Slice/74g	106	143	21.1	1.8	5.8	0.3
Bavarian, Asda*	1 Slice/15g	18	121	21.4	0.5	3.7	0.0
Beechwood Smoked, Morrisons*	1 Slice/20g	32	160	19.5	0.5	9.0	0.0
Black Forest, Waitrose*	1 Slice/7.7g	14	181	25.8	0.6	8.4	0.0

H

	Measure INFO/WEIGHT	per Measure KCAL	Nutrition Values per 100g / 100ml				
			KCAL	PROT	CARB	FAT	FIBRE
HAM,							
Boiled, Average	1 Pack/113g	154	137	20.6	0.6	5.8	0.0
Breaded, Average	1 Slice/37g	57	155	23.1	1.9	6.3	1.6
Breaded, Dry Cured, Average	1 Slice/33g	47	142	22.2	1.4	5.4	0.0
Brunswick, Average	1 Slice/20g	32	160	19.5	0.6	8.8	0.1
Cooked, Sliced, Average	1 Serving/50g	57	115	19.1	0.9	3.9	0.1
Danish, Average	1 Slice/11g	14	125	18.4	1.1	5.4	0.0
Danish, Lean, Average	1oz/28g	26	93	17.9	1.0	1.8	0.0
Dry Cured, Average	1 Slice/18g	26	144	22.4	1.0	5.6	0.2
Dry Cured, Mustard, Sainsbury's*	1 Slice/26.1g	40	153	20.2	1.6	7.3	0.1
Dry Cured, Rosemary &Thyme, Safeway*	1 Slice/28g	37	133	24.8	1.5	3.1	0.0
Extra Lean, Average	1 Slice/11g	10	90	18.0	1.4	1.4	0.0
Gammon Joint, Boiled	1oz/28g	57	204	23.3	0.0	12.3	0.0
Gammon Joint, Raw, Average	1oz/28g	39	138	20.3	0.0	6.3	0.0
Gammon, Cooked, Somerfield*	1oz/28g	45	159	20.0	1.0	8.0	0.0
Gammon, Honey Roast, Average	1 Serving/60g	81	135	22.5	0.5	4.8	0.0
Gammon, Mustard, Cured, Waitrose*	1 Slice/45g	54	120	21.4	0.1	4.0	0.0
Gammon, Oak Smoked, Waitrose*	1 Slice/43g	62	145	24.2	0.0	5.3	0.0
Gammon, Peppered, Waitrose*	1/3 Pack/36g	51	142	20.7	0.3	6.4	0.0
Gammon, Wiltshire, Breaded, British, Marks & Spencer*	1 Pack/95g	128	135	23.6	1.6	3.7	0.0
German Black Forest, Average	½ Pack/35g	93	267	27.2	1.3	17.0	0.5
Glazed With Honey & Muscovado Sugar, Waitrose*	1 Slice/21g	25	119	21.3	0.4	3.6	0.0
Honey & Mustard, Average	1oz/28g	39	140	20.8	4.6	4.3	0.0
Honey Roast, Average	1oz/28g	34	123	20.3	1.6	3.8	0.1
Honey Roast, Dry Cured, Average	1 Slice/33g	46	140	22.7	2.3	4.4	0.2
Honey Roast, Lean, Average	1 Serving/25g	28	111	18.2	2.7	3.1	0.0
Honey Roast, Wafer Thin, Average	1 Slice/10g	11	113	17.4	3.7	3.2	0.3
Honey Roast, Wafer Thin, Premium, Average	1 Serving/75g	112	149	22.0	1.6	6.0	0.0
Italian Rostello, Safeway*	1 Serving/60g	78	130	21.0	0.2	5.0	0.0
Joint, Easy Carve, Asda*	1oz/28g	41	146	22.8	1.2	5.9	0.6
Joint, Honey Roast, Asda*	1oz/28g	35	124	23.9	1.7	2.8	0.7
Lean, Average	1 Serving/100g	104	104	19.5	1.1	2.4	0.3
Maple Drycure, Asda*	1 Slice/37.1g	53	143	22.0	3.0	4.8	0.0
Oak Smoked, Average	1 Pack/160g	208	130	21.0	1.0	4.7	0.3
On The Bone, Breaded, Somerfield*	1oz/28g	45	161	21.0	0.0	9.0	0.0
Parma, Average	1 Serving/10g	21	213	29.3	0.0	10.6	0.0
Parma, Premium, Average	1 Serving/80g	206	258	27.9	0.3	16.1	0.0
Peppered, Average	1 Slice/12g	13	110	18.5	2.1	2.7	0.0
Peppered, Dry Cured, Average	1 Slice/31g	43	140	23.1	1.3	4.7	0.2
Prosciutto, Average	1 Slice/12g	27	227	28.7	0.1	12.4	0.4
Scrumpy Cured, Tesco*	1 Slice/34g	60	176	27.2	0.9	7.1	0.0
Serrano, Spanish, The Best, Safeway*	1 Packet/70g	153	218	32.0	0.0	10.0	0.0
Smoked, Average	1 Pack/150g	175	117	19.7	0.9	3.7	0.0
Smoked, Dry Cured, Average	1 Slice/28g	38	137	23.0	1.5	4.4	0.2
Smoked, Wafer Thin, Average	1 Serving/40g	41	102	17.7	1.2	2.9	0.2
Thick Carved, Finest, Tesco*	1 Serving/75g	89	119	22.8	0.1	3.0	0.0
Thick Cut, Tesco*	1 Serving/85g	119	140	20.6	1.4	5.8	0.0
Turkey, Average	1 Serving/75g	81	108	15.6	2.8	3.9	0.0
Wafer Thin, Average	1 Pack/180g	181	101	17.9	1.4	2.6	0.1
Wiltshire, Average	1oz/28g	41	148	23.1	0.0	6.1	0.0
Wiltshire, Crumbed, Average	1oz/28g	41	145	23.9	1.0	5.0	0.0
Wiltshire, Orange Marmalade Roasted, Finest, Tesco*	1 Slice/40g	67	167	26.0	2.0	6.1	0.3
HARIBO*,							
American Hard Gums	1 Pack/175g	630	360	0.3	85.5	1.9	0.2

H

	Measure INFO/WEIGHT	per Measure KCAL	Nutrition Values per 100g / 100ml				
			KCAL	PROT	CARB	FAT	FIBRE
HARIBO*,							
Cola Bottles	1 Sm Pack/16g	57	358	7.7	78.9	1.3	0.3
Cola Bottles, Fizzy	1 Pack/175g	628	359	6.3	78.3	2.3	0.5
Dolly Mixtures	1 Pack/175g	719	411	1.8	90.2	4.8	0.2
Fantasy Mix	1 Sm Pack/100g	360	360	6.6	79.0	2.0	0.3
Gold Bears	1 Pack/100g	358	358	7.7	78.9	1.3	0.3
Horror Mix	1 Sm Pack/100g	360	360	6.6	79.0	2.0	0.3
Jelly Beans	1 Pack/100g	360	360	3.8	89.2	1.2	0.0
Kiddies Super Mix	1 Pack/100g	401	401	1.1	95.3	1.7	0.8
Milky Mix	1 Pack/175g	644	368	7.1	79.6	2.3	0.4
Mint Imperials	1 Pack/175g	695	397	0.4	98.8	0.5	0.1
Pontefract Cakes, Haribo*	1 Pack/200g	612	306	5.3	68.2	1.3	5.6
Starmix	1 Pack/100g	360	360	6.6	79.0	2.0	0.3
Tangfastics	1 Pack/100g	359	359	6.3	78.3	2.3	0.5
Wine Gums	1 Pack/175g	655	374	6.2	85.9	0.6	0.1
HASH,							
Barbecue Beef, COU, Marks & Spencer*	1 Pack/400g	360	90	7.0	14.0	0.4	1.4
Chicken Salsa, Healthy Eating, Tesco*	1 Pack/350g	291	83	4.1	10.6	2.7	1.1
Corned Beef, Asda*	1 Pack/400g	416	104	6.0	12.0	3.6	1.1
Corned Beef, Chilled, Co-Op*	1 Pack/300g	345	115	9.0	5.0	6.0	1.0
Corned Beef, Marks & Spencer*	½ Pack/320g	368	115	7.6	9.6	5.3	2.8
Corned Beef, Somerfield*	1 Pack/300g	324	108	6.2	8.5	5.5	1.6
Corned Beef, Value, Tesco*	1 Pack/300g	372	124	6.8	12.7	5.1	0.7
Farmhouse, Healthy Eating, Tesco*	1 Serving/300g	264	88	2.2	13.6	2.7	1.1
Vegetable & Lentil, Asda*	1 Pack/289g	254	88	3.2	14.0	2.1	0.0
HASH BROWNS,							
Bird's Eye*	1 Serving/63g	126	200	2.0	21.9	11.6	1.6
Burger King*	1 Serving/102g	318	312	7.2	32.3	19.4	3.8
Deep Fried, McCain*	1oz/28g	69	246	2.0	24.3	15.3	0.0
McDonald's*	1 Portion/56g	138	247	2.5	28.3	13.8	3.1
Oven Baked, McCain*	1oz/28g	55	196	1.7	25.5	8.6	0.0
Tesco*	1oz/28g	43	154	2.4	20.0	7.2	1.7
HASLET,							
Somerfield*	1oz/28g	57	205	15.0	10.0	12.0	0.0
HAZELNUTS,							
Average	10 Whole/10g	66	655	15.4	5.8	63.5	6.5
Chopped, Sainsbury's*	1 Serving/10g	66	660	16.6	5.6	63.5	6.5
HEART,							
Ox, Raw	1oz/28g	29	104	18.2	0.0	3.5	0.0
Ox, Stewed	1oz/28g	44	157	27.8	0.0	5.1	0.0
Pig, Raw	1oz/28g	27	97	17.1	0.0	3.2	0.0
Pig, Stewed	1oz/28g	45	162	25.1	0.0	6.8	0.0
HERB CUBES,							
Basil, Knorr*	1 Cube/10g	47	472	6.1	35.9	33.8	0.6
Parsley & Garlic, Knorr*	1 Cube/10g	42	422	8.6	35.2	27.4	1.8
HERMESETAS,							
Hermes*	1 Tsp/0.78	3	387	1.0	96.8	0.0	0.0
HEROES,							
Miniture, Cadbury's*	1 Hero/8g	40	505	6.0	61.0	27.0	0.0
HERRING,							
Canned, In Tomato Sauce, Average	1oz/28g	57	204	11.9	4.1	15.5	0.1
Dried, Salted	1oz/28g	47	168	25.3	0.0	7.4	0.0
Fillets, In Mustard & Dill Sauce, John West*	1 Can/190g	426	224	11.7	3.7	18.0	0.1
Fillets, In Olive Oil, Succulent, Princes*	1 Serving/50g	108	215	20.0	0.0	15.0	0.0

H

HERRING,

	Measure INFO/WEIGHT	per Measure KCAL	KCAL	PROT	CARB	FAT	FIBRE
Fillets, Raw, Average	1oz/28g	52	185	18.4	0.0	12.6	0.0
Grilled	1oz/28g	51	181	20.1	0.0	11.2	0.0
In Horseradish Sauce, John West*	1oz/28g	64	230	13.0	4.0	18.0	0.0
Oatmeal, Fried In Vegetable Oil	1oz/28g	66	234	23.1	1.5	15.1	0.1
Pickled	1oz/28g	59	209	16.7	10.0	11.1	0.0
Rollmop, With Onion, Asda*	1 Rollmop/65g	89	137	13.2	10.3	4.8	0.8
Rollmops, Tesco*	1 Serving/130g	181	139	7.8	8.6	8.2	0.4
Smoked, Pepper, In Oil, Glyngøre*	1 Can/130g	338	260	21.0	0.0	19.0	0.0

HIGH LIGHTS,

	Measure INFO/WEIGHT	per Measure KCAL	KCAL	PROT	CARB	FAT	FIBRE
Caffe Latte, Made Up, Cadbury's*	1 Serving/200g	40	20	1.0	2.5	0.7	0.0
Choc Malt Hot Chocolate, Made Up, Cadbury's*	1 Serving/200ml	44	22	1.0	2.5	0.7	0.3
Choc Mint, Made Up, Cadbury's*	1 Serving/200ml	40	20	1.0	2.5	0.7	0.3
Chocolate Drink, Dry, Cadbury's	1 Sachet/10g	36	364	17.1	44.7	13.0	4.6
Chocolate Orange, Made Up, Cadbury's*	1 Serving/200ml	40	20	1.0	2.3	0.7	0.3
Dairy Fudge, Made Up, Cadbury's*	1 Serving/200ml	40	20	1.0	2.8	0.5	0.2
Dark Chocolate, Cadbury's*	1 Serving/200ml	35	18	1.3	2.1	0.5	0.0
Espresso, Made Up, Cadbury's*	1 Serving/200ml	35	18	1.3	2.0	0.5	0.0
Made Up, Cadbury's*	1 Cup/200ml	40	20	1.0	2.5	0.7	0.3
Mint, Cadbury's*	1 Serving/200ml	40	20	1.0	2.5	0.7	0.0
Toffee Flavour, Made Up, Cadbury's*	1 Serving/200ml	40	20	1.0	2.6	0.7	0.0

HOKI,

	Measure INFO/WEIGHT	per Measure KCAL	KCAL	PROT	CARB	FAT	FIBRE
Grilled	1oz/28g	34	121	24.1	0.0	2.7	0.0
In Breadcrumbs, Average	1 Piece/156g	298	191	14.5	13.9	8.9	1.2
Raw	1oz/28g	24	85	16.9	0.0	1.9	0.0
Steaks, In Batter, Crispy, Bird's Eye*	1 Steak/123.1g	320	260	12.4	21.3	13.9	0.8

HONEY,

	Measure INFO/WEIGHT	per Measure KCAL	KCAL	PROT	CARB	FAT	FIBRE
Acacia, Tesco*	1 Tsp/4g	12	307	0.4	76.4	0.0	0.0
Australian Eucalyptus, Finest, Tesco*	1 Tsp/4g	12	307	0.4	76.4	0.0	0.0
Canadian Clover, TTD, Sainsbury's*	1 Tsp/5g	17	339	0.1	84.7	0.1	0.3
Florida Orange, Extra Special, Asda*	1 Tbsp/15g	50	334	0.5	83.0	0.0	0.0
Greek, Waitrose*	1 Tsp/6g	18	307	0.4	76.4	0.0	0.0
Mexican, TTD, Sainsbury's*	1 Tbsp/15g	51	339	0.1	84.7	0.1	0.3
Pure, Clear, Average	1 Tbsp/20g	63	314	0.3	79.1	0.0	0.0
Pure, Set, Average	1 Tsp/5g	16	312	0.4	77.6	0.0	0.0
Spanish Orange Blossom, Sainsbury's*	1 Tbsp/15g	51	339	0.1	84.7	0.0	0.3
Tasmanian Leatherwood, TTD, Sainsbury's*	1 Serving/6g	20	339	0.1	84.7	0.1	0.3

HORLICKS,

	Measure INFO/WEIGHT	per Measure KCAL	KCAL	PROT	CARB	FAT	FIBRE
Low Fat Instant Powder, Made Up With Water	1 Mug/227ml	116	51	2.4	10.1	0.5	0.0
Malted Chocolate Drink, Light, Dry, Horlicks*	1 Sachet/32g	123	384	13.7	7.3	4.1	1.7
Malted Drink, Light, Dry, Horlicks*	1 Sachet/32g	123	384	13.7	73.0	4.1	2.7
Powder, Made Up With Semi-Skimmed Milk	1 Mug/227ml	184	81	4.3	12.9	1.9	0.0
Powder, Made Up With Skimmed Milk	1 Mug/227ml	159	70	4.3	12.9	0.5	0.0
Powder, Made Up With Whole Milk	1 Mug/227ml	225	99	4.2	12.7	3.9	0.0
Snoozoo, Chocolate, Dry, Horlicks*	1 Sachet/20g	74	370	8.6	74.2	4.3	4.3

HORSERADISH,

	Measure INFO/WEIGHT	per Measure KCAL	KCAL	PROT	CARB	FAT	FIBRE
Raw	1oz/28g	17	62	4.5	11.0	0.3	6.2

HOT CHOCOLATE,

	Measure INFO/WEIGHT	per Measure KCAL	KCAL	PROT	CARB	FAT	FIBRE
Caramel Flavoured, Instant, Dry, Aldi*	1 Serving/11g	40	363	18.5	40.6	14.1	8.5
Chocolate Break, Dry, Tesco*	1 Serving/21g	110	524	7.9	58.9	28.5	1.7
Chocolate Time, Safeway*	1 Serving/30g	123	411	9.4	67.8	11.4	1.8
Drink, Balanced Lifestyle, Camelot, Aldi*	1 Sachet/11g	40	363	18.5	40.6	14.1	0.5
Galaxy, Mars*	1 Mug/28g	115	411	7.0	68.7	12.1	0.0
Horlicks*	1 Serving/32g	128	400	8.8	72.5	8.1	3.8

H

	Measure INFO/WEIGHT	per Measure KCAL	Nutrition Values per 100g / 100ml				
			KCAL	PROT	CARB	FAT	FIBRE
HOT CHOCOLATE,							
Instant Break, Cadbury's*	1 Sachet/28g	119	426	10.9	64.2	14.0	2.3
Instant, BGTY, Sainsbury's*	1 Sachet/28g	16	56	2.1	10.6	0.6	0.3
Instant, GFY, Asda*	1 Mug/200ml	106	53	1.8	10.0	0.6	0.4
Instant, Galaxy*	1 Serving/28g	115	411	7.0	68.7	12.1	0.0
Instant, Tesco*	1 Serving/32g	132	414	8.0	68.3	12.1	0.7
Low Calorie, Somerfield*	1 Sachet/12g	40	330	18.0	48.0	8.0	0.0
Maltesers, Malt Drink, Instant, Mars*	1 Serving/220ml	104	47	0.9	7.7	1.4	0.0
McDonald's*	1 Reg Cup/32ml	122	380	7.0	79.0	4.0	0.0
Organic, Green & Black's*	1 Tsp/3g	11	376	7.4	66.8	6.6	0.0
Protein, Easy Body*	1 Serving/20g	74	370	70.7	19.2	1.2	0.0
Slim Fast*	1 Serving/59g	203	347	22.2	53.8	4.8	8.4
Soya Milk, EAT*	1 Tall/278ml	115	42	3.5	2.1	2.2	0.0
Value, Tesco*	1 Serving/32g	132	414	8.0	68.3	12.1	0.7
Velvet, Cadbury's*	1 Serving/28g	136	487	8.6	57.8	24.6	2.0
With Marshmallows, Swiss Miss*	1 Mug/25g	103	413	6.0	80.0	9.0	0.0
With Whipped Cream Grande, Starbucks*	1 Mug/473ml	440	93	3.2	9.3	5.1	0.4
HOT DOG,							
& Ketchup, McDonald's*	1 Serving/116g	296	255	9.6	25.8	12.6	1.3
Sausage, American Style, Average	1 Sausage/75g	180	241	11.6	6.2	19.0	0.0
Sausage, Average	1 Sausage/23g	40	175	10.8	4.3	12.8	0.3
HOT DOG VEGETARIAN,							
Meat Free, Sainsbury's*	1 Sausage/30g	70	235	17.8	4.2	16.4	1.9
Tesco*	1 Sausage/30g	81	271	19.0	6.0	19.0	2.0
HOT POT,							
Beef, Ross*	1 Pack/322g	254	79	2.5	9.4	3.5	0.4
Beef, Weight Watchers*	1 Pack/320g	266	83	4.6	10.6	2.4	1.1
Chicken & Cider, Ready Meals, Waitrose*	1 Pack/400g	500	125	6.8	12.9	5.1	1.1
Chicken, Co-Op*	1 Pack/340g	289	85	6.0	9.0	3.0	0.7
Chicken, GFY, Asda*	1 Serving/400g	292	73	5.0	10.0	1.4	0.8
Chicken, Good Choice, Iceland*	1 Pack/400g	276	69	5.0	9.3	1.3	1.0
Chicken, Healthy Living, Tesco*	1 Pack/400g	348	87	5.0	12.0	2.1	1.8
Chicken, Safeway*	1 Pack/400g	292	73	4.2	10.7	1.5	1.6
Chicken, Sainsbury's*	1 Pack/400g	340	85	5.2	9.9	2.8	1.3
Chicken, Weight Watchers*	1 Pack/330g	277	84	5.4	10.1	2.4	0.7
Lamb & Vegetable, Asda*	1 Pot/500g	240	48	4.0	7.0	0.4	0.0
Lamb, Heinz*	1 Pack/340g	337	99	4.9	12.7	3.1	1.7
Lamb, Safeway*	½ Pack/225g	218	97	6.9	8.1	4.1	1.3
Lancashire, Asda*	1 Pack/401g	269	67	3.8	10.0	1.3	0.9
Lancashire, Marks & Spencer*	1 Pack/454g	431	95	10.1	6.7	3.3	1.0
Lancashire, Safeway*	1 Pack/400g	336	84	8.4	6.6	2.7	1.3
Lancashire, Sainsbury's*	½ Pack/225g	203	90	6.7	9.5	2.8	0.5
Lancashire, Tesco*	½ Pack/225g	205	91	6.0	9.7	3.1	0.5
Minced Beef & Vegetable, COU, Marks & Spencer*	1 Pack/400g	380	95	10.3	9.0	1.7	2.4
Minced Beef, Asda*	1 Pack/375g	409	109	7.0	10.0	4.6	1.7
Minced Beef, Classic, Sainsbury's*	1 Pack/450g	491	109	6.1	13.4	3.4	1.0
Minced Beef, Iceland*	1 Pack/500g	505	101	5.5	12.7	3.1	1.3
Minced Beef, Long Life, Sainsbury's*	1 Pack/300g	207	69	3.9	10.0	1.5	0.9
Minced Beef, Marks & Spencer*	½ Pack/227g	227	100	8.0	8.0	3.5	1.7
Minced Beef, Mini Favourites, Marks & Spencer*	1 Pack/300g	210	70	5.0	6.4	2.9	2.5
Minced Beef, Sainsbury's*	1 Pack/300g	174	58	3.6	7.0	1.7	2.1
Minced Beef, SmartPrice, Asda*	1 Pack/300g	199	66	3.7	10.0	1.3	0.4
Minced Beef, Tesco*	1 Pack/400g	352	88	3.6	10.6	3.5	1.7
Sausage With Baked Beans, Heinz*	1 Can/340g	354	104	4.6	14.3	3.2	2.4

H

INFO/WEIGHT	Measure	per Measure KCAL	Nutrition Values per 100g / 100ml KCAL	PROT	CARB	FAT	FIBRE
HOT POT,							
Sausage, SmartPrice, Asda*	1 Pack/300g	239	80	3.7	11.0	2.3	0.4
Vegetable, Ross*	1 Pack/300g	261	87	2.4	11.7	3.5	2.0
Vegetable, Weight Watchers*	1 Pack/335g	228	68	2.6	9.9	1.9	1.5
HOUMOUS,							
30% Less Fat, Asda*	1oz/28g	77	275	8.8	16.4	19.4	2.1
BGTY, Sainsbury's*	1 Serving/50g	100	200	7.3	12.5	13.0	6.4
Co-Op*	1 Tbsp/25g	91	365	9.0	14.0	30.0	3.0
Dip, Reduced Fat, Co-Op*	1 Tbsp/25g	63	250	8.0	12.0	19.0	3.0
Fresh, 25% Less Fat, Tesco*	1 Serving/85g	207	244	7.5	12.9	18.1	4.8
Fresh, Dips, Tesco*	1/3 Pot/94g	271	288	6.8	10.7	24.2	3.0
Fresh, Healthy Choice, Safeway*	1oz/28g	74	264	9.1	13.6	19.2	0.0
Fresh, Tesco*	1oz/28g	83	296	7.8	7.9	25.9	3.3
GFY, Asda*	½ Pot/85g	209	246	9.0	12.0	18.0	4.3
Good Intentions, Somerfield*	½ Pot/85g	201	236	7.5	12.9	17.2	3.3
Greek, Somerfield*	1 Serving/50g	152	304	7.6	8.2	26.8	5.5
Lemon & Coriander, Sainsbury's*	½ Pot/85g	247	291	7.0	9.1	25.1	6.0
Light, Morrisons*	½ Pack/85g	200	235	7.4	10.9	18.0	0.0
Low Fat, Safeway*	1 Serving/10g	26	258	9.0	12.8	19.0	3.3
Marks & Spencer*	1oz/28g	87	310	7.1	9.5	27.3	3.3
Mixed Olive, Sainsbury's*	½ Pot/85g	228	268	6.7	8.4	23.1	7.7
Organic, Marks & Spencer*	1 Serving/42g	139	330	6.9	9.1	29.7	3.3
Organic, Tesco*	1 Pot/170g	544	320	6.5	12.3	27.2	2.4
Red Pepper, Roasted, Sainsbury's*	½ Pot/85.2g	252	297	7.0	7.4	26.6	3.5
Reduced Fat, Fresh, Tesco*	1oz/28g	66	236	7.5	12.9	17.2	3.3
Reduced Fat, Marks & Spencer*	1oz/28g	67	240	7.5	12.9	17.2	3.3
Reduced Fat, Mediterranean Deli, Marks & Spencer*	1 Serving/75g	158	210	7.5	8.3	16.2	9.3
Reduced Fat, Morrisons*	1 Serving/50g	94	188	6.0	14.1	12.6	2.0
Reduced Fat, Safeway*	1 Serving/25g	65	260	9.0	12.5	19.3	3.3
Reduced Fat, Waitrose*	1oz/28g	67	239	7.7	11.3	18.1	2.6
Roasted Red Pepper, 50% Less Fat, Tesco*	½ Pot/85g	156	184	7.3	10.9	12.4	9.5
Roasted Red Pepper, Tesco*	1 Serving/75g	221	294	7.0	9.6	25.3	5.5
Sainsbury's*	½ Pot/85g	265	312	7.3	8.9	27.5	2.2
Somerfield*	1oz/28g	87	309	8.0	11.0	26.0	0.0
Spicy Red Pepper, Marks & Spencer*	¼ Pot/75g	158	210	7.3	14.8	13.7	2.5
Sun Dried Tomato, Chunky, Tesco*	½ Pot/95g	322	339	6.7	14.0	28.4	3.3
Waitrose*	¼ Pot/74.9g	248	331	7.5	9.2	29.3	3.0
With Crunchy Vegetables, Starbucks*	1 Pot/219g	359	164	4.7	26.4	4.4	2.9
HULA HOOPS,							
Bacon & Ketchup Flavour, KP*	1 Bag/27g	140	517	3.4	56.3	30.9	2.0
Barbecue Beef Flavour, KP*	1 Bag/34g	170	500	3.9	58.7	27.5	2.4
Beef & Mustard, KP*	1 Bag/50g	260	519	3.9	55.0	31.5	1.8
Beef, KP*	1 Bag/27g	139	513	3.6	60.5	28.5	1.7
Cheese & Onion, KP*	1 Bag/34g	179	525	3.9	56.8	31.4	2.2
Cheese Toastie, KP*	1 Bag/34g	178	523	3.4	56.7	31.4	2.0
Minis, Original, KP*	1 Tub/140g	752	537	3.0	52.9	34.8	1.7
Original, KP*	1 Bag/34g	177	522	3.2	57.8	30.9	2.0
Salt & Vinegar, KP*	1 Bag/34g	169	497	3.7	58.4	27.4	2.5
Sizzling Bacon, KP*	1 Bag/34g	175	514	3.2	54.7	31.4	2.1
Totally Cheese Flavour Shoks, KP*	1 Bag/55g	285	519	3.8	54.5	31.8	2.1

H

ICE CREAM,

	Measure INFO/WEIGHT	per Measure KCAL	KCAL	PROT	CARB	FAT	FIBRE
After Eight, Nestle*	1 Serving/55.1g	114	207	3.6	27.1	9.4	0.3
Baileys, Haagen-Dazs*	1oz/28g	73	260	4.5	22.2	17.1	0.0
Banana, Thorntons*	1oz/28g	63	225	4.0	23.8	12.6	0.0
Bananas Foster, Haagen-Dazs*	1 Serving/125ml	260	208	3.2	22.4	12.0	0.0
Banoffee Fudge, Sainsbury's*	1/8 Pot/67g	119	178	2.8	28.7	5.9	0.2
Banoffee, Criminally Creamy, Co-Op*	1oz/28g	66	235	3.0	26.0	13.0	0.1
Belgian Chocolate, Haagen-Dazs*	1oz/28g	89	318	4.6	28.4	20.7	0.0
Bounty, Mars*	1oz/28g	77	274	3.3	23.8	18.3	0.0
Bourbon Biscuit, Asda*	1 Dessert/37g	120	324	5.9	48.6	12.2	1.6
Bournville, Cadbury's*	1 Bar/120g	258	215	3.5	26.0	11.6	0.0
Brandy, Luxurious, Marks & Spencer*	1 Serving/100g	228	228	3.8	19.1	13.3	0.2
Cappuccino, Thorntons*	1oz/28g	61	218	4.4	20.7	12.9	0.0
Caramel Craze, Organic, Tesco*	1 Serving/100g	253	253	3.3	25.5	15.3	0.0
Caramel, Carte d'Or*	2 Boules/50g	106	212	2.6	30.8	8.7	0.0
Cherrylicious, Tesco*	1 Serving/57.7g	122	210	2.8	37.0	5.6	0.2
Chilli Red, Purbeck*	1 Serving/50g	99	198	4.8	18.7	11.5	0.0
Choc Chip Cookie Dough, Ben & Jerrys*	1 Serving/100g	230	230	3.0	23.0	14.0	0.0
Choc Chip, Cookie Dough, Haagen-Dazs*	1oz/28g	83	296	4.2	27.7	18.8	0.0
Choc Chip, Haagen-Dazs*	1oz/28g	80	286	4.7	24.8	18.7	0.0
Chocolate & Caramel, Stick, SlimFast*	1 Ice Cream/55g	87	159	4.1	26.3	4.2	2.2
Chocolate & Marshmallow, Swirl, BGTY, Sainsbury's*	1 Sm Scoop/40g	69	173	3.9	33.8	2.5	2.8
Chocolate Brownie With Walnuts, Haagen-Dazs*	1 Cup/101g	290	287	5.0	24.8	18.8	0.0
Chocolate Chip, Baskin Robbins*	1 Serving/75g	170	227	4.0	24.0	13.3	0.0
Chocolate Flavour, Soft Scoop, Sainsbury's*	1 Serving/70g	122	174	3.1	23.6	7.5	0.3
Chocolate Fudge Brownie, Ben & Jerry's*	1 Serving/100g	260	260	0.0	31.0	13.0	2.0
Chocolate Fudge Swirl, Haagen-Dazs*	1oz/28g	77	276	4.6	25.6	17.2	0.0
Chocolate Honeycomb, COU, Marks & Spencer*	1 Serving/100ml	150	150	3.5	31.5	2.6	0.7
Chocolate Honeycomb, Co-Op*	¼ Pot/81g	186	230	4.0	26.0	13.0	0.3
Chocolate Midnight Cookies, Haagen-Dazs*	1oz/28g	81	289	4.9	28.7	17.2	0.0
Chocolate Mint Crisp, COU, Marks & Spencer*	¼ Pot/85.2g	115	135	5.4	21.9	2.9	1.0
Chocolate Orange, Deliciously Dairy, Co-Op*	1oz/28g	55	195	4.0	29.0	7.0	0.8
Chocolate, 98% Fat Free, Too Good, Wall's*	1 Spoonful/20ml	15	75	2.2	14.1	1.0	0.2
Chocolate, COU, Marks & Spencer*	1 Serving/140g	231	165	3.9	35.0	2.9	0.8
Chocolate, Dairy, The Best, Safeway*	1 Serving/82.4g	243	296	4.6	28.1	18.3	2.0
Chocolate, Easy Serve, Co-Op*	1oz/28g	46	165	3.0	22.0	7.0	0.3
Chocolate, On Stick, Green & Black's*	1 Stick/100g	214	214	3.7	19.3	13.6	2.1
Chocolate, Organic, Green & Black's*	1 Serving/20g	35	176	3.5	18.6	9.8	1.3
Chocolate, Organic, Iceland*	1oz/28g	58	208	4.9	28.6	8.2	0.0
Chocolate, Organic, Marks & Spencer*	1oz/28g	71	255	5.0	24.0	16.0	1.5
Chocolate, Soft Scoop, Asda*	1 Scoop/47g	84	179	3.7	23.0	8.0	0.0
Chocolate, Thorntons*	1oz/28g	67	238	4.6	25.1	12.9	0.0
Chocolate, With Chocolate Chips, Milfina, Aldi*	1oz/28g	66	235	3.8	26.7	12.5	0.8
Chocolatino, Tesco*	1 Serving/100g	243	243	4.4	32.2	10.8	0.6
Chunky Chocolate, Giant, Marks & Spencer*	1 Lolly/89.6g	302	335	4.0	28.0	23.0	2.3
Chunky Monkey, Ben & Jerry's*	1 Serving/100g	280	280	4.0	28.0	17.0	1.0
Coconut, Carte D'or*	1 Serving/100ml	125	125	1.8	14.0	7.1	0.5
Coffee, Finest, Tesco*	¼ Pot/93g	236	254	4.9	22.5	16.0	0.0
Coffee, Waitrose*	1 Serving/180ml	256	142	3.2	13.2	8.5	0.0
Cookies & Cream, Haagen-Dazs*	1oz/28g	73	262	4.6	22.6	17.0	0.0
Cornish Clotted, Marks & Spencer*	1 Pot/90g	207	230	2.8	21.8	14.5	0.1
Cornish Dairy, Waitrose*	1 Serving/125ml	161	129	2.3	14.6	6.8	0.0
Cornish Style, Co-Op*	1oz/28g	53	190	4.0	23.0	9.0	0.1
Cornish Vanilla, Organic, Iceland*	1oz/28g	60	214	4.1	21.4	12.4	0.0

ICE CREAM,	Measure INFO/WEIGHT	per Measure KCAL	Nutrition Values per 100g / 100ml				
			KCAL	PROT	CARB	FAT	FIBRE
Cornish Vanilla, Soft Scoop, Marks & Spencer*	1oz/28g	56	199	3.9	21.8	10.7	0.2
Creamy Caramella, Tesco*	1 Serving/54.7g	114	207	3.7	31.4	7.3	0.0
Creamy Chocolate & Nut, Co-Op*	1oz/28g	66	235	4.0	25.0	13.0	0.5
Crunchie, Cadbury's*	1 Pot/500ml	710	142	2.3	19.4	12.5	0.0
Dairy Cornish, Tesco*	1 Serving/49g	112	228	3.2	24.7	12.3	0.1
Dairy Milk, Orange, Cadbury's*	1 Serving/120ml	259	216	3.5	26.0	11.6	0.0
Dairy Milk, Vanilla, Mr Men, Nestle*	1 Lolly/40ml	39	98	2.9	14.7	3.0	0.0
Dairy, Pizza Hut*	1 Portion/141.7g	273	192	4.6	23.3	8.9	0.2
Dark Toffee, Organic, Green & Black's*	¼ Pot/125ml	193	154	2.8	18.1	7.9	0.1
Demon Chocolate, Marks & Spencer*	1 Serving/79g	208	263	3.7	37.1	11.1	0.6
Double Chocolate, Nestle*	1 Serving/77.5g	250	320	4.8	33.7	18.4	0.0
Dream, Cadbury's*	1 Bar/120ml	264	220	3.6	26.0	11.9	0.0
Dulce De Leche, Bar, Haagan-Daaz*	1 Bar/105g	370	352	3.8	32.3	22.9	0.0
Galaxy, Mars*	1 Bar/60ml	203	339	4.7	29.7	22.4	0.0
Get Fruit, Tropical, Solero*	1 Serving/125ml	163	130	1.6	20.6	4.4	0.4
Heavenly Vanilla, Cadbury's*	1 Serving/250ml	355	142	2.5	12.8	9.3	0.0
Honey, I'm Home, Ben & Jerry's*	1 Serving/100g	260	260	0.0	28.0	15.0	0.0
Honeycomb Harvest, Mackies*	1 Serving/100g	209	209	4.0	25.0	10.0	0.0
Knickerbocker Glory	1oz/28g	31	112	1.5	16.4	5.0	0.2
Lemon & White Chocolate, Crackpots, Iceland*	1 Serving/100g	202	202	1.7	29.9	8.4	0.3
Lemon Curd Swirl, Duchy Originals*	¼ Pot/101g	247	245	3.7	25.8	14.1	0.0
Lemon Pie, Haagan-Dazs*	1oz/28g	73	262	3.9	24.5	16.3	0.0
Less Than 5% Fat, Asda*	2 Scoops/80g	111	139	2.7	22.0	4.5	0.0
Light Chocolate Ices, Co-Op*	1 Ice/62g	121	195	2.0	18.0	13.0	0.5
Log, Mint Chocolate, Sainsbury's*	1 Serving/50.75g	100	197	3.0	23.8	10.0	0.2
Log, Viennetta, Mint, Wall's*	¼ Standard/84g	212	252	3.4	22.9	16.4	0.0
Luscious Mint Choc Chip, Morrisons*	1 Serving/50g	99	198	2.9	23.1	10.5	0.7
Luxurious Marshallow, Weight Watchers*	½ Tub/138g	268	194	3.2	34.5	4.7	1.3
Magic Maple, Marks & Spencer*	1 Ice Cream/93g	259	278	2.9	39.0	12.3	0.6
Magnum Moments, Wall's*	1 Serving/18ml	58	323	4.0	30.0	20.8	0.0
Magnum, Almond, Wall's*	1 Serving/95g	329	346	5.3	28.4	23.2	0.0
Mango, 98% Fat Free, Bulla*	1 Serving/70g	94	134	4.2	25.4	1.6	0.0
Maple & Walnut, American, Sainsbury's*	1/8 Pot/68g	121	179	3.1	25.6	7.2	0.2
Maple Brazil, Thorntons*	1oz/28g	66	236	4.1	24.4	13.6	0.0
Mars, Mars*	1 Bar/75g	260	346	5.1	37.2	19.7	0.0
Mince Pie, Finest, Tesco*	¼ Pack/187.5g	478	254	3.9	33.0	11.8	1.1
Mint & Chocolate, Sainsbury's*	1 Serving/80g	154	192	3.4	23.5	9.4	0.4
Mint Choc Chip Soft Scoop, Asda*	1 Serving/46g	86	187	2.9	24.0	9.0	0.3
Mint Choc Chip, Organic, Iceland*	1oz/28g	55	197	4.7	25.8	8.3	0.0
Mint Crisp, Nestle*	1 Serving/75ml	232	309	2.9	25.5	21.9	0.9
Mint Ripple, Good Choice, Iceland*	1 Scoop/50g	59	117	3.0	21.7	2.1	0.1
Mint, Majestic Luxury, Iceland*	1 Serving/79.8g	270	337	3.8	39.3	18.3	1.3
Mint, Thorntons*	1oz/28g	66	237	4.0	25.0	13.4	0.0
Mocha Coffee Indulgence, Sainsbury's*	¼ Pot/82g	178	217	3.2	22.1	12.9	0.1
Monster Mint, Sainsbury's*	1/8 Pot/67g	121	180	3.0	26.3	6.9	0.3
Muddy Pigs, Wall's*	1 Serving/150ml	150	100	1.7	12.1	4.9	0.3
Neapolitan Brick, Co-Op*	1oz/28g	43	155	3.0	20.0	7.0	0.2
Neapolitan Easy Serve, Co-Op*	1oz/28g	42	150	3.0	20.0	7.0	0.2
Neapolitan, Iceland*	1oz/28g	46	164	3.0	21.3	7.4	0.0
Neapolitan, Organic, Iceland*	1oz/28g	55	196	4.2	26.4	8.2	0.0
Neapolitan, Soft Scoop, Asda*	1 Scoop/47g	83	176	3.1	23.0	8.0	0.0
Neapolitan, Soft Scoop, Marks & Spencer*	1 Scoop/65g	120	185	3.8	23.9	8.2	0.1
Neapolitan, Soft Scoop, Sainsbury's*	1 Serving/75g	124	165	2.8	22.8	6.9	0.2

ICE CREAM,

	Measure INFO/WEIGHT	per Measure KCAL	KCAL	PROT	CARB	FAT	FIBRE
Non-Dairy, Mixes	1oz/28g	51	182	4.1	25.1	7.9	0.0
Non-Dairy, Reduced Calorie	1oz/28g	33	119	3.4	13.7	6.0	0.0
Non-Dairy, Vanilla	1oz/28g	50	178	3.2	23.1	8.7	0.0
One Sweet Whirled, Ben & Jerry's*	½ Cup/240ml	280	117	1.7	13.8	6.3	0.0
Organic, Mini, Waitrose*	1 Serving/110g	107	97	2.1	12.9	4.1	2.1
Peach Melba, Soft Scoop, Marks & Spencer*	1oz/28g	46	165	2.8	21.4	7.6	0.3
Picnic, Cadbury's*	1 Cone/125ml	258	207	3.4	28.9	9.4	0.3
Praline & Chocolate, Thorntons*	1oz/28g	87	309	4.6	21.3	22.9	0.6
Praline, Green & Black's*	1 Sm Pot/100g	191	191	3.5	20.0	10.8	0.9
Pralines & Cream, Haagen-Dazs*	1oz/28g	77	276	4.2	26.2	17.2	0.0
Raspberries, Clotted Cream, Waitrose*	1 Tub/500ml	790	158	2.9	18.9	7.9	0.1
Raspberry & Shortcake, Co-Op*	1oz/28g	64	230	3.0	23.0	14.0	0.3
Raspberry Pavlova, Sainsbury's*	1 Serving/100g	202	202	2.7	26.6	9.4	3.3
Raspberry Ripple Brick, Tesco*	1 Serving/48g	71	148	2.6	20.8	6.0	0.2
Raspberry Ripple, Co-Op*	1oz/28g	45	160	3.0	23.0	7.0	0.2
Raspberry Ripple, Organic, Iceland*	1oz/28g	50	180	4.8	22.6	7.8	0.0
Raspberry Ripple, Soft Scoop, Asda*	1 Scoop/46g	75	164	2.5	25.0	6.0	0.0
Raspberry Ripple, Soft Scoop, Sainsbury's*	1 Serving/75g	128	170	2.6	24.2	7.0	0.3
Raspberry Ripple, Soft Scoop, Tesco*	2 Scoops/50g	79	157	2.5	23.0	6.1	0.2
Raspberry, Easy Serve, Co-Op*	1oz/28g	43	152	2.5	22.3	5.9	0.0
Really Creamy After Dinner Mint, Asda*	1 Serving/100g	191	191	3.4	24.0	9.0	0.4
Really Creamy Chocolate, Asda*	1 Serving/100g	227	227	4.1	28.0	11.0	0.4
Really Creamy Toffee, Asda*	1 Serving/120ml	146	122	1.8	17.5	5.0	0.1
Rocky Road, Sainsbury's*	1/8 Pot/67g	137	205	3.8	30.9	7.3	1.0
Rolo, Nestle*	½ Tub/500ml	1180	236	3.4	31.9	10.5	0.2
Rum & Raisin, Organic, Iceland*	1oz/28g	55	195	4.5	28.1	7.2	0.0
Screwball, Asda*	1 Screwball/60.1g	122	203	3.3	25.0	10.0	1.5
Screwball, Co-Op*	1 Lolly/95g	190	200	2.0	31.0	7.0	0.0
Screwball, Safeway*	1 Serving/65g	129	198	3.1	24.5	9.7	0.6
Screwball, Tesco*	1 Screwball/61g	116	190	2.9	25.2	8.6	0.3
Smarties Ice Cream Pot, Nestle	1 Pot	151	218	4.4	33.6	8.2	0.0
Smarties, Nestle*	1 Serving/50g	125	250	3.6	32.3	11.9	0.2
Stem Ginger With Belgian Chocolate, Waitrose*	1 Lolly/109.9g	255	232	2.9	25.5	13.1	1.7
Sticky Toffee, Cream O' Galloway*	1 Serving/30g	80	266	4.7	28.7	14.7	0.0
Strawberries & Cream, Deliciously Dairy, Co-Op*	1oz/28g	46	165	3.0	24.0	6.0	0.3
Strawberry & Cream, Mivvi, Nestle*	1 Serving/60g	118	196	2.6	29.4	7.6	0.2
Strawberry & Cream, Organic, Sainsbury's*	1 Serving/100g	193	193	3.6	22.6	9.8	0.4
Strawberry Cheesecake, Co-Op*	1/6 Pot/86g	163	190	3.0	29.0	7.0	0.2
Strawberry Cheesecake, Haagen-Dazs*	1oz/28g	74	266	3.9	26.5	16.1	0.0
Strawberry, Carte D'Or*	1 Serving/100ml	110	110	1.6	16.2	4.3	0.2
Strawberry, Fromage Frais, Asda*	1 Pot/46g	87	190	3.7	28.0	7.0	0.3
Strawberry, Get Fruit, Solero*	1 Serving/100ml	120	120	1.5	18.8	4.5	1.3
Strawberry, Haagen-Dazs*	1oz/28g	67	241	4.0	21.5	15.5	0.0
Strawberry, Majestic, Luxury, Iceland*	1 Lolly/100g	281	281	2.7	25.8	18.6	0.1
Strawberry, Soft Scoop, Tesco*	1 Serving/45.8g	78	170	2.8	23.1	7.4	0.1
Strawberry, Thorntons*	1oz/28g	52	185	3.2	22.5	9.3	0.1
Strawberry, Weight Watchers*	1 Pot/57g	81	142	2.5	23.4	3.9	0.2
Tantilising Toffee, COU, Marks & Spencer*	¼ Pot/125ml	125	100	0.6	18.0	2.8	0.0
The Full Vermonty, Ben & Jerry's*	1 Serving/100g	280	280	0.0	27.0	18.0	1.0
Toffee & Biscuit, Weight Watchers*	1 Pot/100ml	93	93	1.5	14.9	2.7	0.1
Toffee & Vanilla, Sainsbury's*	1 Serving/71.2g	146	205	3.1	26.7	9.5	0.1
Toffee Creme, Haagen-Dazs*	1oz/28g	74	265	4.5	26.7	15.6	0.0
Toffee Crunch, Handmade Farmhouse, TTD, Sainsbury's*	½ Pot/90g	288	320	2.9	29.7	21.1	0.1

ICE CREAM,

	Measure INFO/WEIGHT	per Measure KCAL	Nutrition Values per 100g / 100ml				
			KCAL	PROT	CARB	FAT	FIBRE
Toffee Fudge, Soft Scoop, Asda*	1 Serving/50g	93	185	2.6	28.0	7.0	0.0
Toffee Ripple, Tesco*	1 Serving/100g	173	173	2.7	24.4	7.2	0.1
Toffee, Deliciously Dairy, Co-Op*	1oz/28g	45	160	3.0	21.0	7.0	0.2
Toffee, Somerfield*	1 Serving/75g	172	229	3.4	33.2	9.2	0.9
Toffee, Thorntons*	1oz/28g	61	218	4.1	24.5	11.6	0.0
Toffee, Too Good To Be True, Wall's*	1fl oz/30ml	23	75	2.2	14.9	0.4	0.1
Totally Toffee, Safeway*	1 Serving/100ml	136	136	1.3	21.1	5.1	0.1
Traditional Cornish Blackberry, Marks & Spencer*	1oz/28g	61	218	2.3	28.0	10.8	0.3
Traditional Cornish Strawberry, Marks & Spencer*	1oz/28g	64	229	2.3	29.7	11.2	0.2
Triple Chocolate, Safeway*	1 Serving/100g	235	235	3.8	30.0	10.8	0.0
Tropical Fruit Sorbet, Waitrose*	1 Lolly/109.8g	90	82	1.5	14.5	2.0	0.2
Vanilla & Chocolate Swirl, Safeway*	1 Serving/125g	250	200	3.3	26.2	9.1	0.1
Vanilla & Cinnamon, Finest, Tesco*	1 Serving/50g	115	229	3.9	20.2	14.7	0.4
Vanilla & Strawberry Swirl, Safeway*	1 Serving/125g	238	190	2.9	27.0	7.5	0.2
Vanilla Bean, Purbeck*	1 Serving/100g	198	198	4.8	18.7	11.5	0.0
Vanilla Brick, Co-Op*	1oz/28g	45	160	3.0	21.0	7.0	0.2
Vanilla Caramel Brownie, Haagen-Dazs*	1 Serving/150g	410	273	4.5	26.8	16.5	0.0
Vanilla Caramel Fudge, Ben & Jerry's*	1 Serving/100g	260	260	4.0	28.0	14.0	0.0
Vanilla Choc Fudge, Haagen-Dazs*	1oz/28g	75	267	4.3	23.5	17.2	0.0
Vanilla Dairy, Finest, Tesco*	1 Serving/92g	227	247	4.5	18.0	17.4	0.3
Vanilla Flavour, Budgens*	1oz/28g	45	159	3.0	21.7	6.7	0.1
Vanilla Flavour, Soft Scoop, Sainsbury's*	1 Serving/70g	111	159	3.0	21.7	6.7	0.1
Vanilla With Strawberry Swirl, Mini Tub, Weight Watchers*	1 Mini Tub/57.0g	81	142	2.5	23.4	3.9	0.2
Vanilla, COU, Marks & Spencer*	¼ Pot/79g	111	140	1.7	25.9	2.8	0.8
Vanilla, Carte D'Or*	1 Serving/100ml	110	110	1.6	15.0	4.9	0.2
Vanilla, Criminally Creamy, Co-Op*	1oz/28g	60	215	3.0	18.0	15.0	0.1
Vanilla, Dairy, Organic, Yeo Valley*	1 Serving/100g	206	206	4.9	21.3	11.2	0.0
Vanilla, Deliciously Dairy, Co-Op*	1oz/28g	49	175	3.0	23.0	8.0	0.2
Vanilla, Easy Serve, Co-Op*	1oz/28g	39	140	3.0	18.0	7.0	0.2
Vanilla, Everyday, Co-Op*	1oz/28g	41	145	3.0	18.0	7.0	0.2
Vanilla, Haagen-Dazs*	1oz/28g	70	250	4.5	19.7	17.1	0.0
Vanilla, Light Soft Scoop, 25% Less Fat, Morrisons*	1 Scoop/50g	75	150	2.9	23.2	5.0	0.2
Vanilla, Light, Carte d'Or, Wall's*	1 Serving/50g	71	142	2.3	23.0	4.4	0.0
Vanilla, Low Fat, Weight Watchers*	1 Scoop/125ml	75	60	1.1	9.7	1.7	0.1
Vanilla, Organic, Green & Black's*	1 Sm Tub/100ml	164	164	3.5	15.2	9.8	0.1
Vanilla, Organic, Iceland*	1oz/28g	61	217	4.5	22.2	12.2	0.0
Vanilla, Organic, Sainsbury's*	1 Serving/85g	176	207	4.3	20.5	12.0	0.1
Vanilla, Organic, Waitrose*	1 Serving/125g	178	142	2.7	12.4	9.0	0.0
Vanilla, Really Creamy, Asda*	1 Serving/50g	98	196	3.5	23.0	10.0	0.1
Vanilla, Safeway*	1 Scoop/50g	85	170	2.8	21.5	7.6	0.2
Vanilla, SmartPrice, Asda*	1 Scoop/40g	55	137	2.8	19.0	6.0	0.2
Vanilla, Soft Scoop, 25% Less Fat, Asda*	1oz/28g	42	149	2.9	23.0	5.0	0.0
Vanilla, Soft Scoop, BGTY, Sainsbury's*	1 Serving/75g	104	139	2.7	21.6	4.6	0.2
Vanilla, Soft Scoop, Marks & Spencer*	1 Scoop/125ml	225	180	2.9	23.8	8.1	0.1
Vanilla, Soft Scoop, Tesco*	1oz/28g	39	138	2.7	21.6	4.5	0.2
Vanilla, Soft Scoop, Wall's*	2 Scoops/100ml	90	90	1.4	11.2	4.4	0.1
Vanilla, Soft Slice, Wall's*	1 Serving/100ml	90	90	1.4	11.2	4.4	0.1
Vanilla, Soft, Non Milk Fat, Waitrose*	1 Serving/125ml	78	62	1.3	8.0	2.7	0.1
Vanilla, Thorntons*	1oz/28g	63	225	4.9	20.5	13.6	0.0
Vanilla, Too Good to be True, Walls*	1 Serving/50ml	35	70	2.0	14.9	0.4	0.1
Vanilla, Value, Tesco*	1 Serving/56g	75	134	2.7	18.3	5.5	0.2
Vanilla, Wth Vanilla Pods, Sainsbury's*	1 Serving/100g	195	195	3.5	22.5	10.1	0.1
Vanilletta, Tesco*	1 Serving/46.8g	82	175	4.0	21.6	8.1	0.0

	Measure INFO/WEIGHT	per Measure KCAL	Nutrition Values per 100g / 100ml				
			KCAL	PROT	CARB	FAT	FIBRE
ICE CREAM,							
Viennetta, Biscuit Caramel, Wall's*	1/6 Serving/58g	183	315	3.3	27.8	20.9	0.0
Viennetta, Cappuccino, Wall's*	1 Serving/75g	191	255	3.5	22.0	17.0	0.0
Viennetta, Chocolate, Wall's*	¼ Pot/80g	200	250	4.1	24.0	15.2	0.0
Viennetta, Forest Fruit, Wall's*	1 Serving/98g	265	270	3.4	27.2	16.2	0.0
Viennetta, Mint, Wall's*	1 Serving/80g	204	255	3.4	23.0	16.6	0.0
Viennetta, Selection Brownie, Wall's*	1 Serving/70g	194	277	4.2	28.5	16.2	0.0
Viennetta, Strawberry Cheesecake Biscuit, Wall's*	1 Serving/100g	305	305	3.5	28.1	20.7	0.0
Viennetta, Strawberry, Wall's*	1 Serving/80g	204	255	3.4	22.1	16.8	0.0
Viennetta, Vanilla, Wall's*	¼ Bar/80gg	204	255	3.3	23.0	16.7	0.0
Virtuous Vanilla & Strawberry, Weight Watchers*	1 Serving/100ml	81	81	1.4	13.3	2.2	0.1
Voluptuous Vanilla, COU, Marks & Spencer*	1 Pot/400g	520	130	4.6	22.0	2.6	0.6
White Vanilla Flavour, Soft Scoop, Sainsbury's*	1oz/28g	38	136	2.9	18.8	5.5	0.2
White Vanilla, Soft Scoop, Tesco*	1oz/28g	46	164	3.1	21.8	7.1	0.1
With Cherry Sauce, Tesco*	1 Serving/57.7g	122	210	2.8	37.0	5.6	0.2
Zesty Lemon Meringue, COU, Marks & Spencer*	¼ Pot/73g	120	165	2.6	33.0	2.5	0.5
ICE CREAM BAR,							
Bailey's, Haagen-Dazs*	1oz/28g	86	307	4.1	24.8	21.2	0.0
Choc Chip, Haagen-Dazs*	1oz/28g	90	320	4.3	27.4	21.5	0.0
Chocolate Covered	1oz/28g	90	320	5.0	24.0	23.3	0.0
Chunky Chocolate, Co-Op*	1 Bar/60g	204	340	5.0	35.0	20.0	1.0
Chunky Toffee, Co-Op*	1 Bar/60g	204	340	4.0	34.0	21.0	1.0
Crunchie, Cadbury's	! Bar	155	260	1.7	26.9	21.6	0.0
Dairy Milk, Lolly, Cadbury's	1 Lolly	270	245	2.8	24.2	15.4	0.0
Dairy Milk, With Caramel, Lolly, Cadbury's	1 Lolly	159	265	2.1	27.2	23.7	0.0
Dream, Cadbury's*	1 Serving/118g	260	220	3.6	26.0	11.9	0.0
Feast, Wall's*	1 Bar/60g	190	317	3.3	24.7	22.8	0.0
Maltesers, Mars*	1 Stick/80g	264	330	3.7	33.6	20.2	0.0
Mars, Mars	1 Bar	177	283	3.6	30.1	16.4	0.0
Peanut, Farmfoods*	1 Bar/60ml	187	360	5.3	36.6	21.4	1.2
Racer, Aldi*	1 Bar/59g	194	328	6.0	34.2	18.6	0.0
Snickers, Mars*	1 Bar/67g	250	373	6.0	37.3	22.4	0.0
Toffee Cream, Haagen-Dazs*	1oz/28g	97	346	4.1	32.2	22.3	0.0
Toffee Crisp, Nestle	1 Bar	197	329	3.8	33.4	20.0	0.0
Twix, Mars*	1 Serving/43.5g	231	524	6.9	52.9	32.2	0.0
Yorkie, Nestle	1 Bar	144	359	4.8	36.5	21.6	0.0
ICE CREAM CONE,							
Average	1 Cone/75g	140	186	3.5	25.5	8.5	0.0
Blackcurrant, GFY, Asda*	1 Cone/67.2g	161	241	3.0	37.0	9.0	0.1
Carousel Wafer Company*	1 Cone/2g	7	342	12.6	65.0	3.7	0.0
Choc 'n' Nut, Farmfoods*	1 Cone/120ml	183	278	5.0	33.0	14.0	1.0
Chocolate & Nut, Co-Op*	1 Cone/110g	307	279	3.9	31.0	15.5	0.6
Chocolate & Vanilla, Good Choice, Iceland*	1 Cone/110ml	161	146	2.7	22.9	6.5	0.8
Chocolate & Vanilla, Marks & Spencer*	1oz/28g	83	295	4.2	31.8	17.0	0.7
Chocolate Flavour, Somerfield*	1 Cone/110ml	329	299	4.0	38.0	15.0	0.0
Chocolate, Marks & Spencer*	1oz/28g	94	335	4.0	28.0	23.0	2.3
Chocolate, Vanilla & Hazelnut, Sainsbury's*	1 Cone/62g	190	306	4.5	33.9	16.9	0.6
Cone, Haagen-Dazs*	1oz/28g	85	303	4.7	25.5	20.3	0.0
Cornetto, Classico, Wall's	1 Cone	200	205	2.7	19.7	12.9	0.0
Cornetto, Flirt, Choc Chip, With Hazelnut, Wall's*	1 Cone/69.7g	224	320	4.0	40.0	16.0	0.0
Cornetto, GFY, Asda*	1 Cone/67.2g	161	241	3.0	37.0	9.0	0.1
Cornetto, Wall's*	1 Cone/75g	195	260	3.7	34.5	12.9	0.0
Creme Egg, Cadbury's*	1 Cone/115ml	270	235	2.9	29.3	11.6	0.0
Extreme Raspberry, Cornetto, Nestle*	1 Cornetto/88g	220	250	2.5	36.0	10.0	0.2

I

ICE CREAM CONE,

Item	Measure INFO/WEIGHT	per Measure KCAL	KCAL	PROT	CARB	FAT	FIBRE
Flake 99, Cadbury's*	1 Cone/125ml	244	195	2.6	23.2	10.0	0.0
McDonald's*	1 Cone/98g	157	160	4.5	24.4	5.0	0.0
Mini, Tesco*	1 Cone/48g	152	316	4.1	31.5	19.3	0.8
Mint Choc Chip, Iceland*	1 Cone/72g	210	292	3.3	40.4	13.0	1.0
Sticky Toffee, Farmfoods*	1 Cone/120ml	177	272	3.2	36.0	12.8	2.0
Strawberry & Vanilla, Asda*	1 Cone/115ml	193	168	1.8	22.6	7.8	0.1
Strawberry & Vanilla, Farmfoods*	1 Cone/120ml	170	257	3.0	32.0	13.0	2.0
Strawberry & Vanilla, Iceland*	1 Serving/70g	182	260	3.3	37.5	10.8	0.7
Strawberry & Vanilla, Marks & Spencer*	1oz/28g	81	290	4.2	30.9	16.5	0.7
Strawberry & Vanilla, Sainsbury's*	1 Cone/62g	153	247	2.8	36.5	10.0	0.3
Strawberry & Vanilla, Tesco*	1 Cone/70g	194	277	3.0	35.9	13.5	0.3
Strawberry, BGTY, Sainsbury's*	1 Cone/69g	151	219	2.6	37.5	6.5	1.3
Strawberry, Co-Op*	1 Cone/110g	283	257	3.5	33.6	12.1	0.5
Strawberry, Marks & Spencer*	1oz/28g	74	263	3.5	31.1	14.0	0.4
Strawberry, Somerfield*	1 Cone/110g	299	272	3.0	40.0	11.0	0.0
Toffee Flavoured, Somerfield*	1 Cone/110ml	320	291	4.0	39.0	14.0	0.0
Tropical, GFY, Asda*	1 Cone/100g	135	135	2.6	20.0	5.0	0.3
With Flake, McDonald's*	1 Cone/107g	204	191	4.8	27.0	7.2	0.0

ICE CREAM ROLL,

Item	Measure INFO/WEIGHT	per Measure KCAL	KCAL	PROT	CARB	FAT	FIBRE
Artic	1 Portion/70g	140	200	4.1	33.3	6.6	0.0
Basics, Somerfield*	1/6 Roll/110ml	233	212	4.0	35.0	6.0	0.0
Marks & Spencer*	1oz/28g	60	215	3.6	35.2	6.7	0.0
Mini, Cadbury's*	1 Roll/45ml	99	220	3.4	24.3	13.1	0.0
Tesco*	¼ Roll/57g	131	230	3.7	34.5	8.6	0.4

ICE LOLLY,

Item	Measure INFO/WEIGHT	per Measure KCAL	KCAL	PROT	CARB	FAT	FIBRE
Assorted, Farmfoods*	1 Lolly/56ml	35	62	0.0	15.6	0.0	0.0
Assorted, Iceland*	1 Lolly/51g	33	65	0.0	16.2	0.0	0.0
Assorted, Safeway*	1 Lolly/31ml	26	85	0.0	20.9	0.0	0.1
Baby, Tesco*	1 Lolly/32.4g	26	80	0.1	20.0	0.0	0.1
Blackcurrant Split, Iceland*	1 Lolly/75g	61	81	1.1	12.0	3.2	0.1
Blackcurrant, Dairy Split, Sainsbury's*	1 Lolly/72.7ml	88	121	1.8	20.4	3.6	0.1
Blackcurrant, Real Fruit Juice, Sainsbury's*	1 Lolly/73ml	67	92	0.2	22.8	0.1	0.1
Blackcurrant, Ribena*	1 Lolly/55ml	43	79	0.0	19.2	0.0	0.0
Bournville, Cadbury's	1 Lolly	270	245	2.5	23.2	15.6	0.0
Choc & Almond, Mini, Tesco*	1 Lolly/31g	103	331	4.4	24.8	23.8	0.9
Choc Lime Split, Morrisons*	1 Lolly/73ml	120	164	1.6	20.4	8.4	0.1
Chocolate, Plain, Mini, Tesco*	1 Lolly/31g	94	304	3.1	24.8	21.4	1.2
Chocolate, Pooh Stick, Nestle*	1 Lolly/40g	36	89	2.1	12.9	3.6	0.0
Cider Refresher, Treats*	1 Lolly/70ml	54	77	0.0	19.2	0.0	0.0
Cola Lickers, Farmfoods*	1 Lolly/56ml	37	68	0.0	17.0	0.0	0.0
Elderflower,Tubes, Frozen, Marks & Spencer*	1oz/28g	23	82	0.1	20.5	0.1	0.2
Exotic Fruit, Tesco*	1 Lolly/31.5g	41	131	1.8	26.4	2.0	0.6
Exotic Split, Bars, Marks & Spencer*	1oz/28g	36	127	2.5	25.0	1.9	0.4
Fab, Nestle*	1 Lolly/57g	82	144	0.8	23.7	4.9	0.0
Feast, Chocolate, Mini, Wall's	1 Lolly	185	310	3.2	23.0	22.0	0.0
Feast, Toffee, Mini, Wall's	1 Lolly	180	305	2.9	23.0	22.0	0.0
Fizzy Cola Lances, Sainsbury's*	1 Lolly/50g	182	364	2.8	79.8	2.6	1.8
Frenzy, Farmfoods*	1 Lolly/92ml	235	255	3.1	23.1	16.8	0.6
Fruit Assorted, Basics, Somerfield*	1 Lolly/56ml	32	58	0.0	15.0	0.0	0.0
Fruit Fusion, Mini, Farmfoods*	1 Lolly/45ml	36	79	0.2	19.2	0.1	0.2
Fruit Ices, Made With Orange Juice, Del Monte*	1 Lolly/75ml	79	105	0.5	25.7	0.0	0.0
Fruit Luxury, Mini, Co-Op*	1 Lolly/45g	59	130	2.0	18.0	6.0	0.2
Fruit Pastille, Rowntree's*	1 Lolly/65ml	59	90	0.0	21.0	0.0	0.0

ICE LOLLY,	INFO/WEIGHT	KCAL	KCAL	PROT	CARB	FAT	FIBRE
Fruit Split, Asda*	1 Lolly/73.9g	85	115	1.7	19.0	3.6	0.0
Fruit Split, Assorted, Co-Op*	1 Lolly/73g	80	110	1.0	20.0	3.0	0.1
Fruit Split, Better For You, Morrisons*	1 Lolly/72.5g	50	69	1.6	13.9	0.7	0.1
Fruit Split, Waitrose*	1 Lolly/73.4g	91	124	2.5	21.7	3.6	0.4
Fruit Splits, Assorted, Somerfield*	1 Split/73ml	74	102	0.0	18.0	3.0	0.0
Fruit Splits, Treats*	1 Lolly/75ml	77	103	1.4	17.6	4.1	0.0
Fruit, Assorted, Waitrose*	1 Lolly/73g	59	81	0.0	20.0	0.0	0.1
Fruit, Red, Tesco*	1 Lolly/31.5g	40	128	1.8	25.6	2.0	0.6
Fruity n Freezy, Asda*	1 Lolly/30ml	24	80	0.1	20.0	0.0	0.0
Fruity, Ice Cream, Morrisons*	1 Lolly/73ml	50	69	1.6	13.9	0.7	0.1
Funny Foot, Wall's	1 Lolly	83	102	2.0	12.5	6.0	0.0
Lemon & Lime, Mini Bar, Marks & Spencer*	1 Lolly/50g	48	95	0.1	23.6	0.1	0.2
Lemon & Lime, Rocket Split, De Roma*	1 Lolly/60ml	65	108	1.0	16.0	4.3	0.2
Lemon & Lime, Tubes, Frozen, Marks & Spencer*	1oz/28g	27	95	0.1	23.6	0.1	0.2
Lemonade & Cola, Morrisons*	1 Lolly/55ml	36	65	0.0	16.2	0.0	0.0
Mango & Passion Fruit, Sainsbury's*	1 Lolly/73ml	76	104	0.2	25.5	0.1	0.6
Mango & Passion Fruit, TTD, Sainsbury's*	1 Lolly/73ml	76	104	0.2	25.5	0.1	0.6
Mega Truffle, Nestle*	1 Lolly/71.1g	217	305	3.2	28.0	20.1	0.8
Milk Chocolate & Crisped Wheat, Co-Op*	1 Lolly/110g	259	235	3.0	28.0	12.0	0.7
Milk Flavour, Farmfoods*	1 Lolly/50ml	91	182	2.8	20.1	10.1	0.1
Milky Bar, Nestle*	1 Lolly/45.1g	156	346	4.3	33.2	21.8	0.1
Mini Milk, Chocolate, Wall's*	1 Lolly/24g	29	125	4.1	20.0	3.2	0.0
Mini Milk, Strawberry, Wall's*	1 Lolly/24g	30	130	3.3	19.0	4.1	0.0
Mini Milk, Vanilla, Wall's*	1 Lolly/24g	30	130	3.8	22.0	3.0	0.0
Morrisons*	1 Lolly/100g	30	30	0.0	7.4	0.0	0.0
Orange & Lemon Splits, Farmfoods*	1 Lolly/56ml	56	124	1.6	19.8	4.3	0.2
Orange Juice, Asda*	1 Lolly/70g	58	83	0.7	20.0	0.0	0.0
Orange Juice, Bar, Marks & Spencer*	1 Lolly/75g	65	86	0.5	21.0	0.0	0.1
Orange Juice, Co-Op*	1 Lolly/73g	51	70	0.4	17.0	0.1	0.1
Orange Juice, Fresh, Eat Smart, Safeway*	1 Lolly/107.1g	75	70	0.4	16.6	0.0	0.1
Orange Juice, Freshly Squeezed, Finest,Tesco*	1 Lolly/80ml	89	111	0.7	27.0	0.0	0.0
Orange Juice, Milfina*	1 Lolly/79.3g	69	87	0.5	23.3	0.0	0.0
Orange Juice, Safeway*	1 Lolly/73ml	62	85	0.7	20.4	0.1	0.0
Orange Juice, Tropicana*	1 Lolly/50g	43	85	0.5	20.7	0.0	0.0
Orange Maid, Nestle*	1 Lolly/73ml	66	91	0.5	21.6	0.0	0.0
Orange, Lidl*	1 Lolly/50g	50	100	0.5	24.4	0.1	0.0
Orange, Real Fruit Juice, Sainsbury's*	1 Lolly/73ml	49	67	0.2	16.5	0.1	0.1
Orange, Real Juice, Sainsbury's*	1 Lolly/72ml	63	88	0.7	21.0	0.1	0.1
Orange, Real Juice, Tesco*	1 Lolly/32g	25	78	0.6	18.7	0.0	0.3
Orange, Tesco*	1 Lolly/77.4g	52	68	0.2	16.8	0.0	0.3
Orange, Water, Iceland*	1 Lolly/75g	74	98	0.2	24.4	0.0	0.0
Pineapple Split, Iceland*	1 Lolly/75g	89	118	1.4	18.5	4.6	0.1
Pineapple, Dairy Split, Sainsbury's*	1 Lolly/72.4ml	84	116	1.8	19.0	3.6	0.1
Pineapple, Real Fruit Juice, Sainsbury's*	1 Lolly/73ml	55	76	0.1	19.0	0.1	0.1
Polar Snappers, Double, Farmfoods*	1 Lolly/60ml	40	66	0.0	16.5	0.0	0.0
Raspberry, Real Fruit Juice, Sainsbury's*	1 Lolly/72g	62	86	0.3	21.0	0.1	0.1
Raspberry, Rocket Split, De Roma*	1 Lolly/60ml	65	108	1.0	16.2	4.3	0.2
Real Fruit Juice, Rocket, Blue Parrot Cafe, Sainsbury's*	1 Lolly/58ml	45	77	0.2	19.1	0.0	0.1
Real Fruit, Dairy Split, Sainsbury's*	1 Lolly/73ml	100	137	2.1	22.8	4.2	0.1
Real Orange, Kids, Tesco*	1 Lolly/31.5g	25	78	0.6	18.7	0.0	0.3
Refresher, Bassett's*	1 Lolly/40g	47	117	2.2	22.2	2.2	0.3
Rocket, Co-Op*	1 Lolly/60g	42	70	0.0	17.0	0.0	0.0
Rolo, Nestle*	1 Lolly/75ml	243	324	3.8	36.5	18.8	0.0

INFO/WEIGHT	Measure	per Measure KCAL	KCAL	PROT	CARB	FAT	FIBRE
			Nutrition Values per 100g / 100ml				

ICE LOLLY,

	Measure	per Measure KCAL	KCAL	PROT	CARB	FAT	FIBRE
Solero, Exotic, Wall's	1 Lolly	104	112	1.5	20.0	3.0	0.0
Solero, Orange Fresh, Wall's	1 Lolly	78	81	0.2	20.0	0.0	0.0
Solero, Red Fruits, Walls	1 Lollie	99	104	1.3	21.0	2.2	0.0
Strawberries 'n' Cream, Tropicana*	1 Lolly/50g	59	117	1.6	25.0	1.2	0.0
Strawberry & Banana, Smoothies, Sainsbury's*	1 Lolly/60g	100	166	1.5	28.0	5.3	0.2
Strawberry & Vanilla, 99% Fat Free, So-Lo, Iceland*	1 Lolly/92g	98	107	2.3	23.5	0.4	2.2
Strawberry Split, Co-Op*	1 Lolly/71ml	75	105	1.0	17.0	3.0	0.1
Strawberry, Dairy Split, Sainsbury's*	1 Lolly/72.9ml	86	118	1.7	19.8	3.6	0.1
Strawberry, Orange & Pineapple, Rocket, Iceland*	1 Lolly/47g	38	81	0.0	20.2	0.0	0.1
Strawberry, So-Lo, Good Choice, Iceland*	1 Lolly/66.4g	84	128	2.4	25.6	1.8	0.1
Strawberry, Sun Lolly*	1 Lolly/65g	55	85	0.0	20.0	0.0	0.0
Tip Top, Calypso*	1 Lolly/20ml	6	30	0.1	7.1	0.1	0.0
Traffic Light, Co-Op*	1 Lolly/52g	55	105	0.4	25.0	0.8	0.0
Tropical Fruit, Starburst, Mars*	1 Lolly/93ml	94	101	0.3	24.8	0.1	0.0
Twister, Wall's*	1 Lolly/80ml	76	95	0.6	18.4	1.9	0.0
Vanilla, Pooh Stick, Nestle*	1 Lolly/40g	34	86	1.9	12.9	3.5	0.0
Vimto*	1 Lolly/73.0ml	84	115	1.3	18.2	4.1	0.1
Wonka Super Sour Tastic, Nestle*	1 Lolly/60ml	84	140	0.0	26.1	3.6	0.0
Zoom, Nestle*	1 Lolly/58.1ml	54	93	0.9	20.6	0.7	0.0

ICE TEA,

	Measure	per Measure KCAL	KCAL	PROT	CARB	FAT	FIBRE
Green Tea & Lemon, Twinings*	1 Serving/250ml	75	30	0.1	7.3	0.1	0.0
Lemon, Diet, Lipton*	1 Bottle/500ml	1	0	0.0	0.0	0.0	0.0
Lemon, Lipton*	1 Can/150ml	48	32	0.0	7.7	0.0	0.0
Lemon, San Benedetto*	1 Sm Bottle/500ml	170	34	0.1	8.3	0.0	0.0
Pickwick*	1 Serving/250ml	33	13	0.0	3.3	0.0	0.0

INDIAN MEAL,

	Measure	per Measure KCAL	KCAL	PROT	CARB	FAT	FIBRE
Banquet, For One, COU, Marks & Spencer*	1 Pack/500g	400	80	6.7	10.2	1.2	3.1
Daal, Sainsbury's*	1 Pack/300g	264	88	3.7	8.4	4.4	0.7
For One, Asda*	1 Pack/550g	919	167	8.0	18.0	7.0	1.3
For One, Eat Smart, Safeway*	1 Serving/600g	690	115	6.5	16.2	2.6	2.0
For One, GFY, Asda*	1 Serving/495g	644	130	8.0	14.0	4.7	1.0
For One, Healthy Eating, Tesco*	1 Pack/420g	437	104	7.4	14.0	2.1	1.4
For One, Vegetarian, Asda*	1 Pack/500g	789	158	3.2	16.0	9.0	1.4
For Two, Hot, Takeaway, Tesco*	1 Pack/825g	1215	147	6.6	13.6	7.3	1.9
For Two, Menu, Tesco*	1 Serving/537g	811	151	6.3	17.0	6.4	0.8
For Two, Peshwari Naan, Finest, Tesco*	½ Pack/200g	612	306	8.3	48.3	8.9	5.2
Menu, COU, Marks & Spencer*	1 Pack/550g	413	75	8.4	7.5	1.2	2.1
Takeaway, Ready Meals, Marks & Spencer*	1oz/28g	42	150	6.7	15.3	7.1	1.5

INDIAN SELECTION,

	Measure	per Measure KCAL	KCAL	PROT	CARB	FAT	FIBRE
Asda*	1oz/28g	234	837	17.4	117.0	33.2	0.0
Snack, Safeway*	1 Serving/170g	347	204	4.0	25.8	9.4	1.9

INSTANT WHIP,

	Measure	per Measure KCAL	KCAL	PROT	CARB	FAT	FIBRE
Chocolate Flavour, Dry, Bird's*	1oz/28g	109	390	3.8	80.5	5.9	0.7
Strawberry Flavour, Dry, Bird's*	1oz/28g	112	400	2.5	85.0	5.4	0.4

IRON BRU,

	Measure	per Measure KCAL	KCAL	PROT	CARB	FAT	FIBRE
Barrs*	1 Can/330ml	142	43	0.0	10.6	0.0	0.0
Diet, Barr's*	1 Can/330ml	2	1	0.1	0.1	0.0	0.0

INFO/WEIGHT	Measure	per Measure KCAL	Nutrition Values per 100g / 100ml				
			KCAL	PROT	CARB	FAT	FIBRE
JALFREZI,							
Chicken & Rice, Healthy Eating, Tesco*	1 Pack/420g	483	115	7.9	17.5	1.6	0.3
Chicken With Basmati Rice, Eat Smart, Safeway*	1 Pack/400g	300	75	6.8	8.5	1.0	1.7
Chicken With Pilau Rice, BGTY, Sainsbury's*	1 Pack/450g	432	96	7.0	14.3	1.2	0.8
Chicken With Pilau Rice, GFY, Asda*	1 Pack/445.9g	495	111	8.0	14.0	2.5	1.2
Chicken With Pilau Rice, Patak's*	1 Pack/400g	556	139	9.8	14.7	4.6	0.9
Chicken With Pilau Rice, Perfectly Balanced, Waitrose*	1 Pack/400g	464	116	8.4	15.4	2.3	1.8
Chicken With Pilau Rice, Safeway*	1 Pack/424.2g	700	165	8.1	20.9	5.0	0.8
Chicken With Rice, COU, Marks & Spencer*	1 Pack/400g	320	80	9.2	8.3	1.1	1.2
Chicken With Rice, Healthy Living, Tesco*	1 Pack/450g	554	123	7.2	21.6	0.9	0.8
Chicken With Rice, Sainsbury's*	1 Serving/200g	220	110	7.4	18.3	0.8	1.3
Chicken, Asda*	1 Pack/340g	415	122	10.0	7.0	6.0	1.6
Chicken, GFY, Asda*	1 Pack/350g	277	79	11.0	6.0	1.2	0.8
Chicken, Marks & Spencer*	1 Pack/350g	385	110	10.8	4.2	5.7	2.0
Chicken, Medium, GFY, Asda*	1 Pack/644g	972	151	6.0	22.0	4.3	0.9
Chicken, Sainsbury's*	1 Pack/400g	436	109	12.1	3.4	5.2	1.7
Chicken, Somerfield*	1 Pack/350g	340	97	11.2	2.6	4.6	1.2
Chicken, Tesco*	1 Pack/350g	459	131	11.9	3.8	7.6	1.2
Chicken, Waitrose*	½ Pack/200g	214	107	12.4	2.3	5.3	1.6
Meal For One, Marks & Spencer*	1 Serving/500g	700	140	6.1	13.4	7.0	3.0
Pilau Rice, Ready Meals, Patak's*	1oz/28g	37	131	7.8	13.5	5.3	0.9
Vegetable, Co-Op*	1 Pack/400g	320	80	1.0	9.0	4.0	2.0
Vegetable, Eastern Indian, Sainsbury's*	1 Pack/400g	208	52	3.4	2.0	3.4	1.7
Vegetable, Take Away Menu For 1, BGTY, Sainsbury's*	1 Pack/148g	43	29	1.8	5.4	0.0	2.3
Vegetable, Waitrose*	1 Pack/400g	256	64	2.2	4.7	4.0	3.7
Vegetable, With Rice, Bird's Eye*	1 Pack/350g	354	101	2.5	20.2	1.1	1.0
JAM,							
Apricot & Peach, 25% Less Sugar, Asda*	1 Tsp/15g	28	184	0.5	45.4	0.1	1.1
Apricot, Average	1 Tsp/15g	37	248	0.2	61.6	0.0	1.5
Apricot, Reduced Sugar, Average	1 Serving/20g	37	187	0.5	46.0	0.3	0.4
Black Cherry, Average	2 Tsp/30g	74	247	0.4	61.2	0.3	0.4
Blackberry, Extra Special, Asda*	1 Tbsp/15.3g	29	190	0.9	45.0	0.7	0.0
Blackcurrant, Average	1 Tbsp/15g	38	250	0.2	62.3	0.0	1.0
Blackcurrant, Reduced Sugar, Average	1 Tsp/5.7g	11	178	0.5	44.4	0.2	1.0
Blueberry & Blackberry, Baxters*	1 Tsp/15g	38	252	0.0	63.0	0.0	1.2
Country Berries, Luxury, Baxters*	1 Tsp/15g	38	252	0.0	63.0	0.0	1.1
Damson, Extra Fruit, Best, Hartley's*	1 Tsp/5g	12	244	0.2	60.8	0.0	0.0
Fruits Of The Forest, Extra Special, Asda*	1 Tbsp/15g	29	192	0.9	45.0	0.9	0.0
Kiwi & Goosberry, 66% Fruit, Asda*	1 Serving/30g	56	187	0.5	45.0	0.5	0.0
Mixed Fruit, Average	1 Tbsp/15g	38	253	0.3	63.5	0.0	0.5
Plum, Tesco*	1 Serving/50g	131	261	0.2	64.4	0.0	0.6
Rasberry, Reduced Sugar, Average	1 Tsp/6.3g	10	160	0.5	39.3	0.2	0.6
Raspberry, Average	1 Tbsp/15.1g	36	239	0.6	58.7	0.1	0.9
Raspberry, Seedless, Average	1 Tsp/10g	26	257	0.5	63.6	0.0	0.3
Rhubarb & Ginger, Baxters*	1 Tsp/15g	32	210	0.0	53.0	0.0	0.6
Strawberry & Redcurrant, Reduced Sugar, Streamline*	1 Tbsp/15g	29	192	0.4	46.8	0.3	0.0
Strawberry, Average	1 Tsp/10g	25	253	0.3	62.8	0.0	0.6
Strawberry, Reduced Sugar, Average	1 Tbsp/15g	28	187	0.4	45.8	0.3	0.2
Wild Blackberry Jelly, Baxters*	1 Tsp/15g	32	210	0.0	53.0	0.0	1.2
JAMBALAYA,							
American Style, Tesco*	1 Serving/275g	432	157	7.7	16.0	7.0	0.5
American, Healthy Eating, Tesco*	1 Pack/450g	477	106	6.4	15.5	2.0	0.9
COU, Marks & Spencer*	1 Pack/400g	340	85	6.5	10.8	2.0	0.9
Cajun Chicken, BGTY, Sainsbury's*	1 Pack/400g	364	91	7.7	11.9	1.4	1.1

J

	Measure INFO/WEIGHT	per Measure KCAL	Nutrition Values per 100g / 100ml				
			KCAL	PROT	CARB	FAT	FIBRE
JAMBALAYA,							
GFY, Asda*	1 Pack/450g	428	95	6.0	12.0	2.5	0.9
Marks & Spencer*	1 Pack/480g	552	115	5.8	14.6	3.5	1.2
JELLY,							
Blackberry, Unprepared, Morrisons*	1 Serving/20g	52	261	0.3	65.0	0.0	0.0
Blackcurrant, Made Up, Rowntree's*	¼ Jelly/140ml	100	71	1.4	16.4	0.1	0.0
Blackcurrant, Made Up, Sainsbury's*	¼ Jelly/150g	98	65	1.2	15.1	0.0	0.0
Blackcurrant, Sugar Free, Unprepared, Rowntree's*	1 Pack/24g	73	305	66.5	0.3	0.0	0.4
Crystals, Blackcurrant, Unprepared, Bird's*	1oz/28g	92	330	57.5	13.0	0.1	0.0
Crystals, Lemon & Lime, Sugar Free, Rowntree's*	¼ Pint/140ml	10	7	1.4	0.1	0.0	0.0
Crystals, Strawberry, Tesco*	1 Serving Made/3g	9	303	63.5	12.0	0.1	0.2
Exotic Fruit, Marks & Spencer*	1 Pot/175g	140	80	0.1	18.9	0.2	0.9
Fresh Fruit, Marks & Spencer*	1 Pot/175g	131	75	0.2	18.4	0.1	0.3
Fruit Cocktail, Marks & Spencer*	1oz/28g	31	110	0.4	16.4	4.7	0.3
Lemon & Lime, Sugar Free, Rowntree's*	1oz/28g	85	305	4.5	60.7	0.0	0.0
Lemon, Rowntree's*	1 Serving/140ml	414	296	4.4	69.6	0.0	0.0
Lemon, Unprepared, Co-Op*	1 Pack/135g	412	305	5.0	71.0	0.0	0.0
Lemon, Unprepared, Somerfield*	1 Pack/135g	393	291	6.0	66.0	0.0	0.0
Lime Flavour, Unprepared, Waitrose*	1 Square/11g	33	296	4.5	69.5	0.0	0.0
Lime, Made Up, Rowntree's*	¼ Jelly/140ml	100	71	1.4	16.4	0.1	0.0
Lime, Unprepared, Somerfield*	1 Pack/135g	392	290	6.0	66.0	0.0	0.0
Made With Water	1oz/28g	17	61	1.2	15.1	0.0	0.0
Mandarin & Pineapple, Sainsbury's*	1 Pot/125g	95	76	0.2	18.9	0.1	1.2
Mandarin, Aroma, Marks & Spencer*	1oz/28g	17	60	0.2	14.6	0.0	0.4
Mixed Berry, WTF, Sainsbury's*	1 Serving/160g	112	70	0.7	16.3	0.2	1.5
Orange Flavour, Somerfield*	1 Pack/128g	379	296	5.0	69.0	0.0	0.0
Orange, Quickset, Rowntrees*	1 Serving/¼ Pint	65	340	0.0	84.0	0.0	3.0
Orange, Rowntree's*	1 Square/11g	33	296	4.4	69.6	0.0	0.0
Orange, Sugar Free, Asda*	1 Serving/12g	36	303	63.6	12.0	0.1	0.2
Raspberry & Rose, Aroma, Marks & Spencer*	1oz/28g	14	50	0.2	11.9	0.2	0.4
Raspberry Flavour, Sugar Free, Made Up, Rowntree's*	1 Portion/140ml	9	6	1.4	0.1	0.0	0.0
Raspberry, Marks & Spencer*	1 Serving/175g	109	62	0.3	14.6	0.3	0.0
Raspberry, Somerfield*	¼ Serving/38g	111	292	6.0	66.0	0.0	0.0
Raspberry, Unprepared, Rowntree's*	1 Serving/135g	405	300	5.6	67.3	0.4	0.0
Strawberry & Raspberry, Sainsbury's*	½ Pot/280g	230	82	0.2	20.2	0.0	1.2
Strawberry Flavour, Sugar Free, Made Up, Rowntree's*	1 Serving/140ml	10	7	1.5	0.1	0.0	0.0
Strawberry Flavour, Sugar Free, Unprepared, Rowntree's*	1oz/28g	84	300	64.9	3.0	0.0	0.0
Strawberry, Basics, Somerfield*	¼ Jelly/32g	95	296	5.0	69.0	0.0	0.0
Strawberry, Pot, Rowntree's*	1 Pot/100g	92	92	0.1	23.0	0.0	1.1
Strawberry, Somerfield*	¼ Jelly/33.75g	99	291	6.0	66.0	0.0	0.0
Summer Fruits, Co-Op*	1 Pack/135g	401	297	5.5	68.7	0.1	0.0
Table, Chivers*	1oz/28g	83	296	4.9	69.1	0.0	0.0
Tangerine, Unprepared, Rowntree's*	1 Serving/33g	99	300	5.6	67.3	0.4	0.0
Tropical Fresh Fruit, Eat Smart, Safeway*	1 Serving/185g	120	65	0.6	14.5	0.3	1.1
Tropical Fruit, WTF, Sainsbury's*	1 Serving/160g	144	90	0.3	19.9	1.0	0.9
JELLY BABIES,							
Bassett's*	1 Baby/6g	20	335	4.0	79.5	0.0	0.0
Mini, Waitrose*	1 Bag/125g	370	296	4.3	68.7	0.4	0.0
Tesco*	1 Baby/6g	20	332	5.3	77.4	0.1	0.1
JELLY BEANS,							
Asda*	1 Bag/100g	364	364	0.1	90.0	0.4	0.2
Rowntree's*	1 Pack/35g	128	367	0.0	91.8	0.0	0.0
JELLY BEARS,							
Co-Op*	1 Sweet/3g	10	325	6.0	76.0	0.1	0.0

J

	Measure INFO/WEIGHT	per Measure KCAL	Nutrition Values per 100g / 100ml				
			KCAL	PROT	CARB	FAT	FIBRE
JELLY TOTS,							
Rowntree's*	1 Pack/42g	145	346	0.1	86.5	0.0	0.0
JUICE,							
Apple & Cranberry, Average	1 Glass/250ml	114	46	0.1	10.2	0.0	0.0
Apple & Elderflower, Copella*	1 Glass/250ml	108	43	0.4	10.2	0.1	0.0
Apple & Mango, Average	1 Glass/200ml	108	54	0.3	12.6	0.0	0.1
Apple & Raspberry, Average	1 Serving/200ml	89	45	0.5	10.2	0.1	0.2
Apple, Concentrate, Average	1Tbsp/15ml	45	302	0.1	73.6	0.2	0.0
Apple, Pure, Average	1 Glass/100ml	47	47	0.1	11.2	0.0	0.0
Apple, Pure, Organic, Average	1 Serving/200ml	93	46	0.1	11.2	0.1	0.1
Apple, Red Grape & Blueberry, Pure, Blends, Del Monte*	1 Serving/250ml	125	50	0.6	11.5	0.0	0.0
Apple, With Calcium, Juice Plus, Tesco*	1 Serving/250ml	118	47	0.1	11.2	0.0	0.0
Apple, With Mango Puree, Safeway*	1 Glass/150ml	80	53	0.3	12.6	0.0	0.0
Breakfast, Del Monte*	1 Glass/200ml	86	43	0.6	9.6	0.0	0.0
Breakfast, Ruby, Tropicana*	1 Glass/200ml	86	43	0.7	9.0	0.0	0.5
Breakfast, Sainsbury's*	1 Serving/200ml	94	47	0.7	11.3	0.1	0.3
Breakfast, Tesco*	1 Glass/200ml	88	44	0.5	9.7	0.0	0.0
Carrot, Average	1 Glass/200ml	46	23	0.6	5.2	0.0	0.1
Clementine, Morrisons*	1 Serving/100ml	48	48	0.5	10.9	0.1	0.1
Cranberry & Raspberry, Low Sugar, Sainsbury's*	1 Glass/250ml	10	4	0.1	0.7	0.1	0.1
Cranberry, Average	1 Bottle/250ml	139	56	0.1	13.4	0.1	0.3
Cranberry, No Added Sugar, Average	1 Glass/200ml	11	6	0.1	0.9	0.1	0.1
Exotic Fruit, Pure, Del Monte*	1 Glass/200ml	96	48	0.3	11.3	0.0	0.0
Grape & Peach, Don Simon*	1 Serving/200ml	94	47	0.4	11.3	0.0	0.0
Grape & Raspberry, Pressed, Marks & Spencer*	1 Bottle/250ml	138	55	0.4	12.9	0.0	0.1
Grape, Purple, Welch's*	1 Serving/200ml	136	68	0.1	16.5	0.0	0.0
Grape, Red, Average	1 Serving/100ml	62	62	0.2	15.2	0.0	0.0
Grape, White, Average	1 Can/160ml	95	60	0.2	14.3	0.1	0.1
Grapefruit, Low Calorie, Natreen*	1 Sm Glass/100ml	18	18	0.5	3.3	0.5	0.0
Grapefruit, Pink, Average	1 Glass/200ml	81	41	0.6	9.0	0.1	0.2
Grapefruit, Pure, Average	1 Glass/200ml	77	38	0.5	8.5	0.1	0.1
Lemon, Co-Op*	1 fl oz/30ml	8	25	0.3	2.0	0.1	0.0
Lemon, Fresh	1 Tsp/5ml	0	7	0.3	1.6	0.0	0.1
Lemon, Made With Concentrated Lemon Juice, Tesco*	1 Serving/100ml	10	10	0.4	2.0	0.0	0.0
Lime, Fresh	1 Tsp/5ml	0	9	0.4	1.6	0.1	0.1
Mango & Apple, Copella*	1 Serving/200ml	86	43	0.4	10.1	0.1	0.0
Mango, Canned	1 Glass/200ml	78	39	0.1	9.8	0.2	0.0
Multivitamin, Fruit, Vitafit, Lidl*	1 Glass/200ml	106	53	1.0	12.0	0.0	0.5
Orange & Grapefruit, Average	1 Serving/200g	85	42	0.8	9.3	0.1	0.4
Orange & Kiwi Fruit, Tropicana*	1 Serving/175ml	90	51	0.5	12.0	0.0	0.0
Orange & Pineapple, Average	1 Glass/120ml	56	47	0.5	10.5	0.5	0.5
Orange & Raspberry, Average	1fl oz/30ml	15	50	0.6	11.4	0.1	0.2
Orange & Strawberry, Average	1 Serving/125ml	64	51	0.6	10.9	0.4	0.8
Orange Banana & Grapefruit, Marks & Spencer*	1 Serving/250ml	125	50	0.8	11.5	0.2	0.3
Orange With Cranberry Juice, Marks & Spencer*	1 Bottle/250ml	138	55	0.5	14.0	0.5	1.0
Orange, Apple & Passionfruit, Del Monte*	1 Glass/200ml	90	45	0.5	10.1	0.0	0.0
Orange, Peach & Apricot, Pure, Blends, Del Monte*	1 Serving/200ml	88	44	0.6	9.9	0.0	0.0
Orange, Pure, Smooth, Average	1 Glass/200ml	88	44	0.7	9.8	0.0	0.2
Orange, Pure, With Bits, Average	1 Glass/200ml	90	45	0.6	10.2	0.1	0.1
Orange, Pure, With Calcium, Tropicana*	1 Glass/250ml	108	43	0.7	9.0	0.0	0.5
Orange, Red, Average	1 Glass/250ml	115	46	0.4	10.7	0.0	0.2
Passion Fruit, Average	1 Glass/200ml	94	47	0.8	10.7	0.1	0.0
Pear, Concentrate, Meridian Foods*	1 Serving/45ml	134	298	0.0	74.6	0.0	0.0
Pear, With A Hint Of Ginger, Pressed, Marks & Spencer*	1 Glass/250ml	125	50	0.3	11.7	0.1	0.0

J

	Measure	per Measure	Nutrition Values per 100g / 100ml				
	INFO/WEIGHT	KCAL	KCAL	PROT	CARB	FAT	FIBRE
JUICE,							
Pineapple & Coconut, Sainsbury's*	1 Glass/250ml	128	51	0.4	11.9	0.1	0.1
Pineapple Mango Crush, Just Juice*	1 Glass/250ml	108	43	0.0	10.6	0.0	0.0
Pineapple, Average	1 Glass/200ml	100	50	0.3	11.7	0.1	0.2
Prune, Average	1 Serving/200ml	123	61	0.6	15.3	0.1	1.8
Raspberry & Black Cherry, Carbonated, Crystal Spring*	1 Glass/200ml	204	102	2.0	7.5	7.1	0.0
Raspberry Cooler, With Mint, Sainsbury's*	1 Serving/250ml	63	25	0.1	6.0	0.1	0.1
Sweet Carrot & Orange, Shapers, Boots*	1 Serving/250ml	100	40	0.9	8.8	0.2	0.4
Tomato, Average	1 Glass/200ml	40	20	0.8	4.0	0.1	0.5
Tropical Fruit, Plenty*	1 Glass/200ml	120	60	0.5	13.7	0.1	0.0
Tropical, No Added Sugar, Safeway*	1 Glass/200ml	10	5	0.1	0.9	0.0	0.0
Tropical, Pure, Sainsbury's*	1 Glass/200ml	104	52	0.5	12.0	0.1	0.1
Tropical, Tropics, Tropicana*	1 Serving/250ml	113	45	0.4	11.0	0.0	0.0
Vegetable, Organic, Evernat*	1 Glass/200ml	36	18	0.9	3.5	0.1	0.2
Vegetable, V8*	½ Can/165ml	31	19	0.8	3.3	0.5	1.0
JUICE DRINK,							
Apple & Blackcurrant, No Added Sugar, Asda*	1 Glass/250ml	13	5	0.0	1.0	0.0	0.0
Apple & Blackcurrant, Robinson's*	1 Glass/250ml	20	8	0.1	1.1	0.0	0.0
Apple & Cranberry, Safeway*	1 Serving/250ml	125	50	0.0	12.1	0.0	0.0
Apple & Raspberry, Tesco*	1 Serving/300ml	138	46	0.0	11.2	0.0	0.0
Apple, No Added Sugar, Asda*	1 Glass/200ml	10	5	0.0	1.0	0.0	0.0
Berry Blast, 5 Alive*	1 Serving/250ml	133	53	0.0	13.0	0.0	0.0
Blackcurrant, Kids, Tesco*	1 Serving/250ml	128	51	0.0	12.4	0.0	0.0
Blackcurrant, Purity*	1 Bottle/500ml	265	53	0.0	13.2	0.0	0.0
Capri Sun, Orange, The Coca Cola Co*	1 Pouch/200ml	90	45	0.0	11.0	0.0	0.0
Cherry, No Added Sugar, Sainsbury's*	1 Carton/250ml	25	10	0.2	1.9	0.0	0.0
Citrus Burst, 5 Alive*	1 Carton/250ml	125	50	0.0	12.8	0.0	0.0
Citrus, Co-Op*	1 Serving/150ml	68	45	0.2	11.0	0.0	0.0
Citrus, Oasis*	1 Bottle/500ml	210	42	0.0	10.0	0.0	0.0
Cranberry & Apple, Ocean Spray*	1 Glass/200ml	92	46	0.0	11.1	0.0	0.0
Cranberry & Blackberry, Ocean Spray*	1 Glass/250ml	120	48	0.1	11.3	0.1	0.2
Cranberry & Blackcurrant, Ocean Spray*	1 Bottle/500ml	265	53	0.2	12.7	0.0	0.0
Cranberry & Lime, Ocean Spray*	1 Glass/250ml	140	56	0.1	13.2	0.0	0.0
Cranberry & Orange, Healthy Eating, Tesco*	1 Glass/200ml	10	5	0.0	0.8	0.0	0.0
Cranberry & Passion Fruit, Ocean Spray*	1 Glass/250ml	135	54	0.1	12.8	0.0	0.0
Cranberry & Raspberry, Asda*	1 Glass/250ml	135	54	0.2	13.0	0.0	0.0
Cranberry & Raspberry, Light, Ocean Spray*	1 Glass/250ml	63	25	0.0	5.8	0.0	0.0
Cranberry & Raspberry, Ocean Spray*	1 Glass/200ml	104	52	0.0	12.7	0.0	0.0
Cranberry & Raspberry, Tesco*	1 Glass/200ml	10	5	0.0	0.8	0.0	0.0
Cranberry Raspberry, Diet, Snapple*	1 Bottle/227ml	10	4	0.0	0.9	0.0	0.0
Cranberry, Asda*	1/5 Carton/200ml	100	50	0.0	12.0	0.0	0.0
Cranberry, Classic, Light, Ocean Spray*	1 Glass/200ml	48	24	0.0	5.5	0.0	0.0
Cranberry, Classic, Ocean Spray*	1 Glass/200ml	98	49	0.0	11.7	0.0	0.0
Cranberry, Del Rivo, Aldi*	1 Glass/100ml	40	40	0.0	9.6	0.0	0.0
Cranberry, Grape & Apple, Ocean Spray*	1 Glass/200ml	108	54	0.1	12.9	0.0	0.0
Cranberry, Juice Burst, Purity*	1 Bottle/500ml	245	49	0.0	12.0	0.0	0.0
Cranberry, Light, Classic, Ocean Spray*	1 Glass/200ml	48	24	0.0	6.0	0.0	0.0
Cranberry, Morrisons*	1 Glass/200ml	92	46	0.0	11.6	0.0	0.0
Cranberry, No Added Sugar, Tesco*	1 Glass/200ml	8	4	0.0	0.7	0.0	0.0
Cranberry, Original, Concentrated, Ocean Spray*	1 Serving/15ml	27	183	0.2	44.1	0.0	0.1
Cranberry, Solevita*	1 Serving/200ml	98	49	0.5	11.7	0.0	0.0
Cranberry, Tesco*	1 Glass/200ml	100	50	0.0	12.0	0.0	0.0
Cranberry, Tropical, Ocean Spray*	1 Glass/200ml	96	48	0.1	11.5	0.0	0.0
Five Fruits, 5 Alive*	1 Carton/250ml	125	50	0.0	12.0	0.0	0.0

JUICE DRINK,	Measure INFO/WEIGHT	per Measure KCAL	KCAL	PROT	CARB	FAT	FIBRE
Fruit Cocktail, Sainsbury's*	1 Glass/200ml	94	47	0.2	11.2	0.1	0.1
Fruit, Really Red, Bertrams*	1fl oz/30ml	14	45	0.3	9.8	0.1	0.1
Grape, Apple & Raspberry, Asda*	1 Glass/200ml	90	45	0.2	11.0	0.0	0.0
Grape, Apple & Raspberry, Co-Op*	1 Serving/150ml	75	50	0.4	12.0	0.0	0.1
Grapefruit & Cranberry, Marks & Spencer*	1 Serving/250ml	125	50	0.2	11.9	0.1	0.0
Grapefruit & Lime, Quest, Marks & Spencer*	1 Bottle/330ml	53	16	0.0	4.0	0.0	0.0
Guava Exotic, Rubicon*	1 Carton/288ml	150	52	0.2	12.8	0.1	0.0
J20, Apple & Mango, Britvic*	1 Bottle/275ml	132	48	0.1	11.3	0.1	0.0
J20, Orange & Passion Fruit, Britvic*	1 Bottle/275ml	132	48	0.1	11.3	0.1	0.0
Lemon & Lime, Light, Oasis*	1 Bottle/250ml	7	3	0.0	0.2	0.0	0.0
Lemon & Mandarin, Diet, Quest, Marks & Spencer*	1 Bottle/330ml	13	4	0.0	1.0	0.0	0.0
Lemon, The Feel Good Drinks Co*	1 Bottle/171.4ml	78	46	0.1	10.8	0.1	0.0
Lemonade, Asda*	1 Glass/200ml	88	44	0.1	11.0	0.0	0.0
Mango Madness, Snapple*	1 Bottle/227ml	104	46	0.0	12.0	0.0	0.0
Mega Green, Smucker's*	1 Serving/473ml	237	50	0.0	12.5	0.0	0.0
Multivitamin, Tropicana*	1fl oz/30ml	16	52	0.5	10.5	0.0	0.1
Orange & Banana, Pure, Average	1 Glass/150ml	79	53	0.7	12.1	0.1	0.2
Orange & Cranberry, Ocean Spray*	1 fl oz/30ml	14	48	0.0	11.5	0.0	0.0
Orange & Mango, Average	1 Bottle/375ml	176	47	0.5	10.7	0.1	0.3
Orange & Tropical, Tesco*	1 Bottle/250ml	15	6	0.1	1.1	0.0	0.0
Orange, Caprisun*	1 Pouch/200ml	89	45	0.0	10.8	0.0	0.0
Orange, Carrot & Lemon, Pago*	1 Serving/200g	90	45	0.2	10.5	0.1	0.0
Orange, Fruitish, Spar*	1 Carton/330ml	13	4	0.1	0.8	0.1	0.0
Orange, Healthy Eating, Tesco*	1 Glass/200ml	56	28	0.3	6.1	0.1	0.0
Orange, Juice Burst, Purity*	1 Bottle/500ml	220	44	1.0	10.2	0.0	0.0
Orange, Morrisons*	1 Serving/250ml	13	5	0.1	0.9	0.1	0.1
Orange, No Added Sugar, Asda*	1 Glass/250ml	13	5	0.1	0.9	0.0	0.0
Orange, Ribena*	1 Serving/288ml	98	34	0.1	8.1	0.0	0.0
Orange, Sainsbury's*	1 Serving/250ml	18	7	0.1	1.4	0.1	0.1
Orange, Value, Tesco*	1 Glass/250ml	33	13	0.0	3.3	0.0	0.0
Peach & Passionfruit Fruit, Sunmagic*	1 Serving/330ml	172	52	0.3	13.0	0.0	0.1
Pineapple & Grapefruit, Shapers, Boots*	1 Bottle/500ml	10	2	0.1	0.2	0.1	0.0
Pink Grapefruit, Fruit & Barley, No Added Sugar, Co-Op*	1fl oz/30ml	3	10	0.2	1.0	0.1	0.1
Pink Grapefruit, Juice Burst, Purity*	1 Bottle/500ml	210	42	0.4	10.0	0.0	0.0
Pomegranate, Pomegreat*	1 Glass/200ml	88	44	0.1	11.1	0.0	0.0
Summer Fruits, Light, Oasis*	1 Bottle/500ml	16	3	0.0	0.4	0.0	0.0
Summer Fruits, Oasis*	1 Bottle/500ml	185	37	0.0	9.0	0.0	0.0
Tropical Fruit, Safeway*	1 Glass/250ml	118	47	0.2	11.2	0.0	0.0
Tropical Fruit, Somerfield*	1 Glass/250ml	130	52	0.0	12.0	0.0	0.0
Tropical Fruit, Tesco*	1 Glass/250ml	125	50	0.1	12.1	0.0	0.0
Tropical Fruit, Waitrose*	1 Glass/250ml	118	47	0.2	11.2	0.0	0.0
Tropical Hit, 5 Alive*	1 Carton/250ml	93	37	0.0	9.3	0.0	0.0
Vimto*	1 Can/330ml	147	45	0.0	11.0	0.0	0.0
White Cranberry & Grape, Oceanspay*	1 Serving/100ml	48	48	0.0	11.6	0.0	0.0
White Grape & Peach, Sainsbury's*	1 Glass/250ml	95	38	0.2	9.0	0.1	0.1

Nutrition Values per 100g / 100ml

J

	Measure	per Measure	Nutrition Values per 100g / 100ml				
	INFO/WEIGHT	KCAL	KCAL	PROT	CARB	FAT	FIBRE
KABANOS,							
Polish, Sainsbury's*	1 Kabanos/25g	91	365	23.0	0.1	30.4	0.1
KEBAB,							
BBQ Pork, Sainsbury's*	1 Serving/90g	65	72	11.0	1.4	2.4	0.9
Barbecue Chicken Tikka, Mini, Somerfield*	1oz/28g	38	134	21.0	4.0	4.0	0.0
Cajun Salmon, Tesco*	1 Kebab/75g	100	133	19.8	3.9	4.2	1.3
Chicken & Pineapple, Aldi*	1 Kebab/85g	89	105	13.9	5.3	3.1	0.0
Chicken & Sausage, With Teriyaki Sauce, Asda*	1 Serving/110g	257	234	17.0	10.0	14.0	1.0
Chicken Mango Flavour, Cooked, Waitrose*	1 Kebab/73g	86	118	24.1	4.5	0.4	0.1
Chicken Tikka, Breast, Safeway*	1 Kebab/88g	127	145	23.8	9.8	1.0	0.7
Chicken With Sweet Chilli Sauce, Finest, Tesco*	½ Pack/175g	242	138	17.9	14.7	0.8	1.2
Chicken With Sweet Chilli Sauce, Marks & Spencer*	1 Serving/165g	228	138	17.9	14.7	0.8	1.2
Chicken, Barbecue, Sainsbury's*	1 Pack/200g	238	119	24.4	1.5	1.7	1.8
Chicken, Honey & Mustard, Marks & Spencer*	1oz/28g	41	145	16.7	8.2	4.8	1.0
Chicken, Mini Fillet, Marks & Spencer*	1 Serving/150g	210	140	20.2	2.0	5.8	0.3
Chicken, Thin Sliced, Heat 'n' Eat, Asda*	½ Pack/50g	92	184	15.0	3.9	12.0	1.1
Chinese Chicken, Mini, Marks & Spencer*	1 Kebab/11g	24	215	19.5	5.1	12.9	0.6
Chinese Salmon, Iceland*	1 Kebab/75g	115	153	23.8	4.1	4.6	1.6
Citrus Tikka Chicken Breast, Sainsbury's*	1 Kebab/61g	79	129	25.6	5.4	0.5	0.9
Citrus Tikka Lamb Kofta, Sainsbury's*	1 Kebab/84g	199	235	18.1	9.8	13.7	2.6
Doner, Heat 'n' Eat Thin Sliced, Asda*	1 Pack/100g	196	196	16.7	8.4	10.6	1.7
Donner, Iceland*	1 Serving/152.3g	268	176	9.2	24.4	4.7	2.4
Green Pesto Chicken Breast, COU, Marks & Spencer*	1 Serving/200g	160	80	15.1	1.5	1.4	1.0
Green Thai Chicken, Waitrose*	1 Serving/180g	223	124	20.5	1.4	4.0	1.4
Honey & Mustard Chicken, Sainsbury's*	1 Serving/50g	66	131	24.5	4.3	1.8	0.0
Indian Chicken, Marks & Spencer*	1 Serving/175g	228	130	22.6	1.1	4.0	2.0
Lamb Kofta With A Mint & Coriander Raita, Safeway*	1 Pack/290g	632	218	16.9	8.4	13.0	1.2
Lamb Kofta, Safeway*	1 Pack/227g	465	205	14.3	5.8	13.4	1.0
Lamb Shami With A Mint Raita Dip, Marks & Spencer*	½ Pack/90g	189	210	12.8	9.7	13.4	3.5
Lamb, Greek Style, Sainsbury's*	1 Kebab/168g	428	255	17.4	7.7	17.0	2.3
Lamb, Shish, Marks & Spencer*	½ Pack/200g	440	220	16.5	0.4	16.9	1.1
Lamb, Shish, Waitrose*	1 Kebab/55.8g	91	163	16.5	6.8	7.7	1.3
Lamb, Shoulder, Marks & Spencer*	½ Pack/250g	313	125	20.4	0.9	4.3	1.7
Lamb, With Halloumi Cheese & Olives, Waitrose*	2 Kebabs/150g	246	164	20.0	2.4	8.3	0.2
Mango & Lime Chicken, Waitrose*	1 Serving/180g	275	153	28.2	2.5	3.3	0.3
Mango Salsa Chicken Breast, Sainsbury's*	1 Kebab/60g	85	142	26.3	5.5	1.6	0.6
Salmon, Hot & Spicy, Tesco*	1 Kebab/75g	89	118	22.0	1.1	2.9	0.0
Shish With Onions & Peppers	1oz/28g	59	212	12.9	3.9	16.2	1.2
Shish in Pitta Bread With Salad	1oz/28g	43	155	13.5	17.2	4.1	1.0
Spicy Tomato Creole King Prawn, Marks & Spencer*	1 Pack/240g	240	100	14.3	2.9	3.3	0.7
Sticky Barbecue Chicken Thigh, Marks & Spencer*	1 Kebab/100g	160	160	15.6	7.4	7.5	0.8
Sweet Oriental Chicken Breast, COU, Marks & Spencer*	½ Pack/200g	220	110	20.8	4.3	1.0	0.1
Sweetcorn, Tesco*	1 Kebab/130g	74	57	2.0	9.9	1.0	0.9
Tandoori, Marks & Spencer*	1oz/28g	34	120	23.3	1.0	2.5	0.0
Thai Style Chicken, Eat Smart, Safeway*	1 Kebab/85g	85	100	15.3	6.4	1.3	1.4
Tiger Prawn, Asda*	1oz/28g	17	59	14.6	0.1	0.0	0.0
Tikka Chicken, Mini, Somerfield*	1oz/28g	38	134	21.0	4.0	4.0	0.0
Tikka, Mini, Marks & Spencer*	1 Kebab/11g	23	205	18.4	4.0	12.7	0.6
Tomato & Basil Chicken, Eat Smart, Safeway*	1 Kebab/71.5g	82	115	18.0	5.0	2.1	1.5
Vegetable, Asda*	1 Kebab/40g	25	63	1.8	4.5	4.3	2.4
Vegetable, Sainsbury's*	1 Kebab/100g	36	36	1.5	6.4	0.5	1.2
Vegetable, Tesco*	1 Kebab/120g	47	39	1.7	6.8	0.6	1.1
KEDGEREE,							
Average	1oz/28g	48	171	15.9	7.8	8.7	0.1

K

INFO/WEIGHT	Measure	per Measure KCAL	Nutrition Values per 100g / 100ml KCAL	PROT	CARB	FAT	FIBRE
KEDGEREE,							
COU, Marks & Spencer*	1 Pack/370g	426	115	7.9	14.4	2.6	0.8
Perfectly Balanced, Waitrose*	1 Pack/400g	368	92	7.0	10.8	2.3	0.6
Smoked Haddock, Big Dish, Marks & Spencer*	1 Pack/450g	585	130	8.5	13.0	5.0	1.9
KETCHUP,							
BBQ, Heinz*	1 Serving/10g	14	137	1.3	31.3	0.3	0.3
Barbeque, Asda*	1 Tbsp/15g	20	136	0.9	33.0	0.0	0.0
Tomato, Average	1 Tsp/5g	6	120	1.5	28.1	0.2	0.8
Tomato, Reduced Sugar, Average	1 Tbsp/10g	9	87	2.0	16.9	1.2	0.9
Wicked Orange, Heinz*	1 Serving/11g	12	108	1.0	24.7	0.1	0.6
KIDNEY,							
Lamb, Raw, Average	1oz/28g	44	156	21.5	0.0	7.7	0.0
Ox, Raw	1oz/28g	25	88	17.2	0.0	2.1	0.0
Ox, Stewed	1oz/28g	39	138	24.5	0.0	4.4	0.0
Pig, Fried	1oz/28g	57	202	29.2	0.0	9.5	0.0
Pig, Raw	1oz/28g	24	86	15.5	0.0	2.7	0.0
Pig, Stewed	1oz/28g	43	153	24.4	0.0	6.1	0.0
KIEV,							
Bacon & Cheese, Moy Park*	1 Kiev/142g	342	241	13.4	11.5	15.7	0.8
Cheese & Ham, Tesco*	1 Kiev/142.5g	313	219	13.6	12.4	12.8	1.2
Cheese & Herb, Mini, Bernard Matthews*	1 Kiev/23g	46	199	15.7	12.1	9.8	0.0
Cheese & Mushroom Chicken, Somerfield*	½ Pack/142g	294	207	14.0	15.0	11.0	0.0
Cheese, Smoked Ham & Chicken, Sainsbury's*	1 Kiev/136g	299	220	15.9	12.0	12.8	0.3
Chicken & Garlic Butter, Healthy Living, Tesco*	1 Kiev/142.5g	286	200	14.3	9.9	11.5	0.6
Chicken Breast, Garlic Butter, Sun Valley*	1 Kiev/141g	436	309	13.2	11.8	23.2	0.9
Chicken With Garlic Butter, Tesco*	1 Kiev/125g	343	274	13.7	8.8	20.4	0.7
Chicken, BGTY, Sainsbury's*	1 Kiev/125g	253	202	14.3	11.3	11.1	1.0
Chicken, Bernard Matthews*	1 Kiev/125g	374	299	10.6	13.9	22.3	2.7
Chicken, Better For You, Morrisons*	1 Kiev/134g	304	227	16.1	11.5	13.0	1.0
Chicken, Breaded, Mini, Family, Bernard Matthews*	1 Kiev/23g	46	199	15.7	12.1	9.8	0.0
Chicken, COU, Marks & Spencer*	1 Kiev/150g	188	125	15.8	10.8	1.8	0.5
Chicken, Cheese & Ham, Tesco*	1 Kiev/142g	338	238	16.3	11.3	14.2	0.6
Chicken, Cheesy Bean, Asda*	1 Kiev/94.0g	202	215	12.0	17.0	11.0	1.9
Chicken, Creamy Garlic, Tesco*	1 Kiev/142g	280	197	12.0	8.0	13.0	0.6
Chicken, Creamy Pepper, Safeway*	1 Kiev/133g	306	230	11.9	11.1	15.4	1.1
Chicken, Creamy Pepper, Tesco*	1 Kiev/142g	270	190	12.0	10.0	11.0	2.0
Chicken, Creamy Peppercorn, Sun Valley*	1 Kiev/140g	382	273	13.3	13.5	18.5	0.0
Chicken, Creamy Peppercorn, Tesco*	1 Kiev/141g	303	215	12.8	8.1	14.6	1.5
Chicken, Finest, Tesco*	1 Kiev/237g	460	194	18.0	9.0	9.5	1.0
Chicken, Garlic & Herb, Reduced Fat, Safeway*	1 Kiev/125g	270	216	13.0	11.4	13.2	1.0
Chicken, Garlic & Herb, Sainsbury's*	1 Kiev/133.5g	318	239	15.0	11.7	14.7	1.3
Chicken, Garlic & Mushroom, Sainsbury's*	1 Kiev/142.4g	345	243	16.2	14.5	13.4	1.4
Chicken, Garlic & Parsley, BGTY, Sainsbury's*	1 Kiev/133g	318	239	15.0	11.7	14.7	1.3
Chicken, Garlic & Parsley, Sainsbury's*	1 Kiev/136.4g	426	313	12.0	9.9	25.4	1.0
Chicken, Garlic Butter, Lower Fat, Asda*	1 Kiev/136g	282	207	13.0	14.0	11.0	0.7
Chicken, Garlic Butter, Safeway*	1 Kiev/115g	316	275	13.3	12.5	19.1	1.1
Chicken, Garlic Butter, Somerfield*	1 Kiev/142g	425	299	12.6	8.5	23.9	1.2
Chicken, Garlic, Asda*	1 Kiev/142.9g	446	312	11.0	13.0	24.0	0.5
Chicken, Garlic, Marks & Spencer*	1 Kiev/150g	375	250	16.5	9.5	16.4	0.5
Chicken, Garlic, Morrisons*	1 Kiev/122g	289	237	14.3	9.8	15.7	0.0
Chicken, Garlic, Safeway*	1 Kiev/147g	413	281	12.9	11.2	20.5	0.9
Chicken, Good Choice, Iceland*	1 Kiev/120g	366	305	12.7	12.6	22.7	0.8
Chicken, In Crispy Breadcrumbs, Sainsbury's*	1 Kiev/116.5g	311	266	12.8	10.6	19.2	1.1
Chicken, Italian Style, Sainsbury's*	1 Kiev/134.8g	342	253	14.3	12.8	16.1	1.3

K

	Measure INFO/WEIGHT	per Measure KCAL	Nutrition Values per 100g / 100ml				
			KCAL	PROT	CARB	FAT	FIBRE
KIEV,							
Chicken, Maitre Jean-Pierre, Lidl*	1 Pack/284g	781	275	13.3	12.7	19.1	0.0
Chicken, Tesco*	1oz/28g	70	251	16.7	8.8	16.5	1.1
Chicken, Tomato & Mozzarella, Tesco*	1 Kiev/143g	339	237	11.4	7.9	17.7	1.4
Cod & Parsley, Safeway*	1 Kiev/160g	310	194	10.6	11.0	9.2	0.0
Garlic & Parsley, TTD, Sainsbury's*	1 Kiev/150g	371	247	15.7	11.1	15.6	0.8
Garlic Butter, Safeway*	1 Kiev/134.6g	394	292	12.3	11.1	22.0	1.0
Garlic Chicken, GFY, Asda*	1 Kiev/138.4g	302	219	15.0	15.0	11.0	1.0
Ham & Cheese Chicken, Somerfield*	½ Pack/142g	294	207	14.0	14.0	11.0	0.0
Lemon Butter Chicken, Somerfield*	½ Pack/142g	409	288	12.0	12.0	21.0	0.0
Mushroom & Cheese, Oven Baked, Safeway*	1 Kiev/100g	305	305	22.6	14.8	17.3	1.9
Salmon, Fillet, Tesco*	1 Kiev/160g	376	235	13.3	18.0	12.2	2.5
Tikka Chicken, Asda*	1 Kiev/150g	326	217	15.6	15.6	10.2	0.8
Tikka, Safeway*	1 Kiev/132g	327	248	11.9	10.5	17.5	1.0
KIEV VEGETARIAN,							
Cheesy Garlic, Meat Free, Sainsbury's*	1 Kiev/123g	263	214	17.3	10.6	11.4	3.0
Garlic Butter, Tesco*	1 Kiev/142g	462	325	14.4	22.1	19.9	0.8
Garlic Butter, Tivall*	1 Kiev/125g	366	293	15.1	10.8	21.0	2.6
Garlic, Safeway*	1 Kiev/142g	423	298	13.2	20.3	18.2	0.7
Vegetable, Marks & Spencer*	1 Kiev/155g	326	210	4.6	17.8	13.4	2.5
KIPPER,							
Baked	1oz/28g	57	205	25.5	0.0	11.4	0.0
Fillets, In Brine, John West*	1 Can/140g	269	192	21.0	0.0	12.0	0.0
Fillets, In Sunflower Oil, John West*	1 Can/140g	321	229	19.0	0.0	17.0	0.0
Fillets, Raw, Average	1 Serving/200g	451	226	17.0	0.0	17.1	0.0
Fillets, With Butter, Farmfoods*	1oz/28g	64	229	17.5	0.0	17.7	0.0
Fillets, With Butter, Scottish, Marks & Spencer*	1 Pack/200g	382	191	16.7	0.0	13.8	0.0
Grilled	1oz/28g	71	255	20.1	0.0	19.4	0.0
Raw	1oz/28g	64	229	17.5	0.0	17.7	0.0
Smoked, Average	1 Serving/150g	322	215	18.9	0.0	15.4	0.0
KIT KAT,							
2 Finger, Nestle*	2 Finger Bar/21g	106	507	5.9	62.0	26.1	0.0
4 Fingers, Nestle*	4 Fingers/48g	244	508	6.0	61.5	26.4	1.1
Chunky, Nestle*	1 Bar/55g	283	514	5.6	61.3	27.4	1.0
Chunky, Snack Size, Nestle*	1 Bar/26g	133	513	6.6	60.4	27.2	1.1
Chunky, White, Nestle*	1 Bar/53g	278	525	8.0	58.3	28.9	0.4
Individual Bars, Nestle*	1 Bar/28g	144	513	6.6	60.4	27.2	0.0
Kubes, Nestle*	1 Pack/50g	258	515	5.9	60.9	27.5	1.0
Kubes, Orange, Nestle*	4 Kubes/12.8g	67	514	5.7	61.1	27.4	1.0
Mini, Nestle*	1 Bar/15g	75	502	7.5	59.4	26.0	0.0
Mint, Nestle*	4 Finger Bar/48g	244	508	6.0	61.5	26.4	1.1
Orange, 2 Finger, Nestle*	2 Finger Bar/20g	101	507	5.9	62.0	26.1	1.1
KIWI FRUIT,							
Fresh, Raw	1oz/28g	14	49	1.1	10.6	0.5	1.9
Weighed With Skin	1 Kiwi/60g	25	42	1.0	9.1	0.4	1.6
KOHL RABI,							
Boiled in Salted Water	1oz/28g	5	18	1.2	3.1	0.2	1.9
Raw	1oz/28g	6	23	1.6	3.7	0.2	2.2
KORMA,							
Chicken & Basmati Rice, Tesco*	1 Pot/350g	588	168	4.3	16.9	9.3	2.3
Chicken & Pilau Rice, BGTY, Sainsbury's*	1 Pack/450g	513	114	9.0	14.6	2.2	1.2
Chicken & Pilau Rice, GFY, Asda*	1 Pack/400g	600	150	8.0	16.0	6.0	1.3
Chicken & Pilau Rice, Good Intentions, Somerfield*	1 Serving/400g	472	118	7.7	15.3	2.9	0.8
Chicken & Pilau Rice, Morrisons*	1 Pack/450g	889	198	9.4	15.9	10.7	1.4

K

	INFO/WEIGHT	KCAL	KCAL	PROT	CARB	FAT	FIBRE
KORMA,							
Chicken & Pilau Rice, New, BGTY, Sainsbury's*	1 Pack/400g	344	86	8.1	10.8	1.2	1.9
Chicken & Pilau Rice, Somerfield*	1 Pack/340g	687	202	9.0	16.0	11.0	0.0
Chicken & Rice, 95% Fat Free, Bird's Eye*	1 Pack/370g	444	120	6.2	19.6	1.9	1.1
Chicken & Rice, COU, Marks & Spencer*	1 Pack/400g	420	105	8.1	13.7	1.7	0.5
Chicken & Rice, Easy Steam, BGTY, Sainsbury's*	1 Pack/400g	448	112	7.9	17.1	1.3	0.6
Chicken & Rice, Good Choice, Iceland*	1 Pack/400g	464	116	5.8	18.4	2.1	0.8
Chicken & Rice, Healthy Eating, Tesco*	1 Pack/420g	487	116	7.2	17.9	1.8	0.3
Chicken & Rice, Healthy Living, Co-Op*	1 Pack/400g	480	120	8.0	17.0	2.0	1.0
Chicken & Rice, Healthy Living, Tesco*	1 Pack/420g	458	109	7.1	16.1	1.8	1.6
Chicken & Rice, Organic, Tesco*	1 Pack/450g	923	205	6.0	21.5	10.6	0.4
Chicken & Rice, Patak's*	1 Pack/370g	466	126	5.9	15.8	4.8	0.4
Chicken & Rice, Tesco*	1 Pack/450g	594	132	6.8	13.7	5.5	2.6
Chicken Coconut, Sainsbury's*	1 Pack/400g	664	166	13.0	5.3	10.3	1.6
Chicken Meal, Restaurant, BGTY, Sainsbury's*	1 Serving/201g	223	111	15.0	4.0	4.1	1.2
Chicken With Basmati Rice, Eat Smart, Safeway*	1 Pack/380g	399	105	7.0	13.8	1.9	1.5
Chicken With Pilau Rice, Perfectly Balanced, Waitrose*	1 Pack/400g	528	132	8.9	18.3	2.6	1.1
Chicken With Pilau Rice, Safeway*	1 Pack/400g	784	196	7.6	16.9	10.9	2.4
Chicken With Pilau Rice, Sharwood's*	1 Pack/375g	566	151	6.7	15.4	7.0	0.9
Chicken, Fresh, Chilled, Tesco*	1 Pack/350g	819	234	13.1	6.3	17.4	2.3
Chicken, Healthy Living, Tesco*	1 Pack/350g	287	82	11.8	4.5	1.9	0.8
Chicken, Indian Meal for 2, Finest, Tesco*	½ Pack/200g	348	174	10.3	6.2	12.0	2.5
Chicken, Indian Takeaway For One, Sainsbury's*	1 Serving/300g	498	166	13.0	5.3	10.3	1.6
Chicken, Indian Takeaway, Iceland*	1 Pack/400g	656	164	11.8	4.5	11.0	1.4
Chicken, Less Than 3% Fat, Bird's Eye*	1 Pack/358g	440	123	6.5	20.4	1.9	0.8
Chicken, Safeway*	1 Pack/350g	648	185	14.1	8.4	10.6	2.0
Chicken, Sainsbury's*	1 Pack/400g	580	145	14.1	3.3	8.4	0.7
Chicken, Tesco*	1 Pack/350g	620	177	10.8	6.8	11.8	0.6
Chicken, Tinned, Asda*	½ Can/196.9g	321	163	8.0	8.0	11.0	2.3
Chicken, Vegetable Curry & Rice, Tesco*	1 Pack/450g	495	110	7.1	15.2	2.4	1.4
Chicken, Waitrose*	1 Pack/399.4g	678	170	13.7	2.4	11.7	1.9
Chicken, With Coriander & Rice, Slim Fast*	1 Pack/375g	394	105	5.7	18.6	0.9	0.7
Chicken, With Pilau Rice, Asda*	1 Serving/350g	735	210	12.0	9.0	14.0	2.0
Creamy, With Pilau Rice, Safeway*	1 Pack/400g	560	140	5.2	15.8	5.7	2.3
Vegetable & Rice, Tesco*	1 Pack/450g	621	138	2.9	18.3	5.9	1.6
Vegetable With Rice, Eat Smart, Safeway*	1 Pack/400g	412	103	3.1	17.5	2.3	1.6
Vegetable, Sainsbury's*	1 Serving/200g	302	151	2.7	6.6	12.6	2.2
KRISPROLLS,							
Cracked Wheat, Original, Pogen*	1 Piece/10g	38	380	12.0	67.0	7.0	9.0
Golden Wheat, Pogen*	1 Serving/10g	41	410	11.0	72.0	8.5	4.0
Golden, Pagen*	1 Serving/25g	100	400	11.0	69.0	8.5	5.0
Organic, Bio, Pagen*	1 Serving/12g	46	380	12.0	67.0	7.0	8.0
Whole Grain, Swedish, Pagen*	1 Toast/12g	44	370	12.0	65.0	7.0	9.5
KULFI,							
Average	1oz/28g	119	424	5.4	11.8	39.9	0.6
KUMQUATS,							
Canned, In Syrup	1oz/28g	39	138	0.4	35.4	0.5	1.7
Raw	1oz/28g	12	43	0.9	9.3	0.5	3.8

K

	Measure	per Measure	Nutrition Values per 100g / 100ml				
	INFO/WEIGHT	KCAL	KCAL	PROT	CARB	FAT	FIBRE
LAGER,							
Alcohol Free, Becks*	1 Serving/275ml	55	20	0.7	5.0	0.0	0.0
Amstel, Heinekin N V*	1 Pint/568ml	227	40	0.5	3.0	0.0	0.0
Average	1 Pint/568ml	165	29	0.3	0.0	0.0	0.0
Becks*	1 Can/275ml	113	41	0.0	3.0	0.0	0.0
Budweiser, Anheuser-Busch*	1 Bottle/330ml	133	40	0.3	2.9	0.0	0.0
Export, Carlsberg*	1 Can/440ml	189	43	0.4	4.0	0.0	0.4
Export, Foster's*	1 Pint/568ml	210	37	0.0	2.2	0.0	0.0
Foster's*	1 Pint/568ml	227	40	0.0	3.1	0.0	0.0
French Premier, Somerfield*	1 Bottle/250ml	108	43	0.0	4.0	0.0	0.0
German, Low Alcohol, Sainsbury's*	1 Bottle/330ml	92	28	0.4	5.9	0.1	0.1
Heineken*, 5%	1 Bottle/250ml	110	44	0.4	3.4	0.0	0.0
Heineken, Heineken N V*	1 Pint/568ml	256	45	0.5	3.0	0.0	0.0
Kaliber, Guinness*	1 Can/440ml	79	18	0.0	3.8	0.0	0.0
Low Alcohol	1 Can/440ml	44	10	0.2	1.5	0.0	0.0
Miller Pilsner*	1 Bottle/500ml	150	30	0.3	2.4	0.0	0.0
Organic, Tesco*	1 Bottle/500ml	215	43	0.2	3.5	0.0	0.0
Pills, Holsten*	1 Can/440ml	167	38	0.3	2.4	0.0	0.0
Pilsner, German, Somerfield*	1 Bottle/250ml	73	29	1.0	1.0	0.0	0.0
Premium	1 Can/440ml	260	59	0.3	2.4	0.0	0.0
Premium, Co-Op*	1 Can/440ml	132	30	0.4	0.9	0.1	0.0
Premium, French, Biere Speciale, Tescor*	1 Serving/250ml	105	42	0.3	3.3	0.0	0.0
Premium, Tesco*	1 Can/440	229	52	0.4	4.0	0.0	0.0
Shandy, Traditional Style, Asda*	1 Serving/200ml	44	22	0.0	4.6	0.0	0.0
Stella Artois*	1 Can/550ml	222	40	0.3	2.9	0.0	0.0
Ultra Low Carb, Michelob*	1 Bottle/275ml	88	32	0.2	0.9	0.0	0.0
Value, Tesco*	1 Can/440ml	75	17	0.2	1.2	0.0	0.0
LAMB,							
Chops, Average	1oz/28g	65	231	20.6	0.4	16.4	0.0
Chops, Leg, With Redcurrant & Rosemary Sauce, Tesco*	1 Pack/325g	605	186	17.6	4.0	11.1	0.5
Chops, Minted, Average	1 Chop/100g	260	260	25.9	5.1	15.1	0.3
Chops, Shoulder, Mango & Mint, Waitrose*	1 Chop/250g	555	222	16.7	2.3	16.2	0.5
Diced, From Supermarket, Healthy Range, Average	½ Pack/200g	277	138	24.6	0.1	4.5	0.0
Escalope, British, Tesco*	1 Piece/95g	105	110	20.1	0.0	3.3	0.0
Grill Steak, Average	1oz/28g	70	251	20.2	4.4	16.9	0.4
Grill Steak, Prime, Average	1 Steak/63g	197	312	18.5	2.1	25.5	0.1
Joint, With Sweet Mint Dressing, Tesco*	1 Serving/50g	97	193	19.9	1.8	11.8	0.6
Leg, Joint, Raw, Average	1 Joint/510g	859	168	20.9	1.4	8.9	0.2
Leg, Roasted, Lean & Fat, Average	1oz/28g	66	237	28.6	0.0	13.6	0.0
Mince, Average	1oz/28g	58	207	17.7	0.5	14.9	0.1
Rack, Raw, Lean & Fat	1oz/28g	79	283	17.3	0.0	23.8	0.0
Rack, Roasted, Lean	1oz/28g	63	225	27.1	0.0	13.0	0.0
Rack, Roasted, Lean & Fat	1oz/28g	102	363	23.0	0.0	30.1	0.0
Shank, With Rosemary Gravy, Sainsburys*	1 Serving/200g	204	102	13.2	3.1	4.1	0.3
Shoulder, Cooked, Lean & Fat	1oz/28g	84	301	24.4	0.0	22.5	0.0
Shoulder, Raw, Average	1oz/28g	70	249	16.8	0.0	20.2	0.0
Steak, Leg, Raw, Average	1 Steak/150g	169	113	20.1	0.0	3.7	0.0
Steak, Minted, Average	1 Steak/125g	212	170	22.7	3.4	7.2	0.9
Steak, Raw, Average	1 Steak/140g	190	136	21.7	0.2	5.4	0.0
Stewing, Raw, Lean & Fat	1oz/28g	57	203	22.5	0.0	12.6	0.0
Stewing, Stewed, Lean	1oz/28g	67	240	26.6	0.0	14.8	0.0
Stewing, Stewed, Lean & Fat	1oz/28g	78	279	24.4	0.0	20.1	0.0
LAMB DINNER,							
Lamb Meal, Roast, Ready Meals, Marks & Spencer*	1 Pack/340g	459	135	7.5	14.1	5.7	1.5

L

LAMB DINNER,

Roast, Bird's Eye*	1 Pack/340g	357	105	6.6	11.2	3.8	1.4

LAMB GREEK,

With Orzo Pasta, Marks & Spencer*	1 Serving/350g	438	125	10.2	9.7	5.0	2.7

LAMB IN,

A Pot, Sainsbury's*	1 Pack/450g	554	123	7.6	14.6	3.8	0.7
A Rich Balsamic Sauce, Shank, Safeway*	½ Pack/705g	1304	185	18.0	3.1	11.0	0.9
Gravy, Minted, Roast, Marks & Spencer*	1 Pack/200g	140	70	6.8	6.6	1.5	0.9
Gravy, Roast, Bird's Eye*	1 Pack/239g	160	67	8.1	3.8	2.2	0.1
Mint Gravy, Sliced, Sainsbury's*	1 Pack/125g	134	107	15.3	2.9	3.8	0.8
Minted Gravy, Shank, Iceland*	1 Pack/400g	824	206	20.1	1.6	13.2	0.7

LAMB KOFTA,

Kleftico, Sainsbury's*	1 Pack/401.2g	654	163	13.5	5.5	9.7	0.5

LAMB MEDITERRANEAN,

Shanks, Finest, Tesco*	1 Serving/404g	671	166	15.0	6.6	8.8	2.0

LAMB WITH,

Carrot & Swede Mash, Braised, Eat Smart, Safeway*	1 Pack/388g	330	85	7.6	7.4	2.4	1.4
Chunky Vegetables, Braised Shank, Marks & Spencer*	½ Pack/425g	808	190	24.7	2.0	9.0	0.7
Redcurrant & Mint Sauce, Steak, Asda*	1 Steak/142.8g	327	229	16.0	8.0	13.0	0.0
Roasted Vegetables, Shank, Marks & Spencer*	½ Pack/420g	660	157	14.9	8.3	7.3	0.7
Rosemary, Ready To Roast, Marks & Spencer*	1 Serving/188g	235	125	17.5	2.0	5.2	0.3

LARD,

Average	1oz/28g	249	891	0.0	0.0	99.0	0.0

LASAGNA,

Frozen, Safeway*	1 Serving/400g	455	114	6.0	11.8	4.6	0.2
Al Forno, Marks & Spencer*	1 Pack/330g	528	160	9.6	12.3	8.3	1.4
Asda*	1 Pack/378g	427	113	6.0	11.0	5.0	1.1
Asparagus, Marks & Spencer*	1 Pack/360g	414	115	4.7	12.1	5.2	1.2
BGTY, Sainsbury's*	1 Pack/400g	420	105	5.9	15.5	2.2	0.5
Balsamic Onion & Chicken, Marks & Spencer*	1 Pack/375g	563	150	9.5	12.5	6.7	1.5
Beef & Chunky Vegetable, Healthy Living, Tesco*	1 Pack/340g	354	104	5.9	13.8	2.8	1.2
Beef Tomato Bechamel, Healthy Eating, Tesco*	1 Pack/425g	472	111	5.9	12.4	4.2	1.3
Beef, 3% Less Fat, Eat Smart, Safeway*	1 Pack/380g	342	90	5.9	11.1	2.3	1.3
Beef, Asda*	1 Pack/400g	372	93	4.2	11.0	3.6	0.6
Beef, BGTY, Sainsbury's*	1 Pack/400g	340	85	5.3	11.3	2.1	0.6
Beef, Bird's Eye*	1 Pack/384g	515	134	7.0	12.5	6.2	0.7
Beef, Chilled, Safeway*	½ Pack/325g	452	139	7.5	11.8	5.9	1.2
Beef, Eat Smart, Safeway*	1 Pack/380g	380	100	7.6	10.9	2.7	1.3
Beef, Frozen, Findus*	1 Pack/330g	363	110	6.1	11.5	4.2	0.7
Beef, Frozen, Tesco*	1 Pack/400g	492	123	5.7	11.4	6.1	0.7
Beef, GFY, Asda*	1 Pack/350g	385	110	9.0	14.0	2.0	1.0
Beef, Less Than 5% Fat, Asda*	1 Pack/400g	460	115	5.0	14.0	4.3	0.6
Beef, Ready Meals, Waitrose*	1 Pack/325g	471	145	6.7	13.1	7.3	1.4
Beef, Reduced Fat, Waitrose*	1 Pack/325g	345	106	5.5	12.1	4.0	0.8
Beef, TTD, Sainsbury's*	1 Serving/450g	648	144	8.7	10.3	7.5	0.6
Beef, Weight Watchers*	1 Pack/300g	288	96	6.3	9.7	3.4	0.3
Bird's Eye*	1 Pack/375g	420	112	6.1	11.6	4.6	0.7
Boiled	1oz/28g	28	100	3.0	22.0	0.6	0.9
COU, Marks & Spencer*	1 Pack/360g	324	90	6.9	11.7	1.7	1.0
Chicken, Italian, Sainsbury's*	1 Pack/450g	549	122	8.4	12.6	4.2	0.5
Chicken, Italiano, Tesco*	1 Serving/450g	491	109	8.6	12.0	3.0	0.6
Chicken, Marks & Spencer*	1 Pack/400g	420	105	7.5	9.7	3.8	1.0
Chicken, Mushroom & Asparagus, Finest, Tesco*	½ Pack/300g	396	132	9.2	11.1	5.7	0.6
Chicken, Ready Meals, Waitrose*	1 Pack/300g	411	137	6.3	13.0	6.6	0.9

L

LASAGNA,	Measure INFO/WEIGHT	per Measure KCAL	Nutrition Values per 100g / 100ml KCAL	PROT	CARB	FAT	FIBRE
Chicken, Safeway*	1 Pack/400g	420	105	7.2	8.6	4.6	1.1
Chilled, Somerfield*	1 Pack/300g	312	104	6.8	12.2	3.1	1.3
Classic, Deep Filled, Marks & Spencer*	1 Pack/400g	760	190	10.0	11.2	11.9	0.6
Dried, Napolina*	1oz/28g	99	352	11.5	73.0	1.5	2.2
Extra Special, Asda*	½ Pack/290.9g	416	143	7.0	13.0	7.0	0.3
Family, Marks & Spencer*	¼ Pack/225g	281	125	10.3	6.9	6.2	1.1
Finest, Tesco*	½ Pack/300g	432	144	7.4	13.1	6.9	0.5
GFY, Asda*	1 Pack/410g	328	80	4.8	11.0	1.9	0.2
Good Choice, Iceland*	1 Pack/400g	444	111	7.7	11.6	3.8	0.2
Good Intentions, Somerfield*	1 Pack/300g	303	101	5.3	13.9	2.7	0.4
Healthy Living, Tesco*	1 Pack/425g	451	106	5.5	13.5	3.3	1.2
Iceland*	1 Pack/400g	548	137	7.5	14.3	5.5	0.9
Italia, Marks & Spencer*	1 Pack/400g	640	160	8.2	10.7	9.5	0.8
Italian, Healthy Living, Tesco*	1 Pack/340g	347	102	6.4	13.6	2.5	1.3
Italian, Sainsbury's*	1 Pack/450g	801	178	8.9	13.2	9.9	0.5
Italiano, Tesco*	1 Pack/800g	1144	143	8.4	17.1	4.6	0.5
Layered, Asda*	1 Pack/300g	444	148	5.0	14.0	8.0	0.3
Less Than 3% Fat, Frozen, BGTY, Sainsbury's*	1 Pack/400g	340	85	5.3	11.3	2.1	0.6
Less Than 5% Fat, Better For You, Morrisons*	½ Pack/350g	227	65	5.9	8.2	2.5	0.7
Low Fat, Co-Op*	1 Pack/300g	255	85	6.0	10.0	3.0	1.0
Marks & Spencer*	1/3 Pack/333g	466	140	8.5	10.4	7.4	0.9
Meat, Somerfield*	1 Pack/600g	768	128	6.0	12.0	6.0	0.0
Mediterranean Vegetable, COU, Marks & Spencer*	1 Pack/360g	306	85	3.4	11.5	2.7	1.4
Mega, Value, Tesco*	1 Pack/600g	726	121	4.7	12.2	5.9	0.5
New, Healthy Living, Tesco*	1 Pack/340g	347	102	6.4	13.6	2.5	1.3
Pizza Hut*	1 Serving/350g	669	191	11.3	17.8	8.3	2.7
Primana, Aldi*	1 Serving/250g	423	169	8.0	14.0	9.0	0.0
Ready Meal, Marks & Spencer*	1 Pack/360g	594	165	11.3	11.7	8.2	1.3
Roasted Mushrooms, Safeway*	1 Serving/400g	440	110	3.9	11.2	5.0	1.4
Roasted Mushroopinach, COU, Marks & Spencer*	1 Pack/360g	288	80	5.0	12.1	1.2	1.1
Safeway*	1 Pack/300g	354	118	5.7	11.5	5.5	0.5
Sainsbury's*	1 Pack/300g	339	113	5.2	12.2	4.8	1.3
Salmon & Spinach, Tesco*	1 Pack/400g	292	73	4.9	10.0	1.5	0.8
Sheets, Cooked, Safeway*	1 Serving/125g	184	147	5.5	28.3	1.4	1.8
Sheets, Dry, Average	1oz/28g	98	349	11.9	72.1	1.5	2.9
Sheets, Fresh, Dry, Average	1 Sheet/21g	56	271	10.9	52.7	2.1	1.9
Sheets, Verdi, Dry, Average	1 Serving/50g	178	356	12.7	71.1	2.3	2.8
Spinach & Cheese, Italian, Sainsbury's*	1 Pack/450g	666	148	6.0	15.5	6.8	0.5
Spinach & Ricotta, Finest, Tesco*	1 Pack/350g	585	167	6.1	11.7	10.6	1.2
Triangles With Chicken, COU, Marks & Spencer*	1 Pack/360g	324	90	7.8	11.9	1.8	1.0
Value, Tesco*	1 Pack/500g	630	126	4.4	13.7	5.9	0.5
Vegetable	1oz/28g	29	102	4.1	12.4	4.4	1.0
Vegetable, BGTY, Sainsbury's*	1 Pack/400g	286	72	4.8	9.5	1.6	1.4
Vegetable, Eat Smart, Safeway*	1 Pack/380g	266	70	3.5	10.8	1.3	1.4
Vegetable, Findus*	1 Pack/330g	314	95	4.0	13.0	2.5	0.0
Vegetable, Italian Three Layer, Sainsbury's*	1 Pack/450g	554	123	4.8	14.3	5.2	0.5
Vegetable, Italian, Somerfield*	1 Serving/400g	372	93	3.3	10.0	4.4	1.3
Vegetable, Italiano, Tesco*	1 Pack/340g	286	84	2.8	11.9	2.8	1.0
Vegetable, Linda McCartney*	1 Pack/320g	374	117	7.0	14.2	3.5	1.9
Vegetable, Low Fat, Co-Op*	1 Pack/300g	195	65	4.0	10.0	2.0	1.0
Vegetable, Luxury Roasted, Safeway*	1 Pack/400g	492	123	3.4	15.8	5.1	1.1
Vegetable, Mediterranean Style, Eat Smart, Safeway*	1 Pack/380g	228	60	3.0	10.1	0.8	1.5
Vegetable, Mediterranean, Linda McCartney*	1 Pack/320g	333	104	3.2	15.8	3.1	1.5

L

	Measure INFO/WEIGHT	per Measure KCAL	Nutrition Values per 100g / 100ml				
			KCAL	PROT	CARB	FAT	FIBRE
LASAGNA,							
Vegetable, Mediterranean, Waitrose*	1 Pack/351g	397	113	3.7	12.7	5.3	1.0
Vegetable, Two Layered, BGTY, Sainsbury's*	1 Pack/400g	288	72	4.8	9.5	1.6	1.4
Vegetable, Value, Tesco*	1 Pack/500g	410	82	4.1	9.7	3.0	2.3
Vegetable, Weight Watchers*	1 Pack/330g	251	76	3.6	11.8	1.7	0.7
Vegetarian, Tesco*	1 Pack/430g	581	135	5.3	13.6	6.6	1.0
LAVERBREAD,							
Average	1oz/28g	15	52	3.2	1.6	3.7	0.0
LEEKS,							
Boiled, Average	1oz/28g	6	21	1.2	2.6	0.7	1.7
Raw, Average	1oz/28g	7	25	1.7	3.7	0.4	2.4
LEMON,							
Fresh, Raw	1 Slice/5g	0	7	0.3	1.6	0.0	1.7
LEMON CURD,							
Average	1 Tbsp/15g	44	294	0.7	62.9	4.7	0.1
Luxury, Average	1 Tsp/7g	23	326	2.8	59.7	8.4	0.1
LEMON SOLE,							
Fillets, Raw, Average	1 Serving/220g	180	82	17.3	0.2	1.3	0.3
Goujons, Average	1 Serving/150g	359	239	13.9	18.5	12.2	1.0
Goujons, With Citrus Mayonnaise, Tesco*	1 Serving/250g	610	244	11.7	19.6	13.2	0.8
In Breadcrumbs, Average	1 Fillet/142g	322	228	13.7	15.7	12.3	1.0
In White Wine, & Herb Butter, Fillets, Marks & Spencer*	1 Pack/220g	385	175	15.1	0.1	12.6	0.0
LEMONADE,							
7-Up, Light, Britvic*	1 Can/330ml	4	1	0.1	0.2	0.0	0.0
Asda*	1 Glass/250ml	83	33	0.0	8.0	0.0	0.0
Average	1 Glass/250ml	53	21	0.1	5.0	0.1	0.1
Cloudy, Diet, Morrisons*	1 Serving/250ml	8	3	0.1	0.2	0.0	0.0
Cloudy, Diet, Sainsbury's*	1 Can/330ml	7	2	0.1	0.2	0.1	0.3
Cloudy, Sainsbury's*	1 Glass/250ml	118	47	0.1	12.0	0.1	0.1
Diet, Asda*	1 Glass/250ml	3	1	0.0	0.1	0.1	0.0
Diet, Schweppes*	1 Bottle/500ml	8	2	0.0	0.0	0.0	0.0
Diet, Traditional Style, Sainsbury's*	1 Glass/250ml	8	3	0.1	0.2	0.1	0.1
Diet, Traditional Style, Tesco*	1 Glass/200ml	6	3	0.0	0.8	0.0	0.0
Fresh Squeezed, Marks & Spencer*	1 Bottle/250ml	113	45	0.1	11.8	0.0	0.0
Lime, Safeway*	1 Can/144ml	63	44	0.0	10.6	0.0	0.0
Low Calorie, SmartPrice, Asda*	1 Glass/250ml	1	0	0.0	0.1	0.0	0.0
Premium, Freeway, Lidl*	1oz/28g	5	17	0.0	4.2	0.0	0.0
Sainsbury's*	1 Serving/250ml	53	21	0.1	4.9	0.1	0.1
Shapers, Boots*	1 Bottle/500ml	13	3	0.0	0.0	0.0	0.0
Somerfield*	½ Pint/284ml	77	27	0.0	7.0	0.0	0.0
Sparkling, Morrisons*	1 Glass/250ml	63	25	0.0	6.1	0.0	0.0
Sparkling, With Spanish Lemon Juice, Waitrose*	1 Serving/250ml	85	34	0.0	8.3	0.0	0.0
Sprite*	1 Bottle/500ml	215	43	0.0	10.5	0.0	0.0
Sprite, Light, Sprite*	1fl oz/30ml	0	2	0.0	0.0	0.0	0.0
Still, Marks & Spencer*	1 Glass/250ml	5	49	0.1	12.9	0.0	0.0
Still, Tesco*	1 Glass/200ml	100	50	0.0	12.0	0.0	0.0
Sugar Free, Value, Tesco*	1 Glass/200ml	2	1	0.1	0.1	0.1	0.0
Tesco*	1 Glass/200ml	30	15	0.0	3.6	0.0	0.0
Traditional Style, Tesco*	1 Glass/200ml	100	50	0.0	12.3	0.0	0.0
LENTILS,							
Green & Brown, Whole, Dried, Boiled in Salted Water	1oz/28g	29	105	8.8	16.9	0.7	3.8
Green Or Brown, Dried, Average	1 Serving/50g	151	301	22.8	49.8	1.5	9.6
Green Or Brown, In Water, Tinned, Average	½ Can/132g	131	99	8.1	15.4	0.6	3.8
Red, Boiled In Unsalted Water, Average	1oz/28g	28	102	7.6	17.5	0.4	2.6

L

	Measure	per Measure		Nutrition Values per 100g / 100ml				
	INFO/WEIGHT	KCAL		KCAL	PROT	CARB	FAT	FIBRE
LENTILS,								
Red, Dried, Average	1oz/28g	88		315	23.8	53.8	1.3	4.9
LETTUCE,								
Chinese Leaf, Tesco*	1 Serving/200g	36		18	3.5	0.3	0.3	2.6
Iceberg, Average	1oz/28g	4		13	0.8	1.8	0.3	0.5
Lamb's, Average	1 Serving/25g	4		15	1.4	1.6	0.3	1.0
Romaine, Average	1oz/28g	4		15	0.9	1.7	0.5	0.7
LILT*,								
Fruit Crush	1 Serving/330ml	66		20	0.0	4.6	0.0	0.0
LINGUINE,								
Dry, Average	1 Serving/100g	352		352	13.1	70.0	2.2	2.8
King Prawn, Meal for One, Marks & Spencer*	1 Pack/400g	380		95	6.6	13.1	1.7	2.2
Pomodoro, Marks & Spencer*	1 Pack/300g	360		120	4.1	17.6	3.5	1.2
Sun Dried Tomato & Egg, Asda*	1 Serving/200g	324		162	7.0	28.0	2.4	3.9
Tomato & Mushroom, Perfectly Balanced, Waitrose*	1 Pack/350g	294		84	2.2	10.6	3.8	1.0
Vegetable & Ham, BGTY, Sainsbury's*	1 Pack/450g	410		91	4.4	11.7	3.0	0.9
LINGUINI,								
Fresh, Dry, Average	1 Pack/250g	681		273	12.3	51.7	2.6	4.0
LINSEED,								
Seeds, Average	1 Serving/5g	23		464	21.7	18.5	33.5	26.3
LION BAR,								
Mini, Nestle*	1 Bar/16g	80		486	4.6	67.7	21.7	0.0
Nestle*	1 Bar/54.9g	279		508	4.9	62.9	26.0	0.0
Peanut, Nestle*	1 Bar/49g	256		522	7.1	56.9	29.6	0.0
LIQUEURS,								
Cream	1 Shot/25ml	81		325	0.0	22.8	16.1	0.0
High Strength	1 Shot/25ml	79		314	0.0	24.4	0.0	0.0
LIQUORICE,								
Allsorts, Average	1 Sm Bag/56g	195		349	3.7	76.7	5.2	2.0
Catherine Wheels, Sainsbury's*	1 Wheel/17g	49		286	3.8	67.2	0.3	0.7
Comfits, Marks & Spencer*	1oz/28g	100		357	2.4	86.2	0.3	0.7
Organic, Laidback Liquorice*	1 Bar/28g	90		320	4.7	75.0	1.0	3.0
Panda*	1 Bar/32g	109		340	3.8	78.0	0.5	0.0
Red, Fresh, 98% Fat Free, RJ's*	1oz/28g	96		342	3.0	75.0	1.7	0.0
Shapes, Average	1oz/28g	78		278	5.5	65.0	1.4	1.9
LIVER,								
Calves, Fried	1oz/28g	49		176	22.3	0.0	9.6	0.0
Calves, Raw	1oz/28g	29		104	18.3	0.0	3.4	0.0
Calves, With Fresh Sage Butter, Marks & Spencer*	1 Serving/116.7g	211		180	12.8	10.1	10.7	1.5
Calves, With Garlic Butter, Marks & Spencer*	1oz/28g	56		200	13.3	7.3	13.5	0.4
Chicken, Fried	1oz/28g	47		169	22.1	0.0	8.9	0.0
Chicken, Raw	1oz/28g	26		92	17.7	0.0	2.3	0.0
Lamb's With Onions, Marks & Spencer*	1oz/28g	52		185	14.1	6.8	11.3	0.1
Lamb's, Fried, Average	1oz/28g	66		237	30.1	0.1	12.9	0.1
Lamb's, Raw, Average	1 Serving/125g	171		137	20.3	0.0	6.2	0.0
Ox, Raw	1oz/28g	43		155	21.1	0.0	7.8	0.0
Ox, Stewed	1oz/28g	55		198	24.8	3.6	9.5	0.0
Pig's, Raw	1oz/28g	32		113	21.3	0.0	3.1	0.0
Pig's, Stewed	1 Serving/70g	132		189	25.6	3.6	8.1	0.0
LIVER &,								
Bacon, British Classics, Tesco*	1 Pack/400g	496		124	10.7	7.1	5.9	0.7
Bacon, Sainsbury's*	1 Serving/250g	303		121	10.9	8.3	4.9	0.4
Bacon, With Creamy Mash, GFY, Asda*	1 Pack/385.9g	355		92	7.0	10.0	2.7	1.8
Bacon, With Fresh Mashed Potato, Waitrose*	1 Pack/400g	512		128	6.9	10.2	6.6	0.8

L

	Measure INFO/WEIGHT	per Measure KCAL	Nutrition Values per 100g / 100ml				
			KCAL	PROT	CARB	FAT	FIBRE
LIVER &,							
Onions, Marks & Spencer*	1 Serving/200g	250	125	7.6	10.5	6.0	0.9
LIVER SAUSAGE,							
Average	1 Slice/10g	22	216	15.3	4.5	15.2	0.2
LOBSTER,							
Boiled	1oz/28g	29	103	22.1	0.0	1.6	0.0
Cooked, Asda*	1oz/28g	32	115	22.1	0.0	3.4	0.0
Dressed, John West*	1 Can/43g	45	105	13.0	2.0	5.0	0.0
Dressed, Marks & Spencer*	1oz/28g	76	273	14.3	0.8	23.6	0.1
Half, Marks & Spencer*	1oz/28g	66	235	12.1	2.4	19.6	0.2
Squat, Youngs*	½ Pack/125g	246	197	9.8	20.1	8.6	1.1
Thermidor, Marks & Spencer*	1 Serving/140g	287	205	10.7	9.7	13.7	0.0
LOGANBERRIES,							
Raw	1oz/28g	5	17	1.1	3.4	0.0	2.5
LOLLIPOPS,							
Assorted Flavours, Asda*	1 Lolly/7g	27	380	0.0	95.0	0.0	0.0
Chupa Chups*	1 Lolly/18g	72	400	0.6	97.2	0.6	0.0
Marks & Spencer*	1oz/28g	107	383	0.0	95.4	0.0	0.0
LOLLY,							
Cookies N Cream, Skinny Cow, Richmond Foods*	1 Lolly/66.9g	89	133	4.7	25.2	1.5	3.6
Fruit, Mini, Tesco*	1 Lolly/31.5g	41	127	1.9	25.7	1.9	0.6
Milk, Blue Parrot Cafe, Sainsbury's*	1 Lolly/30ml	34	113	2.7	18.0	3.3	0.3
Orange N Cream, Tropicana*	1 Lolly/64.5g	84	129	1.4	20.5	4.5	0.3
Sugar Free, Simpkins*	1 Lolly/15g	51	340	0.0	88.0	0.0	0.0
LONGANS,							
Canned, In Syrup, Drained	1oz/28g	19	67	0.4	17.1	0.3	0.0
LOQUATS,							
Raw	1oz/28g	8	28	0.7	6.3	0.2	0.0
LUCOZADE,							
Citrus Clear, Energy, SmithKline Beecham*	1 Bottle/380ml	266	70	0.1	17.0	0.0	0.0
Hydro Active, Smithkline Beecham*	1fl oz/30ml	3	10	0.0	2.0	0.0	0.0
Orange Energy Drink, Smithkline Beecham*	1 Bottle/500ml	350	70	0.0	17.2	0.0	0.0
Original, Smithkline Beecham*	1 Bottle/345ml	252	73	0.0	17.9	0.0	0.0
Sport Isotonic Lemon Body Fuel, Smithkline Beecham*	1 Bottle/500ml	140	28	0.0	6.4	0.0	0.0
Sport, Mixed Berry, Body Fuel, Smithkline Beecham*	1 Bottle/500ml	140	28	0.0	6.4	0.0	0.0
Sport, Orange, SmithKline Beecham*	1 Bottle/500ml	140	28	0.0	6.4	0.0	0.1
Sport, Wild Berry, Smithkline Beecham*	1 Bottle/500ml	140	28	0.0	6.4	0.0	0.0
Tropical, SmithKline Beecham*	1 Bottle/380ml	266	70	0.0	17.2	0.0	0.0
LUNCHEON MEAT,							
Pork, Average	1oz/28g	81	288	13.3	4.0	24.3	0.0
LYCHEES,							
Fresh, Raw	1oz/28g	16	58	0.9	14.3	0.1	0.7
In Juice, Amoy*	1oz/28g	13	46	0.4	10.9	0.0	0.0
In Syrup, Average	1oz/28g	19	69	0.4	17.7	0.0	0.4
Raw, Weighed With Skin & Stone	1oz/28g	10	36	0.5	8.9	0.1	0.4

L

INFO/WEIGHT	Measure	per Measure KCAL	Nutrition Values per 100g / 100ml KCAL	PROT	CARB	FAT	FIBRE
M&M'S,							
Mars*	1 Funsize/20g	97	487	4.7	69.6	21.1	0.0
Mini, Mars*	1 Sm Pack/36g	176	489	6.3	63.6	23.2	0.0
Peanut, Mars*	1 Pack/45g	231	514	10.2	57.3	27.1	0.0
Plain, Mars*	1 Pack/48g	240	499	4.1	70.7	20.8	2.1
MACADAMIA NUTS,							
Salted	6 Nuts/10g	75	748	7.9	4.8	77.6	5.3
MACARONI,							
Dry, Average	1oz/28g	99	354	11.9	73.5	1.7	2.6
Dry, Tesco*, Cooked	1 Serving/135g	269	199	4.8	30.2	6.5	1.3
MACARONI CHEESE,							
Average	1oz/28g	50	178	7.3	13.6	10.8	0.5
Bird's Eye*	1 Pack/302g	374	124	4.2	15.6	5.0	0.4
Canned	1oz/28g	39	138	4.5	16.4	6.5	0.4
Chilled, GFY, Asda*	1 Pack/442.5g	469	106	6.0	14.0	2.9	1.6
Eat Smart, Safeway*	1 Pack/315g	394	125	6.5	19.2	2.1	0.8
Findus*	1 Pack/360g	576	160	6.3	14.3	8.5	0.0
Healthy Eating, Tesco*	1 Pack/340g	252	74	6.6	6.2	2.5	0.6
Healthy Living, Tesco*	1 Pack/340g	391	115	6.2	18.6	1.8	1.0
Heinz*	1 Can/400g	380	95	3.4	9.8	4.7	0.3
Italian, Sainsbury's*	½ Pack/225g	360	160	7.3	15.3	7.7	1.6
Italian, Tesco*	1 Pack/340g	541	159	6.5	14.2	8.5	2.7
Kraft*	1 Serving/50g	205	410	11.0	47.0	17.5	1.0
Marks & Spencer*	1 Pack/400g	680	170	6.9	12.8	9.9	0.6
New, BGTY, Sainsbury's*	1 Pack/400g	432	108	5.5	17.2	1.9	1.1
Perfectly Balanced, Waitrose*	1 Pack/350g	351	100	6.7	11.4	3.1	0.5
Tesco*	1 Can/410g	513	125	4.5	10.1	6.3	0.3
Tinned, Sainsbury's*	1 Can/400g	428	107	5.1	12.2	4.2	0.5
Value, Tesco*	1 Pack/300g	489	163	5.7	17.3	7.9	0.7
Waitrose*	1 Pack/350g	466	133	6.8	5.2	9.4	0.0
MACKEREL,							
Arbroath Hot Smoked Scottish, Spink & Sons*	1 Serving/60g	179	298	22.2	0.0	23.2	0.0
Fillets, In Brine, Average	1 Can/88g	206	234	19.4	0.0	17.4	0.0
Fillets, In Curry Sauce, John West*	1oz/28g	65	233	16.0	4.0	17.0	0.3
Fillets, In Green Peppercorn Sauce, John West*	1 Can/125g	329	263	14.0	4.5	21.0	0.1
Fillets, In Mustard Sauce, Average	1 Can/125g	274	219	14.1	5.4	15.5	0.1
Fillets, In Olive Oil, Average	1 Serving/50g	149	298	18.5	1.0	24.4	0.1
Fillets, In Spicy Tomato Sauce, Average	1oz/28g	56	199	14.3	3.9	14.1	0.0
Fillets, In Sunflower Oil, Average	1 Can/94g	262	279	20.2	0.2	21.9	0.2
Fillets, In Tomato Sauce, Average	1 Can/125g	251	200	14.3	2.7	14.7	0.0
Fillets, In White Wine & Spices, Connetable*	1 Can/120g	169	141	15.5	1.2	8.2	0.0
Fillets, Red Pepper & Onion, Smoked, Asda*	1 Serving/90g	319	354	18.0	0.8	31.0	1.2
Fillets, Smoked, Average	1oz/28g	94	335	19.8	0.5	28.2	0.3
Fried in Blended Oil	1oz/28g	76	272	24.0	0.0	19.5	0.0
Raw, Average	1oz/28g	67	238	19.9	0.0	17.6	0.0
Smoked, Lemon & Parsley, Morrisons*	½ Pack/100g	282	282	20.9	4.6	20.0	1.0
Smoked, Peppered, Average	1oz/28g	87	310	20.4	0.3	25.2	0.2
MADRAS,							
Beef, Tesco*	1 Pack/460g	552	120	5.2	13.1	5.2	1.8
Chicken & Pilau Rice, Asda*	1 Pack/400g	588	147	8.0	13.0	7.0	1.7
Chicken, & Rice, Sainsbury's*	1 Pack/461.3g	572	124	5.9	19.6	2.4	0.7
Chicken, Asda*	1 Serving/350g	431	123	7.0	3.6	9.0	2.3
Chicken, Iceland*	1 Pack/400g	376	94	7.7	4.9	4.8	1.1
Chicken, Improved Recipe, Sainsbury's*	1 Pack/400g	468	117	11.7	2.2	6.8	2.8

	Measure INFO/WEIGHT	per Measure KCAL	Nutrition Values per 100g / 100ml				
			KCAL	PROT	CARB	FAT	FIBRE
MADRAS,							
Chicken, Indian, Tesco*	1 Pack/350g	518	148	11.3	5.6	8.9	1.9
Chicken, Safeway*	1 Pack/350g	469	134	13.4	4.0	7.2	1.8
Chicken, Tesco*	1 Pack/350g	326	93	10.6	3.6	4.1	0.6
Chicken, Waitrose*	1oz/28g	47	168	14.6	3.7	10.5	1.8
MAGNUM,							
Almond, Wall's*	1 Bar/86g	190	221	3.4	19.4	14.4	0.0
Caramel & Nuts Bar, Walls*	1 Bar/60g	132	220	4.0	19.0	15.0	0.0
Classico, Wall's	1 Lolly	275	250	3.4	25.0	15.0	0.0
Gluttony, Wall's*	1 Lolly/110ml	425	386	4.5	32.7	26.4	0.0
Greed, Wall's*	1 Bar/110ml	307	279	3.6	29.1	16.4	0.0
Light, Wall's	1 Lolly	170	154	2.9	15.0	9.0	0.0
White, Wall's*	1 Bar/86g	173	201	2.6	19.4	12.6	0.0
MAKHANI,							
Chicken Tikka & Pilau Rice, BGTY, Sainsbury's*	1 Pack/400g	448	112	8.3	17.5	1.0	1.9
Chicken Tikka, BGTY, Sainsbury's*	1 Pack/251.4g	186	74	11.3	3.0	1.9	1.7
Chicken Tikka, Waitrose*	1 Pack/400g	644	161	13.2	4.2	10.1	1.8
Chicken, Sainsbury's*	½ Pack/199.4g	312	157	12.2	2.9	10.7	2.5
MALTESERS,							
Mars*	1 Sm Pack/37g	183	494	10.0	61.4	23.1	0.0
White Chocolate, Mars*	1 Pack/37g	186	504	7.9	61.0	25.4	0.0
MANDARIN ORANGES,							
Average	1 Mandarin/50g	18	37	0.9	8.4	0.1	1.3
In Juice, Average	1oz/28g	11	39	0.7	9.0	0.0	0.5
In Light Syrup, Average	1 Can/298g	201	68	0.6	16.0	0.1	0.1
MANGE TOUT,							
& Sugar Snap Peas, Tesco*	1 Pack/150g	102	68	7.0	9.2	0.4	3.8
Boiled in Salted Water	1oz/28g	7	26	3.2	3.3	0.1	2.2
Raw, Average	1oz/28g	9	33	3.6	4.2	0.2	1.2
Stir-Fried in Blended Oil	1oz/28g	20	71	3.8	3.5	4.8	2.4
MANGO,							
Dried, Average	1 Serving/75g	199	265	1.3	63.2	1.2	5.4
In Syrup, Average	1oz/28g	22	80	0.3	20.5	0.0	0.9
Raw, Average	1oz/28g	15	55	0.7	13.2	0.2	2.5
MARGARINE,							
Average	1oz/28g	203	727	0.1	0.5	81.0	0.0
Butter Style, Average	1 Serving/25g	157	627	0.7	1.1	68.9	0.0
For Baking, Average	1 Serving/8g	49	607	0.2	0.4	67.2	0.0
Olive, Light, GFY, Asda*	1 Thin Spread/4g	14	344	0.1	0.5	38.0	0.0
Olivio*	1 Serving/10g	56	563	0.2	1.0	59.0	0.0
Reduced Fat, Average	1 Serving/10g	36	356	0.6	3.0	38.0	0.0
Soya, Granose*	1oz/28g	209	745	0.1	0.1	82.0	0.0
MARINADE,							
Barbecue, COU, Marks & Spencer*	1 Serving/35g	53	150	1.2	35.5	0.2	1.0
Barbecue, In Minutes, Knorr*	1 Pack/110g	337	306	6.2	66.4	1.3	3.4
Cajun Spice, EPC*	1 Serving/50g	94	187	1.3	15.3	13.4	1.6
Chinese, Classic, Sharwood's*	1oz/28g	32	113	1.8	16.1	4.8	1.0
Hot & Spicy Barbecue, Marks & Spencer*	1 Serving/18g	23	130	1.0	31.1	0.3	0.8
Lime Curry, Ainsley Harriott*	1oz/28g	26	93	1.4	17.7	1.2	0.0
Sweet Chilli & Garlic, Marks & Spencer*	1 Serving/40g	70	175	0.3	43.2	0.1	0.5
Tequila Chilli Lime, Marks & Spencer*	1 Serving/75ml	116	155	0.6	34.0	1.6	0.5
Thai Coconut, Coriander & Lime, Lea & Perrins*	1oz/28g	45	159	1.3	25.7	6.1	0.0
Tomato & Herb, Lea & Perrins*	1oz/28g	28	100	1.2	24.1	0.5	0.0
Tomato, Basil & Parmesan, Marks & Spencer*	1 Serving/50g	38	75	2.1	10.1	2.5	1.5

INFO/WEIGHT	Measure	per Measure KCAL	Nutrition Values per 100g / 100ml				
			KCAL	PROT	CARB	FAT	FIBRE
MARINADE,							
White Wine, Garlic & Pepper, Lea & Perrins*	1oz/28g	28	99	0.1	23.7	0.7	0.0
MARJORAM,							
Dried	1 Tsp/0.6g	3	271	12.7	42.5	7.0	0.0
MARLIN,							
Smoked, H. Forman & Son*	1 Pack/200g	240	120	29.8	0.0	0.1	0.0
Steaks, Chargrilled, Sainsbury's*	1 Serving/240g	367	153	23.6	0.8	6.1	0.6
Steaks, Raw, Sainsbury's*	1 Steak/110g	109	99	24.3	0.0	0.2	0.0
MARMALADE,							
Christmas Orange & Whisky, Marks & Spencer*	1oz/28g	67	240	0.3	59.5	0.2	1.9
Five Fruit, Tesco*	1 Serving/10g	28	278	0.2	68.2	0.1	0.9
Grapefruit & Cranberry, Marks & Spencer*	1 Tsp/15g	36	240	0.3	60.3	0.0	1.5
Lemon & Lime, Average	1 Tsp/20g	53	267	0.2	66.4	0.1	0.4
Lemon Jelly, No Peel, Tesco*	1 Tsp/15g	39	263	0.1	65.0	0.0	0.4
Lemon, With Shred, Average	1 Serving/20g	50	248	0.2	61.6	0.1	0.6
Lime, With Shred, Average	1 Tbsp/15g	39	261	0.2	65.0	0.1	0.4
Orange & Ginger, Average	1 Serving/10g	26	264	0.2	65.7	0.1	0.3
Orange & Lemon, Reduced Sugar, Zest*	1 Tsp/6g	12	195	0.3	47.1	0.2	0.0
Orange, Lemon & Grapefruit, Baxters*	1 Tsp/15g	38	252	0.0	63.0	0.0	0.1
Orange, Reduced Sugar, Average	1 Serving/28g	48	170	0.4	42.0	0.1	0.6
Orange, Shredless, Average	1 Tsp/10g	26	261	0.2	65.0	0.0	0.1
Orange, With Shred, Average	1 Serving/28g	74	263	0.2	65.2	0.0	0.3
Three Fruit, Diabetic, Thursday Cottage*	1 Serving/5g	8	154	0.4	38.0	0.0	1.0
Three Fruits, Fresh Fruit, Sainsbury's*	1 Tsp/15g	38	250	0.0	61.3	0.0	0.0
MARMITE,							
Yeast Extract, Marmite*	1 Tsp/9g	20	219	38.4	19.2	0.1	3.1
MARROW,							
Boiled, Average	1oz/28g	3	9	0.4	1.6	0.2	0.6
Raw	1oz/28g	3	12	0.5	2.2	0.2	0.5
MARS,							
Bar, 5 Little Ones, Mars*	1 Piece/8g	38	477	4.5	73.6	18.3	0.0
Bar, Mars*	1 Std Bar/62.5	281	449	4.2	69.0	17.4	0.0
Delight, Mars*	1 Pack/39.9g	220	551	4.3	54.8	34.9	0.0
MARSHMALLOWS,							
Average	1oz/28g	92	327	3.9	83.1	0.0	0.0
MARZIPAN,							
Bar, Chocolate, Plain, Thorntons*	1 Bar/46g	206	448	5.2	69.1	17.4	2.0
Dark Chocolate, Thorntons*	1 Serving/46g	207	451	5.2	69.4	17.4	2.1
Plain, Average	1oz/28g	115	412	5.9	67.5	14.2	1.7
MASH,							
Cheddar, Irish, Finest, Tesco*	1 Serving/200g	312	156	7.4	9.4	9.9	1.6
Cheddar, Waitrose*	1 Pack/450g	464	103	3.8	13.4	3.8	1.3
MAYONNAISE,							
50% Less Fat, GFY, Asda*	1 Tbsp/10g	32	322	0.8	10.0	31.0	0.0
Aioli, Finest, Tesco*	1 Tsp/5g	20	408	0.8	8.5	41.2	0.0
Average	1 Tsp/11g	80	724	1.9	0.2	79.3	0.0
Dijonnaise, Hellmann's*	1 Tsp/6g	13	210	2.9	5.1	19.7	0.0
Egg, Reduced Fat, Safeway*	½ Pot/85g	136	160	10.2	1.4	12.2	1.6
Egg, Safeway*	1 Serving/50g	121	241	10.4	0.4	22.0	0.1
Extra Light, Hellmann's*	1 Tbsp/15g	16	105	0.5	11.3	6.4	0.2
Finest, Tesco*	1 Dtsp/22g	155	703	1.1	1.5	77.0	0.0
French Style, BGTY, Sainsbury's*	1 Tbsp/15ml	55	366	0.6	7.5	36.9	0.0
French With Course Ground Mustard, Sainsbury's*	1 Serving/15ml	93	618	0.8	1.7	67.3	0.3
French, Sainsbury's*	1 Tsp/6ml	41	678	1.2	2.4	73.6	1.4

	Measure INFO/WEIGHT	per Measure KCAL	Nutrition Values per 100g / 100ml				
			KCAL	PROT	CARB	FAT	FIBRE
MAYONNAISE,							
Garlic & Herb, Marks & Spencer*	1 Tsp/6g	43	712	3.4	2.4	76.9	0.9
Garlic & Herb, Reduced Calorie, Hellmann's*	1 Serving/25ml	58	233	0.7	13.1	19.3	0.4
Garlic, Asda*	1 Serving/20g	136	678	1.3	6.0	72.0	0.0
Garlic, Morrisons*	1 Tbsp/15ml	55	365	0.7	8.8	36.0	0.0
Garlic, Waitrose*	1 Tsp/6g	21	346	0.6	8.6	34.3	0.0
Good Intentions, Somerfield*	1 Serving/30g	93	309	0.5	7.4	30.8	0.0
Half Fat, Healthy Choice, Safeway*	1 Tsp/11g	35	319	0.8	10.8	30.3	0.0
Heinz*	1 Tbsp/10g	30	295	0.7	6.6	29.4	0.0
Hellmann's*	1 Tsp/11g	79	722	1.1	1.3	79.1	0.0
Lemon, Waitrose*	1 Tsp/8ml	56	694	1.2	1.3	76.0	5.4
Light Dijon, Benedicta*	1 Tbsp/15g	44	292	0.7	6.7	29.2	0.0
Light, Morrisons*	1 Tsp/11g	32	287	1.4	8.5	27.5	0.0
Light, BGTY, Sainsbury's*	1 Tsp/11g	33	296	0.5	7.2	29.3	0.0
Light, Hellmann's*	1 Serving/10g	30	299	0.7	6.7	29.8	0.0
Light, Kraft*	1 Serving/25g	61	245	0.6	15.0	20.0	0.0
Light, Reduced Calorie, Hellmann's*	1 Serving/15ml	43	285	0.7	6.6	29.4	0.0
Light, Squeezable, Hellmanns*	1 Tbsp/15g	44	295	0.7	6.6	29.4	0.0
Low Fat, Belolive*	1 Serving/15ml	45	298	0.8	11.1	29.0	0.0
Made With Free Range Eggs, Marks & Spencer*	1 Tbsp/15g	108	720	1.1	1.2	78.5	0.0
Mediterranean, Hellmann's*	1 Tsp/11g	79	722	1.1	1.3	79.1	0.0
Mustard, Safeway*	1 Tbsp/15ml	105	703	1.4	2.1	76.5	0.0
Onion & Chive, BGTY, Sainsbury's*	1 Tbsp/15ml	19	127	2.0	11.8	8.0	0.7
Organic, Evernat*	1 Tsp/11g	83	752	1.3	2.8	81.0	0.0
Organic, Tesco*	1 Tsp/20g	150	749	1.5	2.4	81.5	0.1
Real, Asda*	1 Serving/10g	72	721	1.3	1.2	79.0	0.1
Real, The Big Squeeze, Hellmann's	1 Tbsp/15ml	101	676	1.0	1.2	74.0	0.0
Reduced Calorie	1 Tsp/11g	32	288	1.0	8.2	28.1	0.0
Reduced Calorie, Healthy Selection, Somerfield*	1 Tbsp/15ml	49	326	0.8	9.8	31.5	0.0
Reduced Calorie, Hellmann's*	1 Serving/30g	90	299	0.7	6.7	29.8	0.0
Reduced Calorie, Iceland*	1 Tbsp/15ml	48	320	0.8	9.7	31.2	0.0
Reduced Calorie, Tesco*	1 Tbsp/15g	49	326	0.8	9.8	31.5	0.0
Reduced Calorie, Waitrose*	1 Tsp/11g	32	287	1.4	8.5	27.5	0.0
Reduced Fat, Safeway*	1 Tbsp/15ml	48	323	0.8	9.7	31.2	0.0
Reduced Fat, Tesco*	1 Tbsp/15ml	44	292	0.8	7.9	28.6	0.0
Sainsbury's*	1 Tsp/11g	75	686	0.4	1.2	75.4	0.0
Tesco*	1 Serving/28g	203	725	1.3	1.2	79.4	0.0
Value, Tesco*	1 Tbsp/15g	73	488	0.8	5.4	51.4	0.0
Vegetarian, Tesco*	1 Tsp/12g	89	738	1.5	0.8	81.0	0.0
Waitrose*	1 Tbsp/15ml	106	709	1.3	0.8	77.8	0.0
Weight Watchers*	1 Tbsp/15g	42	280	1.0	7.3	27.7	0.7
MCFLURRY,							
Creme Egg, Cadbury's, McDonald's*	1 McFlurry/203g	390	192	4.1	29.9	6.5	0.0
Crunchie, McDonald's*	1 McFlurry/183g	319	174	4.1	26.4	6.0	0.0
Dairy Milk, McDonalds's*	1 McFlurry/181g	324	178	4.5	24.3	7.2	0.0
Jammie Dodger, McDonald's*	1 Serving/128g	256	200	3.9	33.6	6.4	0.3
Rolo, McDonald's*	1 McFlurry/205g	390	190	4.0	29.2	6.5	0.1
Smarties, McDonald's*	1 McFlurry/185g	327	177	4.2	26.2	6.2	0.2
MCMUFFIN,							
Bacon & Egg, Double, McDonald's*	1 McMuffin/226g	600	265	15.8	16.9	14.9	1.2
Bacon & Egg, McDonald's*	1 McMuffin/141g	345	245	14.2	18.5	12.8	1.3
Egg, McDonald's*	1 McMuffin/127g	281	221	12.2	20.4	10.1	3.2
Sausage & Egg, Double, McDonald's*	1 McMuffin/227g	572	253	14.7	11.4	16.4	0.8
Sausage & Egg, McDonald's*	1 McMuffin/176g	426	242	13.8	14.7	14.1	1.0

INFO/WEIGHT	Measure per Measure KCAL	Nutrition Values per 100g / 100ml KCAL	PROT	CARB	FAT	FIBRE
MCMUFFIN,						
Scrambled Egg, McDonald's*	1 McMuffin/147g 294	200	10.9	17.5	9.6	1.3
MEAL REPLACEMENT,						
Ny-Tro Pro-40, Cool Vanilla, AST Sports Science*	1 Sachet/72g 250	347	55.6	30.6	2.1	2.8
Ny-Tro Pro-40, Creamy Strawberry, AST Sports Science*	1 Sachet/72g 250	347	55.6	30.6	2.1	2.8
Ny-Tro Pro-40, Chocolate, AST Sports Science*	1 Sachet/72g 250	347	55.6	30.6	2.1	2.8
MEAT LOAF,						
Beef & Pork, Co-Op*	¼ Loaf/114g 314	275	13.0	7.0	22.0	1.0
Iceland*	1 Serving/150g 332	221	10.8	9.3	15.7	0.9
Somerfield*	1 Pack/454g 867	191	10.0	8.0	13.0	0.0
Turkey & Bacon, Tesco*	1 Serving/225g 401	178	14.7	7.4	9.9	1.1
MEATBALLS,						
Aberdeen Angus In Sauce, Perfectly Balanced, Waitrose*	½ Pack/240g 228	95	10.5	6.5	3.0	1.1
Aberdeen Angus, Waitrose*	3 Meatballs/107g 223	208	20.0	1.0	13.8	0.0
Al Forno, Safeway*	1 Pack/450g 684	152	6.0	16.8	6.8	0.4
Beef, Asda*	1 Serving/287g 362	126	11.0	7.0	6.0	0.6
Chicken, In Tomato Sauce, Average	1 Can/392g 580	148	7.7	10.4	8.4	0.0
Galician Style, Cafe Culture, Marks & Spencer*	½ Pack/500g 675	135	5.9	13.2	6.7	1.1
Greek, Marks & Spencer*	1 Serving/350g 403	115	7.7	9.1	5.4	1.5
In Bolognese Sauce, Somerfield*	1 Pack/454g 704	155	7.0	7.0	11.0	0.0
In Gravy, Campbell's*	½ Can/205g 164	80	5.6	8.6	2.6	0.0
In Tomato Sauce, Canned, Average	1 Can/410g 387	95	5.6	9.9	3.7	0.0
Italian Pork, Al Forno, Sainsbury's*	1 Pack/450g 644	143	6.1	17.6	5.3	1.4
Lion's Head, Marks & Spencer*	1 Serving/300g 435	145	10.4	5.1	9.3	1.0
Manhattan Style & Spaghetti, Spicy, Safeway*	1 Pack/450g 540	120	5.7	13.2	4.8	2.0
Marks & Spencer*	1oz/28g 58	208	10.9	10.7	13.5	2.4
Mighty, In Tomato Sauce, Westlers*	1 Tin/400g 424	106	5.8	10.2	4.8	0.0
Roman-Style Sith Basil Mash, COU, Marks & Spencer*	1 Pack/430g 344	80	3.7	10.9	2.2	1.9
Spaghetti, Tesco*	1 Pack/385g 377	98	5.4	9.8	4.2	1.2
Spicy, Benjys*	1 Pack/118g 274	232	15.0	13.1	9.1	0.0
Spicy, Marks & Spencer*	1 Pack/400g 540	135	8.8	12.0	6.0	1.4
Swedish, Average	¼ Pack/88g 198	225	14.0	7.4	15.7	1.3
Turkey, GFY, Asda*	½ Pack/330g 333	101	10.0	7.0	3.7	0.0
MEDAGLIONI,						
Cheese & Red Bell Pepper, Eat Smart, Safeway*	1 Serving/125g 175	140	6.3	21.1	2.9	1.0
Roasted Vegetable & Cheese, Safeway*	½ Pack/125g 297	238	9.3	34.2	7.0	2.7
MELBA TOAST,						
Asda*	1 Toast/5g 20	396	12.0	79.0	3.6	2.8
Buitoni*	1 Serving/33g 130	395	12.1	75.5	4.9	4.6
Dutch, Tesco*	1 Serving/20g 75	377	16.0	73.0	2.3	5.0
Dutch, Wheat Bread, Tesco*	1 Pack/20g 80	399	12.8	80.5	2.9	3.9
Organic, Trimlyne*	1 Pack/28g 109	390	13.0	78.0	2.9	5.5
Original, Van Der Meulen*	1 Slice/3g 12	399	12.8	80.5	2.9	3.9
Safeway*	1 Serving/3g 11	362	12.0	72.0	2.9	3.9
Sainsbury's*	1 Toast/3g 13	399	12.8	80.5	2.9	3.9
With Sesame, Tesco*	1 Slice/3g 11	370	12.8	61.7	8.0	3.8
MELON,						
Galia, Average	1 Serving/240g 60	25	0.8	5.8	0.1	0.2
Honeydew, Raw, Average	1oz/28g 8	30	0.7	6.9	0.1	0.5
Medley, Average	1 Pack/240g 66	27	0.6	6.0	0.1	0.5
MELON SEEDS,						
Average	1oz/28g 163	583	28.5	9.9	47.7	0.0
MELT,						
Cheese, Chilli, Fresh, Asda*	1 Melt/29g 87	301	6.0	31.0	17.0	0.0

	Measure INFO/WEIGHT	per Measure KCAL	Nutrition Values per 100g / 100ml				
			KCAL	PROT	CARB	FAT	FIBRE
MELT,							
Cheesy Fish, Youngs*	1 Pack/340g	418	123	7.6	8.3	6.6	0.9
Chicken, Salsa, Sainsbury's*	1 Pack/400g	516	129	7.2	10.7	6.4	1.6
Chilli With Spicy Potato Wedges, Asda*	1 Pack/450g	540	120	8.0	12.0	4.4	1.2
Mushroom & Broccoli Potato Wedge, Weight Watchers*	1 Pack/310g	285	92	3.3	12.6	3.1	1.0
Salmon & Broccoli Wedge, Weight Watchers*	1 Pack/320g	301	94	5.1	10.2	3.6	0.8
Sausage & Bean, Iceland*	1 Pack/400g	588	147	6.5	17.1	5.8	1.6
Tuna, Go Large, Asda*	1 Roll/175g	509	291	12.0	27.0	15.0	0.0
Tuna, Iceland*	1 Pack/400g	424	106	6.0	11.3	4.2	0.7
Tuna, Marks & Spencer*	1 Pack/218g	621	285	13.0	20.1	17.0	1.0
Vegetable & Potato, Asda*	1 Serving/100g	451	451	17.0	44.0	23.0	6.2
MERINGUE,							
Average	1oz/28g	106	379	5.3	95.4	0.0	0.0
Bombe, Raspberry & Vanilla, Marks & Spencer*	1 Bombe/100g	155	155	3.4	33.3	1.8	2.6
Chocolate, Waitrose*	1 Meringue/76.8g	342	444	2.6	75.3	14.7	0.5
Coffee Fresh Cream, Asda*	1 Meringue/27.5g	111	396	3.8	57.0	17.0	0.3
Cream, Marks & Spencer*	1 Cake/34.1g	145	425	4.1	52.6	22.2	0.3
Cream, Sainsbury's*	1 Meringue/25g	98	392	3.9	59.0	15.7	0.8
Layered, Tesco*	1/5 Meringue/52g	146	280	3.5	63.2	1.5	1.4
Marks & Spencer*	1 Meringue/12g	47	389	5.2	92.0	0.0	0.0
Mini, Marks & Spencer*	1oz/28g	111	395	6.1	91.6	0.0	0.0
Nests, Asda*	1 Nest/15g	59	390	3.7	93.0	0.3	0.0
Nests, Marks & Spencer*	1 Nest/12g	47	395	6.1	91.6	0.0	0.0
Nests, Safeway*	1 Nest/13.9g	55	395	4.2	93.6	0.1	0.0
Nests, Sainsbury's*	1 Nest/15g	58	387	3.9	92.8	0.0	0.0
Nests, Tesco*	1 Nest/13g	51	387	3.9	92.8	0.1	0.0
Nests, Tropical Fruit, Sainsbury's*	1 Nest/95g	234	246	2.0	42.0	7.8	2.4
Raspberry, Marks & Spencer*	1 Serving/105g	215	205	1.8	20.6	13.1	3.1
Shells, Mini, Asda*	1 Shell/4g	16	388	4.8	92.0	0.1	0.0
Shells, Sainsbury's*	2 Shells/24g	93	387	3.9	92.8	0.0	0.0
Strawberry, COU, Marks & Spencer*	1 Meringue/5.2g	19	385	6.4	90.0	0.1	1.4
Summer Fruits, 90% Fat Free, Sara Lee*	1 Meringue/135g	308	228	2.5	35.7	8.5	2.2
Toffee, COU, Marks & Spencer*	1 Mini Meringue/5.1g	20	395	5.0	95.3	1.7	0.7
Toffee, Marks & Spencer*	1 Meringue/30g	125	415	4.1	52.2	20.9	0.8
Tropical, Marks & Spencer*	1 Serving/53g	212	400	3.1	37.0	26.9	0.0
MIDGET GEMS,							
Marks & Spencer*	1 Bag/113g	367	325	6.3	75.1	0.1	0.0
SmartPrice, Asda*	1 Pack/178g	586	329	6.0	76.0	0.1	0.0
MILK,							
Condensed, Semi Skimmed, Sweetened	1oz/28g	75	267	10.0	60.0	0.2	0.0
Condensed, Skimmed, Unsweetened, Average	1 Sm Can/205g	221	108	7.5	10.5	4.0	0.0
Condensed, Whole, Sweetened	1oz/28g	93	333	8.5	55.5	10.1	0.0
Dried Whole	1oz/28g	137	490	26.3	39.4	26.3	0.0
Dried, Skimmed, Average	1oz/28g	99	355	35.4	52.3	0.9	0.0
Evaporated, Average	1 Serving/85g	136	160	8.2	11.6	9.0	0.0
Evaporated, Reduced Fat, Average	1oz/28g	33	118	7.4	10.5	5.2	0.0
Goats, Pasteurised	1fl oz/30ml	18	60	3.1	4.4	3.5	0.0
Goats, Semi-Skimmed, St Helens Farm*	1 Serving/250ml	109	44	3.0	4.3	1.6	0.0
Low Fat, Calcia Extra Calcium, Unigate*	1fl oz/30ml	14	45	4.3	6.3	0.5	0.0
Rice Dream, Imagine Foods Ltd*	1 Serving/250ml	118	47	0.1	9.4	1.0	0.1
Semi Skimmed, Average	1fl oz/30ml	15	49	3.4	5.0	1.7	0.0
Semi Skimmed, Long Life, Average	1fl oz/30ml	15	49	3.4	5.0	1.7	0.0
Semi Skimmed, Low Lactose, Arla*	1 Glass/125ml	56	45	3.4	5.0	1.5	0.0
Skimmed, Average	1fl oz/28ml	10	34	3.3	5.0	0.1	0.0

INFO/WEIGHT	Measure per Measure KCAL		Nutrition Values per 100g / 100ml				
			KCAL	PROT	CARB	FAT	FIBRE
MILK,							
Skimmed, Powdered, Organic, Evernat*	1oz/28g	96	344	34.0	52.0	0.0	0.0
Skimmed, UHT, Average	1fl oz/30ml	10	34	3.4	5.0	0.1	0.0
Soya, Chocolate, So Good*	1 Serving/100ml	71	71	3.0	10.8	1.7	0.0
Soya, Flavoured	1floz/30mls	12	40	2.8	3.6	1.7	0.0
Soya, No Added Sugar, Unsweetened, Average	1 Serving/250ml	85	34	3.3	0.9	1.9	0.4
Soya, Sweetened, Average	1 Glass/200ml	94	47	3.4	3.7	2.1	0.4
Soya, Sweetened, Calcium Enriched, Average	1floz/30ml	14	46	3.4	3.7	2.0	0.3
Soya, Vanilla, Organic, Heinz*	1 Serving/200ml	106	53	2.6	6.9	1.6	0.2
UHT Portions, Kerrygold*	1 Portion/14g	9	66	3.2	4.8	3.9	0.0
Whole, Average	1 Serving/200ml	134	67	3.3	4.7	3.9	0.0
MILK DRINK,							
Banana Flavour, Sterilised, Low Fat, Gulp*	1 Bottle/500ml	315	63	3.8	9.7	1.0	0.0
Choc O Latte, Cafe Met*	1 Bottle/290ml	203	70	3.5	10.0	1.5	0.0
Chocolate Sterilised Skimmed, Happy Shopper*	1 Bottle/500ml	295	59	3.6	10.4	0.3	0.0
Chocolate, Spar*	1 Serving/500ml	290	58	3.6	10.2	0.3	0.0
Mars Extra Milk Chocolate Caramel, Mars*	1 Bottle/330g	224	68	3.5	12.1	0.3	0.0
Strawberry, Yazoo, Campina*	1 Bottle/500ml	325	65	3.1	10.3	1.3	0.0
MILK SHAKE,							
Banana Flavour, Frijj*	1 Bottle/500ml	310	62	3.4	10.1	0.8	0.0
Banana Flavour, Mix, Nesquik*	1 Serving/15g	59	395	0.0	97.3	0.5	0.0
Banana Flavour, Shapers, Boots*	1 Bottle/250ml	201	80	5.6	12.8	0.8	1.9
Banana Flavour, Spar*	1 Bottle/500ml	250	50	3.3	9.1	0.1	0.0
Banana, McDonald's*	1 Regular/336g	396	118	3.2	20.2	3.0	0.0
Banana, Yazoo*	1 Bottle/500ml	325	65	3.1	10.3	1.3	0.0
Chocolate Flavour, BGTY, Sainsbury's*	1 Bottle/500ml	290	58	5.3	8.0	0.5	0.9
Chocolate Flavoured, Fresh, Thick, Frijj*	1 Bottle/500ml	350	70	3.5	11.7	1.0	0.0
Chocolate, Burger King*	1 Serving/336ml	291	87	1.5	12.2	3.9	0.0
Chocolate, Extreme, Frijj*	1 Bottle/500g	425	85	3.9	12.7	2.1	0.0
Chocolate, McDonald's*	1 Regular/336g	403	120	3.4	19.9	3.0	0.0
Measure Up, Asda*	1 Glass/250ml	200	80	6.0	12.0	1.0	2.4
Mount Caramel, Frijj*	1 Bottle/500ml	360	72	3.4	12.7	0.9	0.0
Powder, Made Up With Semi-Skimmed Milk	1 Serving/250ml	173	69	3.2	11.3	1.6	0.0
Powder, Made Up With Whole Milk	1 Serving/250ml	218	87	3.1	11.1	3.7	0.0
Strawberry Flavour, Thick, Low Fat, Frijj*	1 Bottle/250ml	155	62	3.4	10.1	0.8	0.0
Strawberry, Fresh, Nesquik*	1 Glass/250ml	175	70	3.3	10.4	1.6	0.3
Strawberry, McDonald's*	1 Regular/336g	396	118	3.2	20.0	3.0	0.0
Strawberry, Thick, Somerfield*	1 Shake/250ml	275	110	4.0	15.0	4.0	0.0
Syrup, Crusha*	1 Serving/30ml	37	124	0.0	31.0	0.0	0.0
Syrup, Strawberry, Crusha*	1 Serving/20ml	25	125	0.5	30.0	0.5	0.0
Vanilla Flavour, BGTY, Sainsbury's*	1 Bottle/500ml	230	46	5.3	5.9	0.1	0.4
Vanilla, Frijj*	1 Bottle/500ml	320	64	3.4	10.7	0.8	0.0
Vanilla, McDonald's*	1 Regular/336g	383	114	3.2	18.8	3.0	0.0
MILKY BAR,							
Buttons, Nestle*	1 Mini Bag/16g	87	542	7.6	57.5	31.3	0.0
Choo, Nestle*	1oz/28g	131	468	4.1	73.2	17.6	0.0
Crunchies, Nestle*	1 Pack/30g	168	560	7.0	54.9	34.7	0.0
Nestle*	1 Bar/12g	65	542	7.6	57.5	31.3	0.0
MILKY WAY,							
Magic Stars, Mars*	1 Bag/33g	184	557	8.8	51.8	35.0	0.0
Mars*	1 Single Bar/26g	117	449	3.5	71.4	16.7	0.0
MILO,							
Nestle*	1 Serving/20g	76	380	8.2	72.9	6.0	4.7

	Measure INFO/WEIGHT	per Measure KCAL	Nutrition Values per 100g / 100ml				
			KCAL	PROT	CARB	FAT	FIBRE
MINCEMEAT,							
Average	1oz/28g	77	274	0.6	62.1	4.3	1.3
MINSTRELS,							
Galaxy, Mars*	1 Pack/42g	206	491	6.0	69.5	21.0	0.0
MINT,							
Dried	1oz/28g	78	279	24.8	34.6	4.6	0.0
Fresh	1oz/28g	12	43	3.8	5.3	0.7	0.0
Jelly, Baxters*	1oz/28g	74	264	0.0	66.0	0.0	0.0
Jelly, Safeway*	1 Serving/10g	17	174	0.3	41.6	0.0	0.0
Jelly, Sainsbury's*	1 Serving/10g	27	269	0.1	66.6	0.2	0.3
MINTS,							
After Dinner, Dark, Elizabeth Shaw*	1 Chocolate/9g	42	469	2.8	62.5	23.1	0.0
After Dinner, Sainsbury's*	1 Mint/7g	32	456	4.1	62.1	21.2	4.1
After Dinner, Tesco*	1oz/28g	132	471	5.0	70.0	19.0	0.0
After Eight, Nestle*	1 Mint/8g	34	419	2.5	72.9	12.8	1.1
After Eight, Orange, Nestle*	1 Sweet/7g	29	417	2.5	72.6	12.9	1.1
Butter Mintoes, Marks & Spencer*	1 Sweet/9g	35	391	0.0	84.0	6.8	0.0
Clear, Co-Op*	1 Sweet/6g	24	395	0.0	98.0	0.0	0.0
Cool Mint, Smint*	1 Smint/0.2g	0	55	0.6	7.8	1.0	0.0
Cream, Luxury, Thorntons*	1 Chocolate/13g	62	477	4.2	62.3	23.8	2.3
Curiously Strong, Marks & Spencer*	1 Sweet/1g	4	390	0.4	97.5	0.0	0.0
Everton, Co-Op*	1 Sweet/6g	25	410	0.6	92.0	4.0	0.0
Extra Strong, Trebor*	3 Mints/10g	40	396	0.3	98.8	0.0	0.0
Glacier, Fox's*	1 Mint/5g	19	386	0.0	96.4	0.0	0.0
Humbugs, Asda*	1 Sweet/8g	29	362	0.0	86.0	2.0	0.0
Humbugs, Co-Op*	1 Sweet/8g	34	425	0.6	89.9	7.0	0.0
Humbugs, Marks & Spencer*	1 Sweet/9g	37	407	0.6	91.1	4.4	0.0
Humbugs, Thorntons*	1 Sweet/9g	31	340	1.0	87.8	4.4	0.0
Imperials, Co-Op*	1 Sweet/3g	12	395	0.3	98.0	0.2	0.0
Imperials, Marks & Spencer*	1oz/28g	109	391	0.0	97.8	0.0	0.0
Imperials, Sainsbury's*	1 Mint/3g	12	396	0.4	97.9	0.2	0.0
Imperials, Tesco*	1 Mint/3g	12	397	0.6	98.7	0.0	0.0
Mighty, 24-7, Sugar Free, Trebor*	1 Sweet/0.1g	0	277	0.0	94.7	0.0	0.0
Mint Assortment, Marks & Spencer*	1 Sweet/7g	29	414	0.7	85.4	7.7	0.0
Mint Favourites, Bassett's*	1 Sweet/6g	22	367	0.9	77.4	5.9	0.0
Peppermints, Strong, Altoids*	1 Mint/0.8g	4	385	0.5	96.0	0.0	0.0
Soft, Trebor*	1 Pack/48g	182	380	0.0	94.9	0.0	0.0
Softmints, Trebor*	1 Tube/40g	156	391	0.0	93.3	2.0	0.0
MISO,							
Average	1oz/28g	57	203	13.3	23.5	6.2	0.0
MIX,							
Chinese Curry, Youngs*	1 Serving/22g	109	495	8.3	46.4	30.7	0.0
Drink, 100% Egg White Powder, Tropicana*	2 Tbsp/20g	66	328	82.0	0.0	0.0	0.0
For Fish, Smoked Haddock, Schwartz*	1 Pack/35g	154	440	13.8	46.9	21.9	0.0
For Pork, Somerset, Schwartz*	1 Serving/36g	120	334	8.4	71.6	1.6	0.2
Garlic & Herb, Crust for Cod, Schwartz*	1 Serving/10g	36	359	11.5	72.5	2.6	0.0
Pastry, Short Crust, Somerfield*	1oz/28g	134	479	7.0	49.0	28.0	0.0
Scone, Fruit, Asda	1 Scone/47.5g	144	301	7.0	57.0	5.0	3.7
Trifle, Strawberry Flavour, Bird's*	1oz/28g	119	425	2.7	78.0	10.5	1.2
MIXED VEGETABLES,							
Bag, Marks & Spencer*	1 Serving/200g	70	35	2.9	5.6	0.2	0.0
Broccoli & Cauliflower Florets, Baby Carrots, Asda*	1 Serving/113g	28	25	2.2	2.6	0.6	2.4
Canned, Drained, Co-Op*	½ Can/100g	45	45	2.0	9.0	0.1	2.0
Canned, Drained, Sainsbury's*	1 Can/200g	114	57	3.0	10.6	0.3	2.3

M

INFO/WEIGHT	Measure	per Measure KCAL	KCAL	PROT	CARB	FAT	FIBRE
MIXED VEGETABLES,							
Canned, Re-Heated, Drained	1oz/28g	11	38	1.9	6.1	0.8	1.7
Canned, Tesco*	1 Can/195g	103	53	2.6	9.2	0.6	27.0
Chunky, Frozen, Sainsbury's*	1 Serving/85g	31	37	2.9	4.7	0.7	3.1
Farmhouse, Frozen, Four Seasons, Aldi*	1oz/28g	10	34	2.8	4.3	0.7	0.0
Farmhouse, Tesco*	1 Serving/80g	32	40	3.6	4.6	0.8	3.0
Fresh, Asda*	1oz/28g	7	26	1.9	3.0	0.7	1.0
Fresh, Frozen, Tesco*	1 Serving/75g	36	48	3.0	7.2	0.8	3.2
Frozen, Boiled in Salted Water	1oz/28g	12	42	3.3	6.6	0.5	0.0
Frozen, Safeway*	1 Serving/120g	70	58	3.0	9.4	0.9	3.4
Frozen, Sainsbury's*	1 Serving/90g	49	54	2.8	8.4	1.0	3.1
Green, Microwave, Aldi*	1 Serving/300g	189	63	3.5	5.6	3.0	4.1
In Salt Water, Tesco*	1/3 Can/65g	34	53	2.6	9.2	0.6	2.7
In Salted Water, Canned, Asda*	1 Serving/65g	31	48	2.6	9.0	0.2	1.7
In Water, Straight to Wok, Amoy*	½ Pack/110g	27	25	1.8	3.7	0.3	0.0
Micro, Tesco*	1 Packet/100g	48	48	3.0	7.2	0.8	3.2
Organic, Waitrose*	1oz/28g	19	69	4.4	10.0	1.3	2.7
Oriental, Marks & Spencer*	1 Serving/250g	50	20	1.6	3.4	0.3	1.6
Ready To Roast, Asda*	½ Pack/362g	315	87	1.6	13.0	3.2	2.4
Red Peppers & Courgette, Tesco*	1 Pack/250g	68	27	1.7	3.8	0.5	2.0
Roast, Four Seasons, Aldi*	1 Serving/187g	79	42	1.2	8.8	0.2	0.0
Sainsbury's*	1 Serving/230g	55	24	2.1	2.5	0.6	0.0
Spar*	1oz/28g	16	58	2.3	11.5	0.3	3.3
Special, Frozen, Sainsbury's*	1 Serving/80g	54	68	3.4	9.7	1.7	3.2
Special, Tesco*	1 Serving/125g	61	49	3.3	7.2	0.8	3.3
Straight to Wok, Water Selection, Amoy*	½ Pack/110g	25	23	1.8	3.7	0.3	1.5
Supreme, Frozen, Somerfield*	1 Serving/90g	23	25	1.9	4.3	0.0	3.1
Tesco*	1oz/28g	8	27	1.7	3.8	0.5	2.0
MOLASSES,							
Average	1 Tbsp/20g	53	266	0.0	68.8	0.1	0.0
MONKEY NUTS,							
Average	1oz/28g	158	565	25.6	8.2	48.0	6.3
MONKFISH,							
Grilled	1oz/28g	27	96	22.7	0.0	0.6	0.0
Raw	1oz/28g	18	66	15.7	0.0	0.4	0.0
Tails, Asda*	1oz/28g	27	96	22.7	0.0	0.6	0.0
MONSTER MUNCH,							
Baked Bean Flavour, Walkers*	1 Pack/25g	120	480	5.5	58.0	25.0	1.4
Flamin' Hot, Walkers*	1 Bag/25g	123	490	7.0	60.0	25.0	1.5
Pickled Onion, Walkers*	1 Bag/25g	124	495	6.0	62.0	25.0	1.6
Roast Beef, Walkers*	1 Pack/25g	119	475	6.6	58.0	24.0	1.5
Spicy, Walkers*	1 Bag/25g	125	500	5.0	55.0	29.0	1.3
MOUSSAKA,							
Beef, BGTY, Sainsbury's*	1 Pack/400g	300	75	6.1	6.8	2.6	1.2
Beef, GFY, Asda*	1 Pack/400g	300	75	7.0	7.0	2.1	0.7
COU, Marks & Spencer*	1 Pack/340g	272	80	5.3	8.5	2.9	1.4
Cafe Culture, Marks & Spencer*	1 Serving/375g	619	165	9.2	7.8	10.5	0.8
Eat Smart, Safeway*	1 Pack/400g	380	95	5.2	12.6	2.6	1.2
Lamb, Eat Smart, Safeway*	1 Pack/380g	304	80	6.8	6.4	2.7	1.3
Lamb, Finest, Tesco*	1 Pack/330g	521	158	7.7	9.1	10.1	2.0
Lamb, Sainsbury's*	1 Pack/329.1g	497	151	8.4	7.2	9.8	1.0
Perfectly Balanced, Waitrose*	1 Pack/300g	255	85	6.6	7.6	3.1	1.0
Ready Meals, Waitrose*	1 Pack/300g	492	164	8.2	10.9	9.7	1.7
Vegetable, Marks & Spencer*	1 Pack/300g	330	110	4.4	11.8	5.2	1.1

	Measure INFO/WEIGHT	per Measure KCAL	Nutrition Values per 100g / 100ml				
			KCAL	PROT	CARB	FAT	FIBRE
MOUSSAKA,							
Vegetable, Ready Meals, Waitrose*	1oz/28g	38	134	3.7	12.3	7.8	2.3
Vegetable, Roasted, Safeway*	1 Pack/365g	365	100	3.7	7.9	5.7	2.9
MOUSSE,							
Aero Chocolate, Nestle*	1 Pot/59g	109	185	5.1	21.0	8.9	0.5
Aero Mint, Nestle*	1 Pot/100g	218	218	4.1	23.6	11.9	0.0
Aero Twist Cappuccino & Chocolate, Nestle*	1 Pot/75g	135	180	4.2	16.8	10.8	0.2
Apricot, Lite, Onken*	1 Pot/150g	156	104	4.6	18.0	1.5	0.3
Banoffee, COU, Marks & Spencer*	1 Pot/70g	102	145	2.9	28.8	2.1	1.5
Black Cherry, Lite, Onken*	1 Pot/150g	156	104	4.6	17.9	1.5	0.3
Blackcurrant, Onken*	1 Pot/150g	210	140	5.2	14.6	6.8	0.0
Cadbury's Flake, Twinpot, St Ivel*	1 Pot/100g	257	257	5.6	27.4	13.9	0.0
Cadbury's Light Chocolate, St Ivel*	1 Pot/64g	79	123	6.2	17.3	3.2	0.0
Caramel, Meringue, Mousse, Cadbury's*	1 Serving/65g	181	277	4.6	42.4	10.3	1.0
Caramelised Orange, COU, Marks & Spencer*	1 Pot/70g	91	130	2.8	26.3	1.7	3.4
Chocolate	1 Pot/60g	83	139	4.0	19.9	5.4	0.0
Chocolate & Hazelnut Puree, Onken*	½ Pot/185g	222	120	3.4	19.5	3.1	0.0
Chocolate & Hazelnut, Onken*	1 Pot/125g	173	138	3.3	17.8	6.0	0.0
Chocolate & Mint, COU, Marks & Spencer*	1 Pot/70g	84	120	6.2	18.7	2.5	1.0
Chocolate & Orange, COU, Marks & Spencer*	1 Pot/70g	77	110	5.9	16.0	2.6	0.9
Chocolate & Vanilla, Weight Watchers*	1 Pot/80g	106	132	4.4	22.2	2.8	0.9
Chocolate Orange, Low Fat, Cadbury's*	1 Pot/100g	110	110	5.6	15.1	3.0	0.0
Chocolate With Vanilla Layer, Cadbury's*	1 Pot/100g	162	162	4.8	21.9	6.1	0.0
Chocolate, Asda*	1 Pot/61g	134	219	3.7	26.0	10.0	1.0
Chocolate, BGTY, Sainsbury's*	1 Pot/62.5g	78	126	4.0	21.5	2.7	1.1
Chocolate, COU, Marks & Spencer*	1 Pot/70g	81	115	5.8	16.6	2.7	1.0
Chocolate, Eat Smart, Safeway*	1 Pot/62g	81	130	4.1	21.5	2.7	1.1
Chocolate, GFY, Asda*	1 Pot/62.5g	85	136	3.8	24.0	2.7	0.0
Chocolate, Good Choice, Iceland*	1 Pot/62.0g	85	137	5.4	22.7	2.7	0.0
Chocolate, Healthy Living, Tesco*	1 Pot/60g	80	134	4.4	23.2	2.6	1.0
Chocolate, Healthy Selection, Low Fat, Somerfield*	1 Pot/60g	81	135	5.3	18.2	4.6	0.0
Chocolate, Iceland*	1 Pot/62g	113	183	4.0	26.3	6.9	0.0
Chocolate, Italian Style, Tesco*	1 Pot/90g	243	270	5.0	32.8	13.2	2.4
Chocolate, Less Than 3% Fat, BGTY, Sainsbury's*	1 Pot/63g	85	136	3.8	24.0	2.7	1.1
Chocolate, Light, Cadbury's*	1 Pot/55g	69	125	6.2	17.5	3.2	0.0
Chocolate, Organic, Evernat*	1oz/28g	83	296	10.1	21.1	19.1	0.0
Chocolate, Pret A Manger*	1 Pot/110g	314	285	2.7	16.9	22.9	1.3
Chocolate, Safeway*	1 Pot/62g	127	205	4.0	25.3	9.8	1.1
Chocolate, Sainsbury's*	1 Pot/62g	122	197	4.0	25.4	8.8	1.1
Chocolate, Shapers, Boots*	1 Pot/70g	97	138	5.3	23.0	2.7	1.7
Chocolate, Somerfield*	1 Pot/60g	115	192	4.3	24.5	8.5	0.0
Chocolate, Tesco*	1 Pot/60g	74	124	4.4	20.8	2.6	1.0
Chocolate, Value, Tesco*	1 Pot/62.5g	96	152	5.5	20.9	5.2	2.7
Creamy Strawberry, Shapers Boots*	1 Pot/90g	59	66	3.9	6.4	2.8	0.3
Dream, Cadbury's*	1 Pot/53g	100	189	6.0	22.0	8.0	0.0
Fruit Juice, Shape*	1 Pot/100g	115	115	3.5	18.5	2.8	0.0
Layered Lemon, Co-Op*	1 Pot/100g	140	140	3.0	24.0	3.0	0.2
Layered Strawberry, Co-Op*	1 Pot/100g	120	120	3.0	19.0	3.0	0.2
Lemon Fruit Juice, Shape*	1 Pot/100g	116	116	3.5	18.6	2.8	0.0
Lemon, COU, Marks & Spencer*	1 Pot/70g	81	115	2.9	19.4	2.4	3.5
Lemon, Dessert, Sainsbury's*	1 Pot/62.5g	114	182	3.6	20.7	9.4	0.6
Lemon, Eat Smart, Safeway*	1 Pot/70g	95	135	3.4	23.5	2.7	0.4
Lemon, GFY, Asda*	1 Pot/62.5g	72	114	3.4	19.0	2.7	0.0
Lemon, Healthy Eating, Tesco*	1 Pot/60g	57	95	3.4	14.3	2.7	0.7

M

MOUSSE,

INFO/WEIGHT	Measure	per Measure KCAL	KCAL	PROT	CARB	FAT	FIBRE
Lemon, Less Than 3% Fat, BGTY, Sainsbury's*	1 Pot/62g	59	95	3.4	14.3	2.7	0.7
Lemon, Less Than 3% Fat, Healthy Eating, Tesco*	1 Pot/60g	57	95	3.4	14.3	2.7	0.0
Lemon, Lite, Onken*	1 Pot/150g	156	104	4.6	18.0	1.6	0.0
Lemon, Low Fat, Morrisons*	1 Pot/110g	175	159	3.1	30.5	2.7	0.1
Lemon, Onken*	1 Pot/150g	219	146	5.1	15.8	6.9	0.1
Lemon, Perfectly Balanced, Waitrose*	1 Pot/95g	150	158	3.1	30.2	2.7	0.1
Lemon, Somerfield*	1 Pot/62.5g	114	181	3.5	20.7	9.4	0.6
Lemon, Tesco*	1 Pot/60g	67	111	3.4	18.2	2.7	0.0
Mars, Eden Vale*	1 Pot/110g	215	195	6.0	28.2	6.7	0.7
Milky Way, Mars*	1 Pot/50g	115	229	4.5	20.0	14.5	0.0
Orange & Lemon, Light, Muller*	1 Pot/150g	147	98	4.3	19.3	0.4	0.0
Orange & Nectarine, Shape*	1 Pot/100g	47	47	3.0	4.9	1.9	0.0
Orange Fruit Juice, Shape*	1 Pot/100g	116	116	3.5	18.5	2.8	0.0
Orange, Mango & Lime, Onken*	1 Pot/150g	207	138	5.1	15.3	6.3	0.1
Peach & Passion Fruit, Perfectly Balanced, Waitrose*	1 Pot/95g	118	124	3.5	21.2	2.8	0.5
Peach, Onken*	1 Pot/150g	200	133	4.8	13.5	6.6	0.0
Peach, Shape*	1 Pot/100g	43	43	3.0	3.9	1.8	0.1
Pineapple, COU, Marks & Spencer*	1 Pot/70g	84	120	3.3	20.7	2.4	3.5
Pineapple, Lite, Onken*	1 Pot/150g	162	108	4.6	19.0	1.5	0.2
Pineapple, Shape*	1 Pot/100g	43	43	2.9	3.8	1.8	0.1
Plain Chocolate, Low Fat, Nestle*	1 Pot/120g	71	59	2.4	10.4	0.8	0.0
Raspberry Ripple, Economy, Sainsbury's*	1 Serving/50g	39	78	1.3	9.7	3.7	0.3
Raspberry, COU, Marks & Spencer*	1 Pot/70g	81	115	3.0	19.6	2.4	3.9
Raspberry, Lite, Onken*	1 Pot/150g	152	101	4.6	17.3	1.5	1.0
Rhubarb & Vanilla, Onken*	1 Pot/150g	210	140	5.0	15.8	6.3	0.2
Rhubarb, COU, Marks & Spencer*	1 Pot/70g	88	125	2.9	25.7	2.1	4.2
Rhubarb, Lite, Onken*	1 Pot/150g	155	103	4.6	17.8	1.5	0.3
Strawberry Fruity, Organic, Sainsbury's*	1 Pot/125g	129	103	6.2	15.7	3.0	3.6
Strawberry, Asda*	1 Pot/64g	107	167	3.5	18.0	9.0	0.2
Strawberry, BGTY, Sainsbury's*	1 Pot/62.5g	64	101	3.4	15.0	2.8	0.2
Strawberry, Eat Smart, Safeway*	1 Pot/70g	95	135	3.2	24.4	2.7	0.5
Strawberry, Light, Muller*	1 Pot/150g	147	98	4.3	19.4	0.4	0.0
Strawberry, Lite, Onken*	1 Pot/150g	153	102	4.6	17.3	1.6	1.1
Strawberry, Low Fat, Waitrose*	1 Pot/95g	112	118	3.2	20.0	2.8	0.6
Strawberry, Morrisons*	1 Pot/62.5g	107	170	3.5	17.6	9.5	0.2
Strawberry, Onken*	1 Pot/150g	204	136	5.1	14.6	6.3	0.1
Strawberry, Safeway*	1 Pot/63g	106	168	3.5	17.3	9.4	0.1
Strawberry, Sainsbury's*	1 Pot/63g	106	168	3.4	17.5	9.4	0.1
Strawberry, Shape*	1 Pot/100g	44	44	3.0	4.0	1.8	0.0
Strawberry, Weight Watchers*	1 Pot/90g	124	138	3.0	25.5	2.7	0.5
Summer Fruits, Light, Muller*	1 Pot/149g	143	96	4.3	18.7	0.4	0.0
Tropical Fruits, Light, Muller*	1 Pot/150g	150	101	4.3	20.0	0.4	0.0
Tropical, Eat Smart, Safeway*	1 Pot/90g	122	135	3.3	24.5	2.3	3.2
White Chocolate, Finest, Tesco*	1 Pot/92g	436	474	3.9	30.2	37.5	0.0

MOUSSECAKE,

INFO/WEIGHT	Measure	per Measure KCAL	KCAL	PROT	CARB	FAT	FIBRE
Lemon, Weight Watchers*	1 Serving/90g	130	144	3.2	26.7	2.7	0.5
Strawberry, Weight Watchers*	1 Serving/90g	124	138	3.0	25.5	2.7	0.5

MUFFIN,

INFO/WEIGHT	Measure	per Measure KCAL	KCAL	PROT	CARB	FAT	FIBRE
All Butter, TTD, Sainsbury's*	1 Muffin/70.1g	183	261	10.7	40.0	6.5	2.7
Apple, Sultana & Cinnamon, GFY, Asda*	1 Muffin/50g	134	268	6.0	53.0	3.5	3.9
Average	1 Muffin/57g	161	283	10.1	49.6	6.3	2.0
Berry Burst, Asda*	1 Muffin/60g	139	232	6.2	46.7	2.3	1.7
Blueberry Buster, McVitie's*	1 Muffin/95g	408	429	4.3	49.9	23.6	1.1

MUFFIN,	Measure INFO/WEIGHT	per Measure KCAL	Nutrition Values per 100g / 100ml				
			KCAL	PROT	CARB	FAT	FIBRE
Blueberry, American Style, Aldi*	1 Muffin/85g	344	405	4.3	51.2	20.3	0.0
Blueberry, Asda*	1 Muffin/77.3g	272	353	5.0	45.0	17.0	1.3
Blueberry, GFY, Asda*	1 Muffin/58.6g	147	249	6.0	51.0	2.3	3.0
Blueberry, Marks & Spencer*	1 Muffin/75g	282	376	4.8	52.4	16.4	1.2
Blueberry, Martha White*	1 Muffin/38g	170	447	5.3	73.7	11.8	0.0
Blueberry, Mini, Tesco*	1 Muffin/28g	104	370	5.6	43.5	19.3	1.2
Blueberry, Sainsbury's*	1 Muffin/75g	242	322	5.4	46.7	12.6	2.2
Blueberry, Tesco*	1 Muffin/70g	279	398	4.8	39.7	24.4	1.3
Blueberry, Waitrose*	1 Muffin/65g	239	367	4.7	55.2	14.2	1.7
Blueberry, Weight Watchers*	1 Muffin/65g	172	265	6.4	46.9	5.7	2.6
Blueberry, Wild Canadian, Fabulous Bakin' Boys*	1 Muffin/40g	140	349	4.0	39.0	20.0	1.0
Bran	1 Muffin/57g	155	272	7.8	45.6	7.7	7.7
Bran & Sultana, Weight Watchers*	1 Muffin/60g	144	240	4.5	50.7	2.1	2.3
Buttered, McDonald's*	1 Muffin/63g	158	250	8.6	40.7	5.9	2.9
Buttered, With Preserve, McDonald's*	1 Muffin/93g	234	252	5.9	48.1	4.0	2.0
Cafe Latte, Sainsbury's*	1 Muffin/72g	270	375	5.9	43.6	19.7	2.8
Carrot Cake, Cuisine De France*	1 Muffin/105g	373	355	4.7	56.9	12.0	0.0
Carrot Cake, Entenmanns*	1 Muffin/105g	344	328	5.1	45.8	15.1	3.0
Carrot, Asda*	1 Muffin/59.2g	137	233	6.0	47.0	2.3	1.6
Cheese & Black Pepper, Sainsbury's*	1 Muffin/65g	142	218	12.9	34.6	2.0	1.2
Cheese, Tesco*	1 Muffin/75g	183	244	12.5	38.1	4.6	2.0
Choc Chip, BGTY, Sainsbury's*	1 Muffin/75g	282	376	5.2	51.8	16.4	1.6
Choc Chip, Mini, Weight Watchers*	1 Muffin/15g	47	312	6.6	52.1	8.6	3.1
Chocolate Chip, American Style, Sainsbury's*	1 Muffin/75g	328	437	5.9	52.4	22.7	0.6
Chocolate Chip, Black Friar's*	1 Muffin/50g	218	435	6.0	51.0	23.0	4.0
Chocolate Indulgence, McVitie's*	1 Muffin/75g	254	338	5.8	57.9	9.2	1.3
Chocolate, BGTY, Sainsbury's*	1 Muffin/75g	282	376	5.2	51.8	16.4	1.6
Chocolate, Dairy Cream, Safeway*	1 Muffin/109.7g	430	391	7.3	31.9	26.1	3.1
Chocolate, Sainsbury's*	1 Muffin/72.2g	293	407	6.2	49.5	20.5	1.0
Christmas, Weight Watchers*	1 Muffin/63g	173	275	6.8	51.1	4.8	3.0
Chunky Choc n Orange, Fabulous Bakin Boys*	1 Muffin/40g	154	384	5.0	42.0	22.0	1.0
Chunky Chocolate Chip, McVitie's*	1 Muffin/94g	393	418	5.3	50.6	21.6	0.8
Classic Blueberry, Starbucks*	1 Muffin/129g	438	337	4.4	39.7	17.7	1.4
Cranberry & White Chocolate, Sainsbury's*	1 Muffin/72g	253	352	5.7	40.7	18.5	1.5
Dairy Cream Lemon, Safeway*	1 Muffin/110g	409	372	4.4	44.5	19.6	0.0
Double Berry Burst, Entenmann's*	1 Muffin/59g	140	238	4.6	50.1	2.1	1.6
Double Choc Chip, Mini, Asda*	1 Muffin/19g	74	390	6.0	51.0	18.0	0.0
Double Choc Chip, Weight Watchers*	1 Muffin/65g	189	291	6.8	47.2	8.3	3.6
Double Chocolate Chip, Co-Op*	1 Muffin/60g	246	410	6.0	49.0	21.0	3.0
Double Chocolate Chip, Healthier, Tesco*	1 Muffin/72g	272	378	7.0	51.6	16.0	1.4
Double Chocolate Chip, Mini, Weight Watchers*	1 Muffin/15g	45	300	7.0	48.5	8.7	3.5
Double Chocolate Chip, New, Weight Watchers*	1 Muffin/65g	169	260	3.9	52.2	4.0	1.9
Double Chocolate Chip, Sainsbury's*	1 Muffin/72.0g	290	403	4.8	50.0	20.4	1.9
Double Chocolate Chip, Tesco*	1 Muffin/72g	302	419	6.1	48.0	22.5	1.4
Double Chocolate, 95% Fat Free, Entemann's*	1 Muffin/58g	152	262	2.6	52.3	4.7	1.8
Double Chocolate, Chocolate Chip, Mini, Tesco*	1 Muffin/28g	116	414	6.3	45.7	23.0	1.4
Double Chocolate, Marks & Spencer*	1 Muffin/75g	313	417	5.2	48.7	22.4	1.9
Double Chocolate, Mini, Marks & Spencer*	1 Muffin/32g	133	416	5.4	49.8	21.7	1.1
Double Chocolate, Somerfield*	1 Muffin/70g	298	425	6.8	46.5	23.5	0.0
English, Butter, Tesco*	1 Muffin/67.2g	170	253	11.2	39.8	5.4	2.0
English, Marks & Spencer*	1 Muffin/60g	135	225	11.2	43.7	1.9	2.9
English, Plain, Oakrun Bakery*	1 Muffin/57g	139	244	8.4	47.4	1.8	1.4
English, Whole Wheat, Finest, Tesco*	1 Muffin/70g	98	140	7.6	24.6	1.3	3.7

MUFFIN,	Measure INFO/WEIGHT	per Measure KCAL	Nutrition Values per 100g / 100ml				
			KCAL	PROT	CARB	FAT	FIBRE
Finger, Double Chocolate, Bakers Delight*	1 Muffin/25g	104	416	5.8	56.9	18.4	1.7
Galaxy, McVitie's*	1 Muffin/94.0g	358	381	5.1	45.0	20.1	0.0
Iceland*	1 Muffin/76g	173	228	8.6	44.5	1.7	2.0
Irwin's*	1 Muffin/40g	116	291	8.9	50.0	6.2	0.0
Lemon & Blueberry, Tesco*	1 Muffin/110g	411	374	4.0	42.4	20.9	1.1
Lemon & Poppy Seed, Entenmann's*	1 Muffin/105g	417	397	5.6	52.8	19.3	2.5
Lemon & Poppy Seed, Marks & Spencer*	1 Muffin/72g	281	390	6.3	46.1	19.8	1.5
Lemon & Sultana, BGTY, Sainsbury's*	1 Muffin/75g	211	281	4.5	55.6	4.5	1.4
Lemon, Boots*	1 Muffin/110g	424	385	3.6	50.0	19.0	1.3
Magnificent, Kingsmill*	1 Muffin/75g	168	224	9.8	42.3	1.7	2.2
Marks & Spencer*	1 Muffin/56g	126	225	11.2	43.7	1.9	2.9
Mini, Tesco*	1 Muffin/28g	120	428	6.4	50.0	22.6	1.2
Mississipi Mud, Sainsbury's*	1 Muffin/72.1g	274	380	5.2	48.6	18.3	4.2
Mixed Fruit, Low Fat, Abbey Bakery*	1 Muffin/35g	93	267	4.5	55.6	4.5	1.4
Oven Bottom, Aldi*	1 Muffin/68g	173	255	10.0	50.4	1.5	2.2
Oven Bottom, Asda*	1 Muffin/68g	173	255	10.0	50.4	1.5	2.2
Oven Bottom, Lancashire, G.H. Sheldon*	1 Muffin/63g	159	253	10.1	45.8	3.3	0.0
Oven Bottom, Mini, Morrisons*	1 Muffin/42g	107	255	10.0	50.4	1.5	2.2
Oven Bottom, Tesco*	1 Muffin/68g	173	255	10.0	50.4	1.5	2.2
Oven Bottom, Warburton's*	1 Muffin/69g	175	253	10.9	45.8	2.9	0.0
Plain Choc Chip, Tesco*	1 Muffin/72g	302	419	6.2	48.9	22.1	1.1
Plain Chocolate Chip, Sainsbury's*	1 Muffin/75g	313	423	6.4	51.3	21.4	0.6
Plain, Co-Op*	1 Muffin/60g	150	250	13.3	45.0	1.7	1.7
Plain, Morrisons*	1 Muffin/70g	140	200	8.0	41.4	1.1	0.0
Premium White, Sainsbury's*	1 Muffin/65g	135	208	8.0	41.4	1.1	2.0
Raspberry Cream, Sainsbury's*	1 Muffin/90g	314	349	3.9	33.8	22.0	1.3
Rolo, Nestle*	1 Muffin/80g	289	361	5.4	44.3	18.0	0.8
Sausage, Egg & Cheese, American Style, Tesco*	1 Muffin/155g	383	247	12.2	19.9	13.2	1.0
Skinny Blueberry, Starbucks*	1 Muffin/129g	306	236	3.7	47.2	3.2	1.7
Skinny Peach & Raspberry, Starbucks*	1 Muffin/120.2g	286	238	5.1	46.5	3.7	1.4
Skinny Sunrise, Starbucks*	1 Muffin/130g	255	194	4.6	36.7	3.0	1.3
Somerfield*	1 Muffin/60g	130	216	12.2	39.3	1.6	1.9
Spiced Fruit, Co-Op*	1 Muffin/60g	159	265	11.0	52.0	2.0	3.0
Spicy Fruit, Sainsbury's*	1 Muffin/63g	140	222	9.6	43.3	1.2	2.7
Sunblest*	1 Muffin/72.2g	166	230	9.6	43.9	1.8	2.2
Sunrise, Starbucks*	1 Muffin/150g	592	395	5.5	40.8	23.1	1.9
Toffee & Pecan, Finest, Tesco*	1 Muffin/127g	551	434	5.4	51.8	22.8	0.9
Toffee Choo Choo, Tesco*	1 Muffin/95g	402	423	6.4	49.1	22.4	1.0
Toffee Temptation, McVitie's*	1 Muffin/85.5g	295	347	4.7	60.8	9.5	0.8
Toffee, GFY, Asda*	1 Serving/90g	151	168	2.1	34.0	2.6	0.0
Triple Chocolate, Triumph, Fabulous Bakin' Boys*	1 Muffin/40g	160	400	4.5	42.0	24.0	0.0
Truly Madly Chocolatey, Fabulous Bakin' Boys*	1 Muffin/40g	154	386	5.0	41.0	22.0	2.0
Vanilla & Choc Chip, GFY, Asda*	1 Muffin/58.5g	151	260	7.0	53.0	2.2	1.6
White Chocolate & Strawberry, Starbucks*	1 Muffin/142g	583	411	5.7	49.0	23.6	2.3
White Chocolate Chunk Lemon, Mini, Marks & Spencer*	1 Muffin/28g	130	464	6.4	55.4	23.9	2.1
White, Asda*	1 Muffin/72g	174	242	9.0	48.0	1.6	2.0
White, Finest, Tesco*	1 Muffin/70g	159	227	8.4	45.7	1.2	2.1
White, Marks & Spencer*	1 Muffin/60g	135	225	11.2	43.7	1.9	2.9
White, Safeway*	1 Muffin/63g	142	226	10.3	43.2	1.3	2.0
White, Sainsbury's*	1 Muffin/65g	147	226	10.3	43.2	1.3	2.8
White, Tesco*	1 Muffin/60g	143	238	10.2	42.0	3.2	2.1
White, Waitrose*	1 Muffin/60g	128	213	10.7	39.4	1.4	4.2
Wholemeal, Organic, Waitrose*	1 Muffin/65g	129	198	12.4	32.9	1.9	7.6

	Measure	per Measure		Nutrition Values per 100g / 100ml				
	INFO/WEIGHT	KCAL		KCAL	PROT	CARB	FAT	FIBRE
MUFFIN,								
Wholemeal, Perfectly Balanced, Waitrose*	1 Muffin/65g	137		211	11.8	36.1	2.2	5.8
Wholemeal, Tesco*	1 Muffin/65g	134		206	11.1	35.9	2.0	5.2
MUFFIN MIX,								
Banana Nut, Betty Crocker*	1 Serving/30g	130		433	6.7	70.0	16.7	0.0
Corn, Baked, Jiffy*	1 Muffin/38g	180		474	5.3	73.7	10.5	2.6
MULBERRIES,								
Raw	1oz/28g	10		36	1.3	8.1	0.0	0.0
MULLET,								
Grey, Grilled	1oz/28g	42		150	25.7	0.0	5.2	0.0
Grey, Raw	1oz/28g	32		115	19.8	0.0	4.0	0.0
Red, Grilled	1oz/28g	34		121	20.4	0.0	4.4	0.0
Red, Raw	1oz/28g	31		109	18.7	0.0	3.8	0.0
MUNCHIES,								
Milky Bar, Nestle*	1 Pack/35g	196		560	7.0	54.9	34.7	0.1
Mint, Nestle*	1 Pack/61g	267		432	3.8	67.5	16.4	0.0
Nestle*	1 Pack/52g	255		490	4.8	63.7	24.0	0.6
MUSHROOMS,								
Breaded, Average	1oz/28g	42		152	4.3	20.8	5.7	0.7
Breaded, Garlic, Average	1 Serving/50.3g	91		183	5.2	18.7	9.7	1.7
Button, Average	1 Serving/50g	7		15	2.3	0.5	0.4	1.2
Chargrilled & Truffle Sauce, The Best, Safeway*	1 Pot/350g	385		110	3.4	5.8	7.6	0.8
Cheesey, Stuffed, Asda*	1 Serving/290g	322		111	4.3	10.0	6.0	0.0
Chestnut, Average	1 Mushroom/63g	8		13	1.8	0.4	0.5	0.6
Chinese, Dried, Raw	1oz/28g	80		284	10.0	59.9	1.8	0.0
Closed Cup, Average	1oz/28g	5		18	2.9	0.5	0.5	0.6
Common, Boiled in Salted Water	1oz/28g	3		11	1.8	0.4	0.3	1.1
Common, Fried, Average	1oz/28g	44		157	2.4	0.3	16.2	1.5
Common, Raw, Average	1oz/28g	4		13	1.9	0.3	0.5	1.1
Creamed, Average	1oz/28g	23		82	1.3	6.8	5.5	0.5
Dried	1oz/28g	45		159	21.8	4.8	6.0	13.3
Flat, Large, Average	1 Mushroom/52g	10		20	3.3	0.5	0.5	0.7
Garlic, Average	½ Pack/150g	160		106	2.1	3.7	9.3	1.7
Garlic, With BBQ Dip, Pizza Hut*	1 Pack/112.2g	264		234	6.2	30.5	10.0	3.4
Garlic, With Sour Cream & Chive Dip, Pizza Hut*	1 Pack/112.2g	429		380	6.4	20.0	30.8	3.4
Giant, With Tomatoes & Mozzarella, Marks & Spencer*	1 Serving/145g	218		150	6.3	7.1	10.9	5.5
Oyster, Average	1oz/28g	4		15	1.6	1.7	0.3	1.3
Porcini, Dried, Merchant Gourmet*	1 oz/28g	36		128	12.3	5.0	6.5	0.0
Shiitake, Cooked	1oz/28g	15		55	1.6	12.3	0.2	0.0
Shiitake, Dried, Raw	1oz/28g	83		296	9.6	63.9	1.0	0.0
Shiitake, Raw, Finest,Tesco*	1 Serving/28g	7		26	2.2	4.4	0.0	1.1
Sliced, Average	1oz/28g	3		12	1.8	0.4	0.3	1.1
Straw, Canned, Drained	1oz/28g	4		15	2.1	1.2	0.2	0.0
Stuffed With Cheese, Mustard & Herbs, Sainsbury's*	1 Serving/115g	150		130	7.4	6.3	8.3	1.2
Stuffed, Finest, Tesco*	1 Serving/130g	224		172	4.0	7.4	14.0	1.9
Stuffed, With Cheese & Herb Breadcrumbs, Waitrose*	1 Serving/165g	215		130	4.6	16.2	5.2	2.1
MUSSELS,								
Boiled	1 Mussel/7g	7		104	16.7	3.5	2.7	0.0
Cooked & Shelled, Asda*	1 Pack/175g	186		106	17.0	3.5	2.7	0.0
Fresh, With Tomato & Garlic, Marks & Spencer*	1 Serving/650g	455		70	7.9	6.5	1.6	0.1
Greenshell, New Zealand, Sainsbury's*	1 Serving/60g	74		123	19.2	4.3	2.3	0.1
In Garlic Butter Sauce, Average	½ Pack/225g	179		80	6.4	2.0	5.1	0.2
Pickled, Drained, Average	1oz/28g	32		113	20.0	1.5	2.3	0.0
Raw, Average	1oz/28g	24		87	12.7	3.6	2.5	0.2

	Measure INFO/WEIGHT	per Measure KCAL	Nutrition Values per 100g / 100ml				
			KCAL	PROT	CARB	FAT	FIBRE
MUSSELS,							
Thai Fragrant, Marks & Spencer*	½ Pack/325g	358	110	10.6	4.5	5.7	0.1
Vegetable Oil, Smoked, John West*	1oz/28g	58	207	20.0	7.0	11.0	0.0
White Wine Cream Sauce, Cooked, Scottish, Morrisons*	½ Pack/250g	263	105	9.0	5.4	5.3	0.5
MUSTARD,							
American, French's*	1 Tbsp/15g	27	180	6.0	16.0	12.0	0.0
Cajun, Colman's*	1 Tsp/6g	11	187	7.0	23.0	6.5	2.7
Coarse Grain, Frank Cooper*	1 Tsp/6g	12	206	8.9	17.0	11.4	0.0
Coarse Grain, Organic, Simply Delicious*	1 Tbsp/5g	9	170	8.7	11.5	9.1	2.6
Colman's*	1 Tsp/5ml	9	188	7.0	19.0	9.3	1.6
Dijon, Asda*	1 Tsp/7g	11	163	7.7	6.6	11.1	0.0
Dijon, Frank Cooper*	1 Tsp/6g	11	179	7.2	10.0	12.3	0.0
Dijon, Marks & Spencer*	1 Tsp/6g	9	153	10.0	7.2	9.5	1.0
Dijon, Organic, Simply Delicious*	1 Serving/10g	17	166	8.2	6.7	10.6	2.6
Dijon, Tesco*	1 Serving/10g	14	141	8.4	6.4	8.2	0.0
English, Colman's*	1 Tsp/10ml	19	188	7.0	19.0	9.3	1.6
English, Frank Cooper*	1 Tsp/6g	11	188	5.7	22.0	8.6	0.2
English, Marks & Spencer*	1 Tsp/6g	14	226	12.6	8.7	15.9	1.0
English, Powder, Colman's*	1 Tsp/5g	26	518	29.0	24.0	34.0	6.2
English, Safeway*	1 Tsp/6g	10	163	6.1	18.3	6.7	0.0
English, With Chillies, Sainsbury's*	1 Tsp/5g	10	204	8.3	18.1	10.9	6.4
French Classic Yellow, Colman's*	1 Tsp/6g	4	73	4.3	2.6	4.2	0.0
French Mild, Colman's*	1 Tsp/6g	6	104	6.3	4.0	7.0	3.8
French, Frank Cooper*	1 Tsp/6g	7	113	4.6	7.0	7.4	0.0
Honey, Colman's*	1 Tsp/6g	12	208	7.4	24.0	8.2	0.0
Mayonnaise, BGTY, Sainsbury's*	1 Tsp/6g	9	146	2.9	13.4	8.8	0.5
Peppercorn, Colman's*	1 Tsp/6g	11	182	8.8	12.0	10.0	4.9
Powder	1 Tsp/3.3g	14	452	28.9	20.7	28.7	0.0
Powder, Made Up	1oz/28g	63	226	14.5	10.4	14.4	0.0
Smooth	1 Level Tsp/8g	11	139	7.1	9.7	8.2	0.0
Sweet Peppers, Colman's*	1 Tsp/6g	13	218	7.9	20.0	11.0	4.9
Tarragon, Tesco*	1 Tbsp/15ml	59	396	0.9	8.6	39.8	0.2
Whole Grain	1 Level Tsp/8g	11	140	8.2	4.2	10.2	4.9
Whole Grain, Colman's*	1 Tsp/6g	10	173	8.5	8.5	11.0	5.9
Whole Grain, Safeway*	1 Tbsp/15g	27	183	8.0	15.2	9.1	0.0
Whole Grain, Sainsbury's*	1 Tsp/5g	7	137	6.5	4.2	10.5	0.0
Whole Grain, Tesco*	1 Tsp/6g	0	153	8.2	8.7	9.5	5.8
MUSTARD CRESS,							
Raw	1oz/28g	4	13	1.6	0.4	0.6	1.1

INFO/WEIGHT		KCAL	KCAL	PROT	CARB	FAT	FIBRE
NACHOS,							
American Chilli Beef, Asda*	1 Serving/200g	208	104	10.0	4.7	5.0	0.8
Chicken, Safeway*	½ Pack/170g	352	207	10.3	15.7	11.4	1.8
Chilli, Sainsbury's*	½ Pack/250g	695	278	10.9	29.5	12.9	1.3
Kit, Old El Paso*	½ Pack/260g	598	230	4.0	31.0	10.0	0.0
NECTARINES,							
Average	1 Med/140g	53	38	1.3	8.5	0.1	1.2
NESQUIK,							
Chocolate Flavour, Dry, Nestle*	3 Tsp/15g	57	377	4.9	82.5	3.0	5.0
Strawberry, Dry, Nestle*	1 Serving/10g	39	390	0.0	96.7	0.5	0.0
NIK NAKS,							
Cream 'n' Cheesy, Golden Wonder*	1 Bag/34g	185	545	5.1	56.1	33.4	0.0
Nice 'n' Spicy, Golden Wonder*	1 Bag/34g	184	541	4.7	55.5	33.4	1.0
Rib 'n' Saucy, Golden Wonder*	1 Bag/34g	185	545	5.1	55.7	33.5	1.1
Scampi 'n' Lemon, Golden Wonder*	1 Bag/34g	195	573	5.0	49.6	39.4	1.4
NOODLES,							
& Bean Sprouts, Fresh Ideas, Tesco*	1 Pack/250g	310	124	5.4	19.8	2.6	1.9
99% Fat Free, Dry, Heinz*	1 Serving/85g	257	302	9.5	65.3	0.4	2.7
Beef Flavour, Instant, Prepared, Heinz*	1 Pack/384g	257	67	2.1	14.4	0.1	0.6
Beef, Shanghai, Chef's Selection, Marks & Spencer*	1 Pack/352g	440	125	6.0	16.2	4.2	1.6
Char Sui, Cantonese, Sainsbury's*	1 Pack/450g	378	84	6.8	10.5	1.6	1.5
Chicken Flavour, 3 Minute, Dry, Blue Dragon*	1 Pack/85g	403	475	9.3	61.2	21.4	0.0
Chicken Flavour, Dry, Eldorado*	1 Pack/85g	360	423	14.0	61.0	15.0	0.0
Chicken Flavour, Dry, Princes*	1 Pack/85g	395	465	10.0	63.8	18.8	0.0
Chicken Flavour, Instant, Cooked, Sainsbury's*	1 Pack/335g	409	122	2.7	18.0	4.4	0.1
Chicken Flavour, Instant, Cooked, SmartPrice, Asda*	1 Pack/65g	409	629	18.5	93.9	20.0	1.1
Chicken Flavour, Instant, Value, Tesco*	1 Serving/65g	82	126	3.2	20.7	3.4	0.9
Chicken, Chinese Style, GFY, Asda*	1 Pack/393g	295	75	6.0	9.0	1.7	0.6
Chicken, Chinese, Asda*	1 Pot/302g	305	101	6.0	16.0	1.4	0.8
Chicken, Dry, Heinz*	1 Serving/85g	257	302	9.5	65.3	0.4	2.7
Chicken, Instant, Less Than 1% Fat, Heinz*	1 Pack/385g	258	67	2.1	14.4	0.1	0.6
Chicken, Instant, Prepared, Heinz*	1 Pack/384g	257	67	2.1	14.4	0.1	0.6
Chilli Chicken, GFY, Asda*	1 Pack/415g	461	111	6.0	20.0	0.8	1.0
Chilli Chicken, Take Away, Marks & Spencer*	1 Pack/250g	325	130	9.6	15.2	3.1	1.3
Chinese, Egg, Medium, Dry, Sharwood's*	1 Serving/65g	223	343	11.0	70.9	1.8	2.5
Chow Mein Flavour, Princes*	1 Pack/85g	396	466	10.1	64.6	18.6	0.0
Chow Mein, Chicken Bowl, Uncle Ben's*	1 Pack/330g	307	93	6.1	13.5	1.4	0.0
Chow Mein, Instant, Made Up, Tesco*	1 Pack/167.5g	255	152	3.8	23.0	5.0	1.2
Chow Mein, Sainsbury's*	1 Pack/125g	136	109	3.9	19.2	1.8	0.8
Chow Mein, Stir Fry, Tesco*	1 Serving/200g	116	58	2.1	9.7	1.2	1.0
Crab Flavour, Dry, 3 Minute, Blue Dragon*	1 Pack/85g	393	463	9.9	62.6	19.2	0.0
Crispy, Blue Dragon*	1 Box/125g	438	350	2.4	84.0	0.5	0.0
Curry Flavour, Instant, Asda*	1 Serving/65g	415	638	20.0	101.5	16.9	0.9
Curry Flavour, Instant, Sainsbury's*	1 Pack/335g	412	123	2.6	17.8	4.6	0.1
Curry, Instant, Dry, Heinz*	1 Serving/85g	261	307	9.5	66.4	0.4	2.7
Curry, Prepared, Heinz*	1 Pack/85g	58	68	2.1	14.6	0.1	0.6
Egg Fried, Cantonese, Safeway*	1oz/28g	29	104	3.4	10.7	5.3	1.1
Egg, Asda*	1 Pack/184g	280	152	4.8	31.0	0.8	1.3
Egg, Boiled	1oz/28g	17	62	2.2	13.0	0.5	0.6
Egg, Dry	1oz/28g	109	391	12.1	71.7	8.2	2.9
Egg, Fine Thread, Dry, Marks & Spencer*	1 Serving/63g	221	350	14.3	71.6	0.9	5.1
Egg, Fine, Dry, Sharwood's*	1 Serving/75g	257	343	11.0	70.9	1.8	2.5
Egg, Fresh, Tesco*	1 Pack/300g	204	68	2.8	11.8	1.3	0.6
Egg, Medium, Asda*	1 Layer/190g	289	152	4.8	31.0	0.8	1.3

NOODLES,	Measure INFO/WEIGHT	per Measure KCAL	KCAL	PROT	CARB	FAT	FIBRE
Egg, Medium, Dry, Blue Dragon*	1 Sheet/81g	276	341	11.0	70.0	1.9	1.0
Egg, Medium, Dry, Sharwood's*	1 Block/65g	223	343	11.0	70.9	1.8	2.5
Egg, Medium, Sainsbury's*	1 Serving/122.1g	162	133	5.5	25.9	0.7	1.0
Egg, Ramen, Fresh, The Original Noodle Company*	1 Serving/62.5g	188	298	11.3	57.0	2.7	0.0
Egg, Straight To Wok, Amoy*	½ Pack/75g	113	151	4.2	29.0	2.1	1.3
Egg, Thick, Dry, Sharwood's*	1 Serving/250g	850	340	10.8	70.1	1.8	2.9
Egg, Thread, Amoy*	1 Serving/150g	227	151	4.2	29.0	2.1	1.3
Egg, Thread, Sharwood's*	1oz/28g	30	107	3.6	21.8	0.6	1.1
Egg, Tossed In Sesame Oil, Asda*	½ Pack/150g	174	116	2.3	11.0	7.0	0.0
Fine Egg, Marks & Spencer*	½ Pack/150g	143	95	4.1	14.6	2.3	1.4
Fresh, Tesco*	1 Serving/150g	102	68	2.8	11.4	1.3	0.6
Fried	1oz/28g	43	153	1.9	11.3	11.5	0.5
Heinz*	1 Serving/385g	257	67	2.1	14.4	0.1	0.6
Instant, Fat Free, Koka*	1 Piece/80g	143	179	6.2	38.5	0.0	1.0
Japanese Udon, Sainsbury's*	1 Serving/150g	210	140	3.9	27.1	1.8	1.2
Medium, Straight To Wok*	1oz/28g	47	169	6.0	24.5	5.2	0.0
Mung Bean, Dry, Amoy*	1oz/28g	95	341	15.9	66.6	1.2	0.0
Oriental Beef & Sweet Red Pepper, Colman's*	1 Serving/80g	254	317	4.2	73.4	0.7	5.1
Oriental Style, Break, Asda*	1 Pot/57g	218	382	12.3	80.7	1.2	2.5
Peking Duck, Shapers, Boots*	1 Pack/280g	395	141	7.2	25.0	1.4	1.8
Plain, Boiled	1oz/28g	17	62	2.4	13.0	0.4	0.7
Plain, Dry	1oz/28g	109	388	11.7	76.1	6.2	2.9
Prawn Flavour, Instant, Cooked, Sainsbury's*	1 Pack/325g	393	121	2.8	18.1	4.2	0.1
Prawn Satay, Safeway*	1 Serving/400g	460	115	5.3	12.4	4.6	1.8
Ramen, With Chilli Beef, Marks & Spencer*	1 Pack/484g	532	110	8.1	11.9	3.6	0.8
Rice, Dry, Amoy*	1oz/28g	101	361	6.5	86.6	1.0	0.0
Rice, Dry, Blue Dragon*	1 Serving/30g	113	376	6.0	88.0	0.0	0.0
Rice, Oriental, Thai, Stir Fry, Dry, Sharwood's*	1 Serving/62.5g	227	361	6.5	86.8	1.0	2.4
Savoury Vegetable, COU, Marks & Spencer*	1 Pack/450g	270	60	2.9	11.5	0.6	1.2
Sharwood's*	1 Serving/125g	429	343	11.0	70.9	1.8	2.5
Singapore Spicy, Safeway*	1 Serving/225g	270	120	6.0	14.2	4.3	1.7
Singapore Style, Asda*	1 Pack/400g	688	172	7.0	18.0	8.0	1.0
Singapore, Marks & Spencer*	1oz/28g	38	135	5.9	18.7	4.3	0.5
Singapore, New, Marks & Spencer*	1 Pack/400g	540	135	5.3	14.6	5.9	0.6
Singapore, Sainsbury's*	1 Pack/350g	441	126	3.2	11.9	7.3	2.4
Singapore, Somerfield*	1 Pot/300g	261	87	5.0	15.0	1.0	0.0
Singapore, Straight To Wok, Amoy*	1 Serving/150g	233	155	4.8	28.4	2.8	0.0
Singapore, Tesco*	1 Pack/350g	389	111	6.3	16.8	2.1	0.7
Singapore, Waitrose*	1 Pack/400g	476	119	7.3	12.6	4.4	2.1
Special, Chinese Takeaway, Iceland*	1 Pack/340g	422	124	6.5	17.2	3.2	0.6
Spicy Curry Flavour, Princes*	1 Pack/85g	395	465	9.6	64.1	18.8	0.0
Spicy Curry Flavour, Snack, SmartPrice, Asda*	1 Pot/76g	358	471	10.5	65.8	18.4	0.0
Spicy Thai, Instant, Heinz*	1 Packet/385g	262	68	2.1	14.6	0.1	0.6
Straight to Wok, Amoy*	1 Pack/180g	272	151	4.2	29.0	2.1	1.3
Straight to Wok, New, Amoy*	1 Serving/150g	240	160	5.8	31.7	1.5	0.0
Super, Bacon, Dry Weight, Batchelors*	1 Pack/100g	457	457	9.8	60.9	19.7	3.2
Super, Chicken & Ham, Dry Weight, Batchelors*	1 Pack/100g	472	472	9.4	63.2	20.2	1.5
Super, Chicken Flavour, Dry, Batchelors*	1 Serving/100g	449	449	8.7	60.3	19.2	2.5
Super, Chicken Flavour, Made Up, Batchelors*	1 Serving/100g	170	170	3.3	22.9	7.3	0.9
Super, Chow Mein Flavour, Batchelors*	1 Serving/100g	158	158	3.2	20.9	6.8	1.0
Super, Mild Curry Flavour, Made Up, Batchelors*	1 Serving/100g	157	157	3.2	20.9	6.7	1.0
Super, Mild Curry, Dry Weight, Batchelors*	1 Pack/100g	457	457	9.5	60.6	19.7	3.0
Super, Mushroom Flavour, Made Up, Batchelors*	1 Serving/100g	157	157	3.2	20.9	6.8	1.0

	Measure INFO/WEIGHT	per Measure KCAL	Nutrition Values per 100g / 100ml KCAL	PROT	CARB	FAT	FIBRE
NOODLES,							
Super, Southern Fried Chicken, Made Up, Batchelors*	1 Serving/100g	171	171	3.3	23.2	7.2	0.5
Super, Spicy Balti, Made Up, Batchelors*	1 Serving/100g	166	166	3.0	21.5	7.5	1.1
Super, Spicy Salsa, Dry Weight, Batchelors*	1 Pack/105g	474	451	7.0	63.8	18.6	1.7
Sweet & Sour, BGTY, Sainsbury's*	1 Serving/100g	112	112	2.3	18.6	3.1	0.0
Sweet Chilli, Wok, Findus*	1 Pack/300g	300	100	3.0	20.0	0.5	0.0
Sweet Thai Chilli Noodles, 98% Fat Free, Batchelors*	1 Serving/270.4g	292	108	3.3	22.8	0.4	0.9
Szechuan Beef Flavour, Blue Dragon*	½ Pack/100g	350	350	10.5	72.3	1.2	0.0
Szechuan Style Prawn, Tesco*	1 Bowl/400g	376	94	5.5	17.3	0.3	0.9
Thai Stir Fry Rice, Sharwood's*	1 Portion/60g	217	361	6.5	86.8	1.0	2.4
Thai Style, GFY Asda*	1 Pot/237.9g	226	95	3.0	20.0	0.3	0.8
Thai Style, Sainsbury's*	1 Pack/340g	381	112	3.3	19.4	2.3	0.7
Thai, Waitrose*	1 Pack/300g	357	119	6.8	18.4	2.1	1.7
Thread, Fine, Straight To Wok, Amoy*	1 Packet/150g	237	158	5.0	28.7	2.6	0.0
Tom Yum, Hot & Spicy, Tiger Tiger*	1 Pot/90g	407	453	9.5	69.0	15.5	0.2
Traditional, Medium, Amoy*	1 Serving/75g	120	160	5.8	31.7	1.5	0.0
Udon Japanese, & Dashi Soup Stock, Yutaka*	1 Pack/230g	290	126	3.0	26.8	0.5	0.0
Udon, New, Amoy*	1 Portion/150g	212	141	4.4	28.8	1.3	0.0
Whole Wheat, Blue Dragon*	1 Serving/65g	208	320	12.5	63.0	2.0	8.0
Won Ton Flavour, 3 Minute, Dry, Blue Dragon*	1 Serving/80g	370	463	9.1	62.2	19.7	0.0
Yaki Soba, Yutaka*	1 Pack/170g	311	183	4.7	35.1	2.2	0.0
NOUGAT,							
Almond & Cherry, Marks & Spencer*	1 Sweet/7g	28	405	4.5	76.0	9.1	1.1
Average	1oz/28g	108	384	4.4	77.3	8.5	0.9
Bassetts & Beyond, Cadbury's*	1oz/28g	105	375	4.0	82.0	4.0	0.0
Raspberry & Orange Hazelnut, Thorntons*	1 Chocolate/9g	39	433	4.8	60.0	20.0	2.2
NUGGETS,							
Meat Free, Blue Parrot Cafe, Sainsbury's*	1 Nugget/18g	41	228	17.3	12.5	12.1	3.0
Vegetarian, Safeway*	4 Nuggets/80.1g	161	201	16.3	10.5	10.4	3.6
NURISHMENT,							
Dunn's River*	1 Serving/420ml	420	100	5.0	14.6	2.6	0.0
Strawberry, Dunn's River*	1fl oz/30ml	30	100	5.0	14.6	2.6	0.0
NUT ROAST,							
Average	1oz/28g	99	352	13.3	18.3	25.7	4.2
Leek, Cheese & Mushroom, Organic, Cauldron Foods*	½ Pack/143g	343	240	13.2	13.2	14.9	4.1
Lentil	1oz/28g	62	222	10.6	18.8	12.1	3.8
Tomato & Courgette, Organic, Waitrose*	½ Pack/142g	295	208	11.7	12.5	12.3	4.9
Vegetarian, Tesco*	1 Serving/160g	218	136	5.4	11.4	7.6	2.0
NUTMEG,							
Powder	1 Tsp/3g	16	525	5.8	45.3	36.3	0.0
NUTRI-GRAIN,							
Apple, Kellogg's*	1 Bar/37g	130	350	4.0	68.0	8.0	3.0
Blueberry, Kellogg's*	1 Bar/37g	130	350	4.0	68.0	8.0	3.0
Cappuccino, Kellogg's*	1 Bar/37g	137	370	4.5	66.0	10.0	2.5
Cherry, Kellogg's*	1 Bar/37g	133	360	4.0	68.0	9.0	3.0
Chocolate, Kellogg's*	1 Bar/37g	133	360	4.5	63.0	11.0	3.5
Elevenses, Ginger, Kellogg's*	1 Bar/45g	167	370	5.0	68.0	9.0	2.5
Elevenses, Kellogg's*	1 Bar/45g	162	360	5.0	67.0	8.0	3.5
Minis, Apple, Kellogg's*	1 Pack/45g	162	359	3.5	71.0	8.0	3.5
Minis, Blueberry, Kellogg's*	1 Bag/45g	158	350	4.0	69.0	8.0	3.5
Minis, Strawberry, Kellogg's*	1 Pack/45g	158	350	4.0	69.0	8.0	3.5
Orange, Kellogg's*	1 Bar/37g	137	370	5.0	68.0	9.0	4.0
Strawberry, Kellogg's*	1 Bar/37g	133	360	4.0	68.0	9.0	3.0
Tangy Orange, Kellogg's*	1 Bar/38g	141	370	5.0	68.0	9.0	4.0

	Measure INFO/WEIGHT	per Measure KCAL	Nutrition Values per 100g / 100ml				
			KCAL	PROT	CARB	FAT	FIBRE
NUTRI-GRAIN,							
Twists, Forest Fruits & Yoghurt, Kellogg's*	1 Bar/37g	133	360	4.0	69.0	8.0	2.0
Twists, Mixed Fruits, Kellogg's*	1 Bar/37g	133	360	3.5	69.0	8.0	2.0
Twists, Strawberry, Kellogg's*	1 Bar/37g	130	350	4.0	68.0	8.0	3.0
Yoghurty Raspberry, Kellogg's*	1 Bar/37g	134	361	4.5	68.0	9.0	3.5
Yoghurty Strawberry, Kellogg's*	1 Bar/37g	134	361	4.5	68.0	9.0	3.5
NUTS,							
Clusters, Sweet Tomato Salsa, Sensations, Walkers*	1 Serving/35g	187	535	14.0	36.0	37.0	5.0
Honey Roasted, Marks & Spencer*	1oz/28g	175	625	18.1	20.5	52.2	5.1
Luxury, Organic, Marks & Spencer*	1oz/28g	179	640	21.1	11.6	56.6	6.1
Mixed	1 Pack/40g	243	607	22.9	7.9	54.1	6.0
Mixed, Chopped, Safeway*	1 Serving/2g	12	588	22.0	10.3	51.0	5.9
Mixed, Chopped, Tesco*	1 Pack/100g	591	591	23.5	10.5	50.6	6.0
Mixed, Feast, Eat Natural*	1 Bar/50g	278	556	18.8	28.0	41.0	0.0
Mixed, Luxury, Unsalted, Somerfield*	1oz/28g	186	663	18.0	10.0	61.0	0.0
Mixed, Marks & Spencer*	1 Serving/25g	166	665	18.2	4.4	63.7	7.4
Mixed, Natural, Luxury, Tesco*	1oz/28g	179	639	22.6	6.9	57.9	5.6
Mixed, Natures Harvest*	1 Serving/25g	166	662	16.0	5.6	63.9	5.6
Mixed, Roast, Salted, Somerfield*	1oz/28g	175	625	24.0	11.0	54.0	0.0
Mixed, Roasted, Salted, Waitrose*	1 Pack/200g	1252	626	13.7	11.3	58.4	4.4
Mixed, Sainsbury's*	1 Bag/200g	1346	673	18.8	4.6	64.5	5.3
Mixed, Unsalted, Sainsbury's*	1 Serving/50g	311	622	18.5	7.2	57.7	8.7
Natural Assortment, Tesco*	1 Serving/50g	338	676	17.5	6.1	64.6	5.0
Natural, Mixed, Waitrose*	1 Serving/50g	318	635	16.3	18.9	54.9	4.6
Oak Smoke Flavour Selection, Finest, Tesco*	1 Serving/25g	158	633	21.4	11.2	55.8	6.3
Roast Salted, Luxury, KP*	1oz/28g	181	646	21.9	10.1	57.6	5.9
Selection, Salted, TTD, Sainsbury's*	1 Pack/75g	509	678	16.3	8.9	64.2	7.2
Selection, Unsalted, Sainsbury's*	1 Serving/75g	491	655	14.7	5.0	64.0	6.7
NUTS & RAISINS,							
Mixed	1 Pack/40g	192	481	14.1	31.5	34.1	4.5
Mixed, KP*	1 Serving/50g	273	546	21.4	24.4	40.3	5.2
Mixed, Nature's Harvest*	1 Serving/50g	232	463	12.4	32.9	33.7	3.4
Mixed, Safeway*	1 Serving/50g	264	527	18.6	30.7	36.7	4.8
Mixed, Somerfield*	1oz/28g	159	568	18.0	24.0	45.0	0.0
Mixed, Tesco*	1 Serving/50g	256	512	16.1	31.0	36.0	4.8
Mixed, Unsalted, Sainsbury's*	1oz/28g	143	510	16.2	28.0	37.0	4.8
Peanuts, Average	1 Pack/40g	174	435	15.3	37.5	26.0	4.4
Peanuts, Somerfield*	1oz/28g	133	474	19.0	37.0	28.0	0.0

	Measure	per Measure	Nutrition Values per 100g / 100ml				
	INFO/WEIGHT	KCAL	KCAL	PROT	CARB	FAT	FIBRE
OATCAKES,							
Bran, Patersons*	1 Cake/12.5g	53	441	10.7	57.3	18.8	8.2
Cheese, Nairn's*	1 Cake/8g	38	471	13.4	54.0	25.1	6.2
Fine, Nairn's*	1 Oatcake/7g	32	463	10.9	61.3	19.3	6.0
Highland, Organic, Sainsbury's*	1 Oatcake/12.5g	59	456	10.2	59.8	19.5	5.5
No Wheat, No Sugar, Orgainic, Nairns*	1 Oatcake/10g	43	423	8.8	70.2	16.0	9.3
Organic, Safeway*	1 Oatcake/13g	56	445	11.2	56.7	19.3	6.6
Retail	1oz/28g	123	441	10.0	63.0	18.3	0.0
Rough Scottish, Sainsbury's*	1 Oatcake/11g	51	462	12.3	59.9	19.3	6.5
Rough With Bran, Walkers*	1 Oatcake/13g	59	454	10.2	53.3	22.2	7.8
Rough, Nairn's*	1 Oatcake/11g	48	436	10.6	64.7	18.2	7.2
Rough, Organic, Nairn's*	1 Oatcake/11g	47	428	10.9	57.7	17.0	7.6
Rough, Sainsbury's*	1 Cake/10.6g	51	462	12.3	59.9	19.3	6.5
Rough, Scottish, Tesco*	1 Oatcake/11g	48	434	12.3	54.8	18.4	6.6
Rough, Traditional, Nairn's*	1 Oatcake/11g	47	429	11.7	63.5	17.7	7.8
Scottish, Marks & Spencer*	1oz/28g	116	413	9.1	70.0	12.6	8.5
Scottish, Paterson's*	1 Cake/12.5g	49	409	11.1	58.6	14.5	8.5
With Cracked Black Pepper, Walkers*	1 Oatcake/9.5g	39	433	10.4	55.0	19.0	8.5
OATMEAL,							
Medium, Mornflake*	1 Tbsp/12g	43	359	11.0	60.4	8.1	8.5
Raw	1oz/28g	112	401	12.4	72.8	8.7	6.8
OATS,							
Jumbo, Organic, Waitrose*	1oz/28g	101	361	11.0	61.1	8.1	7.8
Porridge, Old Fashioned, Scotts*	1 Serving/45g	160	356	11.0	60.0	8.0	9.0
OCEAN,							
Prawnies, Mini, Asda*	1 Prawnie/11g	9	84	11.0	8.0	0.9	0.5
Sticks, Average	1 Stick/16g	17	109	7.1	19.9	0.2	0.2
OCTOPUS,							
Raw	1oz/28g	23	83	17.9	0.0	1.3	0.0
OIL,							
Again & Again, No Cholesterol, Anglia*	1 Tbsp/15ml	124	828	0.0	0.0	92.0	0.0
Avocado, Olivado*	1 Tsp/5ml	40	802	0.0	0.0	88.0	0.0
Black Truffle Grapeseed, Cuisine Perel*	1 Tbsp/15ml	129	857	0.0	7.1	100.0	0.0
Carotino*	1 Tsp/5ml	40	804	0.0	0.0	92.0	0.0
Chilli, Average	1 Tsp/5ml	41	824	0.0	0.0	91.5	0.0
Chinese Stir Fry, Asda*	1 Tbsp/15ml	123	823	0.0	0.0	91.4	0.0
Coconut	1 Tsp/5ml	45	899	0.0	0.0	99.9	0.0
Corn, Average	1 Tsp/5ml	43	865	0.0	0.0	96.0	0.0
Flax Seed	1 Tbsp/14ml	117	838	0.0	0.0	93.1	0.0
Flora*	1 Tsp/5g	45	900	0.0	0.0	100.0	0.0
Fry Light, Bodyline*	4 Sprays/0.8ml	5	522	0.0	0.0	55.2	0.0
Grapeseed	1 Tsp/5ml	45	899	0.0	0.0	99.9	0.0
Groundnut, Average	1 Tsp/5ml	41	824	0.0	0.0	91.8	0.0
Hazelnut	1 Tsp/5ml	45	899	0.0	0.0	99.9	0.0
Linseed, Organic, Biona*	1 Serving/10ml	84	837	0.0	0.0	93.0	0.0
Olive, Average	1 Serving/5ml	43	855	0.0	0.0	94.9	0.0
Olive, Extra Virgin, Average	1 Serving/15ml	127	848	0.0	0.0	94.5	0.0
Olive, Garlic, Average	1 Serving/15ml	127	848	0.0	0.0	94.3	0.0
Olive, Lemon Flavoured, Sainsbury's*	1 Tbsp/15ml	123	823	0.1	0.0	91.4	0.1
Olive, Light, GFY, Asda*	1 Serving/10g	35	346	1.0	0.0	38.0	0.0
Olive, Mild, Average	1 Tbsp/14.9ml	129	862	0.1	0.0	95.7	0.0
Olive, Spray, Fry Light*	5 Sprays/1ml	5	498	0.0	0.0	55.2	0.0
Palm	1 Tsp/5ml	45	899	0.0	0.0	99.9	0.0
Peanut	1 Tsp/5ml	45	899	0.0	0.0	99.9	0.0

O

	Measure INFO/WEIGHT	per Measure KCAL	Nutrition Values per 100g / 100ml				
			KCAL	PROT	CARB	FAT	FIBRE
OIL,							
Rapeseed, Average	1 Serving/30ml	259	864	0.0	0.0	96.0	0.0
Safflower	1 Tsp/5ml	45	899	0.0	0.0	99.9	0.0
Sesame, Average	1 Tsp/5ml	45	892	0.1	0.0	99.9	0.0
Sesame, Toasted, Sainsbury's*	1 Serving/15ml	124	827	0.1	0.0	91.9	0.0
Soya	1 Tsp/5ml	45	899	0.0	0.0	99.9	0.0
Stir Fry, Sharwood's*	1fl oz/30ml	269	897	0.0	0.0	99.7	0.0
Sunflower, Average	1 Tbsp/15ml	130	869	0.0	0.0	96.6	0.0
Sunflower, Fry Light Spray	1 Spray/0.2ml	1	522	0.0	0.0	55.2	0.0
Ultimate Blend, Udo's Choice*	1 Capsule/1ml	9	900	1.3	0.0	96.8	0.0
Vegetable, Average	1 Serving/15ml	129	858	0.0	0.0	95.3	0.0
Walnut	1 Tsp/5ml	45	899	0.0	0.0	99.9	0.0
Wheatgerm	1 Tsp/5ml	45	899	0.0	0.0	99.9	0.0
OKRA,							
Boiled in Unsalted Water	1oz/28g	8	28	2.5	2.7	0.9	3.6
Canned, Drained	1oz/28g	6	21	1.4	2.5	0.7	2.6
Raw	1oz/28g	9	31	2.8	3.0	1.0	4.0
Stir-Fried in Corn Oil	1oz/28g	75	269	4.3	4.4	26.1	6.3
OLIVES,							
Black, Pitted, Average	½ Jar/82g	135	164	1.0	3.5	16.2	3.1
Green, Garlic Stuffed, Asda*	1 Olive/3.4g	5	174	1.8	3.5	17.0	0.0
Green, Lightly Flavoured With Lemon & Garlic, Attis*	1 Serving/50g	82	164	1.7	2.2	16.5	0.0
Green, Pimiento Stuffed, Somerfield*	1 Olive/3g	4	126	1.0	4.0	12.0	0.0
Green, Pitted, Average	1 Olive/3g	4	130	1.1	0.9	13.3	2.5
Green, Stuffed With Anchovy, Waitrose*	½ Can/40g	38	94	1.5	4.7	7.7	2.3
Kalamata, Gaea*	1 Serving/50g	54	107	0.0	3.8	9.8	3.4
Marinated, Selection, Marks & Spencer*	4 Olives/19.6g	45	225	1.4	3.9	22.6	2.1
Pimento Stuffed, In Brine, Tesco*	1 Serving/25g	38	153	0.8	0.1	16.4	2.1
Pitted, With Anchovy Paste, Safeway*	1/3 Can/50g	70	139	2.7	0.1	14.2	2.0
OMELETTE,							
Cheese, 2 Egg	1 Omelette/180g	479	266	15.9	0.0	22.6	0.0
Cheese, Asda*	1 Omelette/120g	287	239	11.0	3.8	20.0	0.1
Cheese, Findus*	1 Serving/200g	400	200	9.5	14.0	13.0	0.0
Cheese, Tesco*	1 Serving/120g	270	225	11.4	3.7	18.3	0.0
Ham & Mushroom, Farmfoods*	1 Omelette/120g	200	167	8.7	1.8	13.9	0.1
Mushroom & Cheese, Tesco*	1 Omelette/120g	248	207	9.8	1.6	17.9	0.2
Plain, 2 Egg	1 Omelette/120g	229	191	10.9	0.0	16.4	0.0
Spanish	1oz/28g	34	120	5.7	6.2	8.3	1.4
ONION RINGS,							
Asda*	¼ Pack/25g	122	489	6.0	60.0	25.0	2.4
Battered, Sainsbury's*	1 Ring/12g	32	268	3.6	28.9	15.3	2.2
COU, Marks & Spencer*	1oz/28g	95	340	4.7	80.7	1.5	3.7
Maize Snacks, Safeway*	1 Pack/100g	485	485	7.8	58.7	24.3	3.0
Maize Snacks, Sainsbury's*	½ Pack/50g	240	479	8.5	57.8	23.8	3.9
Marks & Spencer*	1 Pack/40g	186	465	5.2	62.1	21.5	4.3
Oven Crisp Batter, Tesco*	1 Onion Ring/17g	40	236	4.2	24.8	13.3	2.5
Pickled, BGTY, Sainsbury's*	1 Bag/10g	34	340	4.7	77.0	1.5	3.7
Pickled, COU, Marks & Spencer*	1 Bag/20g	68	340	4.7	80.7	1.5	3.7
Pickled, Healthy Eating, Tesco*	1 Pack/15g	51	340	6.2	74.7	1.8	6.5
Red Mill*	1 Bag/50g	249	498	7.5	58.8	25.9	2.2
Regular, Burger King*	1 Serving/90g	261	290	4.8	36.4	13.9	3.8
Spar*	1 Bag/40g	178	444	7.0	51.4	23.4	3.1
Value, Tesco*	1 Bag/16g	77	482	7.6	58.3	24.3	2.5

	Measure	per Measure	Nutrition Values per 100g / 100ml				
	INFO/WEIGHT	KCAL	KCAL	PROT	CARB	FAT	FIBRE
ONIONS,							
Baked	1oz/28g	29	103	3.5	22.3	0.6	3.9
Boiled in Unsalted Water	1oz/28g	5	17	0.6	3.7	0.1	0.7
Dried, Raw	1oz/28g	88	313	10.2	68.6	1.7	12.1
Fried, Average	1oz/28g	46	164	2.3	14.1	11.2	3.1
Pickled, Average	1oz/28g	6	23	0.8	4.9	0.1	0.7
Raw, Average	1oz/28g	9	31	1.3	6.0	0.2	1.4
Red, Raw, Average	1 Serving/25g	9	37	1.2	7.9	0.2	1.5
OPTIONS*,							
Belgian Chocolate, Instant	1 Serving/11g	40	363	12.4	54.9	10.4	7.5
Belgian, Ovaltine	3 Tspn/11g	40	363	12.4	54.9	10.4	7.5
Caribbean Coconut	1 Serving/40g	146	364	15.1	50.7	11.2	0.0
Choca Mocha Drink	1 Sachet/10g	36	359	14.1	50.1	11.4	7.0
Chocolate Au Lait Drink	1 Sachet/10g	36	355	11.8	54.5	10.0	7.3
Diet Friendly	1 Sachet/11ml	40	364	14.3	50.6	11.6	7.1
Irish Cream	1 Sachet/10.9g	39	357	13.9	50.0	11.3	8.1
Irish Cream Drink	1 Sachet/10g	36	357	13.9	50.0	11.3	8.1
Mint, Made Up	1 Serving/200ml	40	20	0.8	2.8	0.7	0.4
Mint Drink	1 Sachet/10g	37	365	15.0	50.6	11.4	7.1
Orange Flavour	1 Serving/11ml	40	364	14.2	50.8	11.6	7.1
Outrageous Orange Drink	1 Sachet/10g	36	364	14.2	50.8	11.6	7.1
Pleasure	1 Sachet/18g	68	377	16.7	48.4	13.0	7.8
Toffee Drink	1 Sachet/13g	52	400	10.5	68.9	9.2	0.0
Turkish Delight Drink	1 Sachet/11g	40	364	15.1	50.4	11.3	7.2
Wicked White Chocolate	1 Sachet/11g	45	412	10.9	63.9	12.5	16.3
ORANGE DRINK,							
Active Sport, Tesco*	1 Bottle/500ml	135	27	0.0	6.5	0.0	0.0
Burst, Diet, Safeway*	1 Can/330ml	13	4	0.1	0.5	0.1	0.1
No Added Sugar, Asda*	1 Glass/250ml	13	5	0.1	0.6	0.0	0.0
Orangina*, Light, Cadbury Schweppes*	1 Bottle/500ml	30	6	0.1	1.2	0.0	0.0
Sparkling, Diet, Tesco*	1 Glass/250ml	8	3	0.1	0.5	0.1	0.0
Sparkling, Florida, Diet, Marks & Spencer*	1fl oz/30ml	2	5	0.0	0.5	0.0	0.0
Sparkling, Florida, Marks & Spencer*	1 Serving/500ml	250	50	0.0	12.5	0.0	0.0
Sparkling, Shapers, Boots*	1 Bottle/500ml	15	3	0.1	0.4	0.1	0.0
ORANGES,							
Fresh, Raw	1 Med/160g	59	37	1.1	8.5	0.1	1.7
Segments, In Natural Juice, Tesco*	1oz/28g	14	50	0.7	11.0	0.0	0.3
Weighed With Peel & Pips	1oz/28g	7	26	0.8	5.9	0.1	1.2
OREGANO,							
Dried, Ground	1 Tsp/1g	3	306	11.0	49.5	10.3	0.0
Fresh	1oz/28g	18	66	2.2	9.7	2.0	0.0
OVALTINE*,							
Hi Malt, Light, Instant Drink	1 Sachet/20g	72	358	9.1	67.1	5.9	2.8
Powder, Made Up With Semi-Skimmed Milk	1 Mug/227ml	179	79	3.9	13.0	1.7	0.0
Powder, Made Up With Whole Milk	1 Mug/227ml	220	97	3.8	12.9	3.8	0.0
OXTAIL,							
Raw	1oz/28g	48	171	20.0	0.0	10.1	0.0
Stewed	1oz/28g	68	243	30.5	0.0	13.4	0.0
OYSTERS,							
In Vegetable Oil, Smoked, John West*	1oz/28g	64	230	16.0	10.0	14.0	0.0
Raw	1oz/28g	18	65	10.8	2.7	1.3	0.0

O

	Measure	per Measure	Nutrition Values per 100g / 100ml				
	INFO/WEIGHT	KCAL	KCAL	PROT	CARB	FAT	FIBRE
PAELLA,							
Big Dish Chicken & Chorizo, Marks & Spencer*	1 Pack/450g	630	140	7.9	18.4	3.9	1.6
Bistro, Waitrose*	1 Serving/300g	534	178	7.4	22.2	6.6	0.7
Chicken & Chorizo, Asda*	1 Pack/390g	432	111	9.0	14.1	2.1	2.3
Chicken & Vegetable, Healthy Living, Tesco*	1 Pack/450g	441	98	9.7	11.8	1.3	1.1
Chicken, Healthy Living, Tesco*	1 Pack/400g	432	108	6.7	19.2	0.5	1.7
Chicken, Steam Pack, Healthy Eating, Tesco*	1 Pack/350g	291	83	8.1	11.8	0.4	7.0
Enjoy, Bird's Eye*	1 Pack/500g	620	124	7.7	16.2	3.2	0.6
Seafood, Finest, Tesco*	1 Pack/400g	600	150	6.3	18.9	5.5	2.0
Seafood, Marks & Spencer*	1 Pack/450g	518	115	6.4	13.7	3.8	3.2
Seafood, Sainsbury's*	1 Pack/400g	504	126	8.3	20.3	1.3	0.6
TTD, Sainsbury's*	1 Pack/375g	386	103	8.3	16.9	0.2	3.1
Vegetable, Waitrose*	1 Serving/174g	202	116	2.2	22.7	1.8	1.5
With Prawns, Chicken, Cod & Salmon, Sainsbury's*	1 Pack/750g	773	103	8.3	16.9	0.2	3.1
PAIN AU CHOCOLAT,							
Asda*	1 Serving/23g	106	462	8.0	49.0	26.0	0.0
Marks & Spencer*	1 Pain/60g	210	350	5.9	38.0	19.2	1.6
Mini, Asda*	1 Chocolat/22.8g	97	421	9.0	49.0	21.0	2.2
Sainsbury's*	1 Serving/58g	241	415	7.9	42.5	23.7	3.3
Tesco*	1 Pain/56g	235	420	7.0	46.5	22.9	1.4
Waitrose*	1 Serving/90g	380	422	8.1	34.9	27.8	1.1
PAIN AU RAISIN,							
Marks & Spencer*	1 Serving/74.1g	215	290	5.3	38.7	12.8	1.2
PAK CHOI,							
Tesco*	1 Serving/100g	11	11	1.0	1.4	0.2	1.2
PAKORA,							
Bhajia, Onion, Fried in Vegetable Oil	1oz/28g	76	271	9.8	26.2	14.7	5.5
Bhajia, Potato Carrot & Pea, Fried in Vegetable Oil	1oz/28g	100	357	10.9	28.8	22.6	6.1
Bhajia, Vegetable, Retail	1oz/28g	66	235	6.4	21.4	14.7	3.6
Potato & Spinach, Mini, Indian Snack Selection, Waitrose*	1 Pakora/21g	56	266	5.4	17.0	19.6	4.5
Sainsbury's*	1 Pakora/55g	166	302	7.3	26.8	18.3	1.1
Vegetable, Indian Starter Selection, Marks & Spencer*	1 Pakora/23g	61	265	6.3	19.6	18.1	2.9
Vegetable, Mini, Tesco*	1 Pakora/21g	62	297	5.8	18.0	22.4	3.2
Vegetable, Somerfield*	1 Pakora/15g	46	305	7.0	19.0	23.0	0.0
PANCAKE,							
& Sausage, McDonald's*	1 Portion/262g	686	262	5.4	33.8	10.8	0.5
& Syrup, McDonald's*	1 Pack/209.4g	531	254	2.4	41.9	7.6	0.6
Apple & Sultana, Marks & Spencer*	1 Serving/80g	160	200	2.2	30.2	7.9	1.2
Apple, GFY, Asda*	1 Pancake/85g	114	134	4.2	24.0	2.5	1.0
Aunt Bessie's*	1 Pancake/60g	90	150	6.1	24.6	3.1	1.1
Cherry, GFY, Adsa*	1 Serving/206g	206	100	1.9	18.9	1.8	1.8
Chinatown, Asda*	1 Pancake/10g	34	335	10.9	51.7	9.2	2.4
Chocolate, Marks & Spencer*	1 Pancake/80g	125	156	3.1	22.1	6.1	0.3
Healthy Living, Tesco*	1 Panceake/30g	74	246	7.3	49.9	1.9	1.5
Irish, Marks & Spencer*	1 Pancake/35g	85	243	7.1	53.8	1.4	1.3
Lemon, Marks & Spencer*	1 Pancake/38.3g	89	235	4.5	38.5	7.2	2.8
Maple & Raisin, Marks & Spencer*	1 Pancake/32.7g	89	269	6.5	49.7	5.4	2.2
Mini, Tesco*	1 Pancake/16g	44	277	6.7	50.0	5.6	1.4
Morello Cherry, Iceland*	1 Pancake/129g	204	158	3.1	29.8	2.9	2.9
Perfect, Kingmill	1 Pancake/26.9g	71	264	6.2	49.7	4.5	1.2
Plain, Sainsbury's*	1 Pancake/63g	144	228	8.4	37.3	5.0	1.5
Raisin & Lemon, Safeway*	1 Pancake/35.1g	93	265	5.8	44.5	7.1	1.6
Raisin & Lemon, Sainsbury's*	1 Pancake/35.0g	96	274	5.8	47.8	6.6	2.3
Raisin & Lemon, Tesco*	1 Pancake/36g	99	275	5.8	49.3	6.1	2.7

	Measure INFO/WEIGHT	per Measure KCAL	Nutrition Values per 100g / 100ml				
			KCAL	PROT	CARB	FAT	FIBRE
PANCAKE,							
Sainsburys*	2 Pancakes/92g	256	278	6.1	46.8	7.4	1.8
Savoury, Made With Skimmed Milk	1oz/28g	70	249	6.4	24.1	14.7	0.8
Savoury, Made With Whole Milk	1oz/28g	76	273	6.3	24.0	17.5	0.8
Scotch	1 Pancake/50g	146	292	5.8	43.6	11.7	1.4
Scotch, BGTY, Sainsbury's*	1 Pancake/30g	76	252	5.3	48.5	4.1	1.3
Scotch, Low Fat, Asda*	1 Pancake/32g	87	272	6.0	57.0	2.2	0.0
Scotch, Marks & Spencer*	1 Pancake/34g	95	280	6.5	54.5	4.0	1.6
Scotch, Sainsbury's	1 Pancake/30g	98	337	7.5	54.4	9.9	1.6
Scotch, SmartPrice, Asda*	1 Pancake/35g	107	305	7.0	49.0	9.0	1.4
Sultana & Syrup Scotch, Sainsbury's*	1 Pancake/35g	113	322	6.7	55.2	8.3	1.7
Sweet, Made With Skimmed Milk	1oz/28g	78	280	6.0	35.1	13.8	0.8
Sweet, Made With Whole Milk	1oz/28g	84	301	5.9	35.0	16.2	0.8
Sweet, Raspberry Ripple Sauce, Findus*	1 Pancake/38.1g	80	210	3.9	37.1	4.7	0.9
Syrup, Tesco*	2 Pancakes/60g	175	291	7.0	48.4	7.7	1.9
Toffee Apple, COU, Marks & Spencer	1oz/28g	36	130	2.9	31.5	1.7	1.7
Toffee Apple, Marks & Spencer*	1 Pancake/88.9g	160	180	2.2	32.6	4.7	1.5
Traditional, Tesco*	1 Pancake/62g	137	221	8.4	35.6	5.0	1.5
Vegetable Roll	1 Roll/85g	185	218	6.6	21.0	12.5	0.0
Warburton's*	1 Serving/28g	64	230	6.3	37.7	6.0	0.0
With Syrup, American Style, Large, Tesco*	2 Pancakes/76g	204	268	5.1	54.2	3.4	0.9
PANCAKE MIX,							
Fresh, Marks & Spencer*	1 Pancake/38.3g	89	235	7.5	22.4	13.1	0.5
Traditional, Asda*	1 Pack/256g	545	213	6.0	27.0	9.0	1.8
PANCETTA,							
Average	½ Pack/65g	212	327	17.0	0.1	28.7	0.1
PANINI,							
Chicken & Baby Spinach, Costa*	1 Serving/440g	832	189	9.8	32.5	2.5	0.0
Egg & Bacon, Starbucks*	1 Panini/210g	458	218	11.1	22.0	9.5	0.0
Grilled Chicken Salsa, Lightly Spiced, Starbucks*	1 Pack/237.7g	386	162	7.9	25.0	3.4	2.0
Grilled Chicken Salsa, With Creme Fraiche, Starbucks*	1 Panini/180g	385	214	10.4	32.9	4.5	0.0
Ham & Swiss Cheese, Coffee Republic*	1 Panini/223g	558	250	15.7	20.5	11.7	0.0
Mozarella, Tomato & Pesto, Costa*	1 Panini/209g	487	233	9.6	35.1	7.2	5.0
Mozzarella & Tomato, Coffee Republic*	1 Panini/255g	566	222	11.1	23.6	10.0	0.0
Mozzarella & Tomato, Marks & Spencer*	1 Serving/176g	484	275	11.3	21.3	16.2	2.1
Mozzarella With Sun Dried Tomatoes & Olives, Starbucks*	1 Serving/255g	903	354	6.6	21.6	26.8	0.0
Pastrami, Starbucks*	1 Serving/200g	630	315	15.0	28.5	18.0	0.0
Roasted Vegetables & Cheese, Starbucks*	1 Pack/215g	542	252	8.7	20.6	15.1	0.0
PAPAYA,							
Dried, Sweetened, Tesco*	4 Pieces/25g	59	235	0.4	56.3	0.9	2.9
Pieces, Nature's Harvest*	1 Serving/50g	178	355	0.2	85.4	0.0	2.6
Unripe, Raw	1oz/28g	8	27	0.9	5.5	0.1	1.5
PAPPARDELLE,							
Basil, Fresh, Sainsbury's*	1 Serving/240g	281	117	5.0	21.2	1.4	2.0
Buitoni*	1 Serving/65g	242	373	15.0	67.5	4.8	0.0
Chilli, Fresh, Sainsbury's*	1 Serving/250g	303	121	5.7	20.7	1.7	2.0
Cracked Black Pepper, Safeway*	1 Bowl/120g	173	144	5.7	26.5	1.8	1.9
Salmon, COU, Marks & Spencer*	1 Pack/358g	340	95	6.3	13.0	1.9	0.8
PAPRIKA,							
Average	1 Tsp/2g	6	289	14.8	34.9	13.0	0.0
PARATHA,							
Average	1oz/28g	90	322	8.0	43.2	14.3	4.0
PARCELS,							
Basil & Parmesan, Fresh, Sainsbury's*	1 Pack/250g	550	220	10.0	26.4	8.3	3.3

P

	Measure INFO/WEIGHT	per Measure KCAL	Nutrition Values per 100g / 100ml				
			KCAL	PROT	CARB	FAT	FIBRE
PARCELS,							
Beef Steak, Sainsbury's*	½ Pack/226g	488	216	12.2	6.6	15.6	1.0
Cheese & Ham, Sainsbury's*	1 Pack/250g	445	178	7.4	19.9	7.6	1.5
Chilli Beef, Tex Mex Feast, Asda*	1 Parcel/25g	68	270	9.0	27.0	14.0	2.1
Filo, Brie & Cranberry, Tesco*	1 Parcel/22g	82	373	9.5	29.3	24.2	1.5
Filo, Mushroom, Savoury, Creamy, Somerfield*	1oz/28g	86	308	5.0	24.0	21.0	0.0
Smoked Salmon, Sainsbury's*	1 Pack/115g	269	234	15.8	3.5	17.6	0.2
Thai, Pak Choi, Tied, Sainsbury's*	2 Parcels/77g	17	22	0.9	3.6	0.4	1.9
Tomato & Mozarella, Fresh, Sainsbury's*	1 Serving/175g	340	194	7.5	23.0	8.0	3.4
With Cheese & Sweet Pepper Sauce, Egg, Somerfield*	½ Pack/125g	349	279	12.4	30.7	11.8	2.2
PARSLEY,							
Dried	1 Tsp/1.3g	2	181	15.8	14.5	7.0	26.9
Fresh	1oz/28g	10	34	3.0	2.7	1.3	5.0
PARSNIP,							
Boiled, Average	1oz/28g	18	66	1.6	12.9	1.2	4.7
Raw, Average	1oz/28g	19	66	1.8	12.5	1.1	4.6
Roasting, From Supermarket, Average	1 Serving/50g	68	136	2.1	17.4	6.5	4.5
PARTRIDGE,							
Meat Only, Roasted	1oz/28g	59	212	36.7	0.0	7.2	0.0
PASANDA,							
Chicken, Marks & Spencer*	½ Pack/150g	240	160	11.3	3.8	10.9	1.3
PASSION FRUIT,							
Raw, Fresh	1 Fruit/15g	5	36	2.6	5.8	0.4	3.3
Weighed With Skin	1oz/28g	6	22	1.7	3.5	0.2	2.0
PASTA,							
& Chargrilled Mushrooms, Finest, Tesco*	1 Pot/200g	404	202	5.4	16.7	12.5	1.3
& Flame Grilled Chicken, Marks & Spencer*	1 Pack/180g	414	230	8.2	17.5	14.0	0.8
& Roasted Vegetables, Waitrose*	1oz/28g	43	154	2.4	14.2	9.7	1.0
Amori, Waitrose*	1 Serving/200g	754	377	10.8	82.8	0.3	0.0
Arrabbiata, Vegetable, Roast, Healthy Eating, Tesco*	1 Pack/450g	437	97	3.3	18.4	1.1	1.1
Bean & Tuna, BGTY, Sainsbury's*	1 Serving/200g	176	88	7.3	12.6	0.9	2.8
Blue Cheese, Bacon & Spinach, Marks & Spencer*	1 Pack/400g	640	160	6.5	13.8	8.5	0.7
Carbonara, With Cheese & Bacon, Slim Fast*	1 Serving/70g	240	343	22.7	48.9	6.3	5.7
Chargrilled Chicken Salsa, Healthy Eating, Tesco*	1 Pack/450g	396	88	7.3	11.7	1.3	1.0
Cheese & Broccoli, Pasta Pronto, Safeway*	1 Serving/208g	352	169	5.4	22.2	6.5	0.6
Cheese & Ham, Shapers, Boots*	1 Pack/76g	220	289	23.7	34.2	6.5	6.5
Cheesy Spirals, Curly Whirly, Asda*	1/3 Pack/200g	214	107	6.0	15.0	2.6	0.5
Chicken & Pineapple, Shapers, Boots*	1 Pack/221g	210	95	5.4	15.0	1.5	0.9
Chicken & Spicy Salsa Bowl, Marks & Spencer*	1 Pack/350g	368	105	6.2	17.2	1.4	1.4
Chicken & Spinach, Waitrose*	1 Pack/350g	483	138	7.0	14.0	6.0	0.8
Chicken, Tomato & Basil, Healthy Living, Tesco*	1 Pack/400g	264	66	7.9	7.5	0.5	1.1
Chicken, Tomato & Mascarpone, Heathly Living, Tesco*	1 Pack/450g	504	112	7.5	14.8	2.5	1.1
Chicken, Tomato, & Basil, Asda*	1 Pack/400g	474	119	6.5	17.5	2.5	1.2
Chicken, Tomoato & Basil, GFY, Asda*	1 Serving/400g	420	105	6.0	15.0	2.3	0.9
Egg, Fresh, Somerfield*	1 Serving/125g	148	118	4.4	22.1	1.4	1.4
Eliche, Buitoni*	1 Serving/80g	282	352	11.2	72.6	1.9	0.0
Elicoidali, Waitrose*	1 Serving/200g	682	341	11.5	70.7	1.3	3.7
Fagottini, Wild Mushroom, Sainsbury's*	½ Pack/125g	274	219	10.2	27.7	7.5	2.7
Florentina, With Broccoli & Spinach, Slim Fast*	1 Serving/71g	239	336	23.0	50.5	4.6	5.8
Garlic Mushroom Filled, Extra Special, Asda*	1 Serving/125g	224	179	8.0	21.0	7.0	2.5
Gemelli, Durum Wheat, Tesco*	1 Serving/100g	354	354	13.2	68.5	2.0	2.9
Honey & Mustard Chicken, Somerfield*	1 Serving/200g	280	140	8.5	18.0	3.7	1.0
In Herb Sauce, Sainsbury's*	1 Pack/420g	441	105	3.5	22.4	0.2	0.8
Lumache, Tesco*	1 Serving/100g	345	345	13.2	68.5	2.0	2.9

	Measure	per Measure	Nutrition Values per 100g / 100ml				
	INFO/WEIGHT	KCAL	KCAL	PROT	CARB	FAT	FIBRE
PASTA,							
Meat Feast, Italian, Sainsbury's*	1 Pack/450g	509	113	7.4	11.8	4.0	0.6
Parcels, Basil & Parmesan, Fresh, Sainsbury's*	1 Serving/162g	357	220	10.0	26.4	8.3	3.3
Pepper & Tomato, Asda*	1 Serving/250g	340	136	3.2	15.0	7.0	2.4
Pesto, Asda*	¼ Pack/50g	109	218	5.0	18.0	14.0	0.0
Pomodoro, With Tomato & Herbs, Slim Fast*	1 Serving/71g	235	331	21.5	51.5	4.3	6.0
Quick Cook, Tesco*	1 Serving/80g	276	345	13.2	68.5	2.0	2.9
Riccioli, Buitoni*	1 Serving/75g	264	352	11.2	72.6	1.9	0.0
Seafood, Retail	1oz/28g	31	110	8.9	7.6	4.8	0.4
Spirali, Dry, Average	1 Serving/50g	176	352	12.2	72.6	1.7	2.8
Stortelli, Microwaveable, Dolmio*	1 Serving/220g	299	136	5.3	26.3	1.0	0.0
Tomato & Basil Chicken, Boots*	1 Serving/320g	621	194	9.0	19.0	9.0	1.4
Tomato & Basil, Meal, Shapers, Boots*	1 Serving/76g	214	282	22.4	38.2	4.3	6.8
Tomato & Mascarpone, GFY, Asda*	½ Can/200g	128	64	2.1	9.0	2.2	0.0
Tomato & Pepper, Fireroast, Finest, Tesco*	1 Serving/200g	384	192	3.9	19.4	11.0	1.4
Tomato & Pepper, GFY, Asda*	1 Pack/400g	344	86	3.1	14.0	1.9	1.1
Trottole, Sainsbury's*	1 Serving/90g	321	357	12.3	73.1	1.7	2.5
Tuna & Sweetcorn, Sainsbury's*	1 Pasta/300g	327	109	6.7	14.7	2.6	1.4
Twists, With Tuna, Balanced Lifestyle, Aldi*	1 Can/400g	264	66	4.8	7.8	1.7	1.7
Twists, With Tuna, Italian, Weight Watchers*	1 Can/385g	239	62	4.3	8.2	1.4	0.6
Wheat Free, Delverde*	1 Serving/63g	229	366	0.5	86.9	1.9	1.2
Whole Wheat, Barilla*	1oz/28g	95	340	13.0	67.5	2.0	6.0
Whole Wheat, Tesco*	1 Serving/56g	180	322	12.5	62.5	2.5	10.0
PASTA 'N' SAUCE,							
Bolognese Flavour, Batchelors*	1 Pack/126g	459	364	14.0	71.9	2.3	5.2
Carbonara Flavour, Batchelors*	1 Pack/120g	463	386	14.3	71.0	5.0	3.1
Cheese, Leek & Ham, Batchelors*	1 Pack/126g	478	379	14.1	68.3	5.5	2.3
Chicken & Mushroom, Batchelors*	1 Pack/126g	455	361	12.4	73.5	2.0	2.7
Chicken & Roasted Garlic Flavour, Batchelors*	½ Pack/60g	223	372	12.6	73.8	2.9	3.4
Creamy Tikka Masala, Batchelors*	1 Pack/122.1g	426	349	12.7	69.5	2.2	4.4
Creamy Tomato & Mushroom, Batchelors*	1 Pack/125g	458	366	13.0	71.0	3.3	3.2
Macaroni Cheese, Batchelors*	1 Pack/108g	408	378	17.2	63.6	6.1	2.8
Mild Cheese & Brocolli, Batchelors*	1 Pack/123g	456	371	13.5	69.0	4.5	2.8
Mushroom & Wine, Batchelors*	1 Pack/132g	498	377	12.0	71.3	4.9	2.5
Tomato & Bacon Flavour, Batchelors*	1 Pack/134g	476	355	13.0	70.0	2.6	3.0
Tomato Onion & Herb Flavour, Batchelors*	1 Pack/135g	470	348	13.2	64.5	4.1	5.8
PASTA BAKE,							
Aberdeen Angus Meatball, Waitrose*	½ Pack/350.3g	501	143	5.2	12.5	8.0	0.9
Bacon & Leek, Sainsbury's*	1 Pack/400g	660	165	7.3	18.5	6.9	1.8
Bacon & Leek, Tesco*	1 Pack/450g	774	172	8.1	16.1	8.3	2.0
Bolognese, Asda*	1 Serving/375g	799	213	10.0	14.0	13.0	0.5
Bolognese, Italiano, Tesco*	1/3 Pack/284g	409	144	8.7	15.7	5.1	2.3
Cheese & Bacon, Asda*	1 Serving/60g	80	134	2.7	3.8	12.0	0.7
Cheese & Broccoli, Fish Bakes, Bird's Eye*	½ Pack/200g	264	132	12.5	6.1	6.4	0.3
Cheese & Tomato, Italiano, Tesco*	1 Bake/300g	354	118	3.9	16.1	4.2	1.0
Cheese & Tomato, Tesco*	1 Pack/400g	388	97	3.4	17.8	1.4	1.2
Chicken & Bacon, Tesco*	1oz/28g	46	166	6.9	19.3	6.8	0.5
Chicken & Broccoli, Pasta Presto, Findus*	1 Pack/321g	449	140	7.5	12.0	7.0	0.0
Chicken & Broccoli, Safeway*	1 Pack/340g	405	119	8.1	11.7	4.4	1.3
Chicken & Broccoli, Weight Watchers*	1 Bake/305g	290	95	6.0	14.2	1.5	0.9
Chicken & Courgette, Asda*	½ Pack/387.3g	519	134	6.0	14.0	6.0	0.6
Chicken & Mushroom, Waitrose*	1 Pack/400g	532	133	6.7	9.1	7.7	0.8
Chicken & Roast Mushroom, Healthy Living, Tesco*	1 Pack/390g	413	106	8.6	17.6	0.1	1.3
Chicken & Spinach, GFY, Asda*	1 Pack/335g	281	84	4.9	10.0	2.7	0.6

P

	Measure INFO/WEIGHT	per Measure KCAL	Nutrition Values per 100g / 100ml				
			KCAL	PROT	CARB	FAT	FIBRE
PASTA BAKE,							
Chicken & Spinach, Sainsbury's*	1 Pack/340g	286	84	4.9	10.0	2.7	0.6
Chicken & Sweetcorn, Eat Smart, Safeway*	1 Pack/400g	380	95	6.5	13.0	1.8	1.8
Chicken & Tomato, Tesco*	1 Pack/400g	504	126	7.0	14.7	4.3	1.9
Chicken & Vegetable, Healthy Eating, Tesco*	1 Pack/400g	344	86	6.0	11.8	1.7	0.5
Chicken, BGTY, Sainsbury's*	1 Pack/400g	376	94	8.2	12.4	1.3	0.9
Chicken, GFY, Asda*	1 Pack/400g	424	106	6.0	14.0	2.9	0.7
Chicken, Healthy Living, Tesco*	1 Pack/400g	376	94	8.2	12.4	1.3	0.9
Chicken, Italiano, Tesco*	1 Pack/400g	448	112	9.8	10.3	3.5	1.7
Chicken, Mushroom & Leek, Healthy Eating, Tesco*	1 Pack/450g	468	104	8.6	11.9	2.5	1.4
Chicken, Somerfield*	1 Pack/300g	351	117	8.0	8.0	6.0	0.0
Chicken, Tesco*	1 Serving/400g	344	86	6.0	11.8	1.7	0.5
Chilli & Cheese, American Style, Tesco*	1 Pack/425g	638	150	6.8	21.8	3.9	1.5
Creamy Ham & Mushroom, Homepride*	1 Pack/425g	489	115	1.8	2.8	10.7	0.0
Creamy Mushroom, Dolmio*	½ Jar/245g	267	109	1.1	5.5	9.2	0.0
Creamy Mushroon, Asda*	¼ Jar/118g	204	173	1.8	3.3	17.0	0.5
Creamy Tomato, Dolmio*	1 Serving/125g	141	113	2.3	8.4	7.2	0.0
Creamy Tomato, Safeway*	1 Serving/250g	350	140	1.6	7.9	11.1	3.8
Ham & Broccoli, Asda*	1 Pack/340g	309	91	3.4	10.0	4.1	0.5
Ham & Mushroom, Italiano, Tesco*	1 Pack/425g	646	152	5.8	21.3	4.8	1.7
Italian Bolognese, Asda*	1 Serving/300g	639	213	10.0	14.0	13.0	0.5
Italian Creamy Tomato & Bacon, Asda*	1 Serving/125g	131	105	2.0	3.9	9.0	0.6
Leek & Bacon, Morrisons*	1 Pack/400.7g	553	138	4.8	9.9	9.0	0.2
Meatball, Tesco*	1 Pack/400g	576	144	5.9	19.3	4.8	0.5
Mediterranean Style, Tesco*	1 Pack/450g	423	94	2.9	19.6	0.4	2.0
Penne Mozzarella, Tesco*	1 Pack/340g	408	120	4.7	19.7	2.5	0.6
Pepperoni & Ham, Tesco*	½ Pack/425g	502	118	8.9	19.3	0.6	2.5
Roast Vegetable, Eat Smart, Safeway*	1 Pack/330g	380	115	3.8	19.6	1.9	1.3
Spicy Tomato & Pepperoni, Asda*	1 Pack/440g	431	98	1.1	10.0	6.0	1.2
Spicy Tomato & Pepperoni, Homepride*	1 Jar/450g	324	72	1.5	8.1	3.7	0.0
Sun Dried Tomato, Dolmio*	1 Serving/100ml	83	83	2.2	10.5	3.0	0.0
Three Bean, Asda*	¼ Jar/124.7g	188	150	2.4	8.0	12.0	1.3
Tomato & Cheese, Dolmio*	1 Serving/125g	69	55	2.2	8.8	1.2	0.0
Tomato & Herb, Asda*	1 Jar/436g	715	164	1.8	10.0	13.0	1.2
Tomato & Mozzarella, Italiano, Tesco*	1 Pack/340g	418	123	5.5	17.9	3.3	1.0
Tuna & Sweetcorn, Asda*	1 Serving/250g	333	133	5.0	8.0	9.0	0.9
Tuna & Tomato, BGTY, Sainsbury's*	1 Pack/450g	554	123	8.7	12.6	4.2	0.4
Tuna, Co-Op*	1 Serving/340g	306	90	7.0	12.0	2.0	1.0
Tuna, Eat Smart, Safeway*	1 Serving/400g	340	85	5.6	11.6	1.7	1.2
Tuna, Good Intentions, Somerfield*	1 Serving/400g	400	100	5.9	14.5	2.1	1.2
Tuna, Healthy Living, Tesco*	1 Serving/400g	360	90	8.3	10.7	1.5	0.9
Tuna, Lean Cuisine*	1 Pack/345.5g	380	110	5.0	16.0	2.5	1.5
Tuna, Safeway*	1 Pack/400g	620	155	8.9	12.0	7.9	1.1
Tuna, Somerfield*	1 Bake/300g	411	137	9.0	10.0	7.0	0.0
Tuna, Tesco*	1oz/28g	36	129	6.9	11.7	6.1	0.9
Vegetable, Asda*	1 Serving/300g	231	77	2.4	9.0	3.5	0.8
Vegetable, Findus*	1 Pack/330.8g	430	130	6.0	13.0	6.5	0.4
Vegetable, Marks & Spencer*	1 Pack/350g	455	130	4.8	14.6	5.7	1.6
Vegetable, Ready Meals, Waitrose*	1oz/28g	44	157	5.9	14.4	8.6	1.0
Vegetable, Tesco*	1 Pack/380g	467	123	5.6	12.6	5.6	1.6
PASTA BREAK,							
Cheese & Ham, Asda*	1 Pot/63g	257	408	11.1	58.7	14.3	0.0
Chicken & Herb, Knorr*	1 Pot/347g	382	110	3.7	16.5	3.3	0.9
Chicken & Mushroom Flavour, Asda*	1 Pot/231g	254	110	2.7	19.0	2.6	0.0

	Measure INFO/WEIGHT	per Measure KCAL	Nutrition Values per 100g / 100ml KCAL	PROT	CARB	FAT	FIBRE
PASTA BREAK,							
Korma, Asda*	1 Pot/68g	74	109	2.3	19.0	2.6	0.0
Tomato & Herb, Asda*	1 Pot/66g	180	273	7.1	57.6	1.5	0.0
PASTA QUILLS,							
Co-Op*, Cooked	1 Serving/200g	302	151	5.7	30.2	0.9	1.8
Dry, Average	1 Serving/75g	257	342	12.0	72.3	1.2	2.0
Gluten Free, Salute*	1 Serving/75g	269	359	7.5	78.1	1.9	0.0
Whole Wheat, Morrisons*	1 Serving/100g	362	362	12.5	71.2	2.5	0.0
PASTA SALAD,							
BBQ Bean, Tesco*	1 Pack/850g	1139	134	3.6	18.5	5.1	1.8
Basil & Parmesan, Tesco*	1 Serving/50g	65	130	4.3	20.2	3.6	0.6
Basil Pesto, Caffe Nero*	1 Serving/200g	510	255	5.9	24.1	15.1	0.4
Big Penne, Honey & Mustard Chicken, Marks & Spencer*	1 Pack/380g	646	170	8.1	17.7	7.2	2.6
Caesar & Santa Tomatoes, Marks & Spencer*	1 Serving/220g	495	225	5.2	15.9	15.3	0.8
Carbonara, Waitrose*	1oz/28g	72	257	5.4	8.1	22.6	0.5
Chargrilled Chicken, Italian Style, Fresh, Asda*	1 Pack/200g	318	159	7.0	17.0	7.0	0.4
Chargrilled Chicken, Marks & Spencer*	1 Serving/190g	285	150	9.6	23.6	2.9	1.6
Chargrilled Vegetables & Tomato, Shapers, Boots*	1 Pack/175g	187	107	2.8	17.0	3.1	1.5
Cherry Tomato & Rocket, Healthy Eating, Tesco*	1 Salad/225g	223	99	3.2	15.8	2.5	1.0
Chicken & Smoked Bacon, Marks & Spencer*	1 Salad/380g	817	215	7.5	19.0	12.3	1.9
Chicken & Sweetcorn, Eat Smart, Safeway*	1 Serving/200g	230	115	7.5	16.3	1.8	1.0
Chicken Caesar, Shapers, Boots*	1 Pack/218g	288	132	6.7	18.0	3.8	1.8
Chicken Ceasar, Ginsters*	1 Pack/220g	504	229	7.5	13.6	16.1	0.0
Crayfish, Rocket & Lemon, Finest, Tesco*	1 Serving/250g	728	291	8.9	28.0	15.9	4.2
Crayfish, Shapers, Boots*	1 Pack/280.2g	269	96	6.0	13.0	2.3	0.7
Farfalle, Prawns Tomatoes & Cucumber, Sainsbury's*	1 Serving/260g	270	104	4.5	10.9	4.7	0.7
Feta Cheese, Sun Blush Tomatoes, Marks & Spencer*	1 Serving/190g	361	190	5.5	17.2	11.1	2.1
Fire Roasted Tomato, So Good, Somerfield*	½ Pack/100g	199	199	4.4	21.6	10.6	1.5
Garlic Mushroom, Salad Bar, Asda*	1oz/28g	59	212	2.5	12.5	16.9	0.8
Ham & Pineapple, Salad Bar, Asda*	1oz/28g	62	221	3.3	15.6	16.2	1.4
Honey & Mustard Chicken, Sainsbury's*	1 Pack/260g	447	172	7.3	16.9	8.3	1.4
Honey & Mustard Chicken, Shapers, Boots*	1 Pack/240g	286	119	7.0	18.0	2.0	1.8
Italian Style, Safeway*	1 Serving/225g	234	104	2.9	17.2	2.6	0.6
Italian Style, Sainsbury's*	1/3 Pot/84g	129	153	3.5	20.5	6.3	1.4
Lime & Coriander Chicken, Marks & Spencer*	1 Serving/190g	371	195	7.6	14.4	12.2	0.6
Mediterranean Chicken, Waitrose*	1 Serving/200g	314	157	7.0	16.9	6.8	2.1
Mediterranean Style, Layered, Waitrose*	1 Pot/275g	190	69	2.6	11.8	1.3	1.0
Mediterranean Tuna, Shapers, Boots*	1 Serving/239g	232	97	6.2	15.0	1.3	0.9
Mediterranean Vegetable & Bean, BGTY, Sainsbury's*	1 Serving/66g	53	80	3.2	12.5	1.9	2.8
Mediterranean, Good Intentions, Somerfield*	1 Pack/250g	290	116	2.8	19.8	2.8	1.1
Mediterranean, Tesco*	1oz/28g	24	87	2.1	9.6	4.5	1.4
Mozzarella & Plum Tomatoes, COU, Marks & Spencer*	1 Bowl/255g	204	80	4.6	11.5	1.6	1.7
Mozzarella & Sun Dried Tomato, Waitrose*	1 Serving/150g	312	208	5.8	18.8	12.2	1.3
Pepper, Healthy Eating, Tesco*	1 Salad/210g	139	66	2.4	13.3	0.4	1.0
Poached Salmon, Marks & Spencer*	1 Serving/200g	340	170	7.8	16.2	8.4	1.4
Prawn Cocktail, Improved, Shapers, Boots*	1 Pack/248.5g	256	103	5.0	15.0	2.7	1.6
Prawn, COU, Marks & Spencer*	1 Pack/274g	260	95	5.1	16.4	1.5	0.9
Prawn, Shapers, Boots*	1 Pot/250g	250	100	4.1	14.0	3.1	0.4
Roast Chicken & Pesto, Shaker, Sainsbury's*	1 Box/224g	253	113	8.2	12.3	3.4	0.0
Roasted Mushroom, Spinach & Tarragon, Tesco*	1 Pot/200g	216	108	4.3	17.2	2.4	0.8
Roasted Vegetable, Waitrose*	1 Pack/190g	270	142	6.8	18.2	4.6	1.1
Salmon, Marks & Spencer*	1 Serving/380g	817	215	6.8	12.7	15.2	0.7
Spicy Chicken, Geo Adams*	1 Pack/230g	580	252	5.1	14.9	19.1	2.9
Spicy Chilli Pesto, Sainsbury's*	¼ Pot/62.5g	171	272	3.8	20.1	19.6	1.6

	Measure INFO/WEIGHT	per Measure KCAL	Nutrition Values per 100g / 100ml				
			KCAL	PROT	CARB	FAT	FIBRE
PASTA SALAD,							
Spinach & Nuts, Marks & Spencer*	1oz/28g	64	229	6.9	18.2	15.0	1.6
Sun Dried Tomato Dressing, Sainsbury's*	1 Pack/320g	442	138	3.7	20.8	4.4	3.6
Sweetcorn & Pepper, GFY, Asda*	1 Serving/175g	68	39	1.9	7.0	0.4	0.0
Sweetcorn, Marks & Spencer*	1oz/28g	30	107	2.8	14.9	4.0	1.8
Tiger Prawn & Tomato, GFY, Asda*	1 Serving/200g	250	125	4.6	20.0	2.9	2.0
Tiger Prawn, Waitrose*	1 Serving/225g	545	242	5.4	16.7	17.1	0.4
Tomato & Basil Chicken, Marks & Spencer*	1 Serving/279g	446	160	7.0	14.8	7.9	1.8
Tomato & Basil With Red & Green Pepper, Sainsbury's*	¼ Pot/63g	89	141	3.2	16.4	6.9	3.8
Tomato & Basil, Marks & Spencer*	1 Pot/225g	484	215	2.9	15.0	15.9	1.2
Tomato & Basil, Sainsbury's*	1 Serving/250g	383	153	3.5	20.5	6.3	1.4
Tomato & Chargrilled Vegetable, Tesco*	1 Serving/200g	248	124	3.7	18.6	3.9	1.4
Tomato & Mozzarella, Leaf, Shapers, Boots*	1 Pack/185g	356	192	5.1	16.0	12.0	2.5
Tomato & Mozzarella, Waitrose*	1 Pack/225g	380	169	4.3	10.0	12.4	0.6
Tomato & Tuna, Snack, Sainsbury's*	1 Serving/200g	238	119	5.3	21.7	1.2	0.0
Tomato, Bacon & Cheese, Ginsters*	1 Pack/220g	381	173	7.4	15.6	9.0	0.0
Tuna & Spinach, COU, Marks & Spencer*	1 Pack/270g	257	95	6.8	14.3	1.8	3.8
Tuna & Sweetcorn, COU, Marks & Spencer*	1 Pack/200g	210	105	7.1	18.3	0.9	1.2
Tuna & Sweetcorn, Healthy Eating, Tesco*	1 Pot/200g	230	115	5.7	17.0	2.7	1.3
Tuna Nicoise, Waitrose*	1 Pot/190g	306	161	5.1	14.9	9.0	1.1
Tuna, Eat Smart, Safeway*	1 Pack/220g	220	100	8.0	12.2	1.6	0.5
Tuna, Tesco*	1 Pot/300g	399	133	6.2	10.5	7.3	0.0
Vegetable, Healthy Selection, Somerfield*	1 Pot/200g	180	90	2.8	19.6	0.0	0.7
Vegetable, Somerfield*	1 Salad/200g	288	144	3.0	20.0	6.0	0.0
Wild Mushroom, TTD, Sainsbury's*	1 Serving/259g	464	179	4.6	16.6	10.5	1.5
With Avocado & Cherry Tomatoes, Marks & Spencer*	1 Pack/185g	259	140	2.9	13.9	8.0	1.2
With Italian Style Chicken, Weight Watchers*	1 Pack/185g	237	128	6.7	22.9	1.1	0.7
With Spinach & Pine Nuts, Marks & Spencer*	1 Pack/205g	440	215	7.9	26.6	8.4	2.2
PASTA SAUCE,							
Amatrician, Asda*	1 Jar/320g	496	155	4.4	5.0	13.0	1.0
Amatriciana, Fresh, Safeway*	½ Pot/175g	89	51	2.5	5.6	2.1	1.2
Amatriciana, Fresh, Sainsbury's*	½ Pot/153g	69	45	3.5	3.5	1.9	1.3
Amatriciana, Italiano, Tesco*	½ Pot/175g	124	71	4.1	5.3	3.8	0.9
Arrabbiata, BGTY, Sainsbury's*	1 Jar/150g	107	71	1.3	7.6	3.9	0.7
Arrabbiata, Fresh, Safeway*	½ Pot/176g	58	33	1.2	5.1	0.9	1.0
Arrabbiata, Fresh, Tesco*	1 Serving/110ml	29	26	0.7	3.7	0.9	0.9
Arrabbiata, GFY, Asda*	1 Serving/350g	133	38	1.1	6.0	1.1	0.0
Arrabbiata, Italian, Waitrose*	1 Jar/320g	102	32	1.6	5.6	0.3	0.0
Arrabbiata, Italiano, Tesco*	½ Pot/175g	65	37	1.7	6.1	0.6	1.0
Arrabbiata, Marks & Spencer*	1 Jar/320g	240	75	1.2	6.2	5.3	0.8
Arrabbiata, Sainsbury's*	1oz/28g	13	45	1.4	3.3	2.9	1.6
Aubergine & Pepper, Sacla*	½ Pot/95g	238	250	1.8	5.6	24.5	0.0
Aubergine, Marks & Spencer*	1oz/28g	41	148	1.6	8.4	13.4	3.0
Basil & Oregano For Bolognese, Ragu*	1 Serving/200g	76	38	2.0	7.6	0.0	0.8
Beef Bolognese, Fresh, Asda*	¼ Pot/82g	78	95	4.3	3.4	7.3	0.4
Bolognese With Beef, Tesco*	½ Can/213g	179	84	4.9	5.5	4.7	0.0
Bolognese, Dolmio*	¼ Jar/175g	91	52	1.8	10.3	0.0	0.0
Bolognese, Finest, Tesco*	1 Serving/175g	170	97	7.0	3.8	6.1	0.5
Bolognese, Fresh, Sainsbury's*	½ Pot/150g	120	80	6.0	4.7	4.1	1.2
Bolognese, Marks & Spencer*	1 Jar/100g	115	115	7.0	10.8	4.9	1.2
Bolognese, Original, Asda*	1 Serving/157.5g	73	46	1.4	7.0	1.4	0.8
Bolognese, Original, Light, Dolmio*	1 Serving/125g	48	38	1.6	7.8	0.1	0.0
Bolognese, Original, Sainsbury's*	¼ Jar/136g	90	66	1.9	9.9	2.1	1.3
Bolognese, Somerfield*	1 Pack/300g	243	81	3.0	8.0	4.0	0.0

P

PASTA SAUCE,

	Measure INFO/WEIGHT	per Measure KCAL	KCAL	PROT	CARB	FAT	FIBRE
			Nutrition Values per 100g / 100ml				
Bolognese, Tesco*	1 Serving/175g	100	57	4.2	4.0	2.6	0.8
Bolognese, Traditional, Ragu	1 Jar/515g	345	67	2.0	9.9	2.1	1.2
Cacciatore, Fresh, Sainsbury's*	½ Pot/150g	152	101	5.4	8.1	5.9	1.5
Carbonara, Asda*	½ Pot/175g	359	205	7.0	6.0	17.0	0.1
Carbonara, BGTY, Sainsbury's*	½ Pack/165g	225	136	6.3	23.4	1.9	1.0
Carbonara, Dolmio*	1 Serving/150g	224	149	3.4	4.2	13.2	0.0
Carbonara, Italiano, Tesco*	1 Pot/350g	613	175	5.8	6.1	14.1	0.0
Carbonara, With Cheese & Bacon, BGTY, Sainsbury's*	1 Serving/150g	138	92	5.5	10.1	3.3	1.5
Chargrilled Vegetable With Extra Virgin Olive Oil, Bertolli*	½ Jar/250g	150	60	2.1	8.7	1.9	2.4
Cheery Tomato & Roasted Pepper, Asda*	1 Jar/171.7g	91	53	1.5	5.0	3.0	2.4
Cheese & Bacon Bake, Homepride*	1oz/28g	27	95	2.0	2.5	8.6	0.0
Cheese & Bacon, Asda*	1 Pack/116g	476	410	13.0	67.0	10.0	2.3
Cheese & Tuna, Safeway*	1 Serving/175g	175	100	6.9	4.8	5.7	0.6
Cheese, Fresh, Perfectly Balanced, Waitrose*	½ Pot/175g	144	82	6.1	7.9	2.9	0.5
Cherry Tomato & Basil, Sacla*	1 Serving/96g	90	94	1.2	5.3	7.4	0.0
Chilli With Jalapeno Peppers, Seeds Of Change*	1 Jar/350g	322	92	3.6	16.0	1.5	2.2
Chunky Vegetable, Asda*	1 Serving/250g	123	49	1.4	7.0	1.7	1.2
Cream & Mushroom, Marks & Spencer*	1oz/28g	45	160	1.5	6.6	14.3	0.6
Creamy Mushroom, Chicken Tonight*	¼ Jar/125g	110	88	0.7	2.8	8.2	0.4
Creamy Mushroom, Dolmio*	1 Pack/150g	167	111	1.3	3.7	10.0	0.0
Creamy Mustard, Colman's*	1 Pack/29g	108	374	11.0	46.0	16.0	0.0
Creamy Pepper & Mushroom, Colman's*	1 Pack/25g	82	327	8.1	56.0	9.1	0.0
Creamy Tomato & Bacon Bake, Homepride*	1 Serving/110g	99	90	1.9	6.5	6.3	0.0
Creamy Tomato & Basil, BGTY, Sainsbury's*	½ Jar/250g	173	69	1.7	7.6	3.6	1.0
Creamy Tomato & Herb Bake, Homepride*	1 Jar/455g	464	102	2.0	7.5	7.1	0.0
Extra Mushrooms Bolognese, Dolmio*	1 Jar/500g	235	47	1.6	9.3	0.1	0.0
Extra Spicy Bolognese, Dolmio*	1 Serving/250g	133	53	1.7	9.2	1.1	0.0
Fiorentina, Fresh, Sainsbury's*	½ Pot/157g	165	105	3.2	4.3	8.4	0.9
Four Cheese, BGTY, Sainsbury's*	1 Serving/150g	104	69	2.9	5.5	4.0	0.1
Four Cheese, Fresh, Asda*	½ Pot/162g	309	191	5.4	2.2	17.8	0.5
Four Cheese, GFY, Asda*	½ Pot/175g	144	82	4.0	6.3	4.6	0.5
Four Cheese, Sainsbury's*	1 Serving/150g	296	197	6.6	4.5	17.0	0.8
Garlic, Perfectly Balanced, Waitrose*	1 Jar/440g	330	75	2.3	12.7	1.7	2.3
Ham & Mushroom, Creamy, Stir & Serve, Homepride*	1 Serving/92g	124	135	1.8	5.5	11.7	0.0
Hot & Spicy, Morrisons*	1 Serving/130g	82	63	1.3	9.3	2.4	1.0
Hot Mixed Peppers Bolognese, Sainsbury's*	1oz/28g	18	66	2.0	9.7	2.1	1.5
Hot Pepper & Mozzarella, Stir Through, Sacla*	½ Jar/95g	229	241	4.7	7.2	21.5	0.0
Italian Cheese, Finest, Tesco*	½ Pot/175g	172	98	4.8	8.4	5.1	0.0
Italian Mushroom, Sainsbury's*	1 Serving/85g	56	66	2.0	9.8	2.1	1.7
Italian Tomato & Herb, For Pasta, Sainsbury's*	½ Jar/146g	102	70	2.0	11.1	2.0	1.4
Italian Tomato & Smoked Bacon, Stir-In, Safeway*	½ Jar/75g	152	203	2.9	7.3	18.0	1.2
Italian, Tomato, Mushroom & Pancetta, Sainsbury's*	½ Jar/75g	125	167	2.2	6.1	14.9	1.3
Layered Tomato & Mozarella, Finest, Tesco*	1 Jar/160g	232	145	6.6	6.9	10.1	0.7
Leek & Bacon, Safeway*	½ Pot/170.6g	145	85	4.0	5.7	4.9	0.5
Mascarpone, BGTY, Sainsbury's*	1 Serving/120g	379	316	8.6	2.8	30.0	0.0
Mediterrainean Vegetable Pasta, Tesco*	1 Serving/166g	95	57	1.4	9.0	1.7	1.2
Mediterranean Sizzling, Homepride*	1 Serving/96g	83	86	0.9	6.3	6.4	0.0
Mediterranean Tomato, Asda*	1 Jar/500g	285	57	1.5	10.0	1.2	0.0
Mediterranean Vegetable, Safeway*	1oz/28g	17	60	1.6	10.5	0.9	0.6
Mediterranean, BGTY, Sainsbury's*	1oz/28g	23	82	1.9	9.0	4.3	1.4
Mediterranean, Fresh, Waitrose*	1 Pot/350g	214	61	1.4	5.0	3.9	2.4
Mushroom & Garlic, 98% Fat Free, Homepride*	1 Jar/450g	230	51	1.1	8.9	1.4	0.5
Mushroom & Garlic, Deliciously Good, Homepride*	1/3 Jar/147g	109	74	0.9	6.9	4.8	0.3

PASTA SAUCE,

INFO/WEIGHT	Measure	per Measure KCAL	KCAL	PROT	CARB	FAT	FIBRE
Mushroom & Marsala Wine, Sacla*	½ Pot/85g	165	194	2.2	3.9	18.8	0.0
Mushroom & Mascarpone, Healthy Eating, Tesco*	½ Jar/175g	86	49	2.1	5.3	2.2	0.3
Mushroom & White Wine, Knorr*	1oz/28g	27	98	1.0	4.0	8.0	0.0
Mushroom, BGTY, Sainsbury's*	1 Pack/200g	526	263	12.0	45.9	3.5	2.8
Mushroom, Co-Op*	¼ Jar/125g	75	60	2.0	9.0	2.0	1.0
Mushroom, Colman's*	1 Pack/27g	97	358	14.0	53.0	9.7	0.0
Mushroom, Fresh, Waitrose*	1 Serving/175g	142	81	1.6	5.7	5.7	0.5
Mushroom, GFY, Asda*	1 Serving/175g	112	64	2.7	7.0	2.8	0.0
Mushroom, Marks & Spencer*	1oz/28g	61	218	4.9	5.0	21.3	3.4
Mushroom, Microwaveable, Dolmio*	1 Serving/150g	161	107	1.4	3.8	9.6	0.0
Mushroom, Perfectly Balanced, Waitrose*	1 Jar/440g	330	75	2.6	11.8	1.9	2.2
Napoletana, BGTY, Sainsbury's*	½ Pot/151g	71	47	1.2	5.0	2.5	1.3
Napoletana, Fresh, Asda*	1 Pot/330g	135	41	2.2	6.0	1.3	1.4
Napoletana, Fresh, Safeway*	½ Pot/175g	67	38	1.5	6.1	0.8	1.2
Napoletana, Fresh, Sainsbury's*	1oz/28g	25	91	1.9	7.9	5.8	1.1
Napoletana, GFY, Asda*	1 Serving/175g	58	33	1.0	5.0	1.0	0.0
Napoletana, Sainsbury's*	½ Pot/150g	126	84	1.9	6.6	5.6	0.9
Olive & Tomato, Sacla*	1 Serving/95g	87	92	1.3	3.6	8.0	0.0
Onion & Garlic Bolognese, Extra, Dolmio*	1 Serving/125g	66	53	1.7	9.0	1.0	0.0
Onion & Garlic For Bolognese, Ragu*	1 Serving/125g	80	64	2.2	11.4	1.1	1.2
Onion & Garlic, Tesco*	1 Serving/225g	83	37	1.2	7.6	0.3	0.8
Original, Better For You, Morrisons*	1/3 Jar/200g	100	50	1.6	10.6	0.1	1.2
Original, For Bolognese, Ragu*	1 Jar/525g	268	51	1.7	10.7	0.1	1.0
Original, Healthy Eating, Tesco*	1 Jar/455g	155	34	1.2	6.5	0.1	0.8
Original, With Tomato & Onions, BFY, Morrisons*	1 Serving/125g	51	41	1.4	6.3	1.1	1.2
Pepper & Tomato, Marks & Spencer*	1 Jar/320g	224	70	1.6	6.1	4.2	0.9
Porcini Mushroom & Pepperoni, Asda*	½ Jar/140g	158	113	3.8	11.0	6.0	0.0
Porcini Mushroom Stir In, BGTY, Sainsbury's*	½ Jar/75g	57	76	3.8	5.7	4.2	1.9
Primavera, Fresh, Morrisons*	½ Pot/175g	152	87	2.4	6.1	5.9	0.0
Puttanesca, Marks & Spencer*	1 Jar/320g	256	80	1.5	6.2	5.5	1.9
Puttanesca, Safeway*	1 Serving/170g	179	105	1.5	5.9	8.2	0.0
Puttanesca, Sainsbury's*	1 Serving/110g	132	120	2.0	8.1	8.8	0.0
Roasted Red Pepper & Tomato, Finest, Tesco*	1 Serving/145g	117	81	1.2	6.8	5.4	2.2
Roasted Vegetable, Microwaveable, Dolmio*	½ Pack/190g	103	54	1.4	7.6	2.0	0.0
Roasted Vegetable, Sainsbury's*	½ Pot/151g	103	68	1.6	6.7	3.9	0.4
Roasted Vegetables & Tuna, BGTY, Sainsbury's*	½ Pot/150g	74	49	3.5	4.5	1.9	3.1
Romano, Aldi*	1 Serving/235g	141	60	1.7	8.8	2.0	1.1
Salsina With Onions & Garlic, Valfrutta*	1 Serving/150g	36	24	1.6	4.5	0.0	1.4
Sliced Mushroom, Tesco*	1 Jar/460g	161	35	1.3	7.0	0.2	0.8
Smoky Bacon, Loyd Grossman*	1oz/28g	27	98	3.1	5.4	7.2	0.7
Spicy Italian Chilli, Microwaveable, Dolmio*	1 Sachet/170g	92	54	1.4	7.6	2.0	0.0
Spicy Pepper & Tomato, Sacla*	½ Jar/95g	132	139	1.4	6.8	11.8	0.0
Spicy Red Pepper & Vegetable, Asda*	1 Pot/350g	182	52	1.2	5.0	3.0	1.1
Spicy Roasted Garlic, Seeds Of Change*	1 Serving/195g	123	63	1.5	9.7	2.0	1.2
Spicy With Peppers, Tesco*	1 Jar/455g	177	39	1.2	7.9	0.3	1.1
Spinach & Ricotta, BGTY, Sainsbury's*	1 Serving/150g	74	49	2.7	3.4	2.7	2.2
Spinach & Ricotta, Stir Through, Sacla*	½ Jar/95g	196	206	3.7	3.7	19.6	0.0
Sun Dried Tomato & Basil, Free From, Sainsbury's*	½ Jar/172.2g	124	72	2.9	8.7	2.8	1.5
Sun Dried Tomato & Garlic, Sacla*	1 Serving/95g	177	186	3.0	10.3	14.7	0.0
Sun Dried Tomato & Garlic, The Best, Safeway*	1 Jar/340g	496	146	2.2	6.2	12.5	0.0
Sun Dried Tomato & Olive Oil, Loyd Grossman*	1oz/28g	52	187	0.8	10.3	15.8	0.3
Sun Dried Tomato, Asda*	½ Jar/158.7g	165	104	1.9	6.0	8.0	1.5
Sun Dried Tomato, Garlic & Basil, Finest, Tesco*	1 Serving/72.5g	123	168	2.0	6.8	14.8	2.9

PASTA SAUCE,

	Measure INFO/WEIGHT	per Measure KCAL	KCAL	PROT	CARB	FAT	FIBRE
Sun Dried Tomato, Marks & Spencer*	1oz/28g	102	363	3.6	12.4	34.9	5.7
Sun Dried Tomato, Stir In, Light, Dolmio*	½ Tub/75g	62	83	1.7	9.8	4.7	0.0
Sun Ripened Tomato & Basil, Dolmio*	1 Serving/150g	117	78	1.3	7.9	4.6	0.0
Sun Ripened Tomato & Basil, Microwaveable, Dolmio*	½ Pack/190g	106	56	1.4	7.9	2.1	0.0
Sundried Tomato & Garlic, Marks & Spencer*	½ Jar/95g	147	155	2.9	4.4	13.7	0.8
Sweet Pepper, Dolmio*	1 Serving/150g	239	159	1.6	8.8	13.4	0.0
Sweet Red Pepper, Loyd Grossman*	1oz/28g	24	87	1.7	7.3	5.6	1.2
Three Cheeses, Co-Op*	1 Pack/300g	405	135	6.0	6.0	9.0	0.1
Tomato & Aubergine, TTD, Sainsbury's*	1 Serving/150g	107	71	2.1	7.7	3.5	2.0
Tomato & Basil, Bertolli*	1 Serving/250g	118	47	1.5	7.9	1.1	1.6
Tomato & Basil, Dolmio*	1 Serving/170g	95	56	1.4	7.9	2.1	0.0
Tomato & Chargrilled Vegetable, Loyd Grossman*	1 Serving/150g	134	89	1.8	7.9	5.6	0.9
Tomato & Chilli, Pour Over, Marks & Spencer*	½ Jar/165g	124	75	1.2	6.2	5.3	0.8
Tomato & Chunky Mushroom, Dolmio*	1 Pack/475g	323	68	1.2	7.6	3.7	0.0
Tomato & Herb, Marks & Spencer*	1 Jar/500g	400	80	2.6	10.1	3.1	1.7
Tomato & Herb, Organic, Marks & Spencer*	1 Jar/320g	176	55	1.1	6.8	2.6	1.8
Tomato & Herb, Organic, Sainsbury's*	1 Serving/75g	38	51	1.2	6.6	2.0	0.5
Tomato & Herb, Perfectly Balanced, Waitrose*	½ Pot/175g	86	49	1.2	5.3	2.6	0.9
Tomato & Marscapone, Fresh, Waitrose*	1 Serving/175ml	184	105	1.9	5.5	8.4	1.1
Tomato & Mascapone, Sainsbury's*	½ Pot/150g	137	91	2.1	5.9	6.6	1.2
Tomato & Mascarpone, Asda*	1 Serving/175g	210	120	1.6	6.0	10.0	0.0
Tomato & Mascarpone, BGTY, Sainsbury's*	½ Pot/150g	75	50	2.0	3.6	3.0	3.6
Tomato & Mascarpone, Fresh, Sainsbury's*	1 Serving/150g	177	118	2.2	4.2	10.3	1.1
Tomato & Mascarpone, Marks & Spencer*	½ Pack/175g	175	100	3.3	6.6	6.2	0.8
Tomato & Mascarpone, Sacla*	½ Jar/95g	161	169	2.2	6.2	15.0	0.8
Tomato & Mascarpone, Safeway*	1 Serving/175g	271	155	2.1	7.6	12.9	1.1
Tomato & Mascarpone, Tesco*	1 Serving/175g	194	111	2.8	5.4	8.7	0.6
Tomato & Mushroom, Organic, Sainsbury's*	1 Serving/150g	87	58	1.6	7.1	2.6	1.5
Tomato & Olives, La Doria*	1 Jar/90g	76	84	1.2	5.0	6.6	0.0
Tomato & Parmesan, Seeds Of Change*	1 Serving/150g	101	67	2.5	7.8	2.9	1.1
Tomato & Roasted Garlic, Loyd Grossman*	½ Jar/175g	161	92	2.0	8.8	5.5	0.8
Tomato & Smokey Bacon, Dolmio*	1 Pot/150g	240	160	5.5	5.8	13.1	0.0
Tomato & Spicy Sausages, Marks & Spencer*	1 Jar/330g	215	65	4.0	5.5	3.0	0.8
Tomato & Tuna, Loyd Grossman*	½ Jar/175g	154	88	4.4	7.5	4.4	0.8
Tomato & Wild Mushroom, Waitrose*	1 Serving/175g	65	37	1.7	6.0	0.7	0.9
Tomato Red Wine Shallots, Bertolli*	½ Jar/250g	113	45	1.7	7.2	1.7	1.5
Tomato With Herbs & Garlic, Italian, Safeway*	1 Serving/120g	73	61	1.9	8.7	2.1	1.3
Tomato With Herbs Buon Appetito, Princes*	1 Jar/475g	214	45	0.7	9.6	0.4	0.0
Tomato With Mushrooms, Italian, Safeway*	½ Jar/235g	146	62	2.0	8.8	2.1	1.9
Tomato With Onions & Garlic, Italian, Safeway*	1 Serving/50g	35	69	2.3	10.2	2.1	1.8
Tomato, Bacon & Mushroom, Asda*	½ Pot/50g	33	66	2.5	6.0	3.6	0.0
Tomato, Basil & Parmesan Stir In, BGTY, Sainsbury's*	1 Serving/75g	69	92	2.9	7.8	5.5	1.0
Tomato, Chilli & Onion, Bertolli*	1 Serving/100g	49	49	1.8	6.7	1.7	1.8
Tomato, Kalamata Olive & Pine Nut, The Best, Safeway*	½ Pot/175g	158	90	1.7	5.0	6.7	1.9
Tomato, Organic, Evernat*	1oz/28g	18	64	2.8	10.2	1.3	0.0
Tomato, Pepper & Herb, Somerfield*	1 Serving/186g	233	125	3.0	17.4	4.8	0.8
Tomato, Roasted Garlic & Mushroom, Bertolli*	1 Jar/500g	255	51	1.9	6.4	2.0	1.5
Tomato, Romano & Garlic, Bertolli*	¼ Jar/181g	127	70	2.9	7.6	3.0	1.7
Traditional, Healthy Choice, Safeway*	1 Jar/475g	257	54	1.8	8.2	1.6	1.3
Traditional, Somerfield*	1 Jar/525g	263	50	2.0	8.0	1.0	0.0
Vine Ripened Tomato & Black Olive, Bertolli*	½ Jar/92.5g	146	157	2.3	7.3	13.3	0.0
Whole Cherry Tomato & Red Chilli, Sacla*	1 Serving/96g	85	89	1.5	6.2	6.5	0.1
Whole Cherry Tomato & Roasted Pepper, Sacla*	½ Jar/145g	93	64	1.5	5.2	4.1	0.0

P

	Measure INFO/WEIGHT	per Measure KCAL	Nutrition Values per 100g / 100ml				
			KCAL	PROT	CARB	FAT	FIBRE
PASTA SHAPES,							
Economy, Sainsbury's*	1oz/28g	97	346	12.0	72.2	1.0	2.3
In A Cheese & Broccoli Sauce, Tesco*	1 Serving/84g	317	377	13.1	66.2	6.6	4.1
In Rich Chicken, Garilc & Wine Sauce, Tesco*	1 Pack/110g	393	357	14.0	66.1	4.1	4.2
Postman Pat, HP*	1 Can/410g	279	68	1.8	14.3	0.4	0.7
Safeway*	1 Serving/175g	261	149	5.7	30.1	0.7	1.2
Scooby Doo, HP*	1 Can/410g	279	68	1.8	14.3	0.4	0.7
Teletubbies, Heinz*	1 Can/400g	244	61	2.0	12.3	0.4	0.6
Tesco*, Cooked	1 Serving/260g	356	137	5.1	26.3	0.8	1.1
PASTA SHELLS,							
Dry, Average	1 Serving/75g	265	353	11.1	71.8	2.0	2.0
Egg, Fresh, Average	1 Serving/125g	344	275	11.5	49.8	2.9	3.5
In Bolognese Sauce, Weight Watchers*	1 Pack/395g	280	71	5.2	9.6	1.3	0.7
PASTA SNACK,							
Chicken & Smoked Bacon, Sainsbury's*	1 Pack/190g	490	258	7.2	14.1	19.2	0.0
Chicken, Morrisons*	1 Pack/250g	285	114	3.3	19.3	2.7	0.0
Ham & Mushroom, Tesco*	1 Pack/300g	618	206	4.2	15.0	14.3	1.1
Tomato & Basil, Healthy Living, Tesco*	1 Pack/200g	116	58	1.8	10.4	1.0	1.0
Tomato & Herb, Morrisons*	1 Pot/247g	247	100	3.1	19.5	1.1	0.0
PASTA SPIRALS,							
Co-Op*	1 Serving/100g	350	350	12.0	73.0	1.0	3.0
Glutenfree, Glutano*	1oz/28g	100	357	4.0	83.0	1.0	0.0
Spicy, Tesco*	1oz/28g	20	72	4.5	11.6	0.8	0.8
PASTA TWIRLS,							
Asda*	1 Serving/50g	173	346	12.0	71.0	1.5	3.0
Tri-Colour, Sainsbury's*	1 Serving/75g	268	357	12.3	73.1	1.7	2.5
PASTA TWISTS,							
Dry, Average	1oz/28g	99	354	12.3	71.8	1.5	2.2
Wheat & Gluten Free, Glutafin*	1 Serving/75g	263	350	8.0	75.0	2.0	0.1
PASTA WITH,							
Meatballs, Puglian Style, Marks & Spencer*	½ Pack/500g	600	120	5.5	12.5	5.3	1.2
Meatballs, Sainsbury's*	1 Can/300g	339	113	6.6	10.6	4.9	1.6
Prawns & Tomatoes, COU, Marks & Spencer*	1 Serving/270g	243	90	5.4	13.9	1.3	1.3
Roasted Vegetables & Goats Cheese, Marks & Spencer*	1 Pack/360g	576	160	5.3	19.0	6.8	1.2
Tuna & Roasted Peppers, Marks & Spencer*	1 Serving/220g	308	140	9.1	17.7	3.9	0.9
PASTE,							
BBQ Bean, Princes*	1 Serving/33g	35	106	5.7	19.8	0.4	0.0
BBQ Chicken, Princes*	1oz/28g	69	246	14.3	9.5	16.8	0.0
Bacon & Tomato, Tesco*	1 Serving/20g	46	232	14.0	3.4	18.0	0.1
Beef, Princes*	1 Serving/18g	40	220	14.4	5.2	15.8	0.0
Beef, Sainsbury's*	1 Jar/75g	142	189	16.0	1.5	13.2	1.4
Chicken & Ham, Princes*	1 Jar/100g	233	233	13.6	2.8	18.6	0.0
Chicken & Ham, Sainsbury's*	Thin Spread/9g	14	158	16.0	1.1	10.0	1.1
Chicken & Mushroom, Princes*	1 Serving/50g	94	187	17.1	5.0	11.0	0.0
Chicken & Stuffing, Princes*	1 Jar/100g	229	229	15.7	3.3	17.0	0.0
Chicken, Princes*	Thin Spread/9g	22	240	12.6	5.6	18.5	0.0
Chicken, Tesco*	1 Serving/12g	30	248	14.8	2.3	20.0	0.1
Chicken, Value, Tesco*	Thin Spread/9g	18	196	15.1	1.8	14.3	0.1
Crab, Princes*	1 Pot/35g	36	104	13.4	4.8	3.5	0.0
Salmon & Shrimp, Tesco*	1 Jar/75g	83	111	15.1	5.0	3.4	0.1
Salmon, Princes*	1 Serving/30g	59	195	13.5	6.5	12.8	0.0
Sardine & Tomato, Asda*	Thin Spread/9g	11	123	14.0	3.3	6.0	0.0
Sardine & Tomato, Princes*	1 Jar/75g	110	146	15.4	5.0	7.2	0.0
Sardine & Tomato, Sainsbury's*	1 Mini Pot/35g	60	170	16.9	1.2	10.8	1.3

	Measure INFO/WEIGHT	per Measure KCAL	Nutrition Values per 100g / 100ml				
			KCAL	PROT	CARB	FAT	FIBRE
PASTE,							
Sardine & Tomato, Tesco*	1 Jar/75g	98	130	14.6	4.8	5.8	0.1
Smokey Bacon, Princes*	1 Serving/30g	60	199	17.3	5.4	12.0	0.0
Sun Dried Tomato, Average	1 Heaped Tsp/10g	39	385	3.2	13.9	35.2	0.0
Tuna & Mayonnaise, Princes*	1 Pot/75g	158	210	16.6	1.3	15.4	0.0
Tuna & Mayonnaise, Sainsbury's*	1 Tbsp/17g	41	242	19.2	0.6	18.1	1.6
Tuna & Mayonnaise, Tesco*	1 Serving/15g	31	209	14.9	2.1	15.7	0.1
Vegetable, Sainsbury's*	1 Serving/17g	26	154	7.4	5.9	11.2	3.4
PASTILLES,							
Fruit, Average	1 Tube/33g	108	327	2.8	84.2	0.0	0.0
Fruit, Rowntree's*	1 Tube/53g	186	351	4.4	83.7	0.0	0.0
Wine, Maynards*	1 Pack/52g	161	310	3.9	72.1	0.0	0.0
PASTRAMI,							
Beef, Average	1 Serving/40g	51	128	23.1	1.1	3.6	0.2
Turkey, Average	½ Packet/35g	38	107	21.8	1.7	1.5	0.5
PASTRY,							
Case, From Supermarket, Average	1 Case/230g	1081	470	5.8	55.9	25.6	1.2
Choux, Cooked	1oz/28g	91	325	8.5	29.8	19.8	1.2
Choux, Raw	1oz/28g	59	211	5.5	19.4	12.9	0.8
Filo, Average	1 Sheet/45g	137	304	9.0	61.4	2.7	0.9
Flaky, Chinese	1oz/28g	110	392	5.4	59.3	16.4	0.0
Flaky, Cooked	1oz/28g	157	560	5.6	45.9	40.6	1.8
Flaky, Raw	1oz/28g	119	424	4.2	34.8	30.7	1.4
Flan Case	1oz/28g	152	544	7.1	56.7	33.6	1.8
Greek	1oz/28g	90	322	4.7	40.0	17.0	0.0
Puff, Frozen, Average	1 Shell/47g	188	401	5.1	29.2	25.6	0.0
Shortcrust, Cooked	1oz/28g	146	521	6.6	54.2	32.3	2.2
Shortcrust, Raw, Average	1oz/28g	127	453	5.6	44.0	29.1	1.3
Wholemeal, Cooked	1oz/28g	140	499	8.9	44.6	32.9	6.3
Wholemeal, Raw	1oz/28g	121	431	7.7	38.5	28.4	5.4
PASTY,							
Bite Size Pasties, Food To Go, Sainsburys*	1 Serving/60g	226	377	8.2	31.2	24.4	1.5
Cheese & Onion, Geo Adams*	1 Pasty/150g	420	280	6.9	27.9	15.6	1.1
Cheese & Onion, Safeway*	1 Pasty/165g	482	292	6.5	24.1	18.8	1.0
Cheese & Onion, Sainsbury's*	1 Serving/150g	486	324	7.4	24.5	21.8	1.3
Cheese & Onion, Somerfield*	1 Pasty/145g	419	289	7.0	24.0	18.0	0.0
Corned Beef, Mega, Marks & Spencer*	1oz/28g	87	310	9.5	22.3	20.2	0.9
Cornish Roaster, Ginsters*	1 Pasty/130g	417	321	8.5	29.9	18.6	1.3
Cornish, Asda*	1 Pasty/100g	287	287	7.0	22.0	19.0	1.2
Cornish, BGTY, Sainsbury's*	1 Pasty/135g	308	228	7.7	28.2	9.4	1.6
Cornish, Cheese & Onion, Ginsters*	1 Pasty/130g	511	393	10.4	30.7	25.4	2.3
Cornish, Chicken & Bacon, Ginsters*	1 Pasty/227g	574	253	6.9	22.2	15.2	0.8
Cornish, Chunky Steak, Ginsters*	¼ Pasty/56g	316	565	15.1	52.7	32.7	3.6
Cornish, Marks & Spencer*	1 Pasty/150g	480	320	6.5	27.3	20.3	1.5
Cornish, Mega, Marks & Spencer*	1oz/28g	84	300	6.0	18.7	22.1	1.2
Cornish, Mini, Marks & Spencer*	1 Pastie/72g	227	315	6.7	21.0	22.6	1.0
Cornish, Mini, Sainsbury's*	1 Pasty/70g	280	400	7.3	28.1	28.7	1.5
Cornish, Mini, Tesco*	1 Pasty/24g	66	274	5.6	23.2	17.7	0.5
Cornish, Original, Ginsters*	1 Pasty/227g	568	250	6.0	19.0	15.8	1.1
Cornish, SmartPrice, Asda*	1 Pasty/94g	286	304	8.0	32.0	16.0	1.7
Cornish, Snack, Morrisons*	1 Serving/113g	128	113	2.5	9.4	7.3	0.5
Cornish, Tesco*	1 Pasty/150g	467	311	6.8	21.9	21.8	1.6
Cornish, Traditional Style, Geo Adams*	1 Pasty/165g	488	296	7.1	25.4	18.4	1.3
Steak & Onion, Marks & Spencer*	1 Pasty/164g	459	280	8.7	19.2	18.8	1.4

	Measure INFO/WEIGHT	per Measure KCAL	Nutrition Values per 100g / 100ml				
			KCAL	PROT	CARB	FAT	FIBRE
PASTY,							
Tandoori & Vegetable, Holland & Barrett*	1 Pack/110g	232	211	4.3	29.4	8.5	1.8
Vegetable	1oz/28g	77	274	4.1	33.3	14.9	1.9
Vegetarian, Cornish, Linda McCartney*	1 Pasty/170g	420	247	5.2	25.5	13.8	1.5
PATE,							
Apricot, Asda*	1 Serving/50g	156	312	12.0	3.0	28.0	0.0
Ardennes, Asda*	1 Serving/50g	143	286	13.9	3.6	24.0	1.3
Ardennes, BGTY, Sainsbury's*	1 Serving/50g	95	189	18.1	2.4	11.9	0.1
Ardennes, Healthy Living, Tesco*	1 Serving/50g	116	231	14.6	7.7	15.8	1.5
Ardennes, Improved Recipe, BGTY, Sainsbury's*	¼ Pack/43g	72	169	16.7	2.4	10.3	0.1
Ardennes, Reduced Fat, Good Intentions, Somerfield*	1 Serving/50g	98	195	16.4	2.6	13.2	1.6
Ardennes, Reduced Fat, Safeway*	1 Serving/50g	97	194	18.5	3.1	11.9	0.1
Ardennes, Reduced Fat, Waitrose*	¼ Pack/42g	94	224	15.4	2.6	16.9	0.5
Ardennes, Safeway*	1 Serving/50g	166	331	12.8	6.0	28.4	0.8
Ardennes, Sainsbury's*	1 Serving/20g	60	299	16.5	2.1	24.9	0.1
Ardennes, Tesco*	1 Tbsp/15g	53	354	13.3	0.5	33.2	1.2
Asparagus, Sainsbury's*	½ Pot/57g	88	153	3.4	5.4	13.1	1.0
Breton Course Country With Apricots, Sainsbury's*	1 Serving/21g	60	285	13.5	7.0	22.5	0.5
Brie & Cranberry, Marks & Spencer*	1 Serving/55g	160	290	7.5	18.9	20.5	0.5
Brussels & Garlic, Reduced Fat, Tesco*	1 Serving/65g	135	208	16.2	8.1	12.3	0.6
Brussels & Mushroom, 25% Less Fat, Asda*	1 Serving/40g	88	220	14.0	2.7	17.0	0.0
Brussels With Garlic, Asda*	1 Serving/50g	170	340	10.7	4.0	31.3	2.5
Brussels With Wild Mushrooms, The Best, Safeway*	1 oz/28g	89	319	11.6	2.9	29.0	1.0
Brussels, 25% Less Fat, Morrisons*	¼ Pack/42.5g	107	249	14.2	0.7	20.6	0.0
Brussels, Asda*	1 Serving/50g	175	350	10.7	4.4	32.2	1.7
Brussels, Fat Reduced, Somerfield*	1 Serving/50g	96	192	14.0	2.0	14.0	0.0
Brussels, Healthy Living, Tesco*	1 Serving/29g	66	229	14.4	8.4	15.3	1.3
Brussels, Marks & Spencer*	1 Pot/170g	519	305	13.3	2.8	26.6	1.0
Brussels, Reduced Fat, Asda*	1 Serving/44g	88	199	15.0	2.1	15.0	1.9
Brussels, Reduced Fat, Somerfield*	1 Serving/50g	139	277	14.0	8.0	21.0	0.0
Brussels, Sainsbury's*	1 Pack/170g	663	390	10.6	1.1	38.2	0.1
Brussels, Smooth, Safeway*	1 Pack/170g	553	325	11.5	3.9	29.3	1.6
Brussels, Tesco*	1 Serving/28g	92	330	11.0	3.0	30.5	1.1
Brussels, With Forest Mushroom, Co Op*	1 Serving/57g	180	315	12.0	2.0	29.0	1.0
Carrot, Ginger & Spring Onion, Marks & Spencer*	1 Serving/50g	73	145	1.5	9.6	11.0	0.9
Celery, Stilton & Walnut, Waitrose*	1 Pot/115g	294	256	9.0	3.2	23.0	2.2
Chargrilled Vegetable, BGTY Sainsbury's*	½ Pot/57.3g	43	75	4.9	10.8	1.3	2.7
Chick Pea & Black Olive, Cauldron Foods*	1 Pot/113g	203	180	6.2	15.6	10.3	4.5
Chicken & Brandy, Morrisons*	1 Serving/44g	133	303	10.8	4.3	26.9	0.8
Chicken Liver & Brandy, Asda*	1 Serving/50g	177	353	9.0	5.5	32.8	3.2
Chicken Liver Parfait, TTD, Sainsbury's*	1 Serving/20g	72	359	8.0	2.0	35.0	0.5
Chicken Liver With Brandy, Tesco*	1oz/28g	82	293	11.8	3.5	25.8	1.4
Chicken Liver, Marks & Spencer*	1oz/28g	79	281	14.0	1.9	24.1	0.1
Chickpea, Fragrant Moroccan, Organic, Cauldron Foods*	1 Tsp/15g	27	177	4.9	9.4	13.3	11.8
Coarse Farmhouse, Organic, Sainsbury's*	1 Serving/56g	138	246	13.3	3.7	19.7	0.8
Coarse Pork Liver With Garlic, Asda*	1 Pack/40g	130	326	13.0	1.0	30.0	0.0
Crab, Marks & Spencer*	1oz/28g	63	225	12.1	5.9	17.3	0.0
Duck & Champagne, Luxury, Marks & Spencer*	1oz/28g	106	380	8.3	8.3	35.2	7.8
Duck & Orange, Asda*	1 Serving/40g	94	235	16.0	2.2	18.0	0.0
Duck & Orange, Marks & Spencer*	1oz/28g	88	315	10.6	2.8	29.0	0.5
Duck & Truffle Medallions, Marks & Spencer*	1 Slice/25g	91	365	9.0	4.8	35.0	1.4
Duck Liver With Champagne & Truffles, TTD, Sainsbury's*	1 Serving/50g	212	423	8.2	2.5	42.2	0.0
Farmhouse Mushroom, Asda*	1 Serving/50g	126	252	13.0	5.0	20.0	0.7
Farmhouse Style, Finest, Tesco*	1 Serving/28g	83	295	11.9	3.6	25.9	1.0

	Measure INFO/WEIGHT	per Measure KCAL	Nutrition Values per 100g / 100ml KCAL	PROT	CARB	FAT	FIBRE
Farmhouse Style, Marks & Spencer*	¼ Pack/42g	90	215	14.4	1.9	16.9	1.2
Farmhouse Style, Weight Watchers*	1 Serving/36.8g	49	133	14.8	5.5	5.7	0.5
Farmhouse With Christmas Ale, Sainsbury's*	1oz/28g	67	239	15.4	1.6	19.1	0.0
Farmhouse With Herbes de Provence, Tesco*	1 Serving/50g	137	273	13.9	5.4	21.6	1.0
Farmhouse With Mushrooms & Garlic, Tesco*	1 Serving/90g	257	285	13.8	0.6	25.3	1.3
Forestiere, Marks & Spencer*	1 Serving/20g	61	305	11.5	4.2	26.6	1.4
Garlic & Herb Yeast, Tartex*	1 Serving/10g	23	230	7.0	10.0	18.0	0.0
Herb, Organic, Suma*	1 Serving/25g	59	234	12.0	6.0	18.0	0.0
Isle of Skye Smoked Salmon, TTD, Sainsbury's*	½ Pot/58g	161	277	16.5	0.8	23.1	0.1
Liver & Bacon, Tesco*	1 Serving/10g	28	276	12.9	4.3	23.0	0.4
Liver & Pork, Healthy Eating, Tesco*	1 Serving/28g	64	229	14.4	8.4	15.3	1.3
Liver Spreading, Somerfield*	1oz/28g	77	275	14.0	3.0	23.0	0.0
Liver, Value, Tesco*	1 Serving/50g	151	302	13.0	4.1	26.0	0.5
Luxury Orkney Crab, Castle MacLellan*	1 Serving/15g	27	178	11.1	9.2	10.7	0.8
Mackerel, Smoked	1oz/28g	103	368	13.4	1.3	34.4	0.0
Mackerel, Tesco*	1 Serving/29g	102	353	14.3	0.5	32.6	0.0
Mediterranean Roast Vegetable, Tesco*	1 Serving/28g	31	112	2.4	4.3	9.4	1.2
Moroccan Chick Pea, Cauldron Foods*	½ Pack/57.6g	103	177	4.9	9.4	13.3	11.8
Mushroom & Herb, Somerfield*	1oz/28g	81	289	4.0	8.0	27.0	0.0
Mushroom & Tarragon, Cauldron Foods*	1oz/28g	43	155	2.8	5.5	13.5	1.4
Mushroom, BGTY, Sainsbury's*	½ Pot/58g	29	50	4.6	6.7	0.5	3.0
Mushroom, COU, Marks & Spencer*	1oz/28g	17	60	2.9	7.4	1.9	0.9
Mushroom, Marks & Spencer*	1 Pot/115g	224	195	4.2	4.8	17.5	1.3
Mushroom, New, Tesco*	1 Serving/85g	117	138	3.3	9.8	9.5	1.0
Mushroom, Organic, Cauldron Foods*	1oz/28g	33	119	2.8	4.3	10.1	1.0
Mushroom, Sainsbury's*	1oz/28g	47	168	3.1	5.9	15.2	1.3
Mushroom & Tarragon, Vegetarian, Waitrose*	1 Serving/30g	47	155	2.8	5.5	13.5	1.4
Poached Salmon & Watercress, Tesco*	1 Serving/25g	60	238	19.2	0.4	17.7	0.2
Pork & Garlic, Somerfield*	1oz/28g	83	295	14.0	3.0	25.0	0.0
Pork & Mushroom, Somerfield*	1oz/28g	95	339	11.0	3.0	31.0	0.0
Pork With Port & Cranberry, Tesco*	1 Serving/28g	83	296	12.1	4.3	25.6	0.6
Pork, With Peppercorns, Tesco*	1 Serving/28g	84	300	12.9	1.4	26.8	0.7
Red Pepper, Marks & Spencer*	1oz/28g	52	185	3.0	6.6	16.2	0.9
Ricotta, Subdried Tomato & Basil, Princes*	1 Jar/110g	343	312	5.2	8.3	28.7	0.0
Roasted Carrot, Ginger & Spring Onion, Marks & Spencer*	1 Serving/50g	73	145	1.5	9.6	11.0	0.9
Roasted Parsnip & Carrot, Cauldron Foods*	1 Serving/60g	64	107	3.7	9.8	5.9	2.6
Roasted Red Pepper & Houmous, Princes*	¼ Jar/27g	32	120	4.6	12.4	5.8	0.0
Roasted Red Pepper, Princes*	1 Serving/35g	47	135	4.8	17.6	5.0	0.0
Roasted Vegetable, COU, Marks & Spencer*	1 Pot/115g	86	75	6.2	9.1	1.5	1.4
Salmon Dill, Princes*	1 Serving/70g	124	177	15.4	4.0	11.1	0.5
Salmon, Organic, Marks & Spencer*	1oz/28g	76	270	16.9	0.0	22.5	0.0
Salmon, Smoked, Marks & Spencer*	1oz/28g	74	265	16.9	0.0	22.0	0.0
Salsa, Princes*	1 Serving/25g	21	84	3.6	16.7	0.3	0.0
Scottish Smoked Salmon, Marks & Spencer*	1 Serving/30g	81	270	17.0	0.2	22.3	0.0
Smoked Duck, With Cranberry Coulis, TTD, Sainsbury's*	1 Serving/62g	174	280	10.7	9.3	22.2	1.0
Smoked Mackerel, Marks & Spencer*	1oz/28g	104	370	13.4	0.7	34.7	0.3
Smoked Mackerel, Sainsbury's*	½ Pot/57g	201	352	15.2	1.9	31.5	0.3
Smoked Mackerel, Scottish, Marks & Spencer*	½ Pot/57.5g	160	275	15.9	0.6	23.2	0.1
Smoked Salmon, Healthy Eating, Tesco*	1 Serving/50g	65	130	17.5	2.6	5.5	0.0
Smoked Salmon, Waitrose*	½ Pot/56g	122	217	17.7	1.5	15.6	0.6
Spiced Parsnip & Carrot, Organic, Asda*	½ Pot/58g	63	109	3.7	10.0	6.0	2.6
Spicy Bean, Princes*	½ Pot/55g	46	84	3.6	16.7	0.3	0.0
Spicy Bean, Weight Watchers*	1 Serving/37g	33	89	5.7	12.9	1.6	4.2

	Measure INFO/WEIGHT	per Measure KCAL	Nutrition Values per 100g / 100ml				
			KCAL	PROT	CARB	FAT	FIBRE
PATE,							
Spicy Mexican, Vegetarian, Organic, Waitrose*	1 Serving/50g	58	115	6.2	8.6	6.2	3.5
Spinach & Soft Cheese, Cauldron Foods*	1 Pack/113g	209	185	5.1	6.8	15.4	2.3
Spinach, Parmesan & Almond, Cauldron Foods*	1/3 Pack/38g	66	173	7.2	6.3	13.2	2.3
Spinach, Soft Cheese & Onion, Vegetarian, Co-Op*	1oz/28g	48	170	5.0	3.0	15.0	4.0
Tofu, Spicy Mexican, Organic, GranoVita*	1 Serving/50g	112	224	4.0	7.0	20.0	0.0
Tomato, Lentil & Basil, Cauldron Foods*	1oz/28g	43	154	7.5	15.6	6.8	1.5
Tomato, Organic, GranoVita*	1 Tsp/5g	11	215	5.0	6.0	19.0	0.0
Tuna With Butter & Lemon Juice, Sainsbury's*	½ Pot/58g	209	360	19.0	0.1	31.6	0.3
Tuna, Marks & Spencer*	1oz/28g	99	355	18.0	0.0	31.3	0.0
Tuna, Tesco*	1 Pack/115g	332	289	19.8	0.3	23.2	0.2
Vegetable	1oz/28g	48	173	7.5	5.9	13.4	0.0
Vegetable, Cauldron Foods*	1 Pack/112.8g	220	195	9.2	14.1	11.3	4.4
Yeast With Red & Green Peppers, Vessen*	1 Pot/50g	111	222	6.0	9.0	18.0	0.0
Yeast, Wild Mushroom, Vegetarian, GranoVita*	1oz/28g	60	213	10.0	5.0	17.0	0.0
PAVLOVA,							
Bucks Fizz Mini Champagne, Co-Op*	1 Pavlova/19g	62	325	3.0	38.0	18.0	0.5
Mandarin, Mini, Iceland*	1 Pavlova/22.0g	59	268	2.1	37.9	12.0	1.7
Mixed Berry, Two, COU, Marks & Spencer*	1 Pavlova/100g	140	140	4.9	27.4	1.8	9.3
Raspberry & Lemon, Asda*	1 Serving/43.4g	101	235	2.8	46.0	4.4	0.5
Raspberry, Individual, Marks & Spencer*	1 Pavlova/65g	133	205	4.0	41.8	2.4	0.2
Raspberry, Marks & Spencer*	1 Serving/84g	193	230	2.3	33.3	9.6	0.3
Raspberry, Mini, Co-Op*	1 Pavlova/19g	61	320	3.0	56.0	9.0	0.6
Raspberry, Sara Lee*	1/6 Slice/55.4g	167	303	2.7	38.5	15.3	1.1
Raspberry, Tesco*	1 Serving/65g	191	294	2.7	41.8	12.9	1.1
Sticky Toffee, Sainsbury's*	1/6 Pack/61g	249	415	3.7	63.1	16.4	0.9
Strawberry & Champagne, Mini, Co-Op*	1 Pavlova/19g	65	340	3.0	40.0	19.0	0.8
Strawberry, COU, Marks & Spencer*	1 Pot/95g	147	155	2.4	30.5	2.4	0.8
Strawberry, Co-Op*	1 Serving/52g	177	340	3.0	50.0	14.0	0.4
Toffee Pecan, Marks & Spencer*	1oz/28g	118	420	3.9	41.5	26.6	0.4
Toffee, Co-Op*	1/6 Pavlova/53g	193	365	3.0	52.0	16.0	0.6
PAW-PAW,							
Raw, Fresh	1oz/28g	10	36	0.5	8.8	0.1	2.2
Raw, Weighed With Skin & Pips	1oz/28g	8	27	0.4	6.6	0.1	1.7
PEACHES,							
Dried, Average	1 Pack/250g	473	189	2.6	45.0	0.7	6.9
In Fruit Juice, Average	1oz/28g	13	47	0.5	11.2	0.0	0.7
In Syrup, Average	1oz/28g	19	67	0.4	16.3	0.1	0.4
Pieces In Strawberry Jelly, Fruitini*	1 Can/140g	91	65	0.3	15.3	0.1	0.0
Raw, Average	1oz/28g	9	32	1.0	7.2	0.1	1.4
PEANUT BUTTER,							
Creamy, Smooth, Sun Pat*	1 Tsp/15g	93	620	24.0	17.5	50.2	6.1
Crunchy, Asda*	1 Tsp/10g	61	611	28.0	12.0	51.0	6.0
Crunchy, No Added Sugar, Whole Earth*	1 Tsp/10g	59	592	24.9	10.1	50.2	7.3
Crunchy, Organic, Evernat*	1 Tsp/10g	64	641	29.0	13.0	53.0	7.0
Crunchy, Organic, Tesco*	1 Serving/25g	148	592	23.6	12.5	49.7	6.9
Crunchy, Original, Sun Pat*	1 Tsp/10g	63	630	26.6	12.6	52.8	6.5
Crunchy, Sainsbury's*	1 Tsp/10g	59	594	23.2	12.4	50.2	6.7
Crunchy, Somerfield*	1 Tsp/10g	59	586	24.0	12.0	49.0	0.0
Crunchy, Tesco*	1 Tsp/10g	61	614	27.8	12.0	50.5	6.5
Crunchy, Value, Tesco*	1 Serving/20g	121	606	22.5	11.6	52.2	5.7
Extra Crunchy, Sun Pat*	1 Serving/10g	62	615	25.1	16.3	50.2	6.3
GFY, Asda*	1 Tsp/15g	80	531	28.0	31.0	35.0	0.0
Kraft*	1 Serving/10g	56	557	17.0	37.8	38.0	0.0

	Measure INFO/WEIGHT	per Measure KCAL	Nutrition Values per 100g / 100ml				
			KCAL	PROT	CARB	FAT	FIBRE
PEANUT BUTTER,							
Morrisons*	1 Serving/20g	119	596	23.3	12.4	50.3	0.0
Organic, Whole Earth*	1 Serving/5g	30	595	24.6	9.9	50.8	7.1
SmartPrice, Asda*	1 Tbsp/15g	87	582	23.0	10.0	50.0	6.0
Smooth	1 Tsp/10g	62	623	22.6	13.1	53.7	5.4
Smooth, 25% Less Fat, Tesco*	1 Serving/30g	159	529	22.6	30.7	35.1	6.7
Smooth, BGTY, Sainsbury's*	1 Tsp/10g	53	533	22.6	31.7	35.1	6.7
Smooth, Light, Kraft*	1 Tsp/20g	114	571	16.3	40.1	38.6	0.0
Smooth, Somerfield*	1 Tsp/10g	59	592	24.0	11.0	50.0	0.0
Smooth, Sun Pat*	1 Serving/20g	117	585	27.9	14.4	46.3	7.1
Smooth, Tesco*	1 Tsp/10g	61	614	27.8	12.0	50.5	6.5
Stripy, Sun Pat*	1 Tsp/10g	62	617	13.0	35.0	47.0	3.0
Whole Grain	1 Tsp/10g	61	606	24.9	7.7	53.1	6.0
Wholenut, Sainsbury's*	1 Tbsp/15g	90	598	24.2	9.8	51.3	7.0
Wholenut, Tesco*	1 Tsp/5g	30	590	24.9	10.1	50.0	6.3
PEANUTS,							
Chilli, Average	½ Pack/50g	303	605	28.2	9.3	50.6	6.8
Dry Roasted, Average	1 Serving/20g	117	587	25.7	11.5	48.8	6.5
Honey Roasted, Average	1oz/28g	169	605	26.9	23.6	47.1	5.5
Plain, Average	10 Whole/10g	59	592	24.7	11.0	50.0	6.3
Roast, Salted, Average	1oz/28g	172	614	27.8	7.9	52.4	4.9
Salted, Average	1oz/28g	171	609	27.0	8.3	52.1	5.4
PEARL BARLEY,							
Boiled	1oz/28g	34	120	2.7	27.6	0.6	0.0
Raw	1oz/28g	101	360	7.9	83.6	1.7	0.0
PEARS,							
Comice, Raw, Weighed With Core	1 Med/170g	56	33	0.3	8.5	0.0	2.0
Conference, Average	1oz/28g	14	49	0.3	11.6	0.2	2.3
Dried, Average	1oz/28g	57	204	1.9	48.4	0.5	9.7
In Fruit Juice, Average	1 Serving/225g	102	45	0.3	10.9	0.0	1.2
In Syrup, Average	1oz/28g	16	58	0.2	14.4	0.1	1.4
Prickly, Raw, Fresh	1oz/28g	14	49	0.7	11.5	0.3	0.0
Raw, Average	1oz/28g	11	38	0.3	9.1	0.1	1.4
Red, Tesco*	1 Pear/180g	65	36	0.4	8.3	0.1	2.2
William, Raw	1 Med/170g	58	34	0.4	8.3	0.1	2.2
PEAS,							
& Sweetcorn, Fresh, Marks & Spencer*	1oz/28g	21	75	4.8	11.4	1.5	3.0
Dried, Boiled in Unsalted Water	1oz/28g	31	109	6.9	19.9	0.8	5.5
Dried, Raw	1oz/28g	85	303	21.6	52.0	2.4	13.0
Frozen, Average	1 Serving/85g	55	64	5.4	9.0	0.8	4.9
Frozen, Boiled, Average	1 Serving/75g	51	68	6.0	9.4	0.9	5.1
Garden, Canned, No Sugar Or Salt, Average	1 Can/80g	36	45	4.4	6.0	0.4	2.8
Garden, Canned, With Sugar & Salt, Average	1 Serving/90g	59	66	5.3	9.3	0.7	5.1
Garden, Frozen, Average	1oz/28g	21	74	6.3	9.8	1.1	3.3
Garden, Minted, Average	1 Serving/113g	84	74	6.3	9.7	1.1	5.9
Marrowfat, Average	1 Sm Can/160g	140	88	6.4	14.3	0.6	3.9
Mushy, Average	1oz/28g	24	86	6.2	14.3	0.5	2.2
Processed, Canned, Average	1oz/28g	22	80	6.1	12.3	0.8	3.7
Sugar Snap, Average	1oz/28g	10	34	3.3	4.9	0.2	1.4
Summer Sweet, Green Giant*	3/4 Cup/175ml	107	61	3.4	11.0	0.4	0.0
PECAN NUTS,							
Average	3 Nuts/18g	125	693	10.1	5.7	70.1	4.7
PENNE,							
Arrabbiata, BGTY, Sainsbury's*	1 Pack/450g	414	92	2.9	16.5	1.6	1.9

P

	Measure INFO/WEIGHT	per Measure KCAL	Nutrition Values per 100g / 100ml				
			KCAL	PROT	CARB	FAT	FIBRE
PENNE,							
Chicken & Red Wine, Weight Watchers*	1 Pack/394g	248	63	3.7	10.1	0.7	0.6
Chicken & Tomato, Italian, Sainsbury's*	½ Pack/350g	473	135	7.6	19.0	3.2	1.6
Chilli & Garlic, Asda*	1 Serving/75g	260	346	12.0	71.0	1.5	3.0
Cooked, Average	1 Serving/185g	244	132	4.7	26.7	0.7	1.1
Corn, Free From, Dry, Sainsbury's*	1 Serving/100g	348	348	7.6	74.2	2.3	5.2
Creamy Sun Dried Tomato & Mascarpone, Somerfield*	1 Pack/500g	775	155	5.0	21.0	6.0	0.0
Dry, Average	1 Serving/100g	352	352	12.4	71.3	1.9	2.7
Egg, Fresh, Average	1 Serving/125g	353	282	11.1	52.2	3.2	2.0
Fresh, Dry, Average	1 Serving/215g	383	178	7.3	32.2	1.9	1.6
Hickory Steak, American, Sainsbury's*	1 Pack/450g	545	121	6.5	19.8	1.8	1.5
Hickory Steak, Asda*	1 Pack/443.0g	660	149	8.0	19.0	4.5	1.1
Leek & Bacon, Al Forno, Asda*	½ Pack/300g	531	177	5.0	10.0	13.0	0.5
Mozzarella, Safeway*	1 Serving/400g	480	120	5.2	16.3	3.8	1.5
Napoletana Chicken, Better For You, Morrisons*	1 Pack/350g	252	72	6.4	7.2	1.6	0.2
Organic, Dry, Average	1 Serving/100g	352	352	12.4	71.6	1.8	1.9
Rigate, Dry, Average	1 Serving/50g	177	353	12.3	72.1	1.8	1.8
Roasted Red Pepper, GFY, Asda*	1 Pack/400g	212	53	1.9	10.0	0.6	0.8
Tomato & Basil Sauce, Asda*	½ Pack/314g	185	59	0.8	6.0	3.5	2.0
Tuna, Tomato & Olive, Asda*	1 Pack/340g	173	51	4.2	4.2	1.9	0.6
Wheat, Gluten, Milk & Egg Free, Dry, Trufree*	1 Serving/75g	263	350	8.0	75.0	2.0	0.0
With Chilli & Red Peppers, Asda*	1 Can/400g	224	56	1.3	10.0	1.2	0.6
PEPERAMI,							
Hot, Peperami*	1oz/28g	155	554	19.0	2.5	52.0	1.2
Salami Sausage, Peperami*	1oz/28g	150	536	22.0	1.7	49.0	0.1
PEPPER,							
Black, Freshly Ground	1 Tsp/2g	5	226	10.9	64.8	3.3	0.0
Cayenne, Ground	1 Tsp/1.8g	6	318	12.0	31.7	17.3	0.0
PEPPERONI,							
American Style, Tesco*	1 Piece/5g	19	387	20.0	3.2	32.7	0.0
Asda*	1 Slice/6g	24	405	22.0	6.6	32.3	0.0
Ready to Eat, Sainsbury's*	1 Serving/25g	94	376	24.9	0.1	30.7	0.1
Spicy Italian, Marks & Spencer*	1 Pack/50g	158	316	20.9	1.1	25.3	0.0
PEPPERS,							
Capsicum, Chilli, Green, Raw	1oz/28g	6	20	2.9	0.7	0.6	0.0
Capsicum, Chilli, Red, Raw	1oz/28g	7	26	1.8	4.2	0.3	0.0
Capsicum, Green, Boiled in Salted Water	1oz/28g	5	18	1.0	2.6	0.5	1.8
Capsicum, Green, Raw	1oz/28g	4	15	0.8	2.6	0.3	1.6
Capsicum, Red, Boiled in Salted Water	1oz/28g	10	34	1.1	7.0	0.4	1.7
Capsicum, Red, Raw	1oz/28g	9	32	1.0	6.4	0.4	1.6
Capsicum, Yellow, Raw	1oz/28g	7	26	1.2	5.3	0.2	1.7
Green, Filled, Tesco*	1 Pepper/150g	117	78	2.6	9.0	3.5	0.7
Jalapeno, Co-Op*	1oz/28g	74	265	5.0	31.0	13.0	0.9
Mixed Bag, From Supermarket, Average	1oz/28g	7	25	1.0	4.5	0.4	1.7
Red, Filled Withss & Feta, COU, Marks & Spencer*	1 Pepper/153.8g	200	130	4.1	12.4	7.2	0.6
Red, Filled, Marks & Spencer*	1 Serving/250g	200	80	2.8	12.1	2.1	1.8
Roasted Red & Yellow, in Oil, Marks & Spencer*	1 Serving/40g	34	85	1.1	4.4	6.9	3.5
Stuffed With Rice	1oz/28g	24	85	1.5	15.4	2.4	1.3
Stuffed With Vegetables, Cheese Topping	1oz/28g	31	111	3.4	9.8	6.7	1.5
Stuffed, Fresh, Asda*	1 Pepper/150g	144	96	3.8	9.0	5.0	1.2
Stuffed, Perfectly Balanced, Waitrose*	1 Pack/300g	243	81	3.0	11.8	2.4	1.3
Stuffed, Sainsbury's*	1 Serving/137g	169	123	3.3	11.8	6.9	1.0
Stuffed, Yellow, Italian, Ready to Roast, Sainsbury's*	1 Pack/136g	144	106	5.3	9.9	5.0	1.3
Sweet, Raw	1 Serving/100g	16	16	0.8	2.6	0.3	1.6

INFO/WEIGHT	Measure INFO/WEIGHT	per Measure KCAL	Nutrition Values per 100g / 100ml				
			KCAL	PROT	CARB	FAT	FIBRE
PEPPERS,							
Sweet, Tinned, Sainsbury's*	½ Can/125g	45	36	1.1	7.0	0.4	1.7
PERNOD*,							
19% Volume	1 Shot/50	65	130	0.0	0.0	0.0	0.0
PETIT POIS,							
& Baby Carrots, Safeway*	1 Can/138g	57	41	2.5	7.4	0.0	1.0
& Carrots, Tesco*	1 Serving/110g	63	57	3.0	11.2	0.0	3.0
Average	1 Serving/65g	34	53	5.0	6.8	0.7	3.5
PHEASANT,							
Meat Only, Roasted	1oz/28g	62	220	27.9	0.0	12.0	0.0
Meat Only, Roasted, Weighed With Bone	1oz/28g	32	114	14.5	0.0	6.2	0.0
PICCALILLI,							
Dijon, Sainsbury's*	1 Dtsp/15.4g	14	91	1.8	19.0	0.9	0.7
Haywards*	1 Serving/28g	18	66	1.4	13.9	0.5	0.0
Marks & Spencer*	1 Tbsp/15g	11	70	1.9	13.5	1.2	1.1
Sainsbury's*	1 Dtsp/15g	9	60	1.8	11.9	0.6	0.7
Sweet, Asda*	1 Tbsp/15g	17	112	0.5	27.0	0.2	0.6
Sweet, Somerfield*	1 Tsp/10g	11	107	1.0	24.0	1.0	0.0
Three Mustard, Finest, Tesco*	1 Serving/30g	40	134	1.3	30.7	0.7	1.0
PICKLE,							
Branston, Crosse & Blackwell*	1 Tsp/10g	14	140	0.7	34.2	0.3	1.3
Brinjal, Patak's*	1 Tsp/16g	57	355	2.1	36.5	24.4	0.9
Chilli Tomato, Patak's*	1oz/28g	27	95	2.5	16.0	3.2	1.5
Chilli, Branston*	1 Tsp/16g	21	130	0.7	30.0	0.7	1.5
Chilli, Patak's*	1 Tsp/16g	49	305	4.1	1.4	33.7	0.0
Dill, Cucumbers, Safeway*	1oz/28g	5	19	0.9	3.5	0.2	0.0
Garlic, Patak's*	1 Tsp/16g	43	267	3.6	21.3	18.5	1.6
Lime, Hot, Patak's*	1 Tsp/16g	30	186	2.6	4.2	18.7	0.3
Lime, Marks & Spencer*	1 Tsp/16g	34	215	0.8	42.5	4.8	2.4
Lime, Oily	1oz/28g	50	178	1.9	8.3	15.5	0.0
Lime, Sharwood's*	1 Tsp/16g	24	152	2.2	15.0	9.3	2.9
Mango, Hot, Patak's*	1 Tsp/16g	42	265	2.3	8.0	25.7	1.9
Mild Mustard, Heinz*	1 Tbsp/10g	13	129	2.2	25.7	1.3	0.9
Mixed, Patak's*	1 Serving/30g	78	259	2.3	4.7	25.7	0.8
Original, Tesco*	1 Tsp/25g	33	132	0.8	30.4	0.2	1.1
Ploughman's, Heinz*	1 Tbsp/10g	12	117	0.8	26.7	0.2	0.9
Sandwich, Branston*	1 Tsp/10g	14	140	0.7	34.2	0.3	1.3
Smooth, Branston*	1 Serving/13g	18	139	0.6	34.0	0.1	1.4
Spicy, Branston*	1 Heaped Tsp/15g	21	140	0.7	34.7	0.3	1.3
Sweet	1 Tsp/10g	14	141	0.6	36.0	0.1	1.2
Sweet, Hartley's*	1 Tsp/16g	7	140	0.5	36.2	0.0	0.0
Tangy, Sandwich, Heinz*	1 Tsp/10g	13	134	0.7	31.4	0.2	0.9
Tomato, Tangy, Heinz*	1 Tsp/10g	10	102	2.0	22.0	0.3	1.5
PICKLES,							
Mixed, Salad Bar, Asda*	1oz/28g	11	40	0.5	9.2	0.1	0.0
PICNIC,							
Cadbury's*	1 Bar/48g	228	475	7.5	58.3	23.6	0.0
PIE,							
Aberdeen Angus Minced Beef, Marks & Spencer*	¼ Pie/137g	349	255	9.4	23.9	13.6	1.1
Admiral's, Ross*	1 Pie/340g	357	105	4.8	10.9	4.6	0.7
Admiral, Youngs*	1 Pie/340g	357	105	4.6	10.7	4.9	0.7
Apple & Blackberry, Lattice Topped, BGTY, Sainsbury's*	¼ Serving/100g	256	256	2.8	44.4	7.5	3.1
Apple & Blackberry, Shortcrust, Marks & Spencer*	1 Serving/142g	469	330	4.3	50.2	12.5	1.1
Apple & Blackberry, Somerfield*	¼ Pie/106g	280	264	4.0	36.0	12.0	0.0

P

PIE,	Measure INFO/WEIGHT	per Measure KCAL	Nutrition Values per 100g / 100ml				
			KCAL	PROT	CARB	FAT	FIBRE
Apple & Blackberry, Tesco*	1 Serving/106g	287	271	4.2	38.4	11.2	1.7
Apple & Blackcurrant, Mr Kipling*	1 Pie/66g	228	346	3.4	53.9	13.0	1.6
Apple Meringue, Frozen, Sara Lee*	1/6 Slice/74g	179	242	2.7	37.9	8.8	1.5
Apple Slice, Colonels Pies, KFC*	1 Slice/113g	310	274	1.7	38.9	12.3	0.0
Apple, American, Iceland*	1 Portion/92g	258	280	4.8	39.2	11.6	2.2
Apple, Asda*	¼ Pack/106.7g	288	269	3.6	39.0	11.0	1.7
Apple, Bramley, Individual, Sainsbury's*	1 Pie/53.7g	166	307	3.6	52.2	9.3	1.3
Apple, Cooked, Speedibake*	1 Serving/120g	340	283	3.4	38.5	12.8	1.5
Apple, Deep Filled, Iceland*	1 Portion/116g	332	286	2.5	39.2	13.2	1.1
Apple, Deep Filled, Sainsbury's*	¼ Pie/137g	374	273	3.8	35.6	12.8	1.6
Apple, Family, Morrisons*	1/6 Pie/116g	326	281	3.1	39.9	12.1	3.1
Apple, Individual, Somerfield*	1 Pie/47.2g	178	379	3.5	53.2	16.9	1.3
Apple, Lattice, Tesco*	1 Serving/145g	325	224	2.2	33.2	9.2	1.4
Apple, McDonald's*	1 Pie/78g	225	289	2.8	33.2	16.1	1.4
Apple, McVitie's*	1 Slice/117g	316	270	3.0	39.0	11.0	2.0
Apple, Pastry Top & Bottom	1oz/28g	74	266	2.9	35.8	13.3	1.7
Apple, Puff Pastry, Marks & Spencer*	1 Pie/135g	338	250	2.4	31.3	12.7	1.0
Apple, Ready Baked, Sara Lee*	1/6 Pie/89.9g	249	277	2.8	35.4	13.8	1.2
Apple, Safeway*	1 Serving/80g	241	301	3.3	45.5	11.8	0.0
Apple, Sainsbury's*	1/6/118g	314	266	3.4	37.1	11.5	0.6
Apple, SmartPrice, Asda*	1 Serving/47g	178	379	3.5	53.0	17.0	1.3
Apple, Somerfield*	1oz/28g	110	392	4.0	59.0	16.0	0.0
Apple, Tesco*	1 Pie/47g	191	406	3.3	59.4	17.2	1.5
Apple, Value, Tesco*	1 Pie/47g	179	381	3.4	53.2	17.0	1.3
Apricot Fruit, GFY, Asda*	1 Serving/52g	162	311	3.3	52.0	10.0	0.0
Banoffee Cream, American Dream, McVitie's*	1 Portion/70g	277	396	4.3	36.7	25.5	0.8
Banoffee, Pizza Express*	1 Serving/300g	389	130	2.2	13.4	7.5	0.0
Banoffee, Sainsbury's*	1 pie/104g	383	368	3.7	37.1	22.8	0.7
Banoffee, Shape*	1 Serving/120g	175	146	3.3	28.0	2.3	0.5
Banoffee, Tesco*	1 Pie/112g	381	340	3.7	45.4	15.9	1.2
Beef & Kidney, Farmfoods*	1oz/28g	68	242	5.6	23.9	13.8	1.1
Beef & Vegetable, MacDougalls, McDougalls*	¼ Pie/114g	292	256	5.3	20.6	16.9	0.3
Beef Steak, Aberdeen Angus, Top Crust, Waitrose*	½ Pie/280g	476	170	10.0	13.4	8.6	4.1
Beef, Lean, BGTY, Sainsbury's*	1 Serving/212g	280	132	7.3	12.2	6.0	1.5
Beef, Sainsbury's*	1 Pie/209.8g	536	255	10.3	21.2	14.3	2.0
Blackcurrant, Deep Filled, Sainsbury's*	1 Slice/137g	440	321	5.8	42.6	14.1	2.2
Blackcurrant, Shortcrust, Marks & Spencer*	1 Pie/142g	412	290	3.9	45.6	10.1	1.3
Bramley Apple & Blackberry, Marks & Spencer*	¼ Pie/146g	380	260	3.4	39.8	9.9	1.3
Bramley Apple & Custard, Lattice Topped, Mr Kipling*	1 Pie/64g	236	369	3.8	53.7	15.4	1.1
Bramley Apple & Damson, Marks & Spencer*	¼ Pie/142.3g	369	260	3.3	39.7	9.8	2.1
Bramley Apple, Deep Filled, Mr Kipling*	1 Pie/66g	220	333	3.4	50.7	13.0	1.3
Bramley Apple, Deep Filled, Sainsbury's*	1/6 Pie/120g	329	274	3.7	38.0	11.9	1.9
Bramley Apple, Free From, Tesco*	1 Pie/60g	185	309	2.5	55.4	8.6	1.4
Bramley Apple, Individual, Mr Kipling*	1 Pie/66g	228	346	3.3	53.9	13.0	1.3
Bramley Apple, Marks & Spencer*	1 Pie/55g	184	335	2.9	57.6	11.7	1.6
Bramley Apple, Reduced Fat, Asda*	1 Pie/56g	176	314	3.3	55.1	9.4	1.3
Bramley Apple, Somerfield*	1/6 Pie/70.2g	193	275	3.5	34.0	12.8	2.4
Bramley Apple, Tesco*	1/8 Slice/87g	224	257	3.8	37.4	10.2	1.7
Cheese & Potato	1oz/28g	39	139	4.8	12.6	8.1	0.7
Cherry Bakewell Meringue, Sara Lee*	1 Slice/69.9g	228	326	4.1	51.9	11.3	1.4
Cherry, Deep Filled, Somerfield*	1/6 Pie/90g	259	288	3.0	41.0	12.0	0.0
Cherry, Sainsbury's*	1 Serving/117g	325	278	3.9	39.6	11.6	1.7
Cherry, Shortcrust, Marks & Spencer*	1 Pie/142g	412	290	3.6	43.4	10.9	0.8

PIE,

INFO/WEIGHT	Measure per Measure	KCAL	Nutrition Values per 100g / 100ml KCAL	PROT	CARB	FAT	FIBRE
Chicken & Asparagus, Tesco*	1 Serving/170g	468	275	8.3	22.4	16.9	0.8
Chicken & Bacon, Filo Pastry, Finest, Tesco*	1 Serving/160g	362	226	11.3	18.9	11.7	1.7
Chicken & Basil, Marks & Spencer*	1oz/28g	59	210	8.9	17.0	11.9	1.1
Chicken & Broccoli Lattice, Sainsbury's*	½ Pie/192g	520	271	9.3	22.4	16.0	0.9
Chicken & Broccoli Potato, Top, Asda*	1 Pack/400g	319	80	5.3	10.8	1.8	0.7
Chicken & Broccoli, COU, Marks & Spencer*	1 Serving/320g	272	85	8.1	8.8	1.9	1.3
Chicken & Broccoli, Eat Smart, Safeway*	1 Pack/400g	320	80	6.9	8.5	2.0	1.2
Chicken & Broccoli, GFY, Asda*	1 Pack/400g	340	85	7.0	9.0	2.3	0.5
Chicken & Broccoli, Healthy Living, Tesco*	1 Pie/400g	414	92	5.3	11.3	2.8	1.4
Chicken & Broccoli, Lattice, Tesco*	½ Pie/200g	496	248	8.5	18.9	15.4	2.1
Chicken & Gravy, Deep Fill, Asda*	1 Serving/130g	371	285	10.0	23.0	17.0	0.8
Chicken & Gravy, Tesco*	1 Serving/120g	239	199	7.6	20.5	9.2	2.1
Chicken & Ham, Deep Filled, Sainsbury's*	1 Pie/210g	594	283	8.0	23.0	17.7	1.0
Chicken & Ham, Family, Farmfoods*	1oz/28g	67	241	9.9	19.4	13.8	1.2
Chicken & Ham, Safeway*	1 Pie/134.7g	385	285	9.2	23.0	17.4	1.3
Chicken & Ham, Sainsbury's*	1 Pie/128g	461	360	11.0	28.5	22.4	2.0
Chicken & Ham, Tesco*	1 Serving/113g	293	259	9.4	20.2	15.6	1.2
Chicken & Leek, Deep Filled, Puff Pastry, Sainsbury's*	1/3 Pie/451g	1109	246	10.1	18.7	14.5	1.5
Chicken & Leek, Marks & Spencer*	1oz/28g	70	250	10.1	18.8	15.1	1.1
Chicken & Mushroom, Asda*	1 Pie/ 150g	444	296	7.7	25.4	18.2	1.0
Chicken & Mushroom, Favourites, Morrisons*	¼ Pie/352g	989	281	7.2	23.8	17.4	0.9
Chicken & Mushroom, Fray Bentos*	1 Pie/425g	684	161	6.7	11.5	9.5	0.0
Chicken & Mushroom, Individual, Co-Op*	1 Pie/149g	465	312	8.6	24.5	19.9	1.2
Chicken & Mushroom, Luxury, Marks & Spencer*	½ Pie/275g	880	320	9.9	20.0	22.5	1.0
Chicken & Mushroom, Puff Pastry, Bird's Eye*	1 Pie/152.0g	415	273	11.9	24.9	14.0	1.6
Chicken & Mushroom, Puff Pastry, Sainsbury's*	1 Pie/150g	450	300	7.8	29.6	16.7	0.9
Chicken & Mushroom, Shortcrust, Somerfield*	¼ Pie/125g	410	328	6.2	24.7	22.7	1.2
Chicken & Mushroom, Tesco*	1 Pie/150g	449	299	8.6	22.4	19.4	1.7
Chicken & Vegetable, Asda*	1 Pie/130.7g	329	251	8.0	21.0	15.0	1.4
Chicken & Vegetable, Kids, Tesco*	1 Serving/235g	235	100	5.9	9.1	4.5	0.7
Chicken & Vegetable, Perfectly Balanced, Waitrose*	1 Serving/375g	285	76	5.1	10.8	1.4	1.3
Chicken & Vegetable, Potato Topped, Somerfield*	1 Pack/350g	270	77	3.7	8.8	3.0	2.0
Chicken & Vegetable, Value, Tesco*	1 Pie/150g	378	252	5.5	19.7	16.8	1.0
Chicken Cottage, Tesco*	1 Pack/400g	344	86	3.1	11.7	3.0	1.2
Chicken, Aunt Bessie's*	¼ Pie/200g	452	226	9.5	22.3	11.0	1.3
Chicken, Bacon & Cheddar Cheese, Lattice, Bird's Eye*	1 Lattice/157g	460	293	13.4	21.0	17.3	1.5
Chicken, Bird's Eye*	1 Pie/158g	414	262	7.2	23.1	15.6	1.3
Chicken, Broccoli & White Wine, Waitrose*	1 Serving/200g	605	303	12.6	17.7	20.3	2.3
Chicken, Cheese & Bacon, Healthy Living, Tesco*	1 Pack/450g	401	89	6.2	10.0	2.7	0.1
Chicken, Cheese & Brocolli Lattice, Bird's Eye*	1 Lattice/150g	380	253	10.3	18.4	14.8	1.0
Chicken, Cheese & Leek Lattice, Sun Valley*	1 Lattice/125g	315	252	15.2	8.6	17.5	1.0
Chicken, Deep Filled, Puff Pastry, Sainsbury's*	1 Pie/210g	538	256	10.0	19.9	15.2	3.1
Chicken, Eat Smart, Safeway*	1 Pack/400g	340	85	8.2	9.0	1.7	1.2
Chicken, Individual Shortcrust, Asda*	1 Pie/175g	534	305	10.0	28.0	17.0	1.0
Chicken, Individual, Bird's Eye*	1 Pie/155g	473	305	8.7	25.6	18.6	1.9
Chicken, Roast, Puff Pastry, Deep Fill, Asda*	½ Pie/259g	739	285	10.0	23.0	17.0	0.8
Chicken, Short Crust, Marks & Spencer*	1 Pie/170g	510	300	9.7	26.2	17.4	1.7
Chocolate, Mini, Waitrose*	1 Pie/24.0g	109	455	5.3	51.4	25.3	1.7
Cod & Prawn, Marks & Spencer*	1oz/28g	43	155	10.6	8.7	8.9	0.7
Cod & Smoked Haddock, COU, Marks & Spencer*	1 Serving/300g	195	65	6.8	6.2	1.3	1.4
Cottage, Aberdeen Angus, Finest, Tesco*	½ Pie/360g	403	112	8.2	8.4	5.1	0.7
Cottage, Aberdeen Angus, Waitrose*	1 Pie/350g	340	97	5.3	11.0	3.5	0.9
Cottage, Asda*	1 Pie/300g	258	86	4.3	11.0	2.8	0.9

PIE,	Measure INFO/WEIGHT	per Measure KCAL	Nutrition Values per 100g / 100ml				
			KCAL	PROT	CARB	FAT	FIBRE
Cottage, British Classics, Tesco*	½ Pie/475g	480	101	4.7	11.6	4.0	0.6
Cottage, COU, Marks & Spencer*	1oz/28g	27	95	8.0	11.0	1.9	0.6
Cottage, Classic British, Sainsburys*	1 Pack/450g	500	111	6.3	11.1	4.6	0.6
Cottage, Eat Smart, Safeway*	1 Pack/388g	310	80	5.5	8.7	2.3	1.9
Cottage, Fresh, Marks & Spencer*	1 Pie/400g	460	115	6.8	9.9	5.6	0.6
Cottage, Frozen, Asda*	1 Serving/121g	146	121	4.8	12.0	6.0	0.6
Cottage, GFY, Asda*	1 Pack/414g	302	73	6.0	9.0	1.4	1.3
Cottage, Good Intentions, Somerfield*	1 Serving/300g	261	87	6.2	11.0	2.0	1.2
Cottage, Healthy Living, Co-Op*	1 Pack/400g	340	85	5.0	11.0	2.0	1.0
Cottage, Healthy Living, Tesco*	1 Pack/400g	356	89	5.4	10.7	2.7	1.9
Cottage, Large, Tesco*	1 Pack/475g	575	121	5.5	10.8	6.2	0.5
Cottage, Luxury, Marks & Spencer*	½ Pack/310g	403	130	7.7	9.5	6.9	1.6
Cottage, Meal for One, Marks & Spencer*	1 Pack/445g	356	80	4.7	7.1	3.7	1.2
Cottage, Meatfree, Sainsbury's*	1 Pack/400g	364	91	4.4	11.7	3.0	0.7
Cottage, Mega, Tesco*	1 Pie/500g	470	94	4.1	11.6	3.5	0.7
Cottage, New, Healthy Living, Tesco*	1 Pack/450g	374	83	3.4	11.2	2.7	0.7
Cottage, Ross*	1 Pack/320g	240	75	3.0	10.9	2.2	0.3
Cottage, Safeway*	1 Serving/400g	1000	250	13.6	38.8	4.3	7.8
Cottage, Sainsbury's*	1 Pack/300g	207	69	3.8	10.4	1.4	1.2
Cottage, SmartPrice, Asda*	1 Pie/159g	149	94	3.1	12.0	3.7	0.7
Cottage, Tesco*	1 Pie/300g	300	100	3.3	12.5	4.1	0.5
Cottage, Value, Tesco*	1 Serving/155g	163	105	3.8	11.4	4.9	0.7
Cottage, Vegetarian, Tesco*	1 Pack/400g	432	108	4.4	12.9	4.3	0.9
Cottage, Vegetarien, Safeway*	1 Serving/400g	260	65	3.5	10.0	1.1	2.0
Cottage, Weight Watchers*	1 Pack/320g	230	72	3.8	11.3	1.2	0.5
Cumberland Fish, Healthy Living, Tesco*	1 Serving/450g	396	88	6.0	10.0	2.7	0.8
Cumberland, Asda*	1 Serving/300g	336	112	6.0	12.0	4.4	0.9
Cumberland, British Classics, Tesco*	1 Pack/500g	490	98	5.2	8.2	4.9	1.3
Cumberland, GFY, Asda*	1 Pack/400g	384	96	7.0	12.0	2.2	0.1
Cumberland, Healthy Living, Tesco*	1 Pie/500g	430	86	4.5	10.8	2.7	1.2
Cumberland, Marks & Spencer*	1 Pie/195g	312	160	6.9	10.1	10.4	1.1
Cumberland, Safeway*	1 Pie/450g	608	135	5.9	11.4	7.2	1.3
Cumberland, Tesco*	1 Pie/500g	575	115	6.3	10.9	5.1	1.3
Dutch Apple, Burger King*	1 Pie/113g	339	300	1.7	46.0	12.3	0.8
Festive, BGTY, Sainsbury's*	1 Pie/58g	222	383	6.2	69.9	8.7	2.6
Fish	1 Serving/250g	263	105	8.0	12.3	3.0	0.7
Fish & Prawn, Perfectly Balanced, Waitrose*	1 Serving/375g	379	101	6.8	10.4	3.6	0.7
Fish With Cheese, Ross*	1 Pack/300g	321	107	4.7	12.0	4.5	0.8
Fish With Vegetables, Ross*	1 Pack/300g	255	85	4.4	10.2	2.9	1.3
Fish, Asda*	1 Pack/338g	372	110	6.0	11.0	4.7	1.3
Fish, Better for You, Morrisons*	1 Pack/350g	301	86	5.0	10.0	2.9	0.9
Fish, Creamy, Finest, Tesco*	1 Serving/300g	438	146	10.3	5.7	9.1	0.8
Fish, Frozen, Asda*	1 Pie/400g	504	126	5.0	13.0	6.0	1.1
Fish, GFY, Asda*	1 Pack/356.4g	360	101	6.0	14.0	2.3	0.9
Fish, Good Intentions, Somerfield*	1 Pack/400g	284	71	5.2	10.2	1.0	0.5
Fish, Healthy Living, Co-Op*	1 Pack/400g	280	70	5.0	9.0	1.0	0.6
Fish, Healthy Living, Tesco*	1 Pack/400g	316	79	4.0	10.8	2.2	1.7
Fish, Luxury, Cafe Culture, Marks & Spencer*	1 Pack/660g	627	95	7.1	7.8	4.0	1.1
Fish, Luxury, Marks & Spencer*	1 Pack/300g	330	110	7.3	7.6	5.6	1.5
Fish, Mashed Potato Topped, Asda*	¼ Pie/257g	306	119	6.0	8.0	7.0	0.5
Fish, Topped With Potato, GFY, Asda*	1 Pack/450g	414	92	6.0	9.0	3.6	1.1
Fish, With Grated Cheddar, Asda*	¼ Pie/250g	263	105	7.0	8.0	5.0	1.0
Fisherman's, Asda*	1 Serving/300g	429	143	7.0	13.0	7.0	0.0

PIE,

	Measure INFO/WEIGHT	per Measure KCAL	Nutrition Values per 100g / 100ml				
			KCAL	PROT	CARB	FAT	FIBRE
Fisherman's, Chilled, Co-Op*	1 Pie/300g	345	115	4.0	11.0	6.0	0.7
Fisherman's, Healthy Eating, Tesco*	1 Pie/400g	308	77	5.1	9.2	2.2	1.3
Fisherman's, Healthy Options, Asda*	1 Pie/406g	337	83	5.0	10.0	2.5	0.9
Fisherman's, Morrisons*	1 Serving/300g	246	82	3.8	9.5	3.3	1.0
Fisherman's, Sainsbury's*	1 Pack/300g	195	65	3.9	9.7	1.2	1.2
Fisherman's, Tesco*	1 Pie/400g	400	100	4.2	9.8	4.9	1.1
Fisherman's, Youngs*	1 Pack/375g	499	133	6.2	11.2	7.0	0.8
Fruit, Pastry Top & Bottom	1oz/28g	73	260	3.0	34.0	13.3	1.8
Gala, Tesco*	1 Serving/70g	241	344	10.6	24.5	25.2	0.0
Haddock & Broccoli, Marks & Spencer*	1 Serving/250g	263	105	8.1	9.3	4.0	0.5
Haddock Cumberland, Marks & Spencer*	1 Pie/300g	345	115	7.8	10.1	4.7	0.7
Haddock, Eat Smart, Safeway*	1 Pack/400g	300	75	5.2	10.0	1.4	1.0
Key Lime, Sainsbury's*	¼ Pie/80g	280	350	4.2	51.8	14.0	0.7
Lamb & Mint, Tesco*	¼ Pack/150g	413	275	5.9	23.6	17.4	1.6
Lamb Shepherd's, Waitrose*	1 Pie/350g	448	128	7.1	10.5	6.4	1.0
Lemon Meringue	1oz/28g	89	319	4.5	45.9	14.4	0.7
Lemon Meringue, 90% Fat Free, Sara Lee*	1/6 Slice/75g	204	273	2.4	46.1	8.9	0.9
Lemon Meringue, I Need A, Marks & Spencer*	1 Pot/105g	221	210	2.1	23.3	12.0	2.6
Lemon Meringue, Lyons*	1 Serving/100g	310	310	0.0	45.9	14.4	0.0
Lemon Meringue, Marks & Spencer*	1 Serving/119.4g	399	335	3.2	45.2	15.5	0.3
Lemon Meringue, Mr Kipling*	1 Cake/51g	184	360	2.9	59.9	12.1	3.0
Lemon Meringue, Sara Lee*	1oz/28g	77	276	2.6	46.6	9.2	0.9
Lemon Meringue, Tesco*	1 Pie/385g	989	257	4.0	43.7	7.3	0.5
Lemon Meringue, Weight Watchers*	1 Serving/85g	161	189	2.4	43.1	0.5	0.6
Mariner's, Ross*	1 Pie/340g	435	128	5.0	13.9	5.9	1.0
Mariners, Youngs*	1 Serving/340g	401	118	5.5	12.1	5.3	0.5
Mashed Potato Topped Cumberland, Marks & Spencer*	1/3 Pack/300g	360	120	5.8	9.6	5.9	1.0
Meat & Potato, Shortcrust, Co-Op*	¼ Pie/137g	403	294	7.3	23.3	19.1	1.4
Meat & Potato, Value, Tesco*	1 Pie/95g	274	288	6.9	23.8	18.4	3.5
Meat, Freshbake*	1 Pie/48.6g	153	313	6.6	23.2	21.6	1.0
Mince, Asda*	1 Pie/53.4g	202	382	3.8	58.0	15.0	1.5
Mince, Christmas, Sainsbury's*	1 Pie/37g	147	397	4.5	58.0	16.3	2.6
Mince, Deep Filled, Sainsbury's*	1 Pie/67g	240	358	3.5	55.0	13.8	1.4
Mince, Deep Filled, Tesco*	1 Pie/57g	215	376	3.9	57.8	14.3	1.6
Mince, Extra Special, Asda*	1 Pie/59.5g	243	405	3.4	64.0	15.0	2.5
Mince, Finest, Tesco*	1 Pie/61g	234	384	4.3	59.9	14.1	2.7
Mince, Free From Tesco*	1 Pie/60g	188	314	2.0	58.4	8.0	4.8
Mince, Iced Top, Asda*	1 Pie/57g	214	375	2.8	61.0	12.0	1.1
Mince, Iceland*	1 Pie/38.5g	158	405	4.4	59.6	16.6	3.8
Mince, Individual	1 Pie/48g	203	423	4.3	59.0	20.4	2.1
Mince, Lattice, Marks & Spencer*	1 Pie/51g	204	400	4.4	58.0	16.8	4.1
Mince, Luxury, Deep Filled, Marks & Spencer*	1 Pie/65g	234	360	4.3	55.0	13.8	3.8
Mince, Merry, Mr Kipling*	1 Pie/62g	234	376	3.7	59.2	13.8	1.5
Mince, Mini, Marks & Spencer*	1 Pie/27.6g	106	380	4.3	57.8	14.6	4.0
Mince, Mini, Waitrose*	1 Pie/30g	150	501	5.7	51.3	30.3	1.7
Mince, Mr Kipling*	1 Pie/62g	231	372	3.8	56.8	14.4	1.5
Mince, Organic, Sainsbury's*	1 Pie/46.1g	177	384	5.0	54.5	16.2	5.6
Mince, Safeway*	1 Pie/55g	213	388	3.9	58.8	15.2	1.6
Mince, Shortcrust, Waitrose*	1 Pie/54.5g	212	385	3.6	60.0	14.6	20.9
Mince, Somerfield*	1oz/28g	111	398	4.0	56.0	17.0	0.0
Mince, Tesco*	1 Pie/47g	180	383	3.9	54.7	16.5	1.5
Mince, Value, Tesco*	1 Pie/45g	185	410	4.3	58.4	17.7	1.6
Minced Beef & Onion, Aberdeen Angus, Somerfield*	1 Serving/240g	732	305	8.6	25.8	18.6	1.0

P

PIE,	Measure INFO/WEIGHT	per Measure KCAL	KCAL	PROT	CARB	FAT	FIBRE
Minced Beef & Onion, Bird's Eye*	1 Pie/145g	419	289	7.1	26.3	17.3	0.7
Minced Beef & Onion, Sainsbury's*	1 Pie/150g	410	273	6.8	27.8	15.0	0.9
Minced Beef & Onion, Tesco*	1 Pie/150g	455	303	5.7	27.4	19.0	1.7
Minced Beef & Vegetable, Pot, Marks & Spencer*	1/3 Pie/183g	366	200	7.8	9.1	14.5	7.1
Minced Beef, Plate, Marks & Spencer*	1oz/28g	71	253	7.6	20.7	16.0	2.0
Minced Steak & Onion, Sainsbury's*	1/3 Pie/172.9g	524	303	11.7	24.8	17.4	2.0
Mississippi Mud, Tesco*	1 Serving/104g	399	384	5.3	33.1	25.6	1.8
Moroccan, Filo, Marks & Spencer*	1 Serving/125g	181	145	4.9	16.4	6.5	2.6
Mushroom & Parsley Potato, Waitrose*	1 Pack/350g	347	99	2.5	10.9	5.0	1.2
Ocean, BGTY, Sainsbury's*	1 Pack/350g	270	77	5.4	10.5	1.5	1.1
Ocean, Frozen, BGTY, Sainsbury's*	1 Pack/350g	319	91	7.0	12.4	1.5	0.9
Ocean, Marks & Spencer*	1 Pie/650g	532	95	8.2	7.6	3.5	0.9
Ocean, Weightwatchers*	1 Pack/295g	221	75	4.7	10.4	1.6	0.5
Ocean, With Cod, Weight Watchers*	1 Pack/295g	251	85	5.4	10.0	2.6	0.8
Ocean, With White Fish, Weight Watchers*	1 Pack/295g	221	75	4.7	10.4	1.6	0.5
Ocean, Youngs*	1 Serving/187.5g	250	133	6.2	11.2	7.0	0.8
Pork, & Egg, Marks & Spencer*	1/4 Pie/108g	379	351	9.7	19.8	25.9	0.8
Pork, & Pickle, Pork Farms*	1 Pie/50g	185	370	8.5	30.1	24.0	0.0
Pork, Buffet, Bowyers*	1 Pie/60g	217	362	10.4	24.9	24.5	0.0
Pork, Cheese & Pickle, Mini, Tesco*	1 Pie/49g	191	389	9.2	29.3	26.1	1.2
Pork, Crusty Bake, Mini, Sainsbury's*	1 Pie/43g	165	384	11.5	26.0	26.0	1.5
Pork, Crusty Bake, Sainsbury's*	1 Pie/75g	293	390	10.5	27.0	26.7	1.0
Pork, Geo Adams*	1 Pie/125g	488	390	11.8	23.1	27.8	0.9
Pork, Medium, Pork Farms*	1/6 Pie/51g	188	369	10.2	20.8	27.2	0.0
Pork, Melton Mowbray, Cured, Marks & Spencer*	1 Pie/290g	1044	360	10.1	25.9	24.5	1.0
Pork, Melton Mowbray, Cured, Mini, Marks & Spencer*	1 Pie/50g	193	385	9.8	32.6	24.4	1.0
Pork, Melton Mowbray, Ginsters*	1 Pie/75g	317	423	12.3	25.2	30.3	0.9
Pork, Melton Mowbray, Medium, Somerfield*	1/4 Pie/70g	275	393	11.0	27.0	27.0	0.0
Pork, Melton Mowbray, Mini, Morrisons*	1 Pie/50.1g	197	393	10.9	31.3	24.9	0.9
Pork, Melton Mowbray, Mini, Tesco*	1 Pie/50g	196	392	12.6	20.8	28.7	2.9
Pork, Melton Mowbray, Safeway*	1 Pie/50g	197	393	10.9	31.3	24.9	0.9
Pork, Melton Mowbray, Small, Somerfield*	1/2 Pie/64g	237	371	12.0	30.0	23.0	0.0
Pork, Melton Mowbray, Tesco*	1 Sm Pie/148g	679	459	10.0	29.0	33.7	1.3
Pork, Melton, Mini, Pork Farms*	1 Pie/50g	200	399	8.9	26.2	29.2	0.0
Pork, Mini, Tesco*	1 Pie/45g	162	359	10.2	25.9	23.8	1.0
Pork, Somerfield*	1 Pie/110g	442	402	11.0	24.0	29.0	0.0
Potato & Meat, Farmfoods*	1 Pie/158g	416	263	5.4	22.0	17.0	1.0
Potato Topped Cottage, Marks & Spencer*	1 Pack/190g	238	125	5.8	10.0	6.8	0.7
Potato Topped Salmon, Marks & Spencer*	1 Pie/300g	285	95	6.2	10.3	3.3	1.1
Rhubarb, Sara Lee*	1 Serving/89.6g	225	250	2.9	28.7	13.8	1.3
Roast Chicken & Vegetable, Pot, Marks & Spencer*	1/3 Pie/183g	366	200	7.7	13.5	12.5	4.5
Roast Chicken, COU, Marks & Spencer*	1 Pack/320g	272	85	9.4	9.7	1.0	0.8
Roast Chicken, Marks & Spencer*	1 Serving/170g	451	265	9.9	23.4	14.4	1.0
Roast Chicken, Sainsbury's*	1/3 Pie/173g	535	311	10.5	27.2	17.8	0.9
Roast Chicken, Shortcrust, Sainsbury's*	1 Pie/200g	1012	506	19.2	44.4	28.0	2.4
Salmon & Broccoli Lattice Bar, Asda*	1/3 Bar/133g	360	271	6.0	28.0	15.0	0.8
Salmon & Broccoli Lattice, Marks & Spencer*	1/3 Lattice/120g	300	250	8.7	14.9	17.4	4.4
Salmon & Broccoli, Bird's Eye*	1 Pie/351g	449	128	6.6	11.4	6.2	0.7
Salmon & Broccoli, Filo Pastry, Finest, Tesco*	1 Pie/170g	386	227	7.9	18.9	13.3	2.1
Salmon & Broccoli, Premium, Tesco*	1 Serving/170g	425	250	6.1	17.7	17.2	0.7
Salmon Cottage, Sainsbury's*	1 Pack/218g	159	73	4.6	10.4	1.4	1.3
Salmon, Value, Tesco*	1 Pack/300g	312	104	4.5	11.3	4.5	1.0
Sausage & Onion, Tesco*	1 Pack/300g	333	111	2.3	11.7	6.1	0.5

PIE,

INFO/WEIGHT	Measure	per Measure KCAL	Nutrition Values per 100g / 100ml				
			KCAL	PROT	CARB	FAT	FIBRE
Scotch, Co-Op*	1 Pie/132g	408	309	7.3	27.3	18.9	1.5
Scottish Steak, Topcrust Puff Pastry, Marks & Spencer*	1 Portion/240g	432	180	13.1	12.1	8.5	0.7
Shepherd's	1oz/28g	31	112	6.0	9.3	5.9	0.7
Shepherd's Pie, Safeway*	1 Serving/200g	200	100	6.5	11.4	2.9	1.1
Shepherd's With Lamb, Weight Watchers*	1 Pack/320g	234	73	3.8	11.6	1.2	0.5
Shepherd's, Asda*	1 Pie/153g	193	126	5.0	13.0	6.0	0.8
Shepherd's, BGTY, Sainsbury's*	1 Pack/300g	225	75	3.6	10.2	2.2	1.7
Shepherd's, Baked Bean Cuisine, Heinz*	1 Pie/340g	299	88	4.1	11.6	2.8	1.5
Shepherd's, British Classics, Tesco*	1 Pack/500g	715	143	4.8	10.5	9.1	1.4
Shepherd's, COU, Marks & Spencer*	1 Pack/300g	210	70	5.2	8.6	1.3	1.6
Shepherd's, Classic British, Sainsbury's*	1 Pack/450g	500	111	6.6	10.8	4.6	0.7
Shepherd's, Finest, Tesco*	1 Pack/350g	364	104	7.2	9.5	4.1	0.6
Shepherd's, Frozen, Tesco*	1 Pack/400g	508	127	4.2	11.7	7.1	1.0
Shepherd's, Great Value, Asda*	1 Pack/400g	376	94	4.7	12.0	3.0	0.6
Shepherd's, Marks & Spencer*	1 Pack/400g	380	95	5.3	9.7	3.9	1.4
Shepherd's, Mashed Potato Topped, Marks & Spencer*	½ Pack/200g	220	110	7.1	8.9	4.7	0.5
Shepherd's, Perfectly Balanced, Waitrose*	1oz/28g	24	87	5.8	10.5	2.4	1.0
Shepherd's, Sainsbury's*	1 Pie/300g	225	75	3.6	10.2	2.2	1.7
Shepherd's, Tesco*	1 Pie/400g	380	95	6.0	10.5	3.2	0.7
Shepherd's, Weight Watchers*	1 Pack/326g	290	89	5.8	12.7	1.5	0.8
Shepherd's, Welsh Hill Lamb, Marks & Spencer*	½ Pack/310g	295	95	5.4	10.2	3.5	1.5
Smoked Haddock, Eat Smart, Safeway*	1 Pack/400g	376	94	8.1	10.1	2.4	1.2
Steak & Ale, British Classics, Tesco*	1 Serving/150g	380	253	7.8	22.8	14.5	3.3
Steak & Ale, Deep Filled, Somerfield*	1 Pie/200g	550	275	12.0	22.0	16.0	0.0
Steak & Ale, Fray Bentos*	1 Pie/425g	697	164	7.6	13.0	9.1	0.0
Steak & Ale, Pub Style, Co-Op*	1 Pie/250g	538	215	9.0	17.0	12.0	2.0
Steak & Gravy, Somerfield*	1oz/28g	67	239	13.0	23.0	11.0	0.0
Steak & Guinness, Sainsbury's*	¼ Pie/137g	399	291	8.7	22.2	18.6	1.0
Steak & Kidney, Bird's Eye*	1 Pie/146g	419	287	9.5	24.4	17.1	1.7
Steak & Kidney, Family, Co-Op*	1/6 Pie/87g	278	320	9.0	26.0	20.0	0.9
Steak & Kidney, Individual	1 Pie/200g	646	323	9.1	25.6	21.2	0.9
Steak & Kidney, Marks & Spencer*	1 Serving/170g	459	270	8.8	24.7	15.1	1.3
Steak & Kidney, Premium, Tesco*	1 Serving/170g	428	252	9.9	18.3	15.5	1.2
Steak & Kidney, Princes*	½ Pack/212g	379	179	8.8	14.8	9.4	0.0
Steak & Kidney, Puff Pastry, Sainsbury's*	1 Pie/150g	423	282	8.2	26.9	15.7	0.9
Steak & Kidney, Tinned, Fray Bentos*	½ Pie/212g	346	163	8.2	12.9	8.8	0.0
Steak & Mushroom, Asda*	1 Pack/300g	270	90	5.0	10.0	3.3	0.7
Steak & Mushroom, Bird's Eye*	1 Pie/142g	389	274	7.5	22.7	17.0	2.0
Steak & Mushroom, Deep Fill, Asda*	1/3 Pie/175g	476	272	11.0	21.0	16.0	1.1
Steak & Mushroom, Family, Iceland*	¼ Pie/164g	366	223	10.5	15.4	13.3	2.9
Steak & Mushroom, Healthy Eating, Tesco*	1 Serving/200g	380	190	10.5	24.2	5.7	1.9
Steak & Mushroom, Sainsbury's*	¼ Pie/130g	372	286	8.6	26.0	16.4	1.0
Steak & Onion, Farmfoods*	1 Pie/127g	382	301	6.0	26.4	19.1	1.0
Steak & Red Wine, Puff Pastry, Pub, Sainsbury's*	1 Pie/240g	497	207	7.2	16.8	12.3	2.1
Steak, Asda*	1 Pie/150g	453	302	9.2	25.1	18.3	1.0
Steak, Au Gratin, Tesco*	1 Pack/450g	594	132	8.7	10.7	6.0	1.1
Steak, Classic British, Shortcrust Pastry, Sainsbury's*	¼ Pie/130g	519	299	9.9	27.1	16.8	0.9
Steak, Marks & Spencer*	1oz/28g	64	230	10.0	19.0	12.7	1.2
Steak, Puff Pastry, Deep Filled, Sainsbury's*	1 Pie/210g	536	255	10.3	21.4	14.3	2.0
Steak, Puff Pastry, Deep Filled, Somerfield*	½ Pie/275g	715	260	10.0	23.7	13.9	0.8
Steak, Safeway*	¼ Pie/130g	381	293	9.4	27.4	16.2	1.1
Steak, Short Crust, Sainsbury's*	¼ Pie/131g	392	299	9.9	27.1	16.8	0.9
Steak, Shortcrust Pastry, Tesco*	1/3 Pie/300g	693	231	10.7	21.9	11.2	1.0

	Measure	per Measure		Nutrition Values per 100g / 100ml				
	INFO/WEIGHT	KCAL		KCAL	PROT	CARB	FAT	FIBRE
PIE,								
Steak, Tesco*	1 Serving/205g	556		271	7.2	23.3	16.5	1.4
Strawberry Creme, Slice, KFC*	1 Slice/78g	279		358	5.4	41.0	19.2	2.5
Summer Fruits, Orchard Tree, Aldi*	1/8 Pie/75g	242		323	3.0	46.6	13.8	1.2
Teviot, Minced Beef, Morrisons*	½ Pie/250g	383		153	8.0	14.5	6.9	1.6
Tuna & Sweetcorn, Healthy Living, Tesco*	1 Pack/450g	392		87	7.1	8.6	2.7	2.0
Turkey & Ham, Shortcrust, Marks & Spencer*	1/3 Pie/183g	494		270	11.9	19.5	15.9	1.0
Vegetable	1oz/28g	42		151	3.0	18.9	7.6	1.5
Vegetable & Cheddar Cheese, Waitrose*	1 Pie/210g	475		226	4.9	17.8	15.0	1.2
Vegetable & Cheese, Asda*	1 Pie/131g	346		264	6.0	24.0	16.0	1.8
Vegetable, Healthy Eating, Tesco*	1 Pack/450g	360		80	2.7	11.1	2.7	0.8
Vegetarian, Deep Country, Linda McCartney*	1 Pie/176g	375		213	5.5	25.1	10.0	3.4
Vegetarian, Shepherd's, Linda McCartney*	1 Pack/340g	317		93	4.6	13.9	2.1	1.6
Vegetarian, Vegetable Cumberland, Marks & Spencer*	½ Pack/211.1g	190		90	2.8	13.4	2.6	1.6
Welsh Lamb, Sainsbury's*	¼ Pie/120g	290		242	9.1	19.2	14.3	0.8
West Country Chicken, Sainsbury's*	1 Serving/240g	614		256	11.9	17.1	15.6	2.1
PIE FILLING,								
Apple, Sainsbury's*	1 Serving/75g	67		89	0.1	22.1	0.1	1.0
Black Cherry, Fruit, Sainsbury's*	1 Serving/100g	73		73	0.3	17.7	0.1	0.3
Blackcurrant, Fruit, Sainsbury's*	1 Serving/100g	82		82	0.4	20.0	0.1	1.6
Cherry	1oz/28g	23		82	0.4	21.5	0.0	0.4
Fruit	1oz/28g	22		77	0.4	20.1	0.0	1.0
Lemon, Sainsbury's*	1 Sachet/280g	218		78	0.1	18.6	0.4	0.0
Summer Fruits, Fruit, Tesco*	1 Can/385g	377		98	0.4	24.1	0.0	0.9
PIGEON,								
Meat Only, Roasted	1oz/28g	52		187	29.0	0.0	7.9	0.0
Meat Only, Roasted, Weighed With Bone	1oz/28g	25		88	13.6	0.0	3.7	0.0
PIKELETS,								
Less Than 2% Fat, Marks & Spencer*	1 Pikelet/35g	70		200	7.3	39.1	1.3	1.6
Tesco*	1 Pikelet/35g	68		193	5.8	40.9	0.7	1.7
PILAF,								
Forest Mushroom & Pine Nut, Bistro, Waitrose*	1 Serving/225g	338		150	7.0	15.8	6.5	1.5
With Tomato	1oz/28g	40		144	2.5	28.0	3.3	0.4
PILCHARDS,								
Fillets, In Tomato Sauce, Average	1 Can/120g	158		132	16.2	2.2	6.5	0.1
Fillets, In Virgin Olive Oil, Glenryck*	1 Serving/92g	223		242	23.3	2.0	15.7	0.0
In Brine, Average	½ Can/77g	114		148	20.8	0.0	7.3	0.0
PIMMS*,								
19% Volume	1fl oz/30ml	44		146	0.0	0.0	0.0	0.0
PINE NUTS,								
Average	1oz/28g	195		695	15.7	3.9	68.6	1.9
PINEAPPLE,								
& Papaya, Dried, Garden Gang, Asda*	1 Pack/50g	142		283	2.8	64.0	1.7	8.0
Dried, Tesco*	1 Serving/15g	35		230	0.4	52.9	1.9	1.7
In Juice, Average	1 Can/106g	57		53	0.3	12.9	0.0	0.6
In Syrup, Average	1 Can/240g	158		66	0.3	16.1	0.0	0.8
Pieces, Yoghurt Coated, Holland & Barrett*	1 Pack/100g	344		344	2.1	46.8	19.3	0.6
Raw, Average	1 Serving/200g	99		49	0.4	11.6	0.2	0.9
PINK GRAPEFRUIT,								
Segments, Waitrose*	¼ Can/134ml	43		32	0.6	7.3	0.0	0.4
PISTACHIO NUTS,								
Plain, Average	1 Serving/15g	91		607	20.6	8.4	54.5	7.1
Roasted & Salted, Average	1 Serving/25g	152		608	19.6	9.9	54.5	6.1
Unsalted, Roasted, KP*	1oz/28g	179		640	20.8	14.2	55.5	6.0

P

	Measure INFO/WEIGHT	per Measure KCAL	Nutrition Values per 100g / 100ml				
			KCAL	PROT	CARB	FAT	FIBRE
PITTA BREAD,							
Coronation Chicken, COU, Marks & Spencer*	1 Serving/207g	269	130	9.2	20.4	1.2	2.0
Sweet Chilli Chicken, Shapers, Boots*	1 Pack/177.5g	246	138	9.2	19.0	2.8	2.2
With Chicken, Nando's*	1oz/28g	55	196	8.8	24.5	7.4	0.0
PIZZA,							
American Hot, Chicargo Town, Chicago Town*	1 Pizza/170g	445	262	8.2	30.8	11.8	0.9
American Hot, Pizza Express*	½ Pizza/264g	517	196	10.6	26.8	5.1	1.1
BBQ Chicken Stuffed Crust, Asda*	½ Pizza/245g	613	250	13.0	27.0	10.0	2.7
BBQ Chicken, Chicago Town*	1 Pizza/172.4g	373	217	7.0	30.9	7.3	1.0
BBQ Chicken, Thin & Crispy, Sainsbury's*	½ Pizza/147g	384	261	13.8	33.1	8.2	1.6
BBQ Chicken, Thin & Crispy, Tesco*	1 Serving/165g	355	215	11.9	31.6	4.5	1.2
BBQ Chicken, Weight Watchers*	1 Pizza/224g	412	184	11.5	26.5	3.5	2.7
Bacon & Mushroom Pizzeria, Sainsbury's*	1 Pizza/355g	880	248	11.7	34.5	7.0	3.7
Bacon & Mushroom, Deep Pan, Big Bite, Goodfella's*	¼ Pizza/104g	241	232	11.3	27.3	8.6	3.6
Bacon & Mushroom, Stone Bake, Marks & Spencer*	1 Pizza/375g	750	200	9.9	27.2	6.4	1.6
Bacon & Mushroom, Thin & Crispy, Sainsbury's*	½ Pizza/150g	396	264	12.9	29.2	10.6	1.7
Bacon And Mushroom, Stonebaked, Tesco*	1 Serving/157g	352	224	10.5	24.3	9.4	3.3
Bacon, Mushroom & Tomato, Stonebaked, Tesco*	1 Serving/173g	351	203	9.9	24.1	7.4	2.0
Balsamic Roast Vegetable & Mozzarella, Sainsbury's*	½ Pizza/200g	444	222	8.5	29.4	7.8	2.4
Bianca, Bistro, Waitrose*	½ Pizza/618g	1842	298	12.9	26.2	15.7	2.3
Big American, Dr Oetker*	1 Serving/225g	572	254	9.7	28.9	11.0	0.0
Bistro Caramelised Onion, Feta & Rosemary, Waitrose*	½ Pizza/229.9g	607	264	8.6	26.1	13.9	2.4
Bistro Cheese & Tomato, Waitrose*	½ Pizza/205g	488	238	10.0	27.6	9.7	1.2
Bistro Salami & Pepperoni, Waitrose*	½ Pizza/190g	492	259	12.9	28.8	10.2	1.5
Cajun Chicken, BGTY, Sainsbury's*	½ Pizza/165g	363	220	11.0	36.0	3.6	1.7
Cajun Chicken, Pizzatilla, Marks & Spencer*	½ Pizza/240g	636	265	10.5	21.8	15.1	1.3
Cajun Chicken, Sainsbury's*	½ Pizza/146g	285	195	12.9	31.8	1.8	2.6
Cajun Style Chicken, Stonebaked, Tesco*	1 Pizza/561g	1318	235	11.9	24.8	9.8	1.4
Capricciosa, Pizza Express*	1 Serving/300g	753	251	13.6	29.1	9.8	0.0
Caprina, Pizza Express*	1 Pizza/300g	635	212	8.0	31.0	7.3	0.0
Charged Up Chilli Beef, Goodfella's*	½ Pizza/357g	857	240	12.8	26.4	9.2	1.6
Chargrilled Chicken & Bacon, Pizzeria, Sainsbury's*	½ Pizza/181g	554	306	12.8	35.4	12.6	1.2
Chargrilled Chicken & Vegetable, GFY, Asda*	½ Pizza/166g	355	214	13.0	36.0	2.0	2.0
Chargrilled Chicken, Thin & Crispy, Asda*	1 Pizza/373g	780	209	9.0	32.0	5.0	1.6
Chargrilled Vegetable, COU, Marks & Spencer*	1 Pizza/294g	397	135	6.0	23.4	2.4	1.9
Chargrilled Vegetable, Eat Smart, Safeway*	1 Pizza/206g	361	175	10.2	27.6	2.1	2.6
Chargrilled Vegetable, Frozen, BGTY, Sainsbury's*	1 Pizza/290g	548	189	10.2	26.7	4.6	3.0
Chargrilled Vegetable, Healthy Eating, Tesco*	½ Pizza/143g	320	224	10.4	39.6	2.7	1.1
Chargrilled Vegetable, Thin & Crispy, GFY, Asda*	1 Serving/188.3g	290	154	6.0	28.0	2.0	3.1
Cheese & Tomato	1oz/28g	66	237	9.1	25.2	11.8	1.4
Cheese & Tomato French Bread, Findus*	1 Piece/143g	336	235	9.1	32.2	7.7	1.5
Cheese & Tomato Range, Italiano, Tesco*	1 Pizza/380g	969	255	11.4	31.7	9.2	3.3
Cheese & Tomato Slice, Ross*	1 Slice/77g	148	192	6.5	22.2	8.6	2.0
Cheese & Tomato Thin & Crispy, Stonebaked, Tesco*	1 Pizza/155g	355	229	11.6	28.1	7.8	1.3
Cheese & Tomato, 9.5", Domino's Pizza*	1 Slice/52g	125	241	12.8	34.9	5.6	3.2
Cheese & Tomato, Basics, Somerfield*	1 Serving/80g	194	242	9.7	35.1	7.0	1.9
Cheese & Tomato, Big Value, Ross*	1 Pizza/716g	1446	202	7.8	32.2	4.7	2.7
Cheese & Tomato, Blue Parrot Cafe, Sainsbury's*	¼ Pizza/87.5g	218	248	12.7	29.5	8.8	1.2
Cheese & Tomato, Deep & Crispy, Safeway*	1 Pizza/510g	1214	238	10.2	33.3	7.1	1.5
Cheese & Tomato, Deep & Crispy, Tesco*	1oz/28g	65	231	10.8	31.7	6.8	1.2
Cheese & Tomato, Deep Pan, Goodfella's*	¼ Pizza/102.4g	258	253	11.5	29.6	10.5	3.7
Cheese & Tomato, Deep Pan, Sainsbury's*	1 Pizza/182g	470	258	11.7	33.1	8.7	1.9
Cheese & Tomato, Eat Smart, Safeway*	1 Pizza/165g	355	215	11.5	40.1	0.7	1.9
Cheese & Tomato, Economy, Sainsbury's*	1 Pizza/60g	142	237	11.2	34.1	6.2	1.8

PITZA,

INFO/WEIGHT	Measure	per Measure KCAL	KCAL	PROT	CARB	FAT	FIBRE
Cheese & Tomato, French Bread, Co-Op*	1 Pizza/135g	270	200	9.0	27.0	6.0	2.0
Cheese & Tomato, Marks & Spencer*	1oz/28g	63	225	11.5	29.3	6.9	1.3
Cheese & Tomato, Micro, McCain*	1 Slice/135g	420	311	11.7	29.5	16.2	0.0
Cheese & Tomato, Mini, Marks & Spencer*	1 Pizza/95g	233	245	10.0	38.7	5.8	1.6
Cheese & Tomato, Retail, Frozen	1oz/28g	70	250	7.5	32.9	10.7	1.4
Cheese & Tomato, Sainsbury's*	1 Pizza/247g	706	286	13.7	35.4	9.9	2.4
Cheese & Tomato, Small, Tesco*	1 Pizza/102g	226	222	9.5	31.9	6.3	1.2
Cheese & Tomato, SmartPrice, Asda*	1 Pizza/125g	356	285	13.0	38.0	9.0	0.0
Cheese & Tomato, Square, Sainsbury's*	1 Square/160g	435	272	14.0	37.6	7.3	2.1
Cheese & Tomato, Stonebaked, Organic, Co-Op*	1 Pizza/330g	677	205	9.0	26.0	7.0	4.0
Cheese & Tomato, Stonebaked, Safeway*	½ Pizza/190g	437	230	12.0	32.3	5.9	1.5
Cheese & Tomato, Stonebaked, Thin & Crispy, Tesco*	½ Pizza/161g	388	241	11.6	29.4	8.6	2.1
Cheese & Tomato, Thin & Crispy, Asda*	1 Pizza/366g	827	226	11.0	23.0	10.0	2.0
Cheese & Tomato, Thin & Crispy, Organic, Tesco*	½ Pizza/147g	369	251	10.6	30.1	9.8	1.3
Cheese & Tomato, Thin & Crispy, Safeway*	1 Serving/365g	949	260	11.7	37.2	7.0	4.7
Cheese & Tomato, Thin & Crispy, Sainsbury's*	1 Serving/135g	329	244	11.4	26.0	11.1	1.5
Cheese & Tomato, Thin & Crispy, Stonebaked, Tesco*	1/3 Pizza/212g	509	240	10.1	29.2	9.2	1.4
Cheese & Tomato, Thin & Crispy, Waitrose*	½ Pizza/118g	245	208	9.2	25.0	7.9	1.3
Cheese & Tomato, Value, Tesco*	1 Serving/140g	319	228	10.0	28.7	8.1	2.4
Cheese Feast, Deep Pan, Asda*	½ Pizza/210g	500	238	11.4	26.7	9.5	1.1
Cheese Feast, Grand Pan, Pizza Hut*	1 Serving/97g	270	278	11.3	27.8	13.4	1.0
Cheese Feast, Tesco*	1 Serving/228g	577	253	10.7	29.8	10.1	1.9
Cheese Suprema, Freschetta, Schwan's*	½ Pizza/150g	392	261	12.4	32.4	9.3	1.8
Cheese Supreme, New Recipe, Goodfella's*	¼ Pizza/102g	269	264	12.3	31.2	10.0	2.2
Cheese Triple, Chicago Town*	1 Serving/170g	418	246	9.9	27.6	10.7	0.0
Cheese, Onion & Garlic, Pizzeria, Waitrose*	½ Pizza/245.2g	684	279	10.8	29.8	11.8	2.5
Cheese, Stuffed, Crust, Sainsbury's*	1 Pizza/525g	1428	272	14.0	31.5	10.0	2.0
Cheese, Thin & Crispy, Goodfella's*	1 Serving/275g	729	265	15.7	27.6	10.1	1.8
Cheesefeast, Deep & Crispy 12", Takeaway, Iceland*	1 Slice/132g	342	259	13.1	32.8	8.4	1.5
Chicken & Bacon, Loaded, Tesco*	1 Serving/258g	622	241	12.8	25.4	9.8	1.9
Chicken & Maple Bacon Carbonara, Asda*	½ Pizza/195g	484	248	11.0	33.0	8.0	2.2
Chicken & Pesto, Californian Style, Asda*	½ Pizza/234.8g	533	227	10.0	31.0	7.0	2.0
Chicken & Red Pepper Tapenade, TTD, Sainsbury's*	¼ Pizza/39.0g	103	264	12.3	25.5	12.5	2.1
Chicken & Red Pepper, Healthy Eating, Tesco*	1 Pizza/260g	608	234	12.7	40.1	2.5	0.7
Chicken & Spinach, Eat Smart, Safeway*	1 Pizza/165g	322	195	19.0	24.0	2.1	2.5
Chicken & Sweetcorn, Stonebaked, Tesco*	1 Serving/177g	354	200	11.9	26.0	5.4	2.0
Chicken & Vegetable, Stone Baked, GFY, Asda*	½ Pizza/160.8g	349	217	13.0	36.0	2.3	1.7
Chicken Arrabbiata, Marks & Spencer*	1 Pizza/325g	618	190	11.6	26.5	4.2	1.1
Chicken Arrabiata, Sainsbury's*	½ Pizza/191.4g	443	232	12.1	31.4	6.4	1.7
Chicken Provencal, Goodfella's*	½ Pizza/142.5g	389	272	13.7	25.9	12.6	2.1
Chicken Salsa, Healthy Choice, Safeway*	½ Pizza/177g	437	246	13.3	40.9	3.2	1.6
Chicken Salsa, Healthy Living, Tesco*	½ Pizza/169g	313	185	13.0	30.3	1.3	1.5
Chicken Supreme, Medium Pan, Pizza Hut*	½ Pizza/300g	810	270	13.0	29.0	12.0	2.0
Chicken, Thin & Crispy, Somerfield*	½ Pizza/159g	356	224	11.1	29.0	7.1	2.9
Chilli Beef, Stone Bake, Marks & Spencer*	1 Pizza/395g	790	200	9.6	26.7	5.8	1.9
Chorizo & CherryBell Peppers, TTD, Sainsbury's*	½ Pizza/194.7g	589	302	13.8	33.0	12.8	2.2
Chorizo & Sweet Pepper, Stonebaked, Safeway*	1 Serving/190g	466	245	9.9	35.5	6.8	3.8
Cream Cheese & Pepperonata, Calzone, Waitrose*	½ Pizza/165g	383	232	7.0	29.4	9.6	1.5
Deep South, Chicago Town*	1 Pizza/171g	363	212	6.9	30.0	7.1	0.0
Delicata Four Season Ultra Thin, TTD, Sainsbury's*	½ Pizza/168g	445	265	13.3	24.3	12.9	2.3
Delicia, Mediterranean, Goodfella's*	½ Pizza/150.2g	371	247	9.1	25.3	12.2	2.1
Deluxe, 9.5", Domino's Pizza*	1 Slice/66g	171	259	12.8	29.1	10.1	2.4
Double Cheese, Chicago Town*	1 Pizza/405g	932	230	11.7	30.6	6.7	0.0

PIZZA,

INFO/WEIGHT	Measure per Measure KCAL		Nutrition Values per 100g / 100ml				
			KCAL	PROT	CARB	FAT	FIBRE
Double Cheese, Square Snacks, Food Explorer, Waitrose*	1 Pizza/145.5g	415	286	12.4	40.2	7.5	1.9
Fajita Chicken, COU, Marks & Spencer*	1 Pizza/255g	434	170	9.9	25.5	2.4	1.2
Fajita Vegetable, BGTY, Sainsbury's*	1 Pizza/214g	366	171	8.9	30.8	1.4	2.9
Fingers & Curly Fries, Marks & Spencer*	1 Pack/211.8g	360	170	7.9	22.9	4.9	1.6
Fingers, McCain*	1 Finger/33g	76	230	11.8	28.9	7.5	0.0
Fire Roasted Pepper, Sainsbury's*	1 Pizza/344g	605	176	5.3	35.3	1.5	1.6
Five Cheese & Pepperoni, Deep & Crispy, Waitrose*	1/3 Pizza/200g	560	280	11.7	32.3	11.6	1.3
Flamed Chicken & Vegetables, BGTY, Sainsbury's*	1 Pizza/260g	660	254	14.2	39.3	4.4	2.3
Flamin' Hot, Deep Dish, Chicago Town*	1 Pizza/170g	454	267	8.6	31.1	12.0	0.0
Focaccia Tomato & Black Olive, TTD, Sainsbury's*	½ Pizza/222g	515	232	9.3	28.7	8.9	2.9
Four Cheese & Tomato, Pizzatilla, Marks & Spencer*	1 Serving/69.3g	224	324	10.5	26.0	19.9	1.5
Four Cheese, Deep Pan, Tesco*	½ Pizza/253g	741	293	14.6	33.6	11.1	1.5
Four Cheese, Freschetta, Schwan's*	¼ Slice/75g	205	273	11.3	34.8	9.8	1.4
Four Cheese, Marks & Spencer*	1oz/28g	67	240	13.2	30.3	7.5	1.2
Four Cheese, Thin & Crispy, Sainsbury's*	1 Pizza/265g	729	275	11.8	29.3	12.3	3.5
Four Cheese, Thin Crust, Tesco*	½ Pizza/142g	386	272	14.5	31.8	9.6	1.8
Four Cheese, Weight Watchers*	1 Pizza/186g	400	215	10.8	34.9	3.8	1.6
Four Seasons, Pizza Express*	1 Serving/300g	720	240	11.6	29.2	9.6	0.0
French Bread, Blue Parrot Cafe, Sainsbury's*	1 Pizza/132g	271	205	10.7	30.8	4.3	1.3
Frutti Di Mare, Express, Pizza Express*	1 Pizza/373g	500	134	9.1	20.1	2.6	0.0
Full House, 9.5", Domino's Pizza*	1 Slice/74g	183	247	12.5	25.5	10.5	1.8
Funghi, Pizzaroma, Safeway*	½ Pizza/205g	506	247	10.8	29.3	9.6	2.9
Garden Style, Hot Stuff*	1 Slice/188g	370	197	0.0	21.3	11.2	1.6
Garlic & Mushroom, Thin & Crispy, Sainsbury's*	1 Pizza/260g	829	319	11.1	31.2	16.6	1.7
Garlic Chicken & Spinach, Perfectly Balanced, Waitrose*	½ Pizza/172g	351	204	13.3	30.8	3.1	2.3
Garlic Chicken, Deep Pan, Sainsbury's*	½ Pizza/214g	464	217	11.2	28.3	6.5	3.3
Garlic Mushroom, BGTY, Sainsbury's*	½ Pizza/123g	262	213	11.6	37.2	2.0	2.7
Garlic Mushroom, Ciabatta Style, Stonebake, Goodfella's*	½ Pizza/186.6g	475	254	10.0	27.9	12.3	2.2
Garlic Mushroom, Classico, Tesco*	½ Pizza/207.5g	415	200	10.0	24.9	6.7	2.6
Garlic Mushroom, Italian Style, Somerfield*	½ Pizza/175g	460	263	9.0	33.0	10.0	0.0
Garlic Mushroom, Safeway*	½ Pizza/155g	482	311	9.4	39.2	12.9	1.7
Garlic Mushroom, Tesco*	1 Pizza/425g	829	195	9.3	21.6	8.0	5.3
Giardiniera, Pizza Express*	1 Pizza/300g	735	245	10.2	34.5	8.4	0.0
Giardino, Wood Fired, Dettori's*	½ Pizza/205g	433	211	8.0	28.5	7.2	3.0
Grilled Pepper, Weight Watchers*	1 Pizza/220g	392	178	10.0	29.3	2.3	1.8
Ham & Cheese, Chunky, Asda*	1 Serving/90g	211	234	12.0	39.0	3.3	4.7
Ham & Cheese, Mini, Tesco*	1 Serving/92g	228	248	13.6	31.3	7.6	3.2
Ham & Mushroom Calzone, Waitrose*	½ Pizza/145g	363	250	10.0	31.6	9.3	1.6
Ham & Mushroom Slices, Farmfoods*	1 Slice/89g	170	191	8.0	34.0	2.6	0.9
Ham & Mushroom, BGTY, Sainsbury's*	½ Pizza/158g	291	184	10.2	26.4	4.2	2.9
Ham & Mushroom, COU, Marks & Spencer*	1 Pizza/245g	404	165	8.8	25.4	2.4	1.2
Ham & Mushroom, Deep & Crispy, Tesco*	1 Serving/210g	420	200	9.7	29.2	4.9	1.1
Ham & Mushroom, Deep Pan, Asda*	½ Pizza/223g	444	199	9.0	25.0	7.0	1.2
Ham & Mushroom, Healthy Eating, Tesco*	1 Pizza/252g	491	195	10.4	35.6	1.2	2.0
Ham & Mushroom, New, BGTY, Sainsbury's*	1 Pizza/248g	526	212	12.1	37.8	1.4	2.9
Ham & Mushroom, Stone Baked, Goodfella's*	½ Pizza/175g	439	251	9.6	27.6	11.4	1.2
Ham & Mushroom, Stonebaked, Stateside Foods*	¼ Pizza/101g	225	223	9.9	31.9	6.2	1.4
Ham & Mushroom, The Italian, Medium 12", Pizza Hut*	1 Slice/96g	270	281	13.6	35.4	10.6	2.6
Ham & Mushroom, Thin & Crispy, Asda*	1 Pizza/360g	760	211	11.0	26.0	7.0	2.4
Ham & Mushroom, Thin & Crispy, Tesco*	1 Serving/166g	349	210	13.0	23.9	6.9	2.4
Ham & Onion, Tesco*	1 Serving/181g	453	250	11.8	29.0	9.6	2.2
Ham & Pineapple, American Deep Pan, Sainsbury's*	1 Pizza/412g	1001	243	10.5	32.6	7.8	1.7
Ham & Pineapple, Chicago Town*	1 Pizza/435g	866	199	10.0	29.7	4.5	0.0

	Measure INFO/WEIGHT	per Measure KCAL	Nutrition Values per 100g / 100ml				
			KCAL	PROT	CARB	FAT	FIBRE
PIZZA,							
Ham & Pineapple, Deep Dish, Chicago Town*	1 Serving/170g	403	237	8.0	26.1	11.2	0.0
Ham & Pineapple, Deep Pan, Ciabatta, Iceland*	½ Pizza/185g	440	238	11.6	30.3	7.8	0.8
Ham & Pineapple, Deep Pan, Tesco*	1 Pizza/237g	437	184	9.8	29.8	2.9	1.9
Ham & Pineapple, Eat Smart, Safeway*	1 Serving/151g	279	185	13.6	27.2	2.4	2.5
Ham & Pineapple, Healthy Eating, Tesco*	1 Serving/169g	343	203	11.9	35.4	1.5	1.3
Ham & Pineapple, Loaded, Tesco*	½ Pizza/265g	557	210	11.3	28.7	5.5	1.4
Ham & Pineapple, Stone Bake, Marks & Spencer*	1 Pizza/345g	690	200	10.1	28.3	5.7	1.6
Ham & Pineapple, Stonebaked, Tesco*	1 Pizza/161g	293	182	9.2	23.5	5.7	3.5
Ham & Pineapple, Thin & Crispy, Goodfella's*	1 Serving/163g	333	204	10.6	22.8	7.8	2.4
Ham & Pineapple, Thin & Crispy, Safeway*	½ Pizza/182g	455	250	13.6	29.9	7.9	4.0
Ham & Pineapple, Thin & Crispy, Sainsbury's*	1 Pizza/305g	824	270	13.5	29.8	10.7	1.7
Ham & Pineapple, Thin & Crispy, Somerfield*	½ Pizza/192g	405	211	10.7	21.5	9.1	2.4
Ham & Pineapple, Thin Base, Sainsbury's*	½ Pizza/150g	321	214	11.8	23.0	8.3	3.8
Ham & Roast Onion, Classico, Italiano, Tesco*	1 Serving/181.5g	455	250	11.8	29.0	9.6	2.2
Ham, Mushroom & Gruyere, Sainsbury's*	¼ Pizza/169.0g	404	239	10.2	31.3	8.1	3.7
Ham, Mushroom & Tomato, BGTY, Sainsbury's*	½ Pizza/150g	307	206	11.8	30.4	4.1	1.2
Ham, Pepperoni & Milano, Marks & Spencer*	1 Pizza/290g	696	240	14.0	23.3	9.8	1.1
Hawaiian, Healthy Living, Tesco*	½ Pizza/175g	301	172	7.5	30.0	2.5	2.9
Hawaiian, Medium Pan, Pizza Hut*	1 Slice/96g	241	251	12.6	29.2	9.3	1.4
Hawaiian, Tesco*	1 Pizza/264g	649	246	12.1	32.4	7.6	1.5
Hawaiian, Thin Crust, Tesco*	½ Pizza/205g	398	194	8.4	28.3	5.3	2.1
Hickory Steak, Marks & Spencer*	1 Pizza/400g	820	205	9.9	25.7	6.7	1.4
Honey Roast Salmon & Broccoli, BGTY, Sainsbury's*	1 Serving/280g	613	219	12.0	34.4	4.5	3.5
Hot & Spicy Chicken, Marks & Spencer*	1oz/28g	59	210	15.5	20.9	7.3	1.9
Hot & Spicy, Deep Dish, Chicago Town*	1 Pizza/177g	434	245	8.6	30.4	9.9	0.9
Hot & Spicy, Deep Pan, Tesco*	1 Serving/221g	423	191	10.5	30.0	3.3	2.1
Hot & Spicy, Thin & Crispy, Somerfield*	1 Pizza/305g	918	301	12.0	25.0	17.0	0.0
Hot Chicken, Stone Bake, Marks & Spencer*	1 Pizza/380g	798	210	11.5	25.1	6.8	1.3
Italian Bacon, Mushroom & Parmesan, Marks & Spencer*	1 Pizza/315g	819	260	10.1	27.0	12.3	0.9
Italian Cheese & Ham, The Little Big Food Company*	1 Pizza/95g	236	248	11.0	36.3	6.6	1.0
Italian Meat Feast, Thin & Crispy, Waitrose*	1 Pizza/182g	477	262	10.7	26.5	12.6	1.8
Italian Meat, So Good, Somerfield*	½ Pizza/200g	468	234	14.0	32.4	5.4	2.4
Italian Meats, Finest, Tesco*	½ Pizza/217g	449	207	13.6	29.4	3.9	1.3
Italian Meats, TTD, Sainsbury's*	½ Pizza/223.7g	587	262	12.8	25.6	12.0	2.4
Italian Mozzarella & Black Forest Ham, Asda*	¼ Pizza/110g	227	206	10.0	28.0	6.0	2.7
La Reine, Pizza Express, Sainsbury's*	½ Pizza/155g	361	233	12.3	29.8	7.2	1.9
La Reine, Takeaway, Pizza Express*	¼ Pizza/138g	324	235	12.4	30.0	7.3	1.9
Leek & Rosemary, Prince Carlo, Pizza Express*	1 Pizza/400g	708	177	8.0	24.5	6.0	0.0
Loaded Cheese, Goodfella's*	1 Pizza/410g	1037	253	11.5	28.9	10.2	3.6
Margherita Cheese & Tomato, San Marco*	½ Pizza/200g	454	227	10.7	29.8	7.2	1.2
Margherita Classico, Italiano, Tesco*	½ Pizza/191g	414	217	11.2	29.1	6.2	2.5
Margherita, 12", Finest, Tesco*	½ Pizza/254.5g	434	170	8.1	26.4	3.6	2.7
Margherita, BGTY, Sainsbury's*	½ Pizza/128.9g	254	197	11.8	32.5	2.2	2.0
Margherita, Classico, Tesco*	1 Serving/150g	383	255	11.4	31.7	9.2	3.3
Margherita, Healthy Living, Tesco*	1 Serving/165g	300	182	8.4	29.7	3.3	3.1
Margherita, Italian Stone Baked, Somerfield*	1 Pizza/290g	554	191	10.0	22.0	7.0	0.0
Margherita, Italian Style, Somerfield*	½ Pizza/190g	424	223	10.0	32.0	6.0	0.0
Margherita, Italiano, Tesco*	1 Serving/172.5g	336	194	9.5	30.1	4.0	2.5
Margherita, Medium Pan, Pizza Hut*	1 Slice/85g	239	281	12.7	31.1	11.8	2.1
Margherita, Pizza Express*	½ Pizza/135g	263	195	10.2	30.5	3.6	1.4
Margherita, Pizzeria, Sainsbury's*	½ Pizza/165g	450	273	13.9	34.5	8.8	2.9
Margherita, So Good, Somerfield*	½ Pizza/220.2g	513	233	9.9	29.5	8.4	2.2
Margherita, Stone Baked, GFY, Asda*	¼ Pizza/73g	158	217	11.0	39.0	1.9	1.8

	Measure INFO/WEIGHT	per Measure KCAL	Nutrition Values per 100g / 100ml				
			KCAL	PROT	CARB	FAT	FIBRE
PIZZA,							
Margherita, Stone Baked, Goodfella's*	1 Slice/36g	95	263	10.9	31.9	11.4	7.6
Margherita, Stonebaked Ciabatta, Goodfella's*	½ Pizza/149.5g	405	270	11.3	32.8	11.5	2.6
Margherita, Stuffed Crust Original, Pizza Hut*	1 Slice/125.3g	330	262	14.9	28.5	9.8	1.0
Margherita, The Italian, Medium, Pizza Hut*	1 Slice/95g	292	307	15.2	39.5	9.8	2.3
Marinated Tomato & Mascarpone, Piccadella, Tesco*	1 Pizza/260g	634	244	6.4	31.6	10.2	2.2
Massive On Meat, Deep Pan, Goodfella's*	1 Serving/106g	259	244	10.4	30.6	8.9	3.0
Meat Feast, American Style, Sainsbury's*	½ Pizza/263g	642	244	12.6	26.2	9.9	2.9
Meat Feast, Asda*	¼ Pizza/100g	316	316	14.0	38.0	12.0	2.0
Meat Feast, Big Fill, Somerfield*	1 Pizza/455g	1019	224	11.0	26.0	8.0	0.0
Meat Feast, Deep & Crispy, Iceland*	1/6 Pizza/136g	345	254	11.2	33.7	8.3	2.0
Meat Feast, Deep & Loaded, Sainsbury's*	½ Pizza/297.5g	817	275	13.2	32.7	10.1	2.6
Meat Feast, Loaded, Deep Pan, Tesco*	½ Pizza/282g	776	275	12.0	26.1	13.6	1.9
Meat Feast, Medium Pan, Pizza Hut*	1 Slice/114g	324	284	14.6	24.4	14.2	0.9
Meat Feast, The Italian, 12", Pizza Hut*	1 Slice/113g	341	302	15.4	30.3	14.3	2.3
Meat Feast, Thin & Crispy, Asda*	½ Pizza/183g	410	224	11.0	27.0	8.0	1.4
Meaty, The Edge, Pizza Hut*	1 Slice/64g	207	323	16.6	23.3	18.2	0.0
Mediterranean Madness, Goodfella's*	¼ Pizza/108.8g	235	216	9.1	27.0	8.0	3.9
Mediterranean Vegetable, Good Intentions, Somerfield*	1 Pizza/375.2g	604	161	7.3	30.2	1.2	1.7
Mediterranean Vegetable, Pizzeria, Sainsbury's*	1 Serving/211.3g	430	204	8.4	28.7	6.2	2.4
Mexican Chicken, COU, Marks & Spencer*	1 Pizza/248g	384	155	10.3	25.0	2.0	2.0
Mexican Style, Morrisons*	½ Pizza/180g	437	243	13.7	26.0	9.4	2.0
Mexican, Deep Pan, Farmfoods*	1oz/28g	53	188	8.4	31.7	3.1	0.9
Micro, McCain*	½ Serving/133g	388	292	12.4	26.9	15.0	0.0
Mighty Meaty, 9.5", Domino's Pizza*	1/6 Pizza/71g	177	249	13.9	25.5	10.2	2.8
Mixed Grill, 9.5", Domino's Pizza*	1 Slice/75g	178	237	12.0	26.2	9.3	2.3
Mozarella & Tomato, Gluten Free, Dietary Specials*	1 Pizza/320g	646	202	6.7	33.1	4.7	1.3
Mozzarella & Cherry Tomato, Stonebaked, Safeway*	½ Pizza/262.5g	618	235	10.6	30.3	7.8	3.5
Mozzarella, Lidl*	1 Serving/175g	436	249	10.1	22.7	13.1	0.0
Mushroom & Roasted Onion, Waitrose*	½ Pizza/187.4g	402	215	9.8	28.9	6.7	1.3
Mushroom, Pizza Express*	1 Pizza/400g	627	157	7.5	21.9	5.2	0.0
Napoletana, TTD, Sainsbury's*	1 Pizza/374g	1070	286	11.1	28.5	12.2	2.0
Napoli Ham & Mushroom, San Marco*	½ Pizza/219g	449	205	10.0	27.5	6.1	2.8
Napoli, Tesco*	½ Pizza/183.5g	432	235	11.9	32.6	6.3	1.4
Neptune, Pizza Express*	1 Pizza/300g	604	201	10.9	29.9	5.3	0.0
Pepper Steak, Deep Dish, Chicago Town*	1 Pack/365g	372	102	6.1	13.4	2.7	0.0
Pepperonata, Delicata, Sainsbury's*	1 Pizza/330g	917	278	12.9	24.3	14.4	2.6
Pepperoni & Jalapeno Chill, Asda*	1 Pizza/277g	742	268	10.0	39.0	8.0	1.8
Pepperoni & Onion, 9", Sainsbury's*	½ Pizza/207g	615	297	13.4	31.7	13.0	1.9
Pepperoni Bacon, Primo*	½ Pizza/111g	360	324	10.5	42.5	13.1	0.0
Pepperoni Classico, Italiano, Tesco*	1 Pack/419g	1060	253	11.6	26.1	11.4	2.4
Pepperoni Passion, 9.5", Domino's Pizza*	1 Slice/65g	186	286	13.6	31.5	11.6	1.4
Pepperoni Style, Italiano, Tesco*	1 Serving/215g	495	230	9.3	28.4	8.8	2.4
Pepperoni, Chicago Town*	1 Sm Pizza/170g	471	277	11.5	28.8	12.9	0.0
Pepperoni, Chilli & Vegetable, Fresh, Tesco*	1 Pizza/260g	660	254	9.5	35.1	8.4	1.7
Pepperoni, Classico, Tesco*	½ Pizza/205g	586	286	11.6	27.3	14.5	1.9
Pepperoni, Deep & Crispy, Somerfield*	¼ Slice/101g	236	234	10.7	31.6	7.2	1.6
Pepperoni, Deep & Crispy, Tesco*	1 Pizza/375g	881	235	10.1	31.8	7.5	1.2
Pepperoni, Deep Filled, Chicago Town*	1 Serving/202.3g	620	307	11.5	28.0	16.6	1.3
Pepperoni, Deep Pan, Goodfella's*	¼ Slice/109g	294	270	12.7	28.9	11.6	1.6
Pepperoni, Deep Pan, Safeway*	½ Pizza/198g	558	283	13.9	28.9	12.4	2.5
Pepperoni, Deluxe, American Deep Pan, Sainsbury's*	1 Pizza/424g	1077	254	13.3	28.7	9.5	2.7
Pepperoni, Extra, Chicago Town*	1 Pizza/460g	994	216	9.6	27.7	7.4	0.0
Pepperoni, Freschetta, Schwan's*	1 Pizza/310g	846	273	10.8	31.6	11.5	0.0

	Measure INFO/WEIGHT	per Measure KCAL	Nutrition Values per 100g / 100ml				
			KCAL	PROT	CARB	FAT	FIBRE
Pepperoni, Goodfella's*	1 Pizza/337g	900	267	13.2	26.3	12.9	1.7
Pepperoni, Hot & Spicy, Stuffed Crust, Asda*	1 Pizza/245g	666	272	13.9	26.5	12.2	2.4
Pepperoni, Individual, Chicago Town*	1 Pizza/168g	496	295	9.9	30.9	14.6	0.8
Pepperoni, Italian Style, Somerfield*	1 Pizza/380g	920	242	11.0	32.0	8.0	0.0
Pepperoni, Micro, McCain*	1 Serving/135g	405	300	12.1	26.5	16.2	0.0
Pepperoni, Oven Rising, Safeway*	1 Serving/95g	259	273	8.2	39.9	9.0	1.9
Pepperoni, Pizzeria, Sainsbury's*	½ Pizza/197g	528	268	12.5	34.7	8.8	1.3
Pepperoni, Stateside Foods*	½ Pizza/370g	988	267	12.2	32.3	9.8	1.4
Pepperoni, Stone Baked, Pizzaroma, Safeway*	½ Pizza/178.4g	479	269	12.9	30.6	10.6	2.2
Pepperoni, Stonebaked Ciabatta, Goodfella's*	½ Pizza/181g	503	278	11.9	27.4	14.4	2.4
Pepperoni, Stonebaked, Tesco*	1 Serving/290g	771	266	11.7	25.9	12.8	2.7
Pepperoni, The Insider, Pizza Hut*	1 Slice/137g	360	263	12.4	25.5	12.4	1.5
Pepperoni, Thin & Crispy, Asda*	½ Pizza/180g	436	242	11.0	27.0	10.0	1.7
Pepperoni, Thin & Crispy, Goodfella's*	1 Pizza/593g	1595	269	13.8	26.9	11.8	2.3
Pepperoni, Thin & Crispy, Safeway*	½ Pizza/133.1g	394	296	11.8	33.9	12.6	1.5
Pepperoni, Thin & Crispy, Sainsbury's*	½ Pizza/132g	395	299	13.7	27.0	15.1	5.1
Pepperoni, Thin & Crispy, Tesco*	¼ Pizza/132g	379	287	11.5	30.3	13.3	2.3
Pepperoni, Thin Crust, Tesco*	1 Pizza/148g	281	190	7.8	27.0	5.7	2.6
Pepperoni, Zingy, Asda*	1 Serving/90g	255	283	12.0	43.0	7.0	4.0
Pleasure With Fire Roasted Vegetables, Heinz*	½ Pizza/200g	418	209	9.5	24.8	8.0	2.4
Pork, American Style Tennesse BBQ, Asda*	1 Pizza/248.7g	563	226	11.0	32.0	6.0	2.5
Prosciutto & Fresh Rocket, TTD, Sainsbury's*	½ Pizza/164.2g	541	330	11.9	39.9	13.6	2.5
Prosciutto & Mascarpone, Safeway*	½ Pizza/200g	522	261	12.3	29.8	10.3	2.2
Prosciutto Con Funghi, Lidl*	½ Pizza/200g	454	227	9.5	31.5	7.0	0.0
Prosciutto, Classico, Tesco*	½ Pizza/205g	461	225	11.7	33.6	4.9	2.5
Prosciutto, Pizzaria, Sainsbury's*	1 Pizza/325g	806	248	11.4	34.7	7.1	3.2
Quattro Formaggi Pizzeria, Sainsbury's*	½ Pizza/175g	490	280	12.8	30.8	12.1	2.5
Quattro Formaggi, Pizza Express*	1 Pizza/528g	723	137	6.1	19.1	4.2	0.0
Quattro Formaggio, Tesco*	½ Pizza/219.2g	572	261	12.5	27.0	11.4	2.3
Roasted Vegetable, For One, GFY, Asda*	1 Pizza/96.0g	190	198	9.0	32.0	3.8	1.5
Roasted Vegetable, Italian Style, Stone Baked, Safeway*	1 Serving/185g	339	183	8.6	31.1	2.7	1.5
Roasted Vegetable, Waitrose*	1 Pizza/300g	609	203	8.8	39.7	1.0	3.3
Roasted Vegetable, Wood Fired, Pizzaroma, Safeway*	½ Pizza/175g	350	200	7.9	27.0	6.3	5.1
Salami & Ham, Pizzeria, Waitrose*	½ Pizza/205g	443	216	10.1	28.7	6.7	1.8
Salami, Ultra Thin Italian, Tesco*	1 Serving/263g	692	263	12.0	31.9	9.7	1.0
Sicilian, Premium, Co-Op*	1 Pizza/600g	1320	220	9.0	27.0	8.0	2.0
Siciliana, Frozen, Finest, Tesco*	1 Serving/247.5g	432	174	8.5	21.9	5.8	3.2
Simply Cheese, Goodfella's*	¼ Pizza/81.9g	226	276	16.3	22.5	13.4	1.9
Slice Selection, Marks & Spencer*	1 Serving/52g	120	230	9.4	30.3	7.8	1.9
Sloopy Giuseppe, Pizza Express*	½ Pizza/181g	310	171	8.4	27.7	3.0	1.9
Smoked Ham & Mushroom, Thin & Crispy, Co-Op*	1 Pizza/400g	792	198	9.0	30.3	4.5	1.7
Smoked Ham & Peppers, Healthy Living, Tesco*	1 Serving/282g	386	137	8.7	21.1	2.0	1.8
Smoked Ham & Pineapple, Deep Pan, Co-Op*	1 Pizza/395g	1142	289	11.6	36.7	10.6	1.7
Smoked Ham & Pineapple, Weight Watchers*	1 Pizza/241g	429	178	10.3	27.6	2.9	1.5
Spicy Beef, Goodfella's*	½ Pizza/147.5g	392	265	12.4	26.5	12.1	2.2
Spicy Chicken, Micro, McCain*	1 Pizza/133g	388	292	12.4	26.9	15.0	0.0
Spicy Chicken, Somerfield*	1 Serving/132.5g	305	229	13.4	29.7	6.3	0.0
Spicy Pepperoni, Tesco*	1 Pizza/380g	756	199	8.9	27.7	5.8	2.6
Spicy Vegetable Nacho, GFY, Asda*	1 Pizza/282.7g	637	225	10.0	36.0	4.5	3.3
Spicy Vegetable, Low Fat, Bertorelli*	1 Pizza/180g	243	135	6.0	23.4	2.4	1.9
Spinach & Bacon, Thin & Crispy, Marks & Spencer*	1 Pizza/290g	740	255	10.6	26.8	12.1	1.0
Spinach & Goats Cheese, BGTY, Sainsbury's*	½ Pizza/160g	304	190	6.8	31.8	3.9	2.4
Spinach & Ricotta, BGTY, Sainsbury's*	1 Pizza/265g	535	202	10.4	34.4	2.5	2.6

PIZZA,

	Measure INFO/WEIGHT	per Measure KCAL	Nutrition Values per 100g / 100ml				
			KCAL	PROT	CARB	FAT	FIBRE
Spinach & Ricotta, Classico, Tesco*	½ Pizza/215g	434	202	9.4	27.8	5.9	2.0
Spinach & Ricotta, Extra Special, Asda*	1 Pizza/400g	940	235	9.0	34.0	7.0	1.9
Spinach & Ricotta, GFY, Asda*	1 Pizza/160g	375	234	8.8	40.0	4.4	1.8
Spinach & Ricotta, Healthy Living, Tesco*	1 Pizza/304g	429	141	8.3	21.1	2.6	1.9
Spinach & Ricotta, Pizzaroma, Safeway*	1 Pizza/420g	1042	248	10.9	31.4	8.8	3.6
Spinach & Ricotta, Pizzeria, Sainsbury's*	1 Pizza/390g	1002	257	11.4	30.8	10.7	2.1
Spinach With Bacon & Mushroom, GFY, Asda*	1 Serving/270g	618	229	13.0	34.0	4.5	2.6
Steak, Stone Bake, Marks & Spencer*	1 Pizza/400g	820	205	9.9	25.7	6.7	1.4
Sunblushed Tomato & Mascarpone, Pizzadella, Tesco*	1 Serving/275g	894	325	8.5	36.7	16.0	1.5
Super Supreme, Family, Chicago Town*	¼ Pizza/225g	527	234	9.6	24.5	10.8	0.0
Supreme, Deep Dish, Individual, Chicago Town*	1 Pizza/170g	456	268	9.2	30.8	12.0	1.0
Supreme, Deep Pan, Safeway*	1 Serving/189g	450	238	10.8	27.0	9.6	4.7
Supreme, McCain*	1 Serving/125g	267	214	10.9	27.0	6.9	0.0
Supreme, Medium Pan, Pizza Hut*	1 Slice/105.7g	292	275	12.6	25.1	13.8	1.2
Supreme, The Italian, Medium, Pizza Hut*	1 Slice/106g	297	280	13.0	33.4	11.4	2.1
Supreme, Vegetable, Italian Pan, Pizza Hut*	1 Slice/112g	180	161	7.1	21.4	5.4	1.8
Sweet Chilli Chicken, BTGY, Sainsbury's*	½ Pizza/138g	276	200	13.0	33.2	1.7	2.1
Sweet Chilli Chicken, Stonebaked, Goodfella's*	½ Pizza/170g	423	249	12.9	22.3	12.1	3.0
Tandoori Hot, 9.5", Domino's Pizza*	1 Slice/67g	137	205	12.2	27.8	5.2	2.8
The Big Cheese, Deep Pan, Goodfella's*	1/6 Pizza/118g	295	250	12.2	25.9	10.8	1.1
The Big Eat Meat X-Treme, Deep Pan, Goodfella's*	½ Pizza/352g	806	229	11.6	27.1	8.2	3.6
The Works, The Edge, Pizza Hut*	1 Slice/64g	161	252	12.9	22.0	12.5	0.0
Three Cheese Calzone, Waitrose*	1 Calzone/265g	747	282	10.4	33.0	12.0	1.4
Three Cheese, Ultra Thin, Sodebo*	1 Pizza/180g	450	250	10.9	28.5	10.2	1.8
Three Cheeses & Tomato, Stonebaked, Co-Op*	1 Pizza/415g	888	214	10.0	25.2	8.1	1.5
Three Meat, Thin & Crispy, Sainsbury's*	½ Pizza/147g	344	234	12.5	23.4	10.7	1.3
Tomato	1oz/28g	54	193	3.3	22.6	10.6	1.4
Tomato & Cheese, Stone Bake, Marks & Spencer*	1 Pizza/340g	782	230	10.8	30.1	8.4	1.6
Tomato & Cheese, Thin & Crispy, Marks & Spencer*	1 Pizza/300g	705	235	11.0	27.7	9.4	1.2
Tomato & Red Pepper, Perfectly Balanced, Waitrose*	½ Pizza/163g	313	192	6.6	38.1	1.5	1.9
Tomato & Ricotta, Waitrose*	½ Pizza/207.5g	443	214	7.8	25.7	8.9	2.2
Tomato, Aubergine & Spinach, Pizzeria, Waitrose*	½ Pizza/193g	403	209	7.8	35.4	4.0	3.6
Tomato, Basil & Garlic, Weight Watchers*	1 Serving/85g	169	199	12.3	29.8	3.4	1.6
Tomato, Mushroom & Bacon, Deep Pan, Co-Op*	1 Pizza/420g	882	210	9.0	25.0	8.0	2.0
Triple Cheese, Deep Dish, Chicago Town*	1 Serving/170g	418	246	9.9	27.6	10.7	0.0
Tuna & Caramelised Red Onion, COU, Marks & Spencer*	1 Pizza/245g	429	175	9.6	26.7	2.3	1.2
Tuna Sweetcorn, BGTY, Sainsbury's*	1 Pizza/304g	602	198	13.5	31.7	1.9	2.7
Tuscan Vegetable & Mozzarella, Way To Five, Sainsbury's*	1 Pizza/317g	552	174	5.7	26.6	5.0	2.3
Vegetable Feast, Thin & Crispy, Iceland*	1 Slice/63g	148	237	7.8	26.5	11.1	1.8
Vegetable Supreme, Safeway*	¼ Pizza/170g	352	207	10.4	25.9	6.9	2.9
Vegetable, Asda*	1 Pizza/368.7g	554	150	7.0	24.0	2.9	3.4
Vegetable, COU, Marks & Spencer*	1 Pizza/294g	397	135	6.4	23.2	2.4	1.9
Vegetable, Frozen, Healthy Living, Tesco*	1 Pizza/400g	604	151	8.1	23.5	2.7	4.4
Vegetable, GFY, Asda*	¼ Pizza/94g	141	150	7.0	24.0	2.9	3.7
Vegetable, Healthy Living, Tesco*	1 Serving/200g	302	151	8.1	23.5	2.7	4.4
Vegetable, Stone Bake, Marks & Spencer*	1 Serving/465g	837	180	7.8	25.0	5.6	1.5
Vegetable, Thin & Crispy, Iceland*	½ Pizza/200g	442	221	8.3	23.2	10.6	1.7
Vegetarian, Organic, Evernat*	1oz/28g	59	212	7.5	36.4	4.0	0.0
Vegetarian, Original Medium, Pizza Hut*	1 Slice/93.5g	227	241	11.2	28.0	9.4	1.9
Vegetarian, Supreme, 9.5", Domino's Pizza*	1 Slice/71g	137	193	10.8	27.0	4.6	2.4
Veggie, The Edge, Pizza Hut*	1 Slice/60g	137	228	11.4	24.6	9.3	0.0
Veneziana, Pizza Express*	1 Pizza/300g	614	205	8.8	30.9	6.2	0.0
Verona, Frozen, Finest, Tesco*	1 Serving/237.5g	543	228	11.6	23.2	9.8	2.7

P

	Measure INFO/WEIGHT	per Measure KCAL	Nutrition Values per 100g / 100ml				
			KCAL	PROT	CARB	FAT	FIBRE
PIZZA BASE,							
Deep Pan, Italian, Sainsbury's*	1 Pizza/220g	684	311	7.0	59.5	5.0	1.4
Deep Pan, Napolina*	1 Base/260g	757	291	7.9	58.0	3.0	0.2
Gluten & Wheat Free, Glutafin*	1 Base/110g	309	281	3.0	56.0	5.0	6.0
Gluten & Wheat Free, Sainsbury's*	1 Serving/75g	188	250	3.0	57.4	0.9	4.0
Gluten Free, Glutafin*	1 Base/110g	278	253	3.0	49.0	5.0	4.5
Italian, Sainsbury's*	1 Base/150g	452	301	7.6	57.0	4.8	1.5
Medium, Standard Recipe, Pizza Two Four*	1oz/28g	63	225	7.0	48.7	0.2	0.0
Mini, Napolina*	1 Base/75g	218	291	7.9	58.0	3.0	0.2
Thin & Crispy, 9", Sainsbury's*	½ Pizza/70.1g	176	251	8.4	47.3	3.1	4.4
Thin & Crispy, Napolina*	1 Base/150g	437	291	7.9	58.0	3.0	0.2
Thin & Crispy, Safeway*	1 Base/140g	393	281	9.0	54.0	3.2	2.4
Thin & Crispy, Sainsbury's*	1 Base/140g	421	301	9.9	62.8	1.1	1.1
Thin & Crispy, Tesco*	1 Serving/110g	348	316	9.2	52.9	7.5	1.5
PIZZA BASE MIX,							
Morrisons*	1 Serving/77g	313	407	12.7	77.9	5.0	3.6
Sainsbury's*	1 Pack/145g	486	335	12.8	62.3	3.8	2.9
Tesco*	1 Serving/36g	99	272	10.2	43.0	6.6	3.8
PIZZA POCKET,							
Chargrilled Chicken & Veg, Healthy Eating, Tesco*	1 Pack/190g	304	160	11.4	23.1	2.4	2.8
Hot, Healthy Eating, Tesco*	1 Serving/190g	304	160	11.4	23.1	2.4	2.8
PLAICE,							
Filled With Mushrooms, Somerfield*	1 Plaice/169.8g	338	199	10.2	15.7	10.6	1.2
Filled With Prawns & Garlic, Somerfield*	1 Plaice/171g	366	214	12.0	14.8	11.9	0.7
Fillets, In Breadcrumbs, Average	1 Serving/150g	331	221	12.8	15.5	11.9	0.8
Fillets, Lightly Dusted, Average	1 Fillet/113g	188	166	12.9	10.5	8.2	0.6
Fillets, Raw, Average	1oz/28g	24	87	18.3	0.0	1.5	0.0
Fillets, With Prawns, Asda*	1oz/28g	24	86	11.0	0.4	4.5	0.7
Goujons, Baked	1oz/28g	85	304	8.8	27.7	18.3	0.0
Goujons, Fried in Blended Oil	1oz/28g	119	426	8.5	27.0	32.3	0.0
In Batter, Fried in Blended Oil	1oz/28g	72	257	15.2	12.0	16.8	0.5
PLAICE FLORENTINE,							
Fillets, Sainsbury's*	½ Pack/180g	222	123	11.7	2.7	7.3	0.7
Fillets, With Spinach & Cheddar Cheese, Sainsbury's*	1 Serving/154g	222	144	13.6	3.1	8.6	0.8
PLAICE WITH,							
A Lightly Seasoned Coating, Whole, Filleted, Waitrose*	1 Fillet/88g	162	185	11.9	11.7	10.1	0.5
Mushrooms & Prawns, Sainsbury's*	1 Serving/170g	354	208	12.0	15.9	10.7	1.7
Spinach & Ricotta Cheese, Whole, Sainsbury's*	1 Fillet/159g	334	210	11.6	17.2	10.5	0.8
PLANTAIN,							
Boiled in Unsalted Water	1oz/28g	31	112	0.8	28.5	0.2	1.2
Raw	1oz/28g	33	117	1.1	29.4	0.3	1.3
Ripe, Fried in Vegetable Oil	1oz/28g	75	267	1.5	47.5	9.2	2.3
PLUMS,							
Average	1oz/28g	10	36	0.6	8.6	0.1	1.6
Average, Stewed Without Sugar	1oz/28g	8	30	0.5	7.3	0.1	1.3
Soft Dried, Blue Parrot Cafe, Sainsbury's*	1 Pack/50g	119	237	2.6	55.6	0.5	7.1
POLENTA,							
Gourmet Merchant*	1 Serving/65g	232	357	7.4	78.8	1.4	1.3
Organic, Kallo*	1 Serving/150g	543	362	8.5	78.0	1.8	0.0
POLO,							
Citrus Sharp, Nestle*	1 Tube/34g	134	393	0.0	96.6	1.0	0.0
Fruits, Nestle*	1 Tube/37g	142	383	0.0	96.0	0.0	0.0
Mints, Clear Ice, Nestle*	1 Polo/4g	16	390	0.0	97.5	0.0	0.0
Mints, Original, Nestle*	1 Mint/2g	8	404	0.0	98.9	1.1	0.0

	Measure INFO/WEIGHT	per Measure KCAL	KCAL	PROT	CARB	FAT	FIBRE
			Nutrition Values per 100g / 100ml				

POLO,

	Measure INFO/WEIGHT	per Measure KCAL	KCAL	PROT	CARB	FAT	FIBRE
Mints, Sugar Free, Nestle*	1oz/28g	67	238	0.0	99.1	0.0	0.0
Smoothies, Nestle*	1 Sweet/4g	16	408	0.1	86.9	6.8	0.0
Spearmint, Nestle*	1 Tube/35g	141	402	0.0	98.2	1.1	0.0
POMEGRANATE,							
Raw, Fresh	1oz/28g	14	51	1.3	11.8	0.2	3.4
Weighed With Skin	1oz/28g	9	33	0.9	7.7	0.1	2.2
POP TARTS,							
Chocolate, Kellogg's*	1 Pop Tart/50g	198	395	6.0	68.0	11.0	2.0
Cream Cheese & Cherry Swirl, Kellogg's*	1 Serving/62g	250	403	3.2	59.7	17.7	1.0
Frosted Brown Sugar Cinnamon, Kellogg's*	1 Serving/50g	210	420	6.0	68.0	14.0	2.0
Strawberry Sensation, Kellogg's*	1 Pop Tart/50g	198	395	4.0	70.0	11.0	2.0
POPCORN,							
94% Fat Free, Orville, Redenbacher's*	1 Bag/76g	220	289	13.2	65.8	0.0	0.0
Air Popped, Plain	1 Serving/28g	108	382	12.0	77.7	4.2	0.0
Butter Flavour, Microwave, Popz*	1 Serving/100g	504	504	7.0	51.5	30.0	9.2
Butter Toffee, Asda*	1 Serving/100g	364	364	2.1	71.0	8.0	4.1
Butter Toffee, Marks & Spencer*	1 Serving/100g	495	495	5.7	59.0	26.3	2.3
Butter Toffee, Tesco*	1 Pack/350g	1418	405	2.2	81.7	7.7	4.3
Cakes, Caramel, Orville Redenbacher's*	1 Cake/12g	47	392	7.2	89.0	0.9	6.0
Chocolate Toffee, Mini Bites, Marks & Spencer*	1 Bite/9g	44	490	4.9	68.4	22.1	1.2
Honey, Organic, Pret A Manger*	1 Bag/35g	157	449	4.0	75.7	17.4	6.3
Plain	1oz/28g	166	593	6.2	48.7	42.8	0.0
PlayTime Popcorn, Salt, Sold at Cinema	1 Serving/100g	519	519	8.3	45.9	33.6	0.0
Popping Corn, Organic, Evernat*	1oz/28g	165	588	6.2	44.4	42.8	6.6
Ready Salted, Microwave, Popz*	1 Serving/20g	101	504	7.0	51.5	30.0	9.2
Salted, Blockbuster*	1 Bowl/25g	121	482	8.2	57.8	24.3	5.5
Sea Salt, Organic, Pret A Manger*	1 Bag/35g	138	394	11.1	52.0	15.7	13.1
Sea Salt, Sainsbury's*	1 Serving/10g	46	460	10.2	60.2	19.8	5.7
Super, Perri*	1 Packet/30g	139	464	8.4	55.5	23.2	8.5
Sweet, Blockbuster*	1 Serving/100g	470	470	6.2	67.2	17.9	6.0
Sweet, Microwave, Cinema, Popz*	1 Bag/85g	420	494	6.0	60.0	25.5	8.2
Toffee, 90% Fat Free, Butterkist*	1 Pack/35g	142	406	2.8	77.7	9.3	0.0
Toffee, Blockbuster*	¼ Pack/50g	221	441	2.2	77.4	13.7	2.9
Toffee, Sainsbury's*	1 Pack/100g	423	423	2.6	80.8	9.9	1.5
Vanilla, Cinema Sweet Microwave, Act II*	½ Pack/50g	234	468	9.0	71.0	16.0	12.0
POPPADOM BITES,							
Cool Yoghurt & Mint, Walkers*	1 Serving/35g	170	485	7.0	58.0	25.0	4.5
Spicy Tandoori Masala, Sensations, Walkers*	1 Sm Bag/18g	88	490	7.5	59.0	25.0	4.0
POPPADOMS,							
Extra Large, Sharwood's*	1oz/28g	78	279	21.3	44.7	1.7	10.3
Fried in Vegetable Oil	1oz/28g	103	369	17.5	39.1	16.9	0.0
Garlic & Coriander, Sharwood's*	1oz/28g	130	464	17.7	37.9	26.8	7.7
Indian Spiced, Sharwood's*	1 Serving/12g	32	267	20.2	43.0	1.5	13.0
Madras Spiced, Sharwood's*	1oz/28g	79	281	20.4	45.6	1.9	10.3
Marks & Spencer*	1 Poppadum/9g	42	467	17.4	39.3	26.6	8.4
Mercifully Mild, Phileas Fogg*	1 Serving/30g	150	499	14.8	36.8	32.6	6.0
Mildly Spiced, Sharwood's*	1 Poppadum/13g	58	444	18.4	35.5	25.3	10.5
Mini, Sainsbury's*	½ Pack/50g	249	498	14.9	36.9	32.3	7.6
Patak's*	1 Serving/10g	28	275	21.5	43.2	1.9	0.0
Plain, Asda*	1 Poppadum/9g	44	484	18.0	40.0	28.0	0.0
Plain, Indian To Go, Sainsbury's*	1 Poppadum/8.4g	32	405	18.4	43.4	17.5	9.0
Plain, Sharwood's*	1oz/28g	136	484	17.3	36.3	28.4	5.0
Plain, Tesco*	1 Serving/30g	145	484	16.3	36.1	30.5	3.1

P

	Measure INFO/WEIGHT	per Measure KCAL	Nutrition Values per 100g / 100ml				
			KCAL	PROT	CARB	FAT	FIBRE
POPPADOMS,							
Sharwood's*	1 Serving/10g	41	408	21.0	39.3	18.6	9.1
Spicy, COU, Marks & Spencer*	1 Pack/26g	85	325	23.5	51.9	2.4	8.1
POPPETS*,							
Chocolate Raisins	1 Box/100g	409	409	4.8	66.0	14.0	0.0
Mint Cream	1oz/28g	119	424	2.0	75.0	13.0	0.0
Peanut	1 Box/100g	544	544	16.4	37.0	37.0	0.0
Toffee, Milk Chocolate	1 Box/100g	484	484	4.6	67.0	22.0	0.0
POPPY SEEDS,							
Asda*	1 Serving/2g	11	556	21.0	19.0	44.0	0.0
PORK,							
BBQ, Chunky, Tesco*	1 Pack/170g	226	133	23.3	4.6	2.4	0.2
Chop, Average	1oz/28g	67	240	29.2	0.0	13.7	0.0
Diced, Average	1oz/28g	31	109	22.1	0.0	1.8	0.0
Escalope, Average	1oz/28g	40	145	31.1	0.0	2.3	0.0
Escalope, Lean, Healthy Range, Average	1 Escalope/75g	80	107	22.0	0.0	2.1	0.0
Joint, Crackling, Tesco*	¼ Joint/125g	284	227	22.0	0.0	15.4	0.0
Joint, Ready To Roast, Average	½ Joint/254.2g	375	148	19.3	2.3	7.1	0.2
Leg, Joint, Healthy Range, Average	1 Serving/200g	206	103	20.1	0.6	2.2	0.0
Lemon & Thyme, TTD, Sainsbury's*	1 Serving/67g	159	238	19.8	5.6	15.2	0.3
Loin, Cured, British, Roast, Marks & Spencer*	1 Slice/10g	14	140	25.2	0.7	4.4	0.0
Loin, Honey Roast, Sainsbury's*	1 Slice/12g	20	165	23.6	2.7	6.6	0.1
Loin, Joint, Lean, Roast	1oz/28g	51	182	30.1	0.0	6.8	0.0
Loin, Oak Smoked, Sainsbury's*	1 Slice/12.5g	21	163	24.0	0.9	7.0	0.1
Loin, Smoked, Cured, Marks & Spencer*	1oz/28g	43	155	18.1	0.0	9.1	0.0
Loin, Steak, Fried, Lean	1oz/28g	53	191	31.5	0.0	7.2	0.0
Loin, Steak, Fried, Lean & Fat	1oz/28g	77	276	27.5	0.0	18.4	0.0
Loin, Stuffed, Roast, Marks & Spencer*	1 Slice/12g	22	180	24.4	2.4	7.9	0.0
Medallions, Average	1 Pack/220g	179	163	35.1	0.1	2.5	0.5
Mince, Lean, Healthy Range, Average	1 Pack/400g	504	126	19.8	0.4	5.1	0.3
Mince, Raw	1oz/28g	46	164	19.2	0.0	9.7	0.0
Mince, Stewed	1oz/28g	53	191	24.4	0.0	10.4	0.0
Raw, Lean, Average	1oz/28g	42	151	28.6	0.0	4.1	0.0
Roast, Average	1oz/28g	34	121	22.7	0.3	3.3	0.0
Roast, Slices, Average	1 Slice/30g	40	134	22.7	0.5	4.5	0.0
Shoulder, Slices, Cured	1oz/28g	29	103	16.9	0.9	3.6	0.0
Shoulder, Steak, Hot & Spicy, Waitrose*	1 Steak/100g	207	207	19.5	1.3	13.7	0.0
Shoulder, Steaks, Barbecue, Safeway*	1 Serving/130g	306	235	27.0	1.6	13.3	0.0
Shoulder, Steaks, Chinese Style, Safeway*	1 Steak/132g	409	310	24.8	6.2	20.5	0.0
Shoulder, Steaks, Chinese, Sainsbury's*	1 Steak/100g	243	243	28.6	1.6	13.6	1.1
Sliced, Chinese, Marks & Spencer*	1 Serving/140g	224	160	26.4	6.1	3.1	0.0
Steak, Lean & Fat, Average	1oz/28g	61	219	23.8	0.0	13.7	0.1
Steak, Lean, Stewed	1oz/28g	49	176	33.6	0.0	4.6	0.0
Steaks, Chinese, Asda*	1 Serving/250g	508	203	22.0	4.0	11.0	1.3
Strips, For Stir Fry, Healthy Range, Average	¼ Pack/113g	118	104	21.3	0.0	2.0	0.0
Tenderloin, Roulade, Waitrose*	1 Pack/171g	282	165	18.4	5.9	7.5	1.8
PORK &,							
Apricots, Aromatic, Cafe Culture, Marks & Spencer*	½ Pack/420g	672	160	10.3	12.5	7.4	2.1
Chestnut Stuffing, Marks & Spencer*	1oz/28g	64	230	5.3	12.6	17.1	3.7
PORK CHAR SUI,							
In Cantonese Sauce, Asda*	1 Pack/360g	623	173	9.8	28.4	2.2	0.5
Takeaway, Iceland*	1 Pack/400g	412	103	7.9	12.5	2.4	1.2
PORK DINNER,							
Roast, Bird's Eye*	1 Pack/362g	348	96	7.4	11.2	2.4	1.3

P

	Measure INFO/WEIGHT	per Measure KCAL	Nutrition Values per 100g / 100ml				
			KCAL	PROT	CARB	FAT	FIBRE
PORK IN,							
Creamy Cider Sauce With Apple, Asda*	1 Serving/250g	1395	558	56.0	25.0	26.0	0.0
Light Mustard Sauce, COU, Marks & Spencer*	1 Serving/390g	312	80	12.2	3.2	2.1	0.4
Mustard & Cream, Chops	1oz/28g	73	261	14.5	2.4	21.6	0.3
Mustard Sauce With Colcannon Mash, BGTY, Sainsbury's*	1 Pack/450g	369	82	6.2	10.0	1.9	0.6
PORK SCRATCHINGS,							
KP*	1 Pack/20g	125	624	47.3	0.5	48.1	0.5
Pork Crunch, Low Carb, Top Notch, Freshers*	1 Bag/42g	211	502	66.2	0.9	26.0	0.6
PORK WITH,							
Bramley Apple, Medallions, Marks & Spencer*	1 Serving/380g	418	110	17.7	2.5	3.4	0.5
Cheese & Pineapple, Loin Steaks, Marks & Spencer*	1 Steak/141g	240	170	14.0	6.3	9.9	0.0
Herbes De Provence, Joint, Sainsbury's*	¼ Joint/200g	302	151	19.2	0.1	8.2	0.6
Honey & Mustard Sauce, Steaks, Tesco*	½ Pack/160g	258	161	16.3	7.3	7.4	1.4
Sage & Onion Stuffing, Joint, BGTY, Sainsbury's*	1 Serving/150g	246	164	29.5	3.3	3.6	1.3
Sage & Onion Stuffing, Joint, Tesco*	1 Serving/200g	208	104	17.1	2.7	2.8	0.0
Sage, Onion & Lemon Stuffing, Joint, Sainsbury's*	1 Serving/260g	699	269	27.4	2.2	16.7	1.4
Thai Style Butter, Steaks, Asda*	4 Steaks/300g	810	270	26.0	1.0	18.0	0.0
PORT,							
Average	1 Serving/50ml	79	157	0.1	12.0	0.0	0.0
POT NOODLE*,							
Balti Curry, Made Up	1 Pot/301.1g	268	89	3.1	17.8	0.5	0.5
Beef & Tomato, Made Up	1 Pot/300g	378	126	3.1	18.1	4.7	1.1
Beef & Tomato, Mini	1 Pot/190g	254	134	3.5	18.7	5.0	1.7
Bombay Bad Boy, Hot, Made Up	1 Pot/300g	378	126	3.0	16.9	5.2	1.1
Chicken & Mushroom, King	1 Pack/401g	513	128	3.2	18.1	4.8	1.1
Chicken & Mushroom, Made Up	1 Pot/300g	384	128	3.2	18.0	4.7	1.1
Chicken & Mushroom, Mini, Made Up	1 Pot/189.8g	243	128	3.8	18.2	4.5	1.4
Chicken Curry, Hot, Made Up	1 Pot/300g	384	128	2.8	18.7	4.7	1.1
Chow Mein, Made Up	1 Pot/300g	381	127	3.0	18.0	4.8	1.1
Hot Dog & Ketchup, Fun Pots, Made Up	1 Pot/189.8g	243	128	3.6	18.3	4.5	1.5
Korma Curry, Made Up	1 Pot/300g	273	91	2.9	17.4	1.1	0.4
Nice & Spicy, Made Up	1 Pot/300g	381	127	2.8	18.3	4.7	1.1
Noodle, Hot, Made Up	1 Pot/300g	378	126	3.0	16.9	5.2	1.1
Seedy Sanchez, Made Up	1 Pot/300g	396	132	3.1	19.1	4.8	1.1
Spicy Chilli, Posh, Made Up	1 Pot/300.9g	337	112	1.8	15.6	4.7	0.5
Spicy Curry, Made Up	1 Pot/300g	393	131	2.9	19.1	4.8	1.1
Sweet & Sour, King	1 Serving/105g	473	450	8.8	60.0	19.1	4.8
Sweet & Sour, Made Up	1 Pot/86g	376	437	12.1	60.9	16.1	3.1
Tikka Massala, Made Up	1 Pot/298.8g	245	82	3.1	17.5	0.8	0.3
POT RICE*,							
Chicken & Sweetcorn	1 Pot/68g	243	357	13.1	65.8	4.6	4.0
Chicken Curry	1 Pot/74g	253	342	11.0	67.2	2.3	3.3
Meal, Tomato, Barkat*	1 Pack/260g	260	100	1.7	19.8	1.5	0.7
POTATO BAKED,							
& Butter Bakes, BGTY, Sainsbury's*	1 Serving/50g	176	351	7.1	75.4	2.3	4.7
Average	1 Potato/200g	260	130	3.7	19.9	4.1	2.2
Leek & Cheese, Marks & Spencer*	1 Serving/206g	206	100	3.8	13.4	3.1	3.2
With Bacon, Finest, Tesco*	1 Pack/400g	484	121	3.7	15.1	5.2	0.9
With Cheddar Cheese, COU, Marks & Spencer*	1 Potato/164g	164	100	2.9	17.3	1.9	2.0
With Cheese & Bacon, Finest, Tesco*	1 Potato/245g	360	147	6.0	12.7	8.0	2.5
With Cheese, Healthy Living, Tesco*	1 Potato/200g	178	89	3.1	14.0	2.2	3.1
With Cheese, Tesco*	1 Pack/400g	448	112	2.7	18.7	2.9	1.0
With Chilli Con Carne, Eat Smart, Safeway*	1 Serving/300g	225	75	6.1	8.9	1.3	1.9
With Chilli, COU, Marks & Spencer*	1 Pack/300g	270	90	6.0	11.0	2.1	1.2

P

	Measure INFO/WEIGHT	per Measure KCAL	Nutrition Values per 100g / 100ml				
			KCAL	PROT	CARB	FAT	FIBRE
POTATO BAKED,							
With Tuna & Sweetcorn, COU, Marks & Spencer*	1 Pack/300g	270	90	5.1	12.8	1.8	1.4
POTATO BITES,							
Barbecue, Baked, COU, Marks & Spencer*	1 Pack/26g	92	355	7.1	76.7	2.4	4.2
Butter & Chive, Baked, COU, Marks & Spencer*	1 Serving/26g	92	355	7.6	77.2	2.0	4.7
POTATO BOMBAY,							
Asda*	½ Can/196.0g	198	101	2.0	12.0	5.0	1.1
Average	1oz/28g	33	117	2.0	13.7	6.8	1.2
Canned, Sainsbury's*	½ Can/200g	160	80	2.4	13.3	1.9	1.8
Canned, Tesco*	1 Can/400g	296	74	1.6	11.9	2.2	0.7
Eat Smart, Safeway*	1 Serving/225g	124	55	1.3	7.3	1.9	2.3
Indian Takeaway For 1, Sainsbury's*	1 Serving/200g	202	101	1.8	11.8	5.2	1.7
Marks & Spencer*	1 Pack/300g	300	100	1.5	12.1	4.8	1.6
Medium, Chilled, Tesco*	1oz/28g	29	103	1.7	8.4	7.0	0.8
Mild, Flavour Of India, Sainsbury's*	½ Can/200g	166	83	2.0	13.0	2.5	1.4
Sainsbury's*	1 Pack/300g	303	101	1.8	11.8	5.2	1.7
Tesco*	1 Pack/350g	413	118	1.8	13.5	6.4	1.1
POTATO CAKES,							
Average	1 Cake/70.4g	126	180	3.9	37.5	1.7	2.4
Fried, Average	1oz/28g	66	237	4.9	35.0	9.1	0.8
POTATO CHIPS,							
Hand Fried Mature Cheddar, Burts*	1 Serving/40g	202	504	6.4	57.4	27.7	0.0
Lighly Salted, Organic, Kettle*	1 Serving/40g	189	472	6.2	53.6	25.8	5.1
Ready Salted, Sainsbury's*	¼ Pack/33g	174	526	5.6	51.7	33.0	3.8
Reduced Fat, Cape Cod*	1 Bag/140g	664	474	7.9	53.5	25.4	6.4
POTATO CREAMED,							
With Cabbage, Asda*	1 Pack/350g	256	73	1.3	11.0	2.6	0.0
POTATO FARLS,							
Marks & Spencer*	1 Farl/55g	79	144	4.2	33.8	0.4	4.7
Sunblest*	1 Slice/100g	156	156	3.8	33.2	0.9	1.9
POTATO FRITTERS,							
Crispy, Bird's Eye*	1 Fritter/20g	29	145	2.0	16.3	8.0	1.2
With Sweetcorn, Marks & Spencer*	1 Pack/135g	304	225	4.4	24.1	12.6	2.3
POTATO INSTANT,							
Made Up With Water, Average	1 Serving/180g	118	66	1.7	14.5	0.2	1.3
Mash, Dry, SmartPrice, Asda*	½ Pack/60g	209	349	8.0	78.0	0.5	7.0
POTATO JACKET,							
Baked Bean & Sausage, Asda*	1 Pack/300g	447	149	5.0	25.0	3.2	2.7
Baked Bean Toppers, Safeway*	1 Topper/91.7g	166	180	5.0	22.1	7.8	4.5
Beef Chilli, Asda*	1 Pack/300g	372	124	5.0	22.0	1.8	2.1
Cheese & Beans, Somerfield*	1 Pack/338.9g	305	90	4.1	13.8	2.0	2.2
Cheese & Butter, Tesco*	1 Potato/200g	214	107	4.2	14.6	3.5	1.0
Cheese, Marks & Spencer*	1oz/28g	24	85	4.5	11.1	2.5	1.6
Cheesy, GFY, Asda*	1 Serving/155g	129	83	2.6	16.0	1.0	2.1
Chilli Con Carne, Somerfield*	1 Pack/340g	319	94	5.5	10.3	3.4	1.2
Halves, Marks & Spencer*	1 Serving/250g	188	75	2.0	14.2	1.1	1.7
Ham & Cheddar Cheese, Asda*	1 Pack/300g	435	145	7.0	21.0	3.7	1.6
Marfona, Marks & Spencer*	1 Serving/125g	106	85	2.6	16.8	1.0	2.9
Oven Baked, McCain*	1oz/28g	29	105	2.3	23.8	0.1	0.0
Tuna & Sweetcorn, Deep Filled, Marks & Spencer*	1 Pack/300g	270	90	4.9	13.1	2.2	1.2
Tuna & Sweetcorn, Somerfield*	1 Pack/340g	333	98	3.2	12.5	3.9	1.0
With Baked Beans & Mozzarella, Eat Smart, Safeway*	1 Pack/283g	255	90	5.8	12.8	1.4	2.3
With Cheese Mash, GFY, Asda*	1 Potato/200g	194	97	2.9	17.0	1.9	0.0
With Cheese, Safeway*	1 Potato/200g	165	83	2.1	16.3	0.9	2.1

P

	Measure INFO/WEIGHT	per Measure KCAL	Nutrition Values per 100g / 100ml KCAL	PROT	CARB	FAT	FIBRE
POTATO JACKET,							
With Chicken Tikka, COU, Marks & Spencer*	1 Serving/300g	240	80	5.4	10.9	1.6	1.3
With Chilli Con Carne, COU, Marks & Spencer*	1 Potato/300g	270	90	6.0	11.0	2.1	1.2
With Chilli Con Carne, Eat Smart, Safeway*	1 Pack/300g	225	75	6.1	8.9	1.3	1.9
With Chilli, BGTY, Sainsbury's*	1 Pack/350g	319	91	5.3	14.3	1.4	1.2
With Garlic Butter, Mini, Safeway*	1 Pack/450g	495	110	1.8	14.6	4.6	2.4
With Garlic Mushrooms, BGTY, Sainsbury's*	1 Pack/350g	263	75	2.3	14.4	0.9	1.2
With Garlic Mushrooms, Eat Smart, Safeway*	1 Pack/300g	210	70	2.7	8.1	2.7	1.6
With Garlic, Mini, Asda*	1 Serving/65g	59	91	2.2	13.0	3.3	0.0
With Herb & Rock Salt Seasoning, Marks & Spencer*	1 Pack/500g	375	75	2.0	14.2	1.1	1.7
With Spicy Mushroom & Onion, Marks & Spencer*	1 Pack/300g	210	70	2.2	13.9	0.8	1.2
With Tuna & Sweetcorn, BGTY, Sainsbury's*	1 Pack/350g	361	103	6.5	13.2	2.7	1.3
With Tuna & Sweetcorn, COU, Marks & Spencer*	1 Pack/300g	270	90	5.1	12.8	1.8	1.4
With Tuna & Sweetcorn, Eat Smart, Safeway*	1 Pack/300g	240	80	5.3	10.3	1.9	1.4
POTATO MASH,							
Bacon & Spring Onion, Finest, Tesco*	½ Pack/200g	214	107	4.3	10.8	5.2	1.6
Cabbage & Spring Onion, COU, Marks & Spencer*	1 Serving/225g	180	80	1.7	11.8	2.5	1.9
Cabbage & Spring Onion, Sainsbury's*	½ Pack/225g	279	124	2.0	14.8	6.3	1.1
Carrot & Swede, Sainsbury's*	½ Pack/225g	230	102	1.9	11.7	5.3	1.5
Cheddar Cheese, Marks & Spencer*	½ Pack/225g	248	110	4.6	12.6	5.3	1.0
Cheddar, Tesco*	1 Pack/500g	555	111	2.7	13.0	5.4	1.0
Leek & Cheese, COU, Marks & Spencer*	½ Pack/225g	180	80	3.0	12.0	2.1	1.3
Mustard, With Caramelised Onions, Finest, Tesco*	1 Serving/200g	232	116	2.6	16.0	4.6	1.8
Olive Oil, Healthy Eating, Tesco*	1 Serving/100g	90	90	2.1	15.5	2.2	0.9
Savoy Cabbage & Spring Onion, Marks & Spencer*	1 Serving/225g	250	111	2.0	10.2	6.9	1.3
Sun Dried Tomato & Basil, COU, Marks & Spencer*	1 Serving/170g	128	75	1.0	14.4	1.5	1.2
With Carrot & Swede, COU, Marks & Spencer*	1oz/28g	17	60	1.0	12.2	1.2	1.9
With Carrot & Swede, Marks & Spencer*	1 Serving/225g	214	95	1.6	8.3	6.4	1.4
With Leeks, Creamy, Bird's Eye*	1 Pack/300g	300	100	2.0	7.3	7.0	0.8
With Smoked Bacon, Smash*	1 Serving/169g	137	81	1.7	13.6	2.2	0.6
With Vegetables, Sainsbury's*	½ Pack/229.0g	142	62	1.8	11.4	1.0	3.1
POTATO MASHED,							
From Supermarket, Average	½ Pack/200g	197	98	1.8	13.3	4.1	1.5
From Supermarket, Healthy Range, Average	1 Serving/200g	160	80	1.8	14.6	1.6	1.3
From Supermarket, Premium, Average	1 Serving/225g	305	136	1.7	14.4	7.9	1.1
Old, Homemade, Average	1oz/28g	29	104	1.8	15.5	4.3	1.1
POTATO RINGS,							
Ready Salted, Marks & Spencer*	1 Serving/75g	375	500	3.5	58.9	28.1	2.6
Salt Vinegar, Sainsbury's*	1 Pack/25g	114	456	3.6	65.6	19.6	2.8
POTATO ROAST,							
Frozen, Average	1oz/28g	42	149	2.6	23.5	5.0	1.4
Frozen, Healthy Range, Average	1 Serving/300g	300	100	2.6	18.2	2.4	2.1
Old, Average	1oz/28g	42	149	2.9	25.9	4.5	1.8
Pepper & Basil Layer, Safeway*	1 Pack/260g	195	75	1.7	8.8	3.4	1.9
POTATO SAUTE,							
Deep Fried, McCain*	1oz/28g	47	167	2.6	23.3	7.0	0.0
Oven Baked, McCain*	1oz/28g	56	199	4.4	36.9	3.8	0.0
POTATO SKINS,							
1/4 Cut, Oven Baked, McCain*	1oz/28g	53	190	3.7	33.1	4.8	0.0
Cheddar & Bacon Snack Chips, T.G.I. Friday's*	1 Serving/28g	42	150	0.0	17.0	9.0	1.0
Cheese & Bacon, Sainsbury's*	1 Serving/140g	349	249	10.3	17.3	15.4	2.5
Cheese & Bacon, Tesco*	1 Serving/95g	241	254	9.2	19.5	15.5	3.0
Jacket, Pizza Hut*	1 Portion/ 223.5g	571	255	3.4	23.0	16.6	2.1
Jacket, With Sour Cream & Chive Dip, Pizza Hut*	1 Portion/223.5g	311	139	1.4	9.3	10.8	0.8

P

	Measure INFO/WEIGHT	per Measure KCAL	Nutrition Values per 100g / 100ml				
			KCAL	PROT	CARB	FAT	FIBRE
POTATO SKINS,							
Loaded, American, Asda*	1 Serving/78.4g	293	375	15.0	27.0	23.0	2.4
Loaded, Healthy Eating, Tesco*	1 Serving/340g	425	125	7.7	17.9	2.5	0.6
Loaded, New York Style, Tesco*	1 Burger/35g	89	254	9.2	19.5	15.5	3.0
Loaded, With Cheese & Bacon, Asda*	1 Serving/253.2g	314	124	6.0	16.0	4.0	2.3
Loaded, With Soured Cream, Marks & Spencer*	½ Pack/150g	308	205	9.1	15.8	11.9	0.9
POTATO SLICES,							
Crispy, Marks & Spencer*	1oz/28g	55	195	3.2	20.2	11.3	2.8
Garlic & Herb, Heinz*	1oz/28g	23	82	1.7	10.2	3.9	0.7
Spicy Coated, Safeway*	½ Pack/150g	305	203	2.5	19.7	12.4	2.5
POTATO SMILES,							
McCain*	1 Piece/14g	27	192	3.2	29.2	6.9	0.0
POTATO WAFFLES,							
Bird's Eye*	1 Waffle/56g	94	167	2.0	20.7	8.5	1.5
Frozen, Cooked	1oz/28g	56	200	3.2	30.3	8.2	2.3
Oven Baked, Mini, McCain*	1oz/28g	62	221	3.9	32.0	8.6	0.0
POTATO WEDGES,							
& Dip, Marks & Spencer*	1 Pack/450g	698	155	2.5	20.4	7.4	1.8
Asda*	1 Wedge/40g	57	142	3.4	21.0	4.9	1.7
BBQ Chicken Spicy, Good Intentions, Somerfield*	1 Pack/400g	380	95	7.4	13.6	1.2	1.4
BGTY, Sainsbury's*	½ Pack/190g	179	94	3.0	16.4	1.8	3.4
Baked, GFY, Asda*	1 Pack/450g	617	137	3.4	25.0	2.6	3.4
Bombay, With Yoghurt & Mint Dip, Healthy Living, Tesco*	1 Serving/170g	139	82	1.3	14.5	2.1	0.9
Chunky, McCain*	10 Wedges/175g	242	138	2.4	23.3	4.7	0.0
Crispy, Marks & Spencer*	1 Serving/200g	340	170	1.3	25.3	7.1	1.7
Domino's Pizza*	1 Serving/198g	428	216	4.1	30.3	8.7	0.0
Frozen, Tesco*	1 Serving/200g	262	131	2.0	22.4	3.7	1.8
Garlic & Herb, COU, Marks & Spencer*	1 Pack/300g	300	100	2.3	16.4	2.6	3.2
Garlic & Herb, Kitchen Range Foods*	1oz/28g	42	151	1.6	18.5	7.8	0.0
Hot & Spicy With Salsa Dip, Healthy Living, Tesco*	1 Serving/170g	112	66	1.1	12.4	1.3	1.4
Hot & Spicy, Frozen, Sainsbury's*	1 Serving/70g	98	140	2.8	23.7	3.8	2.0
In BBQ Sauce, Micro, McCain*	1 Box/200g	234	117	2.2	23.5	2.4	0.0
Jacket, Sainsbury's*	1 Serving/100g	151	151	3.0	27.3	3.3	2.6
McDonald's	1 Portion/176g	368	208	3.3	26.1	10.1	2.2
Micro, Tesco*	1 Pack/100g	170	170	2.6	24.5	6.8	2.3
New York Style, Healthy Eating, Tesco*	½ Pack/125g	124	99	2.3	16.4	2.7	1.3
Oven Baked, Waitrose*	1oz/28g	46	165	2.4	29.2	4.3	2.1
Savoury, McCain*	1 Serving/200g	300	150	2.9	22.7	6.2	0.0
Savoury, Waitrose*	1/3 Bag/250g	350	140	2.3	22.9	4.3	1.9
Sour Cream & Chives, McCain*	1 Serving/100g	132	132	2.4	24.0	4.1	0.0
Southern Fried Flavour, Champion, Aldi*	1oz/28g	41	147	2.1	20.8	6.2	2.8
Southern Fried Style, Tesco*	1 Serving/155g	233	150	3.0	14.1	9.1	2.0
Southern Fried, Asda*	1 Serving/188g	263	140	2.9	23.0	4.0	1.8
Spicy With Soured Cream & Chives, Tesco*	½ Pack/86.9g	385	443	5.4	28.4	34.2	2.7
Spicy, & Garlic Dip, Linda McCartney*	1 Pack/300g	366	122	2.6	15.3	5.6	3.1
Spicy, American Style, Sainsbury's*	½ Pack/155.7g	190	122	3.0	20.1	3.3	3.5
Spicy, Deep Fried, McCain*	1oz/28g	52	187	3.6	27.3	8.1	0.0
Spicy, Marks & Spencer*	½ Pack/225g	349	155	2.4	21.8	6.5	1.3
Spicy, Oven Baked, McCain*	1oz/28g	61	219	4.2	34.8	8.4	0.0
Spicy, Simple Solutions, Tesco*	1 Serving/150g	141	94	4.6	12.2	3.0	1.4
Tesco*	1 Serving/110g	135	123	3.0	18.4	4.2	1.5
With Broccoli & Mozzerella Cheese, Weight Watchers*	1 Pack/320g	294	92	3.1	13.3	3.0	1.0
With Soured Cream & Chive Dip, Safeway*	1 Pack/450g	639	142	3.1	22.1	4.6	2.1

P

	Measure INFO/WEIGHT	per Measure KCAL	Nutrition Values per 100g / 100ml				
			KCAL	PROT	CARB	FAT	FIBRE
POTATOES,							
Alphabites, Bird's Eye*	9 Bites/56g	75	134	2.0	19.5	5.3	1.4
Baby, New, With Mint Butter, The Best, Safeway*	½ Pack/190g	162	85	1.2	15.4	1.8	2.2
Baby, With Butter & Herbs, Sainsbury's*	¼ Pack/141g	135	96	1.4	14.7	3.5	1.5
Baby, With Herb Butter, Safeway*	1 Serving/200g	158	79	1.4	15.6	1.2	1.4
Baked, Flesh Only	1 Med/160g	123	77	2.2	18.0	0.1	1.4
Baking, Average	1 Med Size/250g	193	77	2.0	16.8	0.2	1.4
Boiled, Average	1oz/28g	20	72	1.8	17.0	0.1	1.2
Boulangere, Marks & Spencer*	½ Pack/225g	180	80	2.8	15.9	0.9	0.9
Charlotte, Average	1 Serving/184g	139	76	1.6	17.4	0.3	3.3
Dauphinoise, Average	1 Serving/200g	335	168	2.2	12.8	12.0	1.5
Desiree, Safeway*	1 Serving/200g	146	73	2.1	15.7	0.2	0.0
Garlic, Tapas Selection, Sainsbury's*	1 Serving/22g	49	224	2.6	10.4	19.1	0.7
Hasselback, Average	1 Serving/175g	182	104	1.9	22.0	0.9	2.9
Jersey Royal, Canned, Average	1 Can/186g	116	62	1.4	14.0	0.1	1.2
Jersey Royal, New, Raw, Average	1oz/28g	21	75	1.7	17.2	0.2	1.5
Juliette, Sainsbury's*	1 Serving/250g	200	80	1.4	19.7	0.1	1.0
Lemon & Rosemary, Finest, Tesco*	½ Pack/200g	200	100	2.1	14.7	3.7	2.0
Maris Piper, In Salted Water, Asda*	1 Serving/95g	67	70	1.5	15.0	0.1	0.8
New, Baby, Canned, Average	1oz/28g	16	59	1.4	13.2	0.2	1.4
New, Baby, Raw, Average	1 Serving/180g	135	75	1.7	17.1	0.3	1.6
New, Crushed, The Best, Safeway*	1 Pack/400g	440	110	2.2	12.6	5.2	1.3
New, In A Herb Marinade, Tesco*	¼ Pack/150g	152	101	1.3	13.0	4.9	1.5
New, In Herbs & Butter, Asda*	1 Pack/590g	637	108	1.6	17.0	3.3	1.2
New, With English Churned Butter, Marks & Spencer*	1 Pack/180g	261	145	1.3	29.5	2.2	2.1
New, With Parsley Butter, TTD, Sainsbury's*	1 Serving/150g	126	84	2.2	13.3	2.4	1.0
New, With Sunblush Tomato, Marks & Spencer*	1 Pack/385g	347	90	1.6	17.2	1.8	1.3
Parmentier, With Shallot Butter, Marks & Spencer*	¼ Pack/125g	200	160	2.5	21.1	7.1	4.0
Red, Average	1 Serving/300g	218	73	2.0	16.4	0.2	1.3
Roasting, Average	1 Serving/150g	203	135	2.5	23.4	3.5	1.7
Roasting, Washed And Peeled, Partly Cooked, Iceland*	1oz/28g	40	142	2.9	25.5	3.1	1.4
Rosemary & Garlic, Waitrose*	1 Serving/150g	237	158	3.8	30.7	2.2	2.9
Vivaldi, Boiled in Unsalted Water, Sainsbury's*	1 Serving/200g	160	80	1.4	19.7	0.1	1.0
White, Raw, Average	1oz/28g	21	75	2.0	16.8	0.2	1.3
With Garlic & Parsley Butter, Herb Oil Dressed, Co-Op*	1 Serving/178.3g	205	115	1.0	15.0	5.0	2.0
POUSSIN,							
Raw, Meat & Skin	1oz/28g	57	202	19.1	0.0	13.9	0.0
POWERADE,							
Citrus Charge, Coca-Cola Co*	1 Bottle/500ml	120	24	0.0	6.0	0.0	0.0
Ice Storm, The Coca Cola Co*	1 Bottle/500ml	120	24	0.0	6.0	0.0	0.0
Lemon & Grapefruit, Coca Cola*	1 Bottle/500ml	120	24	0.0	6.0	0.0	0.0
PRAWN COCKTAIL,							
20% More Prawns, Marks & Spencer*	½ Pack/100g	330	330	8.9	2.2	31.6	0.2
Asda*	1oz/28g	124	443	8.6	3.3	43.6	0.0
BGTY, Sainsbury's*	1oz/28g	45	160	7.5	2.3	13.4	0.5
COU, Marks & Spencer*	1oz/28g	24	85	11.6	4.9	2.2	0.5
Half Fat, Safeway*	1 Serving/200g	362	181	8.0	6.4	13.8	0.6
Healthy Living, Tesco*	1 Serving/200g	276	138	6.8	2.3	11.3	0.6
Light, Asda*	1oz/28g	45	160	9.9	4.8	11.2	0.0
Marks & Spencer*	1oz/28g	97	345	8.7	3.0	33.1	1.2
Reduced Fat, Marks & Spencer*	1oz/28g	43	152	9.1	2.9	11.6	1.1
Reduced Fat, Tesco*	1 Serving/200g	304	152	7.6	6.5	10.6	0.4
Reduced Fat, Waitrose*	1 Serving/200g	510	255	5.7	6.6	22.9	1.3
Safeway*	½ Pot/100g	373	373	7.6	3.4	36.5	0.2

	Measure	per Measure	Nutrition Values per 100g / 100ml				
	INFO/WEIGHT	KCAL	KCAL	PROT	CARB	FAT	FIBRE
PRAWN COCKTAIL,							
Sainsbury's*	1 Serving/200g	706	353	7.9	2.7	34.5	0.5
Tesco*	1 Tub/200g	834	417	7.3	3.5	41.5	0.1
PRAWN CRACKERS,							
Asda*	1 Serving/25g	134	535	2.0	53.0	35.0	0.0
Cooked In Sunflower Oil, Sharwood's*	5 Crackers/10g	48	479	0.7	68.3	22.6	0.8
Food To Go, Sainsbury's*	1 Bag/40g	214	534	2.9	60.2	31.3	0.4
Marks & Spencer*	1 Pack/15g	83	550	3.0	62.3	32.0	0.0
Ready To Eat, Sharwood's*	1 Bag/60g	316	527	0.5	62.0	30.8	1.2
Sainsbury's*	1 Cracker/3g	16	537	2.4	60.4	31.7	0.8
Tesco*	1/3 Pack/20g	114	568	3.7	44.0	41.9	0.5
Thai Green Curry, MS*	1 Packet/50g	250	500	3.2	62.2	25.8	1.6
Uncooked, Sharwood's*	1oz/28g	136	487	0.7	52.7	29.7	1.7
PRAWN PINWHEEL,							
Oriental Style, BGTY, Sainsbury's*	1 Pack/189.0g	274	145	6.0	26.7	1.1	0.0
PRAWN TOAST,							
Chinese Snack Selection, Mini, Tesco*	1 Toast/11g	36	330	9.4	18.8	24.2	1.9
Dim Sum Selection, Sainsbury's*	1 Toast/8g	23	283	9.9	19.2	18.5	2.0
Marks & Spencer*	1oz/28g	78	280	11.5	18.4	18.1	2.2
Oriental Selection, Waitrose*	1 Toast/14g	38	272	11.1	18.3	17.2	2.1
Sesame, Marks & Spencer*	1 Toast/28g	84	300	10.6	15.3	21.5	3.2
Sesame, Occasions, Sainsbury's*	1 Toast/12g	34	283	9.9	19.2	18.5	2.0
Waitrose*	1 Toast/21g	47	223	9.7	7.4	17.2	5.8
PRAWNS,							
Batter Crisp, Lyons*	1 Pack/160g	350	219	8.0	18.2	12.7	1.1
Boiled	1 Prawn/3g	3	99	22.6	0.0	0.9	0.0
Brine, John West*	½ Can/60g	58	97	21.0	1.0	1.0	0.0
Chilli & Coriander, Marks & Spencer*	1 Serving/70g	67	95	17.9	0.6	2.2	0.6
Chilli, Battered, Marks & Spencer*	1oz/28g	63	225	7.2	23.8	11.5	0.5
Chilli, Marks & Spencer*	1oz/28g	22	79	17.9	0.6	0.5	0.6
Cooked & Peeled, Average	1oz/28g	21	77	17.6	0.2	0.6	0.0
Dried	1oz/28g	79	281	62.4	0.0	3.5	0.0
Filo Wrapped & Breaded, Marks & Spencer*	1 Serving/19g	45	235	9.5	20.4	13.0	1.4
Hot & Spicy, Average	1 Serving/170g	461	271	9.4	22.9	15.8	2.2
Icelandic, Raw, Average	1oz/28g	30	106	22.7	0.0	1.6	0.0
King, Chilli & Coriander, Sainsbury's*	1 Pack/140g	133	95	13.8	0.5	4.2	0.5
King, Crevettes, Sainsbury's*	1 Pack/225g	205	91	21.8	0.1	0.5	0.3
King, In Filo, Finest, Tesco*	1 Prawn/20g	38	189	13.0	27.8	2.9	1.6
King, Raw, Average	1 Bag/200g	145	72	15.8	0.2	1.0	0.1
Lemon & Pepper, Marks & Spencer*	1 Serving/70g	67	95	17.5	0.0	2.7	0.5
North Atlantic, Peeled, Cooked, Average	1oz/28g	22	80	17.5	0.0	1.1	0.0
North Atlantic, Raw, Average	1oz/28g	17	62	14.4	0.0	0.4	0.0
Raw, Average	¼ Pack/112g	88	79	17.8	0.2	0.7	0.0
Thai, Marks & Spencer*	1oz/28g	29	103	5.2	13.6	3.1	1.3
Tiger, Cooked & Peeled, Average	1 Pack/180g	151	84	18.4	0.1	1.1	0.0
Tiger, Jumbo, Average	1 Serving/50g	39	78	18.3	0.3	0.5	0.0
Tiger, Raw, Average	1oz/28g	18	64	14.2	0.1	0.7	0.0
Tiger, Wrapped, Marks & Spencer*	1 Pack/190g	477	251	11.3	20.7	13.6	1.3
PRAWNS BHUNA,							
Tandoori, Indian, Sainsbury's*	½ Pack/200g	152	76	5.5	4.5	4.0	1.7
PRAWNS CHILLI,							
With Spicy Chilli Dip, King, Sainsbury's*	½ Pack/150g	282	188	8.6	22.2	7.2	1.0
PRAWNS CHINESE,							
Oriental Express*	1 Serving/320g	218	68	3.2	13.8	0.6	1.9

	Measure INFO/WEIGHT	per Measure KCAL	Nutrition Values per 100g / 100ml				
			KCAL	PROT	CARB	FAT	FIBRE
PRAWNS CREOLE,							
Spicy, BGTY, Sainsbury's*	1 Pack/350g	382	109	4.2	20.9	0.9	0.4
With Vegetable Rice, King, COU, Marks & Spencer*	1 Pack/400g	300	75	4.5	13.3	0.6	0.7
PRAWNS GULNARI,							
With Rice, COU, Marks & Spencer*	1 Pack/400g	400	100	4.0	18.7	0.8	1.6
PRAWNS IN,							
Creamy Garlic Sauce, Youngs*	1 Serving/158g	261	165	8.5	0.3	14.5	0.0
Red Thai Curry Sauce, Youngs*	1 Pack/255g	197	77	4.8	6.5	3.4	0.8
Sweet Chilli Sauce, Asda*	1 Pack/360g	500	139	4.1	15.0	6.9	0.3
PRAWNS JAPANESE,							
King, Noodle Box, Marks & Spencer*	1 Pack/300g	330	110	5.8	16.0	2.7	1.6
PRAWNS MASALA,							
King, Waitrose*	1 Pack/350g	385	110	7.1	3.8	7.4	1.8
PRAWNS ORIENTAL,							
Marks & Spencer*	1 Pack/200g	440	220	11.9	16.9	11.7	0.9
PRAWNS SZECHUAN,							
Spicy, COU, Marks & Spencer*	1 Pack/400g	380	95	4.5	16.9	0.9	1.5
PRAWNS WITH,							
A Spicy Cajun Dip, King, Sainsbury's*	1 Pack/240g	254	106	14.8	9.1	1.8	1.4
A Sweet Chilli Sauce, Crispy, Maks & Spencer*	1 Pack/240g	444	185	6.6	23.1	7.4	1.6
Garlic & Herb Butter, King, Fresh, Marks & Spencer*	1 Serving/200g	330	165	12.5	9.1	9.0	0.5
Ginger & Spring Onion, King, Budgens*	1 Pack/350g	151	43	5.9	2.1	1.2	0.7
Ginger & Spring Onion, Sainsbury's*	1 Pack/300g	198	66	4.7	4.7	3.1	0.3
Noodles, King, Debenhams*	1 Serving/370g	537	145	5.4	20.2	4.8	0.0
Rice, Sweet Chilli, Tesco*	1 Pack/460g	488	106	2.4	19.2	2.2	0.5
With Creamy Lime Dip, King, Waitrose*	1 Pot/230g	518	225	15.8	0.8	17.7	0.2
PRETZELS,							
American Style, Salted, Sainsbury's*	1 Serving/50g	191	381	9.6	81.8	4.0	5.2
Lightly Salted, Tesco*	1 Serving/25g	99	395	9.3	73.4	7.1	5.5
Marks & Spencer*	1 Serving/100g	375	375	10.4	73.7	4.2	4.7
Mini, 99% Fat Free, Free Natural*	1 Serving/50g	188	376	10.1	81.7	1.0	0.0
Mini, Eat Smart, Safeway*	1 Bag/25g	90	360	9.6	79.7	2.5	5.5
Mini, Marks & Spencer*	1 Pack/45g	194	430	10.4	66.6	13.4	4.9
New York Style, Salted, Mini, Shapers, Boots*	1 Bag/25g	94	375	10.0	79.0	2.1	4.2
New York Style, Shapers, Boots*	1 Bag/24g	94	391	11.0	81.0	2.5	3.8
Pret A Manger*	1 Serving/175g	371	212	7.5	35.4	4.0	1.7
Salt & Cracked Black Pepper, COU, Marks & Spencer*	1 Pack/25g	95	380	9.7	83.3	2.4	2.7
Salted, Safeway*	1 Serving/50g	192	383	10.3	76.0	4.2	4.6
Sea Salt & Black Pepper, Tesco*	1 Serving/50g	192	383	10.6	76.7	3.7	2.3
Sea Salt & Cracked Black Pepper, Sainsbury's*	1 Serving/50g	191	381	9.5	79.0	4.0	3.8
Selection Tray, Marks & Spencer*	1oz/28g	112	401	9.7	75.5	6.7	3.4
Snacks, Fabulous Bakin Boys*	1 Pack/24g	96	401	9.0	79.5	4.9	2.5
Sour Cream & Chive Flavour, Penn State*	1 Serving/25g	114	454	12.7	70.3	14.4	0.8
Sour Cream & Onion, Marks & Spencer*	1 Pack/150g	683	455	11.0	70.9	14.5	0.7
Sour Cream & Onion, Tesco*	1 Serving/25g	114	457	8.4	67.7	17.0	2.3
With Sea Salt, Giant, Marks & Spencer*	1 Pretzel/8g	31	390	9.7	77.3	6.8	5.4
PRINGLES*,							
Barbecue	1 Serving/50g	267	533	4.9	48.0	36.0	5.1
Cheese & Onion	1 Serving/50g	271	541	4.7	50.0	36.0	3.6
Curry	1 Serving/50g	266	531	5.2	46.0	36.0	3.4
Dippers, Original	1 Serving/100g	519	519	5.1	54.0	32.0	4.1
Hot & Spicy	1 Serving/50g	273	546	5.0	49.0	37.0	3.3
Original	1 Serving/50g	274	547	4.7	47.0	38.0	5.1
Paprika	1 Serving/50g	273	545	5.1	49.0	36.0	3.4

P

	Measure	per Measure		Nutrition Values per 100g / 100ml				
	INFO/WEIGHT	KCAL		KCAL	PROT	CARB	FAT	FIBRE
PRINGLES*,								
Pizza	1 Serving/50g	268		536	5.1	43.0	37.0	4.8
Salt & Vinegar	1 Serving/50g	265		530	4.5	47.0	36.0	4.8
Sour Cream & Onion	1 Serving/50g	270		539	5.3	46.0	37.0	4.9
Sour Cream & Onion, Light	1 Serving/50g	233		466	5.4	56.0	25.0	4.6
Spanish Salsa	1 Serving/35g	193		550	5.0	48.0	37.0	3.5
Texas Barbecue Sauce	1 Serving/50g	272		544	4.4	50.0	36.0	3.4
PROBIOTIC DRINK,								
Lidl*	1 Serving/125g	94		75	2.6	12.3	1.7	0.0
Orange, Health, Tesco*	1 Serving/100g	67		67	1.5	13.4	0.9	1.3
Orange, Pianola*	1 Serving/125ml	105		84	2.5	14.7	1.6	0.0
Pianola*	1 Serving/125ml	105		84	2.5	14.7	1.6	0.0
Yoghurt, Original, Tesco*	1 Bottle/100g	68		68	1.7	13.1	1.0	1.4
PROFITEROLES,								
Asda*	1 serving/64g	218		343	5.0	20.0	27.0	0.0
Chocolate, Co-Op*	1Pot/91g	260		285	6.0	33.0	15.0	3.0
Choux & Chocolate Sauce, Tesco*	1 Serving/76.5g	297		386	5.1	26.9	28.7	0.5
Choux Fourres Nappes De Chocolat, Ed Marche*	1 Serving/90g	262		291	5.9	42.0	11.0	0.0
Classic French, Sainsbury's*	1 Serving/90g	284		316	6.6	33.7	17.2	0.1
Dairy Cream, Safeway*	¼ Pack/67.1g	275		410	5.5	35.3	26.9	2.2
Sainsbury's*	1 Profiterole/22g	62		289	3.9	36.5	14.1	1.8
Stack, Sainsbury's*	¼ Pack/74g	301		407	5.4	38.3	25.8	2.1
PROVAMEL*,								
Soya Dessert, Caramel, Alpro Soya*	1 Pot/125g	103		82	3.0	13.7	1.7	0.3
Soya Dessert, Chocolate, Alpro Soya*	1 Pot/125g	110		88	3.0	13.8	2.3	0.9
Soya Dessert, Fruits Of The Forest, Alpro Soya*	1 Serving/125g	98		78	3.0	11.9	1.8	0.3
Soya Dessert, Hazelnut, Alpro Soya*	1 Pot/125g	126		101	3.0	16.0	2.8	1.2
Soya Dessert, Peach, Alpro Soya*	1 Pot/125g	109		87	3.8	12.4	2.2	0.3
Soya Dessert, Vanilla, Alpro Soya*	1 Pot/125g	108		86	3.0	14.4	1.8	1.0
Soya Dream, Alpro Soya*	1 Carton/250ml	445		178	3.0	1.7	17.7	1.1
Soya Milk, Banana Flavour, Alpro Soya*	1 Carton/250ml	188		75	3.6	10.5	2.1	1.2
Soya Milk, Chocolate, Alpro Soya*	1 Serving/100ml	82		82	3.8	10.7	2.4	1.2
Soya Milk, Rice, Alpro Soya*	1 Serving/100g	50		50	0.1	9.9	1.1	0.0
Soya Milk, Strawberry Flavour, Alpro Soya*	1 Carton/250ml	160		64	3.6	7.7	2.1	1.2
Soya Milk, Vanilla, Organic, Alpro Soya*	1 Serving/250ml	153		61	3.8	6.5	2.3	0.3
Yofu, Black Cherry, Alpro Soya*	1 Pot/125g	106		85	3.7	12.9	2.1	1.2
Yofu, Organic, Alpro Soya*	1oz/28g	15		53	4.5	2.8	2.6	1.5
Yofu, Peach & Mango, Organic, Alpro Soya*	1 Pot/125g	116		93	3.7	14.7	2.1	1.2
Yofu, Peach & Pear, Junior, Alpro Soya*	1 Pot/125g	105		84	3.8	12.4	2.2	0.0
Yofu, Peach, Alpro Soya*	1 Pot/125g	109		87	3.8	13.3	2.1	1.2
Yofu, Red Cherry, Organic, Alpro Soya*	1 Pot/125g	116		93	3.7	14.8	2.1	1.2
Yofu, Strawberry & Banana, Junior, Alpro Soya*	1 Pot/125g	106		85	3.8	12.7	2.2	0.0
Yofu, Strawberry, Alpro Soya*	1 Pot/125g	106		85	3.8	12.6	2.1	1.3
Yofu, Vanilla, Alpro Soya*	1 Pot/125g	96		77	4.1	10.0	2.3	1.3
PROVENCALE,								
Cabillaud à la, Weight Watchers*	1 Pack/380g	327		86	5.1	10.3	2.7	0.0
Chicken, Marks & Spencer*	1 Pack/430g	366		85	13.2	2.3	2.7	0.6
Chicken, Steam Cuisine, Marks & Spencer*	1oz/28g	34		120	9.6	12.7	3.8	1.4
Cod, Cote Table*	1 Serving/281g	185		66	8.6	3.4	2.0	0.0
King Prawn & Mushroom, Marks & Spencer*	½ Pack/185g	120		65	7.2	3.9	2.5	0.9
Mushroom, Fresh, COU, Marks & Spencer*	½ Pack/150g	60		40	2.6	4.1	1.5	1.8
Prawn & Mushroom With Pasta, COU, Marks & Spencer*	1 Pack/400g	360		90	5.9	15.7	0.5	0.0
Raratouille, Asda*	½ Can/195g	98		50	1.0	7.0	2.0	1.0
Ratatouille, Tesco*	½ Can/195g	72		37	1.1	4.2	1.8	0.9

	Measure INFO/WEIGHT	per Measure KCAL	Nutrition Values per 100g / 100ml				
			KCAL	PROT	CARB	FAT	FIBRE
PROVENCALE,							
Ratatouille, Waitrose*	½ Can/195g	107	55	1.5	7.8	2.1	0.8
PRUNES,							
Average	1 Serving/50g	79	158	2.5	36.4	0.4	5.8
In Apple Juice, Average	1 Serving/90g	76	84	0.8	19.8	0.1	1.4
In Fruit Juice, Average	1oz/28g	25	88	0.9	21.4	0.2	3.0
In Syrup, Average	1oz/28g	26	92	1.0	22.1	0.2	2.6
Stewed With Sugar	1oz/28g	29	103	1.3	25.5	0.2	3.1
Stewed Without Sugar	1oz/28g	23	81	1.4	19.5	0.3	3.3
PUDDING,							
Apple & Blackberry Crumble, Custard Style, Somerfield*	1oz/28g	34	123	3.0	17.0	5.0	0.0
Apple & Custard, Sainsbury's*	1 Serving/115g	132	115	5.4	19.0	1.9	0.1
Apple Pie, Custard Style, Somerfield*	1oz/28g	34	123	3.0	17.0	5.0	0.0
Banana Fudge Crunch, Bird's*	1oz/28g	125	445	5.4	75.0	14.0	0.8
Blackberry & Bramley Apple, Marks & Spencer*	¼ Pudding/152g	365	240	3.3	38.2	8.2	2.0
Bread	1oz/28g	83	297	5.9	49.7	9.6	1.2
Butterscotch, Instant, Fat Free, Jell-O*	1 Serving/7.5g	27	333	1.3	78.7	1.3	0.0
Cherry Cobbler, GFY, Asda*	1 Cobbler/100g	158	158	2.1	33.0	2.0	0.9
Chocolate Marks & Spencer*	1 Serving/105g	401	382	6.2	40.7	21.6	1.1
Chocolate Sponge, Healthy Eating, Tesco*	1 Pudding/102.5g	197	191	4.4	34.7	3.8	0.9
Chocolate With Chocolate Sauce, BGTY, Sainsbury's*	1 Pudding/110.3g	161	146	3.5	28.6	1.9	2.3
Chocolate With Chocolate Sauce, Heinz*	¼ Can/77g	221	287	3.1	47.7	9.3	1.4
Chocolate, BGTY, Sainsbury's*	1 Pot/110g	161	146	3.5	28.6	1.9	0.0
Chocolate, Delice*	1 Pot/100g	136	136	2.5	18.9	5.4	0.0
Chocolate, Fat Free, Snacks, Jell-O*	1 Pudding/99g	90	91	2.0	20.2	0.0	0.0
Chocolate, Perfectly Balanced, Waitrose*	1 Pot/105g	196	187	3.8	36.0	3.1	0.8
Creamed Sago, Ambrosia*	1 Serving/200g	158	79	2.5	13.6	1.6	0.2
Creamy Brioche With Apricot Compote, Co-Op*	1 Pack/230g	391	170	6.0	22.0	6.0	0.9
Creme aux Oeufs a la Vanille, Weight Watchers*	1 Pot/100g	116	116	4.8	17.0	3.2	0.0
Creme aux Oeufs au Chocolat, Weight Watchers*	1 Pot/100g	136	136	4.7	19.7	4.3	0.0
Eve's	1oz/28g	67	241	3.5	28.9	13.1	1.4
Eve's, 5% Fat, Marks & Spencer*	1 Pudding/223g	323	145	3.0	23.5	4.4	0.6
Eve's, BGTY, Sainsbury's*	1 Pudding/145g	164	113	2.2	23.4	1.2	0.7
Eve's, Eat Smart, Safeway*	1 Pudding/87g	131	150	2.3	30.6	1.8	0.9
Eve's, Marks & Spencer*	1 Serving/118g	254	215	2.7	32.3	8.3	0.4
Eve's, With Custard, Snack, Marks & Spencer*	1 Serving/230g	437	190	3.2	22.6	9.2	0.7
Forest Fruit Sponge, Eat Smart, Safeway*	1 Pot/88.2g	150	170	4.2	33.5	1.8	2.6
Jam Roly Poly & Custard, Co-Op*	1 Serving/105g	263	250	3.0	44.0	7.0	0.8
Lemon Crunch , Bird's*	1oz/28g	125	445	5.5	74.0	14.0	0.7
Lemon Sponge With Lemon Sauce, Eat Smart, Safeway*	1 Pudding/90g	135	150	2.2	29.0	2.6	1.4
Lemon, Marks & Spencer*	1 Pudding/105g	328	312	4.3	39.4	15.2	2.3
Lemon, Perfectly Balanced, Waitrose*	1 Serving/105g	212	202	3.4	41.7	2.4	0.6
Low Fat Chocolate Pudding, Good Intentions, Somerfield*	1 Pudding/110g	200	182	3.0	37.6	2.2	2.4
Macaroni, Creamed, Ambrosia*	1 Can/425g	374	88	3.6	14.6	1.7	0.3
Pease, Canned, Re-Heated, Drained	1oz/28g	26	93	6.8	16.1	0.6	1.8
Plum, Spiced, Safeway*	1 Pudding/125g	275	220	2.7	45.7	2.5	0.9
Queen of Puddings	1oz/28g	60	213	4.8	33.1	7.8	0.2
Rhubarb Crumble, Custard Style, Somerfield*	1oz/28g	33	119	3.0	16.0	5.0	0.0
Spotted Dick, Asda*	1 Serving/105g	282	269	2.9	34.3	13.3	1.3
Spotted Dick, Sainsbury's*	¼ Pudding/82g	270	329	4.1	50.9	12.1	1.6
Spotted Dick, With Custard, Individual, Sainsbury's*	1 Pudding/205g	505	246	3.3	32.6	11.4	0.7
Sticky Toffee & Sticky Toffee Sauce, BGTY, Sainsbury's*	1 Serving/130g	319	245	5.0	49.3	4.1	2.2
Sticky Toffee, Bread, Marks & Spencer*	1oz/28g	83	295	4.1	46.3	10.6	2.2
Sticky Toffee, Marks & Spencer*	1 Pudding/105g	337	321	3.5	51.9	11.0	1.1

P

	Measure INFO/WEIGHT	per Measure KCAL	Nutrition Values per 100g / 100ml				
			KCAL	PROT	CARB	FAT	FIBRE
PUDDING,							
Sticky Toffee, Tesco*	1 Serving/110g	287	261	3.3	31.8	13.4	0.7
Sticky Toffee, With Custard, Somerfield*	1 Pack/245g	576	235	3.0	38.0	8.0	0.0
Strawberry Jam With Custard, Farmfoods*	1 Serving/145g	525	362	3.2	35.5	23.9	0.9
Summer Fruits, Marks & Spencer*	1oz/28g	25	90	2.0	20.9	0.2	4.1
Summer Pudding, BGTY, Sainsbury's*	1 Pot/110g	223	203	3.2	40.9	4.6	2.4
Summer Pudding, Safeway*	1 Pudding/135g	196	145	2.5	32.9	0.4	3.1
Summer Pudding, Waitrose*	1 Pot/120g	125	104	2.0	23.1	0.4	1.4
Summerfruit, Healthy Eating, Tesco*	1 Pudding/100g	72	72	1.3	16.3	0.2	2.9
Syrup Sponge, Iceland*	1 Serving/72.8g	228	312	5.1	54.1	8.4	0.9
Syrup, Individual, Co-Op*	1 Pudding/170g	604	355	3.0	38.0	21.0	1.0
Syrup, Marks & Spencer*	1 Serving/105g	370	352	3.9	61.7	10.0	0.8
Treacle Sponge, Heinz*	1 Serving/160g	445	278	2.5	48.9	8.1	0.6
Truffle, Chocolate Amaretto, Gu*	1 Pot/80g	272	340	3.3	34.9	19.4	1.6
Truffle, Chocolate, With Rasberry Compote, Gu*	1 pot/80g	250	313	2.8	28.8	18.3	1.8
Truffle, Double Chocolate, Gu*	1 Pot/50g	220	440	3.5	25.9	25.0	2.7
PULSES,							
Mixed, In Water, Sainsbury's*	½ Can/120g	131	109	8.7	13.6	2.2	4.6
PUMPKIN,							
Boiled in Salted Water	1oz/28g	4	13	0.6	2.1	0.3	1.1
Raw	1oz/28g	4	13	0.7	2.2	0.2	1.0
PUMPKIN SEEDS,							
Average	1 Tbsp/10g	57	568	27.9	13.0	45.9	3.9

P

	Measure INFO/WEIGHT	per Measure KCAL	Nutrition Values per 100g / 100ml				
			KCAL	PROT	CARB	FAT	FIBRE
QUAVERS,							
Cheese, Walkers*	1 Bag/20g	103	515	3.0	61.0	29.0	1.2
Prawn Cocktail, Walkers*	1 Bag/16g	82	510	2.6	61.0	28.0	1.2
Salt & Vinegar, Walkers*	1 Bag/16g	80	500	2.3	58.0	29.0	1.1
Streaky Bacon, Walkers*	1 Pack/19.6g	103	515	2.2	62.0	29.0	1.3
QUICHE,							
Asparagus & Cheese, Safeway*	¼ Quiche/100g	260	260	7.5	18.2	17.4	1.4
Baby Spinach & Gruyere, Sainsbury's*	¼ Quiche/93g	228	245	7.4	15.1	17.2	1.0
Bacon & Cheese, Pork Farms*	1 Pack/120g	378	315	11.1	20.8	20.0	0.0
Bacon & Tomato, Asda*	1 Serving/106.9g	201	188	8.0	21.0	8.0	1.1
Bacon & Tomato, Good Intentions, Somerfield*	1 Serving/145g	255	176	5.7	5.1	14.8	0.1
Bacon, Leek & Mushroom, Marks & Spencer*	¼ Quiche/100g	250	250	8.7	14.2	17.9	2.1
Bacon, Mushroom & Tomato, Somerfield*	¼ Quiche/100g	264	264	7.6	19.6	17.2	1.0
Brie & Smoked Bacon, Asda*	¼ Quiche/90g	249	277	8.9	17.8	18.9	1.0
Broccoli & Cheddar Cheese, Safeway*	1 Pack/300g	813	271	7.7	19.8	17.9	1.9
Broccoli & Cheese, Healthy Choice, Safeway*	1oz/28g	49	176	7.8	18.3	10.0	1.8
Broccoli & Stilton, Mini, Sainsbury's*	1 Quiche/14g	52	369	8.8	35.2	21.4	3.3
Broccoli & Tomato, Marks & Spencer*	1oz/28g	59	210	6.7	14.7	13.8	1.6
Broccoli, Extra, Value, Tesco*	1 Serving/125g	341	273	10.0	15.1	19.2	0.8
Broccoli, Healthy Eating, Tesco*	1 Quiche/175g	308	176	6.7	21.5	7.0	1.4
Broccoli, Tesco*	1 Quiche/175g	340	194	7.0	20.9	9.2	1.4
Broccoli, Tomato & Cheese, BGTY, Sainsbury's*	1 Quiche/390g	632	162	6.4	15.7	8.2	1.3
Broccoli, Tomato & Cheese, Sainsbury's*	1 Serving/125g	274	219	6.1	15.5	14.7	1.3
Cheddar Cheese, & Onion, Safeway*	¼ Quiche/100g	293	293	8.3	21.6	19.3	1.5
Cheese & Bacon, Healthy Eating, Tesco*	1 Serving/155g	307	198	9.1	19.9	9.1	1.4
Cheese & Bacon, SmartPrice, Asda*	¼ Quiche/82g	208	257	6.0	20.0	17.0	0.7
Cheese & Broccoli, Good Intentions, Somerfield*	1 Quiche/145g	409	282	6.9	27.7	15.9	1.8
Cheese & Chive, Healthy Eating, Tesco*	1 Serving/86g	169	197	10.4	22.1	7.4	1.2
Cheese & Egg	1oz/28g	88	314	12.5	17.3	22.2	0.6
Cheese & Ham, Somerfield*	1 Quiche/325g	835	257	7.0	18.0	18.0	0.0
Cheese & Mushroom, Budgens*	½ Quiche/170g	474	279	7.8	18.4	19.3	1.4
Cheese & Onion, Marks & Spencer*	1 Slice/100g	250	250	8.2	16.1	17.2	1.5
Cheese & Onion, Mini, Somerfield*	1oz/28g	110	394	9.0	27.0	28.0	0.0
Cheese & Onion, Morrisons*	¼ Quiche/112g	364	325	10.1	20.3	22.6	1.1
Cheese & Onion, Reduced Fat, Safeway*	¼ Flan/100g	212	212	9.6	20.8	10.0	1.5
Cheese & Onion, Safeway*	1 Serving/310g	797	257	7.2	25.2	14.2	1.0
Cheese & Onion, Sainsbury's*	1 Quiche/390g	956	245	8.0	15.0	17.0	0.9
Cheese & Onion, Somerfield*	1 Quiche/300g	696	232	8.0	14.0	16.0	0.0
Cheese & Onion, Tesco*	1 Serving/90g	230	256	8.2	18.1	16.8	2.5
Cheese & Onion, Value, Tesco*	½ Quiche/200g	526	263	8.6	16.1	18.2	0.7
Cheese & Onion, Waitrose*	1 Serving/85g	182	214	6.4	13.9	14.8	3.6
Cheese & Tomato, Asda*	¼ Quiche/105g	274	261	8.0	19.0	17.0	0.9
Cheese & Tomato, Morrisons*	½ Quiche/64g	195	304	7.3	22.8	20.5	1.0
Cheese & Tomato, Somerfield*	1 Quiche/135g	416	308	10.0	23.0	19.0	0.0
Cheese Potato & Onion, Safeway*	1/3 Quiche/115g	361	314	8.8	24.1	20.3	1.5
Cheese, Broccoli & Tomato, Nisa Heritage*	1 Serving/85g	234	275	7.3	17.5	19.5	1.4
Cheese, Onion & Chive, Healthy Eating, Tesco*	1 Slice/100g	202	202	10.9	21.2	8.2	1.3
Cheese, Onion & Chive, SmartPrice, Asda*	¼ Quiche/83g	213	257	6.0	20.0	17.0	0.7
Cheese, Onion & Chive, Somerfield*	1oz/28g	87	310	9.0	16.0	23.0	0.0
Cheese, Onion & Chive, Tesco*	1oz/28g	90	320	10.6	15.5	24.0	0.6
Chicken & Basil, Finest, Tesco*	1 Serving/134g	381	284	9.3	19.8	18.6	1.3
Chicken & Mushroom, Somerfield*	1oz/28g	90	320	12.0	22.0	21.0	0.0
Chicken, Bacon & Mushroom, Asda*	1 Quiche/425g	1131	266	9.0	17.0	18.0	0.8
Chicken, Garlic & Herb, Asda*	1/8 Quiche/52g	137	264	10.0	20.0	16.0	1.2

Q

	Measure	per Measure	Nutrition Values per 100g / 100ml				
	INFO/WEIGHT	KCAL	KCAL	PROT	CARB	FAT	FIBRE
QUICHE,							
Cumberland Sausage & Onion, Sainsbury's*	1 Serving/180g	486	270	7.0	18.8	18.5	1.3
Davidstow Cheddar Cheese & Caramelised Onion, Asda*	1/3 Quiche/117g	369	315	7.0	20.0	23.0	1.0
Egg, Bacon & Cheese, Iceland*	1 Serving/90g	299	332	7.7	23.5	23.0	1.9
Gammon, Leek & Cheddar Cheese, Somerfield*	¼ Quiche/95g	251	264	7.6	19.9	17.1	0.9
Garlic Mushroom, Asda*	¼ Quiche/105g	273	260	7.0	22.0	16.0	0.7
Goats Cheese & Red Pepper, Tesco*	1 Serving/87g	271	312	5.8	19.2	23.6	0.9
Ham & Mustard, GFY, Asda*	1 Quiche/155g	327	211	9.0	19.0	11.0	3.9
Ham & Soft Cheese, Tesco*	¼ Quiche/100g	280	280	7.4	17.5	20.1	1.9
Ham & Tomato, Marks & Spencer*	½ Pack/200g	440	220	8.1	12.4	15.5	2.9
Ham, Cheese & Chive, GFY, Asda*	1 Serving/78g	186	239	8.0	27.0	11.0	1.0
Leek & Sweet Potato, Waitrose*	½ Quiche/200g	440	220	5.3	17.0	14.5	2.3
Leek, Cheese & Chive, Sainsbury's*	1/3 Quiche/125g	293	234	7.1	14.9	16.2	1.3
Lincolnshire Sausage & Whole Grain Mustard, Somerfield*	¼ Quiche/100g	282	282	6.7	17.7	20.5	0.8
Lorraine	1oz/28g	109	391	16.1	19.8	28.1	0.7
Lorraine, Asda*	1 Serving/106g	318	300	9.0	21.0	20.0	2.3
Lorraine, BGTY, Sainsbury's*	1 Serving/128g	273	213	10.9	17.7	10.9	0.7
Lorraine, Finest, Tesco*	1 Serving/100g	330	330	8.4	17.5	25.1	1.5
Lorraine, Healthy Eating, New Improved Recipe, Tesco*	¼ Quiche/100g	202	202	13.0	20.9	7.4	1.3
Lorraine, Healthy Living, Tesco*	1 Serving/200g	404	202	13.0	20.9	7.4	1.3
Lorraine, Improved Recipe, Marks & Spencer*	1oz/28g	78	280	12.5	14.9	18.9	0.9
Lorraine, Marks & Spencer*	1oz/28g	85	305	13.7	12.0	22.5	0.9
Lorraine, Mini, Marks & Spencer*	1oz/28g	95	340	11.6	21.0	23.6	1.6
Lorraine, Quiche Selection, Marks & Spencer*	1 Slice/56g	160	285	12.8	12.3	20.6	2.1
Lorraine, Reduced Fat, Safeway*	¼ Quiche/100g	231	231	11.0	18.9	12.4	1.4
Lorraine, Sainsbury's*	1/3 Quiche/128g	341	265	9.3	14.4	19.0	0.9
Lorraine, Somerfield*	¼ Quiche/87g	260	299	10.1	17.1	21.1	0.7
Lorraine, TTD, Sainsbury's*	1/3 Pie/158g	482	305	10.2	15.1	22.7	0.9
Lorraine, Tesco*	1 Serving/81g	220	272	9.1	18.7	17.9	1.2
Lorraine, With A Creamy Filling, Safeway*	1 Quiche/485g	1576	325	9.8	19.4	22.7	1.2
Mediterranean Pepper, Good Intentions, Somerfield*	1/3 Quiche/130g	264	203	7.9	22.2	9.2	1.3
Mediterranean Vegetable, BGTY, Sainsbury's*	½ Quiche/90g	160	178	7.3	19.2	8.0	1.7
Mediterranean Vegetable, Mini, Marks & Spencer*	1oz/28g	78	280	6.8	23.9	17.5	1.6
Mediterranean Vegetable, Sainsbury's*	1 Serving/200g	482	241	6.3	14.6	17.5	2.2
Mediterranean, GFY, Asda*	1 Serving/25g	54	217	9.0	25.0	9.0	2.4
Mediterranean, Marks & Spencer*	1oz/28g	64	230	6.6	16.6	15.3	0.9
Mushroom	1oz/28g	80	284	10.0	18.3	19.5	0.9
Mushroom Medley, Waitrose*	¼ Quiche/100g	222	222	6.4	15.0	15.2	2.9
Mushroom, Bacon & Leek, Marks & Spencer*	1 Pack/170g	425	250	8.7	13.4	18.1	1.6
Mushroom, Marks & Spencer*	¼ Quiche/100g	235	235	6.1	14.6	16.7	2.8
Mushroom, Sainsbury's*	1/3 Quiche/125.2g	283	226	7.1	15.9	14.9	1.2
Mushroom, Somerfield*	¼ Quiche/82g	212	258	9.0	20.0	16.0	0.0
Roast Sweet Potato, Carrot & Coriander, Asda*	½ Quiche/207.5g	524	252	7.0	20.0	16.0	1.0
Salmon & Asparagus, Healthy Eating, Tesco*	1 Quiche/345g	621	180	7.5	20.2	7.7	1.2
Salmon & Broccoli, Asda*	¼ Quiche/106g	289	273	10.0	20.0	17.0	2.6
Salmon & Broccoli, Sainsbury's*	1 Serving	346	260	7.9	18.5	17.1	0.8
Salmon & Broccoli, Tesco*	1 Serving/133g	355	267	8.8	17.0	18.0	1.8
Salmon & Spinach, Sainsbury's*	1/3 Quiche/125g	318	254	8.2	15.9	17.5	1.0
Spinach & Gruyere, Mini, Somerfield*	1oz/28g	108	384	11.0	25.0	27.0	0.0
Spinach & Gruyere, Sainsbury's*	¼ Quiche/100g	258	258	7.7	13.9	19.1	1.0
Spinach & Ricotta, Marks & Spencer*	1oz/28g	73	260	8.0	14.9	18.8	1.7
Spinach & Ricotta, Safeway*	¼ Quiche/85g	193	227	7.9	22.6	11.7	1.7
Spinach Ricotta Cheese & Red Pepper, Safeway*	1 Serving/120g	304	253	6.2	20.2	16.4	1.2
Spinach, Ricotta & Gruyere Slice, Somerfield*	1 Slice/130g	348	268	7.0	15.0	20.0	0.0

	Measure INFO/WEIGHT	per Measure KCAL	Nutrition Values per 100g / 100ml				
			KCAL	PROT	CARB	FAT	FIBRE
QUICHE,							
Summer Vegetable, Marks & Spencer*	¼ Quiche/100g	225	225	4.9	14.5	16.5	1.7
Sunblush Tomato, Basil & Mozzarella, Somerfield*	¼ Quiche/88g	221	251	7.7	17.9	16.5	1.0
Sweet Cherry Pepper & Fontal Cheese, Finest, Tesco*	¼ Slice/100g	293	293	6.7	16.9	22.1	0.9
Three Cheese & Onion, GFY, Asda*	1 Serving/73g	188	258	10.0	23.0	14.0	3.1
Tomato & Cheese, Sainsbury's*	1/3 Quiche/133g	374	281	7.9	20.9	18.4	1.5
Tomato Cheese & Courgette, GFY, Asda*	1 Serving/155g	333	215	7.0	22.0	11.0	3.3
Tomato, Broccoli & Cheese, Sainsbury's*	1 Serving/180g	437	243	6.7	19.6	15.3	1.5
Tomato, Cheese & Courgette, Asda*	1 Quiche/100g	333	333	11.0	34.0	17.0	5.0
Tomato, GFY, Asda*	¼ Quiche/50g	94	188	8.0	21.0	8.0	0.8
Tomato, Mushroom & Bacon, Sainsbury's*	1 Serving/187g	447	239	7.5	15.2	16.5	1.1
Tuna, Tomato & Basil, Asda*	1 Serving/125g	305	244	9.0	16.0	16.0	1.5
Vegetable, Tesco*	1 Serving/100g	257	257	6.9	17.5	17.7	1.5
QUICK SNACK,							
Chicken & Mushroom Flavour, Value, Tesco*	1 Pot/80g	274	342	14.9	60.6	4.5	7.0
Mash, Roasted Onion, Sainsbury's*	1 Pot/58g	75	130	1.8	14.8	7.1	0.0
Rice, Chilli, Sainsbury's*	1 Pack/280g	241	86	2.5	18.6	0.2	0.0
QUINCE,							
Average	1oz/28g	7	26	0.3	6.3	0.1	0.0
QUINOA,							
Average	1oz/28g	87	309	13.8	55.7	5.0	0.0
QUORN*,							
Bacon*	1 Rasher/30g	42	141	13.5	8.1	6.1	3.0
Balls, Al Forno	1 Serving/400g	348	87	4.7	13.1	1.8	1.8
Balls, Swedish Style	3 Balls/50g	72	144	22.0	5.4	3.8	3.2
Balls, Swedish Style, In Chunky Tomato & Basil Sauce	1 Pack/400g	296	74	8.2	5.0	2.3	2.0
Burger, Premiere, McDonald's*	1 Burger/210g	311	148	9.1	24.2	2.9	2.7
Burgers, Original	1 Burger/50g	109	219	24.0	13.8	7.4	9.8
Burgers, Premium	1 Burger/81g	96	118	11.4	7.1	4.9	3.5
Burgers, Southern Style	1 Burger/63g	125	199	10.7	17.0	9.8	3.1
Casserole, With Dumplings	1oz/28g	36	127	4.5	14.2	5.8	1.7
Chicken Slices, Deli Style	3 Slices/33g	36	108	16.9	4.0	2.7	3.2
Chilli	1oz/28g	23	81	4.7	6.9	4.2	2.5
Curry, Red Thai	1 Pack/400g	464	116	4.6	15.5	3.9	4.0
Enchiladas	1 Pack/400g	384	96	5.3	11.7	3.1	1.9
Enchiladas, Marlow Foods*	1 Pack/401g	405	101	5.3	11.7	3.7	1.9
Escalopes, Garlic & Herb	1 Escalope/140g	293	209	8.9	16.9	11.8	3.8
Fajita, Ready Meal	1oz/28g	41	148	6.9	22.1	3.5	2.7
Fillets	2 Fillets/102g	92	90	12.6	5.9	1.8	4.7
Fillets, Chargrilled Tikka Style, Mini	½ Pack/85g	110	129	12.5	14.4	2.4	5.0
Fillets, Chinese Style Chargrilled, Mini	1 Serving/85g	115	135	12.1	15.6	2.7	4.7
Fillets, Garlic & Herb	1 Fillet/100g	198	198	10.7	16.7	9.8	4.1
Fillets, Hot & Spicy	1 Fillet/100g	176	176	10.9	14.7	8.2	6.4
Fillets, In A Mediterranean Marinade	1 Fillet/80g	90	112	12.5	8.8	3.0	4.0
Fillets, In A White Wine Sauce With Mushrooms & Chives	1 Fillet/162.5g	142	87	6.2	4.4	5.0	1.5
Fillets, In Breadcrumbs	1 Fillet/94g	184	196	11.0	14.2	10.6	3.8
Fillets, In Mushroom & White Wine Sauce	1 Pack/325g	218	67	5.1	4.9	3.0	2.1
Fillets, Lemon & Black Pepper	1 Fillet/100g	195	195	11.6	17.2	8.9	3.3
Fillets, Oriental, Sainsbury's*	1 Serving/294g	353	120	4.0	24.6	0.6	1.8
Fillets, Provencale, Morrisons*	1 Serving/165g	94	57	5.4	5.8	1.4	1.1
Fillets, Thai	1 Serving/79.4g	85	107	14.9	6.1	2.5	3.6
Fillets, With A Crispy Seasonal Coating	1 Fillet/100g	197	197	8.8	18.4	9.8	3.0
Goujons, With Chunky Salsa Dip	1oz/28g	57	204	10.4	17.0	10.5	3.0
Grills, Lamb Flavour	1 Grill/90g	104	116	11.4	10.4	3.2	4.2

	Measure INFO/WEIGHT	per Measure KCAL	Nutrition Values per 100g / 100ml				
			KCAL	PROT	CARB	FAT	FIBRE
QUORN*,							
Ham	1 Slice/12.5g	18	139	18.3	6.1	4.6	3.1
Ham, Wafer Thin, Deli	1 Serving/18g	23	130	19.3	6.1	3.1	3.1
Korma	1oz/28g	39	140	3.7	16.7	7.0	0.0
Lasagne	1 Pack/300g	249	83	4.1	9.9	3.0	1.3
Mince	1 Pack/350g	329	94	14.5	4.5	2.0	6.0
Moussaka	1 Pack/400g	364	91	3.6	9.8	4.1	1.2
Myco-Protein	1oz/28g	24	86	11.8	2.0	3.5	4.8
Noodles, Sweet Chilli	1 Pack/400g	352	88	4.2	12.7	2.3	1.5
Nuggets	1 nugget/20g	38	191	10.6	15.7	9.5	3.5
Nuggets, Southern Style	1 Nugget/20g	39	197	12.1	15.7	9.5	3.5
Pate, Brussels Style	1 Pack/130g	150	115	10.8	5.7	5.4	3.4
Pate, Country Style Coarse	½ Pot/65g	68	104	9.2	7.3	4.2	2.7
Pate, Deli	1oz/28g	32	115	10.8	5.7	5.4	3.4
Pie, Cottage	1 Pie/300g	213	71	2.7	10.7	1.9	1.3
Pie, Creamy Mushroom	1 Pie/134g	362	270	4.1	22.8	18.0	1.3
Pie, Mince & Onion	1 Pie/141g	368	261	5.3	27.1	14.6	1.5
Pie, Quorn & Vegetable	1oz/28g	52	186	6.9	14.7	11.5	2.0
Pieces	1 Pack/300g	309	103	14.0	5.8	2.6	6.0
Pork Ribsters	2 Ribsters/83.9g	99	118	15.9	4.8	3.9	2.8
Roast	2 Slices/90g	97	108	16.9	4.0	2.7	4.0
Sausage & Mash, Sainsbury's*	1 Pack/394g	339	86	3.8	11.0	3.0	0.7
Sausage & Mash, Tesco*	1 Pack/400g	292	73	4.1	8.8	2.4	1.3
Sausage, Leek & Pork Style	1 Sausage/44g	56	127	13.3	7.5	4.9	2.1
Sausage, Vegetarian	1 Sausage/42g	47	111	13.4	5.9	3.8	3.0
Slices, Roast, With Sage & Onion Stuffing	¼ Pack/70g	47	67	7.5	4.9	1.9	3.0
Spaghetti Bolognese	1 Pack/400g	292	73	5.7	9.4	1.4	2.4
Spaghetti Carbonara	1 Pack/400g	460	115	5.0	9.1	6.5	1.1
Steaks, Peppered	1 Steak/98.2g	107	109	11.4	7.4	3.8	4.0
Stir Fry, Spicy Chilli With Vegetables & Rice	½ Pack/170g	162	95	5.9	15.6	1.0	1.8
Tikka Masala, With Rice	1 Pack/400g	476	119	4.3	13.5	5.3	1.6
Turkey Flavour, With Stuffing, Deli	1 Slice/13g	15	114	15.1	8.3	2.3	4.7

Q

	Measure INFO/WEIGHT	per Measure KCAL	Nutrition Values per 100g / 100ml				
			KCAL	PROT	CARB	FAT	FIBRE
RABBIT,							
Meat Only, Raw	1oz/28g	38	137	21.9	0.0	5.5	0.0
Meat Only, Stewed,	1oz/28g	32	114	21.2	0.0	3.2	0.0
Meat Only, Stewed, Weighed With Bone	1oz/28g	19	68	12.7	0.0	1.9	0.0
RADDICCIO,							
Raw	1oz/28g	4	14	1.4	1.7	0.2	1.8
RADIATORE,							
Sainsbury's*	1 Serving/75g	268	357	12.3	73.1	1.7	2.5
RADISH,							
Red, Average	1oz/28g	3	12	0.7	1.9	0.2	0.9
White, Mooli, Raw	1oz/28g	4	15	0.8	2.9	0.1	0.0
RAISINS,							
& Sultanas, Jumbo, Marks & Spencer*	1 Pack/50g	133	265	2.4	62.4	0.5	2.6
Seedless, Average	1 Serving/75g	215	287	2.2	68.5	0.5	3.2
Yoghurt Coated, Holland & Barrett*	1 Bag/100g	404	404	2.6	66.6	16.5	1.0
RAITA,							
Cucumber & Mint, Patak's*	1oz/28g	33	117	3.9	12.9	5.5	0.1
Plain	1oz/28g	46	166	2.6	5.5	15.3	0.0
RASPBERRIES,							
Average	1oz/28g	7	26	1.3	4.7	0.3	3.5
In Fruit Juice, Average	1oz/28g	9	32	0.9	6.7	0.2	1.7
In Syrup, Canned	1oz/28g	25	88	0.6	22.5	0.1	1.5
RATATOUILLE,							
Chicken, Finest, Tesco*	1 Pack/550g	407	74	7.8	5.9	2.1	0.0
Princes*	1 Can/360g	86	24	1.0	4.2	0.4	0.0
Safeway*	1 Serving/200g	78	39	1.0	3.0	2.5	1.6
Sainsbury's*	1 Pack/300g	99	33	1.5	5.5	0.6	1.6
RAVIOLI,							
Amatriciana, TTD, Sainsbury's*	1 Serving/125g	390	312	16.6	33.3	12.5	3.5
Asparagus & Ham, Healthy Eating, Tesco*	½ Pack/125g	203	162	8.2	26.5	2.6	0.6
Asparagus, Waitrose*	1 Serving/150g	303	202	10.5	26.4	6.0	2.0
Basil & Parmesan, Organic, Sainsbury's*	½ Pack/192g	290	151	7.4	21.1	5.2	2.1
Beef, Fresh, Safeway*	1 Serving/137g	352	257	10.0	39.4	6.6	3.0
Beef, In Tomato Sauce, Asda*	1 Serving/400g	352	88	3.6	14.0	2.0	3.0
Beef, Tesco*	1 Serving/194g	175	90	4.3	12.3	2.6	1.5
Blue Cheese & Bacon, Safeway*	½ Pack/125g	288	230	10.5	24.9	9.6	1.6
Cheese & Sun Dried Tomato, Co-Op*	½ Pack/125g	356	285	12.0	38.0	9.0	2.0
Cheese & Tomato, Fresh, Organic, Tesco*	1 Serving/125g	343	274	12.5	30.8	11.2	1.1
Cheese & Tomato, Heinz*	1 Can/410g	332	81	2.7	14.1	1.5	0.6
Cheese, Garlic, & Herb, Safeway*	½ Pack/125g	263	210	9.1	26.5	7.6	2.0
Cheese, Tomato & Basil, Italiano, Tesco*	½ Pack/125g	304	243	13.6	24.1	10.2	0.5
Cherry Tomato & Mushroom, Somerfield*	1 Pack/400g	436	109	3.5	9.8	6.2	1.2
Chicken & Mushroom, Finest, Tesco*	½ Pack/125g	268	214	11.6	25.8	7.1	1.1
Chicken & Rosemary, Perfectly Balanced, Waitrose*	½ Pack/125g	266	213	14.9	30.4	3.5	2.1
Chicken & Tomato, Perfectly Balanced, Waitrose*	1 Serving/125g	265	212	13.5	33.4	2.7	2.8
Five Cheese, Weight Watchers*	1 Pack/330g	271	82	3.2	11.1	2.8	0.8
Florentine, Weight Watchers*	1 Serving/241g	220	91	3.7	14.1	2.1	1.2
Four Cheese, Good Intentions, Somerfield*	1 Pack/353g	367	104	4.1	14.0	3.5	1.7
Four Cheese, Italia, Marks & Spencer*	1 Pack/360g	432	120	6.7	13.1	4.6	1.0
Free Range Duck, TTD, Sainsbury's*	½ Pack/161g	314	195	11.5	21.0	7.3	2.3
Fresh, Bolognese, Safeway*	1 Serving/120g	200	167	8.8	22.6	4.6	2.0
Fresh, Pasta Reale*	1 Serving/150g	459	306	13.1	53.3	5.9	0.0
Goat's Cheese & Pesto, Asda*	½ Pack/150g	204	136	6.0	20.0	3.6	0.0
In Tomato Sauce, Heinz*	1 Can/410g	299	73	2.6	13.0	1.1	0.6

R

	Measure INFO/WEIGHT	per Measure KCAL	Nutrition Values per 100g / 100ml				
			KCAL	PROT	CARB	FAT	FIBRE
RAVIOLI,							
In Tomato Sauce, Meat Free, Heinz*	1 Can/410g	308	75	2.4	14.4	0.8	0.5
In Tomato Sauce, Sainsbury's*	1oz/28g	23	83	3.1	15.5	1.0	0.5
In Tomato Sauce, Tesco*	1 Can/400g	276	69	2.7	14.2	0.1	1.3
Meat, Italian, Fresh, Asda*	½ Pack/150g	261	174	8.0	26.0	4.2	0.0
Meditteranean Vegetable, Healthy Eating, Tesco*	1 Serving/125g	199	159	6.7	27.2	2.6	0.9
Mozzarella Tomato & Basil, Tesco*	1 Serving/125g	304	243	13.6	24.1	10.2	0.5
Mushroom & Mascarpone, The Best, Safeway*	1 Pack/175g	466	266	9.9	31.8	11.0	1.0
Mushroom, Italian, Fresh, Somerfield*	½ Pack/125g	336	269	10.8	34.4	9.8	1.8
Mushroom, Italiano, Tesco*	1 Serving/125g	333	266	10.4	27.0	12.9	3.0
Mushroom, Ready Meals, Marks & Spencer*	1oz/28g	38	135	8.1	22.0	1.9	2.2
Mushroom, Safeway*	½ Pack/125g	243	194	7.5	25.5	6.9	1.8
Mushroomi, Tesco*	½ Pack/125g	333	266	10.4	27.0	12.9	3.0
Prosciuttoi, Ready Meal, Marks & Spencer*	1 Pack/100g	195	195	13.3	17.0	8.1	1.0
Red Onion & Brunello Wine, TTD, Sainsbury's*	1 Serving/125g	235	188	7.5	23.0	7.3	2.5
Rich Beef & Red Wine, Morrisons*	1 Serving/150g	396	264	12.1	40.6	7.2	3.0
Roast Garlic & Herb, Tesco*	½ Pack/125g	343	274	12.8	31.1	10.9	1.1
Roasted Pepper, Marks & Spencer*	1 Pack/400g	540	135	5.4	11.0	7.7	1.1
Roasted Vegetable, Asda*	½ Pack/150g	218	145	6.0	29.0	0.5	0.0
Salmon, Open, Finest, Tesco*	1oz/28g	37	131	6.8	15.5	4.6	0.5
SmartPrice, Asda*	1 Can/400g	272	68	2.7	14.0	0.1	1.3
Smoked Ham, Bacon & Tomato, Italiano, Tesco*	1 Can/125g	303	242	10.8	32.3	7.7	2.9
Spinach & Ricotta, Waitrose*	1 Serving/125g	309	247	10.5	35.0	7.2	1.9
Sweet Pepper & Chilli, Tesco*	½ Pack/125g	324	259	12.5	27.1	11.2	2.7
Tomato Cheese & Meat, Sainsbury's*	1 Serving/125g	314	251	12.4	21.4	12.9	2.2
Vegetable In Tomato Sauce, Italiana, Weight Watchers*	1 Can/385g	266	69	1.7	11.0	2.1	0.5
Vegetable, Sainsbury's*	1 Can/400g	328	82	2.6	16.3	0.7	0.7
Vegetable, Tesco*	½ Can/200g	164	82	2.6	16.3	0.7	0.7
Wild Mushroom, Al Forno, TTD, Sainsbury's*	1 Pack/300g	459	153	7.0	14.0	7.7	1.2
RED BULL*,							
Regular	1 Can/250ml	113	45	0.0	11.3	0.0	0.0
Sugar Free	1 Can/250ml	8	3	0.0	1.0	0.0	0.0
REDCURRANT JELLY,							
Average	1oz/28g	70	250	0.2	64.4	0.0	0.0
REDCURRANTS,							
Raw	1oz/28g	6	21	1.1	4.4	0.0	3.4
REHYDRATION DRINK,							
Citrus Flavour, Still, Low Calorie, Shapers, Boots*	1 Bottle/500ml	10	2	0.1	0.1	0.1	0.0
Still Pink Grapefruit Sports, Shapers, Boots*	1 Bottle/500ml	10	2	0.1	0.2	0.1	0.0
RELISH,							
Barbeque, Sainsbury's*	1 Serving/50g	50	100	1.0	19.3	2.1	1.1
Caramelised Onion & Chilli, Marks & Spencer*	1 Serving/20g	47	235	1.4	55.1	1.1	1.0
Caramelised Red Onion, Tesco*	1 Serving/10g	28	280	0.6	69.1	0.1	0.7
Hamburger, Bick's*	1oz/28g	27	96	1.3	22.3	0.2	0.0
Onion, Marks & Spencer*	1oz/28g	46	165	1.0	32.1	3.0	1.1
Sweetcorn, Bicks*	1 Tbsp/22g	23	103	1.3	24.3	0.2	0.0
Sweetcorn, Safeway*	1 Serving/50g	69	137	1.0	32.4	0.4	0.5
Tomato & Chilli Texan Style, Tesco*	1 Tbsp/14g	20	140	1.7	32.0	0.1	1.1
Tomato, Marks & Spencer*	1oz/28g	36	130	1.8	30.2	0.3	1.5
REVELS,							
Mars*	1 Sm Bag/35g	173	495	6.2	65.6	23.1	0.0
RHUBARB,							
Raw, Average	¼ Can/133g	9	7	0.9	0.8	0.1	1.4
Stewed With Sugar	1oz/28g	13	48	0.9	11.5	0.1	1.2

	Measure INFO/WEIGHT	per Measure KCAL	Nutrition Values per 100g / 100ml				
			KCAL	PROT	CARB	FAT	FIBRE
RHUBARB,							
Stewed Without Sugar	1oz/28g	2	7	0.9	0.7	0.1	1.3
RIBENA*,							
Apple Juice Drink	1 Carton/287ml	132	46	0.0	11.1	0.0	0.0
Blackcurrant Juice Drink	1 Carton/288ml	164	57	0.0	14.0	0.0	0.0
Blackcurrant Juice Drink, Toothkind	1 Carton/288ml	12	4	0.0	0.7	0.0	0.0
Blackcurrant, Diluted With Water	1 Serving/180ml	81	45	0.0	11.0	0.0	0.0
Light	1 Carton/288ml	26	9	0.1	2.1	0.0	0.0
Orange Tropical Juice Drink, Toothkind	1 Carton/288ml	9	3	0.0	0.6	0.0	0.0
Strawberry Juice Drink	1 Carton/288ml	156	54	0.0	13.2	0.0	0.0
Strawberry Juice Drink, Toothkind	1 Carton/288ml	12	4	0.0	0.7	0.0	0.0
RIBS,							
Pork, Barbecue, Average	1 Serving/100g	275	275	21.4	7.2	17.9	0.3
Pork, Chinese Style, Average	1 Serving/300g	736	245	17.9	10.0	14.9	0.7
Pork, Raw, Average	1oz/28g	47	169	18.6	1.8	9.9	0.2
Spare, Sticky, Glazed, Marks & Spencer*	½ Pack/150g	263	175	13.6	5.4	11.1	0.4
RIBSTEAKS,							
Chinese Style, Dalepak*	1 Steak/75g	184	245	20.3	11.6	13.1	1.1
Smokey Barbecue Style, Dalepak*	1 Serving/75g	164	219	16.1	8.8	13.1	0.8
RICE,							
Arborio, Dry, Average	1 Serving/80g	279	348	7.1	78.3	0.8	0.8
BBQ & Spicy, Marks & Spencer*	1 Pack/250g	463	185	6.1	23.7	7.2	1.2
Balti Style, Quick, Sainsbury's*	1 Serving/228g	192	84	4.3	15.7	0.5	2.0
Balti, Break, Asda*	1 Serving/60g	209	348	13.3	70.0	1.7	0.0
Basmati, & Wild, Easy Cook, Tilda*	1oz/28g	98	349	9.4	77.0	0.4	0.9
Basmati, & Wild, Marks & Spencer*	1 Pack/180g	189	105	2.8	22.5	0.4	1.2
Basmati, Boil In The Bag, Dry, Average	1 Serving/50g	176	352	8.4	77.9	0.8	0.5
Basmati, Brown, Dry, Average	1oz/28g	99	353	9.5	71.8	3.0	2.2
Basmati, Cooked, Average	1 Serving/140g	189	135	3.6	26.0	1.8	0.7
Basmati, Dry Weight, Average	1 Serving/100g	353	353	8.1	77.9	1.0	0.6
Basmati, Easy Cook, Dry Weight, Average	1 Serving/40g	135	338	8.0	75.5	0.5	0.8
Basmati, Indian, Dry, Average	1 Serving/75g	260	347	8.4	76.1	0.9	0.1
Basmati, Microwave, Cooked, Average	1 Serving/125g	182	146	2.7	30.1	1.9	0.0
Basmati, Pilau, Rizazz, Tilda* Cooked	1 Serving/125g	183	146	2.5	28.7	2.4	0.0
Basmati, Savory Mushroom, Tilda*	1 Pack/250g	353	141	2.6	27.5	2.3	0.0
Basmati, Spicy Mexican, Tilda*	1 Serving/125g	188	150	2.9	28.1	2.9	0.5
Basmati, Thai Lime & Coriander, Tilda*	½ Pack/125g	185	148	2.4	28.4	2.8	0.1
Basmati, White, Dry, Average	1 Serving/75g	262	349	8.1	77.1	0.6	2.2
Brown, American, Easy Cook, Dry, Average	1 Serving/100g	350	350	7.4	75.3	2.2	1.5
Brown, Cooked, Average	1 Serving/140g	173	123	2.6	26.6	1.1	0.9
Brown, Dry, Average	1 Serving/75g	267	355	7.5	76.2	3.0	1.4
Brown, Long Grain, Dry, Average	1 Serving/50g	182	364	7.6	76.8	2.9	2.1
Brown, Whole Grain, Cooked, Average	1 Serving/170g	223	132	2.7	27.8	1.1	1.3
Brown, Whole Grain, Dry, Average	1 Serving/40g	138	344	7.4	71.6	2.9	3.0
Chicken & Sweetcorn Savoury, Asda*	½ Pack/60g	195	325	10.0	65.0	2.8	10.0
Chicken, Savoury, Cooked, Safeway*	1 Serving/151g	213	141	3.6	28.3	1.5	2.2
Chinese Five Spice, Special Recipe, Sainsbury's*	1oz/28g	37	133	2.9	29.9	0.3	0.9
Chinese Savoury, Batchelors*	1 Serving/50g	177	354	9.9	73.1	2.4	2.8
Chinese Style, Express, Uncle Ben's*	1 Pack/250g	338	135	3.1	27.3	1.5	0.0
Coconut & Lime, Asda*	1 Pack/360g	695	193	4.5	32.7	4.9	0.9
Coconut, Marks & Spencer*	½ Pack/124g	217	175	3.1	31.8	4.0	0.3
Coriander & Herbs, Batchelors*	1/3 Pack/76g	280	369	7.9	79.6	3.5	5.0
Easy Cook, Cooked, Average	1 Serving/100g	139	139	2.8	29.3	1.2	0.2
Egg Fried	1oz/28g	58	208	4.2	25.7	10.6	0.4

	Measure INFO/WEIGHT	per Measure KCAL	Nutrition Values per 100g / 100ml				
			KCAL	PROT	CARB	FAT	FIBRE
RICE,							
Egg Fried, Asda*	1oz/28g	43	152	4.2	23.4	4.4	1.8
Egg Fried, Cantonese, Sainsbury's*	½ Pot/260g	465	179	4.0	27.4	8.0	1.3
Egg Fried, Chinese Style, Tesco*	1 Portion/250g	418	167	4.4	27.9	4.2	0.7
Egg Fried, Chinese Takeaway, Tesco*	1 Serving/200g	250	125	4.7	23.3	1.5	1.8
Egg Fried, Chinese, Sainsbury's*	1 Pack/200g	350	175	4.5	27.8	5.1	1.2
Egg Fried, Express, Uncle Ben's*	1 Pack/250g	440	176	4.1	30.5	4.2	0.0
Egg Fried, Healthy Eating, Tesco*	1 Serving/250g	285	114	3.5	22.2	1.3	1.8
Egg Fried, Marks & Spencer*	1 Pack/200g	420	210	4.1	32.4	7.0	0.3
Egg Fried, New, Tesco*	1 Serving/250g	365	146	4.0	23.9	3.8	3.1
Egg Fried, Oriental Express*	1 Pack/425g	531	125	4.0	22.2	2.3	1.3
Egg Fried, Original, Asda*	1 Pack/250g	425	170	4.0	25.0	6.0	1.6
Egg Fried, Rizazz, Tilda*	1 Pack/250g	358	143	3.3	25.4	3.1	0.0
Egg Fried, Tesco*	1 Pack/250g	313	125	4.7	23.3	1.5	1.8
Egg Fried, Waitrose*	1 Pack/300g	426	142	3.0	20.6	5.2	1.0
Fried, Chicken, Chinese Takeaway, Iceland*	1 Pack/340g	510	150	6.5	20.7	4.6	0.6
Fried, Duck, Chicken & Pork Celebration, Sainsbury's*	1 Pack/450g	545	121	7.9	14.2	3.6	1.5
Garlic & Butter Flavoured, Batchelors*	1 Serving/50g	175	350	8.0	79.8	2.8	5.0
Garlic & Coriander Flavoured, Patak's*	1 Serving/125g	186	149	2.6	28.9	2.2	0.0
Garlic & Herb, Sainsbury's*	¼ Pack/50g	66	132	2.3	28.8	0.8	1.1
Golden Savoury, Batchelors*	½ Pack/62g	226	364	10.1	74.7	2.8	2.4
Golden Savoury, Cooked, Tesco*	1 Serving/178g	219	123	3.0	25.0	1.0	1.0
Golden Savoury, New Improved Flavour, Batchelors*	1 Pack/120g	439	366	9.3	78.9	1.5	4.5
Golden Savoury, Safeway*	1 Serving/205g	221	108	2.6	22.6	0.8	1.2
Golden Vegetable, Express, Uncle Ben's*	1 Pack/250g	350	140	2.9	28.2	1.8	0.0
Golden Vegetable, Tesco*	1 Serving/125g	135	108	2.6	21.9	1.1	0.6
Imperial Red, Merchant Gourmet*	1oz/28g	85	305	8.6	61.2	2.5	8.6
Lemon Pepper Speciality, Asda*	1 Serving/52g	67	129	2.0	27.0	1.4	0.1
Lemon Pepper, In 5, Crosse & Blackwell*	½ Pack/163.4g	200	123	2.7	25.2	1.3	4.0
Lentil & Roast Aubergine, Marks & Spencer*	1oz/28g	1	125	3.8	15.4	5.3	2.3
Long Grain, & Wild, Dry, Average	1 Serving/75g	254	338	7.6	72.6	2.0	1.7
Long Grain, American, Cooked, Average	1 Serving/160g	229	143	3.1	28.8	1.8	0.3
Long Grain, American, Dry, Average	1 Serving/50g	175	350	7.2	77.9	1.1	0.6
Long Grain, Dry, Average	1 Serving/100g	337	337	7.4	75.5	1.0	1.7
Long Grain, Microwavable, Cooked, Average	1 Serving/150g	180	120	2.7	25.8	0.6	0.7
Mediterranean Tomato, Rizazz, Tilda*	½ Pack/125g	194	155	2.7	28.6	3.3	0.0
Mexican Style, Old El Paso*	1 Serving/75g	268	357	9.0	78.0	1.0	0.0
Mexican, Ready Meals, Waitrose*	1 Pack/300g	432	144	2.6	27.8	2.5	0.5
Mushroom & Coconut, Organic, Waitrose*	1 Pack/300g	474	158	3.7	24.5	5.0	1.4
Mushroom & Pepper, Savoury, Safeway*	½ Pack/194g	227	117	2.7	25.4	0.5	0.7
Mushroom Savory, Bettabuy, Morrisons*	1 Serving/128.4g	131	102	2.3	21.5	0.8	0.0
Mushroom, Express, Uncle Ben's*	1 Pack/250g	380	152	3.1	30.9	1.8	0.0
Peri Peri Spicy, Nando's*	1 Pot/100g	204	204	3.6	42.8	1.5	0.0
Pilau, Cooked, Average	1oz/28g	49	174	3.5	30.3	4.4	0.8
Pilau, Dry, Average	1oz/28g	101	362	8.5	78.2	2.4	3.4
Pudding, Short Grain, Morrisons*	1oz/28g	36	129	3.9	19.9	4.3	0.0
Risotto, Dry, Average	1oz/28g	97	348	7.8	76.2	1.3	2.4
Saffron, Cooked, Average	1 Serving/150g	209	139	2.6	25.3	3.2	0.5
Savoury, Beef, Batchelors*	½ Pack/62g	222	358	9.4	74.9	2.3	3.2
Savoury, Chicken, Batchelors*	1 Pack/124g	443	357	9.9	74.5	2.2	2.9
Savoury, Chicken, SmartPrice, Asda*	½ Pack/168g	210	125	3.2	26.0	0.9	2.4
Savoury, Chicken, Tesco*	1 Serving/87g	177	204	6.4	39.4	2.2	6.7
Savoury, Curry, Somerfield*	½ Pack/160g	194	121	2.2	26.0	0.9	1.3
Savoury, Golden Vegetable, Asda*	½ Pack/176g	208	118	2.6	25.0	0.8	2.5

RICE,	Measure INFO/WEIGHT	per Measure KCAL	KCAL	PROT	CARB	FAT	FIBRE
Savoury, Golden Vegetable, Sainsbury's*	¼ Pack/100g	122	122	2.9	25.4	1.0	0.3
Savoury, Mild Curry, Batchelors*	½ Pack/61g	217	355	8.4	76.0	1.9	1.8
Savoury, Mixed Vegetable, Tesco*	1 Serving/63g	219	347	8.8	71.1	3.0	6.4
Savoury, Mushroom & Pepper, Cooked, Morrisons*	1 Serving/200g	204	102	2.3	21.5	0.8	0.0
Savoury, Mushroom, Asda*	½ Pack/168g	207	123	3.2	26.0	0.7	2.9
Savoury, Mushroom, Batchelors*	1 Sachet/122g	439	360	10.9	74.3	2.1	2.5
Savoury, Paella, Tesco*	1 Serving/60g	220	367	8.4	72.7	4.7	4.5
Savoury, Spicy Mexican Style, Tesco*	1 Serving/164g	584	356	9.0	69.9	4.5	6.0
Savoury, Sweet & Sour, Batchelors*	1 Serving/135g	419	310	9.4	75.6	2.1	3.1
Savoury, Sweet & Sour, Cooked, Tesco*	½ Pack/153g	214	140	2.7	29.1	1.4	2.3
Savoury, Sweet & Sour, Somerfield*	1 Pack/120g	127	106	2.0	23.0	1.0	0.0
Savoury, Tandoori, Batchelors*	1 Serving/120g	430	358	10.3	73.5	2.5	3.0
Savoury, Vegetable, Marks & Spencer*	½ Pack/250g	313	125	3.4	23.9	1.9	1.2
Short Grain, Organic, Evernat*	1oz/28g	41	146	5.6	30.1	0.3	0.0
Spanish Paella, Special Recipe, Sainsbury's*	1 Pack/125g	134	107	2.1	22.5	0.9	0.2
Spanish Style Savoury, Safeway*	1 Pack/394g	449	114	2.7	23.7	0.9	1.4
Special Fried, Asda*	1oz/28g	42	149	5.4	21.0	4.9	1.5
Special Fried, Marks & Spencer*	1 Pack/450g	923	205	6.2	27.2	7.8	0.5
Special Fried, Sainsbury's*	1 Serving/166g	272	164	5.1	25.5	4.6	0.7
Special Fried, Somerfield*	1 Pack/200g	316	158	5.0	25.0	4.0	0.0
Special Fried, Tesco*	1 Pack/250g	333	133	7.6	17.6	3.6	1.7
Spicy, Nando's*	1oz/28g	66	234	4.2	50.6	2.6	0.0
Sticky Thai, Safeway*	1 Pack/200g	260	130	2.5	25.6	1.8	1.4
Sweet & Sour Savoury, Cooked, Asda*	½ Pack/126g	154	122	2.5	26.0	0.9	3.0
Sweet & Sour, Rice Bowl, Uncle Ben's*	1 Pack/350g	364	104	5.2	19.5	0.6	0.0
Thai, Chicken, Enjoy, Bird's Eye*	1 Pack/500g	535	107	6.9	13.2	3.0	0.7
Thai, Cooked, Average	1 Serving/100g	136	136	2.5	27.4	1.8	0.3
Thai, Dry, Average	1oz/28g	97	348	7.1	78.9	0.5	0.9
Thai, Fragrant, Dry, Average	1 Serving/75g	272	363	7.2	82.0	0.7	0.3
Thai, Fragrant, Waitrose*, Cooked	1 Serving/175g	243	139	2.7	28.7	1.5	0.3
Tomato & Basil, Express, Uncle Ben's*	1 Pack/250g	450	180	3.9	31.5	4.3	0.0
Valencia For Paella, Asda*	1 Serving/125g	435	348	6.0	79.0	0.8	0.0
Vegetable Pilau, Express, Uncle Ben's*	1 Pack/250g	445	178	3.4	33.8	3.2	0.0
Vegetable, Golden, Safeway*	1 Serving/125g	111	89	2.9	18.2	0.5	1.9
Vegetable, Original, Bird's Eye*	1oz/28g	29	105	4.0	20.8	0.6	1.1
White, Cooked, Average	1oz/28g	36	130	2.6	28.7	0.8	0.2
White, Cooked, Frozen, Average	1 Serving/150g	168	112	2.9	23.9	0.6	1.2
White, Dry, Average	1 Serving/50g	181	362	7.1	79.1	1.9	0.4
White, Flaked, Raw	1oz/28g	97	346	6.6	77.5	1.2	0.0
White, Fried	1oz/28g	37	131	2.2	25.0	3.2	0.6
White, Microwave, Cooked, Average	1 Serving/150g	158	105	2.7	22.4	0.5	1.1
Whole Grain, Dry, Average	1 Serving/50g	171	342	8.2	72.0	2.3	4.1
Wild, Raw, Tilda*	1 Serving/40g	140	350	11.5	74.2	0.8	1.9
Yellow, Ready Cooked, Tesco*	1oz/28g	32	113	2.7	27.1	1.3	0.1
RICE &,							
Reed Kidney Beans, Average	1oz/28g	49	175	5.6	32.4	3.5	2.5
Vegetables, Marks & Spencer*	1 Serving/125g	125	100	3.1	18.8	1.6	1.9
RICE BOWL,							
Beef With Black Bean Sauce, Uncle Ben's*	1 Pack/350g	368	105	5.6	17.4	1.4	0.0
Chicken & Mushroom, Sharwood's*	1 Pack/350g	392	112	4.8	17.1	2.7	0.7
Chicken Tikka Masala, Uncle Ben's*	1 Pack/350g	382	109	5.9	15.9	2.4	0.0
Free From, Sainsbury's*	1 Serving/182g	146	80	1.6	17.1	0.6	1.4
Honey BBQ Chicken, Uncle Ben's*	1 Pack/350g	420	120	5.4	23.1	0.6	0.0

R

	Measure INFO/WEIGHT	per Measure KCAL	Nutrition Values per 100g / 100ml				
			KCAL	PROT	CARB	FAT	FIBRE
RICE BOWL,							
Sweet N Sour, Sharwood's*	1 Serving/350g	438	125	4.8	18.6	3.5	0.8
Thai Green, Sharwood's*	1 Bowl/350g	550	157	4.8	17.3	7.6	0.9
Thai Red, Sharwood's*	1 Bowl/350g	487	139	4.7	18.1	5.3	1.0
RICE CAKES,							
& Oats, High Fibre, Kallo*	1 Cake/8g	27	356	10.6	75.0	5.5	9.0
Apple & Cinnamon Flavour, Kallo*	1 Cake/11g	41	376	6.2	83.1	2.2	3.9
Bacon, Asda*	1 Cake/9g	42	462	8.0	67.0	18.0	0.0
Barbeque, Tesco*	1 Cake/9g	28	328	9.6	66.8	2.5	6.2
Black & White Sesame, Clearspring*	1 Cake/8g	31	385	7.4	82.2	2.9	0.0
Brink*	1 Cake/15g	56	370	8.8	78.8	2.2	0.0
Caramel Flavour, Kallo*	1 Cake/9.9g	38	383	6.2	78.9	4.8	3.9
Caramel, Jumbo, Tesco*	1 Cake/10g	36	364	6.5	73.9	2.5	5.1
Caramel, Snack Size, Tesco*	1 Bag/35g	133	379	5.5	82.7	2.9	0.9
Caramel, Tesco*	1 Serving/2.3g	8	379	5.5	98.2	2.9	0.9
Cheese & Onion, Namchow*	1 Serving/38g	141	377	7.2	79.5	3.3	0.0
Cheese, Jumbo, Free From, Tesco*	1 Serving/10g	44	439	8.1	62.1	17.6	3.8
Chocolate, Fabulous Bakin' Boys*	1 Biscuit/17g	83	490	6.4	66.7	22.0	1.6
Co-Op*	1 Cake/20g	80	402	8.0	84.0	3.1	0.0
Crispy, Somerfield*	1oz/28g	134	479	5.0	77.0	17.0	0.0
Dark Chocolate, Organic, Kallo*	1 Cake/12g	57	471	6.8	57.2	24.1	7.4
Five Grain, Finncrisp*	1 Piece/10g	36	356	9.8	73.9	1.7	9.7
Honey, Puffed, Kallo*	1 Serving/50g	182	364	7.0	80.0	2.0	6.7
Lightly Salted, Thick Slice, Low Fat, Kallo*	1 Cake/8g	30	372	8.0	78.7	2.8	5.1
Low Fat, Kallo*	1 Cake/10g	38	375	6.2	83.1	2.2	3.9
Milk Chocolate, Kallo*	1 Cake/15g	77	511	6.5	56.2	28.7	3.5
Oat, Kallo*	1 Slice/7.7g	28	351	10.6	75.3	5.5	9.1
Oat, Lightly Salted, Thick Slice, Kallo*	1 Cake/7.6g	28	356	10.6	75.0	5.5	9.0
Organic, Organix*	3 Cakes/5.9g	22	370	6.5	83.0	1.4	3.2
Rice Bites, Asda*	1 Cake/8.8g	42	466	8.0	68.0	18.0	0.0
Rice Crunchies, Safeway*	1 Small Pack/25g	95	378	7.4	84.2	1.3	1.5
Ryvita*	1 Cake/7g	28	394	8.1	83.1	3.2	1.2
Salt & Vinegar, Snack, Tesco*	1 Pack/35g	116	332	7.5	71.5	1.8	1.1
Salt 'n' Vinegar, Jumbo, Tesco*	1 Cake/8.8g	28	306	8.4	62.5	7.5	6.0
Savoury With Yeast Extract, Kallo*	1 Slice/11g	40	364	12.7	72.0	2.8	4.7
Savoury, Kallo*	1 Cake/8g	28	355	14.2	67.5	3.2	4.4
Savoury, Thick Slice, Organic, Kallo*	1 Slice/9g	31	364	12.7	72.0	2.8	4.5
Sesame Garlic, Clearspring*	1 Serving/8g	29	382	7.8	82.3	2.4	0.0
Sesame Teriyaki, Clearspring*	1 Cake/8g	28	377	6.5	82.8	2.2	0.0
Sesame, Ryvita*	1 Slice/7.3g	28	396	8.2	82.3	3.8	1.3
Slightly Salted, Thick Slice, Organic, Kallo*	1 Cake/8g	30	372	8.0	78.7	2.8	5.1
Slightly Salted, With Cracked Pepper, Snack Size, Kallo*	1 Rice Cake/2g	8	372	8.0	78.7	2.8	5.1
Tesco*	1 Serving/35g	116	332	7.5	71.5	1.8	1.1
Thin Slice, Organic, Kallo*	1 Cake/5g	19	372	8.0	78.7	2.8	5.1
Thin Slice, Organic, Waitrose*	1 Cake/6g	23	391	9.0	81.3	3.3	3.8
White Cheddar, Quaker*	1 Cake/11g	45	409	9.1	72.7	4.6	0.0
Whole Grain, No Added Salt, Thick Slice, Organic, Kallo*	1 Cake/9g	33	365	7.6	80.0	3.1	3.4
With Sesame, Organic, Evernat*	1 Cake/4g	15	368	8.5	74.5	4.0	0.0
With Sesame, Organic, Kallo*	1 Cake/7.5g	30	373	8.0	78.0	3.2	5.4
With Sesame, Thick Sliced, No Added Salt, Kallo*	1 Cake/10g	37	373	8.0	78.0	3.2	5.4
With Yeast Extract, Snack Size, Kallo*	1 Cake/2g	7	364	12.6	71.1	2.8	4.7
RICE CRACKERS,							
Barbecue, Sakata*	½ Pack/50g	204	407	7.3	85.2	2.6	1.6
Brown, Wakama*	1 Cracker/5g	19	375	8.0	84.8	0.4	0.0

R

RICE CRACKERS,	Measure INFO/WEIGHT	per Measure KCAL	KCAL	PROT	CARB	FAT	FIBRE
Choco Noir, Bonvita*	1 Cracker/18g	79	440	6.8	64.0	18.5	0.0
Cracked Pepper, Sakata*	½ Pack/50g	200	400	7.3	84.4	3.0	2.0
Crispy, Chilli & Lime, Go Ahead, McVities*	1 Serving/25g	101	405	7.1	83.6	3.6	2.1
Crispy, Sea Salt & Vinegar, Go Ahead, McVitie's*	1 Serving/25g	102	408	6.6	80.6	5.4	1.8
Crispy, Sour Cream & Herbs, Go Ahead, McVitie's*	1 Serving/25g	106	422	7.1	78.2	8.0	1.8
Japanese, Holland & Barrett*	1oz/28g	111	397	9.0	79.7	4.7	0.3
Japanese, Mini, Sunrise*	1 Serving/50g	180	360	7.0	83.0	0.0	7.0
Mix, Marks & Spencer*	½ Pack/62.5g	227	360	6.5	82.9	0.1	1.6
Paprika Flavour, Namchow*	1 Serving/38g	141	375	7.5	78.9	3.3	0.0
Salt & Vinegar, Namchow*	1 Serving/38g	139	370	6.7	77.5	3.7	0.0
Thai Chilli, Nature's Harvest*	1 Pack/75g	401	535	4.6	61.5	29.7	4.2
Thai, Sesame & Soy Sauce, Marks & Spencer*	1 Pack/54.5g	212	385	7.6	77.8	4.8	1.4
Thai, Wakama*	1 Cracker/2g	8	400	6.9	86.9	2.7	0.5
Thin, Blue Dragon*	3 Crackers/5g	20	395	6.1	84.4	3.7	0.0
With Tamari, Clearspring*	1 Bag/50g	190	380	8.2	83.4	1.5	0.3
RICE PUDDING,							
& Conserve, Marks & Spencer*	1oz/28g	53	190	2.3	17.4	12.5	0.3
50% Less Fat, Asda*	½ Can/212g	170	85	3.3	16.2	0.8	0.2
Apple, 99% Fat Free, Mullerice, Muller*	1 Pot/150g	125	83	3.5	15.3	0.9	0.0
Apple, Mullerice, Muller*	1 Pot/200g	244	122	3.3	21.7	2.4	0.0
BGTY, Sainsbury's*	½ Can/212g	180	85	3.3	16.2	0.8	0.2
Canned	1oz/28g	25	89	3.4	14.0	2.5	0.2
Caramel, Mullerice, Muller*	1 Pot/200g	210	105	3.5	17.4	2.4	0.0
Chocolate, Mullerice, Muller*	1 Pot/200g	246	123	3.4	21.5	2.6	0.0
Clotted Cream, Marks & Spencer*	1 Pudding/185g	431	233	3.0	19.2	16.6	0.2
Co-Op*	1oz/28g	49	175	5.0	20.0	9.0	2.0
Creamed With Sultanas & Nutmeg, Ambrosia*	½ Can/200g	210	105	3.2	16.6	2.9	0.1
Creamed, Asda*	1 Serving/215.4g	196	91	3.2	16.0	1.6	0.0
Creamed, Canned, Ambrosia*	1 Can/425g	383	90	3.1	15.2	1.9	0.0
Creamed, Co-Op*	1 Can/170g	153	90	3.0	16.0	1.5	0.0
Creamed, Healthy Eating, New, Tesco*	1 Can/215g	146	68	3.6	11.4	0.9	0.0
Creamed, Low Fat, Ambrosia*	1 Serving/150g	129	86	3.3	16.1	0.9	0.0
Creamed, Morrisons*	1 Can/212g	189	89	3.1	15.7	1.6	0.0
Creamed, Pot, Ambrosia*	1 Pot/150g	152	101	3.2	16.5	2.5	0.0
Creamed, Sainsbury's*	1 Serving/213g	202	95	3.2	16.2	1.5	0.1
Creamed, Weight Watchers*	1 Pot/130.1g	108	83	3.2	16.0	0.7	0.3
Creamy Rice With Tropical Crunch, Ambrosia*	1 Pack/210g	307	146	3.6	23.4	4.2	0.6
Creamy Rice, Shape*	1 Serving/175g	149	85	3.5	15.4	1.0	0.4
Creamy With Strawberry Crunch, Ambrosia*	1 Pack/205g	297	145	3.9	23.0	4.2	0.7
Eat Smart, Safeway*	1 Serving/212g	138	65	3.4	10.3	0.8	0.0
Everyday, Co-Op*	1 Can/396	333	84	3.4	15.5	0.9	0.1
GFY, Asda*	1 Pudding/119g	115	97	4.2	17.0	1.4	0.5
Libby's*	1 Serving/200g	180	90	3.3	16.2	1.6	0.2
Light, Mullerice, Muller*	1 Pot/100g	72	72	3.5	12.2	0.9	0.0
Low Fat, Canned, Ambrosia*	½ Can/200g	162	81	3.2	15.2	0.8	0.0
Low Fat, Good Intentions, Somerfield*	½ Can/212g	164	77	3.0	15.1	0.6	0.2
Low Fat, Healthy Selection, Somerfield*	1 Pot/213g	173	81	4.0	15.0	1.0	0.0
Low Fat, No Added Sugar, Weight Watchers*	½ Can/212g	155	73	3.7	11.4	1.5	0.0
Low Fat, Pot, Ambrosia*	1 Pot/150g	129	86	3.3	16.1	0.9	0.0
Milk, Economy, Sainsbury's*	½ Can/198g	139	70	3.2	12.6	0.8	0.2
Organic, Ambrosia*	1 Can/425g	455	107	3.4	15.1	3.7	0.0
Organic, Co-Op*	1 Can/425g	446	105	3.0	16.0	3.0	0.2
Organic, Evernat*	1oz/28g	39	141	5.5	22.9	3.0	0.0

R

	Measure INFO/WEIGHT	per Measure KCAL	Nutrition Values per 100g / 100ml				
			KCAL	PROT	CARB	FAT	FIBRE
RICE PUDDING,							
Original, 99% Fat Free, Mullerice, Muller*	1 Pot/150g	108	72	3.9	11.8	1.0	0.0
Original, Mullerice, Muller*	1 Pot/200g	232	116	3.7	19.1	2.7	0.0
Raisin & Nutmeg, Muller*	1 Pot/200g	244	122	3.3	22.0	2.3	0.0
Raspberry, Mullerice, Muller*	1 Pot/200g	228	114	3.4	20.0	2.3	0.0
Strawberry, 99% Fat Free, Mullerice, Muller*	1 Pot/150g	107	71	3.5	12.2	0.9	0.0
Strawberry, Mullerice, Muller*	1 Pot/200g	230	115	3.4	20.0	2.4	0.0
Thick & Creamy, Co-Op*	1 Can/425g	531	125	3.0	16.0	6.0	0.0
Thick & Creamy, Nestle*	1 Can/425g	527	124	3.1	15.4	5.6	0.2
Toffee, 99% Fat Free, Mullerice, Muller*	1 Pot/150g	119	79	3.3	14.3	1.0	0.0
Value, Tesco*	½ Can/212g	178	84	3.3	15.5	0.9	0.2
Vanilla Custard, Mullerice, Muller*	1 Pot/200g	250	125	3.3	22.1	2.6	0.0
Venetian, Cafe Culture, Marks & Spencer*	1 Serving/120g	300	250	3.4	21.8	16.4	0.2
With Cream, Sainsbury's*	1 Can/229.5g	242	105	3.1	9.8	5.9	0.0
With Jam, Kosy Shack, Costcutters*	1 Serving/150g	173	115	3.5	19.8	2.5	0.9
With Sultanas & Nutmeg, Ambrosia*	1 Pack/425g	446	105	3.2	16.6	2.9	0.1
With Sultanas & Nutmeg, Co-Op*	1 Can/425g	446	105	3.0	18.0	3.0	0.1
RICE STICKS,							
Mediterranean Tomato, Weight Watchers*	1 Bag/20g	72	360	7.3	77.7	2.2	2.8
Salt & Vinegar, Weight Watchers*	1 Serving/20g	73	365	7.7	79.7	1.7	2.4
Thai Sweet Chilli Flavour, Weight Watchers*	1 Serving/20g	73	363	7.6	79.5	1.6	2.2
RIGATONI,							
Carbonara, Tesco*	1 Serving/205g	236	115	5.2	10.6	5.8	1.2
Dry, Average	1 Serving/80g	272	340	11.4	68.5	1.5	2.7
Tomato & Cheese, Perfectly Balanced, Waitrose*	1 Pack/400g	664	166	7.6	28.6	2.3	2.3
RISOTTO,							
Balls, Mushroom, Occasions, Sainsbury's*	1 Ball/25g	76	304	3.8	41.2	13.8	1.7
Balls, Sun Dried Tomato, Occasions, Sainsbury's*	1 Ball/25g	71	285	6.8	30.8	15.0	2.9
Caramelised Onion & Gruyere Cheese, Marks & Spencer*	1 Pack/200g	350	175	3.0	17.8	10.3	1.7
Chargrilled Chicken, Ready Meal, Marks & Spencer*	1 Pack/365g	493	135	6.4	11.6	6.9	0.7
Cherry Tomato, COU, Marks & Spencer*	1 Pack/400g	320	80	1.9	16.6	0.9	1.8
Chicken & Asparagus, Eat Smart, Safeway*	1 Pack/380g	418	110	6.2	16.8	1.5	0.6
Chicken & Bacon, Italiano, Tesco*	1 Pack/450g	653	145	5.9	20.2	4.5	1.5
Chicken & Lemon, Weight Watchers*	1 Pack/330g	317	96	5.9	12.3	2.6	0.5
Chicken & Mushroom, Finest, Tesco*	1 Pack/400g	496	124	7.4	17.2	2.8	0.5
Chicken & Mushroom, Good Intentions, Somerfield*	1 Pack/300g	345	115	5.7	19.0	1.8	0.3
Chicken & Sun Dried Tomato, Waitrose*	1 Pack/350g	385	110	6.0	7.2	6.3	0.3
Chicken, BGTY, Sainsbury's*	1 Pack/327g	356	109	7.5	15.5	1.9	1.0
Chicken, Co-Op*	1 Pack/340g	442	130	6.0	16.0	5.0	2.0
Chicken, Enjoy, Bird's Eye*	1 Pack/500g	735	147	8.5	14.0	6.3	0.5
Chicken, Lemon & Wild Rocket, Sainsbury's*	1 Pack/360g	683	190	16.2	5.6	11.4	0.1
Chicken, Ready Meal, Marks & Spencer*	1 Pack/360g	450	125	6.7	14.4	4.4	0.9
Haddock & Mushroom, COU, Marks & Spencer*	1 Pack/400g	320	80	6.4	12.1	0.8	2.0
Hot Smoked Salmon & Spinach, Marks & Spencer*	½ Pack/300g	420	140	6.4	11.0	8.0	0.6
Italian Red Wine With Creamed Spinach, Sainsbury's*	1 Pack/400g	596	149	2.4	19.3	6.9	0.4
King Prawn & Snow Crab, Marks & Spencer*	1 Pack/365g	402	110	4.1	12.7	4.5	0.5
King Prawn, Pea & Mint, Marks & Spencer*	½ Pack/300g	405	135	3.8	15.9	6.2	0.9
Lemon & Mint, Perfectly Balanced, Waitrose*	1 Pack/350g	462	132	3.9	20.7	3.7	1.0
Mushroom, Asda*	1 Pack/340g	340	100	2.3	15.0	3.4	0.6
Mushroom, BGTY, Sainsbury's*	1 Pack/400g	320	80	2.6	15.6	0.8	0.6
Mushroom, COU, Marks & Spencer*	1 Pack/330g	314	95	2.9	15.3	2.3	1.0
Mushroom, Finest, Tesco*	1 Pack/350g	550	157	3.1	16.4	8.8	1.2
Mushroom, Healthy Living, Tesco*	1 Pack/400g	320	80	2.6	15.6	0.8	0.6
Mushroom, Italiano, Tesco*	1 Pack/340g	367	108	2.4	20.0	2.0	4.6

R

	Measure INFO/WEIGHT	per Measure KCAL	Nutrition Values per 100g / 100ml				
			KCAL	PROT	CARB	FAT	FIBRE
RISOTTO,							
Mushroom, Ready Meals, Marks & Spencer*	1 Pack/360g	450	125	2.8	16.9	4.9	1.0
Mushroom, Waitrose*	1 Pack/350g	277	79	1.9	6.9	4.9	0.5
Roasted Vegetable & Sunblush Tomato, Finest, Tesco*	½ Pack/200g	306	153	3.7	14.5	9.0	1.4
Roasted Vegetables, Stir-in, Uncle Ben's*	½ Pack/75g	86	115	1.7	5.0	9.7	0.0
Seafood, Youngs*	1 Pack/350g	424	121	4.5	17.4	3.7	0.1
Spring Vegetable, Marks & Spencer*	1 Serving/330g	330	100	2.0	14.2	4.0	0.9
Tomato & Cheese, GFY, Asda*	1 Pack/400g	428	107	3.1	17.0	3.0	0.7
Tomato & Mascarpone, Marks & Spencer*	1 Pack/360g	468	130	2.7	17.5	5.3	0.9
Vegetable	1oz/28g	41	147	4.2	19.2	6.5	2.2
Vegetable, Brown Rice	1oz/28g	40	143	4.1	18.6	6.4	2.4
Wild Mushroom & Garlic, Tesco*	1 Pack/320g	522	163	3.6	27.2	4.4	1.6
RISPINOS,							
Apple & Cinnamon, Uncle Ben's*	1 Bag/60g	230	383	4.7	90.0	0.5	0.0
Barbecue, Uncle Ben's*	1 Pack/50g	182	363	8.4	82.0	0.2	0.0
Caramel, Uncle Ben's*	1 Pack/60g	229	382	5.1	89.0	0.7	0.0
Cheese & Onion, Uncle Ben's*	1 Pack/50g	181	361	8.4	81.0	0.4	0.0
Chocolate, Uncle Ben's*	1oz/28g	108	385	5.3	89.0	1.1	0.0
Coconut, Uncle Ben's*	1oz/28g	111	396	6.7	86.0	2.8	0.0
Hot & Spicy, Uncle Ben's*	1 Bag/50g	183	366	7.5	83.0	0.6	0.0
Pizza, Uncle Ben's*	1 Pack/50g	182	363	8.4	82.0	0.2	0.0
Vanilla, Uncle Ben's	1oz/28g	107	383	7.7	87.0	0.5	0.0
ROAST,							
Vegetarian, Chicken Style, Tesco*	1 Serving/113g	214	189	22.1	4.8	9.0	1.7
Veggie, Chicken Style, Realeat*	1 Pack/454g	844	186	23.0	3.2	9.0	0.0
ROCKET,							
Fresh, Average	1 Serving/50g	10	21	2.6	1.7	0.4	0.8
ROE,							
Cod, Average	1 Can/100g	96	96	17.1	0.5	2.8	0.0
Cod, Hard, Coated in Batter, Fried	1oz/28g	53	189	12.4	8.9	11.8	0.2
Herring, Soft, Fried in Blended Oil	1oz/28g	74	265	26.3	4.7	15.8	0.2
Herring, Soft, Raw	1oz/28g	25	91	16.8	0.0	2.6	0.0
ROGAN JOSH,							
Chicken & Rice, Sainsbury's*	1 Pack/500g	730	146	7.9	16.6	5.3	1.3
Chicken, Patak's*	1oz/28g	34	123	8.1	17.2	2.4	0.7
Chicken, With Pilau Rice, Farmfoods*	1 Pack/325g	354	109	5.3	17.1	2.1	0.4
Lamb With Basmati Rice, Eat Smart, Safeway*	1 Pack/380g	380	100	6.9	14.0	1.5	1.9
Lamb, Marks & Spencer*	1 Pack/300g	360	120	14.4	3.9	5.1	1.2
Lamb, Safeway*	1 Pack/350g	515	147	13.0	2.5	9.3	3.0
Lamb, Sainsbury's*	1 Pack/400g	660	165	11.3	4.9	11.1	1.9
Lamb, Tesco*	1 Pack/350g	504	144	12.2	6.7	7.6	2.4
Lamb, Waitrose*	1 Serving/60g	79	131	12.3	3.0	7.8	1.3
Lamb, With Pilau Rice, Eastern Classics, Aldi*	1 Pack/400g	604	151	5.6	19.9	5.4	1.0
Prawn & Pilau Rice, BGTY, Sainsbury's*	1 Pack/401g	353	88	4.8	15.3	0.8	1.9
Prawn, COU, Marks & Spencer*	1 Pack/400g	360	90	4.9	16.2	0.6	0.8
ROLL,							
All Day Breakfast, Asda*	1 Roll/220g	581	264	10.0	29.0	12.0	0.0
Bacon & Sausage, Marks & Spencer*	1oz/28g	88	315	13.3	3.4	27.7	0.7
Bacon With Brown Sauce, McDonald's*	1 Roll/118g	289	245	12.8	31.2	8.4	1.4
Bacon, Marks & Spencer*	2 Rolls/18g	40	220	14.2	0.4	18.3	0.0
Bacon, McBacon, McDonald's*	1 Roll/122g	349	286	13.5	30.5	11.5	1.7
Beef, Weight Watchers*	1 Roll/174g	276	159	10.8	23.1	2.5	1.0
Brie & Grapes, Marks & Spencer*	1 Roll/57g	174	306	11.1	24.5	18.2	1.4
Cheese & Chutney, Marks & Spencer*	1 Roll/165g	256	155	13.9	23.1	0.7	1.2

R

ROLL,	Measure INFO/WEIGHT	per Measure KCAL	Nutrition Values per 100g / 100ml KCAL	PROT	CARB	FAT	FIBRE
Cheese & Onion, Asda*	1 Serving/66.8g	224	334	8.0	26.0	22.0	3.9
Cheese & Onion, Co-Op*	1 Roll/66g	195	295	7.0	26.0	18.0	2.0
Cheese & Onion, Iceland*	1 Roll/66.9g	222	332	7.5	29.6	20.4	1.5
Cheese & Onion, Marks & Spencer*	1 Roll/25g	80	320	9.6	24.7	20.5	1.3
Cheese & Onion, Sainsbury's*	1 Roll/67g	205	306	8.0	22.9	20.3	1.9
Cheese & Onion, Somerfield*	1 Roll/70g	242	345	8.0	28.0	22.0	0.0
Cheese & Onion, Tesco*	1 Roll/66.6g	212	317	7.5	27.9	19.4	2.3
Cheese & Pickle, Sainsbury's*	1 Roll/136g	359	264	10.6	35.1	10.0	0.0
Cheese & Tomato, Benjys*	1 Pack/263g	742	282	12.2	29.8	12.7	0.0
Cheese Ploughman's, Malted Wheat, BGTY, Sainsbury's*	1 Roll/171.7g	310	180	10.9	29.3	2.1	3.8
Cheese, Tomato & Onion, Sainsbury's*	1 Pack/100g	518	518	18.4	47.9	28.1	0.0
Chicken & Beef Duo, Marks & Spencer*	1 Serving/146.9g	235	160	12.0	22.1	2.6	2.7
Chicken & Herb, Shapers, Boots*	1 Roll/167.6g	291	173	12.0	25.0	2.8	1.7
Chicken & Sun Dried Tomato, Weight Watchers*	1 Pack/170g	272	160	12.9	22.7	1.9	1.2
Chicken Salad, Healthy Eating, Tesco*	1 Serving/224g	289	129	10.3	16.0	2.6	1.1
Chicken Salsa, BGTY, Sainsbury's*	1 Pack/197g	323	164	11.1	24.8	2.3	0.0
Chunky Cheese & Mustard, Finest, Tesco*	1 Roll/88g	260	295	10.9	40.0	10.2	2.4
Chunky Herbes de Provence, Finest, Tesco*	1 Roll/82g	196	239	7.4	45.2	3.2	2.6
Cornish, In Pastry, Pork Farms*	1 Roll/75.1g	226	301	6.6	24.5	20.1	0.0
Egg & Bacon, Sub, Shapers, Boots*	1 Serving/169.3g	319	189	11.0	27.0	4.3	1.3
Egg & Cress, Healthy Living, Tesco*	1 Pack/175g	322	184	9.6	27.7	3.9	1.2
Egg & Tomato, Shapers, Boots*	1 Roll/166.3g	300	181	8.0	30.0	3.2	2.6
Egg Mayo & Cress, Fullfillers*	1 Roll/125g	266	213	10.0	25.7	9.4	0.0
Egg Mayonnaise & Cress, Sub, Shapers, Boots*	1 Pack/156.9g	306	195	9.5	30.0	4.0	1.7
Ham & Cheese, In Pastry, Pork Farms*	1 Roll/70.1g	216	308	8.0	28.8	17.9	0.0
Ham & Pineapple, Eat Smart, Safeway*	1 Serving/180g	225	125	11.2	17.2	1.1	2.6
Ham & Tomato, Taste!*	1 Serving/112.2g	211	188	10.4	27.0	4.3	0.0
Ham Salad, BGTY, Sainsbury's*	1 Roll/178g	292	164	10.0	23.3	3.4	0.0
Ham Salad, Good Intentions, Somerfield*	1 Pack/213.8g	325	152	8.7	24.3	2.2	1.6
Leicester Ham & Cheese, Sub, Waitrose*	1 Pack/206.4ml	581	282	12.6	24.0	15.1	13.0
Mushroom & Bacon, Crusty, Marks & Spencer*	1 Roll/160g	424	265	8.7	29.0	12.6	2.3
Oak Smoked Salmon, Marks & Spencer*	1 Roll/55g	139	252	14.6	23.1	11.3	1.2
Roast Chicken & Mayonnaise, Big, Sainsbury's*	1 Pack/185g	479	259	9.6	21.8	14.8	0.0
Roast Chicken & Sweetcure Bacon, Boots*	1 Pack/244.7g	691	282	13.0	26.0	14.0	1.6
Roast Chicken Salad, Improved, Shapers, Boots*	1 Pack/187.6g	303	161	11.0	25.0	1.9	1.6
Roast Pork, Stuffing & Apple Sauce, Boots*	1 Roll/218.1g	602	276	10.0	32.0	12.0	1.8
Smoked Ham & Free Range Egg, Marks & Spencer*	1 Serving/208.3g	499	240	11.1	20.5	12.4	1.0
Spicy Chicken, Crusty, Marks & Spencer*	1 Roll/150g	383	255	12.8	25.8	11.1	2.0
Steak & Onion, Marks & Spencer*	1 Serving/150g	308	205	11.0	24.5	7.0	3.8
Taiko California, Waitrose*	4 Pieces/120g	196	163	4.4	26.8	4.1	1.5
Tomato & Basil, Sub, COU, Marks & Spencer*	1 Roll/35g	93	265	11.0	48.7	2.7	2.4
Tuna & Sweetcorn With Mayonnaise, Shell*	1 Pack/180g	536	298	13.1	28.6	14.6	0.0
Tuna Cheese Melt, Boots*	1 Roll/198.7g	613	308	13.0	23.0	18.0	1.2
Tuna Mayo & Cucumber, Taste!*	1 Serving/110.9g	274	247	9.0	27.3	11.3	0.0
Turkey Salad, Northern Bites*	1 Roll/230.7g	323	140	8.6	19.6	3.6	3.0
Turkey, Stuffed, GFY, Asda*	1 Pack/197g	280	142	14.0	12.0	4.2	0.8
White, Cheese & Onion, Shell*	1 Roll/178g	554	311	14.5	30.2	14.8	0.0
ROLO,							
Giant, Nestle*	1 Rolo/9g	42	471	3.2	68.5	20.5	0.3
Minis, Nestle*	1 Pack/26g	123	471	3.2	68.5	20.5	0.3
Nestle*	1 Rolo/5g	24	471	3.2	68.5	20.5	0.3
ROLY POLY,							
Jam & Custard, Sainsbury's*	1 Pack/205g	521	254	3.3	34.1	11.6	0.5

	Measure INFO/WEIGHT	per Measure KCAL	Nutrition Values per 100g / 100ml				
			KCAL	PROT	CARB	FAT	FIBRE
ROLY POLY,							
Jam, & Custard, Co-Op*	¼ Pack/100g	235	235	4.0	36.0	8.0	0.7
Jam, Marks & Spencer*	¼ Pudding/107g	326	305	3.1	47.1	11.5	5.5
Jam, Tesco*	1 Serving/82g	308	375	4.7	51.5	16.7	1.2
Strawberry Jam, Tryton Foods*	1oz/28g	108	384	5.4	53.9	16.3	1.7
Syrup, With Fresh Custard, Sainsbury's*	1 Pack/225g	524	233	3.4	29.9	11.1	0.4
ROOT BEER,							
Average	1 Can/330ml	135	41	0.0	10.6	0.0	0.0
ROSEMARY,							
Dried	1 Tsp/1g	3	331	4.9	46.4	15.2	0.0
Fresh	1oz/28g	28	99	1.4	13.5	4.4	0.0
ROSTI,							
Garlic & Mushroom, Finest, Tesco*	1 Serving/200g	346	173	5.7	15.4	9.8	1.7
Oven Baked, McCain*	1 Rosti/95g	234	246	3.7	29.7	12.8	0.0
Peppered Steak, British Classics, Tesco*	1 Pack/450g	599	133	9.0	10.7	6.2	1.7
Potato & Leek, Sainsbury's*	½ Pack/190g	296	156	4.5	9.8	11.0	0.3
Potato & Root Vegetable, COU, Marks & Spencer*	1 Cake/100g	85	85	1.6	13.3	2.7	1.5
Potato Cakes, Baby, Marks & Spencer*	1 Rosti/22.9g	40	175	3.5	25.1	6.7	1.6
Potato, Chicken & Sweetcorn Bake, Asda*	1 Serving/400g	440	110	7.0	10.0	4.7	0.6
Potato, Fresh, Safeway*	1 Rost/100g	138	138	2.8	19.2	5.5	2.8
Potato, McCain*	1 Rosti/95g	161	169	2.2	19.6	9.1	0.0
Potato, Mini, Party Range, Tesco*	1 Rosti/16.7g	33	193	2.1	20.6	11.4	3.3
Potato, Onion & Gruyere, Finest, Tesco*	1 Pack/350g	403	115	3.5	11.9	5.9	1.4
Vegetable, Waitrose*	1 Pack/400g	248	62	1.4	8.8	2.3	1.3
Waitrose*	½ Pack/200g	190	95	1.1	15.1	3.3	1.4
ROUGHY,							
Orange, Raw	1oz/28g	35	126	14.7	0.0	7.0	0.0
ROULADE,							
Chocolate, Finest, Tesco*	1 Serving/80g	222	277	3.4	53.2	5.6	2.3
Lemon Meringue, Marks & Spencer	1 Serving/74g	230	311	3.2	46.6	12.5	0.3
Mini, Marks & Spencer*	1 Serving/62.5g	202	321	8.5	3.0	30.5	0.0
Orange & Lemon Meringue, Co-Op*	1 Serving/82g	287	350	3.0	57.0	12.0	0.3
Passion Fruit, Marks & Spencer*	1oz/28g	83	295	2.8	50.0	9.2	0.2
Raspberry & Vanilla, Somerfield*	1oz/28g	118	420	3.0	56.0	20.0	0.0
Raspberry, Marks & Spencer*	1oz/28g	88	315	3.3	50.3	11.0	0.1
Toffee & Walnut, Somerfield*	1oz/28g	130	465	4.0	50.0	28.0	0.0
Toffee, Marks & Spencer*	1oz/28g	104	371	4.1	56.0	14.5	0.3
RUM,							
21% Volume, Malibu*	100ml	200	200	0.0	29.0	0.0	0.0
37.5% Volume	1 Shot/25ml	52	207	0.0	0.0	0.0	0.0
40% Volume	1 Shot/25ml	56	222	0.0	0.0	0.0	0.0
Southern Comfort, 37.5% Volume	1 Shot/25ml	52	207	0.0	0.0	0.0	0.0
White	1 Shot/25ml	52	207	0.0	0.0	0.0	0.0
RUSKS,							
Banana, Farleys*	1 Serving/17.1g	70	409	7.3	75.1	8.8	2.9
Mini, Farleys*	1 Serving/30g	122	405	7.0	77.7	7.3	2.1

R

	Measure INFO/WEIGHT	per Measure KCAL	Nutrition Values per 100g / 100ml				
			KCAL	PROT	CARB	FAT	FIBRE
SAAG,							
Aloo, Canned, Tesco*	½ Can/200g	124	62	1.8	9.3	1.9	2.0
Aloo, Fresh, Sainsbury's*	1 Pack/400g	388	97	2.0	14.7	3.3	4.8
Aloo, North Indian, Sainsbury's*	1 Pack/300g	354	118	2.4	9.0	8.0	1.6
Aloo, Sainsbury's*	½ Pack/150g	177	118	2.4	9.0	8.0	1.6
Aloo, Tesco*	1 Serving/200g	144	72	2.1	8.0	3.5	2.0
Chicken, Marks & Spencer*	½ Pack/175g	192	110	11.3	4.1	5.2	1.2
Chicken, Masala, Sainsbury's*	1oz/28g	80	284	30.2	10.8	13.3	1.0
Chicken, Safeway*	1 Pack/350g	504	144	11.6	5.4	8.4	1.4
Gobi Aloo, Indian Takeaway, Sainsbury's*	1 Pack/334g	164	49	1.7	8.0	1.1	1.5
Gobi Aloo, Marks & Spencer*	1 Pack/225g	270	120	1.9	9.3	8.5	2.4
Gobi Aloo, Tesco*	1 Serving/175g	182	104	2.3	7.3	7.3	1.4
Paneer, Sainsbury's*	½ Pack/200g	380	190	8.5	4.5	15.3	1.2
SAFFRON,							
Average	1 Tsp/0.7g	3	310	11.4	61.5	5.9	0.0
SAGE,							
Dried, Ground	1 Tsp/1g	3	315	10.6	42.7	12.7	0.0
Fresh	1oz/28g	33	119	3.9	15.6	4.6	0.0
SAGO,							
Raw	1oz/28g	99	355	0.2	94.0	0.2	0.5
SALAD,							
Alfresco Style, Tesco*	1 Serving/200g	40	20	0.9	3.3	0.3	1.4
All Seasons, Sainsbury's*	1oz/28g	3	12	1.0	1.5	0.2	1.2
American Ranch, Asda*	1 Serving/220g	253	115	2.5	6.0	9.0	2.0
American Style, Morrisons*	1 Serving/25g	5	22	1.1	3.9	0.3	2.3
Aromatic Herb, Waitrose*	¼ Pack/27g	4	15	0.9	1.7	0.5	1.0
Baby Leaf With Watercress, Tesco*	¼ Bag/25g	5	19	2.0	1.3	0.7	1.4
Baby Leaf & Herb, Asda*	1 Serving/50g	7	14	2.3	0.7	0.2	2.4
Baby Leaf, Fully Prepared, Sainsbury's*	½ Bag/63g	10	16	1.3	1.9	0.4	1.5
Baby Leaf, Italian Style, Marks & Spencer*	1 Serving/55g	74	135	1.6	2.7	13.1	1.4
Baby Leaf, Marks & Spencer*	1 Pack/100g	15	15	2.1	1.4	0.3	1.4
Baby Leaf, Organic, Sainsbury's*	1 Serving/20g	3	14	1.5	1.4	0.3	1.1
Baby Leaf, Sainsbury's*	1 Serving/60g	13	21	1.3	1.7	1.0	3.3
Baby Spinach & Red Mustard, Marks & Spencer*	1 Pack/170g	264	155	1.7	1.1	15.7	0.1
Baby Tomato, Tesco*	1 Pack/205g	35	17	0.8	2.8	0.3	0.9
Bacon Caesar, Marks & Spencer*	1oz/28g	48	170	5.5	5.7	14.0	1.2
Bacon Caesar, Sainsbury's*	1 Pack/256g	415	162	4.7	7.3	12.7	1.4
Bacon Ranch, With Chicken Premiere, McDonald's*	1 Salad/329g	447	136	10.1	5.0	8.5	0.9
Bacon Ranch, With Classic Chicken, McDonald's*	1 Salad/342.9g	360	105	10.4	2.1	6.1	1.1
Bagel Egg, Tesco*	1 Pack/185g	474	256	10.2	29.5	10.8	1.7
Bean & Chorizo, Tapas Selection, Sainsbury's*	1 Serving/22g	29	132	8.1	10.7	6.3	1.9
Bean & Sweetcorn, Side, Marks & Spencer*	1 Serving/125g	131	105	2.5	7.0	7.2	1.3
Bean, & Mexican Rice, COU, Marks & Spencer*	1 Serving/250g	250	100	6.0	15.6	1.4	1.2
Bean, Marks & Spencer*	1 Serving/80g	72	90	6.4	14.3	0.9	3.9
Bean, Mint & Coriander, Somerfield*	1 Pack/250g	288	115	7.0	19.4	1.1	4.7
Bean, Retail	1oz/28g	41	147	4.2	12.8	9.3	3.0
Bean, Three, Marks & Spencer*	1 Pack/225g	225	100	5.8	16.7	1.3	3.9
Bean, Vinaigrette Mixed, Tesco*	1 Can/400g	280	70	3.2	13.1	0.5	1.9
Beetroot	1oz/28g	28	100	2.0	8.4	6.8	1.7
Beetroot & Lettuce, Asda*	1 Serving/30g	5	16	1.4	2.7	0.0	2.5
Beetroot, 1% Fat, Marks & Spencer*	1 Serving/225g	131	58	1.1	7.7	2.7	1.7
Beetroot, Co-Op*	1 Pack/250g	100	40	0.9	8.0	0.3	2.0
Beetroot, GFY, Asda*	1 Serving/84g	46	55	1.0	12.0	0.3	1.8
Beetroot, Healthy Eating, Tesco*	1 Tub/200g	204	102	1.4	22.6	0.6	1.4

S

SALAD,

	Measure INFO/WEIGHT	per Measure KCAL	Nutrition Values per 100g / 100ml				
			KCAL	PROT	CARB	FAT	FIBRE
Beetroot, Marks & Spencer*	1 Serving/225g	124	55	1.0	12.0	0.3	3.0
Beetroot, Organic, Marks & Spencer*	1oz/28g	20	73	1.5	9.1	3.4	1.9
Beetroot, Pots, Healthy Living, Tesco*	1 Serving/200g	110	55	1.7	11.5	0.2	1.3
Beetroot, Sainsbury's*	1 Tub/200g	160	80	0.9	11.7	3.3	2.1
Bistro, Asda*	1 Serving/180g	29	16	1.4	2.7	0.0	2.5
Bistro, Sainsbury's*	1 Pack/150g	33	22	1.1	3.6	0.4	1.3
Bistro, Somerfield*	1/2 pack/50g	7	14	0.8	1.6	0.5	1.4
Bistro, Washed Ready To Eat, Tesco*	1 Pack/140g	22	16	1.1	1.7	0.5	1.0
Bowl, French Style, Way to Five, Sainsbury's*	1 Pack/264g	103	39	0.7	4.2	2.2	2.2
Bowl, Large, Sainsbury's*	1 Pack/300g	51	17	1.1	2.9	0.2	2.3
Burger King*	1 Serving/165g	34	21	1.2	3.5	0.2	2.6
Cabbage & Leek, Crunchy Mix, Sainsbury's*	½ Pack/126.3g	24	19	1.2	2.1	0.6	1.9
Caesar Kit, New Improved, Tesco*	½ Pack/138g	279	202	4.7	4.5	18.3	1.3
Caesar Kit, Safeway*	2 Servings/295g	504	171	3.8	4.9	15.1	1.1
Caesar, BGTY, Sainsbury's*	1/3 Pack/75g	78	104	3.6	9.8	5.6	1.7
Caesar, Bistro, Waitrose*	½ Pack/112.5g	172	152	6.4	6.3	11.2	7.6
Caesar, Chicken, JD Wetherspoon*	1 Serving/150g	634	423	12.1	9.4	37.3	0.7
Caesar, Chicken, McDonald's*	1 Serving/150g	333	222	31.7	2.5	8.8	3.3
Caesar, Co-Op*	¼ Pack/50g	88	175	3.0	6.0	15.0	2.0
Caesar, Finest, Tesco*	1 Lge Bowl/220g	532	242	5.2	4.7	22.5	0.9
Caesar, GFY, Asda*	½ Pack/87.4g	76	87	8.0	7.0	3.0	1.5
Caesar, Improved Recipe, Marks & Spencer*	1 Pack/290g	551	190	5.0	1.3	18.1	1.3
Caesar, Kit, Asda*	½ Pack/113g	154	136	5.0	11.0	8.0	1.4
Caesar, Kit, Healthy Living, Tesco*	½ Pack/132.5g	149	112	3.3	5.9	8.3	1.4
Caesar, Marks & Spencer*	1 Serving/100g	151	151	2.6	8.0	12.1	0.7
Caesar, No Meat, McDonald's*	1 Salad/213g	149	70	4.6	5.1	3.4	1.0
Caesar, Sainsbury's*	½ Bag/128g	227	177	3.6	6.7	15.1	1.0
Caesar, Somerfield*	1 Pack/255g	339	133	4.6	5.1	10.5	1.3
Caesar, Waitrose*	1 Serving/115g	175	152	6.4	6.3	11.2	0.8
Caesar, Washed & Ready to Eat, Somerfield*	½ Bag/125g	155	124	5.0	6.5	8.7	0.8
Cajun Chicken, David lloyd leisure*	1 Pack/300g	429	143	11.7	17.7	3.3	1.0
Californian Crunch, GFY, Asda*	1 Pack/160g	75	47	0.9	8.0	1.3	1.8
Cannelini Bean & Chorizo, Sainsbury's*	1 Pack/250g	228	91	5.3	10.2	3.2	1.6
Cannellini Bean & Chicken, Marks & Spencer*	1 Serving/225g	250	111	5.9	7.4	6.5	3.1
Cannellini Bean & Tuna, Marks & Spencer*	1 Serving/255g	215	84	5.3	5.4	4.5	2.1
Caribbean Chicken, Shapers, Boots*	1 Pack/220g	222	101	5.8	14.0	2.3	1.2
Carrot & Nut With Dressing, Retail, French's*	1oz/28g	61	218	2.1	13.7	17.6	2.4
Carrot & Sultana, BGTY, Sainsbury's*	½ Pack/100g	55	55	0.6	12.4	0.3	0.0
Carrot & Sultana, Healthy Living, Tesco*	1 Tub/225g	142	63	1.2	13.2	0.6	2.5
Carrot, Marks & Spencer*	1 Pack/215.4g	280	130	3.1	22.4	3.4	2.7
Carrot, Orange & Ginger, Good Intentions, Somerfield*	1 Serving/250g	275	110	2.0	22.4	1.4	1.4
Carrot, Peanut & Sultana, Asda*	1 Serving/20g	54	272	8.0	15.0	20.0	4.5
Ceasar, Bacon, Marks & Spencer*	1 Serving/250g	400	160	7.1	4.1	12.5	1.3
Celery, Nut & Sultana, Asda*	1oz/28g	76	272	2.9	11.2	23.9	1.9
Celery, Nut & Sultana, Waitrose*	1oz/28g	54	192	2.8	8.4	16.4	1.0
Chargrilled Chicken & Bacon, Tesco*	1 Pack/300g	657	219	7.8	18.7	12.6	0.9
Chargrilled Chicken Wholefood, Marks & Spencer*	1 Pot/219g	230	105	10.1	11.6	1.9	4.8
Chargrilled Chicken, Safeway*	1 Serving/200g	280	140	8.9	17.9	3.6	1.4
Chargrilled Chicken, Tesco*	1 Serving/300g	384	128	6.1	15.0	4.8	2.4
Chargrilled Pepper With Cous Cous, Asda*	1 Pack/325.2g	426	131	4.3	21.0	3.3	0.0
Chargrilled Vegetable Tortellini, Snack, Tesco*	1 Serving/300g	492	164	5.1	18.7	7.7	1.7
Cheddar Cheese & Pasta, Tesco*	1 Pot/215g	546	254	5.7	12.0	20.4	0.8
Cheese Coleslaw, Sainsbury's*	1oz/28g	61	218	5.1	6.0	19.3	0.1

S

	Measure INFO/WEIGHT	per Measure KCAL	Nutrition Values per 100g / 100ml				
			KCAL	PROT	CARB	FAT	FIBRE
SALAD,							
Cheese Layered, Marks & Spencer*	1 Pack/450g	923	205	4.3	9.0	17.0	0.7
Cheese Layered, Tesco*	1 Serving/165g	264	160	4.4	9.9	11.4	1.0
Cheese Potato, Sainsbury's*	1 Serving/125g	200	160	2.7	7.9	13.1	3.4
Chef's, EAT*	1 Serving/200g	414	207	8.5	1.8	18.4	0.9
Cherry Tomato, All Good Things*	1 Pack/185g	31	17	0.8	2.8	0.3	1.4
Cherry Tomato, Fresh, Safeway*	1 Pack/170g	31	18	0.8	2.9	0.3	0.9
Cherry Tomato, Large, Fresh, Safeway*	1 Serving/245g	49	20	1.0	3.1	0.4	1.9
Chick Pea & Cous Cous, Tesco*	1 Serving/250g	245	98	3.2	15.5	2.6	0.0
Chick Pea & Spinach, Marks & Spencer*	1 Serving/260g	299	115	7.3	12.5	4.1	2.7
Chicken & Bacon, Asda*	1 Pack/381.0g	480	126	7.0	11.0	6.0	0.0
Chicken & Caesar, Boots*	1 Serving/200g	144	72	4.9	2.8	4.6	1.4
Chicken & Rice, Safeway*	1 Serving/200g	220	110	6.4	17.6	1.3	1.4
Chicken Caesar Bistro, Marks & Spencer*	½ Pack/135g	189	140	5.0	6.5	10.6	0.6
Chicken Caesar, Shapers, Boots*	1 Serving/200g	316	158	6.6	19.0	6.2	1.1
Chicken Caesar, Snack, Sainsbury's*	1 Pack/182.2g	164	90	5.9	5.3	5.0	1.0
Chicken Caesar, Starbucks*	1 Serving/233g	403	173	8.7	18.0	7.9	1.2
Chicken Caesar, TTD, Sainsbury's*	1 Serving/190g	308	162	11.1	1.6	12.3	1.5
Chicken Caesar, Tesco*	1 Pack/300g	330	110	6.8	10.6	4.5	0.8
Chicken Ceasar, Marks & Spencer*	½ Pack/140g	266	190	6.7	8.7	14.3	0.8
Chicken Noodle & Sweet Chilli, Shapers, Boots*	1 Pack/197g	266	135	12.0	16.0	2.6	0.9
Chicken Pesto Pasta, Royal London Hospital*	1oz/28g	37	132	10.4	15.3	3.5	0.0
Chicken Tikka & Rice, COU, Marks & Spencer*	1 Pack/390g	410	105	5.1	18.7	1.0	0.6
Chicken With Mayonnaise, Waitrose*	1 Pack/208g	406	195	10.3	17.1	9.5	2.5
Chicken, Avacado & Bacon, Marks & Spencer*	1 Serving/235g	235	100	8.5	2.8	5.8	2.8
Chicken, Burger King*	1 Salad/237g	135	57	9.3	2.6	1.1	1.8
Chicken, Healthy Eating, Tesco*	1 Salad/216g	296	137	8.4	22.6	1.4	1.2
Chicken, Healthy Option, Mattessons*	1 Pack/200g	344	172	11.1	20.0	5.3	2.9
Chicken, Safeway*	1 Serving/200g	279	140	8.9	17.9	3.6	1.4
Chicken, Sweetcorn & Pasta, Safeway*	1 Serving/200g	230	115	7.5	16.3	1.8	1.0
Chicken, Tesco*	1 Serving/300g	348	116	5.3	7.0	7.4	1.0
Chicken, Tomato, & Basil, Safeway*	1 Serving/200g	330	165	6.9	14.2	8.9	0.6
Chilli Chicken & Spicy Cous Cous, Healthy Eating, Tesco*	1 Serving/190g	251	132	6.5	21.1	2.4	1.5
Chilli, Tomato, Chick Pea & Butterbean, Tesco*	1 Pack/130g	146	112	3.4	14.3	4.6	0.5
Chunky, Somerfield*	1 Serving/250g	40	16	1.0	3.0	0.0	0.9
Classic Caesar, Marks & Spencer*	½ Pack/112g	174	155	2.9	6.8	12.7	0.5
Classic Caesar, Reduced Fat, Marks & Spencer*	1 Serving/115g	132	115	4.8	12.7	4.9	0.5
Club, Safeway*	1 Serving/215g	226	105	1.3	6.0	8.4	1.3
Coleslaw & Potato, 3% Fat, Marks & Spencer*	1oz/28g	20	72	2.7	7.7	3.4	1.5
Coleslaw Layered, Fresh, Asda*	1 Tub/197g	209	106	1.2	5.0	9.0	0.0
Coleslaw, Deli Style, Marks & Spencer*	1 Serving/320g	336	105	3.5	1.5	9.7	1.4
Coleslaw, Sainsbury's*	1 Serving/150g	191	127	0.9	6.8	10.7	1.9
Complete Hot Greek, Sainsbury's*	1 Pack/299g	287	96	4.3	2.9	7.5	1.7
Continental Four Leaf, Sainsbury's*	1oz/28g	5	18	1.6	2.1	0.3	0.8
Continental Leaf, Asda*	1oz/28g	4	16	1.4	1.4	0.5	1.4
Continental Style, Co-Op*	1 Bag/100g	15	15	1.0	2.0	0.3	0.5
Coronation Chicken & Rice, Asda*	1oz/28g	67	241	6.7	15.2	17.0	0.4
Coronation Chicken, Sainsbury's*	1 Serving/62.4g	180	290	6.3	14.4	23.0	1.4
Coronation Chicken, Salad Bar, Asda*	1oz/28g	82	293	5.7	16.4	22.7	0.7
Coronation Rice, Tesco*	1 Serving/50g	104	207	2.0	15.9	15.1	0.8
Country Style, Co-Op*	½ Pack/100g	20	20	1.0	3.0	0.4	2.0
Cous Cous With Chargrilled Chicken, Sainsbury's*	1 Pack/240g	446	186	7.4	19.6	8.7	0.0
Cous Cous, Better For You, Morrisons*	½ Pot/113g	164	145	4.6	23.8	3.5	0.5
Cous Cous, Tesco*	1 Serving/25g	35	141	4.8	26.9	1.6	0.6

SALAD,

	Measure INFO/WEIGHT	per Measure KCAL	KCAL	PROT	CARB	FAT	FIBRE
Cous Cous, With Mixed Peppers & Cucumber, GFY, Asda*	¼ Pot/56g	66	117	3.9	25.0	0.2	1.5
Couton & Mediterranean Herb, Rochelle*	1 Serving/15g	77	510	8.5	62.7	25.0	2.5
Crayfish & Avocado, EAT*	1 Pack/100g	387	387	12.1	2.7	36.7	2.8
Crayfish, Pret a Manger*	1 Av Pack/320g	200	63	3.0	0.8	5.2	0.3
Creamy Potato With Onion & Chives, Sainsbury's*	¼ Pot/62.5g	96	153	1.3	9.0	12.4	2.7
Crisp & Crunchy, Asda*	1 Pack/250g	55	22	0.8	3.3	0.6	1.4
Crisp & Crunchy, Marks & Spencer*	1oz/28g	6	20	1.4	2.9	0.1	1.3
Crisp & Cruncy With French Dressing, GFY, Asda*	1/3 Pack/116g	26	22	0.8	3.3	0.6	1.4
Crisp & Light, Marks & Spencer*	1 Serving/170g	51	30	0.5	5.4	0.8	1.0
Crisp Mixed, Safeway*	1 Serving/60g	12	20	1.2	3.0	0.3	2.0
Crisp Mixed, Tesco*	1 Pack/200g	38	19	1.1	2.8	0.3	1.5
Crispy Duck & Herb, Marks & Spencer*	½ Pack/140g	378	270	20.7	3.7	18.3	1.4
Crispy Green, Safeway*	1 Bag/165g	21	13	1.0	1.6	0.3	1.1
Crispy Green, Sainsbury's*	1 Serving/70g	8	12	0.9	1.6	0.2	0.8
Crispy Leaf, Asda*	1oz/28g	4	14	0.8	1.6	0.5	0.9
Crispy Leaf, Sainsbury's*	½ Pack/75g	9	12	1.0	1.2	0.4	1.5
Crispy Medley, Waitrose*	1 Serving/50g	8	15	0.8	1.7	0.5	0.9
Crispy, Somerfield*	1 Pack/140g	17	12	1.0	2.0	0.0	0.0
Crispy, Tesco*	1oz/28g	6	20	1.2	3.0	0.3	1.6
Croutons With Garlic & Basil, Safeway*	1 Bag/60g	284	473	12.7	50.8	24.3	3.3
Crunchy Coleslaw Bowl, Marks & Spencer*	1 Pack/325g	455	140	1.0	2.5	13.8	2.0
Crunchy Layered, Tesco*	1 Serving/54g	15	27	1.1	4.9	0.3	1.7
Crunchy Mix, Co-Op*	1oz/28g	7	25	1.0	4.0	0.3	2.0
Crunchy Shredded, Safeway*	1 Serving/50g	10	19	1.2	2.9	0.3	1.5
Crunchy Spring, Side, Marks & Spencer*	1 Serving/160g	32	20	0.9	4.1	0.2	1.3
Crunchy, Fully Prepared, Sainsbury's*	½ Pack/150g	24	16	1.1	3.0	0.1	1.7
Crunchy, Waitrose*	½ Pack100g	18	18	1.0	2.6	0.4	1.5
Eat Me Keep Me, Tesco*	1 Serving/80g	14	18	0.8	3.0	0.3	1.7
Egg & Baby Spinach, Waitrose*	1 Pack/215g	168	78	3.5	1.8	6.3	1.0
Egg & Coleslaw, Boots*	1 Pot/233g	405	174	3.0	4.6	16.0	1.0
Egg & Potato, Fresh, Marks & Spencer*	1 Serving/250g	150	60	3.0	4.6	2.9	0.9
Egg & Potato, GFY, Asda*	1 Serving/290g	206	71	2.6	5.0	4.5	0.0
Egg Layered Bowl, Tesco*	1 Pack/410g	726	177	4.2	8.4	14.1	1.3
Endive & Radicchio, Somerfield*	1 Pack/150g	20	13	2.0	1.0	0.0	0.0
English Garden, Tesco*	1 Serving/180g	22	12	0.7	1.8	0.2	0.7
Family, Somerfield*	1 Serving/67g	12	18	0.8	2.9	0.4	1.3
Feta Cheese & Pasta, McDonald's*	1 Pack/250g	240	96	3.8	11.2	3.9	0.9
Feta Cheese & Sunblushed Tomato, Marks & Spencer*	1 Serving/190g	361	190	5.5	17.2	11.1	2.1
Feta, Lentil & Rice, EAT*	1 Pack/120g	525	438	17.6	53.3	17.1	6.8
Fine Cut, Asda*	1oz/28g	7	24	1.2	4.1	0.3	2.1
Fine Noodle With Duck Breast, COU, Marks & Spencer*	1 Pack/280g	294	105	5.5	18.9	1.1	1.1
Florida, Retail	1oz/28g	63	224	0.9	9.7	20.5	1.0
Four Leaf, Marks & Spencer*	1 Serving/130g	26	20	1.9	3.2	0.2	3.7
Four Leaf, Tesco*	1oz/28g	4	15	0.8	1.8	0.5	0.9
French Goat's Cheese, Extra Fine, Asda*	1 Pack/185g	463	250	8.4	11.4	19.0	0.8
French Style, Marks & Spencer*	1 Pack/140g	140	100	1.0	2.5	9.7	0.9
French Style, Morrisons*	1 Pack/200g	28	14	0.8	1.7	0.5	0.0
French Style, Waitrose*	½ Pack/82g	149	182	5.1	7.2	14.8	1.8
Fusion, Fully Prepared, Sainsbury's*	½ Pack/62.5g	15	24	3.7	0.3	0.8	3.4
Garden With Watercress, Marks & Spencer*	1 Salad/80g	10	12	1.5	1.4	0.1	1.4
Garden With Yoghurt & Mint Dressing, GFY, Asda*	1 Serving/195g	51	26	1.1	3.2	1.0	0.0
Garden, Fresh, Safeway*	½ Pack/105g	27	26	1.1	4.8	0.3	1.1
Garden, Safeway*	1oz/28g	6	23	1.1	4.0	0.3	2.0

	Measure INFO/WEIGHT	per Measure KCAL	Nutrition Values per 100g / 100ml				
			KCAL	PROT	CARB	FAT	FIBRE
SALAD,							
Garden, Shapers, Boots*	1 Pack/237.3g	159	67	1.5	8.8	2.9	1.5
Garden, Side, McDonald's*	1 Salad/93g	13	14	0.8	2.2	0.3	1.4
Garden, Side, With Balsamic Dressing, McDonald's*	1 Salad/124g	86	69	0.6	4.6	2.2	1.0
Garden, Sweet And Crispy, Tesco*	1 Bag/225g	54	24	1.0	4.2	0.4	1.4
Garden, Tesco*	1 Serving/225g	34	15	1.0	2.0	0.3	0.9
Goats Cheese & Roasted Pepper, Gourmet, Benjys*	1 Pack/400g	412	103	3.4	12.4	3.8	0.0
Gourmet Nicoise, Marks & Spencer*	1 Serving/500g	575	115	4.8	3.9	8.9	0.0
Gourmet Chargrilled Chicken & Bacon, Atkins*	1 Pack/245g	311	127	12.0	2.5	8.2	1.0
Gourmet Continental, Waitrose*	1 Serving/150g	23	15	0.8	1.6	0.5	0.9
Gourmet Crayfish & Salsa, Atkins*	1 Pot/262.5g	126	48	5.9	2.4	1.4	0.6
Gourmet Goats Cheese & Roast Vegetable, Atkins*	1 Pot/243g	243	100	5.0	3.8	6.7	1.6
Greek	1oz/28g	36	130	2.7	1.9	12.5	0.8
Greek Style Collection, Marks & Spencer*	1 Pack/328.6g	461	140	4.4	8.8	9.9	1.2
Greek Style Feta, Marks & Spencer*	1 Serving/255g	268	105	3.5	1.5	9.7	1.4
Greek Style Feta, Tip & Mix, Marks & Spencer*	1 Pack/195g	215	110	4.0	2.5	9.4	1.6
Greek Style Layered, Perfectly Balanced, Waitrose*	1 Pack/280g	134	48	2.4	3.2	2.8	0.7
Greek Style, Marks & Spencer*	½ Pack/120.8g	145	120	3.7	3.7	11.3	0.7
Greek, BGTY, Sainsbury's*	1 Serving/198.5g	133	67	2.0	9.0	2.5	0.8
Greek, Marks & Spencer*	1 Serving/125g	119	95	2.5	2.4	8.2	0.7
Green	1oz/28g	3	12	0.7	1.8	0.3	1.0
Green Side, Marks & Spencer*	1 Serving/200g	30	15	0.9	2.5	0.2	0.0
Green Side, Sainsbury's*	1 Pack/200g	28	14	0.8	2.1	0.3	0.8
Green With Chives, Tesco*	½ Pack/90g	13	14	1.0	1.6	0.4	1.7
Green With Honey & Mustard Dressing, Marks & Spencer*	1 Pack/200g	120	60	0.9	2.7	4.8	0.8
Green With Sweetcorn & Radish, Fresh, Safeway*	1 Pack/210g	55	26	1.1	4.8	0.3	1.1
Green, Fresh, Safeway*	½ Pack/98g	14	14	0.9	1.9	0.3	0.8
Green, Marks & Spencer*	1oz/28g	4	13	0.8	1.7	0.3	0.9
Grilled Chicken, Nando's*	1oz/28g	17	60	9.1	2.5	1.5	0.0
Herb Garden, Morrisons*	1 Serving/28g	4	14	0.9	1.7	0.5	0.0
Herb, Marks & Spencer*	1 Pack/100g	20	20	2.9	1.4	0.4	1.9
Herb, Sainsbury's*	1 Serving/40g	10	26	1.9	2.0	1.1	1.7
Herb, Tesco*	1oz/28g	4	16	1.1	1.8	0.5	0.9
Honey Smoked Salmon & New Potato, Marks & Spencer*	1 Pack/270g	270	100	5.5	7.5	5.3	1.5
Hot Smoked Salmon & Rice, Deli Meal, Marks & Spencer*	1 Pack/380g	570	150	6.5	15.1	6.9	0.2
Houmous & Pitta Bread, Pot, Pret a Manger*	1 Pot/200g	393	197	4.8	12.0	14.4	3.4
Iceberg & Cabbage, Asda*	½ Pack/125g	24	19	1.0	3.1	0.3	1.5
Italian Style Pasta, Iceland*	1 Serving/75g	97	129	2.6	16.2	6.0	1.6
Italian Style Side, Waitrose*	1 Serving/160g	32	20	1.1	3.1	0.3	2.6
Italian Style, Asda*	1 Serving/20g	2	12	1.5	1.3	0.1	1.2
Italian Style, Marks & Spencer*	1 Bag/100g	18	18	1.3	1.8	0.5	1.4
Italian Style, Sainsbury's*	1/3 Pack/60g	80	134	2.1	8.0	10.9	1.1
Italian Style, Tesco*	1oz/28g	4	14	1.1	1.4	0.4	1.3
Italian Wild Rocket & Parmesan, Sainsbury's*	1 Serving/50g	89	177	7.5	3.4	14.8	0.5
Italian, Complete, Sainsbury's*	1 Pack/160g	203	127	3.6	9.0	8.5	1.5
Italian, Organic, Marks & Spencer*	1oz/28g	5	17	1.3	1.8	0.5	0.1
Jardin, Tesco*	1 Serving/25g	4	14	0.8	1.7	0.5	0.9
King Prawn & Pasta, COU, Marks & Spencer*	1 Pack/270g	284	105	5.9	15.1	2.4	2.7
King Prawn, Thai Style, Marks & Spencer*	1 Pack/295g	266	90	4.4	12.6	2.5	1.3
Layered Tuna, Tesco*	1 Serving/370g	466	126	4.4	9.4	7.9	1.0
Layered With Egg, Somerfield*	1 Pot/300g	543	181	3.0	3.0	18.0	0.0
Layered With Tuna, Somerfield*	1 Pot/255g	599	235	5.0	5.0	22.0	0.0
Leafy Mixed, Co-Op*	1 Bag/200g	40	20	1.0	4.0	0.3	1.0
Leafy, Tesco*	1oz/28g	4	14	1.2	1.5	0.4	1.9

SALAD,

INFO/WEIGHT	Measure	per Measure KCAL	KCAL	PROT	CARB	FAT	FIBRE
Lemon Chicken, Snack, Good Intentions, Somerfield*	1 Pot/200.8g	249	124	8.0	17.0	2.7	1.3
Lemonss & Roasted Pepper, COU, Marks & Spencer*	1 Pack/340g	306	90	3.2	14.6	2.3	1.8
Luxury Potato, Asda*	1 Serving/50g	119	237	1.0	11.0	21.0	0.0
Marinated Seafood, Waitrose*	1 Tub/160g	331	207	15.7	3.1	14.6	0.0
Mediterranean Style Side, Way to Five, Sainsbury's*	1 Serving/244g	61	25	0.9	3.0	1.0	0.0
Mediterranean Style, Asda*	½ Pack/135g	22	16	1.0	3.0	0.0	0.0
Mediterranean Style, Morrisons*	1 Serving/90g	13	14	1.5	1.9	0.2	0.0
Mediterranean Style, Safeway*	1 Serving/25g	5	20	1.7	1.9	0.6	2.0
Mediterranean Style, Tesco*	½ Pack/100g	141	141	2.7	9.4	10.3	1.7
Mediterranean Tuna, John West*	1oz/28g	30	106	8.0	5.0	6.0	2.0
Mexican Style Bean & Cheese, Marks & Spencer*	½ Pot/150g	150	100	6.1	11.2	3.5	4.8
Mixed Bean With Onions & Peppers, Safeway*	½ Can/210g	141	67	4.0	11.4	0.6	2.7
Mixed Bean, Asda*	½ Can/145g	129	89	5.8	13.7	1.2	6.3
Mixed Bean, Tesco*	1 Serving/70g	49	70	3.2	13.1	0.5	1.9
Mixed Bean, Waitrose*	1 Serving/210g	229	109	8.7	13.6	2.2	4.6
Mixed Bean, Way To Five, Sainsbury's*	1 Can/270g	227	84	5.4	13.5	0.9	3.8
Mixed Crunchy, Safeway*	1oz/28g	7	25	1.1	4.0	0.3	2.0
Mixed Leaf Medley, Waitrose*	1 Serving/25g	4	15	0.8	1.7	0.5	0.9
Mixed Leaf With Olive Oil Dressing, Pizza Express*	1 Pack/240g	326	136	0.9	2.1	14.1	0.7
Mixed Leaf, Tomato & Olive, Tesco*	1 Serving/170g	150	88	1.0	3.4	7.8	0.0
Mixed Leaf, Tomato, Feta, Boots*	1 Pack/179g	218	122	3.7	5.4	9.5	1.0
Mixed Leaves, Somerfield*	1 Pack/140g	17	12	1.0	2.0	0.0	0.0
Mixed Leaves, Tesco*	1 Serving/20g	3	14	0.9	1.6	0.4	0.9
Mixed Pepper, Asda*	½ Pack/100g	24	24	1.0	4.3	0.3	1.7
Mixed Vegetable, Aldi*	1 Serving/200g	120	60	0.6	10.0	2.0	0.0
Mixed With Peppers & Iceberg Lettuce, Somerfield*	1 Pack/200g	50	25	1.0	5.0	0.0	0.0
Mixed With Tatsoi, Safeway*	1 Serving/34g	5	15	1.1	1.5	0.4	1.2
Mixed, Including Dressing, Benjys*	1 Pack/315g	151	48	0.8	3.5	3.4	1.2
Mixed, Sweet & Crispy, Tesco*	1 Serving/200g	48	24	1.0	4.2	0.3	2.0
Moroccan Styless, COU, Marks & Spencer*	½ Pack/100g	160	160	5.0	32.8	1.2	4.8
Mozzarella & Cherry Tomato, Shapers, Boots*	1 Bowl/194g	184	95	4.1	3.3	7.3	0.9
Mozerella & Tomato, Marks & Spencer*	1 Serving/310g	400	129	5.5	15.5	4.8	0.9
Mozzarella & Sunkissed Tomato, Tesco*	1 Bag/160g	270	169	4.6	4.3	14.3	2.1
Nantaise, Waitrose*	1 Pack/160g	34	21	1.5	2.9	0.4	2.0
New Potato & Free Range Egg, Marks & Spencer*	1 Pack/305g	214	70	2.5	7.0	3.8	0.8
New Potato & Free Range Egg, Side, Sainsbury's*	1 Pack/315g	189	60	2.5	3.1	4.2	1.4
New Potato & King Prawn, Marks & Spencer*	1 Pack/210g	221	105	5.6	10.2	4.5	1.7
New Potato & Sweet Chilli Prawn, Marks & Spencer*	1 Pack/210g	147	70	2.8	14.0	0.5	0.7
New Potato, Co-Op*	1 Serving/50g	98	195	1.0	10.0	16.0	2.0
New Potato, Less Than 3% Fat, Marks & Spencer*	1 Pot/190g	143	75	1.7	14.4	1.3	1.2
New Potato, Marks & Spencer*	1 Serving/60g	63	105	1.6	15.0	4.5	1.0
New World, Finest, Tesco*	1 Bag/125g	15	12	1.2	0.5	0.6	1.1
Nicoise Style, Layered, Waitrose*	1 Bowl/275g	129	47	2.7	5.8	1.4	1.0
Nicoise, FTG, Marks & Spencer*	1 Pack/350g	473	135	5.9	7.5	9.0	0.5
Nicoise, Lunch Pot, Marks & Spencer*	1 Pot/330g	330	100	5.6	4.9	6.7	1.0
Nicoise, Pizza Express*	1 Salad/400g	729	182	10.0	16.3	9.3	0.0
Noodle & King Prawn, Perfectly Balanced, Waitrose*	1 Pack/225g	272	121	4.3	17.3	3.9	1.1
Noodle With Thai Style Chicken, Marks & Spencer*	½ Pot/145g	160	110	5.2	11.6	4.9	1.4
Pancetta, Express, Pizza Express*	1 Salad/90g	200	223	7.4	3.3	20.0	0.0
Pasta & Cheese, Asda*	1 Serving/125g	319	255	6.0	15.0	19.0	1.2
Pasta & Cheese, Somerfield*	½ Pack/225g	342	152	3.6	11.8	10.4	1.5
Pasta & Chesse, Safeway*	1 Serving/225g	554	246	4.8	15.2	18.4	0.0
Pasta & Garlic, Iceland*	1 Serving/75g	149	199	2.2	15.4	14.3	1.6

SALAD,	Measure INFO/WEIGHT	per Measure KCAL	KCAL	PROT	CARB	FAT	FIBRE
			Nutrition Values per 100g / 100ml				
Pasta & Ham, Safeway*	1 Pot/225g	284	126	4.5	16.9	4.5	0.3
Pasta & Mushroom, Waitrose*	1 Pack/200g	320	160	4.1	14.0	9.7	0.6
Pasta & Pepper Side, Tesco*	1 Pack/230g	278	121	2.4	13.0	6.6	1.3
Pasta & Sweetcorn, Less Than 3% Fat, Marks & Spencer*	½ Pack/100g	85	85	2.8	14.7	1.4	1.5
Pasta & Tomato, GFY, Asda*	1 Pack/300g	348	116	3.0	19.0	3.1	1.6
Pasta & Tuna, McDonald's*	1 Pack/244g	217	89	4.5	12.5	2.2	0.9
Pasta, Spinach & Pinenut, Safeway*	1 Serving/200g	295	148	5.3	15.2	7.2	1.7
Pasta, With Chicken, McDonald's*	1 Serving/190g	266	140	6.6	19.6	3.5	0.2
Pesto Pasta, Pret a Manger*	1 Pot/320g	425	133	2.7	6.9	10.7	0.9
Potato & Cheese, Pasta & Mixed Leaf, Waitrose*	1 Serving/205g	267	130	3.2	10.1	8.5	1.1
Potato & Egg Side, Tesco*	1 Pack/300g	192	64	2.5	4.2	4.1	1.1
Potato & Egg, Fresh, Safeway*	1 Serving/105g	84	80	8.4	3.0	3.6	1.6
Potato & Egg, Somerfield*	½ Pack/157.9g	90	57	2.5	5.1	3.0	1.2
Potato Layered, Tesco*	1 Pack/350g	284	81	1.3	7.8	4.9	1.3
Potato With Mayonnaise	1oz/28g	67	239	1.6	12.2	20.8	0.9
Potato With Reduced Calorie Dressing, Retail	1oz/28g	27	97	1.3	14.8	4.1	0.8
Potato, 50% Less Fat, Asda*	½ Pot/62g	47	76	1.6	11.2	2.7	1.5
Potato, Asda*	¼ Pot/57g	67	117	0.9	12.5	7.0	1.1
Potato, Chunky, Somerfield*	1oz/28g	59	212	1.0	3.0	22.0	0.0
Potato, Creamy, Asda*	1oz/28g	61	219	1.0	11.9	18.6	0.7
Potato, Eat Smart, Safeway*	½ Pack/121g	85	70	1.7	10.2	2.0	1.9
Potato, GFY, Asda*	½ Pack/125g	145	116	1.3	12.0	7.0	0.0
Potato, Good Intentions, Somerfield*	1 Serving/50g	50	100	1.2	14.0	4.4	1.0
Potato, Half Fat, Safeway*	1 Serving/125g	175	140	0.9	11.6	9.5	1.1
Potato, Healthy Eating, Tesco*	1 Pot/250g	218	87	2.2	12.0	3.4	0.9
Potato, Heinz*	½ Can/97g	137	141	1.4	14.8	8.5	0.8
Potato, Iceland*	1 Serving/75g	162	216	1.1	8.9	19.6	0.6
Potato, KFC*	1 Portion/160g	229	143	2.5	14.3	8.7	1.8
Potato, Less Than 4% Fat, Safeway*	1 Serving/250g	213	85	2.1	13.1	2.7	0.9
Potato, Less Than 5% Fat, Somerfield*	1oz/28g	24	86	2.0	11.0	4.0	0.0
Potato, Marks & Spencer*	1oz/28g	55	195	1.2	8.5	17.3	1.3
Potato, Perfectly Balanced, Waitrose*	½ Pot/125g	99	79	2.4	10.5	3.0	1.0
Potato, Reduced Calorie, Waitrose*	1oz/28g	22	77	2.2	10.4	2.9	0.9
Potato, Reduced Fat, Sainsbury's*	1oz/28g	34	121	1.0	11.8	7.3	1.6
Potato, Salad Bar, Asda*	1oz/28g	52	187	0.6	11.6	15.4	1.1
Potato, Savers, Safeway*	1 Serving/113g	122	108	0.9	10.6	6.9	1.5
Potato, Tesco*	1 Pot/125g	219	175	1.5	12.2	13.3	0.9
Prawn & Avacado, Marks & Spencer*	1 Serving/220g	176	80	3.0	2.0	6.8	3.1
Prawn & Egg, Leaf, Shapers, Boots*	1 Pack/182g	193	106	6.7	2.1	7.9	1.0
Prawn Cocktail, Boots*	1 Pack/202g	234	116	4.4	2.1	10.0	1.2
Prawn Cocktail, Healthy Eating, Tesco*	1 Serving/300g	279	93	5.7	15.3	1.0	2.0
Prawn Cocktail, Tesco*	1 Pack/300g	360	120	5.7	10.9	6.0	0.8
Prawn Layered, Asda*	1 Sm Box/190.6g	265	139	3.6	11.0	9.0	0.0
Prawn Layered, Food To Go, Marks & Spencer*	1 Pack/220g	176	80	4.8	9.6	2.4	1.1
Prawn Layered, Marks & Spencer*	1 Pack/450g	338	75	4.1	10.0	2.3	0.7
Prawn Satay & Noodle, Tesco*	1 Serving/250g	320	128	7.1	9.5	6.8	1.2
Primavera, Finest, Tesco*	1 Pack/100g	25	25	2.4	2.4	0.6	1.3
Rainbow Rice, Marks & Spencer*	1 Serving/261.5g	341	130	2.5	23.3	3.2	1.5
Ranch, Crispy Chicken, With Dressing, McDonald's*	1 Salad/401g	501	125	8.3	6.6	7.2	1.1
Ranch, Crispy Chicken, Without Dressing, McDonald's*	1 Salad/299g	394	132	10.2	5.5	7.4	1.2
Ranch, Grilled Chicken, With Dressing, McDonald's*	1 Salad/400g	396	99	9.8	3.1	5.0	1.1
Ranch, Grilled Chicken, Without Dressing, McDonald's*	1 Salad/298g	289	97	12.2	1.4	4.5	1.1
Ranch, No Meat, Mcdonald's*	1 Salad/219g	177	81	4.8	2.3	5.9	0.9

	Measure INFO/WEIGHT	per Measure KCAL	Nutrition Values per 100g / 100ml KCAL	PROT	CARB	FAT	FIBRE
Red Leaf & Rocket, Sainsbury's*	1 Serving/50g	11	21	3.5	1.6	0.1	1.7
Red Rice & Feta, Marks & Spencer*	1 Pack/244.4g	439	180	4.8	21.0	8.5	1.3
Red Thai Chicken With Noodles, Tesco*	1 Pack/300g	342	114	7.2	20.2	0.5	1.4
Ribbon, Marks & Spencer*	1oz/28g	5	17	0.8	3.2	0.2	1.7
Rice, Average	1oz/28g	46	166	3.1	23.1	7.5	0.7
Rice, Courgette & Pine Nut, BGTY, Sainsbury's*	1/3rd Pot/65g	68	105	2.7	20.0	1.6	1.5
Rice, Lentil & Roast Aubergine, Marks & Spencer*	1 Serving/270g	405	150	4.6	18.2	6.8	1.7
Roast Chicken & Coleslaw, Boots*	1 Serving/245g	392	160	4.5	3.9	14.0	1.3
Roast Chicken, Snack, Tesco*	1 Pack/300g	324	108	6.0	4.8	7.2	1.0
Roast Chicken, Tesco*	1 Salad/300g	348	116	5.3	7.0	7.4	1.0
Roasted Artichoke & Pepper, Marks & Spencer*	1 Serving/220g	638	290	4.1	12.8	24.5	5.1
Roasted Vegetable, Feta & Cous Cous, Somerfield*	1 Pack/299.4g	490	164	5.0	22.9	5.8	1.6
Roasted Vegetables & Cous Cous, Sainsbury's*	1 Pot/225g	349	155	5.5	26.3	3.1	0.0
Rocket, Leafy, Asda*	1 Serving/75g	10	13	1.5	1.4	0.1	1.8
Rocket, Tesco*	1oz/28g	4	16	1.3	1.7	0.5	1.2
Rocket, Wild, Safeway*	1 Serving/25g	6	25	3.3	2.3	0.3	1.7
Salmon & Roquette, Marks & Spencer*	1 Serving/255g	306	120	3.9	8.5	8.0	1.0
Santa Plum Tomato & Avocado, Marks & Spencer*	1 Pack/240g	348	145	1.7	4.1	13.4	0.2
Santa Plum Tomato With Dressing, Marks & Spencer*	1 Pack/225g	135	60	0.9	3.1	4.8	0.9
Santa Tomato, Side, Marks & Spencer*	1 Pack/225g	146	65	0.8	3.3	5.5	0.9
Seafood, Marinated, Marks & Spencer*	1 Serving/90g	108	120	13.4	2.3	6.4	0.8
Seasonal, Organic, Waitrose*	¼ Pack/25g	4	15	0.8	1.7	0.5	0.9
Selection, Fresh, Marks & Spencer*	1 Pack/230g	32	14	0.7	2.1	0.3	0.9
Selection, Side, Marks & Spencer*	1 Serving/255g	153	60	1.1	2.5	5.0	1.3
Shredded Beetroot, Asda*	1 Serving/140g	29	21	1.1	3.5	0.3	1.5
Side, Fresh & Crispy, Tesco*	1 Salad/230g	30	13	0.7	1.9	0.3	0.7
Simple, Marks & Spencer*	1oz/28g	3	10	1.1	1.2	0.3	1.6
Simply Chicken, Ginsters*	1 Pack/186.5g	316	170	11.4	22.7	3.7	0.0
Skipjack Tuna, John West*	1 Can/192g	190	99	7.3	3.7	6.1	0.0
Smoked Ham, Weight Watchers*	1 Pack/181g	233	129	11.0	16.6	2.0	3.0
Spanish Style Rice, Marks & Spencer*	1 Serving/220g	319	145	5.8	17.4	5.8	0.5
Spicy Bean, Tesco*	1 Serving/125g	111	89	4.9	12.1	2.3	2.5
Spicy Chick Pea, Feta & Chilli, Marks & Spencer*	1oz/28g	56	200	7.2	13.1	13.4	2.9
Spicy Rice, Waitrose*	1 Serving/200g	318	159	3.2	21.7	6.6	0.9
Spinach, Watercress & Rocket, Safeway*	1 Serving/60g	14	24	3.0	1.5	0.7	1.8
Spring, American Style, Marks & Spencer*	1 Serving/60g	9	15	1.9	1.4	0.2	1.3
Sugar Plum Tomato, Fresh, Safeway*	1 Serving/160g	46	29	1.1	3.2	1.3	1.2
Summer Bean, Marks & Spencer*	1 Pack/225g	225	100	5.8	16.7	1.3	3.9
Summer, Marks & Spencer*	1oz/28g	6	20	0.8	3.6	0.4	1.2
Super Club, Pret a Manger*	1 Av Pack/200g	213	107	10.8	1.6	6.3	0.6
Sweet & Crispy, Fresh, Safeway*	1 Serving/90g	19	21	0.9	3.7	0.3	1.5
Sweet & Crispy, Marks & Spencer*	1 Serving/140g	49	35	1.7	4.7	1.0	1.6
Sweet & Crispy, Side, Sainsbury's*	1 Serving/74g	32	43	1.3	8.2	0.5	1.3
Sweet & Crispy, Somerfield*	1 Pack/100g	25	25	1.0	5.0	0.0	0.0
Sweet & Crunchy, Safeway*	1 Serving/175g	33	19	0.7	3.4	0.3	1.3
Sweet & Crunchy, Sainsbury's*	1 Serving/125g	21	17	0.8	2.9	0.2	1.3
Sweet & Crunchy, Tesco*	1 Pack/285g	51	18	0.8	3.0	0.3	1.7
Sweet & Sour Prawn Noodle, Healthy Eating, Tesco*	1 Pack/190g	122	64	5.0	9.4	0.7	0.4
Sweet Carrot, 3% Fat, Marks & Spencer*	1oz/28g	21	75	1.3	16.7	1.2	1.4
Sweet Chilli Chicken Noodle, COU, Marks & Spencer*	1 Pack/340g	408	120	6.8	17.4	2.3	1.2
Sweet Crispy, Eat Smart, Safeway*	1 Serving/220g	59	27	1.0	4.9	0.4	1.3
Sweet Crispy, Safeway*	1 Serving/220g	132	60	2.2	10.8	0.9	2.9
Sweet Crunchy, Sainsbury's*	1oz/28g	6	20	1.1	3.5	0.3	1.4

S

	Measure INFO/WEIGHT	per Measure KCAL	Nutrition Values per 100g / 100ml				
			KCAL	PROT	CARB	FAT	FIBRE
SALAD,							
Sweet Green, Marks & Spencer*	1 Serving/150g	23	15	1.5	1.3	0.3	2.0
Sweet Leaf & Carrot, Asda*	½ Pack/164g	34	21	0.9	3.6	0.3	1.4
Sweet Leaf, Fully Prepared, Fresh, Sainsbury's*	¼ Pack/75g	12	16	0.8	3.0	0.1	2.1
Sweet Leafy, Organic, Tesco*	1 Serving/250g	45	18	0.8	2.7	0.4	1.9
Sweet Pepper Side, Tesco*	1 Serving/54g	22	41	1.3	8.0	0.4	2.1
Sweet Pepper With Corn, Tesco*	1 Pack/270g	103	38	1.3	7.2	0.5	1.5
Sweet Pepper, Medley, Waitrose*	½ Pack/100g	22	22	0.9	3.8	0.4	1.5
Sweet, Baby Leaf Mix, Co-Op*	1 Serving/50g	8	15	0.8	2.0	0.5	2.0
Sweet, Layered, Tesco*	1 Serving/285g	117	41	1.9	7.4	0.5	2.1
Sweet, Shredded, Tesco*	1 Serving/100g	20	20	1.1	2.9	0.4	1.9
Sweet, Waitrose*	1 Serving/160g	27	17	0.7	2.8	0.3	1.7
Tabbouleh Feta, Finest, Tesco*	1 Pack/225g	266	118	4.2	13.7	5.2	0.6
Tabbouleh Style, Perfectly Balanced, Waitrose*	1 Pack/225g	234	104	2.8	14.3	3.9	2.6
Tatsoi, Fully Prepared, Sainsbury's*	1 Pack/115g	21	18	1.7	2.2	0.3	1.3
Tender Leaf, With Mizuna, Tesco*	1 Serving/30g	5	15	1.6	1.4	0.3	1.7
Tenderleaf, Waitrose*	1 Serving/200g	30	15	0.9	1.6	0.5	1.1
Thai Prawn, Snack, Good Intentions, Somerfield*	1 Serving/215g	230	107	5.0	17.9	1.7	1.1
Thai Style Chicken, Marks & Spencer*	1 Serving/195g	205	105	6.7	15.1	1.9	1.9
Thai Style Noodle With King Prawns, Marks & Spencer*	1 Serving/425g	425	100	5.2	17.5	1.0	1.8
Three Bean, Pots, Tesco*	1 Pot/210g	200	95	4.6	10.5	3.9	3.7
Three Bean, Sainsbury's*	1 Serving/125g	108	86	4.2	6.0	5.0	0.0
Three Bean, Tesco*	1 Can/300g	330	110	7.7	17.6	1.0	5.3
Three Leaf Blend, Sainsbury's*	1 Pack/50g	10	19	1.7	1.8	0.6	1.2
Tiger Prawn & Pasta, GFY, Asda*	1 Serving/200g	250	125	4.6	20.0	2.9	2.0
Tomato & Mozarella Cheese, Marks & Spencer*	½ Pack/110g	155	141	10.0	3.2	9.6	0.5
Tomato & Onion	1oz/28g	20	72	0.8	4.0	6.1	1.0
Tomato, Avocado & Rocket, Marks & Spencer*	1 Pack/350g	508	145	1.7	4.1	13.4	0.2
Tuna & Pasta, Snack, BGTY, Sainsbury's*	1 Pack/260g	255	98	5.7	13.9	2.2	1.3
Tuna & Sweetcorn, Snack, Good Intentions, Somerfield*	1 Pot/215g	219	102	6.6	12.7	2.8	0.9
Tuna & Tomato, Boots*	1 Pack/171g	150	88	6.5	2.0	6.0	1.0
Tuna In a Tomato & Herb Dressing, John West*	1 Can/192g	190	99	7.3	3.7	6.1	0.0
Tuna Layered, COU, Marks & Spencer*	1 Tub/450g	360	80	6.7	8.3	2.0	0.8
Tuna Layered, Waitrose*	1 Bowl/300g	636	212	4.0	4.8	19.6	1.0
Tuna Nicoise, BGTY, Sainsbury's*	1 Pack/300g	315	105	6.3	15.5	2.0	2.5
Tuna Nicoise, Finest, Tesco*	1 Serving/250g	430	172	8.5	13.3	9.4	0.8
Tuna Nicoise, Marks & Spencer*	½ Pack/255g	306	120	6.0	3.7	8.8	0.2
Tuna Nicoise, No Mayonnaise, Shapers, Boots*	1 Pack/276.4g	132	48	4.0	5.0	1.3	0.8
Tuna Nicoise, Pret a Manger*	1 Av Pack/300g	194	65	8.9	1.0	2.8	1.0
Tuna Nicoise, Sainsbury's*	1 Pack/183g	234	128	11.3	1.8	8.4	0.0
Tuna Snack, Health Living, Tesco*	1 Serving/300g	252	84	7.6	11.5	0.9	0.9
Tuna, Healthy Eating, Tesco*	1 Serving/300g	399	133	6.2	10.5	7.3	0.9
Tuna, Pret a Manger*	1 Serving/150g	237	158	13.8	4.0	9.7	1.0
Tuscan Style Bean & Sunblush Tomato, Waitrose*	1 Pot/225g	308	137	5.6	17.9	4.8	1.0
Vegetable, Canned	1oz/28g	40	143	1.6	13.0	9.8	1.2
Vegetable, Heinz*	1 Can/195g	259	133	1.5	12.6	8.5	1.3
Waldorf	1oz/28g	54	193	1.4	7.5	17.7	1.3
Waldorf Style Side, Waitrose*	1 Pack/195g	189	97	1.8	5.5	7.5	1.9
Waldorf, Waitrose*	1 Serving/50g	161	321	2.6	7.6	31.1	1.3
Watercress & Spinach, Asda*	1 Serving/50g	8	16	2.1	1.7	0.1	1.7
Watercress, Morrisons*	1 Bag/100g	17	17	1.7	1.2	0.7	0.0
Watercress, Mustard Leaf & Mizuna, Marks & Spencer*	½ Pack/60g	9	15	2.4	0.4	0.3	3.0
Watercress, Spinach & Rocket, Sainsbury's*	1oz/28g	7	25	3.0	1.2	0.9	1.7
Watercress, Spinach & Rocket, Tesco*	1 Serving/30g	7	22	3.0	0.8	0.8	1.9

	Measure INFO/WEIGHT	per Measure KCAL	Nutrition Values per 100g / 100ml				
			KCAL	PROT	CARB	FAT	FIBRE
SALAD,							
Watercress, Spinach & Rocket, Waitrose*	1 Bag/135g	28	21	2.2	1.2	0.8	1.5
Wheat With Roasted Vegetables, Sainsbury's*	1 Pack/220g	339	154	3.3	17.0	8.3	4.5
Wild Rocket, Safeway*	1 Serving/75g	14	18	1.3	2.1	0.5	1.1
With Sweetcorn, Side, Tesco*	1 Serving/135g	51	38	1.3	7.2	0.5	1.5
SALAD BOWL,							
Avocado & Tomato, Sainsbury's*	1 Pack/180g	97	54	1.0	6.7	2.6	1.3
Coleslaw, Budgens*	1 Pack/162.5g	221	135	1.5	7.1	11.2	1.4
Coleslaw, Marks & Spencer*	1 Pack/325g	293	90	1.3	4.9	7.4	1.3
Coleslaw, Somerfield*	½ Pack/162.6g	227	139	1.2	6.6	12.0	1.8
Coleslaw, Tesco*	1 Bowl/300g	327	109	1.3	3.4	10.1	1.3
Crispy, Marks & Spencer*	1 Serving/250g	88	35	1.3	6.6	0.5	1.2
French Style, Sainsbury's*	1oz/28g	15	55	1.0	4.8	3.5	1.5
Fruit Crunch, Marks & Spencer*	½ Pack/120g	174	145	3.1	25.5	3.4	0.6
Greek Style, Marks & Spencer*	1 Bowl/255g	242	95	2.5	2.4	8.2	0.7
Greek Style, Somerfield*	1 Bowl/225g	178	79	2.2	3.5	6.2	1.1
Italian Avocado & Tomato, Sainsbury's*	1 Bowl/180g	97	54	1.0	6.7	2.6	1.3
Large, Sainsbury's*	1/6 Pack/52g	12	23	0.9	4.3	0.3	1.1
Marks & Spencer*	1oz/28g	4	13	1.4	1.2	0.3	2.0
Mixed, Medley, Waitrose*	¼ Pack/60g	9	15	0.9	1.7	0.5	1.0
Mozzarella & Sweet Baby Plum Tomato, WTF, Sainsbury's*	1 Pack/153g	193	126	5.9	2.3	10.3	1.1
New Potato, Tuna & Egg, Marks & Spencer*	1 Pack/340g	255	75	3.8	6.7	3.8	0.7
Pasta With Sun Dried Tomato Dressing, WTF, Sainsbury's*	1 Bowl/320g	470	147	3.2	20.0	6.0	1.5
Pasta, Somerfield*	1 Pack/320g	541	169	3.3	20.8	8.1	1.5
Red Cheddar & Edam, Way to Five, Sainsbury's*	½ Pack/224g	240	107	4.4	12.8	4.2	1.1
Ribbon, Marks & Spencer*	1oz/28g	4	15	1.2	2.0	0.1	1.5
Tomato & Basil, Marks & Spencer*	1 Serving/225g	225	100	0.8	3.7	10.1	1.1
Tomato, Sainsbury's*	½ Bowl/150g	93	62	0.9	4.4	4.5	1.6
Tomato, WTF, Sainsbury's*	1 Bowl/300g	174	58	0.8	4.5	4.1	2.8
Tuna, Fresh, Asda*	1 Serving/160g	184	115	8.0	5.0	7.0	0.0
SALAD CREAM,							
Average	1 Tsp/5g	17	335	1.7	18.6	27.9	0.1
Reduced Calorie, Average	1 Serving/14g	18	130	1.0	12.9	7.9	0.2
SALAMI,							
Ardennes Pepper, Waitrose*	2 Slices/14g	60	429	18.6	1.9	38.5	1.1
Average	1 Slice/5g	18	360	28.4	1.9	26.2	0.0
Continental Peppered, Marks & Spencer*	1 Slice/8.3g	33	415	21.6	3.0	34.9	0.0
Danish, Average	1 Serving/17g	89	524	13.2	1.3	51.7	0.0
German, Average	1 Serving/60g	200	333	20.3	1.6	27.3	0.1
German, Peppered, Average	3 Slices/25g	86	342	22.2	2.5	27.1	0.2
Healthy Range, Average	4 Slices/25g	55	221	22.4	0.7	14.3	0.0
Milano, Average	1 Serving/70g	278	397	25.9	0.9	32.2	0.0
Napoli, Average	1 Slice/5g	17	342	27.1	0.8	25.5	0.1
SALMON,							
Appetisers, Smoked, Tesco*	1 Pack/100g	224	224	15.1	0.7	17.9	1.7
Blinis, Smoked, Marks & Spencer*	1oz/28g	67	240	11.9	18.9	13.0	1.8
Crunchies, Tesco*	1 Serving/112g	268	239	11.4	13.6	15.4	1.0
Crusted, Mediterranean Style Crusted, Sainsbury's*	1 Serving/166g	322	194	18.0	5.3	11.5	0.8
Fillets, & Butter, Marks & Spencer*	1oz/28g	64	230	16.7	0.0	18.0	0.0
Fillets, Cajun, Waitrose*	1 Serving/150g	215	143	20.6	0.4	6.5	0.0
Fillets, Chargrilled, Sainsbury's*	1 Serving/270 g	270	243	20.9	0.2	17.6	0.0
Fillets, In White Wine & Parsley Dressing, Tesco*	1 Fillet/150g	291	194	17.5	0.3	13.6	0.6
Fillets, Lime & Coriander, Tesco*	1 Pack/250g	368	147	21.4	7.0	3.7	0.7
Fillets, Raw, Average	1 Fillet/79g	149	189	20.9	0.1	11.7	0.1

S

	Measure INFO/WEIGHT	per Measure KCAL	Nutrition Values per 100g / 100ml				
			KCAL	PROT	CARB	FAT	FIBRE
SALMON,							
• Fillets, With Lemon & Herb Butter, Asda*	1 Fillet/125g	305	244	20.0	0.4	18.0	0.0
Fillets, With Orange & Dill Dressing, Tesco*	1 Serving/300g	540	180	17.7	4.1	10.3	0.7
Fillets, With Sea Salt & Black Pepper Butter, Safeway*	1 Fillet/115g	288	250	20.4	0.1	18.7	0.0
Fillets, With Sicilian Citrus Glaze, Sainsbury's*	1 Fillet/144.9g	371	256	21.9	2.3	17.8	0.0
Fillets, With Tarragon, BGTY, Sainsbury's*	1 Pack/402g	350	87	6.9	9.1	2.6	1.0
Flakes, Honey Roast, Average	1oz/28g	56	198	24.0	1.9	10.7	0.2
Goan, Limited Edition, Sainsbury's*	1 Pack/351g	358	102	11.1	2.3	5.4	2.4
Goujons, Average	1 Pack/150g	321	214	16.4	12.4	11.0	1.1
Hot Smoked, Average	1 Serving/62g	103	166	24.0	0.9	7.2	0.1
In Crust, Wild Alaska, Youngs*	1 Serving/160g	224	140	19.5	7.2	3.6	0.2
Lime & Coriander, Tesco*	1 Serving/120g	176	147	21.4	7.0	3.7	0.7
Lunchbox, COU, Marks & Spencer*	1 Pack/235g	200	85	5.1	13.1	1.4	0.9
Mild Oak Smoked, Average	1 Slice/25g	46	182	22.6	0.1	10.2	0.0
Pink, Average	1 Serving/50g	65	130	19.5	0.1	5.8	0.1
Pink, In Brine, Average	1oz/28g	43	153	23.5	0.0	6.6	0.0
Poached, Average	1 Serving/90g	176	195	22.5	0.2	11.7	0.3
Potted, Marks & Spencer*	1 Serving/75g	184	245	17.1	0.5	19.4	1.2
Red, Average	½ Can/90g	141	156	20.5	0.1	8.2	0.1
Red, In Brine, Average	1oz/28g	47	169	22.4	0.0	8.9	0.0
Rillettes, John West*	½ Can/62g	169	272	14.9	0.1	23.5	0.0
Smoked, Average	1 Serving/70g	126	179	21.9	0.5	10.0	0.1
Tail Joint, Lemon & Herb Butter, Marks & Spencer*	1 Pack/480g	864	180	18.8	0.8	11.4	0.2
Wafer Thin, Scottish, Marks & Spencer*	1oz/28g	52	187	22.4	0.0	10.8	0.0
SALMON &,							
Dill Sauce, Youngs*	1 Pack/435g	265	61	6.1	4.2	2.3	0.1
Pasta, Youngs*	1 Pack/300g	411	137	7.8	16.6	4.4	1.2
Spinach, Roulade, Tesco*	1 Serving/60g	155	258	9.5	1.7	23.7	0.2
Thai Noodles, Healthy Eating, Tesco*	1 Pack/350g	231	66	6.7	7.1	1.2	1.5
Vegetables, Marks & Spencer*	1 Serving/200g	220	110	6.0	5.2	6.9	0.8
SALMON EN CROUTE,							
Iceland*	1 Serving/170g	476	280	8.5	20.1	18.4	1.0
Luxury, Marks & Spencer*	1oz/28g	59	210	11.9	9.4	13.7	2.2
Marks & Spencer*	½ Pack/185g	574	310	10.4	17.3	21.9	0.6
Retail	1oz/28g	81	288	11.8	18.0	19.1	0.0
Sainsbury's*	1 Serving/179g	533	298	9.7	18.4	20.0	1.2
Tesco*	1 Serving/205g	568	277	9.7	15.4	19.6	0.6
Youngs*	1 Serving/200g	330	165	5.3	9.2	11.9	0.4
SALMON FLORENTINE,							
Asda*	1 Serving/190g	306	161	16.0	1.8	10.0	0.0
SALMON IN,							
A Watercress Sauce, Marks & Spencer*	1 Pack/400g	480	120	7.1	8.1	6.8	1.7
Creamy Dill Sauce, Fillets, Bird's Eye*	1 Pack/340g	333	98	5.6	8.7	4.5	1.3
Creamy Watercress Sauce, Fillets, Sainsbury's*	1 Serving/180g	292	162	13.0	2.2	11.3	0.4
Creamy Watercress Sauce, Fillets, Scottish, Seafresh*	1 Pack 300g	528	176	13.7	1.2	12.9	0.1
Lemon Mayonnaise, Weight Watchers*	1 Can/80g	130	163	10.2	6.4	10.6	0.1
Lime & Coriander, Fillets, Good Choice, Iceland*	½ Pack/150g	189	126	19.8	5.1	2.9	0.8
Tomato & Mascarpone Sauce, Fillets, Asda*	½ Pack/181.0g	219	121	13.0	1.4	7.0	0.0
Watercress Sauce, Somerfield*	1 Serving/212g	585	276	14.1	3.2	23.3	0.5
SALMON MORNAY,							
With Broccoli, Weight Watchers*	1 Pack/290g	261	90	9.6	9.0	1.7	0.7
SALMON MOROCCAN,							
Style, Fillets, Asda*	1 Serving/240g	454	189	19.0	1.3	12.0	0.0

S

	Measure INFO/WEIGHT	per Measure KCAL	Nutrition Values per 100g / 100ml				
			KCAL	PROT	CARB	FAT	FIBRE
SALMON PARCELS,							
& Garlic Butter, Finest, Tesco*	1 Serving/164g	321	196	16.8	0.6	14.1	0.5
In Lemon Sauce, Marks & Spencer*	1 Serving/185g	350	189	12.1	1.4	15.1	0.5
Smoked, Marks & Spencer*	1 Parcel/55g	151	275	15.4	0.7	23.6	0.0
Smoked, Scottish, Marks & Spencer*	1 Parcel/58g	130	226	16.7	1.2	17.6	0.0
Smoked, Tesco*	1 Serving/50g	147	293	16.4	0.0	25.3	0.2
With Light Creamy Mousse Filling, Smoked, Tesco*	1 Parcel/56.5g	99	177	17.5	1.7	11.1	0.1
SALMON PLATTER,							
GFY, Asda*	1 Pack/400g	376	94	7.0	8.0	3.8	1.4
SALMON WITH,							
A Cream Sauce, Scottish Fillets, Marks & Spencer*	1 Serving/200g	360	180	13.8	1.0	13.0	0.1
Coriander & Lime, Pacific, Asda*	1 serving/113g	154	137	27.0	0.5	3.0	0.0
Herb Vegetables, Healthy Eating, Tesco*	1 Pack/350g	228	65	6.6	3.8	2.6	0.9
Potatoes & Vegetables, Scottish, Marks & Spencer*	1 Pack/400g	460	115	7.9	5.8	6.9	0.9
Spinach & Cheese, Atlantic, Bird's Eye*	1 Serving/241g	415	172	9.8	4.2	12.9	0.1
SALSA,							
Chicken, Morrisons*	½ Sm Pot/85g	89	105	9.0	11.2	3.0	0.0
Chunky Tomato & Avocado, COU, Marks & Spencer*	½ Pot/85g	30	35	0.8	5.4	1.4	1.4
Chunky, Marks & Spencer*	½ Jar/132g	92	70	1.2	12.0	2.4	1.5
Cool, Tesco*	1oz/28g	11	38	0.9	7.1	0.3	0.8
Extra Hot, Fresh, Somerfield*	1oz/28g	13	47	1.0	8.0	1.0	0.0
Fire Roasted Pepper, Somerfield*	1 Pot/120g	50	42	1.2	8.1	0.5	1.3
Fresh, Asda*	1oz/28g	10	35	1.2	6.2	0.6	2.0
Fresh, Sainsbury's*	1oz/28g	15	54	1.7	7.0	2.1	0.9
Fresh, Waitrose*	1oz/28g	16	57	1.2	6.9	2.7	1.0
GFY, Asda*	½ Pot/236g	85	36	1.0	7.0	0.4	2.0
Hot, Fresh, Tesco*	1oz/28g	17	62	1.8	7.9	2.6	0.9
Hot, Primula*	1oz/28g	10	35	1.8	6.6	0.2	0.0
Hot, Tesco*	1 Serving/75g	43	57	1.4	7.5	2.4	1.2
King Prawn, Marks & Spencer*	1 Pack/160g	176	110	12.2	1.0	6.4	1.3
Marks & Spencer*	½ Jar/136g	95	70	1.2	12.0	2.4	1.5
Medium Hot, Discovery*	1oz/28g	16	58	1.1	8.1	2.4	2.1
Mild, Amigos, Safeway*	1oz/28g	10	34	1.0	6.1	0.3	0.0
Red Onion & Tomato, Tapas Selection, Sainsbury's*	1 Serving/22g	17	77	3.0	6.0	4.5	0.9
Red Pepper, Sainsbury's*	1 Serving/85g	31	37	1.7	3.8	1.7	1.5
Sainsbury's*	1 Serving/50g	24	48	1.7	7.7	1.1	0.0
Smokey BBQ, Weight Watchers*	1 Serving/56g	20	36	1.1	7.6	0.1	2.3
Spiced Mango, Ginger & Chilli, Weight Watchers*	½ Pot/50g	43	85	1.0	19.9	0.2	2.6
Spicy Mango & Lime, Morrisons*	½ Pot/85g	62	73	1.0	15.9	0.4	1.3
Spicy, Less Than 3% Fat, Marks & Spencer*	½ Pot/85g	30	35	1.3	5.6	0.8	0.8
Spicy, Marks & Spencer*	1oz/28g	17	60	1.3	7.2	2.7	1.2
Taco, Old El Paso*	¼ Pack/29g	13	46	1.5	10.0	0.0	0.0
Tomato & Avocado, Marks & Spencer*	½ Pack/85.7g	30	35	0.8	5.4	1.4	1.4
Tomato, Chunky, Tesco*	1 Pot/170g	68	40	1.1	5.9	1.3	1.1
Tomato, Chunky, Tex Mex, Tesco*	1 Serving/50g	26	52	1.0	6.4	2.5	1.0
Tomato, Marks & Spencer*	1 Tbsp/25g	9	35	1.0	4.7	1.2	0.9
Tomato, Reduced Fat, Waitrose*	1 Serving/1g	0	27	1.5	4.7	0.2	1.4
Tomato, Spicy, Worldwide, Aldi*	1 Serving/25g	8	30	1.2	5.9	0.2	1.2
Tomato, Waitrose*	1 Serving/50g	24	47	1.5	5.0	2.3	1.7
Tuna, Good Intentions, Somerfield*	1 Pack/51g	142	278	17.4	47.4	2.1	2.7
SALT,							
Cooking, Sainsbury's*	1oz/28g	0	0	0.0	0.0	0.0	0.0
Table	1 Tsp/5g	0	0	0.0	0.0	0.0	0.0

S

	Measure per Measure		Nutrition Values per 100g / 100ml				
	INFO/WEIGHT	KCAL	KCAL	PROT	CARB	FAT	FIBRE
SAMOSAS,							
Chicken Tikka, Sainsbury's*	2 Samosas/100g	239	239	8.3	22.5	12.9	3.1
Chicken, Mumtaz*	1 Serving/105g	177	169	19.6	4.9	7.9	0.0
Co-Op*	1oz/28g	70	250	6.0	34.0	10.0	2.0
Dim Sum Selection, Sainsbury's*	1 Samosas/12g	24	196	3.4	28.6	7.6	2.8
Indian Style Selection, Co-Op*	1 Samosa/20.8g	50	240	5.0	27.0	13.0	3.0
Lamb, Morrisons*	1 Samosa/50g	144	288	9.8	27.0	15.7	1.5
Lamb, Waitrose*	1oz/28g	87	310	8.5	18.1	22.6	0.8
Mini, Sainsbury's*	1 Serving/28g	82	294	6.9	33.2	14.8	2.7
Vegetable	1oz/28g	132	472	3.1	22.3	41.8	1.8
Vegetable, Marks & Spencer*	1 Samosa/45g	115	255	5.1	24.8	15.3	2.8
Vegetable, Mini, Tesco*	1 Samosa/32g	79	247	5.0	30.0	11.9	1.6
Vegetable, Mini, Waitrose*	2 Samosas/59.8g	146	244	4.5	28.7	12.4	2.8
Vegetable, Northern Indian, Sainsbury's*	1 Samosa/50g	126	252	5.8	30.6	11.8	2.6
Vegetable, Retail	1oz/28g	61	217	5.1	30.0	9.3	2.5
Vegetable, Tesco*	1 Samosa/50g	126	252	5.0	28.4	13.2	2.7
Vegetable, Waitrose*	1 Samosas/50g	107	214	3.3	26.3	10.6	0.8
SANDWICH,							
All Day Breakfast, BGTY, Sainsbury's*	1 Pack/188g	294	156	9.6	22.7	2.4	0.0
All Day Breakfast, Eat Smart, Safeway*	1 Pack/157g	236	150	10.0	21.6	2.1	2.2
All Day Breakfast, Finest, Tesco*	1 Pack/275g	660	240	9.7	16.4	15.1	1.6
All Day Breakfast, Ginsters*	1 Pack/241.3g	537	223	10.8	20.3	11.0	0.0
All Day Breakfast, Healthy Living, Tesco*	1 Pack/223.1g	328	147	11.9	16.8	3.6	2.7
All Day Breakfast, Pret A Manger*	1 Pack/300g	679	226	10.7	19.3	11.6	2.2
All Day Breakfast, Shapers, Boots*	1 Pack/207.1g	323	156	11.0	23.0	2.5	2.2
All Day Breakfast, The Big Eat Street, Safeway*	1 Pack/213.1g	584	274	12.1	23.1	14.8	2.1
All Day Breakfast, Walls*	1 Pack/225.1g	610	271	9.2	24.3	15.4	1.4
All Day Breakfast, Weight Watchers*	1 Pack/157.7g	299	189	11.0	30.2	2.7	1.9
Apple, Cheese & Celery, Asda*	1 Pack/173.0g	244	141	8.0	21.0	2.8	2.7
Asian Chicken, Shapers, Boots*	1 Pack/189.6g	274	144	12.0	19.0	2.4	2.9
Avocado & Alfalfa Sprout, Pret A Manger*	1 Av Pack/250g	329	132	3.4	11.6	8.0	2.4
Avocado & Spinach, Marks & Spencer*	1 Pack/241.7g	581	240	4.5	24.7	13.6	2.2
Avocado, Mozzarella & Tomato, Marks & Spencer*	1 Pack/272.9g	655	240	8.8	21.7	13.2	2.3
BBQ Chicken & Ranch Coleslaw, Big, Sainsbury's*	1 Pack/276.6g	474	171	9.2	22.7	4.8	0.0
BBQ Chicken On Malted Bread, Fresh Bite*	1 Pack/225.8g	341	151	9.0	23.4	2.4	0.0
BBQ Chicken Wedge, Tesco*	1 Pack/195g	321	165	10.2	27.4	1.6	1.0
BBQ Rib, Rustlers*	1 Pack/170g	444	261	14.6	23.8	11.9	0.0
BBQ Ribsteak, Snack Express*	1 Serving/145g	410	283	14.6	26.2	13.3	0.0
BLT, Classic, Taste!*	1 Serving/150g	345	230	9.3	25.2	9.9	0.0
BLT, Deep Fill, Spar*	1 Pack/165.9g	408	246	10.7	35.1	7.0	0.0
BLT, Max, Shell*	1 Pack/249.1g	665	267	10.8	24.1	14.1	0.0
Bacon & Free Range Egg, Daily Bread*	1 Serving/175g	425	243	10.1	21.5	13.1	0.0
Bacon & Tomato, COU, Marks & Spencer*	1 Pack/168.8g	270	160	9.5	25.6	2.7	2.5
Bacon, Chicken & Avocado, Ultimate, Marks & Spencer*	1 Pack/241g	552	229	10.7	17.9	12.7	2.8
Bacon, Chicken, Cheese Triple, BGTY, Sainsbury's*	1 Pack/263g	534	203	11.7	19.4	7.6	4.4
Bacon, Chicken, Cheese, Big, Sainsbury's*	1 Pack/254g	734	289	11.7	18.0	17.9	0.0
Bacon, Lettuce & Tomato & Chicken Salad, Co-Op*	1 Pack/230g	472	205	10.0	21.0	9.0	2.0
Bacon, Lettuce & Tomato, Asda*	1 Pack/262g	618	236	12.2	20.3	12.0	3.0
Bacon, Lettuce & Tomato, BGTY, Sainsbury's*	1 Pack/180g	268	149	10.8	20.8	2.5	1.6
Bacon, Lettuce & Tomato, Boots*	1oz/28g	75	268	10.0	21.0	16.0	2.2
Bacon, Lettuce & Tomato, COU, Marks & Spencer*	1 Pack/174g	278	160	9.5	25.6	2.7	2.5
Bacon, Lettuce & Tomato, Daily Bread*	1 Pack/171.1g	344	201	9.1	21.6	11.0	0.0
Bacon, Lettuce & Tomato, Deep Filled, Asda*	1 Pack/206g	606	294	13.3	21.8	17.0	3.0
Bacon, Lettuce & Tomato, Eat Smart, Safeway*	1 Pack/165g	231	140	9.8	21.8	1.4	2.4

SANDWICH,

	Measure INFO/WEIGHT	per Measure KCAL	KCAL	PROT	CARB	FAT	FIBRE
			Nutrition Values per 100g / 100ml				
Bacon, Lettuce & Tomato, GFY, Asda*	1 Pack/171g	294	172	9.0	26.0	3.5	1.6
Bacon, Lettuce & Tomato, Ginsters*	1 Pack/192g	516	269	15.6	21.2	15.6	0.0
Bacon, Lettuce & Tomato, Healthy Eating, Tesco*	1 Pack/165g	221	134	10.3	19.8	1.5	2.0
Bacon, Lettuce & Tomato, Healthy Living, Tesco*	1 Pack/190g	287	151	10.1	24.5	1.4	1.6
Bacon, Lettuce & Tomato, Healthy Selection, Budgens*	1 Pack/183g	388	212	10.1	21.3	9.6	2.8
Bacon, Lettuce & Tomato, Marks & Spencer*	1 Serving/181g	534	295	10.3	22.4	18.2	1.9
Bacon, Lettuce & Tomato, New, Healthy Eating, Tesco*	1 Pack/188.0g	312	166	10.4	22.2	4.0	1.6
Bacon, Lettuce & Tomato, Platter, Marks & Spencer*	¼ Sandwich/49g	159	325	11.7	21.2	21.4	1.3
Bacon, Lettuce & Tomato, Safeway*	1 Pack/230g	529	230	15.9	35.4	2.3	3.9
Bacon, Lettuce & Tomato, Shapers, Boots*	1 Pack/171g	328	192	10.0	22.0	7.1	2.3
Bacon, Lettuce & Tomato, Starbucks*	1 Pack/190g	437	230	7.7	28.3	9.6	0.0
Bacon, Lettuce & Tomato, Sutherland*	1 Pack/216g	654	303	10.6	27.3	16.8	0.0
Bacon, Lettuce & Tomato, Taste!*	1 Pack/168.9g	353	209	8.5	22.4	9.5	0.0
Bacon, Lettuce & Tomato, Tesco*	1 Pack/203g	629	310	8.0	18.4	22.7	1.4
Bacon, Lettuce & Tomato, Waitrose*	1 Pack/210g	578	275	9.3	25.6	15.0	2.3
Bacon, Lettuce & Tomato, Weight Watchers*	1 Pack/171g	267	156	9.8	23.5	2.5	2.4
Bacon, Lettuce & Tomato, With Mayo, Safeway*	1 Pack/168g	462	275	10.4	20.7	16.7	2.3
Bacon, Lettuce, & Tomato, Deep Fill, Safeway*	1 Pack/202g	565	280	14.0	29.2	12.0	2.2
Bap, Ham Salad, Co-Op*	1 Bap/163.9g	295	180	8.0	30.0	3.0	2.0
Bap, Malted, Chargrilled Chicken, Co-Op*	1 Bap/201g	492	245	9.0	23.0	13.0	2.0
Bap, Malted, Tuna & Sweetcorn, Co-Op*	1 Bap/212g	530	250	9.0	24.0	13.0	2.0
Barm, White, Corned Beef & Onion, Open Choice Foods*	1 Roll/144g	331	230	12.7	30.7	6.1	0.0
Beef & Horseradish Mayonnaise, Shapers, Boots*	1 Pack/159.3g	266	167	12.0	25.0	2.1	2.6
Beef & Horseradish, Deep Filled, BGTY, Sainsbury's*	1 Pack/202g	313	155	11.4	22.0	2.4	2.4
Beef & Horseradish, Pret A Manger*	1 Av Pack/250g	382	153	11.2	17.7	4.4	2.5
Beef & Onion, American Style, The Big One, Sainsbury's*	1 Pack/386g	737	191	11.7	21.2	6.6	0.0
Beef & Onion, Co-Op*	1 Sandwich/221g	530	240	11.0	24.0	11.0	1.0
Beef & Pate, Marks & Spencer*	1 Pack/187.9g	310	165	11.2	21.6	3.9	2.4
Beef & Roast Onion, Healthy Living, Tesco*	1 Pack/185.3g	278	150	13.3	20.0	1.9	2.7
Beef Salad, Gibsons*	1 Pack/185g	348	188	10.6	23.5	5.7	0.0
Beef, Tomato & Horseradish, Asda*	1 Pack/168.9g	255	151	10.0	22.0	2.6	2.7
Big BLT, Pret A Manger*	1 Serving/200g	481	241	11.1	20.5	12.3	2.9
Black Pepper Chicken, Bloomer, Pret A Manger*	1 Av Pack/250g	642	257	13.0	29.5	9.7	1.8
Bloomer, Tuna Salad, Marks & Spencer*	1 Pack/230.8g	601	260	11.8	17.8	16.0	2.6
Breakfast, Mega Triple, Co-Op*	1 Pack/267g	750	281	11.6	25.5	15.0	3.4
Brie & Bacon, Asda*	1 Pack/181g	603	333	13.3	22.9	21.1	1.3
Brie & Bacon, Finest, Tesco*	1 Pack/201.1g	571	284	14.1	19.4	16.7	2.1
Brie & Grape, Finest, Tesco*	1 Pack/209g	527	252	8.5	20.6	15.1	1.5
Brie With Apple & Grapes, Sainsbury's*	1 Pack/220g	515	234	8.4	21.7	13.6	0.0
British Roast Chicken With Fresh Herb Salad, Asda*	1 Pack/213.9g	447	209	11.0	21.0	9.0	2.0
Brunch, Eat Smart, Safeway*	1 Pack/250g	363	145	9.4	21.6	1.9	2.9
Brunch, St Ivel*	1 Pack/225g	581	258	10.2	26.0	12.6	0.0
Chargrilled Chicken & Roasted Peppers, BHS*	1 Pack/183.2g	295	161	11.5	22.0	3.1	3.1
Chargrilled Chicken & Tomato Relish, Shapers, Boots*	1 Pack/190g	295	155	12.0	20.0	3.0	3.1
Chargrilled Chicken & Tomato Salsa, BGTY, Sainsbury's*	1 Pack/225g	218	97	1.5	15.9	1.8	2.9
Chargrilled Chicken & Watercress, BGTY, Sainsbury's*	1 Pack/172g	318	185	14.5	24.1	3.4	0.0
Chargrilled Chicken & Watercress, Marks & Spencer*	1 Pack/173g	285	165	12.8	23.9	1.7	2.1
Chargrilled Chicken Caesar, Big, Sainsbury's*	1 Pack/216g	657	304	12.2	25.3	17.1	0.0
Chargrilled Chicken Salad, Weight Watchers*	1 Pack/186g	296	159	9.9	20.4	4.2	1.9
Chargrilled Chicken With Honey Mustard Mayo, Spar*	1 Pack/168g	428	255	13.1	25.0	11.4	0.0
Chargrilled Chicken With Mango, TTD, Sainsbury's*	1 Pack/217g	352	162	11.0	22.2	3.2	0.0
Chargrilled Chicken With Salad, Debenhams*	1 Pack/250g	325	130	7.6	18.0	3.6	0.0
Chargrilled Chicken, Budgens*	1 Pack/192.8g	483	250	10.3	24.9	12.1	1.8

S

SANDWICH,	Measure INFO/WEIGHT	per Measure KCAL	Nutrition Values per 100g / 100ml				
			KCAL	PROT	CARB	FAT	FIBRE
Chargrilled Chicken, Ginsters*	1 Pack/209g	431	206	11.3	21.6	8.3	0.0
Chargrilled Chicken, No Mayo, Rustlers*	1 Pack/150g	228	152	16.0	20.1	0.8	0.0
Chargrilled Vegetable, Eat Smart, Safeway*	1 Pack/183g	265	145	7.4	23.4	2.3	2.8
Cheddar Cheese & Celery, Marks & Spencer*	1 Pack/200g	540	270	9.7	22.4	15.9	1.5
Cheddar Cheese & Celery, Somerfield*	1oz/28g	78	280	10.0	16.0	20.0	0.0
Cheddar Cheese Ploughman's, Deep Fill, Asda*	1 Pack/228.6g	472	206	9.0	20.0	10.0	4.3
Cheddar Cheese Ploughman's, Gibsons*	1 Sandwich/198g	467	237	9.8	23.7	11.5	0.0
Cheddar Cheese Ploughman's, Marks & Spencer*	1 Pack/185g	435	235	9.6	23.7	12.4	2.5
Cheddar Cheese Ploughman's, Platter, Marks & Spencer*	¼ Sandwich/49g	125	255	9.1	25.1	13.4	3.0
Cheese & Carrot, Somerfield*	1oz/28g	50	180	11.0	24.0	4.0	0.0
Cheese & Celery, Marks & Spencer*	1 Pack/180g	466	259	10.8	14.7	17.4	2.9
Cheese & Coleslaw, Asda*	1 Pack/262g	799	305	10.1	22.1	19.6	3.3
Cheese & Coleslaw, Eat Smart, Safeway*	1 Pack/169.0g	245	145	10.1	20.7	2.2	4.0
Cheese & Coleslaw, Safeway*	1 Pack/187g	501	268	8.4	22.9	17.1	0.5
Cheese & Coleslaw, Shapers, Boots*	1 Pack/224g	338	151	11.0	22.0	2.1	3.2
Cheese & Coleslaw, Sutherland*	1 Pack/185g	376	203	10.7	29.9	4.5	0.0
Cheese & Marmite, No Mayonnaise, Boots*	1 Pack/156g	420	269	12.2	26.3	12.8	1.7
Cheese & Onion With Mayo, Somerfield*	1oz/28g	111	395	12.0	17.0	31.0	0.0
Cheese & Onion, GFY, Asda*	1 Pack/156g	253	162	13.0	23.0	2.0	0.0
Cheese & Onion, Good Intentions, Somerfield*	1 Pack/171.9g	294	171	10.8	24.8	3.2	2.1
Cheese & Onion, Healthy Living, Tesco	1 Pack/168g	314	187	10.3	23.2	5.9	1.7
Cheese & Onion, Heinz*	1 Pack/197g	563	286	11.2	24.0	16.1	3.2
Cheese & Onion, Safeway*	1 Pack/183.9g	594	323	12.7	19.5	21.6	2.2
Cheese & Onion, Tesco*	1 Pack/178g	621	349	11.5	17.1	26.1	2.2
Cheese & Onion, Waitrose*	1 Pack/176g	579	329	12.5	20.2	22.0	2.8
Cheese & Pickle, BHS*	1 Pack/177.7g	504	283	12.5	29.6	12.7	1.8
Cheese & Pickle, Shapers, Boots*	1 Pack/165g	342	207	9.8	31.0	4.9	2.3
Cheese & Pickle, Virgin Trains*	1 Sandwich/158g	444	281	11.5	31.1	12.4	0.0
Cheese & Salad, COU, Marks & Spencer*	1 Pack/188g	244	130	12.1	17.0	1.6	2.4
Cheese & Spring Onion, Asda*	1 Pack/159.6g	578	361	13.0	21.0	25.0	1.9
Cheese & Spring Onion, Co-Op*	1 Pack/164g	607	370	12.0	21.0	26.0	3.0
Cheese & Spring Onion, Sutherland*	1oz/28g	104	371	12.0	21.4	26.4	0.0
Cheese & Tomato, Asda*	1 Pack/154g	388	252	11.0	23.2	12.8	3.7
Cheese & Tomato, Co-Op*	1 Pack/161g	394	245	10.0	23.0	12.0	2.0
Cheese & Tomato, Freshmans*	1 Pack/111g	248	223	11.0	8.0	16.8	0.0
Cheese & Tomato, Organic, Marks & Spencer*	1 Pack/165g	559	339	11.8	24.8	21.4	1.9
Cheese & Tomato, Spar*	1 Pack/124g	294	237	11.1	24.4	10.5	0.0
Cheese & Tomato, Tesco*	1 Pack/182g	582	320	9.2	22.6	21.4	1.1
Cheese Coleslaw, Marks & Spencer*	1 Pack/186g	498	268	10.2	17.6	17.4	3.2
Cheese Ploughman's, BGTY, Sainsbury's*	1 Pack/216.7g	365	168	9.7	24.5	3.5	0.0
Cheese Ploughman's, Boots*	1 Pack/260g	640	246	7.8	20.0	15.0	1.9
Cheese Ploughman's, Deep Fill, Sutherland*	1 Pack/219.6g	528	240	10.1	22.6	12.1	0.0
Cheese Ploughman's, Deep Filled, Safeway*	1 Pack/231.4g	589	255	11.4	20.7	14.1	2.8
Cheese Ploughman's, Healthy Living, Tesco*	1 Pack/186g	279	150	11.2	22.3	1.8	0.9
Cheese Ploughman's, Marks & Spencer*	1 Pack/192.3g	499	260	9.1	25.1	13.4	3.0
Cheese Salad, Bugdens*	1 Pack/168.9g	250	148	10.9	21.9	1.8	1.6
Cheese Salad, Shapers, Boots*	1 Pack/205g	308	150	9.7	22.0	2.5	2.2
Cheese Tomato Spring Onion, Shapers, Boots*	1 Pack/179g	344	192	11.0	22.0	6.7	3.3
Cheese, Apple & Grape, COU, Marks & Spencer*	1 Pack/186.2g	270	145	8.5	24.9	1.2	2.0
Cheese, Asda*	1 Pack/262g	618	236	12.2	20.3	12.0	3.0
Cheese, Ham & Pickle, Tesco*	1 Serving/215g	497	231	11.7	20.3	11.5	1.8
Cheese, Ham, BLT, Triple Pack, Asda*	1 Pack/260g	614	236	12.2	20.3	12.0	3.0
Cheese, Pickle & Tomato, Somerfield*	1 Pack/166.5g	317	191	12.5	25.6	4.3	3.5

	Measure INFO/WEIGHT	per Measure KCAL	Nutrition Values per 100g / 100ml				
			KCAL	PROT	CARB	FAT	FIBRE
Cheese, Salad & Mayonnaise, Reduced Fat, Waitrose*	1 Pack/180g	301	167	9.8	20.8	5.0	3.1
Cheese, Tomato & Apple Chutney, Half Fat, Starbucks*	1 Pack/200g	318	159	8.8	21.3	4.2	0.0
Cheese, Tomato & Spring Onion, Shapers, Boots*	1 Pack/178.2g	319	179	12.0	24.0	3.9	1.5
Chicken & Avocado, Pret A Manger*	1 Av Pack/250g	523	209	8.4	15.9	12.4	3.4
Chicken & Bacon, BGTY, Sainsbury's*	1 Pack/211.4g	314	149	11.7	20.8	2.3	0.0
Chicken & Bacon, COU, Marks & Spencer*	1 Pack/181g	244	135	12.2	17.1	2.2	3.8
Chicken & Bacon, Club, Starbucks	1 Pack/252g	590	234	11.5	12.8	15.3	0.0
Chicken & Bacon, Deep Filled, Co-Op*	1 Pack/166g	556	335	16.0	23.0	20.0	3.0
Chicken & Bacon, Deep Filled, Eat Street, Safeway*	1 Pack/206.5g	476	230	14.6	23.6	8.5	1.9
Chicken & Bacon, Deep Filled, Ginsters*	1 Pack/200g	540	270	13.1	18.3	16.1	0.0
Chicken & Bacon, Good Intentions, Somerfield*	1 Pack/168g	282	168	10.7	24.9	2.9	2.3
Chicken & Bacon, Healthy Eating, Tesco*	1 Pack/155g	240	155	10.4	24.6	1.7	1.7
Chicken & Bacon, Marks & Spencer*	1 Pack/173g	450	260	14.1	23.8	12.1	3.4
Chicken & Bacon, Mattessons*	1 Pack/190g	604	318	13.3	26.0	17.9	1.1
Chicken & Bacon, Sainsbury's*	1 Pack/214.9g	548	255	12.7	21.0	13.0	13.0
Chicken & Bacon, Shapers, Boots*	1 Pack/179g	317	177	14.0	19.0	5.0	3.1
Chicken & Bacon, Sub, Compass Foods*	1 Pack/165g	450	273	12.2	28.7	12.2	0.0
Chicken & Bacon, Sutherland*	1 Pack/170.9g	535	313	15.3	21.4	18.4	0.0
Chicken & Bacon, Tesco*	1 Pack/195g	538	276	11.2	18.7	17.4	1.3
Chicken & Basil, Safeway*	1 Pack/179g	303	169	12.3	20.7	4.9	1.7
Chicken & Mayo, The Sandwich Company*	1 Pack/72g	251	348	17.8	35.9	14.8	0.0
Chicken & Pepperonata, COU, Marks & Spencer*	1 Pack/171.4g	239	140	10.4	20.9	1.7	1.3
Chicken & Pesto, Shapers, Boots*	1 Pack/181g	311	172	12.0	26.0	2.3	1.7
Chicken & Roast Ham, Tesco*	1 Pack/228g	561	246	13.3	16.6	14.0	1.2
Chicken & Roast Tomatoes, COU, Marks & Spencer*	1 Pack/195g	273	140	12.0	21.7	2.1	4.2
Chicken & Salad, COU, Cafe, Marks & Spencer*	1 Pack/193g	261	135	9.8	19.0	1.9	1.6
Chicken & Salad, Low Fat, Waitrose*	1 Pack/188g	291	155	10.4	18.6	4.3	2.1
Chicken & Salad, Marks & Spencer*	1 Pack/200g	408	204	9.2	17.6	10.8	1.5
Chicken & Stuffing, Co-Op*	1 Pack/201g	503	250	12.0	22.0	13.0	7.0
Chicken & Stuffing, Marks & Spencer*	1 Pack/166g	412	248	12.2	20.1	13.2	2.9
Chicken & Stuffing, Shapers, Boots*	1 Serving/184.7g	327	177	13.0	25.0	2.8	2.2
Chicken & Stuffing, Sutherland*	1 Pack/201.2g	505	251	11.9	22.1	12.8	3.0
Chicken & Stuffing, Tesco*	1 Pack/323g	1043	323	10.4	29.4	18.2	1.0
Chicken & Stuffing, Waitrose*	1 Pack/183g	450	246	12.8	25.6	10.3	1.5
Chicken & Sweetcorn, Marks & Spencer*	1 Pack/186g	394	212	10.9	19.8	10.0	2.0
Chicken & Sweetcorn, Shapers, Boots*	1 Pack/180g	324	180	12.0	25.0	3.5	2.0
Chicken & Sweetcorn, Somerfield*	1oz/28g	71	252	10.0	28.0	11.0	0.0
Chicken & Sweetcorn, Tesco*	1 Pack/194g	433	223	9.4	22.1	10.8	1.7
Chicken & Watercress, BGTY, Sainsbury's*	1 Pack/170g	284	167	14.2	22.9	2.1	2.0
Chicken & Watercress, COU, Marks & Spencer*	1 Pack/164g	266	162	12.8	23.9	1.7	2.1
Chicken & Watercress, Healthy Eating, Tesco*	1 Pack/160g	253	158	13.8	21.7	1.8	1.7
Chicken BLT, Taste!*	1 Pack/238.5g	459	192	10.3	19.0	8.3	0.0
Chicken Breast, BGTY, Sainsbury's*	1 Pack/165g	251	152	12.2	24.7	0.5	0.0
Chicken Breast, Bacon & Lettuce, Tesco*	1 Pack/195g	515	264	15.4	16.0	15.4	1.6
Chicken Caesar & Bacon, Club, TTD, Sainsbury's*	1 Pack/246.6g	662	268	14.0	21.2	14.1	0.0
Chicken Caesar Salad, Sainsbury's*	1 Pack/186g	299	161	11.2	20.4	3.8	0.0
Chicken Caesar Salad, Somerfield*	1oz/28g	71	255	15.0	20.0	13.0	0.0
Chicken Caesar Style Salad, GFY, Asda*	1 Pack/163g	289	177	11.0	27.0	2.8	2.1
Chicken Caesar, Boots*	1 Pack/226.0g	531	235	9.8	22.0	12.0	1.7
Chicken Caesar, COU, Marks & Spencer*	1 Pack/181g	244	135	12.2	19.9	2.4	4.3
Chicken Caesar, Finest, Tesco*	1 Pack/199g	454	228	15.4	19.2	10.0	1.4
Chicken Caesar, No Bread, Pret A Manger*	1 Pack/233g	195	84	10.1	2.0	3.9	0.6
Chicken Caesar, Pret A Manger*	1 Serving/400g	481	120	5.6	10.2	6.1	1.4

	Measure INFO/WEIGHT	per Measure KCAL	Nutrition Values per 100g / 100ml				
			KCAL	PROT	CARB	FAT	FIBRE
SANDWICH,							
Chicken Caesar, The Best, Safeway*	1 Pack/198g	505	255	14.3	20.8	12.3	2.6
Chicken Club, Burger King*	1 Pack/242g	620	256	12.3	22.3	13.2	1.6
Chicken Cordon Bleu, Somerfield*	1oz/28g	78	279	14.0	19.0	17.0	0.0
Chicken Coriander, Taste!*	1 Serving/159.4g	227	143	5.6	23.3	2.9	0.0
Chicken Harvester, Taste!*	1 Pack/200g	295	148	7.7	20.3	4.0	0.0
Chicken Jalfrezi Naan, Ready To Go, Marks & Spencer*	1 Pack/288g	576	200	9.8	26.3	6.3	2.9
Chicken Kashmir, French Cuisiniers*	1 Pack/145g	204	141	12.9	20.3	1.6	2.9
Chicken Mayonnaise, Country Harvest*	1 Pack/120.2g	268	223	13.1	27.6	7.5	0.0
Chicken No Mayo, Marks & Spencer*	1 Pack/142g	220	155	15.0	17.5	3.0	3.1
Chicken Pesto With Rocket, Woolworths*	1 Pack/195g	326	167	5.0	16.9	8.8	0.0
Chicken Salad & Mayonnaise, Woolworths*	1 Serving/183g	337	184	11.3	19.3	6.8	0.0
Chicken Salad On Malted Bread With Mayo, Safeway*	1 Pack/195g	392	201	10.9	18.7	9.2	2.1
Chicken Salad Wedge, Tesco*	1 Pack/220g	458	208	9.4	18.2	10.8	1.2
Chicken Salad With Mayo. BGTY, Sainsbury's*	1 Serving/200g	314	157	12.0	21.9	2.4	0.0
Chicken Salad, BGTY, Sainsbury's*	1 Pack/197g	278	141	10.3	18.6	3.0	0.0
Chicken Salad, Baxter & Platts*	1 Pack/165g	254	154	11.4	17.8	4.2	2.8
Chicken Salad, Bernard Matthews*	1 Pack/162g	269	166	7.0	22.7	5.2	0.0
Chicken Salad, Big Fill, Somerfield*	1 Pack/247.8g	513	207	11.5	20.4	8.8	2.0
Chicken Salad, Big, Marks & Spencer*	1 Pack/283g	509	180	9.8	19.4	7.3	1.5
Chicken Salad, COU, Marks & Spencer*	1 Pack/194g	256	132	9.8	19.0	1.9	1.6
Chicken Salad, Co-Op*	1 Pack/195g	429	220	10.0	20.0	11.0	3.0
Chicken Salad, Deep Filled, Asda*	1 Pack/247g	551	223	18.1	22.2	7.4	1.3
Chicken Salad, Deep Filled, Co-Op*	1 Pack/213g	437	205	10.0	20.0	9.0	1.0
Chicken Salad, Deep Filled, Safeway*	1 Pack/211.9g	445	210	11.0	21.1	8.8	3.7
Chicken Salad, Deepfill, Woolworths*	1 Pack/180g	284	158	9.6	22.4	3.4	0.0
Chicken Salad, EAT*	1 Pack/250g	436	174	9.3	19.3	6.6	2.1
Chicken Salad, Eat Smart, Safeway*	1 Pack/183g	265	145	13.7	17.1	2.3	0.8
Chicken Salad, Eat Street, Safeway*	1 Pack/200g	330	165	10.3	22.2	3.4	1.8
Chicken Salad, Food To Go, Marks & Spencer*	1oz/28g	48	172	9.0	19.5	7.0	0.0
Chicken Salad, GFY, Asda*	1 Pack/194g	239	123	11.0	19.0	0.9	2.8
Chicken Salad, Ginsters*	1 Pack/186.5g	316	170	11.4	22.7	3.7	0.0
Chicken Salad, Good Intentions, Somerfield*	1 Pack/186g	294	158	10.4	23.5	2.5	1.5
Chicken Salad, Healthy Choice, Safeway*	1 Pack/185g	287	155	10.7	20.5	3.4	1.9
Chicken Salad, Healthy Living, Co-Op*	1 Pack/180g	297	165	10.0	23.0	4.0	3.0
Chicken Salad, Healthy Living, Tesco*	1 Pack/195g	257	132	10.7	16.8	2.5	4.0
Chicken Salad, Heinz*	1 Pack/165.5g	246	148	11.8	22.3	1.3	5.3
Chicken Salad, Homestyle, Somerfield*	1oz/28g	56	201	13.0	20.0	7.0	0.0
Chicken Salad, Low Fat, Healthy, Spar*	1 Pack/191g	300	157	7.9	21.2	4.5	0.0
Chicken Salad, Mattessons*	1 Pack/193g	313	162	11.2	18.8	4.7	2.8
Chicken Salad, Millers*	1 Pack/200g	310	155	11.3	16.3	4.9	0.0
Chicken Salad, Montagu's*	1 Pack/162g	275	170	10.5	20.9	5.3	0.0
Chicken Salad, Prawn Mayo, Egg & Bacon, Waitrose*	1 Pack/246g	608	247	9.8	17.8	15.2	2.4
Chicken Salad, Scottish Slimmers*	1 Pack/168.7g	275	163	9.5	22.8	3.8	1.8
Chicken Salad, Shell*	1 Pack/201.0g	404	201	8.7	19.4	9.8	0.0
Chicken Salad, Somerfield*	1oz/28g	48	171	10.0	24.0	4.0	0.0
Chicken Salad, Superdrug*	1 Pack/181g	257	142	10.1	18.7	2.6	68.6
Chicken Salad, Sutherland*	1 Pack/181g	302	167	10.3	23.1	3.7	0.0
Chicken Salad, Waitrose*	1 Pack/208g	406	195	10.3	17.1	9.5	2.5
Chicken Salad, Wild Bean Cafe*	1 Pack/210g	273	130	12.4	18.9	0.5	2.8
Chicken Tandoori, Waitrose*	1 Pack/181g	302	167	11.6	23.0	3.1	4.1
Chicken Teriyaki, Subway*	6" Sub/269g	370	138	9.7	21.9	1.9	1.5
Chicken Tikka & Salad Pack, COU, Marks & Spencer*	1 Pack/253g	215	85	9.7	9.6	1.0	3.2
Chicken Tikka & Yoghurt, Taste!*	1 Pack/215.3g	436	203	8.2	20.4	9.8	0.0

SANDWICH,	Measure INFO/WEIGHT	per Measure KCAL	Nutrition Values per 100g / 100ml				
			KCAL	PROT	CARB	FAT	FIBRE
Chicken Tikka Masala, GO Foods Wonderfill*	1 Pack/136g	343	252	11.4	23.5	12.8	0.0
Chicken Tikka Naan, Ready To Go, Marks & Spencer*	1 Pack/298g	641	215	9.9	26.5	7.8	4.0
Chicken Tikka, Asda*	1 Pack/186g	316	170	11.0	21.0	4.7	1.5
Chicken Tikka, COU, Marks & Spencer*	1 Pack/185g	268	145	12.1	20.5	1.8	3.2
Chicken Tikka, Eat Smart, Safeway*	1 Pack/159g	240	151	11.8	21.6	1.9	2.5
Chicken Tikka, Garlic & Herb Bread Pocket, Somerfield*	1 Pack/168g	341	203	11.0	30.0	4.3	2.0
Chicken Tikka, Healthy Eating, Tesco*	1 Pack/159g	270	170	14.5	21.9	2.7	1.8
Chicken Tikka, Improved Recipe, COU, Marks & Spencer*	1 Pack/186g	270	145	12.1	20.5	1.8	3.2
Chicken Tikka, Marks & Spencer*	1 Pack/180g	391	217	10.4	19.5	10.9	2.0
Chicken Tikka, On Pepper Chilli Bread, Shapers, Boots*	1 Pack/172.1g	296	172	13.0	25.0	2.6	2.5
Chicken Tikka, Open, COU, Marks & Spencer*	1 Pack/190g	260	137	9.6	21.8	1.2	2.2
Chicken Tikka, Sayers*	1 Pack/203g	315	155	10.8	19.8	3.7	2.8
Chicken Tikka, Taste!*	1 Pack/195.7g	368	188	11.7	21.7	6.0	0.0
Chicken Tikka, Thai Style, Korma, Big, Sainsbury's*	1 Pack/268g	581	217	11.9	20.5	9.7	0.0
Chicken Tikka, Weight Watchers*	1 Pack/158g	289	183	12.8	23.4	4.3	1.6
Chicken, Bacon & Sweet Chilli, Feel Good, Shell*	1 Pack/173.5g	365	211	14.1	29.2	5.0	0.0
Chicken, Bacon & Tomato, BGTY, Sainsbury's*	1 Pack/190g	270	142	11.4	19.0	2.3	0.0
Chicken, Basil & Sunblush Tomato, Harry Mason*	1 Pack/163.9g	272	166	13.0	21.8	3.2	0.6
Chicken, Breast, Millers*	1 Pack/162g	343	212	13.8	19.3	8.9	0.0
Chicken, Burger King*	1 Pack/224g	659	294	11.2	23.6	17.4	1.3
Chicken, Eat Smart, Safeway*	1 Pack/141g	240	170	14.9	22.2	2.0	0.6
Chicken, Flame Grilled, Rustlers*	1 Pack/150g	347	231	16.3	20.1	9.5	0.0
Chicken, Healthier Choice, Ginsters*	1 Pack/183g	247	135	10.2	20.5	1.4	0.0
Chicken, Healthy, BHS*	1 Pack/250g	840	336	21.9	41.4	9.2	6.0
Chicken, Honey & Mustard, BGTY, Sainsbury's*	1 Pack/171g	296	173	13.1	24.0	2.7	0.0
Chicken, Honey & Mustard, Safeway*	1 Pack/167g	399	239	12.7	23.6	10.4	2.5
Chicken, Lightly Spiced, Starbucks*	1 Pack/200g	286	143	11.2	18.2	2.4	0.0
Chicken, Lime & Coriander, BP*	1 Pack/154.5g	291	189	12.5	25.2	4.2	0.0
Chicken, Low Fat, BHS*	1 Pack/200g	336	168	11.0	20.7	4.6	3.0
Chicken, No Mayo, Cafe Revive, Marks & Spencer*	1 Pack/153g	230	150	14.1	17.9	2.4	3.1
Chicken, No Mayo, Daily Bread*	1 Pack/160.3g	278	174	8.6	23.8	4.4	0.0
Chicken, No Mayonnaise, Waitrose*	1 Pack/173g	332	192	11.6	24.0	5.5	2.1
Chicken, Prawn & Egg, Triple Pack, Ginsters*	1 Pack/300g	2010	670	27.3	56.7	37.1	0.0
Chicken, Prawn Mayo, Mixed, Shapers, Boots*	1 Pack/220g	416	189	12.0	20.0	6.8	2.8
Chicken, Rustlers*	1 Pack/150g	347	231	16.3	20.1	9.5	0.0
Chicken, Safeway*	1 Serving/200g	350	175	10.7	20.6	5.6	2.5
Chicken, Shell*	1 Pack/121g	334	276	13.9	25.9	13.0	0.0
Chicken, Sutherland*	1 Pack/220g	465	211	10.4	22.9	8.7	0.0
Chicken, Triple, GFY, Asda*	1 Pack/230g	453	197	13.0	25.0	5.0	1.6
Chicken, Triple, Shapers, Boots*	1 Serving/228g	440	193	13.0	23.0	5.4	2.3
Chicken, Woolworths*	1 Pack/120g	331	276	13.9	25.9	13.0	0.0
Chilli Chicken, Fresh, Taste!*	1 Pack/154.5g	223	145	5.6	23.4	3.2	0.0
Chilli Chicken, Woolworths*	1 Pack/155g	225	145	5.6	23.4	3.2	0.0
Chinese Chicken, Esso*	1 Pack/177.8g	409	230	13.0	22.8	9.0	4.0
Chinese Chicken, Low Calorie, Tesco*	1 Pack/169g	270	160	11.8	22.6	2.5	2.0
Chinese Chicken, Malted Brown Bread, Waitrose*	1 Pack/164g	333	203	13.5	21.9	6.8	3.3
Chinese Chicken, Treat Yourself, Shell*	1 Pack/178g	409	230	13.0	22.8	9.6	0.0
Christmas Cheddar, Pret A Manger*	1 Av Pack/270g	671	249	8.8	18.3	15.5	2.0
Christmas Lunch 2003, Pret A Manger*	1 Av Pack/270g	599	222	11.3	19.0	11.2	2.3
Christmas Special, Ginsters*	1 Pack/220g	583	265	9.5	23.2	15.6	0.0
Christmas, BGTY, Sainsbury's*	1 Pack/186.4g	370	199	14.6	27.3	3.5	0.0
Christmas, Shell*	1 Pack/182.7g	414	226	11.1	25.5	8.2	2.1
Christmas, Weight Watchers*	1 Pack/173.1g	296	171	12.2	28.8	2.8	2.1

	Measure INFO/WEIGHT	per Measure KCAL	Nutrition Values per 100g / 100ml				
			KCAL	PROT	CARB	FAT	FIBRE
SANDWICH,							
Ciabatta, Chicken & Herb, Shapers, Boots*	1 Pack/168g	290	173	11.9	25.0	2.8	1.7
Ciabatta, Ham & Cheese, Asda*	¼ Bread/74g	231	312	11.6	38.9	12.2	1.2
Ciabatta, Italian Ham With Plum Tomato & Rocket, Costa*	1 Serving/50g	115	231	23.1	24.9	4.4	0.0
Classic, Triple Pack, Somerfield*	1 Serving/250g	653	261	10.2	22.1	14.6	2.5
Club, Pret A Manger*	1 Av Pack/250g	542	217	12.8	18.7	10.1	2.3
Coriander Chicken, On Rye, Pret A Manger*	1 Sandwich/200g	500	250	10.8	22.1	13.9	2.0
Corned Beef With Onion & Tomato, The Salad Garden*	1 Pack/137g	338	247	14.2	23.0	10.8	0.0
Coronation Chicken & Mild Curry Mayo, Somerfield*	1oz/28g	82	294	10.0	24.0	18.0	0.0
Coronation Chicken, Marks & Spencer*	1 Pack/210g	420	200	11.2	20.2	9.7	3.1
Coronation Chicken, Pret A Manger*	1 Av Pack/250g	415	166	7.9	21.2	5.4	0.2
Coronation Chicken, Woolworths*	1 Serving/159g	396	249	9.1	26.5	11.8	0.0
Cottage Cheese & Tomato, Shapers, Boots*	1 Pack/150g	219	146	7.8	18.0	4.8	2.4
Crab Marie Rose, Brown Bread, Royal London Hospital*	1 Pack/158g	293	185	9.7	22.0	7.1	0.0
Crayfish & Lemon Mayonnaise, Daily Bread*	1 Pack/173.0g	391	226	9.5	31.0	6.6	0.0
Crayfish & Rocket, EAT*	1 Sandwich/200g	519	260	11.3	21.9	14.1	2.6
Crayfish & Rocket, Pret A Manger	1 Av Pack/250g	435	174	9.4	16.7	7.8	1.5
Crayfish & Rocket, Shapers, Boots*	1 Pack/172.2g	291	169	11.0	26.0	2.2	2.5
Crayfish & Rocket, So Good, Somerfield*	1 Pack/205.5g	486	237	9.5	25.8	10.6	1.0
Cream Cheese & Cucumber, Gourmet Express*	1 Pack/104g	267	257	8.9	39.5	7.0	0.0
Cream Cheese & Peppers, Taste!*	1 Pack/154.2g	296	192	7.3	25.5	6.8	0.0
Cream Cheese Salad, The Sandwich Box*	1 Pack/138g	250	181	5.6	26.3	5.8	0.0
Cream Cheese, Red Pepper & Spinach, Daily Bread*	1 Pack/156g	273	175	7.4	24.0	5.2	0.0
Creole Chicken & Italian Leaves, Northern Bites*	1 Pack/189.8g	298	157	13.1	22.1	2.4	2.4
Danish Ham Salad, COU, Marks & Spencer*	1 Pack/138g	181	131	9.3	17.4	2.7	1.9
Danish Ham Salad, Lean, COU, Marks & Spencer*	1 Pack/192g	250	130	10.6	19.5	0.9	1.4
Edam Cheese, Oldfields*	1 Pack/175g	326	186	9.8	23.9	5.7	0.0
Egg & Bacon, Bacon & Tomato, Sausage & Egg, Tesco*	1 Pack/256g	778	304	9.7	19.4	20.8	1.2
Egg & Bacon, Boots*	1 Pack/179g	480	268	12.0	19.0	16.0	1.4
Egg & Bacon, Burger King*	1 Pack/139g	296	213	11.1	21.7	9.1	1.9
Egg & Bacon, Co-Op*	1 Pack/188g	536	285	13.0	20.0	17.0	2.0
Egg & Bacon, Deep Fill, Ginsters*	1 Pack/210g	590	281	11.5	18.8	18.2	0.0
Egg & Bacon, Deep Fill, Spar*	1 Pack/191g	579	303	12.2	18.7	19.9	0.0
Egg & Bacon, Felix Van Den Berghe*	1 Pack/137.9g	382	277	8.9	22.2	17.0	0.0
Egg & Bacon, Ginsters*	1 Pack/210g	523	249	13.2	22.0	11.6	0.0
Egg & Bacon, Marks & Spencer*	1 Pack/215g	525	244	13.4	15.8	14.2	2.1
Egg & Bacon, Scottish Slimmers, Tesco*	1 Pack/139g	279	201	13.6	26.3	4.6	1.2
Egg & Bacon, Shell*	1 Pack/191g	579	303	12.2	18.7	19.9	0.0
Egg & Bacon, Taste!*	1 Pack/186.8g	496	265	12.8	19.1	15.3	0.0
Egg & Bacon, Tesco*	1 Pack/179g	530	298	10.6	20.2	19.4	1.3
Egg & Cress, BGTY, Sainsbury's*	1 Pack/166g	281	169	9.7	23.1	4.2	3.8
Egg & Cress, COU, Marks & Spencer*	1 Pack/192g	240	125	9.8	15.5	2.7	2.8
Egg & Cress, Co-Op*	1 Pack/159g	398	250	9.0	21.0	15.0	2.0
Egg & Cress, EAT*	1 Pack/200g	530	265	11.0	23.2	14.3	2.9
Egg & Cress, Free Range, Eat Smart, Safeway*	1 Sandwich/300g	235	78	5.2	11.3	1.3	1.9
Egg & Cress, Free Range, Marks & Spencer*	1 Pack/192g	374	195	9.7	16.7	10.1	1.5
Egg & Cress, Free Range, Safeway*	1 Pack/190.4g	473	249	9.4	19.5	14.9	2.1
Egg & Cress, Free Range, Tesco*	1 Pack/195g	402	206	10.4	12.9	12.5	3.0
Egg & Cress, Heinz*	1 Pack/162g	241	149	9.6	22.7	2.2	5.4
Egg & Cress, Marks & Spencer*	1 Pack/182g	331	182	10.1	13.6	9.7	3.2
Egg & Cress, On Whole Grain Bread, Cafe Life*	1 Pack/154.7g	250	162	6.2	15.4	8.3	1.2
Egg & Cress, Organic, Marks & Spencer*	1 Pack/185g	444	240	9.6	18.0	14.2	3.6
Egg & Cress, Reduced Fat, Waitrose*	1 Pack/162g	262	162	9.7	16.5	6.4	6.4
Egg & Cress, Sainsbury's*	1 Pack/170g	357	210	9.2	22.1	9.5	0.0

SANDWICH,

	Measure INFO/WEIGHT	per Measure KCAL	Nutrition Values per 100g / 100ml				
			KCAL	PROT	CARB	FAT	FIBRE
Egg & Cress, Tesco*	1 Pack/174g	445	256	10.0	20.3	15.0	1.7
Egg & Tomato, Deep Fill, Spar*	1 Serving/183.2g	348	190	8.2	22.8	7.4	0.0
Egg & Tomato, On Rye, Pret A Manger*	1 Pack/350g	476	136	6.3	13.1	6.5	1.6
Egg & Tomato, On Softgrain Bread, Daily Bread*	1 Pack/160.3g	278	174	8.6	23.8	4.4	0.0
Egg & Tomato, Organic, Waitrose*	1 Pack/192g	359	187	9.7	15.3	9.7	4.0
Egg & Tomato, Tesco*	1 Pack/172g	341	198	8.8	22.0	8.3	1.9
Egg & Tomato, With Salad Cream, Big, Sainsbury's*	1 Pack/266g	463	174	9.1	21.3	5.8	0.0
Egg & Watercress, Free Range, Marks & Spencer*	1 Pack/191.9g	355	185	9.2	18.1	8.2	2.9
Egg Florentine, No Bread, Pret A Manger*	1 Pack/232g	263	113	5.7	4.9	7.9	0.7
Egg Mayo, On Malted Wheatgrain, Taste!*	1 Serving/169g	394	233	10.6	20.0	12.3	0.0
Egg Mayonnaise & Cress, BHS*	1 Serving/187.8g	462	246	10.0	24.7	12.7	1.9
Egg Mayonnaise & Cress, Co-Op*	1 Pack/159g	405	255	8.8	20.8	15.1	1.9
Egg Mayonnaise & Cress, Go Simple, Asda*	1 Pack/169g	370	219	10.0	20.0	11.0	1.7
Egg Mayonnaise & Cress, Millers*	1 Pack/166g	369	222	9.4	18.8	12.2	0.0
Egg Mayonnaise & Cress, Shapers, Boots*	1 Pack/161g	304	189	9.4	24.0	6.1	0.0
Egg Mayonnaise & Cress, Somerfield*	1oz/28g	71	252	10.0	18.0	16.0	0.0
Egg Mayonnaise & Cress, Starbucks*	1 Pack/202g	450	223	9.5	18.5	12.3	0.0
Egg Mayonnaise & Cress, Wheatgerm Bread, Asda*	1 Pack/158g	371	235	9.7	21.3	12.4	1.9
Egg Mayonnaise & Cress, Wheatgerm, Tesco*	1 Pack/146g	368	252	9.8	18.4	15.5	1.3
Egg Mayonnaise & Cress, Wholemeal Bread, Oldfields*	1 Pack/128g	301	235	9.7	24.0	11.2	3.6
Egg Mayonnaise & Salad, Superdrug*	1 Pack/169g	286	169	7.6	18.3	7.3	2.4
Egg Mayonnaise With Cress, Reduced Fat, Waitrose*	1 Pack/162g	300	185	10.4	18.1	7.9	3.4
Egg Mayonnaise, Boots*	1 Pack/183.6g	449	244	9.7	22.0	13.0	2.3
Egg Mayonnaise, Good Intentions, Somerfield*	1 Pack/150.3g	263	175	10.8	23.7	4.1	3.0
Egg Mayonnaise, Healthy Living, Tesco*	1 Pack/162.2g	253	156	9.3	21.4	3.7	2.8
Egg Mayonnaise, On Hi Bran Bread, Ginsters*	1 Pack/143g	343	240	10.7	17.6	15.2	0.0
Egg Mayonnaise, Pret A Manger*	1 Av Pack/250g	394	158	6.5	15.1	7.9	1.5
Egg Mayonnaise, Shell*	1 Pack/189g	522	276	9.8	24.7	15.4	0.0
Egg Mayonnaise, Snack & Shop, Esso*	1 Pack/240g	624	260	9.4	25.5	13.4	0.0
Egg Mayonnaise, Waitrose*	1 Pack/180g	396	220	10.1	19.1	11.4	3.4
Egg Salad With Mayonnaise Wholemeal, Waitrose*	1 Pack/180g	257	143	8.3	16.5	4.9	3.6
Egg Salad, Co-Op*	1 Pack/190g	285	150	7.0	22.0	4.0	4.0
Egg Salad, Deep Filled, Asda*	1 Pack/231g	404	175	7.3	18.5	7.9	1.3
Egg Salad, Free Range, Good Intentions, Somerfield*	1 Pack/173g	260	150	7.2	21.6	3.9	2.9
Egg Salad, Free Range, Sainsbury's*	1 Pack/224.5g	450	200	8.5	24.5	7.5	0.0
Egg Salad, Free Range, Waitrose*	1 Pack/180g	257	143	8.3	16.5	4.9	3.6
Egg Salad, GFY, Asda*	1 Pack/156.8g	229	146	8.0	22.0	2.9	2.9
Egg Salad, Healthy Eating, Tesco*	1 Pack/169g	279	165	7.6	22.5	4.9	2.0
Egg Salad, Healthy Living, Tesco*	1 Pack/182g	264	145	7.2	18.6	4.2	1.8
Egg Salad, Malted Brown Bread, Healthy Eating, Tesco*	1 Pack/182g	264	145	7.2	19.6	4.2	1.8
Egg Salad, Shapers, Boots*	1 Pack/184g	304	165	6.9	24.0	4.6	1.1
Egg Salad, Weight Watchers*	1 Pack/171.6g	255	148	7.5	22.8	3.0	1.4
Egg, Co-Op*	1 Pack/190g	285	150	6.8	22.1	3.7	3.7
Egg, Delilite*	1 Pack/179.7g	337	187	8.0	22.0	7.2	3.0
Eggstatic, Cranks*	1oz/28g	72	257	8.7	20.9	9.1	2.3
Gammon & Egg, Safeway*	1 Pack/233.3g	489	210	12.9	20.4	8.0	0.0
Goat's Cheese & Cranberry, Shapers, Boots*	1 Pack/149.7g	293	195	8.6	31.0	4.1	3.3
Gourmet Prawn, Pret A Manger*	1 Av Pack/250g	454	182	7.8	15.2	10.2	1.8
Ham & Cheddar, Marks & Spencer*	1 Pack/165g	396	240	15.1	20.0	11.3	1.7
Ham & Cheddar, Platter, Marks & Spencer*	¼ Sandwich/42g	101	240	15.1	20.0	11.3	1.7
Ham & Cheese Toasted, Coffee Republic*	1 Pack/160g	429	268	15.7	24.4	12.7	0.0
Ham & Cheese, Baxter & Platts*	1 Pack/168g	408	243	11.3	20.5	13.0	1.7
Ham & Cheese, Eat Smart, Safeway*	1 Pack/170g	230	135	11.3	19.3	1.3	3.2

S

	Measure INFO/WEIGHT	per Measure KCAL	Nutrition Values per 100g / 100ml				
			KCAL	PROT	CARB	FAT	FIBRE
Ham & Chicken, Healthy Living, Co-Op*	1 Pack/150g	285	190	12.0	28.0	4.0	3.0
Ham & Cream Cheese, Tesco*	1 Pack/212g	655	309	11.0	27.2	17.3	1.2
Ham & Dijon Mustard, Healthy Selection, Budgens*	1 Pack/120g	190	158	9.7	21.9	2.5	2.0
Ham & Egg, Asda*	1 Pack/262g	590	225	10.4	16.8	12.8	2.1
Ham & Mustard Salad, EAT*	1 Pack/85g	363	427	26.8	54.9	11.2	6.1
Ham & Mustard, Eat Smart, Safeway*	1 Pack/139g	250	180	13.7	26.3	2.2	2.0
Ham & Mustard, Eat Street, Safeway*	1 Pack/150g	285	190	12.3	25.2	4.2	1.0
Ham & Mustard, Tesco*	1 Pack/147g	437	297	10.6	20.8	19.0	1.2
Ham & Salad, British, COU, Marks & Spencer*	1 Pack/183g	265	145	10.5	19.9	2.6	1.8
Ham & Salad, Fullfillers*	1 Pack/180g	290	161	7.3	22.9	4.4	0.0
Ham & Swiss Cheese, BIG, Sainsbury's*	1 Pack/218g	652	299	11.6	25.4	16.7	0.5
Ham & Swiss Cheese, Marks & Spencer*	1 Pack/159g	393	247	14.7	18.9	12.6	3.3
Ham & Swiss Cheese, Safeway*	1 Pack/201.1g	533	265	14.5	19.7	14.3	1.5
Ham & Tomato, GFY, Asda*	1 Pack/173g	254	147	10.0	23.0	1.7	1.4
Ham & Turkey Salad, Co-Op*	1 Pack/188g	263	140	9.0	21.0	3.0	2.0
Ham & Turkey, Asda*	1 Pack/190g	393	207	12.9	15.8	10.2	2.3
Ham Salad Wedge, Healthy Eating, Tesco*	1 Pack/198g	269	136	7.1	23.0	1.7	1.0
Ham Salad, Big Fill, Somerfield*	1 Pack/222g	515	232	9.4	22.9	11.4	2.3
Ham Salad, Co-Op*	1 Pack/193g	299	155	9.0	19.0	5.0	1.0
Ham Salad, Coffee Republic*	1 Pack/224g	309	138	8.6	19.9	2.7	0.0
Ham Salad, Ginsters*	1 Pack/179g	220	123	8.8	16.4	2.5	0.0
Ham Salad, Good Intentions, Somerfield*	1 Pack/178g	287	161	9.5	23.8	3.1	1.1
Ham Salad, Healthy Eating, Tesco*	1 Pack/163g	215	132	10.6	17.5	2.2	2.0
Ham Salad, Healthy Options, Oldfields*	1 Pack/156g	229	147	8.7	24.0	1.9	0.0
Ham Salad, Healthy, Spar*	1 Serving/181g	286	158	8.4	22.7	3.7	0.0
Ham Salad, Safeway*	1 Pack/272g	403	148	8.3	24.5	1.8	1.9
Ham Salad, Select*	1 Serving/180g	266	148	8.0	23.2	2.6	0.0
Ham Salad, Snack & Shop, Esso*	1 Pack/191.2g	304	159	9.2	22.9	3.4	5.0
Ham Salad, Woolworths*	1 Pack/181g	286	158	8.4	22.7	3.7	0.0
Ham, Asda*	1 Pack/262g	618	236	12.2	20.3	12.0	3.0
Ham, Cheese & Pickle, Healthy Choice, Sutherland*	1 Pack/185g	368	199	13.4	27.4	4.0	0.0
Ham, Cheese & Pickle, Healthy Living, Co-Op*	1 Pack/185g	370	200	13.0	27.0	4.0	3.0
Ham, Cheese & Pickle, Marks & Spencer*	1 Pack/197g	459	233	13.0	15.9	13.1	2.4
Ham, Cheese & Pickle, Platter, Marks & Spencer*	¼ Sandwich/56g	146	260	11.9	19.3	14.9	5.3
Ham, Cheese & Pickle, Pret A Manger*	1 Av Pack/250g	592	237	11.9	25.0	11.0	2.4
Ham, Cheese & Pickle, Sutherland*	1 Pack/230g	727	316	11.3	20.6	20.9	0.0
Ham, Cheese & Pickle, Taste!*	1 Pack/173.9g	414	238	11.1	20.3	12.5	0.0
Ham, Emmental Cheese & Mustard Mayonnaise, Classic*	1 Pack/163.8g	444	271	19.5	21.4	14.2	0.0
Ham, Marks & Spencer*	1 Pack/200g	220	110	17.2	3.2	2.6	0.0
Ham, Subway*	1 6" Pack/223g	288	129	8.1	20.6	2.3	1.8
Ham, Tomato & Lettuce, Oldfield's*	1 Pack/215.9g	393	182	12.3	19.0	8.1	3.5
Honduran King Prawn & Wild Rocket, Marks & Spencer*	1 Serving/195.7g	451	230	9.4	20.3	12.2	1.4
Honey Roast Ham & Tomato, Feel Good, Shell*	1 Pack/170.9g	388	227	9.8	22.1	11.0	0.0
Houmous & Crunchy Salad, Oldfields*	1 Pack/180g	256	142	6.3	20.0	4.2	0.0
Houmous & Oven Roasted Tomato, Pret A Manger*	1 Pack/350g	404	115	3.5	13.6	5.2	3.1
Houmous With Crunchy Vegetables, Starbucks*	1 Pack/218.9g	359	164	4.7	26.4	4.4	2.9
Houmous With Mixed Leaves & Carrot, BGTY, Sainsbury's*	1 Pack/175g	275	157	6.1	26.7	2.9	0.0
Houmous, Costa*	1 Pack/165g	263	160	6.4	25.9	2.8	0.0
Houmungously Crunchy, Cranks*	1oz/28g	58	206	2.2	24.3	7.8	3.1
Italian Style Mozzarella, Taste!*	1 Pack/183.1g	390	213	9.2	20.1	10.6	2.0
King Prawn, Sainsbury's*	1 Pack/203.8g	424	208	11.6	22.3	8.0	0.0
Kippered Salmon & Horseradish, Pret A Manger*	1 Pack/300g	462	154	9.0	14.2	6.7	1.8
Lean Danish Ham & Salad, COU, Marks & Spencer*	1 Pack/182g	255	140	10.6	18.7	2.4	1.9

S

SANDWICH,	Measure INFO/WEIGHT	per Measure KCAL	Nutrition Values per 100g / 100ml				
			KCAL	PROT	CARB	FAT	FIBRE
Leicester Ham, Cheese & Pickle, Waitrose*	1 Pack/205g	513	250	11.9	23.7	11.9	2.1
Lemon & Mint Chicken, Delilite*	1 Pack/178.6g	326	182	12.3	23.1	3.6	1.7
Lemon Chicken & Relish, Perfectly Balanced, Waitrose*	1 Pack/151g	243	161	12.3	21.4	2.9	3.5
Lime & Coriander Chicken, BGTY, Sainsbury's*	1 Pack/168g	282	168	10.6	23.5	3.5	0.0
Lovely Stuff, Cranks*	1 Pack/209.5g	353	169	5.2	26.1	4.9	2.7
Maple Flavoured Ham & Pineapple Salsa, Waitrose*	1 Pack/193.5g	330	170	8.4	23.8	4.6	3.1
Mature Cheddar & Pickle, Sainsbury's*	1 Pack/171g	588	344	14.3	38.7	15.8	7.0
Mature Cheddar Cheese & Tomato, Big, Sainsbury's*	1 Pack/233g	596	256	12.9	26.3	11.0	0.0
Mature Cheddar Cheese Salad, Upper Crust*	1 Pack/225.1g	466	207	9.5	20.3	9.8	0.0
Mature Cheddar, Soft Cheese & Celery, Sainsbury's*	1 Pack/183g	576	315	10.2	21.8	19.3	0.0
Mediterranean Style, Triple, GFY, Asda*	1 Pack/211g	352	167	11.0	26.0	2.1	2.3
Mediterranean Tuna Salad, Waitrose*	1 Pack/207g	253	122	7.2	17.1	2.8	2.6
Mediterranean Tuna, COU, Marks & Spencer*	1 Pack/260g	364	140	10.3	19.6	2.2	1.6
Mediterranean Tuna, Scottish Slimmers*	1 Pack/147.2g	259	176	8.5	27.8	3.6	3.2
Mixed Seafood, Tesco*	1 Pack/184g	502	273	7.3	23.2	16.8	0.8
More Than Mozzarella, No Bread, Pret A Manger*	1 Pack/311g	398	128	5.9	2.7	10.5	1.5
Moroccan Chicken, Sainsbury's*	½ Pack/99.5g	184	186	10.6	27.9	3.6	0.0
Mozarella & Salad, Coffee Republic*	1 Pack/242g	477	197	8.6	14.4	11.8	0.0
Mozzarella, Tomato & Basil, Healthy Options, Oldfields*	1 Pack/175g	285	163	8.1	22.1	4.8	3.3
Mozzarrella & Tomato Calzone, Waitrose*	1 Pack/175g	410	234	10.8	22.7	11.1	2.2
New York Deli, Boots*	1 Pack/245g	603	246	11.0	19.0	14.0	2.2
Oriental Chicken Triple, Shapers, Boots*	1 Pack/215g	398	185	12.0	22.0	5.4	2.6
Paprika Chicken, Bacon & Tomato, Shapers, Boots*	1 Pack/184g	296	161	11.0	19.0	4.6	2.3
Parmesan & Rocket, Egg, Cheese & Tomato, Boots*	1 Pack/241g	422	175	8.7	23.0	5.4	2.1
Pastrami & Gherkin, BGTY, Sainsbury's*	1 Pack/230g	357	155	9.8	23.1	2.6	3.0
Pastrami, On Rye, Pret A Manger*	1 Sandwich/200g	391	196	10.3	22.6	7.7	1.9
Peking Duck no Mayo, Boots*	1 Pack/221.7g	400	180	7.7	27.0	4.6	1.7
Peppered Beef, Shell*	1 Pack/181.0g	400	221	7.3	29.0	8.4	1.3
Philadelphia Salad, The Classic Sandwich Co*	1 Pack/135g	264	196	6.2	22.1	9.1	0.0
Pitta Pocket, Chargrilled Chicken, Marks & Spencer*	1 Pack/208g	279	134	11.2	14.5	3.5	1.6
Plain Salad, Northern Bites*	1 Pack/210g	193	92	4.1	15.3	2.0	3.0
Ploughman's & Onion Mayonnaise, Somerfield*	1oz/28g	77	275	10.0	30.0	13.0	0.0
Ploughman's Wedge, Tesco*	1 Pack/269.1g	705	262	10.5	26.9	12.5	1.4
Ploughman's, Cheese, Marks & Spencer*	1 Pack/185g	451	244	9.3	21.5	13.4	1.5
Ploughman's, Deep Fill, Ginsters*	1 Pack/232g	636	274	9.6	20.8	17.6	0.0
Ploughman's, Deep Filled, Asda*	1 Pack/254g	650	256	10.3	21.3	14.5	2.9
Ploughman's, Healthy Eating, Tesco*	1 Pack/180g	261	145	11.6	21.0	1.6	2.0
Ploughman's, Shell*	1 Pack/225.9g	540	239	9.0	19.4	13.9	1.0
Ploughmans, Taste!*	1 Pack/205g	492	240	9.5	20.6	13.3	0.0
Poached Salmon & Rocket, Marks & Spencer*	1 Pack/180g	495	275	13.5	21.2	14.9	2.1
Poached Salmon & Rocket, Pret A Manger*	1 Av Pack/260g	516	198	10.3	14.9	10.7	1.9
Poached Salmon & Spinach, Shapers, Boots*	1 Pack/168.0g	284	169	9.2	23.0	4.5	3.1
Poached Salmon With Salad On Oatmeal, Costa*	1 Pack/151g	224	148	7.7	22.9	2.8	0.0
Poached Salmon, Coffee Republic*	1 Pack/191g	350	183	10.3	18.4	7.6	0.0
Poached Salmon, Marks & Spencer*	1 Pack/180g	495	275	13.5	21.2	14.9	2.1
Poached Salmon, Prawn & Rocket, Waitrose*	1 Pack/165.6g	309	186	11.2	23.5	5.2	2.1
Prawn & Egg, Deep Filled, Asda*	1 Pack/250g	570	228	12.0	17.0	12.0	2.3
Prawn & Egg, Safeway*	1 Pack/216g	400	185	9.4	18.8	8.0	1.0
Prawn & Mayonnaise, COU, Marks & Spencer*	1 Pack/141g	162	115	10.2	22.9	2.3	1.7
Prawn & Mayonnaise, Healthy Selection, Budgens*	1 Pack/143g	296	207	11.0	22.0	8.3	1.8
Prawn & Mayonnaise, Reduced Fat, Waitrose*	1 Pack/146g	276	189	9.2	24.1	6.2	2.5
Prawn & Mayonnaise, Safeway*	1 Pack/168g	402	239	9.0	21.1	13.2	3.1
Prawn & Mayonnaise, Tesco*	1 Serving/88g	259	294	11.9	17.4	19.9	2.2

S

SANDWICH,	Measure INFO/WEIGHT	per Measure KCAL	Nutrition Values per 100g / 100ml KCAL	PROT	CARB	FAT	FIBRE
Prawn & Rocket, Pret A Manger*	1 Pack/280g	435	155	8.4	14.9	6.9	1.3
Prawn & Salmon, Waitrose*	1 Pack/154g	345	224	12.5	22.0	9.5	2.8
Prawn & Smoked Salmon, Marks & Spencer*	1 Pack/445g	1135	255	11.7	19.3	14.3	1.4
Prawn Cocktail Salad, Shapers, Boots*	1 Pack/167g	296	177	10.0	18.0	7.2	2.9
Prawn Cocktail, Classic, Heinz*	1 Pack/193g	409	212	8.4	25.0	8.7	2.5
Prawn Cocktail, Healthy Eating, Tesco*	1 Pack/154g	245	159	11.0	22.0	2.7	1.8
Prawn Cocktail, Platter, Marks & Spencer*	¼ Sandwich/50g	115	230	8.1	22.3	12.8	2.2
Prawn Cocktail, Weight Watchers*	1 Pack/168g	252	150	8.9	18.1	4.6	2.8
Prawn Marie Rose, Fulfilled*	1 Pack/149g	292	196	13.4	26.3	4.1	0.0
Prawn Marie Rose, Waitrose*	1 Pack/164g	303	185	9.4	17.3	8.7	2.7
Prawn Mayo, Ham Salad Triple Pack, Sutherland*	1 Pack/253g	620	245	9.8	24.8	11.9	0.3
Prawn Mayonaise, Healthy Living, Tesco*	1 Pack/157g	245	156	10.2	21.8	3.1	0.5
Prawn Mayonnaise Oatmeal Bread, Co-Op*	1 Pack/159g	445	280	11.0	28.0	14.0	2.0
Prawn Mayonnaise On Oatmeal Bread, Weight Watchers*	1 Pack/158g	254	161	10.4	23.7	2.7	2.3
Prawn Mayonnaise, BGTY, Sainsbury's*	1 Pack/175g	275	157	12.3	21.1	2.6	0.0
Prawn Mayonnaise, COU, Marks & Spencer*	1 Pack/154.8g	240	155	10.2	22.9	2.3	2.8
Prawn Mayonnaise, Co-Op*	1 Pack/154g	285	185	9.7	27.3	3.9	3.2
Prawn Mayonnaise, Daily Bread*	1 Pack/156.5g	373	239	11.9	23.0	11.0	0.0
Prawn Mayonnaise, Deep Filled, Eat Street, Safeway*	1 Pack/225g	450	200	10.7	23.6	6.5	2.1
Prawn Mayonnaise, Eat Smart, Safeway*	1 Pack/165g	256	155	10.4	23.0	2.3	2.0
Prawn Mayonnaise, GFY, Asda*	1 Pack/160g	270	169	10.0	22.0	4.6	2.1
Prawn Mayonnaise, Ginsters*	1 Pack/152g	415	273	12.4	17.8	17.8	0.0
Prawn Mayonnaise, Healthy Eating, Tesco*	1 Pack/154g	270	175	11.9	22.7	4.1	1.9
Prawn Mayonnaise, Heinz*	1 Pack/180g	493	274	8.9	24.0	15.8	2.5
Prawn Mayonnaise, Marks & Spencer*	1 Pack/156g	382	245	10.5	20.2	13.5	2.7
Prawn Mayonnaise, New, Shapers, Boots*	1 Pack/188.8g	287	152	10.0	22.0	2.4	2.7
Prawn Mayonnaise, Oatmeal Bread, Waitrose*	1 Pack/180g	463	257	10.2	20.4	15.0	3.2
Prawn Mayonnaise, On Oatmeal Bread, Taste*	1 Pack/144.1g	320	222	12.6	24.3	8.3	1.5
Prawn Mayonnaise, Platter, Marks & Spencer*	¼ Sandwich/42g	111	265	8.6	23.2	15.4	1.8
Prawn Mayonnaise, Reduced Fat, Waitrose*	1 Pack/155g	284	183	8.9	20.0	7.5	2.8
Prawn Mayonnaise, Sainsbury's*	1 Pack/150.9g	323	214	11.6	20.9	9.3	0.0
Prawn Mayonnaise, Shapers, Boots*	1 Pack/161g	291	181	10.0	25.0	4.6	1.9
Prawn Mayonnaise, Triple, Asda*	1 Pack/248.0g	635	256	9.0	19.0	16.0	3.4
Prawn Mayonnaise, Upper Crust*	1 Pack/207.9g	343	165	9.2	20.9	5.0	0.0
Prawn Mayonnaise, Waitrose*	1 Pack/178g	309	174	9.3	20.1	6.2	2.2
Prawn Mayonnaise, Woolworths*	1 Pack/144g	321	223	12.6	24.3	8.3	0.0
Prawn With Citrus Mango, Healthy Options, Oldfields*	1 Pack/220g	275	125	9.0	18.5	1.8	0.0
Prawn, Shell*	1 Serving/209.2g	523	250	9.4	23.7	13.1	0.0
Rare Roast Beef & Horseradish, Marks & Spencer*	1 Pack/168g	311	185	14.8	21.1	4.3	2.4
Red Salmon & Cucumber, 2 Pack, Tesco*	1 Pack/144g	284	197	11.1	23.8	6.4	1.9
Red Salmon & Cucumber, BGTY, Sainsbury's*	1 Pack/178.1g	276	155	10.9	22.7	2.3	0.0
Red Salmon & Cucumber, Healthy Choice, Asda*	1 Pack/149g	285	191	10.6	19.9	7.7	2.1
Red Salmon & Cucumber, Marks & Spencer*	1 Pack/183g	375	205	11.1	18.5	9.3	1.4
Red Salmon & Cucumber, Tesco*	1 Pack/144g	251	174	11.3	24.2	3.5	1.9
Roast Beef & Horseradish, Starbucks*	1 Pack/200g	546	273	18.7	23.1	11.1	1.0
Roast Beef & Onion, Deep Filled, Asda*	1 Pack/258g	550	213	11.3	22.6	10.8	1.1
Roast Beef On White, No Cheese Or Sauce, Subway*	1 Pack/222g	289	130	8.5	20.0	2.3	1.8
Roast Beef With Cheese, Subway*	6" Pack/222g	291	131	8.6	20.3	2.3	1.8
Roast Beef With Horseradish Mayonnaise, Finest, Tesco*	1 Pack/222.8g	439	197	12.5	20.7	7.1	1.6
Roast Beef, Daily Bread*	1 Pack/199.3g	281	141	8.7	20.0	2.7	0.0
Roast Beef, Deep Fill, Woolworths*	1 Pack/191g	283	148	10.5	17.9	3.9	0.0
Roast Beef, English Mustard Mayonnaise, Oldfields*	1 Pack/150g	405	270	16.0	29.0	11.9	0.0
Roast Beef, Feel Good, Shell*	1 Pack/153g	390	255	17.6	24.2	9.7	0.0

SANDWICH,	Measure INFO/WEIGHT	per Measure KCAL	KCAL	PROT	CARB	FAT	FIBRE
			Nutrition Values per 100g / 100ml				
Roast Beef, Healthy, Woolworths*	1 Pack/191g	283	148	10.5	17.9	3.9	0.0
Roast Beef, Sainsbury's*	1 Pack/173.9g	426	245	9.4	29.3	10.0	0.0
Roast Chicken & Bacon, Boots*	1 Pack/250g	599	240	11.6	16.8	14.0	1.4
Roast Chicken & Bacon, Marks & Spencer*	1 Pack/173.1g	450	260	14.1	23.8	12.1	3.4
Roast Chicken & Bacon, Sainsbury's*	1 Pack/167g	433	259	14.1	18.6	14.2	0.0
Roast Chicken & Coleslaw, Sainsbury's*	1 Pack/186g	348	187	11.4	21.0	7.9	0.0
Roast Chicken & Ham, Ginsters*	1 Pack/180g	425	236	11.2	18.5	13.6	0.0
Roast Chicken & Oak Smoked Ham, Big, Sainsbury's*	1 Pack/244g	461	189	12.3	18.8	7.2	0.0
Roast Chicken & Salad With Mayo, Big, Sainsbury's*	1 Pack/268.8g	560	208	11.0	20.9	8.9	9.0
Roast Chicken & Salad, COU, Marks & Spencer*	1 Pack/196g	265	135	10.2	17.8	2.1	3.5
Roast Chicken & Salad, Marks & Spencer*	1 Pack/200g	430	215	8.5	19.5	9.5	2.6
Roast Chicken & Stuffing, Boots*	1 Pack/234.7g	670	285	12.0	22.0	17.0	1.9
Roast Chicken & Stuffing, Marks & Spencer*	1 Pack/182g	519	285	13.2	23.4	15.3	3.0
Roast Chicken & Stuffing, Platter, Marks & Spencer*	¼ Sandwich/46g	131	285	13.2	23.4	15.3	3.0
Roast Chicken & Stuffing, Tesco*	1 Pack/164g	313	191	14.6	20.3	5.7	1.7
Roast Chicken Breast, BGTY, Sainsbury's*	1 Pack/161.0g	277	172	14.9	22.2	2.6	0.0
Roast Chicken Salad, Feel Good, Shell*	1 Pack/190.6g	327	171	9.8	22.4	4.7	0.0
Roast Chicken Salad, Healthy Selection, Budgens*	1 Pack/168.3g	244	145	11.7	21.1	1.9	1.0
Roast Chicken Salad, Improved, Shapers, Boots*	1 Pack/230.4g	340	148	11.0	23.0	1.8	1.7
Roast Chicken Salad, Marks & Spencer*	1 Pack/221g	420	190	10.4	23.4	6.3	1.1
Roast Chicken Salad, Shapers, Boots*	1 Pack/193g	284	147	11.0	19.0	3.0	2.3
Roast Chicken Salad, Waitrose*	1 Pack/217g	482	222	9.4	21.1	11.1	2.0
Roast Chicken Salad, Weight Watchers*	1 Pack/186g	266	143	10.3	15.8	4.3	2.8
Roast Chicken Triple, Perfectly Balanced, Waitrose*	1 Pack/254g	356	140	8.7	19.2	3.2	2.8
Roast Chicken With Black Pepper Mayo, Boots*	1 Pack/160g	296	185	15.0	20.0	5.0	1.8
Roast Chicken, Bacon & Salad, Big, Sainsbury's*	1 Pack/249g	610	245	11.1	21.7	12.7	0.0
Roast Chicken, Healthy Living, Tesco*	1 Pack/155.1g	276	178	14.6	26.8	1.4	0.8
Roast Chicken, Improved, Shapers, Boots*	1 Pack/174.2g	277	159	16.0	21.0	1.3	2.4
Roast Chicken, No Mayo, COU, Marks & Spencer*	1 Serving/147g	250	170	14.5	21.1	2.6	1.4
Roast Chicken, Prawn Mayo, BLT, Shapers, Boots*	1 Pack/221g	402	182	12.0	22.0	5.1	2.9
Roast Chicken, Prawn, Triple Pack, BLT, Waitrose*	1 Pack/241g	653	271	9.2	18.8	17.7	1.6
Roast Chicken, Shapers, Boots*	1 Pack/163g	289	177	15.0	19.0	4.6	1.5
Roast Lamb, Pea & Mint Relish, Pret A Manger*	1 Sandwich/250g	938	375	21.8	44.1	12.7	7.4
Roast Peppers & Goats Cheese Focaccia, Finest, Tesco*	1 Focaccia/150g	419	279	7.0	21.5	18.3	1.7
Roasted Vegetable & Chilli Bean, Marks & Spencer*	1 Pack/200g	340	170	5.2	24.5	5.7	2.1
Roasted Vegetable Open, COU Marks & Spencer*	1 Pack/150g	260	173	8.4	31.3	1.5	4.4
Salad & Pepper Salsa, Hackens*	1 Pack/157.0g	197	126	5.1	21.8	2.0	0.0
Salad & Salad Cream, Fulfilled*	1 Pack/172g	244	142	4.9	21.5	4.1	0.0
Salad, Taste!*	1 Serving/200g	246	123	4.4	18.9	3.3	0.0
Salmon & Cucumber, BGTY, Sainsbury's*	1 Pack/161g	266	165	9.7	21.0	3.0	3.5
Salmon & Cucumber, Brown Bread, Waitrose*	1 Pack/150g	296	197	10.5	22.7	7.1	1.4
Salmon & Cucumber, Healthly Choice, Sutherland*	1 Pack/164g	321	196	9.8	26.6	5.6	0.0
Salmon & Cucumber, Healthy Living, Co-Op*	1 Pack/159g	286	180	10.0	24.0	5.0	2.0
Salmon & Cucumber, Marks & Spencer*	1 Pack/168g	329	196	11.0	19.5	8.3	2.6
Salmon & Cucumber, Safeway*	1 Serving/173g	346	200	11.1	19.8	8.3	1.9
Salmon & Cucumber, Shapers, Boots*	1 Pack/164.9g	310	188	12.0	23.0	5.3	3.4
Salmon & Cucumber, White Bread, Waitrose*	1 Pack/161.4g	304	189	9.8	25.5	5.3	1.7
Salmon & Soft Cheese, Feel Good, Shell*	1 Pack/174.1g	404	232	13.5	28.0	7.4	1.0
Salt Beef, Gherkins & Mustard Mayo, Sainsbury's*	1 Pack/242g	486	201	9.3	24.1	7.5	3.1
Sausage & Egg Wedge, Tesco*	1 Pack/269g	699	260	9.1	23.6	14.4	1.1
Sausage, Bacon & Egg, Burger King*	1 Pack/182g	430	236	13.2	17.5	12.7	1.7
Sausage, Egg & Bacon, Boots*	1 Pack/325g	887	273	9.3	23.0	16.0	2.2
Sausage, Triple Pack, GFY, Asda*	1 Pack/215g	424	197	9.0	30.0	4.5	2.3

S

SANDWICH,

	Measure INFO/WEIGHT	per Measure KCAL	Nutrition Values per 100g / 100ml				
			KCAL	PROT	CARB	FAT	FIBRE
Seafood Cocktail, Asda*	1 Pack/190g	486	256	6.7	21.3	15.8	1.6
Seafood Cocktail, Marks & Spencer*	1 Pack/226g	463	205	7.2	16.3	12.4	3.5
Seafood Cocktail, Waitrose*	1 Pack/210.2g	267	127	7.3	17.6	3.0	8.1
Seafood Medley, Marks & Spencer*	1 Pack/227g	468	206	7.2	16.3	12.4	3.5
Simply Cheddar Cheese & Coleslaw, Boots*	1 Pack/185g	538	291	9.2	23.0	18.0	1.8
Simply Cheese Ploughman's, Boots*	1 Pack/260g	640	246	7.8	20.0	15.0	1.9
Simply Chicken, Eat Smart, Safeway*	1 Pack/147g	250	170	14.5	23.0	2.2	1.4
Simply Chicken, Healthy Selection, Budgens*	1 Pack/148.2g	286	193	14.3	28.4	2.5	2.1
Simply Egg Mayonnaise, Boots*	1 Pack/181g	449	248	9.2	19.0	15.0	2.9
Simply Egg Mayonnaise, Ginsters*	1 Pack/161g	309	192	8.5	24.1	6.8	0.0
Simply Ham & Mustard, Ginsters*	1 Pack/157.1g	399	254	11.7	23.5	12.6	0.0
Simply Prawn Mayonnaise, Boots*	1 Pack/261g	736	282	11.0	19.0	18.0	2.2
Simply Salad, Shapers, Boots*	1 Pack/216g	300	139	5.2	23.0	2.9	1.8
Simply Smoked Ham, Cheese & Pickle, Boots*	1 Pack/225g	551	245	11.0	21.0	13.0	2.4
Simply Tuna Mayonnaise & Cucumber, Boots*	1 Pack/200g	498	249	12.0	21.0	13.0	2.4
Simply Tuna, Ginsters*	1 Pack/167.0g	466	279	12.8	22.9	15.1	0.0
Smoked Cheese Folded Focaccia, TTD, Sainsbury's*	¼ Focaccia/220g	607	276	13.1	34.6	9.4	2.9
Smoked Ham & Cheese, Ciabatta Style, Shapers, Boots*	1 Pack/179.3g	329	184	13.0	25.0	3.6	1.6
Smoked Ham & Cheese, Co-Op*	1 Pack/167g	334	200	15.0	24.0	5.0	2.0
Smoked Ham & Cheese, Tesco*	1 Pack/204g	620	304	14.1	19.7	18.7	1.6
Smoked Ham & Edam, Shapers, Boots*	1 Pack/183g	315	172	9.3	19.0	6.5	2.7
Smoked Ham & Mustard, Marks & Spencer*	1 Pack/149g	347	233	10.1	18.8	13.0	2.0
Smoked Ham & Mustard, Sainsbury's*	1 Pack/175g	406	232	10.6	21.9	11.3	0.0
Smoked Ham Salad, Taste!*	1 Serving/188g	286	152	9.1	18.4	4.8	0.0
Smoked Ham Salad, Weight Watchers*	1 Pack/190.9g	252	132	10.2	19.1	1.6	3.5
Smoked Ham, Cheese & Pickle, COU, Marks & Spencer*	1 Pack/174g	270	155	14.4	20.0	1.8	3.7
Smoked Ham, Cheese & Pickle, Shapers, Boots*	1 Pack/172g	296	172	13.0	19.0	4.9	2.9
Smoked Ham, Fresh, Taste!*	1 Pack/186.9g	286	153	9.1	18.4	4.8	0.0
Smoked Salmon & Black Pepper, Fulfilled*	1 Pack/120g	293	244	13.8	29.0	8.6	0.0
Smoked Salmon & Cream Cheese, Marks & Spencer*	1 Pack/162g	437	270	11.7	19.3	16.2	2.5
Smoked Salmon Creme Fraiche, Safeway*	1 Pack/171.4g	359	210	11.0	23.6	7.8	2.5
Smoked Salmon With Soft Cheese, Waitrose*	1 Pack/154g	300	195	14.8	19.2	6.5	4.2
Smoked Salmon, Daily Bread*	1 Pack/121.8g	296	243	13.5	28.0	8.7	0.0
Smoked Salmon, Felix Van Den Berghe*	1 Pack/118.8g	292	245	13.9	29.4	6.2	0.0
Smoked Salmon, Luxury, Marks & Spencer*	1 Pack/137g	333	243	15.0	19.0	11.9	1.8
Smoked Salmon, Pret A Manger*	1 Av Pack/250g	370	148	3.8	20.3	5.8	1.8
Smoked Tomato Ham, Starbucks*	1 Pack/206g	297	144	5.2	22.0	3.9	0.0
Smoked Turkey Summer Salad, Starbucks*	1 Pack/198g	303	153	10.8	22.3	2.4	1.5
Smokey Chicken, BGTY, Sainsbury's*	1 Pack/178g	276	155	11.1	25.6	1.0	0.0
Soft Cheese & Roast Tomato, Extra Light, Starbucks*	1 Pack/186g	283	152	8.0	24.0	2.7	3.1
Soft Cheese & Roasted Pepper, Weight Watchers*	1 Pack/158g	289	183	9.4	27.7	3.8	1.5
Southern Amercian Style, Boots*	1 Pack/270.0g	548	203	9.9	24.0	7.5	1.3
Southern Spiced Chicken, Marks & Spencer*	1 Pack/179g	421	235	11.2	21.7	13.0	3.1
Spicy Aubergine & Soft Cheese, Pret A Manger*	1 Av Pack/250g	319	128	4.6	21.2	2.7	2.8
Spicy Cajun Vegetable, Sandwich King*	1 Pack/140.5g	287	205	6.0	30.3	6.7	0.0
Spicy Chicken, Deep Filled, Co-Op*	1 Pack/216g	421	195	10.0	24.0	7.0	3.0
Sub, Beef & Onion, Marks & Spencer*	1 Pack/207g	611	295	13.3	25.6	15.3	1.5
Sub, Chargrilled Chicken Caesar, Sainsbury's*	1 Pack/216g	611	283	13.4	25.6	14.1	0.0
Sub, Chicken & Stuffing, Safeway*	1 Roll/275g	605	220	10.3	21.3	10.4	4.2
Sub, Chicken & Stuffing, Shell*	1 Serving/182.8g	437	239	13.3	32.0	6.4	0.0
Sub, Chicken Salad, Asda*	1 Sub/200g	460	230	9.4	17.4	13.6	0.9
Sub, Egg Mayonnaise, Daily Bread*	1 Pack/165.2g	441	267	9.6	29.6	13.5	0.0
Sub, Meatball With Cheese & Salad, Subway*	1 Pack/286g	526	184	8.4	18.5	9.1	2.1

SANDWICH,

	Measure INFO/WEIGHT	per Measure KCAL	KCAL	PROT	CARB	FAT	FIBRE
Sub, Nacho Style Chicken Sub, Global, Somerfield*	1 Roll/226g	513	227	7.4	30.8	8.3	4.2
Sub, Roast Chicken & Bacon, Marks & Spencer*	1 Pack/212g	583	275	16.3	23.9	12.7	1.1
Sub, The Big Chicken & Bacon, Marks & Spencer*	1 Pack/218g	545	250	15.6	24.9	10.0	1.4
Super Club, Pret A Manger*	1 Av Pack/200g	542	271	16.0	23.4	12.6	2.9
Tandoori Chicken, Finest, Tesco*	1 Pack/224g	421	188	10.8	19.2	7.5	1.4
Tangy Lime & Ginger Chicken, Shapers, Boots*	1 Pack/168g	319	190	12.0	21.0	6.4	5.1
Thai Chicken, Tesco*	1 Pack/244g	634	260	8.5	21.1	15.7	1.5
Thai Style Prawn, Ginsters*	1 Pack/183.0g	313	171	9.2	22.5	4.9	0.0
Three Cheese & Onion, New Style, Weight Watchers*	1 Pack/148g	275	186	14.8	26.2	2.4	1.4
Three Cheese & Roasted Tomato, Pret A Manger*	1 Pack/350g	417	119	3.8	11.5	6.2	1.5
Three Cheese & Spring Onion, Shell*	1 Pack/168g	672	400	11.1	20.8	30.3	0.0
Tiger Prawn & Thai Dressing, Waitrose*	1 Pack/200g	342	171	9.6	23.6	4.3	2.2
Tomato & Basil Chicken, Healthy Eating, Tesco*	1 Pack/176g	266	151	11.5	21.1	2.3	2.0
Tomato, Edam & Spring Onion, BHS*	1 Serving/184.1g	313	170	8.6	22.5	5.1	3.2
Tuna & Celery, Perfectly Balanced, Waitrose*	1 Pack/172g	272	158	11.7	20.5	3.2	3.9
Tuna & Chargrilled Vegetables, BGTY, Sainsbury's*	1 Pack/196g	329	168	10.7	21.5	4.4	0.0
Tuna & Cucumber, BGTY, Sainsbury's*	1 Pack/164g	275	169	12.0	21.6	3.9	3.0
Tuna & Cucumber, Feel Good, Shell*	1 Pack/214.0g	518	242	12.6	31.2	7.5	0.0
Tuna & Cucumber, GFY, Asda*	1 Pack/169.3g	275	163	12.0	24.0	2.1	2.7
Tuna & Cucumber, Ginsters*	1 Pack/171g	238	139	9.9	19.4	3.2	0.0
Tuna & Cucumber, Healthy Choice, Asda*	1 Pack/164g	315	192	10.9	22.3	6.6	1.1
Tuna & Cucumber, Healthy Choice, Sutherlands*	1 Pack/179g	344	192	12.2	22.0	6.2	0.0
Tuna & Cucumber, Healthy Living, Co-Op*	1 Pack/186.8g	355	190	12.0	25.0	5.0	2.0
Tuna & Cucumber, Heinz*	1 Pack/183.4g	276	151	12.3	21.6	1.6	6.8
Tuna & Cucumber, Marks & Spencer*	1 Pack/170g	430	253	12.0	18.0	14.8	2.4
Tuna & Cucumber, New, BGTY, Sainsbury's*	1 Pack/160g	218	136	10.3	20.9	1.2	0.0
Tuna & Cucumber, On Malted Wheatgrain, Ginsters*	1 Pack/175g	319	182	14.1	21.8	4.3	0.0
Tuna & Cucumber, Shapers, Boots*	1 Pack/179g	322	180	11.0	24.0	4.4	1.7
Tuna & Cucumber, Shell*	1 Pack/188g	431	229	12.3	21.9	10.2	0.0
Tuna & Cucumber, Weight Watchers*	1 Pack/173.3g	279	161	11.4	25.1	1.7	1.4
Tuna & Green Pesto, BGTY, Sainsbury's*	1 Pack/211.4g	279	132	11.0	17.0	2.2	0.0
Tuna & Lemon Mayo, Shapers, Boots*	1 Pack/206g	318	154	10.0	18.0	4.7	1.7
Tuna & Peppers, Virgin Trains*	1 Pack/177.5g	338	191	9.9	26.5	5.0	0.0
Tuna & Sweetcorn, Asda*	1 Pack/205g	592	289	11.5	21.8	17.2	2.7
Tuna & Sweetcorn, COU, Marks & Spencer*	1 Pack/180g	270	150	12.6	19.0	2.4	3.8
Tuna & Sweetcorn, Eat Smart, Safeway*	1 Pack/204.2g	537	263	11.7	21.9	14.3	1.5
Tuna & Sweetcorn, Ginsters*	1 Pack/163.3g	306	188	10.5	25.2	5.0	0.0
Tuna & Sweetcorn, Healthy Eating, Tesco*	1 Pack/154g	263	171	11.4	25.6	2.5	2.1
Tuna & Sweetcorn, Heinz*	1 Pack/208g	528	254	10.4	23.5	13.2	1.6
Tuna & Sweetcorn, Marks & Spencer*	1 Pack/185g	453	245	11.0	20.9	13.0	2.1
Tuna & Sweetcorn, New Recipe, Healthy Living, Tesco*	1 Pack/209.6g	330	157	13.0	22.5	1.7	2.3
Tuna & Sweetcorn, Safeway*	1 Pack/154.5g	256	165	12.8	23.2	1.8	1.7
Tuna & Sweetcorn, Sainsbury's*	1 Pack/183g	441	241	10.6	23.2	11.7	0.0
Tuna & Sweetcorn, Shapers, Boots*	1 Pack/170g	306	180	12.0	27.0	2.7	2.1
Tuna & Sweetcorn, Tesco*	1 Pack/174g	432	248	11.3	24.4	11.7	1.8
Tuna Crunch Ciabatta, Eat Smart, Safeway*	1 Serving/200g	280	140	10.7	21.7	1.1	1.5
Tuna Crunch, Healthy Living, Tesco*	1 Pack/180g	261	145	11.0	19.9	2.4	0.5
Tuna Crunch, Shapers, Boots*	1 Pack/200g	290	145	9.1	20.0	3.2	3.2
Tuna Mayo, No Bread, Pret A Manger*	1 Pack/233g	312	134	8.3	5.8	8.7	0.7
Tuna Mayo, Pret A Manger*	1 Av Pack/250g	622	249	11.7	24.4	11.6	1.6
Tuna Mayonnaise With Spring Onions, Starbucks*	1 Pack/209g	318	152	9.0	19.9	4.0	1.5
Tuna Mayonnaise, White Bread, Open Choice Foods*	1 Pack/120g	298	248	12.0	29.6	8.4	0.0
Tuna Mayonnaise, With Cucumber, Classic*	1 Serving/185g	429	232	10.6	19.8	12.3	0.0

S

	Measure INFO/WEIGHT	per Measure KCAL	KCAL	PROT	CARB	FAT	FIBRE
SANDWICH,							
Tuna Melt, Swedish Bread, Shapers, Boots*	1 Pack/163g	254	156	14.0	20.0	2.2	2.1
Tuna Nicoise, Taste!*	1 Pack/218.4g	403	185	11.3	20.1	6.6	0.0
Tuna Pepper & Sweetcorn Salad, Shapers, Boots*	1 Pack/204g	345	169	9.2	24.0	4.0	1.9
Tuna Salad Wedge, Tesco*	1 Pack/204.9g	291	142	8.1	23.9	1.5	0.8
Tuna Salad With Sour Cream Dressing, Weight Watchers*	1 Pack/201g	260	129	9.8	17.7	2.1	2.8
Tuna Salad, Marks & Spencer*	1 Pack/250g	575	230	12.5	16.8	12.6	2.1
Tuna Salad, On White, Tesco*	1 Pack/190g	352	185	9.8	20.8	7.0	1.1
Tuna Salad, Tesco*	1 Pack/197g	427	217	9.5	20.9	10.6	1.1
Tuna Salad, Weight Watchers*	1 Pack/191g	248	130	10.6	15.8	2.7	2.6
Tuna With Salad, Debenhams*	1 Pack/249g	309	124	7.7	16.9	3.4	0.0
Tuna, Healthy Options, Spar*	1 Pack/150g	269	179	14.3	24.9	2.4	0.0
Tuna, Tomato & Onion, COU, Marks & Spencer*	1 Pack/177g	250	141	11.1	18.8	2.4	2.2
Turkey & Bacon, COU, Marks & Spencer*	1 Pack/165g	256	155	12.0	21.0	2.4	1.7
Turkey & Coleslaw, Cafe, Asda*	1 Pack/193g	457	237	10.0	20.0	13.0	0.0
Turkey & Cranberry Salad, Fullfillers*	1 Serving/180g	319	177	13.0	23.3	3.2	0.0
Turkey & Cranberry, COU, Marks & Spencer*	1 Pack/180g	279	155	12.1	22.8	1.7	2.9
Turkey & Ham Salad, Sutherland*	1 Pack/185g	303	164	9.8	25.2	2.6	0.0
Turkey & Stuffing, Marks & Spencer*	1 Pack/190g	352	185	12.3	23.1	4.9	1.9
Turkey & Sun Dried Tomato, Festive Feast, Taste!*	1 Pack/159.1g	401	252	8.8	23.0	13.9	0.0
Turkey Breast & Ham Sandwich, Subway*	1 Pack/235g	294	125	8.5	19.6	2.1	1.7
Turkey Salad, Fullfillers*	1 Serving/218g	320	147	10.3	18.6	3.2	0.0
Turkey, Gibsons*	1 Pack/138g	260	188	12.5	26.0	3.8	0.0
Turkey, Lettuce & Tomato, Shapers, Boots*	1 Pack/217g	310	143	9.8	21.0	2.2	2.9
Turkey, Northern Bites*	1 Pack/200g	354	177	11.9	22.8	4.3	0.0
Turkey, Pork & Herb, Starbucks*	1 Pack/198g	465	235	11.7	22.6	10.8	2.1
Turkey, Stuffing & Cranberry Sauce, Shapers, Boots*	1 Pack/167g	316	189	10.0	26.0	5.0	1.5
Two Cheese & Pickle, Heinz*	1 Pack/178g	543	305	13.8	28.4	15.1	3.8
Vegetable, Grilled, Safeway*	1 Pack/150g	236	157	5.6	24.9	3.9	2.4
Vegetable, Marks & Spencer*	1 Serving/180g	252	140	6.1	23.5	2.3	2.1
Vegetarian, Salad, Waitrose*	1oz/28g	74	266	9.8	19.6	16.5	1.9
Veggie Delite, Subway*	1 Pack/166g	226	136	5.4	26.5	1.8	2.4
Wensleydale & Carrot, Marks & Spencer*	1 Pack/183g	430	235	9.9	21.4	12.3	2.8
White Crab & Crayfish, Pret A Manger*	1 Pack/250g	391	156	5.0	16.8	7.7	2.2
York Ham, Starbucks*	1 Pack/208g	341	164	10.4	21.2	4.2	2.9
SANDWICH FILLER,							
Beef & Onion, Deli, Asda*	1 Serving/50g	79	157	10.0	0.1	13.0	1.1
Chargrilled Vegetable, Sainsbury's*	½ Pot/85g	192	226	3.4	2.2	22.7	0.6
Cheese & Onion, Safeway*	1 Serving/50g	260	520	10.6	2.6	51.4	1.3
Cheese & Onion, Sainsbury's*	1 Serving/85g	463	545	10.8	1.1	55.3	0.4
Cheese & Spring Onion, Healthy Eating, Tesco*	1 Serving/85g	185	218	13.2	6.8	15.4	0.6
Cheese & Spring Onion, Marks & Spencer*	1 Serving/56g	199	355	8.5	5.0	33.6	0.2
Cheese & Spring Onion, Morrisons*	1 Serving/28g	119	426	12.8	3.1	44.6	0.0
Chicken & Bacon With Sweetcorn, Sainsbury's*	1 Serving/60g	187	312	13.2	2.6	27.6	1.1
Chicken & Sweetcorn, Deli, Marks & Spencer*	1 Pot/170g	306	180	11.6	4.2	12.9	1.5
Chicken Caesar, BGTY, Sainsbury's*	½ Jar/85.4g	116	137	15.6	2.5	7.2	2.2
Chicken Tikka & Citrus Raita, COU, Marks & Spencer*	½ Pot/85g	77	90	12.6	4.9	2.0	0.9
Chicken Tikka, BGTY, Sainsbury's*	½ Pot/85g	99	117	16.5	6.0	3.0	1.0
Chicken Tikka, Mild, Heinz*	1 Serving/52g	102	196	5.2	12.3	14.0	0.7
Chicken With Salad Vegetables, Heinz*	1 Filling/56g	114	203	5.1	11.7	15.1	0.5
Chicken, Coronation, Deli, Asda*	1 Serving/56.1g	171	305	13.0	7.0	25.0	0.8
Chicken, Stuffing & Bacon, COU, Marks & Spencer*	1 Pack/170g	170	100	13.1	6.2	2.2	1.3
Chicken, Sweetcorn & Sage, Healthy Eating, Tesco*	1 Serving/125g	105	84	9.4	8.8	1.3	1.3
Chicken, Tikka, Deli, Asda*	1 Serving/40g	114	284	13.0	13.0	20.0	0.7

SANDWICH FILLER,

INFO/WEIGHT	Measure per Measure		Nutrition Values per 100g / 100ml				
		KCAL	KCAL	PROT	CARB	FAT	FIBRE
Chicken, Tomato & Sweetcure Bacon, Marks & Spencer*	1 Pot/170g	502	295	11.4	2.8	26.4	0.7
Chunky Egg & Smoked Ham, Tesco*	1 Serving/100g	234	234	11.8	0.2	20.7	0.3
Chunky Seafood Cocktail, Tesco*	1 Serving/100g	347	347	5.6	3.3	34.6	1.7
Corned Beef & Onion, Deli, Asda*	1 Serving/50g	170	340	12.0	3.3	31.0	0.7
Coronation Chicken, Somerfield*	1 Serving/85g	326	383	8.4	9.7	34.5	0.8
Coronation Chicken, Tesco*	1 Tbsp/30g	84	279	14.7	6.1	21.8	0.7
Creamy Chicken Tikka, Sainsbury's*	1 Serving/85g	184	217	14.6	1.1	17.1	1.4
Egg & Bacon, Fresh, Tesco*	1 Serving/45g	112	248	12.7	4.2	20.1	0.6
Egg & Bacon, Safeway*	1 Serving/85g	302	355	12.2	1.0	33.5	0.0
Egg Mayonaise, Better for You, Morrisons*	1 Spread/50g	71	142	10.0	1.7	10.6	0.0
Egg Mayonnaise & Bacon, Free Range, Co-Op*	1 Pot/200g	500	250	13.0	0.9	22.0	0.6
Egg Mayonnaise, BGTY, Sainsbury's*	1 Serving/85g	102	120	10.9	0.9	7.1	1.2
Egg Mayonnaise, Chunky Free Range, Tesco*	1 Serving/50g	104	208	12.3	0.2	17.6	0.3
Egg Mayonnaise, Deli, Asda*	1 Serving/50g	114	227	11.0	0.8	20.0	0.3
Egg Mayonnaise, Deli, Somerfield*	1 Serving/40g	120	301	9.7	0.2	29.2	0.0
Egg Mayonnaise, Marks & Spencer*	1oz/28g	62	220	10.1	0.8	19.7	1.1
Egg Mayonnaise, Sainsbury's*	1 Serving/50g	138	275	10.1	1.1	25.6	0.5
Egg Mayonnaise, Tesco*	1 Serving/50g	120	239	10.6	0.5	21.6	0.5
Egg Mayonnaise, safeway*	1 Serving/300g	960	320	9.6	1.1	30.5	1.8
Ham & Salad Vegetables, Heinz*	1oz/28g	57	204	5.3	10.0	15.9	0.4
Poached Salmon & Cucumber, Deli, Marks & Spencer*	1 Pot/170g	349	205	14.0	1.0	16.3	0.5
Prawn Mayonaise, Deli, Asda*	1 Serving/50g	170	339	9.0	1.6	33.0	0.4
Prawn Mayonnaise, Marks & Spencer*	½ Pack/170g	502	295	10.6	0.6	28.0	0.3
Prawn Mayonnaise, Waitrose*	1 Pot/170g	537	316	8.9	0.2	31.1	0.0
Red Leicester & Bacon, Tesco's*	1 Serving/125g	518	414	13.1	8.0	36.6	1.1
Roast Beef, Onion & Horseradish, Sainsbury's*	1 Serving/100g	372	372	6.4	3.7	36.8	1.2
Seafood Cocktail, Marks & Spencer*	1oz/28g	76	272	6.4	8.2	23.8	0.2
Seafood, BGTY, Sainsbury's*	1oz/28g	36	128	8.7	7.6	7.0	0.5
Smoked Ham, Roasted Onion & Mustard, Sainsbury's*	1 Serving/100g	343	343	7.3	3.4	33.4	0.0
Smoked Salmon & Soft Cheese, Marks & Spencer*	1 Pack/170g	451	265	11.1	4.9	23.9	0.0
Tex-Mex Chicken, Tesco*	1 Pack/250g	255	102	12.3	11.2	0.9	1.2
Tuna & Sweetcorn With Salad Vegetables, Heinz*	1oz/28g	53	191	5.8	12.1	13.2	0.7
Tuna & Sweetcorn, COU, Marks & Spencer*	½ Pot/85g	77	90	11.6	5.7	2.0	1.3
Tuna & Sweetcorn, Deli, Asda*	1 Serving/50g	148	296	12.0	3.4	26.0	1.4
Tuna & Sweetcorn, Marks & Spencer*	1oz/28g	70	250	14.2	2.3	20.7	1.3
Tuna Crunch, Tesco*	1 Serving/100g	336	336	12.1	2.6	30.8	0.4
Tuna Mayonnaise & Sweetcorn, BGTY, Sainsbury's*	1 Serving/100g	92	92	13.8	5.9	1.5	1.1
Tuna Mayonnaise, BGTY, Sainsbury's*	1 Serving/100g	114	114	17.6	3.5	3.4	0.1
Tuna, Tomato & Black Olive, BGTY, Sainsbury's*	1 Pack/100g	88	88	12.6	5.9	1.6	1.2

SANDWICH FILLING,

INFO/WEIGHT	Measure per Measure		Nutrition Values per 100g / 100ml				
Big Breakfast, Asda*	1 Serving/125g	314	251	12.0	3.5	21.0	0.5
Cheese & Onion, Asda*	1 Serving/56g	288	515	9.8	4.4	50.9	0.3
Cheese & Onion, Co-Op*	1 Serving/56g	269	480	10.0	4.0	47.0	0.5
Cheese & Onion, GFY, Asda*	1 Serving/80g	206	257	11.0	6.0	21.0	0.8
Cheese & Spring Onion, Better For You, Morrisons*	½ Pot/85g	216	254	10.4	7.0	20.0	2.2
Chicken & Bacon, Asda*	1 Serving/100g	359	359	18.0	2.0	31.0	1.0
Chicken & Sweetcorn, Asda*	1 Serving/60g	187	312	11.0	4.0	28.0	2.0
Chicken & Sweetcorn, Low Fat, Morrisons*	1 Serving/56g	101	180	8.8	8.5	12.3	1.6
Chicken Tikka, Asda*	1 Serving/28g	80	284	13.0	13.0	20.0	0.7
Chicken Tikka, Less Than 5% Fat, Asda*	1 Serving/56g	65	116	11.0	7.3	4.7	1.2
Crab, BGTY, Sainsbury's*	1oz/28g	36	128	8.7	7.6	7.0	0.5
Egg Mayonnaise With Chives, Asda*	1oz/28g	92	327	9.1	1.1	31.8	0.0
Egg Mayonnaise, Asda*	1oz/28g	72	258	10.3	1.9	23.3	0.7

S

	Measure INFO/WEIGHT	per Measure KCAL	Nutrition Values per 100g / 100ml				
			KCAL	PROT	CARB	FAT	FIBRE
SANDWICH FILLING,							
Egg Mayonnaise, Co-Op*	1oz/28g	69	245	11.0	3.0	21.0	0.8
Houmous & Vegetable, Asda*	1/3 tub/57g	133	233	8.0	12.0	17.0	3.5
Prawn Mayonnaise, GFY, Asda*	1 Serving/57g	101	177	12.0	3.0	13.0	0.1
Prawns With Seafood Sauce, Asda*	1oz/28g	107	382	11.7	1.4	36.8	0.0
Tuna & Sweetcorn With Mayonnaise, Morrisons*	1 Serving/25g	72	289	13.1	5.9	23.7	0.6
Tuna & Sweetcorn, Asda*	1oz/28g	83	295	8.2	6.0	26.5	0.6
Tuna & Sweetcorn, GFY, Asda*	1/3 Pot/57g	73	128	11.0	12.0	4.0	0.3
Tuna & Sweetcorn, Reduced Fat, Co-Op*	1 Serving/50g	103	205	13.0	7.0	14.0	0.9
Tuna & Sweetcorn, Reduced Fat, Morrisons*	1oz/28g	50	178	13.0	7.8	10.5	1.2
Tuna & Sweetcorn, Tesco*	1 Serving/60g	172	287	9.4	10.0	23.3	0.9
SANDWICH SPREAD,							
Chicken & Bacon, Asda*	1 Jar/170g	610	359	18.0	2.0	31.0	1.0
Chicken Tikka, Asda*	1 Serving/50g	77	154	7.0	9.0	10.0	0.2
Cucumber, Heinz*	1oz/28g	46	164	1.7	12.7	11.6	0.6
Original, Heinz*	1oz/28g	66	237	1.7	15.2	18.6	0.7
Somerfield*	1oz/28g	59	212	1.0	26.0	11.0	0.0
SARDINES,							
Boneless, John West*	1 Can/62g	102	164	17.0	1.5	10.0	0.0
Cook!, Marks & Spencer*	1 Serving/128g	262	205	16.4	1.2	14.1	0.1
Grilled	1oz/28g	55	195	25.3	0.0	10.4	0.0
Headless, Somerfield*	1oz/28g	46	165	21.0	0.0	9.0	0.0
In Barbecue Sauce, Princes*	1 Can/120g	182	152	15.1	5.0	8.0	0.0
In Brine, Asda*	1 Can/84g	160	191	23.0	0.0	11.0	0.0
In Brine, Canned, Drained	1oz/28g	48	172	21.5	0.0	9.6	0.0
In Brine, John West*	1 Can/90g	156	173	23.0	0.0	9.0	0.0
In Brine, Portuguese, Sainsbury's*	1 Can/90g	165	183	22.4	0.1	10.3	0.1
In Brine, Tesco*	½ Can/42g	79	189	22.8	0.0	10.9	0.0
In Brine, Waitrose*	1 Can/120g	170	142	20.2	0.0	6.8	0.0
In Extra Virgin Olive Oil, Drained, Princes*	1 Can/90g	203	226	24.2	0.0	13.9	0.0
In Oil, Canned, Drained	1oz/28g	62	220	23.3	0.0	14.1	0.0
In Olive Oil, John West*	1 Can/96g	243	253	25.0	0.0	17.0	0.0
In Olive Oil, Portuguese, Marks & Spencer*	1 Can/90g	176	195	23.0	0.0	11.3	0.0
In Olive Oil, Portuguese, Sainsbury's*	1 Can/90g	194	216	25.5	0.1	12.6	0.3
In Olive Oil, Skinless & Boneless, Sainsbury's*	1 Can/90g	165	183	28.2	0.1	7.8	0.1
In Salsa, Norwegian, Canned, Finest, King Oscar*	1 Can/106g	180	170	13.2	2.8	11.3	0.0
In Smoky Barbecue Sauce, Princes*	1 Can/120g	182	152	15.1	5.0	8.0	0.0
In Spring Water, Portuguese, Sainsbury's*	1 Can/90g	165	183	22.4	0.0	10.3	0.0
In Sunflower Oil, Drained, Princes*	1 Can/90g	189	210	22.0	0.0	13.9	0.0
In Sunflower Oil, John West*	1 Can/96g	209	218	23.0	0.0	14.0	0.0
In Sunflower Oil, Portuguese, Sainsbury's*	1 Can/90g	167	186	25.1	0.1	10.3	0.1
In Tomato Sauce, Asda*	1 Can/120g	218	182	18.0	0.5	12.0	0.0
In Tomato Sauce, Canned	1oz/28g	45	162	17.0	1.4	9.9	0.0
In Tomato Sauce, John West*	1oz/28g	46	164	17.0	1.5	10.0	0.0
In Tomato Sauce, Ocean Rise*	1 Can/120g	194	162	17.0	1.4	9.9	0.0
In Tomato Sauce, Portuguese, Marks & Spencer*	1 Can/120g	160	133	19.4	1.2	5.6	0.2
In Tomato Sauce, Portuguese, Sainsbury's*	1 Can/120g	212	177	17.4	2.2	11.0	0.4
In Tomato Sauce, Princes*	1 Can/120g	228	190	19.0	1.6	11.9	0.0
In Tomato Sauce, Skinless & Boneless, Sainsbury's*	1 Can/120g	143	119	22.1	1.0	3.0	0.1
In Tomato Sauce, Tesco*	1 Can/120g	214	178	17.8	0.5	11.6	0.0
In Tomato Sauce, Waitrose*	1 Tin/120g	251	209	18.8	0.7	14.6	0.0
Raw	1oz/28g	46	165	20.6	0.0	9.2	0.0
SARSAPARILLA,							
Baldwins*	1fl oz/30ml	35	117	0.0	27.8	0.0	0.0

	Measure INFO/WEIGHT	per Measure KCAL	Nutrition Values per 100g / 100ml				
			KCAL	PROT	CARB	FAT	FIBRE
SATAY,							
Chicken & Turkey, Co-Op*	1 Pack/120g	264	220	20.0	4.0	14.0	0.1
Chicken & Turkey, Sainsbury's*	1 Stick/20g	44	222	20.0	4.0	14.0	1.9
Chicken Tikka, Cocktail Selection, Somerfield*	1oz/28g	48	171	24.0	4.0	7.0	0.0
Chicken, A Taste Of Indonesia*	1 Serving/160g	232	145	22.0	3.0	5.0	0.0
Chicken, GFY, Asda*	1 Serving/168.1g	242	144	22.0	6.0	3.6	0.8
Chicken, Marks & Spencer*	1 Satay/43g	90	210	19.1	4.4	12.7	0.7
Chicken, Mini, Iceland*	1 Satay/8g	19	236	23.0	4.5	14.0	0.7
Chicken, Morrisons*	1 Satay/10g	17	171	23.5	3.5	7.0	0.7
Chicken, Occasions, Sainsbury's*	1 Satay/10g	15	150	22.0	2.0	6.0	0.7
Chicken, Sainsbury's*	1 Pack/350g	301	86	7.6	7.8	2.7	0.4
Chicken, Sticks, Asda*	1 Stick/20g	43	216	18.0	4.5	14.0	0.0
Chicken, Taste Original*	1 Serving/20g	33	164	23.0	2.5	6.5	0.7
Chicken, Tesco*	1 Serving/350g	483	138	13.4	5.1	7.1	0.7
Chicken, Thai Cocktail Sel & Peanut Sauce, Somerfield*	1oz/28g	43	152	23.0	2.0	6.0	0.0
Chicken, Waitrose*	1 Serving/350g	679	194	17.1	6.7	11.0	1.3
Chicken, With Jasmin Rice, Eat Smart, Safeway*	1 Pack/400g	380	95	5.3	14.3	1.5	0.7
Selection, Safeway*	1 Satay/10g	20	200	26.0	9.0	8.0	3.0
Szechuan Style, Occasions, Sainsbury's*	1 Satay/10g	20	196	22.8	6.4	8.8	0.5
SATSUMAS,							
Fresh, Raw	1oz/28g	10	36	0.9	8.5	0.1	1.3
Weighed With Peel	1 Med/80g	21	26	0.6	6.0	0.1	0.9
SAUCE,							
Amatricana, Asda*	1 Serving/155g	240	155	4.4	5.0	13.0	1.0
Apple & Brandy, Asda*	1 Serving/125g	56	45	0.2	11.0	0.0	0.0
Apple, Baxters*	1 Tsp/15g	7	49	0.1	11.1	0.4	0.7
Apple, Bramley, Asda*	1 Tsp/15g	14	94	0.2	23.0	0.1	0.9
Apple, Bramley, Colman's*	1 Tsp/15ml	16	108	0.2	26.0	0.0	0.0
Apple, Bramley, Marks & Spencer*	1 Serving/50g	53	106	0.3	25.0	0.1	0.8
Apple, Bramley, Morrisons*	1 Tsp/15g	21	139	0.2	34.5	0.0	1.2
Apple, Bramley, Safeway*	1 Serving/50g	61	121	0.2	29.9	0.1	1.0
Apple, Bramley, Sainsbury's*	1 Tsp/15g	17	111	0.2	27.2	0.1	1.8
Apple, Bramley, Tesco*	1 Serving/50g	70	140	0.3	33.7	0.1	1.1
Apple, Heinz*	1 Tsp/15g	8	56	0.3	13.4	0.2	1.5
Apple, Shoprite*	1 Pot/113g	57	50	0.0	12.0	0.0	0.0
Apricot & Almond Tagine, Sainsbury's*	1/3 Jar/120g	98	82	2.0	17.9	1.6	2.5
Aromatic Cantonese, Express, Uncle Ben's*	1 Serving/170g	172	101	0.6	24.6	0.1	0.0
Arrabbiata, Don Pomodoro*	½ Pot/185g	231	125	0.5	6.0	11.0	0.0
Arrabbiata, Lazio, Sainsbury's*	1/3 Jar/113g	154	136	2.2	7.2	10.9	0.0
Arrabiata, Italiano, Tesco*	1 Pot/350g	126	36	1.4	7.1	0.2	1.1
Arrabiata, Safeway*	½ Pot/175g	250	143	2.9	14.1	8.3	2.9
Au Poivre, TTD, Sainsbury's*	1 Serving/150g	300	200	2.5	6.2	18.4	0.6
BBQ Original, Heinz*	1 Serving/9.5g	12	137	1.3	31.0	0.3	0.3
BBQ, HP*	1 Serving/20ml	29	143	0.8	33.1	0.2	0.0
BBQ, Smokey Tomato, HP*	1oz/28g	40	143	0.8	33.1	0.2	0.0
BBQ, Spicy Mayhem, HP*	1 Serving/2g	3	156	0.9	36.7	0.1	0.0
Balti Indian, Marks & Spencer*	1oz/28g	25	90	1.4	9.2	5.5	1.1
Balti, 97% Fat Free, Homepride*	1 Serving/230g	133	58	1.1	9.1	1.9	1.8
Balti, Cooking, Asda*	¼ Jar/145g	155	107	1.9	9.0	7.0	1.1
Balti, Cooking, BGTY, Sainsbury's*	¼ Jar/129g	98	76	1.1	10.9	3.1	0.6
Balti, Cooking, Eat Smart, Safeway*	1 Serving/88g	66	75	1.1	10.0	2.9	0.8
Balti, Cooking, Organic, Perfectly Balanced, Waitrose*	1 Jar/450g	257	57	0.9	7.6	2.6	0.9
Balti, Cooking, Organic, Sainsbury's*	1 Serving/225g	158	70	2.2	10.0	2.3	0.5
Balti, Cooking, Sharwood's*	1 Jar/420g	370	88	1.1	9.1	5.2	0.5

S

SAUCE,	Measure INFO/WEIGHT	per Measure KCAL	Nutrition Values per 100g / 100ml				
			KCAL	PROT	CARB	FAT	FIBRE
Balti, Cooking, Shere Khan*	1 Jar/425g	261	61	0.9	3.9	4.7	0.0
Balti, Cooking, Tesco*	1 Serving/500g	575	115	2.3	8.6	7.8	1.6
Balti, Curry, Asda*	¼ Jar/125g	155	124	1.6	7.0	10.0	1.7
Balti, Curry, Loyd Grossman*	1 Serving/212g	346	163	1.7	8.8	13.4	1.4
Balti, Curry, Sharwood's*	1 Serving/140g	123	88	1.1	9.1	5.2	0.5
Balti, Deliciously Good, Homepride*	1/3 Jar/153g	89	58	1.1	9.1	1.9	0.6
Balti, Indian Style, Iceland*	1 Serving/220g	154	70	1.6	10.1	2.6	0.5
Balti, Sizzle & Stir, Chicken Tonight*	1/3 Jar/168g	195	116	1.3	6.3	9.5	2.9
Balti, Tomato & Coriander, Patak's*	1 Serving/70g	58	83	0.8	6.5	6.0	1.2
Barbecue, Asda*	1 Serving/135g	128	95	1.2	22.0	0.2	0.6
Barbecue, Chicken Tonight*	¼ Jar/125g	76	61	2.0	12.4	0.4	0.9
Barbecue, Cooking, BGTY, Sainsbury's*	¼ Jar/124g	46	37	0.4	8.4	0.2	0.7
Barbecue, Tesco*	1 Tbsp/15ml	21	143	2.2	31.3	0.1	0.5
Barbeque, Cook In, Homepride*	1 Serving/130g	96	74	0.8	14.0	1.6	0.0
Barbeque, McDonald's*	1 Portion/32g	55	173	2.2	38.3	1.2	0.0
Barbeque, Simply Sausages Ranch, Colman's*	1 Serving/130g	96	74	1.8	16.6	0.1	1.1
Beef In Ale, Cooking, Asda*	1 Jar/500g	160	32	1.6	6.0	0.2	0.0
Bhuna Cooking, Shere Khan*	1 Jar/425g	244	57	1.3	4.5	3.8	0.0
Bhuna, Sharwood's*	1 Jar/420g	361	86	0.8	8.4	5.4	0.6
Black Bean & Chillli, Stir Fry, Asda*	½ Jar/97g	158	163	3.7	10.0	12.0	0.8
Black Bean & Green Pepper, Stir Fry, Sharwood's*	1 Serving/150g	83	55	2.0	11.0	0.3	0.5
Black Bean, Amoy*	1oz/28g	42	150	10.0	23.0	2.0	0.0
Black Bean, Aromatic, Stir Fry, Amoy*	1 Serving/150g	228	152	3.8	33.7	0.2	0.0
Black Bean, Asda*	1 Serving/55g	55	100	2.9	19.0	1.4	0.0
Black Bean, Canton, Stir Fry, Blue Dragon*	1 Pack/100g	88	88	2.8	14.8	2.0	1.5
Black Bean, Cantonese, Sainsbury's*	1 Serving/50ml	83	166	2.6	33.4	2.4	2.6
Black Bean, Finest, Tesco*	1 Jar/350g	252	72	0.8	16.1	0.5	0.8
Black Bean, Fresh, Sainsbury's*	1 Sachet/50ml	78	156	6.7	27.5	2.6	1.7
Black Bean, Iceland*	¼ Jar/125g	131	105	1.3	15.3	4.2	0.7
Black Bean, Lloyd Grossman*	1 Serving/175g	177	101	2.4	12.6	4.5	0.7
Black Bean, Sharwood's*	1 Serving/97.5g	98	100	2.0	20.3	1.2	0.6
Black Bean, Stir Fry Additions, Tesco*	1 Sachet/50g	69	138	4.1	23.6	3.0	0.0
Black Bean, Stir Fry, Amoy*	1oz/28g	29	104	1.8	12.0	5.6	0.0
Black Bean, Stir Fry, Asda*	1 Serving/50ml	54	108	2.9	21.0	1.4	0.0
Black Bean, Stir Fry, Fresh Ideas, Tesco*	½ Sachet/25g	33	132	4.2	22.6	2.8	0.8
Black Bean, Stir Fry, Marks & Spencer*	1 Serving/60g	108	180	6.3	20.0	8.0	2.0
Black Bean, Stir Fry, Morrisons*	½ Jar/237g	135	57	1.7	11.2	0.6	0.0
Black Bean, Stir Fry, Safeway*	1/3 Pack/33g	43	129	3.7	20.2	3.7	0.9
Black Bean, Stir Fry, Sainsbury's*	1 Serving/70ml	107	153	6.7	25.8	2.6	1.7
Black Bean, Stir Fry, Sharwood's*	1 Jar/160g	149	93	0.3	19.9	1.3	1.2
Black Bean, Stir Fry, Straight To Wok, Amoy*	1 Pack/220g	411	187	2.7	42.7	0.6	0.0
Black Bean, Stir Fry, Tesco*	½ Jar/220g	216	98	2.3	17.9	1.6	0.7
Black Bean, Uncle Ben's*	1 Serving/125g	89	71	2.0	12.8	1.3	0.0
Black Bean, Wing Yip*	½ Jar/61g	75	123	3.2	17.3	4.9	0.0
Black Pepper, Hong Kong, Straight To Wok*	1oz/28g	40	142	2.2	20.5	5.7	0.0
Black Pepper, Lee Kum Kee*	1 Serving/90g	107	119	3.2	19.0	3.3	1.3
Black Pepper, Stir Fry, Blue Dragon*	½ Sachet/60g	47	79	1.6	8.4	4.4	0.1
Bolognese, Emilia Romagna, Fresh, Sainsbury's*	½ Pot/150g	99	66	5.9	3.4	3.2	1.7
Bolognese, Fresh, Safeway*	½ Pot/153g	182	119	7.3	6.3	7.2	1.6
Bolognese, Lloyd Grossman*	¼ Jar/106g	80	75	2.0	10.2	2.9	1.4
Bolognese, Original, Deliciously Good, Homepride*	¼ Jar/112g	39	35	1.3	7.1	0.2	0.8
Bolognese, Original, Dolmio*	1 Serving/250g	130	52	1.7	8.7	1.2	0.0
Bolognese, Waitrose*	1 Serving/175g	151	86	5.4	5.3	4.9	2.0

SAUCE,

INFO/WEIGHT	Measure	per Measure KCAL	KCAL	PROT	CARB	FAT	FIBRE
Brandy Flavour, Kraft*	1oz/28g	25	91	2.5	15.5	1.4	0.0
Branston Smooth, Crosse & Blackwell*	1 Serving/25g	35	139	0.6	34.0	0.1	1.4
Brazilian Chicken, Chicken Tonight*	1 Serving/125g	49	39	1.2	7.0	0.7	1.3
Bread, Luxury, Marks & Spencer*	1 Serving/115g	196	170	3.2	8.1	14.1	2.2
Bread, Made With Semi-Skimmed Milk	1 Serving/45g	42	93	4.3	12.8	3.1	0.3
Bread, Marks & Spencer*	1 Serving/85g	153	180	3.1	8.7	14.6	0.2
Brown, Bottled	1 Tsp/6g	6	99	1.1	25.2	0.0	0.7
Brown, Daddies Favourite, HP*	1 Tsp/6g	6	102	0.9	24.3	0.1	0.0
Brown, Tesco*	1 Tsp/10g	10	104	0.7	25.1	0.1	0.6
Burger, Hellmann's*	1 Tbsp/15g	36	240	1.1	12.0	21.0	0.0
Butter & Tarragon, Chicken Tonight*	1oz/28g	30	106	1.0	2.1	10.4	0.7
Buttermilch Banane, Lifestyle, Co-Op*	1 Serving/250ml	65	26	2.1	4.0	0.2	0.0
Cajun, Sizzle & Stir, Chicken Tonight*	1/3 Jar/150g	189	126	0.8	12.0	8.3	0.0
Cantonese, Sizzling, Uncle Ben's*	½ Jar/270g	416	154	0.7	24.0	6.1	0.0
Cantonese, Sweet & Sour, Stir Fry, Sainsbury's*	1 Pack/100ml	211	211	0.9	38.0	6.2	1.2
Carbonara, BGTY, Sainsbury's*	1 Serving/150g	110	73	3.5	4.5	4.5	0.5
Carbonara, Co-Op*	1 Pack/300g	555	185	8.0	7.0	14.0	0.1
Carbonara, Creamy, Loyd Grossman*	1oz/28g	52	186	3.8	8.9	15.0	0.3
Carbonara, Creamy, Microwaveable, Dolmio*	1 Serving/75g	116	155	3.3	4.0	13.5	0.0
Carbonara, Fresh, Safeway*	1 Serving/175g	285	163	7.1	5.2	12.6	0.5
Carbonara, Fresh, Sainsbury's*	½ Pot/150g	333	222	5.9	2.2	21.1	0.8
Carbonara, GFY, Asda,*	1 Serving/170g	167	98	5.0	6.0	6.0	0.0
Carbonara, Healthy Eating, Tesco*	1 Serving/175g	121	69	5.2	6.2	2.6	0.0
Carbonara, Less Than 5% Fat, Safeway*	1 Serving/175g	130	74	4.1	4.8	4.2	0.2
Carbonara, Pasta, Tesco*	1 Serving/150g	182	121	2.8	3.2	10.8	0.0
Carbonara, Perfectly Balanced, Waitrose*	½ Pot/175g	154	88	7.8	6.0	3.6	1.2
Carbonara, Stir In, Dolmio*	1 Serving/75g	140	186	6.5	3.7	15.8	0.0
Carmelised Onion & Red Wine, Marks & Spencer*	1 Serving/52g	31	60	1.9	6.7	3.1	0.6
Casserole, Sausage, Cook In , Homepride*	1 Jar/720g	504	70	0.8	16.0	0.2	0.0
Chasseur, Classic, Chicken Tonight*	1 Serving/100g	45	45	0.7	3.9	2.9	1.3
Chasseur, Cook In, Homepride*	1 Can/390g	156	40	0.7	9.2	0.1	0.0
Cheddar Cheese, Knorr*	1 Serving/10g	47	469	7.8	38.0	31.8	0.3
Cheddar Cheese, Schwartz*	1 Pack/40g	50	124	5.0	12.2	6.2	0.3
Cheese, Asda*	1 Serving/27g	101	373	4.4	64.0	11.0	7.0
Cheese, Cheddar, Colman's*	1 Pack/40g	158	394	19.7	45.2	14.9	1.5
Cheese, For Broccoli, Creamy, Schwartz*	1 Pack/40g	144	361	8.1	66.5	6.9	1.4
Cheese, Fresh, Italiano, Tesco*	½ Tub/175g	236	135	6.8	6.2	9.2	0.0
Cheese, Fresh, Waitrose*	1 Pot/350g	459	131	5.1	5.7	9.8	0.0
Cheese, Granules, Bisto*	1 Serving/200ml	168	84	1.2	7.4	5.4	0.2
Cheese, Granules, Made Up, Bisto*	1floz/30ml	30	100	1.2	6.4	7.6	0.0
Cheese, Instant, Morrisons*	1 Serving/14g	38	272	7.9	14.3	20.3	0.0
Cheese, Italian Style, Finest, Tesco*	½ Pot/175g	355	203	10.1	14.0	11.9	0.0
Cheese, Italiano, Tesco*	1 Pot/350g	368	105	5.3	8.0	5.7	0.0
Cheese, Made With Semi-Skimmed Milk	1 Serving/60g	107	179	8.1	9.1	12.6	0.2
Cheese, Made With Whole Milk	1 Serving/60g	118	197	8.0	9.0	14.6	0.2
Cherry Tomato & Fresh Basil, Marks & Spencer*	1 Serving/175g	131	75	1.2	5.5	5.3	1.1
Chicken, Sizzling, Dolmio*	1 Serving/100g	102	102	1.2	7.5	7.5	0.0
Chicken, Spanish, Chicken Tonight*	1 Serving/250g	123	49	1.7	8.0	1.3	1.0
Chili & Garlic, Amoy*	1oz/28g	31	112	12.0	27.0	0.0	0.0
Chili Soy, Amoy*	1 Tbsp/15g	8	54	4.2	9.2	0.0	0.0
Chilli & Garlic, Lea & Perrins*	1 Tsp/6g	4	60	1.0	14.9	0.0	0.0
Chilli & Garlic, Stir Fry, Marks & Spencer*	1 Serving/82.5g	120	145	0.7	32.4	1.2	1.1
Chilli Con Carne, 2 Step Season, Discovery*	½ Jar/185g	176	95	3.8	17.6	1.2	3.1

S

SAUCE,	Measure INFO/WEIGHT	per Measure KCAL	Nutrition Values per 100g / 100ml				
			KCAL	PROT	CARB	FAT	FIBRE
Chilli Con Carne, Asda*	1 Large Jar/570g	371	65	2.6	12.0	0.7	0.0
Chilli Con Carne, Cook In, Homepride*	1 Can/390g	234	60	2.5	11.2	0.6	0.0
Chilli Con Carne, Cooking, BGTY, Sainsbury's*	1 Jar/500g	190	38	0.8	8.2	0.2	0.6
Chilli Con Carne, Hot, Sainsbury's*	1 Serving/116g	66	57	2.4	11.3	0.2	1.6
Chilli With Kidney Beans, Old El Paso*	1 Serving/115g	92	80	4.3	14.8	0.4	0.0
Chilli, Amoy*	1 Tsp/6g	2	25	1.0	5.2	0.0	1.0
Chilli, Cooking, SmartPrice, Asda*	1 Serving/140g	80	57	2.5	11.0	0.3	1.1
Chilli, HP*	1 Tsp/6g	8	134	1.2	32.3	0.1	0.0
Chilli, Hot, Co-Op*	1 Jar/440g	242	55	2.0	10.0	0.5	2.0
Chilli, Iceland*	1 Serving/115g	75	65	2.7	12.0	0.7	1.6
Chilli, Medium, Deliciously Good, Homepride*	1 Jar/460g	258	56	2.3	10.4	0.5	1.2
Chilli, Mild, Colman's*	1 Pack/35g	113	322	9.2	60.0	3.9	0.0
Chilli, Mild, Healthy Eating, Asda*	½ Jar/250g	173	69	2.1	10.0	2.3	1.7
Chilli, Mild, Safeway*	1 Serving/250g	188	75	2.4	11.3	2.2	1.2
Chilli, Seeds Of Change*	1 Jar/400g	408	102	4.0	18.2	1.5	2.2
Chillil, Mild, Asda*	1 Pack/128g	88	69	2.1	10.0	2.3	1.7
Chinese 5 Spice, Stir It Up, Chicken Tonight*	1 Jar/80g	478	597	2.4	34.1	50.1	6.6
Chinese Orange, Honey & Ginger, Cooking, Sainsbury's*	1 Serving/125g	91	73	0.3	17.2	0.3	0.3
Chinese Style, Stir Fry, Fresh, Asda*	½ Sachet/50ml	93	186	1.5	18.0	12.0	0.0
Chinese Sweet & Sour, Cooking, Sainsbury's*	¼ Jar/125g	109	87	0.7	20.1	0.1	0.7
Chinese, Curry, Farmfoods*	1 Sachet/200g	220	110	0.6	7.1	8.8	0.7
Chinese, Stir Fry, Sachet, Fresh, Sainsbury's*	½ Sachet/51ml	83	163	1.7	14.1	11.1	1.8
Chinese, Stir Fry, Tesco*	1 Pack/50g	170	340	0.8	17.3	29.7	0.0
Chip Shop Curry, Bisto*	1 Serving/10.7g	51	468	4.3	72.6	17.8	2.7
Chocolate Flavour, Lyle's*	1 Serving/10g	31	305	1.0	74.0	0.5	0.0
Chocolate, Sainsbury's*	1 Serving/30g	108	360	1.3	62.8	11.6	0.9
Chop Suey, Blue Dragon*	½ Sachet/60g	34	57	0.5	8.3	2.4	0.5
Chop Suey, Cantonese, Sharwood's*	1 Serving/200g	146	73	0.6	14.4	1.4	0.4
Chop Suey, Cooking, Asda*	1 Serving/240g	214	89	0.6	17.0	2.1	0.2
Chop Suey, Stir Fry, Sharwood's*	1 Jar/160g	120	75	0.7	14.6	1.5	0.2
Chow Mein, Sainsbury's*	1 Serving/50g	36	71	1.8	10.5	2.4	0.0
Chow Mein, Stir Fry, Asda*	½ Jar/97.5g	97	99	1.6	21.0	1.0	0.1
Chow Mein, Stir Fry, Blue Dragon*	1 Sachet/120g	110	92	1.1	15.4	2.9	0.4
Chow Mein, Stir Fry, Safeway*	1 Serving/75ml	128	170	1.3	29.0	5.1	0.7
Chunky Onions & Garlic, Ragu*	¼ Jar/129g	66	51	1.9	7.6	1.4	2.0
Coconut, Chilli & Lime, Cook-In, Homepride*	1 Serving/115g	110	96	1.1	5.9	7.5	0.0
Coronation Chicken, Cook In, Homepride*	1 Serving/250g	233	93	0.8	13.2	4.2	0.0
Coronation, Heinz*	1 Tbsp/10g	33	334	0.8	13.1	31.0	0.9
Country French, Chicken Tonight*	¼ Jar/125g	123	98	0.7	3.3	9.1	0.7
Country French, Low Fat, Chicken Tonight*	1 Serving/125g	58	46	0.9	4.2	2.8	0.7
Country Mushroom, Ragu*	¼ Jar/129g	88	68	2.0	9.5	2.1	1.2
Cowboy Joe BBQ, Eazy Squirt, Heinz*	1 Serving/10ml	11	114	0.5	27.4	0.2	0.2
Cracked Black Pepper, Marks & Spencer*	1 Jar/300g	345	115	2.7	6.7	8.9	0.4
Cracked Black Pepper, Stir Fry, Amoy*	1 Serving/60g	151	251	1.9	49.4	5.1	0.0
Cranberry & Port, Marks & Spencer*	1 Serving/75g	71	95	2.3	20.2	0.4	2.1
Cranberry & Red Onion, Sizzling, Homepride*	1 Serving/100g	83	83	0.5	17.7	1.0	0.0
Cranberry Jelly, Baxters*	1 Tsp/15g	40	268	0.0	67.0	0.0	0.0
Cranberry, Safeway*	1 Tsp/15g	25	168	0.2	41.0	0.3	1.3
Cranberry, Sainsbury's*	1 Tsp/15g	23	154	0.8	37.1	0.3	1.3
Cranberry, Tesco*	1 Tsp/15g	23	156	0.1	38.8	0.0	0.9
Creamy Garlic & Herb, Schwartz*	1 Serving/75g	83	110	3.6	11.6	5.5	0.4
Creamy Ham, Knorr*	1 Pouch/100ml	163	163	0.3	4.0	16.0	0.3
Creamy Horseradish With Garlic, So Good, Somefield*	1 Tsp/6g	19	317	4.1	25.0	22.3	0.0

SAUCE,	Measure INFO/WEIGHT	per Measure KCAL	Nutrition Values per 100g / 100ml				
			KCAL	PROT	CARB	FAT	FIBRE
Creamy Lemon & Dill, Fresh, Sainsbury's*	½ Pot/150g	242	161	1.6	4.2	15.3	1.5
Creamy Mushroom Stroganoff, Marks & Spencer*	1 Serving/75g	86	115	3.3	4.8	9.2	0.6
Creamy Mushroom, Cooking, Marks & Spencer*	1 Jar/510g	663	130	1.3	5.4	11.3	0.5
Creamy Mushroom, Knorr*	1 Serving/125g	111	89	0.4	4.5	7.7	0.4
Creamy Mushroom, Low Fat, Chicken Tonight*	1 Serving/250g	108	43	1.3	2.9	2.9	1.0
Creamy Peppercorn & Whisky, Baxters*	1 Pack/320g	422	132	1.9	6.7	10.8	0.2
Creamy Peppercorn, Asda*	¼ Jar/137g	137	100	1.1	6.0	8.0	0.2
Creamy Peppercorn, Chicken Tonight*	¼ Jar/125g	114	91	0.3	5.3	7.6	1.0
Creamy White Wine & Herb, 95% Fat Free, Homepride*	1 Serving/220g	150	68	0.6	6.3	4.5	0.7
Creamy, Curry, BGTY, Sainsbury's*	¼ Jar/125g	84	67	1.4	6.8	3.8	0.5
Creamy, Curry, Chicken Tonight*	¼ Jar/125g	106	85	1.5	4.6	6.7	0.8
Creole Recipe, Discovery*	¼ Jar/66g	62	94	0.9	17.9	1.8	0.7
Creole Style, Aldi*	1 Serving/160g	158	99	1.3	18.6	2.2	0.0
Cumberland Sausage, Colman's*	¼ Jar/126g	43	34	0.7	7.4	0.2	0.8
Curry Moglai Passanda, Asda*	½ Jar/170g	277	163	2.9	10.0	12.4	1.1
Curry, 98% Fat Free, Homepride*	1oz/28g	15	54	1.4	9.2	1.5	0.6
Curry, Bettabuy, Morrisons*	1 Jar/440g	295	67	0.7	10.8	2.3	1.0
Curry, Chinese Style, Asda*	1 Serving/184.2g	140	76	1.6	7.0	4.6	2.5
Curry, Cook In, Homepride*	½ Can/250g	270	108	0.7	9.1	7.6	0.6
Curry, Cooking, Savers, Safeway*	1 Jar/440g	295	67	1.4	7.4	3.5	0.9
Curry, Deliciously Good, Homepride*	1/3 Jar/149g	91	61	1.1	10.0	1.8	0.5
Curry, Medium, Uncle Ben's*	1 Serving/100g	66	66	0.9	11.1	2.0	0.0
Curry, Mild, Tesco*	1 Jar/500g	420	84	1.1	13.4	2.8	0.8
Curry, SmartPrice, Asda*	¼ Jar/110g	58	53	0.7	9.0	1.6	0.6
Curry, Sweet	1oz/28g	25	91	1.2	9.6	5.6	1.4
Curry, Sweet, McDonald's*	1 Portion/32g	61	192	1.2	41.1	2.5	0.0
Curry, Thai Red, Sizzle & Stir, Chicken Tonight*	1 Jar/485g	873	180	1.5	4.5	17.3	1.7
Dark Soya, Amoy*	1 Serving/10g	9	85	1.2	20.0	0.0	0.0
Dhansak, Medium, Sharwood's*	1 Jar/420g	370	88	3.6	11.1	3.2	1.0
Dhansak, Sharwood's*	1 Jar/445g	668	150	4.7	15.2	7.8	1.4
Diane, Safeway*	½ Pot/85g	40	47	0.8	3.3	3.5	0.3
Dill, Gravalax, Ikea*	1 Serving/17g	26	150	4.2	20.0	5.0	0.0
Dill, Sainsbury's*	1 Tsp/5g	23	466	1.9	19.7	42.2	0.9
Dipping For Dim Sum, Amoy*	1 Tbsp/15ml	29	190	0.0	48.0	0.0	0.0
Dopiaza, Patak's*	1 Serving/212g	235	111	1.7	9.1	7.6	1.3
Dopiaza,Medium, Cook In, Sharwood's*	½ Bottle/210g	193	92	1.4	10.2	5.1	0.6
Enchilada, Medium, Old El Paso*	1 Can/270g	92	34	0.0	5.0	1.7	0.0
Exotic Curry, Heinz*	1 Serving/15ml	41	271	0.7	15.3	22.8	0.6
Extra Creamy Mushroom, Chicken Tonight*	1 Serving/250g	218	87	0.4	5.5	7.0	0.5
Fajita, Asda*	¼ Jar/125g	79	63	1.0	5.0	4.3	1.0
Fajita, Marks & Spencer*	1oz/28g	24	85	1.3	6.4	6.1	2.2
Fajita, Stir It Up, Chicken Tonight*	1 Jar/80g	494	617	4.6	25.1	55.4	2.8
Fish, Nam Plam, Blue Dragon*	1 Tbsp/15ml	12	80	13.4	6.7	0.0	0.0
Flour, Sainsbury's*	1 Serving/20g	69	343	9.8	73.0	1.3	3.0
For Bolognese, Extra Onion & Garlic, Dolmio*	1 Serving/125g	66	53	1.7	9.0	1.0	0.0
For Bolognese, Light, Original, Ragu*	1 Jar/515g	196	38	1.4	8.2	0.1	1.2
For Bolognese, Original, Ragu*	1 Jar/515g	242	47	1.4	8.2	0.9	1.2
For Lasagne, Tomato, Ragu*	1 Jar/515g	191	37	1.5	7.4	0.2	1.0
For Lasagne, White, Dolmio*	1 Serving/140g	154	110	2.1	3.7	9.6	0.0
For Lasagne, White, Light, Ragu*	¼ Jar/122g	88	72	0.5	6.3	5.0	0.2
For Lasagne, White, Ragu	¼ Jar/123g	205	167	0.5	4.7	16.3	0.3
Four Cheese, Asda*	½ Jar/155g	242	156	3.5	3.9	14.0	0.1
Four Cheese, Less Than 5% Fat, Safeway*	½ Pot/175g	140	80	4.9	5.8	4.1	0.2

S

	Measure INFO/WEIGHT	per Measure KCAL	Nutrition Values per 100g / 100ml				
			KCAL	PROT	CARB	FAT	FIBRE
SAUCE,							
Four Cheese, Safeway*	1 Serving/175g	261	149	5.7	6.4	11.2	0.5
Fruity, HP*	1 Tsp/6g	8	141	1.2	35.1	0.1	0.0
Garlic, Heinz*	1 Serving/10ml	32	323	1.0	12.1	29.9	1.2
Garlic, Lea & Perrins*	1 Tsp/6g	20	337	1.8	17.8	29.0	0.0
Granules, White, Bisto*	1 Serving/10g	50	499	3.3	58.6	28.0	1.0
Green Peppercorn, Sainsbury's*	1 Tbsp/15ml	68	455	0.4	3.8	48.5	0.1
Green Tandoori, Marks & Spencer*	1 Jar/385g	501	130	3.6	6.8	9.9	1.5
Green Thai, Curry, Asda*	1 Jar/340g	309	91	0.5	4.3	8.0	0.2
Green Thai, Loyd Grossman*	½ Jar/175g	228	130	2.3	10.1	9.0	1.2
Green Thai, So Good, Somerfield*	1 Jar/350g	413	118	1.2	7.0	9.5	0.5
Green Thai, Stir Fry, Fresh Ideas, Tesco*	1 Pack/50g	91	182	2.1	6.2	16.6	0.1
Green Thai, Stir Fry, Safeway*	1 Serving/75ml	259	345	1.2	12.2	32.0	2.1
HP*	1oz/28g	33	119	1.1	27.1	0.2	0.0
Ham & Mushroom, Safeway*	½ Pot/154g	149	97	6.5	6.5	5.0	0.7
Hoi Sin & Plum, Chinatown, Knorr*	¼ Jar/131g	96	73	0.8	15.8	0.7	1.2
Hoi Sin & Plum, Finest, Tesco*	1 Serving/50g	78	156	2.3	35.3	0.6	1.4
Hoi Sin & Plum, Sweet & Fruity Stir Fry, Sharwood's*	1 Serving/136g	126	93	0.9	19.3	1.3	0.7
Hoi Sin & Spring Onion, Stir Fry, Sharwood's*	1 Jar/165g	223	135	2.6	27.8	1.5	0.9
Hoi Sin, Marks & Spencer*	½ Pot/50ml	80	160	3.2	31.8	2.0	2.2
Hoi Sin, Sharwood's*	1 Tbsp/20g	42	211	2.7	49.5	0.3	0.6
Hollandaise, Colman's*	1 Pack/27g	102	379	10.0	54.0	13.0	0.0
Hollandaise, Full Fat, Marks & Spencer*	1 Tbsp/20g	67	336	1.1	4.5	34.9	0.1
Hollandaise, Maille*	1 Serving/30g	149	495	1.0	10.8	50.6	0.0
Hollandaise, Marks & Spencer*	1oz/28g	56	200	1.6	2.4	20.5	0.1
Hollandaise, Pour Over, Knorr*	1oz/28g	44	158	0.0	7.0	14.0	0.0
Hollandaise, Sainsbury's*	1 Tbsp/15ml	77	515	0.5	4.2	55.0	0.0
Hollandaise, Schwartz*	1 Pack/25g	98	392	11.3	61.5	11.2	0.0
Honey & Coriander, Stir Fry, Blue Dragon*	1 Pack/120g	115	96	0.5	22.1	0.6	0.3
Honey & Mustard, COU, Marks & Spencer*	½ Jar/160g	112	70	2.3	9.2	2.9	0.7
Honey & Mustard, Chicken Tonight*	¼ Jar/130g	139	107	1.6	13.5	5.2	1.3
Honey & Mustard, For Cooking, Asda*	1 Serving/200g	234	117	0.6	13.0	7.0	0.0
Honey n Chilli, Stir Fry, Discovery*	½ Pack/75g	123	164	1.1	37.3	1.1	1.9
Hong Kong Curry, Loyd Grossman*	1 Jar/350g	371	106	1.3	7.8	7.7	0.8
Horseradish, Asda*	1oz/28g	38	135	2.2	14.0	7.0	2.0
Horseradish, Creamed, Colman's*	1 Tsp/16g	37	229	4.3	21.4	13.3	0.0
Horseradish, Creamed, Marks & Spencer*	1 Tsp/5g	16	325	2.4	12.1	29.3	2.5
Horseradish, Creamed, Safeway*	1 Serving/10g	18	184	2.4	19.6	9.8	2.3
Horseradish, Creamed, Tesco*	1 Serving/15g	30	202	2.4	23.0	10.3	1.9
Horseradish, Creamed, Waitrose*	1 Tbsp/16g	30	185	2.4	19.6	9.9	2.3
Horseradish, Hot, Colman's*	1 Tbsp/15ml	16	105	1.8	9.7	5.7	0.0
Horseradish, Hot, Tesco*	1 Serving/10g	15	150	1.8	20.1	6.0	3.3
Horseradish, Mustard, Sainsbury's*	1 Tsp/5g	4	82	5.3	2.3	5.8	0.0
Horseradish, Sainsbury's*	1 Dtsp/10g	15	145	1.5	17.8	6.6	2.4
Hot Chilli, Asda*	¼ Jar/126g	82	65	2.0	8.0	2.8	1.2
Hot Chilli, Deliciously Good, Homepride*	1 Serving/120g	62	52	1.3	10.6	0.5	1.1
Hot Chilli, Sharwood's*	1fl oz/30ml	36	120	0.5	29.4	0.6	1.3
Hot Chilli, Uncle Ben's*	1 Jar/500g	250	50	2.0	9.6	0.4	0.0
Hot Onion, TTD Sainsbury's*	1 Serving/10g	17	167	0.2	41.0	0.1	0.1
Hot Pepper	1oz/28g	7	26	1.6	1.7	1.5	0.0
Hot Pepper, Encona*	1 Tsp/5ml	3	52	0.5	10.5	1.2	0.0
Indian Tikka, Chicken Tonight*	1 Serving/250g	320	128	1.3	10.0	9.2	1.2
Italian Hot Chili, Dolmio*	½ Pack/150g	104	69	1.3	7.1	3.9	0.0
Italian Onion & Garlic, Sainsbury's*	1 Jar/500g	375	75	2.2	12.1	2.0	1.7

SAUCE,	Measure INFO/WEIGHT	per Measure KCAL	Nutrition Values per 100g / 100ml				
			KCAL	PROT	CARB	FAT	FIBRE
Italian Tomato & Herb, For Pasta, BGTY, Sainsbury's*	½ Jar/250g	138	55	2.1	10.9	0.3	0.0
Italian Tomato & Herb, Sainsbury's*	¼ Jar/126g	88	70	2.0	11.1	2.0	1.4
Italian With Onion, Garlic & Herb, Safeway*	1 Serving/210g	143	68	2.1	11.5	1.6	1.8
Jalfrezi Hot, Cooking, Sharwood's*	1 Jar/440g	264	60	1.4	7.8	2.6	1.5
Jalfrezi, Cooking, Asda*	1 Jar/500g	470	94	1.0	9.0	6.0	0.7
Jalfrezi, Cooking, Sainsbury's*	1 Serving/250g	160	64	1.0	9.6	2.4	1.7
Jalfrezi, Cooking, Shere Khan*	1 Jar/425g	202	48	0.8	3.9	3.2	0.0
Jalfrezi, Cooking, Tesco*	¼ Jar/125g	144	115	2.6	11.4	6.5	1.6
Jalfrezi, Curry, Loyd Grossman*	1 Jar/425g	540	127	2.1	8.2	9.5	1.2
Jalfrezi, Curry, Patak's*	1 Serving/135g	157	116	1.7	11.3	7.0	1.4
Jalfrezi, Hot, Tesco*	1 Serving/220g	125	57	1.1	8.3	2.1	0.8
Jalfrezi, Marks & Spencer*	1 Jar/385g	308	80	1.7	6.6	5.2	1.9
Jalfrezi, Mild, Sharwood's*	1 Jar/420g	315	75	1.1	8.1	4.2	1.2
Jalfrezi, Piri Piri, Finest, Tesco*	1 Serving/175g	145	83	1.2	5.7	6.2	1.5
Jalfrezi, Stir Fry, Patak's*	1 Jar/250g	260	104	1.4	7.6	7.5	1.4
Kaffir Lime Chilli & Basil, Stir Fry, Sainsbury's*	1 Serving/150g	158	105	1.2	10.6	6.4	1.0
Karai Tomato & Coriander, Patak's*	1 Serving/135g	170	126	4.0	15.7	5.2	1.1
Kashmiri, Butter, Patak's*	1 Jar/420g	533	127	2.1	14.4	7.1	0.7
Kashmiri, Sharwoods*	½ Bottle/210g	231	110	3.0	13.0	5.1	1.5
Korma, Asda*	1 Serving/225g	434	193	2.5	12.0	15.0	2.2
Korma, Coconut & Cream, Patak's*	1 Serving/135g	235	174	1.3	9.1	14.7	0.8
Korma, Cooking, BGTY, Sainsbury's*	¼ Jar/129g	119	92	1.1	10.8	4.9	1.4
Korma, Cooking, Healthy Eating, Tesco*	¼ Jar/125g	120	96	1.9	7.4	6.4	0.6
Korma, Cooking, Sainsbury's*	¼ Jar/125g	159	127	1.4	8.0	9.9	1.0
Korma, Deliciously Good, Homepride*	1 Jar/450g	396	88	1.4	10.6	4.4	1.4
Korma, GFY, Asda*	1 Serving/240g	312	130	3.0	7.0	10.0	1.6
Korma, Homepride*	1 Serving/160g	110	69	1.3	11.6	2.0	0.0
Korma, Indian Style, Iceland*	¼ Jar/112g	150	134	1.5	11.4	9.1	1.0
Korma, Indian, Marks & Spencer*	1oz/28g	60	215	3.8	11.7	17.3	0.9
Korma, Loyd Grossman*	½ Jar/222g	542	244	3.6	19.1	17.0	0.6
Korma, Mild Curry, Better For You, Morrisons*	¼ Jar/118g	150	127	1.3	16.8	6.1	1.5
Korma, Organic, Patak's*	¼ Jar/106g	148	140	1.9	5.9	12.0	0.9
Korma, Patak's*	1 Jar/540g	751	139	2.4	11.4	9.4	1.0
Korma, Safeway*	½ Jar/250g	213	85	2.0	13.6	2.5	1.7
Korma, Seeds Of Change*	½ Jar/175g	231	132	1.2	12.8	8.4	1.3
Korma, Sharwood's*	1 Serving/105g	150	143	1.4	12.2	9.8	1.8
Korma, Sizzle & Stir, Knorr*	1 Serving/152g	365	240	1.2	11.2	21.2	2.7
Korma, Tesco*	1 Serving/125g	230	184	2.4	10.2	14.7	0.6
Korma, Tin, Patak's*	1 Can/283g	478	169	3.6	8.5	13.4	2.3
Korma, Uncle Ben's*	1 Jar/500g	625	125	1.2	11.4	7.8	0.0
Lamb Hot Pot, For Cooking, Asda*	1 Pack/42g	147	351	7.0	65.0	7.0	3.3
Lemon & Ginger, Stir Fry, Safeway*	1 Serving/110g	182	165	0.2	40.7	0.2	0.2
Lemon & Sesame, Sharwood's*	1 Serving/100g	118	118	0.2	28.9	0.2	0.1
Lemon Butter, Schwartz*	1 Serving/9g	35	388	10.2	61.4	11.3	0.0
Lemon Pepper, Stir It Up, Chicken Tonight*	1 Jar/80g	527	659	5.2	26.1	59.3	2.7
Lemon, Amoy*	1 Tsp/5ml	5	104	0.0	26.0	0.0	0.0
Lemon, Stir Fry, Straight to Wok, Amoy*	½ Sachet/50g	81	162	0.3	40.0	0.2	0.0
Lemon, Stir Fry, Tesco*	1 Jar/450g	369	82	0.1	19.3	0.2	0.1
Lime Honey & Ginger, Stir Fry, Sharwood's*	1 Serving/50g	35	69	0.3	16.6	0.1	0.2
Madras Cumin & Chilli, Patak's*	1/4 Jar/135g	162	120	2.1	11.9	7.1	1.8
Madras, Aldi*	1 Serving/113g	68	60	1.5	9.0	2.0	0.0
Madras, Cooking, Asda*	¼ Jar/141.6g	109	77	1.3	8.0	4.4	1.0
Madras, Cooking, Sharwood's*	1 Tsp/2g	2	86	1.5	6.9	5.8	1.3

	Measure	per Measure	Nutrition Values per 100g / 100ml				
	INFO/WEIGHT	KCAL	KCAL	PROT	CARB	FAT	FIBRE
SAUCE,							
Madras, Curry, Sharwood's*	1 Jar/420g	521	124	1.7	8.9	9.1	1.4
Madras, Curry, Somerfield*	1 Serving/110g	106	96	1.7	8.3	6.1	0.7
Makhani, Sharwood's*	1 Jar/420g	399	95	0.9	7.2	6.9	0.4
Mediterranean Vegetable, Roasted, Sainsbury's*	½ Pot/150g	102	68	1.6	6.7	3.9	0.4
Mediterranean Vegetable, Waitrose*	1/3 Pot/120g	60	50	1.3	4.5	3.0	1.6
Mediterranean Vegetables, Stir In, BGTY, Sainsbury's*	1 Jar/150g	123	82	1.9	9.0	4.3	1.4
Mexican Fajita, Stir It Up, Knorr*	1/3 Jar/26.7g	161	596	4.4	22.6	54.2	7.8
Mexican Recipe, Discovery*	1 Jar/265g	355	134	1.5	18.2	5.5	1.4
Mexican Style, Cooking, Eat Smart, Safeway*	1 Serving/178g	134	75	1.3	15.8	0.6	1.2
Mint Garden, Fresh, Tesco*	1 Tsp/5g	2	40	2.6	3.6	0.4	1.5
Mint Jelly, Sweet, Colman's*	1 Serving/14ml	35	249	0.2	61.0	0.0	0.0
Mint Raita, Patak's*	1 Jar/270g	340	126	3.9	13.6	5.5	0.1
Mint, Baxters*	1oz/28g	17	62	1.7	13.2	0.3	0.0
Mint, Classic, Colman's*	1 Serving/5ml	6	122	0.8	26.0	0.1	0.0
Mint, Sainsbury's*	1 Dtsp/10g	13	126	2.5	28.7	0.1	4.0
Mint, SmartPrice, Asda*	1 Serving/5g	3	52	0.1	13.0	0.0	1.2
Mornay, Cheese, Asda*	¼ Pot/71g	114	161	6.8	6.6	12.7	0.4
Moroccan Seven Vegetable Cous Cous, Sainsbury's*	1 Serving/50g	89	178	2.6	5.9	16.0	0.0
Moroccan Tagine, Pan Fry, Loyd Grossman*	1oz/28g	15	53	0.9	5.4	3.1	0.4
Morrocan Chicken, Chicken Tonight*	1 Jar/500g	365	73	0.4	14.7	1.3	1.4
Mushroom & Garlic, 95% Fat Free, Homepride*	1 Serving/220g	154	70	0.9	7.0	4.2	0.3
Mushroom & Herb, Cooking, BGTY, Sainsbury's*	¼ Jar/125g	68	54	1.8	6.6	2.3	0.5
Mushroom & White Wine, Knorr*	1 Serving/100ml	99	99	1.0	4.0	8.0	0.6
Mushroom, Creamy, Tesco*	½ Pot/175g	128	73	1.3	6.4	4.7	0.4
Mushroom, For Pasta, Organic, Safeway*	1 Serving/220g	130	59	1.4	7.8	2.5	1.2
Mushroom, TTD, Sainsbury's*	1 Serving/150g	251	167	2.6	3.5	15.8	1.4
Mustard, Mild, McDonald's*	1 Portion/30g	64	212	1.0	24.8	12.1	0.0
Napoletana, Fresh, Sainsbury's*	½ Pot/150g	95	63	1.7	7.3	3.0	2.3
Napoletana, Italiano, New Improved Recipe, Tesco*	½ Pot/175g	126	72	1.6	8.7	3.4	1.1
Napoletana, Safeway*	1 Serving/175g	107	61	1.3	6.1	3.5	1.4
Napoletana, Tesco*	¼ Lge Tub/125g	90	72	1.6	8.7	3.4	1.1
Napoletana, Waitrose*	½ Pot/175g	88	50	1.2	5.2	2.7	1.8
Nasi Goreng, Indonesion, Sainsbury's*	1 Tbsp/15g	24	162	3.3	11.8	11.3	2.1
Olive & Tomato, Stir Through, Sacla*	½ Jar/95g	189	199	2.1	4.1	19.4	0.0
Onion, Colman's*	1 Sachet/35g	111	318	9.8	67.7	0.9	400.0
Onion, Made With Semi-Skimmed Milk	1 Serving/60g	52	86	2.9	8.4	5.0	0.4
Onion, Made With Skimmed Milk	1 Serving/60g	46	77	2.9	8.4	4.0	0.4
Orange & Green Ginger, Blue Dragon*	1 Pack/120g	118	98	0.5	20.4	1.6	0.5
Oriental Orange & Ginger, Homepride*	1 Serving/100g	68	68	0.7	15.9	0.1	0.0
Oriental Sweet & Sour, Express, Uncle Ben's*	1 Serving/170g	221	130	0.8	27.5	1.9	0.0
Oyster & Garlic, Stir Fry, Straight To Wok, Amoy*	½ Pack/50g	98	195	4.9	37.0	3.0	0.0
Oyster & Spring Onion, Stir Fry, Blue Dragon*	1 Serving/80g	74	92	1.6	19.9	0.7	1.1
Oyster Flavoured, Amoy*	1 Tsp/5ml	5	108	2.0	25.0	0.0	0.0
Oyster, Stir Fry, Sainsbury's	1 Tbsp/15g	9	61	1.6	13.3	0.1	0.2
Pad Thai, Blue Dragon*	1 Serving/50g	117	234	1.0	44.0	6.0	0.0
Paprika Chicken, Chicken Tonight*	1 Serving/250g	240	96	0.9	3.5	8.7	1.4
Parsley & Chive ,For Cod, Schwartz*	1 Serving/19g	74	388	9.4	64.1	10.4	0.0
Parsley, Colman's*	1 Sachet/20g	64	320	10.4	66.0	1.7	0.0
Parsley, Fresh, Sainsbury's*	½ Pot/150g	183	122	2.5	7.0	9.3	1.3
Parsley, Instant, Asda*	1 Serving/23g	82	355	7.0	66.0	7.0	4.4
Parsley, Made Up, Semi Skim Milk, Sainsbury's*	¼ Sachet/51ml	34	67	3.5	8.6	2.1	0.1
Pasanda, Almond & Yogurt, Patak's*	1 Jar/420g	634	151	2.2	8.5	12.0	0.5
Passata, Basil, Del Monte*	1 Jar/500g	160	32	1.4	5.9	0.2	0.0

S

SAUCE,

	Measure INFO/WEIGHT	per Measure KCAL	KCAL	PROT	CARB	FAT	FIBRE
Passata, Classic Italian With Onion & Garlic, Sainsbury's*	1oz/28g	10	37	1.4	7.7	0.1	1.3
Passata, Italian, Sainsbury's*	¼ Jar/175g	51	29	1.1	6.0	0.1	0.8
Passata, Italian, Tesco*	1 Pack/500g	170	34	1.1	6.4	0.2	1.0
Passata, Napolina*	1 Bottle/690g	173	25	1.4	4.5	0.1	0.0
Passata, Onion Garlic & Herbs, Safeway*	1 Serving/138g	47	34	1.4	5.7	0.6	1.2
Passata, SmartPrice, Asda*	1 Serving/15g	4	25	1.4	4.5	0.1	0.2
Passata, Valfrutta*	1 Serving/50g	13	25	1.4	4.5	0.1	0.0
Passata, With Garlic & Italian Herbs, Tesco*	1 Serving/165g	53	32	1.2	6.4	0.2	1.1
Peking Lemon, Stir Fry, Blue Dragon*	1 Serving/35g	58	166	0.3	36.8	1.9	0.1
Peking, Sizzle & Stir, Chicken Tonight*	1 Jar/510g	617	121	0.8	9.4	8.9	1.6
Pepper & Brandy, Pour Over, Knorr*	1oz/28g	29	104	1.0	4.0	9.0	0.0
Pepper, Creamy, Colman's*	1 Pack/25g	88	352	13.0	50.0	11.0	0.0
Pepper, Creamy, Schwartz*	1 Serving/25g	92	368	17.6	61.0	5.9	0.0
Peppercorn, Creamy, Chicken Tonight*	¼ Jar/125g	100	80	1.0	3.8	6.7	0.5
Peppercorn, Marks & Spencer*	1oz/28g	38	135	1.8	7.1	10.8	0.2
Peppercorn, Mild, Creamy, Cooked, Schwartz*	1 Serving/125g	133	106	4.7	8.7	5.9	0.8
Peppercorn, Milk, Creamy, Schwartz*	1 Pack/25g	93	373	12.9	64.7	6.9	0.0
Peppercorn, Safeway*	1 Serving/150g	221	147	1.9	6.9	12.4	0.6
Peri-Peri, Hot, Nando's*	1oz/28g	18	63	0.1	4.5	2.7	1.4
Pesto Rosso, Bertolli*	¼ Jar/47g	179	380	6.8	9.5	35.0	2.0
Pesto, Basil, Stir In, Waitrose*	½ Bottle/85g	394	463	12.8	8.2	42.1	1.4
Pesto, Bertolli*	1 Serving/20g	78	391	5.6	4.4	39.0	1.4
Pesto, Black Olive, Sacla*	1oz/28g	115	409	2.9	4.3	42.2	0.0
Pesto, Chargrilled Aubergine, Sacla'*	3 Tbsp/30g	102	339	2.4	3.8	34.9	0.0
Pesto, Classic Green, Sacla' *	1oz/28g	142	507	4.1	8.5	50.7	0.0
Pesto, Classsic, Sacla*	1 Serving/45g	209	465	5.5	5.6	46.7	0.0
Pesto, Creamy, Pasta Reale*	1 Pack/200g	302	151	2.1	4.5	13.8	0.2
Pesto, Fresh, Waitrose*	1 Tbsp/26g	120	463	12.8	8.2	42.1	1.4
Pesto, Green, Asda*	1 Tsp/5g	21	429	4.7	3.5	44.0	1.4
Pesto, Green, BGTY, Sainsbury's*	1 Hpd Tsp/20g	60	299	13.0	5.9	24.8	0.1
Pesto, Green, Bertolli*	1 Serving/47g	202	429	5.4	4.2	43.0	1.3
Pesto, Green, Free From, Sainsbury's*	1/3 Jar/70g	298	425	4.1	5.4	43.0	2.8
Pesto, Green, Fresh, Tesco*	1oz/28g	141	505	6.5	12.2	48.0	0.1
Pesto, Green, Half the Fat, Grandissimo*	1 Serving/48g	85	177	4.4	2.2	16.7	0.0
Pesto, Green, Italian, Safeway*	¼ Jar/50g	215	429	5.4	4.2	43.4	1.3
Pesto, Green, Morrisons*	1 Serving/50g	255	510	10.7	4.7	49.8	0.0
Pesto, Green, Romano*	½ Jar/50g	234	467	5.1	7.8	46.2	0.0
Pesto, Green, Sainsbury's*	1oz/28g	120	430	5.4	8.3	41.7	0.0
Pesto, Italian, Co Op*	1 Tsp/10g	43	430	5.0	4.0	44.0	2.0
Pesto, Marks & Spencer*	1oz/28g	115	411	3.2	3.5	43.3	3.9
Pesto, Red Pepper, Barilla*	1 Serving/25g	91	364	2.8	22.9	29.0	0.0
Pesto, Red Pepper, Sainsbury's*	1 Serving/37g	118	320	4.3	5.0	31.4	0.0
Pesto, Red, BGTY, Sainsbury's*	1 Serving/30ml	26	85	2.9	13.3	2.3	1.4
Pesto, Red, Fresh, Sainsbury's*	1 Serving/60g	233	389	4.5	8.6	37.4	0.7
Pesto, Red, Marks & Spencer*	1oz/28g	93	331	3.6	6.9	33.2	3.5
Pesto, Red, Sacla*	1 Serving/25g	82	327	4.3	8.9	30.4	0.0
Pesto, Red, Sainsbury's*	1 Serving/60g	242	404	4.8	17.0	35.5	0.8
Pesto, Rich Tomato With Basil, Dolmio*	1 Jar/170g	146	86	2.0	6.2	5.9	0.0
Pesto, Roasted Pepper, Sacla' *	1 Serving/47.6g	115	239	4.5	6.0	23.0	0.0
Pesto, Spinach & Parmesan, Sainsbury's*	½ Heap Tsp/16g	63	396	5.6	3.4	40.0	0.0
Pineapple & Red Pepper, Kwazulu, New World, Knorr*	1 Pack/500g	260	52	0.2	12.4	0.1	0.5
Pineapple Juice & Sweet Chilli, Stir Fry, Marks & Spencer*	1 Pot/120g	192	160	1.6	36.8	0.5	0.5
Plum & Ginger, Stir Fry, Asda*	½ Jar/97g	94	97	0.7	22.0	0.7	0.3

S

SAUCE,	Measure INFO/WEIGHT	per Measure KCAL	KCAL	PROT	CARB	FAT	FIBRE
Plum & Sesame, Stir Fry, Marks & Spencer*	½ Jar/115g	138	120	0.9	29.0	0.1	1.8
Plum, Sharwood's*	1 Serving/50g	121	241	0.5	59.4	0.2	0.6
Prawn Cocktail, Frank Cooper*	1 Tbsp/15g	47	316	0.8	18.3	26.7	0.1
Primavera, Loyd Grossman*	¼ Jar/88g	86	98	1.4	6.3	7.4	0.9
Puttanesca, Fresh, Waitrose*	½ Pot/176.1g	118	67	1.8	6.2	4.4	1.2
Raspberry, Dessert, Marks & Spencer*	1 Serving/20g	24	120	0.5	28.7	0.3	2.6
Real Oyster, Sharwood's*	1 Jar/150ml	113	75	1.3	17.0	0.2	0.3
Red & Yellow Pepper, Roasted, Sacla*	1 Serving/290g	232	80	1.1	5.5	5.9	0.0
Red Pepper, Fresh, Asda*	¼ Pot/82g	35	43	1.4	6.8	1.2	1.1
Red Thai Curry, Asda*	½ Jar/158g	248	157	2.0	8.0	13.0	2.5
Red Thai Curry, Finest, Tesco*	1 Jar/350g	389	111	1.3	6.2	9.0	0.9
Red Thai, Cooking, Perfectly Balanced, Waitrose*	1 Jar/430g	267	62	1.1	6.2	3.6	1.6
Red Thai, Curry, Worldwide Sauces*	1 Jar/450g	630	140	1.5	10.9	10.0	0.0
Red Thai, Loyd Grossman*	1oz/28g	34	123	2.6	11.7	7.3	1.1
Red Wine & Herb, Safeway*	1 Jar/680g	347	51	1.1	8.3	1.5	0.5
Red Wine & Herbs, Ragu*	¼ Jar/130g	81	62	2.1	8.8	2.0	1.1
Red Wine & Onion, Rich, Simply Sausages, Colman's*	¼ Jar/125g	49	39	0.9	8.5	0.2	1.3
Red Wine, Cook In, Homepride*	¼ Can/98g	47	48	0.5	10.1	0.6	0.0
Red Wine, Cooking, BGTY, Sainsbury's*	1 Serving/125g	53	42	0.5	8.8	0.5	0.8
Redcurrant, Colman's*	1 Tsp/12g	44	368	0.7	90.0	0.0	0.0
Risotto, Mushroom & White Wine, Sacla' *	1 Serving/95g	151	159	3.7	6.9	13.0	0.0
Roasted Peanut Satay, Stir Fry, Amoy*	1 Serving/75g	221	294	7.9	25.5	17.8	0.0
Roasted Vegetable, Finest, Tesco*	1 Serving/175g	102	58	1.4	7.8	2.4	1.0
Roasted Vegetable, Stir In, Dolmio*	1oz/28g	38	135	1.5	9.1	10.3	0.0
Rogan Josh, 99% Fat Free, Homepride*	1/3 Jar/153g	92	60	1.8	11.6	0.7	2.0
Rogan Josh, Asda*	¼ Jar/125g	135	108	0.9	8.0	8.0	0.6
Rogan Josh, Loyd Grossman*	½ Jar/212.5g	413	194	2.4	10.5	15.8	1.5
Rogan Josh, Medium, Sharwood's*	½ Jar/210g	151	72	1.4	8.6	3.6	0.5
Rogan Josh, Patak's*	1 Serving/270g	192	71	1.8	9.4	2.9	1.9
Rogan Josh, Tesco*	½ Can/220g	130	59	1.5	11.5	0.6	0.9
Rogan Josh, Worldwide, Aldi*	1 Serving/150g	92	61	1.5	12.4	0.6	0.9
Royal Korma, Tilda*	1 Pack/400ml	824	206	1.9	8.4	18.3	0.7
Saffron Tikka Masala, Patak's*	1 Serving/140g	147	105	1.3	7.9	7.5	1.0
Salmon, Oriental, Schwartz*	1 Serving/105g	138	131	2.0	27.5	1.5	0.0
Satay, Amoy*	1 Tsp/5ml	10	198	10.2	11.6	12.3	0.0
Satay, Indonesian, Sharwood's*	1oz/28g	31	112	2.8	11.8	6.0	0.6
Seafood, 25% Less Fat, Tesco*	1 Tsp/5g	17	344	2.7	18.2	28.5	0.3
Seafood, Asda*	1 Serving/10g	47	474	1.2	16.0	45.0	0.0
Seafood, BGTY, Sainsbury's*	1 Serving/15ml	23	150	0.8	15.1	9.3	0.1
Seafood, Baxters*	1oz/28g	149	533	1.5	9.9	54.2	0.7
Seafood, Colman's*	1 Serving/14ml	47	335	0.9	20.0	28.0	0.0
Seafood, GFY, Asda*	1 Dstp/10ml	31	313	0.6	17.0	27.0	0.0
Seafood, Organic, Simply Delicious*	1 Serving/35g	192	549	2.3	13.6	53.9	0.3
Seafood, Sainsbury's*	1 Tbsp/15g	50	330	0.7	17.6	28.2	0.1
Seafood, Somerfield*	1oz/28g	97	345	2.0	12.0	32.0	0.0
Seafood, Tesco	1 Serving/10g	47	465	1.8	15.6	43.5	0.3
Sichuan, Marks & Spencer*	1 Serving/120g	192	160	1.6	36.8	0.5	0.5
Singapore, Curry, Blue Dragon*	1 Sachet/120g	89	74	1.8	9.0	3.4	3.7
Sizzling Szechuan, Uncle Ben's*	1 Serving/260g	289	111	0.9	10.8	7.1	0.0
Smoked Ham & Cheese, For Pasta, Eat Smart, Safeway*	1 Serving/125g	94	75	5.8	6.1	2.5	0.9
Smoked Paprika & Tomato, Marks & Spencer*	1 Serving/300g	135	45	1.3	6.1	1.7	0.9
Smokey Bacon & Tomato, Stir In, Dolmio*	1 Pot/150g	248	165	5.5	6.9	12.8	0.0
Smokey Texan, Sizzle & Stir, Chicken Tonight*	1 Serving/150g	149	99	1.1	5.8	7.9	1.8

	Measure	per Measure	Nutrition Values per 100g / 100ml				
	INFO/WEIGHT	KCAL	KCAL	PROT	CARB	FAT	FIBRE
Soy	1 Tsp/5ml	3	64	8.7	8.3	0.0	0.0
Soy Ginger & Garlic, Stir Fry, Asda*	1 Pack/100ml	82	82	0.8	19.0	0.3	0.0
Soy, Dark, Amoy*	1 Tsp/5ml	4	73	1.9	16.3	0.0	0.0
Soy, Light, Amoy*	1 Tsp/5ml	3	55	3.2	11.5	0.0	0.0
Soy, Light, Asda*	1 Tbsp/15ml	7	47	0.8	11.0	0.0	0.0
Soy, Light, Sharwood's*	1 Tsp/5ml	1	18	4.4	0.2	0.0	0.3
Soy, Reduced Salt, Amoy*	1 Tsp/5ml	3	56	4.0	10.0	0.0	0.0
Soy, Rich, Sharwood's*	1 Tsp/5ml	2	48	4.6	7.5	0.0	0.3
Soy, Superior Dark, Amoy*	1 Tsp/5ml	3	63	1.9	16.3	0.0	0.0
Soya, Japanese, Waitrose*	1 Tbsp/15ml	11	74	7.7	9.4	0.6	0.8
Soya, Tamari, Meridian Foods*	1oz/28g	37	132	16.2	12.1	0.5	0.0
Spaghetti Bolognese, Colman's*	1 Pack/45g	149	330	8.9	66.5	3.1	6.2
Spiced Tomato Tagine, Sainsbury's*	1 Jar/355g	227	64	1.7	10.6	1.6	4.3
Spicy Bolognese, Cooking, Ragu*	1 Jar/510g	326	64	1.6	9.3	2.3	1.2
Spicy Durban, New World, Knorr*	1 Pack/500g	305	61	0.6	8.7	2.7	0.4
Spicy Peanut, Sharwood's*	1oz/28g	29	103	2.5	12.1	5.0	0.6
Spicy Pepper & Tomato, Stir Through, Marks & Spencer*	½ Jar/95g	166	175	1.6	7.5	15.4	0.0
Spicy Pepper, Eat Smart, Safeway*	1 Serving/84g	42	50	1.4	7.0	1.7	1.3
Spicy Red Pepper & Roasted Vegetable, For Pasta, Asda*	1 Serving/175g	140	80	1.2	9.0	4.4	1.0
Spicy Red Pepper & Roasted Vegetable, Sainsbury's*	1 Pot/302g	220	73	1.5	8.9	3.4	1.0
Spicy Sweet & Sour, Sharwood's*	1 Serving/138g	142	103	0.7	23.8	0.5	0.4
Spicy Szechuan Tomato, Stir Fry, Sharwood's*	1/3 Jar/140g	73	52	1.1	10.2	0.8	0.9
Spicy Tikka, Cooking, Sharwood's*	1oz/28g	27	95	1.3	9.4	5.9	0.8
Spicy Tomato, Fresh, Somerfield*	1/3 Pot/100g	41	41	0.8	6.4	1.3	1.1
Spicy Tomato, Italian, Somerfield*	½ Pot/149.1g	79	53	1.2	6.1	2.6	0.8
Spinach & Ricotta, Fresh, Perfectly Balanced, Waitrose*	½ Pot/175g	59	59	2.7	4.9	3.1	1.0
Stir Fry, Black Bean, Safeway*	½ Sachet/37.5ml	70	185	4.1	17.3	10.8	1.5
Stir Fry, Chow Mein, Safeway*	1 Serving/105g	79	75	1.1	16.2	0.6	1.3
Stroganoff, Asda*	1 Serving/285g	305	107	1.5	5.0	9.0	0.3
Stroganoff, Marks & Spencer*	1oz/28g	30	107	3.8	4.9	8.0	0.6
Sun Dried Tomato & Basil, Free From, Sainsbury's*	1 Serving/175g	126	72	2.9	8.7	2.8	1.5
Sun Dried Tomato With Vodka & Chilli, TTD, Sainsbury's*	½ Pot/150g	99	66	1.7	6.9	3.5	0.5
Sun Dried Tomato, Heinz*	1 Serving/10ml	7	73	1.5	14.9	0.6	0.9
Sun Dried Tomato, Mozzarella & Basil, Safeway*	½ Pot/159.1g	175	110	3.5	8.7	6.7	1.4
Sun Dried Tomato, Stir In, Light, Dolmio*	1 Serving/75g	62	83	1.7	9.8	4.7	0.0
Sun Dried Tomato, Stir-In, Dolmio*	1 Serving/75g	124	165	1.5	9.3	14.0	0.0
Swedish Mustard & Dill, Safeway*	1 Serving/20g	32	162	17.1	1.5	9.8	0.2
Sweet & Sour, Chinese, Sainsbury's*	½ Jar/150g	222	148	0.2	36.6	0.1	0.1
Sweet & Sour, Colman's*	1 Pack/40g	134	334	3.4	78.0	0.1	0.0
Sweet & Sour, Cook In, NEW, Homepride*	1 Serving/125g	115	92	0.3	22.5	0.1	1.0
Sweet & Sour, Cooking, GFY, Asda*	1 Jar/500g	310	62	0.9	14.0	0.3	0.6
Sweet & Sour, Cooking, Healthy Choice, Asda*	1 Jar/500g	175	35	0.6	8.0	0.1	0.5
Sweet & Sour, Cooking, Organic, Sainsbury's*	1/3 Jar/150g	150	100	0.8	22.1	0.9	0.5
Sweet & Sour, Extra Pineapple, Asda*	¼ Jar/148.4g	138	93	0.5	22.0	0.3	0.3
Sweet & Sour, Extra Pineapple, Chinatown, Knorr*	1 Jar/525g	441	84	0.4	20.4	0.1	0.6
Sweet & Sour, Extra Pineapple, Uncle Ben's*	1 Serving/165g	144	87	0.3	21.4	0.0	0.0
Sweet & Sour, Fresh Ideas, Tesco*	1 Serving/50ml	77	154	1.1	34.3	1.4	0.5
Sweet & Sour, Fresh, Safeway*	1 Sachet/50g	101	201	0.9	37.8	5.1	0.3
Sweet & Sour, Fresh, Sainsbury's*	1 Sachet/50ml	103	205	0.8	31.2	8.6	0.3
Sweet & Sour, Homepride*	1 Serving/195g	193	99	0.4	24.4	0.1	0.0
Sweet & Sour, Light, Uncle Ben's*	1 Serving/200g	128	64	0.5	15.5	0.0	0.0
Sweet & Sour, McDonald's*	1 Portion/32g	59	183	0.4	43.5	0.8	0.0
Sweet & Sour, Oriental, Chicken Tonight*	½ Jar/262g	0	92	0.6	20.9	0.7	0.9

S

SAUCE,	INFO/WEIGHT	KCAL	KCAL	PROT	CARB	FAT	FIBRE
Sweet & Sour, Original, Uncle Ben's*	1 Pack/300g	264	88	0.5	21.7	0.0	0.0
Sweet & Sour, Peking Style, Safeway*	1 Jar/340g	214	63	0.6	14.9	0.1	0.9
Sweet & Sour, Seeds Of Change*	1 Serving/200g	174	87	0.3	21.3	0.0	0.7
Sweet & Sour, Sizzle & Stir, Chicken Tonight*	1 Jar/465g	693	149	0.6	19.5	7.7	1.6
Sweet & Sour, Sizzle & Stir, Knorr*	1 Serving/460g	676	147	0.6	15.6	9.0	0.2
Sweet & Sour, Sizzling, Homepride*	¼ Jar/125g	88	70	0.4	16.8	0.1	0.0
Sweet & Sour, Sizzling, Uncle Ben's*	½ Jar/270g	375	139	0.6	19.2	6.7	0.0
Sweet & Sour, Spicy, Stir Fry, Sainsbury's*	1 Jar/500g	430	86	0.7	20.0	0.1	0.7
Sweet & Sour, Spicy, Uncle Ben's*	1 Jar/400g	364	91	0.6	22.1	0.1	0.0
Sweet & Sour, Stir Fry Additions, Tesco*	1 Sachet/50g	84	167	0.8	38.7	1.0	0.5
Sweet & Sour, Stir Fry, Asda*	1 Serving/63g	146	232	0.8	46.0	5.0	0.0
Sweet & Sour, Stir Fry, Blue Dragon*	1 Serving/120g	137	114	0.6	25.6	1.1	0.6
Sweet & Sour, Stir Fry, GFY, Asda*	½ Pack/51ml	43	85	0.9	11.0	4.1	3.4
Sweet & Sour, Stir Fry, Healthy Eating, Tesco*	1 Jar/440g	167	38	0.6	8.0	0.1	0.8
Sweet & Sour, Stir Fry, Marks & Spencer*	1 Serving/165g	215	130	0.6	32.0	0.2	0.7
Sweet & Sour, Stir Fry, Sharwood's*	1 Jar 160g	160	100	0.8	24.1	0.1	1.0
Sweet & Sour, Stir Fry, Straight To Wok, Amoy*	1 Pack/220g	486	221	0.5	54.6	0.2	0.0
Sweet & Sour, Stir Fry, Tesco*	½ Jar/222g	164	74	0.6	17.0	0.2	0.4
Sweet & Sour, Straight To Wok*	1oz/28g	52	186	0.3	45.5	0.3	0.0
Sweet & Sour, Take-Away	1oz/28g	44	157	0.2	32.8	3.4	0.0
Sweet & Sour, Two Stage, Uncle Ben's*	½ Jar/200g	314	157	1.0	18.1	9.1	0.0
Sweet & Sour, Uncle Ben's*	1 Serving/200g	168	84	0.4	21.7	0.0	0.0
Sweet & Sour, With Mango, Sharwood's*	1/3 Jar/138g	134	97	0.7	23.3	0.1	1.3
Sweet Barbecue, 97% Fat Free, Homepride*	1 Serving/230g	166	72	1.4	11.7	2.7	2.3
Sweet Barbecue, Deliciously Good, Homepride*	1/3 Jar/149g	110	74	1.4	12.0	2.2	1.2
Sweet Chilli & Coriander, Sharwood's*	1 Pack/370g	407	110	0.3	24.4	1.2	0.1
Sweet Chilli & Garlic Noodle, Sharwood's*	1oz/28g	30	107	0.9	18.9	3.1	0.4
Sweet Chilli & Garlic, Stir Fry & Dipping, Tesco*	½ Jar/95ml	78	82	0.3	20.1	0.0	0.1
Sweet Chilli & Ginger, Stir Fry, Marks & Spencer*	1 Serving/60ml	207	345	0.5	44.9	18.1	0.6
Sweet Chilli & Lemon Grass, Sharwood's*	1 Serving/155g	119	77	0.4	18.3	0.2	0.3
Sweet Chilli & Lime, Chinatown, Knorr*	1 Jar/525g	635	121	0.6	22.0	3.3	0.5
Sweet Chilli & Red Pepper, Sharwood*	1 Serving/250g	178	71	0.8	16.4	0.2	1.1
Sweet Chilli Dipping, Blue Dragon*	1 Tsp/5ml	12	230	0.0	56.0	0.0	0.0
Sweet Chilli Dipping, Marks & Spencer*	1 Tbsp/15g	37	245	0.2	61.1	0.1	0.5
Sweet Chilli, Asda*	1 Tbsp/15ml	18	123	0.4	30.0	0.1	0.8
Sweet Chilli, Sharwood's*	1 Jar/150ml	281	187	0.6	44.4	0.8	1.5
Sweet Curry, Eazy Squirt, Heinz*	1 Serving/10ml	12	124	0.7	29.0	0.3	0.5
Sweet N Sour, Sauces From Afar, Princes*	1 Jar/475g	485	102	0.1	25.2	0.1	0.0
Sweet Pepper, Stir In, Dolmio*	½ Pot/75g	103	137	1.5	9.7	10.3	0.0
Sweet Soy & Sesame, Uncle Ben's*	1 Serving/100g	110	110	0.7	23.0	1.7	0.0
Sweet Soy Chow Mein, Stir Fry, Amoy*	½ Pack/75g	146	195	0.3	35.0	6.0	0.0
Szechuan Spicy Tomato, Stir Fry, Blue Dragon*	1 Sachet/120g	151	126	1.3	17.6	5.6	2.0
Szechuan Style, Stir Fry, Fresh Ideas, Tesco*	1 Sachet/50g	114	228	1.9	33.4	9.7	0.1
Szechuan Sweet & Sour, Sainsbury's*	½ Jar/100g	151	151	0.5	37.0	0.1	0.1
Szechuan, Cooking, Safeway*	1 Jar/440g	458	104	1.3	13.0	5.0	1.2
Szechuan, Hot n Spicy, Safeway*	1 Jar/225g	281	125	1.2	17.9	5.4	0.9
Szechuan, Stir Fry, Sharwood's*	1 Jar/150g	126	84	3.0	15.5	1.1	0.4
Szechuan, Stir Fry, Tesco*	½ Jar/220g	205	93	1.0	14.7	3.2	0.9
Tagine, Cooking, Perfectly Balanced, Waitrose*	1 Jar/430g	258	60	1.0	9.6	2.0	1.5
Tamarind & Lime, Stir Fry, Sainsbury's*	1 Serving/75g	88	117	1.1	11.4	7.4	0.8
Tartar, Kraft*	2 Tbsp/30ml	162	539	1.3	0.0	58.3	0.0
Tartare	1oz/28g	84	299	1.3	17.9	24.6	0.0
Tartare, Baxters*	1oz/28g	144	515	1.0	8.0	53.3	0.3

S

	Measure INFO/WEIGHT	per Measure KCAL	Nutrition Values per 100g / 100ml				
			KCAL	PROT	CARB	FAT	FIBRE
Tartare, Colman's*	1 Serving/14ml	37	263	1.1	14.0	21.7	0.0
Tartare, Sainsbury's*	1 Serving/20ml	94	469	0.4	5.8	49.0	1.0
Tartare, Tesco*	1 Tbsp/15g	43	287	1.5	19.6	21.8	0.3
Tartare, With Olives, EPC*	1 Tbsp/15g	64	425	2.2	5.7	43.7	0.7
Teriyaki, Asda*	1 Serving/98g	99	101	2.1	23.0	0.1	0.0
Teriyaki, Blue Dragon*	½ Pack/60g	104	173	2.0	28.6	0.0	0.0
Teriyaki, Stir Fry, Fresh Ideas, Tesco*	1 Serving/25g	33	133	1.1	26.9	2.3	0.0
Teriyaki, Stir Fry, Sharwood's*	1 Jar/150g	137	91	0.9	19.7	1.0	0.3
Texan Barbeque, Stir It Up, Chicken Tonight*	½ Pot/40g	241	602	4.4	33.8	52.5	5.8
Texan Honey & Hickory, Safeway*	1 Serving/110g	173	157	1.7	17.7	8.8	1.3
Thai Chilli, Dipping, Sainsbury's*	1 Tbsp/15g	30	201	0.2	49.8	0.0	5.0
Thai Chilli, Sharwood's*	1 Serving/10g	16	164	1.8	39.1	0.0	0.3
Thai Coconut, Curry, Uncle Ben's*	1 Serving/125g	128	102	1.4	13.2	4.8	0.0
Thai Fish, Amoy*	1 Tbsp/15ml	12	80	13.4	6.7	0.0	0.0
Thai Green Curry, Sharwood's*	1 Serving/403g	431	107	1.1	8.4	7.6	0.1
Thai Green, Barts*	½ Pack/150ml	210	140	2.0	6.0	12.0	0.0
Thai Green, Curry, Express, Uncle Ben's*	1 Pack/170g	131	77	1.1	5.4	5.8	0.0
Thai Green, Curry, Stir Fry, Blue Dragon*	1 Sachet/120g	98	82	1.6	6.5	5.5	2.8
Thai Green, Sainsbury's*	¼ Pack/125g	170	136	1.8	10.8	9.5	2.1
Thai Panang, Sainsbury's*	1/3 Pack/166g	229	138	1.4	6.6	11.8	1.4
Thai Red, Curry, Sainsbury's*	½ Pouch/250g	390	156	1.7	5.0	14.3	1.5
Thai Red, Curry, Sharwood's*	1 Serving/138g	150	109	1.2	7.9	8.0	0.2
Thai Red, Curry, Stir Fry, Blue Dragon*	1 Serving/60g	55	91	1.0	7.3	6.4	1.2
Thai Satay, Sharwood's*	1oz/28g	160	573	17.2	18.0	48.0	6.3
Thai Sweet Chilli, Dipping, Blue Dragon*	1 Serving/30ml	65	215	0.8	52.3	0.0	0.9
Thai Sweet Chilli, Sizzle & Stir, Chicken Tonight*	1 Jar/510g	694	136	0.6	7.5	11.4	2.9
Thai Yellow, Curry Cooking, Sainsbury's*	1 Jar/500g	785	157	2.3	5.4	14.0	2.3
Thai, Ginger & Lemon Grass, Stir Fry, Sainsbury's*	½ Pack/150g	159	106	0.9	9.2	7.3	3.2
Thai, Stir Fry, Sainsbury's*	1 Serving/53g	66	124	2.5	6.9	9.6	0.2
Thai, Stir Fry, Sainsbury's*	½ Sachet/50ml	95	189	2.4	11.2	15.0	0.3
Tikka Bhuna, Sizzle & Stir, Chicken Tonight*	1 Jar/460g	561	122	1.1	7.2	9.9	2.7
Tikka Masala For One, Express, Uncle Ben's*	1 Sachet/170g	168	99	1.5	9.0	6.3	0.0
Tikka Masala Lemon & Coriander, Patak's*	1 Jar/270g	265	98	2.6	10.8	4.9	0.0
Tikka Masala, 25% Fat Reduced, Asda*	1 Jar/500g	380	76	2.9	9.0	3.2	0.5
Tikka Masala, 98% Fat Free, Homepride*	1oz/28g	14	49	1.4	7.9	1.7	0.8
Tikka Masala, COU, Marks & Spencer*	½ Pack/100g	80	80	4.5	9.9	2.6	1.7
Tikka Masala, Cooking, BGTY, Sainsbury's*	1 Jar/516g	516	100	1.5	12.1	4.9	1.3
Tikka Masala, Cooking, Budgens*	1oz/28g	27	96	1.6	10.1	5.5	0.2
Tikka Masala, Cooking, Eat Smart, Safeway*	½ Jar/180g	117	65	1.9	9.9	1.7	1.1
Tikka Masala, Cooking, Healthy Eating, Tesco*	1 Serving/250g	220	88	2.1	8.1	5.1	0.8
Tikka Masala, Cooking, Sharwood's*	1 Tsp/2g	2	122	1.2	11.9	7.8	0.9
Tikka Masala, Cooking, Tesco*	1 Jar/735g	1095	149	2.0	9.6	11.2	0.7
Tikka Masala, Deliciously Good, Homepride*	¼ Jar/149g	121	81	2.1	10.0	3.6	1.5
Tikka Masala, Fresh, Somerfield*	1 Pack/250g	308	123	3.0	10.0	8.0	0.0
Tikka Masala, GFY, Asda*	½ Jar/250g	190	76	2.9	9.0	3.2	0.5
Tikka Masala, Jar, Sharwood's*	1 Jar/435g	492	113	1.4	9.6	7.6	1.4
Tikka Masala, Lemon & Coriander, Cooking, Patak's*	1 Serving/70g	119	170	2.8	10.3	13.0	1.6
Tikka Masala, Lemon & Coriander, Original, Patak's*	1 Serving/125g	111	89	1.2	6.2	6.6	0.5
Tikka Masala, Organic, Seeds Of Change*	1 Jar/385g	343	89	1.7	9.1	5.5	0.7
Tikka Masala, Organic, Tesco*	½ Jar/220g	229	104	1.9	9.4	6.2	0.8
Tikka Masala, Shere Khan*	1 Serving/213ml	177	83	1.3	3.9	6.9	0.0
Tikka Masala, Sizzle & Stir, Chicken Tonight*	1/3 Jar/168g	336	200	2.0	8.4	17.3	2.6
Tikka Masala, Sizzle & Stir, Knorr*	1 Jar/455g	851	187	1.2	8.3	16.5	3.9

S

SAUCE,	INFO/WEIGHT	KCAL	KCAL	PROT	CARB	FAT	FIBRE
Tikka Masala, Spicy, Sharwood's*	1 Jar/420g	449	107	1.2	9.6	7.1	0.1
Tikka Masala, Uncle Ben's*	1 Serving/200g	212	106	1.3	8.7	7.3	0.0
Tikka, Better for You, Morrisons*	½ Jar/237.5g	259	109	2.3	17.2	3.4	1.3
Tikka, Creamy, Chicken Tonight*	1oz/28g	36	129	1.7	12.1	8.2	0.7
Tikka, Indian Style, Iceland*	1 Serving/225g	284	126	1.7	12.9	7.5	2.2
Toffee, GFY, Asda*	1 Serving/5g	15	306	2.2	68.0	2.8	0.0
Tomato & Basil For Pasta Stir & Serve, Homepride*	1 Jar/480g	278	58	1.2	6.7	2.9	0.0
Tomato & Basil, Cooking, BGTY, Sainsbury's*	1 Jar/500g	335	67	2.6	11.3	1.3	0.7
Tomato & Basil, Cooking, Marks & Spencer*	1 Serving/130g	78	60	1.4	5.7	3.4	1.2
Tomato & Basil, Eat Smart, Safeway*	1 Serving/250g	150	60	1.7	7.4	2.5	1.4
Tomato & Basil, Fresh, Organic, Waitrose*	¼ Pot/175g	77	44	1.0	6.2	1.7	0.8
Tomato & Basil, Sun-Ripened, Microwaveable, Dolmio*	1 Sachet/170g	95	56	1.4	7.9	2.1	0.0
Tomato & Basil, Tesco*	½ Jar/175g	84	48	0.7	3.8	3.3	0.8
Tomato & Chilli, Loyd Grossman*	½ Jar/175g	154	88	1.7	7.3	5.7	0.9
Tomato & Chorizo Sausage, Tesco*	1 Serving/175g	131	75	3.4	6.1	4.1	1.0
Tomato & Garlic, For Pasta, Asda*	¼ Jar/125g	80	64	2.7	8.0	2.3	1.1
Tomato & Herb, Fresh, Perfectly Balanced, Waitrose*	1 Pot/353g	173	49	1.2	5.3	2.6	0.9
Tomato & Herbs, Italienne, Stir It Up, Chicken Tonight*	1/3 Pot/26g	164	632	4.8	18.3	60.0	4.4
Tomato & Marscapone, Italiano, Tesco*	1 Serving/175g	194	111	2.8	5.4	8.7	0.6
Tomato & Mascarpone, BGTY, Sainsbury's*	1 Pot/300g	150	50	2.0	3.6	3.0	3.6
Tomato & Mascarpone, Fresh, Sainsbury's*	1/3 Pot/100g	118	118	2.2	4.2	10.3	1.1
Tomato & Mascarpone, Fresh, Tesco*	½ Pot/175g	207	118	2.8	7.1	8.7	0.6
Tomato & Mascarpone, Safeway*	½ Pot/175g	258	147	2.0	7.3	12.3	1.0
Tomato & Mozarella, Finest, Tesco*	1 Serving/175g	89	51	1.6	4.1	3.2	0.6
Tomato & Onion, Cook In, Homepride*	1 Can/390g	183	47	0.9	9.8	0.5	0.0
Tomato & Roasted Garlic, Stir In, Dolmio*	½ Pack/75g	94	125	1.2	7.7	10.2	0.0
Tomato & Wild Mushroom, Organic, Fresh, Sainsbury's*	1 Serving/152g	102	67	1.9	3.9	4.9	1.7
Tomato & Worcester, Table, Lea & Perrins*	1 Serving/10g	10	102	0.8	23.0	0.5	0.7
Tomato Base For Recipes, Salsina*	1oz/28g	7	24	1.6	4.5	0.0	1.4
Tomato Frito, Heinz*	1oz/28g	20	73	1.3	7.7	4.1	0.8
Tomato, Fresh, Marks & Spencer*	1oz/28g	11	40	1.4	6.5	0.6	0.8
Tomato, Indian, Sizzling, Homepride*	1 Serving/240g	82	34	0.9	7.0	0.2	0.0
Tomato, Mozarella & Wild Rocket, Bistro, Waitrose*	½ Pot/175g	96	55	1.6	7.0	2.9	1.5
Tomato, Olive & Rosemary, Schwartz*	1 Serving/50g	45	90	2.8	6.3	6.0	1.0
Tomato, Organic, Heinz*	1 Tsp/5g	5	105	1.3	24.0	0.1	0.9
Tomato, Parmesan & Dill, Tesco*	1 Serving/70g	81	115	3.1	4.8	9.2	0.7
Tomato, Roasted Garlic & Mushroom, Bertolli*	¼ Jar/125g	68	54	1.9	6.4	2.0	1.5
Tomato, Value, Tesco*	1 Serving/10g	14	139	2.3	32.2	0.1	1.4
Vegetable & Garlic, For Pasta, Dolmio*	1 Serving/150g	108	72	1.3	7.4	4.1	0.0
Vegetables, Hoi Sin & Plum, Stir Fry, Sharwood's*	1 Pack/360g	367	102	1.1	21.4	1.3	0.2
Vine Ripened Tomato & Mascarpone, Stir Through, Sacla*	½ Jar/100g	171	171	1.4	5.9	15.8	0.0
Vodka & Chilli, Finest, Tesco*	1 Serving/350g	343	98	2.2	9.4	5.7	2.1
Watercress, Marks & Spencer*	1oz/28g	32	115	3.4	6.5	8.2	0.7
White Granules, Sauce In Seconds Asda*	1 Pack/57g	237	415	3.7	73.0	12.0	0.9
White Wine & Cream, Homepride*	1 Jar/500g	405	81	1.1	9.0	4.5	0.0
White Wine & Mushroom, BGTY, Sainsbury's*	1 Serving/166g	93	56	1.2	4.9	3.5	0.5
White Wine Mushroom & Herb, 98% Fat Free, Homepride*	1 Jar/450g	180	40	0.8	7.0	1.2	0.5
White Wine, Chardonnay, Marks & Spencer*	1 Serving/160ml	184	115	1.4	4.6	10.0	0.9
White Wine, Cooking, Iceland*	1 Serving/220g	198	90	1.1	8.3	5.8	0.2
White, Savoury, Colman's*	1 Pack/25g	86	343	12.1	53.3	9.0	6.0
White, Savoury, Made With Semi-Skimmed Milk	1oz/28g	36	128	4.2	11.1	7.8	0.2
White, Savoury, Made With Whole Milk	1oz/28g	42	150	4.1	10.9	10.3	0.2
Wild Mushroom, Finest, Tesco*	½ Pack/175g	158	90	1.9	5.2	6.8	0.4

S

	Measure INFO/WEIGHT	per Measure KCAL	Nutrition Values per 100g / 100ml				
			KCAL	PROT	CARB	FAT	FIBRE
SAUCE,							
Worcestershire	1 Tsp/5g	3	65	1.4	15.5	0.1	0.0
Worcestershire, Lea & Perrins*	1 Tsp/5ml	4	88	1.1	22.0	0.0	0.0
Yellow Bean & Cashew, Tesco*	½ Jar/210g	170	81	1.6	11.9	2.9	0.3
Yellow Bean & Ginger, Stir Fry, Finest, Tesco*	1 Jar/350g	319	91	2.1	18.3	1.0	1.1
Yellow Bean, Sharwood's*	1 Jar/160g	128	80	0.3	19.2	0.2	0.3
Yellow Bean, Stir Fry, Sainsbury's*	½ Jar/100g	126	126	1.8	26.7	1.3	0.8
Yellow Bean, Stir Fry, Sharwood's*	1 Jar/195g	156	80	0.3	19.2	0.2	0.3
Yellow Bean, Stir Fry, Straight To Wok, Amoy*	1oz/28g	44	159	1.6	36.9	0.5	0.0
Yellowbean & Cashew Nut, Asda*	1 Serving/50g	60	119	2.7	21.0	2.7	0.9
SAUCE MIX,							
Bearnaise, Knorr*	1 Serving/2.5g	10	400	0.0	80.0	0.0	0.0
Beef Stroganoff, Colman's*	1 Pack/40g	160	399	12.4	48.4	17.3	6.4
Bread, Colman's*	1 Pack/40g	130	325	12.0	66.0	1.3	0.0
Bread, Knorr*	½ Pint/40g	177	442	7.9	49.9	23.3	2.1
Cheddar Cheese, Colman's*	1 Serving/40g	158	394	19.7	45.2	14.9	1.5
Cheddar Cheese, Lidl*	1 Pack/40g	140	350	18.6	43.0	11.5	0.0
Cheese, Instant, Safeway*	1 Pack/54g	202	374	4.1	62.0	12.2	8.5
Cheese, Knorr*	1 Pack/58g	132	227	7.8	38.0	4.9	1.8
Cheese, Made Up With Skimmed Milk	1 Serving/60g	47	78	5.4	9.5	2.3	0.0
Cheese, Made Up, Crosse & Blackwell*	1 Pack/30g	26	86	5.1	9.2	3.2	0.7
Chicken Chasseur, Colman's*	1 Pack/45g	123	273	12.0	53.0	1.0	0.0
Chicken Chasseur, Schwartz*	½ Pack/20g	64	322	9.1	64.5	3.1	0.0
Chicken Korma, Colman's*	½ Pack/50g	230	459	6.6	38.8	30.8	13.2
Chicken Supreme, Colman's*	½ Pack/20g	72	362	12.1	53.2	11.2	6.5
Chilli Con Carne, Asda*	1 Sachet/50g	157	314	7.0	68.0	1.6	2.5
Chilli Con Carne, Colman's*	1 Serving/13g	40	305	7.5	58.4	4.6	7.7
Chilli Con Carne, Schwartz*	1 Serving/10g	31	308	8.2	64.6	1.9	0.5
Coq Au Vin, Colman's*	1 Pack/50g	141	281	7.5	59.0	1.0	0.0
Creamy Cheese & Bacon, For Pasta, Colman's*	1 Pack/50g	197	394	16.6	44.6	16.6	5.7
Creamy Parsley & Lemon, Schwartz*	1 Serving/100g	113	113	3.6	10.3	6.4	0.6
Creamy White Wine With Herbs, Schwartz*	1 Serving/100g	102	102	4.4	10.4	4.7	0.5
Four Cheese, Colman's*	1 Pack/35g	145	414	17.8	40.5	20.1	3.8
Garlic Mushrooms, Creamy, Schwartz*	1 Pack/35g	109	310	7.1	60.1	4.6	0.0
Hollandaise, Schwartz*	1 Serving/100g	106	106	6.0	8.1	5.5	0.5
Lamb Hot Pot, Colman's*	1 Serving/13.5g	37	282	7.3	59.8	1.5	2.7
Mediterranean Roasted Vegetables, Schwartz*	½ Pack/15g	47	311	7.0	64.3	2.9	0.8
Mushroom Stroganoff, Schwartz*	1 Pack/35g	41	117	3.3	21.7	1.9	0.0
Parsley, Colman's*	1 Serving/20g	61	307	8.1	65.3	1.5	3.7
Parsley, Instant, Made Up, Sainsbury's*	¼ Sachet/75ml	42	56	1.2	11.1	0.8	0.1
Parsley, Knorr*	1 Sachet/48g	210	437	4.2	50.6	24.2	0.8
Parsley, Somerfield*	1 Sachet/24g	17	72	4.0	9.0	2.0	0.0
Pepper, Instant, Safeway*	1 Serving/22g	77	348	3.2	66.3	7.5	4.1
Pork Casserole, Morrisons*	1 Pack/36g	118	327	8.1	70.6	1.4	0.0
Rum Flavour, Kraft*	1oz/28g	116	415	6.1	76.5	9.5	0.0
Satay, Thai Chicken, Schwartz*	1 Serving/9g	29	321	3.8	72.5	1.8	0.8
Spaghetti Bolognese, Knorr*	1 Serving/15g	17	111	3.7	9.7	6.4	0.0
Spaghetti Bolognese, Schwartz*	1 Serving/40g	122	306	10.0	63.0	1.0	0.0
Spanish Roasted Vegetables, Schwartz*	1 Pack/15g	43	287	8.1	45.8	7.9	9.3
Tuna & Mushroom Pasta Melt, Schwartz*	1 Pack/40g	133	332	9.9	54.8	8.1	0.5
Tuna & Pasta Bake, Colman's*	1 Pack/45g	144	319	10.4	57.1	5.4	5.2
Tuna Napolitana, Schwartz*	1 Sachet/29g	107	368	9.7	53.0	13.0	0.0
White, Instant, Sainsbury's*	1 Serving/90ml	65	72	0.8	10.9	2.8	0.1
White, Made Up With Semi-Skimmed Milk	1oz/28g	20	73	4.0	9.6	2.4	0.0

S

INFO/WEIGHT	Measure	per Measure KCAL	Nutrition Values per 100g / 100ml				
			KCAL	PROT	CARB	FAT	FIBRE
SAUCE MIX,							
White, Made Up With Skimmed Milk	1oz/28g	17	59	4.0	9.6	0.9	0.0
White, Savoury, Knorr*	½ Pint Pack/16g	46	290	7.8	52.2	5.6	5.2
SAUERKRAUT,							
Average	1oz/28g	4	13	1.3	1.9	0.1	1.1
SAUSAGE,							
Beef, Average	1 Sausage/60g	151	252	14.5	7.0	18.5	0.6
Beef, With Onion & Red Wine, Finest, Tesco*	1 Sausage/63g	117	185	13.2	8.5	10.9	1.2
Bockwurst, Average	1 Sausage/45g	114	253	10.8	0.8	23.0	0.0
Cambridge Gluten Free, Waitrose*	1 Sausage/121g	258	213	14.6	1.9	16.3	1.3
Chicken & Tarragon, Butchers Choice, Sainsbury's*	1 Sausage/47g	106	225	18.1	5.8	14.4	0.2
Chicken, Manor Farm*	1 Sausage/65g	126	194	13.7	6.6	12.5	1.2
Chilli Beef, Boston Style, Waitrose*	1 Sausage/66.5g	136	203	14.7	3.4	14.6	0.9
Chipolata, Average	1 Sausage/28g	81	291	12.1	8.7	23.1	0.7
Chipolata, Cumberland, Average	1 Chipolata/28g	74	264	15.3	7.2	19.3	0.9
Chipolata, Lamb & Rosemary, Tesco*	1 Sausage/31.6g	69	218	11.3	8.3	15.5	0.0
Chipolata, Pork & Tomato, Organic, Tesco*	1 Chipolata/28g	79	283	12.2	4.3	24.1	0.9
Chipolata, Pork, Extra Lean, BGTY, Sainsbury's*	1 Chipolata	46	189	16.9	10.9	8.6	0.5
Chipolata, Premium, Average	1 Serving/80g	187	234	14.9	4.7	17.3	1.2
Chorizo, Average	1 Serving/80g	250	313	21.1	2.6	24.2	0.2
Chorizo, Bites, Mini, Sainsbury's*	½ Pack/32.6g	141	426	25.5	2.3	35.0	0.7
Chorizo, Lean, Average	1 Sausage/67g	131	195	15.7	2.3	13.7	0.8
Classic Sicilian Style, TTD, Sainsbury's*	1 Sausage/49g	135	275	16.8	0.5	22.5	0.9
Classic Toulouse, TTD, Sainsbury's*	1 Sausage/44.5g	138	310	23.2	2.1	23.3	0.9
Cocktail, Average	1oz/28g	90	323	12.1	8.6	26.7	0.9
Cumberland, Average	1 Sausage/57g	167	293	13.8	8.6	22.7	0.8
Cumberland, Healthy Range, Average	1 Sausage/52.6g	75	142	17.4	9.0	4.1	0.9
Duck & Orange, TTD, Sainsbury's*	1 Sausage/40.9g	123	301	13.8	3.2	25.9	0.9
Extra Special Toulouse, Asda*	1 Sausage/65g	212	326	15.0	8.0	26.0	0.6
French Saucisson, Tesco*	1 Slice/5g	19	379	26.7	4.1	28.4	0.0
Garlic, Average	1 Slice/11g	25	227	15.7	0.8	18.2	0.0
German Extrawurst, Waitrose*	1 Slice/12.5g	39	303	13.8	0.8	27.2	0.0
Glamorgan With Cheese & Leek, TTD, Sainsbury's*	1 Sausage/53g	171	323	18.9	3.3	26.0	0.6
Glamorgan, Organic, Waitrose*	1 Sausage/41.8g	81	194	14.5	11.2	10.1	1.7
Hot & Spicy Pork Cocktail, Cooked, Asda*	1 Sausage/10g	31	312	13.0	11.0	24.0	1.3
Hot Mustard Porker, Tesco*	1 Sausage/52g	143	275	16.1	8.1	19.8	3.1
Irish Recipe, Average	1 Sausage/40g	119	298	10.7	17.2	20.7	0.7
Lamb & Mint, Marks & Spencer*	1oz/28g	63	225	13.3	6.6	16.3	1.7
Lincolnshire, Average	1 Sausage/42g	122	291	14.6	9.2	21.8	0.6
Lincolnshire, Healthy Range, Average	1 Sausage/50g	89	177	15.8	9.0	8.6	0.8
Lorne, Average	1 Sausage/25g	78	312	10.8	16.0	23.1	0.6
Mediterranean Style Paprika, Waitrose*	1 Sausage/67g	190	283	12.1	4.6	24.0	1.9
Mediterranean Style, 95% Fat Free, Bowyers*	1 Sausage/50g	60	120	13.9	8.9	3.2	0.0
Pistachio, Waitrose*	1 Slice/12g	32	267	14.0	1.0	23.0	0.1
Polony Slicing, Asda*	1oz/28g	60	214	11.0	11.0	14.0	0.0
Pork & Apple, Average	1 Sausage/57g	146	256	14.5	7.5	18.8	1.9
Pork & Apple, Lean Recipe, Wall's*	1 Sausage/57g	79	139	14.5	9.4	4.5	2.3
Pork & Beef, Average	1 Sausage/45g	133	295	8.7	13.7	22.7	0.5
Pork & Herb, Average	1 Sausage/75g	231	308	13.2	5.5	26.0	0.4
Pork & Herb, Healthy Range, Average	1 Sausage/59g	75	127	16.1	10.8	2.4	1.1
Pork & Leek, Average	1oz/28g	73	262	14.6	6.0	19.9	1.1
Pork & Onion, Gluten Free, Asda*	1 Sausage/40.9g	105	257	20.0	6.0	17.0	1.8
Pork & Smoked Bacon, Finest, Tesco*	1oz/28g	76	271	13.9	4.8	21.8	0.2
Pork & Stilton, Average	1 Sausage/57g	180	317	13.2	5.9	26.7	0.3

	Measure INFO/WEIGHT	per Measure KCAL	Nutrition Values per 100g / 100ml				
			KCAL	PROT	CARB	FAT	FIBRE
SAUSAGE,							
Pork & Tomato, Average	1 Sausage/46.5g	126	273	13.9	7.5	20.8	0.4
Pork With Mozzarella, Italian Style, Tesco*	1 Sausage/75.6g	206	271	12.0	10.1	20.3	1.0
Pork, Apricot & Lovage, Waitrose*	1 Sausage/67g	165	246	11.2	12.9	16.6	1.3
Pork, Average	1 Sausage/24g	73	305	12.8	9.8	23.8	0.8
Pork, Bacon & Cheese, Asda*	¼ Pack/114g	329	289	18.0	7.0	21.0	0.4
Pork, Chilli & Coriander, Grilled, Sainsbury's*	1 Sausage/54g	123	228	18.9	3.5	15.4	1.8
Pork, Extra Lean, Average	1 Sausage/54g	84	155	17.3	6.1	6.9	0.9
Pork, Garlic & Herb, Average	1 Sausage/75.6g	204	269	12.0	6.0	21.9	1.2
Pork, Ham & Asparagus, Tesco*	1 Sausage/75.7g	173	228	14.9	3.8	17.0	1.1
Pork, Honey Roast, Westaways*	1 Sausage/75g	183	244	13.1	12.8	15.6	0.0
Pork, Hungarian Style Smoked Paprika, Finest, Tesco*	1 Sausage/100g	207	207	16.1	0.0	15.8	0.4
Pork, Premium, Average	1 Sausage/74g	191	258	14.9	8.3	18.4	1.0
Pork, Reduced Fat, Healthy Range, Average	1 Sausage/57g	86	151	15.7	9.0	6.0	0.9
Pork, Roasted Pepper & Chilli, COU, Marks & Spencer*	1 Sausage/57g	57	100	15.2	7.1	2.0	2.1
Pork, Skinless, Average	1oz/28g	81	291	11.7	8.2	23.6	0.6
Pork, Thick, Average	1 Sausage/38.8g	116	296	13.3	10.0	22.4	1.0
Pork, Thick, Reduced Fat, Healthy Range, Average	1 Sausage/52g	90	173	14.1	12.3	7.4	0.8
Red Thai & Lemon Grass, Extra Special, Asda*	1 Sausage/65.3g	159	245	18.0	5.0	17.0	1.3
Rich Venison & Redcurrant, Grilled, TTD, Sainsbury's*	1 Sausage/46g	138	299	21.2	3.0	22.5	1.8
Round, Breakfast Pack, Healthy Choice, Asda*	1 Sausage/53g	85	160	23.0	6.0	4.9	0.0
Saveloy, Unbattered, Takeaway	1 Saveloy/65g	192	296	13.8	10.8	22.3	0.8
Smoked Pork, Reduced Fat, Mattessons*	1 Sausage/75g	191	255	14.0	7.0	19.0	0.9
Smoked, Average	1 Sausage/174g	498	286	13.3	2.0	25.6	0.6
Smoky Cajun, TTD, Sainsbury's*	1 Sausage/46.4g	115	250	24.2	1.6	16.3	0.9
Spanish, Wafer Thin, Asda*	1 Slice/4g	12	298	25.4	4.1	20.0	0.0
Spicy Pork, Polenta & Sun Dried Tomato, Waitrose*	1 Sausage/67g	165	247	11.8	9.8	17.8	0.9
Sticky, Marks & Spencer*	1oz/28g	62	220	7.1	18.2	12.8	1.5
Toulouse, Marks & Spencer*	1 Sausage/57g	123	215	12.4	5.8	15.6	1.3
Tuna & Herb, Sainsbury's*	1 Sausage/47g	109	231	19.6	10.0	12.5	1.5
Tuna & Smoked Salmon, Healthy Living, Tesco*	1 Sausage/67g	90	134	17.9	2.8	5.7	2.0
Tuna, Mediterranean Style, Sainsbury's*	1 Serving/50g	102	204	15.1	14.7	9.5	1.2
Turkey & Chicken, Average	1 Sausage/56.7g	126	222	14.5	8.2	14.6	1.8
Turkey & Pork, Bernard Matthews*	1 Sausage/55g	137	249	10.2	13.1	17.3	0.0
Turkey, Average	1 Sausage/57g	90	157	15.7	6.3	8.0	0.0
Tuscan, Marks & Spencer*	1 Sausage/66g	145	220	14.9	4.6	16.0	0.6
Wiener Schnitzel, Average	1oz/28g	62	223	20.9	13.1	10.0	0.4
SAUSAGE & MASH,							
British Classic, Tesco*	1 Pack/450g	648	144	4.6	14.3	7.6	1.1
Eat Smart, Safeway*	1 Pack/400g	340	85	4.6	12.4	1.8	1.3
GFY, Asda*	1 Pack/400g	324	81	3.5	11.0	2.6	2.9
Healthy Living, Tesco*	1 Pack/450g	369	82	4.6	11.3	2.1	1.0
Iceland*	1 Pack/440g	484	110	3.8	10.4	5.9	1.6
Onion, Marks & Spencer*	1 Pack/300g	315	105	4.1	9.0	5.7	1.5
Safeway*	1 Pack/486.1g	875	180	5.9	9.3	12.9	2.2
Vegetarian, GFY, Asda*	1 Pack/400g	292	73	4.2	9.0	2.2	2.1
Vegetarian, Safeway*	1 Pack/450g	450	100	5.5	8.9	4.7	1.8
Vegetarian, Tesco*	1 Pack/410g	398	97	4.6	11.2	3.8	2.0
With Onion Gravy, Healthy Eating, Tesco*	1 Pack/450g	369	82	4.6	11.3	2.1	1.0
With Onion Gravy, Tesco*	1 Pack/500g	525	105	3.0	11.1	5.4	1.6
SAUSAGE MEAT,							
Pork, Average	1oz/28g	96	344	9.9	10.2	29.5	0.7
SAUSAGE MEAT FREE,							
Asda*	1 Sausage/43g	81	189	20.0	7.0	9.0	2.9

S

INFO/WEIGHT	Measure	per Measure KCAL	KCAL	PROT	CARB	FAT	FIBRE
SAUSAGE MEAT FREE,							
Premium, Realeat*	1 Sausage/50g	71	142	14.8	3.7	7.5	3.0
SAUSAGE ROLL,							
Asda*	1 Roll/64g	248	388	8.0	26.0	28.0	1.0
BGTY, Sainsburys*	1 Roll/65g	200	308	9.6	27.9	17.6	1.4
Basics, Party Size, Somerfield*	1 Roll/13g	45	343	7.0	29.0	22.0	0.0
Buffet, Healthy Eating, Tesco*	1 Roll/30g	83	278	9.6	31.2	12.8	1.5
Co-Op*	1 Roll/66g	244	370	8.0	25.0	27.0	2.0
Cocktail, Sainsbury's*	1 Roll/15g	57	381	8.2	26.4	27.0	1.0
Farmfoods*	1 Lge Roll/34g	101	297	6.7	22.9	19.8	0.4
Ginsters*	1 Roll/140g	753	538	13.0	33.7	39.1	2.2
Healthy Eating, Tesco*	1 Roll/70g	195	278	9.6	31.2	12.8	1.5
Jumbo, Sainsbury's*	1 Roll/145g	492	339	8.2	23.2	23.7	1.5
Kingsize, Pork Farms*	½ Roll/49.9g	242	483	10.5	39.9	31.8	0.0
Large, Sainsbury's*	1 Roll/43g	164	382	7.3	28.1	26.7	1.2
Lincolnshire, COU, Marks & Spencer*	1 Roll/175g	280	160	10.0	23.2	2.7	2.6
Lincolnshire, Geo Adams*	1 Serving/130g	475	365	8.3	28.2	24.3	1.1
Marks & Spencer*	1 Roll/32g	130	405	9.2	21.4	31.2	0.9
Mini, Tesco*	1 Roll/15g	53	356	9.0	23.9	24.9	1.5
Party Size, Tesco*	1 Roll/12g	39	327	6.2	26.2	21.9	1.3
Party, Sainsbury's*	1 Roll/12g	54	422	8.7	26.7	31.1	1.2
Party, Value, Tesco*	1 Roll/12g	33	274	6.8	35.9	11.5	0.6
Pork Farms*	1 Roll/54g	213	395	9.6	21.6	30.0	0.0
Pork, Large, Marks & Spencer*	1 Roll/63g	236	375	9.0	22.5	27.9	0.7
Pork, Morrisons*	1 Roll/70g	195	278	9.6	31.2	12.8	1.5
Puff Pastry	1oz/28g	107	383	9.9	25.4	27.6	1.0
Puff Pastry, Large, Marks & Spencer*	1 Roll/63g	236	375	9.0	22.5	27.9	0.7
Puff Pastry, Sainsbury's*	1 Roll/65g	250	384	8.3	25.0	27.9	0.9
Snack Size, Safeway*	1 Roll/28.8g	106	365	7.7	30.0	23.4	1.6
Snack, GFY, Asda*	1 Roll/34g	112	329	9.4	26.5	20.6	0.9
Snack, Sainsbury's*	1 Roll/33g	125	378	7.5	25.5	27.3	1.0
Tesco*	1 Roll/67g	221	330	9.1	23.8	22.0	2.6
Waitrose*	1 Roll/75g	287	383	10.1	27.0	26.1	1.3
SAUSAGE ROLL VEGETARIAN,							
Linda McCartney*	1 Roll/51g	133	260	10.9	23.1	14.5	1.6
SAUSAGE VEGETARIAN,							
Cumberland, Grilled, Cauldron Foods*	1 Sausage/50g	80	160	12.6	12.3	6.7	2.4
Cumberland, Waitrose*	1 Sausage/50g	80	160	12.6	12.3	6.7	2.4
Garlic & Oregano, Roasted, Cauldron Foods*	1 Sausage/50g	90	179	13.1	9.0	10.1	2.1
Hot Dog, Tesco*	1 sausage/30g	81	271	19.0	6.0	19.0	2.0
Leek & Cheese, Organic, Cauldron Foods*	1 Sausage/41g	80	194	14.5	11.2	10.1	1.7
Lincolnshire, Cauldron Foods*	1 Sausage/50g	106	212	14.7	14.5	10.6	2.2
Lincolnshire, Tesco*	1 Sausage/50g	85	170	10.0	10.5	9.8	1.8
Linda McCartney*	1 Sausage/35g	88	252	23.2	8.6	13.8	1.2
Mushroom & Herb, Waitrose*	1 Sausage/50g	62	123	10.2	8.1	5.4	0.5
Mushroom & Tarragon, Wicken Fen*	1 Sausage/47g	82	175	10.1	17.0	7.4	2.4
Smoked Paprika & Chilli, Cauldron Foods*	1 Sausage/50g	76	152	7.8	11.8	8.2	2.6
Spinach, Leek & Cheese, Gourmet, Wicken Fen*	1 Sausage/46g	92	201	10.3	17.0	10.2	1.9
Sun Dried Tomato & Herb, Linda McCartney*	1 Sausage/35g	93	266	21.8	10.1	15.4	1.7
Vegetable, Granose*	1oz/28g	63	226	8.5	17.5	13.5	0.0
SAVOURY EGGS,							
Mini, Asda*	1 Egg/19g	58	303	10.3	17.7	21.2	1.5
Mini, Iceland*	1 Egg/20g	66	327	11.0	17.5	23.7	1.1
Mini, New Improved Recipe, Tesco*	1 Egg/20g	65	323	12.5	18.3	22.2	1.3

S

	Measure INFO/WEIGHT	per Measure KCAL	Nutrition Values per 100g / 100ml				
			KCAL	PROT	CARB	FAT	FIBRE
SAVOURY EGGS,							
Mini, Tesco*	1 Egg/20g	68	342	11.2	23.0	22.8	0.9
SCALLOPS,							
Coquille, St Jacques, Marks & Spencer*	1 Serving/150g	165	110	5.0	8.8	6.1	1.1
Hotbake Shells, Sainsbury's*	1 Serving/140g	241	172	9.5	8.4	11.2	0.8
King, Finest, Tesco*	1 Serving/170g	129	76	16.9	0.1	0.9	0.0
King, Marks & Spencer*	1 Serving/260g	182	70	15.5	1.2	0.1	1.2
King, Trimmed by Hand, Sainsbury's*	1 Pack/200g	142	71	16.0	1.4	0.1	0.2
Lemon Grass & Ginger, Tesco*	½ Pack/112g	90	80	15.2	2.5	1.0	0.6
Meat, Asda*	1oz/28g	33	118	23.2	1.4	1.4	0.0
Queen, Scottish, Sainsbury's*	1 Pack/200g	350	175	30.4	0.8	5.5	0.0
Steamed	1oz/28g	33	118	23.2	3.4	1.4	0.0
Thai Style Breaded With Plum Sauce, Finest, Tesco*	1 Serving/210g	401	191	11.5	20.6	7.0	0.8
With Lemon Pepper Butter, Cook, Marks & Spencer*	1 Serving/105g	158	150	13.9	1.6	9.8	0.3
SCAMPI,							
Breaded, Average	½ Pack/255g	565	222	10.7	20.5	10.7	1.0
SCAMPI &,							
Chips, Tesco*	1 Serving/450g	689	153	5.1	22.4	4.8	1.6
Chips, Youngs*	1oz/28g	42	150	5.0	20.3	5.4	1.7
SCONE,							
3% Fat, Marks & Spencer*	1 Scone/65g	179	275	7.2	55.1	2.5	2.3
All Butter, Tesco*	1 Scone/41g	126	308	7.2	52.3	7.8	1.6
Blueberry, Starbucks*	1 Serving/128g	460	359	3.9	53.1	14.1	2.3
Cheese	1 Scone/40g	145	363	10.1	43.2	17.8	1.6
Cheese & Black Pepper, Mini, Marks & Spencer*	1 Scone/18g	67	370	10.2	41.1	18.3	1.7
Cheese, Finest, Tesco*	1 Scone/70g	250	357	11.3	41.5	16.2	1.2
Cheese, Marks & Spencer*	1 Scone/60g	237	395	10.3	38.9	21.9	1.6
Cherry, Marks & Spencer*	1 Scone/60g	202	337	6.9	49.7	12.2	1.9
Cream, Sainsbury's*	1 Scone/50g	173	345	4.6	42.5	17.4	3.1
Derby, Asda*	1 Scone/59g	202	342	7.0	56.0	10.0	0.0
Derby, Mothers Pride*	1 Scone/60g	208	347	5.2	49.8	14.0	1.5
Derby, Somerfield*	1 Scone/60g	208	347	5.3	49.9	14.0	1.9
Derby, Tesco*	1 Scone/60g	201	335	7.2	53.7	10.2	2.0
Devon, Sainsbury's*	1 Scone/54g	201	372	7.1	51.1	15.5	1.6
Devon, Waitrose*	1 Scone/71.8g	269	373	7.5	56.0	13.2	2.3
Fresh Cream, Tesco*	1 Scone/79.5g	244	304	15.8	32.3	12.5	0.9
Fruit	1 Scone/40g	126	316	7.3	52.9	9.8	0.0
Fruit, Economy, Sainsbury's*	1 Scone/34g	111	326	7.9	52.5	9.4	1.7
Fruit, SmartPrice, Asda*	1 Scone/41g	139	338	7.0	55.0	10.0	3.0
Fruit, Somerfield*	1 Scone/35g	116	332	8.0	53.0	10.0	0.0
Plain	1 Scone/40g	145	362	7.2	53.8	14.6	1.9
Potato	1 Scone/40g	118	296	5.1	39.1	14.3	1.6
Potato, Mothers Pride*	1 Scone/37g	77	207	4.7	42.0	2.2	4.3
Potato, Warburton's*	1 Scone/48g	123	256	5.6	35.1	10.1	0.0
Strawberry, Fresh Cream, BGTY, Sainsbury's*	1 Scone/50g	155	309	5.1	47.0	11.2	1.1
Strawberry, Marks & Spencer*	1 Scone/55g	132	240	3.2	23.0	14.9	0.7
Sultana, BGTY, Sainsbury's*	1 Scone/63g	178	283	7.7	56.7	2.8	2.4
Sultana, Finest, Tesco*	1 Scone/70g	225	321	8.9	46.7	10.9	2.1
Sultana, Less Than 5% Fat, Asda*	1 Scone/60g	198	330	7.0	62.0	6.0	1.8
Sultana, Low Fat, Marks & Spencer*	1 Scone/65g	179	275	7.2	55.1	2.5	2.3
Sultana, Marks & Spencer*	1 Scone/60g	235	392	7.0	58.7	13.8	2.8
Sultana, Reduced Fat, Waitrose*	1 Scone/65g	187	287	6.6	53.2	5.3	2.6
Sultana, Safeway*	1 Scone/34.8g	110	313	6.0	55.1	8.8	0.0
Sultana, Sainsbury's*	1 Scone/53.8g	177	327	6.9	50.2	11.0	6.5

S

	Measure INFO/WEIGHT	per Measure KCAL	Nutrition Values per 100g / 100ml				
			KCAL	PROT	CARB	FAT	FIBRE
SCONE,							
Sultana, Somerfield*	1 Scone/34g	108	318	5.7	55.4	8.2	0.0
Sultana, Tesco*	1 Scone/70g	215	307	6.8	53.8	7.2	2.0
Wholemeal	1 Scone/40g	130	326	8.7	43.1	14.4	5.2
Wholemeal, Fruit	1 Scone/40g	130	324	8.1	47.2	12.8	4.9
SCOTCH EGGS,							
Asda*	1 Egg/114g	286	251	11.2	13.7	16.8	1.4
Bar, Ginsters*	1 Bar/90g	256	284	11.8	20.1	17.4	1.7
Finest, Tesco*	1 Egg/114g	280	247	11.6	10.4	17.7	1.1
Ginsters*	1 Egg/95g	228	240	15.3	9.7	15.9	0.6
Marks & Spencer*	1 Egg/125g	344	275	11.7	15.0	18.7	0.5
Mini, 40% Less Fat, Sainsbury's*	1 Egg/20g	46	231	12.8	15.3	13.2	1.4
Mini, Sainsbury's*	1 Egg/12.2g	39	329	10.9	18.9	23.3	1.0
Retail	1 Egg/120g	301	251	12.0	13.1	17.1	0.0
Sainsbury's*	1 Egg/116g	287	247	11.4	13.2	16.5	0.6
Tesco*	1 Egg/114g	309	271	11.5	17.0	17.4	0.9
SEAFOOD COCKTAIL,							
Average	1oz/28g	24	87	15.6	2.9	1.5	0.0
SEAFOOD STICKS,							
Average	1 Stick/15g	16	106	8.0	18.4	0.2	0.2
With Cocktail Dip, Asda*	1 Pot/95g	126	133	6.0	16.0	5.0	0.1
With Garlic & Lemon Dip, Asda*	1 Pot/97.9g	184	188	7.0	13.0	12.0	0.0
SEASONING,							
Aromat, Knorr*	1oz/28g	46	164	12.4	20.5	3.6	1.0
Sushi, Mitsukan*	2 Tbsp/30ml	50	167	0.0	36.7	3.3	0.0
SEASONING CUBES,							
For Potato, Garlic Parsley, Knorr*	1 Serving/10g	55	550	6.0	22.0	48.0	2.0
For Potato, Mint, Perfect Potato, Knorr*	1 Cube/10g	56	560	5.1	21.2	50.5	1.8
For Rice, Pilau, Knorr*	1 Cube/10g	31	305	11.4	13.9	22.6	1.4
For Rice, Saffron, Knorr*	1 Cube/10g	29	291	13.8	17.5	18.4	2.2
For Stir Fry, Oriental Spices, Knorr*	1 Cube/10g	41	414	9.7	25.0	30.6	1.1
Oriental Spice, Knorr*	1 Cube/10g	41	409	9.5	23.7	30.7	0.0
Perfect Pasta, Knorr*	1 Cube/10g	28	278	10.3	5.2	24.0	0.0
Wild Mushroom, Knorr*	1 Cube/10g	37	365	10.3	21.3	26.5	0.2
SEASONING MIX,							
Beef Taco, Colman's*	1 Pack/30g	76	252	9.1	26.9	12.0	14.0
Chili, Old El Paso*	1 Pack/39g	117	301	7.0	57.0	5.0	0.0
Chinese Style Stir Fry, Budgens*	1 Serving/300g	81	27	1.9	4.2	0.3	1.6
Fajita, Asda*	1 Serving/8g	20	251	6.0	41.0	7.0	0.9
Fajita, Chicken, Colmans*	1 Pack/40g	149	373	10.8	13.3	30.7	13.8
Fajita, Old El Paso*	1oz/28g	88	313	11.0	56.0	5.0	0.0
Garlic & Herb Potato Wedge, Schwartz*	½ Serving/337g	546	162	3.4	26.4	4.7	0.0
Mediterranean Roast Vegetable, Schwartz*	1oz/28g	92	330	7.0	65.6	4.4	0.0
Shepherd's Pie, Colman's*	1 Pack/50g	131	262	14.3	48.6	1.1	4.1
Shepherd's Pie, Schwartz*	1 Pack/38g	110	289	9.3	58.5	2.0	0.0
Taco, Old El Paso*	¼ Pack/9g	30	334	5.5	69.0	4.0	0.0
Whole Grain Mustard & Herb Potato Mash, Colman's*	1 Pack/30g	153	510	9.7	19.1	44.1	0.0
SEAWEED,							
Crispy, Average	1oz/28g	182	651	7.5	15.6	61.9	7.0
Irish Moss, Raw	1oz/28g	2	8	1.5	0.0	0.2	12.3
Kombu, Dried, Raw	1oz/28g	12	43	7.1	0.0	1.6	58.7
Nori, Dried, Raw	1oz/28g	38	136	30.7	0.0	1.5	44.4
Wakame, Dried, Raw	1oz/28g	20	71	12.4	0.0	2.4	47.1

S

	Measure INFO/WEIGHT	per Measure KCAL	Nutrition Values per 100g / 100ml				
			KCAL	PROT	CARB	FAT	FIBRE
SEMOLINA,							
Average	1oz/28g	98	348	11.0	75.2	1.8	2.1
Pudding, Creamed, Ambrosia*	1 Can/425g	344	81	3.3	13.1	1.7	0.2
Pudding, Creamed, Co-Op*	1 Can/425g	383	90	4.0	15.0	2.0	0.0
SHAKE,							
Chocolate, Nutrition, Myoplex*	1 Serving/76g	279	367	55.0	31.0	2.2	1.1
Chocolate, Ready To Drink, Advantage, Atkins*	1 Carton/330ml	172	52	6.0	0.6	2.8	1.2
Chocolate, Ready To Drink, Myoplex*	1 Shake/330ml	150	45	7.6	1.5	1.1	0.0
Herbalife*	1 Serving/250ml	245	98	10.0	8.8	2.6	1.0
Strawberry, Ready To Drink, Myoplex*	1 Shake/330ml	150	45	7.6	1.5	1.1	0.0
Vanilla, Advant Edge, Ready To Drink, EAS*	1 Serving/250ml	150	60	4.5	7.6	1.3	0.4
Vanilla, Ready To Drink, Advantage, Atkins*	1 Carton/330ml	175	53	6.2	0.6	2.7	0.9
Vanilla, Ready To Drink, Myoplex*	1 Shake/330ml	150	45	7.6	1.5	1.1	0.0
SHAKE MIX,							
Chocolate, Advantage, Atkins*	1 Serving/33.5g	123	361	49.0	8.1	12.5	15.5
Get Up & Go, Higher Nature*	1 Serving/30g	104	346	20.0	53.0	3.3	13.3
SHALLOTS,							
Raw	1oz/28g	6	20	1.5	3.3	0.2	1.4
SHANDY,							
Bitter, Original, Ben Shaws*	1 Can/330ml	89	27	0.0	6.0	0.0	0.0
Homemade	1 Pint/568ml	148	26	0.2	2.9	0.0	0.0
Lemonade, Schweppes*	1 Can/330ml	76	23	0.0	5.1	0.0	0.0
Lemonade, Traditional Style, Tesco*	1 Can/330ml	63	19	0.0	4.7	0.0	0.0
SHARK,							
Raw	1oz/28g	29	102	23.0	0.0	1.1	0.0
SHARON FRUIT,							
Average	1oz/28g	20	73	0.8	18.6	0.0	1.6
SHERRY,							
Dry	1 Serving/50ml	58	116	0.2	1.4	0.0	0.0
Medium	1 Serving/50ml	58	116	0.1	5.9	0.0	0.0
Sweet	1 Serving/50ml	68	136	0.3	6.9	0.0	0.0
SHORTBREAD,							
All Butter, Assorted, Parkwood, Aldi*	1oz/28g	143	511	6.5	61.0	26.8	2.0
All Butter, Deans*	1 Biscuit/15g	77	511	4.9	65.7	25.4	1.2
All Butter, McVitie's*	Twin Finger/40g	216	541	6.3	62.6	29.5	1.9
All Butter, Petticoat Tails, Co-Op*	1 Tail/13g	68	520	5.0	60.0	29.0	2.0
All Butter, Petticoat Tails, Gardiners Of Scotland*	1 Wedge/12g	64	514	5.2	62.1	27.2	0.0
All Butter, Royal Edinburgh, Asda*	1 Finger/18g	93	519	5.8	60.3	28.3	1.8
All Butter, Scottish, Marks & Spencer*	1 Biscuit/34g	173	510	5.7	58.9	27.8	1.8
All Butter, Thins, Marks & Spencer*	1 Biscuit/10.3g	49	485	5.8	68.4	21.1	3.5
All Butter, Trufree*	1 Biscuit/11g	58	524	2.0	66.0	28.0	0.9
Average	1oz/28g	139	498	5.9	63.9	26.1	1.9
Butter, Extra Special, Asda*	1 Serving/19g	101	531	7.0	56.0	31.0	1.8
Choc Chip, Fair Trade, Co-Op*	1 Biscuit/19g	100	526	5.3	57.9	31.6	2.6
Chocolate & Caramel, TTD, Sainsbury's*	1 Serving/55g	245	446	4.7	45.0	27.7	1.3
Chocolate Caramel, Co-Op*	1 Cake/49g	245	500	4.1	61.2	26.5	1.0
Chocolate Chip, Jacob's*	1 Biscuit/17g	87	513	5.2	61.2	27.5	1.8
Chocolate, Waitrose*	1oz/28g	144	516	5.5	61.2	27.7	1.8
Clotted Cream & Choc Chip, Furniss*	1 Biscuit/8g	43	516	6.2	60.7	27.7	0.0
Clotted Cream, Finest, Tesco*	1 Biscuit/20g	109	543	5.2	58.0	32.2	1.7
Clotted Cream, Furniss*	1 Biscuit/8g	42	511	6.3	60.1	27.6	0.0
Cookie, Choc Chip, Low Carb, Carbolite*	1 Cookie/30g	120	400	13.3	19.0	30.0	13.3
Crawfords*	1 Biscuit/12.5g	64	533	6.6	65.0	27.4	2.0
Farmhouse, TTD, Sainsbury's*	1 Finger/20g	106	528	5.1	61.6	29.0	1.7

S

	Measure INFO/WEIGHT	per Measure KCAL	Nutrition Values per 100g / 100ml				
			KCAL	PROT	CARB	FAT	FIBRE
SHORTBREAD,							
Fingers, All Butter, Co-Op*	1 Finger/16g	85	520	6.0	58.0	30.0	2.0
Fingers, All Butter, Londis*	1 Finger/13g	66	525	5.9	59.2	29.2	1.9
Fingers, All Butter, Royal Edinburgh Bakery*	1 Biscuit/17g	88	519	5.8	60.3	28.3	1.8
Fingers, All Butter, Tesco*	1 Finger/13g	67	519	5.8	60.3	28.3	1.8
Fingers, All Butter, Traditional, Scottish, Tesco*	1 Finger/17.8g	94	520	6.0	58.5	29.1	1.8
Fingers, Asda*	1 Finger/18g	93	519	5.8	60.3	28.3	18.0
Fingers, Clotted Cream, Furniss*	1 Finger/15g	70	464	5.9	56.9	23.8	0.0
Fingers, Cornish Cookie*	2 Fingers/50g	249	498	6.4	61.0	25.5	0.0
Fingers, Deans*	1 Finger/24g	115	488	5.1	60.1	24.8	1.4
Fingers, Highland, Sainsbury's*	1 Finger/20g	106	528	5.6	57.8	30.5	1.9
Fingers, Light & Buttery, TTD, Sainsbury's*	1 Finger/20g	105	528	5.1	61.6	29.0	0.7
Fingers, Marks & Spencer*	1oz/28g	143	510	5.9	60.8	27.0	1.6
Fingers, Safeway*	1 Finger/21g	109	520	5.8	58.5	29.2	18.9
Fingers, Scottish, Marks & Spencer*	1oz/28g	143	510	5.9	60.8	27.0	1.6
Free From, Sainsbury's*	1 Biscuit/20g	98	490	6.0	58.0	26.0	6.0
Highland Demerara Rounds, Sainsbury's*	1 Biscuit/20g	113	565	5.5	70.5	29.0	2.0
Highland, Organic, Duchy Originals*	1 Biscuit/16g	80	515	5.2	61.8	27.4	1.7
Highland, Petticoat Tails, Sainsbury's*	1 Segment/12.5g	67	518	5.7	60.8	28.0	1.8
Luxury Spices, Extra Special, Asda*	1 Biscuit/20g	97	486	4.9	67.0	22.0	2.1
Mini Bites, Co-Op*	1 Biscuit/10g	53	530	7.0	59.0	30.0	2.0
Mini Bites, Country Table*	1 Biscuit/10g	53	525	7.1	59.3	29.5	1.5
Orange Marmalade & Oatflake, Deans*	1 Biscuit/20g	105	524	6.7	59.3	29.6	3.2
Pecan & Caramel, TTD, Sainsbury's*	1 Slice/52g	259	497	5.1	53.1	29.4	1.6
Pecan All Butter, Sainsbury's*	1 Biscuit/18g	99	548	5.3	49.9	36.3	2.5
Petticoat Tails, Sainsbury's*	1 Segment/13g	68	520	5.4	60.5	28.5	1.8
Pure Butter, Jacob's*	1 Biscuit/20g	105	525	5.7	58.6	29.7	1.8
Raspberry & Oatmeal, Deans*	1 Biscuit/20g	103	514	4.7	63.1	28.6	1.4
Rounds, Safeway*	1 Biscuit/19.9g	108	538	5.4	59.2	31.1	1.6
Rounds, TTD, Sainsbury's*	1 Biscuit/20g	108	538	5.0	59.5	31.1	1.6
Royal Edinburgh*	1 Piece/11g	56	507	6.1	61.1	26.5	4.5
Scottish, Marks & Spencer*	1oz/28g	143	512	4.4	59.7	27.9	2.6
Shrewsbury, Marks & Spencer*	1oz/28g	128	458	7.5	63.9	23.3	4.5
St. Clements Farmhouse Style, TTD, Sainsbury's*	1 Biscuit/20.2g	105	526	4.8	58.4	30.3	2.0
The Best, Safeway*	1 Finger/20g	100	500	4.8	65.5	23.9	2.0
Wheat & Gluten Free, Free From Range, Tesco*	1 Biscuit/20g	98	490	6.0	58.0	26.0	6.0
SHRIMPS,							
Boiled	1oz/28g	33	117	23.8	0.0	2.4	0.0
Dried	1oz/28g	69	245	55.8	0.0	2.4	0.0
Frozen	1oz/28g	20	73	16.5	0.0	0.8	0.0
In Brine, Canned, Drained	1oz/28g	26	94	20.8	0.0	1.2	0.0
SKATE,							
Grilled	1oz/28g	22	79	18.9	0.0	0.5	0.0
In Batter, Fried in Blended Oil	1oz/28g	47	168	14.7	4.9	10.1	0.2
Raw	1oz/28g	18	64	15.1	0.0	0.4	0.0
SKIPS,							
Bacon, KP*	1 Pack/17.1g	81	474	6.5	62.1	22.2	2.3
Buzzboltz Bacon Flavour, KP*	1 Bag/17g	81	474	6.5	62.1	22.2	2.3
Corn Snacks, Prawn Cocktail, KP*	1 Pack/25g	88	352	2.4	40.8	20.0	0.8
Easy Cheesy, KP*	1 Bag/19g	100	525	3.9	59.5	30.1	0.9
Pickled Onion, KP*	1 Pack/13.1g	67	512	3.4	56.4	30.3	1.4
Prawn Cocktail, KP*	1 Bag/17g	88	517	3.3	59.8	29.4	1.3
Tangy Tomato, KP*	1 Bag/17g	88	517	3.2	59.6	29.5	1.2

INFO/WEIGHT	Measure per Measure KCAL		KCAL	Nutrition Values per 100g / 100ml PROT	CARB	FAT	FIBRE
SKITTLES,							
Fruits, Mars*	1 Pack/18g	72	399	0.0	90.4	4.2	0.0
Mars*	1 Pack/55g	220	400	0.0	90.5	4.2	0.0
SLICES,							
Bacon & Cheese, Savoury, Somerfield*	1 Slice/165.0g	490	297	7.4	21.2	20.3	1.5
Beef, Minced Steak & Onion, Tesco*	1 Slice/150g	425	283	8.7	21.3	18.1	1.6
Beef, Minced With Onion, Sainsbury's*	1 Slice/120g	328	273	6.8	24.5	16.4	1.1
Beef, Minced, Morrisons*	1 Slice/143g	457	320	8.8	24.6	20.7	1.0
Beef, Pepper Steak, Ginsters*	1 Slice/155g	415	268	9.9	21.5	15.8	1.9
Cheddar Cheese & Onion, Ginsters*	1 Slice/180g	583	324	7.1	22.8	22.7	1.0
Cheese & Garlic, Safeway*	1 Slice/31g	123	398	11.4	44.1	19.5	2.2
Cheese & Ham, Sainsbury's*	1 Slice/112g	313	280	6.6	25.3	16.9	1.5
Cheese & Ham, Savoury, Somerfield*	1 Slice/150g	399	266	7.0	23.0	16.0	0.0
Cheese & Onion, Savoury, Somerfield*	1 Slice/165g	518	314	7.4	24.0	20.9	0.6
Cheese & Onion, Tesco*	1 Slice/150g	503	335	8.0	20.1	24.7	1.4
Cheese, Potato & Onion, Taste!*	1 Serving/155.1g	501	323	8.6	28.1	19.6	0.0
Chicken & Ham, Taste!*	1 Slice/154.8g	357	230	10.8	24.2	9.9	0.0
Chicken & Leek, Taste!*	1 Slice/155g	406	262	10.1	27.6	12.3	0.0
Chicken & Mushroom, Asda*	1 Serving/127.8g	355	277	7.0	24.0	17.0	2.1
Chicken & Mushroom, Ginsters*	1 Slice/155g	420	271	6.6	21.8	17.5	1.7
Chicken & Mushroom, Sainsbury's*	1 Slice/164g	427	259	7.3	21.3	16.1	1.0
Chicken & Mushroom, Tesco*	1 Slice/165g	457	277	9.2	20.6	17.5	0.9
Ham & Cheese, Ginsters*	1 Slice/155g	625	403	9.8	31.9	28.2	4.2
Ham & Cheese, Sainsbury's*	1 Slice/118g	352	298	7.8	22.5	19.7	1.8
Minced Steak & Onion, Sainsbury's*	1 Slice/165g	475	288	15.2	16.0	18.1	2.5
Smoked Cheese With Ham, Aldi*	1 Slice/21g	66	313	21.0	1.0	25.0	0.1
Spicy Chicken, Deep Fill, Ginsters*	1 Slice/180g	499	277	9.2	21.8	17.0	1.4
Spinach & Ricotta, Safeway*	1 Slice/165g	487	295	6.0	21.2	20.4	2.9
Vegetable, Tesco*	1 Slice/165g	452	274	5.6	21.4	18.5	3.3
SLIMFAST*,							
Banana Deluxe Meal Replacement Drink	1 Serving/325ml	215	66	4.2	11.3	0.8	1.4
Chocolate Royale, Ready To Drink, Ultra	1 Serving/11floz	220	71	3.2	12.8	0.9	1.6
Chocolate Shake	1 Can/325ml	218	67	4.2	10.6	0.8	1.8
Coffee Mocha, Ready to Drink	1 Shake/325ml	215	66	4.2	10.6	0.8	1.5
French Vanilla, Ready To Drink	1 Can/325ml	215	66	4.2	10.6	0.8	1.5
Shake, Chocolate, Dry	1 Serving/35g	123	351	13.6	54.3	9.3	17.1
Shake, Peach	1 Can/325ml	215	66	4.2	10.6	0.8	1.5
Shake, Strawberry	1 Can/327.3ml	216	66	4.2	10.6	1.0	1.5
Shake, Vanilla, Dry	1 Serving/35g	123	351	12.7	57.0	7.5	17.1
Shake, Vanilla, Ready to Drink	1 Can/325ml	215	66	4.2	10.6	0.8	1.5
Strawberry Supreme, Ready To Drink	1 Can/325ml	215	66	4.2	10.6	0.8	1.5
SMARTIES,							
Biscuits, Nestle*	1 Biscuit/5g	26	519	7.7	57.6	28.6	0.0
Giants, Nestle*	1 Pack/186g	882	474	4.6	70.4	19.3	0.7
Mini Cones, Nestle*	1 Serving/44g	145	330	4.5	45.0	13.1	0.0
Mini Eggs, Nestle*	1 Lge Bag/112g	535	478	4.8	69.6	20.0	0.7
Minis, Nestle*	1 Serving/14.8g	69	458	4.1	73.5	16.4	0.6
Nestle*	3 Smarties/3g	14	458	4.1	73.5	16.4	0.6
Tree Decoration, Nestle*	1 Decoration/18g	95	529	5.6	58.9	30.1	0.8
SMOOTHIE,							
Apple, Grapes & Blackcurrant, P & J*	1 Bottle/250ml	125	50	0.8	11.1	0.3	0.7
Apple, Kiwi & Lime, SunJuice*	1 Serving/250ml	133	53	0.5	13.4	0.1	0.8
Apple, Raspberries & Banana, P & J*	1 Bottle/330ml	188	57	0.7	12.2	0.3	0.0
Apple, Strawberry, Cherry & Banana, Marks & Spencer*	1 Bottle/250ml	125	50	0.5	11.2	0.3	0.6

S

SMOOTHIE,

	Measure INFO/WEIGHT	per Measure KCAL	KCAL	PROT	CARB	FAT	FIBRE
Apricot & Peach, COU, Marks & Spencer*	1 Serving/250ml	100	40	0.9	8.3	0.4	0.4
Banana, Marks & Spencer*	1 Bottle/500ml	270	54	1.7	12.2	0.1	0.8
Banana, Measure Up, Asda*	1 Serving/61g	203	333	17.0	55.0	5.0	14.0
Blackberry & Blueberry, Innocent*	1 Bottle/250ml	120	48	0.6	11.5	0.1	0.0
Blackberry & Blueberry, Wild Orchard*	1 Bottle/250ml	110	44	0.6	10.8	0.0	1.9
Blackcurrants & Gooseberries, For Autuman, Innocent*	1 Bottle/250ml	118	47	0.5	12.5	0.1	0.0
Blueberry & Raspberry, Smoothie Smile*	1 Bottle/250ml	135	54	0.6	11.6	0.2	0.0
Boysenberry & Raspberry, Fruit, Sainsbury's*	1 Bottle/250ml	108	43	0.7	10.0	0.1	1.6
Cherries & Strawberries, Innocent*	1 Bottle/250ml	123	49	0.6	12.6	0.1	0.0
Cranberries & Rasperries, Pure Fruit, Innocent*	1 Serving/250ml	103	41	0.5	9.5	0.2	0.0
Cranberries & Strawberries, Innocent*	1 Serving/250ml	103	41	0.5	9.5	0.2	0.0
Daily Detox, P & J*	1 Bottle/250ml	143	57	0.8	13.1	0.2	0.0
Ginseng & Ace Vitamins, Marks & Spencer*	1 Bottle/250ml	138	55	0.7	13.0	0.2	0.9
It's Alive, P & J*	1 Bottle/250ml	150	60	0.7	13.6	0.3	0.0
Mango & Orange, Smoothie Smile*	1 Bottle/250ml	130	52	0.4	11.7	0.4	0.0
Mango & Passion Fruit, Innocent*	1 Bottle/250ml	138	55	0.4	12.8	0.2	0.0
Mango & West Indian Cherry, Plus, Tesco*	1 Serving/250ml	133	53	0.6	12.2	0.2	0.5
Mango, Pineapple & Passion Fruit, Eat Smart, Safeway*	1 Bottle/250ml	135	54	0.5	12.6	0.0	1.1
Mango, Pineapple & Passionfruit, Marks & Spencer*	1 Bottle/500ml	290	58	0.7	12.1	0.5	0.9
Orange & Mango, Fruit, Morrisons*	1 Serving/250ml	145	58	0.5	14.0	0.0	0.7
Orange & Mango, Safeway*	1 Bottle/250ml	130	52	0.5	12.1	0.2	0.7
Orange, Banana & Pineapple, Innocent*	1 Bottle/250ml	120	48	0.6	10.8	0.4	0.0
Orange, Mango & Apricot, COU, Marks & Spencer*	1 Bottle/250ml	130	52	0.6	11.0	0.6	0.6
Orange, Mango, Banana & Passion Fruit, Asda*	1 Serving/100ml	55	55	0.8	12.0	0.2	1.1
Orange, Strawberry & Guava, Sainsbury's*	1 Serving/300ml	159	53	0.3	12.0	0.2	0.8
Oranges & Mangoes, Get Your Vits, P & J*	1 Bottle/250ml	128	51	0.6	11.6	0.2	0.0
Oranges Mangos & Bananas, P & J*	1 Bottle/330ml	195	59	0.9	13.6	0.2	0.7
Passionfruit Lychee, SunJuice*	1 Sm Bottle/250ml	145	58	0.5	13.5	0.2	0.8
Peach, Mild & Fruity, Campina*	1 Bottle/330ml	211	64	2.7	13.1	0.0	0.0
Peaches & Bananas, P & J*	1 Bottle/330ml	188	57	0.7	13.6	0.3	0.0
Pineapple, Banana & Coconut, P & J*	1 Bottle/330ml	234	71	0.8	12.3	1.4	0.0
Pineapple, Banana & Mango Fruit, Finest, Tesco*	1 Glass/200ml	94	47	0.1	11.2	0.2	0.0
Pineapple, Banana & Pear, Asda*	1 Bottle/250ml	147	59	0.5	13.6	0.1	0.3
Pineapple, Banana & Pear, Princes*	1 Bottle/250ml	153	61	0.5	13.9	0.2	0.5
Pineapple, Mango & Lime, Way To Five, Sainsbury's*	1 Bottle/250g	120	48	0.4	11.3	0.1	0.3
Pineapple, Mango & Passion Fruit, Extra Special, Asda*	½ Bottle/250ml	100	40	0.5	9.0	0.2	1.3
Pineapple, Mango & Passionfruit, 100% Fruit, Sainsbury's*	1 Bottle/250ml	163	65	0.7	15.2	0.1	1.0
Pineapple, Strawberries & Passion Fruit, P & J*	1 Bottle/330ml	152	46	0.6	10.8	0.1	1.3
Raspberry & Bio Yogurt, Marks & Spencer*	1 Bottle/500ml	275	55	2.0	10.8	0.3	0.9
Raspberry & Blueberry, Plus, Tesco*	1 Serving/100ml	59	59	2.6	11.6	0.3	0.5
Raspberry, Banana & Peach, Sainsbury's*	1 Bottle/250.9ml	138	55	0.8	12.8	0.1	1.5
Raspberry, Marks & Spencer*	1 Serving/250ml	138	55	1.7	12.2	0.6	1.9
Strawberries & Bananas, Innocent*	1 Bottle/250ml	118	47	0.4	10.7	0.2	0.0
Strawberries & Bananas, P & J*	1 Bottle/330ml	172	52	0.9	11.5	0.3	0.0
Strawberry & Banana Fruit, Finest, Tesco*	1 Bottle/250ml	135	54	0.3	12.5	0.3	0.5
Strawberry & Banana, Morrisons*	1 Serving/250ml	135	54	0.5	13.0	0.0	0.6
Strawberry & Cherry, Organic, Marks & Spencer*	1 Bottle/250ml	138	55	0.8	12.3	0.3	0.4
Strawberry & Raspberry, COU, Marks & Spencer*	1 Bottle/250ml	113	45	0.6	10.2	0.2	0.9
Strawberry & Raspberry, Shapers, Boots*	1 Bottle/250ml	110	44	0.6	10.0	0.2	0.6
Strawberry & Raspberry, The Best Safeway*	1fl oz/30ml	15	49	0.6	10.2	0.2	0.6
Strawberry & White Chocolate, Marks & Spencer*	1 Serving/250ml	100	40	2.5	5.5	1.0	0.1
Strawberry Dairy, Shapers, Boots*	1 Bottle/250ml	120	48	1.7	9.7	0.3	0.5
Strawberry, Dairy, Finest, Tesco*	1 Bottle/250ml	163	65	2.9	13.2	0.1	0.1

S

	Measure INFO/WEIGHT	per Measure KCAL	Nutrition Values per 100g / 100ml				
			KCAL	PROT	CARB	FAT	FIBRE
SMOOTHIE,							
Strawberry, Raspberry, Apple & Banana, P & J*	1 Bottle/250ml	133	53	0.8	11.9	0.3	0.7
Strawberry, Raspberry, Bio Yoghurt, Eat Smart, Safeway*	1 Bottle/250ml	163	65	2.0	12.5	0.6	0.6
Strawberry, Wild Orchard*	1 Bottle/250ml	120	48	0.6	11.8	0.0	1.4
Vanilla & Honey, Sainsbury's*	1 Bottle/250ml	238	95	3.2	14.8	2.4	0.3
Vanilla Bean, Marks & Spencer*	1 Bottle/500ml	450	90	3.3	13.9	2.6	0.0
SNACK EGGS,							
Mini, Tesco*	1 Serving/20g	65	323	12.5	18.3	22.2	1.3
Tesco*	1 Egg/45g	133	295	9.2	18.5	20.5	1.1
SNACK SALAD,							
Chargrilled Chicken & Pesto Pasta, Sainsbury's*	1 Pack/240g	454	189	7.2	19.4	9.2	0.0
Chargrilled Chicken, Tesco*	1 Pot/300g	384	128	6.1	15.0	4.8	2.4
Cheese Layered, Sainsbury's*	1 Pack/190g	397	209	5.4	12.4	15.3	0.0
Chicken & Bacon, Tesco*	1 Pack/300g	501	167	7.2	10.9	10.5	3.2
Chicken Noodle, Sainsbury's*	1 Snack/240g	278	116	5.2	12.4	5.1	1.4
Greek Style, BGTY, Sainsbury's*	1 Pack/198.5g	133	67	2.0	9.0	2.5	0.8
Ham & Mushroom, Tesco*	1 Pot/300g	600	200	4.7	21.2	10.7	1.4
Hoi Sin Chicken & Noodle, TTD, Sainsbury's*	1 Pack/230g	214	93	4.7	15.2	1.5	1.8
Honey & Mustard Chicken Pasta, Sainsbury's*	1 Pack/190.1g	344	181	7.1	18.0	8.9	0.0
Honey & Mustard Chicken, Tesco*	1 Pot/300g	585	195	8.4	20.4	8.9	1.1
Pasta & Tuna, ., Healthy Living, Co-Op*	1 Tub/225g	146	65	5.0	10.0	0.4	1.0
Pasta & Tuna, BGTY, Sainsbury's*	1 Pack/260g	218	84	6.0	11.5	1.6	2.3
Pasta & Tuna, Healthy Selection, Somerfield*	1 Pot/190g	194	102	6.5	13.0	2.7	1.1
Pasta, Cheese, Somerfield*	1 Salad/200g	422	211	8.0	14.0	14.0	0.0
Pasta, Egg Mayo, Asda*	1 Serving/180g	364	202	4.0	12.8	15.0	0.3
Pasta, Tuna, Asda*	1 Serving/180g	196	109	5.5	13.2	3.8	0.9
Pasta, Tuna, Sainsbury's*	1 Pot/260g	218	84	6.0	11.5	1.6	2.3
Salmon & Dill, Tesco*	1 Pack/300g	600	200	7.7	13.4	12.8	0.8
Tuna Pasta With Balsamic Dressing, GFY, Asda*	1 Pack/199.2g	263	132	5.0	20.0	3.6	1.5
Tuna, Tesco*	1 Pack/300g	252	84	7.6	11.5	0.9	0.9
SNACK STOP,							
Bolognese Style, Big, Crosse & Blackwell*	1 Pot/407.1g	403	99	2.8	19.5	1.1	0.0
Chicken & Mushroom Flavour Pasta, Crosse & Blackwell*	1 Pot/60g	251	418	10.3	74.3	8.8	0.0
Creamy Cheese Pasta, Crosse & Blackwell*	1 Pot/218.3g	251	115	3.0	19.2	2.9	0.0
Creamy Chicken Pasta, Crosse & Blackwell*	1 Pot/247g	210	85	2.7	15.7	1.6	0.0
Macaroni Cheese, Light, Crosse & Blackwell*	1 Pack/248g	260	105	3.2	16.4	3.0	0.9
Melting Cheese & Pepperoni, Crosse & Blackwell*	1 Pack/237g	237	100	2.9	13.3	4.1	0.0
Mushroom Pasta Twirls, Crosse & Blackwell*	1 Pot/248g	248	100	3.1	15.9	2.7	0.9
Roast Onion & Potato, Crosse & Blackwell*	1 Pot/210g	210	100	1.7	14.4	3.7	0.0
Roast Parsnip & Potato, Crosse & Blackwell*	1 Pot/210g	200	95	1.7	13.6	3.6	0.0
Spicy Tomato Pasta, Crosse & Blackwell*	1 Pot/412g	358	87	2.4	15.9	1.5	0.0
Sun Ripened Tomato & Herb, Crosse & Blackwell*	1 Pot/ 237g	201	85	2.6	16.1	1.1	0.0
SNACK-A-JACKS,							
Apple & Cinnamon Flavour, Quaker*	1 Jumbo/10g	38	376	6.2	83.1	2.2	3.9
Barbecue Flavour, Quaker*	1 Pack/30g	126	421	6.5	77.0	10.0	1.0
Barbecue, Invidual Bag, Quaker*	1 Bag/30g	122	407	7.0	79.0	6.5	1.0
Caramel, Quaker*	1 Bag/35g	140	401	5.5	86.0	3.5	0.5
Cheddar Cheese Flavour, Quaker*	1 Bag/30g	128	427	8.0	73.0	10.0	1.0
Chocolate Flavour, Quaker*	1 Cake/14g	57	406	5.5	85.0	4.5	1.0
Creamy Lemon Flavour, Quaker*	1 Pack/35g	137	390	5.0	87.0	2.5	1.0
Crispy Caramel, Quaker*	1 Pack/35g	140	400	5.4	86.0	3.4	0.6
Crispy Cheese, Quaker*	1 Bag/30g	123	409	8.0	75.0	8.5	1.0
Crispy Chocolate Flavour, Quaker*	1 Pack/30g	122	407	5.5	85.0	4.5	1.0
Crispy Vanilla Flavour, Quaker*	1 Pack/35g	137	390	5.0	87.0	2.5	1.0

S

	Measure INFO/WEIGHT	per Measure KCAL	Nutrition Values per 100g / 100ml				
			KCAL	PROT	CARB	FAT	FIBRE
SNACK-A-JACKS,							
Jumbo, Apple Danish Flavour, Quaker*	1 Serving/13g	51	392	5.4	86.9	2.3	0.8
Jumbo, Barbecue Flavour, Quaker*	1 Serving/10g	38	376	7.0	80.0	2.5	1.0
Jumbo, Caramel Flavour, Quaker*	1 Cake/13g	52	397	5.0	87.0	2.5	1.0
Jumbo, Cheddar Cheese Flavour, Quaker*	1 Cake/10g	38	383	8.0	81.0	3.0	1.0
Jumbo, Chocolate, Quaker*	1 Cake/12g	49	406	5.5	85.0	4.5	1.0
Jumbo, Sour Cream & Chive, Quaker*	1 Cake/10g	38	380	8.0	82.0	3.0	2.0
Mini Bites, Mature Cheddar & Red Onion, Quaker*	1 Bag/28g	116	415	7.5	76.0	9.0	2.0
Mini Bites, Sour Cream & Sweet Chilli, Quaker*	1 Packet/28g	114	408	6.5	77.5	8.0	2.0
Mini Bites, Tangy Tomato & Red Pepper, Quaker*	1 Bag/28g	114	406	6.0	77.5	8.0	2.0
Salt & Vinegar, Quaker*	1 Bag/30g	123	410	6.5	77.0	8.0	1.0
Savoury Salted, Quaker*	1 Bag/30g	124	414	7.5	77.0	8.0	1.0
Sour Cream & Chive, Quakers*	1 Pack/30g	123	410	7.5	77.0	8.0	1.0
Spudz, Oriental Barbecue, Quaker*	1 Bag/20g	79	395	6.0	73.0	8.5	1.5
Spudz, Smoked Bacon & Cheese, Quaker*	1 Bag/20g	80	398	7.5	76.5	10.0	1.5
Spudz, Sour Cream & Sweet Chilli, Quaker*	¼ Pack/30g	118	394	6.5	75.0	7.5	2.0
Tomato & Herb Flavour, Quaker*	1 Pack/30g	125	415	6.5	78.0	8.5	1.0
Vanilla, Quaker*	1 Pack/35.1g	137	390	5.0	87.0	2.5	1.0
SNAPPER,							
Red, Fried in Blended Oil	1oz/28g	35	126	24.5	0.0	3.1	0.0
Red, Raw	1oz/28g	25	90	19.6	0.0	1.3	0.0
SNAPS,							
Spicy Tomato Flavour, Walkers*	1 Bag/17.9g	91	508	1.5	65.5	26.8	0.0
SNICKERS,							
Cruncher, Mars*	1 Bar/40g	209	523	9.0	57.0	30.0	2.3
Mars*	1 Standard/64.5g	294	501	9.3	52.9	28.1	0.0
SODA,							
Appleade, Sugar Free, Tesco*	1 Serving/200ml	2	1	0.0	0.0	0.0	0.0
Cherryade, Sugar Free, Tesco*	1 Glass/200ml	2	1	0.0	0.0	0.0	0.0
Cream, Traditional Style, Tesco*	1 Can/330ml	139	42	0.0	10.4	0.0	0.0
Dandelion & Burdock, Ben Shaws Original*	1 Can/440ml	128	29	0.0	7.0	0.0	0.0
Orange & Strawberry, Freekee, Britvic*	1 Bottle/330ml	20	6	0.0	1.0	0.0	0.0
Raspberryade, Blue, Panda Pops*	1 Bottle/330ml	86	26	0.0	6.2	0.0	0.0
SORBET,							
Blackcurrant, Del Monte*	1oz/28g	30	106	0.4	27.1	0.1	0.0
Blackcurrant, Iceland*	¼ Pot/100g	100	100	0.0	25.0	0.0	0.0
Kiwi & Papaya, World Fruit, Del Monte*	1 Lolly/90ml	61	68	0.2	16.2	0.3	0.0
Lemon	1 Scoop/60g	79	131	0.9	34.2	0.0	0.0
Lemon Harmony, Haagen-Dazs*	1 Serving/90ml	214	238	1.5	32.5	11.3	0.0
Lemon, Del Monte*	1 Sorbet/500g	570	114	0.1	29.2	0.1	0.0
Lemon, Organic, Evernat*	1oz/28g	27	96	0.1	22.8	0.5	0.0
Lemon, Sticks, Haagen-Dazs*	1oz/28g	67	238	1.5	32.5	11.3	0.0
Lemon, Tesco*	1 Serving/75g	80	106	0.0	26.2	0.0	0.4
Mango, Del Monte*	1 Sorbet/500g	575	115	0.2	29.6	0.1	0.0
Mango, Sainsbury's*	¼ Pot/88.9g	104	117	0.2	28.9	0.1	0.7
Mango, Tropicale, Haagen-Dazs*	1oz/28g	32	116	0.2	28.6	0.1	0.0
Mango, Waitrose*	1 Pot/100g	90	90	0.1	22.1	0.0	0.6
Orange, Del Monte*	1 Sorbet/500g	625	125	0.2	32.1	0.1	0.0
Passion Fruit, Fat Free, Marks & Spencer*	1 Sorbet/125g	129	103	0.4	25.0	0.0	0.4
Peach & Strawberry, Haagen-Dazs*	1oz/28g	30	108	0.0	27.0	0.0	0.0
Peach & Vanilla Fruit Swirl, Healthy Living, Tesco*	1 Pot/73g	93	127	1.1	28.9	0.8	0.5
Pear, Organic, Evernat*	1oz/28g	33	119	0.0	28.3	0.6	0.0
Pineapple, Del Monte*	1 Sorbet/500g	600	120	0.3	30.6	0.1	0.0
Raspberry & Blackberry, Fat Free, Marks & Spencer*	1 Sorbet/125g	140	112	0.4	27.5	0.0	0.6

S

	Measure INFO/WEIGHT	per Measure KCAL	Nutrition Values per 100g / 100ml				
			KCAL	PROT	CARB	FAT	FIBRE
SORBET,							
Raspberry, Häagen-Dazs*	½ Cup/105g	120	114	0.0	28.6	0.0	1.9
Raspberry, Select, Safeway*	½ Cup/105g	100	95	0.0	27.6	0.0	1.0
Raspberry, Sticks, Haagen-Dazs*	1oz/28g	28	99	0.2	24.2	0.1	0.0
Raspberry, Tesco*	1 Serving/70ml	97	138	0.5	34.0	0.0	0.0
Strawberry & Champagne, Sainsbury's*	¼ Pot/89g	95	107	0.2	25.5	0.0	0.6
Strawberry, Fruit Ice, Starburst, Mars*	1 Stick/93ml	99	106	0.1	26.7	0.1	0.0
Strawberry, Marks & Spencer*	1oz/28g	27	95	0.3	23.4	0.1	0.5
Summer Berry, Swirl, Asda*	¼ Pack/89g	97	109	3.0	26.0	0.4	0.0
Swirl, Raspberry & Blackcurrant, Safeway*	1 Serving/50g	58	115	0.6	27.0	0.0	1.6
Tropical, Really Fruity, Asda*	1 Scoop/75g	90	120	0.1	30.0	0.0	0.3
Zesty Lemon, Haagen-Dazs*	1 Serving/125ml	120	96	0.0	24.8	0.0	1.0
SORBET CONE,							
Raspberry, Yoghurt & Sorbet, BGTY, Sainsbury's*	1 Cone/69g	151	219	2.6	37.5	6.5	1.3
Sorbet, Sainsbury's*	1 Serving/70g	153	219	2.6	37.5	6.5	1.3
SOSMIX,							
Direct Foods*	1oz/28g	124	443	18.5	27.0	29.0	0.0
Organic*	1oz/28g	122	435	20.0	37.0	23.0	0.0
SOUFFLE,							
Cheese	1oz/28g	71	253	11.4	9.3	19.2	0.3
Lemon, Finest, Tesco*	1 Pot/80g	270	338	2.9	24.1	25.6	0.2
Plain	1oz/28g	56	201	7.6	10.4	14.7	0.3
Raspberry & Amaretto, Marks & Spencer*	1oz/28g	83	298	2.8	33.1	16.7	0.1
Ricotta & Spinach, Marks & Spencer*	1 Serving/120g	186	155	8.0	6.2	11.1	2.1
Strawberry, Marks & Spencer*	1 Serving/95g	171	180	1.6	19.5	10.6	0.9
SOUP,							
Asparagus & Chicken, Waitrose*	1 Can/415g	166	40	2.1	5.3	1.1	0.7
Asparagus With Croutons, In a Cup, Sainsbury's*	1 Serving/200ml	103	52	1.0	6.4	2.5	1.7
Asparagus, Batchelors*	1 Serving/223g	143	64	0.5	9.2	2.8	0.4
Asparagus, Fresh, Marks & Spencer*	1 Serving/300g	135	45	1.1	2.5	3.6	0.9
Asparagus, Fresh, New Covent Garden Food Co*	1 Carton/600g	324	54	2.1	1.8	4.3	0.9
Asparagus, Healthy Eating, Tesco*	1 Serving/19g	67	351	3.6	60.3	10.6	3.2
Asparagus, Knorr*	1 Serving/300ml	114	38	0.7	4.8	1.7	0.1
Asparagus, Less Than 60 Cals, Waitrose*	1 Serving/204ml	51	25	0.4	4.3	0.7	0.7
Asparagus, Marks & Spencer*	1 Serving/300g	180	60	1.1	3.3	4.5	0.7
Asparagus, New Covent Garden Food Co*	½ Carton/300g	162	54	2.1	1.8	4.3	0.9
Asparagus, Slim Choice, Safeway*	1 Serving/15ml	58	386	8.1	68.4	8.9	8.1
Aubergine & Red Pepper, New Covent Garden Food Co*	½ Pint/284ml	68	24	0.9	4.8	0.1	0.4
Autumn Vegetable With Mild Spice, Baxters*	1 Can/415g	199	48	2.2	9.2	0.3	1.5
Autumn Vegetable, Baxters*	1 Can/425g	170	40	1.8	8.0	0.2	1.5
Autumn Vegetable, Vie, Knorr*	1 Pack/500ml	190	38	0.7	4.3	2.0	0.7
Bean, Italian Style, Tesco*	1 Can/300g	153	51	2.8	7.3	1.2	1.1
Beef & Tomato, Cup A Soup, Batchelors*	1 Serving/215g	71	33	0.6	7.3	0.2	0.5
Beef & Vegetable Big, Heinz*	½ Can/200g	90	45	2.4	7.3	0.7	0.9
Beef & Vegetable Broth, Marks & Spencer*	1 Can/415g	166	40	1.9	6.4	0.8	0.6
Beef & Vegetable Mighty, Asda*	½ Can/81g	32	40	2.3	6.0	0.8	0.6
Beef & Vegetable, Tesco*	1 Serving/410g	312	76	2.0	5.3	4.8	0.6
Beef Broth Big, Heinz*	½ Can/200g	82	41	2.0	6.8	0.6	0.7
Beef Chilli Baked Potato Big, Heinz*	1 Can/400g	232	58	3.4	9.1	0.9	1.3
Beef Consomme, Sainsbury's*	1 Can/415g	46	11	2.0	0.7	0.0	0.0
Beef, Big, Heinz*	1 Can/400g	180	45	2.4	7.2	0.7	0.9
Beetroot & Rosemary, New Covent Garden Food Co*	1 Pack/600g	138	23	1.3	4.0	0.2	1.2
Big Red Tomato, Heinz*	½ Can/210g	63	30	0.5	6.4	0.4	0.0
Black Bean Chilli Con Carne, EAT*	1 Serving/450ml	358	80	7.1	7.1	2.6	1.3

SOUP,

	Measure INFO/WEIGHT	per Measure KCAL	Nutrition Values per 100g / 100ml				
			KCAL	PROT	CARB	FAT	FIBRE
Blended Autumn Vegetable, Heinz*	½ Can/200g	114	57	1.2	6.4	3.0	0.7
Blended Carrot & Coriander, Heinz*	½ Can/200g	104	52	0.7	6.2	2.7	0.6
Blended Leek & Bacon, Heinz*	½ Can/200g	108	54	1.9	5.0	2.9	0.5
Blended Red Pepper With Tomato, Heinz*	½ Can/200g	102	51	0.8	5.2	2.9	0.7
Blended Sweetcorn & Yellow Pepper, Heinz*	½ Can/200g	98	49	0.9	6.6	2.1	0.6
Bloody Mary, Sainsbury's*	1fl oz/30ml	7	22	0.4	4.3	0.3	0.9
Broccoli & Blue Stilton, New Covent Garden Food Co*	1 Carton/600g	378	63	3.5	2.9	4.2	1.2
Broccoli & Cauliflower, Cup, Better For You, Morrisons*	1 Sachet/15g	56	376	4.9	57.2	14.2	4.9
Broccoli & Cheddar, Heinz*	1 Can/430g	340	79	2.6	4.4	5.6	0.6
Broccoli & Cheddar, Snack, Weight Watchers*	1 Serving/26g	124	477	11.2	78.1	13.5	1.9
Broccoli & Dolcelatte Cheese, Soupreme, Aldi*	½ Carton/250g	60	24	3.3	1.1	1.0	1.0
Broccoli & Melton Mowbray Stilton, Marks & Spencer*	½ Pot/300g	240	80	2.8	3.3	6.4	0.9
Broccoli & Potato, Organic, Baxters*	1 Can/425g	162	38	1.5	6.2	0.8	0.7
Broccoli & Stilton, Asda*	1 Pack/302g	172	57	2.2	6.0	2.7	0.0
Broccoli & Stilton, Canned, Sainsbury's*	½ Can/207g	126	61	1.7	4.8	3.9	0.4
Broccoli & Stilton, Canned, Tesco*	1 Can/400g	224	56	1.8	4.2	3.5	0.3
Broccoli & Stilton, Fresh, Safeway*	1 Serving/300g	180	60	2.7	3.7	3.6	0.6
Broccoli & Stilton, Fresh, Sainsbury's*	½ Bottle/300ml	156	52	2.1	3.9	3.1	0.9
Broccoli & Stilton, Fresh, Tesco*	½ Pot/300g	207	69	3.2	3.8	4.5	0.7
Broccoli & Stilton, Homestyle, Somerfield*	1 Pack/500g	350	70	2.0	5.0	4.0	0.0
Broccoli & Stilton, Somerfield*	½ Pack/250g	140	56	1.6	3.5	3.9	1.5
Broccoli & Stilton, Special Recipe, Sainsbury's*	½ Can/208g	127	61	1.7	4.8	3.9	0.4
Broccoli & Stilton, Tesco*	1 Pack/600g	564	94	2.9	2.5	8.1	0.7
Broccoli With Mustard, New Covent Garden Food Co*	1 Carton/568g	204	36	1.3	3.3	1.9	1.2
Broccoli With Stilton, New Covent Garden Food Co*	1floz/30ml	14	47	2.0	2.5	3.2	1.0
Broccoli, Baxters*	1 Can/425g	191	45	1.3	5.9	1.8	0.4
Brocoli & Stilton, Fresh, Safeway*	1 Serving/500g	290	58	3.5	4.8	2.8	0.7
Butternut Squash & Red Pepper, Baxters*	1 Can/425g	153	36	0.7	6.1	1.0	0.6
Butternut Squash, Fresh, Waitrose*	½ Pot/300g	153	51	0.5	5.8	2.9	0.8
Butternut Squash, With Parmesan, EAT*	1 Can/400ml	127	32	1.9	1.7	2.0	0.5
Cajun Spicy Vegetable, Slim A Soup, Batchelors*	1 Sachet/211g	57	27	0.8	5.0	0.5	0.6
Cantonese Chicken & Sweetcorn, Fresh, Sainsbury's*	½ Bottle/300ml	135	45	2.1	7.9	0.5	0.5
Cantonese Hot & Sour Noodle, Baxters*	1 Serving/215g	133	62	1.4	11.1	1.3	0.5
Carrot & Butterbean, Baxters*	1 Can/425g	230	54	1.6	7.7	1.9	1.7
Carrot & Coriander, 'a' Meal, Feeling Great, Findus*	1 Serving/371g	130	35	1.5	5.5	1.0	1.5
Carrot & Coriander, Asda*	1 Pack/297g	92	31	1.0	6.0	0.3	0.0
Carrot & Coriander, BGTY, Sainsbury's*	½ Can/200g	48	24	0.3	4.8	0.4	0.1
Carrot & Coriander, Baxters*	1 Can/425g	174	41	0.8	6.0	1.5	0.8
Carrot & Coriander, Benjys*	1 Serving/300g	162	54	0.4	5.4	3.5	0.0
Carrot & Coriander, COU, Marks & Spencer*	1oz/28g	7	25	0.4	4.3	0.7	0.5
Carrot & Coriander, Can, Marks & Spencer*	½ Can/210g	95	45	0.8	6.3	1.9	0.9
Carrot & Coriander, Carton, Campbell's*	1 Serving/250ml	110	44	0.7	5.4	2.2	0.0
Carrot & Coriander, Classic Homestyle, Marks & Spencer*	1 Can/425g	170	40	0.6	5.6	2.0	0.7
Carrot & Coriander, EAT*	1 Serving/82.7ml	141	169	2.2	11.5	13.0	3.0
Carrot & Coriander, Eat Smart, Safeway*	1 Serving/300g	105	35	0.7	4.8	1.4	1.1
Carrot & Coriander, Fresh, Co-Op*	½ Pot/300g	120	40	0.4	3.0	3.0	1.0
Carrot & Coriander, Fresh, Improved, Sainsbury's*	½ Bottle/300ml	84	28	0.5	3.0	1.6	2.6
Carrot & Coriander, Fresh, Marks & Spencer*	½ Pot/300g	90	30	0.4	4.2	1.5	0.5
Carrot & Coriander, Fresh, Organic, Simply Organic*	1 Serving/250g	83	33	0.6	3.3	2.0	1.0
Carrot & Coriander, Fresh, Sainsbury's*	½ Bottle/300ml	150	50	1.4	4.1	3.1	0.6
Carrot & Coriander, Fresh, Tesco*	1 Pack/600g	246	41	0.6	4.5	2.3	1.2
Carrot & Coriander, Fresh, Waitrose*	½ Pot/300g	117	39	0.5	5.4	1.7	0.9
Carrot & Coriander, GFY, Asda*	½ Pot/251g	88	35	1.2	4.0	1.6	0.4

S

SOUP,	INFO/WEIGHT	KCAL	KCAL	PROT	CARB	FAT	FIBRE
Carrot & Coriander, GFY, Asda*	1 Can/400g	100	25	0.4	4.1	0.8	0.8
Carrot & Coriander, Heinz*	1 Can/400g	208	52	0.7	6.2	2.7	0.6
Carrot & Coriander, Less Than 5% Fat, Asda	1 Serving/300g	96	32	1.0	6.0	0.3	0.8
Carrot & Coriander, Morrisons*	½ Pot/251.2ml	103	41	0.6	4.9	2.1	1.2
Carrot & Coriander, New Covent Garden Food Co*	1floz/30ml	13	42	0.8	3.9	2.6	0.6
Carrot & Coriander, Packet, Sainsbury's*	1oz/28g	7	24	0.7	3.9	0.6	0.7
Carrot & Coriander, Perfectly Balanced, Waitrose*	1 Can/413ml	66	16	0.5	3.1	0.2	1.0
Carrot & Coriander, Safeway*	1 Carton/600g	450	75	0.8	6.5	4.8	1.1
Carrot & Coriander, Sainsbury's*	½ Bottle/300ml	84	28	0.5	3.0	1.6	2.6
Carrot & Coriander, Seeds Of Change*	1 Pack/500g	210	42	0.5	5.7	1.9	0.9
Carrot & Coriander, Selection, Campbell's*	1 Carton/500ml	185	37	0.6	6.4	1.0	0.6
Carrot & Coriander, Somerfield*	½ Pot/300g	108	36	0.5	2.3	2.7	2.2
Carrot & Coriander, Soup-A-Cup, Asda*	1 Serving/26g	102	392	4.6	62.0	14.0	4.5
Carrot & Coriander, Special Recipe, Sainsbury's*	1 Can/415g	170	41	0.7	4.7	2.1	0.7
Carrot & Coriander, Tesco*	½ Can/210g	92	44	0.7	5.4	2.2	0.8
Carrot & Coriander, Vie, Knorr*	1 Pack/500ml	190	38	0.6	3.9	2.2	1.0
Carrot & Coriander, Waistline, Crosse & Blackwell*	1 Sachet/300g	111	37	0.7	6.8	0.8	1.0
Carrot & Ginger, Perfectly Balanced, Waitrose*	½ Pot/300g	66	22	0.4	3.1	0.9	1.0
Carrot & Lentil, Microwave, Heinz*	1 Can/303.2g	94	31	1.5	6.1	0.1	0.8
Carrot & Lentil, Weight Watchers*	1 Can/295g	91	31	1.4	6.0	0.1	0.7
Carrot & Orange	1oz/28g	6	20	0.4	3.7	0.5	1.0
Carrot & Orange, Baxters*	1 Can/415g	174	42	1.0	8.3	0.5	0.4
Carrot & Orange, Finest, Tesco*	½ Tub/300g	150	50	0.7	7.5	1.9	1.1
Carrot & Orange, Pouch, Heinz*	½ Pack/300g	165	55	0.6	8.3	2.2	1.0
Carrot & Parsnip, Marks & Spencer*	1oz/28g	9	32	0.5	4.9	1.2	0.9
Carrot With Creme Fraiche, Baxters*	1 Can/415g	170	41	0.5	5.9	1.7	0.7
Carrot, Eat Smart, Safeway*	½ Pot/225g	79	35	0.6	5.5	1.3	0.4
Carrot, Honey & Ginger, EAT*	1 Serving/474ml	268	57	0.7	4.7	3.9	1.0
Carrot, Onion & Chick Pea, Healthy Choice, Baxters*	1 Can/425g	174	41	1.8	7.7	0.3	1.0
Carrot, Orange & Coriander, COU, Marks & Spencer*	1 Pack/415g	145	35	0.6	6.9	0.6	1.2
Carrot, Parsnip & Nutmeg, Organic, Baxters*	1 Can/425g	145	34	0.7	6.6	0.5	1.1
Carrot, Potato & Coriander, Weight Watchers*	1 Can/295g	74	25	0.5	5.5	0.1	0.6
Cauliflower Cheese, Safeway*	1 Serving/300g	135	45	2.3	3.7	2.3	0.8
Cauliflower Cheese, Somerfield*	1 Pack/500g	345	69	3.0	3.0	5.0	0.0
Celeriac & Bacon, New Covent Garden Food Co*	1 Serving/300g	228	76	1.1	3.0	7.1	1.6
Cheese, Leek & Bacon, Somerfield*	1 Carton/300g	441	147	5.0	5.0	12.0	0.0
Chicken & Asparagus, Eat Smart, Safeway*	1 Pack/450g	248	55	3.3	3.2	2.7	0.7
Chicken & Broccoli Cup A Soup, Asda*	1 Serving/16g	55	341	7.0	58.0	9.0	6.0
Chicken & Broccoli, Soup a Cups, GFY, Asda*	1 Cup/226.1ml	52	23	0.5	4.0	0.6	0.4
Chicken & Broccoli, Soup-a-Slim, Asda*	1 Sachet/16g	55	341	7.0	58.0	9.0	6.0
Chicken & Ham, Big, Heinz*	½ Can/200g	92	46	2.3	6.9	1.0	0.7
Chicken & King Prawn Noodle, Tesco*	1 Pot/400g	180	45	4.7	5.5	0.4	0.4
Chicken & Leek, Big, Heinz*	½ Can/200g	118	59	2.3	7.8	2.0	0.5
Chicken & Leek, Cup A Soup, Batchelors*	1 Serving/213g	77	36	0.6	6.7	0.9	0.3
Chicken & Leek, Cup, Co-Op*	1 Cup/18g	64	355	3.0	55.0	14.0	8.0
Chicken & Leek, In A Mug, Slim Choice, Safeway*	1 Sachet/12g	53	439	7.2	55.9	20.7	10.0
Chicken & Leek, In a Cup, Symingtons*	1 Serving/225ml	110	49	0.5	6.0	2.5	1.2
Chicken & Leek, TTD, Sainsbury's*	½ Bottle/300ml	177	59	4.7	2.1	3.5	0.3
Chicken & Mushroom In A Cup, Sainsbury's*	1 Sachet/223ml	107	48	0.7	7.1	1.9	0.1
Chicken & Mushroom In A Cup, Tesco*	1 Sachet/15g	9	57	1.4	8.5	2.0	0.2
Chicken & Mushroom, Better For You, Morrisons*	1 Serving/14g	47	337	16.0	54.8	6.1	2.5
Chicken & Mushroom, Slim A Soup, Batchelors*	1 Sachet/203g	59	29	0.7	4.1	1.1	0.3
Chicken & Mushroom, Soup-a-Slim, Asda*	1 Sachet/14g	51	362	10.0	58.0	10.0	4.2

S

	Measure INFO/WEIGHT	per Measure KCAL	Nutrition Values per 100g / 100ml				
			KCAL	PROT	CARB	FAT	FIBRE
SOUP,							
Chicken & Pasta Big, Heinz*	½ Can/200g	68	34	1.8	5.9	0.4	0.8
Chicken & Red Pepper Noodle, Fresh, Tesco*	1 Serving/400ml	200	50	3.6	8.5	0.3	0.4
Chicken & Sweet Corn, Cup, Morrisons*	1 Serving/14g	48	341	14.0	57.5	6.1	2.5
Chicken & Sweetcorn With Croutons, Sainsbury's*	1oz/28g	17	60	1.4	8.2	2.4	0.4
Chicken & Sweetcorn, BGTY, Sainsbury's*	1 Serving/200g	42	21	1.2	3.5	0.2	0.1
Chicken & Sweetcorn, Baxters*	1 Can/425g	166	39	1.6	6.2	0.9	0.6
Chicken & Sweetcorn, Fresh, Asda*	1 Pack/500g	260	52	2.6	6.0	1.9	0.0
Chicken & Sweetcorn, Fresh, Morrisons*	1 Pot/500g	205	41	2.1	6.7	0.6	0.2
Chicken & Sweetcorn, Fresh, Sainsbury's*	½ Bottle/300ml	135	45	2.1	7.9	0.5	0.5
Chicken & Sweetcorn, GFY, Asda*	1 Can/400g	108	27	1.5	4.2	0.5	0.2
Chicken & Sweetcorn, Healthy Eating, Tesco*	1 Serving/200ml	64	32	1.5	5.3	0.5	0.2
Chicken & Sweetcorn, In A Cup, BGTY, Sainsbury's*	1 Sachet/200ml	50	25	0.7	3.8	0.8	0.6
Chicken & Sweetcorn, In A Mug, Tesco*	1 Sachet/28g	122	434	4.8	63.4	17.9	1.1
Chicken & Sweetcorn, New Improved, Sainsbury's*	½ Bottle/300g	138	46	3.1	8.1	0.3	0.7
Chicken & Sweetcorn, Slim A Soup, Batchelors*	1 Sachet/203g	59	29	0.6	4.5	0.9	0.1
Chicken & Sweetcorn, Slim Choice, Safeway*	1 Sachet/13g	47	363	12.2	48.8	13.2	5.1
Chicken & Sweetcorn, Soupreme*	1 Serving/250g	90	36	2.7	5.6	0.3	1.7
Chicken & Sweetcorn, Tesco*	1 Can/400ml	128	32	1.5	5.3	0.5	0.2
Chicken & Tarragon, Thick & Creamy, Batchelors*	1 Sachet/281g	118	42	0.8	5.7	2.3	0.3
Chicken & Vegetable Broth, Morrisons*	1 Serving/200g	50	25	1.2	4.5	0.2	0.5
Chicken & Vegetable, Big, Heinz*	1 Can/400g	188	47	2.4	7.3	1.0	0.9
Chicken & Vegetable, Cup A Soup, Batchelors*	1 Sachet/30g	131	437	4.8	62.7	18.6	1.1
Chicken & Vegetable, Cup, Tesco*	1 Sachet/29ml	122	422	5.6	61.3	17.1	0.5
Chicken & Vegetable, Eat Smart, Safeway*	1 Serving/300g	165	55	4.5	5.2	1.6	0.8
Chicken & Vegetable, Fresh, Somerfield*	½ Pot/300g	177	59	2.9	5.6	2.8	3.0
Chicken & Vegetable, Healthy Choice, Baxters*	1 Can/426g	153	36	1.7	6.1	0.5	1.2
Chicken & Vegetable, Loyd Grossman*	1 Pouch/420g	126	30	1.8	2.6	1.4	0.6
Chicken & Vegetable, Marks & Spencer*	1oz/28g	17	59	5.3	5.7	1.7	1.1
Chicken & Vegetable, Mighty, Asda*	1 Can/410g	176	43	2.5	6.8	1.3	0.7
Chicken & Vegetable, Perfectly Balanced, Waitrose*	1 Can/68g	23	34	1.8	5.4	0.6	1.0
Chicken & Vegetable, Simply, Kwik Save*	1 Serving/22g	83	379	4.6	56.4	15.0	7.8
Chicken & Vegetable, Thick, Heinz*	1 Can/400g	152	38	1.2	6.2	0.9	0.6
Chicken & White Wine, Campbell's*	1 Serving/295g	145	49	1.0	4.0	3.3	0.0
Chicken Broth, Baxters*	1 Can/425g	145	34	1.2	5.3	0.9	0.6
Chicken Broth, Fresh, Baxters*	1 Serving/300g	117	39	4.9	2.1	1.2	0.7
Chicken Broth, Traditional, Baxters*	½ Can/207g	64	31	1.5	5.4	0.4	0.6
Chicken Flavour, Calorie Counter, Co-Op*	1 Serving/10g	32	320	6.0	49.0	11.0	7.0
Chicken Fusion, Fresh, New Covent Garden Food Co*	½ Carton/300g	162	54	2.6	4.8	2.7	0.4
Chicken Mulligatawny, Asda*	1 Serving/300g	150	50	3.8	7.0	0.8	0.8
Chicken Mulligatawny, Perfectly Balanced, Waitrose*	1 Serving/300g	138	46	1.7	5.3	2.0	0.4
Chicken Mulligatawny, Tesco*	1 Pack/600g	570	95	3.6	5.4	6.6	0.4
Chicken Noodle & Vegetable, Slim A Soup, Batchelors*	1 Serving/203g	55	27	0.8	4.8	0.5	0.6
Chicken Noodle, Asda*	1 Can/400g	80	20	0.8	3.4	0.4	0.1
Chicken Noodle, Batchelors*	1 Pack/284g	71	25	1.6	4.2	0.2	0.3
Chicken Noodle, Cup A Soup, Batchelors*	1 Serving/217g	89	41	1.7	7.4	0.6	0.2
Chicken Noodle, Cup, Asda*	1 Sachet/13g	40	305	9.0	63.0	1.9	3.6
Chicken Noodle, Healthy Eating, Tesco*	1 Pack/500g	215	43	1.6	6.6	1.1	0.4
Chicken Noodle, Heinz*	1oz/28g	8	27	1.1	4.9	0.3	0.2
Chicken Noodle, In a Mug, Safeway*	1 Sachet/100g	325	325	8.4	69.5	1.5	0.0
Chicken Noodle, Morrisons*	1oz/28g	11	39	1.7	7.4	0.3	0.7
Chicken Noodle, Nissin*	1 Pack/85g	364	428	9.5	62.0	16.6	3.3
Chicken Noodle, Old Fashioned, EAT*	1 Can/400ml	240	60	6.0	5.5	1.6	0.6
Chicken Noodle, Safeway*	1 Can/425g	111	26	1.4	3.5	0.7	0.3

SOUP,

INFO/WEIGHT	Measure per Measure	KCAL	Nutrition Values per 100g / 100ml				
			KCAL	PROT	CARB	FAT	FIBRE
Chicken Noodle, Sainsbury's*	1 Sachet/600ml	102	17	0.8	3.0	0.2	0.1
Chicken Noodle, Symingtons*	½ Pack/15g	48	318	8.6	65.4	2.4	2.4
Chicken Noodle, Weight Watchers*	1 Can/295g	50	17	0.7	3.1	0.1	0.2
Chicken Pot Pie, EAT*	1 Serving/343g	298	87	5.4	7.8	3.9	1.3
Chicken, Campbell's*	1 Can/295g	142	48	1.1	3.5	3.6	0.0
Chicken, Coconut & Lemon Grass, Fresh, Waitrose*	½ Pot/300g	303	101	2.6	4.1	8.3	0.8
Chicken, Coconut & Sweet Potato, EAT*	1 Pack/343g	235	69	2.0	7.0	3.8	1.1
Chicken, Condensed, 99% Fat Free, Campbell's*	1 Can/295g	100	34	1.6	5.0	0.9	0.0
Chicken, Cream Of, Canned	1oz/28g	16	58	1.7	4.5	3.8	0.0
Chicken, Cup A Soup, Batchelors*	1 Serving/213g	77	36	0.7	3.5	2.1	0.6
Chicken, Cup A Soup, Original, Batchelors*	1 Pack/213g	98	46	0.7	5.8	2.2	0.3
Chicken, Cup, Calorie Counter, Co-Op*	1 Sachet/12.5g	42	320	6.0	49.0	11.0	7.0
Chicken, In A Cup, Symingtons*	1 Serving/22g	93	424	7.0	57.7	18.4	11.7
Chicken, In a Cup, Sainsbury's*	1 Serving/221ml	86	39	0.7	5.3	1.7	0.1
Chicken, Leek & White Wine, Finest,Tesco*	1 Pack/300g	216	72	2.8	5.7	4.2	0.3
Chicken, Marks & Spencer*	1 Pack/213g	196	92	1.6	5.5	7.2	0.2
Chicken, Mushroom & Potato, Big, Heinz*	½ Can/200g	122	61	2.9	7.3	2.2	0.4
Chicken, Mushroom & Rice, Chilled, Marks & Spencer*	½ Pot/300g	240	80	3.4	8.6	3.8	0.6
Chicken, Our Best, New Covent Garden Food Co*	1 Carton/600ml	804	134	4.7	12.2	7.4	0.9
Chicken, Sainsbury's*	1 Serving/300g	126	42	2.3	3.2	2.2	0.7
Chicken, Sweetcorn & Potato, Heinz*	1 Can/400g	204	51	1.2	5.5	2.8	0.3
Chicken, Thick & Creamy, Marks & Spencer*	1oz/28g	31	110	5.8	3.9	8.0	0.5
Chicken, Weight Watchers*	1 Can/295g	89	30	1.2	4.1	1.0	0.1
Chilli Bean, Marks & Spencer*	½ Carton/300g	150	50	2.5	4.7	2.5	2.7
Chilli Pumpkin, Sainsbury's*	1 Serving/300g	120	40	0.6	4.0	2.4	1.3
Chilli Tomato & Pasta, COU, Marks & Spencer*	1 Serving/300g	150	50	1.3	7.2	1.9	0.9
Chinese Chicken Noodle, Cup A Soup, Extra, Batchelors*	1 Sachet/281g	101	36	1.3	6.8	0.4	0.7
Chinese Chicken Noodle, Knorr*	1 Pack/45g	138	307	15.1	51.8	4.4	2.9
Chorizo & Tomato With Vegetables, Sainsbury's*	1 Pack/400g	228	57	2.6	4.9	3.0	0.3
Chunky Beef & Vegetable, Sainsbury's*	1 Can/400g	176	44	2.7	7.0	0.6	0.0
Chunky Chicken & Vegetable Meal, Tesco*	1 Can/410g	176	43	2.3	7.2	0.5	0.7
Chunky Chicken & Vegetable, Marks & Spencer*	1 Can/425g	276	65	5.2	6.6	1.8	0.6
Chunky Chicken & Vegetable, Sainsbury's*	1 Can/400g	188	47	3.3	6.9	0.7	0.0
Chunky Chicken Noodle, Campbell's*	½ Can/200g	86	43	2.8	6.5	0.6	0.0
Chunky Chicken, Leek & Potato, Heinz*	1 Can/400g	236	59	2.3	7.8	2.0	0.5
Chunky Minestrone Meal, Tesco*	½ Can/205g	78	38	1.3	6.8	0.6	0.9
Chunky Roasted Vegetable, Marks & Spencer*	1 Can/400g	140	35	1.3	5.8	0.6	1.1
Chunky Tomato, New Covent Garden Food Co*	½ Pack/300g	135	45	1.8	5.3	1.8	1.1
Chunky Tuscan Style Bean & Sausage, Marks & Spencer*	1 Can/415g	249	60	2.4	7.7	2.2	1.0
Chunky Vegetable & Chicken, Safeway*	1 Can/400g	156	39	2.5	6.2	0.5	0.6
Chunky Vegetable & Lentil, Good Intentions, Somerfield*	1 Pack/22.5g	77	333	7.1	61.8	6.7	8.0
Chunky Vegetable, Big, Heinz*	1 Serving/400g	208	52	1.5	8.7	1.3	1.2
Chunky Vegetable, Eat Smart, Safeway*	1 Can/415g	95	23	0.7	4.6	0.2	1.2
Chunky Vegetable, Fresh, Baxters*	1 Serving/300ml	117	39	1.6	7.8	0.2	1.1
Chunky Vegetable, Fresh, Sainsbury's*	½ Bottle/296ml	77	26	0.5	4.8	0.5	1.2
Chunky Vegetable, Fresh, Tesco*	1 Serving/300g	123	41	0.6	5.5	1.9	1.0
Chunky Vegetable, Organic, Tesco*	1 Serving/250g	135	54	2.1	7.8	1.7	1.8
Chunky Vegetable, Sainsbury's*	½ Carton/297.8g	137	46	1.3	7.6	1.1	1.6
Chunky Winter Vegetable, Marks & Spencer*	1 Can/415ml	166	40	1.5	7.5	0.3	0.4
Chunky With Pasta Minestrone, Co-Op*	1 Pack/400g	140	35	1.0	6.0	0.6	0.7
Classic Tomato, Pret A Manger*	1 Serving/336g	179	53	0.9	7.5	2.1	0.7
Cock-a-Leekie, Traditional, Baxters*	1 Can/425g	98	23	0.9	4.1	0.3	0.3
Country Garden, Baxters*	1 Can/425g	149	35	0.9	6.6	0.6	0.8

S

INFO/WEIGHT	Measure	per Measure KCAL	Nutrition Values per 100g / 100ml				
			KCAL	PROT	CARB	FAT	FIBRE
Country Mixture, Sainsbury's*	1 Serving/75g	83	110	6.6	20.1	0.4	3.9
Country Mushroom, Baxters*	1 Pot/600g	378	63	0.9	5.5	4.1	0.1
Country Mushroom, Selection, Campbell's*	1 Serving/250ml	80	32	0.6	3.4	1.8	0.5
Country Vegetable, Chilled, Marks & Spencer*	½ Pot/300g	105	35	0.5	3.2	2.1	1.0
Country Vegetable, Fresh, Asda*	1 Carton/500g	195	39	1.9	7.0	0.4	0.0
Country Vegetable, Fresh, Chilled, Marks & Spencer*	1 Pot/600g	210	35	0.5	3.2	2.1	1.0
Country Vegetable, Fresh, Morrisons*	½ Pot/250g	108	43	1.0	6.3	1.5	1.2
Country Vegetable, Fresh, Somerfield*	½ Pack/300g	123	41	1.1	4.6	2.0	1.2
Country Vegetable, Fresh, Waitrose*	1 Serving/300g	165	55	2.1	7.1	2.0	1.6
Country Vegetable, Heinz*	1oz/28g	14	51	2.3	9.3	0.5	1.1
Country Vegetable, Marks & Spencer*	1oz/28g	14	50	1.8	7.0	1.4	1.0
Country Vegetable, Slim Choice, Safeway*	1 Serving/16.5g	59	345	6.7	63.6	7.3	9.1
Country Vegetable, Thick, Asda*	1 Pack/410g	164	40	1.6	7.0	0.6	1.2
Country Vegetable, Vie Knorr*	1 Pack/500ml	160	32	0.9	5.5	0.7	1.2
Country Vegetable, Weight Watchers*	1 Can/295g	89	30	1.1	5.9	0.2	1.0
Courgette & Parmesan, Sainsbury's*	1 Pack/300ml	198	66	1.5	2.5	5.6	0.4
Courgette, Parmesan & Bacon, Somerfield*	1 Pack/500g	255	51	2.0	2.0	4.0	0.0
Cream Of Asparagus, Campbell's*	½ Can/150g	68	45	0.5	4.6	2.8	0.0
Cream Of Asparagus, Cup A Soup, Batchelors*	1 Sachet/223g	143	64	0.5	9.2	2.8	0.4
Cream Of Asparagus, Heinz*	1oz/28g	13	46	1.1	4.5	2.6	0.2
Cream Of Celery, Campbell's*	1 Serving/150g	71	47	0.6	3.2	3.4	0.0
Cream Of Chicken & Mushroom, Heinz*	1oz/28g	14	49	1.3	4.6	2.9	0.1
Cream Of Chicken & Mushroom, Sainsbury's*	1 Can/400g	232	58	1.1	5.1	3.7	0.1
Cream Of Chicken, Asda*	1 Can/410g	209	51	1.2	4.0	3.4	0.1
Cream Of Chicken, Batchelors*	1 Pack/289g	165	57	1.1	5.6	3.3	0.3
Cream Of Chicken, Cambell's*	1 Can/590g	295	50	3.7	1.0	3.5	0.0
Cream Of Chicken, Condensed, Made Up, Heinz*	1oz/28g	12	42	1.1	3.1	2.8	0.0
Cream Of Chicken, Fresh, Waitrose*	1 Serving/300g	180	60	2.6	3.7	3.9	0.2
Cream Of Chicken, Heinz*	1oz/28g	14	51	1.3	4.4	3.2	0.1
Cream Of Chicken, Sainsbury's*	½ Can/200g	130	65	1.5	6.2	3.8	0.1
Cream Of Corn, EAT*	1 Pack/343g	316	92	1.7	8.4	5.8	0.8
Cream Of Mushroom Condensed, Made Up, Heinz*	1oz/28g	12	42	0.9	3.5	2.7	0.1
Cream Of Mushroom In A Bottle, Homepride*	¼ Bottle/250ml	110	44	0.5	3.5	3.1	0.0
Cream Of Mushroom, Cup A Soup, Batchelors*	1 Serving/219g	125	57	0.6	7.5	2.8	0.4
Cream Of Mushroom, GFY, Asda*	1 Serving/250g	93	37	2.1	6.0	0.5	0.3
Cream Of Mushroom, Heinz*	1oz/28g	14	51	1.4	5.1	2.7	0.1
Cream Of Mushroom, Tesco*	1 Serving/200g	108	54	0.9	4.6	3.5	0.1
Cream Of Tomato, Asda*	½ Can/205g	150	73	0.8	9.0	3.7	0.5
Cream Of Tomato, Condensed, Made Up, Heinz*	1oz/28g	15	55	0.9	7.1	2.6	0.4
Cream Of Tomato, EAT*	1 Can/400ml	247	62	1.5	3.9	4.3	0.9
Cream Of Tomato, For One, Heinz*	1 Can/300g	192	64	0.9	7.1	3.6	0.4
Cream Of Tomato, Fresh, Waitrose*	½ Pot/300g	210	70	1.0	4.9	5.1	0.5
Cream Of Tomato, Heinz*	1oz/28g	18	64	0.9	7.1	3.6	0.4
Cream Of Tomato, Homepride*	¼ Bottle/250ml	138	55	0.9	7.7	2.6	0.0
Cream Of Tomato, Improves, Tesco*	½ Can/200g	142	71	0.9	8.7	3.6	0.5
Cream Of Tomato, Microwave, Heinz*	1 Pack/300g	204	68	0.9	7.5	3.8	0.4
Cream Of Tomato, Microwaveable Cup, Heinz*	1 Cup/275ml	169	61	0.8	6.9	3.4	0.4
Cream Of Tomato, Organic, Heinz*	1 Can/400g	220	55	0.9	7.2	2.5	0.4
Cream Of Tomato, SmartPrice, Asda*	1 Can/408g	290	71	0.7	9.0	3.6	0.0
Cream Of Vegetable, Cup A Soup, Batchelors*	1 Sachet/33g	134	406	5.8	59.8	16.0	6.2
Cream of Asparagus In Seconds, Knorr*	1 Pack/61g	320	524	6.5	42.2	36.6	1.1
Cream of Asparagus Soup in a Cup, Sainsbury's*	1 Serving/230ml	129	56	0.7	8.2	2.3	0.1
Cream of Asparagus, Baxters*	1 Can/415g	278	67	1.1	6.0	4.3	0.2

SOUP,	Measure INFO/WEIGHT	per Measure KCAL	Nutrition Values per 100g / 100ml				
			KCAL	PROT	CARB	FAT	FIBRE
Cream of Celery, Asda*	1 Can/410g	189	46	0.6	4.8	2.7	0.2
Cream of Chicken & Mushroom, Campbell's*	1 Can/250g	108	43	0.5	3.5	3.1	0.0
Cream of Chicken, Baxters*	½ Can/209g	144	69	1.8	6.1	4.2	0.1
Cream of Chicken, Co-Op*	½ Can/200g	120	60	0.8	5.0	4.0	0.1
Cream of Chicken, Fresh, Somerfield*	1 Carton/450g	234	52	2.0	4.0	3.0	0.0
Cream of Chicken, Fresh, Tesco*	1 Serving/300g	294	98	3.3	6.3	6.6	0.2
Cream of Chicken, Homepride*	¼ Bottle/250ml	113	45	1.3	4.0	2.9	0.0
Cream of Chicken, In Seconds, Knorr*	1 Pack/58g	300	518	11.2	36.0	36.6	0.3
Cream of Chicken, Simmer, Sainsbury's*	1 Pack/500ml	182	36	0.8	4.9	1.5	0.8
Cream of Chicken, Somerfield*	1 Serving/215g	129	60	1.5	4.4	4.1	0.1
Cream of Leek In Seconds, Knorr*	1 Pack/64g	326	509	5.9	45.2	33.8	1.4
Cream of Leek, Traditional, Baxters*	1 Can/425g	196	46	0.7	5.2	2.5	0.4
Cream of Mushroom & Garlic, The Best, Safeway*	1oz/28g	19	68	1.6	1.5	6.2	0.7
Cream of Mushroom With Croutons, Special Cup, Aldi*	1oz/28g	129	459	4.9	52.6	25.5	0.6
Cream of Mushroom, Asda*	1 Can/410g	258	63	1.0	6.0	3.9	0.3
Cream of Mushroom, Co-Op*	1 Pack/400g	240	60	1.0	5.0	4.0	0.0
Cream of Mushroom, Condensed, Campbell's*	1 Can/295ml	204	69	1.7	5.3	4.5	0.0
Cream of Mushroom, Fresh, Tesco*	½ Pot/250g	108	43	1.0	4.0	2.6	0.2
Cream of Mushroom, Fresh, Waitrose*	½ Pot/300g	210	70	1.3	3.7	5.5	0.5
Cream of Mushroom, Knorr*	1 Serving/25g	125	500	5.2	47.8	31.8	1.0
Cream of Mushroom, Sainsbury's*	1 Can/400g	220	55	0.6	1.4	5.2	0.1
Cream of Potato & Leek, Sainsbury's*	½ Can/200g	116	58	0.9	6.8	3.0	0.4
Cream of Tomato & Basil, Somerfield*	1 Pack/450g	279	62	1.0	5.0	4.0	0.0
Cream of Tomato, Campbell's*	1 Can/295g	195	66	0.8	8.5	3.2	0.0
Cream of Tomato, Fresh, Sainsbury's*	½ Bottle/300ml	126	42	0.9	7.0	1.2	0.5
Cream of Tomato, Fresh, Tesco*	½ Pot/250g	153	61	1.6	8.3	2.4	0.4
Cream of Tomato, Knorr*	1 Pack/90g	392	435	4.3	51.3	23.6	3.3
Cream of Tomato, Lidl*	1oz/28g	19	69	1.2	9.4	3.0	0.6
Cream of Tomato, Morrisons*	1 Serving/205g	141	69	1.2	9.4	3.0	0.6
Cream of Tomato, Tesco*	1 Pack/600g	474	79	2.2	5.7	5.3	0.5
Cream of Tomato, Traditional, Baxters*	1 Can/415g	315	76	1.4	11.6	2.7	0.6
Creamed Asparagus, Asda*	1 Sachet/30g	131	451	6.0	55.0	23.0	1.1
Creamed Asparagus, Cup a Soup, Symingtons*	1 Serving/28g	108	384	11.6	34.6	22.1	15.0
Creamed Tomato, In A Cup, Sainsbury's*	1 Sachet/233ml	112	48	0.7	9.3	0.9	0.1
Creamed Vegetable, In A Mug, Safeway*	1 Sachet/29g	117	405	5.6	57.9	16.8	3.2
Creamy Carrot, In a Mug, Thick, Safeway*	1 Sachet/28g	105	375	2.9	60.7	13.6	5.4
Creamy Chicken & Vegetables, For One, Wattie's*	1 Can/300g	115	38	0.9	3.8	2.1	0.0
Creamy Leek With Croutons In A Cup, Sainsbury's*	1 Serving/228g	130	57	1.1	7.2	2.6	0.1
Creamy Mushroom, Asda*	1 Pot/500g	228	46	1.1	4.0	2.8	1.3
Creamy Mushroom, Safeway*	1 Pack/300ml	137	46	1.1	3.8	2.9	0.5
Creamy Mushroom, Somerfield*	1 Pack/450g	225	50	1.0	4.0	3.0	0.0
Creamy Potato & Leek, Cup A Soup, Batchelors*	1 Sachet/280ml	132	47	0.8	7.4	1.5	1.1
Creamy Potato, Bacon & Onion, Cup A Soup, Batchelors*	1 Sachet/280ml	106	38	0.9	7.3	1.0	0.5
Creamy Tomato, Fresh, Asda*	1 Pot/500g	202	40	0.7	4.0	2.4	0.5
Creamy Tomato, Seeds Of Change*	1 Pack/500g	320	64	1.1	10.9	1.8	0.5
Crofter's Thick Vegetable, Knorr*	1 Pack/66g	240	364	10.8	52.9	12.2	3.3
Cucumber Pea & Mint, New Covent Garden Food Co*	1 Serving/200ml	90	45	1.8	4.7	2.1	0.6
Cullen Skink, Baxters*	1 Can/415g	357	86	6.4	7.7	3.3	0.4
Dutch Curry & Rice Cup A Soup, Continental*	1 Serving/250ml	125	50	0.7	8.8	1.3	0.0
English Asparagus, New Covent Garden Food Co*	½ Pack/300g	114	38	0.7	5.5	1.5	0.1
English Broccoli & Stilton, Knorr*	1 Pack/65g	331	509	11.7	30.3	37.9	1.6
Extra Chicken & Mushroom, Slim A Soup, Batchelors*	1 Serving/257.1g	90	35	1.4	5.9	0.6	0.3
Farmhouse Chicken Leek, Knorr*	1 Pack/54g	248	459	10.3	39.3	29.0	1.5

S

SOUP,

	Measure INFO/WEIGHT	per Measure KCAL		KCAL	PROT	CARB	FAT	FIBRE
Farmhouse Vegetable, BGTY, Sainsbury's*	1 Serving/200ml	52		26	0.5	4.4	0.8	0.9
Farmhouse Vegetable, Soup-a-Cup, GFY, Asda*	1 Sachet/218.5ml	59		27	0.6	4.9	0.5	0.4
Farmhouse Vegetable, Thick, Co-Op*	1 Can/400g	140		35	1.0	7.0	0.4	0.3
Fire Flamed Tomato & Red Onion, Sainsbury's*	½ Bottle/300ml	129		43	0.8	5.0	2.2	1.0
Fire Roasted Tomato & Red Pepper, Asda*	½ Tub/265.1g	114		43	0.7	4.1	2.6	1.0
Fish, Frozen, Findus*	1 Serving/85g	128		150	11.0	13.0	5.5	0.0
Flame Roasted Red Pepper & Tomato, Baxters*	½ Can/207.1g	116		56	0.9	6.8	2.8	0.6
Florentine Pea, The Best, Safeway*	½ Pot/300g	165		55	2.5	4.9	2.5	1.4
Florida Spring Vegetable, Knorr*	1 Pack/36g	104		290	7.8	52.2	5.6	5.2
Forest Mushroom, Heinz*	1oz/28g	12		43	1.0	4.5	2.3	0.1
Forest Mushroom, Microwaveable Cup, Heinz*	1 Cup/275g	146		53	1.0	4.7	3.3	0.1
Four Mushroom, Loyd Grossman*	1 Pack/420g	202		48	0.8	2.5	3.9	0.2
French Onion	1oz/28g	11		40	0.2	5.7	2.1	1.0
French Onion & Cider, Waitrose*	1 Can/425g	94		22	0.5	4.8	0.1	0.4
French Onion & Croutons, Tesco*	1 Serving/30g	106		353	7.3	63.7	7.7	2.0
French Onion & Gruyere Cheese, Finest, Tesco*	½ Pot/300g	210		70	1.4	4.7	5.1	0.5
French Onion, Baxters*	1 Can/425g	94		22	0.6	4.3	0.2	0.4
French Onion, Chilled, Marks & Spencer*	½ Pot/300g	150		50	2.0	7.2	1.5	1.0
French Onion, Eat*	1 Serving/360ml	237		66	1.7	6.5	3.5	0.5
French Onion, Fresh, Morrisons*	1 Serving/500g	155		31	0.8	5.0	0.9	0.5
French Onion, GFY, Asda*	½ Pot/253g	91		36	1.9	6.0	0.5	0.4
French Onion, Heinz*	1 Pack/400g	100		25	0.5	5.7	0.1	0.4
French Onion, Knorr*	1 Pack/40g	118		296	6.0	62.5	2.5	6.6
French Onion, Made Up, Sainsbury's*	1/3 Serving/205g	39		19	0.4	4.0	0.1	0.1
French Onion, Safeway*	½ Pot/250g	85		34	0.8	3.9	1.7	0.5
French Onion, Sainsbury's*	1 Serving/300ml	153		51	0.5	5.7	3.0	0.5
French Onion, Tinned, Marks & Spencer*	½ Can/200g	40		20	0.4	3.9	0.2	0.3
Garden Vegetable, Heinz*	1 Can/400g	160		40	0.9	7.2	0.8	0.9
Garden Vegetable, SlimFast*	1 Serving/60g	224		373	23.8	45.0	10.3	7.0
Gazpacho, Average	1oz/28g	13		45	0.8	2.6	3.6	0.6
Gazpacho, Fresh, New Covent Garden Food Co*	1 Pack/284g	68		24	0.8	2.6	1.2	0.6
Gazpacho, Marks & Spencer*	½ Pack/390g	98		25	1.1	4.4	0.1	1.0
Giant Minestrone, Big, Heinz*	1oz/28g	12		44	1.7	8.1	0.5	1.0
Giant Minestrone, Big, New Recipe, Heinz*	½ Can/200g	98		49	1.5	9.3	0.7	1.1
Goats Cheese & Rocket, Sainsbury's*	1 Serving/300g	180		60	2.0	3.2	4.4	0.3
Golden Vegetable With Croutons Cup Soup, Co-Op*	1 Sachet/25g	120		480	4.0	56.0	26.0	2.0
Golden Vegetable With Croutons, Instant, Morrisons*	1 Sachet/27g	118		438	5.3	60.7	19.3	0.0
Golden Vegetable, Asda*	1 Pack/300g	150		50	1.9	6.0	2.0	0.0
Golden Vegetable, Calorie Counter, Cup, Co-Op*	1 Sachet/12g	40		335	7.0	54.0	10.0	5.0
Golden Vegetable, Cup A Soup, Batchelors*	1 Serving/212g	70		33	0.4	5.7	0.9	0.4
Golden Vegetable, Cup, Calorie Counter, Co-Op*	1 Sachet/10.9g	35		320	7.0	50.0	10.0	9.0
Golden Vegetable, Instant, Tesco*	1 Sachet/17g	60		351	8.2	62.0	7.8	3.7
Golden Vegetable, Knorr*	1 Pack/76g	299		394	10.4	45.4	19.0	3.3
Golden Vegetable, Slim A Soup, Batchelors*	1 Sachet/207g	58		28	0.5	4.7	0.8	0.7
Golden Vegetable, Soup-A-Slim, Asda*	1 Sachet/15g	50		336	6.0	60.0	8.0	1.9
Green Pea & Mint, Fresh, Waitrose*	1oz/28g	27		97	1.8	5.5	7.7	1.2
Green Thai Chicken, Waitrose*	1 Pack/400g	324		81	3.8	5.7	4.8	0.3
Green Vegetables & Lentil, Lima*	1 Serving/300g	96		32	1.6	3.7	1.2	0.5
Haddock, Chowder, Smoked, Asda*	1 Serving/300g	135		45	2.4	6.0	1.3	0.7
Haggis Broth, Baxters*	1 Can/425g	221		52	1.8	6.8	1.9	0.7
Harvest Carrot & Lima Bean, Heinz*	1oz/28g	11		40	0.8	6.9	1.0	1.3
Harvest Vegetable, In A Cup With Croutons, Sainsbury's*	1 Sachet/226.3ml	86		38	1.0	5.9	1.2	0.9
Hearty Vegetable, 99% Fat Free, Campbells*	1 Can/295g	91		31	0.8	6.1	0.4	0.0

SOUP,

	Measure INFO/WEIGHT	per Measure KCAL	KCAL	PROT	CARB	FAT	FIBRE
Highlanders Broth, Baxters*	1 Can/425g	208	49	1.9	7.0	1.5	0.6
Hot & Sour Mushroom, New Covent Garden Food Co.*	1 Carton/600g	72	12	0.7	1.9	0.2	0.4
Italian Bean & Pasta, Baxters*	1 Can/425g	179	42	2.0	7.9	0.3	1.1
Italian Chicken & Pasta, Big, Heinz*	½ Can/200g	108	54	2.5	9.4	0.7	0.7
Italian Chicken Broth, Healthy Choice, Baxters*	½ Can/210g	84	40	1.5	6.6	0.8	0.8
Italian Chunky, New Covent Garden Food Co*	½ Carton/300g	135	45	1.8	5.3	1.8	1.1
Italian Minestrone, Knorr*	1 Pack/62g	193	311	11.5	57.1	4.1	7.8
Italian Minestrone, Marks & Spencer*	1 Can/425g	191	45	2.2	9.0	0.5	0.8
Italian Minestrone, Sainsbury's*	1 Can/415g	212	51	2.0	6.6	1.8	1.1
Italian Plum Tomato & Basil, Perfectly Balanced, Waitrose*	½ Pot/300g	69	23	0.9	3.8	0.5	0.9
Italian Style Tomato & Basil, Co-Op*	1 Pack/500g	200	40	1.0	4.0	2.0	0.6
Italian Style Tomato & Chicken, BGTY, Sainsbury's*	1 Can/400g	148	37	3.1	5.5	0.3	0.4
Italian Style Tomato, Safeway*	½ Pot/248g	134	54	1.3	5.7	2.9	0.9
Italian Tomato With Basil, Baxters*	1 Can/425g	217	51	2.4	8.4	0.9	0.9
Jamaican Jerk Chicken & Pumpkin, Sainsbury's*	1 Pack/600g	282	47	2.7	5.1	1.7	0.2
Lamb & Cous Cous, Marks & Spencer*	½ Can/208g	100	48	2.1	6.2	1.8	0.9
Lamb & Vegetable, Big, Heinz*	1/2 Can/200g	112	56	2.4	9.2	1.0	1.2
Lamb & Vegetable, Mega, Morrisons*	1 Pack/410g	172	42	1.9	6.3	1.0	0.8
Leek & Chicken, Knorr*	1 Serving/300ml	82	27	0.6	2.4	1.7	0.1
Leek & Potato, Chilled, Marks & Spencer*	1 Serving/300g	240	80	0.9	5.2	6.2	0.6
Leek & Potato, Cup A Soup, Batchelors*	1 Sachet/28g	121	432	5.2	63.2	17.6	1.8
Leek & Potato, EAT*	1 Serving/355ml	156	44	0.8	4.4	2.6	0.6
Leek & Potato, Eat Smart, Safeway*	½ Pot/225g	113	50	1.1	6.0	2.4	0.6
Leek & Potato, Fresh, Morrisons*	½ Pot/250g	185	74	2.0	6.4	4.5	0.7
Leek & Potato, Fresh, Sainsbury's*	1 Bowl/300ml	189	63	1.1	3.9	4.8	0.5
Leek & Potato, Fresh, Somerfield*	½ Pot/300g	186	62	1.2	4.7	4.3	1.6
Leek & Potato, Fresh, Tesco*	½ pack/300g	201	67	1.4	6.3	4.0	0.8
Leek & Potato, Fresh, Waitrose*	½ Pot/300g	150	50	1.0	5.9	2.5	1.0
Leek & Potato, GFY, Asda*	1 Sachet/220g	55	25	0.3	5.0	0.4	0.3
Leek & Potato, In A Cup, BGTY, Sainsbury's*	1 Sachet/196ml	55	28	0.3	4.9	0.8	0.8
Leek & Potato, In A Cup, Tesco*	1 Sachet/15g	51	343	5.3	66.4	6.2	3.5
Leek & Potato, New Covent Garden Food Co*	½ Carton/284g	142	50	1.3	5.0	2.8	0.6
Leek & Potato, Organic, Sainsbury's*	½ Can/200g	84	42	1.6	5.7	1.4	0.9
Leek & Potato, Reduced Calorie Quick, Waitrose*	1 Sachet/190ml	51	27	0.4	5.3	0.5	0.4
Leek & Potato, Slim A Soup, Batchelors*	1 Serving/204g	57	28	0.4	5.0	0.7	0.2
Leek & Potato, Smooth, Vie, Knorr*	1 Pack/500ml	155	31	0.9	4.8	0.9	1.0
Leek & Potato, Tastebreaks, Knorr*	1 Pot/225g	162	72	1.1	9.1	3.4	0.5
Leek & Potato, Weight Watchers*	1 Sachet/214.8ml	58	27	0.5	5.1	0.5	0.1
Lentil	1 Serving/220g	218	99	4.4	12.7	3.8	1.1
Lentil & Bacon, Baxters*	1 Can/425g	255	60	2.7	7.9	1.9	0.8
Lentil & Bacon, Gluten Free, Baxters*	1 Can/207g	114	55	2.9	7.8	1.3	0.8
Lentil & Bacon, Marks & Spencer*	1oz/28g	18	63	4.1	8.6	1.6	0.7
Lentil & Bacon, Safeway*	1 Can/400g	160	40	2.7	6.3	0.4	2.9
Lentil & Bacon, Sainsbury's*	½ Can/200g	90	45	3.3	7.3	0.3	1.5
Lentil & Bacon, Tesco*	1 Serving/200g	96	48	3.2	7.2	0.7	0.5
Lentil & Chick Pea, Organic, Tesco*	1 Serving/300ml	117	39	1.9	6.1	0.8	0.5
Lentil & Smoked Bacon, Marks & Spencer*	1 Pack/415g	228	55	2.8	8.5	0.9	1.2
Lentil & Tomato, New Covent Garden Food Co*	½ Pack/284g	162	57	3.6	8.1	1.1	0.7
Lentil & Vegetable With Bacon, Organic, Baxters*	½ Can/211.4g	93	44	1.9	7.6	0.7	1.0
Lentil & Vegetable, Baxters*	1 Can/423g	165	39	2.0	7.1	0.3	0.9
Lentil & Winter, New Covent Garden Food Co*	1 Serving/250ml	133	53	3.1	7.7	1.1	0.9
Lentil, Asda*	½ Can/202g	89	44	2.6	8.0	0.2	0.7
Lentil, Bacon & Mixed Bean, Low Fat, Aldi*	1 Meal/400g	260	65	4.7	9.5	0.9	1.6

S

	Measure INFO/WEIGHT	per Measure KCAL	Nutrition Values per 100g / 100ml				
			KCAL	PROT	CARB	FAT	FIBRE
SOUP,							
Lentil, Campbell's*	1 Can/295g	139	47	2.6	7.7	0.6	0.0
Lentil, Canned	1 Serving/220g	86	39	3.1	6.5	0.2	1.2
Lentil, Carrot & Cumin, BGTY, Sainsbury's*	1 Pack/400g	204	51	2.3	8.4	0.9	0.1
Lentil, Farmfoods*	1 Can/225g	304	135	8.4	16.9	3.7	3.2
Lentil, Heinz*	1 Can/300g	117	39	2.3	7.1	0.2	1.0
Lobster Bisque, Baxters*	1 Can/415g	187	45	3.0	3.6	2.1	0.2
Londoner's Pea Souper, New Covent Garden Food Co*	½ Carton/300g	153	51	4.3	4.1	2.0	1.1
Luxury Game, Baxters*	1 Can/415g	187	45	3.7	5.9	0.7	0.5
Malaysian Chicken & Sweetcorn, Knorr*	1 Pack/57g	211	370	10.6	56.3	11.4	1.8
Manhattan Clam Chowder, EAT*	1 Can/400ml	262	66	5.2	5.5	2.6	1.0
Manhattan Prawn Chowder, Sainsbury's*	1 Pack/300ml	177	59	1.6	7.9	2.3	0.1
Mediteranean Vegetable, Homepride*	1 Serving/250ml	83	33	0.9	4.3	1.3	0.0
Mediterranean Fish, Waitrose*	½ Pot/300g	108	36	3.4	3.5	0.9	0.7
Mediterranean Minestrone, Campbell's*	½ Carton/250ml	95	38	0.9	6.1	1.1	0.6
Mediterranean Style Tomato, Healthy Eating, Tesco*	1 Serving/22g	78	353	9.7	64.3	6.3	3.0
Mediterranean Tomato & Vegetable, Weight Watchers*	1 Can/295g	47	16	0.4	3.0	0.3	0.4
Mediterranean Tomato, Baxters*	1 Can/425g	140	33	1.0	6.8	0.2	0.7
Mediterranean Tomato, COU, Marks & Spencer*	1 Pack/415g	104	25	0.7	4.8	0.5	0.6
Mediterranean Tomato, Campbell's*	1 Can/295g	83	28	0.6	6.4	0.0	0.0
Mediterranean Tomato, Fresh, Baxters*	1 Can/300g	171	57	2.2	8.1	1.8	1.4
Mediterranean Tomato, Fresh, Organic, Sainsbury's*	1 Serving/250ml	78	31	1.3	3.3	1.4	1.0
Mediterranean Tomato, In A Cup, BGTY, Sainsbury's*	1 Serving/200ml	60	30	0.7	5.7	0.4	0.7
Mediterranean Tomato, In A Cup, Sainsbury's*	1 Serving/214ml	60	28	0.7	5.3	0.4	0.2
Mediterranean Tomato, Instant, Weight Watchers*	1 Serving/200ml	50	25	0.7	5.2	0.1	0.1
Mediterranean Tomato, Reduced Calorie, Waitrose*	1 Serving/200ml	52	26	0.7	4.2	0.7	0.3
Mediterranean Tomato, Slim A Soup, Batchelors*	1 Serving/207g	54	26	0.5	4.7	0.6	0.4
Mediterranean Tomato, SlimFast*	1 Sachet/62g	213	343	22.6	39.8	9.0	10.7
Mediterranean Vegetable, GFY, Asda*	½ Pot/250g	80	32	0.5	3.6	1.7	1.6
Mediterranean Vegetable, Perfectly Balanced, Waitrose*	½ Pot/300g	57	19	0.8	2.8	0.8	0.8
Mediterranean Vegetable, Tesco*	½ Can/200g	76	38	0.6	6.8	0.9	0.5
Mediterraniean Vegetable, Aldi*	1 Serving/250g	78	31	5.2	2.0	0.2	0.9
Melon & Carrot, New Covent Garden Food Co*	1 Serving/300g	60	20	0.6	3.6	0.4	0.6
Mexican Beef Chilli, Mighty, Asda*	1 Can/400g	192	48	3.3	7.0	0.7	0.9
Mexican Black Bean, Extra Special, Asda*	½ Pot/262.5g	195	74	2.3	7.0	4.1	1.7
Minestrone	1oz/28g	18	63	1.8	7.6	3.0	0.9
Minestrone With Croutons, Soup in a Cup, Sainsbury's*	1 Sachet/225ml	72	32	0.9	6.3	0.4	0.5
Minestrone With Ribbon Noodles, Extra, Aldi*	1 Serving/34g	107	315	11.0	62.8	2.2	2.0
Minestrone With Wholemeal Pasta, Baxters*	1 Can/415g	133	32	0.9	6.6	0.2	0.8
Minestrone, Asda*	½ Can/200g	54	27	0.9	4.4	0.6	0.6
Minestrone, Baxters*	1 Can/425g	145	34	1.3	5.9	0.6	0.9
Minestrone, Calorie Counter, Low Calorie Cup, Co-Op*	1 Sachet/13g	40	310	7.0	66.0	2.0	3.0
Minestrone, Canned	1oz/28g	9	32	1.4	5.1	0.8	0.6
Minestrone, Chilled, Marks & Spencer*	½ Pot/300g	66	22	1.4	2.5	0.7	1.2
Minestrone, Cup A Soup, BGTY, Sainsbury's*	1 Serving/200ml	54	27	0.8	6.0	0.1	0.6
Minestrone, Cup A Soup, Batchelors*	1 Serving/217g	100	46	0.9	8.3	1.1	0.5
Minestrone, Delicious, Tesco*	1 Serving/300g	129	43	1.1	7.2	1.1	0.6
Minestrone, For One, Heinz*	1 Can/300g	96	32	1.4	5.2	0.7	0.7
Minestrone, Fresh, Baxters*	1 Box/568ml	233	41	1.8	6.2	1.0	0.6
Minestrone, Fresh, Morrisons*	1 Pot/506ml	182	36	1.9	6.4	0.4	0.2
Minestrone, Fresh, Safeway*	½ Pot/250g	83	33	1.0	6.2	0.5	0.8
Minestrone, Fresh, Sainsbury's*	½ Bottle/300ml	93	31	1.2	4.4	0.9	0.9
Minestrone, Fresh, Tesco*	1 Serving/300g	126	42	1.4	6.9	1.0	0.6
Minestrone, Fresh, Waitrose*	1 Pack/600g	240	40	1.1	5.8	1.4	0.8

S

INFO/WEIGHT	Measure	per Measure KCAL	Nutrition Values per 100g / 100ml KCAL	PROT	CARB	FAT	FIBRE
Minestrone, Healthy Choice, Baxters*	½ Can/207.5g	67	32	0.9	6.7	0.2	1.2
Minestrone, Healthy Eating, Tesco*	1 Pack/500g	140	28	1.0	4.4	0.7	0.6
Minestrone, Heinz*	1 Can/300g	96	32	1.4	5.2	0.7	0.7
Minestrone, In a Cup, BGTY, Sainsbury's*	1 Serving/200ml	54	27	0.8	6.0	0.1	0.6
Minestrone, In a Mug, Healthy Eating, Tesco*	1 Sachet/21g	72	342	3.6	67.7	6.3	3.2
Minestrone, Instant With Croutons, Value, Tesco*	1 Sachet/21g	68	325	6.4	60.2	6.5	1.7
Minestrone, Instant, Under 60 Calories, Tesco*	1 Sachet/19g	58	307	7.3	63.6	2.6	2.3
Minestrone, Marks & Spencer*	½ Pot/300g	120	40	1.3	5.7	1.1	1.2
Minestrone, Mighty, Asda*	1 Serving/38.2g	130	343	9.0	74.0	1.2	2.4
Minestrone, New Covent Garden Food Co*	1 Serving/250ml	83	33	1.7	5.8	0.4	0.7
Minestrone, Organic, Marks & Spencer*	1 Pack/208g	83	40	1.4	8.9	0.5	1.1
Minestrone, Organic, Seeds Of Change*	1 Sachet/500g	325	65	1.3	7.5	3.2	0.9
Minestrone, Packet, Knorr*	1 Pack/61g	178	292	9.2	53.9	4.4	6.5
Minestrone, Pret A Manger*	1 Serving/455g	140	31	1.3	4.2	1.0	1.1
Minestrone, Safeway*	1 Pack/425g	132	31	1.1	6.4	0.1	0.5
Minestrone, Simmer, Asda*	1 Pack/50g	131	262	6.0	57.0	1.1	15.0
Minestrone, Slim A Soup, Batchelors*	1 Serving/203g	53	26	0.6	4.5	0.6	0.3
Minestrone, Soup a Slim, Asda*	1 Serving/17g	53	311	6.0	69.0	1.2	4.5
Minestrone, Tesco*	1 Pack/600g	222	37	0.9	4.0	2.0	0.6
Minestrone, Weight Watchers*	1 Can/295g	59	20	0.8	3.3	0.4	0.5
Minestrone, With Croutons, Cup A Soup, Batchelors*	1 Serving	93	37	0.7	7.3	0.5	0.3
Minestrone, With Pasta, Cup A Soup, Extra, Batchelors*	1 Pack/286g	123	43	1.4	8.5	0.4	0.8
Minestrone, With Pesto, EAT*	1 Pack/400ml	276	69	2.8	9.2	2.4	2.2
Minestrone, in a Cup, Sainsbury's*	1 Serving/227ml	84	37	1.4	6.3	0.7	0.2
Minted Lamb Hot Pot, Big, Heinz*	1oz/28g	14	51	2.2	8.5	1.0	0.9
Mixed Bean & Pepper, Organic, Marks & Spencer*	1 Pack/208g	94	45	2.3	7.7	0.3	1.8
Mixed Vegetable, Gallina Blanca*	1 Pack/20g	76	378	4.0	68.0	10.0	0.0
Moroccan Chick Pea, Marks & Spencer*	1oz/28g	20	70	3.6	8.8	2.1	2.0
Moroccan Chicken, New Covent Garden Food Co*	1 Serving/300g	108	36	2.1	2.7	1.9	0.4
Moroccan Lentil, Waitrose*	½ Pot/300g	153	51	3.5	8.2	0.5	3.4
Mulligatawny	1 Serving/220g	213	97	1.4	8.2	6.8	0.9
Mulligatawny Beef Curry, Heinz*	1oz/28g	17	60	1.8	7.2	2.7	0.5
Mulligatawny, Asda*	1 Can/400g	172	43	2.2	6.0	1.1	0.3
Mulligatawny, In A Cup, Symingtons*	1 Serving/232ml	95	41	0.7	8.3	0.6	0.5
Mulligatawny, Tesco*	1 Can/400g	144	36	1.2	6.8	0.5	0.3
Mushroom & Chestnut, Finest, Tesco*	1 Serving/250g	130	52	1.1	4.7	3.3	0.7
Mushroom & Chicken, Co-Op*	1 Pack/400g	220	55	0.9	5.0	4.0	0.0
Mushroom & Garlic, Slim Choice, Safeway*	1oz/28g	108	384	8.3	61.4	11.7	6.2
Mushroom & Garlic, Slimming Cup A Soup, Tesco*	1 Serving/16g	58	360	5.8	61.1	10.3	3.2
Mushroom & Garlic, Tesco*	1 Sachet/16g	58	360	5.8	61.1	10.3	3.2
Mushroom & Madeira Flavour, Soup In A Mug, Safeway*	1 Sachet/28g	114	406	3.2	67.3	13.8	1.0
Mushroom & Mascarpone, TTD, Sainsbury's*	½ Bottle/300ml	108	36	0.6	2.8	2.5	0.4
Mushroom Creme Fraiche, Waistline, Crosse & Blackwell*	1 Carton/300g	69	23	1.2	2.8	0.8	0.3
Mushroom Noodle, Mighty, Asda*	1 Serving/42g	171	407	8.0	69.0	11.0	1.9
Mushroom Potage, Baxters*	1 Can/415g	320	77	1.5	6.1	5.2	0.3
Mushroom, 98% Fat Free, Baxters*	1 Can/425g	170	40	0.9	5.6	1.6	0.3
Mushroom, 99% Fat Free, Campbell's*	1oz/28g	7	24	0.6	3.5	0.9	0.0
Mushroom, Budgens*	1 Can/400g	284	71	1.2	6.6	4.5	0.1
Mushroom, Chilled, Marks & Spencer*	1 Pack/300g	135	45	1.9	3.3	2.6	0.5
Mushroom, Condensed, Campbell's*	1 Can/300g	207	69	1.7	5.3	4.5	0.0
Mushroom, Cream of, Canned	1 Serving/220g	101	46	1.1	3.9	3.0	0.1
Mushroom, Delicious, Tesco*	1 Serving/300g	111	37	1.2	3.1	2.2	0.4
Mushroom, For One, Heinz*	1 Tin/290g	148	51	1.4	5.1	2.7	0.1

S

	Measure INFO/WEIGHT	per Measure KCAL	Nutrition Values per 100g / 100ml				
			KCAL	PROT	CARB	FAT	FIBRE
SOUP,							
Mushroom, Fresh, Sainsbury's*	1 Serving/300g	204	68	1.6	4.7	4.8	0.8
Mushroom, Marks & Spencer*	1oz/28g	15	52	0.6	4.4	3.5	0.3
Mushroom, Morrisons*	1 Serving/500g	250	50	1.3	3.2	3.6	0.3
Mushroom, Quick, Knorr*	1 Serving/100g	85	85	2.0	8.5	4.5	0.0
Mushroom, Symingtons*	1 Serving/23g	80	348	17.8	48.4	9.2	6.7
Mushroom, Weight Watchers*	1 Can/295g	86	29	1.2	5.6	0.2	0.1
New England Clam Chowder, Select, Campbell's*	1 Cup/240ml	221	92	2.5	6.0	6.0	0.8
Oxtail, Canned	1 Serving/220g	97	44	2.4	5.1	1.7	0.1
Oxtail, Condensed, Classics, Diluted, Campbell's*	1 Can/590g	236	40	1.4	5.3	1.5	0.0
Oxtail, Cup A Soup, Batchelors*	1 Serving/211g	76	36	0.8	6.5	0.8	0.5
Oxtail, Cup Soup, Co-Op*	1 Sachet/19g	67	355	7.0	63.0	9.0	1.0
Oxtail, Heinz*	1oz/28g	11	41	1.9	6.7	0.8	0.3
Oxtail, Marks & Spencer*	1 Serving/415g	208	50	2.1	6.9	1.4	0.5
Oxtail, Sainsbury's*	½ Can/200g	66	33	2.3	5.1	0.4	0.2
Oxtail, Soup in A Cup, Sainsbury's*	1 Serving/223ml	69	31	1.0	5.7	0.5	0.2
Oxtail, Tesco*	1 Can/400g	152	38	2.0	5.9	0.7	0.3
Parsnip & Apple, COU, Marks & Spencer*	1 Can/415g	187	45	0.7	5.4	2.5	1.2
Parsnip & Honey, Sainsbury's*	½ Bottle/300g	192	64	1.1	5.4	4.2	1.5
Parsnip, Carrot & Sweet Potato, Baxters*	1 Serving/150g	93	62	0.9	8.5	2.7	1.4
Parsnip, Fresh, Morrisons*	½ Pot/250g	100	40	0.9	5.8	1.5	1.4
Parsnip, Honey & Ginger, COU, Marks & Spencer*	1 Can/415g	125	30	0.7	5.3	0.6	0.7
Parsnip, Leek & Ginger, New Covent Garden Food Co*	1 Carton/600g	162	27	1.2	4.9	0.3	1.3
Pasta, Tomato & Basil, Bertolli*	1 Serving/100g	47	47	1.5	7.9	1.1	1.6
Pea & Ham	1oz/28g	20	70	4.4	9.2	2.1	1.4
Pea & Ham, Asda*	½ Can/205g	107	52	2.6	9.0	0.6	0.6
Pea & Ham, Baxters*	1 Can/425g	234	55	3.0	8.3	1.1	1.2
Pea & Ham, Fresh, Sainsbury's*	½ Bottle/302ml	136	45	2.6	4.9	1.7	1.1
Pea & Ham, Marks & Spencer*	1oz/28g	17	62	4.0	9.2	1.0	1.2
Pea & Ham, Morrisons*	1 Serving/250g	93	37	2.0	4.8	1.1	1.2
Pea & Ham, Tesco*	1 Serving/300g	207	69	3.4	6.6	3.2	1.0
Pea & Ham, Thick, Heinz*	1 Can/400g	204	51	3.2	8.7	0.4	1.0
Pea & Mint, Baxters*	1 Serving/300g	186	62	2.3	6.1	3.2	1.5
Pea & Mint, Fresh, Marks & Spencer*	1 Serving/164g	49	30	1.8	6.3	0.1	1.5
Pea & Mint, Fresh, Tesco*	1 Serving/300g	207	69	2.4	5.1	4.4	0.0
Pea & Mint, Sainsbury's*	1 Serving/200g	86	43	2.1	6.7	0.9	0.5
Pea & Mint, Tesco*	½ Pouch/250g	198	79	2.0	5.6	5.4	1.5
Pea, In a Cup, Symingtons*	1 Sachet/30.5g	97	311	7.2	54.1	7.2	6.9
Peking Shiitake Mushroom Noodle, Baxters*	1 Serving/215g	90	42	1.3	7.5	0.8	0.2
Pepper & Chorizo, Sainsbury's*	1 Bowl/400ml	172	43	7.0	2.0	1.0	0.0
Pepper & Tomato, Safeway*	½ Pot/100g	100	100	2.6	11.9	4.2	2.5
Porcini Musroom, Pret A Manger*	1 Serving/455g	210	46	1.4	5.6	1.8	0.9
Pork, Chinese Dumpling, New Cultural Revolution*	1 Serving/250ml	156	62	6.4	6.0	1.6	0.4
Potato & Leek	1oz/28g	15	52	1.5	6.2	2.6	0.8
Potato & Leek With Peppers & Chicken, Stockmeyer*	½ Can/200g	118	59	2.6	6.7	2.4	0.8
Potato & Leek, Asda*	½ Pack/292ml	158	54	1.2	6.0	2.8	0.7
Potato & Leek, Baxters*	1 Can/425g	191	45	1.1	8.1	0.9	0.8
Potato & Leek, Fresh, Asda*	½ Pot/250g	98	39	1.2	7.0	0.7	0.0
Potato & Leek, Thick, Heinz*	1 Can/400g	136	34	0.7	6.5	0.6	0.5
Potato, Leek & Chicken, BGTY, Sainsbury's*	1 Can/400g	152	38	2.1	5.4	0.9	0.5
Provencal Vegetable, Marks & Spencer*	1 Serving/300g	150	50	1.0	6.0	2.5	1.1
Pumpkin & Bramley Apple, New Covent Garden Food Co*	½ Carton/300g	99	33	1.1	5.9	0.6	0.8
Pumpkin & Ginger, In a Aup, Symington's*	1 Serving/200ml	66	33	0.4	4.7	1.4	0.4
Pumpkin, New Covent Garden Food Co*	½ Pint/284ml	91	32	1.1	4.8	0.9	1.0

SOUP,

	INFO/WEIGHT	KCAL	KCAL	PROT	CARB	FAT	FIBRE
Red Pepper & Tomato, Perfectly Balanced, Waitrose*	1 Can/415g	154	37	0.8	4.5	1.8	0.9
Red Pepper & Tomato, Vie, Knorr*	1 Pack/500ml	195	39	0.8	6.4	1.2	1.0
Red Pepper & Tomato, Weight Watchers*	1 Serving/295g	35	12	0.4	2.4	0.1	0.4
Red Pepper, Tomato & Basil, Marks & Spencer*	1 Can/415g	83	20	1.3	2.7	0.3	0.8
Rich Tomato & Basil, Batchelors*	1 Serving/280g	104	37	0.5	6.7	0.9	0.6
Rich Woodland Mushroom, Cup A Soup, Batchelors*	1 Pack/280g	123	44	0.6	5.8	1.9	0.5
Roast Pumpkin, EAT*	1 Can/400ml	260	65	1.1	5.9	4.2	0.8
Roasted Parsnip, Chunky Carrot & Sweet Potato, Baxters*	½ Pot/300g	186	62	0.9	8.5	2.7	1.4
Roasted Pepper, Eat Smart, Safeway*	½ Pot/225g	79	35	0.8	3.7	1.8	1.4
Roasted Red Pepper & Tomato, Marks & Spencer*	1 Serving/150g	105	70	1.4	5.0	4.9	0.6
Roasted Red Pepper, Fresh, Waitrose*	1 Pack/600g	172	29	0.8	3.0	1.5	1.0
Roasted Vegetable, Eat Smart, Safeway*	1 Serving/450g	180	40	0.8	4.1	2.2	2.0
Roasted Vegetable, Fresh, Sainsbury's*	½ Pot/273ml	71	26	0.5	4.8	0.5	1.2
Roasted Vegetable, TTD, Sainsbury's*	½ Pack/297.7g	128	43	0.5	3.4	3.0	1.0
Roasted Winter Vegetable, Sainsbury's*	1 Serving/300ml	129	43	0.5	3.4	3.0	1.0
San Marzano Tomato & Mascarpone, Marks & Spencer*	1 Serving/150g	98	65	1.4	5.7	4.3	2.0
Scotch Broth	1 Serving/220g	180	82	8.3	5.0	3.4	1.2
Scotch Broth, Asda*	½ Can/205g	90	44	1.6	6.0	1.5	0.6
Scotch Broth, Baxters*	1 Can/415g	195	47	1.9	7.5	1.0	0.9
Scotch Broth, Fresh, Baxters*	1 Serving/300g	108	36	1.6	5.9	0.7	0.6
Scotch Broth, New Covent Garden Food Co*	½ Pint/284ml	114	40	1.6	2.8	2.5	0.5
Scotch Broth, Sainsbury's*	½ Can/200g	108	54	1.9	8.2	1.5	0.8
Scotch Broth, Tesco*	1 Can/400g	152	38	1.5	6.7	0.6	0.8
Scotch Broth, Thick, Heinz*	½ Can/200g	94	47	2.1	8.1	0.7	0.9
Scotch Vegetable, Baxters*	1 Can/425g	183	43	1.9	7.4	0.6	1.2
Scottish Vegetable With Lentils & Beef, Heinz*	1 Can/403.8g	210	52	3.4	8.2	0.7	1.2
Seasoned Chicken With Sweetcorn & Croutons, SlimFast*	1 Pack/60g	211	351	23.7	36.8	10.6	9.7
Sicilian Tomato, New Covent Garden Food Co*	½ Pint/284ml	114	40	1.6	4.8	1.6	0.8
Snack, Golden Chicken, With Noodles, Weight Watchers*	1 Serving/27g	89	330	6.7	71.9	1.9	1.1
Snack, Mushroom, With Pasta, Weight Watchers*	1 Serving/27g	127	470	10.0	77.0	13.3	1.9
Soupe Des Pecheurs, Royco*	1 Pack/18g	71	392	7.1	65.4	11.4	0.0
Spiced Chickpea & Fresh Red Pepper, Marks & Spencer*	1 Serving/300g	165	55	2.2	5.8	2.3	2.5
Spiced Spinach & Green Lentil, Asda*	½ Pot/250g	123	49	2.7	5.0	2.0	0.0
Spicy Corn Chowder, New Covent Garden Food Co*	½ Pint/284ml	134	47	1.4	5.9	2.0	0.9
Spicy Gumbo, Sainsbury's*	1 Carton/600ml	240	40	1.5	4.5	1.8	0.9
Spicy Lentil & Tomato, Soup A Slim, Asda*	1 Serving/17g	56	327	12.0	63.0	3.0	4.6
Spicy Lentil & Vegetable, Chilled, Marks & Spencer*	½ Serving/600g	300	50	2.7	8.0	0.8	1.1
Spicy Lentil, COU, Marks & Spencer*	1 Pack/415g	187	45	2.6	6.7	0.9	1.2
Spicy Lentil, Seeds Of Change*	1 Pack/500g	345	69	2.8	9.4	2.2	0.8
Spicy Mixed Bean & Vegetable, Eat Smart, Safeway*	1 Can/415g	183	44	2.3	7.5	0.5	3.1
Spicy Parsnip, Aldi*	1 Serving/250g	133	53	0.6	4.9	3.4	1.4
Spicy Parsnip, BGTY, Sainsbury's*	1 Pack/400g	180	45	2.2	7.1	0.9	1.0
Spicy Parsnip, Baxters*	1 Can/425g	217	51	1.1	6.1	2.5	1.5
Spicy Parsnip, Fresh, Tesco*	1 Serving/300g	102	34	0.6	4.5	1.6	1.6
Spicy Parsnip, Perfectly Balanced, Waitrose*	1 Can/415g	125	30	1.0	4.8	0.7	1.1
Spicy Pumpkin, Sainsbury's*	½ Bottle/300ml	96	32	0.4	3.8	1.7	0.6
Spicy Red Curry, Blue Dragon*	1 Serving/205g	97	47	0.4	5.8	2.5	0.3
Spicy Red Lentil & Tomato, Marks & Spencer*	½ Pack/300g	150	50	2.7	8.0	0.8	1.1
Spicy Sausage & Bean Meal, Tesco*	1 Can/500g	265	53	2.8	6.4	1.4	1.2
Spicy Thai Chicken, Baxters*	1 Can/415g	278	67	1.8	7.1	3.5	0.3
Spicy Tomato & Lentil, Asda*	1 Can/410g	156	38	1.0	6.0	1.1	0.4
Spicy Tomato & Lentil, BGTY, Sainsbury's*	1 Can/400g	240	60	3.2	10.4	0.7	0.1
Spicy Tomato & Lentil, Tesco*	1 Can/400g	180	45	2.1	8.7	0.2	0.8

S

INFO/WEIGHT	Measure	per Measure KCAL	KCAL	PROT	CARB	FAT	FIBRE
			Nutrition Values per 100g / 100ml				
Spicy Tomato & Rice With Sweetcorn, Baxters*	½ Can/207g	93	45	1.3	9.2	0.3	0.5
Spicy Tomato & Vegetable, Healthy Living, Co-Op*	1 Can/400g	180	45	2.0	8.0	0.8	2.0
Spicy Tomato, Cup A Soup, Batchelors*	1 Sachet/23g	74	322	7.6	65.8	3.2	3.2
Spicy Tomato, EAT*	1 Can/400ml	137	34	0.7	3.6	1.8	0.8
Spinach & Ricotta, EAT*	1 Pack/400ml	224	56	2.1	3.0	4.0	0.7
Spinach & Watercress, New Covent Garden Food Co*	½ Carton/298g	60	20	1.3	2.8	0.4	0.8
Split Pea & Ham, Asda*	1 Serving/300g	129	43	3.5	6.9	0.2	0.7
Split Peas, Yellow, Simply Organic*	1 Pot/500g	270	54	3.5	9.7	0.2	2.5
Spring Vegetable, Condensed, Campbell's*	1 Can/295g	62	21	0.5	4.5	0.1	0.0
Spring Vegetable, Heinz*	1 Can/400g	124	31	0.8	6.2	0.4	0.7
Stilton & White Port, Baxters*	1oz/28g	25	88	2.5	5.4	6.3	0.3
Stilton, Celery & Watercress, Morrisons*	1 Serving/250g	273	109	3.9	3.1	9.2	0.3
Sugar Snap Pea & Mint, New Covent Garden Food Co*	½ Pack/300g	87	29	1.7	3.0	1.1	1.4
Summer Minestrone, With Basil Pesto, Marks & Spencer*	½ Pot/300g	240	80	1.9	5.7	5.4	1.2
Summer Vegetable, With Pasta, Cup A Soup, Batchelors*	1 Serving/33g	17	50	1.4	8.5	1.1	1.0
Sun Dried Tomato & Basil, Heinz*	1 Serving/275ml	124	45	0.6	6.5	1.9	0.1
Sun Dried Tomato & Basil, Microwaveable Cup, Heinz*	1 Cup/275ml	124	45	0.6	6.5	1.9	0.1
Super Chicken Noodle in Seconds, Knorr*	1 Pack/37g	111	299	17.9	46.1	4.7	0.3
Super Chicken Noodle, Knorr*	1 Pack/56g	182	325	14.3	56.0	4.9	1.8
Sweet Cherry Tomato, TTD, Sainsbury's*	1 Pack/300g	120	40	0.7	6.0	1.5	1.0
Sweet Pepper & Tomato, EAT*	1 Serving/473ml	107	23	0.7	4.3	0.3	0.8
Sweet Potato & Coconut, COU, Marks & Spencer*	1 Can/415g	166	40	0.7	6.7	1.3	0.8
Sweetcorn & Chicken Chowder, Heinz*	1 Serving/200g	108	54	1.5	5.2	3.0	0.3
Sweetcorn & Chicken, Cup, Calorie Counter, Co-Op*	1 Sachet/11.1g	35	315	5.0	49.0	11.0	11.0
Sweetcorn & Chilli, COU, Marks & Spencer*	½ Can/275g	138	50	0.9	6.1	2.4	0.4
Sweetcorn Chowder, New Covent Garden Food Co*	½ Carton/250ml	118	47	1.4	5.9	2.0	0.9
Tangy Tomato, Slim A Soup, Batchelors*	1 Serving/230ml	81	35	1.1	6.7	0.4	0.5
Thai Chicken & Coconut, Safeway*	1 Serving/300g	235	78	3.4	4.6	5.2	0.9
Thai Chicken Fusion, New Covent Garden Food Co.*	1 Carton/111g	59	54	2.6	4.8	1.8	0.4
Thai Chicken Noodle, Baxters*	1 Serving/430g	202	47	1.7	6.8	1.4	0.3
Thai Chicken With Ginger & Coconut, EAT*	1 Serving/340g	244	72	3.4	4.4	4.6	0.6
Thai Chicken, GFY, Asda*	1 Serving/200g	85	43	1.7	5.5	1.5	0.5
Thai Chicken, Safeway*	1 Serving/200g	178	89	4.1	2.5	7.0	1.3
Thai Pumpkin Coconut, New Covent Garden Food Co*	1 Carton/568ml	182	32	1.3	3.5	1.3	1.1
Thai Red Chicken, Fresh, Sainsbury's*	½ Pot/300ml	159	53	1.9	5.0	2.8	0.5
Thai Style Chicken, Morrisons*	1 Serving/250g	205	82	3.3	4.6	5.6	0.0
Thai Style Chicken, Sainsbury's*	½ Can/200g	106	53	2.9	5.5	2.1	0.7
Thai Style Chicken, Soupreme, Aldi*	1 Tin/400g	200	50	2.5	3.8	2.7	1.1
Three Bean, Chunky, Marks & Spencer*	1 Can/415g	208	50	2.3	7.5	1.2	1.8
Three Bean, Organic, Seeds Of Change*	1 Pack/500g	285	57	1.7	9.9	1.2	1.1
Tomato & Basil With Onion, Waistline, Crosse & Blackwell*	1 Serving/300g	87	29	0.9	5.1	0.6	0.3
Tomato & Basil, 1% Fat, Marks & Spencer*	1 Can/400g	152	38	0.6	9.0	0.4	1.4
Tomato & Basil, 99% Fat Free, Baxters*	½ Can/207g	75	36	0.7	6.1	1.0	0.6
Tomato & Basil, Campbell's*	1 Pack/500ml	205	41	0.7	6.7	1.3	1.1
Tomato & Basil, Cup, Co-Op*	1 Sachet/45g	158	350	2.0	76.0	4.0	4.0
Tomato & Basil, Delicious, Tesco*	1 Serving/300ml	150	50	1.0	7.4	1.9	0.7
Tomato & Basil, EAT*	1 Serving/455g	123	27	1.0	4.1	0.7	0.9
Tomato & Basil, Finest, Tesco*	½ Pot/300g	204	68	1.0	4.1	5.2	0.6
Tomato & Basil, Fresh, Improved, Sainsbury's*	½ Bottle/300ml	105	35	1.4	4.1	1.4	0.6
Tomato & Basil, Fresh, Morrisons*	1 Serving/500g	210	42	2.5	4.9	1.4	0.0
Tomato & Basil, Fresh, Sainsbury's*	1 Pack/300ml	78	26	0.8	4.0	0.7	0.7
Tomato & Basil, Fresh, Somerfield*	1 Serving/294.7g	112	38	0.7	4.4	1.9	1.4
Tomato & Basil, Fresh, Tesco*	1 Pack/300g	129	43	1.0	5.7	1.8	0.7

	Measure INFO/WEIGHT	per Measure KCAL	Nutrition Values per 100g / 100ml				
			KCAL	PROT	CARB	FAT	FIBRE
Tomato & Basil, Fresh, The Fresh Soup Company*	½ Pot/250g	85	34	1.3	5.1	0.9	0.6
Tomato & Basil, GFY, Asda*	1 Serving/250ml	103	41	1.4	3.9	2.2	0.4
Tomato & Basil, Loyd Grossman*	½ Pack/210g	88	42	0.8	5.3	2.0	0.3
Tomato & Basil, Marks & Spencer*	1oz/28g	7	24	0.8	4.4	0.4	0.6
Tomato & Basil, New Covent Garden Food Co*	1 Pack/568g	187	33	1.8	5.7	0.4	0.5
Tomato & Basil, Organic, Sainsbury's*	1 Serving/200g	96	48	0.4	7.0	2.0	0.3
Tomato & Basil, Pret A Manger*	1 Serving/453.6g	147	32	0.6	4.7	1.4	0.7
Tomato & Basil, Safeway*	½ Pot/285g	137	48	0.8	5.9	2.3	0.8
Tomato & Basil, Soup-a-Slim, Asda*	1 Sachet/16g	52	326	7.0	70.0	2.0	3.9
Tomato & Basil, Thick & Creamy, Batchelors*	1 Serving/281g	104	37	0.5	6.7	0.9	0.6
Tomato & Basil, Vie, Knorr*	1 Pack/500ml	145	29	0.8	5.5	0.4	0.9
Tomato & Basil, Waitrose*	1 Serving/300ml	123	41	0.6	4.5	2.3	0.6
Tomato & Brown Lentil, Baxters*	1 Can/400g	216	54	2.7	10.4	0.2	1.0
Tomato & Butterbean, Baxters*	1 Can/425g	225	53	1.9	8.6	1.2	1.8
Tomato & Fresh Basil, Marks & Spencer*	½ Pot/300g	105	35	0.8	5.2	1.2	1.5
Tomato & Herb, Campbell's*	1 Carton/500ml	180	36	1.0	5.0	1.3	0.0
Tomato & Herb, Marks & Spencer*	1oz/28g	20	72	1.3	7.9	4.0	0.4
Tomato & Lentil, Heinz*	1 Can/400g	216	54	2.7	10.4	0.2	1.0
Tomato & Lentil, Marks & Spencer*	½ Can/211.1g	95	45	2.3	8.4	0.2	1.5
Tomato & Lentil, Slim Choice, Safeway*	1oz/28g	95	341	13.9	59.4	5.4	6.1
Tomato & Mountain Wheat, Pret A Manger*	1 Serving/455g	220	48	1.3	8.1	1.3	0.7
Tomato & Orange, Baxters*	1 Can/425g	179	42	1.0	8.3	0.5	0.4
Tomato & Orange, Healthy Eating, Tesco*	1 Pack/400g	132	33	0.6	7.1	0.2	0.4
Tomato & Red Pepper, Campbell's*	1 Can/590g	366	62	0.5	7.7	3.3	0.0
Tomato & Red Pepper, Soupreme*	1 Serving/250ml	90	36	1.1	5.7	1.0	1.7
Tomato & Red Pepper, Weight Watchers*	1 Serving/205g	25	12	0.4	2.5	0.1	0.4
Tomato & Roast Red Pepper, COU, Marks & Spencer*	½ Can/207.5g	73	35	1.0	7.6	0.1	0.9
Tomato & Spinach, Organic, Waitrose*	1 Serving/300g	126	42	1.4	4.9	1.9	0.7
Tomato & Three Bean, BGTY, Sainsbury's*	1 Can/400g	216	54	2.9	8.5	0.9	0.8
Tomato & Vegetable, Cup A Soup, Batchelors*	1 Serving/218g	107	49	1.1	8.5	1.2	0.6
Tomato & Vegetable, Cup, Soupreme*	1 Sachet/24g	87	361	6.0	64.6	8.7	1.4
Tomato & Vegetable, Organic, Baxters*	1 Can/400g	200	50	1.6	9.2	0.8	0.8
Tomato Rice, Campbell's*	1oz/28g	13	46	0.9	8.3	1.0	0.0
Tomato, 99% Fat Free, Campbell's*	1 Can/200g	88	44	0.7	8.0	1.0	0.0
Tomato, 99% Fat Free, Watties*	1 Serving/105g	32	31	1.0	5.6	0.4	1.1
Tomato, Cannellini & Borlotti Bean, Marks & Spencer*	½ Pot/300g	195	65	2.1	6.7	3.3	2.5
Tomato, Cream of, Canned	1oz/28g	15	52	0.8	5.9	3.0	0.7
Tomato, Creme Fraiche & Basil, The Best, Safeway*	1/3 Pot/200g	130	65	1.0	5.0	4.2	1.0
Tomato, Cup A Soup, Batchelors*	1 Serving/212g	76	36	0.3	6.7	0.9	0.3
Tomato, Fresh Country, New Covent Garden Food Co*	1 fl oz/30ml	12	40	1.9	6.4	0.8	0.8
Tomato, Fresh, Tesco*	1 Serving/100g	44	44	0.7	5.2	2.3	0.4
Tomato, In A Cup, Gluten Free, Symingtons*	1 Serving/19.1g	68	356	5.2	45.8	16.9	13.0
Tomato, In A Cup, Tesco*	1 Serving/23g	75	328	6.4	68.5	3.2	0.1
Tomato, In a Cup, Symingtons*	1 Sachet/31.5g	99	308	3.5	62.0	5.0	3.8
Tomato, Mediterranean, Rich, Fresh, Baxters*	1 Carton/600g	318	53	1.8	7.7	1.7	1.1
Tomato, Mixed Bean & Vegetable, Chunky, Sainsbury's*	1 Can/400g	232	58	2.2	11.5	0.3	1.6
Tomato, Mixed Bean & Vegetable, Tesco	1oz/28g	18	64	2.4	9.8	0.3	1.6
Tomato, Onion & Basil, GFY, Asda*	1 Can/400g	116	29	0.8	5.0	0.6	0.3
Tomato, Pasta & Basil Cup, Good Intentions, Somerfield*	1 Serving/26g	92	355	5.4	69.1	6.3	5.1
Tomato, Pepper & Basil, Eat Smart, Safeway*	1 Can/415g	162	39	0.9	4.8	1.7	1.8
Tomato, Pepper & Basil, Safeway*	1 Can/415.4g	162	39	0.9	4.8	1.7	1.8
Tomato, Weight Watchers*	1 Pack/300g	74	25	0.7	4.6	0.5	0.3
Tuscan Bean & Sausage, Pret A Manger*	1 Serving/340g	267	79	4.8	8.1	3.3	3.8

S

SOUP,	Measure INFO/WEIGHT	per Measure KCAL	KCAL	PROT	CARB	FAT	FIBRE
Tuscan Bean, GFY, Asda*	1 Carton/400ml	224	56	2.9	9.0	0.9	0.8
Tuscan Bean, New Covent Garden Food Co*	½ Carton/300g	171	57	3.9	8.8	0.7	2.4
Tuscan Bean, Organic, Sainsbury's*	1 Pack/400g	148	37	2.2	5.2	0.8	1.3
Tuscan Bean, Perfectly Balanced, Waitrose*	½ Pot/300g	147	49	2.0	6.1	1.8	1.8
Vegetable	1oz/28g	15	52	0.9	3.2	4.0	0.9
Vegetable & Beef, Sainsbury's*	1 Can/400g	260	65	2.1	8.5	2.5	1.3
Vegetable & Lentil, Fresh, Somerfield*	½ Pack/300g	183	61	2.7	8.4	1.9	1.5
Vegetable & Lentil, Somerfield*	1 Serving/300g	120	40	1.6	4.9	1.5	2.4
Vegetable Broth, Healthy Eating, Tesco*	1 Can/400g	148	37	1.2	7.4	0.2	1.0
Vegetable Broth, Marks & Spencer*	1 Pack/213g	85	40	1.0	6.3	1.4	0.8
Vegetable Chowder, New Covent Garden Food Co*	½ Carton/300g	159	53	2.9	6.6	1.7	1.1
Vegetable, 99% Fat Free, Watties*	1 Serving/105g	30	29	0.8	5.9	0.2	0.8
Vegetable, Asda*	1 Can/400g	144	36	1.1	7.0	0.4	0.8
Vegetable, Bean & Pasta, Organic, Baxters*	1 Can/415g	212	51	2.2	8.7	0.8	1.4
Vegetable, Canned	1oz/28g	13	48	1.4	9.9	0.6	1.5
Vegetable, Chunky, Simply Organic*	1 Pot/500g	200	40	1.6	5.3	1.4	1.4
Vegetable, Condensed, Campbell's*	1 Can/295g	103	35	0.8	6.2	0.8	0.0
Vegetable, Cup, Soupreme*	1 Sachet/26g	111	444	8.1	49.7	23.6	2.3
Vegetable, Extra Thick, Sainsbury's*	1 Can/400g	176	44	1.6	8.0	0.6	1.3
Vegetable, Fresh, Co-Op*	1 Pack/600g	150	25	0.6	4.0	1.0	1.0
Vegetable, Heinz*	1 Can/400g	188	47	1.4	8.4	0.9	1.1
Vegetable, In A Cup, BGTY, Sainsbury's*	1 Sachet/200g	52	26	0.5	4.4	0.8	0.9
Vegetable, In A Mug, Healthy Eating, Tesco*	1 Mug/18g	66	365	7.0	66.3	8.0	2.6
Vegetable, Instant, Weight Watchers*	1 Sachet/219.2ml	57	26	0.5	4.8	0.5	0.2
Vegetable, New Covent Garden Food Co*	½ Pint/284ml	88	31	1.1	5.9	0.4	1.1
Vegetable, Safeway*	1 Can/295g	109	37	1.5	7.1	0.3	1.2
Vegetable, Sainsbury's*	1 Can/400g	184	46	1.5	8.3	0.7	1.2
Vegetable, Soup-a-Cups, Asda*	1 Sachet/200ml	59	30	0.7	5.5	0.6	0.5
Vegetable, Tesco*	½ Can/200g	88	44	1.3	9.3	0.2	1.0
Vegetable, Vie, Knorr*	1 Pack/500ml	160	32	0.9	5.5	0.7	1.2
Vegetable, Weight Watchers*	1 Serving/295ml	83	28	0.9	5.6	0.2	0.8
Vegetable, in a Cup, Healthy Living, Tesco*	1 Sachet/18g	66	367	7.2	66.1	7.8	2.8
Vegetarian Chilli, Eat*	1 Serving/450ml	205	46	2.5	7.3	0.7	2.8
Watercress & Cream, Soup Chef*	1 Jar/780g	413	53	0.8	5.9	2.9	0.3
Watercress, Marks & Spencer*	½ Pot/300g	75	25	1.3	1.5	1.7	0.6
Wild Mushroom & Maderia, Finest, Tesco*	1 Serving/300g	156	52	1.4	5.0	2.9	0.3
Wild Mushroom & Porcini Pieces, BGTY, Sainsbury's*	1 Serving/196.4g	55	28	0.5	4.7	0.8	0.6
Wild Mushroom & Truffle, The Best, Safeway*	½ Pot/300g	180	60	1.1	3.5	4.5	0.9
Wild Mushroom Cup, Good Intentions, Somerfield*	1 Serving/20g	74	369	4.1	68.9	8.5	4.5
Wild Mushroom in a Cup, BGTY, Sainsbury's*	1 Serving/200ml	56	28	0.5	4.7	0.8	0.6
Wild Mushroom, EAT*	1 Serving/500ml	192	38	1.5	2.2	2.7	0.6
Wild Mushroom, Fresh, Tesco*	1 Serving/300g	159	53	1.3	4.7	3.2	0.3
Wild Mushroom, New Covent Garden Food Co*	1 fl oz/30ml	15	51	2.3	3.8	2.9	0.3
Wild Mushroom, SlimFast*	1 Pack/60g	209	349	23.3	37.5	10.2	10.4
Wild Mushroom, Soupreme*	1 Carton/500g	135	27	1.1	2.9	1.2	0.5
Winter Vegetable & Lentil, New Covent Garden Food Co*	1 Serving/300g	243	81	5.1	12.0	1.4	2.6
Winter Warmer, New Covent Garden Food Co*	1 Serving/300g	180	60	2.5	10.5	0.9	2.3
Won Ton, Blue Dragon*	1 Can/410g	62	15	1.4	2.1	0.1	0.0
SOUP MIX,							
Chicken & Leek, Sainsbury's*	1/3 Sachet/203ml	75	37	0.5	6.1	1.2	0.5
Leek & Potato, Sainsbury's*	½ Pack/204g	39	19	0.6	3.6	0.2	0.5
Minestrone, 1 Pint Simmer, Somerfield*	½ Pint/23.5g	69	298	11.9	61.4	0.5	4.5
Minestrone, Sainsbury's*	1 Serving/200ml	44	22	0.3	6.0	0.0	0.3

S

	Measure INFO/WEIGHT	per Measure KCAL	Nutrition Values per 100g / 100ml				
			KCAL	PROT	CARB	FAT	FIBRE
SOUP MIX,							
Scotch Broth, Sainsbury's*	1 Serving/175g	32	18	0.2	3.8	0.2	0.6
SOYA,							
Bolognese Style, Sainsbury's*	½ Pack/168g	113	67	3.1	13.9	0.7	2.7
Chunks, Dried, Sainsbury's*	1oz/28g	27	98	14.0	9.8	0.3	1.1
Mince, Dried, Cooked, Sainsbury's*	1 Serving/200g	164	82	11.8	8.3	0.2	0.9
Mince, Dry Weight, Sainsbury's*	1 Serving/50g	164	328	47.2	33.2	0.8	3.6
Mince, Granules	1oz/28g	74	263	43.2	11.0	5.4	0.0
Mince, Organic*	1oz/28g	101	359	46.0	28.0	7.0	0.0
Mince, With Onion, Sainsbury's*	½ Pack/180g	122	68	5.4	8.0	1.6	1.8
Protein Powder, Holland & Barrett*	1oz/28g	109	390	88.0	0.5	4.0	0.0
SPACE RAIDERS*,							
Beef Flavour	1 Pack/17g	82	482	8.3	61.0	22.7	2.6
Cheese	1 Bag/16g	76	473	7.1	61.6	22.0	3.1
Pickled Onion	1 Bag/16g	77	479	7.4	61.5	22.6	2.4
Salt & Vinegar	1 Bag/16.9g	81	478	6.9	61.7	22.6	2.2
SPAGHETTI,							
Canned in Tomato Sauce	1oz/28g	18	64	1.9	14.1	0.4	0.7
Chicken, BGTY, Sainsbury's*	1 Serving/300g	281	94	9.8	11.6	0.9	2.3
Cooked, Average	1oz/28g	33	119	4.1	24.8	0.7	1.1
Dry, Average	1oz/28g	98	350	12.1	72.1	1.5	2.4
Durum Wheat, Dry, Average	1oz/28g	97	348	12.4	71.8	0.4	1.5
Fresh, Cooked, Average	1 Serving/125g	182	146	6.1	26.9	1.7	1.8
Fresh, Dry, Average	1 Serving/100g	278	278	10.8	53.0	3.0	2.2
In Rich Tomato Sauce, Asda*	1 Serving/200g	128	64	1.6	14.0	0.2	0.5
In Tomato Sauce With Parsley, Weight Watchers*	1 Can/400g	196	49	1.8	10.0	0.2	0.6
In Tomato Sauce, HP*	1 Can/410g	247	60	1.5	13.1	0.2	0.4
In Tomato Sauce, Heinz*	1 Can/400g	244	61	1.7	13.0	0.2	0.5
In Tomato Sauce, Organic, Sainsbury's*	½ Can/205g	133	65	1.8	13.9	0.2	1.0
In Tomato Sauce, Sainsbury's*	1 Can/410g	262	64	1.9	13.3	0.4	0.5
In Tomato Sauce, Tesco*	1 Can/410g	246	60	1.6	12.9	0.2	0.5
In Tomato Sauce, Value, Tesco*	½ Can/205g	131	64	1.9	13.3	0.4	0.5
In Tomato Sauce, Weight Watchers*	1 Serving/200g	98	49	1.8	10.0	0.2	0.6
In Tomato Sauce, Whole Wheat, Sainsbury's*	1 Serving/205g	125	61	2.0	11.9	0.6	1.1
Quick Cook, Dry, Average	1 Serving/50g	176	351	12.8	70.8	1.9	2.7
Weight Watchers*, Cooked	1 Serving/200g	99	50	1.8	10.0	0.2	0.6
Whole Wheat, Dry, Average	1 Serving/100g	326	326	13.5	62.2	2.6	8.0
Wholemeal, Boiled	1oz/28g	32	113	4.7	23.2	0.9	3.5
Wholemeal, Raw	1oz/28g	91	324	13.4	66.2	2.5	8.4
With Cheese & Broccoli, GFY, Asda*	1 Pack/369.8g	477	129	4.3	20.0	3.5	0.8
With Sausages, Heinz*	1 Can/400g	328	82	3.7	11.0	2.6	0.5
With Tomato & Cheese, Tesco*	½ Pack/250g	280	112	4.0	18.1	2.6	1.1
With Tomatoes & Mozzerella, GFY, Asda*	1 Pack/120g	542	452	16.0	79.0	8.0	3.0
SPAGHETTI & MEATBALLS,							
American, Superbowl, Asda*	1 Pack/453.4g	593	131	11.0	13.0	3.9	1.1
BGTY, Sainsbury's*	1 Pack/300g	249	83	5.9	12.7	0.9	3.1
COU, Marks & Spencer*	1 Pack/360g	360	100	6.8	14.2	1.9	1.9
Chicken in Tomato Sauce, Heinz*	1 Can/400g	352	88	4.1	11.0	3.0	0.5
Healthy Living, Tesco*	1 Pack/400g	332	83	4.2	11.4	2.3	2.2
Italian, Sainsbury's*	1 Pack/450g	495	110	5.0	11.9	4.7	2.7
Sainsbury's*	1 Serving/260g	226	87	5.7	12.6	1.5	1.5
Somerfield*	1 Pack/900g	1035	115	5.0	15.0	4.0	0.0
Vegetarian, Safeway*	1 Pack/350g	382	109	5.0	13.7	3.8	0.5

S

	Measure INFO/WEIGHT	per Measure KCAL	Nutrition Values per 100g / 100ml				
			KCAL	PROT	CARB	FAT	FIBRE
SPAGHETTI BOLOGNESE,							
Al Forno, Sainsbury's*	1 Pack/400g	460	115	7.8	10.0	4.9	1.1
Asda*	1 Pack/400g	432	108	6.0	17.0	1.8	0.9
Average	1oz/28g	36	129	7.8	12.5	5.6	0.9
BGTY, Sainsbury's*	1 Pack/450g	392	87	4.7	14.8	1.0	1.1
Bean & Mushroom, Safeway*	1 Pack/435.3g	370	85	3.7	12.8	2.1	3.7
Bird's Eye*	1 Pack/362g	404	112	4.8	13.4	4.4	0.9
COU, Marks & Spencer*	1 Pack/360g	378	105	7.3	13.9	2.2	1.0
Canned, Asda*	½ Can/205g	174	85	4.2	10.7	2.8	0.6
Canned, Garlini, Aldi*	1 Can/410g	324	79	3.7	10.2	2.6	1.2
Co-Op*	1 Pack/300g	285	95	4.0	11.0	4.0	1.0
Cost Cutter, Costcutters*	1 Pack/600g	504	84	5.7	11.2	1.9	0.9
Eat Smart, Safeway*	1 Pack/393g	350	89	5.9	13.1	1.4	1.3
Finest, Tesco*	1 Pack/400g	548	137	9.5	12.3	5.5	1.2
Flavour, Sainsbury's*	1 Serving/233g	231	99	2.9	19.1	1.2	2.1
GFY, Asda*	1 Serving/250g	220	88	5.0	13.0	1.8	0.7
Good Intentions, Somerfield*	1 Serving/400g	380	95	6.2	12.4	2.3	1.4
HP*	1 Pack/410g	312	76	3.8	11.3	1.9	0.7
Healthy Choice, Iceland*	1 Pack/400g	428	107	6.8	17.8	1.0	1.1
Healthy Eating, Tesco*	1 Pack/340g	326	96	5.3	13.7	2.2	1.5
Heinz*	1 Can/400g	296	74	2.7	12.9	1.4	0.5
In Tomato & Beef Sauce, Carlini, Aldi*	1 Can/410g	324	79	3.7	10.2	2.6	1.2
Italia, Marks & Spencer*	1 Pack/400g	600	150	8.8	14.0	6.3	1.1
Italiano, Pro-Cuisine, Pro Cuisine*	1 Pack/600g	522	87	5.7	11.7	1.9	0.0
Italiano, Tesco*	1 Pack/340g	367	108	9.8	9.8	3.3	1.3
Lean Cuisine, Findus*	1 Pack/320g	275	86	4.5	11.5	2.3	1.1
Loved by Kids, Marks & Spencer*	½ Pack/200g	250	125	6.6	15.3	4.4	1.9
Meat Free, Heinz*	1 Serving/200g	162	81	3.3	13.1	1.7	0.6
Meat Free, Sainsbury's*	1 Can/400g	280	70	3.4	12.0	0.9	1.2
Morrisons*	1 Pack/300g	306	102	5.8	12.2	3.3	1.4
Perfectly Balanced, Waitrose*	1 Pack/350g	319	91	4.2	10.0	3.8	1.0
Ready Meals, Marks & Spencer*	1 Pack/360g	576	160	8.8	12.7	8.1	1.2
Ross*	1 Serving/320g	288	90	4.2	15.7	1.1	0.9
Safeway*	1 Pack/650g	780	120	9.5	13.1	3.3	1.7
Sainsbury's*	1 Pack/300g	237	79	4.9	10.5	1.9	0.9
SmartPrice, Asda*	½ Can/205g	215	105	3.2	12.0	4.9	0.8
Somerfield*	1 Pack/300g	339	113	5.3	18.0	2.2	2.0
Spar*	1 Pack/500g	440	88	5.6	8.6	3.5	1.5
Tesco*	1 Pack/257g	339	132	6.5	14.1	5.5	1.2
Value, Tesco*	1 Pack/300g	294	98	5.2	11.8	3.3	0.5
Vegetarian, Tesco*	1 Pack/340g	374	110	5.1	13.7	3.9	1.2
Weight Watchers*	1 Pack/320g	301	94	5.8	14.6	1.3	1.0
SPAGHETTI CARBONARA,							
COU, Marks & Spencer*	1 Pack/330g	347	105	5.7	15.5	2.0	1.8
Cappelletti, Balanced Lifestyle, Carlini, Aldi*	1 Can/400g	328	82	4.1	10.0	2.8	0.6
GFY, Asda*	1 Pack/120g	151	126	4.4	20.0	3.2	0.7
Italian Express*	1 Pack/320g	310	97	4.3	11.6	3.7	1.1
Italiano, Tesco*	1 Pack/450g	702	156	6.9	14.8	7.7	1.7
Marks & Spencer*	1 Pack/360g	630	175	7.6	14.3	9.5	0.1
Safeway*	1 Pack/360g	569	158	7.9	15.7	7.1	1.2
Sainsbury's*	1 Pack/450g	558	124	7.3	14.2	4.2	0.9
Tesco*	1 Pack/450g	612	136	5.9	15.2	5.7	1.3
SPAGHETTI HOOPS,							
'N' Hot Dogs, Heinz*	1 Can/400g	304	76	2.8	11.0	2.4	0.4

S

	Measure	per Measure	Nutrition Values per 100g / 100ml				
	INFO/WEIGHT	KCAL	KCAL	PROT	CARB	FAT	FIBRE
SPAGHETTI HOOPS,							
In Tomato Sauce, Heinz*	1 Can/400g	224	56	1.9	11.7	0.2	0.6
Tesco*	½ Can/205g	123	60	1.6	12.9	0.2	0.5
SPAGHETTI LOOPS,							
SmartPrice, Asda*	1 Serving/205g	127	62	1.7	13.0	0.3	0.4
SPAGHETTI MARINARA,							
GFY, Asda*	1 Pack/400g	520	130	8.0	15.0	4.2	0.9
SPAM*,							
Pork & Ham, Chopped	1 Serving/100g	296	296	14.5	3.2	24.2	0.0
SPICE BLEND,							
Balti, Sharwood's*	1oz/28g	34	122	1.8	7.1	9.6	1.2
Thai, Sharwood's*	1 Pack 260g	424	163	1.8	12.0	11.9	1.0
Tikka, Sharwood's*	1 Pack/260g	263	101	2.7	10.2	5.4	1.7
SPICE MIX,							
Chicken Tikka Masala & Pilau Rice, Colman's*	1 Pack/85g	309	364	11.5	39.9	18.0	11.2
Chili Mix for Chilli, Schwartz*	1oz/28g	96	344	9.6	63.6	5.7	1.0
Chilli & Garlic Seed, The Food Doctor*	1 Serving/15g	88	584	30.5	3.7	49.7	11.0
Chilli Con Carne, Colman's*	1 Pack/50g	154	308	8.6	62.0	1.7	0.0
Chilli Con Carne, Hot, Schwartz*	1 Pack/41g	141	344	10.8	59.0	7.2	0.0
Green Thai Chicken Curry, Schwartz*	1 Pack/41g	137	334	11.3	67.6	3.2	0.3
Mexican Chili Potato Wedges, Schwartz*	1oz/28g	45	162	3.4	26.1	4.9	0.0
Nacho Cheese Wedges, Schwartz*	1 Serving/10g	15	153	3.6	20.8	6.2	2.0
SPINACH,							
& Carrot Pilau, Waitrose*	1oz/28g	44	158	5.8	22.9	5.8	0.0
Baby, Average	1 Serving/90g	23	25	2.8	1.6	0.8	2.1
Boiled Or Steamed, Average	1oz/28g	6	21	2.6	0.9	0.8	2.1
Canned, Average	1oz/28g	6	23	3.1	1.5	0.5	3.0
Raw, Average	1oz/28g	7	24	2.9	1.3	0.8	2.1
SPIRA,							
Cadbury's*	2 Twists/40g	210	525	7.8	56.8	29.4	0.0
SPIRITS,							
37.5% Volume	1 Shot/25ml	48	207	0.0	0.0	0.0	0.0
40% Volume	1 Shot/25ml	51	222	0.0	0.0	0.0	0.0
SPLIT PEAS,							
Dried, Average	1oz/28g	89	319	22.1	57.4	1.7	3.2
Dried, Boiled, Average	1 Tbsp/35g	40	115	8.3	19.8	0.6	3.9
SPONGE FINGERS,							
Boudoir, Sainsbury's*	1 Biscuit/5g	20	396	8.1	82.8	3.6	0.4
Tesco*	1 Finger/5g	19	386	7.6	80.6	3.7	1.0
SPONGE PUDDING,							
Average	1oz/28g	95	340	5.8	45.3	16.3	1.1
Banoffee, Heinz*	¼ Can/78g	239	307	2.8	46.6	12.2	0.6
Banoffee, Morrisons*	1 Pudding/109.8g	316	287	3.0	59.6	2.9	0.7
Blackberry & Apple, Healthy Eating, Tesco*	1 Pot/102.5g	159	155	3.1	32.6	1.4	0.7
Blackcurrant, BGTY, Sainsbury's*	1 Serving/110g	277	252	2.8	50.0	4.5	1.4
Blackcurrant, Low Fat, Iceland*	1 Pudding/90g	159	177	2.2	39.5	1.1	1.6
Canned	1 Portion/75g	214	285	3.1	45.4	11.4	0.8
Cherry & Almond Flavour, Sainsbury's*	¼ Pudding/110g	334	304	3.5	40.3	14.3	0.7
Cherry & Chocolate, Eat Smart, Safeway*	1 Serving/86g	151	175	2.7	35.6	2.4	0.8
Chocolate & Chocolate Sauce, Healthy Eating, Tesco*	1 Pudding/90g	186	207	3.9	38.7	4.1	2.1
Chocolate & Sauce, Co-Op*	1 Pack/225g	608	270	5.0	34.0	13.0	0.6
Chocolate & Sauce, Iceland*	1 Serving/130.0g	407	313	3.8	35.4	17.4	1.9
Chocolate Chip, Healthy Eating, Tesco*	1 Serving/103g	197	191	4.4	34.7	3.8	0.9
Chocolate Custard, Muller*	1 Pot/175g	305	174	3.4	31.0	4.0	0.0

S

SPONGE PUDDING,

	Measure INFO/WEIGHT	per Measure KCAL	KCAL	PROT	CARB	FAT	FIBRE
Chocolate, Asda GFY*	1 Serving/105.8g	254	240	5.0	46.0	4.0	2.3
Chocolate, GFY, Asda*	1 Pudding/105g	252	240	5.0	46.0	4.0	2.3
Chocolate, Healthy Eating, Tesco*	1 Pudding/90g	184	204	4.2	45.4	0.6	1.3
Chocolate, Healthy Living, Tesco*	1 Pudding/102.5g	197	191	4.4	34.7	3.8	0.9
Chocolate, Heinz*	1 Serving/50g	150	300	4.8	45.0	11.2	1.2
Chocolate, Marks & Spencer*	¼ Pudding/131g	524	400	6.1	38.6	24.6	1.8
Chocolate, Somerfield*	¼ Pudding/100g	369	369	5.0	35.0	23.0	0.0
Chocolate, Tesco*	1 Pudding/110g	337	306	4.7	37.7	15.1	1.8
Chocolate, Weight Watchers*	1 Serving/102.5g	202	196	4.5	35.6	3.9	0.9
Chocolate, With Cadburys Caramel Sticky Sauce, Heinz*	1 Serving/200g	762	381	3.5	52.3	16.9	0.6
Circus, & Custard, Weight Watchers*	1 Serving/140g	239	171	4.2	32.1	2.9	0.9
Citrus, BGTY, Sainsbury's*	1 Pudding/110g	230	209	3.5	39.7	4.0	0.7
Double Chocolate, BGTY, Sainsbury's*	1 Pot/110g	293	266	4.3	51.5	4.7	0.6
Fruit, Co-Op*	1 Can/300g	1110	370	3.0	53.0	16.0	2.0
Fruited With Brandy Sauce, Sainsbury's*	1 Pudding/125g	261	209	3.6	33.6	6.7	0.8
Fruits Of The Forest, Asda*	1 Pudding/115g	323	281	2.8	59.0	3.8	1.3
Ginger, Asda*	Per ½ Pudding/153g	614	402	3.1	75.0	10.0	3.2
Ginger, With Plum Sauce, Waitrose*	1 Pudding/120g	424	353	3.1	51.7	14.9	0.7
Golden Syrup, Co-Op*	1 Can/300g	945	315	2.0	47.0	13.0	0.6
Jam & Custard, Co-Op*	1 Pack/244g	598	245	3.0	37.0	9.0	0.3
Jam & Custard, Somerfield*	¼ Pudding/62g	143	231	3.0	38.0	8.0	0.0
Jam Custard, Muller*	1 Pot/175g	291	166	2.7	30.1	3.9	0.0
Jam, Marks & Spencer*	1oz/28g	87	311	3.6	51.5	10.1	1.6
Jam, Safeway*	1 Serving/110g	396	360	3.6	55.6	13.7	2.3
Jam, Tesco*	1 Pudding/110g	367	334	3.3	53.3	11.9	0.5
Lemon Curd, Heinz*	¼ Can/78g	236	302	2.6	46.7	11.7	0.6
Lemon, COU, Marks & Spencer*	1 Pudding/100g	157	157	2.0	32.1	2.3	1.9
Lemon, Healthy Eating, Tesco*	1 Pudding/102g	195	191	3.7	40.1	2.0	0.5
Lemon, Marks & Spencer*	1 Pudding/105g	326	310	4.3	39.4	15.2	2.3
Lemon, Waitrose*	1 Serving/105g	212	202	3.4	41.7	2.4	1.4
Raspberry Jam, Asda*	½ Pudding/147g	481	327	3.1	54.0	11.0	4.1
Spotted Dick, Average	1oz/28g	92	327	4.2	42.7	16.7	1.0
St Clements, GFY, Asda*	1 Pudding/116g	332	286	2.6	60.0	3.9	1.2
Sticky Toffee Custard, Muller*	1 Pot/175g	306	175	2.8	29.1	5.3	0.0
Sticky Toffee, COU, Marks & Spencer*	1 Pack/150g	240	160	2.4	33.7	1.7	1.6
Sticky Toffee, Heinz*	¼ Can/77g	235	305	3.1	45.2	12.5	0.7
Sticky Toffee, Mini, Somerfield*	1 Pudding/110g	349	349	3.0	54.0	13.0	0.0
Sticky Toffee, SmartPrice, Asda*	½ Can/150g	452	301	2.0	44.0	13.0	0.0
Sticky Toffee, Somerfield*	1 Pudding/440g	1456	364	3.0	56.0	14.0	0.0
Strawberry Jam, Heinz*	¼ Can/82g	230	281	2.6	50.4	7.6	0.6
Strawberry, Co-Op*	1 Can/300g	960	320	2.0	48.0	13.0	0.8
Sultana, With Toffee Sauce, Healthy Eating, Tesco*	1 Serving/80g	223	279	3.3	60.3	2.8	1.0
Summer Fruits, BGTY, Sainsbury's*	1 Serving/110g	243	221	2.7	42.9	4.3	1.0
Syrup & Custard, Morrisons*	1 Serving/125g	290	232	3.4	39.1	6.9	0.8
Syrup, & Custard, Iceland*	1 Pudding/130g	410	315	3.6	38.8	16.2	0.4
Syrup, & Custard, Marks & Spencer*	1oz/28g	76	271	3.3	44.9	8.7	1.1
Syrup, BGTY, Sainsbury's*	1 Pudding/110g	338	307	2.8	64.6	4.1	0.4
Syrup, GFY, Asda*	1 Sponge/105g	256	244	3.0	50.0	3.6	0.6
Syrup, Marks & Spencer*	1oz/28g	104	370	4.1	65.9	10.2	1.1
Syrup, Sainsbury's*	¼ Pudding/110g	404	371	2.7	63.5	11.8	0.4
Syrup, Tesco*	1 Pudding/110g	375	341	3.2	55.8	11.7	0.4
Treacle, With Custard, Farmfoods*	1 Serving/145g	539	372	3.2	38.4	22.8	0.8
Very Fruity Cherry, Marks & Spencer*	1 Pot/110g	286	260	3.5	38.6	10.3	1.8

S

	Measure	per Measure	Nutrition Values per 100g / 100ml				
	INFO/WEIGHT	KCAL	KCAL	PROT	CARB	FAT	FIBRE
SPONGE PUDDING,							
With Dried Fruit	1oz/28g	93	331	5.4	48.1	14.3	1.2
With Jam or Treacle	1oz/28g	93	333	5.1	48.7	14.4	1.0
With Lyles Golden Syrup, Heinz*	½ Pudding/95.3g	367	386	3.1	53.3	15.1	0.5
SPRATS,							
Fried	1oz/28g	116	415	24.9	0.0	35.0	0.0
Raw	1oz/28g	48	172	18.3	0.0	11.0	0.0
SPREAD,							
63% Fat, Benecol*	1 Serving/12g	69	573	0.6	1.0	63.0	0.0
Beef, Classic, Shippam*	1 Pot/75g	133	177	15.5	2.2	11.8	0.0
Blackcurrant, Weight Watchers*	1 Tsp/5.7g	6	106	0.2	26.3	0.0	0.9
Butter & Olive, Olivio, Bertolli*	Thin Spread/7g	38	536	0.2	1.0	59.0	0.0
Butterlicious, Sainsbury's*	Thin Spread/7g	44	628	0.6	1.1	69.0	0.1
Buttery Gold, Somerfield*	1 Tbsp/15g	94	627	0.5	1.0	69.0	0.0
Buttery Taste, Benecol*	1 Tsp/7g	40	573	0.6	1.0	63.0	0.0
Chicken, Classic, Shippam*	1 Serving/35g	64	182	15.5	1.8	12.5	0.0
Chocolate Hazelnut, Tesco*	1 Tsp/10g	54	542	7.0	50.8	34.5	3.7
Crab, Classic, Shippam*	1 Jar/35g	48	138	14.1	6.0	6.4	0.0
Diet, Delight*	1oz/28g	64	228	3.6	1.6	23.0	0.0
Diet, Flora*	1 Tbsp/10g	23	227	3.5	1.6	23.0	0.0
Fat, Carapelli, St Ivel*	Thin Spread/7g	38	537	0.6	0.8	59.0	0.0
Flora Buttery, Flora*	Thin Spread/7g	45	637	1.1	0.5	70.0	0.0
Flora Light, Flora*	1 Serving/10g	37	366	0.1	6.0	38.0	0.0
Flora Original, Flora*	1 Serving/10g	53	531	0.1	0.1	59.0	0.0
Flora Pro-Activ, Flora*	1 Serving/10g	33	328	0.1	3.2	35.0	0.3
Flora, Low Salt, Flora*	1oz/28g	176	630	0.1	0.1	70.0	0.0
From Soya, Kallo*	1 Tsp/7g	27	380	7.0	6.0	37.0	0.0
Gold, Low Fat, St Ivel*	Thin Spread/7g	26	365	2.1	2.9	38.0	0.0
Gold, Lowest, Low Fat, St Ivel*	Thin Spread/7g	18	259	0.7	3.3	27.0	0.0
Gold, Semi Skimmed, St Ivel*	1 Serving/5g	18	359	0.9	3.3	38.0	0.0
Gold, Unsalted, Low Fat, St Ivel*	Thin Spread/7g	25	360	0.7	3.9	38.0	0.0
Golden, Light, Healthy Eating, Tesco*	1 Serving/10g	35	354	1.5	1.5	38.0	0.0
Hazelnut & Chocolate, Organic, Green & Black's*	1 Serving/28g	155	553	5.9	53.0	35.0	0.0
Light, Benecol*	2 Tsp/12g	38	318	2.8	0.2	34.0	0.0
Light, Olivio*	Thin Soread/7g	34	486	0.0	0.0	55.0	0.0
Low Fat 32%, Benecol*	1 Serving/12g	36	300	2.8	0.2	32.0	0.0
Low Fat, Better By Far, Morrisons*	1 Serving/10g	63	630	0.0	1.0	69.0	0.0
Low-Fat	Thin Spread/7g	27	390	5.8	0.5	40.5	0.0
Morning Gold, Low Fat, Morrisons*	1 Tbsp/15g	56	372	7.5	0.0	38.0	0.0
Olive Gold, Reduced Fat, Co-Op*	1oz/28g	150	535	0.2	1.0	59.0	0.0
Olive Gold, With Olive Oil, Low Fat, Asda*	1 Serving/10g	54	537	0.2	1.2	59.0	0.0
Olive Light, Low Fat, BGTY, Sainsbury's*	Thin Spread/ 7g	25	356	2.0	1.5	38.0	0.0
Olive Light, Low Fat, Tesco*	1 Serving/15g	52	348	1.5	0.0	38.0	0.0
Olive Light, Safeway*	1 Tsp/10g	35	346	1.0	0.0	38.0	0.0
Olive Oil, 55% Reduced Fat, Benecol*	Thin Spread/7g	35	498	0.3	0.5	55.0	0.0
Olive Oil, 59% Reduced Fat, Safeway*	Thin Spread/7g	37	532	0.1	0.1	59.0	0.0
Olive Oil, 59% Vegetable Fat, Olivio*	Thin Spread/7g	38	536	0.2	1.0	59.0	0.0
Olive, BGTY, Sainsbury's*	1 Tsp/14g	50	356	2.0	1.5	38.0	0.0
Olive, Marks & Spencer*	Thin Soread/7g	38	536	0.2	1.2	59.0	0.0
Olive, Reduced Fat, Asda*	Thin Spread/7g	38	537	0.2	1.2	59.0	0.0
Olive, Reduced Fat, Morrisons*	Thin Spread/7g	38	537	0.9	0.0	59.3	0.3
Olive, Reduced Fat, Organic, Sainsbury's*	Thin Spread/7g	37	531	0.0	0.0	59.0	0.0
Olive, Reduced Fat, Sainsbury's*	1 Serving/10g	54	536	0.1	1.2	59.0	0.0
Olive, Tesco*	1 Serving/28g	150	537	0.2	1.2	59.0	0.0

S

	Measure	per Measure	Nutrition Values per 100g / 100ml				
	INFO/WEIGHT	KCAL	KCAL	PROT	CARB	FAT	FIBRE
SPREAD,							
Olivio, Van Den Bergh Foods Ltd*	Thin Spread/7g	38	536	0.2	1.0	59.0	0.0
Olivite, Low Fat, Weight Watchers*	Thin Spread/7g	25	351	0.0	0.2	38.9	0.0
Organic, Dairy Free, Marks & Spencer*	1 Serving/5g	27	531	0.0	0.0	59.0	0.0
Pure Gold, GFY, Asda*	1 Serving/10g	35	353	1.7	1.0	38.0	0.0
Pure Gold, Light, 65% Less Fat, Asda*	1 Serving/10g	24	239	2.5	1.0	25.0	0.0
Salmon, Classic, Shippams*	1 Serving/35g	60	172	14.8	4.9	10.4	0.0
Soft, Dairy Free, Free From, Sainsbury's*	1 Serving/30g	89	296	2.5	4.0	30.0	0.0
Soft, Economy, Sainsbury's*	1oz/28g	126	450	0.2	1.0	50.0	0.0
Soft, Reduced Fat, SmartPrice, Asda*	1 Serving/7g	32	455	0.2	1.0	50.0	0.0
Sunflower, Asda*	1 Serving/10g	64	635	0.2	1.0	70.0	0.0
Sunflower, Co-Op*	Thin Spread/7g	44	635	0.2	1.0	70.0	0.0
Sunflower, Light, 38% Less Fat, Asda*	Thin Spread/7g	24	342	0.0	0.0	38.0	0.0
Sunflower, Light, BGTY, Sainsbury's*	1 Serving/10g	35	352	1.0	1.5	38.0	0.0
Sunflower, Light, Better For You, Morrisons*	1 Tsp/5g	17	342	0.0	0.0	38.0	0.0
Sunflower, Light, GFY, Asda*	1 Serving/10g	35	351	0.0	0.0	39.0	0.0
Sunflower, Light, Healthy Eating, Tesco*	1 Serving/6g	21	347	0.3	1.0	38.0	0.0
Sunflower, Light, Summerlite, Aldi*	1 Serving/10g	34	344	0.2	0.3	38.0	0.0
Sunflower, Light, Tesco*	Thin Spread/7g	24	348	1.4	0.0	38.0	0.0
Sunflower, Low Fat, Good Intentions, Somerfield*	1 Serving/10g	35	347	0.0	0.0	38.6	0.0
Sunflower, Low Fat, Marks & Spencer*	1 Serving/14g	48	342	0.0	0.0	38.0	1.0
Sunflower, Low Fat, Somerfield*	1 Serving/10g	34	342	0.0	0.0	38.0	0.0
Sunflower, Marks & Spencer*	Thin Spread/7g	44	635	0.2	1.0	70.0	0.0
Sunflower, Probiotic, Tesco*	1 Serving/15g	52	347	0.2	1.0	38.0	0.0
Sunflower, Reduced Fat, Asda*	Thin Spread/7g	37	531	0.2	1.0	58.5	0.0
Sunflower, Reduced Fat, Suma*	1 Serving/25g	134	537	0.0	0.4	59.5	0.0
Sunflower, Sainsbury's*	Thin Spread/7g	44	631	0.2	0.1	70.0	0.1
Sunflower, Substitute, Low Fat, Tesco*	1 Tsp/10g	11	109	2.0	14.0	5.0	10.0
Sunflower, Tesco*	1 Serving/15g	95	631	0.0	0.2	70.0	0.0
Sunflower, Value, Tesco*	Thin Spread/7g	31	439	0.1	0.4	48.6	0.0
Tuna & Mayonnaise, Shippam's*	1 Pot/75g	189	252	18.3	3.1	18.5	0.0
Vegetable, Dairy Free, Free From, Sainsbury's*	1 Serving/10g	63	630	0.0	0.0	70.0	3.0
Vegetable, Soft, Tesco*	1 Tbsp/15g	99	661	0.1	1.0	73.0	0.0
Vitalite, Lite, St Ivel*	Thin Spread/7g	24	348	1.5	0.0	38.0	0.0
Vitalite, St Ivel*	Thin Spread/7g	40	578	0.4	1.2	63.0	0.0
With Garlic & Herb, Soft, Free From, Sainsbury's*	1 Serving/30g	91	302	2.5	5.5	30.0	0.1
With Pure Olive Oil, Bertolli*	1 Serving/10g	54	536	0.2	1.0	59.0	0.0
With Soya, Dairy Free, Pure*	1 Serving/10g	53	531	0.0	0.0	59.0	0.0
SPRING GREENS,							
Boiled, Average	1oz/28g	6	20	1.9	1.6	0.7	2.6
Raw	1oz/28g	9	33	3.0	3.1	1.0	3.4
SPRING ONIONS,							
Bulbs Only, Raw	1oz/28g	10	35	0.9	8.5	0.0	1.7
Raw, Average	1oz/28g	7	24	2.0	3.0	0.5	1.5
SPRING ROLLS,							
Cantonese Chicken & Chilli, Sainsbury's*	1 Roll/51g	85	166	9.7	19.4	5.5	0.6
Char Sui Pork & Bacon, Marks & Spencer*	1 Pack/220g	528	240	4.8	33.9	9.4	0.6
Chicken & Chilli, Sainsbury's*	1 Roll/50g	93	185	9.6	15.6	9.3	2.8
Chicken, Asda*	1 Roll/58g	115	199	4.6	25.0	9.0	3.4
Chicken, Oriental, Asda*	1 Roll/59.6g	107	178	3.7	25.0	7.0	0.4
Chicken, Safeway*	1 Roll/50g	125	250	10.0	30.4	9.2	2.0
Chicken, Tesco*	1 Roll/50g	116	231	8.1	24.5	11.2	1.5
Chinese Takeaway, Tesco*	1 Roll/50g	101	201	4.4	26.4	8.6	1.5
Co-Op*	1oz/28g	67	240	6.0	29.0	11.0	0.4

	Measure	per Measure	Nutrition Values per 100g / 100ml				
	INFO/WEIGHT	KCAL	KCAL	PROT	CARB	FAT	FIBRE
SPRING ROLLS,							
Dim Sum, Sainsbury's*	1 Spring Roll/12g	26	216	4.1	28.2	9.6	2.9
Duck With Sweet Chilli Sauce, Waitrose*	1 Roll/72g	66	92	5.1	14.0	1.9	0.9
Marks & Spencer*	1 Pack/180g	333	185	3.5	24.2	8.4	2.3
Mini, Asda*	1 Roll/20g	35	175	3.5	33.6	3.0	1.9
Mini, Safeway*	1 Serving/30g	63	210	4.0	30.3	8.0	1.9
Mini, Sainsbury's*	1 Roll/12g	27	221	4.2	28.7	9.9	1.6
Mini, Tesco*	1 Roll/18g	47	263	3.9	24.9	16.5	1.9
Prawn, Chinese, Sainsbury's*	1 Roll/30g	65	217	9.6	21.8	10.2	1.3
Prawn, Marks & Spencer*	1oz/28g	62	220	9.4	21.4	10.8	1.6
Prawn, Tesco*	3 Rolls/100g	211	211	8.7	22.8	9.4	1.4
Roast Duck, Marks & Spencer*	1 Spring Roll/31g	85	275	7.8	26.2	15.7	1.4
Thai Prawn, Waitrose*	1 Roll/50g	110	219	8.0	25.4	9.5	2.4
Vegetable, Asda*	1 Roll/62g	126	203	3.5	27.0	9.0	2.7
Vegetable, Chinese Takeaway, Sainsbury's*	1Roll/59g	100	170	4.0	24.4	6.3	2.8
Vegetable, Chinese, Sainsbury's*	1 Roll/26g	69	193	4.1	26.9	7.7	1.4
Vegetable, Cocktail, Tiger Tiger*	1 Roll/15g	38	254	6.4	26.7	13.4	2.0
Vegetable, Marks & Spencer*	1 Roll/29g	70	240	3.0	29.5	12.2	1.3
Vegetable, Mini, Nirvana, Aldi*	1 Roll/26g	54	208	3.5	25.1	10.4	1.7
Vegetable, Mini, Occasions, Sainsbury's*	1 Roll/24g	52	216	4.1	28.2	9.6	2.9
Vegetable, Mini, Oriental Selection, Waitrose*	1 Roll/18.2g	35	192	4.2	28.6	6.8	1.7
Vegetable, Mini, Party Food, Marks & Spencer*	1 Spring Roll/17g	35	205	3.5	26.3	9.7	2.0
Vegetable, Occasions, Sainsbury's*	1 Roll/25g	52	206	3.7	24.4	10.4	2.1
Vegetable, Oriental Style, Party, Tesco*	1 Spring Roll/20g	47	233	2.9	28.8	11.8	1.3
Vegetable, Safeway*	1 Serving/117g	242	207	3.5	27.1	9.4	2.7
Vegetable, Somerfield*	1 Roll/60g	107	179	3.8	26.1	6.6	1.6
Vegetable, Tempura, Marks & Spencer*	1 Pack/140g	280	200	2.8	27.9	8.6	1.8
Vegetable, Tesco*	1 Roll/60g	100	166	4.0	21.2	7.2	2.0
Vegetable, Waitrose*	1 Roll/57g	107	187	3.7	22.1	9.3	3.4
SQUARES,							
Marshmallow, Rice Krispies, Chewy, Kellogg's*	1 Med Bar/18g	74	410	3.0	78.0	10.0	1.0
Rice Krispies, Chocolate Caramel, Kellogg's*	1 Bar/21g	90	430	4.5	71.0	14.0	2.0
Rice Krispies, Chocolate, Kellogg's*	1 Bar/18g	74	410	4.0	75.0	11.0	1.5
SQUASH,							
Acorn, Baked	1oz/28g	16	56	1.1	12.6	0.1	3.2
Acorn, Raw	1oz/28g	11	40	0.8	9.0	0.1	2.3
Apple & Blackcurrant, No Added Sugar, Somerfield*	1fl oz/30ml	2	8	0.1	0.5	0.0	0.0
Apple & Blackcurrant, No Added Sugar, Tesco*	1 Serving/75ml	6	8	0.1	1.0	0.0	0.0
Apple & Blackcurrant, Special R, Diluted, Robinson's*	1fl oz/30ml	2	8	0.1	1.1	0.1	0.0
Apple & Strawberry High Juice, Sainsbury's*	1 Serving/250ml	83	33	0.1	8.2	0.1	0.1
Apple, Hi Juice, Tesco*	1fl oz/30ml	53	176	0.3	42.7	0.1	0.0
Blackcurrant, Cordial, Jucee, Diluted, Princes*	1fl oz/30ml	3	11	0.0	1.6	0.0	0.0
Blackcurrant, High Juice, Marks & Spencer*	1 Glass/250ml	50	20	0.1	5.2	0.0	0.1
Blackcurrant, Sainsbury's*	1 Serving/250ml	8	3	0.1	0.5	0.1	0.1
Butternut, Baked	1oz/28g	9	32	0.9	7.4	0.1	1.4
Butternut, Courgette & Mange Tout, Marks & Spencer*	1 Pack/80g	24	30	2.0	5.8	0.2	2.3
Butternut, Raw, Average	1oz/28g	11	38	1.1	8.3	0.1	1.6
Forest Fruits, High Juice, Undiluted, Robinson's*	1 Serving/25ml	52	206	0.2	50.0	0.1	0.0
Fruit & Barley Orange, Diluted, Robinson's*	1 Av Serving/50ml	8	16	0.3	2.6	0.0	0.0
Grape & Melon, High Juice, Undiluted, Robinson's*	1fl oz/30ml	68	225	0.0	53.0	0.1	0.0
Lemon, High Juice, Tesco*	1 Serving/80ml	141	176	0.3	43.6	0.1	0.0
Lemon, No Sugar, Asda*	1 Serving/200ml	5	3	0.1	0.3	0.1	0.1
Lemon, Whole, Low Sugar, Sainsbury's*	1 Glass/250ml	5	2	0.1	0.2	0.1	0.1
Lemon, Whole, Tesco*	1 Serving/75ml	6	8	0.3	0.4	0.0	0.0

S

	Measure INFO/WEIGHT	per Measure KCAL	Nutrition Values per 100g / 100ml				
			KCAL	PROT	CARB	FAT	FIBRE
SQUASH,							
Mixed Fruit, Low Sugar, Sainsbury's*	1 Glass/250ml	5	2	0.1	0.2	0.1	0.1
Mixed Fruit, Tesco*	1 Serving/75ml	13	17	0.0	3.5	0.0	0.0
Orange & Mango, Low Sugar, Sainsbury's*	1 Serving/250ml	5	2	0.1	0.2	0.1	0.1
Orange & Mango, Special R, Diluted, Robinson's	1 Serving/250ml	20	8	0.2	0.9	0.0	0.0
Orange & Pineapple, No Added Sugar, Asda*	1 Serving/55ml	5	9	0.2	0.9	0.0	0.1
Orange & Pineapple, Original, Diluted, Robinson's*	1 Serving/200ml	18	9	0.2	0.9	0.0	0.0
Orange & Pineapple, Original, Undiluted, Robinson's*	1 Serving/250ml	138	55	1.0	13.0	0.0	0.0
Orange, Barley, Diluted, Asda	1 Serving/250ml	8	3	0.0	0.4	0.0	0.0
Orange, Hi Juice, Tesco*	1 Serving/75ml	140	187	0.3	45.0	0.1	0.0
Orange, High Juice, Undiluted, Robinson's*	1 Serving/200ml	364	182	0.3	44.0	0.1	0.0
Orange, Kia Ora*	1fl oz/30ml	16	55	0.1	12.3	0.0	0.0
Orange, Lemon & Pineapple, Low Sugar, Sainsbury's*	1fl oz/30ml	0	1	0.1	0.1	0.1	0.1
Orange, Lemon & Pineapple, No Added Sugar, Tesco*	1oz/28g	3	9	0.2	0.8	0.0	0.0
Orange, No Added Sugar, Asda*	1fl oz/30ml	2	7	0.0	0.6	0.0	0.0
Orange, Original, Undiluted, Robinson's*	1fl oz/30ml	14	45	0.1	10.0	0.0	0.0
Orange, Sainsbury's*	1 Glass/250ml	8	3	0.1	0.5	0.1	0.1
Orange, Special R, Diluted, Robinson's*	1fl oz/30ml	2	8	0.2	0.7	0.1	0.0
Peach, High Juice, Undiluted, Robinson's*	1fl oz/30ml	54	181	0.5	43.0	0.1	0.0
Pink Grapefruit, Barley, Asda*	1 Serving/250ml	8	3	0.0	0.4	0.0	0.0
Pink Grapefruit, Fruit & Barley, Diluted, Robinson's*	1fl oz/30ml	5	15	0.3	2.1	0.0	0.0
Pink Grapefruit, High Juice, Low Sugar, Tesco*	1 Serving/75ml	12	16	0.2	3.7	0.1	0.0
Pink Grapefruit, High Juice, Sainsbury's*	1 Serving/250ml	103	41	0.1	9.9	0.1	0.1
Pink Grapefruit, High Juice, Undiluted, Robinson's*	1 Glass/250ml	455	182	0.2	43.3	0.1	0.0
Spaghetti, Baked	1oz/28g	6	23	0.7	4.3	0.3	2.1
Spaghetti, Raw	1oz/28g	7	26	0.6	4.6	0.6	2.3
Summer Fruits, High Juice, Undiluted, Robinson's*	1fl oz/30ml	61	203	0.1	49.0	0.1	0.0
Summer Fruits, No Added Sugar, Diluted, Robinson's*	1fl oz/30ml	4	14	0.2	2.3	0.0	0.0
Tropical Fruits, High Juice Sainsbury's*	1 Serving/250ml	95	38	0.1	9.3	0.1	0.1
Whole Orange, No Added Sugar, Tesco*	1fl oz/30ml	2	7	0.1	0.6	0.0	0.0
Whole Orange, Spar*	1 Serving/250ml	10	4	0.0	0.8	0.0	0.0
SQUID,							
Dried	1oz/28g	88	313	63.3	4.8	4.6	0.0
In Batter, Fried in Blended Oil	1oz/28g	55	195	11.5	15.7	10.0	0.5
Raw, Average	1oz/28g	23	81	15.4	1.2	1.7	0.0
STAR FRUIT,							
Average, Tesco*	1oz/28g	9	32	0.5	7.3	0.3	1.3
STARBAR,							
Cadbury's*	1 Bar/53g	286	540	9.1	55.0	31.6	0.0
STARBURST,							
Fruit Chews, Tropical, Mars*	1 Tube/45g	168	373	0.0	76.9	7.3	0.0
Joosters, Mars*	1 Pack/45g	160	356	0.0	88.8	0.1	0.0
Juicy Gums, Mars*	1 Pack/45g	139	309	5.9	71.0	4.1	0.0
Mars*	1 Pack/45g	185	411	0.3	85.3	7.6	0.0
STARS,							
Chargrilled Chicken & Herb, Shapers, Boots*	1 Pack/12.0g	46	382	6.4	83.0	2.7	3.3
Chicken Flavour, Healthy Eating, Tesco*	1 Serving/12g	43	357	5.1	81.0	1.4	3.4
Spicy, COU, Marks & Spencer*	1 Bag/20g	69	345	4.2	82.6	1.6	4.0
STEAK &,							
Vegetable Medley, Healthy Eating, Tesco*	1 Pack/400g	264	66	7.6	5.3	1.6	0.8
STEAK & KIDNEY PUDDING,							
Fray Bentos*	1 Tin/213g	477	224	7.8	19.8	12.6	0.0
Marks & Spencer*	1 Pudding/100g	215	215	10.5	18.1	11.3	1.0
Waitrose*	1 Pudding/223g	497	223	8.9	20.4	11.7	1.2

	Measure INFO/WEIGHT	per Measure KCAL	Nutrition Values per 100g / 100ml				
			KCAL	PROT	CARB	FAT	FIBRE
STEAK CHASSEUR,							
Healthy Eating, Tesco*	1 Pack/450g	347	77	10.0	5.3	1.8	0.5
STEAK PEPPERED,							
With Potato Gratin, Healthy Living, Tesco*	1 Pack/450g	459	102	9.8	9.7	2.7	1.0
STEAK STEWED,							
& Onions With Gravy, John West*	½ Can/205g	269	131	14.0	3.0	7.0	0.0
With Gravy, John West*	1oz/28g	37	131	16.5	5.0	5.0	0.0
With Rich Gravy, Extra Lean, Sainsbury's*	1 Sm Can/220g	249	113	20.3	1.6	2.8	1.6
STEAK WITH,							
Red Wine & Portobello Mushrooms, Marks & Spencer*	½ Pack/240g	240	100	14.0	2.4	4.1	0.9
STEAMED PUDDING,							
Apple With Wild Berry Sauce, BGTY, Sainsburys*	1 Pudding/110g	308	280	2.6	59.7	3.4	1.4
Chocolate Flavour, BGTY, Sainsbury's*	1 Serving/110g	300	273	3.3	58.4	2.5	1.3
Chocolate Fudge, Aunty's*	1 Pudding/110g	314	285	3.0	59.0	4.2	1.8
Chocolate, BGTY, Sainsbury's*	1 Pudding/110g	308	280	3.0	59.0	3.6	1.8
Golden Syrup, Aunty's*	1 Pudding/110g	366	333	2.6	69.0	5.0	2.3
Lemon, BGTY, Sainsbury's*	1 Pudding/110g	307	279	3.0	60.2	2.9	0.7
Toffee & Date, Aunty's*	1 Serving/110g	320	291	2.6	59.1	4.6	1.1
STEW,							
Beef & Dumplings, Asda*	1 Pack/400g	392	98	6.0	11.0	3.3	0.8
Beef & Dumplings, Bird's Eye*	1 Pack/320g	275	86	6.4	10.2	2.2	0.7
Beef & Dumplings, Countryside*	1 Pack/300g	246	82	8.1	7.3	2.3	0.5
Beef & Dumplings, Eat Smart, Safeway*	1 Pack/394g	335	85	8.1	6.8	2.5	1.1
Beef & Dumplings, Farmfoods*	1 Pack/300g	312	104	4.0	12.0	4.4	1.1
Beef & Dumplings, Frozen, Asda*	1 Pack/400g	392	98	6.0	11.0	3.3	0.8
Beef & Dumplings, Iceland*	1 Serving/400g	468	117	4.5	13.5	5.0	0.5
Beef & Dumplings, Morrisons*	1 Serving/300g	354	118	5.3	14.0	4.5	0.7
Beef & Dumplings, Plumrose*	½ Can/196g	143	73	6.1	9.0	2.0	0.0
Beef & Dumplings, Ready Meals, Waitrose*	1oz/28g	38	136	8.0	13.3	5.6	0.8
Beef & Dumplings, Traditional English Meals, Bird's Eye*	1 Pack/338g	355	105	6.7	11.5	3.6	0.0
Beef & Dumplings, Weight Watchers*	1 Pack/327g	262	80	5.2	10.0	2.1	0.8
Beef With Dumplings, COU, Marks & Spencer*	1 Pack/454g	431	95	8.9	9.1	2.6	0.8
Beef With Dumplings, Classic British, Sainsbury's*	1 Pack/450g	531	118	7.7	10.2	5.2	0.5
Beef With Dumplings, GFY, Asda*	1 Pack/400g	429	107	11.5	10.3	2.3	0.9
Beef With Dumplings, Morrisons*	1 Pack/700g	686	98	5.3	7.0	5.5	0.4
Beef With Dumplings, Sainsbury's*	1 Pack/450g	545	121	7.1	10.9	5.4	0.7
Beef With Dumplings, Tesco*	½ Pack/360g	641	178	5.7	14.0	12.1	0.8
Beef, Asda*	½ Can/196g	178	91	10.0	7.0	2.5	1.5
Beef, Meal for One, Marks & Spencer*	1 Pack/440g	350	80	7.0	8.7	1.9	2.0
Chicken & Dumplings, Bird's Eye*	1 Pack/320g	282	88	7.0	8.9	2.7	0.5
Chicken & Dumplings, Tesco*	1 Serving/300g	402	134	7.4	11.0	6.7	0.6
Chicken, Morrisons*	1 Pack/400g	492	123	17.6	8.9	1.9	0.5
Irish, Plumrose*	1 Can/392g	318	81	7.5	7.2	2.5	0.0
Irish, Sainsbury's*	1 Pack/450g	275	61	5.7	4.8	2.1	0.5
Irish, SmartPrice, Asda*	1 Can/392g	298	76	3.0	8.0	3.6	0.9
Irish, Tesco*	1 Can/400g	308	77	7.0	5.9	2.8	0.8
Lentil & Winter Vegetable, Organic, Pure & Pronto*	1 Pack/400g	364	91	3.6	14.0	2.4	4.0
Lentil & Winter Vegetable, Simply Organic*	1 Pack/400g	364	91	3.6	14.0	2.4	4.0
Mixed Vegetable Topped With Herb Dumplings, Tesco*	1 Pack/420g	508	121	1.9	14.5	6.2	1.3
Vegetable & Dumplings, Linda McCartney*	1 Pack/340g	384	113	2.5	13.7	1.8	0.5
STIR FRY,							
Baby Leaf, Marks & Spencer*	1 Serving/125g	31	25	1.7	4.6	0.3	1.9
Baby Vegetable & Pak Choi, Two Step, Tesco*	½ Pack/95g	29	31	2.1	4.0	0.8	2.3
Bean Sprout & Vegetable, Asda*	½ Pack/175g	63	36	1.8	4.7	1.1	2.3

S

	Measure INFO/WEIGHT	per Measure KCAL	Nutrition Values per 100g / 100ml				
			KCAL	PROT	CARB	FAT	FIBRE
STIR FRY,							
Bean Sprout & Vegetable, Tesco*	1 Serving/150g	47	31	2.1	4.8	0.4	1.9
Bean Sprout Mix, Safeway*	1 Serving/175g	123	70	2.5	4.6	4.6	1.9
Bean Sprout, Morrisons*	1 Serving/150g	47	31	2.0	4.8	0.4	1.8
Bean Sprout, Sainsbury's*	1 Pack/300g	144	48	1.9	5.1	2.8	1.5
Bean Sprouts & Vegetables, Asda*	½ Pack/173g	107	62	2.0	4.5	4.0	1.8
Bean Sprouts, Asda*	½ Pack/175g	56	32	2.9	4.0	0.5	1.5
Beef & Black Bean, Sizzling, Oriental Express*	1 Pack/400g	420	105	7.2	14.0	2.1	2.1
Beef, BGTY, Sainsbury's*	½ Pack/125g	156	125	22.0	0.1	4.1	0.0
Beef, Less Than 10% Fat, Asda*	1 Pack/227g	275	121	24.0	0.0	2.8	0.8
Beef, Less Than 3% Fat, BGTY, Sainsbury's*	½ Pack/125g	134	107	22.1	0.1	2.1	0.1
Cherry Tomato & Noodle, Waitrose*	1 Pack/400g	304	76	2.1	8.5	3.8	1.5
Chicken Chow Mein, Fresh, Heathly Living, Tesco*	1 Pack/400g	312	78	5.5	11.5	1.1	1.4
Chicken Chow Mein, Orient Express, Oriental Express*	1 Pack/400g	384	96	7.3	10.7	2.7	2.2
Chicken Noodle, GFY, Asda*	1 Pack/330g	403	122	7.0	16.0	3.3	2.4
Chicken, Safeway*	1 Serving/200g	204	102	22.0	0.0	1.6	0.0
Chinese Bean Sprout, Sainsbury's*	½ Pack/313g	150	48	1.9	5.1	2.8	1.5
Chinese Chicken, Iceland*	1 Pack/298g	262	88	6.2	12.7	1.4	2.9
Chinese Chicken, Sizzling, Oriental Express*	1 Pack/400g	400	100	6.6	13.8	2.0	1.7
Chinese Chop Suey Veg, Sharwood's*	1 Pack/310g	223	72	1.5	13.9	1.1	0.6
Chinese Exotic Vegetable, Sainsbury's*	1 Pack/350g	133	38	1.7	2.8	2.2	1.8
Chinese Mixed Vegetable, Sainsbury's*	1 Serving/150g	75	50	1.7	4.7	2.7	0.0
Chinese Mushroom, Sainsbury's*	1 Serving/175g	67	38	1.7	2.4	2.4	1.7
Chinese Noodles, Oriental Express*	1oz/28g	20	70	2.7	14.7	0.5	1.4
Chinese Prawn, Asda*	1 Serving/375g	345	92	3.6	18.0	0.6	1.8
Chinese Prawn, Farmfoods*	1oz/28g	31	110	4.1	20.3	1.4	2.7
Chinese Prawn, Iceland*	1 Pack/340g	235	69	3.1	11.1	1.3	2.1
Chinese Prawns, Sizzling, Oriental Express*	1 Pack/400g	384	96	3.9	14.7	2.4	1.6
Chinese Style Chicken, GFY, Asda*	1 Pack/338.3g	362	107	6.0	17.0	1.7	1.5
Chinese Style Prawn, GFY, Asda*	1 Pack/400g	324	81	3.6	13.0	1.6	1.6
Chinese Style Rice With Vegetables, Tesco*	1 Serving/550g	495	90	2.2	14.8	2.5	0.3
Chinese Style, Asda*	1oz/28g	19	68	1.7	4.1	5.0	0.0
Chinese Style, Co-Op*	1 Pack/300g	105	35	3.0	6.0	0.4	2.0
Chinese Style, Marks & Spencer*	1oz/28g	7	25	2.5	3.6	0.4	1.5
Chinese Style, Somerfield*	1 Serving/50g	27	54	1.9	6.3	2.3	0.7
Chinese Style, Tesco*	1 Pack/350g	140	40	2.5	6.6	0.4	1.4
Chinese Vegetable & Oyster Sauce, Asda*	1 Serving/150g	93	62	1.9	8.0	2.5	0.0
Chinese Vegetables, Oriental Express*	½ Pack/200g	44	22	1.4	3.7	0.2	2.2
Chinese Vegetables, Tesco*	1 Serving/175g	93	53	1.6	10.8	0.4	1.3
Chinese, Eastern Inspirations*	½ Pack/170g	49	29	2.7	3.5	0.5	1.8
Chinese, Family, Sainsbury's*	1 Serving/150g	60	40	2.3	3.3	2.0	3.6
Chow Mein, Safeway*	1 Pack/400g	536	134	3.8	15.2	6.4	1.9
Creamy Coconut & Lime, The Best, Safeway*	½ Pack/165g	231	140	3.4	14.4	7.2	2.1
Crunchy Vegetable, Tesco*	1 Serving/100g	31	31	2.1	4.0	0.8	2.3
Exotic, Asda*	1 Serving/250g	90	36	1.9	2.7	1.9	2.6
Exotic, Tesco*	1 Pack/191g	42	22	1.3	3.8	0.2	1.5
Family, Safeway*	1 Serving/150g	83	55	2.1	4.2	3.3	2.1
Family, Tesco*	1 Serving/150g	51	34	2.2	5.4	0.4	1.7
Green Vegetable, Marks & Spencer*	1 Pack/220g	165	75	3.1	2.5	5.9	2.2
Imperial Noodles, Fresh, Amoy*	1oz/28g	31	112	1.6	17.0	4.4	0.0
Mediterranean Style, Eastern Inspirations*	½ Pack/153g	41	27	1.6	4.0	0.4	2.2
Mediterranean Style, Waitrose*	1 Pack/305g	82	27	1.6	4.6	0.4	2.2
Mixed Pepper & Sweet Chilli Sauce, Asda*	1 Pack/300g	180	60	1.6	9.0	2.0	2.6
Mixed Pepper, Tesco*	½ Pack/170g	114	67	1.8	5.3	4.3	1.8

S

INFO/WEIGHT	Measure	per Measure KCAL	KCAL	PROT	CARB	FAT	FIBRE
			Nutrition Values per 100g / 100ml				
Mixed Vegetable, Safeway*	1 Serving/150g	105	70	2.1	6.2	3.6	2.5
Mixed Vegetables, Asda*	1oz/28g	7	26	1.1	3.1	1.0	2.6
Mixed Vegetables, Sainsbury's*	½ Pack/140g	70	50	1.7	7.7	2.7	3.0
Mushroom & Vegetables, Asda*	1oz/28g	19	68	2.2	3.8	4.9	0.0
Mushroom, 2 Step, Tesco*	½ Pack/180g	34	19	2.3	2.1	0.2	0.7
Mushroom, Safeway*	1 Pack/350g	210	60	2.3	4.2	3.6	2.1
Mushroom, Sainsbury's*	1 Serving/175g	67	38	1.7	4.0	2.4	1.7
Mushroom, Somerfield*	1 Serving/175g	89	51	2.2	3.0	3.4	1.0
Mushroom, Tesco*	1 Pack/360g	68	19	2.3	2.1	0.1	0.7
Mushroom, Tesco*	1 Pack/350g	102	29	2.4	4.0	0.4	1.7
Mushroom, Waitrose*	1oz/28g	8	28	1.8	4.9	0.3	1.8
Noodles & Bean Sprouts, Tesco*	1 Serving/125g	155	124	5.4	19.8	2.6	1.9
Orient Inspired, Marks & Spencer*	1 Serving/250g	50	20	1.6	3.4	0.3	1.6
Oriental Chinese, Waitrose*	1 Serving/150g	41	27	2.2	3.9	0.4	1.4
Oriental Leaf, Marks & Spencer*	½ Pack/125g	25	20	1.9	2.5	0.5	2.2
Oriental Style Pak Choi, Marks & Spencer*	1 Pack/220g	165	75	2.2	3.5	5.7	2.4
Oriental Style Vegetables, Sainsbury's*	1oz/28g	17	62	1.5	5.2	3.9	1.5
Oriental Vegetables, Frozen, Asda*	1 Serving/150g	116	77	2.1	7.0	4.5	1.7
Oriental, Marks & Spencer*	½ Pack/150g	45	30	3.1	2.5	0.6	1.8
Pineapple, Safeway*	1 Pack/300g	237	79	3.6	4.7	5.1	0.5
Plum Hoisin Noodle, Tesco*	1 Carton/400g	392	98	3.6	17.5	1.5	1.8
Prawns, Chinese Sizzling, Oriental Express*	1 Pack/400g	384	96	3.9	14.7	2.4	1.6
Singaporean Noodle, Sainsbury's*	½ Pack/160g	202	126	3.2	11.9	7.3	2.4
Spicy Oriental Vegetable, Sainsbury's*	½ Pack/175g	112	64	1.3	4.9	4.4	1.7
Spicy Thai Style Noodle, Tesco*	1 Pack/500g	335	67	2.6	8.4	2.6	1.3
Sweet & Sour Vegetable, Somerfield*	1 Pack/350g	249	71	2.0	14.0	1.0	0.0
Sweet & Sour, Marks & Spencer*	1oz/28g	19	68	1.1	15.2	0.3	0.5
Sweet & Sour, Tesco*	1 Pack/350g	161	46	1.8	9.1	0.3	1.3
Sweet Pepper, Marks & Spencer*	1 Pack/400g	160	40	2.3	3.5	1.8	0.6
Szechuan Spicy Oriental Vegetable, Sainsbury's*	1 Pack/350g	224	64	1.3	4.9	4.4	1.7
Tatsoi & Sugar Snap Pea, Marks & Spencer*	½ Pack/125g	25	20	2.0	3.0	0.3	1.9
Thai Style, Eastern Inspirations*	1 Pack/330g	92	28	2.9	3.2	0.5	1.3
Thai Style, Marks & Spencer*	1 Serving/150g	75	50	2.3	3.0	3.0	1.2
Thai Style, Tesco*	1 Pack/350g	322	92	3.8	8.4	4.8	1.8
Thai, Vegetable, Safeway*	1 Serving/300g	220	73	2.6	5.6	4.3	2.3
Turkey, Fresh, Good Intentions, Somerfield*	½ Pack/150g	246	164	31.0	0.0	4.5	0.0
Vegetable & Bean Sprout Mix, Safeway*	1 Serving/160g	96	60	2.3	4.6	3.4	2.3
Vegetable & Mushroom, Asda*	½ Pack/160g	59	37	2.4	3.4	1.5	3.4
Vegetable & Noodle, Asda*	1 Pack/330g	465	141	4.0	21.0	4.5	3.0
Vegetable & Noodle, Tesco*	1 Pack/300g	243	81	3.5	13.2	1.6	2.1
Vegetable & Sprouting Beans, Waitrose*	1 Pack/300g	213	71	4.8	10.4	1.1	2.7
Vegetable Mix, Fried in Vegetable Oil	1oz/28g	18	64	2.0	6.4	3.6	0.0
Vegetable Noodles, BGTY, Sainsbury's*	1 Pack/455g	391	86	3.2	14.0	2.0	1.4
Vegetable, Asda*	1 Pack/300g	132	44	1.6	4.2	2.3	3.1
Vegetable, Cantonese, Sainsbury's*	1 Serving/150g	90	60	2.8	4.2	3.5	2.7
Vegetable, Chinese Style, Asda*	1 Pack/300g	81	27	1.6	3.6	0.7	2.8
Vegetable, Crispy, Oriental Inspired, Marks & Spencer*	1 Pack/300g	81	27	3.1	2.5	0.6	1.8
Vegetable, Mixed, Sainsbury's*	1 Pack/600g	240	40	2.3	3.3	2.0	3.6
Vegetable, Premium, Sainsbury's*	½ Pack/150g	90	60	2.8	4.2	3.5	2.7
Vegetable, Safeway*	½ Pack/150g	68	45	1.1	3.2	3.1	1.6
Vegetable, Tesco*	1 Pack/300g	90	30	1.7	4.9	0.4	2.1
Vegetables & Bean Sprout, Marks & Spencer*	1 Pack/350g	105	30	1.8	4.6	0.4	2.0
Vegetables With Oyster Sauce, Asda*	1 Serving/150g	93	62	1.9	8.0	2.5	0.0

S

INFO/WEIGHT	Measure per Measure KCAL	Nutrition Values per 100g / 100ml				
		KCAL	PROT	CARB	FAT	FIBRE
STIR FRY,						
Vegetables, Amoy*	1 Can/250g	30	12	1.0	2.1	0.0	2.7
Vegetables, Asda*	1oz/28g	7	26	1.1	3.1	1.0	2.6
Vegetables, Cantonese Style, Tesco*	1 Serving/125g	40	32	2.0	4.1	0.9	1.4
Vegetables, Family Pack, Co-Op*	½ Pack/300g	90	30	2.0	5.0	0.4	5.0
Vegetables, Fresh, Asda*	½ Pack/150g	107	71	1.7	4.9	5.0	1.7
Vegetables, Somerfield*	1 Pack/300g	93	31	2.0	5.0	0.0	0.0
Vegetables, Tesco*	1oz/28g	8	27	1.7	4.4	0.3	1.9
STOCK,						
Chicken, Asda*	½ Pot/150g	26	17	1.8	0.7	0.9	0.2
Chicken, Concentrated, Marks & Spencer*	1 Serving/5g	16	315	25.6	12.2	18.1	0.8
Chicken, Fresh, Sainsbury's*	½ Pot/142ml	23	16	3.7	0.1	0.1	0.3
Chicken, Knorr*	1 Pack/150g	348	232	13.1	36.5	3.7	0.4
Chicken, Slowly Prepared, Sainsbury's*	1 Pot/300g	27	9	0.6	1.3	0.1	0.5
Fish, Fresh, Finest, Tesco*	1 Serving/100g	10	10	0.6	1.8	0.0	0.5
Fresh, Finest, Tesco*	1 Pot/300g	33	11	1.9	0.8	0.0	0.2
Vegetable, Campbell's*	1 Serving/250ml	38	15	0.3	2.0	0.7	0.0
Vegetable, Concentrated, Vecon*	1 Serving/5g	9	171	25.0	17.5	1.5	3.5
Vegetable, Knorr*	1 Serving/9g	18	199	8.5	39.9	0.6	0.9
Vegetable, Waitrose*	1 Serving/50g	3	6	0.4	1.2	0.0	0.0
STOCK CUBES,						
Beef, Dry, As Sold, Bovril*	1 Cube/5.9g	12	197	10.8	29.3	4.1	0.0
Beef, Dry, As Sold, Oxo*	1 Cube/5.8	15	265	17.3	38.4	4.7	1.5
Beef, Just Bouillon, Kallo*	1 Pack/500ml	32	6	0.4	0.5	0.3	0.0
Beef, Knorr*	1 Cube/10g	33	326	11.1	21.0	22.0	0.2
Beef, Organic, Kallo*	1 Cube/12g	25	208	16.7	16.7	8.3	0.0
Beef, SmartPrice, Asda*	1 Cube/11g	31	279	10.0	8.0	23.0	0.0
Beef, Toro*	1 Cube/60g	90	150	27.0	1.0	4.0	0.0
Beef, Value, Tesco*	1 Cube/10g	19	189	11.2	17.0	8.5	0.1
Chicken	1 Cube/6g	14	237	15.4	9.9	15.4	0.0
Chicken, Dry, As Sold, Oxo*	1 Cube/6g	15	243	15.6	36.6	3.4	1.4
Chicken, Just Bouillon, Kallo*	1 Cube/12g	30	247	11.8	26.1	10.6	1.0
Chicken, Knorr*	1 Cube/10g	30	301	10.1	23.6	18.5	0.2
Chicken, Organic, Knorr*	1 Cube/10g	7	70	1.0	4.0	5.0	1.0
Chicken, Sainsbury's*	1 Cube/200ml	16	8	0.3	1.4	0.1	0.1
Chinese, Dry, As Sold, Oxo*	1 Cube/6g	16	263	11.0	40.9	6.1	3.6
Fish, Knorr*	1 Cube/10g	32	321	18.9	15.9	20.2	0.7
Garlic, Dry, As Sold, Oxo*	1 Cube/6g	18	298	13.4	48.5	5.5	3.6
Ham, Knorr*	1 Cube/10g	31	313	11.8	24.4	18.7	0.0
Indian, Dry, As Sold, Oxo*	1 Cube/6g	17	291	11.5	43.9	7.7	6.7
Italian, Dry, As Sold, Oxo*	1 Cube/6g	19	309	11.9	48.9	7.3	4.6
Lamb, Knorr*	1 Cube/10g	30	301	14.7	12.9	21.2	0.2
Mexican, Dry, As Sold, Oxo*	1 Cube/6g	15	248	11.8	36.8	6.0	3.7
Pork, Knorr*	1 Cube/24g	8	34	1.2	1.8	2.5	0.0
Vegetable	1 Cube/7g	18	253	13.5	11.6	17.3	0.0
Vegetable Bouillon, Yeast Free, Marigold*	1 Serving/250ml	19	8	0.0	0.5	0.6	0.0
Vegetable, Dry, As Sold, Oxo*	1 Cube/6g	15	253	11.2	41.9	4.5	1.7
Vegetable, Knorr*	1 Pack/80g	246	308	11.9	21.7	19.3	1.3
Vegetable, Organic, Evernat*	1oz/28g	2	6	0.3	0.0	0.5	0.0
Vegetable, Premium, Made Up, Kallo*	1 Serving/125ml	7	6	0.4	0.4	0.3	0.1
Vegetable, Safeway*	1 Serving/500ml	18	4	0.2	0.3	0.2	0.0
Vegetable, Tesco*	½ Cube/4.8g	10	207	8.0	25.7	8.0	0.3
STRAWBERRIES,						
Fresh, Average	1oz/28g	8	28	0.8	6.0	0.1	0.9

	Measure INFO/WEIGHT	per Measure KCAL	Nutrition Values per 100g / 100ml				
			KCAL	PROT	CARB	FAT	FIBRE
STRAWBERRIES,							
In Fruit Juice, Average	1/3 Can/127g	58	46	0.5	11.0	0.0	1.0
In Light Syrup, Sainsbury's*	1oz/28g	17	62	0.4	15.0	0.1	1.0
In Raspberry Sauce, WTF, Sainsbury's*	1 Serving/170g	111	65	0.7	15.3	0.1	2.3
STRAWBERRY LACES,							
Co-Op*	1 Sweet/6g	21	345	7.0	79.0	0.0	1.0
Fizzy, Somerfield*	1 Pack/100g	380	380	3.0	86.0	2.0	0.0
Somerfield*	1 Pack/100g	374	374	3.0	86.0	0.0	0.0
STREUSEL,							
Baked Apple & Plum, Healthy Eating, Tesco*	1 Serving/120g	161	134	1.9	29.4	1.0	2.0
STROGANOFF,							
Beef, Asda*	1 Serving/120g	276	230	16.0	3.3	17.0	0.6
Beef, Finest, Tesco*	1 Pack/200g	200	100	13.4	3.9	3.4	
Beef, Rice Meal for One, COU, Marks & Spencer*	1 Pack/400g	440	110	9.1	13.6	2.1	1.2
Beef, Sainsbury's*	1 Can/200g	232	116	12.5	3.0	6.0	0.2
Beef, TTD, Sainsbury's*	1 Pack/300g	491	164	11.9	5.2	10.6	0.4
Beef, The Best, Safeway*	1 Serving/250g	400	160	19.6	2.2	7.8	0.8
Beef, With Long Grain & Wild Rice, Somerfield*	1 Pack/400g	485	121	7.3	13.8	4.1	1.6
Beef, With Mixed Rice, Tesco*	1 Pack/450g	558	124	7.5	15.2	3.7	1.5
Beef, With Rice, Eat Smart, Safeway*	1 Pack/385.7g	405	105	7.4	12.0	2.5	1.4
Beef, With Rice, Tesco*	1 Pack/475g	518	109	5.6	13.7	3.5	3.4
Chicken & Mushroom, COU, Marks & Spencer*	1 Serving/400g	360	90	8.6	9.0	2.0	1.0
Chicken, Healthy Living, Tesco*	1 Pack/450g	491	109	7.7	13.5	2.7	0.6
Mushroom With Rice, Eat Smart, Safeway*	1 Pack/400g	280	70	2.7	11.3	1.3	1.6
Mushroom With Rice, Healthy Eating, Tesco*	1 Pack/450g	396	88	3.8	13.3	2.2	1.2
Mushroom With Rice, Tesco*	1 Pack/450g	500	111	3.0	12.8	5.3	1.3
Mushroom, BGTY, Sainsbury's*	1 Pack/451g	392	87	3.2	17.4	0.5	0.5
Mushroom, GFY, Asda*	1 Pack/450g	339	75	2.9	12.4	1.6	0.7
Mushroom, With Rice, Eat Smart, Safeway*	1 Serving/400g	320	80	2.6	14.3	1.1	1.0
Pork With Rice, Healthy Eating, Tesco*	1 Pack/450g	482	107	7.0	15.8	1.8	0.5
STRUDEL,							
Apple, Co-Op*	1 Slice/100g	225	225	3.0	28.0	12.0	3.0
Apple, Safeway*	1/4 Strudel/150g	414	276	3.1	35.7	14.4	2.4
Apple, Sainsbury's*	1/6 Portion/90g	269	299	3.6	36.4	15.4	1.9
Apple, Tesco*	1 Serving/150g	432	288	3.3	36.4	14.4	2.8
Wooland Fruit, Sainsbury's*	1/6 Strudel/95.2g	276	290	3.7	34.0	15.5	2.0
STUFFING,							
Chestnut & Pork, Marks & Spencer*	1oz/28g	67	240	6.6	16.3	16.7	2.9
Olde English Chestnut, Sainsbury's*	1 Serving/110g	216	196	9.4	13.5	11.6	2.1
Parsley & Thyme, Co-Op*	1 Serving/28g	95	340	10.0	67.0	3.0	6.0
Parsley, Thyme & Lemon Stuffing, Paxo*	1 Serving/45g	68	150	4.3	28.4	2.1	2.4
Pork, Sage & Onion, Marks & Spencer*	1 Serving/85g	183	215	11.2	10.5	14.3	2.4
Sage & Onion, Somerfield*	1oz/28g	100	358	6.0	74.0	5.0	0.0
Sage and Onion, Made Up, Safeway*	1 Serving/60g	90	150	4.5	30.8	0.7	3.2
Sausage Meat, Balls, Aunt Bessie's*	1 Ball (Baked)/26g	56	214	7.5	29.6	7.3	2.4
Sausagemeat & Thyme, Celebrations, Paxo*	1 Serving/50g	80	160	6.3	25.8	3.5	4.0
STUFFING MIX,							
Apple & Herb, Special Recipe, Sainsbury's*	1 Serving/41g	68	165	3.8	32.4	2.2	2.2
Apple Mustard & Herb, Paxo*	1 Serving/50g	83	166	4.2	32.8	2.0	4.0
Apricot & Walnut, Celebration, Paxo*	1 Serving/50g	81	161	4.3	28.0	3.5	2.8
Chestnut & Cranberry, Celebration, Paxo*	1 Serving/25g	35	141	4.0	26.7	2.0	2.4
Chestnut, Morrisons*	1 Serving/20g	33	165	4.6	29.1	3.4	3.7
Date, Walnut & Stilton, Special Recipe, Sainsbury's*	1 Serving/25g	49	196	5.2	25.0	8.4	2.0
Parsley, Thyme & Lemon, Sainsbury's*	1 Pack/170g	240	141	4.2	28.2	1.3	1.3

S

	Measure	per Measure	Nutrition Values per 100g / 100ml				
	INFO/WEIGHT	KCAL	KCAL	PROT	CARB	FAT	FIBRE
STUFFING MIX,							
Sage & Onion, Asda*	1 Serving/27g	29	107	3.4	22.0	0.6	1.3
Sage & Onion, Balls, Aunt Bessie's*	1 Stuffing Ball/26g	56	214	7.5	29.6	7.3	2.4
Sage & Onion, Balls, Meat-Free, Aunt Bessie's*	1 Ball/28g	54	193	5.4	28.0	6.7	1.7
Sage & Onion, Made Up, Paxo*,	1 Serving/60g	74	123	3.6	23.0	1.8	1.7
Sage & Onion, SmartPrice, Asda*	¼ Pack/75g	262	349	11.0	68.0	3.7	4.7
Sage & Onion, Tesco*	1 Pack/85g	295	347	11.3	71.0	2.0	4.4
Sage, Red Onion & Lemon TTD, Sainsbury's*	1 Serving/50g	53	106	3.8	23.9	1.3	4.2
SUET,							
Beef, Tesco*	1 Serving/100g	854	854	0.6	6.2	91.9	0.1
Shredded Vegetable, Atora Light*	1oz/28g	197	704	3.8	28.5	63.9	1.2
Shredded, Original, Atora*	1oz/28g	232	828	1.6	9.4	87.1	0.4
Vegetable	1oz/28g	234	836	1.2	10.1	87.9	0.0
SUET PUDDING,							
Average	1oz/28g	94	335	4.4	40.5	18.3	0.9
SUGAR,							
Brown, Soft, Average	1 Tsp/4g	15	382	0.0	96.5	0.0	0.0
Caster, Average	1 Serving/100g	399	399	0.0	99.8	0.0	0.0
Dark Brown, Muscovado, Average	1 Tsp/7g	27	380	0.3	94.8	0.0	0.0
Dark Brown, Soft, Average	1 Tsp/5g	18	369	0.1	92.0	0.0	0.0
Demerara, Average	1 Tsp/5g	18	368	0.3	99.2	0.0	0.0
For Making Jam, Silver Spoon*	1oz/28g	111	398	0.0	99.5	0.0	0.0
Golden, Unrefined, Average	1 Tsp/4g	16	399	0.0	99.8	0.0	0.0
Granulated, Organic, Average	1 Tsp/4g	16	398	0.2	99.7	0.0	0.0
Icing, Average	1 Tsp/4g	16	395	0.0	102.2	0.0	0.0
Light Or Diet, Average	1oz/28g	110	394	0.0	98.5	0.0	0.0
White, Granulated, Average	1 Tsp/5g	20	397	0.0	100.7	0.0	0.0
SULTANAS,							
Average	1oz/28g	82	292	2.5	69.7	0.4	2.0
SUMMER FRUITS,							
Asda*	1 Serving/30g	8	28	0.9	6.0	0.0	2.5
Frozen, Safeway*	1oz/28g	8	30	1.0	5.4	0.2	2.8
Frozen, Sainsbury's*	1 Serving/80g	26	33	0.9	7.4	0.1	2.4
In Syrup, Sainsbury's*	1 Pudding/289g	188	65	0.5	15.6	0.1	1.2
Mix, Marks & Spencer*	1oz/28g	9	33	1.0	6.7	0.3	2.5
Mix, Sainsbury's*	1 Serving/80g	26	32	0.9	7.4	0.0	2.4
Shearway*	1oz/28g	10	34	0.9	6.9	0.1	0.0
SUNDAE,							
Banoffee, Healthy Living, Tesco*	1 Sundae/77.2g	122	158	2.6	31.6	2.7	0.7
Blackcurrant, Marks & Spencer*	1 Sundae/49g	196	400	4.5	51.7	19.5	1.9
Butter Toffee, Mini, Eat Smart, Safeway*	1 Pot/62.5g	101	160	2.9	32.5	1.8	3.7
Chocolate & Orange, Weight Watchers*	1 Pot/102g	137	134	1.2	25.2	2.2	0.2
Chocolate & Vanilla Ice Cream, Tesco*	1 Sundae/70.2g	139	199	2.8	27.5	8.6	0.5
Chocolate Brownie, Finest, Tesco*	1 Serving/215g	808	376	3.1	30.1	27.0	0.4
Chocolate Mint, COU, Marks & Spencer*	1 Pot/90g	108	120	5.4	17.8	2.6	0.5
Chocolate Nut	1 Portion/70g	195	278	3.0	34.2	15.3	0.1
Chocolate, Eat Smart, Safeway*	1 Serving/97g	150	155	3.5	29.0	2.7	4.3
Chocolate, Healthy Eating, Tesco*	1 Serving/130g	199	153	4.5	24.9	3.9	0.6
Chocolate, Individual, Marks & Spencer*	1oz/28g	69	247	4.1	28.5	12.9	0.6
Chocolate, Marks & Spencer*	1oz/28g	80	285	3.1	27.2	18.2	0.0
Galaxy Caramel, Eden Vale*	1 Serving/128g	300	234	4.8	26.5	12.4	0.7
Hot Caramel, McDonald's*	1 Sundae/189g	357	189	3.8	33.9	4.4	0.0
Hot Fudge, McDonald's*	1 Sundae/187g	352	188	4.5	30.0	5.7	0.0
Mango & Passionfruit, Tesco*	1 Pot/78g	112	143	1.1	32.7	0.8	0.4

S

	Measure INFO/WEIGHT	per Measure KCAL	Nutrition Values per 100g / 100ml				
			KCAL	PROT	CARB	FAT	FIBRE
SUNDAE,							
No Topping, McDonald's*	1 Sundae/149g	219	147	4.2	21.6	5.1	0.0
Peach & Apricot, Perfectly Balanced, Waitrose*	1 Pot/175ml	142	81	1.7	17.7	0.4	0.0
Raspberry, Eat Smart, Safeway*	1 Serving/97g	150	155	3.0	30.9	2.1	2.8
Raspberry, Perfectly Balanced, Waitrose*	1 Pot/175ml	151	86	1.7	18.9	0.6	0.0
Strawberry & Vanilla Ice Cream, Tesco*	1 Serving/68g	120	177	2.0	29.5	5.7	0.1
Strawberry & Vanilla, Weight Watchers*	1 Pot/105g	148	141	1.2	29.1	2.1	0.3
Strawberry, Co-Op*	1 Pot/155g	279	180	3.0	24.0	8.0	0.5
Strawberry, Marks & Spencer*	1 Sundae/45g	173	385	3.4	53.3	17.8	1.0
Strawberry, McDonald's*	1 Sundae/186g	296	159	3.4	27.5	4.1	0.0
Toffee, Asda*	1 Serving/120g	322	268	2.1	29.0	16.0	0.0
SUNFLOWER SEEDS,							
Average	1 Tbsp/10g	59	585	23.4	15.0	48.7	5.7
SUNNY DELIGHT*,							
Apple & Kiwi Kick	1 Glass/200ml	15	7	0.2	1.3	0.2	0.2
Light	1 Glass/200ml	16	8	0.1	1.0	0.2	0.0
Original	1 Glass/200ml	88	44	0.1	10.0	0.2	0.0
Tropical Tornade	1fl oz/30ml	3	10	0.1	1.5	0.2	0.1
SUSHI,							
Advent, Medium, Tesco*	1 Serving/210g	307	146	3.8	25.7	3.1	0.9
Aya Set, Waitrose*	1 Pack/110g	200	182	5.4	31.7	3.9	1.5
California Roll Box, Marks & Spencer*	1 Box/230g	391	170	7.0	22.0	5.2	1.1
California Rolls, Waitrose*	1 Pack/120g	196	163	4.4	26.8	4.4	1.5
Californian, Yakatori, Marks & Spencer*	1 Serving/200g	340	170	6.4	25.0	4.7	1.0
Deluxe, Pret A Manger*	1 Pack/350g	522	149	5.8	26.2	2.4	0.9
Fish Nigiri, Adventurous, Tesco*	1 Med Pack/200g	270	135	7.1	21.7	2.2	0.5
Fish Selection Box, Marks & Spencer*	1 Serving/220g	396	180	6.6	27.1	4.5	0.9
Fish Selection, Marks & Spencer*	1 Serving/210g	315	150	6.5	25.8	2.3	1.0
Fish, Large Box, Tesco*	1 Box/290g	423	146	4.9	25.8	2.6	0.8
Fish, Medium Box, Tesco*	1 Box/195g	281	144	5.1	25.7	2.3	0.7
Fish, Small, Tesco*	1 Serving/105g	148	141	5.9	23.9	2.4	0.6
Fish, Tesco*	1 Pack/105g	155	148	6.2	25.1	2.5	0.6
GFY, Asda*	1 Pack/220g	352	160	4.9	32.0	1.4	0.0
Hana Set, Waitrose*	1 Serving/175g	324	185	5.4	35.7	2.3	1.4
Komachi Set, Waitrose*	1 Box/235g	425	181	6.1	31.3	3.5	1.4
Large Box, Food To Go, Marks & Spencer*	1oz/28g	41	145	5.1	27.4	1.5	0.5
Large, Boots*	1 Pack/324g	480	148	5.0	28.0	1.8	0.7
Maki Selection, Shapers, Boots*	1 Pack/158g	225	142	3.5	29.0	1.3	1.1
Medium Box, Marks & Spencer*	1 Serving/215g	366	170	9.7	24.3	2.8	0.9
Medium Selection Pack, Tesco*	1 Pack/195g	312	160	5.6	27.9	2.9	1.4
Mini Selection, Improved, Shapers, Boots*	1 Pack/104.2g	173	166	5.8	26.0	4.4	0.9
Mini, Boots*	1 Serving/182g	269	148	4.2	29.0	1.7	1.2
Mixed Box, Somerfield*	1 Pack/220g	339	154	4.6	31.4	1.1	0.0
Nigiri, Marks & Spencer*	1 Serving/190g	285	150	5.2	25.7	2.5	0.9
Oriental Fish Box, Marks & Spencer*	1 Box/205g	318	155	6.1	23.3	4.1	0.9
Prawn & Salmon Selection, Marks & Spencer*	1 Serving/175g	255	146	5.5	27.4	1.7	0.6
Prawn Feast, Marks & Spencer*	1 Box/219g	350	160	5.7	25.8	3.7	1.1
Roll Selection, Tesco*	1 Pack/140g	221	158	4.6	30.5	1.9	1.9
Salmon & Roll Set, Small. Sainsbury's*	1 Serving/101g	167	165	4.9	30.4	2.6	0.8
Salmon Feast Box, Marks & Spencer*	1 Pack/200g	330	165	5.6	27.0	2.9	1.0
Selection, Boots*	1 Pack/268g	434	162	5.5	27.0	3.6	1.6
Selection, Californian, Marks & Spencer*	1 Pack/191.2g	325	170	4.6	27.9	4.6	1.2
Selection, Marks & Spencer*	1 Pack/210g	756	360	15.7	62.0	5.5	2.3
Selection, Shapers, Boots*	1 Pack/189g	293	155	5.1	28.0	2.5	2.2

S

	Measure INFO/WEIGHT	per Measure KCAL	Nutrition Values per 100g / 100ml				
			KCAL	PROT	CARB	FAT	FIBRE
SUSHI,							
Taiko Hagi Set, Waitrose*	1 Box/370g	688	186	7.1	33.6	2.6	1.1
Taiko Vegetable Set, Waitrose*	1 Serving/135g	254	188	4.4	37.1	2.4	1.4
Tesco*	1 Pack/195g	285	146	5.1	25.9	2.3	0.7
Tokyo Set, Marks & Spencer*	1 Pack/150g	240	160	7.3	25.3	3.1	0.6
Trial Pack, Asda*	1 Pack/115g	186	162	4.1	31.0	2.4	0.0
Tuna, To Snack Selection, Food To Go, Marks & Spencer*	1 Serving/150g	225	150	5.2	26.4	2.6	2.3
Vegetarian, Marks & Spencer*	1 Pack/223g	290	130	4.1	25.5	1.5	1.3
Vegetarian, Sainsbury's*	1 Serving/151.0g	222	147	3.2	29.0	2.0	0.9
Vegetarian, Tesco*	1 Pack/132g	185	140	3.1	27.2	2.1	0.9
Yo!, Bento Box, Sainsbury's*	1 Pack/208g	530	255	8.4	48.7	3.0	0.9
Yo!, Salmon Lunch Set, Sainsbury's*	1 Pack/150g	242	161	5.9	28.1	2.8	0.8
SWEDE,							
Boiled, Average	1oz/28g	3	11	0.3	2.3	0.1	0.7
Mash, COU, Marks & Spencer*	1oz/28g	15	55	1.1	9.5	1.2	2.1
Raw, Average	1oz/28g	6	21	0.8	4.4	0.3	1.9
SWEET & SOUR,							
Beef, Feeling Great, Findus*	1 Pack/350g	385	110	4.0	19.0	2.0	1.5
Beef, Feeling Great, New, Findus*	1 Pack/350g	420	120	4.5	20.0	2.5	1.3
Chicken & Egg Fried Rice, BGTY, Sainsbury's*	1 Pack/450g	513	114	5.5	19.5	1.6	0.7
Chicken & Fried Rice, GFY, Asda*	1 Pack/400g	580	145	6.0	23.0	3.2	1.1
Chicken & Noodles, BGTY, Sainsbury's*	1 Pack/400g	356	89	7.5	13.3	0.6	0.7
Chicken & Noodles, Chinese Takeaway, Tesco*	1 Pack/350g	350	100	5.7	18.8	0.2	0.2
Chicken & Rice, Mega, Value, Tesco*	1 Pack/500g	675	135	4.4	25.0	1.9	1.9
Chicken & Rice, Morrisons*	1 Pack/400g	452	113	3.6	18.8	2.6	0.8
Chicken Cantonese, Sainsbury's*	1 Pack/350g	368	105	10.4	14.6	0.6	0.6
Chicken In Crispy Batter, Cantonese, Sainsbury's*	1 Pack/300g	546	182	9.0	21.4	6.7	1.1
Chicken With Egg Fried Rice, BGTY, Sainsbury's*	1 Pack/400g	456	114	5.5	19.5	1.6	1.0
Chicken With Egg Fried Rice, Healthy Eating, Tesco*	1 Pack/450g	468	104	7.4	15.5	1.4	1.2
Chicken With Egg Fried Rice, Somerfield*	1 Pack/400g	428	107	8.5	16.7	0.7	2.0
Chicken With Noodles, Healthy Eating, Tesco*	1 Pack/350g	277	79	8.3	10.4	0.4	0.8
Chicken With Noodles, Steamed, Healthy Eating, Tesco*	1 Pack/370g	289	78	8.3	10.8	0.2	0.6
Chicken With Noodles, Tesco*	1 Pack/350g	441	126	5.7	24.4	0.6	1.4
Chicken With Rice, Asda*	1 Pack/400g	440	110	4.7	22.0	0.3	0.6
Chicken With Rice, BGTY, Sainsbury's*	1 Pack/450g	675	150	8.1	21.1	3.7	0.9
Chicken With Rice, Eat Smart, Safeway*	1 Pack/390g	312	80	5.4	12.2	0.9	1.2
Chicken With Rice, Farmfoods*	1 Pack/300g	324	108	5.9	19.2	0.9	0.7
Chicken With Rice, Healthy Eating, Tesco*	1 Pack/450g	450	100	8.0	16.3	0.3	0.8
Chicken With Rice, Iceland*	1 Pack/400g	516	129	5.4	25.7	0.5	0.4
Chicken With Rice, Kwik Save*	1 Pack/500g	520	104	4.0	21.9	0.3	0.7
Chicken With Rice, Nisa, Heritage, Nisa Heritage*	1 Pack/600g	606	101	6.0	17.4	0.8	0.4
Chicken With Rice, Oriental Express*	1 Pack/340g	350	103	4.4	21.3	0.6	0.7
Chicken With Vegetable Rice, COU, Marks & Spencer*	1 Pack/400g	320	80	6.7	10.7	1.2	1.0
Chicken, Asda*	1oz/28g	28	99	9.2	14.5	0.5	1.4
Chicken, Battered, Chinese, Sainsbury's*	1 Pack/350g	532	152	9.1	22.5	2.9	0.7
Chicken, Battered, Healthy Living, Tesco*	1 Pack/350g	434	124	7.6	18.4	2.2	0.5
Chicken, COU, Marks & Spencer*	1oz/28g	34	120	6.9	20.5	0.9	0.9
Chicken, Cantonese, Sainsbury's*	½ Pack/200g	176	88	8.2	11.8	0.9	0.8
Chicken, Chinese Takeaway, Sainsbury's*	1 Pack/264g	515	195	13.1	21.3	6.4	1.0
Chicken, Crispy, Iceland*	1 Serving/125g	221	177	18.3	14.2	5.2	1.2
Chicken, GFY, Asda*	1 Serving/165g	213	129	16.0	15.0	0.5	1.6
Chicken, Good Choice, Iceland*	1 Pack/400g	488	122	4.5	25.6	0.2	0.5
Chicken, Healthy Choice, Safeway*	1 Pack/400g	580	145	6.5	25.6	1.8	1.4
Chicken, Low Fat, Iceland*	1 Pack/400g	444	111	8.1	15.7	1.7	1.1

S

	Measure INFO/WEIGHT	per Measure KCAL	Nutrition Values per 100g / 100ml				
			KCAL	PROT	CARB	FAT	FIBRE
SWEET & SOUR,							
Chicken, Marks & Spencer*	1 Pack/300g	465	155	6.6	24.4	3.6	0.8
Chicken, Somerfield*	1 Serving/175g	156	89	9.5	12.6	0.1	0.6
Chicken, Take It Away, Marks & Spencer*	1 Pack/200g	200	100	9.4	13.2	0.8	1.2
Chicken, Tesco*	1 Pack/350g	319	91	6.4	12.9	1.5	4.0
Chicken, Tinned, Marks & Spencer*	1 Serving/481g	553	115	11.4	7.8	4.2	1.9
Chicken, Weight Watchers*	1 Pack/320g	304	95	5.2	17.4	0.4	0.3
Pork	1oz/28g	48	172	12.7	11.3	8.8	0.6
Pork, Battered, Sainsbury's*	½ Pack/175g	306	175	7.3	25.1	5.0	0.6
Pork, Cantonese, & Egg Fried Rice, Farmfoods*	1 Pack/327g	520	159	4.8	22.0	5.8	0.1
Pork, In Crispy Batter, Sainsbury's*	½ Pack/150g	293	195	10.0	20.0	8.3	1.1
Prawns, Cantonese, Microwave Easy Steam, Sainsbury's*	1 Pack/400g	424	106	4.3	16.8	2.4	3.0
Quick Snack, Rice, Sainsbury's*	1 Serving/237g	230	97	2.5	20.5	0.5	0.0
Roasted Vegetables, Cantonese, Sainsbury's*	1 Pack/348g	327	94	1.1	19.6	1.2	0.9
Vegetables With Rice, Waitrose*	1 Pack/400g	384	96	1.9	19.5	1.1	1.1
SWEET POTATO,							
Baked	1oz/28g	32	115	1.6	27.9	0.4	3.3
Boiled in Salted Water	1oz/28g	24	84	1.1	20.5	0.3	2.3
Raw	1oz/28g	24	87	1.2	21.3	0.3	2.4
Steamed	1oz/28g	24	84	1.1	20.4	0.3	2.3
SWEETBREAD,							
Lamb, Fried	1oz/28g	61	217	28.7	0.0	11.4	0.0
Lamb, Raw	1oz/28g	37	131	15.3	0.0	7.8	0.0
SWEETCORN,							
& Petit Pois, Marks & Spencer*	1oz/28g	20	73	4.6	10.8	1.3	3.6
Baby, Canned, Drained	1oz/28g	6	23	2.9	2.0	0.4	1.5
Baby, Frozen, Average	1oz/28g	7	24	2.5	2.7	0.4	1.7
Boiled, Average	1oz/28g	31	111	4.2	19.6	2.3	2.2
Canned, In Water , No Sugar & Salt, Average	½ Can/125g	99	79	2.7	14.9	1.1	1.6
Canned, With Sugar & Salt, Average	½ Can/71g	79	111	3.2	21.9	1.2	1.9
Carrot Batons & Broccoli Florets, Microsteam, Bird's Eye*	1 Serving/113.2g	60	53	2.6	8.5	0.9	2.2
Fritters With Chilli Dip, Sainsbury's*	1 Fritter/40g	60	151	3.0	27.0	3.4	3.0
Frozen, Average	1 Sachet/115g	121	105	3.8	17.9	2.1	1.8
Savers, Safeway*	1 Serving/143g	169	118	3.0	23.0	1.5	2.3
With Peppers, Canned, Average	1 Serving/50g	40	79	2.7	16.5	0.3	0.6
SWEETENER,							
Aspartamo, Artificial Sugar, Zen*	1 Tbsp/2g	8	383	1.8	94.0	0.0	0.0
Canderel*	1 Tsp/0.53	2	379	24.7	7.0	0.0	5.3
Canderel, Spoonful, Canderel*	2 Tsp/1g	4	384	2.9	93.0	0.0	0.0
Granulated, Asda*	1 Tsp/1g	4	400	3.0	97.0	0.0	0.0
Granulated, Aspartame, Safeway*	1 Tsp/0.5g	4	392	3.0	95.0	0.0	0.0
Granulated, Safeway*	1 Tsp/1g	4	392	3.0	95.0	0.0	0.0
Granulated, Splenda*	1 Tsp/1g	4	391	0.0	97.7	0.0	0.0
Granulated, Tesco*	1 Tsp/1g	4	400	3.0	97.0	0.0	0.0
Low Calorie, Somerfield*	1 Tsp/0.5g	4	380	3.0	92.0	0.0	0.0
Silver Spoon*	1 Tablet/0.05g	0	325	10.0	71.0	0.0	0.0
SlendaSweet, Sainsbury's*	1 Tsp/1g	4	395	1.8	97.0	0.0	0.1
Spoonfull, Low Calorie, SupaSweet*	1 Tsp/1g	4	392	3.0	95.0	0.0	0.0
Sweet N Low*	1 Sachet/1g	3	368	0.0	92.0	0.0	0.0
Tablets, Splenda*	1 Tablet/0.1g	0	345	10.0	76.2	0.0	1.6
Tablets, Tesco*	5 Tablets/5g	1	20	2.0	2.0	0.5	0.0
SWEETS,							
Aquadrops, Mars*	1 Pack/32g	84	262	0.0	95.7	1.0	0.0
Banana, Baby Foam, Marks & Spencer*	1/3 Pack/34g	131	385	4.1	92.7	0.0	0.0

S

	Measure INFO/WEIGHT	per Measure KCAL	Nutrition Values per 100g / 100ml				
			KCAL	PROT	CARB	FAT	FIBRE
SWEETS,							
Body Parts, Rowntree's*	1 Pack/42g	146	348	4.3	82.9	0.0	0.0
Bursting Bugs, Rowntree's*	1 Pack/175g	583	333	4.8	78.1	0.2	0.0
Candy Butter, Werther's Original*	1 Sweet/5g	22	430	1.0	86.0	9.0	0.0
Chew	1oz/28g	107	381	1.0	87.0	5.6	1.0
Cola Bottles, Fizzy Wizzy, Woolworths*	1 Bag/100g	336	336	3.5	77.2	0.0	0.0
Cola Bottles, Fizzy, Marks & Spencer*	1 Pack/200g	650	325	6.4	75.0	0.0	0.0
Cola Sticks, Fizzy Wizzy, Woolworths*	1 Stick/5.5g	21	358	2.8	79.8	2.7	0.0
Eclair, Marks & Spencer*	1 Sweet/14g	65	465	3.3	69.8	19.3	0.2
Fizzy Lemon Fish, Asda*	1 Sweet/4.3g	13	325	5.0	76.0	0.1	0.0
Fizzy Mix, Tesco*	½ Bag/50g	166	332	5.2	75.2	0.0	0.0
Flying Suacers, Asda*	1 Serving/23.1g	82	355	0.1	83.0	2.5	0.8
Fruit Gums & Jellies	1 Tube/33g	107	324	6.5	79.5	0.0	0.0
Fruities, Liquorice, Weight Watchers*	1oz/28g	35	125	0.0	51.6	0.0	33.0
Kisses, Hershey*	1 Kiss/5g	28	561	7.0	59.0	32.0	0.0
Lances, Fizzy, Strawberry, Somerfield*	1 Lance/3.7g	14	362	2.8	79.8	2.7	1.5
Maynards Sours, Trebor Bassett's*	1 Pack/52g	166	320	3.9	74.9	0.1	0.0
Refreshers, Bassett's*	1oz/28g	106	377	4.3	78.1	0.0	0.0
Rhubarb & Custard, Marks & Spencer*	1 Pack/113g	424	375	0.0	93.9	0.0	0.0
Sherbert Cocktails, Sainsbury's*	1 Sweet/9g	36	400	0.0	83.1	7.5	0.0
Sherbert Lemons, Marks & Spencer*	1 Serving/20g	76	380	0.0	93.9	0.0	0.0
Sherbet Lemons, Marks & Spencer*	1oz/28g	107	382	0.0	93.9	0.0	0.0
Sour Apple Sticks, Fizzy Wizzy, Woolworths*	1 Stick/5g	18	358	2.8	79.8	2.7	0.0
Squidgy Cars, Shannon*	1 Sweet/8g	27	342	5.3	80.0	0.1	0.0
Sweetshop Favourites, Bassett's*	1 Sweet/5g	17	340	0.0	84.3	0.0	0.0
Tooty Frooties, Rowntree's*	1oz/28g	113	402	0.4	92.1	3.6	0.0
Winders, Real Fruit, Kellogg's*	1 Serving/18g	67	370	0.5	77.0	7.0	3.0
York Fruits, Terry's*	1 Sweet/9g	30	328	0.0	81.4	0.0	1.0
SWORDFISH,							
Grilled	1oz/28g	39	139	22.9	0.0	5.2	0.0
Raw, Average	1oz/28g	42	149	21.1	0.0	7.2	0.0
SYRUP,							
Coffee, Caramel, Lyle's*	2 Tsps/10ml	33	329	0.0	83.0	0.0	0.0
Corn, Dark	1 Tbsp/20g	56	282	0.0	76.6	0.0	0.0
Golden, Average	1 Tbsp/20g	61	304	0.4	78.3	0.0	0.0
Hazelnut Flavoured, Starbucks*	1 Pump/10g	20	200	0.0	50.0	0.0	0.0
Maple	1 Tbsp/20g	52	262	0.0	67.2	0.2	0.0

S

	Measure INFO/WEIGHT	per Measure KCAL	Nutrition Values per 100g / 100ml				
			KCAL	PROT	CARB	FAT	FIBRE
TABOULEH,							
Average	1oz/28g	33	119	2.6	17.2	4.6	0.0
Share The Taste, Marks & Spencer*	1oz/28g	31	110	3.4	15.1	4.0	2.0
TACO SHELLS,							
Corn, Crunchy, Old El Paso*	1 Taco/10g	51	506	7.0	61.0	26.0	0.0
Old El Paso*	1 Taco/12g	57	478	7.4	60.8	22.8	0.0
Traditional, Discovery*	1 Shell/11g	51	448	6.7	51.0	24.1	6.4
TAGINE,							
Apricot & Coriander, Al'fez*	1 Serving/175g	224	128	1.4	19.0	5.1	1.2
Vegetable, Filo Topped, Marks & Spencer*	1 Serving/281.8g	310	110	3.3	18.7	2.3	3.9
TAGLIATELLE,							
Basil, Marks & Spencer*	1 Serving/100g	365	365	15.1	69.0	2.8	4.0
Bicolore, Asda*	¼ Pack/125g	203	162	7.0	28.0	2.4	1.4
Carbonara, Frozen, Tesco*	1 Pack/400g	480	120	4.2	12.5	5.9	1.4
Carbonara, Italiano, Tesco*	1 Serving/325g	757	233	8.6	23.8	11.5	1.2
Carbonara, Low Fat, Bertorelli*	1 Pack/350g	301	86	5.3	12.0	2.2	0.9
Carbonara, Naturally Less 5% Fat, Asda*	1 Pack/400g	440	110	4.2	18.0	2.4	0.8
Carbonara, Perfectly Balanced, Waitrose*	1 Pack/350g	357	102	5.3	12.1	3.6	0.7
Carbonara, Reduced Fat, Waitrose*	1 Pack/350g	399	114	5.0	12.1	5.1	0.6
Carbonara, Safeway*	1 Serving/298g	277	93	3.7	13.2	2.8	0.6
Chicken & Mushroom, GFY, Asda*	1 Pack/400g	359	90	7.3	11.3	1.8	0.7
Chicken & Tomato, Eat Smart, Safeway*	1 Pack/400g	360	90	7.5	10.8	1.4	1.1
Chicken & Tomato, Italiano, Tesco*	1 Pack/400g	416	104	6.6	14.8	2.1	0.8
Chicken, Italia, Marks & Spencer*	1 Pack/360g	342	95	8.1	12.1	1.8	1.2
Chicken, Italian, Sainsbury's*	1 Pack/450g	567	126	6.5	17.0	3.5	2.6
Dry, Average	1 Serving/100g	357	357	12.6	72.4	1.8	1.1
Egg & Spinach, Finest, Tesco*	1oz/28g	75	268	11.7	47.5	3.5	2.7
Egg & Spinach, Marks & Spencer*	1 Serving/100g	365	365	15.5	69.6	2.7	3.0
Egg, Dry, Average	1 Serving/75g	272	362	14.3	68.8	3.3	2.3
Egg, Fresh, Dry, Average	1 Serving/125g	345	276	10.6	53.0	2.8	2.1
Fresh, Dry, Average	1 Serving/75g	211	281	11.4	53.3	2.6	2.6
Garlic & Herb, Cooked, Sainsbury's*	1oz/28g	41	147	6.5	26.3	1.8	1.9
Garlic & Herb, Fresh, Asda*	½ Pack/150.7g	202	134	3.5	21.0	4.0	2.1
Garlic & Herb, Fresh, Sainsbury's*	1 Serving/125g	184	147	6.5	26.2	1.8	1.9
Garlic & Herb, Fresh, Tesco*	1 Serving/125g	361	289	12.0	51.8	3.7	1.5
Garlic & Herb, Fresh, Waitrose*	1 Serving/125g	353	282	11.9	49.8	3.9	2.1
Garlic & Herb, Italian, Asda*	1 Serving/100g	134	134	3.5	21.0	4.0	2.1
Garlic & Herbs, Cooked, Pasta Reale*	1 Pack/250g	390	156	6.2	30.4	1.1	1.0
Garlic Mushroom, BGTY, Sainsbury's*	1 Pack/400g	420	105	4.8	15.9	2.5	2.8
Garlic Mushroom, Italiano, Tesco*	1 Pack/450g	738	164	5.2	15.2	9.1	0.6
Ham & Mushroom, Asda*	1 Pack/340g	469	138	6.0	20.0	3.8	0.2
Ham & Mushroom, BGTY, Sainsbury's*	1 Pack/450g	486	108	5.3	14.5	3.2	0.8
Ham & Mushroom, Better For You, Morrisons*	1 Pack/350g	326	93	5.3	9.4	3.8	0.8
Ham & Mushroom, COU, Marks & Spencer*	1 Serving/360g	342	95	5.4	13.1	2.3	1.1
Ham & Mushroom, Eat Smart, Safeway*	1 Pack/400g	380	95	5.0	13.0	2.5	1.2
Ham & Mushroom, GFY, Asda*	1 Pack/400g	304	76	3.8	9.0	2.7	0.4
Ham & Mushroom, Good Intentions, Somerfield*	1 Serving/300g	333	111	5.6	15.6	2.9	0.3
Ham & Mushroom, Healthy Choice, Safeway*	1 Pack/400g	400	100	5.5	12.1	3.3	0.3
Ham & Mushroom, Healthy Eating, Tesco*	1 Meal/340g	306	90	4.3	13.6	2.0	0.9
Ham & Mushroom, Italiano, Tesco*	1 Pack/380g	475	125	5.4	13.3	5.6	0.4
Ham, Ready Meals, Marks & Spencer*	1 Pack/360g	414	115	5.8	10.5	5.7	1.0
Meditarranean Style Chicken, Eat Smart, Safeway*	1 Pack/400g	320	80	5.6	8.7	2.5	1.4
Mushroom & Bacon, Sainsbury's*	1 Pack/450g	585	130	7.1	13.8	5.2	0.5
Mushroom & Tomato, Asda*	1 Pack/340g	211	62	2.5	10.0	1.3	1.2

T

	Measure INFO/WEIGHT	per Measure KCAL	Nutrition Values per 100g / 100ml				
			KCAL	PROT	CARB	FAT	FIBRE
TAGLIATELLE,							
Nests, Dry, Napolina*	1oz/28g	93	332	11.5	68.0	1.5	3.7
Prawn, Eat Smart, Safeway*	1 Pack/380g	304	80	5.1	10.1	2.1	0.8
Red Pepper, Organic, Sainsbury's*	½ Bag/125g	183	146	5.4	27.8	1.5	1.4
Salmon & Prawn, Perfectly Balanced, Waitrose*	1 Pack/401.2g	341	85	6.8	7.1	3.3	1.1
Smoked Salmon, Ready Meals, Marks & Spencer*	1 Pack/360g	612	170	6.2	10.6	11.2	0.9
Sundried Tomato, Fresh, Morrisons*	1 Packet/250g	748	299	11.1	56.4	3.3	3.5
Tomato & Basil Chicken, Weight Watchers*	1 Pack/330g	254	77	5.9	11.8	0.6	0.8
Tricolore, Waitrose*	½ Pack/125g	351	281	12.0	51.6	2.9	1.6
Vegetables, Retail	1oz/28g	21	74	1.6	11.0	3.0	0.7
Verdi, Dry, Barilla*	1 Serving/150g	555	370	14.0	70.5	3.5	0.0
Verdi, Fresh, Average	1 Serving/125g	171	137	5.5	25.5	1.5	1.8
With Chicken, Garlic & Lemon, BGTY, Sainsbury's*	1 Pack/450g	410	91	7.8	14.2	0.3	1.7
With Chicken, Garlic & Lemon, New, BGTY, Sainsbury's*	1 Pack/300g	324	108	9.2	15.1	1.2	1.7
With Ham & Mushroom, New, BGTY, Sainsbury's*	1 Pack/450g	401	89	5.3	11.8	2.3	1.4
With Roasted Vegetables, Good Intentions, Somerfield*	1 Pack/340g	349	103	3.7	16.6	2.4	1.7
Wth Ham, COU, Marks & Spencer*	1 Pack/357.9g	340	95	5.4	13.1	2.3	1.1
TAHINI PASTE,							
Average	1 Hpd Tsp/19g	115	607	18.5	0.9	58.9	8.0
TAMARILLOS,							
Average	1oz/28g	8	28	2.0	4.7	0.3	0.0
TAMARIND,							
Average	1oz/28g	72	256	2.8	60.5	0.3	0.0
Leaves, Fresh	1oz/28g	32	115	5.8	18.2	2.1	0.0
Pulp	1oz/28g	76	273	3.2	64.5	0.3	0.0
TANGERINES,							
Fresh, Raw	1oz/28g	10	35	0.9	8.0	0.1	1.3
Weighed With Peel & Pips	1 Med/70g	18	25	0.7	5.8	0.1	0.9
TANGO*,							
Britvic	1 Serving/100ml	31	31	0.0	7.7	0.0	0.0
TAPENADE,							
Green Olive, Best, Safeway*	1 Tsp/15g	71	470	1.6	10.2	47.0	1.7
Olive With Capers & Anchovy, Safeway*	1 Tbsp/20g	103	513	2.1	1.0	55.6	2.2
Sweet Red Pepper, Finest, Tesco*	1 Serving/100g	202	202	2.4	17.3	13.7	3.8
TAPIOCA,							
Raw	1oz/28g	101	359	0.4	95.0	0.1	0.4
TARAMASALATA,							
Average	1oz/28g	141	504	3.2	4.1	52.9	0.0
Fresh, Healthy Eating, Tesco*	1 Pot/170g	430	253	4.3	13.5	20.2	0.7
Marks & Spencer*	1 Serving/100g	480	480	4.9	6.4	48.9	0.7
Reduced Fat, Waitrose*	1 Pot/170g	598	352	4.2	9.6	33.0	0.6
Tesco*	1 Serving/50g	220	440	7.4	8.8	41.7	0.3
TARRAGON,							
Dried, Ground	1 Tsp/1.6g	6	295	22.8	42.8	7.2	0.0
Fresh	1oz/28g	14	49	3.4	6.3	1.1	0.0
TART,							
Apple, Bistro, Waitrose*	1/6 Tart/100g	183	183	2.2	31.0	5.6	2.1
Apricot Lattice, Sainsbury's*	1 Slice/125g	321	257	3.4	35.3	11.4	2.6
Assorted, Oakdale Bakeries*	1 Serving/26.9g	104	386	3.1	62.0	14.0	1.7
Bakewell	1oz/28g	128	456	6.3	43.5	29.7	1.9
Bakewell, Free From, Tesco*	1 Cake/50g	170	340	1.6	63.0	9.2	4.8
Bakewell, Lemon, Holmefield Bakery*	1 Tart/46.1g	207	449	4.8	52.9	24.6	0.0
Bakewell, Lyons*	1/6 Tart/51.6g	206	397	3.8	56.7	17.2	0.9
Bakewell, Marks & Spencer*	¼ Tart/75g	345	460	7.5	48.1	26.7	2.1

T

	Measure INFO/WEIGHT	per Measure KCAL	Nutrition Values per 100g / 100ml				
			KCAL	PROT	CARB	FAT	FIBRE
TART,							
Bakewell, Weight Watchers*	1 Cake/43.0g	156	363	3.6	65.2	11.7	3.2
Blackcurrant Sundae, Asda*	1 Tart/55g	227	413	3.5	57.0	19.0	2.3
Cherry Tomato Mascarpone, Asda*	1 Tart/160g	290	181	4.4	15.6	11.3	1.1
Chocolate, Co-Op*	1 Tart/22g	102	465	4.0	42.0	31.0	0.7
Coconut & Cherry, Asda*	1 Serving/50g	215	430	4.4	58.0	20.0	4.0
Coconut & Raspberry, Waitrose*	1 Tart/48g	204	426	5.0	45.0	24.0	3.9
Coconut, Marks & Spencer*	1 Tart/53g	220	415	5.8	57.8	18.1	3.6
Congress, Morrisons*	1 Tart/38g	149	393	6.0	59.7	14.4	2.4
Custard, Individual	1 Tart/94g	260	277	6.3	32.4	14.5	1.2
Egg Custard, Marks & Spencer*	1 Tart/85g	243	286	6.3	34.7	14.5	0.7
Egg Custard, Sainsbury's	1 Tart/85g	230	270	6.1	30.1	14.1	0.7
Egg Custard, Somerfield*	1 Tart/85g	206	242	5.1	29.9	11.3	0.7
Egg Custard, Tesco*	1 Cake/82g	214	261	6.2	31.5	12.2	1.1
Feta Cheese & Spinach, Puff Pastry, Tesco*	1 Tart/108g	306	283	7.1	23.5	17.8	0.9
Filo Asparagus Tartlette, Marks & Spencer*	1 Serving/15g	45	300	4.4	25.2	20.4	2.1
Fruit, Safeway*	1 Tart/180g	425	236	2.7	30.6	11.4	0.0
Goats Cheese & Onion, Marks & Spencer*	1 Serving/161g	451	280	5.8	22.4	18.7	1.5
Italian Lemon & Almond, Sainsbury's*	1 Slice/49g	182	371	7.4	31.9	23.7	4.1
Jam	1 Slice/90g	342	380	3.3	62.0	14.9	1.6
Jam, Assorted, Tesco*	1 Tart/35g	123	351	3.4	51.9	14.4	1.2
Jam, Real Fruit, Mr Kipling*	1 Tart/35g	136	389	3.5	61.0	14.5	1.3
Jam, Real Fruit, Sainsbury's*	1 Tart/37g	142	383	3.4	60.9	14.0	1.4
Leek & Stilton, Morrisons*	1 Serving/125g	393	314	6.9	23.1	21.5	0.3
Lemon & Raspberry, Finest, Tesco*	1 Tart/120g	360	300	5.2	38.4	14.0	2.9
Lemon Curd, Asda*	1 Tart/30.1g	121	402	2.8	64.0	15.0	2.2
Lemon Curd, Lyons*	1 Tart/30g	122	406	3.7	59.3	17.0	0.0
Lemon, Marks & Spencer*	1/6 Tart/50g	208	415	5.0	32.7	29.3	0.9
Manchester, Marks & Spencer*	1oz/28g	104	370	4.1	36.0	23.5	1.1
Mixed Fruit, Marks & Spencer*	1oz/28g	59	210	2.8	26.9	10.4	0.8
Mixed Fruit, Waitrose*	1 Tart/146g	318	218	2.3	27.3	11.2	1.0
Normandy Apple & Calvados, Finest, Tesco*	1/6 Tart/100g	256	256	3.2	41.4	7.6	1.9
Pear & Chocolate With Brandy, TTD, Sainsbury's*	1/6 Tart/90g	261	290	3.5	32.0	16.4	1.4
Raspberry Flavoured, Value, Tesco*	1 Tart/29.0g	113	389	3.8	56.6	16.4	1.6
Raspberry, Reduced Sugar, Asda*	1 Tart/34g	129	380	4.6	67.5	10.1	1.2
Red Pepper, Serrano Ham & Goats Cheese, Waitrose*	1 Serving/100g	293	293	8.7	21.3	19.2	3.2
Roasted Vegetable, Finest, Tesco*	1 Serving/130g	250	192	3.0	19.6	11.3	1.2
Strawberry & Fresh Cream, Finest, Tesco*	1 Tart/129g	350	271	3.3	31.1	14.8	1.2
Strawberry Custard, Asda*	1 Tart/100g	335	335	3.1	47.0	15.0	0.0
Strawberry Sundae, Asda*	1 Tart/46g	187	407	3.3	58.0	18.0	1.3
Strawberry, Marks & Spencer*	1 Tart/120g	312	260	2.6	26.4	16.0	0.7
Strawberry, Reduced Sugar, Asda*	1 Tart/37g	141	380	4.6	67.5	10.1	1.2
Toffee Apple, Co-Op*	1 Tart/20g	69	345	3.0	47.0	16.0	0.7
Toffee Bakewell, Sainsbury's*	1 Tart/45.0g	200	444	3.4	64.2	19.3	1.1
Toffee Pecan, Marks & Spencer*	1 Tart/91g	414	455	6.0	48.5	26.5	2.0
Toffee Pecan, Waitrose*	¼ Tart/133.3g	563	423	4.3	69.3	14.3	1.6
Tomato, Mozzarella & Basil Puff, Sainsbury's*	1/3 Tart/120g	318	265	9.2	10.2	20.8	0.9
Treacle	1oz/28g	103	368	3.7	60.4	14.1	1.1
Treacle Lattice, Mr Kipling*	1/6 Tart/70g	256	365	4.4	59.8	12.1	1.1
Treacle, Lattice, Lyons*	1/6 Tart/70g	255	364	4.4	59.3	12.0	1.1
Treacle, Sainsbury's*	1 Serving/100g	369	369	4.3	60.6	12.1	1.2
TARTE,							
Au Chocolat, Finest, Tesco*	1/6 Tarte/85g	421	495	5.1	44.0	33.2	1.6
Aux Fruits, Finest, Tesco*	1 Tart/147g	345	235	3.0	33.4	9.9	1.1

	Measure INFO/WEIGHT	per Measure KCAL	Nutrition Values per 100g / 100ml				
			KCAL	PROT	CARB	FAT	FIBRE
TARTE,							
Bacon, Leek & Roquefort, Bistro, Waitrose*	1/6 Tarte/100g	189	189	6.6	10.8	13.2	2.1
Citron, Marks & Spencer*	1oz/28g	98	350	5.7	36.2	20.9	0.4
Goats Cheese & Spinach Flambe, Sainsbury's*	1/3 Tart/76.8g	223	289	7.4	15.9	21.8	0.9
Normande, French Style, Marks & Spencer*	1/6 Tarte/84.5g	244	290	3.3	26.8	19.0	0.7
Tatin, Sainsbury's*	1 Serving/120g	244	203	2.9	32.8	6.7	1.9
au Citron, TTD, Sainsbury's*	1 Tart/105g	360	343	3.7	36.6	20.2	0.6
TARTLET,							
Caramelised Onion & Gruyere, Sainsbury's*	1 Tart/145g	381	263	5.8	17.3	19.0	1.3
Cherry & Almond, Go Ahead, McVitie's*	1 Tartlette/46.0g	165	359	4.1	67.5	9.8	0.7
Cherry Tomato & Aubergine, Marks & Spencer*	1 Tartlet/160g	320	200	3.1	17.8	12.6	1.7
Mandarin, Mini, Marks & Spencer*	1 Tartlet/28.6g	81	280	3.4	30.4	16.3	0.6
Mushroom, Bacon & Spinach, Safeway*	1 Tartlet/120g	312	260	7.0	13.0	20.0	1.0
Onion, Caramelised, Creamy, Somerfield*	1 Tartlet/105g	310	295	4.0	21.0	22.0	0.0
Raspberry, Mini, Marks & Spencer*	1 Tartlet/27.3g	89	330	4.3	34.4	19.6	0.5
Red Onion & Goats Cheese, Sainsbury's*	1 Tart/112.8g	336	297	7.0	23.7	19.3	1.5
Redcurrant & Blackcurrant, Mini, Marks & Spencer*	1 Tartlet/29.3g	84	290	3.9	30.5	16.8	1.1
Roast Pepper & Mascarpone, Sainsbury's*	1 Tart/100g	232	232	3.5	17.7	16.4	1.5
Roast Vegetable, Filo, Mini, Somerfield*	1oz/28g	71	255	8.0	34.0	10.0	0.0
Sausage & Tomato, Sainsbury's*	1 Tartlet/135g	323	239	4.8	19.5	15.8	1.6
TEA,							
Camomile Lemon, Herbal, Tetley*	1 Serving/175ml	3	2	0.1	0.1	0.0	0.0
Earl Grey, Iced, Twinings*	1fl oz/30ml	10	34	0.1	8.0	0.0	0.0
Fruit, Average, Twinings*	1 Mug/227ml	4	2	0.0	0.4	0.0	0.0
Fruit, Whittards*	1fl oz/30ml	12	40	0.0	1.2	0.0	0.0
Green & Lemon, Iced, Twinings*	1 Serving/250ml	75	30	0.1	7.3	0.1	0.0
Green & Lemon, Twinings*	1 Serving/250ml	65	26	0.0	7.3	0.0	0.0
Green, With Jasmine, Wellbeing Selection, Flavia*	1 Cup/200ml	14	7	0.5	1.2	0.1	0.0
Herbal	1 Mug/227ml	2	1	0.0	0.2	0.0	0.0
Lemon & Limeflower, Infused, Marks & Spencer*	1 Bottle/330ml	99	30	0.0	7.8	0.0	0.0
Lemon Iced, Costa*	1 Bottle/275ml	91	33	0.0	8.0	0.0	0.0
Lemon, Instant Drink, Reduced Sweetness, Lift*	1 Serving/15g	53	352	0.0	87.0	0.0	0.0
Lemon, Original, Instant Drink, Lift*	1 Serving/15g	53	352	0.0	87.0	0.0	0.0
Made With Water	1 Mug/227ml	0	0	0.1	0.0	0.0	0.0
Made With Water With Semi-Skimmed Milk	1 Cup/200ml	14	7	0.5	0.7	0.2	0.0
Made With Water With Skimmed Milk	1 Mug/227ml	14	6	0.5	0.7	0.2	0.0
Made With Water With Whole Milk	1 Cup/200ml	16	8	0.4	0.5	0.4	0.0
Peach Flavour, Lift*	1 Cup/15g	58	384	0.3	95.6	0.0	0.0
Peach, Iced, Twinings*	1 Serving/200ml	60	30	0.1	7.3	0.1	0.0
Pure Peppermint, Herbal, Tetley*	1 Serving/175ml	3	2	0.1	0.2	0.0	0.0
Raspberry & Cranberry, T Of Life, Tetley*	1 Serving/100ml	36	36	0.0	9.0	0.0	0.0
UHT Skimmed Milk, McDonald's*	1 Cup/14ml	10	74	3.7	5.4	4.1	0.0
With 30ml Semi Skimmed Milk, Mug	1 Serving/250ml	15	6	0.4	0.6	0.2	0.0
TEACAKES,							
Chocolate, Tunnocks*	1 Cake/22g	91	413	5.3	61.0	18.1	0.0
Currant, Sainsbury's*	1 Serving/100g	283	283	7.7	50.9	5.4	3.8
Fresh	1oz/28g	83	296	8.0	52.5	7.5	0.0
Fruited, Marks & Spencer*	1 Cake/60g	156	260	8.9	53.4	1.0	2.0
Fruited, Warburton's*	1 Cake/62g	162	261	9.7	48.0	3.4	2.7
Fruity, Warburton's*	1 Teacake/63g	161	256	8.5	48.0	3.2	2.7
Jam, Burton's*	1 Cake/10g	43	429	3.6	66.0	16.7	1.0
Large, Sainsbury's*	1 Cake/100g	291	291	8.3	49.1	6.8	3.4
Mallow, Tesco*	1 Cake/14g	63	450	4.1	65.4	19.1	1.0
Milk Chocolate, Marks & Spencer*	1 Teacake/17.5g	77	430	5.0	65.4	16.7	1.0

T

	Measure INFO/WEIGHT	per Measure KCAL	Nutrition Values per 100g / 100ml				
			KCAL	PROT	CARB	FAT	FIBRE
TEACAKES,							
Milk Chocolate, Tunnock's*	1 Serving/22g	91	413	5.3	61.0	18.1	0.0
Morrisons*	1 Cake/64g	172	268	9.9	50.7	2.9	2.8
Reduced Fat, Marks & Spencer*	1 Cake/17g	68	401	5.0	69.1	11.7	0.9
Richly Fruited, Waitrose*	1 Cake/72g	205	285	7.8	55.0	3.7	2.2
Sainsbury's*	1 Cake/70g	171	244	8.0	45.0	3.6	2.6
Tesco*	1 Cake/61g	163	267	7.8	51.1	3.5	2.4
Toasted	1oz/28g	92	329	8.9	58.3	8.3	0.0
Tunnock's*	1 Cake/22g	91	413	5.3	61.0	18.1	0.0
Value, Tesco*	1oz/28g	74	265	7.5	49.1	4.3	2.3
With Orange Filling, Marks & Spencer*	1 Teacake/20g	80	410	4.5	66.6	14.2	0.9
TEMPEH,							
Average	1oz/28g	46	166	20.7	6.4	6.4	4.3
TERRINE,							
Chicken, With Pork, Sage & Onion Stuffing, Somerfield*	1oz/28g	32	114	25.0	1.0	1.0	0.0
Lobster & Prawn, Slices, Marks & Spencer*	1 Serving/55g	107	195	18.2	0.7	13.4	0.7
Poached Salmon, Tesco*	1 Pack/113g	349	309	15.5	0.8	27.1	0.0
Prawn, TTD, Sainsbury's*	1 Serving/60g	115	192	9.0	3.7	15.7	0.4
Salmon & Crayfish, Slice, Finest, Tesco*	1 Slice/110g	149	135	21.9	0.1	5.2	0.1
Salmon & King Prawn, Waitrose*	1 Serving/75g	98	130	19.3	1.3	5.3	0.0
Salmon, Reduced Fat, Tesco*	1 Serving/56g	100	179	15.5	1.1	12.5	3.5
Salmon, Three, Marks & Spencer*	1 Serving/80g	168	210	17.6	0.8	15.3	0.9
Salmon, With Prawn & Lobster, Marks & Spencer*	1 Serving/55g	107	195	18.2	0.7	13.4	0.7
Scottish Smoked Salmon, Tesco*	1 Slice/25g	56	225	13.9	4.9	16.6	0.5
Trout, TTD, Sainsbury's*	1 Serving/60g	138	230	14.7	2.6	17.9	0.2
THAI BITES,							
Lightly Salted, Jacob's*	1 Pack/25g	94	375	6.9	79.7	3.2	0.1
Mild Thai Flavour, Jacob's*	1 Bag/25g	93	373	6.9	79.0	3.3	1.0
Oriental Spice, Jacob's*	1 Pack/25g	93	373	7.1	78.0	3.6	0.2
Seaweed Flavour, Jacob's*	1 Pack/25g	94	377	7.1	80.0	3.2	0.5
Sweet Herb, Jacob's*	1 Pack/25g	93	372	7.1	78.8	3.2	0.2
THYME,							
Dried, Ground	1 Tsp/1.2g	3	276	9.1	45.3	7.4	0.0
Fresh	1 Tsp/0.8g	1	95	3.0	15.1	2.5	0.0
TIA MARIA,							
Original	1 Serving/25ml	75	300	0.0	0.0	0.0	0.0
TIC TAC,							
Fresh Mint, Ferrero*	2 Tic Tacs/1g	4	390	0.0	97.5	0.0	0.0
Lime & Orange, Ferrero*	2 Tic Tacs/1g	4	386	0.0	95.5	0.0	0.0
Orange, Ferrero*	2 Tic Tacs/1g	4	385	0.0	95.5	0.0	0.0
Spearmint, Ferrero*	1 Box/16g	62	390	0.0	97.5	0.0	0.0
TIDGY PUDS,							
Aunt Bessie's*	4 Puds/16.9g	55	326	9.6	38.4	14.8	2.1
Tryton Foods*	1oz/28g	97	346	11.3	43.5	14.1	2.1
TIDGY TOADS,							
Aunt Bessie's*	1 Serving/45g	125	278	14.7	25.3	13.2	1.1
TIKKA MASALA,							
Cauliflower & Potato, With Pilau Rice, Safeway*	1 Serving/414.3g	435	105	2.4	13.9	4.1	2.2
Chicken & Basmati Rice, Patak's*	1 Pack/400g	580	145	9.9	15.1	5.0	0.2
Chicken & Pilau Rice, Asda*	1 Pack/400g	548	137	7.0	16.0	5.0	1.6
Chicken & Pilau Rice, GFY, Asda*	1 Pack/400g	596	149	8.0	19.0	4.6	1.1
Chicken & Pilau Rice, Safeway*	1 Pack/399g	654	164	7.5	16.5	7.5	1.4
Chicken & Rice, COU, Marks & Spencer*	1 Pack/400g	420	105	7.8	14.6	1.6	2.1
Chicken & Rice, Healthy Living, Tesco*	1 Pack/420g	483	115	7.6	16.2	2.3	1.6

T

	Measure INFO/WEIGHT	per Measure KCAL	Nutrition Values per 100g / 100ml				
			KCAL	PROT	CARB	FAT	FIBRE
TIKKA MASALA,							
Chicken & Rice, Takeaway, Tesco*	1 Pack/350g	525	150	4.4	20.3	5.7	1.2
Chicken With Basmati Rice, Eat Smart, Safeway*	1 Pack/363g	290	80	6.4	9.6	1.4	0.7
Chicken With Golden Rice, Iceland*	1 Pack/500g	885	177	6.2	19.4	8.3	1.1
Chicken With Pilau Rice, BGTY, Sainsbury's*	1 Pack/450g	428	95	7.8	12.7	1.4	0.9
Chicken With Pilau Rice, Eat Smart, Safeway*	1 Pack/400g	396	99	5.7	14.3	2.1	1.6
Chicken With Pilau Rice, New, BGTY, Sainsbury's*	1 Pack/400g	416	104	8.0	16.0	0.9	1.8
Chicken With Pilau Rice, Perfectly Balanced, Waitrose*	1 Pack/400g	520	130	7.7	16.9	3.5	1.1
Chicken With Rice, GFY, Asda*	1 Pack/400g	440	110	6.0	17.0	2.0	0.8
Chicken With Rice, Healthy Eating, Tesco*	1 Pack/400g	472	118	6.1	17.0	2.8	1.8
Chicken With Rice, Healthy Living, Co-Op*	1 Pack/499g	549	110	9.0	17.0	1.0	1.0
Chicken With Rice, Patak's*	1 Carton/350g	571	163	5.1	21.8	6.1	4.4
Chicken With Rice, Sainsbury's*	1 Pack/500g	960	192	8.3	21.2	8.2	0.1
Chicken With Tumeric Rice, BGTY, Sainsbury's*	1 Pack/369g	446	121	6.7	20.5	1.3	0.4
Chicken With White Rice, BGTY, Sainsbury's*	1 Pack/400g	436	109	5.8	16.1	2.4	0.7
Chicken, BGTY, Sainsbury's*	1 Pack/450g	513	114	8.6	17.0	1.3	1.1
Chicken, Boiled Rice & Nan, Meal For One, GFY, Asda*	1 Pack/605g	823	136	6.0	21.0	3.1	0.0
Chicken, COU, Marks & Spencer*	1 Pack/300g	300	100	12.1	6.0	2.8	1.3
Chicken, Feeling Great, Findus*	1 Pack/350g	420	120	5.5	17.0	3.5	2.0
Chicken, Good Choice, Iceland*	1 Pack/398g	486	122	6.6	20.4	1.5	0.6
Chicken, Good Intentions, Somerfield*	1 Pack/400g	612	153	7.6	26.0	2.1	1.7
Chicken, Healthy Choice, Iceland*	1 Pack/399g	431	108	6.5	18.0	1.1	0.9
Chicken, Healthy Living, Tesco*	1 Serving/350g	357	102	12.1	7.7	2.5	0.8
Chicken, Hot, Sainsbury's*	1 Pack/400g	604	151	13.2	3.6	9.3	1.5
Chicken, Indian Meal for One, BGTY, Sainsbury's*	1 Serving/241.0g	200	83	13.9	5.1	0.8	1.0
Chicken, Indian Takeaway, Iceland*	1 Pack/400g	316	79	7.5	6.9	2.4	1.2
Chicken, Indian, Medium, Sainsbury's*	1 Pack/400g	848	212	13.2	5.3	15.3	0.1
Chicken, Low Fat, Iceland*	1 Pack/400g	360	90	7.8	12.5	1.0	0.5
Chicken, Marks & Spencer*	1 Pack/300g	585	195	12.2	5.3	13.8	1.5
Chicken, Medium, Tesco*	1 Pack/350g	532	152	11.2	4.9	9.8	0.6
Chicken, Microwave In Two Minutes, Patak's*	1 Pack/300g	354	118	4.3	17.8	3.3	0.4
Chicken, Microwave Meal, Good Choice, Iceland*	1 Pack/400g	488	122	6.6	20.4	1.5	0.6
Chicken, Morrisons*	1 Pack/340g	388	114	11.9	5.4	5.0	0.0
Chicken, Safeway*	1 Pack/350g	525	150	12.5	6.3	7.8	2.4
Chicken, Sainsbury's*	1 Pack/400g	736	184	12.8	4.6	12.7	0.2
Chicken, Sharwood's*	1 Pack/375g	563	150	7.2	15.1	6.7	0.8
Chicken, SmartPrice, Asda*	1 Pack/300g	405	135	7.0	17.0	4.3	0.3
Chicken, Take Away Menu, BGTY, Sainsbury's*	1 Pack/251g	226	90	13.4	4.2	2.2	1.3
Chicken, Take Away, Tesco*	1 Pack/350g	613	175	11.3	2.0	13.5	1.1
Chicken, Tesco*	1 Pack/350g	511	146	11.1	4.3	9.4	1.5
Chicken, Tinned, Asda*	½ Can/200g	238	119	8.0	6.0	7.0	0.9
Chicken, Tinned, Marks & Spencer*	½ Can/213g	309	145	14.5	2.9	8.5	2.2
Chicken, Waitrose*	½ Pack/200g	298	149	12.8	2.6	9.7	1.6
Green, Asda*	1 Jar/340g	401	118	1.2	8.0	9.0	0.4
Healthy Eating, Tesco*	1 Serving/220g	191	87	1.0	10.2	4.7	0.5
Vegetable & Rice, Patak's*	1 Pack/370g	503	136	2.5	19.0	6.1	0.9
Vegetable, Asda*	½ Can/204g	190	93	2.0	10.0	5.0	2.0
Vegetable, Waitrose*	1 Can/200g	204	102	2.4	6.4	7.4	0.0
Vegetable, With Rice, Tesco*	1 Pack/450g	500	111	2.6	15.5	4.3	0.9
TIME OUT,							
Cadbury's*	2 Fingers/35g	189	540	5.4	61.8	29.9	0.0
Orange, Snack Size, Cadbury's*	1 Finger/11g	61	555	5.0	59.4	32.9	0.0
TIRAMISU,							
Asda*	1 Pot/100g	252	252	4.3	34.0	11.0	0.5

	Measure INFO/WEIGHT	per Measure KCAL	KCAL	PROT	CARB	FAT	FIBRE
			Nutrition Values per 100g / 100ml				
TIRAMISU,							
BGTY, Sainsbury's*	1 Pot/90g	140	156	4.5	28.3	2.7	0.3
COU, Marks & Spencer*	1 Serving/95g	138	145	3.7	26.9	2.7	0.6
Eat Smart, Safeway*	1 Serving/90g	149	165	5.3	29.4	2.6	1.6
Healthy Living, Tesco*	1 Pot/90g	172	191	7.8	27.4	4.3	2.0
Italian, Co-Op*	1 Pack/90g	230	255	5.0	37.0	10.0	0.4
Italian, Safeway*	1 Serving/125g	353	282	4.4	34.4	14.0	1.6
Morrisons*	1 Pot/90g	248	276	4.0	38.0	11.0	0.0
Raspberry, Marks & Spencer*	1 Serving/84g	197	235	3.8	22.9	14.4	0.2
Somerfield*	1 Pot/100g	286	286	5.0	39.0	11.0	0.0
Trifle, Sainsbury's*	1 Serving/100g	243	243	2.3	23.2	15.7	0.6
Waitrose*	1 Pot/90g	221	246	6.4	27.2	12.4	0.0
TOAD IN THE HOLE,							
Asda*	¼ Pack/100g	251	251	11.0	18.0	15.0	2.5
Average	1oz/28g	78	277	11.9	19.5	17.4	1.1
Co-Op*	1 Pack/170g	366	215	7.8	12.3	14.9	2.6
Large, Great Value, Asda*	¼ Pack/81.2g	237	293	10.0	25.0	17.0	2.3
Sainsbury's*	1 Serving/144g	449	312	11.5	23.4	19.2	0.9
Vegetarian, Aunt Bessie's*	1 Pack/190g	481	253	13.1	19.9	13.6	1.2
Vegetarian, Linda McCartney*	1 Pack/190g	359	189	13.6	13.9	8.8	1.1
Vegetarian, Meat Free, Asda*	1 Toad/173g	407	235	9.0	25.0	11.0	3.1
Vegetarian, Tesco*	1 Pack/190g	471	248	13.1	26.5	10.0	2.8
With Three Sausages, Asda*	1 Pack/150g	435	290	10.0	22.0	18.0	1.0
TOAST TOPPERS,							
Chicken & Mushroom, Heinz*	1 Serving/56g	31	56	5.1	5.7	1.4	0.2
Ham & Cheese, Heinz*	1oz/28g	27	96	7.4	7.3	4.1	0.1
Mushroom & Bacon, Heinz*	1 Serving/56g	53	94	6.9	6.6	4.4	0.3
TOASTIE,							
All Day Breakfast, Marks & Spencer*	1 Serving/174.4g	374	215	11.2	25.0	7.9	1.7
Cheese & Pickle, Marks & Spencer*	1 Toastie/136g	320	235	10.4	33.5	6.7	2.6
Ham & Cheddar, British, Marks & Spencer*	1 Pack/128g	269	210	15.5	22.3	6.7	1.3
TOASTIES,							
Cheese & Ham, Coffee Republic*	1 Serving/164g	436	266	13.7	30.1	10.1	0.0
Cheese & Ham, Tayto*	1 Serving/50g	260	519	6.8	58.0	29.7	0.0
Cheese & Onion, Warburton's*	1 Toastie/42g	120	286	7.5	33.1	13.7	0.0
TOBLERONE,							
Milk, Toblerone*	1oz/28g	147	525	5.3	60.7	29.0	2.7
TOFFEE,							
Assorted, Bassett's*	1 Toffee/8g	35	434	3.8	73.1	14.0	0.0
Chocolate Coated, Thorntons*	1 Bag/100g	521	521	3.5	57.9	30.7	0.3
Devon Butter, Thorntons*	1 Sweet/9g	40	444	1.7	72.2	16.7	0.0
Double Devon, Marks & Spencer*	1 Sweet/8g	37	460	1.8	73.1	19.9	0.0
English Butter, Co-Op*	1 Toffee/8g	38	470	2.0	71.0	20.0	0.0
Liquorice, Thorntons*	1 Bag/100g	506	506	1.9	58.8	29.4	0.0
Mixed	1oz/28g	119	426	2.2	66.7	18.6	0.0
No Added Sugar, Boots*	1 Serving/7.1g	23	324	1.3	52.0	14.0	0.0
Original, Thorntons*	1 Bag/100g	514	514	1.8	59.3	30.1	0.0
TOFFEE CRISP,							
Mini, Nestle*	1 Bar/18g	93	511	4.3	60.6	27.9	0.0
Nestle*	1 Bar/48g	243	507	4.5	61.1	27.9	0.0
TOFU,							
Average	1 Pack/250g	297	119	13.4	1.4	6.6	0.1
Fried, Average	1oz/28g	75	268	28.6	9.3	14.1	0.0
Marinated Pieces, Organic, Cauldron Foods*	1oz/28g	64	230	19.3	2.4	15.9	0.7

T

	Measure INFO/WEIGHT	per Measure KCAL	Nutrition Values per 100g / 100ml				
			KCAL	PROT	CARB	FAT	FIBRE
TOFU,							
Savoury Beech, Smoked, Organic, Cauldron Fods*	½ Pack/110g	163	148	16.0	1.0	8.9	0.3
Smoked, Organic, Evernat*	1oz/28g	36	127	16.3	0.8	6.6	0.0
TOMATO PUREE,							
Average	1oz/28g	21	76	4.5	14.1	0.2	2.3
Sun Dried, & Olive Oil, Gia*	1 Serving/20g	41	204	2.6	0.5	21.6	0.0
TOMATOES,							
Chair De Tomate, Sainsbury's*	1 Can/200g	112	56	1.5	6.4	0.4	3.0
Cherry, Average	1 Serving/73g	14	19	0.9	3.3	0.3	1.0
Cherry, On the Vine, Average	1 Serving/50g	9	18	0.7	3.1	0.3	1.0
Chopped, Canned, Average	1 Serving/130g	27	21	1.1	3.8	0.1	0.8
Chopped, Italian, Average	½ Can/200g	47	23	1.3	4.4	0.1	0.9
Chopped, Italian, With Olive Oil & Garlic, Waitrose*	1 Serving/100g	33	33	1.1	3.6	1.6	0.0
Chopped, Italian, With Olives, Waitrose*	1 Can/400g	184	46	1.4	6.0	1.8	0.8
Chopped, Sugocasa, Premium, Sainsbury's*	¼ Jar/172g	59	34	1.6	6.5	0.2	0.9
Chopped, With Chilli & Peppers, Asda*	1 Pack/400g	92	23	1.0	4.0	0.3	0.0
Chopped, With Chilli, Sainsbury's*	½ Can/200g	44	22	1.0	3.5	0.5	0.9
Chopped, With Garlic, Average	½ Can/200g	43	21	1.2	3.8	0.1	0.8
Chopped, With Herbs, Average	1oz/28g	6	21	1.1	3.8	0.1	0.8
Chopped, With Onion & Herbs, Napolina*	1 Can/400g	84	21	1.0	4.0	0.1	0.4
Chopped, With Peppers & Onions, Sainsbury's*	½ Can/200g	40	20	1.2	3.5	0.1	0.9
Creamed, Sainsbury's*	1 Carton/500g	150	30	1.1	6.0	0.1	0.8
Fresh, Raw, Average	1 Med/85g	15	18	0.8	3.2	0.3	1.1
Fried in Blended Oil	1 Av Tomato/85g	77	91	0.7	5.0	7.7	1.3
Grilled	1oz/28g	14	49	2.0	8.9	0.9	2.9
Plum, Baby, Average	1 Serving/50g	9	18	1.5	2.3	0.3	1.0
Plum, In Tomato Juice, Average	1 Can/400g	71	18	1.0	3.3	0.1	0.7
Plum, In Tomato Juice, Premium, Average	1oz/28g	7	23	1.3	3.8	0.3	0.7
Ripened On The Vine, Average	1oz/28g	5	18	0.7	3.0	0.3	0.7
Stuffed With Rice	1oz/28g	59	212	2.1	22.2	13.4	1.1
Sun Blush, Sainsbury's*	1 Serving/65g	79	121	2.9	13.6	7.4	4.3
Sun Dried, Average	3 Pieces/20g	43	214	4.7	13.0	15.9	3.3
Sun Dried, In Seasoned Oil, Asda*	1 Serving/25g	51	205	4.3	11.0	16.0	6.0
Sun Dried, Marinated, Waitrose*	1 Serving/100g	126	126	2.4	8.0	9.4	1.2
Sundried, In Oil, Gia*	1 Serving/10g	15	153	1.9	7.5	13.9	0.0
TONDO'S,							
Lightly Salted, Ryvita*	1 Serving/25g	99	397	7.0	86.1	2.7	0.7
Salsa Flavour, Ryvita*	1 Serving/25g	99	395	7.1	84.8	3.0	0.9
Smokey Barbecue Flavour, Ryvita*	1 Bag/25g	98	393	7.0	84.6	3.0	0.7
TONGUE,							
Lunch, Average	1oz/28g	51	181	20.1	1.8	10.7	0.0
Ox, Wafer Thin, Traditional, Marks & Spencer*	1oz/28g	64	230	22.3	0.0	15.5	0.0
Slices	1oz/28g	56	201	18.7	0.0	14.0	0.0
TONIC WATER,							
Average	1 Glass/250ml	83	33	0.0	8.8	0.0	0.0
Diet, Asda*	1 Glass/200ml	2	1	0.0	0.0	0.0	0.0
Indian, Low Calorie, Tesco*	1 Serving/200ml	2	1	0.0	0.0	0.0	0.0
Indian, Slimline, Schweppes*	1 Serving/188ml	3	2	0.4	0.1	0.0	0.0
Marks & Spencer*	1 Bottle/500ml	100	20	0.0	4.8	0.0	0.0
TOPIC,							
Mars*	1 Bar/47g	232	493	6.0	58.1	26.3	0.0
TOPPING,							
Bruschetta	1serving/115g	30	26	1.2	3.6	0.8	1.1
Bruschetta, Safeway*	1 Serving/100g	26	26	1.2	3.6	0.8	0.0

T

	Measure	per Measure	Nutrition Values per 100g / 100ml				
	INFO/WEIGHT	KCAL	KCAL	PROT	CARB	FAT	FIBRE
TOPPING,							
Bruschetta, Sainsbury's*	1 Sm Tin/230g	60	26	1.2	3.6	0.8	1.1
Mediterranean, For Cod, Schwartz*	½ Jar/147g	128	87	1.7	9.5	4.7	0.0
Pizza, Italian Tomato & Herb, Sainsbury's*	1/5 Jar/50g	19	38	1.6	7.1	0.4	1.1
Pizza, Tomato With Cheese & Onion, Napolina*	1 Jar/250g	195	78	2.9	7.0	4.0	0.8
Pizza, Traditional Tomato With Basil, Napolina*	1 Jar/250g	153	61	1.2	7.8	2.6	0.7
Pizza, With Herbs, Napolina*	1 Serving/100g	49	49	0.9	6.3	2.2	0.6
Tip Top, Nestle*	1 Serving/40g	45	112	4.8	9.0	6.3	0.0
TORTE,							
Chocolate, Safeway*	1/6 Torte/55g	122	221	4.1	27.6	10.5	1.5
Chocolate, Tesco*	1 Serving/50g	126	251	3.6	32.3	11.9	1.0
Lemon & Mango, Waitrose*	1 Serving/80g	142	177	3.9	33.6	3.0	0.6
Lemon, Somerfield*	1 Serving/45g	71	157	0.8	32.6	2.6	0.8
Raspberry, BGTY, Sainsbury's*	1 Serving/100g	154	154	2.6	27.0	3.9	1.2
Raspberry, Safeway*	1/6 Serving/54g	93	172	1.2	25.1	7.4	1.5
TORTELLINI,							
3 Cheese, Sainsbury's*	1 Serving/50g	196	391	14.4	63.8	8.7	3.0
Aubergine & Pecorino, Sainsbury's*	½ Pack/150g	354	236	8.9	40.3	4.3	3.2
Beef & Red Wine, Italian, Asda*	½ Pack/150.3g	242	161	9.0	25.0	2.8	0.0
Cheese & Tomato, Marks & Spencer*	1 Meal/125g	238	190	10.0	29.1	3.6	1.8
Cheese, Weight Watchers*	1 Can/395g	233	59	2.1	8.5	1.8	0.5
Chicken & Mushroom, Asda*	1 Serving/125g	206	165	7.0	21.0	3.9	1.6
Four Cheese & Tomato, Italian, Asda*	1 Serving/150g	249	166	8.0	25.0	3.8	0.0
Four Cheese With Tomato & Basil Sauce, Tesco*	1 Pack/400g	500	125	6.1	16.9	3.7	0.6
Four Cheese, Asda*	1 Serving/150g	201	134	6.0	20.0	3.3	0.0
Four Cheese, Tesco*	1 Serving/125g	351	281	12.0	38.7	8.7	2.2
Garlic & Herb, Fresh, Sainsbury's*	½ Pack/150g	365	243	11.1	32.2	7.8	1.8
Garlic, Basil & Ricotta, Asda*	1 Serving/150g	227	151	6.0	24.0	3.4	0.0
Ham & Cheese, Asda*	1 Serving/125g	191	153	7.0	20.0	5.0	1.8
Ham & Cheese, Tesco*	1 Serving/225g	578	257	13.5	38.1	5.6	1.8
Italian Meat, Tesco*	1 Serving/125g	333	266	10.6	38.9	7.6	2.3
Italiana, Weight Watchers*	1 Can/395g	237	60	2.1	8.5	1.9	0.5
Mozzarella & Tomato Tortellini, Fresh, Asda*	1oz/28g	46	166	8.0	25.0	3.8	0.0
Mushroom, Asda*	1 Serving/125g	218	174	6.0	28.0	4.2	2.3
Mushroom, BGTY, Sainsbury's*	½ Can/200g	180	90	2.2	13.2	3.1	0.7
Mushroom, Perfectly Balanced, Waitrose*	1 Pack/250g	573	229	9.4	39.8	3.6	2.4
Pepperoni, Italian, Asda*	½ Pack/150g	250	167	6.7	26.0	4.0	0.0
Pork & Beef, BGTY, Sainsbury's*	½ Can/200g	142	71	2.3	11.9	1.6	1.2
Smoked Bacon & Tomato, Asda*	1 Pack/300g	591	197	9.0	29.0	5.0	0.0
Smoked Ham & Cheese, Ready Meals, Waitrose*	1oz/28g	73	261	12.9	38.7	6.1	1.3
Spicy Pepperoni, Asda*	½ Pack/150g	252	168	7.0	26.0	4.0	0.0
Spinach & Ricotta, Italian, Asda*	½ Pack/150g	189	126	5.0	21.0	2.4	0.0
Spinach & Ricotta, Sainsbury's*	1oz/28g	109	388	15.0	62.5	8.7	2.2
Spinach & Ricotta, Tesco*	1 Serving/125g	323	258	11.9	36.2	7.3	1.9
Spinach & Ricotta, Verdi, Asda*	1 Serving/125g	186	149	6.0	21.0	4.5	2.4
Tomato & Mozzarella, Fresh, Asda*	½ Pack/150g	236	157	8.0	25.0	2.8	0.0
Trio, Fresh, Tesco*	½ Pack/125g	323	258	12.8	35.8	7.1	2.0
TORTELLONI,							
Arrabbiata, Sainsbury's*	½ Pack/150g	323	215	9.4	26.6	7.9	3.9
Carbonara, Sainsbury's*	1 Serving/154g	416	270	13.1	27.7	12.6	2.5
Cheese & Chive, Safeway*	1 Serving/100g	200	200	8.3	26.4	6.3	1.7
Cheese & Ham, Co-Op*	1 Serving/125g	344	275	12.0	42.0	7.0	3.0
Cheese & Pesto, Somerfield*	1 Pack/250g	788	315	12.0	40.0	12.0	0.0
Cheese & Sun Dried Tomato, Fresh, Safeway*	½ Pack/199g	364	183	7.7	24.2	6.2	2.7

	Measure	per Measure		Nutrition Values per 100g / 100ml				
	INFO/WEIGHT	KCAL		KCAL	PROT	CARB	FAT	FIBRE
TORTELLONI,								
Cheese, Garlic & Herb, Co-Op*	1 Serving/125g	331		265	10.0	43.0	6.0	0.0
Cheese, Heinz*	1 Can/395g	233		59	2.1	8.6	1.8	0.5
Chicken & Ham, Safeway*	1 Serving/125g	203		162	8.8	23.1	3.8	3.8
Five Cheese, Sainsbury's*	1 Serving/125g	285		228	10.8	25.2	9.3	2.9
Four Cheese, Waitrose*	½ Pack/125g	298		238	10.3	34.2	6.7	1.6
Garlic & Herb, Cooked, Pasta Reale*	1 Pack/300g	546		182	6.7	30.1	3.9	0.9
Garlic Mushroom & Onion, Eat Smart, Safeway*	1 Serving/125g	231		185	9.3	31.4	2.0	1.4
Goats Cheese & Pesto, Sainsbury's*	1 Pack/250g	518		207	8.9	24.6	8.1	2.6
Meat & Cheese, Fresh, Sainsbury's*	½ Pack/125g	304		243	13.5	28.3	8.4	2.6
Mediterranean Vegetable, Perfectly Balanced, Waitrose*	½ Pack/125g	286		229	9.1	40.1	3.6	2.5
Mozzarella, Tomato & Basil, Italian, Somerfield*	½ Pack/125g	314		251	10.5	43.1	4.1	1.9
Mushroom, Perfectly Balanced, Waitrose*	½ Pack/125g	286		229	9.4	39.8	3.6	2.4
Parma Ham & Parmesan, Safeway*	1 Serving/125g	269		215	9.9	27.8	6.7	1.5
Porcini & Pancetta, TTD, Sainsbury's*	1 Serving/175g	294		168	7.1	20.8	6.3	3.4
Potato & Rosemary, Fresh, Sainsbury's*	½ Pack/175g	364		208	5.7	26.6	8.8	2.3
Roasted Vegetable, TTD, Sainsbury's*	½ Pack/125g	259		207	8.4	23.3	8.9	4.0
Spinach & Cheese, Italfresco*	1oz/28g	84		299	10.4	43.2	6.8	0.0
Spinach & Ricotta Cheese, Co-Op*	½ Pack/126g	315		250	10.0	41.0	5.0	4.0
Spinach & Ricotta, Fresh, Safeway*	½ Pack/202g	341		169	7.4	24.0	4.8	2.4
Spinach & Ricotta, Fresh, Sainsbury's*	½ Pack/150g	323		215	10.0	31.3	5.5	3.7
Spinach & Ricotta, Italian, Somerfield*	1 Serving/125g	320		256	10.9	38.8	6.3	2.2
Spinach & Ricotta, Waitrose*	½ Pack/125g	328		262	11.3	38.4	7.0	2.4
Taleggio & Leek, Fresh, Sainsbury's*	½ Pack/175g	450		257	9.7	38.8	7.1	2.6
Walnut & Gorgonzola, Fresh, Sainsbury's*	½ Pack/175g	345		197	8.4	27.8	5.8	2.4
Dry, Average	1oz/28g	99		355	12.5	72.2	1.9	2.1
TORTILLA CHIPS,								
Blazing BBQ, Sainsbury's*	1 Serving/50g	237		474	6.8	58.9	23.5	4.6
Blue, Organic, Sainsbury's*	1 Serving/50g	252		504	7.7	65.8	23.4	5.6
Cajun, Organic, Apache*	1 Serving/25g	113		450	6.0	58.0	22.0	0.0
Chilli Flavour, Somerfield*	1 Serving/50g	242		484	6.8	60.1	24.1	5.3
Chilli, Organic, Evernat*	1oz/28g	137		490	8.0	65.0	22.0	0.0
Classic Mexican, Phileas Fogg*	1 Serving/35g	162		464	5.9	67.2	19.1	3.8
Cool Flavour, Sainsbury's*	1 Serving/50g	232		463	5.7	68.1	18.7	3.7
Cool, Asda*	1 Serving/26g	118		454	7.0	57.0	22.0	9.0
Cool, Salted, Sainsbury's*	1 Serving/50g	253		506	6.5	58.6	27.3	4.3
Cool, Tesco*	1 Serving/50g	227		453	6.4	57.4	22.0	8.1
Easy Cheesy!, Sainsbury's*	1 Serving/50g	249		498	7.1	58.7	26.1	4.5
Lightly Salted, Marks & Spencer*	1 Serving/20g	99		495	7.0	62.2	25.0	4.0
Lightly Salted, SmartPrice, Asda*	¼ Bag/50g	251		502	7.0	60.0	26.0	5.0
Lightly Salted, Waitrose*	1 Bag/40g	188		471	6.5	58.6	23.4	4.3
Nacho Cheese Flavour, Marks & Spencer*	1 Serving/25g	126		505	8.0	57.5	26.8	3.0
Nacho Cheese Flavour, Mexican Style, Co-Op*	1 Serving/50g	248		495	7.0	58.0	27.0	4.0
Nachos Kit, Asda*	1 Serving/100g	448		448	7.0	51.0	24.0	0.7
Natural, Evernat*	1oz/28g	137		490	8.0	65.0	22.0	0.0
Phileas Fogg*	1 Serving/50g	243		486	6.1	62.4	10.1	3.3
Salsa Flavour, Somerfield*	1oz/28g	140		499	6.0	62.0	25.0	0.0
Salsa, Asda*	1 Serving/25g	122		488	6.0	62.0	24.0	6.0
Salsa, Marks & Spencer*	½ Bag/75g	364		485	5.7	59.1	25.1	6.1
Slightly Salted, Organic, Sainsbury's*	1 Serving/50g	227		453	10.0	73.3	13.3	13.3
Taco, Tesco*	1 Serving/50g	248		495	7.4	59.3	25.4	4.4
Waitrose*	1 Serving/25g	128		510	7.9	65.5	24.0	4.5
TORTILLAS,								
Asda*	1 Tortilla/34g	106		311	8.0	54.0	7.0	2.5

	Measure	per Measure	Nutrition Values per 100g / 100ml				
	INFO/WEIGHT	KCAL	KCAL	PROT	CARB	FAT	FIBRE
TORTILLAS,							
Corn, Discovery*	1 Serving/15g	36	243	5.4	53.8	2.3	3.8
Corn, Old El Paso*	1oz/28g	88	315	10.0	44.0	11.0	0.0
Corn, Soft, Old El Paso*	1 Tortilla/38g	129	343	10.0	60.0	7.0	0.0
Flour, 10 Pack, Asda*	1 Tortilla/30g	95	315	9.0	54.0	7.0	2.5
Flour, American Style, Sainsbury's*	1 Tortilla/34.5g	110	313	8.6	53.9	7.0	2.5
Flour, Bakery, Asda*	1 Tortilla/42.6g	130	303	9.0	51.0	7.0	2.5
Flour, For Soft Tacos & Fajitas, Old El Paso*	1 Tortilla/25g	80	320	6.0	52.0	9.0	0.0
Flour, Old El Paso*	2 Tortillas/81g	277	342	10.0	60.0	6.6	0.0
Flour, Soft, Plain, Wraps, Pride Valley*	1 Tortilla/63g	171	272	6.9	48.2	5.7	2.0
Flour, Tex "n" Mex 12, Sainsbury's*	1 Tortilla/26g	85	326	8.6	53.9	9.6	2.5
Made With Wheat Flour	1oz/28g	73	262	7.2	59.7	1.0	2.4
Mexican Cheese, Phileas Fogg*	1 Pack/278g	1404	505	6.5	61.4	26.0	3.0
Mexicana Cheddar, Kettle*	1 Serving/50g	249	498	7.9	56.7	26.6	5.1
Plain Wheat, Waitrose*	1 Tortilla/43g	134	311	8.1	51.5	8.1	3.0
Plain, Wheat Flour, Sainsbury's*	1 Tortilla/56g	175	313	8.6	53.9	7.0	2.5
Plain, Wrap, Tesco*	1 Wrap/63g	171	271	6.8	48.3	5.7	2.1
Soft Flour, Discovery*	1 Serving/39g	122	313	8.6	53.9	7.0	2.5
Soft Flour, Garlic & Coriander, Discovery*	1 Tortilla/40g	125	313	8.5	54.0	7.0	2.5
Soft Flour, Old El Paso*	1 Tortilla/41g	141	343	10.0	60.0	7.0	0.0
Wheat Flour, Waitrose*	1 Wrap/62g	203	327	8.5	51.5	9.8	0.0
Wrap, Discovery*	1 Serving/39.9g	125	313	8.6	53.9	7.0	2.5
Wrap, Low Fat, Marks & Spencer*	1 Serving/180g	225	125	6.3	20.6	2.2	1.9
Wrap, Marks & Spencer*	1 Wrap/40g	106	265	9.0	49.9	3.5	3.4
Wrap, Spicy Tomato, Tesco*	1 Wrap/63g	175	278	7.8	49.2	5.6	2.4
Wrap, Tesco*	1 Wrap/63g	171	272	6.9	48.2	5.7	2.0
Wrap, Tomato & Herb, Tesco*	1 Serving/63g	165	262	7.9	45.1	5.5	2.1
Wrap, Tomato & Herbs, Sainsbury's*	1 Tortilla/52g	157	302	7.8	54.1	6.0	2.4
Wraps, Discovery*	1 Serving/56g	166	296	8.1	50.6	6.8	1.9
TRAIL MIX,							
Average	1oz/28g	121	432	9.1	37.2	28.5	4.3
TREACLE,							
Black	1 Tbsp/20g	51	257	1.2	67.2	0.0	0.0
TRIFLE,							
Average	1oz/28g	45	160	3.6	22.3	6.3	0.5
Banana & Mandarin, Co-Op*	¼ Trifle/125g	238	190	2.0	21.0	11.0	0.1
Black Forest, Asda*	1 Serving/100g	237	237	3.1	36.0	9.0	0.0
Blackforest, BGTY, Sainsburyy's*	1 Pot/125g	171	137	2.1	21.9	4.5	1.6
Caramel, Galaxy, Mars*	1 Pot/100g	255	255	4.5	30.0	13.0	1.0
Cherry & Almond, Somerfield*	1 Trifle/125g	230	184	2.0	23.0	9.0	0.0
Chocolate, Asda*	1 Serving/125.3g	271	217	4.1	21.0	13.0	0.5
Chocolate, Healthy Living, Tesco*	1 Serving/150g	189	126	4.0	21.4	2.7	4.6
Chocolate, Light Milk, Cadbury's*	1 Pot/90g	171	190	5.6	25.5	7.3	0.0
Chocolate, Tesco*	1 Serving/125g	313	250	4.3	24.0	15.2	0.7
Cream Mandarin, GFY, Asda*	1 Serving/113g	151	134	1.6	27.0	4.4	0.2
Fruit Cocktail, COU, Marks & Spencer*	1 Trifle/140g	175	125	2.8	23.1	2.3	0.5
Fruit Cocktail, Individual, Shape*	1 Trifle/115g	136	118	3.2	19.6	2.7	1.6
Fruit Cocktail, Individual,Tesco*	1 Pot/113g	175	155	1.7	19.6	7.8	0.6
Fruit Cocktail, Low Fat, Danone*	1 Pot/114.8g	140	122	2.2	24.0	1.8	0.4
Fruit Cocktail, Luxury Devonshire, St Ivel*	1 Trifle/125g	211	169	1.9	22.6	7.9	0.2
Fruit Cocktail, Marks & Spencer*	1 Serving/165g	272	165	2.4	19.6	8.3	0.9
Fruit, Sainsbury's*	1 Serving/125g	233	186	2.3	21.7	10.0	0.3
Mango & Passion Fruit, Danone*	1oz/28g	50	177	2.6	30.7	4.9	0.4
Peach & Zabaglione, COU, Marks & Spencer*	1 Glass/130g	150	115	2.8	20.6	2.3	0.8

T

	INFO/WEIGHT	KCAL	KCAL	PROT	CARB	FAT	FIBRE
TRIFLE,							
Raspberry, Asda*	1 Serving/100g	175	175	1.8	24.0	8.0	0.1
Raspberry, Sainsbury's*	1 Pot/125g	204	163	1.7	21.5	7.8	0.6
Raspberry, Somerfield*	1 Trifle/125g	208	166	2.0	22.0	8.0	0.0
Raspberry, Tesco*	1 Pot/150g	210	140	1.7	18.5	6.5	1.0
Sherry Sainsbury's*	1 Serving/132g	215	162	2.4	20.1	7.5	0.3
Sherry, BGTY, Sainsbury's*	1 Pot/135g	146	108	3.0	20.2	1.7	0.5
Strawberry, COU, Marks & Spencer*	1 Pot/140g	168	120	3.0	21.8	2.3	0.3
Strawberry, Healthy Living, Tesco*	1 Pot/150g	161	107	2.3	19.3	2.3	2.7
Strawberry, Individual, Safeway*	1 Pot/125g	215	172	2.3	22.0	8.0	0.5
Strawberry, Individual, Shape*	1 Pot/115g	137	119	3.3	19.8	2.7	1.6
Strawberry, Individual, Somerfield*	1 Trifle/125g	208	166	2.0	22.0	8.0	0.0
Strawberry, Low Fat, Shape*	1oz/28g	38	137	3.8	22.8	3.1	1.8
Strawberry, Luxury Devonshire, St Ivel*	1 Trifle/125g	208	166	2.0	21.7	7.9	0.2
Strawberry, Marks & Spencer*	1 Trifle/50g	81	161	2.0	17.7	9.2	0.6
Strawberry, Sainsbury's*	¼ Trifle/125g	232	186	2.2	21.7	10.0	0.2
Strawberry, Somerfield*	¼ Trifle/125g	235	188	2.0	21.0	11.0	0.0
Strawberry, St Ivel*	1 Trifle/113g	194	172	2.4	21.0	8.7	0.2
Strawberry, Tesco*	1 Serving/83g	140	169	1.6	17.7	10.2	0.7
Summerfruit, BGTY, Sainsbury's*	1 Trifle/125g	151	121	1.2	19.2	4.4	0.5
Triple Chocolate, Farmfoods*	¼ Trifle/86.25g	223	259	2.1	21.6	18.2	1.2
With Fresh Cream, Average	1oz/28g	46	166	2.4	19.5	9.2	0.5
TRIFLE SPONGES,							
Safeway*	1 Sponge/23g	73	318	5.3	70.8	1.5	1.1
Somerfield*	1 Sponge/24g	81	339	5.0	76.0	2.0	0.0
Tesco*	1 Sponge/24g	78	325	5.4	72.2	1.6	1.1
TRIPE &,							
Onions, Stewed	1oz/28g	26	93	8.3	9.5	2.7	0.7
TROMPRETTI,							
Sainsbury's*	1 Serving/75g	268	357	12.3	73.1	1.7	2.5
Tricolour, Fresh, Tesco*	1 Pack/250g	675	270	11.2	48.6	3.4	4.0
TROUT,							
Fillets, In Lemon & Dill Marinade, Safeway*	1 Fillet/110g	215	195	19.5	0.0	12.7	0.6
Rainbow, Grilled	1 Serving/120g	162	135	21.5	0.0	5.4	0.0
Rainbow, Raw, Average	1oz/28g	36	127	20.5	0.0	5.1	0.0
Rainbow, Smoked, Average	1 Pack/135g	190	141	21.7	0.8	5.7	0.0
Raw, Average	1 Serving/120g	159	132	20.6	0.0	5.4	0.0
Roasting, Lemon & Rosemary, TTD, Sainsbury's*	1 Fish/269.9g	475	176	20.2	0.0	10.6	0.5
Rosemary Crusted, Finest, Tesco*	1 Trout/150g	264	176	16.2	12.2	6.9	1.0
Smoked, Average	1oz/28g	39	139	22.7	0.3	5.2	0.1
TUNA,							
Chunks, In Brine, Average	1oz/28g	30	108	25.9	0.0	0.5	0.0
Chunks, In Spring Water, Average	1oz/28g	30	108	25.4	0.0	0.6	0.1
Chunks, In Sunflower Oil, Average	1 Can/138g	260	189	26.5	0.0	9.2	0.0
Chunks, Skipjack, In Brine, Average	1 Can/138g	141	102	24.3	0.0	0.6	0.0
Coronation Style, Average	1 Can/80g	122	152	10.2	6.5	9.5	0.6
Fillets, In Tomato Sauce, Princes*	1 Can/120g	131	109	19.0	2.5	2.5	0.0
Flakes, In Brine, Average	1oz/28g	29	104	24.8	0.0	0.6	0.0
In A Lime & Black Pepper Dressing, Princes*	1 Can/80g	102	127	16.3	3.5	5.3	0.0
In A Red Chilli & Lime Dressing, Princes*	1 Sachet/85g	102	120	21.5	1.0	3.3	0.0
In A Tikka Dressing, Princes*	1 Sachet/85g	116	137	18.6	5.5	4.5	0.0
In Chilli Sauce, Safeway*	1 Serving/100g	158	158	16.8	4.8	7.9	0.5
In Garlic & Herb Mayonnaise, John West*	½ Can/92g	243	264	12.0	4.0	22.2	0.2
In Light Lemon Mayonnaise, Princes*	1 Can/80g	99	124	16.8	3.5	4.8	0.0

T

	Measure INFO/WEIGHT	per Measure KCAL	Nutrition Values per 100g / 100ml				
			KCAL	PROT	CARB	FAT	FIBRE
TUNA,							
In Light Mayonnaise, Slimming World*	1 Serving/80g	96	120	17.3	3.6	4.1	0.0
In Salted Water, Ready To Go, Princes*	1 Pack/85g	89	105	25.0	0.0	0.5	0.0
In Sweet & Sour Sauce, Safeway*	1 Can/185g	148	80	10.9	5.6	1.6	1.0
In Thousand Island Dressing, John West*	1 Can/185g	287	155	18.0	5.1	7.0	0.2
In Water, Average	1 Serving/120g	126	105	24.0	0.1	0.8	0.0
Lime & Black Pepper, John West*	1 Serving/85g	133	156	15.6	2.8	9.2	0.0
Steaks, Chargrilled, Italian, Sainsbury's*	1 Serving/125g	199	159	25.1	0.2	6.4	0.5
Steaks, In Brine, Average	1 Sm Can/99g	106	107	25.6	0.0	0.6	0.0
Steaks, In Cajun Marinade, Sainsbury's*	1 Steak/100g	141	141	29.8	0.0	2.4	0.0
Steaks, In Olive Oil, Average	1 Serving/111g	211	190	25.8	0.0	9.6	0.0
Steaks, In Oriental Sauce, Good Choice, Iceland*	1 Pack/260g	333	128	22.3	8.1	0.7	0.4
Steaks, In Sunflower Oil, Average	1 Can/150g	276	184	26.7	0.0	8.6	0.0
Steaks, In Vegetable Oil, Heinz*	1oz/28g	53	189	27.1	0.0	9.0	0.0
Steaks, In Water, Average	1 Serving/200g	215	107	25.6	0.0	0.4	0.0
Steaks, Marinated, Sainsbury's*	1 Serving/100g	153	153	25.1	1.3	5.3	0.5
Steaks, Raw, Average	1 Serving/140g	185	132	28.5	0.1	2.0	0.2
Steaks, Skipjack, In Brine, Average	½ Can/75g	73	98	23.2	0.0	0.6	0.0
Steaks, With Lime & Coriander Dressing, Tesco*	1 Serving/150g	156	104	21.6	3.6	0.4	0.6
Steaks, With Sweet Red Pepper Glaze, Sainsbury's*	1 Steak/100g	135	135	28.5	5.0	0.1	0.1
With Basil Butter, Microwave Easy Steam, Sainsbury's*	1 Pack/170g	292	172	23.3	0.5	8.5	0.1
With Light Mayonnaise, Princes*	1 Sachet/100g	112	112	20.5	3.0	2.0	0.0
With Onion, John West*	1oz/28g	33	118	19.0	6.0	2.0	0.0
With Salsa Verde, Sainsbury's*	1 Serving/125g	310	248	25.5	0.6	16.0	0.0
With a Twist, French Dressing, John West*	1 Pack/85g	135	159	15.2	2.8	9.7	0.1
With a Twist, Lime & Black Pepper Dressing, John West*	1 Pack/85g	133	156	15.6	2.8	9.2	0.0
With a Twist, Oven Dried Tomato & Herb, John West*	1 Pack/85g	129	152	16.1	3.9	8.0	0.1
TUNA IN,							
A Chilli Lime Glaze, Steaks, Asda*	1 Pack/290g	374	129	20.0	8.3	1.8	1.0
Tomato & Herb, Weight Watchers*	1 Can/80g	79	99	11.6	5.1	3.6	0.5
TUNA LUNCH,							
French Style, Light, John West*	1 Pack/250g	208	83	7.8	7.6	2.4	1.0
Indian Style, John West*	1 Pack/240g	401	167	7.7	12.3	9.6	0.6
Italian, Light, All Day, John West*	1 Serving/100g	141	141	11.0	13.0	5.0	0.0
Mediterranean, Light, John West*	1 Pack/250g	180	72	8.0	7.5	1.1	1.1
Nicoise Style, Light, John West*	1 Pack/250g	241	96	10.4	8.9	2.1	2.8
Tomato Salsa, Light, John West*	1 Serving/250g	180	72	8.0	7.5	1.1	1.1
TUNA MAYONNAISE,							
And Sweetcorn, BGTY, Sainsbury's*	½ Pack/50g	46	92	13.8	5.9	1.5	1.1
Weight Watchers*	1 Can/80g	114	142	11.5	6.2	7.9	0.1
With Sweetcorn And Green Peppers, GFY, Asda*	1 Pack/100g	103	103	14.0	5.0	3.0	0.8
With Sweetcorn, John West*	½ Can/92g	231	251	12.0	4.5	20.6	0.2
TUNA SNACK POT,							
Italian, Weight Watchers*	1 Pot/240g	245	102	9.1	8.5	3.6	0.5
Oriental, Weight Watchers*	1 Pot/240g	269	112	9.0	12.6	2.9	0.3
Provencale, Weight Watchers*	1 Pot/240g	266	111	9.8	10.2	3.4	0.5
TURBOT,							
Grilled	1oz/28g	34	122	22.7	0.0	3.5	0.0
Raw	1oz/28g	27	95	17.7	0.0	2.7	0.0
TURKEY,							
Breast, Butter Basted, Average	1 Serving/75g	110	146	23.7	1.9	4.9	0.4
Breast, Cured, Tinned, Tesco*	1 Serving/100g	111	111	17.0	1.3	4.2	0.0
Breast, Diced, Asda*	1/3 Pack/150g	216	144	32.0	0.5	1.5	0.9
Breast, Diced, Healthy Range, Average	1oz/28g	30	108	23.9	0.1	1.3	0.1

T

	Measure	per Measure		Nutrition Values per 100g / 100ml				
	INFO/WEIGHT	KCAL		KCAL	PROT	CARB	FAT	FIBRE
TURKEY,								
Breast, Flamegrilled, Bernard Matthews*	1 Serving/100g	126		126	22.5	0.9	3.6	0.0
Breast, Hand Sliced, Butter Roasted, TTD, Sainsbury's*	1 Pack/150g	177		118	24.5	0.3	2.1	0.5
Breast, Honey Roast, Sliced, Average	1 Serving/50g	57		115	24.0	1.6	1.4	0.3
Breast, Joint, Lemon & Pepper Basted, Tesco*	¼ Pack/132g	238		180	19.7	0.0	11.2	0.0
Breast, Joint, Raw, Average	1 Serving/125g	134		108	21.3	0.7	2.1	0.6
Breast, Pieces, Cooked, Ballyfree*	½ Pack/75g	89		119	26.8	0.6	1.0	0.0
Breast, Raw, Average	1oz/28g	33		117	24.1	0.5	2.0	0.1
Breast, Roasted, Average	1oz/28g	37		131	24.6	0.7	3.3	0.1
Breast, Roll, Cooked, Average	1 Slice/10g	9		92	17.6	3.5	0.8	0.0
Breast, Sage & Onion Style, Premium, Bernard Matthews*	1 Slice/20g	21		104	19.6	2.2	2.0	0.0
Breast, Slices, Cooked, Average	1oz/28g	32		114	24.1	1.2	1.4	0.3
Breast, Smoked, Sliced, Average	1 Slice/20g	23		113	23.4	0.7	2.0	0.0
Breast, Spicy Tikka Flavoured, Safeway*	1 Pack/450g	698		155	28.8	5.4	1.7	1.2
Breast, Steaks, In Crumbs, Average	1 Steak/76g	217		286	13.7	16.4	18.5	0.2
Breast, Steaks, Raw, Average	1oz/28g	30		107	24.3	0.0	1.1	0.0
Breast, Steaks, Thai, Bernard Matthews*	1 Serving/175g	280		160	29.4	4.6	2.7	0.0
Breast, Strips, Chinese Style, Sainsbury's*	1 Pack/650g	1274		196	26.4	12.5	4.5	0.5
Breast, Strips, For Stir Fry, Average	1 Serving/175g	205		117	25.6	0.1	1.6	0.0
Breast, Wafer Thin, Chinese Style, Bernard Matthews*	1 Pack/100g	110		110	18.0	6.1	1.5	0.0
Butter Roast, TTD, Sainsbury's*	2 Slices/102g	120		118	24.5	0.3	2.1	0.5
Dark Meat, Raw	1oz/28g	29		104	20.4	0.0	2.5	0.0
Dark Meat, Roasted	1oz/28g	50		177	29.4	0.0	6.6	0.0
Drummers, Golden, Bernard Matthews*	1 Drummer/57g	146		256	12.2	10.1	18.6	0.9
Drumsticks, Tesco*	1 Serving/200g	272		136	19.9	0.0	6.3	0.0
Escalope, Average	1 Escalope/138g	341		247	13.5	16.7	14.0	0.6
Escalope, Lemon & Pepper, Average	1 Escalope/143g	371		260	12.6	16.7	15.8	0.5
Escalope, Spicy Mango, Bernard Matthews*	1 Escalope/136g	354		260	11.6	24.6	12.8	0.0
Fillets, Chinese Marinated, Bernard Matthews*	1 Pack/200g	304		152	23.4	7.2	3.3	0.0
Fillets, Marinated, Lidl*	1 Serving/250g	238		95	19.0	2.5	1.0	0.0
Fillets, Tikka Marinated, Bernard Matthews*	1 Pack/200g	310		155	21.8	5.2	5.2	1.6
Goujons, Bernard Matthews*	1 Goujon/32g	78		245	11.3	18.1	14.1	0.0
Leg, Roast, Bernard Matthews*	1 Leg/567g	777		137	15.4	0.5	5.4	1.2
Leg, Roast, Uncooked, Bernard Matthews*	1 Serving/283g	317		112	15.4	0.5	5.4	0.0
Light Meat, Raw	1oz/28g	29		105	24.4	0.0	0.8	0.0
Meat, For Casseroles, Bernard Matthews*	1oz/28g	33		118	19.3	0.0	4.5	0.0
Mince, Average	1oz/28g	45		161	23.9	0.0	7.2	0.0
Mince, Lean, Healthy Range, Average	1oz/28g	33		118	20.3	0.0	4.1	0.0
On The Bone, Honey Roast, Somerfield*	1oz/28g	42		149	26.0	0.0	5.0	0.0
Rashers, Average	1 Rasher/26g	26		101	19.1	2.3	1.6	0.0
Rashers, Smoked, Average	1 Serving/75g	76		101	19.8	1.5	1.8	0.0
Roast, Meat & Skin	1oz/28g	48		171	28.0	0.0	6.5	0.0
Roll, Dinosaur, Cooked, Bernard Matthews*	1 Slice/10g	17		170	13.6	6.0	10.2	1.1
Schnitzel, Lidl*	1 Schnitzel/115g	210		183	19.0	11.0	7.0	0.0
Strips, Stir-Fried	1oz/28g	46		164	31.0	0.0	4.5	0.0
Thigh, Diced, Average	1oz/28g	33		117	19.7	0.0	4.3	0.0
Wafer Thin, Cooked, Average	1oz/28g	34		122	19.0	3.2	3.7	0.0
Wafer Thin, Honey Roast, Average	1 Serving/50g	55		109	19.2	4.2	1.7	0.2
Wafer Thin, Smoked, Average	1oz/28g	33		119	18.1	3.6	3.7	0.0
Whole, Raw, Average	½ Joint/254g	389		153	22.6	0.9	6.6	0.1
TURKEY DINNER,								
Roast Dinner, New, Bird's Eye*	1 Pack/340g	320		94	6.7	10.0	3.2	1.2
TURKEY IN,								
BBQ Marinade, Steaks, Asda*	1 Serving/225g	356		158	30.0	4.4	2.3	0.9

T

	Measure	per Measure	Nutrition Values per 100g / 100ml				
	INFO/WEIGHT	KCAL	KCAL	PROT	CARB	FAT	FIBRE
TURKEY IN,							
Pepper Sauce, Escalope, Bernard Matthews*	1 Escalope/143g	350	245	9.4	18.2	15.0	1.5
TURKEY WITH,							
A Cheese & Leek Sauce, Escalope, Bernard Matthews*	1 Portion/134g	340	254	9.2	17.6	16.3	0.0
Cranberry & Orange Glaze, Breast Joint, Sainsbury's*	1 Serving/180g	281	156	29.6	3.0	2.9	1.0
Sage & Onion, Breast Joint, Glazed, GFY, Asda*	1 Serving/100g	101	101	19.0	2.5	1.7	1.0
Sausagemeat, Sage & Onion Stuffing, Breast, Tesco*	1 Serving/300g	417	139	17.9	2.8	6.2	0.8
Stuffing, Breast, Cooked, Somerfield*	1oz/28g	29	104	17.0	6.0	2.0	0.0
TURKISH DELIGHT,							
Bar, Marks & Spencer*	1 Bar/55g	219	399	1.6	79.0	8.5	0.0
Bar, Shapers, Boots*	1 Bar/32g	99	310	2.0	76.0	8.0	0.8
Cadbury's*	1 Bar/51g	186	365	2.0	73.3	7.2	0.0
Dark, Thorntons*	1 Chocolate/10g	39	390	2.7	69.0	11.0	2.0
Fry's*	1 Bar/51g	186	365	2.0	73.3	7.2	0.0
TURMERIC,							
Powder	1 Tsp/3g	11	354	7.8	58.2	9.9	0.0
TURNIP,							
Boiled, Average	1oz/28g	3	12	0.6	2.0	0.2	1.9
Raw	1oz/28g	6	23	0.9	4.7	0.3	2.4
TURNOVER,							
Apple, Dairy Cream, Safeway*	1 Turnover/91.8g	350	380	3.8	32.9	25.9	0.9
Apple, Dutch, Sainsbury's*	1 Serving/33g	130	393	3.6	56.9	16.8	1.4
Apple, Tesco*	1 Turnover/88g	294	334	3.2	29.8	22.4	0.9
TWIGLETS,							
Curry, Jacob's*	1 Bag/30g	134	448	8.0	55.7	21.5	6.0
Original, Jacob's*	1 Bag/30g	117	390	12.0	61.3	10.8	6.8
Original, Tub, Jacob's*	1 Tub/200g	802	401	11.8	60.1	12.6	6.7
Tangy, Jacob's*	1 Bag/30g	136	454	8.1	55.9	22.0	5.4
TWIRL,							
Cadbury's*	1 Finger/22g	116	525	8.1	55.9	30.1	0.0
TWIRLS,							
Prawn Cocktail, Bobby's*	1 Pack/26g	116	445	3.4	65.9	18.6	0.0
Salt & Vinegar, Sainsbury's*	½ Bag/40g	167	418	3.0	70.1	14.0	3.0
Salt & Vinegar, Tesco*	1 Bag/80g	349	436	3.9	65.8	17.5	2.4
TWIX,							
Fingers, Mars*	1 Bar/29g	143	494	4.6	64.8	24.1	0.0
Mars*	1 Single Bar/29g	143	494	4.6	64.8	24.1	0.0
Top, Mars*	1 Bar/28g	143	511	5.2	60.2	27.7	0.0
Twixels, Mars*	1 Finger/6g	31	513	5.0	64.0	26.1	0.0
TZATZIKI,							
Average	1oz/28g	18	66	3.7	2.0	4.9	0.2
Fresh, Sainsbury's*	1oz/28g	35	126	4.0	3.7	10.6	0.3
Marks & Spencer*	1oz/28g	41	145	5.6	5.9	10.9	0.4
Safeway*	1 Serving/85g	67	79	7.9	5.6	2.8	0.2
Tesco*	1 Serving/85g	112	132	5.1	4.9	10.2	2.2
Total*	1oz/28g	27	98	4.9	4.1	7.0	0.0
Waitrose*	1 Serving/50g	57	113	6.8	5.0	7.3	0.7

T

	Measure INFO/WEIGHT	per Measure KCAL	Nutrition Values per 100g / 100ml				
			KCAL	PROT	CARB	FAT	FIBRE
VANILLA EXTRACT,							
Pure, Nielsen Massey Vanillas*	1oz/28g	45	160	0.1	39.5	0.2	0.1
VEAL,							
Cutlet, Breaded, Marks & Spencer*	1 Serving/130g	293	225	13.6	18.7	10.7	0.4
Escalope, Fried	1oz/28g	55	196	33.7	0.0	6.8	0.0
Escalope, Marks & Spencer*	1 Serving/115g	121	105	22.7	0.0	1.7	0.0
Mince, Raw	1oz/28g	40	144	20.3	0.0	7.0	0.0
VEGEMITE,							
Australian, Kraft*	1 Tsp/5g	9	173	23.5	19.7	0.0	0.0
Kraft*	Thin Spread/1g	2	180	30.0	14.0	0.0	0.0
VEGETABLE ESCALOPE,							
Italian Style, Dalepak*	1 Escalope/163g	355	218	4.3	26.5	11.9	1.0
Mushroom, Vegetarian, Creamy, Tesco*	1 Pack/300g	765	255	10.0	20.0	15.0	2.0
VEGETABLE FINGERS,							
Crispy Crunchy, Dalepak*	1 Finger/28g	78	277	4.1	25.8	17.5	8.7
Crispy, Bird's Eye*	1 Finger/29g	50	171	3.8	21.0	8.0	1.2
VEGETABLE MASALA,							
Somerfield*	1 Pack/350g	406	116	2.7	11.0	6.8	3.0
With Rice, Feeling Great, Findus*	1 Pack/350g	350	100	3.0	18.0	2.0	1.7
VEGETABLE MEDLEY,							
& Carrot, Waitrose*	½ Pack/100g	28	28	1.5	4.7	0.4	2.2
Asda*	1 Serving/150g	39	26	1.9	3.0	0.7	0.0
Asparagus Tips, Perfectly Balanced, Waitrose*	1 Serving/225g	122	54	1.3	4.6	3.4	1.4
Basil & Oregano Butter, Waitrose*	1 Serving/113g	59	52	1.7	3.7	3.4	1.9
Crunchy, Marks & Spencer*	1 Pack/250g	75	30	3.3	2.7	0.8	2.9
Frozen, Marks & Spencer*	1 Pack/500g	175	35	3.4	3.9	0.8	3.1
Green, Healthy Living, Tesco*	1 Serving/125g	59	47	3.7	4.1	1.8	4.1
Green, Marks & Spencer*	1 Serving/250g	63	25	3.0	1.8	0.5	1.8
Green, Sainsbury's*	1 Pack/220g	178	81	3.0	2.5	6.5	2.9
Green, Tesco*	1 Pack/250g	218	87	3.5	7.4	4.9	1.2
Tesco*	1 Serving/200g	52	26	1.8	3.6	0.5	2.4
Winter, Safeway*	1 Serving/250g	68	27	1.4	3.6	0.8	2.4
With Herby Butter, Marks & Spencer*	1 Pack/300g	180	60	1.4	5.2	3.6	1.5
VEGETABLE SELECTION,							
Casserole, Somerfield*	1 Pack/600g	174	29	1.0	5.7	0.3	1.4
Chefs, Marks & Spencer*	1 Pack/250g	75	30	2.7	3.8	0.6	2.4
Country, Way To Five, Sainsbury's*	½ Pack/125g	36	29	2.1	3.7	0.6	2.2
Garden, Tesco*	1 Pack/275g	124	45	1.2	2.7	3.3	1.2
Green, Fresh, Finest, Tesco*	1 Pack/250g	138	55	3.3	4.8	2.5	2.3
Sainsbury's*	1oz/28g	7	25	1.9	3.0	0.6	2.2
Winter, Marks & Spencer*	1 Bag/400g	80	20	2.2	3.2	0.0	3.1
Winter, Ready to Roast, Safeway*	½ Pack/175g	140	80	0.8	12.4	2.7	3.5
With Herb Butter, Waitrose*	1 Pack/300g	270	90	1.9	8.1	5.6	2.1
VEGETABLES,							
& Feta Cheese, Roasted, BGTY, Sainsbury's*	1 Pack/200g	264	132	6.4	21.7	2.2	0.0
Baby, Frozen, Asda*	1 Serving/100g	25	25	1.9	3.7	0.3	1.9
Broccoli & Cauliflower, Layered, Marks & Spencer*	½ Pack/135g	95	70	1.5	7.6	3.4	1.2
Casserole, Ready To Cook, Sainsbury's*	½ Pack/240g	74	31	0.9	6.2	0.3	1.4
Casserole, With Baby Potatoes, Marks & Spencer*	½ Pack/350g	140	40	1.2	7.8	0.3	2.1
Chargrilled With Tomato Sauce, GFY, Asda*	1 Serving/260g	164	63	1.4	8.0	2.8	0.0
Chinese Inspired, Crisp, Marks & Spencer*	1 Pack/250g	63	25	1.7	4.6	0.3	1.9
Chinese Water, Amoy*	1 Pack/200g	46	23	1.8	3.7	0.3	1.5
Country, Way To Five, Sainsbury's*	1 Serving/250g	73	29	2.1	3.7	0.6	2.2
Crispy, Asda*	1 Serving/50g	18	35	0.1	8.0	0.3	2.2

INFO/WEIGHT	Measure per Measure KCAL	Nutrition Values per 100g / 100ml KCAL	PROT	CARB	FAT	FIBRE

VEGETABLES,

	Measure INFO/WEIGHT	per Measure KCAL	KCAL	PROT	CARB	FAT	FIBRE
Crispy, Ready To Cook, Sainsbury's*	1 Serving/100g	25	25	1.8	3.6	0.3	2.2
Crispy, Tesco*	1 Pack/200g	54	27	1.9	3.9	0.4	2.3
Crudite Selection, Prepared, Marks & Spencer*	1 Serving/250g	75	30	1.4	5.8	0.4	2.0
Farmhouse Mix, Frozen, Asda*	1 Serving/100g	25	25	2.5	2.2	0.8	0.0
Favourite Five Selection, Marks & Spencer*	½ Pack/125g	25	20	1.8	2.4	0.6	2.9
For Roasting, Marks & Spencer*	½ Pack/223.5g	190	85	1.2	7.7	5.6	2.4
Garden, 5 A Day, Tesco*	1 Bag/250g	65	26	3.0	1.9	0.7	0.0
Garden, With Asparagus, Way To Five, Sainsbury's*	1 Serving/230g	55	24	2.1	2.5	0.6	1.9
In Tomato Sauce, Mediterranean, Marks & Spencer*	1 Pack/300g	105	35	2.5	4.3	0.7	2.2
Layered, GFY, Asda*	½ Pack/150g	81	54	1.2	6.0	2.8	2.0
Layered, Marks & Spencer*	1 Serving/100g	85	85	1.6	9.1	4.5	1.8
Mediterranean Roasted, Sainsbury's*	1 Serving/150g	119	79	2.2	9.5	3.6	3.4
Mediterranean Style Vegetables, Safeway*	1 Serving/205g	110	54	1.7	7.4	1.9	2.4
Mediterranean Style, Asda*	½ Pack/205g	172	84	1.4	6.0	6.0	2.8
Mediterranean Style, Finest, Tesco*	1 Serving/150g	153	102	1.9	7.3	7.2	1.2
Mediterranean Style, Marks & Spencer*	½ Pack/200g	170	85	2.0	9.5	4.1	1.2
Mediterranean Style, Ready to Roast, Sainsbury's*	1 Serving/200g	268	134	3.1	6.2	10.8	1.0
Mediterranean Style, Roasting, Tesco*	1 Serving/200g	72	36	1.1	5.7	1.0	1.3
Oriental Inspired, Marks & Spencer*	1 Pack/260g	78	30	1.9	4.6	0.5	2.7
Oriental Stir Fry, Frozen, Sainsbury's*	½ Pack/225g	142	63	1.5	5.4	3.9	1.5
Oven Roasted, Somerfield*	1oz/28g	36	129	1.0	19.0	5.0	0.0
Roast, Marks & Spencer*	1 Pack/420g	273	65	1.4	4.9	4.2	0.4
Roasted Root, Extra Special, Asda*	½ Pack/205g	160	78	1.1	15.0	1.5	6.0
Roasted Winter, Tesco*	1 Serving/200g	170	85	2.2	10.0	4.0	2.0
Roasted, Italian, Marks & Spencer*	1 Serving/95g	219	230	1.8	7.1	21.0	1.7
Roasted, Selection, COU, Marks & Spencer*	1 Pack/250g	88	35	1.2	6.1	0.8	0.6
Root, Honey Roast, BGTY, Sainsbury's*	½ Pack/150g	174	116	2.5	23.1	1.5	5.5
Root, Ready to Roast, Sainsbury's*	½ Pack/200g	188	94	1.3	13.0	4.3	2.2
Special Mix, Sainsbury's*	1 Serving/80g	54	68	3.4	9.7	1.7	3.2
Steam Fresh, Bird's Eye*	1 Bag/121.2g	46	38	3.8	4.5	0.5	2.8
Sun Dried Tomato, Selection, Finest, Tesco*	1 Pack/340g	303	89	1.8	8.9	5.1	1.1
Sweet & Crunchy, Tesco*	1 Serving/50g	22	43	2.3	7.0	0.6	2.4
Sweet Summer, Safeway*	1 Serving/115g	60	52	3.7	7.8	0.7	3.5
Szechuan Style, Ready Prepared, Waitrose*	1 Pack/300g	132	44	2.3	5.7	1.3	1.9
Vietnamese, Wok, Findus*	1 Serving/100g	25	25	1.5	4.5	0.5	0.0
Winter Crunchy, Marks & Spencer*	½ Pack/125g	31	25	2.0	3.1	0.8	2.7
Winter, Fresh, Asda*	1 Bag/250g	75	30	3.0	2.2	1.0	2.3
Winter, Ready to Roast, Fresh, Sainsbury's*	1 Pack/272g	226	83	1.2	13.2	2.8	0.0
Winter, Tesco*	1 Pack/250g	73	29	2.0	3.3	0.8	2.6
With Sun Dried Tomato, Roasted, Finest, Tesco*	½ Pack/150g	153	102	1.9	7.3	7.2	1.2

VEGETARIAN MINCE,

Meat Free, Asda*	1oz/28g	49	176	27.0	7.0	4.4	4.1
Safeway*	1 Pack/454g	781	172	17.3	4.5	9.5	1.8
Vegemince, Realeat*	1 Serving/125g	220	176	15.5	6.0	10.0	2.0
Easy Cook, Linda McCartney*	1oz/28g	35	126	21.4	9.3	0.4	1.7

VENISON,

Grill Steak, Average	1 Grillsteak/150g	179	119	19.0	5.0	2.5	1.0
Roasted	1oz/28g	46	165	35.6	0.0	2.5	0.0
Steak, Raw, Average	1oz/28g	30	108	22.8	0.0	1.9	0.0

VENISON IN,

Red Wine & Port, Average	1oz/28g	21	76	9.8	3.5	2.6	0.4

VERMICELLI,

Dry	1oz/28g	99	355	8.7	78.3	0.4	0.0

V

INFO/WEIGHT	Measure per Measure	KCAL	Nutrition Values per 100g / 100ml KCAL	PROT	CARB	FAT	FIBRE
VERMICELLI,							
Egg, Cooked, Average	1 Serving/185g	239	129	5.0	24.0	1.4	1.0
VERMOUTH,							
Dry	1 Shot/50ml	55	109	0.1	3.0	0.0	0.0
Sweet	1 Shot/50ml	76	151	0.0	15.9	0.0	0.0
VICE VERSAS,							
Nestle*	1 Bag/45.6g	223	485	5.0	69.3	20.9	0.0
VIMTO*,							
Cordial	1 Serving/10ml	3	30	0.0	7.4	0.0	0.0
Grape Blackcurrant & Raspberry Juice Drink	1 Bottle/500ml	223	45	0.0	11.0	0.0	0.0
Light	1 Can/330ml	17	5	0.0	1.2	0.0	0.0
VINAIGRETTE,							
Balsamic Vinegar & Pistachio, Finest, Tesco*	1 Tbsp/15ml	56	370	0.2	2.8	39.2	0.0
Finest, Tesco*	1 Serving/50ml	248	495	0.9	13.2	48.7	0.5
Frank Cooper*	1 Pot/28g	46	163	1.0	14.1	11.4	0.3
French Style, Finest, Tesco*	1 Tbsp/15ml	69	461	0.8	5.9	47.4	0.2
French, Full Flavoured, Fat Free, Kraft*	1 Tbsp/15ml	7	47	0.1	10.5	0.0	0.3
Luxury French, Hellmann's*	1 Tsp/5ml	15	305	0.8	16.0	26.1	0.4
Newman's Own*	½ Tbsp/5g	17	333	0.5	3.9	35.0	0.0
Oil Free, Tesco*	1 Tbsp/15ml	5	30	0.3	6.0	0.1	1.4
Perfectly Balanced, Waitrose*	1 Tsp/5ml	4	89	0.4	20.9	0.4	0.5
Portuguese, Nando's*	1 Tbsp/15g	61	409	1.0	2.1	44.0	0.3
Waistline, 99% Fat Free, Crosse & Blackwell*	1 Tbsp/15ml	1	9	1.0	0.7	0.2	0.2
VINE LEAVES,							
Preserved in Brine	1oz/28g	4	15	3.6	0.2	0.0	0.0
Stuffed With Rice	1oz/28g	73	262	2.8	23.8	18.0	0.0
Stuffed With Rice & Mixed Herbs, Sainsbury's*	1 Leaf/36.7g	44	120	2.6	16.3	4.9	1.2
Stuffed, Marks & Spencer*	1 Vine Leaf/38.1g	40	105	2.6	14.2	4.1	1.2
VINEGAR,							
Balsamic	5ml	0	3	0.3	0.6	0.0	0.0
Balsamic, Dipping Oil, Finest, Tesco*	1 Tsp/5ml	33	668	0.0	4.4	71.7	0.0
Balsamic, Marks & Spencer*	1 Tbsp/20g	24	120	0.9	29.1	0.0	0.3
Balsamic, Of Modena, Fattorie Giacobazzi*	100g	106	106	0.2	21.8	0.1	0.0
Balsamic, Of Modena, Monari Federzoni*	1 Serving/5ml	3	69	0.6	16.0	0.0	0.0
Balsamic, Of Modena, TTD, Sainsbury's*	1 Tbsp/15ml	18	120	2.0	25.0	2.0	2.0
Cider, Tesco*	1 Tbsp/15ml	3	19	0.4	0.6	0.0	0.0
Malt, Heinz*	1 Tsp/5ml	1	18	0.2	0.6	0.0	0.0
Red Wine, Tesco*	1 Tsp/5ml	1	22	0.4	0.6	0.0	0.0
Rice, White, Amoy*	1 Tsp/5ml	0	4	0.0	1.0	0.0	0.0
Wine, White, Heinz*	1 Tsp/5ml	1	21	0.1	0.6	0.0	0.0
VODKA,							
37.5% Volume	1 Shot/25ml	52	207	0.0	0.0	0.0	0.0
40% Volume	1 Shot/25ml	56	222	0.0	0.0	0.0	0.0
VOL AU VENTS,							
Broccoli, Marks & Spencer*	1oz/28g	105	375	6.8	28.5	26.4	1.0
Chicken & Mushroom, Marks & Spencer*	1oz/28g	98	350	7.7	25.2	24.3	2.1
Garlic Mushroom, Mini, Asda*	1 Serving/16.7g	59	347	5.0	21.0	27.0	0.0
Ham & Cheese, Marks & Spencer*	1oz/28g	106	380	8.8	25.7	26.7	1.8
Mushroom, Marks & Spencer*	1oz/28g	94	335	6.3	24.2	23.6	1.5
Mushroom, Sainsbury's*	1 Serving/14g	49	350	6.9	30.8	22.1	1.4
Party Seafood, Youngs*	1 Serving/17g	60	354	8.3	26.0	24.8	1.0
Prawn, Marks & Spencer*	1oz/28g	101	360	8.0	26.2	24.7	1.9
Tomato, Marks & Spencer*	1oz/28g	87	310	4.5	26.7	20.4	1.7

V

	Measure INFO/WEIGHT	per Measure KCAL	Nutrition Values per 100g / 100ml				
			KCAL	PROT	CARB	FAT	FIBRE
WAFERS,							
Cafe Curls, Rolled, Askeys*	1 Curl/5g	21	422	5.8	80.3	8.6	0.0
Cannoli, Sainsbury's*	1 Biscuit/9g	45	496	3.5	71.0	22.0	0.0
Caramel, Dark Chocolate, Tunnock's*	1 Wafer/26g	128	492	5.2	60.7	25.4	0.0
Caramel, Marks & Spencer*	1oz/28g	136	486	5.4	63.1	23.5	0.5
Caramel, Milk Chocolate, Farmfoods*	1 Biscuit/22g	105	475	5.9	61.9	22.8	3.1
Caramel, Milk Chocolate, Marks & Spencer*	1oz/28g	133	475	5.9	61.9	22.8	3.1
Caramel, Tunnock's*	1 Biscuit/26g	118	454	4.6	68.0	20.1	0.0
Caramel, Value, Tesco*	1 Wafer/23.1g	102	443	4.6	64.0	18.7	0.9
Chocolate Curl, Mini, Marks & Spencer*	1 Biscuit/5g	28	550	5.8	56.0	33.6	1.5
Chocolate Mint, Plain, Somerfield*	1oz/28g	151	538	9.0	56.0	31.0	0.0
Chocolate, Cadbury's*	1oz/28g	147	526	7.0	61.2	29.8	0.0
Filled	1oz/28g	150	535	4.7	66.0	29.9	0.0
Ice Cream	1oz/28g	96	342	10.1	78.8	0.7	0.0
Ice Cream, Askeys*	2 Wafers/3g	11	380	11.0	79.0	2.5	0.0
Milk Chocolate, Sainsbury's*	1 Biscuit/10g	51	506	6.2	60.5	26.7	1.4
Orange Break, Somerfield*	1oz/28g	149	531	8.0	57.0	30.0	0.0
Pink, Crawfords*	1 Biscuit/7g	36	521	2.5	68.6	26.5	1.1
WAFFLES,							
Bacon Flavour, Better For You, Morrisons*	1 Bag/12g	41	344	5.6	76.3	1.8	1.5
Barbecue Flavour, American Style, Shapers, Boots*	1 Pack/20g	95	476	4.5	65.0	22.0	3.7
Caramel, Starbucks*	1 Waffle/30g	140	467	4.3	66.7	20.3	1.3
Caramel, The Big Cereal Company*	1 Serving/23g	84	367	7.5	80.1	1.9	2.8
Cheese & Onion, Marks & Spencer*	1 Pack/50g	253	505	5.1	56.0	28.7	2.6
Ready Salted, Marks & Spencer*	1 Bag/40g	194	485	2.1	65.6	23.6	1.6
Smokey Bacon, BGTY, Sainsbury's*	1 Bag/12g	41	344	5.6	76.3	1.8	1.5
Sweet, American Style, Sainsbury's*	1 Waffle/35.0g	153	437	9.5	51.5	21.4	3.3
Toasting, McVitie's*	1 Waffle/23g	108	469	5.9	53.9	25.6	0.9
WAGON WHEEL,							
Burton's*	1 Wheel/36g	159	441	4.9	67.3	16.9	1.3
WALNUT WHIP,							
The Classic, Marks & Spencer*	1 Whip/26g	127	490	7.2	54.9	27.4	1.1
Vanilla, Nestle*	1 Whip/34g	160	486	5.7	60.5	24.6	0.0
WALNUTS,							
Average	6 Halves/20g	138	691	15.6	3.2	68.5	3.5
Halves, Average	1 Serving/25g	167	669	17.4	6.3	65.0	4.7
WATER,							
Barley, Lemon, Robinson's*	1fl oz/30ml	26	88	0.3	19.6	0.0	0.0
Barley, Orange, Robinson's*	1oz/28g	28	101	0.3	23.1	0.0	0.0
Black Cherry Flavoured, Abbey Well*	1 Glass/200ml	1	1	0.0	0.1	0.0	0.0
Blackcurrant Flavour, Still, Danone'*	1 Serving/120ml	25	21	0.0	5.0	0.0	0.0
Grapefruit Flavoured, Balanced Lifestyle, Aldi*	1 Serving/100ml	2	2	0.1	0.4	0.0	0.1
Lemon & Elderflower, Slightly Sparkling, Tesco*	1 Glass/200ml	2	1	0.0	0.1	0.0	0.0
Lemon & Lime Flavoured, Marks & Spencer*	1 Glass/250ml	13	5	0.0	1.0	0.0	0.0
Mandarin & Cranberry, Still, Marks & Spencer*	1 Bottle/500ml	100	20	0.0	5.0	0.0	0.0
Mineral Or Tap	1 Glass/200ml	0	0	0.0	0.0	0.0	0.0
Mineral, Apple & Elderflower, Hedgerow*	1 Serving/250ml	85	34	0.0	8.2	0.0	0.0
Mineral, Touch of Fruit, Still, Volvic*	1fl oz/30ml	7	23	0.0	5.5	0.0	0.0
Orange & Peach, Touch of Fruit, Volvic*	1 Bottle/400ml	93	23	0.0	5.5	0.0	0.0
Peach & Lemon, Still, Marks & Spencer*	1 Bottle/500ml	100	20	0.0	5.0	0.0	0.0
Peach Flavour, Sparkling, Strathmore*	1fl oz/30ml	0	0	0.0	0.1	0.0	0.0
Peach, Perfectly Clear, Silver Spring Mineral Water Co*	1 Bottle/500ml	4	1	0.0	0.0	0.0	0.0
Spring Peach, Safeway*	1 Bottle/500ml	10	2	0.1	0.2	0.1	0.1
Spring, Apple & Blackcurrant, Hadrian*	1 Bottle/365ml	3	1	0.1	0.1	0.0	0.0

W

	Measure INFO/WEIGHT	per Measure KCAL	Nutrition Values per 100g / 100ml				
			KCAL	PROT	CARB	FAT	FIBRE
WATER,							
Spring, Apple & Cherry Flavoured, Sparkling, Sainsbury's*	1 Glass/250ml	5	2	0.1	0.2	0.1	0.1
Spring, Apple & Raspberry Flavoured, Sainsbury's*	1fl oz/30ml	1	2	0.1	0.1	0.1	0.1
Spring, Boysenberry, Shapers, Boots*	1 Bottle/700ml	7	1	0.0	0.1	0.0	0.0
Spring, Elderflower & Pear, Sainsbury's*	1 Glass/250g	5	2	0.1	0.2	0.1	0.1
Spring, Lemon & Lime Flavour, Sparkling, Superdrug*	1 Bottle/500ml	9	2	0.1	0.1	0.1	0.1
Spring, Lemon & Lime Flavoured, Sparkling, Sainsbury's*	1 Lge Bottle/1000ml	17	2	0.1	0.1	0.1	0.1
Spring, Peach Flavour, Shapers, Boots*	1 Bottle/500ml	5	1	0.0	0.0	0.0	0.0
Spring, Peach Flavour, Sparkling, Co-Op*	1 Glass/250ml	2	1	0.0	0.0	0.0	0.0
Spring, Peach Flavoured, No Added Sugar, Asda*	1 Glass/200ml	4	2	0.0	0.2	0.0	0.0
Spring, Peach Flavoured, Sainsbury's*	1 Glass/250ml	5	2	0.1	0.2	0.1	0.1
Spring, Peach, Sparkling, Marks & Spencer*	1fl oz/30ml	2	5	0.0	1.0	0.0	0.0
Spring, Raspberry & Cranberry, Sparkling, Shapers, Boots*	1 Bottle/500ml	10	2	0.0	0.5	0.0	0.0
Spring, Raspberry & Mango, Shapers, Boots*	1 Bottle/500ml	7	1	0.0	0.1	0.0	0.0
Spring, Raspberyy & Cranberry, Shapers, Boots*	1 Bottle/500ml	10	2	0.0	0.0	0.0	0.0
Spring, Stawberry & Vanilla, Sainsbury's*	1 Glass/250ml	5	2	0.1	0.2	0.1	0.1
Spring, Strawberry & Vanilla, Asda*	1 Glass/200ml	2	1	0.1	0.2	0.1	0.1
Spring, White Grape & Blackberry, Tesco*	1 Glass/200ml	4	2	0.0	0.3	0.0	0.0
Spring, White Grape & Jasmine, Marks & Spencer*	1 Bottle/500ml	5	1	0.0	0.2	0.0	0.0
Spring, Wild Berries, The Simpsons*	1oz/28g	0	1	0.0	0.0	0.0	0.0
White Grape & Blackberry, Sparkling, Tesco*	1 Glass/200ml	4	2	0.0	0.5	0.0	0.0
WATER CHESTNUTS,							
Raw, Average	1oz/28g	10	34	1.0	7.8	0.1	0.1
Whole, Crunchy, Sainsbury's*	1 Can/140g	46	33	0.9	7.4	0.1	2.3
WATER ICE,							
Fruit, Iceland*	1 Lolly/75ml	74	98	0.2	24.4	0.0	0.2
Orange, Iceland*	1 Ice/75ml	73	98	0.2	24.4	0.0	0.2
Pineapple, Iceland*	1 Ice/75ml	65	86	0.0	21.5	0.0	0.2
Raspberry, Iceland*	1 Ice/75ml	67	89	0.0	22.2	0.0	0.2
WATERCRESS,							
Raw, Average	1oz/28g	6	23	3.0	0.4	1.0	1.5
WATERMELON,							
Average	1 Serving/250g	75	30	0.4	7.0	0.3	0.4
WHEAT,							
Ebly*	1oz/28g	98	351	12.1	71.9	1.7	5.4
WHEAT CRUNCHIES,							
Bacon, Crispy, Golden Wonder*	1 Bag/35g	172	492	9.7	56.0	25.5	3.9
Golden Wonder*	1 Pack/35g	172	491	11.1	55.9	24.8	0.0
Salt & Vinegar, Golden Wonder*	1 Bag/34g	165	484	10.5	54.5	24.9	2.8
Spicy Tomato, Golden Wonder*	1 Bag/35g	172	491	9.4	56.0	25.5	3.9
Worcester Sauce, Golden Wonder*	1 Bag/35g	172	492	9.3	56.4	25.5	3.9
WHEATGERM,							
Average	1oz/28g	100	357	26.7	44.7	9.2	15.6
WHELKS,							
Boiled	1oz/28g	25	89	19.5	0.0	1.2	0.0
WHISKEY,							
37.5% Volume	1 Shot/25ml	52	207	0.0	0.0	0.0	0.0
40% Volume	1 Shot/25ml	56	222	0.0	0.0	0.0	0.0
Jack Daniels*	1 Shot/25ml	56	222	0.0	0.0	0.0	0.0
Scotch, 37.5% Volume	1 Shot/25ml	52	207	0.0	0.0	0.0	0.0
Scotch, 40% Volume	1 Shot/25ml	56	222	0.0	0.0	0.0	0.0
Teacher's*	1 Shot/25ml	56	222	0.0	0.0	0.0	0.0
WHITE PUDDING,							
Average	1oz/28g	126	450	7.0	36.3	31.8	0.0

	Measure INFO/WEIGHT	per Measure KCAL	Nutrition Values per 100g / 100ml				
			KCAL	PROT	CARB	FAT	FIBRE
WHITEBAIT,							
In Flour, Fried	1oz/28g	147	525	19.5	5.3	47.5	0.2
WHITECURRANTS,							
Raw	1oz/28g	7	26	1.3	5.6	0.0	3.4
WHITING,							
In Crumbs, Fried in Blended Oil	1 Serving/180g	344	191	18.1	7.0	10.3	0.2
Raw	1oz/28g	23	81	18.7	0.0	0.7	0.0
Steamed	1 Serving/85g	78	92	20.9	0.0	0.9	0.0
WINE,							
Mulled, Homemade	1 Glass/120ml	227	196	0.1	25.2	0.0	0.0
Red	1 Glass/120ml	80	68	0.1	0.2	0.0	0.0
Rose, Gently Sparkling, Non Alcoholic, Ame*	100ml	35	35	0.0	5.9	0.0	0.0
Rose, Medium	1 Glass/120ml	83	71	0.1	2.5	0.0	0.0
Sparkling, Alcohol Free, Sainsbury's*	1 Glass/175ml	35	20	0.0	4.9	0.0	0.0
Strong Ale Barley	1 Can/440ml	290	66	0.7	6.1	0.0	0.0
White, Dry	1 Glass/120ml	77	66	0.1	0.6	0.0	0.0
White, Medium	1 Glass/120ml	87	74	0.1	3.0	0.0	0.0
White, Non Alcoholic, Ame*	1 Glass/120ml	46	38	0.0	9.5	0.0	0.0
White, Sparkling	1 Glass/120ml	87	74	0.3	5.1	0.0	0.0
White, Sweet	1 Glass/120ml	110	94	0.2	5.9	0.0	0.0
WINE GUMS,							
Co-Op*	1 Sweet/6g	20	337	3.5	80.8	0.0	0.0
Iceland*	1oz/28g	85	302	6.7	67.8	0.4	0.0
Marks & Spencer*	1oz/28g	94	335	3.9	78.5	0.1	0.0
Maynards*	1 Sweet/5g	17	331	6.0	76.6	0.0	0.0
Mini, Co-Op*	1 Sweet/2g	7	330	6.0	76.0	0.1	0.0
Mini, Rowntree's*	1 Sm Bag/36g	125	348	6.7	80.5	0.0	0.0
Somerfield*	1 Wine Gum/6.3g	21	343	6.4	76.9	0.4	0.5
Sour, Bassett's*	¼ Bag/50g	160	319	3.7	78.0	0.0	0.0
Tesco*	1 Serving/100g	316	316	7.7	70.7	0.2	0.1
WINKLES,							
Boiled	1oz/28g	20	72	15.4	0.0	1.2	0.0
WISPA,							
Bite, With Biscuit In Caramel, Cadbury's*	1 Bar/47g	240	510	6.4	56.9	28.6	0.0
Cadbury's*	1 Treatsize/15g	83	550	7.1	53.9	34.2	0.0
Gold, Cadbury's*	1 Bar/52g	263	505	5.7	57.0	28.0	0.0
Mint, Cadbury's*	1 Bar/50g	275	550	7.0	54.7	33.6	0.0
WOK,							
Chinese, Findus*	1 Serving/250g	113	45	1.5	9.5	0.2	0.0
Classic, Findus*	1 Serving/250g	113	45	2.0	7.5	0.5	0.0
Sambal Oelek, Findus*	1 Serving/200g	170	85	3.0	17.0	0.4	0.0
Thai, Findus*	½ Pack/250g	100	40	1.5	8.0	0.3	0.0
WONTON,							
Chicken, Asda*	1 Wonton/15g	46	306	14.0	18.0	20.0	1.9
Chinese Prawn, Sainsbury's*	1 Wonton/16g	38	252	11.9	16.5	15.4	1.2
Prawn, Dim Sum Selection, Sainsbury's*	1 Wonton/10g	26	259	11.3	26.8	11.8	1.3
Prawn, Oriental Selection, Waitrose*	1 Wonton/17.9g	45	252	9.1	29.2	11.0	1.1
WOTSITS,							
BBQ, Walkers*	1 Bag/21g	109	521	7.2	55.8	29.9	1.2
Cheesy Wafflers, Walkersr*	1 Bag/31g	160	515	6.5	50.0	32.0	1.3
Cheesy, Walkers*	1 Pack/19g	101	530	6.0	55.0	32.0	1.0
Flamin' Hot, Walkers*	1 Pack/19g	99	520	5.0	57.0	30.0	1.2
Mild Cheese, Walkers*	1 Serving/19.1g	102	535	6.0	54.0	33.0	1.0
Prawn Cocktail, Walkers*	1 Pack/21g	109	520	5.5	55.0	31.0	1.1

WRAP,	Measure INFO/WEIGHT	per Measure KCAL	KCAL	PROT	CARB	FAT	FIBRE
All Day Breakfast, Marks & Spencer*	1 Pack/196g	529	270	10.8	21.2	16.0	1.4
American Deli, Shapers, Boots*	1 Pack/171.7g	249	145	9.5	21.0	2.6	2.0
Aromatic Duck, Safeway*	1 Pack/180g	376	209	9.1	21.3	9.7	1.6
Avocado & Salad, Pret A Manger*	1 Serving/200g	605	303	5.3	18.1	23.3	2.9
BBQ Chicken, Shapers, Boots*	1 Serving/165.4g	267	162	10.0	25.0	2.3	1.2
BBQ Steak, Marks & Spencer*	1 Pack/253g	506	200	10.6	24.8	6.8	1.8
Bean & Cheese, Tesco*	1 Pack/105g	258	246	5.5	28.5	12.3	1.0
Beef in Black Bean, Marks & Spencer*	1 Pack/150g	338	225	10.2	20.5	11.4	1.6
Brie & Cranberry, Marks & Spencer*	1 Pack/224.5g	549	245	6.1	27.3	12.4	1.7
Cajun Chicken Louisiana Style, Sainsbury's*	1 Pack/190g	395	209	11.1	23.9	7.6	0.0
Cajun, GFY, Asda*	1 Pack/176.3g	231	131	9.0	21.0	1.2	0.9
Chapati, Patak's*	1 Pack/42g	130	310	11.2	44.9	9.5	0.0
Chargrilled Chicken, Food To Go, Marks & Spencer*	1 Serving/100g	134	134	11.2	14.5	3.5	1.6
Chargrilled Chicken, Perfectly Balanced, Waitrose*	1 Pack/230g	361	157	10.3	22.7	2.9	2.9
Cheese & Bean, Tesco*	1 Pack/209.8g	470	224	7.0	28.6	9.0	1.0
Cheestring & Ham, Attack-a-Snak, Golden Vale*	1 Pack/109.9g	266	242	13.4	28.0	8.2	1.4
Chicken & Bacon Caesar Salad, Asda*	1 Pack/160g	565	353	18.0	20.8	22.0	0.9
Chicken & Bacon, Simple Solutions, Tesco*	1 Pack/300g	474	158	20.7	1.2	7.8	0.5
Chicken & Cous Cous, BGTY, Sainsbury's*	1 Pack/230g	359	156	8.8	21.5	3.9	0.0
Chicken & Cous Cous, Moroccan Style, GFY, Asda*	1 Pack/164g	307	187	12.0	32.0	1.2	1.8
Chicken Caesar, Boots*	1 Pack/160.4g	254	159	13.0	22.0	2.1	2.0
Chicken Caesar, Ginsters*	1 Serving/100g	250	250	10.5	19.6	14.4	0.0
Chicken Caesar, Good Intentions, Somerfield*	1 Pack/184g	357	194	13.0	25.7	4.3	1.1
Chicken Caesar, Healthy Eating, Tesco*	1 Pack/170g	296	174	12.0	26.2	2.4	2.6
Chicken Caesar, Healthy Living, Tesco*	1 Pack/200g	296	148	10.2	22.3	2.0	2.2
Chicken Caesar, Marks & Spencer*	1 Pack/225g	585	260	9.5	22.6	14.3	1.2
Chicken Caesar, Menu, Boots*	1 Pack/225.8g	551	244	11.0	23.0	12.0	1.3
Chicken Caesar, Tesco*	1 Pack/110g	252	229	9.8	25.0	10.0	0.1
Chicken Fajita Red, Yellow Peppers, Weight Watchers*	1 Pack/177g	297	168	9.0	24.7	3.7	1.7
Chicken Fajita, Asda*	1 Pack/180g	369	205	9.4	20.6	9.4	0.4
Chicken Fajita, Tesco*	1 Pack/220g	381	173	9.7	22.6	4.8	0.3
Chicken Fajita, Waitrose*	1 Pack/174g	279	160	8.3	21.2	4.7	2.0
Chicken Fillet With Cheese & Bacon, Asda*	1 Pack/164.1g	366	223	25.0	1.4	13.0	0.0
Chicken Jalfrezi, Boots*	1 Pack/215g	456	212	8.6	28.0	7.3	1.7
Chicken Korma, Patak's*	1 Pack/150g	294	196	7.6	20.0	9.5	0.0
Chicken Salad, Pret A Manger*	1 Av Pack/230g	323	140	7.4	13.6	6.4	0.7
Chicken Salad, Sainsbury's*	1 Pack/211.0g	519	246	10.2	21.6	13.2	0.0
Chicken Salsa, Healthy Eating, Tesco*	1 Pack/240g	348	145	8.3	22.0	2.6	0.5
Chicken Salsa, Taste!*	1 Pack/175.3g	298	170	4.8	22.9	6.6	0.0
Chicken Southern Style, Ginsters*	1 Pack/150g	290	193	9.5	25.1	6.4	0.8
Chicken Sweet & Sour, Ginsters*	1 Pack/150g	378	252	13.4	40.8	3.9	2.4
Chicken Thai Style, Boots*	1 Pack/156g	290	186	11.0	21.0	6.4	2.2
Chicken Tikka Masala, Patak's*	1 Pack/150g	252	168	7.8	19.3	6.6	0.0
Chicken Tikka, French Cuisiniers*	1 Pack/130.0g	185	142	15.4	18.3	1.3	1.5
Chicken Tikka, Ginsters*	1 Pack/150g	278	185	8.9	25.5	5.3	1.6
Chicken Tikka, Mattessons*	1 Pack/150g	284	189	9.8	21.5	7.0	3.2
Chicken With Stilton & Pear, Sainsbury's*	1 Serving/150g	264	176	25.4	2.1	7.3	0.1
Chicken, Eat Smart, Safeway*	1 Pack/153g	230	150	12.5	19.7	1.9	2.0
Chicken, Louisiana Style, GFY, Asda*	1 Pack/195g	355	182	11.0	31.0	1.5	2.0
Chicken, Marks & Spencer*	1 Pack/246.5g	531	215	8.2	23.4	10.1	1.6
Chicken, Meditteranean Style, Waitrose*	1 Pack/182.7g	296	162	8.3	18.6	6.0	2.3
Chicken, Mexican Style, Co-Op*	1 Pack/163g	367	225	11.0	26.0	9.0	3.0
Chicken, Mexican Style, Good Intentions, Somerfield*	1 Pack/220g	387	176	8.3	26.0	4.3	1.4

WRAP,

	Measure INFO/WEIGHT	per Measure KCAL	KCAL	PROT	CARB	FAT	FIBRE
Chicken, Moroccan, BGTY, Sainsbury's*	1 Pack/207.2g	315	152	9.4	25.3	1.5	0.0
Chicken, Morrocan, Shapers, Boots*	1 Serving/154g	271	176	9.6	26.0	3.7	1.7
Chicken, Tandoori Style, Good Intentions, Somerfield*	1 Pack/175g	299	171	10.9	28.8	1.4	1.6
Chicken, Tasties*	1 Pack/148.6g	325	218	11.7	26.5	7.1	0.0
Chilli Beef, COU, Marks & Spencer*	1 Pack/179g	269	150	10.2	23.8	1.5	1.2
Chilli Beef, Co-Op*	1 Pack/163g	310	190	10.0	26.0	6.0	2.0
Chilli Chicken, BGTY, Sainsbury's*	1 Pack/180g	313	174	10.2	28.0	2.4	0.0
Chinese Chicken, Asda*	1 Pack/200g	404	202	9.0	28.0	6.0	0.0
Chinese Chicken, Marks & Spencer*	1 Pack/155g	239	154	14.0	22.3	1.0	2.0
Coronation Chicken, Waitrose*	1 Pack/163.6g	284	173	10.1	21.3	5.1	2.2
Cous Cous, Moroccan Style, Tesco*	1 Serving/240g	370	154	5.3	27.3	2.7	1.3
Dhansak Prawn, Marks & Spencer*	1 Pack/208.1g	385	185	7.1	23.3	7.2	2.4
Duck, Food To Go, Marks & Spencer*	1 Pack/257g	474	185	8.5	25.5	5.4	1.0
Egg Mayonnaise, Tomato & Cress, Sainsbury's*	1 Pack/255g	592	232	7.3	17.7	15.0	0.0
Feta Cheese Flat Bread, COU, Marks & Spencer*	1 Pack/180g	225	125	6.3	20.6	2.2	1.9
Feta Cheese, GFY, Asda*	1 Pack/165g	256	155	7.0	22.0	4.3	2.1
Fiery Mexican Cheese, Ginsters*	1 Pack/150g	291	194	7.4	25.0	7.3	1.8
Garlic & Coriander, Discovery*	1 Pack/55.9g	175	313	8.6	53.9	7.0	2.5
Goats Cheese & Tomato, TTD, Sainsbury's*	1 Pack/204g	420	206	7.0	25.6	8.4	0.0
Greek Feta, Tortilla, Shapers, Boots*	1 Pack/169.4g	270	160	6.7	27.0	2.7	1.6
Greek Salad, COU, Marks & Spencer*	1 Pack/180g	225	125	6.3	20.6	2.2	1.9
Greek Salad, Marks & Spencer*	1 Pack/178.6g	251	140	8.1	21.5	2.5	1.0
Green Thai Chicken, Sainsbury's*	1 Pack/212g	422	199	9.5	25.5	6.5	0.0
Green Thai Chicken, Tortilla, Shapers, Boots*	1 Pack/175.5g	278	159	13.0	21.0	2.6	1.4
Gressingham Duck & Hoi Sin Sauce, TTD, Sainsbury's*	1 Pack/199g	354	178	9.3	24.8	4.6	0.0
Ham, Cheese & Pickle Tortilla, Weight Watchers*	1 Pack/170.1g	296	174	10.9	26.4	2.8	1.2
Ham, Cheese & Pickle, Sainsbury's*	1 Pack/234g	662	283	11.4	23.4	15.8	0.0
Hoisin Duck, Marks & Spencer*	1 Serving/236.1g	425	180	7.7	24.6	5.8	1.9
Houmous & Falafel, Starbucks*	1 Pack/232g	404	174	5.4	28.8	3.9	2.5
Houmous Salad, Pret A Manger*	1 Av Pack/230g	351	153	5.0	17.9	6.8	3.4
Houmous, Royal London Hospital*	1 Pack/200g	318	159	6.3	20.0	6.7	0.0
Houmous, Taste!*	1 Pack/170.2g	291	171	5.4	26.4	4.9	0.0
Italian Chicken, Just Cook, Sainsbury's*	1 Pack/225g	329	146	16.7	3.5	7.2	0.7
Italian Chicken, Sainsbury's*	½ Pack/211g	395	187	15.7	6.2	11.0	0.9
King Prawn, Shapers, Boots*	1 Pack/154.4g	226	147	9.2	24.0	1.4	2.1
Lemon & Lime Chicken, Morrisons*	1 Serving/100g	268	268	11.8	31.1	10.8	0.1
Mediterranean Style, Sainsbury's*	1 Tortilla/56.0g	169	302	7.8	54.1	6.0	2.4
Mexican Bean & Potato In Spinach Tortilla, Daily Bread*	1 Pack/195.8g	329	168	4.9	25.0	5.4	0.0
Mexican Bean, BGTY, Sainsbury's*	1 Pack/216g	313	145	7.9	23.5	2.1	0.0
Mexican Bean, GFY, Asda*	1 Pack/173g	303	175	5.0	31.0	3.4	2.3
Mexican Chicken, Marks & Spencer*	1 Serving/218g	447	205	8.6	19.7	10.3	1.3
Mexican Sweet Potato & Three Bean, Marks & Spencer*	1 Pack/222g	522	235	7.6	26.4	11.0	1.4
Mexican Three Bean, Marks & Spencer*	1 Pack/246.8g	580	235	7.6	26.4	11.0	1.4
Mexican Tortilla, Ainsley Harriott*	1 Pack/230g	421	183	7.1	22.4	7.5	0.0
Mild Chicken Curry, Patak's*	1 Pack/150g	239	159	8.1	21.3	6.0	2.8
Monterey Jack & Ham, Tesco*	1 Pack/200g	522	261	7.9	25.9	14.1	0.2
Nacho Chicken, COU, Marks & Spencer*	1 Pack/181.5g	244	135	9.6	19.7	2.1	1.4
Original, Discovery*	1 Pack/55.9g	175	313	8.6	53.9	7.0	2.5
Parma Ham Chicken, Perfectly Balanced, Waitrose*	½ Pack/198g	212	107	20.1	2.5	1.8	0.9
Peking Duck, Asda*	1 Pack/172g	427	248	9.4	28.5	10.7	1.1
Peking Duck, Boots*	1 Pack/229g	440	192	8.3	30.0	4.3	2.6
Peking Duck, Finest, Tesco*	1 Pack/200g	378	189	8.4	29.5	4.2	0.3
Peking Duck, Shapers, Boots*	1 Pack/161.6g	258	159	9.1	28.0	1.1	1.6

W

Measure / per Measure header — Nutrition Values per 100g / 100ml

WRAP,	Measure INFO/WEIGHT	per Measure KCAL	Nutrition Values per 100g / 100ml				
			KCAL	PROT	CARB	FAT	FIBRE
Peking Duck, Shell*	1 Pack/173g	337	195	8.7	24.2	7.1	0.0
Peking Duck, Waitrose*	1 Pack/182g	319	175	10.0	25.9	3.5	1.6
Pepperoni, Tesco*	1 Pack/153g	271	177	6.4	26.9	4.9	1.4
Plain Tortilla, Morrisons*	1 Pack/35g	84	240	6.8	45.8	3.8	1.9
Pork Caribbean Spicy, Ginsters*	1 Pack/150g	396	264	11.3	34.1	9.1	2.3
Prawn Caesar, Starbucks*	1 Pack/173.1g	464	268	11.4	20.2	15.7	1.1
Red Thai Chicken, BGTY, Sainsbury's*	1 Pack/194g	384	198	11.3	29.3	3.9	1.0
Red Thai Chicken, Shapers, Boots*	1 Pack/158g	254	161	12.0	22.0	2.6	1.4
Red Thai Prawns, Somerfield*	1oz/28g	81	288	10.0	20.0	19.0	0.0
Roasted Vegetable & Feta, BGTY, Sainsbury's*	1 Serving/200g	318	159	5.8	25.0	4.0	0.0
Sausage & Bacon, Asda*	1 Pack/21g	52	249	18.0	15.0	13.0	0.5
Smoked Salmon & Prawn, Finest, Tesco*	1 Serving/58.5g	84	143	14.3	1.0	9.1	0.0
Smoked Salmon, Finest, Tesco*	1 Pack/58g	113	194	15.5	0.6	14.4	0.3
Sushi Salmon & Cucumber, Waitrose*	1 Pack/180g	299	166	6.3	27.2	3.6	1.6
Sweet & Sour Prawn, Eat Smart, Safeway*	1 Pack/204g	275	135	6.4	24.0	1.2	1.4
Sweet Chilli Chicken, Shapers, Boots*	1 Serving/178.9g	297	166	14.0	20.0	3.0	1.3
Tandoori Chicken, GFY, Asda*	1 Pack/167g	281	168	10.0	26.0	2.7	1.7
Thai King Prawn, COU, Marks & Spencer*	1 Serving/185.2g	250	135	6.9	21.7	2.2	1.3
Thai Prawn, COU, Marks & Spencer*	1 Pack/181g	235	130	6.1	22.4	1.3	1.8
Tomato & Chilli, Discovery*	1 Pack/55.9g	161	288	7.9	53.5	5.9	2.5
Tortilla, Chicken Fajita, Sutherland*	1 Pack/158g	379	240	13.0	27.0	9.0	0.0
Tortilla, Chicken, Asda*	1 Pack/125g	253	202	9.6	36.9	1.8	3.3
Tortilla, Vegetable, Asda*	1 Pack/125g	245	196	6.8	37.2	2.2	0.8
Tuna Nicoise, BGTY, Sainsbury's*	1 Pack/181g	273	151	11.0	18.0	3.9	0.0
Tuna Nicoise, Healthy Eating, Tesco*	1 Pack/117g	160	137	8.3	20.6	2.3	0.5
Tuna Nicoise, Pret A Manger*	1 Pack/200g	368	184	8.8	20.4	7.5	1.3
Tuna Salsa, Healthy Eating, Wild Bean Cafe*	1 Pack/159g	245	154	11.3	23.5	1.7	1.5
Tuna, Sweetcorn & Red Pepper, BGTY, Sainsbury's*	1 Pack/178g	306	172	11.5	21.2	4.6	2.1
Turkey, Bacon & Cranberry, COU, Marks & Spencer*	1 Pack/143.8g	230	160	9.6	27.1	1.5	2.3
Twister, KFC*	1 Twister/252g	670	266	10.7	21.8	15.1	1.2
WRAP KIT,							
Chapatis Bread, Tikka Masala, Patak's*	1 Bread/42.2g	121	287	7.5	53.1	6.4	3.2
Cucumber & Mint Raita, Tikka Masala, Patak's*	1 Serving/60g	42	70	2.3	7.7	3.3	0.1
Tikka Masala Paste, Patak's*	1 Serving/40g	58	144	1.4	6.5	12.6	1.3
Tomato Relish, Tikka Masala, Patak's*	1 Serving/60g	35	59	1.4	8.7	2.0	0.9

	Measure INFO/WEIGHT	per Measure KCAL	Nutrition Values per 100g / 100ml				
			KCAL	PROT	CARB	FAT	FIBRE
YAM,							
Baked	1oz/28g	43	153	2.1	37.5	0.4	1.7
Boiled, Average	1oz/28g	37	133	1.7	33.0	0.3	1.4
Raw	1oz/28g	32	114	1.5	28.2	0.3	1.3
YEAST,							
Bakers, Compressed	1oz/28g	15	53	11.4	1.1	0.4	0.0
Dried	1oz/28g	47	169	35.6	3.5	1.5	0.0
Extract	1 Tsp/9g	16	180	40.7	3.5	0.4	0.0
YOGHURT,							
0.1%fat, Lidl*	1 Pot/150g	119	79	4.0	15.6	0.1	0.0
Activa, Danone*	1 Serving/125g	113	90	3.6	12.8	2.8	0.0
Adore Vanilla With Choc Flakes, Ehrmann*	1 Pot/150g	215	143	3.1	17.0	7.0	0.0
Apple & Blackberry, Bio, Sainsbury's*	1 Pot/125g	134	107	4.1	16.6	2.7	0.2
Apple & Blackberry, Custard Style, Co-Op*	1 Pot/150g	195	130	3.7	15.9	5.3	0.1
Apple & Blackberry, Deep Fill Fruit, Ski*	1 Pot/160g	139	87	4.0	14.2	1.6	0.0
Apple & Blackberry, Organic, Yeo Valley*	1 Pot/125g	121	97	4.3	12.5	3.3	0.1
Apple & Blackberry, Perfectly Balanced, Waitrose*	1 Pot/125g	115	92	4.6	18.2	0.1	0.3
Apple & Cinnamon Crumble, Ski*	1 Pot/125g	151	121	3.8	19.6	3.0	0.0
Apple & Cinnamon, COU, Marks & Spencer*	1 Pot/150g	68	45	4.2	6.1	0.1	0.2
Apple & Cranberry, Bio Fruit, Shape*	1 Pot/175g	135	77	3.9	13.2	0.9	0.0
Apple & Cranberry, Fat Free, Bio Fruit, Shape, Danone*	1 Pot/120g	85	71	4.3	13.2	0.1	0.1
Apple & Custard, Low Fat, Sainsbury's*	1 Pot/125g	116	93	4.3	15.5	1.5	0.2
Apple & Pear, Low Fat, Sainsbury's*	1 Pot/125g	115	92	4.3	15.2	1.5	0.2
Apple & Prune, Fat Free, Yeo Valley*	1 Pot/125g	98	78	5.1	14.1	0.1	0.2
Apple & Spice Bio, Virtually Fat Free, Shape*	1 Pot/120g	67	56	5.6	7.3	0.1	0.2
Apple Custard & Crumble, Muller*	1 Pot/190g	287	151	11.6	17.7	3.7	0.0
Apple Danish Fruit Pudding Style, Healthy Eating, Tesco*	1 Pot/125g	99	79	4.1	14.1	0.7	0.2
Apple Strude, Custard Style, Shape, St. Ivel*	1 Pot/100g	58	58	4.1	7.9	0.8	0.2
Apple, Light, Muller*	1 Pot/200g	108	54	4.4	9.0	0.1	0.0
Apricot & Mango Tropical Fruit, Ski*	1 Pot/125g	124	99	4.9	15.7	1.9	0.2
Apricot & Mango, 25% Extra Fruit, Low Fat, Asda*	1 Pot/125g	120	96	4.6	17.0	1.1	0.0
Apricot & Mango, Best There Is, Yoplait*	1 Pot/125g	130	104	4.7	17.4	1.6	0.0
Apricot & Mango, Low Fat, Tesco*	1 Pot/125g	126	101	4.9	16.3	1.8	0.0
Apricot & Mango, Thick & Creamy, Sainsbury's*	1 Pot/150g	179	119	4.3	17.3	3.6	0.2
Apricot & Nectarine, Healthy Eating, Tesco*	1 Pot/175g	79	45	2.1	8.9	0.1	0.3
Apricot & Nectarine, Sunshine Selection, Sainsbury's*	1 Pot/125g	115	92	4.4	15.3	1.5	0.1
Apricot & Passion Fruit, Fat Free, Yeo Valley*	1 Pot/125g	95	76	5.2	13.6	0.1	0.1
Apricot Bio, Healthy Eating, Tesco*	1 Pot/125g	58	46	4.2	7.1	0.1	0.0
Apricot Tart Style, Sveltesse, Nestle*	1 Pot/125g	98	78	4.8	14.2	0.2	0.1
Apricot, Custard Style, Shapers, Boots*	1 Pot/146g	82	56	3.9	8.3	0.8	0.2
Apricot, Fat Free, Bio Live, Rachel's Organic*	1 Pot/142g	81	57	3.5	10.5	0.1	0.0
Apricot, French Style Smooth, Tesco*	1 Pot/125g	123	98	3.6	14.1	3.0	0.0
Apricot, Healthy Living, Tesco*	1 Pot/125g	68	54	5.1	7.9	0.3	1.1
Apricot, Light, Healthy Living, Tesco*	1 Pot/125g	54	43	4.1	6.3	0.2	0.9
Apricot, Low Fat, Organic, Sainsbury's*	1 Pot/125g	103	82	5.3	13.0	1.0	0.1
Apricot, Low Fat, Organic, Somerfield*	1 Pot/150g	153	102	6.0	17.0	2.0	0.0
Apricot, Low Fat, Sainsbury's*	1 Pot/125g	115	92	4.3	15.2	1.5	0.1
Apricot, Low Fat, Tesco*	1 Pot/125g	111	89	4.9	13.4	1.7	0.2
Apricot, Organic, Low Fat, Tesco*	1 Pot/125g	111	89	5.3	14.6	1.0	0.2
Apricot, Organic, Yeo Valley*	1 Pot/150g	146	97	4.3	12.4	3.3	0.1
Apricot, Smooth Set French, Sainsbury's*	1 Pot/125g	100	80	3.5	13.6	1.2	0.0
Apricot, Vitality, Muller*	1 Pot/175g	172	98	4.7	15.8	1.8	0.0
Banana & Orange, Low Fat, 25% Extra Fruit, Asda*	1 Pot/125g	125	100	4.6	18.0	1.1	0.0
Banana Choco Flakes Corner, Muller*	1 Pot/150g	218	145	4.1	22.5	4.3	0.0

	Measure INFO/WEIGHT	per Measure KCAL	Nutrition Values per 100g / 100ml				
			KCAL	PROT	CARB	FAT	FIBRE
YOGHURT,							
Banana Smooth, Marks & Spencer	1 Pot/150g	165	110	4.8	19.3	1.7	0.2
Banana Toffee, Low Fat, Somerfield*	1 Pot/125g	123	98	4.1	18.0	1.1	0.0
Banana, Bio & Cereal Clusters, Rumblers*	1 Pot/167g	261	156	4.2	21.9	5.6	1.1
Banana, Childrens, Co-Op*	1 Pot/125g	124	99	3.7	15.1	2.6	0.2
Banana, Custard Style, Asda*	1 Pot/150g	224	149	3.7	20.0	6.0	0.2
Banana, Light, Muller*	1 Pot/200g	106	53	4.4	8.7	0.1	0.0
Banana, Low Fat, Sainsbury's*	1 Pot/125g	116	93	4.4	15.4	1.5	0.1
Banana, Müllermilch, Müller*	1 Pot/500ml	365	73	3.6	11.8	1.3	0.0
Banoffee, Eat Smart, Safeway*	1 Pot/125g	68	54	4.7	8.5	0.1	0.0
Banoffee, Fat Free, Bio, Eat Smart, Safeway*	1 Pot/125g	69	55	4.7	8.5	0.1	0.0
Banoffee, Low Fat, Asda*	1 Pot/125g	126	101	4.6	18.2	1.2	1.0
Banoffee, Thick & Creamy, Safeway*	1 Pot/150g	189	126	4.3	18.2	4.0	0.1
Berry Crunch, McDonald's*	1 Serving/194.8g	224	115	3.5	18.9	2.6	1.2
Berry Sunshine Grove, Shape*	1 Pot/100g	63	63	4.7	8.3	1.0	0.2
Bio Activia, With Cereals, Danone*	1 Pot/125g	123	98	4.1	15.6	2.1	0.0
Bio Activia, With Prunes, Danone*	1 Pot/125g	124	99	3.3	15.2	2.8	0.0
Bio Activia, With Raspberry, Danone*	1 Pot/125g	113	90	3.6	12.8	2.8	0.0
Bio Activia, With Strawberry, Danone*	1 Pot/125g	124	99	3.9	13.4	3.3	0.0
Bio Fruits With Cherries, 0% Fat, Danone*	1 Pot/125g	65	52	3.6	9.1	0.1	0.0
Black Cherry Live Bio, Perfeclty Balanced, Waitrose*	1 Pot/125g	115	92	4.6	18.3	0.1	0.1
Black Cherry, BGTY, Sainsbury's*	1 Pot/125g	64	51	4.7	7.6	0.2	0.1
Black Cherry, Best There Is, Yoplait*	1 Pot/125g	134	107	4.2	17.8	1.6	0.0
Black Cherry, Bio, Waitrose*	1 Serving/170g	184	108	3.7	17.9	2.4	0.5
Black Cherry, COU, Marks & Spencer*	1 Pot/150g	68	45	4.2	5.9	0.1	0.1
Black Cherry, Economy, Tesco*	1 Pot/125g	85	68	3.0	11.9	1.0	0.1
Black Cherry, Extra Fruit, Low Fat, Ski*	1 Pot/125g	120	96	3.4	17.2	1.5	0.1
Black Cherry, Extremely Fruity, Bio, Marks & Spencer*	1 Pot/150g	165	110	4.9	18.4	1.5	0.2
Black Cherry, Extremely Fruity, Marks & Spencer*	1 Pot/200g	220	110	4.9	18.4	1.5	0.2
Black Cherry, Fat Free, BGTY, Sainsbury's*	1 Pot/125g	71	57	4.8	9.1	0.1	1.1
Black Cherry, Fat Free, Weight Watchers*	1 Pot/120g	55	46	4.2	7.0	0.1	0.1
Black Cherry, Frozen, Marks & Spencer*	1 Pot/125g	164	131	3.1	27.1	1.1	0.5
Black Cherry, Fruit Corner, Low Fat, Muller*	1 Pot/95g	78	82	4.5	12.5	1.5	0.0
Black Cherry, Healthy Living, Tesco*	1 Pot/200g	106	53	4.3	8.7	0.1	0.0
Black Cherry, Low Fat, Asda*	1 Pot/150g	143	95	4.6	17.4	1.0	0.2
Black Cherry, Low Fat, Sainsbury's*	1 Pot/125g	123	98	4.6	17.3	1.1	0.2
Black Cherry, Low Fat, Somerfield*	1 Pot/150g	116	77	3.0	14.0	1.0	0.0
Black Cherry, Low Fat, Tesco*	1 Pot/125g	124	99	4.9	16.0	1.7	0.1
Black Cherry, Low Fat, Value, Tesco*	1 Pot/125g	100	80	2.3	16.0	0.7	0.1
Black Cherry, Marks & Spencer*	1 Pot/150g	149	99	4.8	16.5	1.6	0.2
Black Cherry, Thick & Fruity, Weight Watchers*	1 Pot/120.8g	58	48	4.2	7.5	0.1	0.1
Black Cherry, Variety Selection, Ski*	1 Pot/125g	128	102	4.8	16.7	1.8	0.2
Black Cherry, Virtually Fat Free, Shapers, Boots*	1 Pot/125g	71	57	5.3	8.8	0.1	0.1
Blackberry & Apple, BGTY, Sainsbury's*	1 Pot/122g	61	50	4.7	7.2	0.2	0.3
Blackberry & Apple, Best There Is, Yoplait	1 Pot/124g	133	107	4.7	18.0	1.6	0.0
Blackberry & Apple, Healthy Living, Tesco*	1 Serving/176g	86	49	2.1	10.0	0.1	1.5
Blackberry & Apple, Low Fat, Sainsbury's*	1 Pot/125g	116	93	4.3	15.5	1.5	0.2
Blackberry & Raspberry Flip, Morrisons*	1 Pot/175g	207	118	3.4	15.8	4.6	0.5
Blackberry & Raspberry, Fruit Corner, Muller*	1 Pot/175g	193	110	3.7	15.0	3.9	0.0
Blackberry & Raspberry, Low Fat, Ski*	1 Pot/126g	67	53	5.7	7.2	0.0	2.0
Blackberry & Raspberry, Simply Berries, Shape, Danone*	1 Pot/120g	61	51	4.4	8.1	0.1	1.2
Blackberry, BGTY, Sainsbury's*	1 Pot/150g	107	71	3.4	13.5	0.4	1.6
Blackberry, Boysenberry & William Pear, Marks & Spencer*	1 Pot/150g	188	125	4.0	13.6	6.5	2.4
Blackberry, Elderberry & Lavender, Biowild, Onken*	1 Pot/175g	159	91	4.4	14.7	1.6	0.4

Y

	Measure INFO/WEIGHT	per Measure KCAL	Nutrition Values per 100g / 100ml				
			KCAL	PROT	CARB	FAT	FIBRE
Blackberry, Farmhouse, BGTY, Sainsbury's*	1 Pot/150g	107	71	3.4	13.5	0.4	1.6
Blackberry, Fat Free, BGTY, Sainsbury's*	1 Pot/150g	101	67	3.4	13.6	0.1	1.6
Blackberry, Sveltesse 0%, Nestle*	1 Pot/125g	63	50	4.3	7.9	0.1	0.0
Blackberry, Weight Watchers*	1 Pot/120g	49	41	4.2	5.8	0.1	0.3
Blackcurrant & Vanilla, TTD, Sainsbury's*	1 Pot/143g	136	95	3.6	13.6	2.9	1.0
Blackcurrant Smooth, Ski*	1 Pot/125g	125	100	4.9	15.9	1.9	0.5
Blackcurrant With Liquorice, Tesco*	1 Pot/150g	138	92	4.6	15.8	1.1	0.4
Blackcurrant, BGTY, Sainsbury's*	1 Pot/200g	100	50	4.8	7.3	0.2	0.1
Blackcurrant, Bio Live, Organic, Yeo Valley*	1 Pot/150g	152	101	4.1	12.4	3.9	0.2
Blackcurrant, Bio Live, Rachel's Organic*	1 Serving/225g	167	74	3.6	11.0	1.7	0.0
Blackcurrant, Extra Special, Asda*	1 Pot/100g	163	163	2.6	18.0	9.0	0.0
Blackcurrant, Light, Muller*	1 Pot/200g	110	55	4.7	8.9	0.1	0.0
Blackcurrant, Low Fat, Deliciously Fruity, Somerfield*	1 Pot/125g	116	93	4.6	16.5	1.0	0.5
Blackcurrant, Low Fat, Sainsbury's*	1 Pot/125g	116	93	4.2	15.9	1.4	0.6
Blackcurrant, Low Fat, Tesco*	1 Pot/125g	110	88	4.9	13.2	1.7	0.4
Blackcurrant, Marks & Spencer*	1 Pot/150g	147	98	4.8	16.1	1.6	0.8
Blackcurrant, Munch Bunch, Nestle*	1 Pot/100g	107	107	4.4	15.3	3.1	0.5
Blackcurrant, Thick & Creamy, Sainsbury's*	1 Pot/150g	171	114	4.3	15.9	3.6	0.4
Blueberry Flip, Morrisons*	1 Pot/175g	201	115	3.1	15.1	4.6	0.5
Blueberry Loganberry, Layered, Bio, Sainsbury's*	1 Serving/125g	134	107	4.0	16.6	2.7	0.2
Blueberry Muffin, Fat Free, Eat Smart, Safeway*	1 Pot/125g	66	53	4.7	8.2	0.1	0.3
Blueberry, Fruit Corner, Muller*	1 Pot/175g	196	112	3.7	15.5	3.9	0.0
Blueberry, Light, Muller*	1 Pot/200g	98	49	4.4	7.7	0.1	0.0
Blueberry, Low Fat, Somerfield*	1 Pot/150g	131	87	4.0	16.0	1.0	0.0
Blueberry, Low Lactose, Valio*	2 Servings/200g	160	80	3.2	13.0	2.1	0.0
Blueberry, Marks & Spencer*	1 Pot/150g	141	94	4.7	15.8	1.6	0.4
Blueberry, Starbucks*	1 Pot/130g	116	89	4.4	17.8	0.0	0.0
Blueberry, Wholemilk, Organic, Sainsbury's*	1 Pot/150g	123	82	3.5	9.2	3.5	0.1
Boysenberry, Low Fat, Yoplait*	1 Pot/100g	49	49	5.3	6.7	0.1	0.0
Burst, Strawberry, McDoanld's*	1 Yoghurt/40g	21	52	2.9	11.0	0.0	0.9
Cappuccino, Thick & Creamy, Safeway*	1 Pot/150g	228	152	4.5	20.8	5.6	0.0
Caramel & Praline, Indulgent Greek Style, Somerfield*	1 Pot/125g	245	196	4.0	28.0	8.0	0.0
Caramel, Organic, Onken*	1 Serving/50g	56	111	4.6	15.6	3.3	0.0
Caramelised Orange, COU, Marks & Spencer*	1 Pot/145g	65	45	4.2	6.1	0.1	0.2
Champagne Rhubarb & Vanilla, Marks & Spencer*	1 Pot/150g	195	130	3.8	15.7	5.8	0.8
Champagne Rhubarb, Finest, Tesco*	1 Pot/150g	213	142	3.3	16.8	6.9	0.2
Cherry Bio, Co-Op*	1 Pot/125g	144	115	4.5	17.0	2.8	0.1
Cherry Flip, Better For You, Morrisons*	1 Pot/175g	93	53	3.9	8.7	0.3	0.4
Cherry Morello Bio, Tesco*	1 Pot/124g	51	41	4.4	5.4	0.2	0.9
Cherry Pie Layered, Custard Style, Healthy Eating, Tesco*	1 Pot/125g	99	79	4.1	13.9	0.8	0.2
Cherry Pie, Sveltesse 0%, Nestle*	1 Pot/125g	65	52	4.1	7.7	0.0	0.0
Cherry, 0% Fat, Yoplait*	1 Pot/125g	70	56	3.8	9.8	0.1	0.0
Cherry, Bio Fruit, Shape, Danone*	1 Pot/120g	87	73	4.3	13.6	0.1	0.2
Cherry, Fat Free, Bio, Shape*	1 Pot/120g	90	75	4.5	14.0	0.1	0.0
Cherry, Fruit Corner, Muller*	1 Pot/175g	193	110	3.7	15.0	3.9	0.0
Cherry, Greek Style, Shape*	1 Pot/125.4g	143	114	6.0	16.4	2.7	0.0
Cherry, Healthy Eating, Tesco*	1 Pot/200g	96	48	4.2	7.5	0.1	0.0
Cherry, Light, Muller*	1 Pot/200g	100	50	4.4	7.9	0.1	0.0
Cherry, Low Fat, Asda*	1 Pot/125g	120	96	4.6	17.0	1.1	0.0
Cherry, Low Fat, Benecol*	1 Pot/150g	122	81	3.8	15.2	0.6	0.0
Cherry, Muller*	1 Pot/150g	177	118	3.3	17.0	3.7	0.0
Cherry, Probiotic, Vitality, Muller*	1 Pot/150g	155	103	4.7	17.0	1.8	0.0
Cherry, Somerfield*	1 Pot/125g	61	49	5.0	7.0	0.0	0.0

	Measure INFO/WEIGHT	per Measure KCAL	Nutrition Values per 100g / 100ml				
			KCAL	PROT	CARB	FAT	FIBRE
YOGHURT,							
Cherry, Virtually Fat Free Bio, Morrisons*	1 Pot/200g	120	60	5.4	9.2	0.2	0.0
Chocolate & Orange, COU, Marks & Spencer*	1 Pot/200g	100	50	4.2	6.0	0.4	0.2
Chocolate & Toffee Selection, Shape*	1 Pot/100g	99	99	4.6	15.4	1.8	0.0
Chocolate Chip, Dessert Recipes, Ski*	1 Pot/125g	163	130	3.8	19.3	4.2	0.0
Chocolate, GFY, Asda*	1 Pot/200g	110	55	4.7	8.0	0.5	0.1
Chocolate, Light, Muller*	1 Pot/200g	108	54	4.8	8.1	0.3	0.0
Chocolate, Seriously Smooth, Waitrose*	1 Pot/125g	158	126	6.0	20.1	2.4	0.1
Chocolate, Shape*	1 Pot/100g	111	111	4.9	17.4	2.0	0.2
Citrus Fruit, Fat Free, Weight Watchers*	1 Pot/120g	52	43	4.1	6.3	0.1	0.2
Citrus Fruit, Tesco*	1 Serving/117g	53	45	4.2	6.5	0.1	0.1
Coconut, Greek Style, Bio Live, Rachel's Organic*	1 Pot/450g	702	156	3.6	10.5	11.0	0.0
Coconut, Muller*	1 Pot/150g	156	104	3.4	13.0	3.9	0.0
Coconut, Ski*	1 Pot/125g	126	101	4.9	15.8	2.0	0.0
Country Berries, Virtually Fat Free, Light, Muller*	1 Pot/200g	104	52	4.4	8.3	0.1	0.0
Cranberry & Blackcurrant, Fat Free, Bio, Shape*	1 Pot/120g	54	45	4.6	5.7	0.1	0.3
Cranberry & Blackcurrant, Low Fat Bio, Ocean Spray*	1 Pot/150g	147	98	4.6	17.4	1.1	0.0
Cranberry & Blackcurrant, Shape, Danone*	1 Pot/120g	62	52	4.4	8.4	0.1	1.0
Cranberry & Pink Grapefruit, Low Fat Bio, Ocean Spray*	1 Pot/125g	118	94	4.6	16.5	1.1	0.0
Cranberry & Raspberry, Fat Free Bio, Eat Smart, Safeway*	1 Pot/125g	69	55	4.7	8.2	0.1	0.5
Cranberry & Raspberry, Low Fat Bio, Ocean Spray*	1 Pot/150g	144	96	4.6	17.0	1.1	0.0
Cranberry & Raspberry, Perfectly Balanced, Waitrose*	1 Pot/150g	135	90	4.5	17.8	0.1	0.6
Cranberry Classic, Low Fat Bio, Ocean Spray*	1 Pot/150g	144	96	4.6	17.0	1.1	0.0
Cranberry, Blueberry & Guarana, Probiotic, Ocean Spray*	1 Pot/170g	162	95	4.7	16.6	1.1	0.0
Creamy Cranberry & Raspberry, Shapers, Boots*	1 Pot/150g	86	57	4.0	7.0	1.1	1.1
Dairy Toffee, Shape*	1 Pot/100g	99	99	4.6	15.4	1.8	0.0
Dessert With Honey, Perfectly Balanced, Waitrose*	1 Pot/125ml	128	102	3.5	19.4	1.2	0.1
Devon Toffee, Low Fat, Sainsbury's*	1 Pot/126g	137	109	4.3	19.6	1.5	0.0
Devon Toffee, Shape, Danone*	1 Pot/125g	129	103	4.9	16.2	2.0	1.0
Diet, Yoplait*	1 Pot/125g	100	80	4.0	16.0	0.0	0.0
English Plum, The Best, Safeway*	1 Pot/175g	245	140	3.2	17.4	6.4	0.3
Exotic Fruit, COU, Marks & Spencer*	1oz/28g	13	45	4.3	6.0	0.1	0.2
Exotic Fruits French Set Wholemilk, Asda*	1 Pot/125g	125	100	3.6	14.1	3.2	0.0
Florida Orange, Summer, Onken*	1oz/28g	28	100	3.9	15.1	2.7	0.0
Forest Fantasy, Frozen, Thorntons*	1oz/28g	48	170	1.8	26.2	6.1	0.5
Forest Fruits, French Set Wholemilk, Asda*	1 Pot/125g	125	100	3.6	14.1	3.2	0.0
Forest Fruits, Layered Greek Style, Shapers, Boots*	1 Pot/150g	86	57	3.2	7.9	1.4	2.2
Forest Fruits, Marks & Spencer*	1 Pot/150g	149	99	4.7	16.8	1.6	0.5
French Set, Waitrose*	1 Pot/125g	120	96	3.5	13.4	3.1	0.0
French Style, Tesco*	1 Pot/125g	123	98	3.6	14.1	3.0	0.0
Fruit & Nut Layer, Indulgent Greek Style, Somerfield*	1 Pot/125g	214	171	3.0	24.0	7.0	0.0
Fruit Bio, Low Fat, Sainsbury's*	1 Pot/150g	156	104	4.6	18.9	1.1	0.3
Fruit Halo Strawberry & Vanilla, Light, Muller*	1 Pot/145g	116	80	3.6	15.8	0.3	0.0
Fruit Halo, Raspberry, Light, Muller*	1 Pot/144.0g	121	84	3.7	16.5	0.3	0.0
Fruit Whole Milk	1 Pot/150g	158	105	5.1	15.7	2.8	0.0
Fruit, Deep Fill, Ski*	1 Pot/160g	138	86	4.0	13.8	1.6	0.0
Fruit, Low Fat	1 Pot/120g	108	90	4.1	17.9	0.7	0.0
Fruit, Low Fat, Light, Muller*	1 Pot/200g	100	50	4.4	7.9	0.1	0.0
Fruits Of The Forest, Smooth Set, Co-Op*	1 Pot/125g	95	76	3.7	12.5	0.9	0.0
Fruits of the Forest, Lite, Yoplait*	1 Pot/200g	184	92	5.0	15.9	0.9	0.0
Fruits of the Forest, Nestle*	1 Pot/125g	123	98	3.4	16.7	1.6	0.0
Fruity Favourites, Organic, Yeo Valley*	1 Pot/125g	126	101	4.1	12.4	3.9	0.2
Fudge Layer, Indulgent Greek Style, Somerfield*	1 Pot/125g	226	181	3.0	26.0	7.0	0.0
Fudge, Devonshire Style, Finest, Tesco*	1 Pot/150g	281	187	3.7	22.4	9.2	0.0

Y

YOGHURT,	Measure INFO/WEIGHT	per Measure KCAL	KCAL	PROT	CARB	FAT	FIBRE
			Nutrition Values per 100g / 100ml				
Fudge, Thick & Creamy, Marks & Spencer*	1 Pot/150g	195	130	4.4	17.3	5.0	0.7
Garden Fruit, Wholemilk, Bio Live, Rachel's Organic*	1 Pot/125g	109	87	3.5	10.5	3.4	0.0
Goats Whole Milk	1 Carton/150g	95	63	3.5	3.9	3.8	0.0
Gooseberry & Vanilla, TTD, Sainsbury's*	1 Pot/150g	143	95	3.7	13.6	2.9	0.4
Gooseberry, Custard Style, Shapers, Boots*	1 Pot/151g	106	70	3.9	12.0	0.7	0.2
Gooseberry, Custard Style, Somerfield*	1 Pot/125g	151	121	3.0	17.0	5.0	0.0
Gooseberry, Low Fat, Sainsbury's*	1 Pot/125g	113	90	4.4	14.6	1.5	0.2
Gooseberry, Low Fat, Tesco*	1 Pot/125g	106	85	4.9	12.5	1.7	0.2
Gooseberry, Seriously Fruity, Low Fat, Waitrose*	1 Pot/125g	111	89	4.4	15.7	1.0	0.6
Greek Style With Honey, Asda*	1 Pot/150g	225	150	4.0	13.9	8.7	0.0
Greek Style With Strawberries, Asda*	1 Pot/125g	159	127	3.2	13.6	6.6	0.2
Greek Style With Toffee & Hazelnuts, Asda*	1 Pot/125g	230	184	3.7	23.1	8.6	0.1
Greek Style With Tropical Fruits, Asda*	1 Pot/125g	164	131	3.3	14.5	6.6	0.3
Greek Style, Healthy Living, Tesco*	1 Pot/150g	152	101	5.6	8.1	5.1	0.0
Greek Style, Layered, Honey, Shapers, Boots*	1 Serving/150g	137	91	4.2	14.0	2.0	0.0
Greek Style, Lemon, Low Fat, Bio, Shape*	1 Pot/125g	141	113	6.0	16.2	2.7	0.0
Greek Style, Luxury, Loseley*	1 Pot/175g	226	129	4.8	4.5	10.2	0.0
Greek Style, Orange, Low Fat, Bio, Shape*	1 Pot/125g	143	114	6.0	16.3	2.7	0.0
Greek Style, Sainsbury's*	1 Serving/200g	258	129	4.6	4.8	10.2	0.0
Greek Style, With Honey, Bio Live, Rachel's Organic*	1 Serving/100g	137	137	3.3	13.0	8.0	0.0
Greek, 0% Fat, Total*	1 Pot/150g	84	56	10.0	4.0	0.0	0.0
Greek, Fruits Of The Forest, EAT*	1 Pot/125g	94	75	5.0	12.3	0.8	0.2
Greek, Light, Total*	1 Pot/150g	120	80	6.0	3.0	5.0	0.0
Greek, Original, Total*	1oz/28g	36	130	6.0	4.0	10.0	0.0
Greek, Shape*	1 Serving/100g	108	108	7.1	12.7	2.7	0.0
Greek, With Honey & Nuts, Duettino*	1 Pot/185g	278	150	3.6	15.9	8.0	0.0
Greek, With Mango, EAT*	1 Serving/100g	100	100	6.6	16.6	1.0	0.0
Greek, With Muesli & Mixed Berries, Low Fat, EAT*	1 Serving/100g	161	161	8.1	27.5	2.2	2.7
Greek, With Strawberry, Total*	1 Pot/150g	189	126	4.7	8.7	8.0	0.0
Guava & Orange, Fat Free, Organic, Yeo Valley*	1 Pot/125g	93	74	5.1	13.2	0.1	0.3
Guava & Passion Fruit, Virtualy Fat Free, Tesco*	1 Pot/125g	56	45	4.2	6.7	0.2	1.2
Hazelnut Crunchy, Jordans*	1oz/28g	43	154	5.2	22.2	4.0	1.1
Hazelnut Praline, The Best, Safeway*	1 Pot/175g	302	173	3.7	20.3	8.5	0.2
Hazelnut, Low Fat, Asda*	1 Serving/150g	180	120	4.9	20.0	2.3	0.2
Hazelnut, Low Fat, Sainsbury's*	1 Pot/125g	135	108	4.5	16.4	2.7	0.2
Hazelnut, Low Fat, Tesco*	1 Pot/150g	147	98	4.5	14.0	2.7	0.0
Hazelnut, Seriously Nutty, Waitrose*	1 Pot/150g	179	119	5.3	17.7	3.0	0.2
Hazelnut, Yoplait*	1 Pot/125g	166	133	4.6	19.6	4.0	0.0
Hazlenut, Low Fat, Safeway*	1 Pot/150g	179	119	4.9	19.3	2.5	0.2
Hazlenut, Low Fat, Somerfield*	1 Pot/150g	126	84	4.0	15.0	1.0	0.0
Hint Of Coconut, Bio Activia, Danone*	1 Pot/125g	119	95	3.6	13.2	3.1	0.0
Honey & Ginger, Enhanced, Low Fat, Asda*	1 POT/150g	150	100	4.6	18.0	1.1	0.0
Honey & Ginger, Tesco*	1 Pot/150g	150	100	4.6	18.0	1.1	0.0
Honey & Greek, Total*	1 Pot/150g	245	163	4.8	19.2	8.0	0.0
Honey & Muesli, Breakfast Break, Tesco*	1 Pot/170g	207	122	3.9	20.5	2.7	0.6
Honey & Multigrain, Breakfast Selection, Sainsbury's*	1 Pot/125g	126	101	4.4	17.4	1.5	0.2
Honey, Greek Style, Boots*	1 Pot/140g	204	146	3.1	18.0	6.8	0.0
Honey, Greek Style, Organic, Sainsbury's*	1 Pot/100g	156	156	4.1	15.3	8.7	0.1
Honey, Low Fat, Asda*	1 Pot/125g	130	104	4.6	19.0	1.1	0.0
Italian Lemon, Muller*	1 Pot/150g	210	140	2.3	15.0	7.9	0.0
Jaffa Cakes Corner, McVitie's, Muller*	1 Pot/150g	237	158	4.0	24.6	4.8	0.0
Jaffa Orange, Low Fat, Co-Op*	1 Pot/150g	126	84	3.9	15.0	0.9	0.4
Jaffa Orange, Morrisons*	1 Pot/150g	134	89	3.6	16.2	1.1	0.0

Y

	Measure INFO/WEIGHT	per Measure KCAL	Nutrition Values per 100g / 100ml				
			KCAL	PROT	CARB	FAT	FIBRE
YOGHURT,							
Kellogg's Coco Pops Corner, Muller*	1 Pot/150g	180	120	4.0	19.0	3.1	0.0
Kellogg's Frosties Crunch Corner, Muller*	1 Pot/150g	185	123	4.0	20.1	2.9	0.0
Kellogg's With Rice Krispies, Muller*	1 Pot/150g	185	123	4.1	19.9	3.0	0.0
Layered, Eat Smart, Safeway*	1 Pot/125g	81	65	4.1	11.3	0.1	0.4
Lemon & Lime, Bio, Shape*	1 Pot/120g	54	45	5.7	5.7	0.1	0.1
Lemon & Lime, Fat Free, Shape*	1 Pot/120g	61	51	4.5	7.3	0.1	0.1
Lemon & Lime, Light, Muller*	1 Pot/200g	106	53	4.7	8.2	0.1	0.0
Lemon & Lime, Weight Watchers*	1 Pot/119ml	50	42	4.1	5.9	0.1	0.0
Lemon Cheesecake, Corner, Muller*	1 Pot/150g	224	149	3.7	23.9	4.3	0.0
Lemon Cheesecake, Dessert Recipes, Ski*	1 Pot/125g	154	123	3.8	19.0	3.5	0.0
Lemon Cheesecake, Sveltesse, Nestle*	1 Pot/125g	95	76	4.4	12.9	0.7	0.0
Lemon Curd, Farmhouse, TTD, Sainsbury's*	1 Pot/149.6g	182	121	4.1	17.7	3.7	0.2
Lemon Lime Mousse, Shapers, Boots*	1 Pot/90g	89	99	4.2	11.0	4.2	0.1
Lemon Meringue, Eat Smart, Safeway*	1 Pot/125g	68	54	4.7	8.6	0.1	0.0
Lemon Meringue, Sveltesse 0%, Nestle*	1 Pot/125g	60	48	4.1	7.7	0.1	0.0
Lemon Sunshine Grove, Low Fat, Shape*	1 Pot/100g	64	64	4.6	8.5	1.0	0.0
Lemon, Amore Luxury, Muller*	1 Pot/150g	210	140	2.3	15.0	7.9	0.0
Lemon, COU, Marks & Spencer*	1 Pot/200g	80	40	4.2	5.4	0.1	0.0
Lemon, Fat Free, Weight Watchers*	1 Pot/120g	49	41	4.0	5.8	0.1	0.0
Lemon, Greek Style, GFY, Asda*	1 Pot/150g	125	83	4.1	10.0	2.9	0.1
Lemon, Greek Style, Shape*	1 Pot/100g	115	115	7.6	10.7	3.6	0.0
Lemon, Lite, Biopot, Onken*	1 Serving/100g	44	44	5.2	5.3	0.2	0.1
Lemon, Low Fat, Asda*	1 Pot/125g	130	104	4.6	19.0	1.1	0.0
Lemon, Organic, Evernat*	1oz/28g	27	95	3.9	12.4	3.4	0.0
Lemon, Smooth Set French, Low Fat, Sainsbury's*	1 Pot/125g	100	80	3.5	13.6	1.2	0.0
Lemon, Summer, Biopot, Onken*	1 Pot/150g	155	103	3.9	15.9	2.6	0.1
Lemon, Virtually Fat Free, Morrisons*	1 Pot/200g	118	59	5.4	8.9	0.2	0.0
Light, Muller*	1 Serving/200g	110	55	4.3	9.2	0.1	0.0
Loganberry, Low Fat, Sainsbury's*	1 Pot/125g	111	89	4.2	14.5	1.5	0.2
Loganberry, Sainsbury's*	1 Pot/150g	194	129	3.9	14.2	6.2	0.6
Low Calorie	1 Pot/120g	49	41	4.3	6.0	0.2	0.0
Mandarin, Light, Muller*	1 Pot/200g	108	54	4.3	9.0	0.1	0.0
Mandarin, Low Fat, Safeway*	1 Pot/150g	141	94	4.6	16.4	1.1	0.2
Mango & Guava, Fat Free, Weight Watchers*	1 Pot/120g	55	46	4.1	6.8	0.1	0.3
Mango & Guava, Sunshine Selection, Sainsbury's*	1 Pot/125g	145	116	5.4	19.3	1.9	0.3
Mango & Passionfruit, Biopot, Onken*	1 Serving/100g	101	101	3.9	15.6	2.6	0.2
Mango & Pineapple, BGTY, Sainsbury's*	1 Pot/124g	63	51	4.6	7.6	0.2	0.2
Mango & Vanilla, Organic, Onken*	1 Serving/20g	20	102	3.9	13.5	3.3	0.0
Mango Bio, Healthy Eating, Tesco*	1 Pot/125g	59	47	4.7	6.8	0.1	0.2
Mango Bio, Virtually Fat Free, Shape*	1 Pot/120g	60	50	4.7	6.8	0.1	0.2
Mango Passion, D'lite, Ski*	1 Pot/200g	186	93	5.1	14.9	0.9	0.0
Mango Passionfruit, D'lite 0.2 Ski, Nestle*	1 Pot/125g	103	82	4.6	15.7	0.1	0.1
Mango Smooth, Marks & Spencer*	1 Pot/150g	158	105	4.7	18.0	1.6	0.5
Mango, BGTY, Sainsbury's*	1 Pot/125g	66	53	4.8	8.3	0.1	1.2
Mango, Light, Muller*	1 Pot/200g	110	55	4.3	9.2	0.1	0.0
Mango, Low Fat, Tesco*	1 Pot/125g	111	89	4.9	13.6	1.7	0.3
Mango, Papaya & Passion Fruit, Onken*	1 Serving/100g	101	101	3.9	15.6	2.6	0.2
Mango, Ski*	1 Pot/125g	125	100	4.9	15.8	1.9	0.1
Mango, Virtually Fat Free, Tesco*	1 Pot/125g	56	45	4.1	6.6	0.2	0.9
Mango, Weight Watchers*	1 Pot/120g	54	45	3.9	7.1	0.1	1.1
Melon & Passion Fruit, Weight Watchers*	1 Pot/120g	54	45	4.0	7.0	0.1	0.0
Milchcafe, Onken*	1 Serving/200g	222	111	4.1	15.9	3.4	0.0
Mississippi Mud Pie Corner, Muller*	1 Pot/150g	254	169	4.1	26.3	5.3	0.0

Y

YOGHURT,

INFO/WEIGHT	Measure per Measure KCAL	KCAL	PROT	CARB	FAT	FIBRE
Mississippi Mud Pie, Shape St Ivel*	1 Pot/120g	166	138	3.8	24.5	2.8	0.8
Mixed Berry, Fat Free, Shape*	1 Pot/120g	62	52	4.4	8.2	0.1	1.0
Morello Cherry, Healthy Eating, Tesco*	1 Pot/125g	58	46	4.2	7.1	0.1	0.1
Muesli Nut, Low Fat	1 Pot/120g	134	112	5.0	19.2	2.2	0.0
Multifruits, Yop Petit Déjeuner, Yoplait*	1 Bottle/180g	155	86	2.7	16.0	1.2	0.0
Natural With Honey,Greek Style, Sainsbury's*	1 Sm Pot/150g	243	162	4.0	15.4	9.4	0.0
Natural With Prunes, Bio Activia, Danone*	1 Pot/125g	124	99	3.3	15.2	2.8	0.0
Natural, Bio Activia, Danone*	1 Pot/125g	90	72	4.3	6.0	3.4	0.0
Natural, Bio Activia, Low Fat, Danone*	1 Pot/125g	75	60	4.7	6.1	1.9	0.0
Natural, Bio Live, Organic, Yeo Valley*	1 Pot/100g	82	82	4.5	6.6	4.2	0.0
Natural, Bio Set, Low Fat, Sainsbury's*	1 Pot/150g	78	52	3.9	5.7	1.5	0.0
Natural, Bio Wholemilk, Waitrose*	1 Pot/125g	100	80	4.8	6.9	3.7	0.0
Natural, Bio, Better for You, Morrisons*	1 Serving/100g	65	65	6.5	9.4	0.2	0.0
Natural, Bio, Fat Free, Waitrose*	1 Pot/150g	90	60	6.1	8.6	0.1	0.0
Natural, Bio, GFY, Asda*	1oz/28g	17	62	6.0	9.0	0.2	0.0
Natural, Bio, Low Fat, Sainsbury's*	1 Serving/100g	48	48	4.0	4.6	1.5	0.0
Natural, Bio, Unsweetened, Marks & Spencer*	1 Serving/100g	80	80	6.7	8.5	1.8	0.0
Natural, Bio, Virtually Fat Free, Tesco*	1 Serving/100g	47	47	5.5	5.8	0.2	0.0
Natural, Biopot, Set, Onken*	1 Pot/150g	101	67	3.9	4.8	3.6	0.0
Natural, Biopot, Stirred, Onken*	1 Bowl/200g	118	59	5.9	5.0	1.5	0.0
Natural, Danone*	1 Pot/125g	71	57	3.2	3.8	2.9	0.0
Natural, Farmhouse, Virtually Fat Free, TTD, Sainsbury's*	1 Serving/100g	44	44	4.5	6.6	0.2	0.0
Natural, Fat Free, Organic, Yeo Valley*	1 Serving/100g	58	58	5.9	8.4	0.1	0.0
Natural, Fat Free, Rachel's Organic*	1 Pot/500g	180	36	3.9	4.8	0.1	0.0
Natural, Greek Style, Asda*	1oz/28g	36	129	4.6	4.8	10.8	0.0
Natural, Greek Style, BGTY, Sainsbury's*	1 Serving/50g	48	95	6.2	6.4	5.0	0.0
Natural, Greek Style, Bio Live, Rachel's Organic*	1 Pot/450g	513	114	3.7	4.6	9.0	0.0
Natural, Greek Style, GFY, Asda*	1 Pot/100g	101	101	6.0	8.0	4.8	0.0
Natural, Greek Style, Healthy Eating, Tesco*	1oz/28g	22	79	6.5	4.0	4.1	0.0
Natural, Greek Style, Organic, Tesco*	1oz/28g	37	133	4.5	6.2	10.0	0.0
Natural, Greek Style, Sainsbury's*	1 Serving/100g	78	78	5.5	7.9	2.7	0.0
Natural, Greek Style, Unsweetened, Marks & Spencer*	1 Pot/100g	130	130	5.5	4.6	10.1	0.1
Natural, Greek Style, Waitrose*	1 Pot/150g	210	140	4.8	6.9	10.3	0.0
Natural, Greek Style, With Cow's Milk, Tesco*	1 Pot/150g	215	143	4.5	6.6	10.9	0.0
Natural, Low Fat, Asda*	1oz/28g	17	62	6.1	7.1	1.0	0.0
Natural, Low Fat, Bio, Sainsbury's*	1 Pot/125g	85	68	5.6	7.9	1.5	0.0
Natural, Low Fat, Live, Waitrose*	1 Pot/175g	114	65	5.8	8.2	1.0	0.0
Natural, Low Fat, Onken*	1 Pot/75g	36	48	5.3	6.4	0.1	0.0
Natural, Low Fat, Organic, Yeo Valley*	1 Serving/100g	68	68	5.9	8.5	1.2	0.0
Natural, Low Fat, Somerfield*	1 Pot/150g	78	52	4.5	5.9	1.1	0.0
Natural, Low Fat, TTD, Sainsbury's*	1 Pot/125g	80	64	6.7	4.6	1.8	0.0
Natural, Low Fat, Tesco*	1 Pot/200g	112	56	5.6	5.8	1.1	0.0
Natural, Netto*	1 Serving/50g	40	80	4.8	6.9	3.7	0.0
Natural, Organic, Evernat*	1oz/28g	29	104	3.9	12.9	4.1	0.0
Natural, Organic, Low Fat, Sainsbury's*	1oz/28g	20	71	6.2	8.8	1.2	0.0
Natural, Organic, Yeo Valley*	1 Pot/150g	120	80	4.7	6.9	3.7	0.0
Natural, Set, Asda*	1oz/28g	16	57	5.1	6.8	1.0	0.0
Natural, Set, Low Fat, Waitrose*	1 Pot/150g	99	66	5.7	8.1	1.2	0.0
Natural, Unsweetened, Bio, Marks & Spencer*	1 Pot/225g	135	60	5.6	5.5	1.8	0.0
Natural, Very Low Fat Bio, Somerfield*	1 Pot/150g	98	65	7.0	9.0	0.0	0.0
Natural, Virtually Fat Free, Bio, Safeway*	1 Pot/100g	65	65	6.4	9.4	0.2	0.0
Natural, Vitality Probiotic, Low Fat, Muller*	1 Serving/100g	67	67	5.5	6.9	1.9	0.0
Natural, Weight Watchers*	1 Serving/100g	44	44	4.8	5.3	0.1	1.6

Y

YOGHURT,	Measure INFO/WEIGHT	per Measure KCAL	Nutrition Values per 100g / 100ml				
			KCAL	PROT	CARB	FAT	FIBRE
Natural, Wholemilk, Organic, Sainsbury's*	1 Pot/125g	86	69	3.7	5.0	3.8	0.1
Nectarine & Apricot Bio, Virtually Fat Free, Shape*	1 Pot/120g	53	44	4.8	5.3	0.1	0.1
Nectarine & Orange, Best There Is, Yoplait	1 Pot/122g	131	107	4.7	18.0	1.6	0.0
Nectarine & Orange, Channel Island, Marks & Spencer*	1 Pot/150g	158	105	4.5	14.7	3.3	0.3
Nectarine & Orange, Frozen, Marks & Spencer*	1oz/28g	33	119	3.3	24.3	1.0	0.7
Nectarine & Orange, Marks & Spencer*	1 Pot/150g	147	98	4.9	16.0	1.6	0.3
Nectarine & Orange, Virtually Fat Free, Shape*	1 Pot/120g	55	46	4.7	5.8	0.1	0.1
Nectarine & Orange, Virtually Fat Free, Tesco*	1 Pot/125g	58	46	4.1	7.2	0.1	0.0
Nectarine & Passion Fruit, BGTY, Sainsbury's*	1 Pot/151g	122	81	3.2	16.3	0.4	0.6
Nectarine & Passion Fruit, Fat Free, Weight Watchers	1 Pot/120g	54	45	4.2	6.6	0.1	0.1
Nectarine & Raspberry, Low Fat, Somerfield*	1 Pot/150g	134	89	4.0	17.0	1.0	0.0
Nectarine & Raspberry, Very Low Fat, Somerfield*	1 Pot/125g	60	48	5.0	7.0	0.0	0.0
Nectarines & Greek Style, Food To Go, Marks & Spencer*	1 Pack/200g	100	50	2.9	6.3	2.1	1.0
Orange & Guava Tropical Fruit, Ski*	1 Pot/125g	123	98	4.9	15.5	1.9	0.2
Orange & Lemon, BGTY, Sainsbury's*	1 Pot/125g	63	50	4.7	7.3	0.2	0.2
Orange & Mango, COU, Marks & Spencer*	1 Serving/145g	65	45	4.3	6.0	0.1	0.2
Orange & Nectarine, Weight Watchers*	1 Pot/120g	54	45	4.2	6.5	0.1	0.1
Orange Blossom Honey, Finest, Tesco*	1 Pot/150g	237	158	3.5	20.1	7.1	0.0
Orange With Chocolate Flakes, Shape*	1 Pot/150g	140	93	4.6	11.8	2.8	0.2
Orange With Grains, Good Intentions, Somerfield*	1 Pot/125g	91	73	5.9	11.6	0.3	0.1
Orange, BGTY, Sainsbury's*	1 Pot/125g	66	53	4.8	8.1	0.1	1.2
Orange, Fat Free, Shape*	1 Pot/120g	61	51	4.5	8.7	0.2	0.1
Orange, Greek Style, Boots*	1 Pot/140g	207	148	3.7	14.0	8.6	0.2
Orange, Greek Style, Shape*	1 Pot/100g	105	105	7.7	9.4	3.6	0.1
Orange, Low Fat, Tesco*	1 Pot/125g	111	89	4.9	13.5	1.7	0.2
Orange, Shape, Fat Free, Danone*	1 Pot/119.4g	86	72	4.3	13.5	0.1	0.0
Orange, Truly Fruity, Bio, Shape*	1oz/28g	14	51	4.5	7.2	0.1	0.1
Original, Thick & Creamy, Muller*	1oz/28g	31	109	4.8	11.3	5.0	0.0
Papaya & Banana, COU, Marks & Spencer*	1 Pot/145g	65	45	4.2	5.7	0.1	0.1
Papaya & Passion Fruit, Virtually Fat Free, Shape*	1 Pot/120g	59	49	4.7	6.5	0.1	0.1
Passion Fruit & Peach, Fruit Corner, Muller*	1 Pot/175g	186	106	3.7	14.1	3.9	0.0
Passion Fruit With Elderflower Extract, Tesco*	1 Pot/150g	147	98	4.7	17.3	1.1	0.2
Peach & Apricot, Bio Fruit, Fat Free, Shape, Danone*	1 Pot/119.7g	85	71	4.3	13.1	0.1	0.0
Peach & Apricot, COU, Marks & Spencer*	1 Pot/150g	68	45	4.2	5.7	0.1	0.2
Peach & Apricot, Extremely Fruity, Marks & Spencer*	1 Pot/200g	194	97	4.8	15.8	1.6	0.4
Peach & Apricot, Fat Free, Bio, Shape*	1 Serving/120g	89	74	4.5	13.6	0.1	0.0
Peach & Apricot, Fruit Corner, Muller*	1 Pot/175g	193	110	3.7	15.0	3.9	0.0
Peach & Apricot, Healthy Living, Tesco*	1 Pot/92g	42	46	4.1	7.1	0.1	0.0
Peach & Apricot, Marks & Spencer*	1oz/28g	27	97	4.8	15.8	1.6	0.4
Peach & Apricot, Shape*	1 Pot/120g	54	45	4.6	5.8	0.1	0.1
Peach & Apricot, Smooth, Bio, Fat Free, Shape, Danone*	1 Pot/120g	86	72	4.3	13.7	0.1	0.0
Peach & Apricot, Virtually Fat Free, Bio, Shape*	1 Pot/120g	95	79	4.0	13.7	0.9	0.0
Peach & Lemon Balm, Biowild, Onken*	1 Pot/175g	158	90	4.3	14.9	1.5	0.1
Peach & Mango, Juicy, Shapers, Boots*	1 Pot/150g	89	59	4.0	8.3	1.1	0.5
Peach & Maracuya, Light, Muller*	1 Pot/200g	100	50	4.4	7.9	0.1	0.0
Peach & Papaya, Fat Free, Yeo Valley*	1 Pot/125g	95	76	5.1	13.6	0.1	0.1
Peach & Papaya, Waitrose*	1 Pot/150g	129	86	4.2	17.1	0.1	0.2
Peach & Passion Fruit Flip, Morrisons*	1 Pot/175g	89	51	3.9	8.2	0.3	0.6
Peach & Passion Fruit, Eat Smart, Safeway*	1 Pot/125g	69	55	5.2	8.5	0.1	0.3
Peach & Passion Fruit, Fruit Layered, Bio, GFY, Asda*	1 Pot/126.2g	77	61	4.0	11.0	0.1	0.5
Peach & Passion Fruit, Lite Biopot, Onken*	1 Serving/100g	45	45	4.6	6.0	0.2	0.2
Peach & Passion Fruit, Low Fat, Ski*	1 Pot/125g	124	99	4.9	15.7	1.9	0.2
Peach & Passion Fruit, Low Fat, Somerfield*	1 Pot/150g	132	88	4.0	16.0	1.0	0.0

Y

YOGHURT,	Measure INFO/WEIGHT	per Measure KCAL	Nutrition Values per 100g / 100ml				
			KCAL	PROT	CARB	FAT	FIBRE
Peach & Passion Fruit, Organic, Muller*	1 Pot/150g	147	98	3.9	16.6	1.8	0.0
Peach & Passion Fruit, Very Low Fat, Somerfield*	1 Pot/125g	61	49	5.0	7.0	0.0	0.0
Peach & Pineapple, Fat Free, Weight Watchers*	1 Pot/120g	53	44	4.1	6.5	0.1	0.1
Peach & Pineapple, Light, Ski*	1 Pot/125g	68	54	5.7	7.5	0.1	2.0
Peach & Raspberry, Custard Style, Fat Free, Shape*	1 Pot/170g	77	45	4.1	6.3	0.1	0.2
Peach & Raspberry, Marks & Spencer*	1 Pot/150g	144	96	4.8	15.7	1.6	0.4
Peach & Vanilla, Healthy Eating, Tesco*	1 Pot/125g	55	44	4.8	6.0	0.1	0.1
Peach 'n' Mango, D'lite, Ski*	1 Pot/200g	182	91	5.1	14.5	0.9	0.0
Peach Melba, Everyday Low Fat, Co-Op*	1 Pot/125g	88	70	3.0	13.0	0.7	0.0
Peach Melba, Low Fat, Tesco*	1 Pot/125g	80	64	2.7	11.7	0.7	0.1
Peach Melba, Sveltesse 0%, Nestle*	1 Pot/125.5g	64	51	4.3	8.2	0.1	0.0
Peach, BGTY, Sainsbury's*	1 Pot/125g	61	49	4.7	7.2	0.2	0.2
Peach, Bio Activia 0%, Danone*	1 Pot/125g	64	51	3.7	8.9	0.0	0.0
Peach, Bio, Virtually Fat Free, Shape*	1 Pot/120g	55	46	4.7	5.8	0.1	0.1
Peach, Corner Squeezer, Muller*	1 Serving/64g	65	101	3.2	15.2	3.0	0.0
Peach, Custard Style, Low Fat, Sainsbury's*	1 Pot/125g	110	88	4.4	14.2	1.5	0.1
Peach, D'lite, Ski*	1 Pot/125g	100	80	4.6	15.2	0.1	0.2
Peach, Economy, Sainsbury's*	1 Pot/125g	93	74	2.8	14.7	0.4	0.0
Peach, Extra Fruit, Low Fat, Ski*	1 Pot/125g	114	91	3.5	15.7	1.5	0.1
Peach, Fat Free, Weight Watchers*	1 Pot/118g	53	45	4.2	6.7	0.1	0.2
Peach, Honey & Grain, Eat Smart, Safeway*	1 Serving/200g	120	60	4.7	9.4	0.2	0.3
Peach, Light, Ski*	1 Pot/125g	100	80	4.6	15.2	0.1	0.2
Peach, Low Fat, Asda*	1 Pot/125g	119	95	4.6	17.4	1.0	0.2
Peach, Low Fat, Muller*	1 Pot/150g	152	101	4.8	16.1	1.9	0.0
Peach, Low Fat, Sainsbury's*	1 Pot/125g	114	91	4.3	15.0	1.5	0.1
Peach, Low Fat, Ski*	1 Pot/125g	123	98	4.9	15.5	1.8	0.2
Peach, Low Fat, Yeo Valley*	1 Pot/125g	113	90	4.6	15.3	1.1	0.1
Peach, Organic, Alpro*	1 Serving/125g	109	87	3.8	12.4	2.2	0.3
Peach, Shape*	1 Pot/120g	55	46	4.7	5.8	0.1	0.1
Peach, Smooth, Ski*	1 Pot/125g	128	102	4.9	16.3	1.9	0.0
Peach, Thick & Fruity, Weight Watchers*	1 Pot/120g	55	46	4.2	7.1	0.1	0.2
Peach, Vitality Probiotic, Muller*	1 Pot/150g	113	75	2.6	13.0	1.4	0.0
Peach, Whole Grain, Biopot, Onken*	1 Serving/200g	226	113	4.2	17.9	2.7	0.3
Peaches, Farmhouse, BGTY, Sainsbury's*	1 Pot/150g	134	89	3.2	17.8	0.4	0.3
Peanut Toffee, Low Fat, Somerfield*	1 Pot/150g	131	87	4.0	15.0	1.0	0.0
Pear & Butterscotch, Finest, Tesco*	1 Pot/150g	413	275	5.0	32.3	14.0	0.5
Pear & Ginger, COU, Marks & Spencer*	1oz/28g	13	45	4.0	5.8	0.1	0.3
Pear, Rosehip & Marigold, Biowild, Onken*	1 Pot/175g	161	92	4.4	15.1	1.5	0.3
Pianola, Lidl*	1 Serving/125g	55	44	3.7	7.5	0.1	0.0
Pineapple & Coconut, Weight Watchers*	1 Pot/120g	56	47	3.9	7.4	0.1	0.1
Pineapple & Papaya, Ski*	1 Pot/125g	123	98	4.8	15.5	1.8	0.1
Pineapple & Passion Fruit, Low Fat, Marks & Spencer*	1 Pot/145g	65	45	4.3	5.7	0.1	0.2
Pineapple & Peach, Virtually Fat Free, Light, Muller*	1 Pot/200g	106	53	4.4	8.7	0.1	0.0
Pineapple, BGTY, Sainsbury's*	1 Pot/125g	66	53	4.8	8.3	0.1	1.1
Pineapple, Channel Island, Marks & Spencer*	1 Pot/150g	165	110	4.3	15.9	3.3	0.3
Pineapple, D'Lite 0.2, Ski, Nestle*	1 Pot/125g	100	80	4.4	15.3	0.1	0.1
Pineapple, Eat Smart, Safeway*	1 Pot/125g	66	53	4.5	8.4	0.1	0.1
Pineapple, Extremely Fruity, Marks & Spencer*	1 Pot/200g	200	100	4.3	17.6	1.4	0.2
Pineapple, Finest, Tesco*	1 Pot/200g	220	110	3.5	17.5	2.9	0.2
Pineapple, Healthy Living, Tesco*	1 Pot/125g	69	55	5.1	8.1	0.3	1.1
Pineapple, Low Fat, Bio, Asda*	1 Pot/150g	144	96	4.6	17.0	1.1	0.1
Pineapple, Low Fat, Tesco*	1 Pot/125g	111	89	4.6	13.4	1.7	0.0
Pineapple, Truly Fruity, Shape*	1 Pot/120g	61	51	4.5	7.3	0.1	0.1

YOGHURT,

	Measure INFO/WEIGHT	per Measure KCAL	KCAL	PROT	CARB	FAT	FIBRE
Pineapple, Virtually Fat Free, Tesco*	1 Pot/125g	55	44	4.1	6.5	0.2	0.9
Pineapple, Weight Watchers*	1 Pot/120g	56	47	3.9	7.7	0.1	0.9
Pink Grapefruit Fruit Corner, Muller*	1 Pot/175g	189	108	4.1	13.9	4.0	0.0
Pink Grapefruit With Grains, Good Intentions, Somerfield*	1 Pot/125g	87	70	6.0	10.8	0.3	0.1
Pink Grapefruit, Breakfast Selection, Sainsbury's*	1 Pot/117g	109	93	4.2	15.9	1.4	0.1
Pink Grapefruit, Low Fat, Sainsbury's*	1 Pot/125g	116	93	4.2	15.9	1.4	0.1
Pink Grapefruit, Weight Watchers*	1 Pot/120g	52	43	4.1	6.3	0.1	0.2
Plain, Low Fat	1 Pot/120g	67	56	5.1	7.5	0.8	0.0
Plum & Hop, Biowild, Onken*	1 Pot/175g	158	90	4.3	14.9	1.5	0.3
Plum, Bio Live, Summer Selection, Yeo Valley*	1 Pot/125g	98	78	5.1	14.2	0.1	0.1
Plum, Low Fat, Orchard Grove, Shape*	1 Pot/100g	63	63	4.7	8.3	1.0	0.2
Plum, Low Fat, Ski*	1 Pot/125g	119	95	4.9	14.9	1.8	0.1
Probiotic, Aldi*	1 Serving/200g	178	89	4.1	14.2	1.4	0.0
Prune, Breakfast Selection, Sainsbury's*	1 Pot/125g	119	95	4.2	16.3	1.4	0.2
Rapsberry & White Chocolate, Low Fat, Shape*	1 Pot/100g	101	101	4.7	15.6	1.8	0.1
Rasberry, Fat Free, Bio, Shape, Danone*	1 Pot/120g	84	70	4.3	12.9	0.1	0.4
Rasberry, Orange & Grain, Eat Smart, Safeway*	1 Pot/200g	120	60	4.7	9.1	0.2	0.6
Rashaka, Plain, Danone*	1 Serving/180ml	88	49	5.5	6.5	0.0	0.0
Raspberry & Black Cherry, Virtually Fat Free, Tesco*	1 Pot/125g	54	43	4.2	6.1	0.2	1.1
Raspberry & Blackberry Bio, Fat Free, Shape*	1 Pot/120g	54	45	4.6	5.6	0.1	0.2
Raspberry & Blackberry, Thick & Creamy, Co-Op*	1 Pot/150g	188	125	3.6	17.3	4.6	0.1
Raspberry & Blackcurrant, Ski*	1 Pot/125g	129	103	4.4	14.6	3.0	0.0
Raspberry & Cranberry, Light, Healthy Living, Tesco*	1 Pot/125g	55	44	4.2	6.3	0.2	1.1
Raspberry & Cranberry, Light, Muller*	1 Pot/200g	104	52	4.4	8.3	0.1	0.0
Raspberry & Elderberry, Organic, Onken*	1 Serving/50g	53	106	3.8	15.0	3.1	0.0
Raspberry & Orange, Fat Free, Organic, Yeo Valley*	1 Serving/100g	77	77	5.1	13.7	0.1	0.1
Raspberry & Redcurrant, Low Fat, Sainsbury's*	1 Pot/125g	109	87	4.2	14.5	1.4	0.5
Raspberry, BGTY, Sainsbury's*	1 Pot/125g	64	51	4.4	7.9	0.2	2.0
Raspberry, Bio Pot, Onken*	1 Pot/150g	153	102	4.4	15.1	2.7	0.0
Raspberry, Bio, Virtually Fat Free, Shape*	1 Pot/120g	56	47	4.7	6.1	0.1	0.2
Raspberry, Bio, Virtually Fat Free, Shape, Danone*	1 Pot/120g	91	76	4.0	13.0	0.9	0.5
Raspberry, COU, Marks & Spencer*	1 Pot/150g	68	45	4.2	5.5	0.1	0.3
Raspberry, D'lite 0.2%, Ski*	1 Pot/125g	99	79	4.6	14.9	0.1	0.6
Raspberry, Eat Smart, Safeway*	1 Pot/127g	70	55	5.2	8.5	0.1	0.7
Raspberry, Economy, Sainsbury's*	1 Pot/125g	85	68	3.0	11.9	1.0	0.0
Raspberry, Everyday, Low Fat, Co-Op*	1 Pot/125g	88	70	3.0	13.0	0.7	0.0
Raspberry, Extremely Fruity, Marks & Spencer*	1 Pot/200g	190	95	5.0	15.6	1.5	0.5
Raspberry, Fat Free, Bio Live, Organic, Yeo Valley*	1 Pot/125g	98	78	5.2	14.0	0.1	0.4
Raspberry, Fat Free, Farmhouse, BGTY, Sainsbury's*	1 Pot/150g	101	67	3.4	13.7	0.1	2.0
Raspberry, Fat Free, Weight Watchers*	1 Pot/120g	49	41	4.2	5.7	0.1	0.3
Raspberry, Fimbles, Marks & Spencer*	1 Pot/87.5g	70	80	3.6	11.1	2.6	0.6
Raspberry, French Set Wholemilk, Asda*	1 Pot/125g	125	100	3.6	14.1	3.2	0.0
Raspberry, French Set, Waitrose*	1 Pot/125g	120	96	3.5	13.4	3.1	2.0
Raspberry, Frozen, Handmade Farmhouse, Sainsbury's*	1 Serving/100g	132	132	2.7	21.8	3.8	2.2
Raspberry, Fruit Corner, Muller*	1 Pot/175g	200	114	4.2	15.3	4.0	0.0
Raspberry, Fruit Halo, Muller Light, Muller*	1 Pot/144.0g	121	84	3.7	16.5	0.3	0.0
Raspberry, Greek Style, Layered, GFY, Asda*	1 Pot/150g	123	82	4.3	10.0	2.7	1.3
Raspberry, Healthy Eating, Tesco*	1 Pot/125g	49	39	4.4	5.0	0.2	1.0
Raspberry, Healthy Living, Tesco*	1 Serving/175g	74	42	2.1	8.3	0.1	2.0
Raspberry, Light, Healthy Living, Tesco*	1 Pot/200g	76	38	3.7	5.7	0.1	0.0
Raspberry, Low Fat, Asda*	1 Pot/125g	121	97	4.7	17.0	1.1	0.0
Raspberry, Low Fat, Benecol*	1 Pot/125ml	100	80	3.8	14.5	0.7	0.0
Raspberry, Low Fat, Bio, Sainsbury's*	1 Pot/150g	146	97	4.7	17.0	1.1	0.7

INFO/WEIGHT	Measure	per Measure KCAL	Nutrition Values per 100g / 100ml KCAL	PROT	CARB	FAT	FIBRE
Raspberry, Low Fat, Muller*	1 Pot/150g	152	101	4.8	16.1	1.9	0.0
Raspberry, Low Fat, Organic, Marks & Spencer*	1 Pot/170g	162	95	4.4	16.1	1.4	0.4
Raspberry, Low Fat, Sainsbury's*	1 Pot/125g	115	92	4.4	15.2	1.5	0.2
Raspberry, Low Fat, Ski*	1 Pot/125g	121	97	4.9	15.2	1.9	0.6
Raspberry, Low Fat, Somerfield*	1 Pot/150g	128	85	4.0	16.0	1.0	0.0
Raspberry, Low Fat, Tesco*	1 Pot/125g	123	98	4.9	15.5	1.8	0.3
Raspberry, Marks & Spencer*	1 Pot/150g	144	96	4.9	15.4	1.6	0.6
Raspberry, Meadow Fresh*	1 Sm Pot/125g	130	104	4.5	18.9	1.0	0.0
Raspberry, Organic, Fat Free, Rachel's Organic*	1 Serving/142g	78	55	3.6	10.0	0.1	0.0
Raspberry, Organic, Low Fat, Tesco*	1 Pot/125g	109	87	5.3	14.1	1.0	0.1
Raspberry, Organic, Yeo Valley*	1 Pot/150g	144	96	4.4	12.3	3.3	0.1
Raspberry, Pavlova, Corner, Muller*	1 Pot/150g	230	153	3.4	24.4	4.7	0.0
Raspberry, Probiotic, Vitality, Low Fat, Muller*	1 Bottle/100g	97	97	4.8	15.4	1.8	0.0
Raspberry, Seriously Fruity, Low Fat, Waitrose*	1 Pot/150g	149	99	4.8	16.2	1.7	0.3
Raspberry, Smooth Set, Co-Op*	1 Pot/125g	95	76	3.7	12.5	0.9	0.0
Raspberry, Smooth, Marks & Spencer*	1 Pot/150g	150	100	4.9	16.2	1.6	0.5
Raspberry, Thick & Creamy, Sainsbury's*	1 Pot/150g	179	119	4.4	17.2	3.7	0.2
Raspberry, Virtually Fat Free, Tesco*	1 Pot/125g	51	41	4.1	5.8	0.2	1.1
Raspberry, Vitality, Muller*	1oz/28g	27	97	4.8	15.4	1.8	0.0
Raspberry, Way To Five, Sainsbury's*	1 Pot/151g	104	69	3.3	13.6	0.1	2.1
Red Berry, Blender, Pret A Manger*	1 Av Pack/125g	175	140	5.6	23.0	3.0	2.4
Red Cherries, Bio Activia 0%, Danone*	1 Pot/125g	65	52	3.6	9.1	0.0	0.0
Red Cherry, Bio, Shape*	1 Pot/120g	58	48	4.6	6.4	0.1	0.1
Red Cherry, D'lite, Ski*	1 Pot/125g	101	81	4.5	15.4	0.1	0.1
Red Cherry, Fruit Layered, GFY, Asda*	1 Pot/125g	75	60	3.7	11.0	0.1	0.0
Red Cherry, Light, 99.9% Fat Free, Ski*	1 Pot/125g	73	58	4.9	9.2	0.1	1.2
Red Cherry, Light, Ski*	1 Pot/125g	101	81	4.5	15.4	0.1	0.1
Red Cherry, Organic, Onken*	1 Serving/28g	29	102	3.6	14.8	3.1	0.0
Red Cherry, Simply Berries, Shape, Danone*	1 Pot/120g	64	53	4.4	8.7	0.1	7.4
Red Cherry, Virtually Fat Free, Ski*	1 Pot/125g	64	51	4.5	7.7	0.2	2.0
Red Fruits, Crumble Style, Sveltesse 0%, Nestle*	1 Pot/125g	69	55	4.3	9.0	0.2	0.2
Rhubarb & Orange, Perfectly Balanced, Waitrose*	½ Pot/250ml	218	87	1.9	18.4	0.6	0.2
Rhubarb & Orange, Tesco*	1 Pot/150g	146	97	4.6	17.1	1.1	0.5
Rhubarb & Vanilla, Onken*	1 Serving/100g	106	106	3.8	16.9	2.6	0.3
Rhubarb Crumble Corner, Muller*	1 Pot/150g	222	148	3.3	21.7	5.3	0.0
Rhubarb Crumble, Layered Style, Healthy Eating, Tesco*	1 Pot/125g	93	74	4.1	12.9	0.7	0.2
Rhubarb, Bio, Activia, Danone*	1 Pot/125g	129	103	3.5	15.0	3.2	1.6
Rhubarb, Custard Style, Somerfield*	1 Pot/125g	149	119	3.0	16.0	5.0	0.0
Rhubarb, Eat Smart, Safeway*	1 Pot/125g	69	55	5.1	7.8	0.1	0.2
Rhubarb, Extremely Fruity, Bio, Marks & Spencer*	1 Pot/150g	158	105	4.5	18.2	1.4	0.4
Rhubarb, Extremely Fruity, Marks & Spencer*	1 Pot/150g	158	105	4.5	18.2	1.4	0.4
Rhubarb, Farmhouse, Sainsbury's*	1 Pot/150g	149	99	4.3	13.4	3.1	0.3
Rhubarb, Live Bio, Perfectly Balanced, Waitrose*	1 Pot/151g	131	87	4.6	17.0	0.1	0.2
Rhubarb, Low Fat, Asda*	1 Pot/125g	110	88	4.6	15.0	1.1	0.0
Rhubarb, Low Fat, Bio Live, Rachel's Organic*	1 Pot/100g	73	73	3.5	11.0	1.7	0.0
Rhubarb, Low Fat, Organic, Marks & Spencer*	1 Pot/170g	145	85	4.1	14.7	1.2	0.2
Rhubarb, Low Fat, Ski*	1 Pot/125g	123	98	4.8	15.7	1.8	0.1
Rhubarb, Low Fat, Tesco*	1 Pot/125g	106	85	4.9	12.4	1.7	0.1
Rhubarb, Marks & Spencer*	1 Pot/150g	149	99	4.4	17.4	1.4	0.3
Rhubarb, Very Low Fat, Somerfield*	1 Pot/125g	58	46	5.0	6.0	0.0	0.0
Rum Raisin Crunch Corner, Muller*	1 Pot/150g	219	146	4.2	22.0	4.6	0.0
Sheep's Milk, Total*	1oz/28g	25	90	4.8	4.3	6.0	0.0
Smooth Toffee & Apple, Low Fat, Co-Op*	1 Pot/125g	150	120	6.0	22.0	1.0	0.1

Y

YOGHURT,

INFO/WEIGHT	Measure	per Measure KCAL	KCAL	PROT	CARB	FAT	FIBRE
Smooth Toffee & Orange, Co-Op*	1 Pot/125g	181	145	6.0	27.0	1.0	0.0
Smooth Toffee, Eat Smart, Safeway*	1 Pot/125g	69	55	5.1	8.7	0.1	0.0
Smooth Vanilla, Eat Smart, Safeway*	1 Pot/125g	69	55	5.0	8.3	0.1	0.0
Somerset With Vanilla, TTD, Sainsbury's*	1 Pot/150g	222	148	4.0	18.1	6.6	0.0
Soya	1oz/28g	20	72	5.0	3.9	4.2	0.0
Spanish Lemon, Onken*	1 Serving/100g	100	100	3.9	15.1	2.7	0.0
Spanish Orange, Amore Luxury, Muller*	1 Pot/175g	254	145	2.3	16.3	7.8	0.0
Spiced Rhubarb, COU, Marks & Spencer*	1oz/28g	13	45	4.3	5.5	0.1	0.2
Sticky Toffee Pudding Corner, Muller*	1 Pot/150g	239	159	3.6	24.7	5.1	0.0
Strawberries & Cream, Finest, Tesco*	1 Pot/150g	206	137	3.4	15.4	6.9	0.5
Strawberry & Cornish Clotted Cream, Marks & Spencer*	1 Pot/150g	218	145	3.2	15.4	7.7	0.5
Strawberry & Orange Crunch Corner, Muller*	1 Pot/150g	218	145	4.1	22.5	4.3	0.0
Strawberry & Raspberry, Bio Live, Organic, Yeo Valley*	1 Pot/125g	125	100	4.2	12.0	3.9	0.1
Strawberry & Raspberry, Bio, GFY, Asda*	1 Pot/125g	75	60	3.8	11.0	0.1	0.0
Strawberry & Raspberry, Healthy Eating, Tesco*	1 Pot/125g	58	46	4.2	7.0	0.1	0.0
Strawberry & Raspberry, Layered, Bio, GFY, Asda*	1 Pot/72g	43	60	3.8	11.0	0.1	0.4
Strawberry & Raspberry, Low Fat, Asda*	1 Pot/150g	143	95	4.6	17.4	1.0	0.2
Strawberry & Raspberry, Low Fat, Sainsbury's*	1 Pot/125g	109	87	4.2	14.3	1.4	0.2
Strawberry & Rhubarb, Channel Island, Marks & Spencer*	1 Pot/150g	158	105	3.9	15.4	3.0	0.0
Strawberry & Rhubarb, Low Fat, Sainsbury's*	1 Pot/125g	108	86	4.2	14.1	1.4	0.2
Strawberry & Rhubarb, Low Fat, Somerfield*	1 Pot/125g	108	86	4.1	15.6	0.8	0.1
Strawberry & Rhubarb, Onken*	1 Serving/100g	85	85	4.6	16.2	0.1	0.4
Strawberry & Vanilla, Low Fat, Somerfield*	1 Pot/125g	109	87	4.0	15.9	0.8	0.1
Strawberry & Vanilla, Marks & Spencer*	1 Pot/150g	143	95	4.8	15.4	1.6	0.2
Strawberry & Vanilla, Weight Watchers*	1 Pot/120g	54	45	4.2	6.8	0.1	0.1
Strawberry & Whole Grain, Bio Break, Tesco*	1 Pot/175g	175	100	4.7	17.8	1.1	0.2
Strawberry & Wild Strawberry, Sveltesse 0%, Nestle*	1 Pot/125g	58	46	4.3	7.0	0.1	0.0
Strawberry & Wild Strawberry, Weight Watchers*	1 Pot/120g	49	41	4.2	5.8	0.1	0.1
Strawberry Cheescake Corner, Muller*	1 Pot/150g	233	155	3.7	25.3	4.3	0.0
Strawberry Cheesecake, Eat Smart, Safeway*	1 Pot/125g	64	51	4.7	7.7	0.1	0.3
Strawberry Fruit, Deep Fill, Low Fat, Ski*	1 Pot/159g	137	86	4.0	13.8	1.6	0.0
Strawberry Mousse, Shapers, Boots*	1 Pot/90g	88	97	4.1	11.0	4.1	0.1
Strawberry With Grains, Good Intentions, Somerfield*	1 Pot/125g	86	69	6.0	10.6	0.3	0.2
Strawberry With Real Fruit Chunks, Low Fat, Muller*	1 Pot/150g	149	99	4.8	15.7	1.9	0.0
Strawberry, BGTY, Sainsbury's*	1 Pot/123g	64	52	4.7	7.7	0.2	0.1
Strawberry, Bio & Cereal Clusters, Rumblers*	1 Pot/168g	267	159	4.3	22.4	5.8	1.1
Strawberry, Bio Activia 0% Fat, Danone*	1 Pot/125g	63	50	3.8	8.4	0.0	0.0
Strawberry, Bio Live, Fat Free, Rachel's Organic*	1 Pot/142g	81	57	3.5	10.5	0.1	0.0
Strawberry, Bio Live, Organic, Yeo Valley*	1 Pot/150g	152	101	4.1	12.3	3.9	0.1
Strawberry, Bio Virtually Fat Free, Tesco*	1 Pot/125g	50	40	4.4	5.3	0.2	0.9
Strawberry, Bio, Healthy Eating, Tesco*	1 Pot/125g	61	49	4.7	7.0	0.2	0.2
Strawberry, Bio, Virtually Fat Free, Shape*	1 Pot/120g	55	46	4.7	5.7	0.1	0.1
Strawberry, COU, Marks & Spencer*	1 Pot/125g	63	50	4.3	6.4	0.1	0.1
Strawberry, Childrens, Co-Op*	1 Pot/125g	121	97	3.5	14.9	2.7	0.2
Strawberry, Crisp, Jordans*	1oz/28g	38	137	4.8	22.8	3.3	1.1
Strawberry, Crumble Corner, Muller*	1 Pot/150g	222	148	3.3	21.7	5.3	0.0
Strawberry, Custard Style, Shapers, Boots*	1 Pot/150g	117	78	3.9	14.0	0.7	0.5
Strawberry, Custard Style, Somerfield*	1 Pot/125g	153	122	3.0	17.0	5.0	0.0
Strawberry, D'lite, Ski*	1 Pot/125g	99	79	4.5	14.7	0.1	0.2
Strawberry, Dessert, Frozen, Tesco*	1 Pot/60g	82	136	2.6	26.5	2.2	0.8
Strawberry, Duo, Co-Op*	1 Pot/175g	219	125	3.0	17.0	5.0	0.7
Strawberry, Eat Smart, Safeway*	1 Pot/125g	69	55	5.1	8.3	0.1	0.3
Strawberry, Everyday Low Fat, Co-Op*	1 Pot/125g	88	70	3.0	13.0	0.7	0.0

Y

YOGHURT,

INFO/WEIGHT	Measure	per Measure KCAL	KCAL	PROT	CARB	FAT	FIBRE
Strawberry, Extra Light, 0.1% Fat, Muller*	1 Pot/200g	118	59	5.0	8.8	0.1	0.0
Strawberry, Extremely Fruity, Marks & Spencer*	1 Pot/200g	190	95	4.8	15.4	1.6	0.2
Strawberry, Farmhouse, BGTY, Sainsbury's*	1 Pot/150g	107	71	3.2	13.7	0.4	0.5
Strawberry, Fat Free, Bio Live, Organic, Yeo Valley*	1 Pot/125g	98	78	5.1	14.3	0.1	0.1
Strawberry, Fat Free, Bio, Shape, Danone*	1 Pot/120g	86	72	4.3	13.6	0.1	0.1
Strawberry, Fat Free, Waitrose*	1 Pot/150g	135	90	4.6	17.8	0.1	0.1
Strawberry, Fat Free, Weight Watchers*	1 Pot/120g	52	43	4.1	6.2	0.1	0.1
Strawberry, Frozen, Marks & Spencer*	1oz/28g	35	125	3.1	24.9	1.2	0.6
Strawberry, Frozen, Organic, Yeo Valley*	1 Serving/100g	139	139	4.7	23.9	2.7	0.3
Strawberry, Fruit Corner, Muller*	1 Pot/175g	207	118	3.7	17.1	3.9	0.0
Strawberry, Healthy Living, Tesco*	1 Pot/175g	70	40	2.1	7.7	0.1	0.3
Strawberry, Light & Refreshing, Campina*	1 Pot/125g	110	88	2.5	16.9	1.1	0.0
Strawberry, Light, 99.9% Fat Free, Ski*	1 Pot/125g	60	48	4.7	7.7	0.1	1.0
Strawberry, Light, Healthy Living, Tesco*	1 Pot/200g	96	48	4.1	7.6	0.1	0.0
Strawberry, Light, Muller*	1 Pot/200g	106	53	4.4	8.7	0.1	0.0
Strawberry, Lite, Onken*	1 serving/100g	46	46	4.6	6.5	0.2	0.2
Strawberry, Live, Turner's Dairies*	1 Pot/125g	86	69	4.9	11.9	0.3	0.0
Strawberry, Low Fat, Asda*	1 Pot/125g	114	91	4.4	16.0	1.0	0.0
Strawberry, Low Fat, Benecol*	1 Pot/150g	119	79	3.7	14.8	0.6	0.0
Strawberry, Low Fat, Organic, Marks & Spencer*	1 Pot/170g	153	90	4.8	15.3	1.4	0.4
Strawberry, Low Fat, Organic, Muller*	1 Pot/150g	147	98	3.9	16.6	1.8	0.0
Strawberry, Low Fat, Organic, Sainsbury's*	1 Pot/125g	100	80	5.3	12.6	1.0	0.1
Strawberry, Low Fat, Organic, Somerfield*	1 Pot/150g	153	102	6.0	17.0	2.0	0.0
Strawberry, Low Fat, Safeway*	1 Pot/150g	138	92	4.6	16.0	1.1	0.1
Strawberry, Low Fat, Sainsbury's*	1 Pot/125g	115	92	4.3	15.2	1.5	0.1
Strawberry, Low Fat, Ski*	1 Pot/125g	124	99	4.8	15.8	1.8	0.0
Strawberry, Low Fat, SmartPrice, Asda*	1 Pot/125g	85	68	2.2	13.0	0.8	0.0
Strawberry, Low Fat, Tesco*	1 Pot/125g	110	88	4.8	13.6	1.6	0.1
Strawberry, Low Fat, Value, Tesco*	1 Pot/125g	81	65	2.7	11.8	0.7	0.1
Strawberry, Low Fat, Vitality Probiotic, Muller*	1 Pot/150g	146	97	4.7	15.6	1.8	0.0
Strawberry, Luscious, Shapers, Boots*	1 Pot/150g	83	55	4.0	7.3	1.1	0.6
Strawberry, Marks & Spencer*	1 Pot/150g	143	95	4.8	15.4	1.6	0.2
Strawberry, Organic, Alpro*	1 Serving/125g	104	83	3.8	11.5	2.2	0.3
Strawberry, Organic, Low Fat, Tesco*	1 Pot/125g	104	83	5.3	13.2	1.0	0.1
Strawberry, Organic, Yeo Valley*	1 Pot/150g	144	96	4.3	12.4	3.3	0.1
Strawberry, Perfectly Balanced, Waitrose*	1 Pot/150g	136	91	4.6	17.8	0.1	0.1
Strawberry, Seriously Fruity, Low Fat, Waitrose*	1 Pot/150g	152	101	4.8	16.6	1.7	0.2
Strawberry, Ski*	1 Pot/125g	111	89	3.4	15.3	1.5	0.9
Strawberry, Smooth Set French, Low Fat, Sainsbury's*	1 Pot/125g	100	80	3.5	13.6	1.2	0.0
Strawberry, Smooth Set, Co-Op*	1 Pot/125g	95	76	3.7	12.5	0.9	0.0
Strawberry, Smooth, Fat Free, Shape*	1 Pot/120g	85	71	4.3	13.2	0.1	0.1
Strawberry, Smooth, Shape*	1 Pot/120g	86	72	4.2	13.5	0.1	0.0
Strawberry, Smooth, Ski*	1 Pot/124g	89	72	2.8	13.1	0.9	0.2
Strawberry, So-Good*	1oz/28g	25	90	2.0	16.4	1.4	0.0
Strawberry, Soyage, GranoVita*	1 Pot/145g	112	77	1.8	16.5	0.4	0.0
Strawberry, Sundae Style, Sveltesse %, Nestle*	1 Pot/124.5g	66	53	4.3	8.7	0.1	0.0
Strawberry, Sveltesse*	1 Pot/125g	70	56	4.7	9.1	0.1	0.2
Strawberry, Thick & Fruity, Weight Watchers*	1 Pot/121g	52	43	4.1	6.2	0.1	0.1
Strawberry, Variety Selection, Nestle*	1 Pot/125g	119	95	4.7	15.1	1.8	0.2
Strawberry, Very Low Fat, Bio, Somerfield*	1 Pot/200g	100	50	5.0	7.0	0.0	0.0
Strawberry, Virtually Fat Free, Organic, Yeo Valley*	1 Pot/125g	98	78	5.1	14.3	0.1	0.1
Strawberry, Virtually Fat Free, Shapers, Boots*	1 Pot/125g	67	54	5.2	8.1	0.1	0.1
Strawberry, Virtually Fat Free, Ski*	1 Pot/127g	61	48	4.5	7.1	0.2	2.0

YOGHURT,	INFO/WEIGHT	KCAL	KCAL	PROT	CARB	FAT	FIBRE
Strawberry, Virtually Fat Free, Tesco*	1 Pot/125g	53	42	4.1	6.0	0.2	1.0
Strawberry, Vitality Probiotic, Muller*	1 Pot/175g	138	79	2.6	14.1	1.4	0.0
Strawberry, Whole Grain, Biopot, Onken*	1 Serving/100g	109	109	4.2	16.9	2.7	0.3
Strawberry, Wholemilk, Organic, Sainsbury's*	1 Pot/150g	123	82	3.5	9.2	3.5	0.1
Strawberry, Yoplait*	1 Pot/125g	63	50	4.4	7.9	0.1	0.0
Summer Berries, Fat Free, Shape*	1 Pot/120g	55	46	4.6	6.0	0.1	0.2
Summer Berries, Whole Grain, Lite, Biopot, Onken*	1 Serving/240g	199	83	4.6	15.8	0.2	1.4
Summer Fruits, Strawberry, Light, Healthy Living, Tesco*	1 Pot/125g	53	42	4.1	6.0	0.2	1.0
Summer Selection, Fat Free, Organic, Yeo Valley*	1 Pot/125g	89	71	5.2	12.3	0.1	0.2
Summerfruits Bio, Boots*	1 Pot/150g	140	93	4.1	13.0	2.7	0.4
Summerfruits, Fat Free, Bio Live, Rachel's Organic*	1 Pot/125g	120	96	4.7	15.3	1.8	0.0
Summerfruits, Marks & Spencer*	1oz/28g	27	96	4.8	15.6	1.6	0.5
Timperley Rhubarb, Seriously Fruity, Waitrose*	1 Pot/125g	111	89	4.4	15.5	1.0	0.2
Toffee Apple, COU, Marks & Spencer*	1 Pot/200g	90	45	4.2	6.3	0.2	0.2
Toffee Apple, Indulgent Greek Style, Somerfield*	1 Pot/125g	225	180	3.0	27.0	7.0	0.0
Toffee Caramel, D'lite, Ski*	1 Pot/180g	153	85	4.8	16.3	0.1	0.0
Toffee Fudge, Low Fat, Sainsbury's*	1 Pot/125g	146	117	4.3	20.4	2.0	0.0
Toffee Hoops, Crunch Corner, Muller*	1 Pot/150g	242	161	4.7	22.3	5.9	0.0
Toffee, Benecol*	1 Pot/125g	124	99	3.8	19.3	0.7	0.0
Toffee, COU, Marks & Spencer*	1 Pot/145g	65	45	4.2	7.7	0.2	0.0
Toffee, Economy, Sainsbury's*	1 Pot/126g	91	72	3.0	12.8	1.0	0.0
Toffee, Fat Free, Eat Smart, Safeway*	1 Pot/200g	100	50	4.6	7.7	0.1	0.0
Toffee, Light, Healthy Living, Tesco*	1 Pot/200g	94	47	4.1	7.5	0.1	0.0
Toffee, Light, Muller*	1 Pot/200g	106	53	4.4	8.5	0.1	0.0
Toffee, Light, Ski*	1 Pot/120g	60	50	4.6	7.7	0.2	0.6
Toffee, Live Bio, Perfectly Balanced, Waitrose*	1 Pot/150g	156	104	4.2	21.1	0.3	0.0
Toffee, Low Fat, Asda*	1 Pot/150g	174	116	4.6	22.0	1.1	0.0
Toffee, Low Fat, Marks & Spencer*	1 Pot/150g	180	120	4.9	21.6	1.7	0.0
Toffee, Low Fat, SmartPrice, Asda*	1 Pot/125g	96	77	2.2	15.0	0.9	0.0
Toffee, Low Fat, Somerfield*	1 Pot/150g	149	99	3.0	19.0	1.0	0.0
Toffee, Low Fat, Tesco*	1 Pot/125g	158	126	5.0	22.3	1.9	0.0
Toffee, Seriously Smooth, Low Fat, Waitrose*	1 Pot/150g	156	104	4.7	16.5	2.1	0.1
Toffee, Smooth & Creamy, Fat Free, Weight Watchers*	1 Pot/120g	48	40	3.9	5.9	0.1	0.8
Toffee, Very Low Fat Bio, Somerfield*	1 Pot/200g	100	50	5.0	7.0	0.0	0.0
Toffee, Virtually Fat Free, Boots*	1 Pot/125g	69	55	5.1	8.3	0.1	0.0
Toffee, Weight Watchers*	1 Pot/120g	52	43	4.2	6.2	0.1	0.0
Treacle Toffee, Low Fat, Sainsbury's*	1 Pot/125g	145	116	4.3	20.7	1.8	0.0
Tropical Fruit, Greek Style, Asda*	1 Pot/125g	170	136	3.3	15.0	7.0	0.0
Tropical Fruit, Greek Style, Shapers, Boots*	1 Pot/150g	101	67	3.6	9.8	1.5	0.8
Tropical, Fat Free, Rachel's Organic*	1 Pot/125g	121	97	4.7	15.4	1.8	0.0
Tropical, Smooth, Ski*	1 Pot/125g	126	101	4.9	16.1	1.9	0.1
Valencia Orange, Layered, Bio, GFY, Asda*	1 Pot/125g	80	64	3.7	12.0	0.1	0.0
Valencia Orange, Seriously Fruity, Waitrose*	1 Pot/150g	147	98	4.3	18.0	1.0	0.3
Vanilla & Chocolate Flakes, Low Fat Bio, Shape*	1 Pot/150g	140	93	4.5	12.0	2.7	0.0
Vanilla & Pineapple, Nestle*	1 Pot/125g	120	96	4.2	16.7	1.5	0.0
Vanilla Choco Balls, Crunch Corner, Muller*	1 Pot/150g	218	145	4.1	22.5	4.3	0.0
Vanilla Creme, D'lite, Ski*	1 Pot/200g	192	96	5.1	15.8	0.8	0.0
Vanilla Flavour, Healthy Living, Light, Tesco*	1 Pot/200g	72	36	3.6	5.2	0.1	0.0
Vanilla Flavour, Organic, Low Fat, Tesco*	1 Pot/125g	114	91	5.3	15.3	1.0	0.0
Vanilla Toffee, Low Fat, Sainsbury's*	1 Pot/125g	145	116	4.3	20.6	1.8	0.0
Vanilla, Benecol*	1 Serving/125g	99	79	3.7	14.6	0.6	0.0
Vanilla, Bio, BFY, Morrisons*	1 Pot/150g	83	55	5.7	8.4	0.3	0.0
Vanilla, Blender, Pret A Manger*	1 Pot/250ml	230	92	4.5	12.8	2.7	0.0

Y

	Measure INFO/WEIGHT	per Measure KCAL	Nutrition Values per 100g / 100ml				
			KCAL	PROT	CARB	FAT	FIBRE
YOGHURT,							
Vanilla, Breakfast, Tesco*	1 Pot/150g	108	72	2.9	13.9	0.5	0.0
Vanilla, COU, Marks & Spencer*	1 Pot/200g	90	45	4.1	6.1	0.1	0.0
Vanilla, Channel Island, Marks & Spencer*	1 Pot/150g	173	115	4.5	16.5	3.5	0.0
Vanilla, Frozen, Less Than 5% Fat, Tesco*	1 Pot/120g	179	149	8.1	23.8	2.4	0.7
Vanilla, Light, Muller*	1 Pot/200g	106	53	4.6	8.2	0.1	0.0
Vanilla, Live Bio, Waitrose*	1 Pot/150g	132	88	4.6	17.3	0.1	0.0
Vanilla, Low Fat, Bio, Sainsbury's*	1 Pot/150g	147	98	4.8	17.2	1.1	0.0
Vanilla, Low Fat, Ski*	1 Pot/125g	123	98	5.0	15.5	1.9	0.0
Vanilla, Organic, Low Fat, Sainsbury's*	1 Pot/125g	114	91	5.3	15.3	1.0	0.0
Vanilla, Perfectly Balanced, Waitrose*	1 Pot/150g	132	88	4.6	17.3	0.1	0.0
Vanilla, Seriously Smooth, Low Fat, Waitrose	1 Pot/150g	149	99	4.7	16.3	1.7	0.0
Vanilla, Smooth Set, Co-Op*	1 Pot/125g	95	76	3.7	12.5	0.9	0.0
Vanilla, Thick & Creamy, Waitrose*	1 Pot/150g	188	125	4.2	20.6	2.9	0.0
Vanilla, Thickie, Innocent*	1 Bottle/250ml	200	80	2.4	12.2	2.0	0.0
Vanilla, Very Low Fat Bio, Somerfield*	1 Pot/200g	98	49	5.0	7.0	0.0	0.0
Vanilla, Virtually Fat Free, Shapers, Boots*	1 Pot/125g	66	53	5.0	7.9	0.1	0.0
Vanilla, Virtually Fat Free, Ski*	1 Pot/120g	59	49	4.7	7.2	0.2	0.6
Vanilla, Virtually Fat Free, Yeo Valley*	1 Pot/150g	122	81	5.1	15.0	0.1	0.0
Vanilla, Weight Watchers*	1 Pot/120g	49	41	4.2	5.7	0.1	0.0
Very....Lemon Curd, Morrisons*	1 Pot/150g	263	175	4.1	19.2	9.1	0.0
Walnut & Honey, Amore Luxury, Muller*	1 Pot/150g	227	151	2.3	16.1	8.6	0.0
Whisp, Marks & Spencer*	1 Pot/100g	115	115	4.5	13.9	4.1	0.1
White Peach, Seriously Fruity, Waitrose*	1 Pot/150g	152	101	4.8	16.5	1.7	0.2
Whole Milk, Plain	1oz/28g	22	79	5.7	7.8	3.0	0.0
Wholemilk, Organic, Marks & Spencer*	1fl oz/30ml	27	90	6.1	7.4	3.6	0.0
Wild Blackberry, Seriously Fruity, Waitrose*	1 Pot/125g	120	96	4.4	17.2	1.0	0.4
Wild Blackberry, The Best, Safeway*	1 Pot/175g	254	145	3.3	17.9	6.4	1.2
Wild Blueberry, Finest, Tesco*	1 Pot/150g	212	141	3.4	16.6	6.8	0.5
Wild Blueberry, Sveltesse 0%, Nestle*	1 Pot/125g	59	47	4.3	7.0	0.2	0.0
Winter Medley, COU, Marks & Spencer*	1 Pot/150g	68	45	4.2	6.2	0.1	0.1
With Hazelnut, Low Fat, Safeway*	1 Serving/150g	182	121	4.9	20.1	2.3	0.2
Yellow Fruit, Yoplait*	1 Pot/125g	139	111	3.3	18.0	2.9	0.0
Zingy Lemon, D'lite, Ski*	1 Pot/178.5g	141	79	4.5	14.3	0.1	0.0
YOGHURT DRINK,							
Actimel, Mixed Fruit, Danone*	1 Serving/100ml	88	88	2.7	16.0	1.5	0.0
Actimel, Orange, Danone*	1fl oz/30ml	26	88	2.7	16.0	1.5	0.0
Actimel, Original, 0% Fat, Danone*	1 Bottle/100g	33	33	2.8	6.8	0.1	1.9
Actimel, Original, Danone*	1fl oz/30ml	25	83	2.8	14.3	1.6	0.0
Actimel, Pineapple, Danone*	1 Bottle/100g	35	35	2.7	5.5	0.1	1.8
Actimel, Strawberry, Danone*	1 Bottle/100g	88	88	2.7	15.9	1.5	0.0
Average	1floz/30ml	19	62	3.1	13.1	0.0	0.0
Benecol*	1 Serving/70g	62	88	2.6	14.2	2.3	0.0
Bifidus*	1 Carton/500ml	420	84	2.5	15.0	1.5	0.0
Blueberry & Blackcurrant, Orchard Maid*	1 Carton/250ml	148	59	1.6	13.6	0.0	0.0
Fristi*	1 Carton/330g	191	58	2.6	13.6	0.1	0.0
Light, Yakult*	1 Pot/66ml	31	47	1.3	12.2	0.0	1.8
Orchardmaid*	1 Serving/250g	148	59	1.6	13.0	0.0	0.0
Peach & Mango, Fristi*	1 Carton/330g	191	58	2.6	13.6	0.1	0.0
Peach, Low Fat, Vitality Probiotic, Muller*	1 Bottle/100ml	75	75	2.6	13.0	1.4	0.0
Raspberry & Passion Fruit, Everybody, Yoplait*	1 Bottle/90g	60	67	2.6	12.2	0.9	0.0
Raspberry, Low Fat, Vitality, Probiotic, Muller*	1 Bottle/100g	74	74	2.6	12.8	1.4	0.0
Ski Smooth, Nestle*	1 Bottle/200g	144	72	2.8	13.1	0.9	0.0
Strawberry, Bio, The Best, Safeway*	1 Bottle/250ml	215	86	2.7	13.6	1.9	0.6

Y

	Measure INFO/WEIGHT	per Measure KCAL	Nutrition Values per 100g / 100ml				
			KCAL	PROT	CARB	FAT	FIBRE
YOGHURT DRINK,							
Strawberry, Froop, Muller*	1 Carton/191ml	183	96	2.7	14.0	2.9	0.0
Strawberry, Low Fat, Vitality Probotic, Muller*	1 Bottle/100g	79	79	2.6	14.1	1.4	0.0
Strawberry, Yop, Yoplait*	1 Bottle/330g	261	79	2.8	14.0	1.3	0.0
Tropical, Vitality, Muller*	1oz/28g	11	40	3.4	6.4	0.1	0.0
Vanilla, Activate, Probiotic, Little Town Dairy*	1 Bottle/265.1g	167	63	2.7	10.0	1.4	0.2
Yakult*	1 Pot/65ml	51	78	1.4	17.8	0.1	0.0
YORKIE,							
Honeycomb, Nestle*	1 Bar/65g	331	509	5.7	63.6	25.8	0.0
Nestle*	1 Bar/24g	121	504	6.8	60.4	26.1	1.2
Original, Nestle*	1 Bar/68g	357	525	6.5	58.6	29.4	0.0
Raisin & Biscuit, Nestle	1 Bar/63g	307	487	5.9	60.5	24.6	0.0
YORKSHIRE PUDDING,							
3", Baked, Aunt Bessie's*	1 Pudding/36g	91	252	9.0	36.4	7.9	1.7
4 Minute, Aunt Bessie's*	1 Pudding/18g	59	326	9.6	38.4	14.8	2.1
7", Baked, Aunt Bessie's*	1 Pudding/110g	290	264	8.5	37.4	9.0	2.0
Average	1oz/28g	58	208	6.6	24.7	9.9	0.9
Baked Sage & Onion, Morrisons*	1 Pudding/19.3g	53	280	8.0	35.0	12.0	2.6
Beef Dripping, Marks & Spencer*	1 Pudding/24.7g	106	425	9.2	25.1	32.0	1.2
Chicken & Vegetable, COU, Marks & Spencer*	1 Pudding/150g	195	130	12.2	14.3	2.2	1.3
Filled With Beef & Vegetable, Safeway*	1 Pack/300g	396	132	8.6	15.2	4.1	1.3
Filled With Beef, Tesco*	1 Pudding/300g	408	136	6.1	16.2	5.2	1.1
Filled With Chicken, GFY, Asda*	1 Pack/380.9g	438	115	9.0	14.0	2.6	1.5
Filled With Sausage, Tesco*	1 Pack/300g	417	139	5.1	15.2	6.4	1.1
Filled, Roast Chicken, COU, Marks & Spencer*	1 Pudding/150g	210	140	12.6	15.7	2.7	0.9
Filled, Steak & Red Wine, COU, Marks & Spencer*	1oz/28g	39	140	11.0	14.7	2.5	1.2
Filled, With Beef, Morrisons*	1 Serving/350g	515	147	7.4	15.7	6.0	0.5
Filled, With Sausage, Sainsbury's*	1 Pack/300g	576	192	6.9	17.5	10.4	0.9
Four Minute, Aunt Bessie's*	1 Pudding/18g	59	326	9.6	38.4	14.8	2.1
Frozen, Ovenbaked, Iceland*	1 Pudding/12.4g	35	290	9.7	45.1	7.9	4.1
Fully Prepared, Marks & Spencer*	1 Pudding/22g	63	285	9.4	31.6	13.2	1.2
Giant, Aunt Bessie's*	1 Pudding/110g	290	264	8.5	37.4	9.0	2.0
Individual, Asda*	1 Pudding/30.8g	50	162	5.8	22.7	5.2	0.6
Individual, Aunt Bessie's*	1 Pudding/18g	50	276	9.1	32.6	10.8	1.4
Large, Aunt Bessie's*	1 Pudding/39g	104	267	8.8	32.3	11.4	1.4
Large, Safeway*	1 Pudding/45g	123	273	8.5	41.1	8.3	2.5
Made From Batter Mix, Sainsbury's*	1 Pudding/100g	248	248	9.9	40.1	5.3	4.0
Mini, Asda*	1 Pudding/13g	34	260	10.0	37.0	8.0	2.8
Morrisons*	1 Serving/15.1g	39	259	10.0	39.0	7.0	2.1
Potato & Sausage, Marks & Spencer*	1 Serving/100g	200	200	6.4	14.6	12.9	0.9
Ready Baked, SmartPrice, Asda*	1 Pudding/12g	36	297	10.0	44.0	9.0	2.8
Ready To Bake, Aunt Bessie's*	1 Pudding/17g	42	246	8.5	35.1	8.0	1.7
Ready To Bake, Sainsbury's*	1 Pudding/18g	48	263	9.9	35.9	8.9	1.3
Safeway*	1 Serving/22g	58	265	8.4	38.9	8.4	2.5
Sage & Onion, Tesco*	1 Pudding/19g	53	280	8.0	35.0	12.0	2.6
Sausage & Onion Gravy Filled, Safeway*	1 Pudding/300g	540	180	6.2	18.0	9.2	1.2
Steak & Vegetable, COU, Marks & Spencer*	1 Pudding/150g	188	125	9.6	14.9	2.7	0.9
Traditional Style, Asda*	1 Pudding/35.7g	116	322	10.0	39.0	14.0	0.5
Traditional Style, Small, Asda*	1 Pudding/19g	49	259	10.0	39.0	7.0	2.1
Unbaked, Iceland*	1 Pudding/18g	47	263	9.9	35.9	8.9	1.3
Value, Tesco*	1 Pudding/15.3g	29	196	8.7	35.5	2.1	1.6
With Beef in Gravy, Asda*	1 Serving/290g	406	140	7.0	20.0	3.5	0.7
YULE LOG,							
Chocolate, Sainsbury's*	1/8 Log/48g	186	382	5.1	46.5	19.6	0.7

INFO/WEIGHT	Measure per Measure KCAL		Nutrition Values per 100g / 100ml				
			KCAL	PROT	CARB	FAT	FIBRE
YULE LOG,							
Christmas Range, Tesco*	1 Serving/30g	131	442	4.9	56.8	21.7	2.8
Mini, Marks & Spencer*	1 Cake/35.9g	166	460	5.7	56.9	23.3	1.1

Y

Feedback

If you have any comments or suggestions about the Calorie, Carb & Fat Bible, or would like further information on Weight Loss Resources, please call, email, or write to them:

Email: beky@weightlossresources.co.uk
Tel: 01733 345592
Address: Weight Loss Resources, FREEPOST ANG30222, PE2 9BR

About Weight Loss Resources

"What this does is put you in control with no guilt, no awful groups and no negativity! Fill in your food diary, get support on the boards and watch it fall off!"

LINDAB, Weight Loss Resources Member

How Does It Work?

You simply tap in your height, weight, age and basic activity level - set a weight loss goal, and the programme does all the necessary calculations.

What Does It Do?

The site enables you to keep a food diary which keeps running totals of calories, fat, fibre, carbs, proteins and portions of fruit and veg. You can also keep an exercise diary which adds the calories you use during exercise. At the end of a week, you update your weight and get reports and graphs on your progress.

How Will It Help?

You'll learn a great deal about how your eating and drinking habits affect your weight and how healthy they are. Using the diaries and other tools you'll be able to make changes that suit your tastes and your lifestyle. The result is weight loss totally tailored to your needs and preferences. A method you can stick with that will help you learn how to eat well for life!

Try It Free!

Go to **www.weightlossresources.co.uk** and take a completely free, no obligation, 3 day trial. If you like what you see you can sign up for membership from £7 per month.